Happy Birthday Dad!

Love, Alexa

The Letters of Oscar Hammerstein II

The Letters of Oscar Hammerstein II

COMPILED AND EDITED BY
MARK EDEN HOROWITZ

OXFORD
UNIVERSITY PRESS

OXFORD
UNIVERSITY PRESS

Oxford University Press is a department of the University of Oxford. It furthers
the University's objective of excellence in research, scholarship, and education
by publishing worldwide. Oxford is a registered trade mark of Oxford University
Press in the UK and certain other countries.

Published in the United States of America by Oxford University Press
198 Madison Avenue, New York, NY 10016, United States of America.

CIP data is on file at the Library of Congress
ISBN 978–0–19–753818–0

DOI: 10.1093/oso/9780197538180.001.0001

1 3 5 7 9 8 6 4 2

Printed by LSC Communications, United States of America

Table of Contents

Introduction   vii
Notes on the Letters   xv
Acknowledgments   xix

Chapter One: 1917 through 1929   1

Chapter Two: 1930 through 1936   36

Chapter Three: 1937 through 1939   126

Chapter Four: June 1941 through 1942   183

Chapter Five: 1943   273

Chapter Six: 1944   320

Chapter Seven: 1945 (and Smatterings from 1946 and 1947)   379

Chapter Eight: 1949 (Preceded by a Smattering of Letters from 1948)   445

Chapter Nine: 1950   502

Chapter Ten: 1951   561

Chapter Eleven: 1952   610

Chapter Twelve: 1953   674

Chapter Thirteen: 1954   731

Chapter Fourteen: 1955   778

Chapter Fifteen: 1956   843

Chapter Sixteen: 1957   877

Chapter Seventeen: 1958   918

Chapter Eighteen: 1959   947

Chapter Nineteen: 1960   987

Permissions Acknowledgments   1025
Index   1029

Introduction

Oscar Hammerstein II is, I believe, the most consequential figure in the history of the American musical. His career spanned from 1920 to 1960, and in those forty years he so transformed our understanding of what musicals could be that any post-Hammerstein musical owes him a direct debt. Having spent the last two-and-a-half years working with his correspondence, I am convinced that Hammerstein was not only a great man of the theater—a richly talented writer and an astute businessman—but also a profoundly good human being.

Because it is his songs that are ubiquitous, Hammerstein is primarily categorized as a lyricist. He is usually placed among his contemporaries Irving Berlin, Lorenz Hart, Ira Gershwin, and Cole Porter—heady company, but one in which he is sometimes dismissed as the sentimentalist. Of course he could be as clever and witty as any of them, but he was less interested in showing off than in being true to his characters. He was more concerned with his songs' integration within the context of their shows than he was with their potential for being performed, recorded, or broadcast outside the theater. That's not to suggest he was uninterested in these opportunities—of all of his contemporaries, he was probably the canniest and most successful businessman. But as he wrote in one letter, "The songs are there only to serve the play, and not vice versa."

As a lyricist, Hammerstein is credited with having written (and in a few instances co-written) the lyrics for approximately 850 songs. The majority of them were written for about forty-five musicals. Most of these songs were for Broadway, though some were for films, a few were for London, one—*Cinderella*—was for television. There were also a couple of odd stragglers—a revue at the World's Fair and a show that never made it to Broadway or London. For most stage musicals he wrote between a dozen and nineteen songs that stayed in the show, and a handful that ended-up being cut, if they were ever performed at all. And he wrote a modest number of non-show songs, "The Last Time I Saw Paris" being the most notable. But Oscar was far more than a lyricist.

Oscar wrote (or co-wrote) the scripts to at least fifty dramatic works. Most of these were librettos for stage musicals, but nine are screenplays, three are straight plays, and one is a teleplay. Oscar is credited with directing, staging, or supervising approximately a dozen shows (again, sometimes in collaboration), beginning with

The Letters of Oscar Hammerstein II. Mark Eden Horowitz, Oxford University Press. © Mark Eden Horowitz 2022.
DOI: 10.1093/oso/9780197538180.001.0001

the original productions of *Show Boat* (1927), *Music in the Air* (1932), and *Very Warm for May* (1939). And it is widely believed that he ended up directing several shows for which he was uncredited.

In the theatrical world, "Rodgers and Hammerstein" has a long and impressive reputation (the addition of "Organization" came after Oscar died). But Oscar was an involved and shrewd businessman long before his collaboration with Rodgers. He completed two years at Columbia Law and for a brief time also worked for a law firm. After abandoning law school he convinced his uncle, Arthur Hammerstein (a successful producer in his own right), to hire him. Oscar worked as a production stage manager and, whether actively taught by his uncle, or learning by observing, he mastered the business.

Oscar established a professional relationship with attorney Howard Reinheimer by the mid-1920s. Reinheimer, a few years Oscar's junior, also went to Columbia and graduated from Columbia Law. By 1930 he was not only Oscar's close friend and attorney, but for all intents and purposes, his accountant and business advisor as well. In 1937 Reinheimer famously acquired the rights to seventy-two musical productions from the Florenz Ziegfeld estate on behalf of five clients—Irving Berlin, Jerome Kern, Sigmund Romberg, Otto Harbach, *and* Oscar Hammerstein.

Oscar was a producer in his own right by at least 1933, with *Ball at the Savoy* in London. In 1938 Oscar produced two straight plays on Broadway, although neither was a commercial success. And during his two Hollywood sojourns in the 1930s, Oscar was being courted by movie studios and seriously considered moving into the production side of filmmaking.

In 1942 when Oscar and Richard Rodgers began their collaboration and then formed their business partnership, Reinheimer was all but a third unnamed partner. By my count, Rodgers and Hammerstein produced twelve shows on Broadway. Because of obligations for their own works to the Theatre Guild, the first three were shows they didn't write—the plays *I Remember Mama*, and *John Loves Mary*, plus the Irving Berlin musical *Annie Get Your Gun*, a mega hit. In addition to their twelve original Broadway shows, Rodgers and Hammerstein produced two City Center revivals, one play that closed out-of-town, and the film of *Oklahoma!* Most of these shows were also sent on national tours. Then there was London where, under the name Williamson Music Ltd. (both Oscar's and Richard Rodgers' fathers were named William), they again produced their own productions plus several plays and musicals by other authors. And they managed the leasing of their shows for other productions, both nationally and internationally.

Rodgers and Hammerstein were hands-on producers, concerned with every aspect of their properties, including casting; hiring directors, designers, stage managers, and other artistic and managerial personnel; and overseeing advertising and promotion. Their shows were products they oversaw, regularly visiting productions to make sure standards were maintained. Over time multiple corporations were formed, including a music publishing company, an entity for the leasing of shows, and another for renting theater equipment. In collaboration and with guidance from Reinheimer they were not only major players, but innovators in the business of show business.

With his slow and thoughtful baritone, Oscar embodied gravitas. His opinion and counsel were highly valued. While not officially a play doctor, he read innumerable scripts, and visited rehearsals, out-of-town tryouts, previews, and productions (sometimes as a potential producer, but often just as a friend or colleague). He gave the best, most helpful advice he could. He also received unsolicited lyrics and songs, but (on legal advice), he usually and regretfully declined to look at the songs lest he later be accused of plagiarism.

Oscar was an active member of several boards and committees, and chairman at times for some of them. Most were related to the performing arts, such as ASCAP and the Dramatists Guild, but certainly not all of them. Some organizations he was only briefly involved with—such as the Hollywood Anti-Nazi League, the Writers War Board, and the Music War Committee. Though often approached, he refused invitations to merely have his name used on behalf of various causes (though he may have supported them philosophically and even financially); he believed time and effort should also be requirements for public recognition and solicitation. Among those organizations he publicly supported was the NAACP with which he had a long and close association. Beginning around 1950 Oscar was a passionate member and advocate for the United World Federalists, an organization dedicated to preventing another world war (particularly a nuclear one). And in 1949, in conjunction with their friends and neighbors Pearl S. Buck and James Michener, Oscar and Dorothy Hammerstein founded Welcome House, a child welfare and adoption agency, devoted to children of Asian or part-Asian ancestry. Oscar became its president, and among the first children adopted from the agency was the Hammersteins' first grandchild.

Oscar married Myra Finn in 1917. They had two children, William and Alice. Oscar met Dorothy Blanchard Jacobson in 1927 on a shipboard crossing from New York to England. They fell passionately in love—as his letters attest. They divorced their spouses and married in 1929, remaining together until Oscar's death in 1960.

Dorothy brought her two children, Susan Blanchard and Henry Jacobson, into the fold, although Henry was raised mostly by his father. Oscar and Dorothy had James in 1931. They also provided refuge for other children at times, particularly during the War. But importantly for the future of musical theatre, James brought a school friend home in 1942 or 1943—the twelve-year-old Stephen Sondheim. Sondheim became a frequent visitor. Within a few years, Oscar became his mentor and, as Sondheim describes it, a surrogate father.

Quite surprisingly, the city-born and raised Oscar became a farmer. In the fall of 1940, the Hammersteins bought Highland Farm near Doylestown in Bucks County, Pennsylvania. Although he kept his apartment in Manhattan, Highland Farm became Oscar's primary home and refuge. It was a true working farm that he oversaw to the degree he was able, becoming particularly interested in the breeding of Angus cows. Because of his love of the bucolic, and his lyrics that are rich in images taken from nature (birds in particular), Oscar is sometimes perceived as something of a hayseed. He wasn't. Highly educated, he was an inveterate reader and theater-goer. He was deeply knowledgeable about and interested in history, politics, and finance, and traveled widely.

Having spent years in Oscar's company through his papers and correspondence, I have yet to find even traces of clay feet. Oscar was kind and generous. He was funny. That's not to say he was perfect. He could be testy and did not suffer fools gladly. He was defensive about credit, believing that lyricists and librettists were rarely given their due.

While Oscar's views were quite forward thinking for his times, by today's standards there are comments in his letters that may come across as dated and sexist, and letters to him that are racially insensitive.

Oscar came of age in the 1920s. His early shows alternated between musical comedies and operettas. His early musicals were fairly typical of their time. There were mistaken identities, Cinderella-like stories, villains, heroes, and love stories. There were large choruses—peasants in the village square, Mounties, Riffs—of virtually indistinguishable players. Read the lyrics and you'll find songs or large sections of them assigned to "Men," "Girls" (yes, I note the difference), or the "Ensemble." The only discernable differences seem to be the time and locale—with an eye for color and pageantry.

Then, in 1927, came *Show Boat*. The very fact that it was based on a novel—a serious novel—was, well, novel in itself. (The other hit shows of that year were the comic and slight *Hit the Deck*, *Good News*, and *Funny Face*.) The fact that *Show Boat* dealt with racism, miscegenation, alcoholism, gambling addiction, and the abandonment of a wife and child, was beyond extraordinary. It had a cast that featured both Black and white characters who interacted with each other. It traversed time and geography, covering over thirty years and the length of the Mississippi. But even its broad expanse is secondary in importance to the humanity of the characters. They're not the traditional villains, heroes, and heroines (except for those in the show-within-the-show). Gaylord is as much a victim as a victimizer. Magnolia survives and eventually thrives, not only because of talent and inner grit, but because Julie makes a sacrifice on her behalf.

Show Boat's theatrical importance rests largely on Oscar's libretto, not his lyrics. "Make Believe" is significant, not because it's one of Oscar's love songs that doesn't exclaim its love, but because it's a song where two people who are attracted to each other make a connection and begin to fall in love during the song. "Can't Help Lovin' Dat Man" pretends to be a popular Black song of its day, which is used as a plot point—the first clue that Julie is biracial—but whose substance reflects on most of the ill-fated matches in the show. "Ol' Man River" is the song that's something entirely new . . . and I can think of no other that follows in its footsteps. It's an ambivalent song. Is it a lament or is it an anthem? It's full of complaint but somehow finds solace in a sense that ultimately nothing matters—the river doesn't care and won't remember. But the most important thing is that it puts the suffering of Black people center stage. The white audience must face it and, one hopes, be changed by it. It's not just characters who change and grow through some of Oscar's songs, but the audience, too.

Despite the extraordinary success and acclaim *Show Boat* achieved, Oscar largely reverted to writing shows that were similar in style and content to what he'd written before. There are over twenty stage and film scores that Oscar worked on between *Show Boat* in 1927, and *Oklahoma!* in 1943—sixteen years—yet none of them came close to continuing or fulfilling the promise of *Show Boat*.

It's not entirely fair to make that claim. In most cases, I have only read and played through the songs, and only know the scripts through synopses. Still, I'm fairly confident. I do note one possible exception. In 1938, Oscar collaborated with Otto Harbach on the book and lyrics for *Gentlemen Unafraid*. Jerome Kern supplied the music. The show never made it to Broadway, even after it was revised a few years later and given the equally regrettable title, *Hayfoot, Strawfoot*. Reviewing its songs and story, it's not surprising that it failed, but one senses deeper ambitions— the show focused on the lead-up to the Civil War and the North–South divide. Oscar and his collaborators were crafting their show during the ominous year before the outbreak of war in Europe—again. Tensions were fomenting, and Oscar must have seen connections. There is one particularly thought-provoking song in the score—"I Wish Dat Dere Wasn't No War"—in which a chorus of "Colored Women," Southern soldiers, and "White Women" alternately comment, and the fundamental point is made:

> Ax de boss
> An he don' know.
> Ax de preacher
> And he don' know.
> An' de Lord Hisself don' even know
> Why men want war . . .

Oklahoma! opened in March 1943, generating seismic changes in the theater and in Oscar's life. At the time, Oscar hadn't had a show on Broadway that came close to being a hit since *Music in the Air* in 1932, eleven years previously (*May Wine* in 1935 might be considered a modest success). There had been occasional hit songs—in 1939 *Very Warm for May* produced "All the Things You Are," and "The Last Time I Saw Paris" premiered in 1940—but Oscar's Broadway future did not look bright. Even so, letters he received make clear that Oscar continued to be enormously respected in the entertainment industry. Hollywood was definitely interested in his potential as a producer, organizations and boards craved his involvement, and enthusiasm was building enthusiasm for his updating of the Bizet opera *Carmen*. The show—*Carmen Jones*—set in the contemporary, Black American South was actually written before *Oklahoma!*, but was delayed by casting difficulties. When it finally opened in December 1943 it lived up to the high expectations it had engendered.

   Oklahoma!'s unprecedented success seems to have surprised everyone, including Oscar. But unlike *Show Boat*, its innovations influenced not only Oscar, but his contemporaries and those who followed. While he had doubts and struggles with his subsequent shows, I sense a newfound confidence in his artistic ambitions and faith in audiences' reception of them.

   When people comment on Oscar's innovations they usually focus on what's referred to as the "integrated musical"—how, among other things, songs now grew out of the characters and the story, and how the characters and the story develop through the songs. That was a great achievement. Equal in importance was the substance of the shows Oscar wrote and the subject matter he tackled. His were adult musicals—they respected their audiences. I believe Oscar was capable of manipulating his audiences with an eye toward educating them, sometimes improving them, or at least making them more sympathetic to human imperfection.

His heroes and heroines were flawed, and his "villains" . . . ? Well, his shows came to eschew villains in the traditional sense. Ravenal, Jud, Billy, Joseph Taylor, Nellie, the King, and the Captain are all, to some degree, victims of their own desires, prejudices, and situations. In *Show Boat*, Ravenal and Julie succumbed to the demons of addictions, hurting others, but also hurting themselves; both are also given moments of redemption, Julie through self-sacrifice. In *Oklahoma!*, Jud is a victim of his desires, coupled with an unattractive look and persona he doesn't have the wherewithal to change. Both Nellie Forbush and Cable are the victims of the prejudices with which they were raised. Nellie struggles mightily to change and succeeds, Cable dies. Whatever their flaws, Oscar looked for the humanity in his characters.

Oscar's best works—*Show Boat*, *Oklahoma!*, *Carousel*, *South Pacific*, and *The King and I*—were based on books and plays written by others. But in adapting them as musicals he gave them a power, longevity, subtlety, and influence they would not have otherwise had. In a unique way, songs become the property of the listener. We hear them in our head, we sing them in the shower. When a character in a show sings a song, we then inherit the song and, in a way, we also inherit part of the character who sings it. We take on part of their persona; they become part of us as we think and feel what their words express.

We can't think or sing "Ol' Man River" without identifying with or at least appreciating aspects of Black suffering. Not just Black suffering. Who of any maturity can claim not to have had moments where they were ". . . tired of livin' an' skeered of dyin'"? We can laugh at Ado Annie and her travails in "I Cain't Say No," but the song wouldn't be so effective if we didn't know what it is to have inappropriate urges. One hopes it makes us a bit more forgiving toward those who are less successful at fighting them. You can't go on the journey of the "Soliloquy"—moving through its stages of excitement, pride, terror, and ill-conceived conclusion at the thought of having a child—without acquiring some sympathy (if not forgiveness) for Billy's subsequent acts. "You've Got to Be Carefully Taught" may verge on the polemic, but in its thirteen lines it makes its point so clearly that I can't imagine how one can disagree with its premise without embarrassment. And I think that was Oscar's goal. Can you experience "A Puzzlement" without asking yourself which of your own beliefs might be questionable? "I Enjoy Being a Girl" has fallen out of favor for its perceived sexism, but I'm convinced Oscar wrote the song largely to telegraph to the audience that the Chinese-American woman, Linda Low, was as all-American as any blonde-haired, blue-eyed young woman of the day. The more I think about Oscar's work, the more deeply I believe it's his desire to improve his audience that sets him apart.

In 1953 Oscar received a letter from a college student working on an essay enti-
tled, "The Theme of Brotherhood and Tolerance in the Plays of Oscar Hammerstein
II." He asked Oscar if he could "please send a personal statement on the subject?"
Oscar replied:

> I suppose that my best personal statements on the subject of brotherhood and tol-
> erance are in the plays that you intend to deal with. I am very happy that you are
> writing this essay because none of the references to this theme in my plays is acci-
> dental. They are quite deliberate and conscious. I believe that the introduction of
> this theme in plays is more effective than plays that are written obviously to prop-
> agate these virtues. The public resists direct propaganda – in our country, anyway.

I believe the letters that follow reveal things about all the aspects of Oscar—the lyricist, the collaborator, the writer, the man of the theater, the businessman, the family
man, the believer in causes, the intellectual, the man of good humor, the defensive,
thoughtful, and compassionate man that he was. They're also a fascinating view of
history as it was lived, and the history of forty years of show business.

I close this introduction with a vivid memory. A few months into this project, I was
intently transcribing a long, very rich letter that Oscar wrote to Jerome Kern in 1942
(during World War II). It was full of detailed discussions on four shows. Then, on the
last page, just before the end there was a paragraph that made me feel as though
Oscar was writing directly to me from the past to the future:

> Knowing that you file your letters and I file copies of mine, it is quite possible that
> in a couple of thousand years some archaeologist might dig up either the original
> or the copy and, seeing the date, will be completely puzzled that, during the Great
> War, so long a letter could be written without some reference to it. It will be hard
> enough for him to understand how people could be so dumb as to wage wars
> like this but once in them, how could they possibly be interested in such things
> as I discussed so seriously in this letter. Well, Mr. Archaeologist, that's the way we
> were in these days, feller.

Only eighty years—not two thousand—have transpired since Oscar wrote that, but
I believe his confidence in the rightness of saving his letters and their value to the
future was warranted.

Notes on the Letters

Most of the letters in this book are in the Oscar Hammerstein II Collection in the Music Division of the Library of Congress. One of the blessings of the collection is that Oscar retained carbon copies of a significant amount of his outgoing correspondence. Were that not the case, this book would not have been attempted. Some letters came from other collections within the Library, particularly the Rouben Mamoulian and Josh Logan collections. A few came from other institutions, and some remain in private hands. Unfortunately, there is only a modest amount of correspondence from his early years, and a few significant gaps in the 1940s—suggesting that a file drawer here or there may have been lost or damaged and disposed of before it could make its way safely to the Library. (In fact, just recently an additional carton of Hammerstein papers came to light, too late to consider for this book.) In any case, there is still more than enough to give a rich, well-rounded view of Oscar, his work, his relationships, and his personality.

I estimate that there are approximately 10,000 letters in the Hammerstein Collection. From those, plus the letters from other sources, I selected and transcribed about 4,500 that seemed particularly valuable for research (on a wide variety of topics). Of those I selected between 900 and 1,000 for this book—letters that focus on Oscar personally and on his work. However, as of this writing, the plan is that all of the transcribed letters will go online in a Library of Congress website. This expectation eased my conscience for employing an editorial method that is frowned upon in some quarters: in some cases I elected to include only an excerpt from a letter, rather than a letter in its entirety. There is no censoring here—I did not act as a censor but only as an editor making difficult choices in order to include as much of the best content as possible. There are some long letters that contain only a paragraph or two, or sometimes only a sentence, of real interest. Sometimes I edited out redundant passages that already appeared in other letters in the book. I also left off addresses, return addresses, company names and mottos, variously formatted dates, any manner of letterhead information. Again, I simply did not want to take the space for them here—preferring to be able to include more letters. In instances where I thought it important and useful I included things like company names or locations in the header for a letter.

I did my best to recreate the formatting and style of the original letters. The writers' own idiosyncratic choices for spelling, spacing, and punctuation—as odd and inconsistent as they may be—have been maintained. That is why some letters have paragraphs that begin with indents, and some do not. And why some that have indents have spaces between the paragraphs and some do not. It is why some letters have periods inside quotation marks and some on the outside. Because many of the letters from Oscar came in the form of carbons, those letters do not include signatures, where letters transcribed from originals do.

Within the letters there is a tad less uniformity when it comes to leaving, noting, or correcting "errors." Early in the transcription process I was shocked at some of the misspellings. How was it possible that Oscar did not know that it was *Show Boat* not *Showboat*, or the "Shuberts" not the "Schuberts"? Then I realized, many of Oscar's letters were dictated (he was also an early adopter of the Dictabelt) and the errors were surely made by secretaries who didn't know better. It surprised me to think that Oscar did not proof letters before they were sent, but perhaps he did and corrections were made on the originals not the carbons. Then there are letters Oscar sent while in England, where his secretaries favored British spellings (including "Carrousel" as an alternate spelling of "Carousel"). I have left these various spellings and misspellings, usually confirming the latter with a "[*sic*]"—usually just the first time it appears in a given letter. There are some correspondents whose spellings and grammar are, well, unique; Uncle Arthur's letters are particularly vivid examples. These oddities I, too, have left. But there are typos that I have corrected. Typos such as "hte" for "the" I have corrected without compunction. I fear beyond that I am not always consistent. When I made the original transcripts I inserted "[*sic*]s" regularly. But in preparing this book I found places where, in reading my transcripts, I found typos or missing words that I suspected were errors I made in transcribing. Without ready access to the originals to check against I have made best guesses and sometimes simply made the corrections that seem obvious to me, sometimes with a "[*sic*]", sometimes without. I do not think that any errors I may have made have fundamentally altered the substance of any of the letters.

My dating philosophy for this book was that letters would mostly appear in chronological order, but that I would keep conversations together. It didn't seem worth the risk of a reader having to flip back a page or two or three to remember a letter that this one was responding to. In general I do not like footnotes, but I decided this book would benefit from them. The decision as to whether to include something as a footnote or in the general text was largely determined by three things: length; the shorter the more likely it would find itself in a footnote; if it was a basic fact or required some explanation; and how close its subject was to Oscar;

the further from Oscar the likelier in a footnote. I am sure I was not rigorously consistent. Whether text appears before or after a letter it refers to was also largely determined by whether the text is needed to set up the letter, or to clarify or elaborate a subject in the letter.

In some instances where Oscar's replies made clear what the letter to him had said or asked, I didn't include those letters for reasons of space.

Acknowledgments

My first thank you must go to my wife, Loie Clark, who bore the brunt of the daily realities of this project. Once again she was forced to give up our dining room table to my disorganized spread of papers, reference books, and all the other items that seemed to fill every available space. She shared my frustrations and endured my absences, either real, or simply lost in the world of Hammerstein. Conversely, she was often the first person I had the joy of sharing a great "find" with. She was also the one to whom I would shout to the other room—"How do you spell . . . ?" Or "What's the word for . . . ?" Basically any questions having to do with grammar, history, fact, or fiction (literary and dramatic).

Although Hugh Fordin passed away in 2019, his book, *Getting to Know Him: A Biography of Oscar Hammerstein II* was an invaluable resource. The more I got to know Oscar through his letters, the greater my admiration grew for Fordin's book (with some frustration at letters he quotes that I have been unable to track down). There are several other books that proved invaluable, and where I'm doubly blessed in that they were written by friends, friends who were also generous with direct help. Foremost among these was my dear friend Amy Asch, whose *The Complete Lyrics of Oscar Hammerstein II* proved to be valuable beyond measure. It's a book that impresses me more every time I pick it up (which I have done daily over the past two years) and realize the depth and breadth of the information she captured in its pages. Three good friends also wrote books of correspondence—Nigel Simeone: *The Leonard Bernstein Letters*; Barry Day: *The Letters of Noel Coward*; and Dominic McHugh: *Alan Jay Lerner: A Lyricist's Letters*, and (with Cliff Eisen) *The Letters of Cole Porter*. All three provided help, encouragement, and guidance, and their books stood as models and examples. Frankly, knowing what I now know, I don't know how they did what they did; my admiration approaches awe. Tim Carter wrote two brilliantly researched books: *Oklahoma!: The Making of an American Musical* and *Rodgers and Hammerstein's Carousel*. Todd Purdum authored the thoughtful and thought-provoking *Something Wonderful: Rodgers and Hammerstein's Broadway Revolution*. And while they do not focus on Hammerstein, I found Steven Suskin's books *Show Tunes: The Songs, Shows and Careers of Broadway's Major Composers*, and *Opening Nights on Broadway: A Critical Quotebook of the Golden Era of the Musical Theatre* to be frequently used and useful resources. A final primary reference book (whose author I don't know and who remains uncredited) is the *Richard Rodgers Fact Book with supplement*. It's another remarkable achievement. It seems only fair that I also acknowledge Wikipedia, IMDB, IBDB, and ProQuest Historical Newspapers and Periodicals for providing facts and other information that informed this book.

I became a music specialist in the Music Division of the Library of Congress in June of 1991. It has been one of the great blessings of my life. This book would not have happened were it not for the kindness and assistance of many, many colleagues, past and present. Among the people I must thank are: Sam Brylawski, my first friend at the Library (from before I worked there), who alerted me of the job opening and coached me through the application. Betty Auman, who both hired me and acquired much of the Hammerstein Collection for the Library. Ray White, who became my mentor, a role he still fills. Susan Vita, the chief of the Music Division, who has been a kind supporter, and who gave her blessing for me to take a year's leave of absence from the division to accept a fellowship in the Library's John W. Kluge Center—the Library's office of scholarly programs. Hope O'Keeffe of the Library's Office of General Counsel for being an early and helpful supporter. The helpful staff of the Kluge Center included John Haskell, Travis Hensley, Michael Stratmoen, and my intern Bridget Anderson. Particular thanks and gratitude are due to my friend and colleague Nancy Seeger. Nancy was the archivist for the Oscar Hammerstein II Collection and, were it not for her and her careful processing of the Hammerstein Collection this project would not have been possible.

I have been particularly fortunate in the support of many members of the Hammerstein family, including Patricia Benner, Oscar "Andy" Hammerstein III, William Hammerstein, and Melinda Walsh, as well as Andy Boose, until recently, the attorney for the Hammerstein estate.

Another cheerleader, helpmate, and guide throughout this project and, frankly, throughout my time at the Library, has been Ted Chapin of the Rodgers & Hammerstein Organization.

Among others who provided guidance, assistance, and shared from their vast knowledge were Michael Feinstein, Kurt Gänzl, Alan Gomberg, Brad Hathaway, and Mark Stein.

There are three people whose assistance went so far beyond what I had any right to hope for, that no acknowledgment I write can come close to fully expressing my gratitude. Laurie Winer read through the entire book and provided detailed feedback on both style and substance. Having written her own brilliant book on Oscar, her insights and knowledge were invaluable, and her skill as a writer of elegance helped polish some of my rougher edges. Scott Willis not only read the book in its entirely, he noted every jot, tittle, and space, proofreading in ways that humbled me, as well as making smart suggestions to clarify and improve. A final, unexpected proofreader was David Lahm (who also happens to be the son of the lyricist and librettist Dorothy Fields). David's proofreading in particular benefited from a deep knowledge of the history of the time period, the characters, and their milieu.

While working on this book both my father, Terry Fred Horowitz, and my brother, Evan Reid Horowitz, passed away. This book is dedicated to their memories.

Photo 1 Oscar Hammerstein II, circa 1920. White Studio

Chapter One
1917 through 1929

Oscar Greeley Clendenning Hammerstein—Oscar Hammerstein II and herein-after Oscar—was born on July 12, 1895, in Manhattan. His parents were William and Alice Nimmo Hammerstein. They named him after his German-born grand-father, Oscar Hammerstein, who emigrated to America, alone, in 1864, while still a teenager. Against all reasonable expectations, the elder Oscar became a legendary producer, impresario, and builder of theaters and opera houses—eleven of them. These exploits, along with his ever-present cane, top hat, and cigar, and enlivened by outrageous behavior, quips, and feuds, made him one of the most famous men of his day. His sons, Arthur and William, joined him in the family business, more out of obligation than passion. At least in William's case. Arthur became a producer in his own right. As the more practical businessmen, they helped keep their father afloat, essentially underwriting his often outra-geous projects and ambitious operas with the more popular and less expensive fare that they produced.

William, the less flamboyant of the brothers, was more content working be-hind the scenes as a manager. Oscar's brother, Reggie, was born in 1897. Their mother died in 1910, and a year later their father married her sister, Anna "Mousie" Nimmo. Oscar entered Columbia University in 1912, with the intention of getting a law degree. William died in 1914 at the age of 38, leaving Oscar all but an orphan at the age of nineteen. Oscar remained at Columbia Law for two years, beginning, but not completing, a law degree.

During his time at Columbia, Oscar became involved in its varsity shows, first as a performer in *On Your Way* in 1915. In 1916 he not only appeared in *The Peace Pirate* but contributed his first known lyric to the score. The following year he co-wrote the book and all the lyrics for *Home, James*.

Oscar married Myra "Mike" Finn on August 22, 1917. They had known each other casually for several years, but their courtship was a brief one. At the time of their wedding Oscar was twenty-two and Myra twenty. According to Oscar's

The Letters of Oscar Hammerstein II. Mark Eden Horowitz, Oxford University Press. © Mark Eden Horowitz 2022.
DOI: 10.1093/oso/9780197538180.003.0001

biographer, Hugh Fordin, this is the only letter from Oscar to his stepmother to be found among her possessions when she passed away.

Oscar Hammerstein to Anna "Mousie" Hammerstein, August 21, 1917[1]

Dear Mousie:-

I won the five dollars after all, didn't I? But I won't claim it I know how you felt. I thot about it during the evening and I came to understand your feelings—perhaps better than I ever have before. For, after all, boys are an unappreciative lot, and I suppose it has been only on unusual occasions that Reg and I have realized all that you have been and are to us—and all that we have meant to you. I imagined for myself just what thots passed thru your mind as you saw me start on my honeymoon. To you it was just the latest of a long series of developments which you watched take place thru out my whole life. You have seen and known everything of importance—every experience that I had for the past twenty-two years. The significance of that close and dear relationship has never been borne upon me so keenly as it has in these two days. Perhaps I am already getting older. All this discussion is merely an explanatory preface to a text I want to recite to you, and that is that I haven't broken away from you; that this new step I have taken will result in our living in different houses—but will not draw us any further apart than we have ever been.

As for married life Mouse, I am sure that I was cut out for it. I am very, very happy.

You can write to me if you wish, to Chateau Frontenac Quebec, Canada. I'd love to hear from you. Do not mail a letter later than Saturday. I'll try to write to Reggie later, and you'll hear from me again in a day or two.

Lovingly

Oscar

---

[1] The mystery is that the letter is dated the day before the wedding; the solution may never be known, but it's likely that Oscar either misdated the letter, or the date of the wedding was a couple of days earlier than we have been led to believe.

Photo 2 Oscar and Myra Hammerstein, circa 1925. Photograph courtesy of Oscar Andrew Hammerstein

Oscar was a reliable and gifted writer of thank-you notes. Here is the earliest I've found, possibly to one of Oscar's teachers.

Oscar Hammerstein to Mrs. White, August 23, 1917

Dear Mrs. White:

Of all my wedding gifts, there is none which I appreciate more than your very beautiful present. It shall be a source for constant remembrance of you. I assure you however, that such a reminder was not at all necessary, for I still think of you very often, with your "long pencil" that seemed so much a part of my childhood.

Please convey my sincere gratitude to your sister, also.

I suppose Mousie has told you that I have given up the study of law and entered the theatrical field, with my uncle's firm. I intend eventually to do some play writing, since that is the branch that appeals to me most, and for which I feel I have some talent. I have written some verse to the music of our new show, to be produced next month, and they have been accepted. It is really a very encouraging start.

Thanking you again, and hoping that you'll let me hear from you often, I am

Sincerely yours,

Oscar

The United States entered World War I on April 6, 1917. Oscar tried to enlist but according to Hugh Fordin, he was declared currently ineligible for being underweight. It was after being rejected by the Army that Oscar quit law school.

Oscar's father pressured him into promising that he would not become a part of the theater. However, after his father died, Oscar applied to his uncle Arthur for a job. Arthur was reluctant, knowing of Oscar's promise and feeling similarly bound by his brother's wishes. But Oscar was determined and argued that as a new husband he needed a job; Arthur relented. Although Oscar's goal was to write for the theater, he agreed to Arthur's stipulation that he wait a year before pursuing that aspect of the business, and instead began working as an assistant stage manager. Arthur had already produced a string of some half-a-dozen shows on Broadway entirely under his own name. His first had been the successful operetta, *The Firefly* in 1910, with a score by Rudolf Friml and Otto Harbach.

Oscar's one-year embargo as a writer did not hold. Arthur allowed Oscar to write the lyrics for the show *Furs and Frills*, which opened in October of 1917. The show was not a success (thirty-two performances), but Oscar had his first song in a Broadway musical.

Oscar and Herman Axelrod had been friends from their student days at Columbia, where they had collaborated on *Home, James*. It was with Axelrod, and their mutual friend Herman Mankiewicz (who went on to co-write the screenplay for *Citizen Kane*) that Oscar had gone to the draft board. Axelrod was accepted and, in a jargon-rich (and in places hard to decipher) letter, he apprised Oscar of various doings:

Herman "Ax" Axelrod to Oscar Hammerstein, October 11, 1918[2]

Dear Oc—

Well, Old Jazz, the war are won, she ava[?] [?] just finished the battle of Paris and oh, Madoosha! I, salaam. Well, to make my serial complete, I must relate the good fortune of our hero. Young Gus, the valiant, second Looil, shavetail,[3] if you will, having successfully completed the Artillery course at Saumur, France (that's what the certificate says) and having packed his belongings preparatory to joining a regiment finds his hopes shattered (curses!!!). Upon gazing at the Bulletin now about to finish my first week at this place which puts you through a course of tractors and caterpillars used in drawing artillery It is just a small school for just a few officers. Quite an exclusive affair.

I had quite a wonderful time in Paris. An honest-to-goodness bed at the Hotel de Crillon, (quite Ritz, hey! What). Saw the Follies Bergere— drank everything from chocolate soda and Clover Clubs to Roman candles. My next chance to visit Paris comes two weeks from to-morrow about a week before the end of the course.

I saw Harold before I left Saumur. He came through on his way south to join the regiment he was assigned to.

I've just heard about Milt's being in the Army. It must be a great relief for him to be in uniform.

Is it true that Elliot Sperling died? I don't know how I got that but I believe someone wrote it to Harold.

Received a letter from Kaddy saying your new play "Sometime"[4] may reach New York—sometime. Is it as bad as all that.

Well old dear, that's about all for now. Regards to the gang in mufti and their spouses.

Cheerio,

Ax

---

[2] The letter was sent from the Tractor Artillery School, Amer. Exp. Forces, as World War I was ending.

[3] "Shavetail" is a derogatory term for a 2nd Lieutenant; "Looil" is a term, presumably non-derogatory, for a Lieutenant.

[4] *Sometime* had already opened by October 4. Produced by Oscar's uncle Arthur, Oscar was one of the show's stage managers.

(The following events are not to be equated.) On October 26, 1918, Myra gave birth to William "Billy" Hammerstein. On January 11, 1918, World War I ended. On January 5, 1920, *Always You* opened on Broadway. It was the first show in which the book and lyrics were entirely by Oscar; the music was by Herbert Stothart.

While at Columbia, Oscar became a member of the Pi Lambda Phi fraternity. He maintained at least a temporary connection with the fraternity, writing to the grandmother of fellow fraternity brother, Henry Rosenwald Guiterman.

Oscar Hammerstein to Mrs. Rosenwald, June 16, 1920

My dear Mrs. Rosenwald:

I have been asked by the Alpha Chapter of the Pi Lambda Phi to tell you that we gratefully accept your generous offer to donate a fraternity house in memory on your grandson, Henry Guiterman.[5]

For those of us who were fortunate enough to have been in college while Henry was there, no concrete reminder is necessary to keep him in our thoughts. He was universally esteemed by his comrades as a loyal friend and brother. The qualities in his character were enough to perpetuate our memory of him.

We admire the thought which inspires your donation, and it is a source of genuine gratification to us all that Henry's name will be immortalized throughout the generations of the brethren who are to succeed us.

We are so thankful to you for your gift, Mrs. Rosenwald, that all conventional phrases of gratitude appear to be artificial garments, too thin to drape our sentiment.

I will ask you to imagine our emotions of a body of young men who are suddenly presented with the one, big, necessary thing they most wanted -- the attainment of which seemed impossible to them. And our satisfaction is the greater because you are giving us our home in such a way as to make it a symbol of our ideals of brotherhood.

We shall never forget our debt to you, believe me.

Sincerely yours,

Oscar Hammerstein 2nd

(On behalf of the chapter)

---

[5] Guiterman died in October 1918 at the age of eighteen, not in the war but during training.

Oscar and Myra's daughter, Alice Hammerstein, was born on May 17, 1921. Between 1917 and 1930, Oscar wrote lyrics and/or the script (including for two non-musicals) for some twenty-three Broadway shows. Arthur produced sixteen of them. The most successful were *Wildflower* in 1923, and *Rose-Marie* in 1924. But it was for the show *Tickle Me* in 1920 where Arthur arranged for Oscar to collaborate on the lyrics and book with the seasoned Otto Harbach, twenty-two years Oscar's senior. Harbach's Broadway career began in 1908, and by the time he first worked with Oscar, he'd already worked on twenty-one shows. Harbach became Oscar's mentor; they collaborated on nine shows. Of those, three stand out—*Rose-Marie* with music by Friml and Stothart, *Sunny* with music by Kern, and *The Desert Song* with music by Sigmund Romberg. But before any of those hits they began collaborating on a show to be called *The Poppy Girl* for Arthur.

Arthur Hammerstein to Otto Harbach and Oscar Hammerstein, November 22, 1922

Gentlemen:-

After you two undertakers left my office today, I discovered the coffin in the foyer. It would have been just as appropriate if you had brought it into the office, as you left it in such a conspicuous place.

If ever there was a show buried before it was born, it is the show entitled "The Poppy Girl". In fact after you both left I asked Mr. Grady[6] to be honest and tell me the truth, that I thought my firm of authors were just trying to humor me and I wanted to know whether he also thought I was in that condition. He is still laughing so that I cannot get an answer.

Nevertheless if this funereal atmosphere continues, I shall absolutely lose my enthusiasm, which I consider a big part of my success, and I feel that no matter what is written I will not be able to handle it. So kindly do me a favor, forget the case and everything appertaining to my end of this new production and deliver me the book and score when ready. I will then proceed to produce.

---

[6] Hugh Grady was Arthur's business manager.

If during the rehearsals and after the tryout out of town, I find that the cast is not adequate, then I will be pleased to have the undertakers suggest a remedy or an embalming fluid.

Very truly yours,

Arthur Hammerstein

Photo 3 Arthur Hammerstein, circa 1929. Photograph courtesy of Oscar Andrew Hammerstein

As far as we know, *The Poppy Girl* was either abandoned entirely, or perhaps (given the floral connection) evolved to become the show *Wildflower*, which opened in February 1923, running for 477 performances.

Rose-Marie, a collaboration with Oscar, Harbach, and Romberg, was a certifiable hit. It opened on Broadway in September 1924 and at 577 performances became the longest-running musical in the first half of the 1920s. It spawned several national tours, and opened in London on March 20, 1925, where it was an even bigger hit, running for over 800 performances. The show became the longest running West End show after World War I, a run not to be exceeded until Hammerstein's own *Oklahoma!* in 1947. Its most famous song is "Indian Love Call."

Oscar Hammerstein (in London) to Otto Harbach,
March 15, 1925

Dear Otto:-

I intended to write much sooner but I struck a snag over here. I had an idea that I would pop in at rehearsals once in a while, make a few suggestions, and pop out again. But that has not been the situation. The English crowd, producers, directors and all welcomed us with open arms and were quite willing to turn over complete control to us. And after seeing several English productions we thot we'd better take advantage of the invitation. From what I've seen it seems to me that they allow the actors, especially the comics to run wild with the book. We have one of the biggest comedians over here, Billy Merson. He gets three hundred and fifty pounds a week—more than Edith Day who gets three hundred. So I thot I'd better step in and look after things. The result has been that Arthur, Herb and I have spent more time on this production than any other since the original. We haven't been out of the theatre. In a way it seems like a great waste, but I don't regret it as I feel I have learned a great deal about producing conditions here, and in addition to that, making an assured success doubly sure. In some ways this looks like the best of all Rose Maries. Edith Day is a positive joy. You know how much there is in the part that has never been brought to the surface. She brings it up and shows it off to your heart's content. The comedian about whom I was worried has proved very amenable, and tho he has spent most of his time in the Music Halls and Revues I have kidded him into showing "his public" what a great legitimate actor he can be. He'll play it very well, he's a fine dancer, and they tell me he'll keep the balconies and galleries filled for eight weeks no matter how bad the show is.

I have seen all the costumes and scenery and they are pretty nearly up to our standard — far better than any show I have seen here. All in all a rosy outlook. We open next Friday, March 20th. Arthur'll be home a week later to tell you all about it.

Of course you have heard about your smashing success with "Nanette."[7] I've never heard such raving in my life! They can't say enough about it. They have me so excited that I'm offering mythical sums to buy a seat, but so far unsuccessfully. "Best show since The Merry Widow", "Best show [I] ever saw" are the comments. I am enclosing a Sunday second notice which is typical.

I thot by this time I should have something to say about 'Mariza' but I haven't had a chance to take the 'script out of the envelope. I get glowing reports of the Berlin, Vienna and Budapest productions. I met Jack Haskall the dance producer who saw it in Budapest. He has probably been in touch with you by this time.

Before leaving New York I heard Hope Hampton and was impressed with her just as you were.

Of course the business arrangements seem very informal. Have we a contract? Are we to get an advance? Any arrangements you make are, of course, satisfactory to me.

I assume you'll have some definite agreement on paper before you sail for Europe,—Are you sailing?—and when?

Here are my plans at present—subject to change if you cannot possibly make yours coincide with them. I remain in London until April 20, when my lease expires. Then to Paris until about June 1st. Then I intend to take a seashore cottage either at Camom[?] (near Deauville) or Le Touquet. Myra and the children remain there until the last week in August, but I think I shall have to come back sometime between July 25 and August 15 to clear up things for Mariza[8] rehearsals which I understand are to start in September. If they are to start later I am willing to stay over longer if you want to.

Now then, if you are carrying out your original intention of coming over, I suggest it would be highly desirable for you to come before May 23 which is Louis Dreyfus's[9] date of sailing. Couldn't you precede your family

---

[7] *No, No, Nanette*, had had its London opening a few days prior on March 11. It had lyrics by Harbach and Irving Caesar, music by Vincent Youmans, and hit songs "Tea for Two" and "I Want to Be Happy."

[8] *Mariza* was a 1924 Viennese operetta with music by Emmerich Kálmán. Its American title became *Countess Maritza*. Oscar, Harbach, and Uncle Arthur did not adapt or produce the American production, which was presented by the Shuberts and opened on September 18, 1926.

[9] Louis Dreyfus and his older brother, Max, were music publishers, first with T. B. Harms, and later purchasing Chappell & Co. They became extraordinarily important in Oscar's life, with interests

and stop with me? I make this suggestion because we have no easy job ahead, adapting Mariza and getting well under way with "The Green Peach" as Arthur expects us to do this summer.

I suppose it is wasting time going on with the infinite variety of possibilities until I hear from you. My plans are still flexible and can be made to conform with yours — if you tell me immediately what you would like to do.

In any event, if you book passage, book return passage at the same time as it is almost impossible to get accommodation even now for return in the month of August — I have booked rooms on the "Paris" for Myra and the children on its last August trip. I am holding up my arrangements until I hear from you. So please let me know as soon as possible.

Remember me to Mrs. Harbach, Billy and Bobby —

Sincerely —

Oscar

P.S. Saw "Katza [*sic*], The Dancer"[10] which I believe Dillingham[11] was considering for adaptation. Nothing worth while adapting. Could easily originate a story to beat it. But it's a hit here, largely due to the fact that outside of Nanette there isn't a good show in town

O. H.

Oscar Hammerstein (in London) to Otto Harbach, April 10, 1925

Dear Otto:

Your news about Mariza was welcome. The more I thought about it the less attractive it seemed. A second rate management, a star who had already flopped, and all the foreign rights used up! To cap the climax, Max Dreyfus came along and told me if Hampton did it, it wouldn't have a chance. I was

---

both in the United States and England. They forged a relationship with Rodgers & Hammerstein's music publishing business, Williamson Music, and together produced shows in London.

[10] *Katja die Tänzerin* was an operetta that premiered in Vienna in 1922, and had its London premier as *Katja the Dancer* in February, 1925.

[11] Charles Dillingham was a major Broadway producer with shows from 1903 through 1934. He produced the Kern and Hammerstein musical *Sunny* (1926).

very much discouraged and was on the point of calling you to try to withdraw from the proposition when I received your letter.

I haven't done much on The Green Peach. I first wanted to get the air cleared for Mariza. Accordingly, I spent ten days after the Rose Marie opening, analyzing Mariza and preparing the enclosed outline. Of course this work was wasted, but I am sending it on to you anyway. If the man who is going to adapt it is a nice fellow, give it to him and let him make whatever use of it he can.

I sail May 29 and arrive June 6. In view of my early return I think it best to spend the rest of our time gathering miscellaneous data and collecting disconnected ideas for The Green Peach. I have got hold of lots of Russian books and am keeping all my notes. When I get back we can put our material together, eliminate what we don't want and put the rest into constructive form.

Rose-Marie has broken all London records for eight performances. Last week we did £ 5,306-

I'll phone you as soon as I get back –

Sincerely, --

Oscar

The following letter from Oscar to Otto planning their next show is among the most detailed we have on how their collaboration worked. No show materialized titled *The Green Peach*, but with its Russian background and setting it evolved into *Song of the Flame*, which would open in December 1925. They even share the lead character names Aniuta and Volodya. Despite that, the plot discussed below bears almost no relation to *Song of the Flame*—until the end of the letter when Oscar suddenly veers in another direction, proposing a plot that focuses on the Revolution, rather than an escape to America. Oscar's comments about the amount of research he's already done—having read fifteen books— seems extraordinary; it's hard to imagine another librettist at the time doing something similar. *Song of the Flame* is the one show for which Oscar collaborated with George Gershwin on the score, along with his regular collaborator Herbert Stothart. The only song from the score that seems to have any kind of ongoing life is "Vodka"—not because of any particular merit, but because the very fact of it is amusing.

Oscar Hammerstein (in Paris) to Otto Harbach, May 1, 1925

Dear Otto:

I think it's time I wrote something to you about The Green Peach, but I have no idea where to begin. On the few occasions we met and discussed it, we made many different starts. I took notes on all these and brought them along with me in a separate folio,=.....They don't match!

At one time, our little immigrant is a Spaniard, and she winds up in Southern California with Spanish atmosphere and lots of Melodrama. On cool reflection I am willing to concede that you can not extract novelty from Spain. No matter how much you try, you finish with a sombrero, a shawl and a tortoise shell comb, a couple of knives, a black moustache, and a pair of castanets. I don't think it can be done much better than you did it in Betty Lee, and all those costumes and Spanish threats of violence had a very usual and familiar feeling about them. I move we throw out the Spanish idea as so much Chili Con Carne.

Now then, comes a series of miscellaneous thots which, while they do not constitute a story, are nevertheless the approach to one, and are the things for us to be thinking over prior to our conferences in June. (I arrive June 4th).

During one of our talks, one of us mentioned Chauve Souris[12] and this opened the way to fine possibilities for Russian color and entertainment— the real Russian singing having been proved to be most effective wherever it has been tried—the Ed Wynn Revue for instance, and the gypsy singing in the first Chauve Souris. But it has never been done on a large scale. I remember telling this to Arthur and it appealed to him strongly. He declared his willingness to have two large choruses, Russian men and women, and American Girls. This sounds very "punchy" to me.

Working on this Russian idea, you and I developed the following beginning of a story which I have tried to glean from a confused jumble of notes:

The first scene was in a Russian village, time present. The heroine (Let us call her " Aniuta ", which by the way I consider a very pretty Russian

---

[12] Le Chauve-Souris was a very successful musical revue that originated in Russia, traveled to Paris, and then made its first American tour in 1922.

name) was the daughter of a noble or at least well-born family which had lost its standing in the Revolution. She had promised to marry a young peasant who had gone to the United States to make his fortune, and in a number there was a flashback insert showing the scene a year previous in which they had bid farewell. Meanwhile he has scraped together enough money to pay her passage in the steerage. She is going to America to join him in a tiny caretaker's lodge. He has found employment as a gardener on a big estate. (We'll call him Volodya, which is a nickname for Vladimir).

Her father, Boris (Gorsy) has never acknowledged in his heart the equality established by the Soviet government, and still harbors dreams of a return of power and ancestral estates. He would probably be mixed up in a royalist plot to put a Romanoff back on the throne. But we never went into this. Boris is by no means sympathetic with Aniuta's love affair with Volodya. He has ambitions in the direction of a rich American (Judson) who has taken a fancy to Aniuta. He is a kind of "young Otto Kahn" who is sponsoring an expedition of a troupe like the Chauvre Souris to America. Boris and Judson urge Aniuta to come with them in the first class at Judson's expense, but she prefers the steerage and Volodya waiting at the other end.

Then came three colorful, impressionistic scenes in "one" or "two". The first, a portion of the steerage deck, in which was raised the issue of some trouble about Aniuta's landing, due to a plot hatched by Boris and Judson, who stole her passports or something like that so as to make her acceptance at Ellis island dependent on the influence of Judson. The scene ended with a group of immigrants singing a song of hope as the statue of liberty, illuminated appears in the distance.

The next scene was a drop painted with confused impressions of an immigrant's dream of America. (This reminds me that when we were in Detroit you had a great idea of elaborating this into a scene after the manner of So This Is London, in which the reception of an immigrant at Ellis island should be played with the comic curtesy [sic] and generosity which the immigrant expects to receive, the Western hats, the Indians, the gumchewing, the money being thrown away, and all the illusions which the immigrant has about America, extracted mainly from American-made movies shown in their native lands).

Before this drop is a line of immigrants waiting to come before the immigration officer. They are being huddled about and yelled at and pushed around in a manner very different from the dream we have just seen. Aniuta is one of these. After we have achieved the general effect of confusion and bewilderment, fade out, and thru the darkness hear Aniuta's name called, and light up on a small insert scene, showing an immigration officer at a desk, and Aniuta standing before it. As he fires questions at her, she becomes excited and rattled. The room starts to go around. (Actually, the scene being on a small revolving platform) She stutters and sputters. He shouts something. It brings her out of her trance. The room stops going around. She answers his questions unsteadily. The result is that she is in a lot of trouble, and is in danger of being deported back to Russia. This prospect throws her into a panic, first because we shall have some reason why it is very dangerous for her to return to Russia, and second because she is so anxious to see her Voldya and she knows how heart broken he will be if he doesn't see her. Then Judson comes in with Boris and they place her in the dilemma of being able to come into America at Judson's option if she will consent to stay a certain time at his home with her father. She has the choice then of being sent miles away from her sweetheart or accepting a bargain that that will bring her nearer to him, and yet may be the means of establishing an impassable breach between them. But she takes this latter chance as being the only course open to her.

Then there was the scene where he was setting out to meet her in a new Sears-Roebuck suit, with a little bunch of wildflowers in his hand. She comes in with this merry bunch of wealthy people and bohemian members of the Russian troupe, and they pass on towards the big house at the back. Volodya stands alongside of his little rose-covered lodge house, with the flowers drooping in his hand, listening to the music, and watching silhouettes of dancing figures in the windows of the big house. Curtain. I get a little thrill from describing this last episode.

From there on we are extremely hazy. I remember we were considering the situation of Aniuta scoring a big hit with the troupe and becoming a prominent social figure drifting away from Volodya in spite of them both.

It seems a shame to attack this poor little undeveloped plot in its infancy, but for the sake of helping it grow I'll point out three faults.

First we have no finish. Do you think there is one? I am anxious to have our next show go uphill in the second act, instead of downhill, which Rose Marie most assuredly does. And as soon as we leave colorful Russia and go to Long Island, I feel we're on the toboggan. On the other hand it is difficult to get back to Russia with a full set of characters, and when you get them back you are confronted with a locale where the political and social confusion which actually exists in the country must be taken into consideration. I can not see a happy ending in leaving our hero and heroine in the unsettled Russia of to-day. There is this other possibility of maintaining a Russian atmosphere with a scene in a place like The Russian Eagle in New York or any number of Russian cafes in Paris (All of which I am attending). But here you have your second act restaurant scene which is so often fallen back upon by lazy authors who want dancing teams to do their work.

Second, we have no comedy sub-plot or comedy characters, so far.

Third, I have an instinctive fear that we will never get a real good reason why Aniuta is in Judson's power when it comes to being admitted to the United States. This side of the story has a faky feeling. And yet it would have to be our high spot, our main twist.

I merely submit these destructive comments to provoke thot and discussion and develop new values. I have not for a moment lost confidence in the general direction of our plans. I am convinced we are on very fertile ground. Don't you feel that we are?

Now I have travelled up another street, but I am afraid it is a blind alley. Since seeing you, I have read no less than fifteen books on The Russian Revolution. I was thinking of starting our story there and then combining it with our present one, which would be tacked on later, the arrival at Ellis Island being somewhere along the middle of Act II.

There is undoubtedly great drama wound up in the revolution. Volodya, could be one of the downtrodden peasants or workers, mistreated and tyrannized over by Aniuta's people, she alone treating him as if [he] were a human being. Then the revolution, and Volodya could be one of the leaders of the uprising. Aniuta is humiliated and enraged by a group of rough soldiers and peasants bursting into their palace, perhaps her bedroom and sacking the place, despoiling the treasures of her family home, and in their victorious lust going out of their way to insult the traditions which she reveres by instinct. And these are Volodya's people—and there is real conflict between two lovers - . . ..And I am sorry that I called this a blind alley in the foregoing paragraph, because, as I describe these possibilities they feel rife with genuine drama. What was in my mind in objection to this kind of story was the fear of tampering with political and social problems which are as yet undecided and seem too serious to sing about. Yet, if we stick to the emotional side and keep our problems personal rather than general, we may be able to avoid committing ourselves politically. Another objection, a minor one I think, is that the story would have to start in 1917 when the two revolutions took place. If you are interested in getting some first hand information, the best books I read were:

Six Red Months In Russia—Louis Bryant

The Russian Diary Of An Englishman—Anon.

A Week—Libedinsky

Through The Russian Revolution—Albert Rhys Williams.

I can see a corking satirical comedy character in an American girl who is in Russia—a typical nut radical full of revolutionary phrases like "the downtrodden masses", "the three horned toad, capital", "The people shall arise" etc. I have met any number of them. They do settlement work on the east side, and at night attend labor union meetings, and in the summer they go to foreign countries as representatives of labor organizations. You can imagine little Dorothy Mackaye[13] making stump speeches like these on the slightest provocation. And as a foil, her admirer can be a simple hick like Jack Donohue, who has followed her to Russia and is very sorry he did. He doesn't know what this radical stiff is about. He'd like to marry her and let it go at that, but she doesn't even believe in marriage—which shocks his old-fashioned, simple mind horribly. She is for the freedom of the sexes, and he thinks that the first sex that should be freed should be the males. He is scared to death at all the shooting and bombthrowing that's going on and always wants to go home. . . . .Two funny characters, I think—and easy to wind in with the main plot because of the girl's wild ideas which would involve them both in the very core of the revolution.

Well, there's that possibility. Make what you can of it. I'm so tired writing this letter that nothing I say from now on will have any sense to it.

If you get any ideas on these or other subjects I wish you would write. I sail May 29th and a letter mailed before the twentieth is sure to reach me.

---

[13] Dorothy Mackaye was an actress who had appeared in *Rose-Marie*. Oft-described as a femme fatale, she became part of a Hollywood scandal—a love triangle that ended in a murder.

If you are having occasional meetings with the rest of the Green Peach crowd, I leave it to your discretion to bring up the issues herein submitted.

I hated Paris my first day here, and now I am convinced it's the greatest place on earth.

Love to all,

Oscar

Throughout his career, Oscar evaluated shows by others, reading outlines and drafts of scripts and attending tryouts, previews, and finished productions. He did this for friends and colleagues to provide feedback and advice, and he did it for himself, seeking plays he might adapt as a musical, or plays or musicals he (and later with Rodgers) might take on as a producer. At the time of the letter below, *The Dybbuk* was about ten years old, but seems already to have established itself as a classic. Written by an S. Ansky, first in Russian then in Yiddish, the story of Jewish mysticism, possession, and separated lovers made appealing source material for many authors and composers over the years. George Gershwin considered it for an opera (unrealized) and Leonard Bernstein for a ballet (realized). Oscar's interest seems to presage both the seriousness of *Show Boat* and the operatic ambitions of *Carmen Jones*.

Oscar Hammerstein to Arthur Hammerstein, February 5, 1926

Dear Uncle Arthur:

In reference to The Dybbuk:

I saw the Yiddish version at the Bayes theatre. It does not vary much from the production at the Neighborhood Playhouse—better in some respects, not so good in others.

After seeing it a second time I am convinced more than ever that it would make a fine grand opera, and I am equally convinced that its commercial chances are small. The gloom and oppression which are an essential part of the play's spirit would limit the audience to art lovers and music lovers. These may constitute a sufficient number to give the play a long run in New York, but it is doubtful.

Otto and I are in accord in the opinions:

Our sentimental inclination would be to adapt the play because it would be interesting and enjoyable, and the absence of profitable prospects would not deter us if there [were] some compensating chances of prestige and glory. If the play is an artistic triumph the praise will go to the producer, the composer, Ansky who conceived it, Alsberg who did the already successful version, and Vardi whose direction is admittedly the life and soul of the piece. Otto and I will be away off in some little dark corner.

On the other hand—if something slips up, and the play does not win critical favor you know what they'll say. "Why did Arthur Hammerstein call in two musical comedy hackwriters to spoil this fine thing?"

In approaching such a job, we would want to cast aside all other plays, study up on Jewish lore and tradition, saturate ourselves with the atmosphere of the thing and leave nothing undone to make it perfect. But it is obvious that we have too little to gain to justify such a gamble.

I know that you will see that these are sincere reasons and not mere excuses.

Here's a suggestion: Offer Alsberg 2% and five hundred advance to do a musical version. Otto and I have some good ideas which I will gladly go over with him. If his version is bad you lose five hundred. If it is almost right, Otto or I, or both will be happy to jump in and do some work on it. If you feel like taking this flyer, I will attend to all necessary arrangements. Let me know soon because on February 13 I am sailing with Myra on the Paris. We are just going to spend a few days in Paris and London, returning home on the Majestic, March 3rd. I will see Wildflower in London but I'm afraid I'll miss the opening. Let me know if you want me to attend anything for you over there.

They are giving a good show at the Forty Fourth and business looks very healthy. We are a little off this week because of the worst snow tie up I've ever seen. I stayed in town two days because there was no certainty about Great Neck trains. I don't think the theatres got any trade from New Jersey, Westchester or Long Island. Nevertheless Grady has Herb so worried that he wants to quit the show. He comes to the theatre in good spirits, has a talk with Grady in the lobby and enters the pit a sick man.

I imagine I will be back in New York just about the time you are returning. Meanwhile, I hope you and Dorothy are enjoying your vacation.
Myra joins me in sending our love.

Sincerely,

Photo 4 Oscar Hammerstein and Dorothy Blanchard Jacobson (Hammerstein),
circa 1925. Photo courtesy of Oscar Andrew Hammerstein

After *Rose-Marie*, Oscar scored another hit with *The Desert Song* (1926) and the groundbreaking *Show Boat* (1927). *Show Boat*, with music by Jerome Kern, produced by Florenz Ziegfeld and based on the novel by Edna Ferber, was an adult musical that dealt with serious and difficult issues, including abandonment, alcoholism, and particularly racism and miscegenation. It wasn't only subject matter that distinguished it, but also how the songs were integrated into the script and how

Photo 5 Oscar Hammerstein and Dorothy Blanchard Jacobson (Hammerstein), shipboard, circa 1927. Photo courtesy of Oscar Andrew Hammerstein

specific they were to the characters that sang them. There had never been anything like it, and it would take sixteen more years before Oscar's experiments in *Show Boat* would be, not only repeated, but even more fully realized with *Oklahoma!*, and that would change the notion of musical theater forever. Unfortunately, I have found no significant Hammerstein correspondence contemporary to the original production of *Show Boat*, but there is much related to later productions.

As Oscar's career flourished, his marriage foundered. Myra was known to have had several affairs during their marriage, including one with Oscar's sometime collaborator, librettist Guy Bolton. While unhappy with the situation, Oscar seems to have resigned himself to the status quo. Until, that is, he met Dorothy Blanchard Jacobson. On March 2, 1927, Oscar embarked for England aboard the *S.S. Olympic*, preparing to direct the London premiere of *The Desert Song*. Before he set sail, Oscar's friend and lawyer, Howard Reinheimer, introduced him to a couple he knew who were also making the voyage, Dorothy and Henry Jacobson. As Oscar and Dorothy began to spend time together a love quickly blossomed.

After some difficulty, Oscar was able to persuade Myra to give him a divorce. Dorothy, too, was able to arrange a divorce from her husband. Although their agreement allowed her to take her infant daughter, Susan, with her, their two-year-old son, Henry, remained with his father. In order for Dorothy's divorce to happen as quickly and simply as possible, she took advantage of Nevada's liberal divorce laws that, among other things, provided the extraordinarily brief residency requirement of six weeks (some sources say three months). What follows are several remarkably passionate letters Oscar sent Dorothy while she was in Reno over the course of those six weeks. Although he refers to her as his "wife," it is an aspirational reference.

Oscar Hammerstein to Dorothy Blanchard Jacobson (in Reno, Nevada), February 15, 1928

Dear darling:

I hope it doesn't annoy you when I write with a pencil. I hate a pen. I don't feel as tho I'm quite myself with a pen.

I've put in a call for Chicago at eleven thirty (my time) and while I sit here waiting for it, I'm starting to write. You'll interrupt me, then I'll finish writing—

Before taking the train last night, I went down to the Ritz to meet Howard [Reinheimer]. He was at a wedding (Ell's cousin, by the way,—Jack

Widlberg[?]). I went up to the ballroom to see if I could spot him. They were all at dinner—three hundred I should think, and oh, the cackling! Howard was near the door, and I gave him the high sign. I had not dined, so he came into the main dining room to have his coffee with me. It was the room where you and I were the other night. A little fit of the gloom passed over me. What a poor incomplete thing I felt, sitting there in day clothes, eating my steak in a corner, and thinking how much more brilliant I had been three nights ago—sitting at a front table with a glorious lady in a white frock held up with devilishy provocative shoulder ends.

!!!

(Phone rings and voice says "Ready with Chicago: Confused young scribe drops pencil gingerly, tries to catch breath and yells, "Is that you, Dorothy?" Will not report conversation here, reader being as familiar with it as I.)

Howard and I discussed the movietone situation of Show Boat and a threatened plagiarism suit against us on the Desert Song—(Marjorie will wonder who'd want to steal such a thing). And we settled on how to send your money, and how to help Gertie double-cross you, and how to make separation agreements. And then I left him. I stopped at Grand Central to get a Chicago-Reno time table, and arrived at Penn Station one hour ahead of train time. Lucky for me it was. I had left my tickets home!

I burst into a torrent of expletives which would have done credit to your father on his bridge. Then I thot, "Come boy, Dorothy wouldn't like that much," and I stroked myself figuratively. But self-control did not win an immediate victory. I paced up and down and fermented myself a few dying splutters, then threw back my shoulders, and walked into the subway like a little major. When I got home I figured out a way of justifying the ridiculous delay by changing to my gray raincoat[?] and putting on a sweater jacket. "This will be much better to travel in," I thot. I almost felt clever.

Hurry call from the Alvin Theatre. Arthur [Hammerstein] very anxious to see me. He's paying my fare, and my lodging—and telephone calls. I suppose the decent thing to do is to be nice to him.

I'll continue this diary on the train to-night.

Good-bye for a little while, dear wife.

Oscar Hammerstein to Dorothy Blanchard Jacobson (excerpt), (Reno, Nevada), January 22, 1929

I am glad you feel as I do about never leaving each other. You say you are dead without me. I must steal your thunder and say, so am I—or if I don't die, I change my soul to that of a busy young man who seems the logical successor to the Shuberts.

If we didn't have many beautiful reasons for being together, the economy of it alone would be a strong argument—Reno calls ranging from thirty to a hundred odd dollars, weeks on the road averaging a hundred and fifty a week in phones. Do you know our phone bill for the year, my baby? About three thousand dollars.

But when I think that within two months we shall at last be together for good, and never leave each other's sides for the rest of our lives, this looks like the best of all possible worlds. Dear, we must literally keep the rule of never spending a single night away from each other—even when it involves inconveniences. I mean that until the mineys [?] become eighty, there will be several occasions arise when the male [?] might be required to make sudden overnight business trips, or double tracking across the channel, etc. On such occasions, the physical comfort of the female miney [?] is not to be considered. She must stick to the male and make the trip which is very useless to her. Or if she won't, then the business can just go to hell. Anyway, either her comfort, or my business will always have to give way to the iron-clad rule that one must never awake in the morning without seeing the other there. Nothing is so important, my darling mate. That is why I get so angry when you talk about going on boats at different times and spending whole weeks apart. It's wrong. It's wrong. It's wrong!

I am taking your coat to Joy Thurpes [sic] to be Netherlanded—or was it Austerlanded: I hate to see it go. It looks so nice hanging in the closet next to my things. It always creates the illusion that you are very near, and likely to walk into the room at any moment, and put it on. While it's away, could you send me another old coat that you don't need?

I've been away from "Old Broadway" so long that I am quite thrilled by the activity I have barged into and to realize again how 'portant I evidently am. I know you are unsympathetic with that side of me, but with all my good resolutions about only doing two shows a year, when I see Ziegfeld, or Arthur, or Frank, and they talk of plots, and possible actors and actresses to engage, and where to get the scenery painted, and when I hear Kern, or Gershwin, or Romberg play pretty tunes to me, I start to race ahead breathlessly with the possibilities behind each suggestion. Even if I didn't get any money for it, I'd want to meddle in everything, and get ideas, and watch for the way they hit audiences in their final form. There is no such fun as dabbling with plays before they are produced. They all sound marvelous. My ambition is to be a great artist, but of course, I was born a trouper. Don't worry about me, darling. I won't let one thing stand in the way of the other. I'll make them both work together. My dream is to make the fortune which seems to be piling into my lap (and I've been snubbing that opportunity a little too much lately), and then to settle down to a beautiful life with my beautiful girl, and aim only to write masterpieces, or nothing. It will be lovely if some of them are masterpieces, and if they're not, I'll still be the happiest man in the world. Oh God, how lucky I am. You dear, dear, dear darling prize. I love you so much this minute, that all my veins seem bursting, and I want to cry again. Dear, dear, dear!.....Fly away, month, and bring my wife back to her husband,

Oscar –

Oscar Hammerstein to Dorothy Blanchard Jacobson (excerpt), (Reno, Nevada), circa January 22, 1929

My darling Dorothy:

You were such a dear this afternoon, standing back in a corner of your train platform, looking over Marjorie's shoulder with those sweet, sad eyes. I was proud that they were sad for me. It is uplifting to know that such a beautiful goddess can care so much for a mortal even when he adores her as reverently as I do. You have punctuated the last two years of my life with many, beautiful, breath-taking moments. This afternoon adds to the string. I will never forget kissing you good-bye. I felt so tender, so protective that I didn't dare yield to that funny impulse I have to cry about you. You were being so brave and I knew every word you weren't saying. Oh, Thank God for you and the beauty you bring to me.

As we walked down the platform, Albert said he had just known the sweet sorrow of parting. Like most men in love, I resented another man presuming to approach the outskirts of romance, and I murmured some light comment to the effect that I had stolen the line that follows "Parting is such sweet sorrow", i.e. "Let us say good-night 'til it be morrow"; and written a song in "Sunny" called "Let's Say Good-night 'til it's morning," thereby desecrating the king of all bards. Albert and I then exchanged the usual promise to ring up and have "lunch some time," and I sauntered along with my own thots toward my lawyer's office.

Things were all right there.

Then I walked slowly up to my own office—and in spite of the ache I felt at your leaving I was, (and am now) fundamentally happy—I know a grand fact—I love you and you love me. I just imagine that this emptiness now is only natural- I have voluntarily taken my heart from it's assigned place, sent it out on the twentieth century towards Nevada where it will be nourished as careful and tenderly as Susan will be, and then, in eleven days, I'll get it back all bright and beautiful!

At the office I was met by a young man from Kennilworth who has a prospective purchaser in tow. I hope something comes of it.

Bill McGuire came in. I assured him I was not being high hat, but thot if I worked on "East is West" with him, the show would be a secondary consideration to my personal affairs. To my surprise he said he knew all about my situation, and was in entire sympathy with it. Ziegfeld had told him what I had revealed in strict confidence.

Oscar Hammerstein to Dorothy Blanchard Jacobson (Reno, Nevada), circa January, 1929

My darling Dorothy:

I love you.

I have longed for you so these past three days that I now have a feeling of exhaustion. I am trying to calm down now and wait. I am trying to take hold of myself. Our letters and phones throw us off our chronology, so I must explain that I am writing this letter Friday morning. Yesterday was the first day I did not phone—the day we exchanged three telegrams, mostly in "verse." Darling, I am weak. Don't tell anyone, but I am. If I lost you, I would go to pieces. I've often told you I wouldn't. I feel now that I would. It is two weeks since I left you. Dear, dear, darling, it hasn't been like leaving another person. It has been like "Sawing a man in two". I feel crippled, out of breath, panic-stricken lest I suffocate. Here I am with my guard down, and I confess that I can not do anything without you. My soul's existence depends on you. Believe me, and don't put the usual discount on a lover's protestations. As a matter of fact, there is no essential admiration involved in the dependence. It is just a fact which I state without being able to explain it. When I miss you, I don't say to myself "Oh, I wish I were with her because she is so beautiful, -- or because she is so sweet." I do sometimes say those things, but they do not represent the grip you have on me which hurts me so. The thing I refer to feels almost physical—like the silver chord which binds a mother and child. There is a golden chord which ties me to you, and the longer we are parted, the more it stretches—and hurts me. I feel a vague, but real pain. That is why I cannot sleep—or even work very well. My yearning is the same physical handicap to me as any bodily illness would be. For God's sake, don't say, "There, there, you mustn't be like that, you must get some sleep, and do your work," I can't. Your advice to conquer it would be as annoying as a Christian science healer telling me I had two arms if I had one cut off. Many ills are imaginative. This one is not. And as for work dear, I am not a man who visits his office daily and makes common sense decisions. If I am to do anything worth while it must originate with the heart, and that at the moment is pumping along on one cylinder, with just enough fuel left to last out the next two weeks. How can any real accomplishment result? I know you must think I am dramatizing this. No one can know as I do what a wretched incomplete protoplasm this thing is without its mate, its life force. I had plenty of life force before I met you. I still have it, but most of it is stored in you, now. I don't carry it all within myself. It's like a rich man who can't get at his cash. Oh, my dear, I am not afraid of having my life in your hands. You love me, and you will be kind to me. But you see, it is hell to be away from you.

Your poor darling,

Oscar, The Helpless.

Oscar Hammerstein to Dorothy Blanchard Jacobson
(Reno, Nevada), February 6, 1929

Dearest Girl: This is Tuesday. Last night's telephone call left me depressed again. Once more I felt there was an underlying antagonism in you. When you asked me to bring on your golf clubs, I started to say it would hardly be worth while because you would only have about two weeks after I left, but you didn't even let me finish. You broke in and you said "You're quite right, I can borrow them [?] out here." I hate to be told I'm quite right in saying what I haven't said, and I HATE to be jumped on quickly. I know you can say I'm silly about these things, and even prove to me that I am. But I am inclined to be impressed by my intuitions, and I feel I can always tell when you're all poised for a fight. Oh God, how I worry about you. What a weakling I seem. I've plunged everything on one horse—shot the works on one roll—and of course I watch it anxiously.

I know that in these vague complaints I haven't a leg to stand on. My suspicions are far fetched for a lack of logical bases, but there they are—those instincts that now and then I annoy you with all my love-sick mooning. I don't suppose I can blame you. I'm just not clever enough to stop.

Maybe everything will be all right when we are together. If it is, we shall be romantic Olympians in a world of literal mortals. Oh, let us be that, my Goddess---or nothing. Don't let us be just another married couple.

On my way to school with the children this morning, the traffic signal stopped us in front of the Gotham. Lovely memories, sweet dreams that were hopeless. Now they are not hopeless. Let us live them as we dreamed them.

Darling little Dorothy I mean every wild extravagant thing I've ever told you. I love you with a broad sweep and adoration which I generate with my heart's pulse, and keep it stored up to shower on a Goddess. No woman can take all that. If you are a woman, you leave me with more surplus love than I can hold, and I feel ready to burst, and think it would be as well to die.

I am preparing a banquet of love and happiness for the most lovely guest I know. Don't send me someone in your place for whom a Reuben's sandwich would have sufficed. Come to me in your glory, with graceful robes on your fine, straight back, and your soul that I think the counterpart of my soul shining from your clear, blue eyes. Come to me as I've dreamed of you, and I'll warrant I shall be as you have dreamed of me—or long ago of a man you had never met. Come to me that way, and give me my chance to make it worth your while. And the viands, and the fruits, and the spices we enjoy, and the wine of passion which we drink in deep ecstatic draughts will be sweet to us both, and always, I hope, served to us in dishes and goblets of purest gold. But the highest expression of our union will be those peaceful hours when I hold you in a gentle embrace, silent, contented hours of understanding. I will have my arms around you, and your head will be on my shoulder, and from my eyes, joyful tears of gratitude to God shall well up, and fall down my cheek on to your hair. And you will kiss me on my heart, and we shall think beauty . . . Let us, all our lives.

Your lover

Oscar Hammerstein to Dorothy Blanchard Jacobson (excerpt), circa February, 1929

I have sad news about London Show Boat. The King's illness and the Flu combined were not enough. Mrs. Lee Ephraim[14] steps into the picture. While her husband is in America, she goes over the manuscript and songs of The New Moon with Evelyn Laye, and sends out a notice in the Daily Mail that she is to be the next Prima Donna at the Drury Lane. Edith,[15] whom I don't blame a bit, jumps higher than the tower of London. Her boy friend, Homer, practically owns the Daily Mail, and the next day a much larger column announces that Miss Day has given 1700 performances at the Lane, and is naturally very tired, and at her doctor's orders is going to Madeira [?] for a very long rest. Next day she goes. Naturally the show is knocked flatter than a pancake. The meddlesome Ephraims have cost us all thousands of dollars loss on Show Boat, and hastened the necessary production of New Moon so that neither Larry or I can get over to help. It will probably—with other things added—cost Ephraim his directorship in the United Company. I hope it does. He is a fawning old maid, always professing special friendship for you, and vilifying his own partners.

The next time I come out I may have special research on another show. Frank and I have been discussing the romance of the Mackays and other lowly people finding silver in Nevada, and rising so in two generations that the son thinks the grand-daughter too good to marry a songwriter with only a few million. (Without of course doing the cheap thing of being close enough to the Berlin story to be recognizable). Frank's father and mother kept a store in Virginia City, and tho Mrs. Mandel liked the older Mrs.

[14] Mrs. Lee Ephraim was Irene Wilhelmina Bell, stage name Mademoiselle Renée.
[15] Edith Day starred on Broadway in *Irene* (1919) (which she then opened in London), and Hammerstein's *Wildflower* (1932); she then returned to London where she starred in *Rose-Marie* (1925), *The Desert Song* (1927), and *Show Boat* (1928).

Mackay, she couldn't afford to be too friendly with a woman who took in washing. Isn't that funny? I didn't realize the time was so short—and what an ass Clarence Mackay really is.

Of course the social angle would not be our story—merely a side-light. We really want to write a sort of "Milestone"[?] play dealing with the far west, California and Nevada from 1870 thru three periods to the present day.

Most of the salt has come out of what started to be the Salem story, and I have shifted my scene mainly to New York in the late nineties. I will surely do a sea story, and keep some of my material for another play. I know this shift was necessary if I want a hit with Jerry.

I do get angry when you suggest my sailing on to London with you following. Please stop talking about it. It makes me think you prefer it, and that makes me wild. Oh, Christ, I wish we were married. . . . I have a "header" - - - I hope your telegram is sweet today. Sadly, longingly, I love you.

Oscar

Clarence Mackay grew up in great wealth, his father having been one of three partners in a mining corporation that discovered the Big Bonanza in Virginia City, Nevada, the largest deposit of gold and silver ever found. Clarence Mackay's primary career was as chairman of the board of the Postal Telegraph and Cable Corporation and president of the Mackay Radio and Telegraph Company. Mackay's daughter, Ellin, fell in love with the songwriter Irving Berlin, whom she married in 1926. Mackay was horrified that Ellin, a Roman Catholic debutante, would marry a Russian-born, Jewish immigrant, widower, fifteen years her senior. For a time he disowned her. Mackay lost his fortune in the 1929 stock market crash, which likely contributed toward a rapprochement with his daughter and son-in-law, who remained wealthy despite the crash.

Oscar Hammerstein to Dorothy Blanchard Jacobson, circa February, 1929

Darling baby, I got your letter of last Tuesday this morning. It is almost the nicest one you've ever written to me, because of a few simple statements, to wit: "oh dear, I wish I didn't love you so much." (I know you're very glad you do)—and then "I know you love me so I won't worry about it any more."

Oh, my sweet, I do love you. I do, I do, I do. I'm glad you know it. Always re-member it. Later you say, "I will love you and follow you and be happy with you, whatever you do." That _is_ the loveliest, dearest thing you've ever said my own Ruth, and please carry it out literally, and go whither I go and we'll never have anything but happiness. Cast aside all doubts about whether it is well for us to be in London, or Hollywood, or Melbourne. We will love each other any where.

You must have known what a nice, dear letter it was for you closed by saying "I hope this makes you happy darling"—It does, my Dorothy—and you add: "I want to live with you forever and be your wife and everything exciting and comforting" Exciting and comforting - Shakespeare couldn't have written a more eloquent epitome of all that a wife should be. And as for me, dearest girl, I am not only looking forward to the happy future with the wild heart beats of a demented lover, but I am also deliberately preparing to be a good husband. Every day, many times a day I think of things I'll do to make you happy and make you feel like the queen you were born to be. I can't give you the worldly throne you may have dreamed of when you were a kid, but I will create one more beautiful than any throne of plush and gold could possibly be. You will grace a seat of adoration. I will be-come more specific in my proof that your throne will be finer than any the Prince of Wales can offer you; Instead of a red plush cushion to sit on, you have my lap, and instead of two gold arms to rest on, you will have my arms around you. And instead of a crown of diamonds, you will feel my lips on your head. There is beautiful carving on most golden thrones, and for that I offer a hundred little daily attentions. The red carpet which you tread on as you mount the steps of your dais, is my humility and eagerness to keep your lovely feet free from the shocks of marble floors—the world's inexo-rable hardness. Your scepter is the complete power you have over my heart, and no ruler ever enjoyed such unquestioned control. It is not qualified by a Magna Carta or a Bill of Rights. You are sole despot of my destiny. (Please be a benevolent one, and I shall never rebel). I shall be your court Jester and make you laugh, not only because it is my business to amuse my queen but also because her laugh is the loveliest music in our kingdom, and makes the Jester more joyous than his audience.

I shall of course perform the functions of the Palace guard, as no palace guard ever dared perform this function. For even if the queen sees fit to grant an audience to a visiting Prince, the guard will veto her command, and jolly well throw the prince in the moat if he seeks to gain entrance. And even if the queen desire to leave the palace and walk in the forest alone, nevertheless, the persistent guard will be tagging along, his armor clanking in her ears—irritating them perhaps. But in the end she will always forgive this over zealousness of a guard who is also such a devoted lover. I am crying.

. . . . . I have asked myself what made me cry. I think it is because I know you are in truth a queen. I can not see you as the successor to Queen Mary with a hat, or Queen Marie with a smart hat. You are the embodiment of all the beautiful medieval queens. Your hat is a real crown, and your proper dresses are flowing robes. Even these Guineveres and what nots seem dross beside you. You are more nearly expressed by some of the ladys in the realms of Hans Christian Andersen and Grimm. I know that I am to you, all the surroundings of such an unreal darling. You are the definite vision, and I, lacking a clear cut beauty of that kind, sort of work my way in and around the picture wherever there is space. I am at once a King, and a servant—a jester, a palace guard, a lady in waiting, a knight, a worshipful page, a clandestine lover, all the subjects in the realm, your prime minister, your captive, your gaoler—all these things am I—and yet, only your background. You—you are the real beautiful queen. This is true. It is not true that you are an attractive Mrs. Jacobson who is getting divorced to marry a librettist. That is a dream that a dull world has imagined out of its limited brain. Really you are the lovely Dorothea IV of Hilthegorde, and I am your realm. That, my sweet, is the secret fact that is known only to you, and to me, the people of Hilthegorde. (What a name)

Every morning I have been starting a letter to say certain things, and I never get around to them. I don't know as they are very important. I think I've covered some of the material in our phone conversations. I won't bother about them now, I will stick to the important thing—Bill Mellen. As one who has been disposed to resist the intrusion of another man who has the nerve to adore you—in no matter what way—I must stand up and acknowledge that this man is a real man. In the three short letters you have shown me he has not used one superfluous word, and every word he has used has weight. I am certain, without ever having met him, that he is worth while knowing—and there are few men whom I have met that I can describe thus. You must be proud, as I am, of his confidence in you. I will at the same time admit that a selfish side of me resents his presence in your life, and mail.

However worthy he may be, I can not allow his proprietary and protective interest to have too much sway, nor can I permit you to be subject to it. It is all very beautiful for you to have such a friend, but he'll have to stay in his place, and it must be a comparatively small place. And much as I admire him, I will not hesitate to let him know where he stands, and where I stand—I don't care how many men he's thrown off railroad trains. I am saying these unpleasant things to prevent more unpleasant things in the future. It is largely up to you to behave as my wife first, and his friend second, the first time we meet. I am not going to sit in the background while you two talk over old times. He says "all husbands—semi ex—or otherwise are perfect asses." Well, if he thinks that about this one, he'd better not show it—or he's <u>out</u>! I want you to understand that.

He objects to Henry on the count of not being heavy enough. He may find me absolutely ponderous. You see dear, I know he is in love with you. I know he is not conscious of it. But his flippant comment on husbands is a give-away. And at the end of his letter after wishing that there is "love aplenty in store for you, and that happiness will come to you soon" he adds,

Don't think me a nagger dear. I love you. I am jealous. All the other men in the world must be specks. If they grow to blots, they must be stamped out. That's my platform. If you vote for me, you vote for that policy. Please don't forget that—and don't forget I love you to the exclusion of all else. I want us to give each other EVERYTHING—or the show's no good.

Your uncivilized husband, Oscar.

Oscar Hammerstein to Dorothy Blanchard (excerpt), April 6, 1929

Scene: A Deserted Observation car.

Time: Later that night.

My beautiful self:

That sounds like Narcissus. But it is rather the address of that self of me which seeks beauty, to another self which is the embodiment of beauty; and tho the one "seeking self" is in my body, and the other "beautiful self" is in yours, yet do I possess both selves, for you have drawn unto you an humble mortal—or should I say, "a mortal"?—and you have merged your beauty with his adoration. On the face of it, I get the better of the trade. Indeed the only justification for me is that beauty unadorned and unloved, is no beauty at all. So, beauty, since your importance depended on a lover, you took one. And it was I you took. And whether that be due to the whim of chance or the will of God, or the accident of chemistry—I thank the force.

You and your peach colored bed-sheets, and your peach colored nightie and jacket—you and your soul-filling blue eyes, and your thick chestnut hair—you and your shoulders that are always passively asking to be kissed, as meadows ask (without speaking or moving) for raindrops from a passing cloud. And if your shoulders are meadows, and the raindrops you seek are kisses—then here is a cloud that will never pass, having been sent by nature to hover over you always and shower you with as many osculatory storms as are good for meadows—maybe more than are good for meadows.

Oscar Hammerstein to Dorothy Blanchard (excerpt), circa April, 1929

Yesterday I went over the first act[16] with Jerry. I read it to him, and discussed in on the way, and we solved several problems. But by the time I had come to the curtain, I was absolutely exhausted. It is a terrific strain to me to read a play. Jerry is very enthusiastic about it, and gets all the effect I am striving for. I do like to work with him. I know other good showmen, but when they have an opinion they express themselves so awkwardly that you have to puzzle out what they are driving at. Jerry is an intelligent analyst who can give clear reasons. This lightens my burden considerably. He has some lovely tunes—one in particular which I can already hear being thumped by the troubadours in the Jungle Club and The Lido. I hope I can match it with a lyric.

We knocked off work at five and went out fishing again. This time I caught another Sail Fish—bigger than the other. Old time fishermen of the Florida coast are wagging their heads and saying it is "unnat'ral" for a mere tyro to land two Sail Fish on his first two days out. As soon as I pull them in I feel like phoning you about it. It would be lovely to put down the rod, and

---

[16] The show being discussed is almost certainly *Sweet Adeline*, which opened on Broadway on September 3, 1929. Two of the songs from the score became standards, both introduced by Helen Morgan: the torchy "Why Was I Born?," and the lovely "Don't Ever Leave Me," which Oscar dedicated to Dorothy.

rub my aching arms and hands and turn to get a kiss from you,—maybe you would even kiss the aching hands—that would be lovely.

Oh, my sweet, we're going to be so happy. Just a little wait now, and then we shall really be born—to live the prettiest life in history. Good-bye my dear, dear, dear.

Your lover always—Oscar.

Oscar and Dorothy married on May 14. They moved to Los Angeles in the fall.

Chapter Two
1930 through 1936

Seven films opened in 1930 to which Oscar made significant contributions. Six of the films were adaptations of Oscar's stage musicals and operettas: *Song of the West* (based on *Rainbow*), *The Three Sisters*, *The Song of the Flame*, *Golden Dawn*, *Sunny*, and *New Moon*. *Viennese Nights* was an original screenplay and therefore truly Oscar's "first picture" as noted in the letter below. Produced by Warner Bros. and Vitaphone under the personal supervision of Jack L. Warner, the screenplay and lyrics were by Hammerstein, with music by Sigmund Romberg. The story begins with a love triangle that ends with the wrong couple paired. But the film spans three generations, from 1879 to 1930, and the youngest descendants resolve the mismatch of their grandparents—whose ghosts disappear happily into the ether.

It's not clear how and when Oscar and Howard Reinheimer met, though Hugh Fordin describes them as "boyhood friend[s]." They both went to Columbia law school, but Reinheimer was four years younger, so it's unlikely they crossed paths as fellow students. Reinheimer would prove of incalculable importance to Oscar, as friend, as client and lawyer, and, to some degree, as business partner. Later, with the unparalleled success of Rodgers and Hammerstein as a writing and producing team, Reinheimer not only negotiated on their behalf, but virtually invented several aspects of show *business*. Reinheimer's client list included Jerome Kern, Irving Berlin, Alan Jay Lerner, Mary Martin, Moss Hart, and George S. Kaufman.

Oscar Hammerstein to Howard Reinheimer, March 5, 1930

Dear Howard:

Supplementing my other letter, about adjustments of expenses with Rommy, there was one hundred and seventy five dollars more laid out for presents by me. (That is in addition to the other sums I mentioned in my last letter on this subject.) In addition to Rommy's other claims against my account is one half of the price of a supper we gave the cast at the Embassy Club. I hope all this high finance will not be too complicated for you. Remember that whatever the cost is, you will owe my personal domestic

The Letters of Oscar Hammerstein II. Mark Eden Horowitz, Oxford University Press. © Mark Eden Horowitz 2022.
DOI: 10.1093/oso/9780197538180.003.0002

account out here, whatever I have laid out. We will adjust all that when I come back. I shall probably phone you the day of my arrival in Frisco, altho' I expect to be in New York about a week later.

Neither by phone, nor mail, nor wire, have I properly expressed to you the extent of the good feeling and cooperation which featured our first picture. It is impossible to say whether it will be a popular success but it was surely a success in the taking. There is no question but that we have made a big hit with everyone, from the assistant prop boy up through Crosland, Koenig,[1] Zanuck[2] and Warner. It is also equally certain that they have made a hit with me.

About ten days ago, Koenig sounded me out on how I would feel about supervising all the musical productions of both First National and Warner's, when they move the whole business over to the First National lot. I was non-committal and implied that the whole question, of picture business to me, was a matter of money but I found the work very pleasant and satisfying. The remaining question was to find if I could make as much money here as I can in New York. Of course Koenig was careful to say that this was his own idea and that it did not come from Warner and that he merely wanted to know if it were worth while to mention the idea to Warner. This may have been true or it also may have been diplomacy. Nothing has been said about the matter since and I regard it as premature feeling out without very much importance attached to it. I just mention it to you because I believe it is well for you to be informed of everything that is in the wind. I am giving you a rough idea of my attitude in case the matter ever comes up before you and it is this; in the first place I doubt whether they would pay enough money to claim all my time for a full year this is, in the form of a salary. I would hesitate to relinquish the gambling chance of making more than any set sum that it would necessarily be confined to, and I am most anxious, in fact determined, to keep my identity as an author. I would always have to have time to write at least one original work of my own every year, in addition to what ever administrative duties such a job would entail. As I said before, this is still in a very nebulous state and scarcely worth speaking about at this date. I only thought it would interest you to know that the far off echoings

[1] Koenig is likely Ben Koenig, who became a producer and later an attorney for the Film Censors Board.

[2] Darryl Zanuck was in management at the studio and became head of production the following year.

of such a contingency should have arrived so soon. Rommy knows nothing of my talk with Koenig.

To make up for my previous lack of communication regarding our pleasant association our [*sic*] here, Leighton will be back in about nine days, to grossly exaggerate it for you. I recommend a discount of about forty five percent and then you will get a fair idea of conditions as they really are.

Our love to Elly and yourself from Dorothy and me.

In this letter to Harbach, Oscar recounts his experiences with the filming of *Viennese Nights* to help Harbach prepare for his own upcoming Hollywood adventure, presumably the film version of their show *Sunny*.

Oscar Hammerstein to Otto Harbach, Spring 1930

Dear Otto

Please excuse the pencil and the familiar yellow paper. I am on the set writing this between "takes."

Rommy has written a long letter to Jerry giving him all the low down on what a composer must prepare for out-here. So, not to be out done by composers, I thot I'd better do the same for you.

The first thing to tell you is that there is not much to tell—no mystery, nothing new, the same story requirements in this medium as on the stage which of course, you could figure out for yourself.

One difference is the length. They don't want it to run more than one hour and forty-five minutes. My manuscript in its cut state—the one from which we are producing—runs 82 pages—dialogue, description and all lyrics included. I think it is almost the right length. Therefore, you must stick right on your main story giving only the scantiest, fragmentary strokes to any sub-plot or secondary characters you may have.

I think it is dangerous to let your dialogue run over two pages for any one scene. There may be times, I suppose when the exigencies of your story require you to break this rule. I just say it is dangerous—that's all.

The magic word "set-up" is something you must learn about. A set-up is the arrangement of cameras, lights, and microphones before you take the picture. It takes them anywhere from a half hour to an hour and a half to prepare. This eats up most of your time during the day. When they told me that five minutes of play was a great day's work, I couldn't believe it. But I didn't realize that the bulk of the time consumed was in mechanical preparation rather than dramatic or musical.

There is sometimes more than one set-up for a very short scene. If your characters are grouped in one part of a set-up your natural direction takes them up stage almost ten feet. That will necessitate two vitaphone[3] set-ups. Here is an example—I have a girl, and her father and her sweetheart stepping out of a carriage. They have just returned from the opera. Out on the sidewalk, the father thanks the young man and leaves the young couple alone—about three lines. It took about an hour to set three cameras on that scene, catching the full picture and two close ups, light the scene properly and also arranging the lights so that the shadow of the overhanging microphone would not be visible. The microphone had to be set properly so that we would get good recording. Before actually taking the scene we played it, and then heard it on a wax record, so we would be sure it would sound perfectly before we wasted film on it (Technicolor film costs .41¢ a foot)— about one hour and forty-five minutes to catch their three lines.

Then the girl and boy walk up to the door—ten feet away—the width of a sidewalk. The vitaphone in the first set up could not be stretched over there, so we had to hang another one over the door to catch the three additional lines that passed between the two young people—another set up— another hour and a half of preparation, experiment in sound, and retakes. Three hours for six speeches! You retake a scene anywhere from once to seven times. So many things can go wrong—after all the preparation—a scene concerning three people has the possibility of any one of those performers going up in his lines, or giving a word or delivery you don't like, there can be something wrong with the recording, a film might buckle in the camera. After every "take" you have to wait about fifteen minutes before taking it again. It takes them that time to re-line, get the "A.C." (alternating current) and synchronize the record with the film.

You mustn't misunderstand what I mean by the necessity of making different vitaphone set-ups for scenes that take place within ten feet of each

---

[3] Vitaphone was a method of recording for film using discs as opposed to having the audio as part of the film itself. It was used by Warner Bros. and its sister studio, First National from 1926 to 1931.

other. It doesn't mean your characters must stand in one place all the time. The microphone is held out on a long pole by a man on top of the camera booth, and he moves it around, following the characters. But he doesn't command a radius of much more than eight to ten feet lee-way for movement—and besides if the camera is too far from the microphone you will see it in the picture. The long shots you see are taken without a microphone. That is you make a record without photographing—a "wild" record they call it. Then you play the record on the set, and the chorus and characters synchronize their movements and lips to the record as you photograph them—a "wild" shot.

Glancing over this letter, I am half sorry I wrote it because it may only mix you up. Perhaps I am just showing off my newly acquired technical knowledge. Well, if you don't understand, don't bother about it, because it is not really important to your method of approach in writing your story.

This may help you. You know how we fear to have six or seven characters in a scene on the stage because it is so difficult to keep them all alive during the scene. It's a cinch here. You just cut to close-ups of them when they talk, and cut away from them when they are not interesting, and show a shot of the other scene characters. That is why we have four cameras all taking the same scene at once, trained on certain characters individually and as a group.

I hope you have a simple story with motives that do not require explaining—a few numbers, well plugged and with—well, nothing different from our usual problems except brevity. There's no room at all for a scene that is purely atmosphere. It <u>must</u> be plot and the atmosphere will have to work itself in incidentally.

The lyrics came out beautifully over the orchestra. Every word is heard—never missed. But this is only in duets and solos. The chorus singing is foggy as it is on the stage.

I am so glad you will be out her about the same time I am. Dorothy and I return from Australia May ninth, and save for a quick trip to New York to see the kids, we will be out here from that time until September fifteenth. I hope we can see a great deal of each other. I want you and Ella to know Dorothy better and find out how lovely she is.

Remember me to my friends, Billy and Bobby. And my kindest regards to Ella and yourself.

Sincerely

Oscar

Photo 6 Otto Harbach

Throughout his career, Oscar had a defensive streak about the short shrift generally given lyricists and librettists. In the case of *Ballyhoo of 1930* (starring W. C. Fields), he mostly comes to the defense of others—librettists and lyricists Harry Ruskin and Leighton Brill, and composer Louis Alter. Oscar did pen the lyrics for two songs, one of which is the uncharacteristically provocative, "I'm One of God's Children (Who Hasn't Got Wings)," which includes this rather startling (for Hammerstein) couplet:

> I just want a sweet accommodatin' man to have a sip o' gin with.
> Then we'd have some lovin' 'cause the gin would just be somethin' to begin with.

In Brooks Atkinkson's review he wrote: " 'Ballyhoo' is an uninspired carousel with a score that is reminiscent when it is not flat and a book that no one could ignite with merriment."

Oscar Hammerstein to Brooks Atkinson, *New York Times*, December 21, 1930

My dear Mr. Atkinson:

I think the melodies in "BALLYHOO" are exceptionally strong. You say they are reminiscent. This disturbs me because I hadn't thought they were.

"THROW OUT THE WINDOW" is, of course, a frank paraphrase on a children's song called "GO IN AND OUT THE WINDOW" and is intentionally reminiscent. Outside of this I don't know of any other melodies in the show, which are open to that charge.

Knowing that your criticisms are never carelessly written, I am sure you will be able to tell what earlier tunes are recalled to you by those in "BALLYHOO." Will you take the trouble to make me a list of these songs? Choosing melodies is an important part of my work and I do not like to think I am getting a tin ear. ~~That is why I should be very interested to hear your views.~~

Very truly yours,

Oscar Hammerstein to Brooks Atkinson, *New York Times*, December 27, 1930

Dear Mr. Atkinson:

Thank you very much for your letter. I don't agree with any part of it but that is beside the point. I have a vaguely pleasant feeling of coming closer to a critical mind—a type of mind, which God knows, seems pathetically far away on mornings after my opening nights.

When I can get rid of the tenacious cold that has kept me in bed all week, I should like to have lunch with you some day and find out what you like in the musical play. Please forgive me for being so in earnest about such a trivial subject but somebody ought to be.

Before closing the subject on the "BALLYHOO" score, may I suggest that your impression of having heard music like this before is due, not so much to a recurrence of earlier melodic strains as to repetition of orchestra effects used again and again for dance rhythms in shows and cabarets and over the radio? I believe that you can take ten distinct melodies and, ironing them out under the proper combination of saxophone, clarinet and drum, make them all sound alike. Could go on and on about this but I think I'll put on the brake.

  Sincerely,

Florenz Ziegfeld was the most famous producer, impresario, theater-builder of his day; best known for his lavish, somewhat scandalous, annual *Ziegfeld Follies*. If anyone took on the mantle of Oscar Hammerstein I, it was the similarly flamboyant Ziegfeld. *Show Boat* was the only show by Oscar that Ziegfeld produced; it was also the most prestigious.

British-born Evelyn Laye made her Broadway debut in 1929 in Noel Coward's *Bitter Sweet*, produced by Ziegfeld. Ziegfeld wished to continue to benefit in the association with his new star. He never did.

Oscar Hammerstein to Florenz Ziegfeld, January 14, 1931

Dear Flo:

  I have been working along two tracks for a story suitable for Evelyn Laye. I have been reading four novels a week and also trying to cook up an original plot but so far have been unsuccessful. It's easy enough to build up a conventional ready-made operetta story but I don't think that sort of thing stands a chance today. Unless they can hear of something unique and new, with at least one compelling idea in it, they will not go near the theatre. And unless I can find or create something of this quality, it is useless for us to spend our time and money and risk all the heartbreaks that attend a failure. I assure you that I am continuing the search and as soon as I get a gleam of hope, I'll get in touch with you.

  Sincerely,

Florenz Ziegfeld to Oscar Hammerstein, January 22, 1931

My dear Oscar:

I hope you are having some luck. I understand that Laye is sailing with Goldwyn on the Europe today.

I thoroughly agree with you about a story, and I sincerely hope you will be lucky. I am depending on you and I know you will find something worth while.

I just returned today. I was feeling badly and took ten days rest. They just read me your letter and I am delighted that you are working to try and find something worth while—something that has a good chance of success. I know you will find it!

Of course I am very anxious to satisfy Laye as far as a story is concerned—or give her an idea of one, but naturally I can't do that until we find one, but I know you will keep after it.

I understand that Romberg, through someone else, approached Laye regarding an operetta and story that you and he wrote. Do you know anything about it?

As I said, I am depending on you Oscar, and I do hope we will get another "Show Boat." I know they are hard to get, but I feel sure that if anyone can get one, you can. Please keep me posted. Just had a wire from Jerry and he is anxious to go to work.

Affectionately,

Flo

Florenz Ziegfeld to Oscar Hammerstein, February 13, 1931

My dear Oscar:

I understand you have given up the job on "The Gang's All Here",[4] or is that only Broadway gossip?

---

[4] *The Gang's All Here* was a twenty-three-performance musical revue, with a book by Russel Crouse, Morrie Ryskind, and Oscar.

I am very anxious to get something definite about a show for next Fall, and you know, you and Jerry promised to write it for me.

I regret that Jerry did not think favorably enough of the "Show Boat" revival, just to keep another theatre open in New York, and everyone to do his share towards it. It seems terrible that the Ziegfeld and Amsterdam Theatres should be closed at this time of the year.

I thought, and I still do think, that a "Showboat" revival, with Paul Robeson and an interesting cast at $3.00 prices, would have packed the theatre for a couple of months, but Jerry doesn't seem to think so. What do you really think about, it, Oscar?

You said you were coming in to see me, but I suppose your work on "The Gang's All Here" kept you too busy. Any Sunday that you and your wife are not doing anything, would love to have you come out to Hastings. Just call me at 844 Hastings.

I think we ought to make a definite demand and have all the books and vouchers examined on the "Show Boat" picture.[5] Their figures are ridiculous, but, I suppose, like all moving picture concerns, they charged up the most unheard of things in connection with the studio. I know that from "Whoopee."

Tried to get you on the 'phone but failed. Hope to hear from you.

Sincerely,

Fl

P.S. Let's all concentrate now on a great show for the fall—and start on it now!

Oscar Hammerstein to Jerome Kern, circa February 1931

THINK SHOW BOAT SEQUEL GOOD BUT MORALLY INVOLVES FERBER WOULD NOT IGNORE THIS OBLIGATION NOR WOULD I LIKE TO GIVE HER SLICE FOR DOING NOTHING WOULD PREFER STRAIGHT COLLABORATION WITH HER WHICH IN ADDITION TO BEING FAIR WOULD ALSO BE PRACTICAL REMEDY FOR THE SHORT TIME IN WHICH WE WILL HAVE TO WRITE DIALOGUE

---

[5] Refers to the largely forgotten, mostly silent, 1929 film of *Show Boat*.

AND LYRICS AFTER YOUR RETURN DO YOU WANT ME TO
SEE EDNA

    OSCAR

Oscar Hammerstein to Florenz Ziegfeld, February 16, 1931

Dear Flo:

I've just gone into partnership with Schwab and Mandel,[6] under
conditions too favorable to refuse. This necessarily precludes my doing
plays for any other firm next season and I shall not be able to go ahead with
the Laye piece. I am very sorry about this feature of my new agreement but
the rest of it is so much to my interest, that I have no choice in the matter. At
any rate, I am letting you know in plenty of time so that you can make other
arrangements for a book for Evelyn Laye next season.

Jerry had, what I consider, a wonderful idea in writing a sequel to "SHOW
BOAT" with Kim playing the lead and Robeson playing old Joe's son, now a
successful concert singer. I think this is a germ of a great idea and since Edna
Ferber would have to come in on it any way, having created the characters,
I should think she might be interested in writing the book herself.

Wishing you the greatest success in this and all other ventures, I am,
as ever

    Sincerely,

    OSCAR HAMMERSTEIN 2nd

Florenz Ziegfeld to Oscar Hammerstein, February 18, 1931

My dear Oscar:

Your letter was a terrific shock to me because from a telegram received
from Jerry today, who, by the way, has been trying to get you on the phone
from Palm Beach, we sort of took it for granted that it was definitively understood that [you] and he would do the show for me, even if a story would
not work out for Laye, that you would do a show anyway, and I think Jerry's
idea about "Show boat" [sic] is terrific.

---

[6] Frank Mandel collaborated with Hammerstein on the books to several musicals, and along with
Laurence Schwab, produced *Tickle Me*, *The Desert Song*, *The New Moon*, and *East Wind*. Schwab
alone produced Oscar's play, *Knights of Song*, and collaborated with Oscar on two librettos.

Of course, you know your own business best, but I really think that as far as I was concerned, knowing the talk we all had about it, that you really should have made your arrangements subject to this one show for me, but of course, that is entirely up to you.

I certainly must congratulate Schwab and Mandel, because it is very evident, judging from "America's Sweetheart", that when they had you for "Desert Song" and "New Moon" they were okay, and when they had Desylva [sic] Brown and Henderson for the other two shows they were okay.

I could not get Jerry to enthuse about a revival of "Showboat" [sic] although I think that at the present time with the shows in thos [sic] town that to do "Showboat", and we could get practically the original cast with Robeson and Bledsoe's, and at reduced prices, it would have done a great business, because we closed doing a good business until the expenses of the company made it unprofitable.

I don't suppose there is any chance whatever for you and Jerry to do a show for me, judging from your letter which I exceedingly regret. You can rest assured that if I had any idea of your being willing to make a tie-up such as you did with Schwab and Mandel, I would have been flattered to have such a chance offered to me, but I suppose the thing is all set and there is nothing that can be done about it at this late date. What about the "Show Boat" sequal [sic]. Can you do that?

Please let me hear from you and please communicate with Jerry.

Sincerely yours,

Flo.

Oscar Hammerstein to Florenz Ziegfeld, February 21, 1931

Dear Flo:

It will not be possible for me to work on a sequel to "SHOW BOAT," but as I said in my last letter, I think it is a tremendous idea and if Edna Ferber were interested, I should be very glad to have some talks with her and Jerry and help all I can in giving her a good practical lay-out for a musical play. I would not want any tangible recompense for this, beyond the satisfaction of making up, in some way, for whatever embarrassment I have caused you in your plans for next season.

My decision was entirely in my own selfish interest. I am saddled with a great deal of financial responsibility and I have to follow the course, which seems the most profitable. In the lavish manner in which you must produce to keep up your unique reputation, I don't believe there is so much money to be made as in the more economical productions of Schwab &

Photo 7 Norma Terris (Magnolia Hawks) and Howard Marsh (Gaylord Ravenal)

Mandel. And if I only get royalty out of a success, that is not enough to keep me going, no matter how big the success is. I am sure you must see this point of view.

My arrangement with Larry and Frank is not for any term of years. It is only something I am trying out and if it doesn't turn out satisfactory, I can always become a free lance again.

Have you discussed the "SHOW BOAT" sequel with Jerry? I think it is an idea you should not lose.

Sincerely yours,

OSCAR HAMMERSTEIN 2nd

Photo 8 Cast from the original production of *Show Boat*, circa 1927. Helen Morgan (Julie LaVerne), Francis X. Mahoney (Rubber Face), Charles Ellis (Steve Baker), Norma Terris, Eva Puck (Ellie), and Charles Winninger (Cap'n Andy Hawks)

Jerome Kern to Oscar Hammerstein, March 17, 1931

HAVE AN URGE TO DO A BIG WORK WITH YOU TO WIT MUSICAL VERSION OF MANUEL KOMROFFS TWO THIEVES[7] BUT WHERE HE SKATES ON THIN ICE AND DUCKS ISSUE I PROPOSE SHOWING SOME OF THE MIRACLES OF THE GOOD BOOK TELL ME YOUR IMPRESSION SOON DO YOU REMEMBER CHURCHIN [*sic*] CHOW[8]

JERRY.

930A.

Oscar and Dorothy's son, James Hammerstein was born on March 23, 1931 (a year and a day after his friend-to-be, Stephen Sondheim).

Jerome Kern to Oscar Hammerstein, March 23, 1931

HURRAH AND A COUPLE OF WHOOPS WE ARE SO HAPPY FOR YOU BOTH IS HE REALLY GOING TO BE CHRISTENED JAMES OR DID OSCAR JUST MAKE THAT UP BET TEN BUCKS HE SINGS AND LOOKS BETTER THAN THAT OTHER TENOR HOWARD MARSH[9] AND WITH MUCH MORE HAIR FELICITATIONS AND ALL LOVE

EVA AND JERRY

Oscar Hammerstein to Jerome Kern, March 26, 1931

Dear Jerry:

Yes his name is Jimmie. Do you want to make anything of it?

I read "THE TWO THIEVES" and I think something very unique might be done with that background. The episode in that particular

---

[7] *Two Thieves* was a well-received 1931 novel about the two thieves crucified alongside Jesus.

[8] *Chu Chin Chow* opened in London in 1916 where it ran for 2,238 performances. The first American production opened in 1917. Based on *Ali Baba and the 40 Thieves*, the show caused some scandal for its portrayal of scantily clad slave girls.

[9] Howard Marsh played Gaylord Ravenal in the original Broadway production of *Show Boat*.

narrative emphasized crises that were physical rather than emotional. But there were some grand characters in it. My favorite, of course, being the Babylonian dwarf. I think that using that background and subordinating the two thieves to the love interest of Rongus and the slave girl, we might construct a great show. How about sort of [comic/cameo?] "CHU CHIN CHOW" with mobs and pageantry suggested rather than illustrated? The splendor of a Winthrop Ames rather than a Morris Gest. I wonder, as a matter of fact, if "CHU CHIN CHOW" was not more like that in London. The stage of His Majesty's Theatre would surely never hold one third the ensemble or scenery used at the Manhattan Opera House.

I had a meeting with Arthur Hopkins and Arthur Hammerstein concerning "CAMILLE." Hopkins is very strong for doing a modernized version of it. I have bought the novel and the play and intend to construct a rough outline for a musical version. Hopkins is going to do the same, independent of me. I think it will be a very good idea for you to make a third layout. The plan is to do it later next season, opening in January.

You haven't answered my long letter. I know you have had a sore back but look at me. But a few days ago, I had a child and while not a member of the labor party, I bore the strain in a most unspartan manner.

Dorothy sends her love to all three of you, as do I. And Jimmie is flattered by your offer to do a show for Ziegfeld when he is only sixteen years old. Still perhaps that might be the right age to do a show for Ziegfeld.

Sincerely,

In addition to theater and film, Oscar pitched ideas for radio programs.

Oscar Hammerstein to Mr. McLeod, Musical Supervisor of the National Broadcasting Company (NBC), April 7, 1931

Dear Mr. McLeod:

Following our interview, the outline of my idea is, in brief, as follows:

It is a serial idea. Each week I would write and produce a musical dramatic-comedy episode on the lives of a group of characters living in a Bronx apartment house. My characters would be very much down to earth, even stereotyped to a certain extent. For I don't believe we have time on the radio to go into subtle psychological explanations of why freakish characters are as they are. I would concern myself with the janitor's family in the basement; the newlyweds on the first floor; the mysterious bachelor on the second; the Jewish family on the third; the Irish family that lives across the airshaft from the Jewish family, etc. These examples I'm rattling off quickly without having gone into their respective possibilities very deeply. I might take some of these out and put others in when I get down to actually working the thing out. And even after we have the productions well under way, when we have exhausted the possibilities of any family, we can move them right out, and move another family into their flat.

My weekly musical playlets, all independently entertaining but nevertheless intimate and related to each other would [***?] treat of the love affairs, business ventures and other experiences of these characters, easily recognizable as resembling the every day experiences of the average listener, heightened by the comic or romantic emphasis with which plays underline life.

One very important feature will be the guarantee of introducing one new song every week. I don't mean one new song [that's] already become popular, but a premier of a new song every week. I shall either write the lyric myself, and invite a prominent composer [to] collaborate with me, or I shall take the pick of a group of new songs submitted to me by a publisher.

I shall introduce a variety of songs—one week a comedy song led up to by an appropriate comedy scene, and sung by an appropriate character; another week a love song, mounted on a romantic scene with perhaps some comic interruptions. I believe that when once the listeners are acquainted with the characters the interest in any song is increased a hundredfold as it is on the stage.

I have a great many other thots on the possibilities of the idea which however I shall not go into now. I have given you the substance and the general aim.

I should prefer to carry it out in conjunction with the production firm of Schwab and Mandel with whom I have a very close alliance. We could avail ourselves of their artists and I could work out the whole thing with them. Their name as producers of "THE DESERT SONG," "GOOD NEWS,"

"THE NEW MOON," and "FOLLOW THRU," and their producing ability as attested by the success of these shows would be a valuable acquisition and additional assurance to the enterprise. I believe it would have to be done on a large scale or not at all.

Sincerely,

OSCAR HAMMERSTEIN 2ND

Sigmund Romberg was known for his malapropisms; he also had an intentional sense of humor.

Sigmund Romberg to Oscar Hammerstein, July 12, 1931

My dear Oscar:

This is just to remind you that I have a birthday on the 29th of this month, I don't want you to forget it.

Oh, by the way, my sincere best wishes for your birthday

As ever,

Sincerely,

Romy

Oscar's relationship with his ex-wife, Myra, was often tense. He frequently criticized her excessive spending and disagreed over how best to raise their children, Billy and Alice. By various accounts, Oscar was not an easy father—at least until his children reached adulthood. Although this letter suggests that Myra re-married, there's no other evidence of it, so the marriage was presumably short-lived, and Oscar continued to support Myra through the rest of his life. (She died within a year of Oscar's passing.)

Oscar Hammerstein to Myra Finn, 1931

My apologies for the address on the envelope. I don't know your husband's first name so I just put "R" for "Rusty."

Dear Mike:

After breaking box office records—not to mention the backs of salaaming critics—on the road, East Wind has opened in New York, and is a flop. There are sundry and complicated explanations, but the only important significance is the break-down of a musical-play formula on which I used to make a lot of money. What new device is destined to take its place I don't know, and for the moment I don't intend to find out. I have always had (as you know) higher ambitions than Broadway libretto writing. Whether I should ever have pursued them had I entertained making big money, I don't know. For a while it looked as if Schwab, Mandel, and Hammerstein were headed for Shubertian heights of theatrical power. Now that that prospect has faded, I shudder to think even of its remote imminence. I am certain that my recent succession of musical comedy misfortunes has opened the gates to a career which is more to my liking, and I am embarking on it eagerly and happily—flushed with failure, you might say.

I am writing a novel first. I am canny enough to have chosen a subject that would make good stage material, so that if the publisher rejects it I shall have nonetheless a complete scenario which could be dramatized with an additional month's work. Living on my capital—now a shrunken nugget—I will not continue long on fifth avenue. About the first of the year I hope to be bound for France where rents are cheaper and tempting Ziegfelds and Dillinghams fewer.

I am telling you all this as a preface to an earnest admonition to be economical. You will take $25,000 a year from the children's fund. It is entirely possible that my future contribution to it may be so small that it will be depleted in three years' time. For God's sake, save! Live on 10,000—(I would rather it were six) and save the balance. Create a new fund, and put it in ultra-conservative securities. Don't try to make money with it. Just put it in a very safe place. I do hope you won't try for any brilliant interest rate. On small sums of capital it is not important whether you get 3% or 7%. Safety is all that counts.

The children write enthusiastically about your place in Beverly Hills. It is lovely out there, isn't it? I know that rents are very, very low now, but isn't it rather expensive to run a home as big as that? I sound like an old maid, don't I? I admit to a selfish anxiety. It is essential to my own peace of mind that you and the children are secure. If you spend no more than

10,000 a year, you're taken care of for seven years. By that time Billy and Alice are both grown up. Keep to this rule and nobody will have to worry. Meanwhile I might make a little money, who knows? And if I don't, your husband might—But don't count on either.

Speaking of your husband may I extend my belated congratulations and good wishes to you both? This reads as a much more casual sentence than I intend it to be.

I told Alice that I might have a surprise for her. This "surprise" is the off-chance that I might take a job for a few months in Hollywood, before my pilgrimage to France. There is nothing definite about it yet, so don't say anything to either of them. Their letters are getting better all the time. How is their new school? Does Billy play football?

Howard reports progress on the new agreement which means that what we arranged and understood perfectly in a five minute phone conversation may be expressed by our lawyers about any year now.

Sincerely

Oc

Oscar Hammerstein to Myra Finn, April 14, 1932

Dear Mike:

I am sorry to be so late answering your letter, but I am even more busy than I usually am, and I haven't had the chance.

Your offer of a loan is very generous, but economically unsound. I have plenty of five hundred dollar bills, or the equivalent. But I can't afford to spend five hundred dollars on a trip just now. Whether I borrowed if from you, or from my own funds, would make no difference. I would still be spending five hundred, and I can't afford to.

So I am afraid I shall be unable to go out there this spring. Even if I had the money, it is doubtful if I could come. I have taken on so many commitments that I could scarcely spare three or four weeks. My contract to write a piece for Drury Lane following Noel Coward's Cavalcade has a clause wherein Jerry and I undertake to deliver a manuscript twelve weeks after they give us notice that they want it. I had anticipated that Cavalcade would run forever, like Chu Chin Chow, but to my surprise I have just received the twelve week notice. This means I must drop everything else and finish the English show. I shall probably be required to go over there in July, my expenses shall be paid, of course. Dorothy will go with me, and we'll leave the rest of the family in Great Neck. For a while we had contemplated renting the house for the summer and taking a smaller one, but the possible profit didn't seem to justify all that upheaval. I have such a marvelous study there, with all my reference books catalogued, and the furnishings so cheerful that I really believe my work gains a great deal. I have just finished one act of an "intimate" musical play I am doing for Max Gordon, with Jerry, and I know it is by all odds the best and most subtle play writing I have ever done in my life—no guarantee of commercial success of course.

The rest of the house turned out fine. The fire insurance made it possible to completely redecorate, and the "depression" made it possible to buy gorgeous furniture at auction for next to nothing. And it really looks wonderful.

In addition to the Gordon show next fall, I shall probably do another for Ziegfeld or George White. They both want one from me.

One more prospect is a musical picture adaptation which Thalberg of Metro-Goldwyn told Howard he wanted me to do. This would be for next fall too, but it is, as yet, a vague undertaking. It would have the virtue of paying my expenses to California, but then surely one of these shows should do that.

You are very nice to hang on to all the money you get. When I talk to my friends these days I feel rich and unusually clever to have any money at all. Everyone else I know is in hock—some of the ex-wealthiest.

I heartily applaud your idea of Alice's tour with Fraülein. I think I know her better than you imagine. After all her self-sufficiency and concentrated application to work are qualities which I possess myself—tho perhaps not to so exaggerated a degree. I understand her very well.

I miss them very much, of course, but circumstances took you to California and that fact must be faced. After all the mutual profit the children and I get from each other's society at this time is nothing more than the fun we have in being together. So all we are missing is fun. They are not old enough to have any views on life that I respect. And when I give them my views on life, I am sure I bore them.

As a matter of fact I get more out of their letters than I used to get out of my visits with them. There is of course, however, a pleasure, and a thrill in seeing them and touching them—and this I must do without for several more months.

I always ask for photographs—snapshots—which they never send me. You might encourage them a little along this line.

Sincerely,

Oc

The 1932 revival of *Show Boat* was again produced by Ziegfeld and featured most of the leads from the original cast, including Norma Terris, Helen Morgan, and Charles Winninger, and Paul Robeson joined them as Joe. This time Oscar was the sole director. It ran for 180 performances, from May 19 to October 22.

Oscar Hammerstein to Myra Finn (excerpt), June 12, 1932

Show Boat is doing $25,000 a week and it's [*sic*] success besides being a financial godsend is a great artistic gratification. It seems better now than it did before. Everyone, especially the critics have stated this.

Oscar Hammerstein to Myra Finn, July 21, 1932

Dear Mike:

I don't suppose you were surprised to hear that I liked your plan. It is what I have advised you to do many times. I am so positive of its wisdom because it is a step toward gaining a sense of proportion—something which at the moment you sadly lack. When you talk about "drifting into middle age without first having lived" you are being a melodramatic sophomore. First, you are nowhere near "middle" age. You are a young woman and will remain so for some time. Second, it seems to me you have "lived" a great deal—seen a lot of the world, experienced a lot and learned a lot. Who, of the girls you knew at nineteen, have have [*sic*] "lived" more than you? Edna

Keller? Rose Backer? Ruth Adler? Florence, Lilly, Sue or any of the others you met later? And balancing all things, do you consider that any of these are better off than you now? Maybe you do. It is a question of a sense of values. I would not hesitate in preferring your own outlook, your comparatively comfortable state of wealth, your freedom, your intelligence and your two children to the [?], stodgy assets of the above named.

I am most honest in my belief that you can afford yourself the luxury of the most extravagant anticipations for the success of your latest plan. I think that against new backgrounds—(Italy sounds fine)—you can not help but acquire a new slant on your relations to the world in general. In spite of your tendency to dramatize yourself—I am not [?]ing. I am mentioning a weakness which you know you have—in spite of this tendency you will be pulled out of yourself. A world much bigger than you and your problems will assert it's [sic] existence to you. New places will fill your mind with thots of new things—without any effort on your part. I shall not go on. It will seem too much like "selling" the idea to you. But I do believe it all so sincerely. This all reminds me of several letters I sent you from Hollywood and many talks we have had in New York, all urging you to do the very thing you have decided to do now.

For the children too it seems a great thing. Alice will develop so much more in Europe. She is no "Hollywood in California" type, is she? Bill says her piano playing is making startling strides. Would it be a crazy idea, as long as she is in Europe, to attempt to go after her musical career in a truly energetic and constructive way? How about Leipzig or Vienna instead of Switzerland—under the finest music teachers in the world? The living would be just as cheap. Or is she too young for that yet? I don't know, do you? I think the idea will bear serious consideration. If she has a talent let's plug it for all it's worth. A profession, a useful accomplishment, a knowledge that you are good at any one thing and the ability to apply it for pleasure and profit—that is one of the greatest [?] in the world. I am most anxious that both Billy and Alice develop something of this kind. Billy shows nothing yet. I am worried about that. Few boys of fourteen have any real set ambition. What worries me more about Billy is his conviction that he has no talent for anything. First I must convince him that at the moment he is capable of developing in any one of a hundred directions, later we'll pick a direction. I am working on that now. He's a fine boy. He has several little faults. Carelessness is the chief of these. I am giving a lot of attention to correcting it and can report a little progress. I don't know if I told you that the upstairs maid her who used to work for Arthur at the Elm Point house (personal), and now "does" Billy's room and Reggie's room here, says that "all the Hammerstein men are neat!"

If you have recovered from the shock, you can now proceed with your reading. I promise there will be nothing quite so startling in the rest of the letter.

As for Billy he is very willing to stay here. In fact, a week ago, we had a talk and he was grousing about Hollywood, the people there, and the "dumb" schools. I told him what you proposed doing and he, too thinks it a good idea. I think you can feel absolutely safe about his being well taken care of here. I, of course am very happy to have him near me, after giving up all hope of any such good luck, and he on his part seems really to be having a very good time. He's become great friends with Jack Tyson who is a very nice boy. They are the busiest men in America. Yesterday they built an outrigger canoe—two logs nailed together with three strips of plank, and they were punting all around the water with it—near shore of course. They've laid out the Badminton court and they're both becoming pretty good players. Then there's ukulele practice, bicycle riding odd chores, around the Tyson place and this place—They always pool their jobs and work together. Billy now and then goes in for driving practice. Last night he practiced driving the Plymouth into the garage and executed the maneuver very nicely—all but turning off the battery which remained on all night, and had to be recharged!

He's having lots of fun, and he might as well. Meanwhile I am instilling into him more ambition and sense of responsibility—in small doses, and as painlessly as possible. Whatever ambitions he has are not intellectual ones. They are to do physical and adventurous work. Sir Herbert Wilkins, the explorer was down last weekend with his wife. Billy kept dropping hints to be taken along on the next Antarctic expedition. His offers, however, were not snapped up. His only specific prospect for a job is to become boat [?] boy on Larry Schwab's yacht which he is taking out in August. Billy will put in his bid to work for the same salary as his predecessor, the Ahlken kid—said salary being zero, with an occasional bonus of a package of chewing gum, perhaps.

I have finished one play[10] with Jerry. <u>We</u> like it very much. Two ambitious but insolvent lads—Max Gordon and Floe Ziegfeld—are anxious to do it. Two "dough-boys", Martin Beck and A. C. Blumenthal are also interested. I am afraid we can't be sentimental. We'll have to link up with the dough.

I have another story I am about to start, and a novel I am negotiating for, to adapt. It is "Ballerina" by Lady Eleanor Smith who wrote "Flamenco". I like it very much.

I am flirting with Radio but so far the affair has not progressed beyond a few shy glances.

I hope you have not found me too loquacious. Write and tell me in more detail what you intend doing. Will you store your stuff in L.A? It would be cheaper than transporting it here—even the storage rates are cheaper there. I wouldn't sell it if I were you. You'll get nothing, and in a few years you might want to use it again. Tell me also when you are coming East and how long you will stop off here—and if I can attend to anything for you in connection with it. Meanwhile don't brood, and stick to your plan. It is the best you've had and you will be very glad of it in a short time.

Sincerely

Oc

Oscar was not the only one who could be defensive when it came to credit.

Edna Ferber to Oscar Hammerstein, November 11, 1932

You needn't tell me, dear Oscar, that you had no hand in the Fears billing. I know that perfectly well, knowing you. I'm sorry that you have been involved in the thing at all.

I notified Miss Fears (and Morris Ernst, I think, telephoned Mr. Reinheimer) that the use of the word author in connection with the musical play SHOW BOAT was incorrect. An author is, as you know, the creator of a piece of work. As the background, all the characters, all the important situations and much of the dialogue of SHOW BOAT was taken from the novel of the name, the word author could not be used in that way. I need not say that I know you never intended it to be so used. As the novel SHOW

---

[10] *Music in the Air.*

BOAT still sells, the effect of such use would be confusing to readers of the book, past and future, and unfair to its author and publisher. I assured Miss Fears of my admiration and affection for you, and my eternal gratitude to you and Jerry for your beautiful production of SHOW BOAT. Miss Fears has never replied to my communication. Perhaps she does not know that a book called SHOW BOAT was ever written.

There is life in the musical play SHOW BOAT, and in the book of that name, and perhaps there may be for years to come. One doesn't know. But the confusion resulting from the use of the word author as applied to two separate people must inevitably lead to bad results.

My thanks for your letter. And for the wonderful evening you gave me with MUSIC IN THE AIR.

Yours,

Edna Ferber.

Oscar Hammerstein to Myra Finn (excerpt), circa November 1932

Billy proudly told Alice what a brief time it took to fl̲y̲ to Switzerland. You have taken him in the air against my explicit request not to. You had no right to do it, and you must not do it again.

Despite an obviously higher fatality rate people go on like silly parrots mumbling some fallacious statistics (issued by Airways companies) that the rate of accidents is less than in the other modes of conveyance. It certainly is not. I am aware that thousands are now using planes, but they are a handful compared to the millions that use trains daily. The 14 people who were killed the other day on the Cologne-Croydon plane are equivalent, proportionally to 140,000 in rail travel.

The chance may be a thousand to one, or ten thousand to one that Billy would not be killed on an air trip. I prefer my son to travel by train and have the odds a million to one in his favor.

Furthermore it is unforgivable of you to encourage him to do anything that I have forbidden him to do, and tell him not to tell me. You have not been a bit smart or funny. You have just been very selfish and thotless.

= = =

I have offers to adapt four German operettas for London, at least one of which I am taking.[11]

Oscar Hammerstein to Myra Finn, circa April 1933

Dear Mike:

The fears you expressed in your letter are groundless. I have no desire of snatching your babes from your arms. Indeed I have been as careful to foster their love for you as you have been in fostering their love for me. I recognize the importance that they have for you—so much so that I never will understand why you didn't spend this winter in Vienna with Alice and I am strongly in favor of their being with you as much as possible. It is good for them and it is good for you.

The two children, of course, present such different individual problems, that there is no sense in ever referring to them as "The two children". There is Billy, and there is Alice. Alice is a self-sufficient person, born with just the right equipment to deal with this world. (This is not a 100% compliment). She will thrive in any soil. We can guide her, and love her, and help her. But we don't have to worry about her.

Billy is something else again. He is one of those unfortunate, honest and sincere creatures who believe only what they see, and say only what they think. He is, as you say, very unafraid. He needs lots of work. He needs me very badly. You may not think I have done much with him. Surely I do not submit him to you as a finished article. God knows he's awful in lots of ways—rude, selfish and aimless most of the time. But I know I am making progress. I only wish I had nothing to do but educate him. I'm the one person in the world—and the only one—who can do it perfectly. But I have so many other duties! This is why I must let him go to school in Switzerland now. That's all right. Let him concentrate on languages there. If If [sic] he learns German and French—and nothing else—I will be well satisfied. For the rest, I don't expect much. And I don't much care. I am convinced Billy is no student. He has no sense of theoretical learning—or its value. Yet if you give him a job to do—where he can see some result at the end of it, he is a hard and enthusiastic worker.

---

[11] *Ball at the Savoy.*

My plan is to eventually get him interested in my work. He expresses great interest now, but he doesn't know what it's all about. If I tell him that I am writing a play about Louis XIV and ask him to read up on the subject, he'll learn more French history in a week than he will at college in a year. That's my scheme of educating him in general culture as well as playwriting. But it has much more to it than I have time to explain now.

For the present go ahead with your plans just as you had intended. Only I do think it's worth while waiting a few days so that we can have a good long talk about it. One or two weeks make absolutely no difference. We have done little enough talking about this important subject in the past two years.

I'll let you know as soon as I know when I can come to Paris.

Sincerely,

Oc

When the following letter was written, Hitler's power in Germany was mounting, and the situation for Jews was growing dire, if not fully understood abroad—evidenced by Oscar's somewhat cool response.

Fedor Hammerstein (Berlin) to Oscar Hammerstein (London), July 8, 1933

Dear Sir: --

By the well known condition of the jewish people in Germany particularly the jewish artists I am obliged to go to England for looking out for employment, in the very near future—probably next week.

Having lost any possibility to work here any longer but, however also being not connected at all with any influential person of the English Theatre I can not help writing to you realizing me to be related to you. I know, this is only a distant relation—probably of a very, very great distance—my father is a cousin of the deceased Mr. O. Hammerstein of the former Hammerstein Opera in New York—but I do not see any other way to get in touch with the English theatre unless by you.

Please dear Mr. Hammerstein, I ask you to be convinced that I should not inconvenience you if there would be regular circumstances? It is not up to me at all to go into the relation in order to be managed. I do not ask you for employment in any case. My only wish is when I shall arrive in London that you will be kind enough to welcome me at your office.

Certainly, if there is no possibility to let me work with you, you are in the position to introduce me to some people who might be interested for a young actor (comic and lover parts) and dancer (original steps and grotesques).

But however I should not apply to you unless I should trust my being gifted enough for playing and dancing at a London stage and—your being pleased with me, too.

I speak a rather good English—I am able to follow to every conversation. I have a very good pronunciation which enables me to play any part on the English stage.

For your guidance, please still note that I am playing on the stage for the last 6 years. I am 27 y. old but looking much younger.

Now dear Mr. Hammerstein I have said all I wanted. Please excuse me that I had to bother. Once more I ask you to take it for "force majeur".

Trusting you will not keep me waiting to long for your kind reply

I am

Yours very truly

Fedor Hammerstein

PS. In order not to delay the matter I send this letter to friend in London who will know your address better than I do.

Oscar Hammerstein (London) to Fedor Hammerstein, August 6, 1933

My Dear Mr. Hammerstein,

I am very sorry for the predicament in which you find yourself and if you come to London I shall be pleased to see you and do all I can to secure an engagement for you. At the same time I do not wish you to construe this as an assurance or even as a vague encouragement that you can get work here. It is very difficult here as it is all over the world and of course your accent will be something of a handicap. If, despite these obstacles, you determine to come to London, you will be able to get in touch with me at the Theatre Royal Drury Lane. With best wishes,

Sincerely

Ball at the Savoy opened in London on September 8 at the Drury Lane. It was a German operetta with music by Paul Abraham. Oscar produced the London production and adapted the German script and lyrics, originally written by Alfred Grünwald and Fritz Löhner-Beda. Reggie Hammerstein was credited as director. After 148 performances the show all but disappeared. Hammerstein was later quoted as saying that the show "opened cold in London. When it closed it was even colder."

Leighton K. Brill (nicknamed "Goofy") is one of the most fascinating characters in Hammerstein's life. Their friendship dated from their time as teenagers at summer camp, and Brill would go on to ride Hammerstein's coattails for a large part of his professional life. There are perhaps more letters from Brill to Hammerstein than from any other individual. His letters tend to be long, frequent, frenetic, and self-promotional—if letters could hyperventilate, many of Brill's would. Much of the work Brill did for Hammerstein involved casting, and for a few years he ran a Rodgers & Hammerstein office in Hollywood. Brill's mismanagement of the office ultimately led to their professional separation.

Leighton Brill (London) to Oscar Hammerstein (excerpt), December 16, 1933

Dear Oc,

Thursday saw "Nymph Errant" and was not particularly thrilled. Gertie Lawrence gave a very bad performance in the first act, as did all the cast and nobody really started to work until the Harem scene. Thought Bruce Winston was very good and Lawrence after she warmed up. Doris Carson had a terrible cold—but was very poor anyway. I went round back stage after the performance and everybody told me the reason the first act was so bad was that the stage was so terribly cold they were all very uncomfortable and couldn't get warmed up. Wally Crisham in the oasis scene gave a very good performance and, in fact, I thought that was the best scene in the show.

Last night I had an appointment with Frank Collins and we went and saw "Music in the Air" in the Dress Circle from start to finish. It was a remarkably good show considering it has been running as long as it has. There were several faults from both a technical and an acting end, and at the conclusion of the performance we held the company on the stage and gave them our notes. I again reiterate, on the whole it was a remarkably good performance. Both Ellis and Margestson in the office scene, and I would say throughout, have broadened their characterization and are guilty of a bit of mugging, but as the audience howled at the various little touches they have given, it was of little use to speak to them about it. Our only criticisms were the schoolroom scene, the rush of the singing association to the platform wasn't a rush at all, Margetson and Ellis over-playing and Upman has gotten (if possible) even more dramatic. He has changed from King Lear and is now doing Othello. He is very bad. Lister and Carfax in the Brook scene have lost a lot of the delicacy and were doing the leg and stocking bit in quite a burlesque fashion, getting laughs it is true, but they don't belong there. We spoke to them about that. The tempos of several of the numbers have been let down and that has been corrected. Most of our criticisms were a bit caviling but Frank thought it just as well to snap them up on them. In conclusion, he and I agree that it was an excellent show from start to finish.

I can't say as much for "Ball at the Savoy". Denes and Barsony are even more over-playing and are trying to put in what they think funny Americanisms and what I think are awful. I spoke to Abingdon about this and he is going to have a talk with them, but I doubt if it will be any good. Business, as you know, has been frightful, although there was a very good house and a most appreciative one at "Music in the Air". Frank expects "Music in the Air" to run at His Majesty's until February, and the plan is to have the original company play around London (Golders Green, Streatham) for six weeks. I believe Louis is seeing Ellis and Margetson about that at present writing.

Hammerstein and Kern were at work on *Three Sisters*, an original musical for the West End and focusing on English country life, beginning in 1914. While at work on the show, Hammerstein was stuck in the States, while Brill did research for him in England. The show opened in April of 1934, and closed forty-five performances later. The score introduced "I Won't Dance," but "Lonely Feet" is a particularly tender ballad. This is Brill at his most breathless. It's also revealing of surprising pockets of British social history. (With its multiple "P.S."s it may appear to be more than one letter, but it's one long letter written over a period of time.)

Leighton Brill to Oscar Hammerstein, January 2, 1934

Dear Oc,

This is an official and business letter. The codicil answer has been taken care of by hand, but you should get it at the same time, as the Acquitania is the only boat that is leaving.

As I cabled you, Easter was April 12th 1914 and Whitsun or Whit Monday is always seven weeks later and occurred in 1914 on May 31st. The Derby 1914 was on Wednesday May 27th.

In my letter about fairs I mentioned Hampstead Heath. The three big days for buskers, booths, etc. are Easter Monday, Whitsun Monday and August Bank Holiday. If you're trying to get at what I think you are—a previous meeting of Mary, Gipsy and Charlie—how does Easter Monday, which will be April 13th, fit in? I am trying to dig up some other fairs but as yet haven't had any word.

I am answering the paragraphs in your letter, (which is before me) as they occur, so if I'm skipping around, it's the way your letter reads.

By the way, as your letter was dated 18th December, I sent you dates in a cable to "Operetta", and it was returned, as no such thing has yet been registered. Is this the usual Reinheimer speed?

Louis has already told Mary Ellis there was nothing in the new show for her.

With regard to the three neighbouring villages, Ashstead, Walton and Farleigh, we can find and know of none as Farleigh. If you have by this time substituted Headley, that is all right.

The police (Inspector Ennis no less) informed me that as a rule the village constables are on duty in their villages on Derby Day and the extra police (three hundred of them) are brought up from the Metropolitan Police Force, but it would be entirely O.K. to have a policeman from a neighbouring village take over Eustace's job for that day and have Eustace on the Downs, and if you have used the chicken-stealing episode, it would be perfectly proper to have had Eustace telephone the neighbouring constable that he was going out after the thieves and keep him over on the Downs for one or both days. That is how you can get Eustace over to the Derby.

Expanding a little on cops and enlisting. The police for the greater part, were allowed to resign and enlist and by a special act of Parliament their places were held for them. However, if you need to keep Eustace home, there were some who were not allowed to enlist but were held for some special duty, such as C.I D. work or the Commissioner might say he was unable to replace the man in that special district and hold him, so that leaves you a wide range of choice whether you want to have Eustace enlist or have him at home.

Your next paragraph is about "Sunny". It appears there is only one copy in existence, and I am having that copy copied and will dispatch it to you upon completion.

Your next compels me to weep again, although I have dealt with it in my personal letter. Poor old sweetheart, or rather poor old checque. Please let me know when this is finally settled.

Since you really have a copy of "Good Companions", might I suggest "Red Wagon" by Lady Eleanor Smith, and I left another book at the hospital for you, which in the last half deals with a family that forsake their farm and go travelling around England in a caravan. They meet up with some fair people, although their adventures deal mostly with fruit picking. I can't think of the name at the writing, but if you don't know what I mean, Liverights can check up on this for you.

Since I got this letter Saturday and Sunday being New Year, I haven't had time to go into this fully, as up to the moment of going to press, have been buried at the Imperial War Museum, getting the entertainment dope and photographs, which leave on the same boat with this letter.

Seeing that you are a non-drinking man and never go into pubs, I won't deal with you severely about not seeing pubs on village greens. You're wrong about this. Most every village green has a pub on the edge of it, in fact, most of them have two or three and it is a very common thing.

I have been very careful about what you mentioned about internal politics and have taken no sides at all and ducked from under on any discussion involving Louis, although now there is no reason to do so. The house flag of Dreyfus, with the five-cornered star of David, is again hoisted with the Royal standard on top of the Drury Lane every day.

I have seen and have a copy of the lay-out you sent to Louis and boy, how right you are when you say a scenario is lousy. I'd never send another, but the information contained regarding scene lay-outs and characters has been very useful to Mr Tennet (to be taken up later).

Haven't gone far with the Motleys as they have been very busy with Reggie's show, the American "Richard of Bordeax" and Ivor Novello's production of "Romeo and Juliet", not to mention another Elizabethan thing they are doing, which Gielgud will direct. It is entitled "Spring 1600".

I can't give you any further reports on my tips regarding Knight, Wilcoxon and Doyle, as I have done nothing about it, awaiting word from you. I am afraid Wilcoxon will accept a movie job. I think Knight's height is against him, although he sings well and I think acts well, and as for Jack Doyle's acting, as I couldn't mention any show I had him in mind for and had to be very indefinite, I couldn't give him a part to read. Jimmy Finlayson I know all about. Will have pictures and Jimmy in person for you. He is great in an Old Bill part, a good character actor and a comedian.

So what about Frances Dean? Just that I thought she was a great bet and my judgment was confirmed by Mr Paramount. So what.

The information about the first act being dialogue and coming here of course is, was and will be the biggest thrill. Everybody is waiting for it with bated breath and all that.

You can tell my personal affairs have been temporarily disbanded on account of illness on the part of the party of the second part. They had a show at the Trocadero New Year's Eve, starting at 12. She insisted on going to try to work it and went home to her mother a very sick girl, and today she is no better, even worse. I have at length persuaded her to see a doctor, who will be there this afternoon. She is a pretty sick young lady.

I have been digging wherever possible to get all information regarding everything about the show that you can use and according to your instructions have been sending it to you bit by bit and piece by piece. My short letter going to day, I hope will give you everything on the estaminet scenes that you will need.

Did my first lot of pictures arrive, and did you get the Headley ones? We have just gone through the worst fog London has had in the last fifteen years, and it is impossible to get, as I promised, some pictures around Headley. None of the photo news agencies have them and I will have to make them myself as soon as there is a clear day, if that ever occurs during the winter time here.

Happy New Year to you, that, too, is late I know.

This concludes answering your letter I shall go on from there.

LOVE,

LEIGHTON.

P.S. I have queried, not one but three stenographers, two commissionaires, one telephone operator, Bill Abingdon, two Rabbis, four of the Grenadier Guards and a clergyman. It is absolutely and indubitably necessary to pronounce banns in the Church of England for three successive Sundays before the wedding, not alone in the church of the prospective bridegroom, but also in the church of the bride (if she has one) and is in a different parish, and they won't take off one Sunday regardless, not even for a cash offer. The clergyman I asked is the Rev. Dick Shepherd, of St. Martin's in the Field. So there!

I met Jean Dreyfus yesterday and she asked me to inform you that she has what she thinks is an ideal flat for you. It is the apartment of Lady Humphries at 25 Manchester Square. The flat is on the top floor of a five-story building. The rent is fourteen guineas and everything is there complete. It consists of a large bedroom, with a double bed, a beautiful drawing-room, a kitchen fully equipped, the hot water ready to turn on, and two other bedrooms, one of which is quite small and could be used for a maid living in and the other is fitted up as a study. There is already an upright piano in this apartment. The rent of the outfit is fourteen guineas a week and you can take possession immediately when you come over and have it until Easter, which falls this year on April 1st. The only reason you'd have to get out then is that her little daughter comes home from school on a vacation and she wants to be with her in this apartment. This sound awfully good to me, and I won't do anything further about hunting for others until I hear from you.

Last week I saw "Lilac Time", the revival, with Derek Oldham and Helen Gilliland.

A COURIER HAS JUST DASHED UP, HIS STEED COVERED WITH LATHER AND SALUTING ME HE INFORMS ME IT IS POSSIBLE TO GET MARRIED IN THE CHURCH WITHOUT BANNS BY BUYING A SPECIAL LICENCE. I HAVE SENT FOUR DESPATCH RIDERS OUT AT ONCE TO THE BISHOP OF LONDON TO VERIFY THIS. ONE MAY GET BACK THROUGH A STORM OF SHOT AND SHELL BEFORE THIS LETTER IS OVER.

To continue. Just say a prayer that we didn't have Gilliland in this show. Bad as they think Natalie is, her worst is a darn sight better than Gilliland's best. In "Lilac Time" she has developed a new mannerism. She has gotten very coy and she totters, in fact, I thought she was doing one of the Mincing Misses from the opening of "Show Boat". And as regards my impression of Derek Oldham, the best I can say for him is that to me he seems like a No.3 road company of Dennis King. The comic in the show is W.H. Berry and he is pretty fair. The rest of the cast must have been picked up by Lee Ephraim strolling along the streets and asking all the out of work people "Can you sing?" The scenery and costumes were good in 1912. It is playing at the Alhambra and the audience consisted of myself and a loving couple.

There is a new "Beau Brummell" with music and lyrics by B.B. Hilliam. It is playing at the Saville and I was there, this time without the loving couple. I doubt if there was £10 in the house and strangely enough, I rather liked the show. Harry Welchman played the lead and outside of the fact that he made quite a mess of the production by chewing up parts of the scenery, I thought he did a pretty good job. The show itself did not mean anything, although it was quite pleasant. One of our chorus boys, Bruce Seton, has quite a large part in it and plays and sings it very well. There is a girl in it (I haven't her name before me—it is in the programme at home) who does a French bit, and if you use a bar-maid or French girl in the estaminet scene, she would be very good, as she is young, good-looking and a good actress.

Since your last cables, there has been an absolutely different change in the attitude of everybody connected with the Lane and Chappells. Of course peace, forgiveness and goodwill to men is in the air, and my wild ravings have been completely put to shame. But don't kid yourself that it wasn't touch and go for a while. But now everything is serene. (See note on house flag.) I came down to the Lane this morning for my mail and was greeted by everyone with much enthusiasm. Mr Tennent is now in residence and he called me in his office to discuss everything in connection with the new show. I tried to duck but he came out with the statement "Now that everything is settled" and I said "Before the arrival of the book?" and he said "Practically definitely". He and I have a date to go over cast suggestions tomorrow. In fact, I find he is going so far as to tell certain people not to take other engagements before hearing from him, but you will know all the details after our meeting. He also has a luncheon date with Gladys Calthrop on Thursday, and tells me he has spoken to her -- (over)

THE MOTOR CYCLE COURIER HAS JUST RETURNED FROM THE ARCHBISHOP SHAPIRO OF LONDON AND HERE IS THE DOPE: THERE IS A VERY, VERY, VERY SPECIAL LICENCE GRANTED IN ONLY VERY, VERY RARE OCCASIONS, AND UPON PAYMENT OF A FAIRLY LARGE SUM OF MONEY. THIS HAS TO BEAR THE SIGNATURE OF THE ARCHBISHOP OF CANTERBURY AND IS APPLIED FOR THROUGH THE DIOCESAN AUTHORITIES OF THE DIOCESE CONCERNED. THERE IS ANOTHER LICENCE (often wrongly called a "special" licence) WHICH IS GRANTED BY THE REGISTRAR BY WHICH, IF THE APPLICANTS HAVE BEEN RESIDENT IN THE PARISH FOR FIFTEEN DAYS, THEY CAN BE MARRIED IN CHURCH WITH ONLY ABOUT A COUPLE OF DAYS DELAY NECESSARY FOR THE APPLICATION. This may give you the reason why Mary and Gipsy have stayed at Headley, or wherever the commons is to be, for two weeks before the wedding, and have not been gallivanting around the country at the fairs.

(continued from the previous page)

and her work on the Coward show will be over just in time to let her take this job, if she is not too exhausted.

As this is the third letter I am writing to catch the Aquitania and stenographers are dropping like flies under my slave-driving dictation, I am going to cut this short (??) with the additional information that another motor-cycle courier has just returned with a map of the Epsom Downs district, which I trust will enable you to see your distances and spot your events to greater advantage.

Love,

LEIGHTON.

P.S. Can you let me know by return mail, your lay-out as regards the composition of the chorus, as Bill Abingdon was very eager to get this from me today and I disclaimed all knowledge? He talks about using as many of the "Ball at the Savoy" crowd as we can. Is this agreeable to you? You have told me that it will consist of 70/80 people with just 16 girl dancers. Therefore I figure it out roughly:

> 16 girl dancers
> 16 male dancers
> 12 decorative singing ladies
> 12 decorative singing men
> 8 bit people, male types
> 8 bit people, female types, singers if possible. Is this anywhere near correct?

P.P.S. This is no kid—in order to catch this boat, this letter is dictated and not read.

Leighton Brill to Oscar Hammerstein, January 9, 1934

My dear Oc.

Here is something I have had among my notes for some time but in the rush of getting off to you have always forgotten to mention—to wit—

About a year ago I came back from the Opening Night of "A Gay Divorce" and told you that there were three things I liked about the show, Fred Astaire, the song "NIGHT AND DAY" and the Chorus Routines, which were by Barbara Newberry and Carl Randall [the underlining may be by OH]. These I told you were unique, quite different from the ordinary run of dances and did not consist of girls getting in one line and hoofing like hell, showed imagination, taste and effective dancing.

A couple of weeks ago I saw "A Gay Divorce" with the English chorus put on again by Newbury and Randall, and again I was impressed by the finesse and ideas behind the dances.

Newbury and Randall are here, they are appearing at the Dorchester in their show. I think they would be ideal for the type of dancing that is indicated in the Script of "THREE SISTERS".

I have made discreet enquiries and find they are slated to go to Monte Carlo in February, this however is tentative, and am sure they would stay to do a Lane show. Let me know as soon as possible so the Lane can talk with them in a business way. My own opinion is they are perfect for the imaginative vision scenes and will give us the type of dancing you are looking for.

Love,

Leighton

Arthur Hammerstein to Oscar Hammerstein (excerpt), circa January, 1934

I met Max Gordon at the train as he was in route to Larrys at Miami he told me that he had closed with Jerry Kern for the N. Y. presentation the Three Sisters which you are writing for London. I did expect and I think you said or wrote me that whatever you wrote for London you would reserve the American right for yourself or me. Jerry certainly cannot close a verble [sic] or written understanding without you, but I wouldnt [sic] put anything past him with that ego.

Three Sisters opened at the Drury Lane in London on April 9, and closed thirty-four performances later. Oscar wrote the book and lyrics, and is credited as co-director along with Kern.

Oscar Hammerstein to Myra Finn (excerpt), May 13, 1934

My own affairs are in a poor state as you may gather. "Sweet Adeline" is at last sold to Warners, and after commissions are paid my share is $8000.00 which postpones digging into my small capital a little while longer.

Meanwhile the coast is getting hot about musical pictures again (I wish I knew why). Three deals are pending. The most likely one is with Metro to go out and supervise one of a string of operetta's they plan to do (Naughty Marietta, The Student Prince, etc). We are working on an experimental scheme to go out there for about five weeks at some fair salary (about 1500[?] a week), so that if it doesn't work, it wont cost them too much money or us too much time. This would being me home in time for the children's arrival. I earnestly hope you can clean up your affairs so that you'll be on the boat with them.

The deal, however, is not yet set. And these days Howard has an average of ten deals starting and falling through, each week. Nobody can make up his mind definitely enough to go through with anything. America has again lost her morale, and Roosevelt is no longer the universally acclaimed savior that he was. Tho it sounds paradoxical to be urging your return with the children in times of strife, I believe you will see that a descending dollar and no British earnings forthcoming make the move all the more essential.

If "Three Sisters" is still running when you receive this, don't be deceived. It's a flop. The cast is cut. And we have cut all our royalty to keep it open so that our deal for an American production won't walk away. Don't tell anyone, of course.

Oscar Hammerstein to Myra Finn (excerpt), May 18, 1934

Don't let's make any plans at all. As a matter of fact there are so many other possibilities in my immediate future that we will go nutty if we attempt to be prepared for every eventuality. My six weeks contract (Metro) has much more purpose than meets the naked eye. They have told me frankly that this is an experiment. If they like me and I like them this is a mere prelude to a new contract, and I am to be groomed as supervisor of all their musicals. Big stuff you see, but I am not allowing my hopes to run away with me. So many strange things happen and don't happen out there.

In any event I am convinced that America—not England—is where my work belongs. So I do hope you'll bring the children back for good. They're getting too old for me to see them so little. I must live wherever I can earn the best living. I have no choice. I think everything else must be subordinated to that consideration.

Oscar Hammerstein (from MGM) to Otto Harbach, June 9, 1934

Dear Otto:

I've just signed a years contract to stay out here in California and write and produce pictures for M-G-M.

This means that I can't go ahead with the production of "Three Sisters" with Jerry.

I sincerely believe that with comparatively little work it can be made into not only a good show but a really great show.

Would you be interested in taking it over and splitting fifty-fifty on all author's rights?

I don't want you to look on this as an appeal to help me out on a basis of friendship. I know very well how far you would go for me but I have no intention of taking advantage of that. I want you to approach it as purely a business proposition. Weigh carefully what you consider the prospective profits for the amount of time and work you must put into it and make your decision accordingly.

Furthermore, don't feel for a moment that you're in an embarrassing position. If you don't like the idea at all, don't read it. If you read it and then don't like the play just tell me so frankly. I will understand.

But I think it's a play of fine qualities, lovely music, pretty lyrics and some fine moments. If I didn't have great faith in it, I'd never submit it to you.

I do believe that the main love story needs the addition of one big innovating force for its first climax. I have several theories which I will reserve till you read it - if you do.

I have told Jerry I'd like you to adopt the child and bring it up with the breeding that only you can give it, and he is very enthusiastic about the idea.

I'll see that you get the script and I hope that you like it, and even if you don't I'll always be your greatest admirer, most grateful pupil and dear friend.

Oscar

P. S.

Social and personal

codicil:

Love to Ella.

O.H.

Oscar Hammerstein (from MGM) to Myra Finn, June 11, 1934

Dear Mike:

Supplementing my short note of last week, I agree in substance with all you said in your letter of May 26th, and appreciate your problems in regard to Alice, and the flat.

When you do rent it, what are your plans? Have you any idea about how and when Alice can spend some time with me out here?

Now, finances:

I am getting $1,750 a week for the first six months, and $2000 a week for the second six months. They have options for two additional years at $2250 and 2500. We won't bother about that now.

With this income I can provide enough for you and Billy and Alice, without digging into the fund any more—which I am very happy about. I want to make you as comfortable as possible and at the same time, give myself a break. And by a "break," I mean the chance not only to pay my own current bills, but also to put aside a little so that at the end of the year I can feel I've increased my capital, instead of steadily falling behind myself as I have been doing the past four years—in company with lots of smarter businessmen than I. Large as this salary seems, it is difficult for me to save much of it.

To begin with taxes and insurance start off by taking out a huge lump. I am not pulling the old gag of crying my eyes out prior to driving a hard bargain. I just want you to appreciate my problems.

	1750.00
5% to Howard	87.50
	1662.50
10% of balance to Goofy	166.00
	1496.50
Income tax about 25% of total	437.00
(conservative estimate this year)	1059.50
Insurance (minus what fund	
Income pays.	
More than --------------	150.00
	909.50
Secretary	35.00
	874.50

I won't even start to go into the incidental expenses of moving the whole family out here, and the continual burden of a standard of living absolutely demanded by my business position. In Hollywood above all other places, their psychology is to think a man unimportant and undeserving of big money if he lives in a modest hovel and does no entertaining—this God knows I do as little as possible, since it never entertains me either to give or go to parties.

Well, you're getting about $170 a week now for you and Alice. What do you think is fair? The fund has been supporting Bill. I'll take that over now. That already makes the fund richer by about $2500 a year, so that's one increase for you. I further suggest that I pay you (for you and Alice) $200 a week beginning July 1 until the first six months of my contract have expired, and $225 for the second six months—and if they sign me for further increase, you will be increased accordingly. (In this respect, don't be surprised if it gets back into very big money within two years. I believe it will either be a bust, or I will develop into a four or five thousand a week again.)

I further suggest that you try to continue to live at your present rate and put the balance in the fund—25 a wk. for 6 mons. and 50 a week for the next 6—but this is up to you.

Now, there you have the whole picture. I desire, as I always have, to be fair to you. I have not exaggerated my position. You can easily see that out of $100,000 a year—or nearly that—I'll be lucky if I save 12,000—little enough headway to make for a man who works as hard as I do. This isn't your fault. But it isn't mine, either. It's just what happens to capital these days.

If you have any thoughts to confirm or modify these write to me about it.

I have rented a home for a year. The address is 2003 La Brea Terrace, Hollywood, Calf.

Please, in your letter, discuss the problem of Alice. In three years, I have seen her about four months all told!

I am paying up your storage bill for your books, taking them out of storage, and putting them in my cellar. They will be well looked after, and it will save further expense on them. Write soon, good luck

Oc

Sometimes telegrams are inscrutable, but nonetheless compelling.

Jerome Kern to Oscar Hammerstein, July 2, 1934

SIXTEEN THIRTY TWO LAUREL AVE HOLLYWOOD READ IT JUST
TO SEE IF YOU DON'T THINK HE SHOULD BE ENCOURAGED
STOP IF HOWARD THE MEAN OLD STEAM ROLLER SIGNS ME
WILL LADY COMES TO TOWN BE OUR FIRST TOGETHER HERE
I AM KNOWING NOTHING SECRETS SNIFF MYSTERIES SNIFF
SEND ME A WORK SCHEDULE WILLYA STOP GOT SISTERS
MATERIAL FROM OTTO AND DELIVERED TO FRANKLIN
TODAY THE GUY SEEMS PLAUSIBLE ABOUT EVERYTHING BUT
WITH HIM THERE ARE MORE STALLS THAN HORSES ALL THE
TIME STOP DON'T USE THAT IT GOES INTO THE MOVIE I AM
WRITING ALL ALONE STORY AND MUSIC YOU CAN IMAGINE
LOVE FROM ALL=

JERRY.

Oscar Hammerstein (MGM) to Jerome Kern, July 5, 1934

Dear Jerry:

This is the last time I will ever buy a car from you. After all the trouble
I had with the Chrysler motor number, I now find that in applying for a
California license the actual motor number of the Rolls is 22-21, but it has
been registered 346-HH. I enclose a bill of sale which I would like you to
sign and have acknowledged by a notary. Don't trouble filling it in because
you would put down the wrong number anyway.

Dorothy and I were thrilled by the flowers we received yesterday—
the Fourth. I don't know whether you know how profligate you were.
Every dollar spent on flowers in California buys what ten dollars buys in
New York, so our whole house looks like a bleeding conservatory.

Love to all.

Oscar

Oscar Hammerstein to Myra Finn (excerpt), July 8, 1934

Their chief interest is developing me as a producer. A producer guides a production from its inception, chooses a story, casts it, confers with the writer and director and supervises their work. He is regarded as much more important than a writer. The money I'm getting now is very nearly the maximum for a writer, but if I make good as a producer I can command more. Of course I won't attempt the responsibility of producing a picture until I learn more about them. At present I am working with an established producer (Harry Rapf). I am (with two other motion picture writers and a director) adapting a story by Vicki Baum for Ramon Novarro and Evelyn Laye (all right, Phooey! They're under contract and a vehicle must be provided). Rommy has come out for eight weeks to write the music. Jerry is coming out in November to stay six months and do two pictures with me—as yet unchosen.

Since it is usual to call in several writers on a picture (and I am beginning to see virtue in the idea) it is hard for a writer to build up an individual reputation as he does in the theatre. Hence the producer, as the captain of the team, runs off with the honors. For some reason or other I have made a big hit with Louis B. Mayer. He looks upon me as a kind of protégé and keeps talking about grooming me as a producer, telling me to take my time and learn the business at his expense. So I'm in a very good spot so far and (barring one of those big Hollywood upheavals or fickle switches of sentiment which I imagine are not infrequent) I may remain out here and develop into an important factor. It seems faintly flamboyant to talk that way now when I am only a tyro and woefully lacking in the mere knowledge of the names of pictures, actors, writers and directors (I've only seen about four pictures a year, all my life), nevertheless I feel I have good qualifications for this kind of work.

Jerome Kern to Oscar Hammerstein, August 25, 1934

FINISHED IRENE DUNNE NUMBER[12] SENDING, AIR MAIL SOON AS COPIED STOP DESIGNED FOR THEME MATERIAL FOR BACKGROUND AND SCENE MUSIC IN FRAGMENTS BEFORE USE

---

[12] Kern is likely referring to the song "We Were So Young," written for the film version of *Sweet Adeline.*

AS PRODUCTION NUMBER STOP PERSONALLY THINK IT MIGHT BE KNOCKOUT SO MUCH SO WOULD ALMOST PREFER THAT THEY DO NOT USE IT LOVE=

JERRY.

Oscar Hammerstein to Myra Finn (excerpt), September 10, 1934

How did you find Alice? She was very well and very excited when she left. My first and most important suggestion about her is to have her skin treated at once. I'm scared to death of those blackheads on her chin.

Regarding her letter to you about not seeing me, a great deal of that is bunk. I saw the children much more than the average busy father sees his children. I sat and talked to them nearly every morning at breakfast, I had lunch home every day. I played tennis and badminton with them, and altho I had to go out to dinner very often, my dinner engagements were always at eight or eight thirty, and I used to sit through theirs with them. Like Billy— altho not to nearly so great a degree—she thinks the adult world owes her entertainment.

But on the whole, there is little to complain of with Alice. She's a sweet child of even temper and generous disposition. She has a terrific ego which transcends everything—even her affection for others. This is good I think, and as a matter of fact it makes her very easy to manage, for if you can appeal to her to do anything for the sake of pride in her own accomplishment, she'll move mountains.

Oscar Hammerstein to Myra Finn (excerpt), November 7, 1934

Fox made an awful botch of "Music In The Air." I hope Warner has done better by "Sweet Adeline." If I ever sell a play again to a picture company I shall insist on adapting it. I expect Jerry out next week, and have a new picture well under way (in manuscript) to greet him with.

The "new picture" was probably *Champagne and Orchids*. Intended as a vehicle for Jeanette MacDonald and Nelson Eddy, it was never made, although Hammerstein and Kern did complete four songs for it.

Oscar Hammerstein (MGM) to Myra Finn, November 13, 1934

Dear Mike [Myra Finn]:

I shall take up the points in your letter as they come:

Children being together during summer. Why? They are not companionable to eachother [sic] They have a brotherly and sisterly affection that is sufficiently fed by the several visits a year they have been having together. They have not the same interests. They are always picking on eachother. Why be theoretical about these things? It is hard enough to figure out how each of them can divide time between you and me without adding a third and unessential consideration.

My idea about Billy in a barn theatre was to let him paint scenery, take tickets, hold the script, dress the comedian, pull the curtain up and down and play butlers. As to your fear of turning him loose in a summer theatrical set, it did not occur to me that he might be seduced by the ingénue—and then I surprised myself by realizing that the prospect did frighten me so much. Of course I imagined that you would take a cottage or rooms in a hotel wherever he would be and that you might have a lovely summer together. This may be impractical. God knows I am sure of nothing when it comes to bringing up a boy. The worst things he does may be the best things for him—and vice versa.

Take the question of his school. I'll give you a sketch of the situation, the credit and debit side of the ledger—No, I'll draw two parallels on the next page:

Debit	Credit
Friday and Saturday he has at several times gone out with his crowd and stayed out until one thirty. (I have stopped this—I hope/ The difficulty I will explain later)	This is the first time he has been a member of a "Crowd"—and popular Too.
From what I can gather the academic standing of the school seems indiferent.	Billy, always lackadaisical - always an unimportant factor in the school group is for the first time having

his ego fed by a sense of
accomplishment. His activities
on two papers, in two plays, as cheerleader (God help us), and class treasurer
have stimulated him out of his
old rut of shyness and sense of
inferiority. THIS IS <u>VERY</u> <u>VERY</u>
IMPORTANT!

Debit   Credit?

I am not sure which column to put this in. The boys and girls he goes around with range from seventeen to nineteen. Whether you like it or not, you can't help this. Billy's worldly advantages place him in a position of being bored by kids of his own age and make him sufficiently interesting to older boys and girls to hold their friendship. All his friends have cars. I won't let him have a car. Neither will you. Yet since he hasn't a car, he can't promise me to be home by eleven thirty on Saturday nights because he is dependent on other boys to drive him home. He can't break up the whole party by asking to be taken home by eleven. So he stays. When they finally do start home, they have to drop the girls first. So that's how he came home at 1.30 twice. These occasions were school dances and a party after a Friday night foot-ball game.

Now I am as adamant as you about his getting a car. But you know our purpose is defeated. He is safer driving with these friends than he would be driving himself.

All these details as I give them to you have been crystallized by a talk in which Billy himself was most reasonable and stated all his difficulties without whining. Thinking it over this morning, and writing to you, and realizing how anxious it must make you, I have decided to tell him he must put the soft pedal on his social activities. He will answer that if he obeys my rules his friends will drop him. I will answer that if they drop him for that reason, they're not worth having for friends. But in my heart I will know that is fake logic, and I will feel no assurance that I am doing the right thing.

What to do? I most humbly welcome suggestions. Have you a world-beating school in the east—boarding or day school? No school is better than Exeter. But (1) they won't take him in his present class there—and he's low enough as it is and (2) I am afraid Billy will not thrive in a "good" school. Our ideal of the wholesome scholarly life we think he should lead just bores him to death. He would retire into that old shell of unhappiness and hopelessness—waiting for vacations to come.

In this lousy school he gets there a half hour early every morning. He's happy, enthusiastic and excited about life. What's the use of putting theories up against the fact?

No matter what you think, no matter what anyone might think reading this letter, I am <u>not</u> over-indulgent with Billy. I have studied him very carefully, and he is not an easy problem. You can't dismiss it in the good old-fashioned way saying: "The idea! A boy of sixteen! Pack him off to school—"—He is not just a boy of sixteen. He is a boy with a good mind and an excellent character who suffers from a lack of permanent roots. We can't take any form of insurance against mishap in his life. No school will solve it.

I have developed a bravery about Billy's immediate future. I can think of very little protection for him. He was born an individual. He's never fitted into a world and he never will. His social and extracurricular success in this school is due to its lack of organization. How he loathed what he called the "silly" rules and regulations at Gstaad and Rolle!

In my mind I see Bill—try to follow this obscure symbolism—as a lean Indian boy riding bareback on a galloping horse. Once you put a saddle on the horse, he loses all interest in riding. His saving grace is that his bareback riding is no longer all in play as it used to be. He has become a very hard, ambitious worker—at the things he likes. Have I described Billy—or have I merely described all sixteen year olds?

It's your turn to say something

Oc

Oscar Hammerstein (MGM) to Myra Finn (excerpt), December 6, 1934

Answering your questions:

1. My rating of A-1 despite a mediocre first picture. It isn't "my" picture—as a show is "my" show. I worked on it. The producer gets the blame or praise. A producer is the captain of the team—supervises everything and is responsible.

They want me to be a producer. This first picture I wrote for is just a break-in.

2. The union power prospect is a little understated. It might easily be considered a major power. I have already been offered the job of supervising all musical pictures produced here. I have turned this offer down. I think it premature. Furthermore it would mean my giving up writing. I don't want to do this. My plan is to make another picture with a picture producer, and then write and produce my own as I did on the stage. It is not my ambition to be an office executive. My only interest in becoming a producer is to get control over my own work. As to the time I will stay out here, I can only guess. I can't <u>know</u> until the option dates. In May they are to let me know if they will exercise their option on my services for another year from July first. They have the right to do that for another two years. I can tell you no more for certain.

Oscar may have inherited his interest in opera from his grandfather and namesake. While Oscar was approached for various projects related to operas, the one he instigated was his updating of *Carmen*, setting it in a Black community in the American South. By some accounts that seed was planted a year before this letter, when he attended a concert version of *Carmen* at the Hollywood Bowl.

Oscar Hammerstein to Jack Chertok,[13] January, 1935

Memo (Inter-office at M-G-M)

Subject: Operas

Dear Jack:

I haven't had time to really comb the operatic field for all possibilities, but my first reactions are these:

I think, as a popular operatic subject, "Carmen" stands alone. It has a universally interesting story, fine characterizations and as melodic a score as was ever written. As I say, I put this not merely first on the list, but way out in front, separated from the others. After that I would suggest "Faust," which also has the elements of popular melody and a story which, in various forms, has been popular for many centuries and in all countries.

---

[13] Starting in 1931, Jack Chertok was largely a producer of shorts at MGM. By the mid-1940s he had moved to Warner Bros. In the '50s he moved into television where he produced *The Lone Ranger*, and in the '60s, *My Favorite Martian*.

The Puccini group—"Boheme," "Butterfly" and "Tosca" are also promising possibilities and so, I think is "Pagliacci."

Of the modern French operas I like "Louise," but censorship difficulties might bar this. The only opera I can think of offhand that is really modern—that is, it has been written in the past fifteen years—is Korngold's "Die Tote Stadt," which has a fine story. Perhaps the music is too "modern."

I repeat, these are only random observations, without going very deeply into the long list of possibilities. I am sure I should find more. I am equally sure that there is something in the idea of producing opera on the screen, only it must be handled with great taste and showmanship. Obviously the convention of singing all thoughts in the form of either lyric or recitative would not be acceptable in so realistic a medium as the screen. The stories should be adapted so that they can be told with dialogue, and the music should be handled so it can be introduced in a believable manner.

I am very interested in this whole idea and will be pleased to hear from you how it develops.

Regards.

O.H.

Hammerstein and Kern were passionate about writing a musical based on Brian Oswald Donn-Byrne's fictionalized biography, *Messer Marco Polo* (1921). Although there's a partial draft script, and suggestions that Kern may have toyed with some music, there are no known completed songs. It was sometimes discussed with the working title, *Golden Bells*—the name given Polo's love interest. Kern and Oscar revisited the possibility over the course of several years.

Howard Reinheimer to Oscar Hammerstein, February 18, 1935

JERRY TELLS ME YOU AND HE DEFINITELY DECIDED TO DO MARCO POLO IN FALL STOP IS THIS CORRECT STOP DON'T GET TOO FAR – CONTRACTS ARE SIGNED WHICH MAY TAKE TWO WEEKS STOP WOULD YOU BE INTERESTED IN SUMMER TRYOUT STLOUIS IF SO WHEN AND WHAT ARE YOUR STUDIO PLANS REGARDS=

HOWARD.

Oscar Hammerstein (at MGM) to Howard Reinheimer,
February 19, 1935

Dear Howard:

Jerry and I have an informal understanding with Max Gordon to produce MESSER MARCO POLO at the Centre Theatre next Christmas, after the Stallings play has run its course. That is all there is to that. It is not necessary for us to give Max our definite promise for that date until August. If Metro takes up my option (it still seems to me most likely), I will ask them for a three months leave of absence—October, November, December—and will try to get a substantial advance from Max to partially make up what I would lose were the play a flop. My reason for doing this would be mainly because I want so much to do it, and secondly because I think it would be a good thing to have a play produced on Broadway next season. I realize that, in the event of my staying on here, it is a financial extravagance to take three months off, but there you are. At any rate, there is nothing to worry about at the moment, because it is all very flexible. I don't think a St. Louis tryout would be a good thing for this particular play and anyway, I shouldn't have time to have it written properly. Please expedite the signing of the MESSER MARCO POLO contract and let me know as soon as you have done it.

You ask me about the proper rental for the house. I should think roughly about $3500, unless you think rents may be inflated this summer with everything else, due to the gold decision.[14] Why not consult with some of the local agents and get their opinions about the rentals this summer. Don't turn the house into the agent's control however, until you have first asked the Rube Goldbergs or the Dave Loews if they want it. We might be able to rent it to one of those families without paying an agents' commission.

I think this is all the news for this letter. Love to all.

Oscar

---

[14] The "gold decision" refers to Roosevelt's April 1933 executive order removing the country from the gold standard and the Gold Reserve Act of January 1934. The resulting devaluation of American currency was intended to spur recovery from the Depression.

Oscar Hammerstein to Myra Finn (excerpt), March 14, 1935

I have finished dialoguing my original story. It has been approved by the intellectual giants in the front office and now I shall go ahead on the lyrics. We go into production in May. The date for their taking up my option is May first. But I have heard rumors already that they intend to take it. If they do I shall very likely ask for a leave of absence next fall to come to New York and do a show. Ordinarily I would not do this because it is bad business. I will lose 25 to 30,000 dollars in salary and must take the chance that the show will make that back, maybe more. But the project I have in mind is a labor of love, and I believe I am entitled to leave the grind of strictly commercial writing for three months and gratify my artistic ego. I am sure you will agree with me about that. The story is Messer Marco Polo by Donn Byrne and nothing has ever impressed me so. The production (for about $250,000) will be paid for by the beneficent Rockefellers (via Max Gordon) and will open at The Center Theatre next Christmas—following the run of another show by Rodgers and Hart which opens there in August.

The New Moon, which opened in November 1932, was the last successful Broadway musical Oscar wrote until Oklahoma! opened in March of 1943. It was a difficult ten years, and during much of it Oscar flirted with trying to re-invent himself in Hollywood, as both a writer and producer. It was never a happy match; the letter below encapsulates a lot of Oscar's frustrations. MGM decided not to renew Oscar's contract, letting it expire in May. Until that point, Oscar and Kern had been working on a film musical to star Jeanette MacDonald and Nelson Eddy, with working titles Champagne and Orchids, and Summer Breeze. Four songs were completed and there is at least a scenario for Summer Breeze. In February of 1936, MGM did release a film version of Oscar's Rose-Marie, which became one of MacDonald and Eddy's biggest hits.

Among those mentioned in the letter are: at Metro-Goldwyn-Mayer (MGM), Louis B. Mayer, co-founder and studio head, and his vice president, Irving Thalberg; Sam Katz, musical production chief; and Eddie Mannix, vice-president and general manager, also known as "the Fixer." Max Gordon was a Broadway producer who at this time, was best known for shows that included The Band Wagon, The Cat and the Fiddle, Flying Colors, and Roberta; Gordon went on to produce Oscar's Very Warm for May and Sunny River, and came close to being the original producer of Carmen Jones.

Oscar Hammerstein to Howard Reinheimer, May 6, 1935

Dear Howard:

Mary, Sandy and Janet Carpenter (Betty Axelrod's sister) motored out here together. They are living at The Garden of Allah. They came over here a week ago and played tennis with us. Sandy said he and Mary are going to be married. She put it off as a kind of a joke—not very gracefully—a little embarrassed. Janet as a chaperone, and Sandy as a Gigolo an[d] having a swell time. There is talk of Honolulu and Tahiti. Mary is just what the doctor ordered for both of them. If she ever marries him she will become a terribly unhappy woman. He is kind and courteous now. He will be terrible in a few years. She is too old for him. He will raise hell with her twenty-nine days of the month—all except pay day.

Please do not quote this news and these views as mine—to anyone—not even to Bob. This is just intended as a guide to you in whatever decision you must help Bob make.

Mary talks of getting a job out here—acting. Sandy is a "writer."

As to affairs at Metro-Goldwyn, I can give you only general speculation as to why my option was not taken up. There is no doubt but what I could have stayed here indefinitely had I chosen to do less work—in other words if I had not been anxious to write with Jerry and had rather doubled as a half-writer, half producer in a noncommittal way, I should have remained a man with a big past reputation and a nice fellow.

But I entered the lists. I stuck my chin out. Impatient at sitting around and frightened lest we be forced into doing something we didn't like, I invented an original story. I sold the idea to Katz, Mannix and Mayer at three different sessions—a trial, I assure you. Then I worked at full pressure and turned out a 'script in two months—considered quite an achievement here, single-handed. Katz was enthusiastic, Mannix luke-warm, Mayer didn't like it because it didn't feature MacDonald and Eddy. Inasmuch as I had told them in the very beginning that Eddy couldn't play the part, this was a queer criticism.

I got this news at Palm Springs when I had gone to write lyrics—incidentally I broke more records then, writing six important lyrics in two weeks. Katz and Gordon [?] the only ones who have heard them, raved about them. I saw Mayer at Palm Springs and discussed the story with him.

He was, as usual, fatherly, brotherly, lover-like and vague. Seeping through his talk was an apparent desire to get me "down to earth" and be more "commercial." But again and again he spoke of what "we" ought to do in future musical pictures, as if I was a permanent fixture in the organization, and one with whom he could discuss general policies. This attitude linked to reports that my option was to be taken up—from these sources, Katz, Robbins and Baravale—led me to take that for granted.

At Palm Springs I agreed with Mayer to try and revamp my 'script to feature MacDonald and Eddy more. This I did, but after working two weeks on another line, I decided that my new version did not fit with the old. So I took my new version and wrote a completely new story. I dialogued it in two and a half weeks. Both Jerry and I think it is swell. In fact we have written two original stories since Christmas and we like both of them. I gave the first half of my new script to Katz a week ago. He told Jerry he didn't like it. Jerry wisely asked him not to tell me because I wouldn't finish if I knew. Katz agreed. So I finished last Wednesday and delivered it to him Thursday. I have not yet heard from him. I assume that that script and the other will both be entombed with the huge collection of former M. G. M. extravagances and follies. If so, there will probably be some songs for Jerry and me to write before he goes. After he goes I have half-promised Bernie Hyman one of the producers to write lyrics for the music of Johann Strauss in a biographical picture [*The Great Waltz*], and there are faint rumblings of my going on "Maytime" with Thalberg. Jack Robbins is also submitting the cream of his songs to me anxious for me to give him all I can before I go. This I will do because there is quite a little money to be made in music now with a hit song and with a hustling plugger like Robbins behind it (alongside him, Harms is a joke).

Jerry says he feels that if he had not come out here, I would have done better. I don't admit it to him, but of course it is true. You saw this handwriting on the wall before you left. But, Howard, I am a writer. This is my profession. I am also a producer and director. In these capacities in the theatre I am up with the leaders. I am not a politician. I am not a racketeer. I am not a glorified pimp. And as such, while I might sustain the impression for a time, I would be bound to fail eventually. After that, what? I[t] might be difficult for me to go back to my old tools.

Mind you I have no false illusions about the hazard of the theater, nor is my memory so short that I don't realize what a haven Hollywood seemed last year after being buffeted badly in New York and London. But after being here a year I know that outside of money there is nothing to feed on here. You may say money is a good thing to feed on, and certainly it is an essential. But there are other things a man needs, most of all he needs the impression that he counts for something in the work he's doing. He also must feel that the work is worth doing. The set up here is against that.

I will curb my desire to go into this fascinating discussion further. It would not be a diatribe against the men who run pictures. I have respect for them, but I know they're going in the wrong direction towards eventual self-destruction. All this I will take up with you when we have a few hours. The question goes deeply into psychology, human nature and misdirection of energy and talent. You are not as fond of these explorations as I am. Probably they are futile and it is more profitable to face the simple fact that I must go back to work!

Show business seems to be better than it was two years ago. I think the best ways to make money out of musical shows are two. (1) A big production at The Center (2) a very small, cheap, Princess Theatre musical, making up for small royalties by taking a part of the show—five or six thousand dollars worth.

Jerry and I have made vague arrangements to do both of these things with Max Gordon.

On the big show, Alexander Wolcott sent us an idea of [?] [?] which seems more safely commercial than Marco Polo. We would do that first, and Marco Polo second. Marco Polo is something I love very much and I will do that alone, and not in a rush. On this other idea I have invited Otto to join me. I believe he is more sure-fire at the Box office than I am, and I believe my work has a finer quality than his. The combination gives the product a [?] insurance. If I do a job alone it will be 3%, if with Otto we can each get 2%. The insurance is worth 33 1/3% to me. The collaboration also makes it possible to collaborate on a little show in addition to this big one. Max has brought around Al[l]an Scott, a young writer of great promise. He wrote "Good-bye Again," another play which MacClintock has bought and one which Max is considering. He has been a collaborator in the picture version of Gay-Divorcee, Roberta, and the new Astaire picture, Top-Hat—a very useful asset, a fast and witty dialoguer. I have great hopes from this quarter.

It would surely be fine if you came out for a few days after Ellie's had her daughter and all the anxiety is over. I'd love to have a talk with you and so I know would Charlie. But it is unfair to ask you to do this at your expense, and with the new economy I must adopt for the next six months, I don't feel that I can offer to pay your expenses. Maybe we could make some arrangement to split it up. You could of course stay with us and bunk in my study.

Outside of the financial uncertainty in the future I am, of course, anxious to return, live in Great Neck and get back into the theatre for a while. But I have no sour grape attitude about Hollywood. I love it here, and life would be perfect if I could spend six months (July-November) in N. Y. and six (January-June) in California every year.

I imagine it would be very difficult to arrange at this date to come back next January. The studios don't really know what they'll be doing then. I am, however, letting it be known that "I can be had." An agent? I don't know, Howard. I hate the idea. But that is another thing for us to discuss.

Forgive this long-winded report.

Our love to Elly, Peter and yourself,

Sincerely,

Oscar

Correspondence begins to fly related to the upcoming film version of *Show Boat* to be produced by Universal Studios, which had been founded by Carl Laemmle. The film's actual producer was his son, Carl Laemmle, Jr., often referred to as Junior—just twenty-seven at the time. Ralph Blum was an artist's representative in Hollywood, a partner in the firm Feldman-Blum Corporation, providing: "Exclusive Representation—Artists, Directors, Authors."

Ralph Blum to Oscar Hammerstein and Jerome Kern, August 13, 1935

Dear Oscar and Jerry:-

Before you commit yourselves to a definite decision in connection with the "SHOW BOAT" situation I would like to call your attention to the fact that Junior Laemmle told me, at a recent discussion, that under the terms of the deal by which Universal acquired the right to "SHOW BOAT" and the right to use the music in connection with any motion picture of "SHOW BOAT" which may be made by them, you are entitled to certain percentages and that that deal, of course, would apply to the new picture which goes into production soon.

As I told you in my last wire, the fact that you accept money from them for writing new numbers and the fact that you would write new numbers could not in any wise affect your right to an accounting and the payment over to you of whatever monies may be found to be due to you, and you would not alone protect your property by writing these new numbers but you would, in addition, receive compensation therefor, Junior having agreed that you may write them in the East and submit them to him here, and furthermore, by improving the new production with additional modern numbers you would augment the profits or percentages to which you are entitled.

Please pardon my persistence in this matter. If I could see any benefit which might accrue to you by reason of your refusal I would not attempt to persuade you to act contrary to your wishes, but I would aid and abet you in every respect; I cannot see however how you could possibly profit by your refusal.

I am so anxious about this situation that I threaten you now, that if you both won't act what I consider to be sensibly I will absolutely write Eva and Dorothy and put you right on the spot by telling them the whole situation. Do you give up? Please let me know.

Carmel Meyers joins me in sending our love to all of you including, of course, Eva and Dorothy, Susie and Jimmie, and Betty, and believe me always

Sincerely yours,

Ralph

Give Us This Night was a film with songs by Hammerstein and Erich Korngold. A vehicle for the opera star Glady Swarthout, it's a backstage operetta in which a soprano and two tenors prepare an opera based on Romeo and Juliet.

Oscar Hammerstein to William Lebaron (Paramount Studio), circa August 1935

Dear Bill: please send extra copy of script [*Give Us This Night*] cutting mine up to insert lyrics stop Is Korngold making any musical changes due to Swarthout being mezzo stop Trying to find spots to elaborate her part difficult to avoid danger of throwing scenes off stop Afraid can send no lyrical material before beginning of next week tell Korngold not to worry about this stop they will come easier after I finish Morelli song for which I have already written and torn up three refrains Kindest regards

Oscar

Oscar Hammerstein to Russel Holman, September 1, 1935

Dear Russel:

In regard to Arnold Bennet's "Imperial Palace", Jerry and I suggest buying it merely as a source book for background. Very little of the original story could be used. We would have to conceive a new plot, starting from scratch.

We might make use of many of his characters, but in totally different relationships. Our leads, of course, must be people who can do numbers. This type of character usually forces you into a backstage story. We don't want to write a backstage story. We think a plot centering around a hotel will give us as many musical characters in one place as we desire. We may have any artist we choose as a guest. We may have principals in the band, specialties in the floor show, a chorus of singers and dancers—all the advantages of backstage without going near a theatre. In addition to the floor show we could have Saturday morning musicales much as they used to have at the Biltmore in New York. This would help us introduce operatic and concert singing in contrast with the type of entertainment provided in the cabaret of the big restaurant at night.

It was my experience when I read the novel that the mere revelation of the inside working of the hotel was its chief interest. The various departments of it's complicated organization, their hard-working heads, the problems they faced and how their interests conflicted. Theoretically this sounds dull, and yet I found myself fascinated by it, as you say you were. All this would be subsidiary to whatever plot was developed, but it would still be a valuable support.

As you know, my current duties prevent me from working out a story line at this time but it might be a good idea for one or more of your studio writers to take a crack at it. If it turned out well it would put me that much ahead by the time I am ready to go to work.

I still believe that we should all be digging around for other stories. If we could find a good one, all ready-made, it would of course, be much better than taking what it merely a background and starting on a new plot. But on the assumption that we can't find such a rare treasure, we believe we might develop something very good with this start.

Kindest Regards,

Correspondence regarding the 1936 film of *Show Boat* is the first substantive back-and-forth we have on any Hammerstein show. It establishes a pattern that will continue in later correspondence: the importance of casting to Hammerstein. It may be the first great film adaptation of any Broadway musical. It boasted a screenplay entirely by Oscar, and three new songs by Oscar and Kern (a fourth was written but not used). The director was British-born James Whale, best remembered for the horror films *Frankenstein*, *The Invisible Man*, and *The Bride of Frankenstein*. *Show Boat* was purportedly his favorite among his films. Perhaps because it was his first musical, Whale chose to surround himself with cast members who had been in the original Broadway production, its national tour, its London production, or the 1932 Broadway revival. He also retained orchestrator Robert Russell Bennett and musical director and conductor Victor Baravalle.

Ralph Blum (Feldman-Blum Corp.) to Oscar Hammerstein, September 16, 1935

Dear Oscar:-

I beg to confirm the telegram which I sent to you care of the "Chief" and in which I informed you that I closed the deal for your services with Junior Laemmle this morning, he agreeing to every term and condition which you specified.

The gist of the deal is that you and Jerry are engaged to furnish Universal with a script for "SHOW BOAT" and two new musical numbers and lyrics, therefor, for which you are to be paid the sum of $25,000. The draft of the script is to be delivered within five weeks and you are to make whatever corrections may be required but they are not entitled to your services, for any purpose whatsoever, after December 1, 1935.

The songs are to be furnished within the five week period but if that is too short a time please advise immediately so that I can have the contract corrected accordingly. You are to receive credit upon the screen for the screen play, and you and Jerry are to receive credit, of course, for the additional numbers.

The above amount is to be paid in five equal payments of $5,000.00 each, four of which shall be paid within the five week period and the fifth payment not later than December 1st.

If there is anything about these arrangements which does not meet with your approval please advise me immediately so that I can have the contract corrected accordingly.

When I reached my office at 3:00 o'clock this afternoon I found that George Frank[15] had telephoned me and when I got him on the 'phone he informed me that you had entered into a contract in writing with him by the terms of which he was to be employed as your exclusive agent and he requested me accordingly not to seek to obtain any engagements or employment for you in motion pictures. These statements must be correct or George would certainly not make them and I shall continue to regard them as accurate unless advised by you to the contrary. I regret the fact that you prefer to be represented by George Frank rather than by ourselves but I assure you that so far as I personally am concerned that will make no difference whatsoever in my friendship for you and I know that you will feel the same way about it; and notwithstanding the situation thus created please be assured that if there is anything that I can do to be of service to you that you are at liberty to call upon me at all times.

As soon as the contracts have been approved by me I will forward them on for the approval of yourself, Jerry and Reinheimer.

---

[15] George Frank was Hammerstein's agent in Hollywood.

With kindest and best to you and Dorothy, in which Carmel joins me, believe me

Sincerely yours,

Ralph.

The part of Joe in *Show Boat* was written with Paul Robeson in mind; in fact, Kern wrote that the music for "Ol' Man River" was largely inspired by Robeson's speaking voice. Robeson had been unavailable to play Joe in the original production of *Show Boat*, but he did star in the London premier in 1928 and then in the 1932 Broadway revival. Virtually everyone involved with the film wanted Robeson to play Joe.

Carl Laemmle, Jr. (Universal Pictures) to Oscar Hammerstein, September 24, 1935

Dear Oscar:

I have finally closed with PAUL ROBESON. It was a long hard struggle—I spoke to London twice on the phone and have been cabling back and forth—and the only way we could get Robeson was to finish him by January second. He has to be back in London for a performance at Albert Hall on January 18th—and he has other concerts following that—so there is no way to extend his time.

As you know, he is a very extravagant item—$40,000 for seven weeks—and Whale and I feel it is absolutely essential to give him another big number. SAUNDERS OF THE RIVER (Robeson's English picture) is a smash at the box-office and we want to take advantage of his drawing power.

We have given him a starting date of November 14th, meaning we must finish him between then and January 2nd. I thought I should acquaint you with the facts, so that you will do everything in your power to get us the script as soon as humanly possible. While we are taking a slight gamble on this date, we think we will be able to finish him. He is important to the picture and will be "tops" in the part.

We have the Winninger matter practically straightened out. Am sure you will be delighted with these two additions to our cast.

Kindest personal regards –

Sincerely,

Carl Laemmle Jr

Best regards to Jerome Kern, tell him I am delighted we got together. Regards. CLJ

Oscar Hammerstein to Carl Laemmle, Jr., October 1, 1935

Dear Junior:

I am delighted to hear that you've got Robeson and that you will probably have Winninger. I shall do my utmost to get my first draught of the script out to you at the earliest possible moment.

I have already done a great deal towards plotting it out. It always seems that when I deviate from the structure of the play I get into trouble. This bears out Whale's contention that the screen version should be as nearly as possible, a transcription of the stage version. I have therefore concluded to follow his advice about this except for the finish which we all agree was very weak. I think I have this solved.

The other changes will be the treatment of the new numbers. Jerry has written a new melody which I think is swell, and he's starting on another. Both of us send our kindest regards and best wishes. Please remember me to James Whale.

Sincerely,

<u>P. S.</u>

We had a man playing the small part of "Rubber Face" who was very effective. I think, that in keeping with the original flavor of the play, he would be an additional asset. His name is Francis X. Mahoney. He is out there and I have asked him to get in touch with you.

Oscar Hammerstein to Carl Laemmle, Jr., October 9, 1935

Dear Junior:

I am mailing about thirty pages of my treatment to Ralph Blum today. He will deliver it to you as soon as he gets it. I have gone about twenty pages further but I'm cutting and revising before sending them on at the end of the week.

Please let me know what you think of it as far as I've gone. It will help me as I write the balance of the script.

I read that Edna May Oliver[16] is to play in "Romeo and Juliet" for Thalberg. Does this mean we lose her? I hope not.

For the part of Frank, I believe you should make a test of Sammy White who was so good in the original. If you don't like him, I suggest Buddy Ebsen.[17] He showed great promise in "Broadway Melody" although he and his sister were not handled particularly well in that picture.

I'll keep right after the script and shoot it out to you as fast as I can. I find myself falling in love with the characters all over again, and I'll do all in my power to help you make this a great picture.

Sincerely,

James Whale to Oscar Hammerstein, October 14, 1935

=FIRST PART OF SHOWBOAT SCRIPT EXCELLENT SUGGEST RAVENAL HAS SINGING ENTRANCE WHICH WOULD SELL RAVENAL ON HIS VOICE BEFORE AUDIENCE CAN DISLIKE HIS FACE OR ACTING ABILITY REGARDS=

JAMES WHALE.

Oscar Hammerstein to James Whale, October 16, 1935

Dear James Whale:

Here's the second batch.

Thank you for your wire. I had hoped that Ravenal would be a charming personality but if he has to be played by an actor with a face and manner that no audience could love, I agree with you that it will be safer to give him a singing entrance. This can easily be done. Hoping you like the enclosed.

Sincerely,

---

[16] Edna May Oliver played Parthy—Cap'n Andy's sour, critical wife, and Magnolia's overly protective mother in the original Broadway production of *Show Boat* and its 1932 revival.

[17] Ebsen, who began his career as an eccentric, comedic dancer, and is best remembered for playing Jed Clampett in *The Beverly Hillbillies*, was not cast in *Show Boat*.

Oscar Hammerstein to Edna May Oliver (MGM),
October 17, 1935

Dear Edna:

Is it going to be possible for you to play Parthy in Show Boat? I don't know if Universal has approached you about it, but as I write the screen version I can imagine no one else. I have read that you are playing the nurse in Romeo and Juliet and I hope this will not conflict with the Show Boat production which will be made during the weeks from November twentieth to January twentieth—or thereabouts.

I would appreciate a word from you regarding the probability of your being available between these dates so that I will know what I am talking about when I tell Universal that there is only one Parthy in the world. If we can't have you, then the Show Boat is a ship without a rudder.

With all best wishes to you,

Sincerely,

Edna May Oliver to Oscar Hammerstein, October 21, 1935

My Dear Oscar;

I was so pleased to get your note. Praise from you, my friend, means much to the likes of Me: Unfortunately (it never rains but what it pours) in this world, in other words, all good things come at once. I have wanted all my life to play the nurse in Willie Shakespeare's little Opus, which will make it impossible for me to do Parthy. And I find studio work is pretty strenuous for me these days, and I can only do so much.

However if I am not too fascious [sic], might I suggest Helen Broderick she seems to have many of the ear marks of Parthy.

Best wishes to you Oscar.

Sincerely

Edna.

Oscar Hammerstein to James Whale, October 25, 1935

Dear James Whale:

There has been a serious omission in sequence C page 13. I inadvertently left out a very important direction wherein Steve runs the blade of his knife across the tip of Julie's finger and pressing his lips to the wound, sucks the blood.[18] This is, of course, the whole point of the scene and I can't understand how I missed it when I proofread it. I enclose the corrected page. Will you please insert this in your script, Junior Laemmle's script and any other copies that have been made to date.

I am well into the home stretch now and expect to have the job completed by November First.

Kindest Regards,

James Whale to Oscar Hammerstein, October 25, 1935

Dear Mr. Hammerstein:-

I have now received our script up to the end of sequence "E", the wedding of "Magnolia" and "Ravenal" for which many thanks, and want to tell you how absolutely delighted I am with everything in it. It has all of the play and more-over has an amazing freshness which I feel cannot possibly fail to thrill its waiting public. I am very glad to note that there will be several new musical numbers and think the new scene with duet for "Magnolia" and "Ravenal" after the show where "Ravenal" talks to the stocking is enchanting. I do not care much for the little Zoe Akins "ceegar and cane" scene which you have retained. It seems rather dull and the planting of the cane seems to stick out like a sore thumb. If it is necessary here I think we could get a little more out of it. The only other suggestion I have so far I have already spoken to you about and that is the singing entrance for "Ravenal". I have made many tests so far easily the best is Wilbur Evans, who has a very fine voice, with a very pleasing personality and although quite attractive is

---

[18] Learning that he and Julie, of mixed race, are about to be arrested for breaking Mississippi's law forbidding miscegenation, Steve cuts Julie's hand. Gently tasting her blood, Steve can truthfully claim that he, too, has negro blood in him.

not the ideal "Ravenal" at first glance. The only thing against this entrance is that it was done in NAUGHTY MARIETTA but with such tremendous success and for exactly the same reason that as so much hangs on the first impression the audience get of "Ravenal" I believe we should do this. Quite a different entrance could be devised and I wondered if we could bring him along the river singing his "Good Luck"[19] song, or a new number, what do you think? The "Driftwood"[20] song seems hardly spectacular enough to sell a new Star.

I am coming to New York, leaving Hollywood on Saturday, October 26th on the Chief, so shall be in New York on Wednesday the 30th. I expect to stay at the Waldorf, but if not will let you know and you can always get me through the Universal New York office. I will bring all the interesting tests for you to see. I am looking forward enormously to making the picture and since the arrival of the new script have got back all the thrill I lost over the other one.

All good wishes.

Yours sincerely,

James Whale

James Whale to Oscar Hammerstein, October 28, 1935

Dear Oscar Hammerstein:

Your letter with new page C-13 just [came] in for which many thanks. I had of course noticed that the omitted business of sucking the blood by "Steve" was a mistake and would have rectified it anyway.

It looks as if I will not be able to come to New York after all which is very disappointing as I had hoped to have further talks with you and also to find some new and exciting personalities for the picture. I am looking forward to the rest of the script and if it continues as it has up to now I shall be more than content. It has turned out so well that I am more

---

[19] Gaylord Ravenal's song "Till Good Luck Comes My Way" was not included in the film.
[20] Ravenal's first song, both on stage and in the film, is "Where's the Mate for Me," which includes the lyrics: "The driftwood floating over the sea / Someday finds a sheltering lee, / So somewhere surely there must be / A harbor meant for me."

than ever sure of the wisdom of sticking as near to the original story as you have.

I am very anxious to get the new songs from Jerome Kern as it will be necessary to shoot all Paul Robeson's stuff first to get him away. You are probably sick of hearing all about the super-human difficulties of the studio but I would appreciate it very much if when you send the other stuff it could include the musical numbers, particularly the new Paul Robeson song. Incidentally, I don't quite know where it comes in but it seems to me that with such a terrific personality as Robeson and his magnificent voice it would [be] a very good ending to the picture to have Paul Robeson sing his new number possibly with a production chorus. Don't take this too literally but it just struck me that it might work in to the ending you already have in mind at the Zeigfeld [*sic*] theatre.

Best wishes.

Yours sincerely,

James Whale

Carl Laemmle, Jr. to Oscar Hammerstein, October 31, 1935

HAVE READ YOUR LATEST SEQUENCES THINK THEY MAGNIFICENT CONGRATULATIONS STOP MATTER DISCUSSED WITH YOU ON PHONE WILL GIVE DECISION TO GEORGE FRANK TOMORROW STOP HAVE YOU SEEN HELEN MORGAN STOP ADVISE STRAIGHT YOUR OPINION BUDDY EBSON [*sic*] FOR FRANK WHATS OPINION PATSY KEWLY [*sic*] TO TEAM WITH EBSEN KINDEST REGARDS

CARL LAEMMLE JR

Oscar Hammerstein to Carl Laemmle, Jr., circa November 1, 1935

Junior Laemmle

Glad you liked last sequence. Expect to mail you final sequence tonight. Like Buddy Ebsen for Frank but still favor Sammy white [*sic*] far above all others providing screen test good. Patsy Kelly wrong for Ellie. Consider her very funny comedienne but gives impression of being wise New York rather than quaint down-at-heel river actress. Ellie must also dance to do cake-walk in Trocadero with Frank. Kindest Regards to James Whale and yourself.

Oscar Hammerstein

Oscar Hammerstein to Carl Laemmle, Jr., November 2, 1935

Dear Junior:

Here's the finish. I can't make up my mind whether we should use Irene Dunne in the part of Kim as well as Magnolia, using double exposure devices or whether the stunt would seem too theatrical and artificial taking away from it the quality of sentimental sincerity that this kind of ending needs. I see, of course, certain advantages in the idea for giving Irene Dunne a chance to play a dual part—always an effective stunt for an actress. I wish you would talk this over carefully with James Whale.

I will get busy now on the three new songs and shall try to get them out to you as soon as possible. Jerry and I will have records made here so that you may have our ideas of musical tempo and lyric interpretation.

Kindest Regards

Carl Laemmle, Jr. to Oscar Hammerstein, November 5, 1935

SOME CONFUSION ABOUT DATES IF WE OPEN UP IN 1889 HOW OLD IS KIM IN CHICAGO SEQUENCE AS CHICAGO FAIR IN 1893 THIS WOULD MAKE KIM FORTYTWO[21] ON HER DEBUT=

CARL LAEMMLE JR.

---

[21] In the stage musical Kim was born around 1903 and was a star by 1927.

Oscar Hammerstein to Carl Laemmle, Jr., circa November 6, 1935

Assume we open eighteen ninety I purposely avoided dating marriage or Kim's birth. There is no sign of her being alive during World's Fair stop First clue to her age Sequence G Page two Imagine this about nineteen four she about two Imagine this about nineteen four she about three years old stop Last sequence should be late nineteen twenties but avoided specific dating here too. In original novel dates were so mixed that Magnolia was about nine years old when she had Kim stop I believe that as long as we don't go out of our way to stamp last sequence as nineteen thirty-five we will have no trouble stop In answer to previous wire think Halliday just a little too heavy in voice and personality Have you tested Gregory yet Also think Walter Pidgeon a possibility but don't know how long his play will run here stop How about Elisabeth Patterson for Parthy if we don't get Oliver Regards

Oscar Hammerstein

Oscar Hammerstein to Irene Dunne, November 6, 1935

Dear Irene:

I called you up twice but you were out. This is what I would have said had you been in:

"Jerry and I would like to go over the new songs with you—as soon as we have finished them. This should be about the beginning of next week."

You would have said "Fine! I'd love to hear them!"

So be expecting us.

Kindest regards to you all ("you all" not used as a southern idiom, but meaning yourself, your husband and Mildred, if by some strange chance you bump into her)

Sincerely,

Oscar Hammerstein to James Whale, November 18, 1935

Dear James Whale:

The enclosed new pages for the script are concerned mainly with the introduction of the three new songs.

There are several other revisions the purpose of which I explain on a sheet attached to each one.

The pages are arranged and numbered so that they may be inserted in the script without confusion. The master copies have the changed parts typed in red ink. These are for you so that you may see at a glance what has been added or altered.

Now I will take up categorically several points in your letter:

(A) Admiring Constance Collier as I do, I nevertheless can not subdue a fear that no matter how well she plays it, she'll never seem the real thing.

(B) I discussed your difficulty over "Bill" with Jerry. We both feel that instead of elaborating its production, you should cut it down to one verse and one chorus. Two verses and two choruses are too long to wait for the plot to move on at this point. Whatever you do, please don't let her sit on the piano! She should stay right at the table with that wistful, half-pathetic simplicity which is her virtue.

(C) I read over Zoe Akin's "Captain and Cane" scene which worried you and I think it should be yanked right out. It is unconvincing and really unnecessary. Ravenal's obviously losing money at the table. It is easy to conclude in the following scene that he wants to "bum" his passage to Natchez on the Show Boat because he can't pay to go farther on the River Queen. And we know that he must leave town.

　　Further, it seems good to me after the Pete-Vallon scene which implies a dramatic threat, to go directly to the Show Boat where rehearsals are taking their peaceful, normal course—"little wotting [sic] the blow that is about to fall," etc.

(D) I agree with you about eliminating the superimposing of Robeson's head. I think your device of making him the central figure of the illustrative shots is ever so much better.

(E) Your postscript suggestion regarding the production of the number on D—68 is answered by the enclosed description of Magnolia's banjo number.

I hope you will agree that a naive, old-fashioned "coon number"[22] production is just the thing for the Show Boat, and it seems to us that having Irene Dunne doing a number in blackface is novel and different from anything she's ever done. It "loosens her up". She herself is most enthusiastic about the idea. I think it is one of those things that is sure to be talked about by those who see the picture, and is all in all a good stroke of showmanship.

You will by this time have received two of the new songs. I shudder at the idea of submitting songs in manuscript. It is so hard to get the true conception just having music and words played and sung by someone who happens to be able to read them. We are making records this afternoon, and they may give you a better idea. The third song has been finished and we will send it out as soon as possible.

Now here is a list of miscellaneous matters some of which may seem to you unimportant. They are partly my suggestions and partly Jerry's. You must forgive us if we seem a little over-motherly about our favorite child.

c—15 Vallin's last speech.

"— I warn you, if the folks around here get wind you've got niggers actin' ON THE STAGE with whites, etc."

To avoid any ambiguity or implication that they are "actin' together" off the stage.

d—12 Sixth speech on page.

ANDY: Your missus just sent in a message her sister's took with a FEVER and y' got to drive her over to Centerville.

"Fever" instead of "spell". Fever was in the original and seems better.

d—2 Tenth speech.

Jerry brings up the point that in the warm south, ash-cans were perhaps uncommon things.

This could read:

Ninth speech:

---

[22] The "coon" song added to the film for Irene Dunne to sing is "Gallavantin' Aroun'." While it does show an unexpected side to Irene Dunne, and does "loosen her up," it has now proven to be one of the most difficult aspects of the film.

ELLIE: I feel the same way, Frank. Look at Magnolia. Her picture with Ravenal's on all the posters.

FRANK: An' everybody makin' a fuss over them.

ELLIE: You want to know, etc.

D—10   In addition to Captain Andy's fiddle there are of course other instruments in the orchestra played by members of the brass band, or anyone around the show boat or towboat that can help out. Windy might be very handy with a flute.

D—11   Instead of Rubber Face blowing out a lamp I think it would be interesting to shoot from the wings, obliquely facing the footlights, and show the way a stage was dimmed in those days. Opaque half-cylinders were turned around to cover the lights. I enclose drawings, and Leighton Brill can supplement further details because he did the researche [sic] for me.

I hope you will approve the enclosed changes. Please let me know how you like them.

I am not sending any copies to Junior, assuming that you will show him these and also this letter. That saves me the trouble of writing you both identical letters.

Good Luck!

Sincerely

On November 22, *May Wine* began its out-of-town tryouts in Wilmington, Delaware. With music by Sigmund Romberg, lyrics by Oscar, and a book by Frank Mandel, the show opened on Broadway on December 5, and ran for 213 performances.

James Whale to Oscar Hammerstein, November 30, 1935

Dear Oscar Hammerstein:

I am sorry you didn't like the test of Allan Jones. Of course I know that he is not the Ravenal of Tennessee you have written, but for that matter, neither is Nelson Eddy. Incidentally, there appears to be a very good chance of getting Eddy, so if it is possible to work out the dates, as he has an extensive concert tour booked, we shall seize the chance and sign him pronto. I imagine this would be agreeable to you.

PARTHY: A great many tests of Parthy, all of them disappointing. Jessie Ralph came the nearest, but terribly flabby and common. All New York tests showed actresses think Parthy merely a funny washerwoman type. I am still hoping to get Oliver, but chances are slim, as she is very sick and seems insanely bent on playing the nurse in "Romeo and Juliet". My second choice seems to be Helen Wesley [*sic*].[23] Largely, I must confess, because I think she can do it and we haven't tried her yet. The trouble with her is that she refuses to make a test. I know she is an excellent actress, but I am afraid she would look very old and fat. Also, one can see her 'heart of gold' a bit too clearly, and she'd no doubt be anxious to wear it outside her concrete chest. Would you take her without a test? She has dignity, authority, and I think, intelligence. I know her quite well personally, and I am sure could work with her. However, I am a little scared to take her without test, as Jessie Ralph gave us a disagreeable shock when we saw her today on the screen. Although I knew she was mugging, her commonness was multiplied by ten on the screen. She also had authority and a certain amount of dignity, and completely missed it.

FRANK AND ELLIE: Made test of Sammy White and Queenie Smith yesterday. It looks very good and I am quite happy about both, although Junior isn't at all sold on Sammy White. He thinks he looks too Jewish and has no personality. I agree with the former, but his personality is pleasing on the screen and I think he is almost the perfect Frank.

QUEENIE: I am looking at Ada Brown today, but failing her, Hattie McDaniel[24] will, I think, be admirable.

Paul Robeson has arrived and is, of course, delightful and very keen.

KIM: Definitely feel that although realize the difficulty, a new personality should be found for this part, but great deal depends on number which I understand is on the way.

---

[23] Helen Westley did play Parthy in the film.

[24] Hattie McDaniel, best remembered for playing Mammy in *Gone with the Wind* and being the first Black actor to win an Oscar, did play Queenie in the film of *Show Boat*.

<u>VERA MARSH TEST:</u> This came in today. I thought it was much too shrill and too like comic piping telephone girl. Her tinny voice would be all against her in the letter scene in which Queenie Smith is already very good indeed.

<u>STORY:</u> Very anxious to know your practical reactions to suggestions of singing entrance for Ravenal. Nelson Eddy, although a popular star, I still think should be sold as a lover with his entrance song. If you don't want to write a new one, how about using "If Good Luck Comes My Way?"

In addition, he's anxious to get another spectacular solo.

We are already building levee and Boonsville on back lot, and I am sure that part is going to be excellent.

Best wishes,

James Whale

P.S. In the Y.M.C.A. hut, will Magnolia sing a war song or a "Kern" number?

Leighton Brill to Oscar Hammerstein (excerpts), December 2, 1935

Good old Paul Robeson, the old reliable, made another singing test and it's a pip, so right away everybody is calling for six or seven more songs for Mr. Robeson. I'm fighting valiantly to protect you from that barrage, but as Jerry is arriving tomorrow, I'll let him shoulder that burden . . . not alone Kern songs, but any and every Negro spiritual that has ever been heard.

Charlie Winninger has started to direct, edit costumes, and rewrite script, but I have no fear but that our Mr. Whale will take all that out of him in short order.

Leighton Brill to Oscar Hammerstein, December 3, 1935

TUESDAY BULLETIN

Dear Oc:

At least I can definitely say that Nelson Eddy is a <u>cold</u> <u>turkey</u>. After three weeks of fooling around they have found out that no means <u>no</u>.

Yesterday was engaged in making some real tests of Allan Jones. These were done with Irene Dunne. Haven't seen the rushes on them yet but looking at them on the set they really made a very good pair, Dunne wearing the costume from the piece was surprisingly young looking, and Jones looked very manly. Mr. Whale worked very hard with them, doing the scene on the deck, and in the final rendition we all thought Jones would do a fine job.

Miss Dunne either found out who I was or has a marvelous memory, (because, as you remember, she only met me twice before, first with the road company and once in Louie Shurr's[25] office.) She remembered me—or it was a swell piece of acting, and got very much a "chum". She is wishing for a legitimate actor to play the part opposite her, Fredric March being her choice. But she told me that Jerry was the red flag waver in the case of Jones, not you. I've had a hunch that was so, and asked about it in every letter to you, but as yet have not had an answer. Is this the truth? - Because it looks very much like he's going to get the part.

Boles is still an anathema to Mr. Whale, and I honestly think if you put him in the part it would take a lot of the spirit out of his directing. He really dislikes Boles very much. My honest opinion is that Jones, properly handled, has as good a chance of coming through for us in "Showboat" as Eddy did for M-G-M in "Marietta". He is as good looking, no worse as an actor, and only a couple of shades behind in the singing. What more can you ask for?

Our (Mr. Whale's and mine) two favorite candidates for Frank and Ellie—Sammy White and Queenie Smith—are still in the running, as the front office has offered nobody who are nearly as good. Every test we make is a break for them.

Today we are going on to the small parts. Fred Kohler an enormous movie villain and good actor, is slated to the backwoodsman, and Maude Eburne for Mrs. O'Brien. Whale has a candidate for Steve, a leading man by the name of Kent Taylor. I have never seen him, but I understand that he is very, very good, and it's just a question if we can get him and if he'll play the part.

---

[25] Louie Shurr, famed Hollywood and Broadway casting agent.

The music for "Ah Still Suits Me" has turned up and we are starting to work with Robeson on it.

The latest news is that if we have a leading man we start to shoot Friday, and start with the Showboat coming in to dock at the levee in Boonsville.

What is worrying all concerned is the securing of an ace cameraman for the picture. They have finally succeeded in getting Mescal,[26] who was to shoot it, sobered up, and although the production manager declares he will wash his hands of the production if Mescal shoots it, everybody seems to think that Mescal drunk is better than the ones we can obtain, sober.

I had to stand on my rear legs and do a little violent objecting yesterday. The production manager, Mr. Murphy, is greatly worried as to footage, thinking the picture will run way over in that regard. (NOTE BY SECRETARY: Mr. Murphy always brings up this argument. I think he weighs the scripts then goes into his dance. Think nothing of it.)

I don't blame him for objecting. That seems to be the function of production managers, but Mr. Murphy, after a careful (???) reading of the script, came forward with the bright suggestion of cutting out—(1) Captain Andy's speech explaining the show; (2) The Y.M.C.A. scene, and (3) the school children episode in the opening. I have no objections to him throwing the school children shot in any convenient receptacle, but I argued long and vehemently (but softly) about Andy's speech and the Y.M.C.A. scene, and was backed in this by Mr. Whale, who really understands everything in the script. So those scenes will stay in spite of Mr. Murphy's declaiming that if they are shot they will eventually land on the cutting room floor.

Another thing, Charlie Winninger, in going over the script, felt that what was our old ending of Act I—"Marry a murderer, Oh, my God!"—faint—"She's gone!"—"Let's go on with the wedding!" was stronger than the present one. Whale is about to agree with him, and subject to a violent objection on your part, I am fitting the old scene into the present version. (NOTE: After seeing what is done to some scripts out here by directors, and seeing the care and seeking to preserve everything that Mr. Whale is giving your script, I would say that this is a very, very minor operation.)

I expect this is pretty nearly next to the last letter you will get from me. Will send on Thursday both to your residence and to the boat.

---

[26] John Mescal, cinematographer.

Personal notes: Feel very much better, but have occasional attacks, so today will trek down town, get an Xray and find out what's really wrong.

Oscar Hammerstein to Howard Reinheimer, January 8, 1936

Dear Howard:

Please have Miss Glatterman check the enclosed with other bills you have there to see if it is a duplicate. I note that this one is made out to me and the work is dated December sixth. I believe these plumbers, etc. should be notified that I will not be responsible for work ordered by someone else and not okayed by me.

Please also ask Miss Glatterman to resume my subscription to the New York Sunday Times.

I did not make myself clear in my instructions regarding Mike's allowance. The agreement is that she is to get $225 in cash and the balance of 11½% is to go into the fund.

I have had troubles getting an assignment here. They had nothing that I liked. I turned down several stories and then I went to them and offered to postpone the whole contract until the spring, saying that I could seek and [sic] assignment at another studio or go to Palm Springs to write a play while I was waiting. They thought my attitude very generous and sporting but they wouldn't hear of my leaving. I shall probably go on, to the Count of Luxembourg this week, supplanting Herbert Fields. It is a major production starring W.C. Fields, Gladys Swarthout and a male singer. The idea is that while I'm working on this, they will continue to hustle around for a story for Jerry and me to follow.

I have told George, however, not to depend on them. They have had four months to get a story for Jerry and me and they have flopped. George is exploring among all the other companies and if I can get a commitment for Jerry and me—or me alone—at any studio to follow immediately on the expiration of this contract, I shall take it.

Despite these difficulties, I have, after a great deal of thought, decided that this is the only place for a writer to earn a living. There is so much demand for material that once you are established as a screen author—as

I believe I am now, - there is nothing to stop you from getting as near to an assured income as any man can expect in any business.

Outside of Marco Polo and the thin hope of February Hill I have no immediate interest in the stage or New York.

Dorothy is going to buy a medium sized place here which will not cost as much to run and will be easy to rent at a profit in the event of our being called to New York or London. With my views concerning the future value of the dollar—which are pessimistic indeed—I want her to use the money for a tangible property. I am very set on this point.

So please tell the agents to go after the sale of Great Neck, and tell them I am more in a mood to talk turkey than ever before. I really want to make my home out here.

Can you tell me why the May Wine songs aren't getting a radio plug? Is it because of Rommy's silly idea of holding back? Or is Spitzer just a lousy plugger? Or are the songs no good? Please ask Mac to wire me the week's business every Saturday night.

Will you also please mail Dorothy's newly purchased bonds out here and close out her Irving account and send a check for the full amount so that she can deposit it here?

I guess there are enough of my affairs to bother you with for one letter. I'm looking forward to your coming. Give me the exact date of your arrival when you decide.

Love from both of us to Ellie, the kids, and yourself.

Oscar Hammerstein to Liverights Book Store, January 9, 1936

Dear Miss Liveright:

Kindly send me a copy of "Edna His Wife" by Margaret Ayer Barnes.

Have you anything that might interest me as a possibility for adaptation? I am starving for material with which to make a screen musical. With kindest regards.

Sincerely,

The film version of *Rose-Marie* was released on February 1. It was the second pairing of Jeanette MacDonald and Nelson Eddy, and their duet of the "Indian Love Call" became one of their best-remembered numbers. Oscar had little if any involvement with the film, which largely abandoned his script, and retained only four songs with his lyrics.

Oscar Hammerstein to James Whale, February 24, 1936

Dear James Whale:

The romantic interest at the end of the picture is a reunion of lovers. The dramatic element of this reunion is that a woman, once deserted, has worked hard and conquered life, while the man who deserted her has been punished, has suffered from the very weaknesses in his character that made him run away from the problems they had both faced together. As firmly as she has become established as a success, just so firmly has he become established as a failure. Unless the contrast is sharply drawn, their meeting is a tame, conventional and convenient finish, without flavor, without drama.

The man I saw on the screen Saturday night was more attractive than the man who addressed Magnolia on the levee forty years ago. He is certainly not the kind of stage door man whom the chorus girls would call "Pop." They would call him "Cutie" or "Sweetie." There is nothing pathetic about such a man. When the manager bawls him out you don't have the feeling of a once-proud person now humbled and accustomed to being bullied. You feel rather that he is quite superior to anything the manager might say to him—that he could walk right over to the Savoy-Plaza and get a job as an assistant manager.

Leighton Brill has told me the various justifications advanced for this conception of Ravenal. I don't deny that they are all conceivable and ingeniously logical. But this ingenuity is misdirected into achieving an anemic dilution of the dream that was intended to vitalize the scene. Ingenuity might better be employed to heighten drama. It seems to me no less logical to think of Ravenal as the incurable gambler he always was. Instead of scraping and saving a few dollars to buy a cheap suit for his daughter's opening night, he might easily plunk the meager savings on a "sure thing" at the race track, hoping to buy himself a "real" suit, send his daughter a "real" bunch of flowers—or since she doesn't know he is her father, he might not be concerned about the elegance of his appearance. He might, on the day he was paid, walk into the best florist in New York, a shabbily dressed man, and with a laconic elegance that suggested the old Ravenal, order a large basket of flowers for Kim. It might make a good scene.

But whatever he does with his savings (assuming that he ever saved a penny, which I doubt), don't let him spend it at the tailor's or the barber's. The better he looks, the worse it is for our story.

Magnolia has always loved him. She "can't help lovin' dat man." She will always love him, no matter what he looks like. But her outward behavior on their first meeting would depend a great deal on his appearance. If he looks a serene, well-preserved and attractive man, her impulse would be a formal greeting. She would wait until he made overtures to her. But if his appearance and manner are such as to evoke sympathy, her heart will go out to him. She will want to mother him, take his hand, lift him out of his rut of failure and place him by her side where she feels he has always belonged. That is the ending as written. I can see or feel no other.

Please forgive this long-winded and didactic dissertation. Irrespective of your reaction to it and of your decision, I must repeat my sincere expression of gratitude for your superb treatment of this story and its characters. Your fidelity to the manuscript and the skill with which you have expressed that fidelity is the very boon all authors dream of—and almost never receive. So, in this scene we are discussing, I am equally certain of your fidelity. I write this letter merely to tell you that my conception of the mood and element of drama was different, and to supplement my directions in the script which may have been inadequate. I feel very deeply that the characterization of Ravenal is wrong and that the scene should be done over—without a single change for the other characters, all of whom seem quite perfect to me.

Kindest regards,

Oscar Hammerstein to Paul Robeson, February 25, 1936

Dear Paul:

I have re-read "Black Majesty"[27] and I feel that I can make a fine picture of it. Jerome Kern and I have bought the rights to it.

---

[27] *Black Majesty: The Life of Christophe, King of Haiti* (1928) was written by John W. Vandercook. In the early 1930s, Russian director Sergei Eisenstein was also interested in making a film to star Robeson.

It must be done on a very broad scale or not at all. I discussed it with one big producer who liked it but thought it a great gamble. I think this a very typical reaction.

It has occurred to me that the best auspices under which to produce would be in England under Korda's banner. He has already produced a picture for you and it was successful. Popular as you are here, you are even more popular in England. The picture would cost less to make there. Beyond these considerations, I feel that since it is such an unusual undertaking it would have a better chance with Korda who is a man of taste and courage, untrammelled by the superstitions and conventional convictions of Hollywood producers.

What do you think? I shall do nothing further here until I have heard from you.

With kindest regards to Mrs. Robeson and yourself.

Sincerely,

Oscar Hammerstein to James Whale, March 16, 1936

Dear Jim:

Here is the list of notes you requested last Saturday:

1- THE SCENE IN THE SQUARE after the PARADE—

Some little touches and attempts at light comedy should be cut in favor of pulling story elements closer together.

2- "ONLY MAKE BELIEVE"—

Restore interlude "Your pardon, I pray". Try cutting first refrain and beginning with this.

3- BLOOD TEST SCENE—

Is the camera on Steve sufficiently long to establish his assimilating 'nigger blood'- on which the scene depends?

No film was ever made.

4-   CAPTAIN ANDY'S SPEECH—

I suggest that the camera be on Andy when he says "We ain't never had such a show where virtue ain't won out," which is the feed to "It's been a tight squeeze sometimes."

5-   "BEEN GALLIVANTIN' AROUND"—

At start of refrain Magnolia is in Medium Long, with her back to camera. I feel (maybe because I write lyrics) that all refrains should start with the camera fairly close on the singer. The theme of a refrain is nearly always expressed in the first line. After that it doesn't make so much difference where the camera goes.

6-   "YOU ARE LOVE"—

After seeing the picture through, I feel more strongly that "You Are Love" should be restored.

7-   "SECOND KITCHEN SCENE—

Establish flood raging outside.

8-   "BILL"—

Are the two fat burlesque girls featured just a little too much? Do we come back to them too much after the first shot where they are limbering up?

9-   LAST NUMBER—

I didn't see this out, but I was disturbed by the shots of the scene change from the front of the house. It is unlikely that in a Broadway show the stage management would be so careless as to permit the audience to see the chorus rushing off stage to make their change and the scenery being changed in the semi-darkness. I daresay there will only be a flash of this in the cutting, but I suggest that you use the Reverse Shot from backstage, we don't necessarily feel that the audience can see the same thing out front. This is a very small point, of course. The big point is that I am very doubtful about the second half of the number being any good at all. If I am right, it will not be fatal because it is at least a good enough background for the story to cut into. I only hope that if the number is ineffective, we will be brave enough to recognize it and not keep a lot of dull stuff just because it cost a lot to shoot. What I consider dull is everything that takes place when Kim is not on the stage. There are a lot of dancers, black and white, dancing difficult steps to intricate rhythms, but to me there is very little interest in this. I hope I am wrong.

Speaking of being wrong, I very cheerfully admit that my fears about Ravenal's costume in the last sequence have melted away. He is established so definitely as a down-and-outer in the previous sequence that one still thinks of him as a down-and-outer even if he is dressed a little too sprucely.

I have great confidence in the picture, in fact, from the time "Ol' Man River" is sung right down to Magnolia singing "After the Ball", there seems to be a succession of dramatic, comedy and entertainment punches following each other in continuous succession. In your direction you have sustained the mood and all the characterizations to a degree that approaches perfection. If the picture affects other people as it affected me, I have no doubt about it whatever.

Please let me know when you will be ready for me to come over again.

Kindest regards.

James Whale to Oscar Hammerstein, March 17, 1936

Dear Oscar:

Thank you for your letter with the list of notes with which I agree practically 100%.

(1) I have already trimmed the opening, the shots coming into the square after the parade I have taken out and the handing up of the presents, a few of Parthy's unnecessary hammered reactions, and I think they will take care of that.

(2) "Make Believe". I am rather inclined to think that we really need the whole of this. If we start with "Your pardon I pray", we will lose all the merging of the two and it seems just as sudden as it did with the other cut. However, I will run this again.

(3) The blood test scene. In looking at it again I am quite certain that the camera is on Steve long enough to establish the blood drinking without a shadow of a doubt.

(4) I am putting back the speech "We ain't never had a play where virtue ain't won out" which will take care of that.

(5) The "Gallavantin' Around" is an excellent suggestion and I don't know how I missed it. Of course we must be on Magnolia at the start of the refrain. That has been taken care of.

(6) "You are Love". Baravelle is already putting in the music of "You Are Love" so if we still feel it is needed it will be easy for Dunne to do it when she comes back, in fact I have already made arrangements, and failing positive veto we should have that in the bag soon.

(7) The second kitchen scene. We have three beautiful shots establishing the flood raging outside.

(8) "Bill". The two fat burlesque girls have already been moved to another spot and will take their place in the montage shots. If it still sticks out we shall remove it altogether.

(9) Last number. I entirely agree with you on this. It doesn't seem to belong to "Show Boat" at all. The main fault being that Kim, as per instructions in the script, should have been featured all the time instead of some tap dancing by the chorus and then a solo by Kim. However I see light on it and I think we can use the opening shot, take Kim off to change her dress and as soon as we get our stage full go to Parthy in the taxi. When we come back we get a few spectacular flashes of the dancers, perhaps two from the front and two from the back, after which we bring Parthy in after Kim makes her entrance at the subway. She starts her dance and we play the scene with Magnolia and Ravenal, bring them into the box at which time Kim is just finishing her dance. She has her little speech and gets the audience going on "Gallavantin' Around", we go to the box and see Parthy joining in. Ravenal and Magnolia go out and come back to the curtain in time to see Kim with the audience going full tilt. I think it will take care of that.

(10) I am very glad that you feel happy about Ravenal's looks at the finish. I think it is fully established that he is down and out, but must admit that your criticism of the latter part helped me to get the earlier part right when I shot that after your criticism for which I thank you.

There is still a lot of work to be done on the picture but I have great confidence in it and feel sure that all the work we put into it will knit together into a harmonious and thrilling production.

I want to tell you how very much I have appreciated the valuable help you and Jerry have been, not only on the script but during the production of the picture. Leighton Brill has also been a tremendous asset. It has been, I think, the happiest engagement I have had in Hollywood. I hope that the final result will be completely satisfying as I am very mindful of the terrific responsibility vested in me with this beautiful and important property. There is nothing I would like more than to repeat the experiment with exactly the same set-up and think "Black Majesty" would make a very good follow-up.

I will let you know when we have another running at which time I would like to sit in with you so that we can discuss points as they come up.

Kindest regards,

Jim

Oscar Hammerstein to Harold [?] (excerpt), April 30, 1936

"Show Boat" was previewed last week and it looks great. While, as an old student of "Show Boat", you may say that here and there it falls short of the stage version, you must in the same breath admit that few picture versions have been so faithful to the original as this one. In making the screen version I deliberately transmitted as many of the stage values as I could to the picture and James Whale, the director, stuck very closely to my script, making no changes of any importance. It will be released soon. Watch for it. I am almost sure you will like it.

The film of *Show Boat* opened on May 17 to acclaim and commercial success. It's even more highly regarded today, noted for its faithfulness to the stage version coupled with Whale's cinematic skill.

Oscar Hammerstein to Jerry Watanabe,[28] July 10, 1936

Dear Jerry:

It was kind of you to send me the razor. Unfortunately it comes at a time when I have conceived an undying fidelity to the Schick electrical shaver and while, without telling the Schick, I furtively gave the Redox a trial, I don't feel that at this time I can switch my affections. I don't suppose you know the joy of shaving with your collar on and so I don't expect you to understand me. I have turned the Redox over to Reggie, who has given me an enthusiastic report on it, and I am very grateful to you for thinking of me and also for your kindness to Dorothy during her stay in New York.

We send our love to Doodie, Jennifer and yourself.

---

[28] Jerry Watanabe was Oscar's brother-in-law, married to Dorothy's sister, Eleanor "Doody" Blanchard Watanabe. A graduate of Cambridge University, Watanabe's mother was English and his father was Japanese.

Oscar Hammerstein to Laurence Schwab, July 13, 1936

Dear Larry:

I am returning your script, "Swing It, Susan," under separate cover. I found much in it that was entertaining, some swell line laughs, the basis for a fine comedy scene in the radio broadcasting idea, and a great curtain to Scene 2 of Act 1. These posies I have to throw are however, outweighed by the brickbats.

If there is any family today like the Cabots[29] as you describe them, they are such a rare thing that they seem hardly worth satirizing. They have already been satirized out of existence, or nearly out of existence. This was accomplished some years ago and therefore the subject you are writing about has a faintly old fashioned tinge, despite its modern treatment. I hope as you write your next version you can find a way to put less stress on the exaggerated conservatism of the Cabots and still keep your theme about a girl who, brought up in a more believably conservative family of 1936, steps out into another world to bring herself level with the boy she is interested in. This may be a hard trick to do. I haven't analyzed it very deeply. There is a legal aspect that I don't think can be laughed off;- If you keep the name Cabot and say the things you do about them, that fine old Boston family will come after you with a slander suit that will be hard to defend. However, this is Howard's province, not mine. I also think you exceed the license, even of musical comedy, when you have a chorus dressed in cabaret costumes doing swing steps on the pews of the Little Church Around the Corner.

I have read it only once and this is merely a faithful record of my general reactions. Annoyed as I was by the fundamental proposition of the story, I was nevertheless conscious all through of many big laughs and many chances and suggestions for a good peppy score. I don't feel that the play is "right" yet and I hope you and your collaborator will do a lot more to it before you put it into rehearsal.

---

[29] The Cabot family, one of the "first families of Boston," dated their arrival in the colony to John Cabot in 1700. Descendants Henry Cabot Lodge, and Henry Cabot Lodge, Jr, both became notable U.S. senators.

Dorothy joins me in sending our love to you and Mildred. We are all well out here and things seem to be going well for me professionally. Incidentally, I think it is high time you came out here yourself. I don't know why you worry about ticket speculators and New York critics and financing shows when there are sugar daddies like Metro, Paramount and Twentieth Century to do pictures for you and take away all your worries. Good luck whatever you do.

Sincerely,

In the summer of 1936, Oscar became a founding member and a chairman of the Hollywood Anti-Nazi League (for the Defense of American Democracy). It was later accused of being a Communist front, and it was among the first organizations to be investigated by the House Un-American Activities Committee. Although he left the organization in 1939, Oscar's earlier membership may have been one of the primary reasons the State Department restricted his passport in 1953, during the height of the second "red scare."

Edwin Knopf to Oscar Hammerstein, September 28, 1936

WILL YOU INFORM THE CULTURAL COMMISSION OF THE HOLLYWOOD ANTI NAZI LEAGUE THAT HAVING DULY CONSIDERED THE DISCUSSIONS WHICH TOOK PLACE AT YOUR HOUSE ON FRIDAY NIGHT I FEEL THAT I CANNOT BECOME ACTIVELY ASSOCIATED WITH THE [Anti-Nazi] LEAGUE UNTIL SUCH TIME AS THE TO ME VERY IMPORTANT ISSUES DISCUSSED IN MEETING ARE SETTLED BY THE EXECUTIVE COMMITTEE STOP MAY I AGAIN SAY THAT IF THE LEAGUE IS TO BE ACTIVELY AND SINCERELY PRO DEMOCRACY I WILL NOT ONLY BECOME A MEMBER BUT WILL DO ALL IN MY POWER TO FURTHER ITS ENDS STOP IF IT IS TO BE MERELY ANTI NAZI THEN I FEAR IT IS DOOMED TO BE DEFEATED BY ITS FRIENDS SINCERELY-

EDWIN H KNOPF.

Emma Swift married Oscar Hammerstein I in 1914 (five years before his death)—at the time he was sixty-eight and she was thirty-two. As a result, she became our Oscar's step-grandmother, and over time came to expect his financial support.

Emma Swift Hammerstein to Oscar Hammerstein, November 23, 1936

Dear Oscar 2nd:-

Last July 16th I left NYC + went to Ocean Grove, N.J. to try and recuperate + remained there until Oct 15th last when I returned to NYC. During Sept. + into Oct. I had all my teeth extracted by a dentist in Asbury Park (about 10 minutes walk over) Dr. John G. Campi who does superb work + was born on the Rockefeller estate in Westchester Co., was graduated from Georgetown University, Wash. D.C. + they desired him to remain as a teacher there. For the X Ray of all teeth, extraction, buying both temporary + permanent set he estimated he would have to charge me $220.00. I had promised him a payment Oct. 1st last which I was unable to make leaving me without my teeth (which I can have in about 2 wks. after I pay). He has gone as far as he can because the manufacturer who fills his order has to have money before he will proceed. The duxine [?] shows ones gums though + looks natural. The temporary set gives one teeth with which to eat, looks, + keeps the facial muscles from sagging + in about 5 or 6 mos. the same teeth are put on a new snug fitting. I just had to go through it as I could no longer have them repaired + they did not look nice any longer— too much patchwork.

I am now living on home relief under miserable conditions. I came out of my comfortable hotel room + bath plenty of comfort of every kind + climb 3 flights of stairs to a $3.50 attic room $2.60 per wk. for food. No hot water, no linen, no blanket on my bed and am getting terrible arthritis again from sleeping cold + I haven't enough money for food with which to properly nourish myself + I hear Arthur who justly owes me a lot of money is going to Palm Beach for the winter. I shall soon have to show up this unspeakable situation—because I just cannot stand it any longer. It is not fit for a swine! And my health will not permit it.

In this terrible condition in which Arthur has placed me, I write to ask you if you can help me to get my dentist started so I can get my teeth.

I should be so grateful for whatever degree of assistance you could give me at this time as the present situation is unbearable.

Hoping all is well with you and yours, and with all kind remembrances + deep appreciation, I am,

Very sincerely yours,

(Mrs. Oscar) Emma Swift Hammerstein.

Chapter Three
1937 through 1939

High, Wide and Handsome fulfilled an obligation by Oscar to Paramount Pictures, with him writing both the lyrics and co-writing the script. It was Oscar's first collaboration with the stage and film director Rouben Mamoulian. Mamoulian had directed the original production of the play *Porgy* in 1927 and later its adaptation as an opera with music by George Gershwin and now titled *Porgy and Bess* in 1935. In Mamoulian directed his first film in 1929—*Applause*—one of the earliest "talking" pictures, and a particularly impressive one for the time. In 1932 he directed one of the best original film musicals ever made, *Love Me Tonight*, with songs by Rodgers and Hart. Having worked separately with both Rodgers and Hammerstein, Mamoulian will go on to direct the original Broadway productions of *Oklahoma!* and *Carousel*.

Oscar Hammerstein to Rouben Mamoulian, February 19, 1937

Dear Rouben:

As a neglectful mother might write to the conscientious nurse and tutor of her child I pause in the midst of my selfish pleasures and write to you, and ask, "How is 'High, Wide and Handsome?'" I spoke to Arthur Hamilton on the phone last Sunday, and he seemed very pleased with all that was happening except for the rain which is nearly washing out all your pretty location plans.

Yet, once you get into the Herculean task of staging the famous—though not historic—fight between the circus "razor-backs" and the minions of Brennan (that fiend in human form), I believe you will wish it had rained forever. What a job! If I permitted myself to think of your trouble it would spoil my vacation. Yet, hopefully, my mind is so well disciplined that I find it quite easy to forget other people's troubles. It's a gift! Let me then revert to my pleasures. New York has never seemed so thrilling and stimulating, the theatre never more alive. I've seen eighteen shows in two weeks—holiday matinees helped. Maxwell Anderson's three plays all fall

The Letters of Oscar Hammerstein II. Mark Eden Horowitz, Oxford University Press. © Mark Eden Horowitz 2022.
DOI: 10.1093/oso/9780197538180.003.0003

short of a hundred percent, yet are written in such a distinguished manner as to earn an easy eighty-five. Kaufman and Hart's "You Can't Take It With You" should run forever. It is uproariously funny and adds to its entertainment the additional dimension of a delightfully welcome laissez-faire philosophy—especially attractive to me in my present festive mood.

It is in this same festive mood that Dorothy and I are boarding the Queen Mary next Wednesday for England, for we have no reason whatever for going. But there is that lovely gangplank to walk up, and kippered herring and scrambled eggs for breakfast and the ships auction port[?] and the child-like audience in the London Theatres, the brisk welcome of my tailor, and English oysters and Guinness's Stouts. We will then make a quite unnecessary trip to Paris, become irritated by the confusion, the disdain and the dishonesty of French concierges, waiters and taxi-drivers. Dorothy will buy a few dresses that will seem bargains at the time and we will board The Normandie on March 10th. We'll be back in our Beverly Hills dove-cote about March 23rd. Please have all your problems solved by then, all the scenes shot, assembled—nay, finally cut. Even have the first nerve-wracking preview behind you and present me with a finished, shiny and assembled, full-grown child all dressed up in its party clothes. "Why, High, Wide and Handsome!" I will say, "How you've grown!". And then I'll watch it very closely to see if it still resembles me, its mother or Jerry, (its father)—or whether it has taken on the mannerisms and character of its nurse (you)—I hope it will be a happy combination of the best features of all three. It would be terrible if it combined our worst features - sounding like my singing, for instance—or looking like you after you've missed a shot in tennis! These awful conjectures are intruding on my peace and happiness. With the afore-mentioned well-disciplined mind I hereby wipe them out. Please forgive my wasting your time with this long and pointless essay. In a way, you brought it on yourself by asking me to write.

Good-bye until the end of March—and good luck—and how!

Sincerely,

Oscar

On March 21, Jerome Kern suffered a heart attack. Oscar and Dorothy were in London at the time, but returned to the States and on to California as quickly as they could. Kern remained critically ill for months, during which time Oscar was frequently by his side and was virtually the only person outside his family permitted to visit with him.

Oscar Hammerstein to Louis Dreyfus (Chappell's Ltd., England), May 18, 1937

Dear Louis:

I see by my London Times that Helen Morgan is appearing at the Victoria Palace in a show called "OUR SHOW BOAT." This seems a clear and bold infringement of the title to a valuable theatrical property, and I think something should be done to stop the use of the name. My attitude towards Helen Morgan is most friendly, and I wish to put no obstacles in the way of her London success. I am happy to have her sing our songs, but if they are in a show and produced in any kind of a story situation, it is an improper and unauthorized use of our material. I don't care how often she sings them in a cabaret or a vaudeville show or over the air, but we must always oppose the misuse of theatrical property. Any time we cease to protect a title or any right in a play, we weaken the value of future property. No song plug is worth that sacrifice. I have not taken this up with Jerry because I won't bother him in his sick-bed, but I know he would be even more emphatic than I am in a decision to take whatever steps are necessary to enjoin Mr. Kurt Robitschek from using the title "OUR SHOW BOAT." I will appreciate anything you do for us in this regard, and please let me know how it comes out.

Jerry is getting better every day, and the weight of suspense has definitely been lifted from the household. Eva has lost the constant worried look which she had, and Jerry himself is in high spirits. Of course, he is not altogether well, but he is sitting up in his room a little longer each day and I think there is no doubt that, if he remains patient during his convalescence, he will be in as good shape as ever in a couple of months.

Dorothy sends her love to you and Jeanne and Veevee, and so do I.

Sincerely,

Howard Reinheimer to Oscar Hammerstein, May 18, 1937

Re: "OLD MAN RIVER"

Dear Oscar:

Regarding the above matter, I cannot really give you an authoritative opinion as no case has ever been brought to court involving the precise question as to whether one who originates the name of a song can enjoin the making of a picture bearing that name. It is my opinion that such cannot be enjoined for the following reasons:

There is no ownership in a title and the only restriction against the free use of a title is based upon that vague principle known as "unfair competition". "Unfair competition" was formerly restricted to unfair competition which would deceive the public and an injunction would issue on the theory that the public would be paying to see one motion picture story when in fact they were seeing a different one.

In the last few years, the courts have extended the doctrine of unfair competition so that one who has spent a great deal of money in publicizing and making popular a name or trade name, would have a right to enjoin someone who was unfairly using this name, even though the public might not be misled. For example: "Tiffany & Company" might be able to enjoin a shoe store from operating under the name of "Tiffany & Company", not because the public would be deceived into thinking that Tiffany & Company, the jewelers were making shoes, but because the shoe store would be deemed to have unfairly taken advantage of the capital invested in advertising and building up the goodwill of Tiffany & Company, the jewelers.

When we turn to proprietary rights in titles in the literary and musical field, we are at somewhat of a loss in coming to a definite opinion, since there has never been any litigated case covering the subject, with one exception—the case of "Yukon Jake". This was decided in a lower court and was never appealed. In that case, the author of a poem entitled "The Ballad of Yukon Jake" was awarded damages against a motion picture company arising out of the making of a motion picture having nothing to do with the story contained in the poem but which bore the title "Yukon Jake". The plaintiff showed that he had prepared a scenario based upon his poem and the court's decision was based on two grounds: first, that the saleability of his scenario would no doubt be affected and second, that the public might believe that the picture was based on the poem, which in fact it was not.

A similar case was where an injunction was granted restraining a motion picture company from using the name "Frank Merriwell" as a title for a picture.

In the case of a title to a song, however, I don't believe the same rule would ordinarily apply. In the first place, the most important ground of unfair competition would probably be removed, namely, the confusion to the public. While it is true that many songs tell a story, nevertheless, I am sure no one seeing a motion picture entitled "Old Man River" would be led to believe that the picture was merely an embellishment of the lyrics or idea of your song. True it is, the public may think that "Old Man River" would be a musical number included in the picture, but I don't believe that would be sufficient to make the entire enterprise "a deception on the public".

You will note that the nearest approach to the problem is the "Yukon Jake" case, where the court did say that a motion picture and a poem were close enough to be deemed competitive, but I call attention to the fact that in that case, the poem actually had been made into a motion picture scenario.

Turning to the question as to whether the creators of the title "Old Man River" had created a so-called trade name and that the use of this title in a motion picture would be unfair to the authors as distinguished from the public, I am doubtful if this would be the case, particularly in the case of "Old Man River". The creation of a title to a song does not represent a large capital investment and especially in the case of "Old Man River", the expression was an old one, not originated by you, and was merely taken out of public domain for use as the title of a song. As far as the picture companies are concerned, there might be some trouble, in view of the violent protest that Universal would no doubt make. Frankly, it seems that picture companies are not very much disturbed about similarities between song titles and motion picture titles. They usually ignore the same and any claims based thereon. As a practical matter, they frequently pay a nominal amount to avoid litigation, including the right to use a song in the picture. That is why the matter has been very seldom litigated. For example: Metro paid for the use of the title "Sidewalks of New York" but the payment was primarily for the purpose of acquiring the right to use the song in the picture. This was also the situation on "Music Goes Round and Round".

Well, that is the story, and you can form your own conclusions.

With best regards,

Sincerely,

Howard

Oscar Hammerstein to Howard Reinheimer, May 21, 1937

Dear Howard:

Thank you for your opinion on the situation of the title of "Ol' Man River." Referring to your statement on the last page that the expression was an old one, not originated by me, and was merely taken out of the public domain for the title of a song, I have to violently disagree with that statement even though it is against my interests in this particular case. The expression was originated by me, and if it was an old one and in the public domain, the public seemed blandly unconscious of it up until 1926 when the song was introduced. I had never heard the expression before and neither had you. The only suggestion I ever heard of its previous existence was Ellie's statement that she had heard that some obscure Indian tribe had referred to some obscure river as "Old Man River." I would like to track this down and find out more about it as a matter of curiosity. But it seems odd that what is now a by-word in referring to the Mississippi should never have been used before in newspapers or in common speech. It is such a good name for a river that you would think it would have been used if it had been available. . . . .the aggravated artist speaking.

Love to all.

OSCAR

Gerald Savory was an English actor and writer whose West End play, *George and Margaret*, caught Hammerstein's eye. Oscar signed Savory to write the book for a musical for him and Kern—a show that never came to fruition—but Oscar had a very clear vision of what it should be.

Oscar Hammerstein to Gerald Savory, July 7, 1937

Dear Gerald:

Jerome Kern is now well enough to pitch in with us, and I am writing to pass on to you several suggestions arising from a talk we have had.

Oddly enough, he was not so skeptical about making Tony charming and attractive enough to be the man who eventually gets the girl. He was more concerned about why she falls for Michael in the first place. I explained to him our conception of a strong, homespun young man, and, while he accepted that, his attack forced me into ad libbing some details of a defense which might be helpful in the writing. I told him that the Vessons were the sort of people who felt themselves distinctly superior to anything that came out of New York and London, that they probably gave one concert a year in London, perhaps for the Queen, stopped at the same little pub every year, would give no interviews to newspapers while there nor discuss business, and would invariably take the next train out immediately after the concert. While their violins and other instruments are sold all over the world, they will not deign either to exploit them or fill an order by mail or even deliver them. In other words, the greatest maestros in the world must beat a path to the Vesson home to get their violin, to try it out, to voice their complete approval—or else they just don't get their violin. You might even insert a scene in which a man like Kreisler has sent his secretary or his manager for a violin, and the Vessons refuse to give it to him. If Kreisler wants it, he must come himself.

Jerry kept visualizing Michael as a studious fellow with long hair. I explained that he must be a lusty and husky young man, and he countered with a suggestion for restoring a character whom we once had in the story—Michael's father. After talking with Jerry about this, I strongly urge you to reconsider our elimination of the old man. He would be a mellow, lovable, and amusing character and could epitomize many of the important Vesson attributes, which in Michael might appear stodgy and unromantic. For the situation at the end of Act 1, the old man would be a poignant accent. Let us assume that Michael is the only one of his generation who has inherited the genius for violin making that has gone through the family. Michael's brother is a capable, thorough, plodding technician and craftsman, but Michael alone is achieving that unique tone in fiddles that makes him promise to be one of the most brilliant Vessons of all time. Therefore, when the old man sees him cast aside the beloved instrument he is working on and go up to London to follow the girl he is infatuated with, it is like seeing a hierarchy collapse before his eyes. I am becoming quite overcome as I write this to you. I might add, however, on this point that somewhere during the play there are the makings of a good scene between two very contrasting figures, Michael's father and Helen's.

The next suggestion that arose from this interview was that Helen and her father be Americans. I cannot offhand think of any reason why they shouldn't be, or of any respect in which the play would lose value through this. On the other hand, it would give us a distinct casting advantage and incidentally broaden the appeal of the story for its New York production. As a matter of fact, this disturbs the structure of the story so little that it might almost be left optional. It does, however, affect the dialogue and, all things considered, I think it might be better if you wrote it with Helen as an American. Both she and her father, who are distinctly of a go-getting type, fit in more with the popular idea of Americans, and they would be less likely to understand the Vesson's peculiar attitude about their work than English people would—even English people from Mayfair.

A detail:- When the festival is held in the village, I think it would be very amusing to augment the performers entirely with Vessons from neighboring villages in the county and some cousins and second cousins, each with his own particular instrument or specialty. Their entrance into the Village Green scene might be built up like that endless succession of brothers in "The Barretts of Wimpole Street."

Jerry had one more reaction which I submit to you for consideration. He had an instinctive feeling that this place where the Vessons live should be as remote from London as possible, and he thought it would make a great difference if they were not English but were either Scotch Irish or Welsh— and he preferred the last. In other words, the more remote these people are from those whom Americans meet in their common experience, the more unique, romantic and eccentric they can be made. I seem to feel vaguely a prejudice in the English mind for Welsh people—except for comedy purposes. Am I right about this? There is, of course, none in America because Americans know very little about Welshmen. What do you think about this idea? Aiming for the American production, I am disposed to agree with Jerry about it, but this—as in the case of all other suggestions contained in this letter—is submitted for your approval. We don't want you to attempt to write anything that pleases us if you don't feel it yourself.

I know that when you are writing a play it can be very annoying to have too many people looking over your shoulder and making suggestions, but whatever we write to you during this summer is intended only to help you and to eventually attain an end that we are all seeking. And since we are so far away, I think that your policy should be this:- That whenever a suggestion we make interferes with your peace of mind as an author and with the aims of the script and the context, with which we are not as familiar as you, then you should throw aside whatever of our thoughts are in your way and follow your own impulse about it as you write.

Meanwhile I await eagerly your first draft of the first scene.

Kindest regards.

The film of *High, Wide and Handsome* opened on July 21. Set in the context of an early history of the oil industry, the romance managed to include the building of the first oil pipeline and a feud with a railroad tycoon. The film seems crude by today's standards but at the time was considered rather sophisticated in its integration of songs within the story. It starred Randolph Scott and Irene Dunne, fresh from her star turn in *Show Boat*. The music is by Kern, but only two of the songs became anything close to standards, "Can I Forget You," and "The Folks Who Live on the Hill." The latter was one of Oscar's favorites, and he commented more than once that he wished it were better-known.

Hammerstein's good friend, Hy Kraft, was a screenwriter and playwright with only very modest success. Of his nine Broadway shows, *Top Banana* enjoyed the longest run by far at eleven months, and of the handful of films with which he was involved, *Stormy Weather* is the best remembered—adapting a story that was then taken over by two other screenwriters. Kraft regularly sought Oscar's input and opinions on shows he was working on; with Oscar's later success, Kraft pressed him to produce, or at least invest in some of them.

Hy Kraft to Oscar Hammerstein (excerpt), January 1, 1938

I guess you're right about Kaufman and my play. I got his letter just before writing you and it sent me off into a tirade. I doubt whether I'll do business with The Group Theatre. I've had a talk with Clurman, their director and that old feelin' about directors came back to plague me. I won't go into details about the changes that Clurman wanted (strikes in the play etc), (more direct speeches)—all the things I didn't want. So I've decided to try to promote the money myself and I'm working along those lines now. I've got some interest now and I'm hopeful that I can raise the $25,000. necessary for the production, then turn it over to some responsible management and have them present it. The best shows in town are those that have a social line, Julius Ceasar [*sic*], The Cradle Will Rock (musical) also done by The Mercury Theatre Group and the big hit musical is 'Pins and Needles' presented by the Grament [*sic*] Workers. (And what a hit it is). Saw 'Between the Devil'—pathetic. Buchanan and Laye are old and the book—oi [*sic*].

Oscar Hammerstein to Walter and Marion Knapp,
January 3, 1938

Dear Marion and Walter:

It was good to hear from you. I hope you had a pleasant Christmas. Things were so hectic here that we are just getting over it. Young Henry came out for the holidays and gave the whole family a cold. Reggie took him back to New York. I didn't know which would come out of the train compartment alive but I got a wire from Reggie this morning, saying they had both arrived safely and have apparently became fast friends. The other kids are all fine. I gave Alice a car for Christmas, and for twenty-four hours she didn't believe it. She insisted that I was only kidding. Billy is keeping on with his music and is doing very well, and Jimmy and Susan are going to school and hating it. Dorothy went into the decorating business on her own hook last spring and has brought it into a position where it is well on the profit side and going very strong. Since I saw you I have written a musical screen play for Columbia pictures[1] which will be produced soon and will be simply terrible. I have also written a screen play for Fred Astaire, based on the life of Vernon Castle.[2] I like this very much but what will happen to it when transferred from paper to celluloid is in the lap of the gods. I am at present writing a play[3] with Otto Harbach and Jerome Kern, which we

---

[1] Oscar was at least half wrong, his screenplay for Columbia, *Paris on Broadway*, was never produced—although a draft and a final screenplay exist—but it probably would have been terrible had it been made.

[2] *The Story of Vernon and Irene Castle* was the penultimate Fred Astaire and Ginger Rogers movie, with Oscar only credited for adaptation—to his chagrin.

[3] *Gentlemen Unafraid*, premiered at the Municipal Open Air Theatre ("The Muny") in St. Louis, in June of 1938. It never made it to the Center Theatre . . . or any other Broadway theater.

will try out in St. Louis next summer and probably bring into the Center Theatre next Autumn.

Leighton was married again a few months ago, and this time it really looks good. Mousie is in good health and the same as ever. I have occasional letters from Ax, Kaddy and Walter Redell, but they seem to be getting fewer and farther between. I saw Marjorie Gateson yesterday from a distance. I was at the Tennis Club and she was playing ping-pong, but dressed as if about to go to an afternoon reception at Buckingham Palace. I have a bit of disloyalty to report:- At the Santa Anita race track last week there was a horse called Ruffy. I failed to bet on him and he came in at 8 to 1. Served me right.

We don't expect to go to New York before the Fall but if we do we'll tell you about it first so that we can plan to get together. Meanwhile, break those long silences and let us know what's going on in and around Waterford, even if it's only the latest gossip about the chickens. Love from all.

Gentlemen Unafraid became an obsession with Otto Harbach and, in various permutations, was to be the last show he wrote (a reworking in 1942 was given the pedestrian title, *Hayfoot, Strawfoot*). Based on an original story by Edward Boykin, it told the story of divided loyalties among Southern cadets at West Point during the Civil War, torn between their Southern heritage and their obligations to the Union. There is extensive correspondence between Hammerstein and Harbach (and Kern and several others) that reveals the effort and struggle put into this ambitious, and ultimately frustrating, show.

Oscar Hammerstein to Otto Harbach, January 5, 1938

Dear Otto:

Will you get in touch with our friend Boykin and find out from him the exact details of the sunset gun ceremony every evening, hauling down the flag, etc. My reason for this request is this: In the finale of Act 1, I have an idea that we can accentuate the drama of the seceding students by having the sunset gun fired shortly after the parade and just about the time that the news of Virginia's secession arrives. It would be the mechanical reaction of every cadet to salute the flag as it is being hauled down and carried in the waiting room of the color guard. But if they had just decided to resign from the United States Army service and fight under the opposing confederate flag, what would they do? Would they stand at salute? Would their arms go half up automatically and then drop slowly? Would all of them refuse to salute except Bob? I don't mean to ask Boykin these questions. These are dramatic questions and I am posing them to you to suggest to you the possibilities I see inherent in this situation. All we need get from Boykin is just what happens at any normal sunset gun.

There are several changes Jerry and I are considering submitting to you but these can wait until your arrival. They are rather complicated to describe by mail. In the Ambler home, we would like to confine the musical numbers to "WHAT A PRETTY GIRL," and "THE LAND OF GOOD TIMES." Adding "THE ROAD TO GLORY" as conceived, seems to make it musically top-heavy and to conflict with "THE LAND OF GOOD TIMES." I also have some ideas about the montage in the second act. My chief feeling is that the core of the montage should be a big number, introduced at the beginning of it and serving as the motive for the war. I have already written the lyric to this number and it is to the melody which we had chosen for "THE ROAD TO GLORY." It is really too good to spoil by just mailing the lyric to you. We will have to sing it and explain how it is to be sung when you get here. Now when it is hot off the press, it seems to us both like a terrific thing. I have wired you to-day to send me "GENTLEMEN UNAFRAID" as soon as you can. I have had to do some re-writing in the first scene and I am a little at a loss as to just how to cue the number in without the lyric. What are the other two lyrics you say you have finished, and when do we get them? Are you pushing ahead with the dialogue to the last scenes in the first act? I am confident that I will have all my part written when you get here and if you have yours, we'll have our first version of a complete first act, which is a big part of the play.

After talking to Dick Berger[4] about the St. Louis project, it really seems like a great idea. I imagine you will go over it with him and with Howard before you leave New York. I think it's a very good proposition for us for many reasons.

In closing, let me suggest that you postpone alteration on the house, sell it for what you can get, and then come out here and buy the white house on the hill. Love from all.

---

[4] Richard Berger was the productions manager at the "Muny" and directed *Gentlemen Unafraid*.

The film musical *Paris on Broadway* was never made, but four songs that Oscar wrote for it—along with composer Ben Oakland—ended up in the 1938 film, *The Lady Objects*, produced by William Perlberg. Dolly Haas did not appear in that film, but Lanny Ross did—a singer whose greatest success was in radio. (Haas later married the caricaturist Al Hirschfeld.)

Oscar Hammerstein to William Perlberg (Columbia Pictures), January 11, 1938

Dear Bill:

I just heard that you have returned from your vacation, so I am writing to give you my impression after reading the latest "PARIS ON BROADWAY" script. In general it seems to me that building up the part of Lanny Ross has somehow diminished the importance of the Dolly Haas part. It is not so much the things that have been cut out of her part as the fact that the story with the new prologue seems to be told more from the man's point of view. I question whether she will want to play the part now, and if we must give her up in order to get Lanny Ross, I think we are making a bad trade. You will remember the whole reason for writing this story was Dolly Haas and the very distinctive charm and appeal that I think she has. I thought that a musical capitalizing these qualities would be out of the ordinary run of things. A musical capitalizing [on] Lanny Ross brings it in line with a great many predecessors, and demands a faster pace and a broader type of entertainment than this was designed to be.

I am conscious of your casting difficulties at Columbia, but I am nevertheless reminding you that you may be falling into something which has a very limited chance of success. You are, of course, producing it now and I am out of it. I am just giving you my reactions to your script for what they are worth.

There are two specific features that I am sure you should eliminate. One is that part of the prologue where the various inhabitants of a courtyard play different instruments and take part in a number. This is so exactly like the scene in "ONE NIGHT OF LOVE" that the least sophisticated member in any audience is sure to recognize it, label it a cheap imitation of the real thing, and immediately lose respect for the whole picture. The other item is also an imitation. This is the ventriloquist dummy. When Jane

Murfin[5] first suggested it to me, I was in doubt about it but, because of her enthusiasm for the idea, backed up by Al Hall, I let her go ahead with it. If it was not a mistake then, it certainly is now. The "GOLDWYN FOLLIES"[6] is being cut and will surely be released before your picture. Since Bergen and McCarthy are in this, you would have a tough time following it with your dummy. I think the presence of a second-hand device like this is very injurious to a production and detracts a great deal from whatever is good in it.

I still have to write the lyric of the refrain that I promised you and also a couple of verses. When you are finishing your changes in these numbers, I will be glad to go ahead and write them for you, and also to help in any way that I can.

Remember me to Harry and kindest regards to yourself.

Sincerely,

Oscar Hammerstein to Bruce Winston (London), January 14, 1938

Dear Bruce:

I love the handkerchiefs. I think they are the best lot yet. I would like nothing better than to come over to London and thank you in person, but the chances of a trip in the immediate future are very slim.

I have just finished writing a Fred Astaire picture, based on the life of Mr. and Mrs. Vernon Castle. I like it very much but then I always like them before some director gets hold of them and puts them on the screen in his own individual way. I am now very busy with Jerry and Otto Harbach, writing a play for next season. We shall probably try it out in St. Louis this summer. Writing a play again makes me very homesick for the theatre and makes me realize again the futility of trying to get the same gratification out of screen writing.

I hope that things are going well with you and that by some miracle we can all be together again soon. My love to Ruth, Nora and yourself. Dorothy

---

[5] Jane Murfin wrote dozens of screenplays, including *Alice Adams* and *The Women*.

[6] *The Goldwyn Follies* (1938) boasted the last set of songs composed by George Gershwin before he died, in 1937. The cast included the hugely popular ventriloquist Edgar Bergen, and his dummy, Charlie McCarthy.

is out and very busy buying chintzes and old Chippendale linoleums but if she were here, I am sure she would collaborate on the above. (To wit: Love to Ruth, Nora and yourself.)

Sincerely,

Max Gordon to Oscar Hammerstein, January 19, 1938

My dear Oscar:

I received this letter from Howard Reinheimer and to me it's all out of line.

Instead of paying 7% in royalties and a percentage of the profits, the fair thing—in my opinion—would be to pay eight (8%) per cent of the gross.

If you have a hit in the Center Theatre, you ought to gross $50,000. and that's just as good as if you had 16% with a sensational hit in the average theatre—because you would have to have a sensational hit in the average theatre to gross $25,000. a week on a season of thirty or thirty-five weeks.

The idea of my having to make definite commitments regarding all necessary financing on or before any date is ridiculous, after all the shows I have produced. I am not a fly-by-night manager nor an angel trying to produce a show.

I have never made any announcement about this show and certainly won't until I read the book and I know I am going to produce the play.

I think you boys don't realize how tough it is to get a couple of hundred thousand dollars for a musical show these days. No big musical show has made any real money—due to the expense involved. If this show is a hit at the Center Theatre, your royalty should be $4,000. a week because you ought to play to $50,000. That's certainly enough for any group of authors to hope for.

When we did "Jubilee," Cole Porter and Moss Hart got 6% of the gross and they bought an interest in the show. If you see the play in St. Louis and you think you want to buy an interest in it—after seeing it—it's open to you; so there are enough ways for you to make money.

And let me add this: the picture rights of a hit at the Center Theatre are worth twice as much as the picture rights of a hit in the average musical comedy theatre. All I want you to do is make it possible to put this show on right; and unless you do, you are in for a failure. YOU CAN'T SPARE EXPENSES AT THE CENTER THEATRE. The one thing you and Jerry ought not to worry about is where the money is coming from for this show; the thing to worry about is getting a play. I have never failed to produce any play for which I signed a contract.

Please pass this along to Jerry and let me know your reaction.

And, finally, Oscar, I just want to add that I hope nothing happens about the production of this show because we have been promising each other that we will do one—so let's not permit any foolish capers to upset the applecart.

Kindest regards to all-

Yours,

Max

It appears that the plan was for Max Gordon to take over *Gentlemen Unafraid* after its tryout in St. Louis and produce it on Broadway.

Howard Reinheimer to Oscar Hammerstein, January, 1938

Dear Oscar:

Max Gordon phoned me after receiving my letter. He informed me that he was writing you his comments. I have before me a copy of his letter to you, dated January 19th, which you have no doubt already received.

Frankly, I cannot concur with Gordon's point of view.

Taking up the question of financing first:- What we need is substantial backing—not pin money. If there were only $25,000.00 to $30,000.00 required I would be inclined to take a chance on Gordon, and the probability that he will have no trouble in raising the financing, but when as much as $150,000.00 to $200,000.00 is involved, we are in a slightly different position. I don't quite understand why we should part with our control over the play until we are positive where the money is coming from. What do you think?

Nor, am I in accord on the matter of 8% royalties instead of 7% and a percentage of the profits. Gordon now seems to be putting the shoe on the other foot. He is assuming the position of manager who is buying rights from us and is ready to pay us "a salary" or "a royalty". This is not exactly in accord with our discussion that we would all join in at some sort of profit-sharing basis.

If, for example, the show is financed by the Center Theatre people, I know their purpose is not to make profits and that if they can get their money back they would be most liberal with any percentage of profits over and above the investment. This would mean that if we were on a straight royalty basis with Center Theatre finances, Gordon would hook himself in for the entire profit remaining—which is just what we don't want to do.

Please let me have your further thoughts before I communicate with Max Gordon.

Best regards.

Sincerely,

Howard

cc to Jerome Kern

Oscar Hammerstein to Lloyd Lewis, January 21, 1938

Dear Lloyd:

As the man who wrote the Civil War,[7] can you tell me if there were any negro soldiers in the Confederate army? I know that many went as servants to their masters but, for the purposes of a story I am working on, I hope that some of them served as regular soldiers wearing the gray. If so, were they all volunteers or were some of them pressed into service in one way or another? I assume of course, that they were not scattered among the white battalions but, if they served at all, they must have served in special colored regiments. Is this true? It is hard for me to understand how they served in the southern army at all, but in "GONE WITH THE WIND" there is some

---

[7] Lloyd Lewis's books include one on Lincoln's assassination, and a biography of the Union General, William Tecumseh Sherman.

reference to colored soldiers molesting women. Please tell me whatever you know about this feature of your pet subject and I will be very grateful.

With kindest regards to your wife and yourself from both of us.

Sincerely,

Lloyd Lewis to Oscar Hammerstein (excerpt), January 29, 1938

Dear Oscar:- I have never heard of any negroes in Confederate uniform. The Confederate gov't was considering it as the war ended, but had up to then taken a stand against it. Gen. Cleburne urged it in the direful fall of '64, but he was only an Irish Quaker and didn't understand the soul of aristocracy, so was voted down.

I'm sorry to deny you. Why not make it a sudden decision of a rebellious colonel who says, "Richmond won't face facts—they won't arm the slaves. By god, I'm goin' to do it and the gov't will come around to it later." Wouldn't that solve it? I've no doubt it happened in unrecorded and isolated instances, for there was such sentiment for it in the army during the early months & spring of 1865.

Oscar Hammerstein to Reggie Hammerstein, February 2, 1938

Dear Reg:

Thank you for your letter of no date. Keep on the search for prima donnas and leading men, and if you run across any other talent, specialty dancers or anything at all, let me know about it. I mean unusual talent. I do know that we need a good flashy negro dancer, male, for a short effective spot, and we need a great female negro singer like Ethel Waters. Can you find out what her money is? I mean, without asking an agent and boosting the price right away. Ask somebody like Dan Healy who knows what they all get.

Jack Haskell has returned from Europe and doesn't cook spaghetti any more. He now cooks meats with all kinds of fruit, and cooked one dinner so well in London that an Indian rajah wanted to go to India with him. I am merely reporting his statements without comment. I asked him if he had any message for you and he said to tell you that he had been to Rome and kissed the Pope's ring. "Be sure," he added, "to say ring."

Have you seen any good shows? There is no startling news from this end. I will probably send you a copy of the first act next week,

Love from all.

OSCAR

Encl: Cheque

Oscar Hammerstein to Max Gordon, March 1, 1938

Dear Max:

With the exception of a few lyrics and some incidental scoring, our play will be finished this week. I use the word "finished" with the usual reservations. Perhaps I should say that our first draft is finished. It starts and ends and adds up along the way. Between now and June 3rd we will make improvements and after we see it in St. Louis on that date, we will undoubtedly make more. But fundamentally the story seems to be very solid and the characters come through very well. I am certain that we have some very strong songs and, if we don't look out, you and I will be finally mixed up together in a hit. The last time I heard from you, you said you were going to talk to Audrey Christie. Have you done this? Is she interested? And if so, Jerry would like you to find out for him the range of her voice, and let him know what it is.

I have read in the Hollywood Reporter this morning that your play[8] has just opened and looks very promising. Whoever writes these Reporter criticisms is a gent who hates the theatre and usually lambasts everything that opens in New York. So I take it that your show is good, on which fact I sincerely congratulate you.

Are you coming out here in the middle of March as you had intended? Please let us know. The date you decide upon might influence Otto's plans. Love to Millie and yourself from all of us.

Sincerely,

[8] *Save Me the Waltz.*

Max Gordon to Oscar Hammerstein, March 9, 1938

Dear Oscar:

Your letter to hand. First, my play was a failure and closed last Saturday night—but that's yesterday's newspaper.

Now to the business at hand. Audrey Christie left "The Women" to go with Dwight Wiman's show. She told me that she considered this a temporary engagement and was awaiting the opening of your play.

Ben Boyar informs me that the range of her voice is "A Flat"; and that Otto Harbach heard her sing when she had a cold and said she would be fine for the music. I expect her to be with us.

I don't see now how I will be able to get out to Hollywood at all. As you probably read in the papers, we sold "The Women" to Metro. Conditions were so bad that we couldn't raise the million dollars to produce the picture, so we did the next best thing.

I am happy to hear you are so enthusiastic about the show and hope we will be sweating with it June 3d in St. Louis.

Love to you, Dorothy and all from Millie and me.

As ever,

Max

Oscar Hammerstein to Reggie Hammerstein (excerpt), March 9, 1938

The latest Romberg story is as follows:- Gus Kahn stopped in at the studio on his way to the golf course, wearing a cap that Rommy didn't like. Rommy said: "Take off that cap, Gus. You look like a race trout."

Oscar Hammerstein to Richard Berger (excerpts), March 15, 1938

Now to the two tough parts,- Linda and Bob. You seem to have unearthed no one in the east. We have found only one in the west who might possibly do it. She has a good, strong voice, is pretty, and after trying her out in Scene 3 of Act 1, I am convinced that she has good dramatic feeling. Otto will bear me out in this. It is true, of course, that she has had little stage experience beyond a year's training and coaching as a stock player at M.G.M., and I note in your last letter that statement that it would be fatal to try out an amateur in this part. I am not one for trying amateurs because I have had no luck with them, but it seems certain that the available professionals are all in pictures. Of those who are not, and are really troupers, I can think of only three—Kitty Carlisle, Norma Terris and Vivienne Segal. Kitty Carlisle is definitely wrong for the part, suggesting more a girl from the south of Hungary than one of the Virginia Masons. Norma and Vivienne are neither of them young enough. They are both good enough actresses to play the parts of young girls but there is a definite ingénue requirement, especially in the first act of this part, that eliminates them.

About Bud, I am going to find out as soon as possible whether Buddy Ebsen's contract will be continued at M.G.M. Ray Bolger, another who could play the part very well, seems to be slated to do "THE WIZARD OF OZ" at M.G.M. I have an awful feeling that Buddy will fit in there too. They would be ideal to fill the two Montgomery and Stone roles. The Straw Man and the Tin Man.

The part of Bud ultimately went to Red Skelton. Both Ray Bolger and Buddy Ebsen *were* cast in *The Wizard of Oz*, but Ebsen was ultimately replaced by Jack Haley.

Oscar Hammerstein to Reggie Hammerstein (excerpt), March 15, 1938

I have had several nibbles from M.G.M. lately, one is to do the lyrics of an opera based on the life of Johann Strauss.[9] This would be only a three week job. The only thing that has held up the contract so far is money. They offer $5,000. and I want $7,500. I really don't feel that I should take less than my price, much as I need the money. The other offer is to do the screen play of "TOPSY AND EVA." Mervyn Leroy is producing it and all he needs is an okay from the front office to go ahead. It's about an even chance whether this will go through or not.

---

[9] Oscar would write lyrics for the highly fictionalized biopic of Johann Strauss, *The Great Waltz*.

Oscar Hammerstein to Buddy Ebsen, March 18, 1938

Dear Buddy:

I am very shy of copies of this play, and the script I am sending you is the one that I am working on myself. Therefore I would appreciate it if you would make it your business to read it over the week-end and return it to my house, at above address, not later than Monday morning.

I hope I didn't boost the part too much to you. I happen to like it very much because I like the characterization. He is not a musical comedy clown but a good earthy human character, and in playing the part it is as important for the actor to get sympathy as well as laughs. Then, of course, there are some very vital dancing spots which are fundamental elements in the construction of the role. Enough of these footnotes. I know you are quite capable of making your own analysis and, for your own purposes, it will be much better than mine.

Kindest regards,

Oscar

Oscar Hammerstein to Arthur Hammerstein (excerpt),
March 22, 1938

It seems a very rare case when anyone who has attained any prominence in the theatre can attain any prominence in pictures. It seems that the only people who make good in pictures are those who were nonentities on Broadway. Anyway, Larry [Schwab]'s case is not exceptional. He was with Metro-Goldwyn six months and they gave him nothing to produce, and refused to let him produce anything that he liked. They signed him and then dared him to work for them.

Oscar Hammerstein to Pandro S. Berman (RKO),
March 24, 1938

Dear Pan:

Andre Charlot tells me he is being considered by you for a job at R.K.O.—at any rate he understands that Rufus Lemaire is bringing his name up before you.

I am sending this letter as a "plug" for him, with the sincere conviction that he might prove a genuine and unique asset to you. His career in the theatre was marked by good taste and shrewd showmanship, and while Ziegfeld was spending $200,000. on revues, Charlot was spending $40,000. and drawing the people in by his uncanny ability to choose and assemble entertaining sketches. His access to what must amount to well over a hundred of these sketches out of all his revues would, I think, make him of great value in the Short department alone. He also has a keen faculty for judging new talent and developing it. Bee [sic] Lillie, Gertrude Lawrence and Jack Buchanan were spotted by him when they were just about one cut above the chorus, and he brought them up step by step to stardom. Each has separately acknowledged this to me. It seems to me that there must be a place for such a man in a studio—especially since he has no high-falutin' ideas about salary or credits.

I hope you will not think me presumptuous in making this suggestion. It so happens that, although I have known Charlot for many years, we have never been close friends. I am therefore, writing because I really believe a man of such proven talents should at least get a chance to prove whether or not he could use them in pictures.

Shifting to an entirely different subject, can you tell me when you think you will resume work on the Castle script and, if so, do you think you will want me to go back on it? I am writing one play, producing another, and at the moment, working on a picture at Metro. If you could tell me approximately when and if you will want me this summer, I will try to unravel some of these complex obligations because I am very enthusiastic about the Castle story and want very much to finish it if it is possible for me to do so.

I had better stop writing about myself or you will forget all about Charlot who, after all, was the main purpose of this letter.

Kindest regards. Hope to see you soon.

Sincerely,

Pandro "Pan" Berman was a producer at RKO, at the time of this letter, best known for three Fred Astaire/Ginger Rogers movies, and three starring Katharine Hepburn. André Charlot was a British producer, somewhat akin to Ziegfeld, producing annual revues and introducing many stars to the London stage. Only one of his shows made it to Broadway, *Andre Charlot's Revue of 1924*. Charlot did end up in Hollywood, but as an actor not a producer. Rufus Le Maire was a casting director.

Oscar Hammerstein to Hy Kraft (excerpt), March 29, 1938

As you probably know, the Hollywood Anti-Nazi League is giving a dinner to Thomas Mann this Thursday night at Jack Warner's house. We have thirty-four guests, each of whom are paying $100. a plate. The League is donating one-third of the $3,000. so raised to the Thomas Mann organization to take care of refugees in Prague. The importance of the dinner, beyond the financial benefits, is the probability of activizing [*sic*] the kind of people we have found it so difficult to get into our fold. It is not improbable that this dinner may be a springboard for a new and important development in our work. At any rate, I am going to try to make it so.

Hy Kraft to Oscar Hammerstein (excerpt), April 7, 1938

I've been hitting on all six now and I've got to let up and take it easy for a while. The Spanish situation had been awful. I feed myself on small victories, refusing to believe that this present day world will stand by and watch this terrible slaughter of people and ideals. I'm practically ready to accept any little bit of good news and lull myself into wish fulfillment. This morning's paper announced the defeat of a conservative candidate at a by-election in England and the victory of a labor representative. And I am tickled—even though the victory is small, one representative, but it's a slap at Chamberlain's fascism and Lady Astor's mob . . .

Oscar Hammerstein to Otto Harbach, April 11, 1938

Dear Otto:

I wish you would get your analytical brain busy on that part of our story which concerns the plans for the gun. There is something sour about this and I am not sure what it is. You remember Max picked [up] on it, and I have had Larry Schwab read the play and he put his finger on the same spot although his objections were on a different ground. He thought it was very ten- twenty and thirty. I think that people frequently mislead one by assigning wrong or vague reasons for their objections but when several people object to the same thing, even though on different grounds, it is usually a sign that there is something wrong or at any rate, it makes it well worthwhile looking into. My own feeling about this element is also shaky.

I don't know whether we have told the gun story in too melodramatic a manner, or whether it is too vague because it is entirely an off-stage story, or whether the very nature of the story, where the villain steals the set of papers, is unpalatable these days and a black mark on a production. But I know that when you get your mind rivetted [*sic*] on one spot, you usually bob up with a very sound theory for the reason of the infection, and then the solution or remedy is never hard to find.

I have been confined to my bed with flu but have managed to work out a rather neat refrain for Linda's number in Scene 2—Act 2. When I write the verse I will send it to you and you can let me know if you think it is an improvement on yours or not. I am having Leighton Brill conclude negotiations for Hope Manning to play the lead and I think she is a very likely candidate. I am interested to hear of your enthusiasm for Red Skelton and, although we have a kid out here who might fit the bill, Skelton sounds like a surer proposition.

Getting back to the subject with which I began this letter, the fundamental question would seem to be, can a better story be inserted to take the place of this one and, if not, can this one not be told in a cleverer way. I look forward to hearing from you about this.

Love to Ella and yourself. We've both looking forward to seeing you.

Sincerely,

Oscar Hammerstein to Reggie Hammerstein (excerpt), April 12, 1938

A man went into an English pub and the proprietor said, "Would tha like a chance on a raffle? Only saxpence." The man bought the chance and the next day when he came in, the proprietor came right over to him and said, "Lucky man! Tha has won the second prize." "Indeed?" said the man. "What is it?" "Tha can sleep with the bar maid," said the proprietor. "Oh," said the second prize winner, a little astonished, and as the proprietor went away he called him back and said, "What was the first prize?" "Ah," said the proprietor, his face beaming brightly, "that was a pack of cigarettes."

Len Mence was an actor whose association with Oscar began with *The Wild Rose* in 1926, continued with *Music in the Air* and *Very Warm for May*, and concluded with *The King and I* in 1951. He and Oscar had a particularly warm and teasing relationship.

Len Mence to Oscar Hammerstein, April 26, 1938

My Dear Oscar

Presume you will be surprised to hear from the original creator of many varied roles in many of your admirable plays!! (True they were cut, but, so are diamonds!) At Present I am scintillating for the Schuberts [*sic*] in Three Waltzes, this is our 22nd week 15 in N.Y.C. this is quite a career, my last job with Max Reinhardt lasted a few weeks, the Professor occasionally reminds one of the "Mountain in labour."[10]

Oddly enough the day I got this engagement I had three calls one from Arthur Hammerstein for his play (which I liked very much, but, was afraid of Jack Pearl,) the other from Sidney Harmon, luckly [*sic*] took Schuberts and they've been really very decent to me, even arranged a one man show for my paintings as a publicity stunt! and I had some decent notices etc.

Margaret Sylva is in the show playing a "grand dame" with a dash of Carrrmen [*sic*] does well, Harry Mestaire was with us but, was allowed to resign, and as usual his part was shunted on to me, Ivy Scott too was with us, but, they cut her out on the road, it was almost like old home week when we started, and now "to cut the cackle and come to the 'orses."

Rumor hath it you are going to produce a show in the fall well "<u>my voice is better than ever</u>!" so if Jerry Kern can be persuaded, won't you give me a decent part that needs cutting! I'll hold the script and play Herzig, Emild, Pidgeon Lyppman [?] King of Borovinia all in one for you, any way please keep me in mind.

Give my very best to Reggie, & Goofey, trust your family are all well

Kindest regards to you and to Dorothy.

As always

Your Ays [*sic*]

Len

---

[10] From a Latin poem by Phaedrus: "A mountain had gone into labour and was groaning terribly. Such rumours excited great expectations all over the country. In the end, however, the mountain gave birth to a mouse."

Oscar Hammerstein to Len Mence, April 7, 1938

Dear Len:

I was pleased to hear from you. It's a little early for casting now but it may be we will be able to dig up something for you. Offhand I can think of one or two parts but they are all vital to the play and not likely to be cut down. I only want to engage you for a part out of which I can cut plenty. Until I find a good fat part that can be whittled down to a bit, I will be in no position to make you an offer. Seriously (as though I weren't), it is a little early and I suggest that you write to me again about the 20th of June, enclosing a photograph taken recently, preferably one standing up and without leaning against anything, so that I may determine how well preserved you are.

Dorothy sends her love as do I, and as for Reggie, he has been in New York for the last three months, stopping at the Weylin.

Best wishes

Oscar Hammerstein to Reggie Hammerstein (excerpt), May 4, 1938

Harry Ruby and Sid Silvers were in New York recently and attended Passover services which this year happened to coincide quite closely with Easter. When they entered the Temple, it didn't look like a very good house. Sid Silvers looked around and said "Not many people here," and Harry Ruby said, "Holy Week."

Reggie Hammerstein to Oscar Hammerstein (excerpt), circa 1938

Norma (Show Boat) Terrace [sic; "Terris"] likes the part but does not think it is nearly as good as Magnolia. Dick is negotiating for her to go to St Louis. It's just a matter of dough. But most important of all is, Mousie has gone Hitler.—quote—"He cuts off the heads of all spys." [sic] I told her the best thing to do was to go over to Germany and use her real name of Nimmoberger [?]

Howard Reinheimer to Oscar Hammerstein, June 10, 1938

Dear Oscar:

Just a heart to heart talk.

I personally liked "Gentlemen Unafraid" very much and thought it had good possibilities for a large show. Loads of people (including Larry and Max) seemed to have very little hope for it. But that is merely a matter of opinion and that in itself should not discourage you except as a possible indication of difficulties when it comes to the financing. This last possibility, of course, is not to be laughed off, since the best show is a waste of time if it cannot be financed and put on.

Now that you have a new story line, I think it is perfectly swell for you to see it to a conclusion. I am looking forward anxiously to seeing a summary of this new line of attack, but I sincerely hope that unless the new version rolls off your pen like a "natural" that you won't fuss and fool around with it trying to force a play merely because you have commenced it with Otto and Jerry. I know how you feel towards both of them, but there comes a time when a soft heart must harden. Jerry will manage to exist no matter what happens with the play. Otto certainly is well fixed and if he does not do another play for the rest of his life, he will still be well off. You cannot afford to sit around trying to rehash something merely because you don't want to let your friends down. Neither Jerry nor Otto has your pressing responsibilities.

You and I both know how Otto puttered around with "Forbidden Melody". For three years, he wrote and rewrote and rewrote and even after the play opened and was a failure, he still continued rewriting up to the day it closed. I definitely recall he spent about $500. in extra orchestra rehearsals for a new number the day before the play closed. So please take a tip and if the show does not look right, drop it like a hotcake. You and Jerry can use the music for something else.

I know you think I sound like an awful pessimist but that is not my purpose. I think you might have a perfectly swell new angle, but I am very fearful of the possibility that in discarding so much of the old story, you are practically starting from scratch and may be discarding all of the things which made the whole proposition attractive to you from the beginning.

While I by no means share Larry's feeling that the entire enterprise is hopeless, I do see in KNIGHTS OF SONG a possibility of a good return for a relatively short period of work and I think that unless you come to a quick solution of the "Gentlemen Unafraid" matter, you should concentrate on the "Knights of Song" and lay immediate plans for a picture assignment, shelving "Gentlemen Unafraid" until you are in a more secure financial position.

Best regards,

Sincerely,

Howard

Oscar acquired the rights to the play *Knights of Song* by Glendon Alvine. The play was about the collaboration between W. S. Gilbert and Arthur Sullivan, and was interspersed with numbers from their operettas. Oscar collaborated with Larry Schwab to largely re-write the script.

As Billy begins to make his way in the professional theater, Oscar provides advice.

Oscar Hammerstein to William Hammerstein
(excerpt/the letter is incomplete), June 29, 1938

Dear Bill:

I was very glad to receive your letter and to glean from it that you are coming back in health and thriving on the natural interest your job holds for you. Regarding "THREE SISTERS" we have already spent some time in the past considering the problem of placing it in the United States and using the Kentucky Derby as the central scene, but this has not worked very well. I may bring a script along with me in July and let Dick read it in its present version. I would not be averse to having him put it on in St. Louis and seeing the reaction of an American audience.

I am glad you have the musical assignment of digging out the tenor, bass, soprano, etc. parts from the "KNIGHTS OF SONG" score. In jobs like these and in some of the other assignments you get, like checking up prop and costume plots, a painstaking effort to be accurate is of first importance and of special benefit to you because you are not temperamentally painstakingly accurate. I hope you will bear this in mind and conquer a disposition to go over things too quickly and snappily. That kind of work, although not very interesting, carries with it a great deal of responsibility, and a mistake may be costly and cause a great deal of inconvenience and annoyance to the organization. Lest this sound too much like Lord Chesterfield's letters to his son, I will drop this subject on the assumption that by this time you have got the idea.

I can't tell you how thrilled I was by your social triumph in persuading the illusive singer who would make no dates with anybody else to go out with you. I daresay that if you had smashed up Dick's car I would have heard of it by now, so that anxiety is over. What really has worried me has been to figure out who is a very pretty girl among the singers. As I remember the Municipal Opera troupe, the pulchritude was concentrated pretty well among the dancers, and the lack of pulchritude in about 80 percent of the entire chorus was just short of sensational.

The children's quarantine will be lifted on Saturday, and you can address the batch of letters you send me next week to 1100. Nora has had a litter very nearly resembling the "Birth of a Nation." She has presented the world with 10 Golden Retrievers, which is probably half the population of that breed in this country. Five are dogs and five are bitches, and nothing could be fairer than that. They look a little more like guinea pigs than dogs and I am afraid Alice was very disappointed in them. The weekly bad news bulletin is that Sarah has caught scarlet fever from the children and has gone to the hospital, otherwise the house would have been quarantined for three more weeks. She is doing all right, I understand, but is of course upset at being ill at all, and doubly so because she is missing her big moment, i.e. taking care of Nora and her puppies.

Oscar Hammerstein to William Hammerstein, July 5, 1938

Dear Bill:

I found your letter most interesting and encouraging because from the pages there exudes an enthusiasm which I am glad to see. When you say you find it necessary to stay up a couple of nights a week until four o'clock in the morning, I assume that by the word "couple" you mean five or six. I suggest that in the future you confine it to the conventional two. I know that on Saturday night and also on Sunday you are very likely to stay up that late on dress rehearsals. That only leaves five nights when sleep is available, so don't take too much "relaxation." Looking over the carbon copy of my letter to you of last week, I find it necessary to warn you not always to emulate the spelling of my letters unless they are written in long hand. I have a secretary who apparently thinks the word "elusive" is spelled "illusive." Since she has just told me she prides herself on her spelling, this mixes me all up. As a matter of fact, she is a good speller and probably thought by "illusive" I didn't mean hard to catch but a thing of the illusions.

Going back to a former letter of yours, I note that you say Chester was unpopular with some of the company. Do you not think this is due to the fact that a man in his position must of necessity become unpopular if he is to faithfully perform his duties to Dick Berger, or keep his popularity at the expense of those duties? After all, he is a checker-upper and sometimes in checking up some people are shown up. Of course, there are all sorts of reasons for unpopularity and all sorts of ways of doing things. The main point I want to make it that it is best to be fair and square with everybody and let the popularity take care of itself. It is not nearly so important to be popular as to be efficient. Of course to be both is an art. Here I go being Lord Chesterfield again.

I didn't quite understand what you meant by saying you thought you would soon be qualified to take over Phil Farley's duties, the obvious question being, what happens to Phil? I had a letter from your great-uncle Arthur, who was delighted to hear what you are doing and offers you a job the season after this if we produce the biography of your great-grandfather. Of course, by that time you may be giving him a job so the offer at the moment is of only theoretical interest. My only other questions based on your letter are: (1) What is meant by "practically platonic?" (2) What did you mean by saying "My very best to Sarah. Your very best to Alice."? (3) Muriel wants to know whether you consider "Per M." too intimate or not intimate enough.

Two weeks from to-night I will be aboard the Super-Chief en route to St. Louis, and I am looking forward to the whole thing.

Joanne has arrived, has been tried out on the tennis court and found wanting. She has turned out, however, to be a very sweet kid and I am very fond of her. We've taken her to the Beachcomber's, and I am taking both of them to the races next week. I played singles with Alice to-day, giving her thirty a game. After trailing in the first set 4-1, I beat her 6-4, and the second set she beat me 6-4. I was trying all the time so you can imagine how good she has become. She makes some remarkable shots. Her backhand has especially improved, and so has her serve.

This really does conclude my letter and is next to my last before I arrive myself "under separate cover."

Love,

DAD

Encl: Cheque

Oscar Hammerstein to Myra Finn, August 16, 1938

Dear Mike:

A couple of weeks ago I spent ten dollars to phone you from St. Louis, thinking it would be nice for you to hear Bill's voice and that it would be beneficial for you to be able to tell me the situation regarding your house, that you could tell me about it more clearly on the phone, and that I might advise you about it.

What might have been a pleasure you turned into a most unpleasant experience—for you more than anyone. You did nothing but berate Bill for not writing—a thing you had already covered pretty completely in several letters, and I had also had a talk with him about it. As for me, you preferred to answer all my questions cryptically and melodramatically, in the same manner in which your mother used to annoy you so intensely. The whole phone call was a bust. You didn't even ask me how my new show looked, and you hadn't the common thoughtfulness to see that Alice was near the phone so that she might talk to her father and brother. You were so sealed up in your indignation at Billy, and the world in general, and in some indirect way, at me, that you were deaf, dumb and blind to everything but your resentment.

You say that since my telephone call your nerves have been in a most frightful state. Let me tell you they were in a frightful state before you picked up the receiver. You got yourself worked up for that phone call. You gnawed at yourself and abused yourself and got all wound up - - - Now look!

If Bill is neglectful he is at fault. And he is neglectful. The way to fix that is not to nag him. When will you get that into your head? Don't you see you only make yourself an unwelcome person in his life? Let a few things go. Don't worry and fret yourself—or other people. I know this burns you up, because you are thinking me unjust and too tolerant of Billy. I am not. But you can't fix him by continual scolding. You should know that by now.

<u>YOU WORRY YOURSELF INTO TROUBLE</u> - - - For instance, you started worrying about your new lease last April—then May—as late as June I told you not to do anything—the summer was uncertain. Don't sign any lease I said, "Take Alice for a winter trip. Bill can stay with me." So you signed a lease! You think you have hard luck in being saddled with a lease. It hasn't anything to do with luck. You fretted yourself right into the trap you're in. You fret yourself out of Billy's affection. Next time you feel like writing diatribes, - don't. Try doing some work on yourself, and I guarantee you will find less to complain of in your treatment at the hands of Billy—and everybody. It will be automatic.

Believe me this criticism comes from my interest in you and my constant hope that you can some day shake off this unfortunate and very unattractive habit of complaint and resentment and trouble-stirring for those around you, but principally for yourself. Please do some <u>thinking</u>. God know you've got a good sharp brain to do it with—clogged up by an illusion of persecution, as a motor can be clogged with carbon. Get it out!

Billy has a fine opportunity with Larry. He'll do stage work as well as office work—as I did. And while I did it you will remember I found time to write, to collect gags, to work Sundays, to work at my own ambitions in between my duties at Arthur's office. If Billy is going to write music, don't worry, he'll write it. The one thing he mustn't do, if we can help it, is remain a dilettante student getting a home from his mother and an allowance from his father. That's pernicious!

He'll bunk in with Reg at the Weylin for a few weeks. I'll see that he's all right. His health is wonderful and he's fine in every way—except his thoughtlessness about other people—for which of course he will suffer, if he doesn't change.

Why don't you rent that shack and take a loss on it—take a <u>good</u> loss— $50.00 a month—anything. Send Alice to Great Neck, and come on yourself. Get an apartment, have Billy with you, <u>enjoy</u> life, and snap out of it!

My own plans are so varied and complex that I'm afraid they must await another letter, which I will try to write as soon as possible.

And please don't think me unsympathetic. I am quite the opposite.

Sincerely,

Oc

Nigel Bruce is best remembered for playing Dr. Watson to Basil Rathbone's Sherlock Holmes in a series of films, the first two of which were released in 1939. Playing Gilbert in *Knights of Song* was Bruce's last appearance on Broadway.

Oscar Hammerstein to Nigel Bruce, August 20, 1938

Dear Willy:-

In a few days you will be receiving a new script of "Knights of Song". It is, in our opinion, twice as good as the play we had in St. Louis. Your own part is the least affected because it was nearer to being right than any other part or any element in the show. We have, however, improved it in one respect in which it needed improvement. We have now and then revealed a sympathetic softness and fallibility under the driving force which characterizes the man on the surface and we have strengthened his contact with "Mrs. Ronalds", who is once more living under the alias—"Cynthia Bradley". This return to the former name is designed to avoid any possible law suit from the Ronalds or Lorillard families and also grows out of an earnest desire, on our part, to confuse you as much as possible.

So that you may go along with us as you read the new script, I want to tell you what we are driving at and what main faults we have striven to cure in the new version. In the first scene there is little change except the building up of a good vocal finish by using the actual finale of "Pinafore". In this connection, however, we take the opportunity of illustrating a sympathy and understanding which exists between you and Sullivan underneath all the bickering that is to follow. The orchestrations for the finale are brought in by McManus at the last minute and knowing how eager Sullivan will be to go over it immediately, you stop your rehearsal and turn over the stage to him.

In Scene II we have made some cuts which plunge us into the story immediately and we clarify your attitude about Sullivan and Mrs. Bradley, eliminating all suspicion that you have any interest in her as a kind of glorified song plugger at the Palace, and establishing that you approve of her and her connection with Sullivan because you admire her and because you believe she is a good thing for him.

At the beginning of the scene you may be surprised and chagrined to find Mrs. Gilbert in possession of your line about the success of "Pinafore" going to your waist. We need that reference at the start of the scene so as to establish some connection with the first scene which we have, up to now, lacked. In the other version we went to the trouble of showing a dress rehearsal of "Pinafore" and then went far into the next scene without any feeling of natural and logical continuity. All this, of course, is a lame explanation to veil the truth that we are really out to undermine you and to avenge ourselves for your shabby treatment of Glendon Allvine in St. Louis.

In the third scene we come to our most important development—the new characterization of the "Prince of Wales" and also bringing Mrs. Bradley to life. It was in this third scene that the play started to drop in St. Louis. When you analyze it nothing really happened. The Prince, who was a dull stiff, announced that the audience with "Victoria" was a fait accompli (leaving Mrs. Bradley nothing to do)—then you met Shaw—dinner was announced—you cracked some gags and Mrs. Bradley and Sullivan announced their undying devotion—winding up with a duet from the "Sorcerer", performed in a spirit of elephantine whimsy.

The Prince is now painted as he really was—a fascinating and amusing character—predatory as to females and specifically desirous of Mrs. Bradley. Mrs. Bradley, living up to your description in the previous scene, proves herself to be a clever woman of the world by using the Prince's susceptibility to her charm to achieve an audience with Victoria for Sullivan. We enter the next scene then with an interest in a well conceived intrigue. Mrs. Bradley has said in effect, "I will make your mother believe that I am interested in Sullivan and dispel her suspicions that I am in love with you". The audience, however, knows that she is in love with Sullivan and is using Edward as a dupe. The Queen fools them both by pinning Mrs. Bradley down to a promise not to get a divorce. The Yacht Scene and Dock Scene remain the same with minor improvements and so does the "Pirates of Penzance" Rehearsal Scene, except that we have eliminated the first of the two quarrels because it seemed like very childish bickering and weakened, rather than strengthened, the second quarrel.

The Second Act—well, you wouldn't know the old girl! The first scene takes place in Sullivan's study and will be played about as in St. Louis except for a new opening, establishing Sullivan's enthusiasm for his first Grand Opera "Ivanhoe". The second scene is the New Year's Eve scene—the story of which is exactly the same as it was, there being almost no change from the time you enter, but the opening attack is entirely different—with the stage crowded and Oscar Wilde already on, and a very charming scene in which an ancient Edison Gramophone is brought in and we hear a squeaky rendition of "The Lost Chord" by Mrs. Bradley, which was the first vocal record ever made in England. This is true historically.

After this scene comes our most radical structural change. Despite a certain poetic appeal that it had, we were terribly worried about the scene in which Mrs. Bradley got the psychic message that Sullivan had died. The play seemed definitely to go down-hill from this point on and what alarmed us most of all was not so much the gloom of the Street Scene as the hangover that shadowed the next scene—the one in the ante room, which, of necessity, must be played slowly—so we have substituted for the Street Scene a new one which all of us believe, in many ways, to be the best scene in the play. It takes place in D'Oyly Carte's office—contains some good comedy and, better than that, points up the sentimental tragedy of the breach between the two men. I will not describe this—the scene will speak for itself.

You may wonder why I don't let the whole play speak for itself and why I have sent you this detailed libretto—as if the script itself were written in an old Persian dialect and needed a translation. I have found in my long and varied experience of collaboration with authors, actors, and producers that once one becomes a part of a play all changes are shocking, unless he is forewarned of the reasons and motives which inspired them. Frail and sensitive little thing that you are, I wouldn't shock you for the world!

Larry and I await your comments with interest and you need not tell us that the new version of Edward could not be played in England—we know that. We are certain that he will be an entertaining and lovable character to Americans as he was in real life.

You will be surprised and, I hope, envious when you hear that I am sailing Wednesday on the "Queen Mary". I will spend only four days in

London, mainly in search of a man expertly trained for the production of Gilbert & Sullivan numbers in the D'Oyly Carte tradition. Several of them will be lined up for me on my arrival. I may also do some casting there for whatever characters we are unsuccessful in finding here. If you have any suggestions for me, cable me care of Chappells, 50 New Bond Street. I sail back on the "Paris" on Sept. 3rd, arriving in New York on September 10th. We are going into rehearsal on the 15th—opening in New York October 12th. We will give three dress rehearsals with an audience before this, which means that our first dress rehearsal without an audience will be on October 7th. This, you will see, gives me one day less than three weeks in which to produce the play and it will be a great hardship to me, and I think a serious handicap to the play, if you are not with me from the very first day on—so please make your plans so that you arrive in New York on the 14th, I really believe this is very important.

It was kind of you to get in touch with Dorothy and to tell her about the play. She is, of course, going to London with me and it will be a welcome rest to her after the last hectic month she has had winding things up in Beverly Hills.

My kindest regards to your wife and yourself.

Sincerely,

Oscar Hammerstein to Lloyd Lewis (excerpt), August 20, 1938

Someone forwarded from St. Louis the generously flattering article you wrote about me in the "Daily News". This was a very kind thing for you to do and if I had the talent you believe I have, I could, perhaps, thank you adequately. As it is I find myself vaguely embarrassed and mumbling to you by mail that I am very grateful, indeed.

I must make one correction to straighten you out on the Hammerstein hierarchy. My father's name was William and Oscar, 2nd is—who do you think?—me. Oscar, 3rd is, as yet, unborn and will have to be a grandson unless Dorothy changes her mind about certain avowed intentions.

Author Alice Duer Miller's relationship with Oscar may have dated from her work on the screenplay for *Rose-Marie*. Her novel, *Gowns by Roberta*, was the source for the musical, *Roberta*. In a letter excerpted below she suggested several possible collaborations, none of which came to pass. But here she may have planted the seed for his version of *Cinderella*, which will be realized nine-teen years hence.

Alice Duer Miller to Oscar Hammerstein (excerpt), November 7, 1938

Then another idea I have had for a long time—for a play, but it might do [as] a musical, is nothing more not [*sic*] less than Cinderella. We all keep stealing from the fairy-story. Why not do it straight—fairy godmother, pumpkin and all, with good modernistic dialogue?

Leighton Brill to Oscar Hammerstein (excerpt), November 8, 1938

Seriously, I have been gathering inklings of your plans having had lunch with Mr. George Frank, and in order to make you feel, well—I'll tell you what I heard around and let you judge how you feel. All the positively, definitely, and may-so musicals are doomed, except another Alexander's Ragtime Band. Lyric writers and composers are being lopped off studio rolls as fast as their contracts expire. Warners have let Johnny Mercer and Al Dubin go. Yippy Harburg and Harold Arlen are looking for a job. Ira Gershwin is wandering around Hollywood Boulevard with a script of his brother[']s life under his arm. Ralph Ra[i]nger and Leo Robin are writing tunes for a cartoon. Sig Herzig is writing a grim drama of silent passion and stark reality—and so the story goes. It is a titanic upheaval until the next musical makes a hit.

In his "condolence" letter below, Kern is referring to *Knights of Song*. It opened on Broadway on October 17, and closed after sixteen performances. This was a bad period professionally for Oscar: *Gentlemen Unafraid* had closed in June and hopes it would move to Broadway were dashed. The film *The Lady Objects* opened to little notice. Its song, "A Mist Is Over the Moon" was nominated for an Academy Award, but it didn't win and was quickly forgotten. November brought two plays to Broadway, both of which quickly sank. *Where Do We Go From Here*, produced by Hammerstein, closed after fifteen performances, and *Glorious Morning* directed and co-produced by Hammerstein, closed after nine. *The Great Waltz* was released, but its lyrics were not Oscar's best, and the film is reported to have lost money.

Jerome Kern to Oscar Hammerstein, November 29, 1938

Dear Oscar:

There was an unfavorable reference in yesterday's (Monday's) Hollywood Reporter, so I was not unprepared for your telegram.

I hate to be just perfunctory with a "Too bad, better luck next time" and there is really little one can say—except that perhaps two or three years of dolce far niente[11] out here may have blunted the old, acute sense of dramatic values for the stage, which an incredibly short time spent in and around the theatre will undoubtedly resharpen.

Your character and guts have been tested before this, and I know that these experiments, which just didn't happen to come off, are not going to permanently shake your confidence or cause you to temper your artistic honesty or lower your standards.

Which brings up the point of the Los Angeles Civic Opera Company's proposed revival of SHOW BOAT for one week in May. Mr. Edwin Lester, Managing Director, (the fellow who began last year's three weeks' Romberg festival with John Charles Thomas in BLOSSOM TIME) is again at the helm and telephoned the other day that he definitely wants to do SHOW BOAT. As icily as was possible over the telephone, I received the suggestion, remembering that you and I had decided that unless something might be done about choice of cast, producer, director, etc., we would prefer not to cherish that cup of coffee and doughnut.

Of course, a performance with Winninger, Edna May Oliver, Irene Dunne and Stanley Morner, with perhaps Sammy White, might well be worth seeing, but I tremble to think what he will do for the scenery and costumes. I didn't see ROBERTA except at dress rehearsal, but that was fairly bloody. Of course, it is true that ROBERTA had very little else but Bob Hope and a fashion show and cannot really be compared. Anyway, let me hear what you think.

Best as always.

Hastily yours,

Jerry.

---

[11] "Sweet doing nothing"—pleasant idleness.

Oscar Hammerstein to Jerome Kern, November 30, 1938

Dear Jerry,

Here is the script of "Show Boat". I have no script of "Music In The Air", except the leather-bound script. I should think that this would be as good a model for Jerry Wald's purpose as could be found.

Unless some miracle takes place, I will have to close my third offering this Saturday.

Yesterday morning I took a good long rest of half an hour and then started to work on "Golden Bells". I am writing an entirely new prologue laid in Malachi Campbell's thatched cottage in the county Antrim and I am having the time of my life with it. Instead of waiting until I forward it to you, you might get busy right away on the little song that is being sung as the curtain rises, by Eveleen, Malachi's granddaughter. She is playing a small Irish harp and the winds of the county Antrim, bellying down the glen and whistling through the chimney, accompany the melody which she is singing. Of course the glen is located somewhere in the orchestra pit and the winds are produced from bellows blown by Russell Bennett. I think, offhand, that the melody should be similar to the zither song you had in Otto's picture, although you might think it needs a more plaintive quality. Possibly it should be a version of something that Golden Bells sings later. Anyway, here we are digging into it and I am very happy.

Friday afternoon I am seeing Alice Duer Miller and spending a whole afternoon with her. Friday morning I have promised several hours to Otto who has still another version of "Gentlemen Unafraid" to submit to me. I will write to you again at the end of the week and by the beginning of next week I will send you the new prologue and an elaboration of the old lay-out of "Golden Bells".

Love to all,

Oscar Hammerstein to Arthur Hammerstein (excerpt), December 2, 1938

I have brooded very little over my bad luck this year, because it is all part of the business and I was quite prepared for it. I will have lost comparatively little money on the two dramatic productions, but "Knights of Song" was rather expensive. My biggest loss, of course, was what I didn't make all the weeks that I might have been earning picture money during 1938, but I am still not sorry that I have switched back to the theatre where I want to be. Meanwhile, the fact that I am a Double-A member in A.S.C.A.P. keeps the wolf from the door. I will write you again soon.

Oscar and Kern struggled over a period of months to find a story for their next collaboration. They settled on an original story by Oscar, *Very Warm for May*. However, the show that opened out-of-town in October had been changed dramatically by the time it opened on Broadway in November. The process of finding their show began months earlier.

Oscar Hammerstein to Jerome Kern (excerpt), January 18, 1939

I suspect that if we'd been forced to scenaricize any of the shows we'd done together they would never have been written. I am still a strong believer in the unscientific method of picking up a "Bicycle built for two" and riding it to a destination—without a map. There is then the adventure on the way of trying new paths and byways. Scenarios are like living trial marriages with stories. They sometimes prevent mistakes, but God, how bored you get with the bride before you wed her. Phui on scenarios! Vive la pacing up and down the room and getting excited.

Jerome Kern to Oscar Hammerstein (excerpt), January 18, 1939

Taking your opening sentence at face value, the story of a house, or rather one room of a house, is set forth right enough. But the question arises. Has the public the slightest interest in <u>rooms</u>? I doubt it. On form, the story of a <u>theatre</u> should have knocked 'em cold, but THE FABULOUS INVALID[12] didn't. True, it was only half-baked musically, and dull and stodgy as a play, and will be remembered probably only by the critics. But they are the boys who will review our next venture.

I cannot help but feel that the dramatic and entertainment features of the entire piece are too routine. The large number of principal characters are apt to be burdensome, since you have to <u>tell</u> their careers and adventures. Not seeing them in much action makes excessive gabbiness inevitable. The unpleasant failure of various lives are stressed, without the contrast of

---

[12] *The Fabulous Invalid* was a short-lived 1938 play by Kaufman and Hart, following the thirty-year life of a fictitious Broadway theater.

seeing and believing in their having a shred of glamorous romance. There is no magnetic pole in the central idea (of a house) to attract a section of an audience—as for instance, women were attracted by the gowns in ROBERTA. The recalcitrant husband and father in SHOW BOAT had a swashbuckling attraction, and was only <u>one</u>. Here we see <u>two</u>, and they are both stodgy business men who, if in their youth had had adventure in their blood, reformed (?) and plunged into the dross of dollars and cents and ticker tape.

Don't you feel the imitative and, I fear, unimproved spirit of: the single set of YOU CAN'T TAKE IT WITH YOU, the generations formula of MILESTONES and MAYTIME, and the parade of old tunes in ALEXANDER,[13] etc., etc. pervading the whole piece?

I have a personal distaste of using any of my old catalogue in a piece by us—making me feel like a man reading one of his earlier love letters aloud in public.

Photo 9 Jerome Kern

---

[13] *Alexander's Ragtime Band* was a 1938 film featuring songs by Irving Berlin, with a plot that tracked the evolution of American popular music from 1911 to the (then) present day.

As a member of the audience, I find myself groping without any definite guide because the piece hasn't, thank God, lavender and old lace, nor has it modern youth, verve and gaiety.

Jerome Kern to Oscar Hammerstein, January 23, 1939

Dear Oscar:

This is a hurried acknowledgement of yours of January 18th, which I hope will reach you O.K. as, according to schedule, you and Dorothy are leaving New York probably this very minute.

Jerry Wald turned up yesterday with a 94-page scenario and, as you sagely observed, phui on all scenarios. I have, mirabile dictum,[14] read somewhat more than half and can report that it is still only a bicycle, but I think a corker. I hesitate to send it on to you in its present form because, owing to Wald's and Macauley's[15] inexperience in the theatre and too routine experience in the studio, there is no construction. The scenario is merely a recital of unplanned, sporadic fade-ins and fade-outs.

Maybe I can tell it my way in eleven words, so listen.

Judy is a naïve optimist with an amateur voice, who leaves her native town of Estrellita, Kansas, and boards a train for Hollywood to crash the pictures. She is armed with a letter to Twentieth Century from her mentor and idol, old Mr. Zekwar. She is confident that she can be a glamorous Jeanette MacDonald, only more so, can be a singer like Durbin, only better, and can dance like Ginger Rogers, only better.

In Hollywood, in a stylized auto court, she meets young people who are struggling extras and older performers who are ex-vaudevillians with no vaudeville left to employ them. She also meets the hero, a likable lad, who was by way of being an artist and at one time got himself a job as an animator and, when we pick him up, has now sunk his all in a cartoon studio of his own. His model and target is, of course, Walt Disney.

After typical adventures, she ultimately succeeds in films, but not as a glamour girl and not as a singer, but as the voice behind the drawn character of a successful cartoon. This last is shown in the making, with all the interesting

---

[14] *Mirabile dictum*—wonderful to tell.
[15] Jerry Wald and Richard Macauley were prolific screenwriters and frequent collaborators.

paraphernalia of a cartoon studio—troupes of live actors, entertainers and chorus dancers being employed as models for the animators.

The cartoon, I might add, is also shown as the finished product and, I think, is something of a nifty in that it concerns a happy and contented community of black face sheep, completely demoralized and upset by three aggressor wolves who sow dissension with insidious propaganda against the white face sheep minorities.

The set-up concerns such a varied entertainment, embracing as it does, vaudeville, burlesque and the latest and, to my mind, the most diverting branch of films—animated cartoons—all dished up in our form of musical play, that I find the prospect, once it can be whipped into shape, very exciting.

Now, shall I send you the ninety-four pages, which, with the exception of the character of Judy, is about 80% junk, or shall I wait until I hear from you whether my above eleven words appeal at all? For a long time now I have dreamed of combining a cartoon with a musical play and, with care and devotion, I am sure something good can come of it.

Please give my love to Dorothy and kind regards to Arthur and his Dorothy. Let me hear from you soon.

Ever yours,

Jerry

Disney's *Snow White and the Seven Dwarfs* premiered in December of 1937. It was the first animated feature in color and full sound and, despite the doomsayers, it not only became the progenitor for all animated features that would follow, it became the most commercially successful sound picture to date. Although live action and animation had previously (if rarely) been combined in films, the notion described by Kern seems inventive and unique.

Oscar Hammerstein to Edwin Lester, January 31, 1939

Dear Edwin:

I will assume you could give Show Boat an adequate physical production—costumes and scenery—and let us also say that we have luck with casting. The one thing that disturbs me most is the thing you skip over very lightly in your letter . . . stage direction. The only times Show Boat has been successfully staged have been those times when Jerry and I have done it ourselves. I don't think either of us is free to stage your production, nor do I think you could afford to employ us in this capacity. Strong as the play is it can easily be spoiled by a lack of subtleties in direction that characterized the original production. The Shuberts illustrated this fact very forcibly last summer. It was not the cast that was so wrong. It was the direction. Every time the play has failed—Curran's west coast production, the Paris production—Jerry and I were not there to guide it. But when we did the original, the London show, and the New York revival, the play broke records. You can see, therefore, the reason for our concern.

You must realize I am not under-rating your accomplishments of last season. I saw Roberta and thought it a fine job. I have heard good reports on your other efforts last year. You just have to forgive me for being very squeamish about this pampered baby of ours.

Kindest regards,

Largely to please Uncle Arthur, Oscar worked on and off for almost twenty years to shepherd a biopic of his namesake to the screen. After many *almosts*, followed by many setbacks, the closest he ever came to memorializing his grandfather was the publication of a biography in the 1950s that disappointed both Oscar and Arthur.

Oscar Hammerstein to George Frank (excerpt), February 21, 1939

Meanwhile, I am mailing you a fifty-page manuscript on the life of my illustrious grandfather who, in my version, has turned out to be a combination of Ronald Colman, Boris Karloff and Mickey Rooney. You won't know the old boy—but I think it's very good. I will definitely not sell the story without a contract to write the screen play myself.

Oscar Hammerstein to Carl Van Vechten,[16] March 15, 1939

Dear Carl Van Vechten,

Thank you for the pictures. I am a little disturbed by the supercilious expression that I find in my face, except in one picture where I look

---

[16] Van Vechten was a well-regarded portrait photographer and is now particularly remembered for his documenting of the Harlem Renaissance.

hopelessly worried. If you think it is the artificial light, I will be delighted to try the great outdoors with you when the weather gets nice. How about a sporty type of portrait with a tennis racket held over my shoulder?—or perhaps with my favorite dog and pipe? I am going to California Sunday (two weeks later than I had intended) and when I return, I will call you up.

With kindest regards, I am

Sincerely yours,

OSCAR HAMMERSTEIN

P.S. The more I look at them, the better I think they are as far as likeness is concerned. There's no use blaming it on artificial light—it must be me.

O.H.

As the situation deteriorated for Jews in Nazi Germany, Oscar was contacted by relatives hoping for help to escape the increasingly dire persecution that would lead to the Holocaust.

Alice Nordheimer to Oscar Hammerstein, April 26, 1939

Dear Mr. Hammerstein,

Few days ago we received a letter from the National Council of Jewish Women, giving your address and further informing us, that you so very kindly are prepared to help us. Please let us express our most sincere thanks, and believe, that we cannot find appropriate words to tell you how very happy we feel on receiving the news.

I am asked by the Committee to give you full particulars regarding my husband and myself.

I am the daughter of Gustav Hammerstein, who was a son of Bernhard Hammerstein in Berlin. Bernhard Hammerstein was, as my father often told me, a cousin of yours. I am sorry to say, that my father died in October 1938, otherwise he would have been able to get in touch with you. My husband, who had several important shoestores in Germany is 39 years old. Before leaving Germany he took a course in cooking and took a training as butler, enabling him not to rely on his knowledge acquired in the shoehire [sic]. I am 38 years old, and may state that I am a very good cook, know how to manage a household and I am able to sew and to do any work required. We are lucky in getting a very good job in the country as a married couple and we are running the house, which is pretty big entirely on our own.

We may state that the owners have repeatedly expressed their full satisfaction with our service. I am telling you all these facts, so that you will be assured, that we both can handle a job, once we are over in U.S.A. We fell [sic] confident, that we shall find a suitable position at once, and that there is no risk that we may depend on anybody.

The most important point of my letter as we do not want to fall back on your kind assistance ourselves, having received the necessary affidavits for my husband and myself through a relation, is the question of my mother. It is for here [sic] that I venture to ask you for a[n] affidavit. You can imagine how mothers fate worries us, as she, since father died is alone, and I am her only child. You know how every jew is in constant danger in Germany and how necessary speedy help is needed.

I must try to get mother first of all in England and this step can be facilitated if she has the American affidavit. Besides she wants a guarantee for the time she stays in England. I want to ask you, dear Mr. Hammerstein, if you could see your way to grant us a loan to the amount of many [sic] required for mother, while she stays in England. We cannot get any money out of Germany and it goes without saying, that we would repay you at the very earliest moment once we are in the States. I should feel ever so much gratefull [sic] to you if we could get your answer as soon as possible. You are the only hope for mother as I d'ont [sic] know any other way to get her out of Germany. We expect our American Visa about August this year, this being also the month of our arrival in U.S.A. May I therefore repeat stortly [sic]/

Can you supply a affidavit for mother?

Are you willing to forward the necessary money, whilst she stays in England?

Kindly rest assured that your help would be greatly appreciated and that we would feel ever so thankful for any assistance of [sic] your part.

The dates of mother are:

Clara Hammerstein, born Hess

born April 8th, 1878 in Römhild, Kreis Meiningen.

Thanking you again for your good efforts, I am

Yours sincerely

Alice Nordheimer

Leighton Brill to Oscar Hammerstein, May 6, 1939

Dear Oc:

The force of your vitriolic vituperations entirely lost for the two following reasons. Firstly, the plot offerings were already in the mail when your love letter arrived. Secondly, any force that might have been left was entirely spent by my surprise at your abysmal ignorance. How a man, who has attained, or has he, the position in literature that your biographers give you, can ask a question so elementary that even Romberg would know the answer, is beyond me. It is only my lamentable lack of finances that kept me from telegraphing you the answer post haste. Do not insinuate that I had to look it up.

Connecticut, my dear fellow, is known as the nutmeg state because in its early days its inhabitants were supposedly so shrewd that they were accused of manufacturing nutmegs of wood and selling same. It is with tears in my eyes that I dispatch those facts to you. You can well imagine how one feels when one discovers that one's idol had feet of nutmegs.

Frivolity now off the chest let us get down to moot questions.

1. What do you think of the smuggling device, and the way to put it in the story in the first and second acts?
2. Will you please at once, or as soon as you have arrived at same, send a complete list of characters? As I see the outline, we have

    1. Deanna Dustbin, our heroine.
    2. Charlie Winninger Dustbin, her father.
    3. Humphrey Bogartist, leader of the gang.
    4. Step and Fetchyme, the negro house boy.
    5. May Robson Catwilder, the dowager patron saint of the little theatre.
    6. John Paine Catwilder, her son who Deanna adores.

7. Beryl Carewe, money bags, a young girl of seventeen who sings one song.
8. Matty Melnick's band.
9. Jack Williams, filthy rich, a dancer—up to now no part in the plot.

3. Have you devised any other important characters, and what do they do? I know there will be several adult mr. and mrs. Rich bitches, and a cast of kiddie rich bitches for the play.
4. Do you want to have a lean somber Orson Welles as a director of the opus?
5. Do you want any F.B.I. men lurking about?

In your next docile (I hope) tome will you give me your plot as far as you have developed it, your characters, and I will endeavor to find Brilgenious devices, gags, et cetera. My indignation rises to the fore. All I will say is that to ask a man to devise and gag a plot that isn't formulated is a worthy suggestion from one who has no knowledge of nutmegs.

Hoping that this letter is taken in the spirit it is intended, I remain, sire, your most obedient servant

Leighton

Leighton "Connecticut" Brill

P. S. Indeed sir, it has come to a pretty pass when one has to use secret service operatives to find out that the daughter of the house was in the midst of a dog fight, and bitten. Why do you do this to me?

P. P. S. In the midst of my troubles and travail, in the midst of Probation Officers, Insurance Agents, F.B.I. and S.E.C. operatives, you sire, accuse me of playing badminton! Fie, fie, fie!

Romberg is increasingly determined to find source material for a show on which he and Oscar can collaborate.

Sigmund Romberg to Oscar Hammerstein, May 24, 1939

DEAR OSCAR: IF I REMEMBER CORRECTLY SOME YEARS AGO AN OPERETTA VERSION OF BEAU BRUMMEL WAS DONE FOR J J SHUBERT BY GLADYS UNGER. I DONT THINK IT WAS EVER

FINISHED BECAUSE I NEVER STARTED ON IT FOR HIM AND IT WAS PROBABLY DROPPED HOWEVER HE MUST OWN THE RIGHTS. I DONT KNOW WHETHER HE OWNS THE RIGHTS FOR ENGLAND AND FRANCE BUT IT MIGHT BE WORTH WHILE CHECKING. DONT BOTHER SENDING ME CLYDE FITCH'S PLAY OF BEAU BRUMMEL AS I CAN GET IT HERE. I REMEMBER THE BOOK WELL. ITS VERY DRAMATIC AND IS SOMETHING LIKE MAYTIME. A PLAY WITH MUSIC. IT COULD BE A WONDERFUL LOVE STORY BUT WOULD DEPEND UPON THE TREATMENT YOU GIVE IT IN ORDER TO BRING THE MUSIC IN. SOME OF THE SITUATIONS ARE SO DRAMATIC THAT MUSIC WOULD ONLY INTERFERE WITH THEM UNLESS HANDLED PROPERLY=

I JUST FINISHED READING A NOVEL QUOTE PARVATI UNQUOTE A ROMANCE OF PRESENT DAY INDIA BY ROBERT CHAUVELOT TRANSLATED FROM FRENCH BY HELEN DAVENPORT GIBBONS PUBLISHED BY CENTURY NEWYORK COPYRIGHTED NINETEEN NINETEEN. THIS IS A MARVELOUS STORY FOR AN OPERETTA. IF YOU CANT GET IT AT ONCE WIRE ME AND I WILL SEND IT TO YOU IMMEDIATELY. ALTHOUGH I BORROWED IT MYSELF. NO DOUBT WE COULD BUY THE RIGHTS TO IT. IT IS NOT ONLY A WONDERFUL LOVE STORY BUT HAS ORIENTAL BACKGROUND HAREM STUFF ETCETERA LIKE DESERT SONG WHICH LENDS COLORFUL BACKGROUND TO THE WHOLE STORY. AM VERY ANXIOUS FOR YOU TO READ IT. IT MAY BE JUST THE THING. ARE YOU BY ANY CHANCE GETTING COLD FEET ON THIS THING OR BEING DISCOURAGED BECAUSE WE CANT FIND THE RIGHT SUBJECT BECAUSE YOU DIDN'T SOUND VERY ENTHUSIASTIC ON THE PHONE. BEST REGARDS=

ROMBERG.

Sigmund Romberg to Oscar Hammerstein, May 24, 1939

DEAR OSCAR DO YOU REMEMBER QUEEN CHRISTINE PICTURE WITH GRETA GARBO SEVERAL YEARS AGO. I MENTIONED IT TO YOU. IF NECESSARY YOU CAN ASK SOMEONE IN NEWYORK TO RUN IT FOR YOU. I THINK A DEAL COULD BE MADE WITH

MGM TO GET THE STORY FOR AN OPERETTA. HOW DO YOU FEEL ABOUT IT. AND SHALL I GO AHEAD WITH THE IDEA. JUST FINISHED READING BEAU BRUMMEL AGAIN. A POWERFUL STORY ALTHOUGH SOME DIFFICULT SPOTS TO BRING MUSIC IN WIRE ME YOUR REACTION ON QUEEN CHRISTINE.

LOVE=

ROMBERG.

Oscar Hammerstein to Sigmund Romberg, May 1939

I LIKE CHRISTINA SUGGEST YOU TALK TO METRO ABOUT IT. MAYBE THEY WOULD BACK IT. INQUIRING ABOUT OWNERSHIP OF BRUMMEL. MY ENTHUSIASM NOT LAGGING. JUST WANT TO BE SURE BEFORE WE START ON ANYTHING.

Photo 10 Sigmund Romberg

Oscar Hammerstein to Dorothy Hammerstein, June 4, 1939

Darling:

I must have been in a daze when I left you last Tuesday night. I went straight to a telegram booth and wrote a message to you and gave it to the man. He said, "Who's it going to?" I'd forgotten to put down your name or the boat.

I couldn't get to sleep for a long while, and I slept fitfully all night. I haven't felt rested any morning since you left. Sounds like a sob story, doesn't it?

Leighton and I have stuck close to work and we are getting a good, detailed layout of the Kern play [*Very Warm for May*]. I have been in town only once. That was last Thursday to see Billy for lunch, and then Mike. I put over Chicago University for Alice without much trouble. Mike's apartment is very nice—in a conventional way, of course,—and she seems to have done it very cheaply. Billy's room is the best, I think. He picked out his own things, and there is a marked influence of you in his choices.

Susan, as the miller's daughter in "Rumpelstiltskin" was pretty bloody. She had none of the dramatic fire which she exhibits at home. She was scared and inaudible and in-expressive. So were they all, except one boy— and he was no Mickey Rooney. The children were not helped much by the directrix who had left them standing about the stage with nothing to do, and Susan still had a cold. Let us accept these alibis and hope for the best. In a few weeks I shall discuss her performance with her. She will not be sensitive about it then, and I may be able to guard her against her mistaken attitude towards the next part she gets.

Leighton went to town last night to stop with Ben Hyman and I supped with the Hellmans and talked with them until ten thirty. Lou stayed up later to call for Henry and Patsy at the Movies. I heard him come in at twelve and I am sure he must have been very happy and satisfied to be up at an hour consistent with his advancing years.

It is raining to-day—a timid drizzle, but enough to spoil what promised to be one of Kennilworth's most confused Sunday's. Billy was—maybe he still is—bringing down Dave and Teddy Hecht and a girl friend of Dave's and I believe one other couple. I have the house overflowing with hamburgers and hot dogs—cost me two dollars to supplement your allowance to the steward—and I am not feeding them until six to-night. This cuts out a meal and is not a bad idea for the future. It is so light at six, it should be very pleasant eating out doors then—if it clears.

There are new flowers in the garden and all the bushes on the right side of the drive are now in bloom, but it is all obscured in a milky fog just now, very much as your absence bedims my normal joy of living. You have not done much to brighten this dimness. Since you left you sent me one radiogram, and then a second (after I forced it out of you by my radio to Milton). I don't understand such fundamental neglect. I have worked out several possible explanations but I don't like any of them.

Jimmy is having his lesson downstairs. He has been a very good boy, and so has Henry too. He asked me if he could stay over until to-morrow and of course I said he could. He is probably hoping for a break in the weather. I bought him a pair of swimming trunks in Ninesling's yesterday. We both thought the Kennilworth pool deserved something better than my blue denim shorts tied around him.

Susan's throat is better, but she has a slight headcold and she is staying in bed. She has hung a few dozen trinkets on the wall above her bed, and it looks something like the rack of prizes one gets for ringing canes at a fair. Then there is a large board in front of her bed—about two feet by four, God knows where she got it. And on this is a very fine pencilled portrait of Ferdinand, the bull.

Mousie is coming down Wednesday, principally to see Jimmy I think. She can't go to the fair yet because she has had more teeth out and won't go out until she gets new ones.

I had not heard from Reg and I wired him that I would phone him to-day. But he wired back that he would be out of town. Going social it seems. I am phoning him to-morrow.

I have just read the letters the children wrote to you and we all seem to check up pretty well. I have read none of your other letters because none of them looks interesting.

You are just arriving in England to-day and it seems a long time to wait before you will be here. I hope you will cable me more often while you are in London. Maybe the squirt who made you forget me on the Normandie got off at Cherbourg and went back to his homeland. I hope he is in the minority party, and that he is purged, immediately he steps off the train.

Give my love to Sophie and Milton.

Truly Julius is coming down next Sunday. And the Sunday after that I shall spend in brushing my clothes, washing my hair, shining my shoes, perfuming the back of my ears and preparing to win you back.

All my love and more kisses than you can count.

Ockie

Jerome Kern to Oscar Hammerstein, June 17, 1939

TRIED TO PHONE YOU THIS AFTERNOON AFTER SECOND READING BECAUSE WOULD NOT WANT YOU TO SLEEP TONIGHT WITHOUT KNOWING THAT I THINK IT'S A KNOCK OUT STOP EASILY THE BEST EMBRYO EVER TO COME IN SIGHT AND WHILE I SUPPOSE IT WILL NEVER BE PROPERLY PLAYED IT CANNOT FAIL TO BE ONE OF OUR TOPS CONGRATS SO FAR I HAVE ONLY READ IT FOR ENJOYMENT SHALL WRITE IN DETAIL EARLY NEXT WEEK AFTER STUDY LOVE=

JERRY.

Oscar Hammerstein to Senator Alva Adams of Colorado, June 28, 1939

My dear Senator Adams,

A Sub-Committee of the Senate, of which you are Chairman, is now considering the new WPA[17] appropriation bill passed by the House. In this bill is a provision eliminating the Federal Theatre Project. In common with all conscientious members of the theatrical profession, I feel this to be unfair and discriminatory and a great injustice to artists, musicians, and other theatrical groups who are sorely in need of Federal aid. I hope your committee will consider this feature of the measure very seriously and I here

---

[17] The Works Progress Administration was a New Deal program designed to give people jobs during the Depression. The Federal Theatre Project (FTP) was one of its subsets. Although it employed thousands of theater artists and underwrote a number of important works, it was accused of being a communist front and its support of racial equality rankled some members of Congress. Its funding was pulled on June 30, 1939.

add my earnest plea to the appeal already made by many of my colleagues that the theatre be once again made a beneficiary of the WPA appropriation.

I have the deepest confidence that you will be fair and just.

Very truly yours,

OSCAR HAMMERSTEIN

Emma Swift Hammerstein to Oscar Hammerstein, October 1, 1939

Dear Oscar, 2nd,:-

I am in above my head here, need several things for health and common comfort and am very sick and weak with a cold. I need comfortable walking shoes + arches, my winter coat is in rags. I have been so long without proper nourishment that I am feeling the effect of same and haven't strength to cope with situations. But my most pressing need is to straighten up my bill here tomorrow and, as my week is always up on that day, Monday, to move to a cheaper room—if I can find such an animal. I do not know which way to turn or to whom to go for financial assistance but I need it badly. It takes courage to try to exist under present conditions.

I trust you are very well and happy and that your new presentation will be a great success for you have been very industrious and I know you have a beautiful, understanding mind—and a kind heart. May I hear from you tomorrow, Monday, as I am very much worried and would not want my baggage held here?

With my kindest felicitations,

(Mrs. Oscar) Emma Swift Hammerstein.

Very Warm for May opened on Broadway on November 17, and closed after fifty-nine performances. It included the gorgeous ballad, "All the Things You Are," and was the last complete show Hammerstein wrote with Kern. Brooks Atkinson in the New York Times wrote, "the book is a singularly haphazard invention . . . Mr. Hammerstein's yarn about the gauche antics of a Summer theatre troupe is singularly irrelevant."

Oscar Hammerstein to Alice Hammerstein, November 26, 1939

Darling Alice:

I am so pleased by your letters. You seem more independent and sure of yourself—and if the sureness sometimes extends to cocksureness, I don't mind much, as long as you don't carry it too far.

Taking your last letter categorically, I assume you don't seriously mean the first paragraph in which you say Anderson must be a friend of mine and Lockridge[18] an enemy. Neither has any personal interest in me and each is stating his honest opinion I am sure. Have you seen Benchley's review in The New Yorker? It is very good.

The audiences have liked the show, and while the criticisms seriously affected our business, we are nevertheless doing fairly well and there is enough life at the box office to indicate a possibility of our overriding the bad notices. These weeks between Thanksgiving and Christmas are, of course, the worst theatre weeks in the year, and we don't expect to build into profitable grosses in that time. The trick will be to hold on somehow until the holidays. We must do that anyway so that you can see the show.

Taking your next paragraph: Uncle Reggie is fine. The other night he produced a television version of Three Men On A Horse and it was very well done.

Next paragraph: I do look svelte.

Next: Use your own judgment about getting in touch with Helen Morgan. I am certain she would be delighted to hear from you.

I think you were wise not to join the club.

I can not advise you about dropping math. You are the girl to decide that. And what is a "comp"? That was not part of the campus slang in nineteen twelve to seventeen.

Referring to your postscript, we did get our "traditional turkey" this year.

---

[18] John Anderson was a drama critic for the *New York Journal American*, and Richard Lockridge was a critic for the *New York Sun*.

Yesterday I took Henry, Susan and Jimmy to the Columbia Colgate game. A dull game, but not in the stands with that trio. Billy was to meet us but got lost in the subway.

Great Neck has its beautiful gold and brown cloak of autumn, just turning into the gray-blue of winter and I have walked about fifteen miles this week.

Mousie is much better and may go home to her new apartment this week.

The American Students' Union . . . . . . .All right. Only learn to distinguish between a fair-minded liberal and an intensely bigoted radical who calls himself a liberal. I mean there is as much unreasonable and unintelligent prejudice on the left as there is hard-shelled, blind conservatism on the right. Beware of it.

I am looking forward to seeing you. The time will pass quickly, and before you know it you will be in the midst of a hectic and disorderly Hammerstein Christmas.

Love,

Dad

Chapter Four
June 1941 through 1942

I found hardly any Hammerstein correspondence from 1940 through the first half of 1941, and what I did find was not significant enough to include in this book.

Oscar's fallow period continued through 1940. No Hammerstein shows opened on Broadway, nor were there any original films; MGM did, however, release a film version of *The New Moon* starring Jeanette MacDonald and Nelson Eddy. In Bosley Crowther's *New York Times* review of the film, he complimented the score: "It is pleasant and comforting to hear the old Romberg tunes so nicely sung"—never mentioning Hammerstein at all.

The one new Hammerstein show that did open was not for Broadway but a musical revue for the 1939 New York World's Fair. *American Jubilee*, described as "A panorama of American History . . . ," ran from May until October with multiple shows daily. Oscar wrote both the lyrics and the dialogue, and Arthur Schwartz supplied the music. Brooks Atkinson wrote of it: "As a spectacle it is exuberant— with a good book and rousing score by Oscar Hammerstein 2d and Arthur Schwartz." Of the eight songs we know, "Tennessee Fish Fry" was briefly and mildly popular. Oscar's most significant artistic achievement of 1940 was the writing of his first, and best, song related to World War II—"The Last Time I Saw Paris," with music by Kern. Inspired by the German invasion of Paris in June of 1940, it's one of the few Hammerstein songs not written for a show. Possibly the finest of his pop songs, "Paris" would go on to win the Oscar for best song when it was interpolated into the 1941 film *Lady Be Good*.

In the fall of 1940, Hammerstein purchased Highland Farm near Doylestown in Bucks County, Pennsylvania. It became and remained his primary home and refuge for the rest of his life. The story goes that, while house hunting in the area, Dorothy Hammerstein spotted a rainbow above the main house and "decided immediately that it was a good-luck omen."

During the first half of 1941 Oscar collaborated with Sigmund Romberg on the operetta *Sunny River*. The show's original title was *New Orleans* and it opened in a brief tryout at "the Muny" in St. Louis (St. Louis Municipal Opera Theatre) under that title—June 5 through 10. It was not only Oscar's final collaboration with Romberg,

The Letters of Oscar Hammerstein II. Mark Eden Horowitz, Oxford University Press. © Mark Eden Horowitz 2022.
DOI: 10.1093/oso/9780197538180.003.0004

Photo 11 Highland Farm, circa 1948. Photo courtesy of Oscar Andrew Hammerstein

but the last musical he would write with anyone other than Richard Rodgers (not counting *Carmen Jones*).

   Oscar Hammerstein and Richard Rodgers first met in March of 1917, backstage at the show *Home, James*, produced by the Columbia University Players, with book and lyrics co-written by Oscar who was also in the cast. Rodgers was an impressionable fourteen, Hammerstein, a worldly twenty-one. In 1919, Oscar and Rodgers collaborated on a few songs for an amateur group called the Akron Club. In that same year Rodgers began his partnership with Lorenz Hart. In 1925 Rodgers and Hart became the darlings of Broadway. By June of 1941 they had had some two dozen shows on Broadway, mostly going from hit to hit. At the time of this telegram, Rodgers' career was still soaring, while Hammerstein's had been in general decline for over ten years. Rodgers and Hammerstein's paths must have crossed somewhat regularly over the years, but this is the first communication I have found between them.

Richard Rodgers to Oscar Hammerstein, June 29, 1941

LARRY AND I SIT WITH EVERYTHING CROSSED HOPING THAT YOU WILL DO SARATOGA TRUNK WITH US=

DICK RODGERS

Edna Ferber's novel, *Saratoga Trunk*, had been released earlier in the year. Rodgers' telegram doesn't make clear exactly what part he wants Hammerstein to play in the collaboration, but in the one below from Ferber, it clarifies that Lorenz Hart would be the lyricist, and Hammerstein was only being approached as a librettist.

Edna Ferber to Oscar Hammerstein, June 29, 1941

DEAR OSCAR HAVE YOU READ OR HEARD ABOUT A NEW SERIAL NOVEL OF MINE CALLED SARATOGA TRUNK STOP RICHARD RODGERS WANTS TO MAKE A MUSICAL PLAY OF IT AND WE WOULD BE SO HAPPY IF YOU WERE WILLING TO DO THE BOOK STOP HOW DO YOU FEEL ABOUT IT WIRE REPLY WESTERN UNION=

EDNA FERBER

Edna Ferber to Oscar Hammerstein, July 3, 1941

HAVE JUST TALKED JACOB WILK HE STRONGLY ADVISES YOU TALK JACK WARNER STATING YOUR POSITION COMPLETELY ALSO ADVISES STATING YOU INTEND FOLLOW BOOK IN YOUR LIBRETTO. WOULD EMPHASIZE FACT THAT YOU AND RODGERS AND LARRY HART WOULD MAKE SUPERB MUSICAL. WILK THINKS WARNER WOULD PREFER HEARING ALL THIS FROM YOU PERSONALLY. CONTRACT CHANGE ARRANGEMENT COULD BE MADE BY ME OF COURSE=

EDNA FERBER

Richard Rodgers to Oscar Hammerstein, July 6, 1941

Dear Oscar,

I answer your letter in a very confused state of mind.

Ferber has been "acting up" and has been so impossible on the whole subject of the play that at the moment I am trying to decide whether or not I can afford to let myself in for what appears to be endless aggravation. I will let you know at the earliest possible moment. In the meantime you will probably come to some decision as to your own position.

I can say this, however: I was delighted and warmed by several things in your letter. Even if nothing further comes of this difficult matter it will at least have allowed us to approach each other professionally. Specifically, you feel that I should have a book with "substance" to write to. Will you think seriously about doing such a book?

Let us correspond and when you come east perhaps you and Dorothy will come up here for a week-end.

Love to both of you.

Dick.

Edna Ferber to Oscar Hammerstein, July 14, 1941

That was an unexpected turn in the SARATOGA TRUNK plans, dear Oscar. I feel that, somewhere, something went wrong. Weeks ago Warners were approached with the idea of a musical to be produced before the picture went into production. So far as I know, the plan was well received. Otherwise certainly Dick Rodgers and Larry Hart wouldn't have fallen for it, hard.

*I now learn that Mr. Warner is a temperamental Hollywood genius (ersatz) who must be approached by the forehead-to-the-ground method. He must be made to feel that all ideas originate in his own giant brain. An idea presented as conceived in another person's mind is resented by him. Me, I'd be a great hit in Hollywood if that were the usual method of procedure. It certainly is just as well that I've never written a line in pictures.

I'm disappointed, terribly. I still feel that a superb musical could be made of the book, and that you, Dick, and Larry should do it. Is there any way of putting this again to Warner? I suppose no. Oh, well.

Edna.

*This was told me by someone who has worked with him for many, many years.

After *Sunny River* (then titled *New Orleans*) premiered at the Muny in St. Louis in June, Oscar continued to work diligently on the show over the next several months. He changed the show's structure (from three to two acts), set it about fifty years earlier (beginning in 1806), removed a subplot, and wrote several new songs. It was the second and last Hammerstein show produced by Max Gordon. It had its out-of-town tryout in New Haven in the end of November, opened at the St. James Theatre on December 4, and closed a disappointing thirty-six performances later. It was Hammerstein's final collaboration with Sigmund Romberg. The cast included Joan Roberts, who a little over a year later would star in *Oklahoma!* opposite Alfred Drake.

Max Gordon to Oscar Hammerstein, circa July 24, 1941

Dear Oscar:-

Do you or Rommy know Alfred Drake? I met him in Marblehead yesterday on my trip around the summer theatres + he looked like he might be good for the lead. He played in "Two for the Show" + sang "How high the Moon" beautifully.

You ought to give a script to Buddy De Sylva who may interest Paramount. John Byram told me he would wire you for a script.

I have moved to the Lyceum theatre. It's a good move to have offices over a theatre for rehearsals etc.

Far from giving up I have just started to fight for the dough for the show. I have some ideas I will work on when I get back Friday

Love to you + Dorothy

Max Gordon

Financing *Sunny River* proved difficult.

Oscar Hammerstein to Richard Berger (Municipal Theatre Association of St. Louis), August 6, 1941

Dear Dick:

I have been very inattentive to you this summer, but considering the fact that since I saw you, I have completely rewritten "New Orleans" and nearly finished the screen play of "Very Warm For May," and dashed off another original story, I think you will have to forgive me. I wish now to thank you belatedly for your several communications.

We are now figuring on going into rehearsal the first of September. Max hasn't got all the money yet, but he says he has quite a lot. I am curious to know what happened to Paul Beisman's gang. His first prediction was $40,000, the second was an assurance of $15,000 and he wound up with $3500. Did something happen all of a sudden to create a panic among the angels? Did someone strike a discordant note on the heavenly harp?

The second item of information I would like from you is any report you may be able to get on the Schubert [sic] production of "Mardi Gras" in Dallas. If you have any spies there, put them to work and forward the information to me. I will be here until August 20th. After that all communications addressed to the old manse in Doylestown will reach me.

Dorothy joins in sending out love to you.

Sincerely,

Max Gordon to Oscar Hammerstein, August 13, 1941

Dear Oscar:

Thanks for going into detail to make your point with regard to the character of "Jean." I intend to go over the play very carefully again. As you know, I am not much on the technical end of the drama. All I know is how thing[s] affect me and what my instinct tells me is right.

I am giving practically all my time to digging up the money for the show; and when I tell you that I picked up $5,000. on the Saratoga racetrack on Saturday, you can well imagine that I will do anything to get the dough.

Jake Shubert has the play and I am to know the early part of next week how much they will go in for.

I am stalling on signing Allan Jones because I don't know just when we can get started. I am for him as soon as I have the $100,000. in the bank. We MUST do this one right.

My New Amsterdam friend disappointed me and that blew up in a lot of talk. However, new sources are being tapped and all I can tell you and Rommy is that I am doing everything I can. I hope that Operettas stand a better chance with the public than with people who have money.

Best regards.

Yours,

<u>Max</u>

MG:A

Just came from lunch with Lee Shubert. I am sure they will put in Ten Thousand. Hold Fast. We'll get it.

Billy Rose to Oscar Hammerstein, August 20, 1941

Dear Oscar:

It's a great pity I didn't see the play in St. Louis. As you know, I didn't come out because of the fact that Gordon had agreed to produce it.

I read the script very carefully, of course. Like any script you would write, it's a fine professional job. I wish I knew more about what makes an operetta tick. Its partial similarity to "Bitter Sweet",[1] of course, is something you must have been aware of and there must be some very good reasons why you proceeded to write it in the face of this. I understand that "Bitter Sweet"—one of the most beautifully produced musical plays I ever saw— lost a great sum of money for its American producer. I never knew why, because I remember it as a great night in the theatre.

Several of the lighter musical numbers in no way advance the story line. Again I don't know enough about an operetta to know whether this is the usual thing.

There must be some very good reason why you wrote this without a single comic character—comic in the old sense. As a slam-bang producer

---

[1] Noel Coward's operetta, *Bitter Sweet*, was a West End hit in 1929, a modest success on Broadway later that year, but had a disastrous Broadway revival in 1934. In 1940, Jeannette MacDonald and Nelson Eddy starred in a much-changed film version.

who never budges without a bag full of laughter to lean on, I of course wonder why. In the actual playing at St. Louis, certain scenes or moments in the play may have come across as fun. I wish to hell I had gone to St. Louis.

Is Rommy coming to New York with you? I wish I could hear the music. The lyrics are fine—you always did write the best lyrics.

I am very anxious to do a show with you, of course. I would very much like to discuss it with you. If you feel convinced—especially after having seen it play—that it will be successful, I don't think you'd have much difficulty convincing me of that.

My affectionate regards to Mrs. Hammerstein, Rommy and yourself –

Cordially,

Billy Rose

Sigmund Romberg to Oscar Hammerstein, August 24, 1941

JERRY KERN INFORMED ME CONFIDENTIALLY THAT MAX GORDON HAS 47 THOUSAND AND THAT MAX DREYFUS TELLS HIM THAT HE CAN NOT GET ANY MORE STOP ADVISE YOU SEEING MAX DREYFUS TO GET THE LOW DOWN BEFORE YOU TALK TO MAX GORDON STOP THEN TELEPHONE ME=

ROMMY

Sigmund Romberg to Oscar Hammerstein, August 25, 1941

DEAR OC. SPOKE WITH ORSATTI[2] RIGHT AFTER OUR TELEPHONE CONVERSATION AND HE PROMISED TO HAVE ME IN TOUCH WITH LB WITHIN THE NEXT FORTY EIGHT HOURS. DON'T LET MAX GORDON PUT TOO MUCH FAITH IN THIS MONEY FROM MGM BUT I PROMISE TO DO MY BEST. PLEASE PHONE ME TOMORROW AS SOON AS YOU KNOW THAT THE FIFTEEN THOUSAND DOLLAR DEAL BETWEEN SCENERY AND COSTUME IS MADE. I HAVE NO DOUBT THAT ONCE WE REACH SEVENTY THOUSAND DOLLARS IN THE TILL THE BALANCE OF THE MONEY CAN BE GOTTEN TOGETHER AS WE GO ALONG REHEARSING

---

[2] Frank Orsatti was Oscar's West Coast agent.

ETC. TOM EWELL JUST LEFT. HE LOVES HIS NEW NUMBER.
ALSO READ THROUGH THE BOOK AND THINKS NEW VERSION
IS SO MUCH BETTER. NEVERTHELESS STRONGLY ADVISE MAX
GORDON TO SIGN HIM UP BEFORE THE WEEK IS OUT IF THAT'S
POSSIBLE. HOW DOES MAX LIKE THE NEW TITLE.LOVE=

ROMY.

Highland Farm was not just a country house, it was a working farm. In fact, that was
one of the things that had appealed to Oscar. With the war in Europe and speculation that America might soon join it, people were anticipating food shortages (indeed, rationing books were first issued in April of 1942).

Oscar Hammerstein to Arthur Hammerstein (excerpt), September 6, 1941

Our farm looks wonderful, especially the residential part of it, because the
flowers are still flourishing and the grass doesn't seem to have dried out
at all. The chickens are also doing fine and we have about seven dollars
pouring into our treasury every week from the sale of eggs. I am certainly
thinking of expanding and boosting this amount to fifteen. But I don't want
to push ahead too fast.

Hammerstein first collaborated with the composer Lewis Gensler on songs for the
musical *Queen o' Hearts* in 1922, and later swooped in as an out-of-town play
doctor for Gensler's 1931 revue, *The Gang's All Here*. The patient lingered through
twenty-three performances. They teamed up again in the winter of 1940–1941 to
work on "a film about a British woman who lost her husband in the First World War
and urges her estranged son to stand up for the country's ideals as a second war
begins." They pitched their scenario to several studios, but only one song seems to
have been written—"This Is London"—likely intended to appeal to the public that
so loved "The Last Time I Saw Paris."

Oscar Hammerstein to Lewis Gensler, September 6, 1941

Dear Lew:

I am disappointed that we haven't had quick action from Wanger. Orsatti,
however, in answer to a wire from me, says that he is still interested and that
Zanuck too has entered the field. It seems to me that Frank should continue to
explore all avenues while these people are taking their good time about giving

us an answer. On the other hand, I think he knows more than I do about selling a story and if he thinks it's a bad policy to be dealing with too many people at once, I would bow to his judgment.

The play, "The Heart Of a City",[3] has been called off—at any rate as far as Gordon's and my connection with it is concerned. The man who was handling the American rights became too tough to deal with. This would not necessarily preclude our releasing the song independently and the only thing in the way of that at the moment is the existence of several obligations I have which must precede it.

It looks now as if my operetta with Rommy will go into rehearsal in about three weeks. I still have some things to do on it but the weather is so good in Doylestown it is very difficult to think that dialogue and lyrics can be of any importance at all. So, unless it starts to rain soon I won't be ready to go into rehearsal.

Give my love to Bess and let me hear from you soon.

Sincerely,

Oscar Hammerstein, 2nd.

Oscar Hammerstein to Arthur Hammerstein, October 4, 1941

Dear Uncle Arthur:

I have been long in answering your letter because I wanted to be able to tell you the definite time when the Romberg show will open. It's been on again, off again for several weeks but now at last I can give you a date. We go into rehearsal October 12th. On November 10th we will start giving preview performances in New York, and we will open officially on Saturday night, November 17th. I hope you and Dorothy will be able to be in New York that week.

We are not going out of town because we could not get together the finances necessary to guard against the losses that might be incurred. While I would consider this a very risky undertaking had we not had the St. Louis tryout, I really believe that we are just as well off in this particular case, opening cold.

---

[3] *Heart of a City* was a backstage drama set in London during the Blitz. It opened on Broadway in February 1942 and ran for twenty-eight performances.

I have very carefully rewritten the script and the changes I have made are equivalent to whatever rewriting I might have done if I had the show on the road three weeks after the St. Louis opening. In fact, this is an understatement because I have done much more complete and careful work than I could have done under those circumstances. Furthermore, eighty percent of the cast have already been tried out and know the show.

The news of the family is very sparse. Alice is now going to Columbia University. Billie has been examined by his draft board and because of being underweight and, in general, lacking constitutional stamina, he has been rated for limited service only, meaning clerical work I suppose. It is doubtful whether they will call any boys in this division for a long time. He is now trying to get a job as an assistant stage manager so that he can continue with his music during the day and meanwhile, support himself. Jimmy returned from camp all in from mountain climbing. The dumbells in charge of the camp handled him as if he were fourteen instead of ten. He had a cold and was in a rundown condition and we put him to bed for two weeks, after which Alice took him to Atlantic City for five days. He is now all right and is learning to play the flute so that he can get into the school band. When I gave him my permission to do this I didn't know what flutes cost. Getting twenty percent off I was still stuck for sixty dollars. So far he has been unable to do anything more than achieve a noise resembling the whisper of a three day old sparrow, but I am confident that with his tenacity and self confidence the house will soon be a very undesirable place in which to take an afternoon nap. We have shipped Susan off to Shipley School at Bryn Mawr and that rounds up my report on the children—except for Reggie, whom I am going to take on as assistant director when I go into rehearsal. He is rarin' to go.

Dorothy's business is still flourishing.

What is all this about J. J. Schubert? [sic] All my life I've heard what a tough guy he is. So far, I find him to be sensible and mild mannered and soft spoken—a benign old gentleman. Do you think he has softened up or does he wait until dress rehearsal before he takes off his sheep's clothing?

Dorothy and I look forward to seeing you both. Let us know a few days before you come.

Love from all,

Oscar Hammerstein, 2nd.

Oscar Hammerstein to Tom Girton, Hollywood Bowl Opera Association, October 4, 1941

Dear Mr. Girton:

When you and Mr. Colvan expressed concern with the clause in the "Rose Marie" contract prohibiting changes in the manuscript I told you you could make changes provided you submitted them to me before the production so that I could approve or disapprove of them. You agreed to do this. You did not, however, live up to this agreement. You made whatever changes you pleased and then, after opening the show, you forwarded a very general statement describing the changes made. In other words, I had no chance to approve or disapprove of anything you saw fit to do with my play. This was against both the letter and the spirit of the contract, an obvious and deliberate evasion of my protective clause and an abuse of the concession I made to you.

There is nothing I can do about it now except to express my surprise at such flagrant bad faith.

Very truly yours,

Oscar Hammerstein, 2nd.

Edward Benjamin to Oscar Hammerstein, October 4, 1941

Dear Oscar:

September and October bring me to Miami Beach to avoid hay fever.

Blanche and I are not particularly interested in the stage, but we have come across something here so good in its way I thought it worthwhile bringing it to your attention.

At the Club Bali, a night club here, there is a young French-Syrian girl with an unusually good voice, lovely expressive face, and beautiful lissome figure. This girl sings the current American jazz genre extremely well, but someone has taught her to enunciate Spanish, and actually she out-Mirandas Carmen Miranda in Miranda's own field.

Miranda leers; this girl allures. Miranda has little or no change of pace; the girl offers constant variety of pace and expression, combined with lovely young oomph.

The voice is big enough, I think, to fill a theatre. The girl gives her age as 21. She goes by the name of Lorraine Dewood, which, incredibly enough, is her father's adopted name, taken legally some years ago in court.

I do not usually go for brunettes at all, so you know this girl must be good.

When you acknowledge this, let me know how you are and how things are going. I hope you are fine and send best regards.

Sincerely,

Edward B. Benjamin

Oscar Hammerstein to Edward Benjamin, October 24, 1941

Dear Eddie:

Thank you very much for your kind letter. At the moment I am not on [sic] the market for a French-Syrian girl who vanquishes Carmen Miranda in her own field. But it is more than probable that I may need her in a play I am contemplating for next season. In fact, if I had not had this play in mind I should have made it my business to create one after reading your description.

I am just embarking on the rehearsal of a play about New Orleans which I tried out with the St. Louis Municipal Opera Company last summer. You may have heard of this. There was a deputation of distinguished gentlemen from your city who came to see it while it was there. Among these was Judge Terriberry, who charmed us all with his after-dinner speeches. (Have I spelled his name right?)

I have changed the story a good deal since the St. Louis presentation, moving the period back from 1850 to 1806, and changing the title from "New Orleans" to "Sunny River". I had to do this because there have been so many picture titles recently using New Orleans. As a matter of fact, producers and writers are promoting your town beyond the fondest dreams that the Chamber of Commerce could possibly have. The reason for this is simple. The romantic backgrounds of Europe are denied to us at the moment because of their tragic connotations and therefore we all pounce upon the one city in America that suggests romance and has some of the qualities which a European city might give us.

I am no longer living on Long Island although I still own my house there. It is rented. We bought a farm near Doylestown, Pennsylvania. (This is my address now.) This is a longer drive from New York than Great Neck was, so we maintain a small apartment in New York, spending the middle of the week there and long weekends in the country. This goes on for part of the year and the rest of the time I must spend in California making money out of the movies so that I can come back to New York and lose it on plays.

I keep promising myself to make a detour to New Orleans on my way to the coast and perhaps I will do it this year. Once my play has been produced, it will be interesting to visit its locale and see how far out I was on my research.

This has been a very long letter and was all started by a casual request of yours. You asked me to let you know how I was and how things were going. This reminds me of somebody's definition of a bore, to wit: "A bore is a man who, when you ask him how he feels, tells you."

With all good wishes,

Sincerely,

Oscar Hammerstein, 2nd.

Sunny River opened on Broadway on December 4. The Japanese bombed Pearl Harbor on December 7. The show closed on January 3.

Oscar Hammerstein to Helen Hayes,[4] December 9, 1941

Dear Helen:

Of the telegrams I received last Thursday, none made me as proud as yours did.

Your pre-opening tribute fortified me somewhat against the shower of bricks that were hurled at me the following morning.

---

[4] Helen Hayes, often referred to as "the first lady of American theater," reigned on Broadway for decades, starring in both classic plays and premieres of new works. Hayes' telegram to Hammerstein has not been found.

All of us connected with the show, however, feel that this is one time when we may reverse the judgment of that freakish group of jaded gentlemen who sit on the aisle on opening nights.

All good wishes to you and Charlie.

Sincerely,

Oscar Hammerstein, 2nd.

On December 11 the United States declared war on Germany.

Oscar Hammerstein to Edward Benjamin, December 1941

Dear Eddie:

I heard your protege sing under rather disadvantageous conditions. She had herself booked for one night at a cafe called "The Martinique". She was not spotted very well on the program and I think her reception suffered because of this.

Discounting these circumstances, I found her to have the virtues of youth and beauty and a fair amount of talent. She has the fault of over-confidence and I would say—giving a quick, and not very carefully considered curbstone opinion—that after she has been kicked around a bit and met the reverses that shape stars, and <u>survives</u> them, she might amount to something.

Speaking of being kicked around, I was given a good going over by the critics last week when my play opened, but I feel confident that the audiences we are getting will eventually reverse this decision.

Please don't fail to let me know if you come up north. I know how busy you will be but we must at least have a drink together.

With all good wishes,

Sincerely,

Oscar Hammerstein, 2nd.

Oscar Hammerstein to John Moore, December 30, 1941

Dear John:

Thank you for your kind and welcome letter. Our play is not doing very well. The critics struck us a body blow, and three days later the Japanese followed with another.

I note that yours is leaving town soon but I feel sure you will have a successful tour with it.

Good luck for the New Year and best wishes to Shirley and you—and the new member you are signing up with the troupe.

Sincerely,

Oscar Hammerstein, 2nd

Max Gordon to Oscar Hammerstein, January 2, 1942

Dear Oscar:

I noted the receipts last night, Thursday, following New Year's and, while business is terrible all around, we know that the situation is hopeless. SUNNY RIVER belongs to yesterday. Now, what are we going to do tomorrow? For one thing, I want you to keep your courage because you and I will still do great things in the theatre together but they won't be musical comedies. It is just silly to risk a hundred thousand dollars on what six men are going to say about it in the paper the next day. We must know in our hearts that SUNNY RIVER is a good show. It proved it every time it had a chance and we were murdered by the critics. I will always believe that.

I would like to try to find a play for next season, or to write one. If I have any plays that need an excellent director, you certainly will have a crack at that and, if you set your mind down to write a play, I know you can do it. You cannot afford to waste your time any more with musical shows and I cannot afford to produce them. I know what audiences want but I don't know what critics want.

Let me hear from you and also make use of my office and pick up any plays around there that come from responsible authors or responsible agents.

My love to you and Dorothy and a Happy New Year

Max

Max Gordon

P.S. I know this must be a tough blow to Rommie and I tried to soften it by writing him a letter of explanation. I do wish you would tell him my position regarding the critics and why I will no longer be interested in musical plays.

M.G.

The *River* ran dry, closing on January 3, after thirty-six performances, leaving not even a mildly popular song in its wake.

Oscar Hammerstein to Arthur Freed, January 8, 1942

Dear Arthur:

I saw BABES ON BROADWAY[5] yesterday and feel impelled to write and tell you what a swell job it was. The Music Hall was packed and the large audience seemed to be with the picture every minute. There was spontaneous applause and the right kind of laughs, and now and then a handkerchief came out—including mine. But maybe I'm kind of a softy. I know I'm a pushover for Rooney and Garland. I think Buzz shot the picture superbly, and without straining too much, he built the numbers up in exciting peaks. Altogether it seemed to me to be one of the smartest and most well-rounded of all the musical productions that have come out of Hollywood, and I think you deserve congratulations. You are hereby getting mine.

All good wishes for a happy new year.

Oscar Hammerstein

Max Gordon to Oscar Hammerstein, circa January 1942

Dear Oscar:-

This follows my other letter about not doing musical shows.

---

[5] The film *Babes on Broadway*, directed and choreographed by Busby Berkeley, produced by Arthur Freed for MGM, was the third of the Mickey Rooney and Judy Garland "Let's put on a show" musicals.

There is one type I will do. If you can write a play with music for six outstanding players three of which would have to be stars I'm for that. We could keep that kind on the road indefinitely

Love

Max

Max Gordon to Oscar Hammerstein, circa January 10, 1942

Dear Oscar:

Thank you for your letter. For some reason, I think I have to bolster you. Imagine me in this position—the guy that stood in front of that Dorset Hotel!

Your idea to try to write the great War Song is a good one and I hope you make it. Keep after that idea of a small musical play with stars. Of course, I would rather have you write a straight play and forget this musical show nonsense, but I will take the other if you decide to do it.

Millie will be here in a week and I am terribly lonesome for her.

My love to you and Dorothy.

<u>Max</u>

Oscar became involved with several causes to support the War effort, joining committees and organizations, and helping with fund raising. Billy joined the Navy. Oscar became increasingly obsessed with the notion of writing a "great war song"; it's mentioned frequently in his correspondence. He had already written his best, "The Last Time I Saw Paris," but there were a handful of subsequent attempts. In 1941 he wrote another one other with Kern, "Forever and a Day," an ode to England's inevitable permanence. The more bellicose song suggested below seems never to have been completed.

Jerome Kern to Oscar Hammerstein, January 19, 1942

Dear Oscar:

Fortunately, your wire arrived before the S.D. containing the holograph manuscript. I say 'fortunately' because it prepared me, in a manner of speaking, for something that wouldn't wash.

Since you indicate that you are going to try again, it is only fair that I rush these reactions to you forthwith, even though unsigned. I just don't want to take part in producing a boastful, threatening, jingoistic roundelay. The very word 'jingo' has gravelled the bejezus out of me, ever since I first encountered its doggerel generator. I have literally blushed for Britain every time I have seen or heard

"We don't want to fight,

But, by jingo, if we do,

We've got the ships, we've got the men,

We've got the money, too."

I think the two lines of the burthen[6] 'to call on Tokio and Schickelgruber[7] [*sic*] and his poor Pinocchio' might be nifties [*sic*] with a tune less noble in stature than the H.L., by some composer who doesn't share my revulsion for the whole general scheme. Should another entirely different idea ever strike you, please be certain to end a declarative sentence on a strong word, where at present the word owe occurs, without the necessity of completing the sense by carrying over the second word you. Thus the last line will have three syllable up-beat, at present covered by the three words you, and we, similar to the up-beat in the first line We're on our. If this is not perfectly clear to you, it really doesn't matter much because we can of course clarify it when we meet. And until then, I include me out of any and all Erin Go Braghs.[8] What's say we leave them to the Charlie Tobiasses[9] and other disciples of G.M.C.[10]

Sorry I couldn't thaw out your extremities with my usual warm enthusiasm for your art, indicated with my customary charm.

Ever yours,

Jerry

---

[6] An archaic term for the refrain or chorus of a song, famously used by Kern.

[7] "Schicklgruber" was the original surname of Adolph Hitler's father Alois. Alois was an illegitimate child, therefore Hitler could never prove his own Aryan heritage. Referring to Hitler as Schicklgruber was a way of insulting him as the son of a bastard.

[8] In essence, "Ireland forever."

[9] Immediately after Pearl Harbor, Tobias wrote the song "We Did It Before and We Can Do It Again," making a connection with World War I.

[10] George M. Cohan wrote more than his share of patriotic numbers, including "You're a Grand Old Flag" and, for World War I, "Over There."

This plea to George S. Kaufman is one of several almost identical letters Hammerstein—naively—wrote to neighbors. It quickly became obvious that money and efforts could be better directed.

Oscar Hammerstein to George S. Kaufman,[11] January 26, 1942

Dear George:

Bucks County is faced with a very pressing war obligation. In the event of coast towns being bombed we must be prepared to receive evacuees. We would get them from New York and/or Philadelphia. In the event of such an emergency, the Red Cross could not take over until about forty eight hours had expired, and the county itself would be called on to provide medical care to the wounded, during this period.

However remote and improbable this eventuality may seem to you, I think you will agree that our recent lessons have taught us not to gamble on what we think probable or improbable.

In the way of shelter and temporary hospital units, forty-six buildings have been designated and offered by their owners. These comprises [sic] churches, Elks' halls, fire houses, school auditoriums, etc., and the local doctors have, of course, volunteered their services. But the equipment—cots, medical supplies, surgical instruments, etc.—presents a real financial problem. The sum required has been carefully estimated and comes to $25,000 which Bucks County must raise for itself. Various means are being employed. Plays and benefits, and dances are being held. School children and women's clubs are raising small donations, and I am writing this letter as the member of a committee appointed to raise $5,000 of the total sum required by direct appeal to those members of the community who are deemed to be able to give substantial contributions.

No one realizes more acutely than I do the strain that you must be feeling from an accumulation of appeals of this nature. As a matter of fact, when

---

[11] George S. Kaufman was a leading playwright (often in collaboration with Moss Hart) and director. Among the notable plays and musicals he wrote were *The Royal Family*, *Of Thee I Sing*, *You Can't Take It with You*, and *The Man Who Came to Dinner*.

I consider the way we are all swamped by these daily raids on our dwindling bank balances, I feel self-conscious about writing this letter. But I am writing it and asking you to help out all you can, because in this particular case there is no other way out. This is a definite and inescapable obligation of the residents of Bucks County, and if we don't meet it there is nobody else to meet it. More specifically, I feel that the small group of us who have, in recent years, come from the city and made our home here should do their utmost to make a good showing in a community effort of this kind.

Please forgive me if this letter seems long-winded but I could think of no shorter way to bring the demands of this emergency to your attention.

In answer to the natural question which will come immediately to your mind, "How much are other people giving" donations so far have run between one hundred and five hundred dollars. An enclosed schedule gives you an idea of what can be bought with whatever sums you feel willing and able to donate.

Please let me hear from you as soon as you can.

All good wishes.

Sincerely,

Oscar Hammerstein, 2nd.

P. S.: Checks should be made payable to J. Purdy Weiss, Treasurer. It is the intention of the purchasing committee to place orders for equipment and medicine just as fast as the money comes in. This is necessary because of the almost certain rise in future price, of many of these items.

Oscar Hammerstein to J. Carroll Molloy, February 13, 1942

Dear Mr. Molloy:

Here are two checks. One from Mr. And Mrs. Alan Campbell[12] for $100 and one from George Kaufman for $50.

---

[12] Mrs. Alan Campbell is better known as the author and wit Dorothy Parker.

George writes that it doesn't seem like a pressing cause to him at the moment, and that if the situation seems to call for it later, he will donate more, if he is able to find it at the time. This, I am afraid, is a typical reaction. Mr. and Mrs. Sam Spewack[13] have told me that, later on, if they could see more clearly the necessity of this kind of donation, they would make one. I have not had any answers from any of the others on my list but I will follow them up soon.

The situation is very clear to me. These people are being beset on all sides for emergencies that are more tangible and immediate than our cause, which—at best—is a <u>possible</u> emergency as distinguished from an actual one.

Will you be so kind as to forward these checks to Mr. Weiss and ask him to send acknowledgements so that donors can record them in their income tax reports? The Campbells' present address is 8152 Sunset Boulevard, Hollywood, California. George Kaufman's town address is 14 East 94th Street, New York City.

With all good wishes for the success of your undertaking and the assurance that I will give you whatever further help I can,

Sincerely,

Oscar Hammerstein, 2nd.

The Shubert brothers—Lee, Sam, and Jacob—and their Shubert Organization, became the most powerful and omnipresent theatrical producers of the twentieth century. In addition to several major Broadway theaters, they ultimately "owned, managed, operated, or booked nearly a thousand theaters nationwide." They were notoriously controlling, did not play nicely with the competition, and also played hardball with those who worked for and with them. By most accounts they had minimal interest in the artistic quality of the shows they produced, beyond the extent to which they could be commercially successful.

---

[13] Sam and Bella Spewack were a playwriting team, at the time best known for their play *Boy Meets Girl*, and the Cole Porter musical *Leave it to Me!*, with *Kiss Me Kate* in their future.

Edna Ferber to Oscar Hammerstein, February 2, 1942

After I had talked with you on the telephone, dear Oscar, I decided that I had been much too gabby about the Shuberts. I've had no business dealings with them. You have. I only know what I've heard and observed.

Would they do a real production—lavish and tasteful and authentic? Or would they do one of those cheap cotton-flowers and waving scenery things, with storehouse costumes?

I know they are financially in a position to give SHOW BOAT the kind of production it should have. You know better than I whether they'd be willing and able to do this. Would they let you and Jerry use your own good judgement and taste and theatrical knowledge and experience?

Anyway, call me, there's a dear, when you return to town.

Edna.

Warners just called this afternoon to say they're reviving SO BIG in a new picture. Now if somebody'll just do COME AND GET IT and THE GIRLS I'll be all set for the winter.

Oscar Hammerstein to Ben Hecht,[14] February 2, 1942

Dear Ben:

Dorothy and I saw your play last Tuesday night and we both thought it the most interesting and important play of the season. I have read some of your comments about the critics and, while I agree that most of the things you say are true, I don't believe you're attacking on a broad enough front. It seems to me that the critics are merely the spearheads—or the poison pointed arrows—of a much larger army of people known as the New York theater-going public. These people are all critics. They no longer go to the theater to receive whatever bounty the author and his colleagues can give them. They go there to wistfully imagine how much better they could write and produce a play and they definitely do not want to permit themselves to come under the influence of an author. They will let him regale them with

---

[14] Ben Hecht (1893–1964), playwright and screenwriter, co-wrote the plays *The Front Page* and *Twentieth Century* with Charles MacArthur, and with other collaborators co-wrote screenplays that included *Design for Living, Scarface, Spellbound,* and *Notorious.*

dirty jokes and they will let him exploit the talents of an attractive star, as long as the play is kept well in the background. But once let them suspect that the author is taking his play seriously and they rise up and yell, half in indignation and half in pain. They are not going to have their brains stimulated nor their emotions played upon. It is too trying to the egos to admit that some master mind can do this to them. They are all cowards, afraid to face their own inferiority and deadly afraid of facing any of the problems of life that are dealt with in a play like yours. I have called these people the New York theater-going public. They are not the greater public available to the theater for whom I have the deepest respect. By "theater-going public" I mean the smarties who go to the first nights and the others who follow them and their opinions because not to follow them is not chic. This rather large group, led by the critics, has succeeded not only in destroying many good things in the theater but has created so many bad things that they have kept away and discouraged the greater public—the plain folks who want to go to a show and respect what they have seen and get their money's worth in substance. The trouble is that so many times, when they hear a play is great, they go to it only to find a hollow shell with a few gags rattling around in it and so they just stop going. The things they would really like are often choked off by such an aggressive assault as your play met last week.

"Lily Of The Valley"[15] opened Monday. I came into town Tuesday and ran into a barrage of clattering experts who did their best to tout me off going to your play that night. Some of these had seen it and some had not but had just "heard" that "there was just no reason for it". If I had met an elevator boy and a salesgirl at Altman's and a stage hand and they had told me these things, I might have turned back my tickets. When such people say they don't like a play, I know there is something wrong with it. But the "smart" crowd! There is so much wrong with them that the only thing they can do to make me wary of a play is to give it their silly approbation with the silly adjective they use so frequently—"terrific".

I don't know why I'm saying all this to you, who can say it so much better than I. I think my chief motive in writing to you is to let you know that of the handful of people who were allowed to see your play, there were some who were affected by it as you intended they should be, who understood the

---

[15] Hecht's play, *Lily of the Valley*, opened on December 26, 1942, and closed after eight performances. Perhaps the fact that the setting was a city morgue had something to do with its fast demise.

theme, believed in the characters, and had their hearts broken for the time being and are not ashamed to admit it.

There may be some who would find flaws in this or that characterization or situation or theatrical device. Let us grant that there were such flaws in your play, as there are in all plays. It was, nevertheless, a major effort in the theater, a combination of fine qualities in writing, acting, and production. To sweep it aside with a careless brush of a hand and a feeble wisecrack as if it were a little charade you dashed off for a Lamb's Gambol[16]—this is a high crime. I don't know what can be done about it. I don't think speeches and letters can do it. I don't think your attacks on critics can do it. Some way must be devised to ignore these people, reach around them, and over their heads to that great mass of men and women who are not professionals or semi-professionals but just people who would like to go to the theater and be willing subjects to its hypnotism for two and a half hours.

All good wishes to Rose and yourself,

Oscar Hammerstein, 2nd.

Oscar Hammerstein to Arthur Hammerstein, February 2, 1942

Dear Uncle Arthur:

I am writing to the address on your letterhead on the chance that perhaps you are not living at the house—although it is my impression that you said you were going to. Anyway this seems the safest thing to do.

About Walter O'Keefe, I have not yet been able to get in touch with him since receiving your letters this morning but I expect him to call me back this afternoon and I shall probably wire you when I hear from him.

We will certainly keep our promise and visit the farm after you come back. As a matter of fact, we may see Dorothy before that because I am supposed to spend two days in Chicago, February 18th and 19th, as one of the judges for the operetta contest being conducted by WGN, the Chicago Tribune radio station.

Things are beginning to hum for me. Lee Shubert is calling me up three times a day to get the rights to revive "Showboat", and so is Cheryl

---

[16] The Lambs was a club for theater professionals; "Gambols" were their fund-raising events.

Crawford, the woman who recently revived "Porgy and Bess" with great success. I believe that "Showboat" can also be very successful right now if we get a great cast and a fine production, and my release of the rights to either producer will be conditioned on whatever guarantees I can get in this direction. It looks as if Jerry and I will also adapt Edna Ferber's latest novel "Saratoga Trunk" for next season. The picture rights have already been sold to Warner's but Billy Rose, who wants to produce the play, is willing to risk his hundred grand, or more, and following the example of such courage I am willing to risk my time. The only thing I would be afraid of would be to open against them. If, however, we should open in September and were a big hit, I don't believe that a picture coming into New York later, for three or four weeks, would kill the play. And, on the other hand, if they release in September and we should open at Christmas—(always assuming that we have a great show) I think that the previous production of the picture might even enhance the interest in the play. I have noted that in St. Louis when they play a show that has been done in pictures the preceding winter it always has a much bigger draw than any other. "Roberta" and "Rosalie" were two such cases. We may, of course, be wrong about this but it has never been proven one way or another and it's time it was. My own enthusiasm for the project is based not so much on the length of its run or the money I may make as on the fact that it will be a major production of great merit and quality and will serve to restore some of the respect and standing which I feel I have lost in the past few years.

As for my picture activities, I spoke to MGM last week and they do not think they will need me for another three months. Judy Garland will be in my picture and she must make another one first, so I will probably be going out there in May and that is when we can combine our visit to you with our trip to the coast.

Billy and his wife were down to the farm yesterday and he had a strong hunch that he would go to sea this week. He was not, however, sure of this because they give them no information or warning about these things.

That's about all the news. I will keep after O'Keefe and if there is anything else that comes up in which I can be of some help to you, let me know. I see that my name is now on the committee. I should do something in order to keep my job. I am on so many committees now, - ASCAP and the

Dramatists' Guild, and various organizations connected with raising funds for war activities, that when I see a list of names and my name is absent I feel an involuntary pang of disappointment.

Dorothy sends her love,

Sincerely,

Oscar Hammerstein, 2nd.

Oscar Hammerstein to Leighton Brill, February 2, 1942

Dear Leighton:

I have two items that I know will be of interest to you. One: The success of the revival of "Porgy and Bess" has stimulated interest in "Showboat". Two producers are on my neck and aggressively clamoring for revival rights. One is Cheryl Crawford, who did "Porgy and Bess", and the other is Shubert. The latter set-up does not include J. J. Lee would back it and Milton would be a sort of supervisor. They seem to be the sounder from a financial standpoint but I would prefer to do it with Crawford if she could convince me that she could raise the money. She and her group are, in fact, raising money very rapidly because they are clearing $7,000 a week on "Porgy" at $2.75 top. An irrevelant [*sic*] note: Milton Doublas is one of these backers— for a small share, I think.

The second item of interest is that Billy Rose took a trip to Saratoga two weeks ago, picked up a volume of "Saratoga Trunk" and went nuts. Negotiations are under way—and progressing very smoothly—whereby Jerry and I will acquire the rights and Billy Rose will produce it. All this without regard to when the picture will be released. We have agreed to take our chances on that.

These are only two of the myriad prospects that loom on next year's horizon but I will not mention the others because I do not want to confuse you and, if I remember rightly, you confuse quite easily.

I will keep you posted as things develop.

Love to Jean and yourself,

Oscar Hammerstein, 2nd.

Porgy and Bess, a "folk opera" with music by George Gershwin and libretto by DuBose Heyward and Ira Gershwin opened on Broadway in October 1935, where it ran for 124 performances. While many recognized its genius, it received mixed reviews and its fusion of jazz, gospel, popular music, and opera was ahead of its time. Prospects grew dim that it would enter the standard repertoire: it's a demanding piece, requiring a large cast of black singers with operatic training or vocal abilities. Then in 1942 Cheryl Crawford produced a Broadway revival that was a revelation to many, and prompted a re-evaluation of the show. The production trimmed the opera significantly and replaced much of the recitative with dialogue, making the show closer to a traditional musical. That production ran for 286 performances, more than double the run of the original. The success of that production reinforced Oscar's belief in *Carmen Jones* and added encouragement to his (heretofore unsuccessful) efforts to mount a revival of *Show Boat*.

Oscar Hammerstein to Ira Gershwin, February 2, 1942

Dear Ira:

You have probably heard something of the success of "Porgy and Bess" but I thought you might like to have an intimate eye-witness account of the thrilling goings-on at the Majestic Theater. I went there last Friday night. The big house was jammed (I think the capacity is nearly seventeen hundred). People were dripping over the sides of all the boxes. Before the curtain rose, I could feel an expectant buzz of delighted anticipation like an electric current going through the audience. The people had heard that there was something good in town,—a musical effort that did not consist of a lot of songs, burlesque bits, and comedy specialties thrown together—and it is my belief that they have been starving for quality of this kind.

The tension never diminished but kept increasing during the evening and by the time that Avon Long came out to gool them with "It Ain't Necessarily So", the fever was beginning to express itself in delirium, and one just felt that the top had blown off everything. This may all sound a little incoherent and whacky and you may think I am over-writing the scene. It may be that I am, because the excellence of the performance and the beauty of the opera thrilled me no more than the audience itself. I had begun to think that the New York audience was made up entirely of critics and their relatives. But here was another audience—an entirely different gang—a crowd who knew the songs and loved them and had heard that they could go down to a theater and hear something really good for $2.75. This is about the best thing that has happened in the theater in my memory.

It occurs to me as I write that there is one other musical play[17] in town that has quality and you also happen to be the author of the lyrics of that. I am mighty proud to know you.

Best to Lee.

Sincerely,

Ira Gershwin to Oscar Hammerstein, February 12, 1942

Dear Oscar,

I needn't tell you how much I appreciate your "Porgy and Bess" letter and the nice things you say. I must tell you, however, that the finest thing about it is what it tells me about you. Not that I didn't know it all along.

Love to all the Hammersteins.

Ira.

P.S. Long may you wave!

Edwin Lester founded the Los Angeles Civic Light Opera in 1938 and its affiliate, the San Francisco Civic Light Opera in 1940. Lester became a major impresario on the West Coast, producing revivals of classic musicals and operettas, sometimes bringing in shows directly from Broadway with their original casts, and later co-producing original shows that would go on to Broadway, including *Song of Norway* and *Kismet*. He developed a close professional relationship with Rodgers and Hammerstein, although he sometimes raised their ire with his pushiness and an oversize estimation of his own importance in their world. Oscar's relationship with Lester began before his collaboration with Rodgers, as seen in this Kern letter.

Jerome Kern to Oscar Hammerstein, February 10, 1942

Dear Oscar:

I hate to clutter you up in your present "Show Boat" activity with "Music in the Air," but as Lester has sent you his notions, pursuant to your

---

[17] Hammerstein is referring to *Lady in the Dark*, book by Moss Hart, lyrics by Ira, music by Kurt Weill.

request, I have to bust in on you by a change of view as expressed by Lester to you since our last meeting.

I am afraid we shall have to permit the interpolation of "All The Things You Are" as I have reason to know that John Charles Tomas is mulishly set on doing it, in which case it definitely cannot replace "The Song Is You" in the dressing room scene. The business with Anna in "T.S.I.Y." is too well set and also will not disappoint the audience as much as would the same dirtying up of "A.T.T.Y.A." which the public has undoubtedly appropriated as a classic standard ballad.

For his particular purpose, most of Lester's suggestions seem sound enough, although every reference to the lameness of the original, even though it may be right, makes me bristle. Reminds me of when, at the Savoy, Bruce's saxophonist Saul called the melody of "I Won't Dance" corny. Maybe he, too, was right, but I still could have spat in his eye. Think I should have, anyway.

Still no luck with "We'll work and sweat and suffer." What this country needs is a good five-cent gloom-dispeller. Me, too.

Love,

Jerry.

Oscar Hammerstein to Jerome Kern, February 14, 1942

Dear Jerry:

I will write this letter in four chapters.

CHAPTER I: "GENTLEMEN UNAFRAID"

I am happy to report that Otto has now written a light and very youthful musical play about West Point in 1860; that he has constructed it so that it can be played with a small chorus and a very modest scenery layout; that he has utilized eight of the songs in a very ingenious way and woven them beautifully into his story. I do not believe that the play is in such shape that I could conscientiously recommend it to a producer to put it into rehearsal now with a view to taking it on the road and then bringing it into New York. The comedy needs some work. The dialogue needs the kind of editing that you can imagine. And I know that there is some further story development needed in the second act. Then, you ask, why in hell did

I write that first long sentence? The universities of this country are developing their dramatic societies to such an extent that they are giving very credible performances of good plays and many of them are equipped to give intelligent production of musical shows. It is Otto's belief, and it is mine too, that Otto's new version if played by several of these university companies might be developed into a very unusual stage show for Broadway. This would be especially true if, in the course of the try-outs, we not only found ways to improve the manuscript but also had the luck to uncover several young and charming boy and girl personalities with the very fresh, untheatrical qualities that would be needed to put this play over and make it stand apart from all other musical comedy efforts on Broadway. You may say this is a pipe dream. I will admit it is a long shot. Yet I feel the release of the play with Otto's book and your music and whatever contribution I have made and will make it a project that can't possibly do any harm and has a very good chance of achieving a happy ending to Otto's struggles over the years. He has asked me to put the case before you and I think it is a great idea. Our ambassador to the universities is Dr. Smith of ASCAP whom I believe you have met. In his good will activity for ASCAP, he encountered this situation in the colleges and found so many of their societies anxious to produce new productions of a suitable type that he brought it to Otto's attention. ("Panama Hattie"[18] would obviously not be a suitable type and that is almost the only kind of musical comedy which is now being written.)

CHAPTER II: "SHOWBOAT"

As I wired you, the Crawford deal fell through. She told me that her backers have put up sufficient money, but they did not think it good business to invest in a revival where they would have to gross $18,000 to break even. This was a clear bid to me to come back and say, "Maybe we can hook it up so that we can break on $15,000," but I didn't bite.

Of the other entrants, I think you agree with me that Gordon can be eliminated, that Alex Yokel is unsuited to the responsibility (I don't know that I even told you of his candidacy. He claimed to have all the money.)

---

[18] To give a sense of why Cole Porter's *Panama Hattie* (1940) would not be appropriate for a student production, this is from Brooks Atkinson's review: "Everything is noisy, funny and in order. Not in proper order exactly. Improper order comes closer to the truth. If you go to the theatre, you know what sailors in Panama are interested in. Well, it ain't in battleships. Hewing close to the facts of life, the authors have thrown the sailors at the strumpets in the water-front honky-tonks, taking pains to present La [Ethel] Merman as a coarse-timbred entertainer with a heart of gold."

That leaves Shubert. Knowing your prejudice and realizing that it is well-founded, I am holding him off. I have asked Max Dreyfus to call up Wyman[19] [*sic*] and suggest to him that the property might be available for him to produce although we have already turned down several other bids for one reason or another. If this falls through it is a very simple matter for me to drop in on Vinton Freedley[20] and George Abbott and "Get to talkin'".

Another arrow in my quiver is the prospect of interesting some financing groups in Chicago, which city I am visiting next week to act on a committee of judges who will choose a great American operetta, award it a prize of $10,000, and decree that it be performed on Station WGN in a few weeks. I realize that the earth will not crack asunder if "Showboat" is not produced within the next six or eight months, and yet I have a strong hunch that this is the time to do it. The success of "Porgy and Bess" is an undoubted stimulus to interest in a major revival effort, and while I do not share Max Gordon's belief that a picture can be done this year, it is not at all unlikely that they may make one within the next two years.

CHAPTER III: "SARATOGA TRUNK"

The letter Howard wrote to you expresses a very real fear that he and I share. To work for six months and then have Billy Rose change his mind is a risk we cannot afford to take. It would be even worse for me than for you. A group of melodies might be used with a number of stories but the scenes and lyrics I had written to fit Edna's story would be completely useless. It is not just a question of Billy's proclivity for changing his mind. It might be that he would quite honestly not like our version, or it might be that he would insist on our making changes to suit him or face his abandonment of the production. With an ordinary play originated by ourselves this would be no problem. But with this one I am sure the danger is clear to you. If you approve Howard's idea for the modest insurance policy he suggested in his letter to you, I think we should put it up to Billy immediately in a most frank and friendly manner. I believe he will reject it, in which case I will have to be counted out, as I imagine you will too.

CHAPTER IV: "MUSIC IN THE AIR"

[19] Dwight Deere Wiman was a Broadway producer who within the previous six years had produced Rodgers and Hart's *On Your Toes, Babes in Arms, I Married an Angel*, and *Higher and Higher*.

[20] Vinton Freedley produced several major Broadway musicals, often in partnership with Alex A. Aarons. He produced eight Gershwin musicals, starting with *Lady Be Good* in 1924, and went on to produce four Cole Porter musicals, the first being *Anything Goes* in 1934.

Lester wrote me a long letter, a copy of which is forwarded to you by the same mail. Reading it over quickly, I felt a mounting resistance. It may have been a certain irreverence [?] in his approach. Then I read it a second time. I realized that his confidence and his glibness probably arose from a knowledge of your indorsement [*sic*] of the general policy of the suggested changes. I also realized, on closer analysis, most of them made good sense. When I came down to the country this morning I took out the script, studied the whole thing carefully, and now I feel certain that we can have a better show than we had before, providing that the cast turns out all right.

Will you get Lester's letter out of your files and I will take up the various points in order.

Locale: I think Bohemia, with Prague the "big city" would be best. The action must of course take place a year before the war started, no matter what country we choose?

(2) Who is Petina?

(3) Second paragraph of his letter: This cut is very easy to make. I agree with him that it is something that should be postponed until you and I meet, at which time I am sure we can agree on a sequence after a half hour's talk. I will keep some of the musically synchronized dialogue and cut out some of the things that perhaps we were over-sentimental about. It also occurs to me that we might use Cornelius's entrance stanza, beginning with: "When you're young - " as an exit for the two lovers as they walk off hand in hand. Whom has he in mind for "Sieglinde"? I feel that today there are many girls around who sing better than Kay and who can also meet the simple qualifications of the part.

(4) Page two of Lester's letter. Second paragraph—Office Scene: There should be no dialogue in here. Any interruption of this sequence as a description of Bruno's play would be fatal. My suggestion is a clean-cut substitution of "All The Things You Are" for "I Am So Eager". Then the only constructive change would be that he would have to take an encore before proceeding with the description of his play.

(5) I agree that cuts can be easily made in Scene 2. If you will remember it was necessary for me to pad this scene in order to make the change.

(6) The second Zoo Scene: It should open with the party in full swing—except Sieglinde and Walther have not yet arrived. After the opening number, which, I take it, will be a new one that we will write, Sieglinde and

her father arrive with the excuse that he took a nap and it was very hard for her to awaken him. As a matter of fact, the old man is still pretty sleepy and doesn't become wide-awake until—wonder of wonders, he meets Lilly, the dream girl of his youth. Sieglinde brings the box of cookies which we used to have in the old bedroom scene because Bruno had invited them to what he had described as a "midnight picnic". With the champagne flowing and quail and venison dripping from every fork, her little contribution is indeed bringing "a sandwich to a banquet".

Lilly sings "Egern" and perhaps the chorus <u>does</u> come in as Lester suggests. I don't know. After the number, Bruno brings up the thought of what a charming prima donna Sieglinde might make. With Lilly and Ernst trying to put the brakes on as they did in the first version. But Bruno is wound up and on the make and starts to sing to her "I Hear Music". It is obviously part of his "Line". As he sings to her, Carl enters and is obviously disturbed by what he sees (Sieglinde on her entrance explained that they had tried to get Carl but he had been out and they had left word where he could find them.)

After the number, Sieglinde tells Carl about Bruno's exciting suggestion that she go on the stage and Carl, jealous and in a bad temper, crabs the whole idea—very few line changes from the original required. Now Sieglinde, resenting Carl's attitude and suddenly defiant, falls for Bruno's bait and to prove her talent, shows how she would sing "All The Things You Are" just as she saw Frieda, the professional prima donna, sing it with Bruno when they were doing the new play in the office that afternoon. As she starts to sing a solo, Carl talks against it (something in the way that he talks against her telephone conversation in the present bedroom scene) but she goes on singing to Bruno defiantly. Carl turns to appeal to Walther but the poor old man, sitting next to Lilly, has fallen asleep on her spacious bosom. Bruno takes up the song and so does the chorus and they are all singing like hell as Carl storms out with a defiant shout that he is going to Berlin—or Moscow or Pinsk or Shamokin or wherever Frieda said she was going.

I think this is a very practical and workable lay-out for this scene, told almost entirely by means of music and kept alive and thick with the constant presence and backing of the ensemble.

(7) As to scene four, I don't see why it cannot be eliminated entirely. If the scenery is properly constructed so that the dressing room scene moves out on platform, I don't see why there should be any wait at all. In

this first dressing room scene, Bruno's rendition of "I Hear Music" would now be a reprise which, sung by John Charles Thomas, would, I think, be very welcome. And with the comedy business with the mirror and kneeling down on her skirt would seem not just an effort to get another hand on the number.

(8) I am in complete accord with Lester's idea of bringing Frieda and Bruno down to Edendorf to become a part of the finale.

Knowing that you file your letters and I file copies of mine, it is quite possible that in a couple of thousand years some archaeologist might dig up either the original or the copy and, seeing the date, will be completely puzzled that, during the Great War, so long a letter could be written without some reference to it. It will be hard enough for him to understand how people could be so dumb as to wage wars like this but once in them, how could they possibly be interested in such things as I discussed so seriously in this letter. Well, Mr. Archaeologist, that's the way we were in these days, feller.

I've just finished talking to you on the phone and I'm about to phone you again and I think I've had enough of you for today.

Love to all,

Oscar Hammerstein, 2nd.

Regarding *Gentlemen Unafraid*, Harbach's revised version, re-titled *Hayfoot, Strawfoot*, would premiere at Yale University in October 1942, after which it all but disappeared.

Vinton Freedley to Jerome Kern, February 16, 1942

My dear Jerry Kern:-

"Saratoga Trunk" has been read, digested and carefully analyzed since our pleasant chat on Friday, and for the life of me I cannot see how this book can be translated satisfactorily into a musical. In the first place it lacks a story line, the development of plot being told in the clash between personalities of different temperaments. The entire book is about two people, save for the faithful servants, one of whom I agree with you would be a decidedly unpleasant element on the stage. There are no subsidiary characters of interest, -- no one to supply much-needed comedy or musical sequences. Plot told in terms of action is non-existent, except for the final scene which, while a cinch for the movies, would be impossible for the theatre.

The atmosphere is there; certain incidents, such as the ball at Saratoga, are outstanding, but to compare it to "Show Boat" with its wonderful assortment of spicy characters (your Edna Mae Oliver, your Helen Morgan, the small-time dance team, lusty Captain Andy, etc.) seems to me a far cry.

I am dreadfully sorry to have come to this decision, particularly as I was so enthusiastic about your description of the book. Frankly I consider it one of Miss Ferber's lesser efforts, as the lady distinctly had her eye on that Hollywood gold during its composition. In any event I shall get in touch with Oscar shortly as he may have some ideas which will rekindle my enthusiasm. Unless a great deal is done to the story I fear it would be just another "Sunny River."

If you have not read the book more than once I would suggest that you look through it again and let me have your further reaction. In the meantime, my kindest regards and my hearty congratulations on the quality of your scotch!

Sincerely yours,

VINTON FREEDLEY

Jerome Kern to Oscar Hammerstein, February 20, 1942

Dear Oscar:

After shaking up my Mr. Nat Goldstone ["agent in LA"] in re Metro's ["VWFM"] extension of our contingent contract to February 28th, and admonishing him that the routine of periodic extensions could be protracted indefinitely, he phoned back, stating that Arthur Freed had requested a further extension of ninety days from February 28th.

I objected unless Metro would agree to pay in full at the expiration of the ninety days, whether or not material was accepted, PROVIDED that you would okay such an arrangement. He hung up to notify Orsatti to confer with you. Shortly, Goldstone called back, stating that Orsatti accepted on your behalf. This vicarious acceptance I rejected flatly. Why? Because I consider Orsatti a studio man, not at all solicitous of the best interests of his client. I requested a written plan of procedure from, the [*sic*] which he sent over by hand, and it is hereby enclosed. Your comments, alterations and/or acceptance en bloc will keep our position neat and tidy, and will put the agent where he rightfully belongs, in a spot to earn his commission.

Also enclosed herewith is a douche from Vinton Freedley which anticipates what I had intended to take up with you in answer to your Chapter III, page 2 of yours of February 13th, and almost in answer to Howard's Billy Rose suggestion of February 11th. Freedley puts the bee on what I must confess was a bundle of unspoken misgivings of my own.

In as few words as possible—knowing your distaste for cold water— this is as good a time as any to indicate a terrific uncertainty as to whether you are not taking on far too much of a chore with "S.T.", considering—as Freedley bluntly points out—the non-existence of subsidiary characters, subplot, and broad enough scope of general musical motivation. After all, the thing cannot be a duet with a few occasional side-steps of numbers or numberettes by any of the main three characters. By me, the dwarf is a cupid and has long since been slapped down.

It is as well, too, to mention that I arranged the appointment with Freedley <u>not</u> to discuss "S.T.", but to sound him out on a "Show Boat" revival. From this he shied like a nervous stallion, about to be gelded. When you see him, and please be sure to make a point of seeing him, you can undoubtedly do a better selling job, as I didn't want to press it the other day. But his expressed enthusiasm for "S.B." 'with its wonderful assortment of spicy characters,' etc. seems to be a good enough springboard. You will find his objection rooted in the conviction that a revival must, in truth, be better than the original. Well, that suits us, too. It is one of the reasons why we are leery of the pettifogging Shuberts.

If all this is disjointed and incoherent, it is because Edwin Lester's telephone call interrupted. He was naturally anxious to hear your reaction to his scheme, and is coming here tomorrow morning to analyze both his layout and your Chapter IV. I need all those notes and memos, since it is a matter of ten years since I last saw "Music in the Air" and I cannot recall everything without reminders. Guess I must be slipping.

Joe Pasternak.[21]—This turned out to be, instead of a score for a picture which he outlined in detail and on which I was high, a whittling down to three numbers, the balance to be in public domain, with the typical M-G-M routine of acquiring for doughnuts, everything including birthright.

Before signing off, must revert to Billy Rose, with the hunch that he must be showman enough to be as dubious about the story outcome as are Freedley and Kern. Just cagier, that's all. All this seems to leave you holding two or three bags, which is a-plenty without, at this time, going into "Gentlemen Unafraid."

Best love from us all,

Jerry.

Jerome Kern to Oscar Hammerstein, February 27, 1942

"PARIS" WON THE ACADEMY AWARD CONGRATS LOVE=

JERRY

There were nine songs nominated for best original song that year. In addition to "The Last Time I Saw Paris," they included "Blues in the Night," "The Boogie Woogie Bugle Boy of Company B," "Chattanooga Choo Choo," and "Baby Mine" from *Dumbo*. "Paris" was sung in *Lady Be Good* by Ann Sothern. After the song won the Oscar, Kern worked successfully to have the rules changed so that thereafter all nominated songs had to have been written *for* the film in which they appeared.

Jerome Kern to Oscar Hammerstein, March 3, 1942

WHEN INFORMED OF AWARD HAD NO TIME TO CONSULT YOU SO ON OUR BEHALF TOOK HALF PAGE IN VARIETY AND REPORTER. FAILURE TO DO SO WOULD HAVE MADE US UNCOMFORTABLY CONSPICUOUS SENDING ACCOUNT TO HOWARD LOVE-

JERRY.

---

[21] The producer, Joseph Pasternak, moved from Universal Studios to Metro-Goldwyn-Mayer in June of 1941 where his first film was *Seven Sweethearts* with Kathryn Grayson—probably the film he wanted Oscar to work on.

Oscar Hammerstein to Leighton Brill, March 1, 1942

Dear Leighton:

Things have quieted down a great deal on the two projects I spoke to you about in my last letter. Cheryl Crawford couldn't raise the money to do "Showboat" as we want it done and Jerry and I are both leery of dealing with Shubert. Neither Vinton Friedley [*sic*] nor Dwight Wyman [*sic*]—both of whom I approached—are sufficiently enthusiastic about doing a revival. Alex Yokel said he had all the money but I hear bad reports about him. Gordon called up from the Coast and said he wanted to do it and the next day he cooled off because Sam Katz told him Metro was going to do it soon. I would like to bet that Metro will not do it for three years. Despite all these setbacks, I nevertheless believe that somehow we will get that revival on this year. I have been in touch with Robeson's agent and he assures me that Paul is interested and that he has not yet made his concert bookings for next season. The other key man is Winninger and I think you can help me in the details. Find out if Winninger is still signed with Metro and also if he is interested in doing "Showboat" on Broadway providing I could get Metro to release him. Also try to get some idea of how much money he might want. Use your own discretion as to how you should do this, whether to talk to Leo Fitzgerald or Winninger himself. The ideal I think would be to bump into Winninger himself and sound him out personally. I find that agents usually prefer to keep their clients in Hollywood and that the client is more often the one who wants to change.

"Saratoga Trunk": Two things stand in the way. One is my fear that, after working six months on it, Billy Rose might change his mind or might not agree with me about the adaptation, in which case I am stuck with an unmarketable product—unmarketable because it has been sold for pictures and Billy is the only manager with the courage to produce the play in the face of the imminent picture production. The second obstacle is my growing fear that this is going to be very difficult to adapt for a stage musical. As a picture it is a cinch, but for the stage it requires the invention of many new characters. It is as if we had Magnolia, Ravenal, Joe and Queeny handed to us for "Showboat"—and no one else. And then Julie, Steve, Frank, Ellie, Captain Andy and Parthy all had to be supplied and fitted into sub plots.

At the moment I am devoting all my time to a revue which is being produced by the "FIGHT FOR FREEDOM" crowd. George Kaufman is a kind of editor-producer of the sketches and I have the same duties in regard to the musical material. The contributors to the revue are Kaufman, Hart, Ferber, Krauses[22] [sic], Lindsay, the Spewacks, Mrs. Danny Kaye, Harold Rome, Kurt Weill, Berlin, Johnny Green, Earl Robinson and myself—to name a few. The show is designed to be produced for a run on Broadway and then on the road. The writers contribute their material free of charge. The actors will be asked to work at cut salaries and all the profits are to be devoted to various war reliefs. Robert Alton is doing the dances, Harry Horner the scenery, and Hassard Short is supervising the physical side of the production.

Billy has finished his general training as a seaman and expects to be sent away from Brooklyn any day now. Most of his gang have been assigned to gun crew work on Merchantmen. Some of them were taken away last week and became prompt victims of Nazi torpedoes. I am hoping anxiously that Billy is not assigned to this duty but I am afraid that it is very likely he will be. I would much rather have him on a destroyer or a sub-chaser or something that can give another ship a fight. It is a mystery to me why the Navy sacrifices sailors on merchant vessels, manning those pea-shooters which do no good at all.

We had dinner with Harold Lion the other night and he is very busy raising money for ambulances for the American Field Service. He says that if he fails in his effort to regain his old artillery commission, he will very likely join the service and drive an ambulance. I told him that you had been trying unsuccessfully to get this job with the Red Cross. He said he thought it would be much easier for you to get in the American Field Service. Do you know about this?

I will not go on writing because there is really too much to say about everything in general. It would be great to see you again on either coast and have a good old-time talk.

Please let me know, as soon as you can, what you can learn about Winninger as it would help me materially in lining up a production. Incidentally, if the Winninger situation is discouraging, throw out a feeler for Charlie Ruggles.

---

[22] Probably the playwright Russel Crouse and his first wife, Alison Smith.

I suppose you know that Lester is reviving "Music In The Air" in his Civic Opera Season with John Charles Thomas in the Carminati part. He has suggested some changes, all of which I am doing because I think they are distinct improvements on the original.

That will be all for now.

Love to Jean and yourself,

Oscar Hammerstein, 2nd.

According to Hammerstein's biographer, Hugh Fordin, one day in January 1942, Oscar became gripped by a recording of Bizet's opera *Carmen*, listening to it over and over as he studied its book and score. Knowing of his grandfather's ambition to make opera "livelier and more accessible to the public by using English translations," Oscar was fixated by the idea of doing his own English version of *Carmen*, not just a literal translation, but one written from the point of view of a dramatist and a lyricist who understood how to affect an audience. As his enthusiasm grew, Hammerstein saw parallels between the Spanish gypsies of *Carmen*, and black culture in the South, and with that transplantation began to work intently on the now-titled *Carmen Jones*.

No Broadway orchestrator is more widely respected than Robert Russell Bennett, and none has orchestrated as many iconic shows. Early in his career Russell Bennett became closely associated with Kern, and orchestrated virtually all of the Kern-Hammerstein shows, starting with *Sunny* in 1925. But Russell Bennett's professional relationship with Hammerstein actually pre-dated the Kern collaborations, starting with *Wildflower* in 1923, with music by Vincent Youmans and Herbert Stothart. In the absence of a living composer, Russell Bennett was probably Hammerstein's closest collaborator in the writing/adapting of *Carmen Jones*.

Robert Russell Bennett to Oscar Hammerstein, circa spring, 1942

Dear Oscar,

The changes you write of are most promising. The only argument from me on fidelity to the original Carmen will come from mutilation of music— not from cuts of whole numbers or changes of format.

After all, our aim is to cash in on what we know to be a score that has proven its effectiveness and at the same time has only scratched the edge of its possibilities with the American public.

Here is a short list of things I don't believe in doing to Bizet's music:

1. Making jump arrangements out of melodies that will long outlive jump arrangements.
2. Interpolating songs by Jerome Romberg
3. Building up routines by Bob Alton,[23] with special choruses and fancy exits
4. "Saving" numbers by Hartman methods.

My main question now is the one you have tried to answer by planning August 1 as rehearsal date. Will your new version (incidentally, many things for the prize-fighter!) delay that possibility? I need a month clear after we know what we start with, if I can get it, since not only the piano-score must be O.K., but a large part of the orchestration work has to be done before I start with the main job of getting the folks ready for your staging.

Love to you all from us all,

Robert Russell

Oscar Hammerstein to Laurence Schwab, March 9, 1942

Dear Larry:

It was nice to hear from you. As for Carmen Jones, she has not been gobbled up by Gordon or even submitted to him. I haven't written it yet, either, nor have I found the girl to play Carmen. There is nothing to stop you from producing except one sentence in your letter: "I think I could get some cash for it too." Me, I am looking for a fellow who says he has all the cash. Do you know any such? The idea of doing it with you would be most welcome to me but I would like to keep it free so that if anyone came along who could finance the whole thing, I would not have it committed to you or anyone else who could not give me that kind of delicious assurance. Here I am at

---

[23] Robert Alton was a choreographer who had recently done Cole Porter's *Panama Hattie*, and Rodgers and Hart's *Pal Joey* and *By Jupiter*. He would not choreograph *Carmen Jones*, that job ultimately going to Eugene Loring.

the tender age of forty-six and a half, becoming hard, realistic and selfish. I didn't think I'd make it until I was sixty!

War activities in the North include the enlistment in the Navy of Billy and in the American Field Service of Reggie. I suppose you knew about Billy and also the fact that he got married the same week he enlisted. She is a swell girl. As for Reg, I think he will be headed for Cairo in a couple of weeks where they will give him an ambulance with which to dent the desert sands.

I hope you succeed in your effort to get back into the Navy. I am happy to hear of Mildred's activity. Greater love hath no woman than to spend so much time away from golf for her country.

My own work has been sporadic. I have raised some money for Bucks County Emergency Hospitals (in case we have to take care of evacuees from an air-raided Philadelphia or New York.) I also went well over my quota in getting donations for the American Theater Wing War Service. Incidentally, that Canteen we just opened for service men has turned out to be a big success. It is situated in the old "Little Club" under the 44th Street Theater. The boys get food there and entertainment—by performers from current shows—and dancing with girls from the various choruses. Dorothy goes down there twice a week and works behind the counter and in the kitchen and gets tired but has a hell of a time as the special confidante of all the Anzacs [Australian and New Zealand Army Corps] who drop in there.

With George Kaufman, Bob Alton, Harold Rome and about twenty other fellows who might be described as top-flight authors and song writers, I am working on a show which will be a war revue designed to come into New York for a run. All material contributed free and all profits to be donated to various war reliefs.

My chief aim, however, has been to write a great song, and this I have so far failed to do, although I have devoted nearly all my time to if for the past three months. I don't mean a song like "Goodbye Mamma, I'm Going To Yokohama". I mean an important song. The difficulty of writing an expression of what Americans feel today is a very distressing thing because I find as I try to write it that there is something wrong with the script. We don't all feel the same. We don't all have the same understanding of what are the aims of this war, and the spontaneous emotional unity which was achieved by the sudden blow at Pearl Harbor has now been dissipated into something like the bickering period which existed just before. Colonel McCormick, of the Chicago Tribune, is once more of the opinion that Roosevelt is a better target to shoot at than Hitler and several congressmen think that the President's wife and a handful of entertainers are the real issues behind the conflict. The Catholics are terrified that a military alliance with Russia is an invitation to a dance with Communists and every fifth man you meet is an armchair strategist who wants to know where the Navy is and why isn't the high command doing what he would do if he ever took the trouble to get out of his armchair. Roger DeLisle[24] did not write the Marseillaise and thereby exhort France to revolt against the King. The spirit of revolution was there and, after years of irritation, had been deeply imbedded in the hearts of all Frenchmen. And all he did as a poet was to crystallize this unified purpose. I, as a minor poet of Tin Pan Alley, feel the need for such whole-hearted unity and clarity of aims—and even then I might not do as good a job as DeLisle. I would like, however, to get into the ring with him sometime as equal weights.

This treatise has exhausted me. Let me hear from you again soon. You don't write nearly enough.

Love to Mildred and yourself from both of us,

Oscar Hammerstein, 2nd.

Opened by the American Theatre Wing on March 2, 1942, the Stage Door Canteen was an immediate success. A refuge for off-duty soldiers during the war, it included refreshments, entertainment, and the opportunity to dance with actresses of various degrees of fame. Its success spawned Canteens in several other cities, including London and Paris, and it was immortalized in film, song, and on the radio.

W. C. Handy's autobiography, *Father of the Blues*, was published in 1941. A year later Hammerstein considered adapting it for the stage, incorporating songs written by Handy, whose most famous songs included "Memphis Blues," "St. Louis Blues," and "Beale Street Blues." Hammerstein pursued this project through August, with a letter to his West Coast agent, Frank Orsatti. It appears Oscar rethought the show as something better suited to the screen, but the project quickly disappeared from

---

[24] Claude Joseph Rouget de Lisle wrote the words and music to what became known "La Marseillaise" in 1792. It became identified with the French Revolution and became the French National Anthem in 1795.

his correspondence. The 1958 film titled *St. Louis Blues* was only loosely based on Handy's life.

Oscar Hammerstein to Hy Kraft, March 21, 1942

Dear Hy:

I am not sure whether I have written this letter to you or only composed it in my mind. Anyway, this is what I intended to—or did say to you. I suggest that we each, independently, make a layout for a stage version of "The Handy Biography" and mail it to each other and that neither reads the other's layout until he has mailed his own. I am not suggesting this just to play games but because I think it is a good system. Whatever coincides, that is, whatever appeals to us both, it is probably pretty good. Jerry and I did the original "Showboat" layout this way. It so happened that, in that case, his layout was almost the same as mine and we never deviated from it with the confidence of that double endorsement behind it.

I would prefer not to approach "Handy" until we were sure that we were ready to go ahead. I wouldn't like to get the old boy steamed up and then change our minds. Meanwhile, I am sure he is not going to run away from us.

Now that I have written this letter, I feel more certain that I have never written it before and in that case I ask your forgiveness for the delay.

Love to Reata and yourself from both of us.

Oscar Hammerstein, 2nd.

Hungarian-born Emmerich Kálmán was considered one of the great operetta composers, first finding international fame with *The Gay Hussars* in 1909 (the English title for *Tatárjárás*), and having his greatest Broadway success with *Countess Maritza* in 1926. In 1927 he collaborated with Stothart, Harbach, and Hammerstein on the Arthur Hammerstein-produced *Golden Dawn*, which was made into a film in 1930. Even though Kálmán was Jewish, Hitler was such a fan of his music that he offered to make him an "honorary Aryan." During the war Kálmán escaped to Paris, and moved to the United States in 1940, moving back to Vienna after the war.

There's no indication that Hammerstein and Kálmán were close or maintained an ongoing friendship; that Oscar addressed the letter to "Mr. Kallman" (aside from the misspelling) would seem to confirm that. But the fact that Kálmán sent Hammerstein the script for *Johnny Was a Lady* and Hammerstein's thoughtful response, suggests admiration and respect on both sides. Nothing seems to have become of *Johnny Was a Lady*; its title and story don't align with any of Kálmán's known shows. But its title and Oscar's comments suggest something quite unexpected and provocative—a show ahead of its time.

Oscar Hammerstein to Emmerich Kálmán, March 21, 1942

Dear Mr. Kallman [*sic*]:

Please forgive my long delay in writing and returning the enclosed manuscript. Ten days ago I was suddenly called away to Boston to work on a musical play which was in trouble. It is still in trouble but I am going to try to improve it because it has been produced by a great friend of mine.

I am taking this first opportunity I have had to send you a few notes I made after re-reading "JOHNNY WAS A LADY". I hope they will be of some use to you.

1. Cut Scene 1 completely.

2. I would also cut the ballet (Scene 3). It seems to be enough if, having heard Professor Urosoff's theory and read his circular, she announces her decision to have the transformation performed.

3. Scene 9: Instead of emphasizing the "Johnny-Carmen" story, emphasize the relationship of Johnny and Perkins. After the first shock that Perkin gets when hearing of her transformation, he apparently decides to take her at her word. He takes her out with a group of young men—very gay and boisterous young men. They go to rough places, drink hard liquor, and get into fights. At one point Perkins has to protect her from being beaten up. Nevertheless, if his idea seems to be to test her to see if she has really become a boy, she somehow, in spite of all difficulties, weathers the storm and at the end convinces him that she is a boy. He tries to get her drunk but she can drink more than he can and she seems to be successful in winning the interest of girls and getting them away from the men they are with. In this connection when she meets with Carmen, she might be in a very difficult situation from which Carmen rescues her under the guise of pretending to be in love with her. She goes up to Carmen's rooms and then Carmen—all

curiosity—asks: "Tell me about your operation." I suggest that Johnny say that operations are not an essential part of Professor Urosoff's theory; that masculinity is a state of mind; that, in a series of intensified interviews, Urosoff psycho-analyzes his subject out of being feminine and guides her into the viewpoint and the approach to life of a man. In other words, Johnny had no desire to actually be a man in a physical sense, but, disgusted with the life she had been forced to lead as a woman, had decided to take up the more agreeable superficial habits of a man and not be exposed to other men as she felt she had been when she was a girl. Carmen is interested but skeptical. She shows Johnny some of her new dresses and negligees. Johnny admires them but exhibits no longing to wear those kind of clothes again. Carmen then contrives to get Perkins alone with Johnny to see if her new "masculine state of mind" can resist the charm that Perkins has always had for her. When the three of them are together, Johnny becomes angry and feigns a jealousy over Carmen but the audience begins to suspect that her real jealousy is over Perkins and her anger due to the knowledge that Perkins is apparently in the habit of visiting her friend Carmen. Carmen leaves them alone together for the night (this would have to be through some trick and contrivance).

The curtain would be lowered for lapse of time and rise on the same scene the next morning. Johnny would make her appearance from the bedroom in Carmen's prettiest negligee. She and Perkins have a happy breakfast together. The conclusion seems to be that clothes make the man and Johnny made the mistake of taking off her clothes!

These are only random notes written down as they occurred to me. They probably present many difficulties and perhaps destroy other values in the story that I am not conscious of, but if you and your collaborator can use any of these ideas you are welcome to them.

With kindest regards and all good wishes.

Sincerely,

Jerome Kern to Oscar Hammerstein, March 31, 1942

Dear Oscar:

I am afraid this is going to be a most unsatisfactory reply to your comprehensive letter of March 25th.

What kind of a swap is that—trading a headache with the Shuberts, who, with all their nuisances and pettifoggeries, do have an organization, plenty of capital, many theatres, and are, or were, avid to give us a properly policed, first-class (for them) production, for a headache with the volatile Irving, whose heart is undoubtedly in the right place, but who has none of the Syracuscans' assets, dubious though they be.

Hate to be a killjoy, but after all, we do happen to be men of character, have been in tighter spots before, will probably be in tight spots again, which is no reason why, at this point, that we should lather ourselves up as if this were our last despairing, desperate stand.

I am all for a revival of "Show Boat" that will be as lofty a landmark in the theatre as was the last one, and if, as a means to that end, everything must go into the silence until you and I can talk to Eddie Mannix[25] or L.B. about launching such an enterprise with their support and backing, meaning stars as well as dough, or, if necessary, until after M-G-M releases its "Show Boat" picture, then I say, let us be silent. We had guts enough to pitchfork the unwritten, untried potentialities of Billy Rose's "S.T." right outen [sic] the window, and we surely have common sense enough not to monkey with a property as valuable and as beloved as "S.B."

The same mail which brought your remarks of the 25th re Lester and "Music In The Air," brought Howard's memo of March 25th in re the same property and producer. Howard's memo concerns his demand on Lester for $3150. in advance, if you please. This is all very well if he can get it without calling out the National Guard, but his is a proposal which makes me postpone any thought of sounding Lester out on ponying up for your traveling expenses until after such a time as he comes running to me, pleading for concessions, when a little hoss-tradin' might be promoted.

As a welcome contrast to these unsatisfactory business notes, I thank you for your beautiful summation of our joint joy in fashioning not only "Music In the Air" and "Show Boat" but also "Sweet Adeline" and even the ill-fated "Three Sisters." The same formula so perfectly expressed by you, in which, of course, I whole-heartedly agree, generated all of them. We may have rolled up some faulty craftsmanship somewhere along the line, but the

---

[25] Eddie Mannix was an infamous "fixer" for MGM, covering up and preventing scandals among its stars.

formula was, as you say, simple, honest and true. Simplicity and good taste indelibly marked "Oh Boy"[26] at approximately the same elapsed period in World War I, as now, and much as I dislike agreeing with Lee Shubert when he said that up to then, "O.B." was the best thing ever produced, he hit it on the nose, and there is absolutely nothing to shatter the belief that history doesn't repeat itself.

Ever yours,

Jerry.

David Berg to Oscar Hammerstein, March 31, 1942

Dear Mr. Hammerstein:

I listened intently to your speech at our Ascap Dinner and after analyzing it very carefully, I have come to the conclusion that you are one of those narrow-minded persons who hates to see your brother members get what they justly deserve from our Society.

Of course, you have company. The other selfish members I am speaking of are Mr. Irving Caesar, Mr. Deems Taylor and sad to say, Mr. Otto Harbach. They, too, are as small-minded as you are when the question comes up for a fair distribution of payments to our members.

I also resent the remark that you passed, about writers having other positions, should give up song-writing. I consider that insulting, and out of order at any meeting. I am surprised our good President, Mr. Gene Buck, did not call you on that, because, after all, who are you to tell any individual writer what he should do.

In conclusion, I think you should really feel ashamed of yourself, and I sincerely hope you think this over. In the future, if you can't say anything good and helpful for your brother members, don't say anything at all. I'm sure we'll think more of you.

Respectfully yours,

David Berg

---

[26] *Oh, Boy!* was a 1917 musical by Kern, P. G. Wodehouse, and Guy Bolton, and was the most commercially successful of their intimate "Princess Theatre musicals."

Oscar Hammerstein to David Berg, April 7, 1942

Dear Mr. Berg:

You write very silly letters. I hope your songs are better.

This may be the most eviscerating letter Hammerstein ever wrote, all the more so for its brevity. Far more typical were his letters of encouragement or practical advice, such as in the letter below written the day before.

Oscar Hammerstein to Peter Gladstone, April 6, 1942

Dear Peter:

I have played the enclosed songs and find that they are written in a capable and workmanlike manner and are no worse nor better than the run-of-the-mill songs heard on the radio. I think the writer should be encouraged to go on and I suggest that he step out along more unexplored paths and not ape quite so slavishly the formula of other possible songs. Let him write something that he really feels and means, and not bother about whether it will be popular or not. That is not a sure recipe for success but it is the only way to land on something big.

Reading over this letter I don't know whether I sound more like John J. Anthony[27] or Uncle Don.[28]

Kindest regards,

Oscar Hammerstein, 2nd.

Oscar Hammerstein to George Frank (excerpt), April 6, 1942

In the last few months I have been mixed up with several false alarms that didn't pan out, but it is a lovely day in Doylestown and I feel fine. In fact, we all do except my son Billy who is a sailor, stationed for the moment in Brooklyn. He is laid up with measles but this is a military secret so keep it under your hat. It wouldn't do for the Japs to know that our Navy is under-manned.

---

[27] John J. Anthony was the host of the radio program *Good Will Hour* where he dispensed advice to married couples.
[28] *Uncle Don* was a radio program for children, hosted by Uncle Don Carney (Howard Rice).

Oscar Hammerstein to Arthur Hammerstein, April 6, 1942

Dear Uncle Arthur:

I thought you and Dorothy would be interested in the enclosed portrait of her, clad in a beautiful ermine wrap and looking as if she had just swallowed a swarm of butterflies.

Jerry Watanabe has finally been released[29] and he and Doodie are down here with us now. We are going to give them our city apartment [125 E 53 St.]. I intend to spend only one night a week in town from now on and we will sleep in Dorothy's office. Jennifer, of course, remains down in the country with us. She goes to a Quaker school nearby.

After trying several changes, the most constructive thing I did for Caesar's show was persuade him to close it. He had only half a book and half a cast but if he will rewrite it completely and recast it, I still think he has a very good chance of pulling it out.

Reggie has not yet been called although he has taken all his shots against various tropical fevers, etc. Billy, the Brooklyn Blue-jacket, is laid up in Sick Bay with the measles. I suppose we can count this as the family's first war casualty. Alice is taking a concentrated engineering course at Stevens University of Technology in Hoboken. After three months, she will be qualified to be a foreman in a war plant at $25 or $35 per week. If she likes the work, she can continue with the more advanced course and become an even bigger shot than this. The course is given free by the government. The requirements to get in were very high but Alice was among the top ten percent. Dorothy takes two days a week away from her work to be a hostess and waitress at the American Theater Wing Canteen for soldiers and sailors. This is situated in the old "Little Club" which Shubert donated. They give the boys sandwiches and cake and coffee. Comedians and singers from all the shows drop in continuously to entertain them, and the girls from the various choruses go there and dance with them. It has proved a very successful venture and is probably the best place that an enlisted man from out of town can go when he gets a furlough. I have done my small bit by raising money for this venture and for several other things, and I have written a new lyric for "Stout-hearted Men" and dedicated it to the Navy for which

---

[29] Oscar's brother-in-law, Jerry Watanabe, being of partial Japanese descent, was interned at Ellis Island for a time after America entered the War.

I have had gracious acknowledgement from Admiral Andrews. I have also, on special request, written a new verse to the Marine's Hymn in order to stimulate enlistment in the Aviation Corps of the Marines. I don't think these things amount to very much and I feel that my mission is to write a really important war song but so far the big idea has not come to me.

I am almost positive that in May I shall make a trip to the Coast and whenever I do, I will start a couple of days ahead and spend them on your farm.

Let's hear from you soon. You haven't written in a long time.

Love to all,

Oscar Hammerstein, 2nd,

Jerome Kern to Oscar Hammerstein, April 10, 1942

Dear Oscar:

Following up my hasty night letter, I found, upon shoving up my appointment with Jack Cummings a full day, that what he really wanted, under the guise of a business conference, was my endorsement of the script ideas as set forth by Jack MacGowan.[30] I don't know the exact date on which Jack MacGowan was put on the script, but following that date, here is the sequence of events:

Arthur Freed stubbed his toe badly on the MacGowan version of "Panama Hattie",[31] which, I hear, authoritatively, has to be completely redone, meaning rewritten, reproduced, redirected and reshot; maybe even recast. This mess culminated in a bad rumpus between MacGowan and Freed, and MacGowan, with eighteen months contract still to go, was cut adrift.

Somewhere along the line, they gave him your version of "V.W.F.M."[32] to read, and he alleges (substantiated by Jack Cummings) that he reported he liked it. Whereupon Freed said, "That's good. Now rewrite it." From what

---

[30] Jack McGowan was an actor who switched to writing plays and librettos, most famously for *Girl Crazy* in 1930. He moved to Hollywood where he wrote screenplays, beginning with *Broadway Melody of 1936*.

[31] The 1942 film of *Panama Hattie* was loosely based on the 1940 Cole Porter Broadway musical; the film retained only a handful of the Porter songs.

[32] *Very Warm for May.*

I can piece together from the Cummings and MacGowan narratives, he reluctantly set to work, turned in a treatment, which was greeted with a "That's all, brother, you're through."

Then came the MacGowan-Freed split, and the project was for the time being shelved. Hence the extensions with Hammerstein and Kern. When Hammerstein and Kern got a little tough in granting the last extension, M-G-M—and this is just my theory—hard put to salvage story cost to date, and with another ten thousand bananas staring them in the face, bequeathed the property, plus Jack MacGowan, to Jack Cummings.

Must wander off a trifle at this point by reporting that the MacGowan-Freed row, plus the doghouse yawning for him, so shook MacGowan and preyed on what was left of the MacGowan mind, that one day in the commissary he sponsored a mild stroke. He's not exactly paralyzed, but the use of his left arm is impaired, he has bad headaches, and has the usual accompanying symptoms of nervous eruptions on his good hand. In short, he rates, and is going to take, a good long rest.

ALL OF THESE FACTS MUST BE IN ORSATTI'S POSSESSION AND CERTAINLY SHOULD HAVE BEEN IMPARTED BY HIM TO YOU LONG AGO.

To return to the Cummings interview, in seeking my endorsement, Cummings may have had a slight case of cold feet on the merit of the MacGowan outline, and wanted some moral support, or else it was a furtive plot to get me, by my acquiescence, to sugar-coat the cavalier treatment accorded you by Arthur, who did not wise you up to the real status, but professed what may honestly have been his real enthusiasm for your layout. Naturally I didn't have time enough to read either treatment or script, but from one of those joint recitals, with MacGowan talking and Cummings chipping in, I gather they have dramatized many of your contrivances, and certainly have highlighted the character of the father. I gave them a brief biography of the switch you were forced by Max Gordon to make on tour, deleting the father's jam as the raison d'etre for May's escapades, which, in my opinion, shared by others, was responsible to a large degree for our New York failure.

This apparently was enough moral support for Mr. Cummings who, from the look of it, certainly intends to complete the M-G-M agreement with Kern and Hammerstein by not waiting for the finished MacGowan script, but before the expiration of our latest extension, indicating the type songs he wishes, as far as tempo is concerned, and the general desideratum of getting a new song for Kathryn Grayson and one for Eleanor Powell.

Maybe I have forgotten to mention, either by mail or telephone, that the proposed cast is father: Charles Winninger, brother: Gene Kelly, May: Kathryn Grayson, and a new character based on your Ann Sothern descending Hollywood star, only a dancer instead of an actress: Eleanor Powell. It is to be a musical comedy royal family idea, plus the present real situation of Mickey Rooney, an important Hollywood star, and his father, Joe Yule, still carrying on in the sub-stratum of the burlesque houses. In other words, the brother, a Broadway big shot, who has shelved the old man in softening comfort, not to say affluence, but has hidden him from his public for ten years, insists upon the completion of May's schooling, while the old man, fat and well-fed, is, as far as the footlights are concerned, rotting away.

Nothing much to complain about in all this, except the appalling silence they have maintained up to now, as far as you are concerned. I say up to now, because, with ear-piercing bluntness, I demanded of Cummings "Is Oscar to further hold himself in readiness to come out here?" and the answer was an equally blunt "No."

Before the interview terminated, I had completely sold Cummings our original idea of the hot coloratura number for Grayson. Remember the long megillah you had in your files for months which you returned to me on February 13th? ☉ Naturally, I embellished my sales talk with the fact that I had already run through the coloratura portion of the number with Grayson, right here at my piano. She, of course, will do "All The Things You Are" (which is pretty easy to take) and maybe will even reprise same. This leaves one of those things for Eleanor Powell, on which we shall both probably flop with a satisfying thud. That is, of course, unless you roll around with a superior scene, which I know you will carefully devise, to be eight to a dozen lines of song, and as many minutes of dance routine. Ah well, I suppose in these times, it can be considered pretty good to give Morgenthau[33] a chunk of twenty-two hundred and fifty bucks. So put on

---

[33] Henry Morgenthau, Jr. was Secretary of the Treasury and was responsible (blamed) for increased taxes to counter the deficit spending of the New Deal and to pay for America's war efforts.

your tap shoes, get yourself in the mood, and start thinking. As for me, I now stop ditto on "V.W.F.M."

Left word last evening with Lester to make the proposed changes in "M.I.T.A." and submit them by mail to you. I think perhaps you have heard a two-four melody which Betty likes enormously. You may have heard her ask me to play her what she calls 'the sophisticated number'. Why, Gawd knows, unless it is because it has quite a nice choral counter-melody. I think I had the tentative title, if and when you heard it, of " 'Tain't Fair" or some such junk, this to be finale of zoo scene.

To give "Show Boat" a once-over-lightly here, your notion of rotating stars for a first-class revival, is brilliant. The only thing lacking is the first-classness of the revival. I sense a little scolding in your last reference to "S.B." revival and a disclaimer that your being high on the project is, as you say, from hunger. I told you before, and repeat now, that I am not emptying myself of ice-water. I just think that the impotence of a good-natured Caesar, sans organization, theatres, standing, and general experience and knowledge of how to cope with the many problems involved, including Winninger's right elbow, is too much of a bloody headache for either of us to take on.

Well, you brought all this drool on yourself.

Love:

Jerry

[The addition below is handwritten in Kern's hand, but signed by someone else.]

⊙ You're quite wrong as I write this I hold it in my left hand.

Attested and affirmed 4/10/42

Nancy Kenyon [?]

Oscar Hammerstein to Jerome Kern, April 11, 1942

Dear Jerry:

Without any attempt to urge reconsideration of my belief in the Caesar project I must clear myself of your evident assumption that the suggestion was made on a "strictly-from-hunger" basis. I don't want to throw Show

Boat away or mar it in any way, nor do I think that it is a life or death matter that it be produced within the next six months. I just think this is a good time to do it. But if I didn't think that we could have pulled it off with flying colors with the Caesar set-up I shouldn't have written to you about it. In the first place he would have had nothing to say about the production. We would have complete control. He didn't want any. In the second place he would have raised the money and the investors would have received fifty percent, with the other fifty percent split between you and me and him— and Ferber if we had chosen.

We had evolved an idea—and it would be well to consider this no matter how and when we do it—of cast rotation. Suppose we opened with Robeson and Winninger featured or starred. Suppose you couldn't keep Robeson more than eight weeks on account of concert commitments. When he leaves the cast, you put in another good bass (I've got a great one) and to keep the balance of drawing power you put a star in another part—Mary Martin or Deanna Durbin as Magnolia. Winninger has to quit at the end of twelve weeks on account of picture commitments. So when he drops out and you get a good Captain Andy with no name, you try to get Bing Crosby to appear as Ravenal for six weeks. This system would assure not only a strong cast, drawn from a field of starring names from which you can not ordinarily draw—Pictures and Radio—and the production would be kept alive in the public mind by constant plugging of the new name going in, and by a great deal of controversial argument about who is better in what part. This is new and daring, but I believe it would be not only a great innovation but would become a great institution in show business. The show would not be only a frame in which to place before the public the personal appearances of people they want to see in the flesh, shown off to grand advantage, in great parts. It would also be a proving ground for new talent, playing some of the parts while the stars handled others. If Dinah Shore played Julie during the off months of summer when her radio demands were less, the girl who followed her would have the benefit of her performance and would imitate what would be her admirable singing of Bill, and eventually become a star in her own right. Stars are always made by great parts, and young people have to start following experienced people. This is a great idea, and Show Boat is the one vehicle with which it could be done.

My conviction that Show Boat should be done this year is based on something much stronger than a panicky desire to get it on any which way we can. I think its deep-rooted American feeling gives it a special appeal now. I think that since there have been no plays of this quality written since, and the fact that the public is obviously hungry for them, and that there is no sign of another being written, all make it a perfect pushover. I want to write a new play with you, and I will anyway, but no new play can possibly have the chance that this revival will have. I don't think it's any gamble at all and if I had any money of my own, in it would go. Disagree all you like with any of the production propositions I send on, but don't think I am tossing wild forward passes in the last twenty seconds of the second half. That is not my spirit at all.

Re Music In The Air, Howard's demand for an advance was due to the fact that he had some trouble collecting from Lester before. Do you think it better if I suggest to Lester my coming out to direct for an expense allowance? I would have no hesitation in doing this. Is there any chance that Thomas would give up his concert tour and tour in this play next season? And does Lester think he could finance this? There was a cautious hint at this in one of his letters. Have you had any conversation on the subject? I suppose that by now you have received my rewritten fragments.

If Lester doesn't come through I must, of course, come out anyway. But don't tell him that. It is the only way for us to properly make the changes, and I also feel we should get together and discuss other things—mainly a new play. If Freed's schedule for my coming out in May for V.W.F.M. still held good, the whole thing would work in perfectly, but I haven't heard from him in some time. If he postpones still further, I shall just have to come out at my own expense, and keep said expense down to a minimum.

Has Betty arrived in New York? We haven't heard from her yet. I won't start on news of our family—it takes too long. But none of it is bad. Jerry Watanabe has just been released from his internment in Ellis Island, with the blessing of our government—but God knows how or where he can get a job. Jennifer has been living with us and goes to a Quaker School nearby. Doodie and Jerry are in our New York apartment for the time being—maybe a long time. I'm not going up to town much now, and when I do, we will sleep in Dorothy's office-apartment.

Good-bye and love to both of you.

Hammerstein's idea of "cast rotation" is startling in its seeming obviousness. On the other hand, there were few shows other than *Show Boat* that had so many major parts and, at the time, most actors were migrating from Broadway *to* Hollywood, rarely to return.

Harry Ruby was one of Hammerstein's most reliably funny correspondents. Frustrated in his ambition to be a baseball player, Ruby became a composer, lyricist, and screenwriter. Most of his songs were written with the lyricist Bert Kalmar, including songs used in three Marx Brothers films, and three songs that might now be considered semi-standards: "Who's Sorry Now," "Three Little Words," and "A Kiss to Build a Dream On." Hammerstein was the third collaborator on this last song.

Harry Ruby to Oscar Hammerstein, June 2, 1942

Dear Oscar:

I had no idea you had gone home, but I can understand it. You might have phoned me and asked for the ticket money instead of making me write a letter and waste more paper—a sin in these times—writing a check.

I am sorry that we did not have you for dinner. But we are not set up for entertaining. We have one maid who pays us very little and is sick most of the time. That leaves my wife to cook now and then and although I like her cooking, we do not have guests because we always have sour cream and cottage cheese.

In the good old days, before I lost my fortune betting on the White Sox, it was nothing for me to have big parties. You were at some of them. Yes, it was you who made the snide remark about the shortage of food. Your famous Brandy joke brought you fame, but not for me. Yours is still alive and when I DO have guests, there is a slight pause before they accept. It has become necessary for me to invite people this way: "Will you come to dinner Friday night and don't believe Oscar Hammerstein."

It is our 5th and last week at the studio, unless they keep us on, which they should and I mean it. I believe we are doing a good job. But what a studio will do, no one can foretell. If they keep us on, I'll write you and you and Dorothy can fly out for dinner.

It was good seeing you. Did you hear from Jerry Wald[34]? I will find out what he thinks about the idea.

Best to all.

Sincerely,

Harry

Oscar Hammerstein to Harry Ruby, June 10, 1942

Dear Harry:-

Thank you for the check and the racy letter. I must say your excuses for not inviting me to dinner were pretty lame and the letter was full of contradictions. In one paragraph you said that you never had guests because your wife could only cook cottage cheese with sour cream and in another paragraph you said that when you do have guests you always tell them not to believe what I once said or implied about your food.

It is very foolish for you to practice these petty deceptions when everyone's life in Hollywood is like an open book. It is well known that the shindigs you throw at 805 have sent Ouida Rathbone[35] to her bed with a nervous breakdown. Everyone is talking about that innovation you and Eileen sprang when you strung Chinese lanterns from tree to tree across your lawn. That all happened to take place while I was there, but for some reason I was not among the 600 who were invited.

All this is not stated as a grievance because what the hell do I care if you want to be so God-damned snobbish. I have absolutely no resentment but I just can't let you get away with some of those glib statements in your letter which you expect me to swallow, hook, line, and sinker, the way you expected me to swallow that cold pot roast that you handed out in 1937.

Love and kisses.

---

[34] Wald was a screenwriter who later became a Hollywood producer.
[35] Mrs. Basil Rathbone.

Oscar Hammerstein to Richard Berger[36] (excerpt), June 3, 1942

In the affair of CARMEN JONES, Max Gordon's hot breath is on the back of my neck, and he has so far offered me a share of the Lyceum Theatre, Jr. Miss, My Sister Eileen and all the pictures he ever intends to do for Columbia. It is getting difficult to keep him off. Whatever happens, however, with him or anyone else, I mean to retain full control of the production and sponsorship.

When all these things become more definite, I will tell you about them. Meanwhile, I am going to finish the script of CARMEN JONES. I am resuming work on it with Russell Bennett tomorrow morning. Incidentally, Russell, who is a pretty cold fish, is raving about the first draft of the first act which I left with him before I went to the Coast.

Oscar Hammerstein to Paul Beisman, Municipal Theatre Association, St. Louis, June 11, 1942

Dear Paul:

In your letter graciously acknowledging my telegram, you inserted a throwaway listing of the attractions of the Municipal Opera this season of which, I am proud to note, I have four.

The first is SONG OF THE FLAME, which announces that George Gershwin and Herbert Stothart wrote the music. The next is NEW MOON with a caption, " . . . Some of Sigmund Romberg's best-loved music." The third is WILDFLOWER, which announces Vincent Youman's [sic] inimitable music again. The last is SHOW BOAT, called the Ziegfeld-Kern American classic on a greater scale than ever before.

Thanks for the billing.

Anon.

---

[36] Richard Berger had been the production stage manager for Hammerstein's *May Wine* (1935).

Jerome Kern to Oscar Hammerstein, June 15, 1942

Dear Oscar:

Since your note with the Elsie Janis[37] clipping of the 4th, in which you promised a newsy letter later, I have been waiting to receive it, in order to make my report that I had a long and satisfactory talk with Dinah Shore 'tother night, during which she fairly swooned at the notion of an opportunity to play Julie.

As you undoubtedly know, her status is a fixture with Liggett and Myers. From other sources, one gathers that the lanky lady (no disparagement) really is swinging Eddie Cantor into the fat contracts. Be that as it may, it seems fairly apparent that any idea of casting la Shore means an alternate Julie for Wednesday night, or omitting the Wednesday night performance, instead of the usual Monday night omission, which seems silly. She certainly is a ball of fire with a vivid personality, and not a bit hammy.

Since Sunday, June 7th, when it comes to ham, I know whereof I speak, despite the amusing things you said in yours of June 10th. Well, anyway, glad you liked the music.

Can best answer your "Music In The Air" inquiry by enclosing copy of his letter to Howard, received today from Edwin Lester. Didn't go down to see the thing again, but heard from Frank and Margie that the performance had, as you say, jelled satisfactorily, with the exception of "Good Girl." As I considered the number without anything more done to its production that we saw opening night, an affront to the audience, subscribers and casuals alike, I asked Frank, in the absence of Lester who was in San Francisco, to cut the number and close the scene with Lederer's "Yes, by God, I am" and his stomp off. This, I understand, was done to the improvement of the whole.

Soon after Lester's return, I telephoned him inquiring about the business and reception. He gave me his usual gloomy routine, repeated in his enclosure herewith. During the course of the conversation, he murmured something about the desirability of further dialogue cuts. This was too much for me to be tactful about, so I shriveled and then pulverized him by a plain, unrestrained appraisal of his inattention to the need for adequate

---

[37] Elsie Janis was a singer, actor, writer, songwriter, and director, both on stage and screen, starting in the aughts and teens. During World War I she became known as the "Sweetheart of the AEF" (American Expeditionary Force) for entertaining the troops.

preparation and rehearsal, and invited him to retire as a half-baked editor, and devote more of his time to being a producing manager. After which, I expect, we shall no longer be represented in the repertoire of the Los Angeles Civic Light Opera Association. Which is all right, too. These furbished-up revivals take almost as much concentration and thought as would discussions on new projects.

I suppose we shall be hearing from Howard about Lester's "Hearts and Flowers" supplication. Since his treatment of you was okay, anything you see fit to do in the matter will be endorsed by me. Thrown in here now to save a lot of time and three-cornered correspondence.

Best love from us all,

As ever yours,

Jerry.

Hall Johnson was an important black composer and arranger, and in 1925 founded the Hall Johnson Negro Choir, noted for its performance of spirituals, arranged by Johnson. His choir played a significant part in the play *Green Pastures*, which opened on Broadway in 1930, and its film adaptation in 1936. The play discussed below was undoubtedly Johnson's *Run, Little Chillun*, which opened and closed in August of 1943.

Oscar Hammerstein to Hall Johnson, June 25, 1942

Dear Mr. Johnson:-

I read your play with great interest. The songs are apparently such an integral part of the play's emotional quality that no final opinion upon it would be intelligent without first hearing the music.

My general comment, after making this reservation, would be that the dialogue has an earthy and authentic feeling and that the characterization has a corresponding flavor of honesty. It seemed in the first half of the play that there was a great deal of to-do about matters that were not terribly important. This came from overemphasis on scenes and touches that should have been brushed off much more lightly than they were.

In the second half (I am dividing it into halves arbitrarily. I might be speaking about the last third) the play mounts in importance and interest but I believe there will be confusion in the minds of the audience, when, after believing that Hester has died and hearing a sermon delivered over her body, they are then introduced to a vision which she is having while still alive. Do you think it is necessary for Hester to be thought dead? Could she not merely be in a coma while the services are held for Mary, and then follow with her "vision"?

I have no definite news about CARMEN JONES and I have made no definite commitments about casting (will you please tell this to Miss Shaw?) I have finished the second act and am hard at work on the third.

Mr. Bennett, at this point, feels that he would like to handle the whole musical job which would include the vocal as well as instrumental arrangements.

I would like to tell you how glad I am to have met you on my recent trip to California. I want also to thank you for the great help you were to me while I was there.

If any chance brings you East this summer, I hope that you will let me know when you arrive in town.

All good wishes.

Sincerely,

Oscar Hammerstein to Edna Ferber, June 25, 1942

Dear Edna:-

For three months I have been trying to work out a deal with Metro Goldwyn Mayer to have them back a stage production of SHOW BOAT. I am writing you now to tell you that this is practically assured. They are not putting up all the money but they are putting up so much that it will be quite easy for me to raise the balance.

The next problem is, of course, one of casting. Unless we can get a line up of people who will compare favorably with the original cast, we won't go ahead. The two strikes already called on us are the refusals of both Robeson and Winninger to take their old roles. This is due to concert commitments for one and picture commitments for the other. I am, however, scouring the nation for others to take their place and it may be that we can bolster ourselves up in other parts.

The hottest prospect for a box office name that we have is Dinah Shore for the part of "Julie". Her great radio popularity has made her the #1 draw in the country.

I believe that we can also get Edna Mae Oliver for her original part.

It's not going to be an easy job but I believe it's worth while trying to pull off. I will keep in touch with you and let you know how things are coming—when they start to come.

I don't know if you are still speaking to me after the indecisive and shilly-shallying manner in which I opened and closed a certain trunk, but you can't stop me from writing to you.

All good wishes.

Sincerely,

Jerome Kern to Oscar Hammerstein, June 27, 1942

Dear Oscar:

Well sire, I certainly got snarled up day before yesterday at five p.m. when I had overlapping appointments with Erich Leinsdorf, the Metropolitan conductor, and Werner Janssen. This was bad enough, but lo and behold, enter Miss Grena Sloan with accompanist Miss Lois Mosely, of whom Otto can give you an earful. She was the neurotic, brilliant pianist who did a lot of "Roberta" rehearsal work.

Accompanying the two wenches was a Max E. Gilmore, attorney-at-law, who protects Miss Sloan's legal interests and moreover, is a friend of Hugo Rombert, who telephoned the rendezvous to me, which, of course, I promptly forgot.

Well, we heard Miss Grena Sloan strut her stuff. As you know, she is a beautiful girl and gave pretty good interpretation of a couple of a couple of numbers, and an excellent one of "Bill." But I say to you, as I ruthlessly said to her, privately of course, that I think with her equipment, she'd be the boob of the world, did she attempt to follow Helen Morgan in a revival of "Show Boat". They'd simply shrivel her and we'd be badly injured.

Let's make up our minds that Dinah Shore is our baby, and if things are coming to any kind of a head, get in touch with the William Morris agency in New York, and I shall do the same here, to make a sort of quasi reservation. From my end, I shan't even wait until you give me an approximate date.

Reverting to Miss Sloan, to soften it up a bit, I asked if she thought she could handle Magnolia. (She really is a beautiful girl). With the intrepidity of youth, and confidence born of being not only spoiled, but stuck on herself much as was Frances Mercer, she said "Sure." So I promised I would try to get a script so that she could read the part, either to herself, to me, or to you. Well, I ain't got one. Do you want to waste the poor wretch's time and send her one? Or shall I tell Mr. Gilmore that other arrangements have already been made. Now you give me one.

Shan't sign this myself, because our little Penelope, Nancy Kenyon Young, is welcoming her Ulysses, Corporal Carleton Scott Young, tomorrow, and will close this with my best, while she is still calm and collected. Couldn't dream of busting in on them tomorrow.

Edna Ferber to Oscar Hammerstein, June 28, 1942

Dear Oscar:-

From time to time I've read about the MGM SHOW BOAT possibility. I am, of course, enormously interested to learn from you that things are fairly hopeful so far as production is concerned.

Perhaps others have said to you what I'm now saying: PORGY AND BESS hasn't suffered for lack of the original cast. Robeson was no better than Bledsoe, except vocally, perhaps. Bledsoe was more the negro cook and loafer, though his voice is not the magnificent thing that Robeson has to offer. Robeson is a shade elegant for my taste.

Could Bobby Clark passably do Cap'n Andy. And what's the name of the man who plays the station master in Mrs. Miniver? Though British, I suppose. Of course Winninger's vitality and bounce were so marvelous. It will be hard to duplicate those qualities. But please, please remember how awful Howard Marsh was. And our Magnolia was no dream girl. Something tells me SHOW BOAT will go in a big way.

I wasn't too upset about what happened to SARATOGA TRUNK. Those things don't upset me. Nice if they happen to turn out well, but if they don't, why---what of it!

Edna.

Anyway, that awful stuff between Elly and Whosis (Puck and White[38]) needn't be in it. That's nice.

My casting suggestions (above) aren't very happy ones. But if I have some ideas may I send them along? And if I can be of any help please let me know. I'd love it. And how about coming out here some day, or are you folks wedded to Bucks.

Jerome Kern to Oscar Hammerstein, June 30, 1942

Dear Oscar:

I was so glad to get your nice long letter of June 25th this morning, because I tried desperately to get you on the telephone in New York late yesterday afternoon. I happened to be at Arthur Lyons', when he mentioned somewhat vaguely, it is true, but anyway it was a disquieting mention, that there was some project of a "Show Boat" revival with M. S. Benthem, -- you know, the former agent, and, I think, not much of a guy.

It seems that Arthur's ex-wife, Ila Rhodes, was slated for an audition with Benthem yesterday afternoon, June 29th, for Magnolia. This is so outrageously out of line, that I thought a wholesale madness had come upon all you fellows in the East. Ila is perhaps one of the prettiest girls ever seen. They tell me she can sing, and Arthur, mind you, who is no longer married to her, says that she is a superior actress. But when it comes to Magnolia, even he agreed that it was laughable to suppose that this nineteen year old peacherino could ever play the mature Magnolia. If she has skill, she might skin through the Ontario street scene, and even "After the Ball". But the guitar audition and finale ultimo are out of the question.

And now, to tackle your letter, paragraph by paragraph:

Metro advance, $35,000 cash—okay.

M-G-M present—okay. Shouldn't it be presents?

---

[38] Husband and wife Sammy White and Eva Puck played Ellie and Frank in the original *Show Boat*.

Sharing the load with you of taking on the responsibility of raising the additional $20,000—a reluctant but firm n.g. I am not flush enough to put up any funds myself, and simply cannot violate the creed against trying to interest capital in any venture to which I am not an early stake-holder with my own dough. Would feel more of a guilty poltroon,[39] did you not write off the finances as a very small part of the problem of an "S.B." revival.

As for the proper cast, and a noteworthy production, I have discussed this briefly with you out here, and as Eva is so genuinely worried about the jeopardy attached to my being in New York when the days and nights are an inferno, it is as well not to count on the questionable assistance I would be in the very departments, casting and production, except for consultation over l.d. on the former.

Dinah Shore, Edna May Oliver—enthusiastically okay. Have a strong hunch that, given Dinah Shore, we can scrape by with almost any kind of a competent roster for the others.

Bobby Clark—to me is an unknown quantity, except when behind a trick cigar. But I am certainly prepared to take your appraisal of him as a ten strike. When it comes to unction, there is no comparison between him and what the vats and distilleries have left of Charlie, the sodden old dope.

Lanny Ross has a definite radio drag with a big section of this country's Aunt Hettys. He's a self-opinionated young man, much too good a singer to be classified as pure conceit, and if he doesn't try to <u>act</u> dashing, couldn't contribute less than any of the other C minuses we have drawn hitherto. The whole truth of the matter is that Ravenal should never have been played by a singer. Not only are singers lousy actors congenitally, but the better Ravenal sings, the less one believes in his having to resort to pawning <u>the</u> ring and <u>the</u> walking stick. If the audiences weren't intoxicated with our entrancing words and music (a detonation from the Bronx) they would say, why doesn't the son-of-a-bitch get a job as a singer, to keep his daughter in that beautiful, Urbanesque convent, just as does poor, drab Magnolia, with much inferior singing equipment.

What the hell has happened to you? Are you softening up, that you are impressed by any <u>one</u> or any<u>thing</u> from Gilbert and Sullivan revivals? Am

[39] Coward.

prepared now to underwrite that neither Mary nor Katherine Roach will make anything but a wooden or an arch Nola.

Sammy White—okay except for his bilious over-playing in "The Parson's Bride." His snorts, snarls and bedroom noises, the while the lame-brain tries to be funny, are impossible to take. Incidentally, with him, plus Bobby Clark, we must be on the acutest guard—and this takes in Magnolia, too, and Ellie—against any exaggerated, tongue-in-the-cheek attitude toward the preposterous corn of your burlesque melodrama. Unless it is stiffly and stiltedly serious, it becomes a pain in the neck to the real audience, and makes a monkey of the hillbilly in the box and the stage audience in tot.

Sheriff, Windy, Trocadero manager and Rubberface—okay.

If Gretl Urban hasn't absurd ideas and has Joe's sketches, designs and blueprints, okay, of course, although I am not prepared to go the whole way with you upon your reversal.

Exterior Show Boat, filigreed balustrades and so on, interior and exterior—okay. As for the rest, surely the production can be somewhat simplified. If you remember the army of stagehands and electricians that Zieggy supported, it must strike you that he was as profligate as he was when he saddled us with the Sidell sisters.

It is not very important, and maybe it is only since I have been bitten by the 'Scenario' virus, but I wonder whether, beginning with the overture, Rus couldn't profitably cast a 1942 eye on the orchestral fabric. I don't mean to shove in piano and/or saxophones, but if there are weaknesses, a little not too costly strengthening here and there might be an important improvement. Our ears and Rus', too, after all, are fifteen years older. So much for the "Slowpoke."

[MGM film] Cavalcade—loathsome word. I have neither heard from nor seen Arthur Freed for a couple of weeks, but I just telephoned his office and his secretary tells me he left for New York last Friday, the 26th, and has your New York and Doylestown addresses. Funnily enough, I don't share your apprehension on clearances. Wattenberg, after all, can come out here representing T. B. Harms Company and its interests bound up with collaborators' estates, etc. Howard writes me today that he will be out here soon, and can relieve you and Otto of any embarrassment in the clearing of those numbers we have done together which may be on the list of desiderata. By rights, I suppose this should include everything we have ever done together, and the picture would take nine hours to unroll. If I ever started worrying about this, and my collaborators suddenly getting tough, I would probably call the whole thing off, which I am inclined to do anyway, every odd hour.

Well sir, this is my move, and if I have knocked off M. S. Bentham and put him on the rim, I'll offer a 'double'.

Love to all from us both,

Ever yours,

Jerry.

P.S. Assume you are not counting on Paul Robeson, in which case, grapevine advises investigation of tall, gangling, good-looking negro who gooled 'em with 'Old Man River' at Café Society. Grapevine nothing! It was Dinah the Shore, herself. So long –

Oscar Hammerstein to Edna Ferber, July 1, 1942

Dear Edna:-

Thank you for your letter. Bobbie Clark is one of my candidates, but I am afraid he is pretty well sewed up in a hit—STAR AND GARTER.

I agree with you in principle that a solid play like SHOW BOAT, with characters so definitely drawn should not be hard to cast. I think we have been plagued by the bugbear of Winninger and the rest of the cast long enough. I have some trouble convincing Jerry about this but the only way to get the show on is to keep punching.

I come to town for two days every week and crowd them with auditions. Sooner or later such splendid perseverance will be rewarded, I know.

It will be nice with some of that Puck and White material eliminated, won't it?

It is nice of you to ask us up to Connecticut and we would both love to come. The only trouble is this; we have a big crowd of assorted children at Doylestown, who raise hell with us if we don't come home for weekends and I don't blame them.

Maybe some day, after I obey an impulse I frequently have to drown them all, Dorothy and I will pop in on you.

All good wishes.

Sincerely,

Edna Ferber to Oscar Hammerstein, July 6, 1942

Dear Oscar, I needn't tell you that practically everyone who has ever sat in a theatre, dark or bright, thinks he or she could cast a play—and of course, write one.

I'm no longer sure that I could write one, but I do think I'm a fair caster. Anyway, over the week-end I had some odd ideas. Janet Fox, had an idea or two, too. I send them to you for what they're worth.

I repeat it's nonsense to think that Show Boat can't be as well as it originally was. Terris and Marsh were less than fair. Of course Winninger was marvelous, and no one can replace Morgan. But otherwise------

Allen Jones—Nelson Eddy (too expensive)—a boy named Gregory Peck (unknown, handsome, a good voice but I think an untrained one)— the guy in BY JUPITER but I suppose he's set for the year. RAVENAL.

Is Ernest Truex a crazy idea for a possible for Cap'n Andy?

The Hartmans for Elly and Schultzy? (Well I just though I'd include everyone who came to mind. And Mrs. H. has a kind of engaging quality, and is a pretty good actress.)

I've never seen Helen Gleeson. A possible Magnolia? I wouldn't know.

Anyone in any of these vaudeville shows around town—Cap'n Andy or Steve or Magnolia? Of course, I suppose I shouldn't say that Deanna Durbin would make a rawther [*sic*] nice but expensive Magnolia. Hoping this finds you the same, beg to remain,

Rspctfly,

E. F.

Leighton Brill to Oscar Hammerstein (excerpt), circa July 6, 1942

Pay absolutely no attention to this most beautiful letter head, all it means is that a ream of it was floating around the office at Danmour [?]—Yes, I'm still there—starting on my second serial, a lively lively stinker entitled "The

Batman"—This opus was <u>bought</u> by Columbia—It is I'm told (but don't believe) a comic strip that the young bastards love—The book certainly is issued monthly has a circulation of over a million—Oh the pity of it.

It is about a masked mess who float[s] around accompanied by a younger idiot known as Robin the Boy Wonder.

My first epic now known as The Secret Code goes before the camera next week with Paul Kelly + Anne Nagle as leads.

Oscar Hammerstein to Leighton Brill (excerpt), July 8, 1942

You request in addition to these answers some product you call "Chittle-chattle". Our cow and calf are doing well. Our two dogs killed 115 chickens and now we have no more dogs. The barley has been cut and the wheat is waiting for the combiner to come and if it doesn't come soon, we are going to lose a good field of wheat. The hay has been cut and the oats are coming along. Jimmy is raising rabbits—as if anyone had to—and Alice having finished her course at Stevens is looking for a job that will help in our war effort.

Frank Orsatti to Oscar Hammerstein, July 13, 1942

Dear Oscar:

Do you need any money for CARMEN JONES? Arthur Freed and a few others would like to put some money in it, if you need it.

I talked to L. B. about the property, and inasmuch as they will do "Cabin In the Sky", etc., I have him very interested in it.

I would like very much to see a script, if you could send me one immediately.

Also, can I help you cast it here, from the "Cabin In the Sky" group?

Please let me know if there is anything I can do on this production to help.

On "The Life of Jerome Kern", Freed will let me know in a week or so when he wants you to start on it, but it is definite that you will be on this picture.

Best wishes.

Sincerely,

FOrsatti

Oscar Hammerstein to Frank Orsatti, July 16, 1942

Dear Frank:-

I have arranged with Max Gordon to produce CARMEN JONES. This relieves me of the bother of raising money for it. I would, however, like very much to have Arthur Freed and the group you refer to have an interest in it, because I have great confidence in its success. If you will let me know approximately to what extent they would like to go in, I will take it up with Max.

We haven't any definite figures lined up yet but I am pretty sure the budget will be $50,000. The investors will be paid off with the first money and thereafter share the profits fifty-fifty with the producer. The play will be very inexpensive to run backstage so if it is a success the net will be unusually large.

Will you let me hear from you about this within the next week. I know that Max is raising money for it now and I would like to get your group in before he is all filled up.

Thank you for your offer to help with the production. The thing I am most stuck for now is a tenor. The best one I have heard is Charles Holland, who is out there, but I didn't like his appearance and his manner of dramatizing the song. His voice is wonderful.

I know the CABIN IN THE SKY cast pretty well and there is no one in it whom I could use, except Kenneth Spencer, whom I think I will use in SHOW BOAT.

Kindest regards.

The National Urban League was founded as The Committee on Urban Conditions Among Negroes in 1910, changing to its new name in 1920. Its focus was and is a wide range of civil rights issues, but a fundamental one is to seek fairness and equity in the employment of Black people.

Todd Duncan and Anne Brown to Oscar Hammerstein, July 15, 1942

Dear Mr. Hammerstein:

No group of American people lift their heads with greater pride because of their American nationality than our Negro citizens.

Our constitution gives that right. It is that right for all men, and nothing else, that we now defend with all the resources we can command. Yet thirteen million strong, hard-working, industrious and courageous, we Negro Americans are not being used to the full limits of our capabilities, even in this moment of national crises and despite all-out effort.

It is not fair. Just think of us, Americans, struggling for a chance to help preserve that freedom which we cherish so dearly and being denied the right to help make the planes, tanks, ships and guns and all the equipment that will be <u>needed</u> to win this war. Can America afford this?

The National Urban League is pledged to help dispel this discrimination against the Negro, to help us all—Negro and white—to achieve victory. That is why we ask you to contribute as liberally as you possibly can in order that the League can continue to reason with industrialists, to the end that Negroes may help defend this country which all of us love so well.

Do this that we Negroes may continue to be proud of and may help our nation, and thank you.

Sincerely,

Todd Duncan

Anne Brown

P. S. Please make your check payable to National Urban League.

T. D. and A. B.

A notation on this letter suggests that Hammerstein made a donation of $50.

Hammerstein to Todd Duncan and Anne Brown, August 5, 1942

Dear Miss Brown and Mr. Duncan:-

Due to the pressure of other causes being made upon me, the enclosed check is all I can afford at the moment.

Later in the year, however, I hope I will be able to augment this by a larger one.

Meanwhile, I am so interested in the philosophy behind the movement of your League that I would be delighted to help you in other ways, if you can point out to me what I can do.

All good wishes.

Sincerely,

Oscar Hammerstein to Arthur Freed, July 23, 1942

DEAR ARTHUR: I AM GETTING DESPERATE ON THE CAPN ANDY SITUATION. DO YOU THINK IT CONCEIVABLE THAT I MIGHT GET FRANK MORGAN. I HAVE VERY LITTLE HOPE FOR THIS BUT I HAVE NOW GOTTEN DOWN TO THROWING LONG FORWARD PASSES IN THE LAST THREE MINUTES OF PLAY. REGARDS.

OSCAR HAMMERSTEIN, 2ND.

Lester Granger, the National Urban League,[40] to Oscar Hammerstein, August 6, 1942

Dear Mr. Hammerstein:

Your generous response to the appeal made by Miss Anne Brown and Mr. Todd Duncan in behalf of the National Urban League is acknowledged by the official receipt and membership card herewith enclosed. The official records, however, cannot express the appreciation and encouragement that we feel.

The heroic measures that are being taken in our victory effort are apt to naturally over-shadow long-standing causes and programs such as improving the welfare of our Negro population. Your letter heartens us with a confidence that there are still thoughtful citizens who see the emergency nature of our own work as well.

---

[40] The header on the letter states: "For Social Service Among Negroes." The motto on the bottom of the page reads: "Mobilizing Negro Citizens for Victory and Peace."

There are a number of ways in which you can be of help in our program. Realizing that you are on vacation, I am refraining from pointing these out at this time, but will be sure to remind you of your expression of interest after Labor Day, when some of our fall projects get under way. For instance, I am enclosing the draft of one of our projects, a Manual to Guide Industrial Management in the use of Negro labor now and after the war. We realize that the temporary upsurge of Negro employment can disappear after the war as rapidly as it has begun. Our only protection against this possibility is in wise personnel practices by management, intelligent democratic attitudes by white fellow-workers, and efficient performance and diplomatic relationships by Negro workers themselves. Thus, we hope to produce a triad of manuals: one addressed to Management; one to white labor leaders and similar persons; and the third to Negro workers themselves.

The estimated cost of developing, preparing, publishing and distributing the manuals is approximately $5,000. It may be that you can help in this project by interesting possible contributors or securing the cooperation of key industrial leaders, or in some other way that comes to your mind.

Sincerely Yours,

Lester B. Granger,

Executive Secretary.

Myra Finn to Oscar Hammerstein, August 6, 1942

Dear Oc,

I just finished reading your "Carmen". I believe it is your great play. It thrilled me from start to finish, and I felt that I must tell you so. It has more gusto than anything you've written, + yet that gusto does not overshadow the tenderness with which you always write. I don't see how you can wait to have it produced. It should be a sensation.

I am a bit puzzled about the score in the last scene + wish you would explain it. Knowing the original score + libretto as I do, I got a tremendous kick out of your handling of it, but don't think that knowledge at all necessary for appreciation.

Now I can understand what you meant when you said you had such fun writing it. I had more than fun reading it.

Congratulations

Information Please was a popular radio quiz show which first aired in 1938, and ran into 1951. A panel of celebrities and experts would attempt to (wittily) answer questions submitted by listeners. Submitters would win prizes by stumping the panelists. I don't know if Oscar was invited to submit a question or did it on his own, whether or not it was asked, and, if it was, whether or not anyone answered it successfully.

Oscar Hammerstein to Clifton Fadiman, *Information Please*, August 7, 1942

Dear Clifton Fadiman:-

I am asking INFORMATION PLEASE for the names of the composers and librettists of four operas. I am purposely naming operas of which I am certain your experts will know. I feel equally certain that they will not know the names of the librettists because I believe that librettists are the most anonymous people in the world.

Here are the operas:-

Name	Composer	Librettist
Der Rosenkavalier	Richard Strauss	Hugo Von Hofmannstahl
La Boheme	Giacomo Puccini	Giacosa and Illica
Il Trovatore	Giuseppe Verdi	Cammarano
Louise	Gustave Charpentier	(The composer is also the librettist of this one)

All good wishes.

Sincerely,

Oscar Hammerstein, 2nd

Hammerstein's career can rightly be divided as pre-*Oklahoma!* and post-*Oklahoma!* The same can probably be said for the Broadway musical. The following letter is the first we have that relates to what will become *Oklahoma!* By this time, composer Richard Rodgers and lyricist Lorenz Hart were seemingly indelibly linked, having collaborated on the scores for over thirty stage and film musicals. While the shows and scores were largely successes (and even those that weren't tended to generate standards) the collaboration itself was an increasingly strained one, largely because of Hart's drinking and his resulting disappearances and erratic behavior.

Theresa Helburn and Lawrence Langner were among the founders of The Theatre Guild in 1918. As producers the Guild was less focused on commercial success than on bringing new and important works by American and European playwrights to the Broadway stage. Among the playwrights whose works they first championed and premiered were George Bernard Shaw and Eugene O'Neill. The Guild's first association with musicals came in 1925 with Rodgers and Hart's *Garrick Gaieties*, a revue intended as a two-performance benefit but which was so successful it re-opened a few weeks later for a 211-performance run. The first major musical work they produced was Gershwin-Heyward-and-Gershwin's *Porgy and Bess* in 1935—based on Dorothy and DuBose Heyward's play *Porgy* that the Guild had produced in 1929.

In 1931 the Guild produced a play titled *Green Grow the Lilacs* by Lynn Riggs. The play opened to mixed reviews and a disappointing run of sixty-four performances. Still the play struck a chord in some who saw it. In his *New York Times* review, Brook Atkinson wrote that the play "has no interest in the dramatic significance of its material . . . But it has a warming relish of its characters. How alive they are!" In the summer of 1940, there was a well-received production of the play at the Westport Country Playhouse (a theater owned by Langner and his wife). Although the Guild was not noted for producing musicals, it seems Helburn became passionate and focused on the idea that the time was ripe for the Guild to produce one. The precarious financial state of the Guild appears to have been one of the reasons, but with America at war this was also a time when people were looking for lighter fare. According to Tim Carter's exhaustive study on the making of *Oklahoma!*, that process included considering many works that might be adapted and many possible teams to write the show. After settling on *Green Grow the Lilacs*—whose appeal included its strong sense of Americana—an extraordinary range of composers were considered, including Kurt Weill, Aaron Copland, Woody Guthrie, Earl Robinson,

Ferde Grofé, and Paul Bowles. Sometime in June, Helburn and the Guild seemed to have settled on Richard Rodgers.

On July 23, the New York Times reported that "Richard Rodgers, Lorenz Hart, and Oscar Hammerstein 2d will soon begin work on a musical version of Lynn Riggs' folk-play 'Green Grow the Lilacs.'" What's not clear is how much truth there was in that report. Hart may have already determined he did not want to work on the show, and Rodgers was still trying to convince him. Or Rodgers may have determined he did not wish to collaborate with Hart but wanted to provide an opportunity for him to bow out gracefully. Or perhaps things were still in flux and cover was needed while negotiations continued. It wasn't until mid-September that the announcement came: Hart would not be working on the show.

Oscar Hammerstein to Charlotte Greenwood, August 7, 1942

Dear Charlotte:-

I am working on a musical play with Rodgers and Hart which will be produced by the Theatre Guild later this season. Before going into further details, we would like to know whether you would be interested in playing a part on Broadway later this season or whether you have become inextricably woven into Hollywood and "pitchers".

If you would be interested in our project, I will be glad to tell you more about it, and if you are not, I would like to know as soon as possible so that I won't have my heart set too much on getting you.

I am mapping out the story outline now and have already thought about you so much that I am going to be very disappointed if you turn me down.

Please let me hear from you soon. Dorothy and I send our love to both of you.

Sincerely,

Charlotte Greenwood was a gangly comic actress and dancer who began performing in Vaudeville in the Teens, moving to theater, film, and radio. She starred (as the ironically named Tiny) in Oscar's *Three Sisters* in London in 1934. Oscar wanted her for *Oklahoma!* but film commitments made it impossible, but she ultimately played Aunt Eller in the film. Greenwood's letter below is heavily illustrated with hand-drawn faces of various expressions throughout; I describe the expressions where they appear.

Charlotte Greenwood to Oscar Hammerstein, August 18, 1942

Dear Oscar

If your'n a talking abot thet that Aunt Eller- [quizzical face] 'f it had to be me Ill loose mere'n a leg- [surprised face]. (page 85. (Green Grow the Lilacs). But oh; Oscar it's a purty, kinda thought. At the moment Im waiting for my Nat Goldstone to notify me more definitely about a picture to start in late October or November -.

Ive just finished a not very large part in "Springtime in the Rockies". Miranda, Grable, Horton, Romero, Payne, -.

Im wanted [face looking sideways]? for ten weeks in Detroit but have not been able to clear a date—on this - it is necessary for me to come East for one week—and by the time this happens I should know more—about all this mince meat" [face looking upward] My reservations are around the 19th-.....21st of this month-.

Your letter gave me a real thrill—as once again I pictured the first act of "Three Sisters!-. and still think a grand character could be made out of her.

Highland Farms sound simply lovely—is that your home now—or are you writing there? If all this is any answer it means Im tremendously interested but as to dates not at all clear- love to you both-

Charlotte.

Oscar Hammerstein to Charlotte Greenwood, August 20, 1942

Dear Charlotte:-

I was very pleased to get your not very coherent letter, the gist of which I take to be that if you were free you would like to play AUNT ELLER. This is a good start, anyway.

My answer is that if we do the show we would certainly like to have you, and when our plans become more definite, I will come after you hot and heavy and with high pressure to make you give out with a more specific answer about your plans.

In answer to your question about Highland Farms—"Is that your home now—or are you writing there"—it is my home and I am writing there.

Both of us send our love,

Sincerely,

On August 20, Louella Parsons—the powerful syndicated Hollywood gossip columnist—wrote: "Here is a dilly of an idea, if you will pardon my slang: Jerome Kern and
Oscar Hammerstein want to put on a musical version of 'Rain' on the stage. They will
do it immediately if they can get Marlene Dietrich to play Sadie Thompson . . . "

Oscar Hammerstein to Louella Parsons, August 27, 1942

Dear Louella Parsons:

I recently read a story in your column to the effect that Jerome Kern and
I were writing a musical version of "Rain" for Marlene Dietrich. It made mighty
good reading too. I found myself wishing it were true. Unfortunately it is not.

I have already planned a very full season which includes a stage revival of
"Show Boat," a musical version of "Green Grow The Lilacs" which I am writing
with Rogers [sic] and Hart for the Theatre Guild, and a version of "Carmen"
for an all-negro cast which I call "Carmen Jones." After these three plays are
produced—and following a few weeks in some quiet sanitarium—I look forward to coming out to Hollywood on a screen play assignment which is at the
moment cooling. This will be somewhere around February.

But I am not waiting that long to see the West Coast crowd. I am
flying out on September 7th to preside over the annual ASCAP dinner and
meeting in the place of our President, Deems Taylor, who cannot come because of his radio commitments.

This is a pretty long-winded way of explaining to you why I cannot
write a show for Marlene Dietrich this year. It reminds me of Joe Cook's explanation of why he did not imitate four Hawaiians.[41]

All good wishes to you.

Sincerely,

Oscar Hammerstein, 2nd

[41] Joe Cook: "I will now give an imitation of three Hawaiians. This is one (whistles) this is another
(plays ukulele) and this is the third (marks time with his foot). I could imitate four Hawaiians just as
easily, but I will tell you the reason why I don't do it. You see, I bought a horse for $50 and it turned out
to be a running horse. I was offered $15,000 for him and I took it. I built a house with the $15,000 and
when it was finished a neighbor offered me $100,000 for it. He said my house stood right where he
wanted to dig a well. So I took the $100,000 to accommodate him. I invested the $100,000 in peanuts
and that year there was a peanut famine so I sold the peanuts for $350,000. Now why should a man
with $350,000 bother to imitate four Hawaiians?"

Jerome Kern to Oscar Hammerstein, August 28, 1942

Dear Oscar:

I have an uncomfortable, uneasy feeling that I have been neglectful in my correspondence with you, and yet, when I look at your file, there really is very little dangling, requiring comment, criticism or decision. You have covered the ground so lucidly and so well as far as "Show Boat" revival is concerned, that until you do your refiguring on the old budget, and have your interview with Mr. Rubin, there really is nothing to say.

The only topic upon which I have been acutely neglectful is that of the audition August 16th, held here for Mary Martin's protégé, Dolores Gray, Mary Martin and husband Halliday being present. Also young Mr. Gray, Dolores' brother, also an accompanist. Mary had been so enthusiastic about the Gray, and so determined not to submit her to motion picture studios before she had a whack at the stage—taking a memo leaf out of her own Mary Martin Hollywood biography—that she certainly excited my curiosity.

In three words, Dolores is a helluva singer, in a magnificent, luscious (Helena Mora, the female baritone, if you remember) kind of way. She has a violoncello voice, and curves to match. Not that she's overblown and Mae Westy—she's just a handsome, voluptuous animal, and I bet turns the bald-headed habituees of night clubs dizzy with what she does with her material. She's distinctly a singer of 'arrangements' and looks like a painting of a night club singer by Vargas.

I pulled no punches with her and told her that the vocal requirements for Julie were very simple, that personality and acting were the important ingredients and that there was no opportunity for her to perform trick or hot arrangements. Neither she nor sponsor Mary are dopey ninnies, and they both countered by submitting that Julie would simply be a showcase and a stepping stone to some cabaret or night club job after the "Show Boat" performance, in which she could turn on the heat.

I was noncommittal about this phase of it, but had been so decided, almost brutally so, about the desirable simplicity and naivete of the Julie performance, that it ended up by my packing her off with my blessing, and forty bucks I happened to have in my pocket to pay for her plane trip to and from San Francisco. The fact that she certainly beats the be-jeesus out of a song, and is a little too mannered, and has too much smoldering behind the eyes, makes me and my personal tastes turn eagerly toward Carol Bruce, who is young, slight, engaging, and attractive, or to Nan Wynn, who is young, fairly slight, not so quite attractive, but is a terrific singer, with lovely eyes and well-shaped, thick nigger lips.

If everyone whose opinion you respect, endorses Arthur Lyons or Jim Barton (I have never seen the guy) I'd be inclined to consider that worry stricken off 'n the list. Arthur, I think, is a good showman, and not a has-been good showman in the old palmy vaudeville and Winter Garden days. His current experience in the industry and in the new vaudeville—radio, makes one respect his judgement on present day talent.

This would seem to leave Magnolia and Parthy the only headaches. I can understand how impressive Norma's performance must have been on a big canvas like St. Louis. Her last performance I saw out here in the revival was just a teensy weensy big [*sic*] holier in fragmentary spots than it should have been, as per the crying finish of the Ontario Street scene.

We're having dinner with Mary Martin a week from Friday, and I can find out about her as Magnolia. You don't seem at all worried about Parthy. Since this is a non-singing part, it is the only one that really bothers me in the casting. Or is your complacency because you have connived with Ferber and are going to slip her into it?

I wish, if you come to cases with Metro, that you would keep me posted about Magnolia and Parthy.

Well, this must be all for now. By this time I suppose you will have received the "Hayfoot Strawfoot" agreement.

Love from all of us, which includes Betty to whom we spoke early this week.

Ever yours,

Jerry

P.S. I don't know whether you have been told that on August 20th, the village idiot, L.O.P. [Louella Parsons] ran a story that you and I are making a musical version of—hold tight now—"Rain", for—and hold tight again—Marlene Dietrich. This was repeated by air commentators and other columnists, who couldn't really go for the "Rain" angle, and edited it into angling for Dietrich for the "Show Boat" revival. Well, you pays your money, and you takes your choice. That's enough hysteria for one day.

Mary Martin became one of the biggest stars on Broadway and the performer most closely associated with Rodgers and Hammerstein, but that would be several years in the future. Martin first made a name for herself introducing "My Heart Belongs to Daddy" in Cole Porter's *Leave it to Me* in 1938. From there she made inroads in Hollywood, starring in a handful of now mostly forgotten films. Hammerstein had considered her for his recently hoped-for revival of *Show Boat* and apparently offered her the role of Laurey in his adaptation of *Green Grow the Lilacs*. At the same time Martin was offered a lead in a new musical, *Dancing in the Streets*. She chose the latter show which had its tryout in Boston the same week as *Oklahoma!* According to Martin, Hammerstein sent her roses with a note that read: "I'm going to send you roses for a long time. Had you accepted the role, I would have written a different show." In 1940, Martin married the Paramount Executive, Richard Halliday, who became her very proactive manager.

Richard Halliday to Oscar Hammerstein, September 14, 1942

Dear Mr. Hammerstein:

As you suggested, Mary read a copy of GREEN GROW THE LILACS by Lynn Riggs over the week-end. She very much regrets that she hadn't read the play while you were here so that she could have talked to you about the manner in which you planned to treat it. She confesses that she is deeply puzzled and because of your doing the treatment, is as interested as she is puzzled.

In addition, Mary feels that it would be most necessary, because as I think you will agree this would be a very important step for her, to read a treatment before she could decide. If there is one available, would you let her see it at this time?

I assume that you were unable to get Buddy de Sylva on the phone. In the few days since you have been here, there is no other news to send on regarding the contract situation.

Will all best wishes,

Dick Halliday

Oscar Hammerstein to Richard Halliday, September 17, 1942

Dear Dick Halliday:-

I can understand Mary's bewilderment at reading the original play, GREEN GROW THE LILACS because Dick Rodgers and I are making a very free adaptation of the story. The characterization, on the other hand, will be very much the same.

I called Buddy deSylva long distance two days ago and learned from him that Mary would not be available for a Broadway play before March. Even then, he said, he couldn't guarantee anything definite. He asked me if I had spoken to her about the general idea of doing a play and I said that I hadn't. He said he would speak to her about it.

If at some reasonable time before March, I could be sure that Mary would be available, I would like nothing better than to put off my all-star revival of SHOW BOAT until then. At that time I could get a successful cast, probably Charles Winninger or Frank Morgan for "Cap'n Andy" and Paul Robeson, who will by that time have completed his concert season. With Mary as "Magnolia" this would be a very exciting venture.

Let me know when you have any news. My best wishes to you both.

Sincerely,

Oscar Hammerstein, 2nd.

Len Mence to Oscar Hammerstein, October 21, 1942

Dear Oscar

Even as I write it seems futile, for the few recorded occasions when letters, such as this, have been productive of results, have not been within my experience.

I have reached an all time low in my abortive career, being with J.J. Shuberts garbled monstrosity of the Merry Widow—notices awful JJ—worse.

If you are producing, "How Green was my Valley" I can do Welsh accent, quite creditably, why not give an old disillusioned Hammerstonian a chance at a part (cut later!) I have been too spoiled to remain with this abortion of the Widow.

And so this letter goes forth on its forlorn quest.

Kindest Regards to you and Dorothy.

As always

Len

P.S. I played Apapolus in My Sister Eileen (the Buloff part) lots of fun? Muriel Angelus is very good as a singer and actress

Oscar Hammerstein to Len Mence, October 28, 1942

Dear Len:-

Thank you for your amusing letter anent the MERRY WIDOW. At the moment, I haven't even a part that might be cut which I could offer you. My only theatrical prospects are CARMEN JONES, which is for a negro cast and I never thought you were very attractive in burnt cork, and GREEN GROW THE LILACS, a play I am writing for the Theatre Guild, no part in which seems suited to you. After one or both of these are out of the way, I expect to go to Hollywood.

I do wish, however, that when the MERRY WIDOW returns to the oblivion for which she seems destined, that you would ring Dorothy and me up and come out with us. And remind me to tell you the story about Harry Tate and George Robey.

Sincerely,

Oscar Hammerstein to Laurence Schwab (excerpt), October 28, 1942

I will send you more deathless work from my pen very soon. When I finish the book of GREEN GROW THE LILACS next week, I will send it to you if only because you seem skeptical about the wisdom of my adapting it. I don't guarantee that you will change your mind but I think I should give you the opportunity.

This tantalizing letter to the comic actor Charlie Ruggles hints at a project that never materialized, and that even before *Oklahoma!* opened Rodgers and Hammerstein were intending to continue their partnership, *and* that it might extend beyond the writing of shows to the producing of them. Although best known for his dozens of film roles, in 1928 Ruggles appeared in Hammerstein's *Rainbow*, and in 1929 in Rodgers' *Spring is Here*.

Oscar Hammerstein to Charles Ruggles, November 17, 1942

Dear Charlie:-

The last time you were in New York we had a telephone conversation in which you threw out the attractive news that you and Charlie Winninger would be receptive to a proposition of doing a show together in New York. Dick Rodgers and I have an idea for a musical play in which you and Charlie would be teamed and linked with Vera Zorina in a story which has a strong comedy basis. Because we are at the moment immersed in finishing another play which the Theatre Guild is about to produce, I won't be able to send you a scenario of this story for a few weeks. But meanwhile, Dick and I are most interested to know whether the crack still goes and whether you think you and Charlie would be available for a play to be produced this spring.

Another thing I would have to know is, that if you opened in New York and the play was a success would you both be willing to continue in it through the New York run and for a season on the road. If you didn't feel that you wanted to do this the project would not be worth while for us because the show will be so tightly built around both of you that your withdrawal would abruptly and completely knock it out of commission.

Are you willing to risk leaving those swimming pools for a substantial time? Please have a talk with Charlie and let me know how you both feel about this. As soon as I can, I will write out at least a rough layout of our idea.

All good wishes to you both.

Sincerely,

Oscar Hammerstein, 2nd.

Oscar Hammerstein to Billy Rose, November 19, 1942

Dear Billy:-

Here is my adaptation of CARMEN which I promised to send.

It sounds much better with music but I hope you will get some enjoyment out of it just as it is.

Kindest regards.

Oscar Hammerstein to Ralph Blum, November 19, 1942

Dear Ralph:-

Thank you very much for the very sweet letter you addressed to Dorothy and me. It now makes me feel almost guilty to tell you that we are not coming out. The contract is all drawn up, awaiting my signature but I find that I cannot sign it because in view of the present tax situation, I would make no money.

It is a rather complicated story but the gist of it is this:-

That after paying taxes and expenses, I would wind up with just about as much as I would staying right here and doing nothing. My income from sheet music and records (without new numbers) and from A.S.C.A.P. and stock rights and radio rights on my plays, amounts to about the same as I would net after a year's work in California. The slight balance would be consumed by extra expenses which I do not incur if I remain with my family on the farm. The only way for me to substantially increase my static income is to have a successful play on which there is no ceiling and against which there is no extraordinary charge, commissions or living expenses. This probably sounds fantastic to you but that is the way it adds up.

I have informed Frank of my decision but I don't know whether he has told the studio yet so I would appreciate it if you accepted this as confidential information for the time being.

Dorothy and I miss you both very much and we regret that we cannot take advantage of your invitation which we appreciate deeply.

Love to you both.

Oscar Hammerstein, 2nd

Oscar Hammerstein to Arthur Freed, MGM, November 27, 1942

Dear Arthur:-

I have recently written to Frank Orsatti telling him why I am unable to go ahead with the proposed two-year deal at Metro. I am anxious for you to understand the circumstances that force me to this decision, because I am deeply appreciative of the confidence you and L.B. have expressed in me and I would not lightly throw aside the opportunity you offer.

The core of the trouble is that after moving to the Coast and working at the studio for two years, I would wind up by making no money at all! This is a fantastic statement but it is mathematically true. It has nothing to do with the proposed "ceiling on incomes". The $65,000 a year the studio offered is just within the limit. The problem arises because I have a fairly substantial income without working. This consists of royalties from A.S.C.A.P., sheet music, records and the stock and radio rights of my old plays (I am not considering any new plays or songs I may write—just the income of my old catalogue which goes along at a surprisingly steady and non-fluctuating rate) These earnings, added to whatever dividends and interest I receive from securities, nets me, after taxes, a sum that is only a few thousand dollars less than I get when I add to it the income I would receive from Metro and subtract commissions and taxes. Even this small balance would be consumed by the expense of moving my large family to California and maintaining them there while still owning two homes here in the East.

I hate to take up your time with this lengthy recitation of my personal problems but it is the only way I can make clear to you why I cannot possibly go ahead on the proposed basis. The only way I can substantially add to my normal static income is (1) writing a successful show, against which I don't have to incur these extra expenses and (2) taking separate assignments in Hollywood not involving a permanent change in residence so that I can deduct the travelling and living expenses involved.

There is another not inconsiderable item and that is the fact that while living at Pennsylvania I have no state income tax. At any rate, this has all been computed carefully. My lawyer, Howard Reinheimer and I have spent many hours with pad and pencil figuring every possible angle and this is the way it adds up. You see, if I had no source of income here in the East it would be profitable for me to move to the West and work under a contract like this. But having an income the increased earnings under the new tax situation become so ridiculously small that it just isn't worth while.

Again I want to thank you and L.B. and I hope you will both understand that, much as I enjoy working with you, I cannot afford to give up so much time with no hope of financial reward. The tax situation is at present full of crazy, paradoxical cases and I just happen to be one of them. I have told Frank that if you want me to come out there on any specific job, either as a writer or as your associate in any particular production, I will be very happy to come. I would particularly like to work on the Kern "Cavalcade" or on my grandfather's biography.

I have just finished the adaptation of GREEN GROW THE LILACS for the Theatre Build [*sic*]. (as a matter of fact, my script has been sent out to your studio. I would like you to read it) I am now working with Dick Rodgers on the songs and we expect to go into rehearsal next month, opening in New York about Feb. 1.

I hear extravagent [*sic*] reports about your production of CABIN IN THE SKY. What a great achievement if this finally cracks the old prejudice against negro pictures—a great thing for pictures and a great thing for the colored people.

My best wishes to you and L.B. Please explain my position to him.

As ever,

Oscar

Although *Carmen Jones* was written before *Oklahoma!* it opened eight months after. The primary reason for the delay was difficulty in casting the show. Napoleon Reed was working in the Chicago stockyards when he auditioned for Oscar. Reed was cast as an alternate to play Joe, then won the part entirely when it was revived at City Center in 1945.

Oscar Hammerstein to Napoleon Reed, December 22, 1942

Dear Mr. Reed:-

I was sorry that you had to rush off so quickly the other day under conditions which may have depressed you.

Billy Rose was as enthusiastic about your voice as I am but he had, as I told you, serious reservations about clarity of diction. This is a department about which I am not so worried because I feel confident that rehearsals can cure troubles of this sort. If I were producing the play myself, I would not give the subject a second thought and you would have a contract by this time. But I have been unable to finance the project myself and it is quite likely that Mr. Rose will be the producer. In this case, I cannot guarantee that I can convince him that you are the best man in the country for the part but I can assure you that I will try, and also state my belief that, after looking around as I have done, Mr. Rose will agree with me.

I want to thank you for taking the trouble to come on all the way from Chicago to sing for us and I take this opportunity of extending my best wishes for a Merry Christmas and a Happy New Year.

Very sincerely,

Chapter Five

1943

Facing increasing difficulties in casting *Carmen Jones*, Oscar approached the baritone, Todd Duncan, the original Porgy in *Porgy and Bess*, for the male lead—a tenor part.

Oscar Hammerstein to Todd Duncan (*Porgy and Bess* Company, Chicago), January 4, 1943

Dear Mr. Duncan:-

As you may have read in the paper, Billy Rose is going to present my adaptation of CARMEN, to be sung by a negro cast. I have been searching in vain for a tenor to play the leading role (Don Jose in the original). Those few who possessed the right vocal equipment have not convinced me that they could meet the dramatic requirements of the role. Robert Russell Bennett, my musical consultant in this work, tells me that it is not at all inconceivable to lower this part to the baritone range—and this is where you come in. Would you be interested in playing the role for us after you have concluded your engagement with PORGY AND BESS? If you are interested, Mr. Rose and I will come out to Chicago next week. He has never heard you sing and that will be the main object of our visit, and while we are there we could have a talk with you about the general idea.

I assume you realize that, contrary to some false reports, this is in no sense a "swing Carmen." From the auditions I have had in Los Angeles, Chicago, and New York during the past eight months, I am confident that my version of CARMEN will be sung every bit as well as it is sung at the Metropolitan Opera House. And while it may sound bizarre to transplant to a negro community in North Carolina a story original laid in Spain, I have done this job so honestly that the result can be nothing less than distinguished, and a credit to the American negro singing actor.

The Letters of Oscar Hammerstein II. Mark Eden Horowitz, Oxford University Press. © Mark Eden Horowitz 2022.
DOI: 10.1093/oso/9780197538180.003.0005

Please let me hear from you as soon as possible as our trip to Chicago next week will hinge upon your answer.

All good wishes,

Sincerely,

Todd Duncan to Oscar Hammerstein, January 7, 1943

Dear Mr. Hammerstein:-

It seems unwise for Todd Duncan to say he is not interested in whatever Oscar Hammerstein has written or adapted, I am, therefore interested. The question of time element, importance of role, suitability of role, producer, other commitments are however necessary constituents which would or would not allow me to participate. I should be pleased to have you and Mr. Rose hear a performance of "PORGY" next week and have a talk after. I am absent one performance a week (off my knees) so that I would appreciate your letting me know the day you see the show. I will be certain to perform.

I can understand very well that you have had a great difficulty in finding a Negro tenor with the vocal equipment, physical appearance, dramatic feeling as well as box office value to do Don Jose. "It's a needle in a haystack", I fear.

I do not agree with you that "it sounds bizarre to transplant to a Negro community in North Carolina a story originally laid in Spain". To the contrary, the warm sunny soil of Spain, the temperament of the Spaniard is certainly not too far distant to the South Carolina Negro. Further, the fundamental emotions that surge from a Bull fight in Spain are surely akin to the brawls, cock-fights, sprees and picnics of the palmetto islands off South Carolina. Surely, your integrity of the theatre as well as your genius spoke to you thusly.

Harold Gumm of Goldie and Gumm, 545 fifth ave is my legal advisor, does all my business and knows my promises as to the immediate future. I suggest that you give him a ring to ascertain what ever you'd like to know. He and you could pretty much decide whether you should come out to Chicago to hear me sing and to talk with me.

Bravo and good luck for your Carmen. Best wishes.

Sincerely,

Todd Duncan

Oscar Hammerstein to Leighton Brill, January 11, 1943

Dear Leighton:-

I feel very guilty because I have not written to you much sooner. My professional career and the Christmas holidays have crowded you out but this is no excuse for not sending word of cheer to the only Red Cross angel of mercy whom I know intimately. Knowing that you are a very practical and realistic angel, I will get right down to the business of news.

Billy Rose will present CARMEN JONES. The date is still indefinite due to casting difficulties and the precedence of GREEN GROW THE LILACS on my schedule. But the fact that I [sic] will produce it is very definite indeed and his ability to meet the budget without passing the hat is well known to you. In fact if CARMEN JONES doesn't get his $75,000, Morgenthau will. I am going to Chicago with him tomorrow to interview TODD DUNCAN on the theory (approved by Russell Bennett) that we might lower the tenor role to a high baritone in order to meet the crisis of finding no colored tenor.

GREEN GROW THE LILACS—still in search of a new title—will probably go into rehearsal about February 1st but we have not yet a full cast. The only people engaged so far being Alfred Drake, Joan Roberts and Betty Card [sic; Garde].

Along about May, I expect to go out to MGM on one of several possible assignments. The most recent one indicated is SHOW BOAT which they intend to remake this year. This seems to me inadvisable if not wholly incredible but who am I to question the wisdom of L.B. Mayer especially if he intends to pay me for his mistakes.

This looks like a very full year but I am nevertheless, anxious to add something else to it. I would very much like to do something in connection with the war beyond keeping up civilian morale by entertaining the home folk. There is always the possibility that I might be lowering the morale. Perhaps you can suggest to me something that I might do. You know that

I don't want to get mixed up in a lot of brawling committees. I am pessimistic about the achievements of the Writer's War Board and all such things. In fact, in the past year, I have already dissipated a good deal of my time and energy toward these sort of things, an investment which I begrudge only because it brought so little return to the nation. I imagine there is some way I might be of assistance to the O.W.I. [The United States Office of War Information] and I will try this by writing to Bob Sherwood but of course, nothing could be as effective as just sitting down and writing a good song. The trouble is, you can't sit down and grit your teeth and say you will write a good song. The idea must in some way jump up at you—as "Paris" did.

Billy is still in Boston. His only achievement since you left is in having a humorous letter published in P.M. yesterday. Alice has just left the hospital after an operation of an essentially female nature which has been highly successful. Next week she is going down to Florida to visit Mike's aunts for ten days before going back to her job which is being held for her. All the rest of the kids are as healthy and troublesome as usual—which means that sometimes they are not healthy and now and then not troublesome. Dorothy's business has, for some unaccountable reason, kept up very nicely. When you were here, did I tell you that Pete Moen has taken over the farm and due to his industry, the Rhose [sic] Island Reds[1] are putting us in the black.

Dorothy and Herb Fields with Cole Porter have turned out a new musical hit starring Ethel Merman called SOMETHING FOR THE BOYS. It is produced by Michael Todd and makes his second hit on Broadway—the fifth for the Fields family. Dorothy and Herb have this one and LET'S FACE IT and Joe with MY SISTER EILEEN, JUNIOR MISS and his new one, THE DOUGHGIRLS which opened three weeks ago and is a substantial success.

Now you tell me your news which I am sure is much more interesting. I suggest that you write on only one side of the paper because, if I know you, the censor will be cutting out two thirds of the letter and that m[a]y affect some uncensorable material on the other side. I hope this remark does not in itself get you in bad with the authorities. I am really very eager to hear from you and if you have not already written please find time and come through.

Love from all,

---

[1] Rhode Island Reds are a breed of chicken.

The Writers' War Board was born in December 1941 as a child of the Authors League. Rex Stout, best known for his Nero Wolfe mysteries, was its chairman. Hammerstein was a founding and active member, though one report suggests he didn't join the leadership of the organization until April of 1943. It was privately organized and run as a domestic propaganda organization, yet it was sponsored and subsidized by the government. Among its missions, as described in its first annual report, were to:

> Serve as liaison between American writers and U.S. government agencies seeking written work that will directly or indirectly help win the war; and place ideas or work submitted to the board with appropriate government agencies. Examples include fiction, articles and songs; radio material for broadcast; speeches and style manuals; scripts for troop shows; radio broadcasts and personal appearances by writers.

Oscar founded a sub-organization, the Music War Committee. After the War, the Writers' War Board evolved to become the Writers' Board for World Government, with which Oscar continued his close association.

Oscar Hammerstein to Leighton Brill, February 15, 1943

Dear Leighton:-

To my great amazement, I have heard not a word from you and the only purpose in my writing this letter is to tell you that I wrote you a long letter sometime ago and the reason this cannot be long is that I am in rehearsal for a week now with the Theatre Guild show and I still have three songs to write. Please have Joe Stalin take care of the war for a few moments and sit down and write me a full report.

I will write to you after the Boston opening—how long will depend on how the show goes. Bill has finally shipped and is about to be rated a 3rd Class Petty Officer, Quartermaster. Reggie is stage-managing Joe Fields' DOUGHGIRLS—the newly formed Chicago Company. The New York Company is a big hit.

We all send our love.

Ralph Blum to Oscar Hammerstein, March 3, 1943

BUDDY DE SYLVA[2] INTERESTED IN YOU AND DICK RODGERS DOING SCORE FOR IMPORTANT FORTHCOMING MUSICAL[3] FOR FRED MACMURRAY AND DOROTHY LAMOUR WHICH WOULD MEAN YOU WOULD HAVE TO COME TO THE COAST WITHIN THE NEXT COUPLE OF WEEKS. IF YOU ARE INTERESTED WOULD YOU PLEASE ADVISE ME. AM ALSO WIRING DICK. BEST

RALPH H. BLUM

Oklahoma! began its out-of-town tryouts in New Haven on March 11, with the title *Away We Go!* From there it moved to Boston, through March 27. Changes made out-of-town included cutting, replacing, and adding songs. Audience and critical reactions were largely positive. Friends, colleagues, and theater professionals traveled to see the show and sometimes to offer advice. Among them was Max Gordon, also one of the show's investors.

Max Gordon to Oscar Hammerstein (Ritz Hotel, Boston), March 22, 1943

Dear Oscar:

Did I tell you I thought you ought to try to bring the girls out sooner in Act I? You might do this by some judicious cutting without disturbing your story thread.

The business in Boston certainly shows they want the show there. I only hope they are nice to you the opening night. At least, with the Theatre Guild audience there you won't have that usual first night tough gang.

All best.

Yours,

Max

---

[2] Songwriter Buddy DeSylva also became a Hollywood producer. His films ranged from Shirley Temple vehicles to the screwball comedies of Preston Sturges, to the film noir *Double Indemnity*.
[3] The "forthcoming musical" film was *And the Angels Sing*, which starred Betty Hutton.

Oscar Hammerstein to Anne Glatterman (Reinheimer office), March 22, 1943

Dear Miss Glatterman:

Here are the bills. The show looks fine so you can pay them.

Best Regards,

Very truly yours,

Oscar Hammerstein.

Oscar Hammerstein (Ritz Carlton, Boston) to Siegfried Herzig (MGM), March 23, 1943

Dear Sig:

Thank you for your kind letter. We are a big hit in Boston and next week we open in New York and I almost wish there were no place called New York and that plays could be produced and shown only to the nice people in other cities, who go to the theatre to enjoy themselves.

All good wishes to you. I may come to California in May and if I do, you will see me whether you like it or not.

As ever

Oscar Hammerstein (Ritz Carlton, Boston) to Lynn Riggs (Company C, Photo Battalion, Wright Field, Ohio), March 23, 1943

Dear Lynn Riggs:

I have not forgotten my promise to send you the songs but I am waiting another week until we get our full set of published compositions, with the new title page and the new title of the play "Oklahoma".

The show is a solid success in Boston and now if we can just make the hurdle over the first night grave diggers in New York, we will all be home.

You will hear from me again soon.

All good wishes

Sincerely,

Oscar Hammerstein.

Photo 12 Rouben Mamoulian directs Joseph Buloff (Ali Hakin) and Celeste Holm (Ado Annie) in *Oklahoma!*, 1943

Oscar Hammerstein to William Hammerstein (excerpt), March 25, 1943

I said I would write to you after the opening in N.Y. and I will. But the show is in such fine shape that I find myself with sufficient leisure and repose to write you from here. This is Thursday. Last Monday we suffered a relapse. The show was slow and low-keyed because of the cast concentrating on changes had lost the pace of the unchanged scenes. So we gave them a good drilling and the result was so successful that in one night we suddenly took on the aura of a hit. People have come up from N.Y. and are swooning. I now believe that here is the nearest approach to "Show Boat" that the theatre has attained. I don't believe it has as sound a story or that it will be as great a success. But it is compatable [*sic*] in quality, and may have a very long life. All this is said in the hope that a handful of beer-stupefied critics may not decide that we have tried to write a musical comedy and failed. If they see that this is different and higher in its intent, they should rave. I know this is

Photo 13 Alfred Drake (Curly) and Joan Roberts (Laurey) in *Oklahoma!*,
circa 1943

a good show. I cannot believe it will not find a substantial public! There
my neck is out.

In an article by syndicated columnist Walter Winchell, he claimed that he had
been sent a telegram (usually credited to Mike Todd) from out-of-town that said
of the show: "No jokes, no legs, no chance." Whoever wrote it, they were wrong.
Oklahoma! opened in New York on March 31. Its success was instantaneous, and it
became more influential than its creators could have imagined. According to Hugh

Fordin, a few hours before the show opened, Oscar said to Dorothy: "I don't know what to do if they don't like this. I don't know what to do because this is the only kind of show I can write."

Betty Garde to Oscar Hammerstein, March 31, 1943

Dear Oscar

You have my lifelong admiration for the beautiful show—a great part of which is due to your knowledge and taste. Thank you for your help. I feel better for it and above all—there's one thing I love—you made that little brown maverick a girl—only you would do it that way!

Sincerely,

Betty

Betty Garde was the original Aunt Eller. In the show's opening number, "Oh, What a Beautiful Mornin'," Curly sings:

> All the cattle are standin' like statues.
> They don't turn their heads as they see me ride by,
> But a little brown mav'rick is winkin' her eye.

Jerome Kern to Oscar Hammerstein, April 17, 1943

Dear Oscar:

This is not the letter you tried to wheedle out of me. In order to come across with that one, I shall have to have more repose, serenity, and news. I don't suppose I have to set forth the reasons why you and Dorothy didn't get telegrams of good wishes before "Oklahoma"'s premiere, or of congratulations after. The general restrictions barring social messages prevented them, and my personal superstition of jinxing the works, did also. But now that you and Dick are riding on one of those steam roller smashes, I can no longer withhold congratulations, in which Betty and Eva heartily join. We are all as delighted as you.

Thanks for the concentrated excerpts from the notices. Sig Herzig showed all the unexpurgated press to me the other day. It was glorious. He, too, takes proprietary pride in the success and is fairly gloating about it.

We had a swell visit, though a short one, with Milton, and found him, under the circumstances, in a splendid frame of mind.

Fine chance of our mulcting Columbia on this job. Don't forget that this time we have a producer who knows many, if not all, the answers. When you run down the list of the Hollywood producers of musical pictures, I'll take Arthur Schwartz every time, inexperience and all. Apart from his unquestioned musical talent, he is conscientious, a good showman, considerate and courteous. He knows entertainment values, and having traveled along not too easy a road, is sympathetic toward our problems.

Someone asked him the other day how he liked having Kern work for him, to which he quipped: "Fine. I'd just order him to 'tote dat barge, lift dat tune', preferably from himself." And there is no nonsense of his approaching the score with sickly awe and reverence. Everything does not go. All of this sounds like whistling in the dark—not dancing. Maybe it is, but I am betting that "Cover Girl" turns out a better picture than "You Were Never Lovelier", which, despite its big box office, was a sickening disappointment.

Lee's accident might have been very serious. As it turned out, barring a few stitches in her temple and a badly bruised knee, nothing more serious has developed up to now. Ira's secretary was also a passenger in the car and had a slight concussion and was badly shaken up. The spot Mank is in is none too good. He was arraigned on a felony charge, if you please, not a misdemeanor, and at the first hearing, the immediately preceding case of drunk driving drew a sentence of 180 days in jail, 90 days actual and 90 days suspended. The Hearst papers have overplayed Mank's share in this, in revenge, one supposes for his ditto in "Citizen Kane." Herman has retained Jerry Geisler, the tricky one who gets all the criminals off. And speaking of mulcting, he is one gazabo who Herman will have to pay.

This seems to take care of your question feelers, so with renewed congrats from us all, I shall return to my art. Where Arthur has flopped so far is in his childish faith that the 97 pages of Virginia Van Opp's script here on the desk will ever be read by

As ever, yours,

Jerry.

This letter requires several explanations and definitions. "Mulcting" means "extracting money" or "swindling." Although Arthur Schwartz had produced several major Broadway shows, his most recently produced show closed in 1932 after twenty-eight performances. Kern composed songs for two film musicals for Columbia Pictures, both starring Rita Hayworth: *You Were Never Lovelier* in 1942, co-starring Fred Astaire, and *Cover Girl* in 1944, co-starring Gene Kelly. The latter featured the song "Long Ago and Far Away" and was produced by the composer Arthur Schwartz. "Lee" is Leonore Gershwin, Ira's wife. "Mank" is Herman Mankiewicz, co-screenwriter of *Citizen Kane*, which was a thinly veiled and unflattering portrait of the newspaper publisher William Randolph Hearst. "Gazabo" is a slang term for "guy" or "fellow" but with a derogatory connotation.

With *Oklahoma!* successfully behind him, Oscar returned his attention to *Carmen Jones*.

Arthur Hammerstein to Oscar Hammerstein, circa April 1943

Dear Oscar

Received notices but before yours came three other sets sent by friends of yours have been read.

You should be happy if you had written the notices yourself they couldn't have been better, they certainly gave me a kick.

Now that you are sane again will you answer my last letter wherein I request you to give me the name or names of publishers of music who I could send whatever I may write for their consideration, I mean some one who would put themselves out to consider what I would send; also is there any answer from the other two pieces I sent you?

In your phone conversation the other day you said that Billy Rose was going in the Army. If you wish you can tell him that if he wants me to assist in producing Carmen Jones "if he cannot see to it himself" I would gladly come to N. Y. I want nothing but expenses [?] no billing. I offer myself because that would be up my street "as you know" and secondly I love what you did, had it been other days no body would have done it but me. I feel as you do if Carmen isn't handled in the right way it could be an awful flop, I don't think it could happen if I was there.

Again I say such notices or rather such criticisms.

Love to all

Your uncle

Jerome Kern to Oscar Hammerstein, May 3, 1943

Dear Oscar:

Yours of April 26th just received, and I lose no time to acknowledge and answer.

Freddie Ahlert[4] spoke to me at great length the other night, and said that you would be writing me in regard to the Mills meeting out here, so I was not unprepared for the diplomatic restraint of the tone of your communiqué. Having retained much from my early training, I can still grasp sub-tones and over-tones as well as the indications on paper. Irving and I are going to the meeting tomorrow to absorb whatever ensues like blotting paper, and with about as much combativeness.

That's mighty exciting news about the Stadium, and particularly about my darling Mary Martin. It is unnecessary to go any further than your three names, Magnolia Martin, Dinah LaVerne and Charlie Hawkes. What the hell you mean by their ilk, I don't know. They ain't got no ilk. Give us those three and a better than middling Parthy, and there will be no further worries. About Ravenal, for instance. We have never had a good one yet, and until Clark Gable plays it and cuts out all the music except "Make Believe" in the convent scene, I suppose we never shall.

Of course, it's possible for me to get in with Winninger, but asking him would he be interested in doing Cap'n Andy is a sheer waste of time. Leo Fitzgerald, his handler, is the stumbling block. No sir, there's only one way to get Winninger and that is via the knout of L. B. Mayer. Once the czar declares in, all the parts will fall in line.

FLASH! Metro has a handsome stripling under contract named John Tyres, who has sung for Dick Berger in St. Louis. I don't know how he fared

---

[4] Songwriter Fred Ahlert became a Director of ASCAP in 1933. "Mills" refers to the Mills Music Publishing Company, and Irving may be either Irving Mills, or Irving Berlin.

with Dick, but I do know he stampeded them at a Victory Rally 'tother night with a new song by Ira, Yip and self entitled "Make Way For Tomorrow."

Come across with some more anons space. So long—Here it is, 4:55 p.m., and I haven't been shaved.

J---

V- - - --MAIL

Oscar Hammerstein to Arthur Freed (MGM), May 21, 1943

Dear Arthur:-

You asked me to let you know as soon as Billy and I had made a definite decision about CARMEN and at that time expressed an interest in Metro's participating in the production. Here are the details.

We will go into rehearsal on October 1st. John Murray Anderson will stage the production, Charles Friedman will stage the book (with me kibitzing) and Agnes de Mille will probably do the dances.

The physical production will be much more elaborate than I had originally planned when I was going to do it myself. Billy is budgeting it at $125,000. This means on the usual arrangement of the manager taking 50% and the investors 50% that $62,500 would cover 25% participation in profits. This, I believe, is all he is willing to sell and I am passing it on to you to find out if Metro would be interested. Billy's attitude is not the usual one of going out to get outside money. He has the money and is not afraid of losing it but on the other hand, he is making so much that he has very little to gain by owning the 100% instead of 75%.

If you think it would be a good property for Metro to own please let me or Billy know.

All good wishes,

Sincerely,

Oscar

As it turned out, *Carmen Jones* was staged by Hassard Short, the libretto ("book") was directed by Charles Friedman, and Charles Loring was the choreographer.

Myra Finn to Oscar Hammerstein, May 26, 1943

Dear Oc;

I am afraid that you are going to think me crazy, or senile, or at the very least—a great nuisance, but I have felt uncomfortable ever since our conversation of yesterday, so I must discuss the matter with you further, and rely on your usual kind understanding.

The fact is, I am not satisfied with the arrangement we made. Not in a sense of the amount of money involved, but my feelings about it. I shall try to make myself clear. You see, all these years that I have been living on your bounty, the only thing that has kept me from feeling a complete social pariah has been the fact that I was convinced that I had a vested interest in your genius, and the practical results of that genius. You, in fact, at least once to my knowledge, admitted as much, though not to me. Therefore the percentage arrangement has been a great sop to my ego and self-respect. Therefore also, when things were not going well for you, I never made any untoward demands. I have always felt that I was not taking anything, but merely receiving my due rights, previously arranged for in a business like manner. So now, if you cancel the percentage business and just <u>give</u> me money to live on, I must reclassify myself and join the regiment of divorced women who, simply because they lived with a man for a number of years, feel entitled to support by him for the rest of their lives. If you can cast your mind back so far, you will remember a period of weeks when you were impatiently waiting for me to start divorce proceedings. That delay was caused by my great reluctance to the word alimony and its connotations. Finally one night you called from Pittsburgh and I hit on the idea of percentages.

My vague and mostly futile attempts to get jobs at various times has not been caused by my desire to work. I don't <u>really</u> want to work. I am physically lazy and hate the thought of being at a place of employment every day at the same time. I want lots of time to read, and listen to good talk and hear good music. But I equally hate the thought of being an object of largesse.

This all may seem to you like creating a mountain out of a molehill. Perhaps it is. I don't even have a solution in mind. Your offer was very generous and would certainly help solve the immediate problem. But I should be miserable. I feel this deeply. Perhaps going back on the percentage basis with some sort of temporary and mutual sharing of the tax burden might be a solution.

As far as the bookkeeping and trouble caused to Howard, I can't get very worked up about that. In the first place a child of twelve can figure percentages, secondly, as there is no more custodian fund for him to worry about, no division of the money would be necessary, and thirdly, if a coin flipped many years ago, had landed differently all the legal theatrical headaches so proudly being suffered by Howard, would now be being borne by Horace Manges.

And speaking of legality there is an unpleasant but obvious aspect of the new arrangement which should be borne in mind. Should you die, leaving active works resulting in income, I wouldn't have a legal leg to stand on. You can rest assured I wouldn't attempt such a thing, but please try to understand my feelings and put me on a more business-like basis.

As ever yours,

Mike

Stella Hammerstein was the daughter of Oscar Hammerstein I, from a late second marriage, making her Oscar II's half-aunt, about thirteen years his senior. She had a brief career on stage and in silent films. She regularly sent pleading letters to Oscar, who provided modest support. The original letter is difficult to decipher, lacks punctuation, and features idiosyncratic grammar, but I think the fundamental points are clear.

Stella Hammerstein to Oscar Hammerstein, circa May, 1943

Dear Oscar—Last week I walked thru 44th St. and looked up and saw the Name—I was very proud of you—But I have always said. He did it before he'll do it again—and again—and now for my—shall I say trouble—

I came out of the Hospital over three months ago. Another operation on my eye—no good—the eye is dead—I had no place to go and no money—And no money [?] I had—so I got in touch with a friend who had a room here—Mrs. Burke—she said come right here—and share what I have—it isn't much. Well I am here—I share a small room sleep on a cot—in exchange for a little food—and a roof—I take care of the room and cook her food—she has a job at $22 a week—so she hasn't a great deal to do with—[?] Rose has been giving me $1 a week so I had something—I tried to get work—Had two days at Gimbels—no good—my eye—hurt too much. The one good one—I went to my eye Doctor and he sad I must do nothing that will strain that eye—and it's not very strong—nothing under electric lights. So I am out of luck—Now—this is my real trouble. I would never [have] written you Oscar. If this hadn't happened. Mrs. Burke is leaving here in a few weeks. She wrote her sick mother in Jersey and also to take a war job there—I will have no place to go—

I don't want any money from you Oscar—But if you could only let me have a little each week to get a small room here and some food—it's all I ask—you could let me come to the theatre and get it and none need know that Mrs. Pope is who I am. Maybe you could take it off your income tax—I can get a room here without bath for $8.50 a week I don't mind not having a bath room—I don't want anymore from you. [?] just enough to get by—the $8.50 will get the room and a little more for food. Can you do this for me? Not because I'm Oscar's daughter - or your father's sister. But just because you feel you would like to do it—and that I am worthy of a little help.

I have tried so hard to keep my chin up—But it's hard—with the bad eyesight—and other things You know Rose died in July—and fourth months ago Cliff married again. He sent me her old clothes. I sold nearly all for a little spending money.

I can't thank you - But I know you know how I feel—you are a fine person I'm only sorry papa didn't know you - Carry on the name Oscar and please—as everyone asks me—do "Show Boat"

Always

Stella

Agnes de Mille to Oscar Hammerstein, June 7, 1943

Dear Oscar—

My man of business informs me that I am and have been committed past retraction for some time to Kurt Weil [sic]. That's alright except that the show has no story. And I want with all my heart to do "Carmen." But I still feel maybe I can. I do hope so. It's all a question of dates—and very likely these can be adjusted. Let's try. I most earnestly want to do your show. I believe I could do some quite lovely things with it.

The guy I'm gonna marry nearly beat my head on the wall when he heard I was certainly going to do Weil's show and not certainly yours. He's not seen any of my work ever and for that matter any of yours:- But he's got a nose. He understands what's what. He was very mad. I'm very mad too. It's all Billy Rose's fault for being coy at the wrong moment. Well- let's hope.

I'm having a good time. I hope you are.

Affectionately

Agnes

De Mille married Walter Prude on June 14, one week after sending her letter. The Kurt Weill show she choreographed in lieu of *Carmen Jones* was *One Touch of Venus*. It opened October 7, 1943 and ran sixty-four performances longer than *Carmen Jones*. It was Mary Martin's second Broadway show.

Oscar Hammerstein to Arthur Freed (MGM), June 7, 1943

Dear Arthur:-

Thank you for your letter regarding CARMEN JONES. I have told Billy of the situation and that you would get in touch with him this week after you have talked to Mayer.

Regarding the Judy Garland picture you spoke to Dick and me about, we are looking forward to receiving a story layout whenever you have one. Meanwhile, we have nearly concluded a deal with 20th Century Fox which also contemplates writing a picture in the East. While this in no way affects our desire to do a Garland picture with you, it would necessarily postpone our work on it for a few months.

I saw CABIN IN THE SKY a couple of nights ago and thought it a very beautiful picture. The audience seemed to love it. Please congratulate Vincente for me on his first directorial assignment. I thought he did a fine job. The whole thing was intelligently produced and for the first time

I realized the double-barreled courage that it needed because it was not only a negro picture but a fantasy as well, and both these elements have been on the taboo list for some time.

I may be in California for just two days in the early part of July and if I come, I will ring you up. Meanwhile all the best to you.

Sincerely,

Oscar

Cabin in the Sky had opened on Broadway in October 1940—with an all-black cast, and a lovely score by Vernon Duke and John Latouche. The film opened in April 1943 with a cast including Ethel Waters, Rex Ingram, Louis Armstrong, and Lena Horne. Harold Arlen and Yip Harburg wrote additional songs. It was the first feature film directed by Vincente Minnelli; his last Broadway show had been Oscar's *Very Warm for May*.

Despite the disagreements evidenced below, Rouben Mamoulian would direct Rodgers and Hammerstein's next show, *Carousel* in 1945.

Richard Rodgers (and Oscar Hammerstein) to Theresa Helburn and Lawrence Langner (Theatre Guild), June 15, 1943

Dear Terry and Lawrence:-

I am writing this letter on behalf of Oscar and myself, with Oscar's full approval of its contents.

We wish to register our objection to articles on Mamoulian appearing in the New York Post, the Daily Mirror, The Christian Science Monitor and P.M. We understand that Mamoulian is employing his own press agent, but we do not feel that this relieves the Guild of the managerial responsibility of protecting its authors.

We feel that we have been seriously damaged by this contemptible practice of credit-stealing, which you have tacitly condoned, and we will therefore make two demands:

1. That Mamoulian be stopped (and you will be able to stop him, unless you wish to continue your policy of appeasement).

2. That you institute a vigorous campaign to rectify the harm already done and see that proper credit for the success of "Oklahoma" is granted to Oscar and me.

We hesitate to go to the press ourselves with this matter and start an unpleasant controversy and, at the moment, we do not expect to do so. If, however, we cannot obtain immediate assurance from you that the situation will be corrected, we will be unable to face you on the same basis of pleasant informality and the Thursday sessions, for instance will be enlivened by our absence. Mamoulian, of course, will oblige.

With deep regret at having to write you in this manner and with, believe it or not, my love, I am

Yours sincerely,

RICHARD RODGERS

Theresa Helburn and Lawrence Langner (Theatre Guild) to Richard Rodgers and Oscar Hammerstein, enclosing a letter to Rouben Mamoulian, June 19, 1943

Dear Oscar and Dickie

Enclosed is a copy of the letter we plan to send to Mamoulian. Will you advise us at once if you have any criticism or objection.

Theresa Helburn

Lawrence Langner

Dear Rouben:

We are informed that you have engaged a private press agent who is sending out stories to the newspapers and arranging interviews for you which are directly related to the exploitation of "Oklahoma!". The musical play, "Oklahoma!" is the property of The Theatre Guild and the exploitation of this play is solely in the hands of The Theatre Guild Press Department. The property can be damaged by improper exploitation.

The article appearing in the Daily Mirror of June 13th and arranged by your press agent, is based on an interview exploiting the play "Oklahoma!" and should not have been arranged except at the request of The Theatre Guild Press Department. The Theatre Guild Press Department is responsible for the allocation of interviews and the arrangement of such interviews or the sending out of stories regarding "Oklahoma!" by you or your press agent constitutes an interference with our well-considered exploitation of "Oklahoma!"

Moreover, the article appearing in the Mirror on "Oklahoma!" contains a number of untrue statements which are derogatory to The Theatre Guild and to other parties employed in the production of the play. In this article, you claim credit, or your press agent claims credit in your behalf, for the quiet opening of the play, the period of the costumes, and the position of the two first songs—all of which were clearly set by the authors in the script. And you also claim credit for the casting of Alfred Drake and Joan Roberts in the leads when these two players were already picked and their contracts signed, long before you ever came into the picture. Such untrue statements reflect upon the Guild and upon the contribution made by the other artists engaged in the production, that is, Mr. Rodgers and Mr. Hammerstein. This is not the only article instigated by you in which such untrue statements or implications are present.

We therefore call upon you and your press agent to cease from these practices which are extremely damaging and also, in our opinion, are unethical. It is our belief that you do not wish to interfere with our exploitation of our property or to claim credit for yourself which belongs to other parties. We therefore believe that you will cooperate with us in the future, otherwise, for the protection of the other parties concerned, we shall have to deny publicly any statements hereafter made by you which are untrue.

Very truly yours,

THE THEATRE GUILD, INC.

BY: _____

Theresa Helburn

_____

Lawrence Langner

Dear Mr. Mamoulian:[5]

_____

[5] "Roub" is penciled in as a possible salutation.

We have read the above letter and concur with the contents thereof and shall join with The Theatre Guild, if necessary, in issuing denials of untrue statements.

Very truly yours,

BY:_____

Richard Rodgers

_____

Oscar Hammerstein

Rouben Mamoulian to Theresa Helburn and Lawrence Langner (Theatre Guild), June 23, 1943

Dear Terry and Lawrence:

This is in reply to your extraordinary letter of June 19th, delivered to me yesterday. The motivation behind it is not obscure to me, and it is consistent with your behavior during the past few months.

As you well know, in spite of the disingenuous assumptions of your letter, I have not been exploiting "Oklahoma!" but have been discussing for the press my own professional activities, which are what I have to offer, and the means of my livelihood.

"Oklahoma!" happens to be only one of the many notable and successful productions which I have directed on the stage and on the screen; as the direction of the entire production of "Oklahoma!" is my most recent work, it is perfectly obvious and natural that in any discussion of my professional activities with the press, "Oklahoma!" has its proper place.

As Mr. Langner was himself careful to point out to me when it seemed in your interest to do so, that fact is that newspapers are not under the control of those they interview and write about. The form, phraseology and content of their articles and their selection or omission of material are under their own control. But except under an unfriendly and carping misinterpretation of what has appeared in connection with me, nothing that has appeared is exceptionable in any way. In addition, as to the Daily Mirror article to which you allude at such length, I had no prior knowledge of it whatsoever until I saw it in print.

I consider the whole tone of your letter, and the phrases attributing to me untruthful statements and unethical practices offensive and insulting.

The privilege of issuing untrue statements I leave to you. It is evident that you yourselves realize that your accusations are baseless and false, as in the same letter you say "it is our belief that you do not wish to interfere with our exploitation of our property, or to claim credit for yourself which belongs to other parties." Thus you have honestly answered yourselves.

Your letter has in fact attributed to me as the very wrongs and course of conduction of which you have yourselves been concertedly guilty. I have protested repeatedly in the past and I protest against the manner in which stories and interviews on "Oklahoma!" arranged by the Theatre Guild's Press Department minimize my contribution to the production of "Oklahoma!", suppressing and distorting facts in that regard, even so far as to make it appear that persons other than the director were responsible for the work which was mine. In spite of your promises and assurances, nothing was done to correct this.

Moreover, it has come to my attention from a number of sources that you have been making false, defamatory and derogatory statements about me generally, and in connection with my work on "Oklahoma!" Not only is this a wrong against me personally but my livelihood depends on my reputation as a director. I can be damaged in that and in other respects by false statements about me and I will not countenance it.

This letter also covers my answer to Mr. Rodgers and Mr. Hammerstein, and I am sending copies of it to both of them.

Very truly yours,

Rouben Mamoulian

Stella Hammerstein to Oscar Hammerstein, June 20, 1943[6]

In all sincerity Oscar this letter is much harder to write than for you to read.

I want to thank you personally for the check—it did tide me over—now the d-tide is catching up with me again—I have just $6 left. Martha (Mrs Burke) who has shared everything with me—left for her war job Monday—and that wonderful friend has paid for a weeks rent here—so I wouldn't be out.

---

[6] On the back of the envelope is written: "Please read this—thru".

You said in your note to me you couldn't help me with the allowance because of the taxes. And one more burden would be too much. Would it be possible to keep me if you could list me as a dependent? it might help you with those taxes.

I need so little Oscar I know its not the money. But for you to remember to send it each week would be a nuisance. am I wrong? I have no one to turn to no place to go after this week—that's why (please <u>don't</u> get annoyed at me) Could your lawyer send it to me. I am really desperate—or I wouldn't humiliate myself to ask again for help Its too horrible. You who have never known what I am going thru—no room no money, no future—I just cant go on—the worry and crying have done enough damage to my eyes—I don't want any more handouts. One day I eat and when the hand-out is gone—I'm in the same fix. You do understand. I know-

I met charming [?] outside of this place many many months ago. He said Do you live in this dump I said yes—then I told him about myself—He was shocked He said If only Willie were alive you would be allright how about Oscar. He seems a fine man—I said you were helping me. And you <u>are</u> a fine man—Then [?] said. Here Stella buy yourself something. I said [?] I don't want a hand-out. He just laughed—the next day I had $25 in the mail from him saying no hand-out just a friendly gift- So I mean it about hand-outs—I wont bother you anymore Oscar. What I am going to do I don't know yet. But whatever it is I am not going to <u>be afraid</u>. I am not Oscar's Daughter for nothing He had <u>guts. So have I.</u>

If anything <u>should</u> happen to me—<u>cremate</u> me—<u>thats all I ask</u>

With all my heart I thank you for past kindnesses—My wish is for your continued success. Happiness <u>and health</u>

Stella

I got your address a <u>long</u> time ago from friends in Churchville, Pa,) forgive blots - they are tears.)

Howard Reinheimer to Oscar Hammerstein, July 16, 1943

Dear Oscar:

Just a note regarding your minimum tax requirements for the year 1943.

It looks to me roughly as though your net income for the year, after expenses, will be approximately $80,000 (including past and prospective ASCAP, small rights and music royalties, but not including any possible returns from CARMEN JONES). The tax on this is approximately $42,000.[7]

Under the new tax law, the $4,000 which you have already paid this year on your 1942 tax is credited against your 1943 tax. That leaves approximately $38,000. Due. Of this $19,000 must be paid on September 15th—and the remaining $19,000 on December 15th, 1943.

Now, how to get it! You have $17,000 in the bank, of which $3,000 will be needed on July 30th for OKLAHOMA. This will leave approximately $14,000. I would like to put this entire $14,000 into a special account and just not touch it. The entire next Fox payment of $12,500 should likewise be put into the special account. That will make $26,500. You will still be about $11,500 shy. Therefore, I suggest that we set aside religiously each week out of the OKLAHOMA royalties $500. and in the twenty-two weeks remaining of this year, we will just about pay up your tax bill in full.

In other words, commencing with the day you get home, you will be starting off with an approximately empty bank account; you will be getting about $500.00 net a week from the show for yourself, plus ASCAP, music and other miscellaneous income. If CARMEN JONES gets under way, we will have to keep out each week a proper proportion based upon the extra income.

Sincerely,

Howard.

HOWARD E. REINHEIMER.

Henry Blanchard Jacobson (Duke University) to Oscar Hammerstein, August 6, 1943

Dear Ockie,

I miss you also. No longer do I hear a calm and measured voice doling out derogatory remarks to my right at the dinner table. The nightly patter

---

[7] According to one inflation calculator, $80,000.00 in 1943 would be worth $1,256,397.69 in 2021; $42,000.00 would be worth $659,608.79.

of feet to the kitchen for milk is something I love to hear again. When my roomate [sic] is writing a composition and I interrupt him, the glance I get reminds me of you, peering out of the confines of your study, yelling hoarsely to "turn off that <u>damn</u> victrola." Tell me, do you think Roosevelt packed, or tried to pack to be correct, the Surpreme [sic] court? I miss the debates we had when I was cut down by the sharp edge of your wit. However I shall rise again in all my glory to attempt a rebuttle [sic] someday.

Every day at six, we arise, rub the sleepiness from our eyes, and stumble down into the cold morning for exercises. Half naked we run around a road in formation. At seven o'clock we again line up, clean shaven and in white uniforms for inspection. A cold eyed CPO inspects us and then we wait in line for an hour for breakfast.

As so the day continues. At night we fall exhausted on our beds to sleep. My bed is 1 ½ times my width and 9/10 my length. So I have lots of room to move around in.

Write and give my sister's boy friend's description. What ever became of B. Harback?

Thanks for a swell letter,

<u>Henry</u>

Oscar Hammerstein to William Hammerstein, September 23, 1943

Dear Bill:-

I haven't got time to write a full length letter today but I am enclosing two clippings which I know will interest you. One is the answer to Eva Paul. I don't know whether she is your Eva Paul or not but her eccentric letter would warrant the inference. I am nevertheless grateful to her for giving me the cue for saying something I wanted to say anyway because secretly although I denied her accusation, I felt there was some justice in it.

The other clipping must be the world's record for giving a show a good notice even before it has opened.

On the other hand, I cannot say that I am pleased with rehearsals. We are in the middle of the third week now and I don't feel we have made enough progress to justify looking forward to anything like a smooth opening. The material looks wonderful but so far I wouldn't say that 30% of its possibilities are being realized. With this note of pessimism I close.

Love,

Dad

PS. I am writing a report to Betty of your talk with Artie Shaw but the report will not be too literal. . . . .

Enclosed clipping:

From the Drama Mailbag

To the Drama Editor

In a recent issue of THE TIMES Eva Paul of Provincetown, Mass., complained that "the perpetrators of "Oklahoma!" eliminate all mention of Lynn Riggs, the man who wrote "Green Grow the Lilacs." As a perpetrator of "Oklahoma!" I deny this.

Mr. Riggs has been frequently mentioned and always with great admiration. Nevertheless, to please Miss Paul, I should like to mention him again and go on record as saying that Mr. Riggs' play is a wellspring of almost all that is good in "Oklahoma!" I kept many of the lines of the original play without making any changes in them at all for the simple reason that they could not be improved on—at any rate, not by me. But more important than this, "Green Grow the Lilacs" had a strange combination of qualities—lusty melodrama, authentic folk characters and a sensitive quality pervading the whole story. I feel that in some measure we were able to preserve these values in the musical version and they comprise a very important contribution to its success.

Lynn Riggs and "Green Grow the Lilacs" are the very soul of "Oklahoma!" Okay, Miss Paul?

Oscar Hammerstein 2d.

New York.

Frank Orsatti to Oscar Hammerstein, October 4, 1943

DEAR OSCAR: PLEASE DO ME A FAVOR AND HAVE LARRY HART CALL OR WIRE ME HIS NEW PHONE NUMBER AND ADDRESS STOP ADVISE HIM THAT FREED WANTS HIM FOR "YOLANDE,

THE THIEF" ALSO THE FOLLIES. I WIRED HIM BUT TELEGRAM
RETURNED UNDELIVERED. REGARDS

=FRANK ORSATTI.

The last thing Lorenz Hart worked on before he died was writing additional songs—
with Rodgers—for a revival of *A Connecticut Yankee* which opened on November
17. He died on November 22, seven weeks after the above telegram. Freed himself
went on to write the lyrics for *Yolanda and the Thief* and at least one of the songs
for *Ziegfeld Follies*

During the war Leighton Brill joined the Red Cross, where he became Assistant
Director of Entertainments to the American Red Cross in charge of field zones, which
meant the entire British Isles outside of the London area. One of the performers
working with him in England was Oscar's daughter-in-law Maggie—William's wife.

Leighton Brill to Oscar Hammerstein, October 6, 1943

DEAR OSCAR:

IT CERTAINLY WAS GRAND TO GET YOUR NEWSY
INFORMATIVE LETTER. I FEEL TERRIBLE ABOUT POOR MACKIE
AND I NEVER THOUGHT LOU MEANT SO MUCH TO HIM.

TERRIBLY THRILLED ABOUT THE CONTINUED TERRIFIC
TRIUMPHANT CAREER OF "OKLAHOMA" AND EXCITED NO END
ABOUT "CARMEN JONES", BECAUSE TO ME THAT IS THE GREATEST
THING YOU HAVE EVER DONE. DO KEEP ME INFORMED ABOUT
EVERYTHING IN CONNECTION WITH IT.

MAGGIE AND I WENT TO BAT THIS MORNING. SHE WAS
RIDING A LOVELY WHITE CHARGE ON BEHALF OF A COLOURED
GIRL I HAVE DO MY SHOW. I HAVE GIVEN THIS GIRL EVERY BREAK
IN THE WORLD AND PUT HER IN THE MIDST OF A WHITE UNIT
AND TOLD THE RED CROSS THAT I WOULD GET OUT IF SHE DID
NOT STAY THERE. BUT OUR MAGGIE WANTED HER TO COME IN
ON THE OPENING AS THE AMERICAN FLAG BEARER AND FROM
PURELY SHOWMAN STAND POINT I DID NOT BELIEVE IN THIS.
ANYWAY IT TOOK ME SOMETIME TO CONVINCE OUR MAGGIE
THAT I WAS DOING THIS TO HELP THE SHOW AND NOT TO HURT
THE GIRL. DWIGHT WIMAN AND I HAD TO FIRE ALL OUR BIG
GUNS AT THE TWO TO PUT THE POINT OVER AND BELIEVE ME

WE HAVE BOTH STUCK OUT OUR NECKS PLENTY IN LOOKING FOR TROUBLE BY HAVING A MIXED UNIT.

YOU DID NOT KNOW I WAS A CRUSADER DID YOU? NEITHER DID I! BUT THINGS OVER HERE ON THE COLOURED QUESTION ARE SO—WELL—MIXED UP AND DWIGHT WIMAN AND I STRANGELY ENOUGH ARE BOTH LIBERALS. SO WE ON OUR CHARGERS TOO, ALTHOUGH OURS ARE NOT PURE WHITE BUT JUST A BIT ON THE GRAY SIDE.

I HAVE TO RUSH OFF NOW TO BE BEST MAN AT THE WEDDING OF LIEUTENANT ROBERT LIGHT AND PEGGY DODGESON (ONE OF MY DANCERS) AS THE CEREMONY STARTS AT 4.0.P.M. AND IT IS NOW 3.45.PM.

LOVE,

LEIGHTON.

V- - ----MAIL

John Latouche was a lyricist with more than a hint of the Southern poet in his work. At the time of this letter he had found his greatest success with the songs for *Cabin in the Sky*. (His letterhead reads "LaTouche.")

John LaTouche to Oscar Hammerstein, October 7, 1943

Dear Oscar:

Thank you so much for the tickets to Oklahoma. Used as I am to the theatre, the thrill of getting two aisle seats, and such good ones, at the last minute, was only a small item when the charm of the production completely swept me off my feet. I knew it would be new and captivating, but I was not prepared for the tremendous beauty and—I hate to use the word—intellectual depth of certain of the scenes. Naturally, the audience did not realize they were being stirred in this manner—they only realized they were being constantly delighted.

I have rarely seen a production in which everything was at a top standard of excellence—and done with such an abundant joy in living. You have made another enduring contribution to our musical theatre, which has needed a new one for so long.

I shall see you when I come back on furlough. Thank you again for arranging the tickets.

Sincerely,

John

John LaTouche

Edna Ferber to Oscar Hammerstein, October 8, 1943

Dear Oscar:-

This is written for two reasons—both academic, really, rather than technical. I want to go on record; and I want to keep clear my feeling of friendship and admiration for you.

You already know that on the opening night of OKLAHOMA I recognized the lunch box auction scene as having derived from my novel SO BIG.[8] I was startled, but I resolved immediately that I would not speak of this to you or to anyone else unless it first was mentioned by you or by someone else.

You will recall that after SHOW BOAT became a successful musical play Jerome Kern wanted to make a musical play from SO BIG. He wrote a score for it which I heard at his house in Bronxville. He had asked you to do the book and lyrics, but you couldn't see it. Neither could I. A book was done by an Englishman whose name I've forgotten, and I remember I thought it pretty bad. The project never went through.

As I saw the scene on the stage I realized, after my first shock, that this sort of thing can quite innocently happen to a writer. SO BIG was written twenty years ago. A reader may be impressed by a scene or a character or a situation and, years later, if his profession is that of writing, can use it or something resembling it under the impression that it is his own, freshly thought up.

At Jules Glaenzer's party on the opening night of OKLAHOMA I told you how enchanting I had found the whole production and how fine your lyrics. To my amazement you said, "And how did you like my steal from SO BIG?"

So then, this is just to go on record as saying that I didn't like it at all, and that I think you should not again deliberately use the original idea of

---

[8] *So Big* was published in 1924—two years before *Show Boat*—and won the Pulitzer Prize. There's no evidence that Hammerstein or Kern ever did any work on a libretto or score to be based on the novel.

another writer in one of your own works, without the knowledge or consent of that writer.

A number of people have spoken to me about this lunch box auction scene. And, of course, it is not to be found in the play on which the musical's book is based.

For a long time I have wanted to write you thus, but I shrank from doing so. I wanted to clear my feelings regarding it, and I shall not refer to it again, nor shall I do anything further about it.

Sincerely,

Edna Ferber.

Oscar Hammerstein to Edna Ferber, October 13, 1943

Dear Edna:

My crack at Jules Glaenzer's party was facetious and not at all literal in its intent. Not for a moment had I considered that I'd "stolen" the "box social" scene from you. In your letter you say "I recognized the lunch box auction scene as having derived from my novel SO BIG". As a matter of fact, it derives from American life. In another paragraph you speak of it as an "original idea" of yours. I don't understand this statement. The "box social" is a very well known folk custom practiced for many years in the midwestern states from Nebraska down to Texas. I knew of it before I read SO BIG and so, of course, did you.

It would be strange if one author's use of an existing custom should preclude forever its use by another author who wanted to write a story about a locality to which that custom was indigenous. I felt completely free to use the box social as I would feel free to use a game of "post office" or a "charade party" or a "strawberry festival". Despite its inclusion in GREEN GROW THE LILACS, I would feel free to use a "shivoree" in a different story.

I appreciate the clear intention in your letter to be gentle with me, the more so because your inner feelings about the situation seem to be far from gentle. I just happen to think, Edna, that your inner feelings in this case are slightly cock-eyed and I don't like being slapped on the wrist—however gently—when I feel sure I don't deserve it. I understand your point but I just don't agree with you. My opinion about it is as honest as yours. So is my wish to maintain our friendship as genuine as the wish you express in this connection. I sincerely hope that this friendship will not be jeopardized by my firm and permanent conviction that I have as much right to a "box social" scene as you.

Sincerely,

Deems Taylor to Oscar Hammerstein, October 12, 1943

Dear Oscar:

I wonder if people realize how important "Oklahoma!" is. It's supposed to be very bad form to praise one show by comparing another unfavorably with it; but I can't help remembering all the caterwauling that has gone on about "Porgy and Bess". If they are really looking for the "significant", "American", "Folk" opera—"Oklahoma" is it. It's so much more than a musical comedy, even though it's cast in that form. It's a vivid and moving picture of one phase of American life, and a triumph of stagecraft (sounds as if I were sounding off about some opus by Paul Green, doesn't it?).

Granted that you had a solid foundation in a charming, if slight play, I'm lost in admiration of the superb job you and Dick have done with the adaptation. The whole thing hangs together so beautifully---book, lyrics, music, stage and dance direction. Everything belongs in the picture. The piece establishes a mood at the very start and that is never falsified or broken.

Your lyrics are beyond comparison. They are so brilliant, without ever being smarty-pants, and, when the situation calls for poetry, so poetic. I couldn't help thinking that they are so utterly right and apparently effortless, so easy to put over, that the singers probably get more credit for them than you do.

The staging is completely honest (never before, so far as I remember, have I seen actors in a musical show addressing each other instead of the audience). DeMille, of course, is a genius. As for the casting---I did something last night that I almost never do; I carried my program home. I want to remember those lovely people.

Thank you for a heart-warming evening.

Sincerely yours,

Deems Taylor

Arthur Freed to Oscar Hammerstein, October 14, 1943

Dear Oscar:

Please excuse the delay in answering you letter, but it took me this long to be able to give you an intelligent answer regarding SHOWBOAT. I believe you would be perfectly safe in going ahead with the production this time, because under no circumstances could we have the picture ready for release within eighteen months. That would be a miracle. I believe it will be closer to two years. We have not started to work on the script, which would take at least four or five months, again with optimism. Preparation and shooting—six months, cutting, editing and scoring—two months, previews etc.—another month, prints, color work, release prints etc. —two or three months, trade showings, advertising etc.—another three or four months; so add this up and you can see how long it takes to make a picture of this magnitude. I have very interesting ideas on SHOWBOAT that I will tell you the first time we meet. I believe we can get the most important picture of its kind ever made. Let me know your plans on SHOWBOAT. I would love, as you once suggested, to be associated in some way with you in this venture.

Regarding THE BELLE OF NEW YORK.[9] We have a fine outline for the story and I am still counting on you and Dick Rodgers to do the score. When would you and Dick have time to go to work on this along the lines we spoke about? The way I feel about you, Oscar, "people will say we're in love."

Kindest regards,

Arthur Freed

Rodgers and Hammerstein famously kept tabs on their shows throughout their runs—on Broadway, London, and their national tours—in person when they could and with surrogates when they couldn't. In Rodgers' autobiography he wrote: "Another first for me was that the Guild sent out a road company while the New York company was still performing. The tour began in New Haven in October 1943 and ended ten and a half years later in Philadelphia."

---

[9] Harry Warren and Johnny Mercer ended up writing the score for *The Belle of New York*. The Freed-produced film wasn't released until 1952.

Richard Rodgers to Oscar Hammerstein, October 15, 1943

Dear Oscar,

I am dictating this to Lillian over the telephone so don't look for much composition. What you can look for is good news.

The opening last night in New Haven was nothing short of terrific. At no point in the show has the audience reaction been comparable to last night's. The applause was infinitely greater and I would say, conservatively, the laughs were twice as big and let me point out that this was in no way a "lead" audience. I only saw one agent myself. They, apparently, expect to see a good show and are not prepared to see a wonderful one.

The cast was not uniformly good. Jud got off to a bad start because he couldn't open the drawer containing the gun. He eventually did, of course, but that seemed to throw him. Aunt Eller yelled too much as did Davey Burns, but Jerry Whyte[10] is there for the rest of the week and will take care of that. Walter Donahue was not very effective and I suspect that he is never going to be terribly good. He seems to lack humor although he has projection. Pamela Britton was really wonderful and missed no points. Stockwell and Wyckoff couldn't have been better, and we have another excellent conductor. He was handicapped by pretty poor musicians, but did a magnificent job.

Leonard Sang, the house manager, tells me that he could have disposed of the house for two weeks without running an ad in the paper. I am sorry I haven't a copy of the Courier Journal notice, but it is just as well because it would only embarrass you. I remember that one sentence said that the company was at least as good as the New York company except in one respect and that was the singing. He likes the second company's singing a little better. Let's buy it, put it away, and not forget about it.

I hope everything is going well with the show. I will know in twenty four hours whether or not Dick Foran has pneumonia. Otherwise, everything is fine here.

Love,

Dick.

---

[10] Jerry Whyte was Rodgers and Hammerstein's chief stage manager ("brought over from the George Abbott office") and "on-the-scene producer." Whyte became nearly indispensable to Rodgers and Hammerstein.

Photo 14 Richard Rodgers and Oscar Hammerstein II, circa 1949. Photograph courtesy of Oscar Andrew Hammerstein

Carmen Jones began its out-of-town tryout in Philadelphia on October 19. From there it moved to Boston on November 9.

A. P. Waxman to Oscar Hammerstein ("Carmen Jones Company," Philadelphia), October 20, 1943

Dear Oscar:

Last night's premiere of "Carmen Jones" was one of the most enjoyable evenings that I have ever spent in the theatre. It was well worth the trip to Philadelphia.

After the show, I told Deems Taylor that you had made a two-fold contribution to American culture. You are the first one to make Opera in English 100% entertainment for the general public. You have also broadened the horizon for Negro talent, and gained for them the increased recognition they are entitled to. Deems agreed with me completely. In fact, he also agreed when I ventured the opinion that "Carmen Jones" was ten times better than "Porgy and Bess".

I'll swap you right now a piece of the musical version of "Rain"[11] — which is being done for me by Howard Dietz and Vernon Duke—for a piece of "Carmen Jones". And that goes, regardless of your problem of getting a theatre in New York.

Yours very sincerely,

Abe

A. P. Waxman

Frank Mandel to Oscar Hammerstein, circa October, 1943

Dear Oscar:-

I'm writing you more as a fiery young fan than an old friend. I went nuts! You owe me a lot of hair on the back of my head. Your Carmen is a new element from a distant planet—by long long odds it must prove your sweetest satisfaction and justification for your life's work; and, all that, with due respect for Show Boat.

Do you know I'm ashamed to admit it, but I was stunned that anything so thoroughly fine, so nobly conceived, could prove to be so completely entertaining. Possibly, a little more than the average theatre-goer, I can estimate the many thousands of tricky decisions that must be made in the making of one piece, and when I realize that those thousands were all made in terra incognita, and apparently without one error - - - well I'm still stunned.

Sincerely

Frank.

---

[11] The musical version of *Rain* was titled *Sadie Thompson*. Produced by Waxman, it opened on Broadway November 16, 1944, and closed after sixty performances.

Oscar Hammerstein to Rouben Mamoulian, November 4, 1943

Dear Rouben:-

Telepathic vibrations have been travelling across the continent because for the few days preceding the receipt of your welcome letter to Dorothy and me I was contemplating writing to you. And my only motive was to say "hello". I have some news to be sure and that is that CARMEN JONES has opened in Philadelphia and looks like a certain hit for New York. The New Yorkers who have come down to see it—and it seems that a good portion of the population has—are all ecstatic and unstinting in their praise and the Philadelphians are coming to pack the house each night. In addition to these there is a fellow from Doylestown who likes it very much himself.

Next week we go to Boston where we are booked for six weeks marking time and hoping that some New York show will flop so that we can get in. Among these desired victims is of course, one exception—OKLAHOMA. This is going along at the same pace—the second company (which Lawrence likes to euphemize as the "national company") sells out weeks in advance of wherever it plays. It opens in Chicago the week after next and will probably stay there a long time. Jerry Whyte staged this company as a very faithful carbon copy of all your directions and its success even in your absence is a great tribute to the directorial mould [sic] which you created for the play. Answering your question "do you still live in the country or have we come to town" we are living in town and in the country and in Philadelphia and on trains. Dorothy has been visiting me in Philadelphia and I have been visiting her in New York. I have persuaded her to retreat from the cares of her business because there is little satisfaction in it these days. She can make lots of money (which she can't keep) but the aggravation of labor and material scarcity takes away all her fun. It will take about three months to finish her current jobs and after that I hope we can spend more time in Doylestown.

Let me hear from you again soon. We both send our love to you and Azadia. As ever,

Oscar

Arthur Hammerstein to Oscar Hammerstein (excerpt),
November 5, 1943

Now getting into Carmen Jones that was the biggest loss to me that I ever experienced in my life. If I would have had the money nobody could have produced it but me, I had a long talk with Dorothy after we read it as to trying to raise the necessary money to do it we found that that wasn't possible for should it be a failure it would have left us high + dry. You may not know it but when I walked out of my theatre I didn't have five cents to my name and if it wasn't for Dorothy I would have had to find a job, so you see Carmen Jones was out of the question It all happened for the best for you for I could of never given it the production Rose gave it, so lets forget it my consolation is your success.

You say you are getting a nice swelled head your success is giving you, you have a right to have two swelled heads you didn't just succeed you set a standard that nobody can follow for Carmen Jones will live long after your gone, I think Carmen is now 78 years old and just as new as though it was written yesterday you have made it a masterpiece for the public, before it was for the musical minded. Yes I did worri [sic] about you I couldn't understand why for the past years you were slipping I knew your ability and felt sure with the right subject you would find your feet back where they belonged. Dorothy can tell you how I always preached that you were only in a slump.

Dont worri about Bill he's a Hammerstein he'll come back

Despite being out-of-town with *Carmen Jones*, Oscar took the time to respond to an updated script for the now-titled, *Hayfoot, Strawfoot*. This letter is from an original manuscript in the Hammerstein Collection, not a carbon, so it's possible it was never sent.

Oscar Hammerstein (Ritz-Carlton, Boston) to Otto Harbach,
November 19, 1943

Dear Otto:

Again it seems to me that you have improved the play. But with each new, improved version I become more convinced that I have no interest in the basic subject matter, or characters. It's like that old Moran and Mack[12]

---

[12] George Moran and Charles Mack made up the blackface comedy team Two Black Crows. In one bit Moran would blast a note on a kazoo. Mack, annoyed, would say: "Boy, even if dat was *good*, I wouldn't like it!" To which Moran countered, "I can play *anything* on dis." Mack, "You caint play *piano* on dat!"

gag—"Even if dat was <u>good</u>, I wouldn't like it". I would give a great deal to be able to say I could see what you see in it. I'd like nothing better than to take off my coat and pitch in with you and get the play into rehearsal. But I haven't the kind of enthusiasm one ought to have to work on a play. It's tough enough to put them over when you <u>are</u> enthusiastic. But when you're half-hearted, there isn't a chance. This doesn't apply to you. You <u>do</u> like these people and their problems and somehow or other you'll get them on the stage and they'll come to life under your hand—but not under mine. I haven't your faith in them nor your affection for them. It has become your play by every right. I have no business sharing either its success or failure—whatever its future may be. I am being very definite about this because I think you are being unfair to yourself and the play, dragging two anchors along with you—Jerry and me. I think you should cut away from us, get another composer to set the lyrics and really go after getting it produced. I think it should be produced and I think it has a fine chance—if you can cast it with fresh, young people. God knows, no one could wish you more luck with it than I. You have poured so much good thought and effort into it that there is no limit to the success it deserves.

Specifically, I urge you not to call it "Dance, Little Lady". It's such a well-known Noel Coward song and its connotation is so different from your play. I also have reservations about some of the ballets. They seem wedged in and against the simplicity you have mapped out in the scenic scheme. Another note I made was that I couldn't quite understand Bob's attitude on singing "De Land o' Good Times." On pages 1-1-, 10-12 I still feel too much reminiscence, and that it isn't essential.

I thought the new character of the Freudian doctor, ahead of his time, was productive of many laughs, although his influence on Bob's behavior at the end of the story was not as clear to me as it was when you told me what you intended to write in this spot.

I am so anxious, Otto, that you understand my attitude about this play. I know I've left no doubt about my feeling for it, but I want it to be equally clear to you how unwelcome this decision is, how grateful I am for all the work you've done, carrying my name on it all along, and being willing to share royalties I never could deserve. Please understand this and be assured of my gratitude, for this and—lots of other things, for instance the foundation of a career, which I owe to you more than anyone else.

You know I stand ready to give any help in this venture that you ask of me, and, of course, it goes without saying, that the few lines of mine that remain in the script are yours, for keeps.

I'll be coming back to town next week, for a few days. I'll phone you then.

Love to Ella, the family and yourself,

As ever,

Oscar

Deems Taylor to Oscar Hammerstein, November 30, 1943

Dear Oscar:

My claque rates for "CARMEN JONES" are two on the aisle—or two, period.

I am happy to inform you that they are on the way, so you needn't worry your little head about them any more.

Thanks a lot.

See you on the night of triumph.

Ever yours.

Deems

Saw the old version of "Carmen" at the Met, on Monday night. Did you know? They're doing it in white-face!

Arthur Hammerstein to Oscar Hammerstein, circa November, 1943

Dear Oscar

So long as I paid $42.35 for my tickets to see Oklahoma I am at liberty to give you my opinion. What I've known for a long time certainly came forcibly Monday night when I found myself seated three rows from the back, when your through in the show business your through.

The construction of book, the meeting of music to book, the lyrics and the natural introduction of dances, makes Oklahoma the finest musical entertainment that has ever been produced. I must give all credit to you your lyrics makes Rogers [sic] music masterful, in all it was a great night in the theatre for me. I am besieged for tickets, so many of my friends want to buy and cant get them as you know, will you ask the Guild if they can arrange that I obtain at times those set aside seats.

Love to all

Your

Uncle

P.S. Let me know as soon as you can about the seats

After seeing *Oklahoma!*, Darryl Zanuck, head of Twentieth Century-Fox, determined that Rodgers and Hammerstein would be ideal to write the score for a musical remake he was planning of the 1933 film *State Fair*. They signed the contract in the summer and Oscar began writing the screenplay in January 1944.

Oscar Hammerstein to William Perlberg (Twentieth Century-Fox Films), December 6, 1943

Dear Bill:-

Dick and I heard Grayson[13] in THOUSANDS CHEER and we were very much impressed with her. The picture, however, does not show whether she can handle a song in a simple, straight way. All her renditions had coloratura fireworks in them. Do you know if there is any film on her which demonstrates her ability to put a song over simply and sincerely?

In other words, if she has to rely on her vocal brilliance we don't think she would be the one to play the part of "Marjorie." I have started work and am well into the first sequence now.

Kindest regards.

Sincerely.

---

[13] Kathryn Grayson was an MGM star, beautiful with an impressive coloratura soprano.

With the extraordinary success of *Oklahoma!*, Helburn and Langner—representing the Theatre Guild—were eager to again catch lightning in a bottle. At a November luncheon they proposed the Ferenc Molnár play *Liliom*. Molnár's play premiered in Hungary in 1901, where it was not well received. The Guild produced its America premiere in 1921, where it ran a gratifying 300 performances. Initially, Rodgers and Hammerstein said no, but Helburn was dogged, suggesting ways the show might be changed to meet their objections.

Theresa Helburn (Theatre Guild) to Oscar Hammerstein and Richard Rodgers, December 17, 1943

Dear Oscar and Dick,

Enclosed is the memorandum of our talk. Since last week I've been doing the Inquiring Reporter stunt. I've asked a number of people about Liliom himself and they all say they liked him enormously. When I say "Why? He was such a bastard", their replies vary, but it's usually, "Yes, but he was so human" or

"Such a cute bastard" or

"Such and insolent and charming devil" or

"I agree after you were married to him he wouldn't supply milk for the baby, but you couldn't help loving him."

I'm sure he gets over much closer to Clark Gable than to Pal Joey.

By the way, two Liliom fans told me they remembered the end of the love scene, where Liliom and Julie sit on the bench and smell the acacia blossoms, and it has remained in their minds as high spots in the theatre— so I guess Oscar put his finger on something really lyric.

If you can remember more things we talked about will you add them to this, or telephone them to Miss Lewis who will take them down and send your postscripts.

We're working on the option from Fox.

Here's to our next meeting.

Sincerely,

Terry

P.S. It seems to me that much of the third scene can be eliminated or drastically changed if need be, and that probably Oscar may re-conceive the heaven scene in quite different terms.

MEMO. FROM MISS HELBURN to MR. RODGERS & MR. HAMMERSTEIN

Re. Conference held December 7, 1943

In Mr. Hammerstein's house.

* * * * * * *

We considered the idea of setting the play in America or different European countries but the final feeling was that it belonged in a Central European setting, whether that was Czecho-Slovakian or Hungary, or what have you.

It was felt that the present prologue should be enlarged into a long scene in the amusement park, in which the characters are introduced and developed somewhat and that this could flow right into the park scene by some scenic contrivance. This scene might include both a dancing and chorus number.

The problem of the play, for musical purposes, seems to be what Mr. Hammerstein called "the tunnel" of the gloomy scenes in the Hollander house, followed by the culvert scene and the death. It was felt that the Hollander house didn't need to be too drab an affair but could be attractive scenically.

It was also suggested by Mr. Hammerstein that the second scene in the Hollander house which in the play is the third scene and which in the musical would probably be the fourth scene, should not necessarily be in that setting at all. Miss Helburn suggested that it could be transferred, possibly to a tavern at which Sparrow and his like hang out, and that there Liliom and the Sparrow could be plotting the robbery. This would allow for the introduction of a crown number if needed and Mrs. Muskat would come there to tempt Liliom back, and Julie to tell him the news of the baby. I can see no reason why the photographer shouldn't have come down there to take pictures, if we want to use him in this scene.

Mr. Hammerstein suggested that if we wanted to keep the scene of the Hollander house and yet make it gayer, that Marie's friends in this scene could be assembled to give a shower to Julie for her baby, and that against the background of their sewing and gossip Liliom and the Sparrow should be plotting and go out to commit the robbery. Julie, worried, might follow him later.

It was felt that the culvert scene could be assumed to be near the fair grounds and that after the suicide Liliom's body should be taken to the fair grounds, either to the carousel or some place belonging to Mrs. Muskat. Then the death scene would be played there and group players would be used as needed.

Mr. Hammerstein felt that the ballet should begin with the entrance of the heavenly policeman, that Liliom should be left on stage while the scenery disappeared, and his entrance into heaven should be part of the ballet number.

Miss Helburn suggested that the last scene need not take place in the little house but that it might be laid in the discarded fair grounds, with Julie and Louise, and Wolf and Marie picnicking there. Liliom could re-appear there at the carousel he loved so much, and if needed, the ghosts or echo of the other characters could be seen or heard.

MUSICAL IDEAS:

Mr. Hammerstein felt that the love scene (scene one of the play) was almost too beautiful and too tight to tamper with in any way, but he did feel that the curtain with the falling acacias might lend itself to a beautiful number.

A possible musical number for Mrs. Muskat was suggested for Scene 3 by the lines: (pages 68 and 69) "As for you, you're an artist and you belong among artists. All the beer you want, cigars, a krone a day and a guilden on Sunday—and the girls, Liliom, the girls –".

Mr. Rodgers suggested a fine musical number for the end of the scene where Liliom discovers he is to be a father, in which he sings first with pride of the growth of a boy, and then suddenly realizes it might be a girl, and changes completely with that thought. It was felt this might be the end of the first act.

Mr. Hammerstein suggested that the fourth scene, the railroad embankment, might be played entirely in musical pantomime.

It was felt that Julie's speech to Liliom's body would make a beautiful song.

Mr. Rodgers felt that the time was ripe for a new and brilliant use of modern orchestration and instrumentation along the lines of the orchestra in the Air Force show, but more closely integrated with the play.

CAST SUGGESTIONS:

Cast suggestions for the play included—Alfred Drake for
Liliom,   Pamela Britton
For Marie,   Evelyn Wyckoff
For Julie,   Charlotte Greenwood
or Vivienne Segal for Mrs. Muskat.

It was suggested that the Sparrow could be played by a real low comedian
and that comedic possibilities could be developed between Mrs. Muskat and
the Sparrow in the antagonism which is just indicated in the play.

Meanwhile, Oscar continued his participation in the Rex Stout-led Writers' War
Board. Demaree Bess's article discussed below, "Let's Quit Pretending," appeared
in *The Saturday Evening Post*, on December 18. In the article Bess provided a detailed accounting of how the American Government had been working behind
the scenes with foreign governments and factions prior to Pearl Harbor and before
the United States entered the War. He was angry about misleading propaganda
and gave voice to the fears of many that the consequences of our joining the War
might be dire in the loss of American lives and treasure. McCormick, Wheeler, and
Nye were well-known isolationists. Robert McCormick was a key member of the
America First Committee, whose spokesperson had been Charles Lindbergh. After
Pearl Harbor, Congressman Gerald Nye did vote (reportedly with reluctance) for the
U.S. to join the War.

Oscar Hammerstein to Rex Stout, December 28, 1943

Dear Rex:-

The main purpose of this letter is to give you my reactions to the Post
article by Demaree Bess. First, however, I want to tell you we have missed
you and it will be good to see you back at your accustomed and proper
place at the head of our table. I was horribly disappointed that you could
not attend the CARMEN JONES first night. I hope when you are once
more gadding about the town you will make one of your first gads to the
Broadway Theatre as my guest.

Now about "Let's Quit Pretending," I read it with the knowledge that
you liked it and hailed it as a step forward for the Post. I also knew that

several members of the Board who had read it didn't like it at all. If they are right and you are wrong, then I, like you, have been "taken in" by it.

The chief objection, as I understand it, is that the article tends to create confusion about our war aims. But I think there is equal danger in the over-simplification of war issues that certain propagandists impose on us. It would be nice if we could label this war simply a war against Fascism. We want it to be exactly that and we want the peace to be a permanent merging of anti-fascist power. But, unfortunately, there are other complications hanging around the edges and some time somebody has got to tell the over-propagandized and misled people of the United States that this is not an anti-empire war—certainly not in the minds of many of our allies. The question of whether the Bess article is good or bad is the question of whether we should acknowledge existing imperfections in the characters of nations and men and try to build up as good a world as possible, or whether we should aim at a millennium objective and be bargained down to less. I feel that some members of the [Writers' War] Board—including you, perhaps—are in favor of the latter course. I am not. I am not in favor of covering up any of the difficulties of the coming peace. If we want our ideals to prevail later, we cannot now take positions that will later be discredited. We can't have people saying, "See! [Robert] McCormick was right about this fact or that, and you were wrong. Therefore, he is probably right about everything and we'll follow him instead of you."

It is a mistake to treat the public like very small children and tell them only what seems good for them. They are growing up faster than some of us realize. If we don't tell them the facts of life, someone else will—and it might be [Senator Burton] Wheeler or [Senator Gerald] Nye.

So I say the question is not whether it is right for Bess to say these things at this time but whether the things he says are true. If they are true the second question is, has he expressed these truths in a way that will build up or tear down morale? His article may be vulnerable to the latter charge. In that case, our job is not to discourage further statement of the facts but to restate the facts many times and in _our_ way. Good propaganda is a matter of creating opinion based on fact. Propaganda that depends on suppressing or distorting facts is phoney and will always come home to roost. It is the German kind and it is no good.

I found myself annoyed by Demaree Bess at several points in his article. He was unfair in revealing certain deceptions on the public which had obviously been demanded by military considerations at the time they were practiced. He was too smug over hind-sight exposition. But the article adds up to a good lusty attack at the growing custom of telling the American people fairy tales at a time when it is most important to tell them truths. I, as one of those people, am good and God-damn sick of fairy tales and I was glad to see someone expressing an irritation that has been churning up my insides for some time.

Happy New Year to you and come back soon.

Sincerely,

Oscar Hammerstein to Frank Adams, December 31, 1943

Dear Mr. Adams:-

Thank you for your welcome and gracefully written letter. As to your desire to hear what I have done to the defenseless Bizet, I will be delighted to help you get seats for CARMEN JONES if and when you come to New York. If you can't come, you may get some fun out of the album which Decca is preparing. It will be along the lines of the OKLAHOMA album and will be out in about two months.

This is beginning to look like an advertisement and to alleviate my own self-consciousness about this, I will first send you a published folio of the CARMEN songs and this will help you make up your mind as to whether an investment in the album is worthwhile. The follow-up will be out in a few weeks. This will be my rather awkward appreciation of your letter.

I had no intention of being so expansive when I started this letter but it is the only way I can think of for arriving at a good finish. In fact, these halting words should be an answer to your first sentence; "I don't know how much fan mail a lyric writer gets under the Roosevelt Administration." Obviously, he doesn't get much because when it comes, he doesn't know what to say.

All good wishes to you.

Sincerely,

Chapter Six
1944

The success of *Oklahoma!* brought forth an onslaught of offers to film it. As brilliant an actor and song-and-dance man as James Cagney was, it's hard to imagine him playing Curly. Cagney was short, intense, with an aura of city smarts. Though he won the Oscar for playing George M. Cohan in the 1942 biopic, *Yankee Doodle Dandy*, he was best known for playing gangsters. Curly was the good-looking, easygoing, cowboy—at home on the range—and meant to have a voice for ballads.

William Cagney to Oscar Hammerstein, January 5, 1944

A REPRESENTATIVE OF CAGNEY PRODUCTIONS WILL PRESENT A PLAN PROVIDING DISTINCT ADVANTAGES TO ALL CONCERNED IN THE PRODUCTION OF OKLAHOMA AS A MOTION PICTURE STARRING JAMES CAGNEY WILL YOU PLEASE ADVISE WHETHER YOU FIND THIS PLAN INTERESTING OR NOT REGARDS=

WILLIAM CAGNEY

William Cagney (via Joseph Shea) to Oscar Hammerstein, January 5, 1944

Dear Mr. Hammerstein:

The following is an offer to the owners of OKLAHOMA, an offer setting forth what we believe to be the most advantageous and profitable deal possible to all concerned.

FIRST: We recommend the formation of a corporation to be known as Oklahoma Pictures, Inc. This corporation will issue 100 shares of common stock and these shares will be purchased at $100.00 per share in the following manner; 60 shares by the owners of OKLAHOMA, 20 shares by William Cagney and 20 shares by James Cagney.

The Letters of Oscar Hammerstein II. Mark Eden Horowitz, Oxford University Press. © Mark Eden Horowitz 2022. DOI: 10.1093/oso/9780197538180.003.0006

Oklahoma Pictures, Inc., will star James Cagney in a production of OKLAHOMA.

Formation of the corporation in the manner described above is to permit all parties to enjoy the benefits of the capital gains tax, at 25%, instead of having to pay the straight income tax figure of 80 or 90%. Payment of the smaller, capital gains tax, can be achieved by dissolving the corporation upon completion of the motion picture.

SECOND: We believe the motion picture OKLAHOMA, starring James Cagney, will gross at least $5,000,000. The picture can be produced for $1,000,000. This cost, together with the costs of distribution, prints and advertising, will reach a total of $2,000,000. This would result in a net profit, to Oklahoma Pictures, Inc., of $3,000,000.

Cost of distribution may seem remarkably low, but this is because our present company enjoys the lowest distribution terms in the motion picture business.

This $3,000,000 net profit, under the plan we propose, would be taxable on a capital gains basis of 25%.

The 60% of the common stock held by the present owners of OKLAHOMA would bring a net return of $1,800,000. When a capital gains tax of 25% is paid there will be a sum of $1,350,000 left as "take home" money.

All of the present owners of OKLAHOMA have been extremely successful during the past year. We believe they will understand this amount of "take home" money, $1,350,000, can be realized only through the formation and the dissolution of a corporation that had been established to make a single motion picture. In view of the heavy income taxes the owners of OKLAHOMA have had to pay on their respective incomes from the stage production, we believe they will appreciate the advantages inherent in the proposal we are offering.

THIRD: James Cagney and William Cagney were the star and the producer, respectively, of "Yankee Doodle Dandy," the motion picture version of the life of George M. Cohan. Due to the combined efforts of the star and the producer "Yankee Doodle Dandy" will gross approximately $8,000,000. We therefore feel that we are not being too optimistic in setting the figure of $5,000,000 as the possible gross on the motion picture OKLAHOMA.

FOURTH: While the advantage exists—of earning a large amount of money immediately and placing it on a capital gains basis—we believe that any further decision to delay the motion picture production of OKLAHOMA may be a serious financial mistake.

We therefore propose that we make this motion picture for Fall release with an agreement to withhold its distribution in the New York and Chicago metropolitan areas, or wherever the stage production is playing at the time of the release of the picture.

FIFTH: Presently we are enjoying the greatest box office boom in the history of motion pictures. The owners of OKLAHOMA can cash in on this boom only by allowing the stage production to be made into a motion picture as soon as it is possible to prepare a shooting script. Throughout this year—1944—the box office should remain extremely healthy. As the war progresses in favor of the Allied Nations there is the constant threat of an economic decline that will throw thousands of so-called defense workers out of their jobs and that will, most certainly, serve as a depressant at the box office.

The urgency for immediate motion picture production OKLAHOMA lies not only in the existence of a remarkable box office boom, but also in the fact that all participants in the venture may take advantage of the capital gains tax feature, which, at the present time, still provides the extremely low taxation rate of 25%

Respectfully,

CAGNEY PRODUCTIONS, INC.

By William Cagney

President

Oscar Hammerstein to Joseph Shea of William Cagney Productions, January 19, 1944

Dear Mr. Shea:

Please forgive my not answering sooner. I have just come back from my farm where I was doing some work.

As far as OKLAHOMA is concerned, Mr. Rodgers and I and the Theatre Guild all feel that there is no basis on which we can sell OKLAHOMA for pictures. Its theatrical career is too prosperous at the moment and there is no telling how long it will last.

Very truly yours,

At the time, Oscar couldn't have imagined how successful *Oklahoma!* would become. The normal run for hit musicals in the 1930s and 40s could be less than a year. *Show Boat*, Oscar's longest running show to date, had a run of 577 performances. *Oklahoma!* ran for 2,212 performances—over five years—becoming the longest running musical in Broadway history, not to be bested until *My Fair Lady* overcame it in 1961—thirteen years and two months after *Oklahoma!* closed.

Lillian Hellman wrote Oscar on behalf of the Dramatists Guild Council (and co-council member, Richard Rodgers), urging him to serve on a committee on "new problems which have come up since signing of the last contract, most of them concerned with the sale of motion pictures."

Oscar Hammerstein to Lillian Hellman, January 10, 1944

Dear Lillian:-

I would like to serve on this committee. The trouble with me is I would like to serve on all committees. The result is I am becoming progressively useless as I join more each week.

How often do you think this one would meet? My answer will have to depend on that.

All good wishes to you.

Sincerely,

The Revuers (Betty Comden, Adolph Green, Alvin Hammer, Judy Holliday née Tuvim) to Oscar Hammerstein, January 9, 1944

Dear Mr. Hammerstein –

We are now out at Twentieth Century-Fox, finishing work on "Greenwich Village", our first picture. Remembering how wonderful it was meeting you, and working—however briefly—on that show that shall remain nameless, we were hoping we might be able to work together with you again. Would there be anything for us in "State Fair"?

As you may or may not know, Judy is now a contract player at Fox, having been signed on an individual contract—and there is a good possibility that the rest of us may also be signed in a short time.

As for "Greenwich Village"—we do a version of our operetta, "The Baroness Bazooka", and we also wrote a number specifically for the picture. In addition to this we have an occasional line with Don Ameche. We're not quite sure how or if we could fit into "State Fair", but the fact that we do write and perform special material might lead to conceiving something to fit in, since there are numerous carnival scenes.

Either way—we would love to hear from you.

Sincerely,

The Revuers

Adolph Green

Alvin Hammer

Betty Comden

and

Judy Tuvim

Oscar Hammerstein to the Revuers, January 18, 1944

Dear Revuers:

Thank you for your letter. It's a good idea and as I write the script of STATE FAIR, I will try to think of some way of working you in.

All good wishes to you.

Sincerely,

The Revuers did not appear in *State Fair*. By year's end Betty Comden and Adolph Green had a hit Broadway musical of their own—*On the Town*. With its urban setting and modern sounding score it was definitively *not* in the mold of *Oklahoma!* (or *State Fair*), but equally American and also perfect for a country at war. Comden and

Green wrote the book and lyrics and played two of the show's six leads. Judy Tuvim became Judy Holliday.

Oscar Hammerstein to Reggie Hammerstein, January 1944

Dear Reggie:-

I am sorry I have taken so long to answer your letter and the enclosed clippings which I appreciated very much. I keep saying I am coming out to Chicago soon and therefore it's unnecessary to write to you. I still intend to come out soon but I thought I better write to you anyway to convince you that you have not been forgotten. The kids were all very grateful for your generosity at Christmas and I believe letters of thanks will be dribbling in to you. We had sixteen at the house over the Christmas week-end and I don't need to describe to you the details because you could probably write all the dialogue and stage directions without having been there.

This year was notable because the game of chess seemed to dominate. I must warn you not to play Jimmy when you come back—anyway not until you have had a few games to warm up with me first. He is becoming a real menace. Susan had her appendix out last week and this week she is dancing. I had a long letter from Billy today. He is well and has just received the watch we gave him. The letter was written on Christmas day so the timing must be pretty good. I take it that he has seen quite a little action but that so far he has not been in any grave danger. The other day, however, I read that the APC 21 had been sunk by the Japanese. Billy's boat is the APC 20.

You probably read that Billy Rose bought the Ziegfeld Theatre. He is going to put on a super revue there next September for which he wanted Dick and me to write the music and lyrics and other material. We are turning him down because we would rather spend that time creating a book of a show we could copyright and own. A revue would only mean increased income for next year only a very small part of which I can keep. Billy wants Dorothy to help him redecorate the theatre and offices and it seems that every time she decides to get out of the business things like this keep coming up. She is right now one of the hottest chintz slingers in town.

I am going to try very hard to come out within the next ten days or two weeks. I am very anxious to see the show and sit down and talk to you. I will let you know at least a few days in advance of my arrival. We all send our love.

Oc

Oscar Hammerstein to Timothy Adams,[1] Franklin County Hospital, January 18, 1944

Dear Tim:-

Your father told me about your being whipped off to a hospital and as one who is an old appendicitis man himself I thought I would like to write and welcome you into our club. Last May I was whipped off in much the same way. The only difference in my case was that after they got in there they found that my appendix was perfectly all right. They took it out anyway and told me I had something else called Diverticulitis (?)—a sickness of which I had never heard of and of which I am very proud.

All good wishes to you for a quick recovery.

Sincerely,

Oscar Hammerstein to Laurence Schwab, (excerpt) January 20, 1944

I am trying to write STATE FAIR with my right hand and handle five or six committees with my left. This week the committees won.

Notes re. conference between Theresa Helburn and Lawrence Langner of the Theatre Guild, and Richard Rodgers, and Oscar Hammerstein, January 20, 1944

Re. LILIOM

Mr. Rodgers and Mr. Hammerstein said they didn't have time to do much work on it.[2]

Discussing the character of Julie, Mr. Langner thought that she showed fight and aggressiveness in her first scene with Mrs. Muskat and that the second scene in the photographer's office would also be made a conflict between the two women. There was no reason for her to take Mrs. Muskat's attempt to get Liliom back lying down. Julie should show a lot of spirit.

Lawrence also suggested that Julie might go out and get herself a job. Also that the theme of their wanting to go to America would make an

---

[1] Timothy Adams was the son of columnist and wit, Franklin P. Adams.
[2] Hammerstein penciled a star next to this sentence.

amusing and cheerful motif. Dickie felt there was a good song in what she expected to find in America.

It was suggested to Oscar that Julie's attitude in the beginning keep more like her attitude at the end. That is, instead of confessing all Liliom's faults to Marie she would hide them and play up the fact that they were going to America, and put on a very gallant mask.

The general feeling at the end of the conference seemed to be that while the play was a challenge it would be an inspiring one to meet.

Oscar also felt that Mrs. Hollander could be developed amusingly and there could be good comedy made of the conflict between Mrs. Muskat and Mrs. Hollander, also the carpenter could be developed comedically.

It was suggested that the party given for Marie and her offspring should be given on or near the fair grounds, possibly a little cafe on the fair grounds, or that Mrs. Muskat might give it as a lure for Liliom.

Miss Helburn reiterated that upon re-reading the book she felt the play halfway between CARMEN JONES and OKLAHOMA! in tone—more serious than the latter and not as serious as the former—that the underlying emotional theme had great audience appeal. It seemed to her clearer than ever that a strong love motif underlay everything Liliom did, and that the Heavenly Judge understood this completely, even to understanding that his striking of his child, which left no feeling except that of a caress, was again nothing but a thwarted gesture of love.

Casting suggestions included: Mady Christians, Jessie Royce Landis, and Evelyn Varden as Mrs. Muskat—Margaret Douglas as Mother Hollander, Patricia Peardon for Marie, Walter Sleazak for The Sparrow, George Rasely and George Meador, Natalie Hall and Miss McWatters for what you will.

P.S. MR. RODGERS later suggested that Liliom's entire dream of heaven should be identified with his dream of America and that this would lend itself to excellent comedic and pictorial and musical treatment.

Oscar Hammerstein to Reggie Hammerstein, February 1, 1944

Dear Reg:

You must think you're the forgotten man out there in Chicago in a lonely exile—or are things better socially than they were last year? Anyway

I owe you a letter for a long time. I've kept expecting to come out there but so far, it's been impossible to get away. I am far behind my schedule in writing State Fair and I'm pretty well weighted down with various committee's [*sic*]. This week I came down to the farm to get away from committee's and really get some work done. It was a good idea. I'm really rolling along down here.

Last week-end came a Life Photographer and a writer. They are writing one of those "close-ups" of me. The writer has spent three sessions with me and has also consulted people who know me. They do a thorough job, but God knows how it will turn out. It makes you think back and wonder if perhaps you didn't commit some crime in the past when you were un[con]scious and they'll dig it up. The story will come out in two or three weeks. At about the same time it is very likely that I will have a "profile" in the New Yorker and they are doing a similar type of spread in P.M. Everyone will swear I have a publicity man engaged in a big public relations campaign, but all these things came un-solicited, and they just happened to come at the same time.

I suppose you know all about Arthur. In case you don't, I'll tell you. About two weeks ago I got a letter from him, from Palm Beach. The doctor down there believed he had a prostate cancer. Arthur took the news bravely, as he does everything, and went into the hospital to have them take out a piece and examine it. He wrote to me on the eve of this ordeal and said: "I am looking at this through a lifetime of seventy one years, and I have done all the things I wanted to do."

A couple of days later Dorothy called me from Chicago. The doctor had wired her to come down. His condition was critical. He had a stomach hemorrhage on the operating table, and the doctor thought there might be cancer there, too. Dorothy got down there and a few days later the diagnosis came up—no cancer! She expects him to be out of the hospital in ten days! Harold Hyman told me he should never have gone to a doctor who didn't know all about his condition there. If Arthur would let himself alone—at seventy one—he'd be much better off. Harold said when men have a can-cerous prostate, the cure is castration. I said Arthur would much rather have his head cut off or his heart cut out. He never would have let them!

Carmen Jones is now doing $45,000 a week. Capacity. I saw the show last week and Oklahoma, too and took very few notes on either. How is your company out there? Are you snapping the whip on them?

I have a great many things to talk to you about when I get out there. There are things afoot. Dick found a book we both think will make a good straight play. R.K.O was about to make a picture of it. We unraveled a complicated business situation and secured the dramatic rights. We are now looking for an author. I could do it, but I prefer to do a musical with him, after State Fair—especially since he's the one who found this property and let me in.

Another possibility—more remote—is that I may be about to buy back Arthur's theatre! Don't worry. It would be on almost a free ride basis. Meanwhile don't breathe it to anyone. As I say, it's remote.

Anyway, if you bide your time out there a while, I know something is going to come along for you to come in on with me.

I had a long letter from Bill to-day. He is fine and in good spirits, apparently. I had a gloomy letter from Goofy. They've taken away his appropriations and he can't put on his Showmobile units anymore. This will effect Maggie, too.

We are putting on a big show as a tribute to Larry Hart. So far we have Mary Martin, Gertrude Lawrence, Morton Gould, Paul Wightman [sic], Clifton Fadiman, Vivienne Segal and a crowd of others I can't remember. I'm going to have Jimmy Walker as M.C. conduct the show like the narrator in Our Town. Did you ever see it?

In case you have heard of the "plagiarism" suit against me for Carmen Jones, don't worry about it. It is another of those screwball cases.

We saw Colette—your Colette—at The Stork a few weeks ago. She looked phenomenal—about twenty four. Or maybe my old eyes are growing dim and have lost their sense of proportion about these things. She said she had seen you a little while before you left for Chicago. I think you made a mistake there.

That's all the news, I think. We all send our love.

Oscar Hammerstein to William Perlberg, Twentieth Century-Fox Film Corp., February 4, 1944

Dear Bill:-

Dick and I had an interview with Kathryn Grayson. It was a very unofficial one because her agent, due to her contract with Metro, didn't want to have any part in arranging an interview which concerned a picture being made by another studio. So we put it in on the terms of our being interested in her for a play—which we certainly would be. When we got her into our office, however, we told her about the picture.

The more we get into the picture—and you will be glad to know that we are really into it now—the better Grayson looks for the part of "Margie". Before she leaves town she is going to sing for us so that we have an idea of her range and her effectiveness when deprived of the showy cadenzas with which Metro has always finished up her refrains.

More later. All good wishes,

Sincerely,

Theresa Helburn to Richard Rodgers and Oscar Hammerstein, February 4, 1944

Dear Dickie and Oscar,

Here's a belated memo on our last conference, brought up to date with Dickie's new suggestion.

After seeing "Mexican Hayride"[3] last night I feel more strongly than ever how foolish it is to pour all the elaborate superstructure of costumes, scenery, etc. on an empty framework. It can't help but be a relief to musical comedy audiences to start with real people.

Maybe we're just spoiled by OKLAHOMA!—but so are a lot of other people (even George Jean Nathan[4]—forgive me for bringing up the name!)

Love and à bientôt.

Yours,

Terry

---

[3] *Mexican Hayride* was a musical comedy co-starring Bobby Clark (on the run in a series of disguises) and June Havoc (as a female bullfighter). The lavish production—produced by Michael Todd—was the star of the evening. The Cole Porter score was a weak one. Escapism made the show a wartime hit.

[4] George Jean Nathan was a theater critic, known for being harshly judgmental. He was the purported model for the character of Addison De Witt in *All About Eve*.

Oscar Hammerstein to Harlan Fiske Stone, Chief Justice, U.S. Supreme Court, February 17, 1944

Dear Justice Stone:-

At a meeting of the Writers' War Board, yesterday, I was delegated to ask a favor of you. We have a "brief items" activity in which we supply material to Army Camp papers, "house organ" magazines in factories, etc. One of the most useful of brief items which we could send out now would be a short (200 or 300-word) comment exploding the myth of racial distinctions and alleged superiorities and inferiorities. Such an article if signed by you would be printed by many editors who are too unaware of the importance of such subject matter to carry it in their papers for its own sake.

We would not make such a request of you if we didn't think it absolutely essential that this theme be brought home forcefully to this kind of reader. We assume also that you agree with our concern on this subject.

I am enclosing an example of the kind of publication in which these "brief items" appear.

This has nothing to do with the subject but I cannot help asking you if you remember a very thin and sallow boy who studied trusts under you in 1916. That was me. I made little use of what I learned and turned out to be an author of musical comedies.

All good wishes to you.

Sadly, later that year Stone joined the, now discredited, majority opinion in *Korematsu v. United States*, which ruled that putting Japanese Americans in internment camps was constitutional.

The song "Boys and Girls Like You and Me" was cut from *Oklahoma!* and replaced with a reprise of "People Will Say We're in Love". The cut song was then sold to MGM for use in their film *Meet Me in St. Louis*.

Oscar Hammerstein to Arthur Freed (MGM), February 29, 1944

Dear Arthur:

Dick and I happened to look at a communication from your music department to our publisher. It contained this description:

"The trolley arrives at the place where the World's Fair is to be built and the people get off the trolley. Esther wanders by herself and John tries to find her so she won't be late for the return trolley. John sees Esther in a romantic setting—he comes up and they walk and talk. As they come to a puddle John picks up Esther in his arms then she sings 'Boys and Girls Like You and Me.'"

We wouldn't presume to make any criticism three thousand miles away but for whatever the comment is worth, we were disturbed by the incongruous feeling of going into a song which talks about girls and boys walking through the world with a girl held in the arms of a boy and the public distracted by marveling at his feat of strength, listening to the lyric and music and being enthralled thereby.

For all we know, the number may never have been shot like this or maybe it hasn't been shot at all yet. In case it hasn't been, we are hereby recording our fears for this way of going into it.

I hear you are coming to town soon. Am looking forward to seeing you.

As ever,

Oscar

Arthur Freed (MGM) to Oscar Hammerstein, March 4, 1944

Dear Oscar:

I hasten to reply to your letter about the rendition of BOYS AND GIRLS, and also to allay your fears that the song was shot according to the notice sent to the publishers, which you quoted.

I am sure that you will be very happy when you see the rendition which we have photographed. It is done very simply, without any superhistrionics, by Judy Garland to her boy friend. The camera is on Judy's face throughout the whole rendition and all she does is sing the tender philosophy of your lyric.

Again I repeat I am sure that you and Dick will feel very gratified at the manner in which Vincente Minnelli so simply and eloquently presented this wonderful song. I am anxious for you to see it.

As always,

Arthur

ARTHUR FREED

"Boys and Girls Like You and Me" was cut from *Meet Me in St. Louis* after the film's first preview.

Oscar Hammerstein to Reggie Hammerstein (excerpt), March 3, 1944

As to your scathing comments about my suggestions for your financial recklessness I will discuss those when I see you and whoever is the cause of it get her out of your rooms before I arrive.

Oklahoma! boasted the first original-cast recording of a Broadway musical—the first to preserve a near complete recording of a score, performed by its original cast, with its original orchestrations, under the direction of its musical director. The album was released by Decca in December 1943 as a boxed-set of six 78 rpm records and became an immediate best-seller.

Pfc D. Gregory, Camp McCoy, Wis. To Oscar Hammerstein, March 17, 1944

My dear Mr. Hammerstein–

I know of <u>no</u> subtle reasoning with which to justify the impertinence of my request, but because I would value it inserted in my album of <u>Oklahoma</u>—may I have your autograph?

If you do not reply, I will consider myself justly rebuked, and will remain an admirer of your work.

Sincerely–

Oscar Hammerstein to Pfc. D. Gregory, March 23, 1944

Dear Mr. Gregory:-

Far from regarding your request as impertinent, I feel highly complimented.

I think it would be more fitting if I were asking you for your autograph. Anyway, here's mine.

Sincerely.

Josef Israels, 2nd /Lt. USMS, At Sea, to Richard Rodgers and Oscar, March 25, 1944

GENTLEMEN:

THIS NOTE WILL BE MAILED IN A FEW DAYS AT ONE OF OUR MORE DISTANT SOUTH PACIFIC BASES. IT'S A FAN LETTER PRIMARILY ON MY OWN BEHALF, BUT ALSO FOR MOST OF THE 100 ODD MEN ON THIS MERCHANT SHIP. WE HAVE BEEN TALKING ABOUT THE "OKLAHOMA" MUSIC AND LYRICS AND HOW MUCH PLEASURE THEY HAVE GIVEN US. THE SONGS ARE OF SUCH UNUSUAL QUALITY AND SO LASTING IN OUR MINDS THAT I FELT IT MIGHT GIVE YOU SOME RECIPROCAL PLEASURE TO KNOW OF ONE MORE PLACE WHERE YOUR WORK IS ESPECIALLY APPRECIATED.

I HAPPEN TO BE THE ONLY ONE ABOARD WHO HAS SEEN "OKLAHOMA" IN NEW YORK. WHEN I BROUGHT AN ALBUM OF THE MUSIC ON BOARD AND PLAYED IT FOR THE FIRST TIME MANY OF THE MEN PRICKED UP AN EAR AT "PEOPLE WILL SAY" AND PERHAPS "SURREY" BECAUSE OF HAVING HEARD IT PLUGGED ON THE AIR. (AT SEA WE HAVE NO BROADCAST RECEPTION-WE HAVEN'T BEEN ABLE TO GET ONE OF THE SAFE NON RADIATING RECEIVERS) BUT AFTER A FEW PLAYINGS THE RECORDS HAVE BECOME THE TOP FAVORITE OF EVERY ONE ON BOARD. IT NOW SEEMS DOUBTFUL IF OUR PRESENT ALBUM WILL OUTLAST THIS TRIP AND WE WILL HAVE TO GET MORE OF THEM

NEXT TIME WE REACH THE U.S. LIKEWISE WE KNOW WE WILL HAVE TO STRENUOUSLY RESIST ATTEMPTS BY SHORE UNITS ON THE LITTLE ISLANDS OUT HERE TO SEIZE, BORROW OR BUY OUR "OKLAHOMA" ALBUM.

WE KNOW YOU'VE HEARD MUCH PRAISE FOR "OKLAHOMA" FROM THE PROFESSORIAL CRITICS. JUST WHAT ITS QUALITIES MUSICALLY AND LYRICALLY ARE TO MAKE IT SO HAUNTING AND LIFTING AN EXPERIENCE IS HARD TO DEFINE. BUT I THINK THERE'S LITTLE DOUBT OF THESE SONGS TAKING THEIR PLACE WITH THOSE OF "SHOW BOAT", "PORGY AND BESS" TO BELONG TO THE SELECT CATALOGUE OF GENUINE AMERICAN FOLK OPERA. LEAVING ART OUT OF IT ENTIRELY THERE IS SOMETHING CLEAN WASHED AND BRIGHT ABOUT THE TUNES, THE LYRICS ARE SO LITERATE THAT LISTENERS QUICKLY KNOW THE WORDS AND CHUCKLE AT THEM. THERE IS NOSTALGIA FOR ANYONE WHO HAS EVER EVEN VISITED AN AMERICAN FARM IN "BEAUTIFUL MORNING" AND THE LESS PLUGGED SONGS LIKE "MANY A NEW DAY" ARE MEMORABLE WHEN YOU LEARN TO LISTEN TO THEM.

I HOPE YOU'LL BE INTERESTED TO KNOW WHAT A WORKOUT "OKLAHOMA" HAS HAD OVER 10,000 MILES OF THE OCEAN. WE ON BOARD THANK YOU FOR WRITING THE SHOW AND ALL HOPE TO SEE IT WHEN THE OPPORTUNITY PRESENTS ITSELF. WE EVEN FEEL IT WILL BE RUNNING AFTER THE WAR, WHENEVER THAT MAY BE.

SINCERELY

JOSEF ISRAELS 2ND, RADIO OFFICER

MS AMERICAN PACKER

Oscar Hammerstein to Josef Israels, April 14, 1944

Dear Lt. Israels:-

I WANT TO THANK YOU FOR YOUR VERY KIND LETTER WRITTEN AT SEA AND IT GIVES MR. RODGERS AND ME GREAT

PLEASURE AND GRATIFICATION TO KNOW THAT WE HAVE BEEN ABLE TO MAKE SOME SMALL CONTRIBUTION TO MEN WHO ARE DOING SO MUCH FOR US. IT WAS THOUGHTFUL OF YOU TO WRITE TO US. IF YOU LET US KNOW WHERE WE CAN SEND YOU A FRESH ALBUM WHEN YOU HAVE WORN THIS ONE OUT WE SHALL BE GLAD TO DO IT

ALL GOOD WISHES TO YOU

SINCERELY,

William Perlberg (Twentieth Century-Fox Film Corp.) to Oscar Hammerstein, March 28, 1944

Dear Oscar:

I read the seventy-four pages of the script, and can't tell you how delighted I am with it. I agree with you it may be a little long, but even that will be hard to tell until you have completed the entire script and we can judge the length from viewing the whole. In that way we can decide better, between us, how much and what to cut.

The only major criticism I have is on Page 71, in the scene between Pat and Margie where you make reference to the volcano which is just about to bust in Europe. I think we must decide to avoid all reference to the war—tell our story as of 1939, and not worry too [much about current events]. In "COVER GIRL", I personally disliked the alibi that Gene Kelly had just returned from the wars, a hero and discharged. It is altogether too obvious an excuse and, in my opinion, wholly unnecessary.

The three songs I heard are still ringing in my ears, and I want to tell you how thrilled I am.

My best to Dick and yourself.

Sincerely,

Bill

Oscar Hammerstein to Herbert Stothart (excerpt), March 30, 1944

I am just finishing up a picture for Fox which has been written here in the East and I am coming out there for the month of May to do all I can to keep the shooting script on the same track as my first draft. This will probably be a vain endeavor because once June comes and I return to the East, they will immediately call in four authors to fix it.

In Richard Rodgers' autobiography he wrote that Lawrence Langner's wife discovered John Raitt in California and "sent him East to audition for *Oklahoma!* He was a big, brawny fellow with a magnificent baritone who would be perfect either for Curly in *Oklahoma!* or Billy Bigelow . . . in *Carousel*—so we agreed to cast him as both. Since we weren't yet ready to begin rehearsals for *Carousel*, we put him in the Chicago company of *Oklahoma!* just to keep him busy."

Reggie Hammerstein (in Chicago) to Oscar Hammerstein, circa March, 1944

Dear Oc:

Agree with you that John Raitt should develope [*sic*] into the best Curly of all. I have been very busy breaking him in. Tell Alice as soon as things let up I will write her.

Love to all

Reggie

Oscar Hammerstein to Robert Pollak, *Chicago Daily Times* (excerpt), April 3, 1944

About FALSTAFF, I cannot report an intelligent reaction because the performance was so inept that there is no way of judging the text. Neither Mr. Tibbett nor Sir Thomas Beecham seemed to care whether it was written in English or some Mongolian dialect. I understand the later performances were very much better.

Oscar Hammerstein to Hy Kraft, April 14, 1944

Dear Hy:-

20th Century Fox is providing us with a suite at the Beverly Wilshire. The swimming pool and the tennis courts will be of little compensation for the society of THAT superior establishment but it looks now as if I am going to be in a state of very busy confusion during the short month that we shall be there and I would not subject you to this unpleasant atmosphere. It is all right to say, "treat our house as if it were your own" but I wouldn't treat my own house the way I intend to treat the Beverly Wilshire.

We hope, however, that there will be no ill feeling and that the salami and white radish will be available on several midnights.

Looking forward to seeing you. As for your brother, Reggie, I don't see how you stand him.

Love,

Oscar Hammerstein to Jerome Kern, April 18, 1944

Dear Jerry:-

It's a funny thing that I, too, picked up my very incomplete treatment of Marco Polo a few weeks ago and while several things about it troubled me I still felt the enchantment of its inner beauty. The most important and the worst thing I have to say at this point is that I wouldn't be able to do any work on it for a full year. I expect to finish the picture I am working on early in June then I am going back to Doylestown to keep a promise I have faithfully made myself to rest for from four to six weeks and do nothing at all. After that I start working on the adaptation of LILIOM which I am doing with Dick for the Theatre Guild. This will go into rehearsal sometime in February and that would bring its New York opening not very much before a year from now.

On the vague and remote project of Serlin's RIP VAN WINKLE I had luncheon with him last week and I am very favorably impressed so far. I also think there is probably a great musical play to be written about RIP VAN WINKLE but this is a hunch rather than a conviction based on detailed study.

We arrive at the Beverly Wilshire May 4th. We will be there for about a month and you and I will be able to talk these things over. How about going to the opening of SHOW BOAT which I believe is on May 6th? Would you and Eva have dinner with us? And will you make sure that Edwin Lester gets us seats together? (This of course, on the assumption that you have not already booked yourself with someone else that evening.)

I have two more items to take up before I close and they both concern Rommy. He asked me if it wasn't true that Lena Horne was octane? He also has a theory that that Dewey will not run for president this time but will wait for four years so that he will be sure of a re-election.

Hoping this will hold you until I see you and with love to all,

Sincerely,

Jerome Kern to Oscar Hammerstein (excerpt), April 24, 1944

I think Marco Polo is well worth waiting for. So I'm knocking together some tunes. None of this rushing business next year!

On May 2, *Oklahoma!* was awarded a "special" Pulitzer Prize. According to Rodgers, "The reason for this unusual citation was that word had spread that I was to be the recipient of the prize in music, an honor that I did not feel I could accept without sharing it with Oscar. Therefore the special award to *Oklahoma!* was given as something of a compromise." This might be taken with a grain of salt. The very first Pulitzer for music had only been given the year before. To date no musical has won the Pulitzer in the category of Music. At the time, only one musical had won under the category of drama—*Of Thee I Sing* in 1932—and in that case the show's composer, George Gershwin, was not included in the prize, though its lyricist, Ira Gershwin, was. Oscar provides another explanation as to why they weren't awarded the prize in drama in his May 8 letter to Maggie Hammerstein.

Arthur Schwartz to Oscar Hammerstein, May 3, 1944

Dear Oscar,

I'm quite thrilled that you and Dick were recognized by the Pulitzer boys, even tho they didn't go all-out.

Do they suppose they're defending the dray-ma or something, by such a childish verdict?

Get well in a hurry, and come out here to recuperate.

All the best from us both.

Arthur

Alfred Drake to Oscar Hammerstein, May 3, 1944

Dear Oscar,

Both Harvey and I were taken aback to read of your illness and glad to hear from Reggie that you are much improved. We hope you'll be up and out soon.

Anyway, this letter gives me the opportunity to say a few things that have been on my chest.

First—I'm delighted about the Pulitzer award and may I add my congratulations to the many others you must have received. It couldn't have gone to two more deserving people than you and Dick. As a matter of fact, it was one of the few good decisions the Pulitzer Prize Committee made.

Second—and this one I've been meaning to tell you for some time— Harvey[5] and I saw "Carmen Jones" while on our week-end honey-moon. The night before we had seen "Othello" which was a bitter disappointment. We came to "Carmen Jones" with the expectation, that, since the critics' judgments were not to be relied on, your show might easily have been blown up, too.

Well, we had one of the best evenings we've ever had in the theatre. Your adaptation has almost everything one could ask for, - humor, highly-colored characters (no racist pun intended) and honest-to-God poetry. I shan't forget the line about being like a "leaf that's lost its tree"—an inferior writer would have found it so easy to reverse it—and be banal.

So from Harvey and me, this is thank you for helping to make our honeymoon memorable.

Get well quick.

Alfred.

[5] Drake's wife's name was Esther Harvey Brown, ergo the "Harvey."

Oscar Hammerstein to Margaret "Maggie" Hammerstein
(excerpt), May 8, 1944

It will surprise you to hear unless Alice has written to you that I have just gotten out of the Doctors Hospital after an emergency appendectomy which didn't turn out to be appendix trouble at all but there was something wrong inside and the doctors fixed it up and closed me up and I feel fine now. This postponed our trip to California and State Fair. I am going down to the farm now to recuperate and soon after that I will start working on the adaptation of LILIOM. Did you hear that Dick Rodgers and I were given a special Pulitzer award for OKLAHOMA. We are both very happy about it. The Committee gave no Pulitzer prize to a play and sort of substituted this special award. We could not have gone under the heading of the definition of "Pulitzer Prize Play" because OKLAHOMA is the adaptation of another play and they sort of created something special for us.

Oscar Hammerstein to Stella Applebaum, *Parents' Magazine*
(excerpt), May 8, 1944

I am squarely against a new national anthem. I believe that the Star Spangled Banner has inspiring words and an uplifting melody and it has been doing fine for us. I know it would be difficult to get a more smoothly written poem but I can't as an American imagine anything that could take the place of this song which has become so traditional with us and which seems to me to have such splendid vitality.

William Perlberg (Twentieth Century-Fox Film Corp.) to Oscar
Hammerstein, May 16, 1944

Dear Oscar:

I am so glad you are out of the hospital and down on the farm resting.

Now that the script is completed and in such good shape, I am anxious to have the music, so I would appreciate it very much if you would have the recordings made as soon as possible. This is very important, as Metro is willing to give us Kathryn Grayson but I have to read the script and play the music for both her and some executives of Metro before they will okay the loan-out. Then, if they approve, they will give me the date of her availability, and on whatever that date is we will start the picture.

I am pretty sure we will get her, so we will have her, and Dick Haymes for Wayne. I am scouting around now for a good Emily and Pat. Alice Faye has just left the hospital with her new baby, and I am hoping to talk her into playing the part. I am also scouting around for a good director, but no name has presented itself as yet with which I am entirely satisfied. What do you think of Bob Burns for the part of Abel? I was thinking of making a test of him for the role.

Please let me know when you expect to record, so I will know when to expect the sound tracks, and I can't impress on you too much what a help it will be to me to get them as soon as possible. It will be a great influence with Alice Faye, also, to hear the numbers she will do. I would like to get these people committed before they are set for other pictures.

All the best to you,

As ever,

Bill

William Perlberg

Of the names Perlberg suggests only Dick Haymes ended up in the film. Fay Bainter ended up in the part for which Oscar suggests Spring Byington in the letter below.

Oscar Hammerstein to William Perlberg, Twentieth Century-Fox Film Corp., May 20, 1944

Dear Bill:-

I am sorry that the sound tracks have been so delayed. At the time that I went to the hospital there was one more song to write and Dick and I didn't want to start on the sound tracks until we had a full score. I am well enough now to go back to work and I have already started on this song. I expect to send the lyric to Dick within a few days and if he has the luck to set the melody to it with his usual speed we ought to be able to make the tracks sometime during the week beginning May 28th. We have our singers lined up and we will push it through as fast as possible realizing from your letter how important it is to get the material out to you.

I think Kathryn Grayson is just the right girl for the part and I hope you can get her. With Alice Faye I imagine you will have a selling job on your hands because while it is a very good part and might even turn out to be the best part in the picture, it is not the central part or star part. This picture, however, has no other part that can be described that way either. It is merely about six people (not including Blue Boy and Esmerelda) I think that Bob Burns is a very interesting "Abel". I have never seen him do anything like this but I think that under the right kind of direction and with cooperation on his part that would lead him to turn in a characterization rather than a consciously comic performance he is a by no means impossible candidate.

And have you thought of anyone for "Melissa"? I have a feeling that what she definitely must not be is a typical character woman. I would like her to be a middle-aged woman who is still pretty and not too weather-beaten by the farm. How about Spring Byington? My only objection to her would be that she's been in too many pictures but I think she would be able to play the part well.

After I get this number written I will spend some time trying to think up some suggestions for you. I will try to think in terms of people I know from the stage because when it comes to picture people you will be a few lengths ahead of me anyway.

I guess that's all I can talk about now. As soon as you have any further news or ideas shoot them on to me. I am very steamed up about this picture.

Kindest regards.

As ever,

Oscar Hammerstein to Hy Kraft (excerpt), May 20, 1944

In the next issue of LIFE (the one that comes out Friday, May 26th) there will be what they call a "close-up" of me. From what I have heard of it, it is a kind of vulgar account of all the money I am making and will be followed up the ensuing months by a swarm of people putting a swarm of bees on me on the theory that anything from 100 to 1000 bucks would mean very little to me and a whole lot to them. I am getting several thousand copies of the tax schedule to send them in reply.

Oscar was more directly involved in the running of his farm than is generally assumed.

Oscar Hammerstein to H. H. Hackney, May 31, 1944

Dear Mr. Hackney:-

Thank you for your letter. There is no need to be worried about your lack of information concerning me. As a matter of fact up to a few weeks ago I had never heard of Jock of Wheatland and this is a much more unforgivable ignorance.

I would like, however, to take advantage of your contrite mood and impose on you for some advice. From the little I have learned about Angus breeding it seems to me that in my present position starting a new herd that it would be better to buy a few first class heifers instead of the kind that most people are culling from their herds. It also seems to me that the best way for me to get good cows is to buy them at sales when the bidding is not lively. Am I right in these assumptions? I ask these questions with the greatest humility because I know next to nothing about this subject on which you are so well informed.

My kindest regards to Mrs. Hackney and yourself.

Very truly yours,

Oscar Hammerstein to H. H. Hackney, June 15, 1944

Dear Mr. Hackney:-

This is not so much to answer your last letter (which required no answer) but to tell you that last weekend I was stopping in Libertyville which is about twenty miles from Chicago and I visited Mr. Sidney Florsheim who has a fine herd of Angus. Two of his heifers stood out from the rest in such a manner that even my inexpert eye was attracted by them and they both turned out to be daughters of your Pride Eric. There was nothing in the meadow that could touch them.

I thought you might be interested to hear this. All good wishes to you.

Sincerely,

Oscar Hammerstein to Lena Horne, May 31, 1944

Dear Miss Horne:-

My son, who is in the Navy somewhere in the South Pacific, writes to me that a friend of his, a colored boy who is in his crew, would like nothing better in the world than to have an autographed picture of you. His name is Nick. I don't know his last name. You could send the picture to me and I would forward it or if you wish you could send it to

Nick

c/o William Hammerstein, QM 1/c

USSAPc 20

Fleet Post Office

San Francisco, California

I hope you will forgive me for bothering you about this but Bill's report of Nick's ardor was something that I thought should be rewarded with specific action.

All good wishes to you.

Sincerely,

Philanthropist, businessman, and Broadway "angel" Howard Cullman contacted Oscar about plans to purchase what was then called the Manhattan Theatre. The theater was built between 1924 and 1927 by Arthur Hammerstein who named it Hammerstein's Theatre after his father, the first Oscar. Cullman wanted to restore the theater to its original glory and thought it appropriate for Oscar (and Rodgers) to take at least some small part in the investment. Cullman's plan never came to fruition. It's currently the Ed Sullivan Theatre.

Oscar Hammerstein to Howard Cullman, May 31, 1944

Dear Howard:-

Thank you for your nice letter of May 26th.

I agree with you that the right name to give the theatre would be its original name. I know you would have no objections from any of the family and it would be particularly gratifying to Arthur Hammerstein who built it, as it would be to me.

I share your confidence in the theatre as an investment and my only reason for staying out of the deal is a new and very determined desire to simplify my life. I want to spend most of the time in Doylestown thinking up rhymes and jokes and once a year go through the rigors of rehearsing them and taking them out prior to their New York debut. This seems enough for any man to do if he wants any spare time to read an occasional book and stay on reasonably intimate terms with his family so my reason for giving up this opportunity is a social and not a business one.

All good wishes.

Sincerely

Oscar Hammerstein to Jerome Kern, May 31, 1944

Dear Jerry:-

There was a story about me in LIFE last week and while it was gratifying to know that they thought I was important enough to write about, the contents of the story were very distressing because of many inaccuracies and misquotations and false emphasis. You are one of a few people who are close to me whom I feel impelled to write to and explain that I had no control over the writing of the article and that it didn't come out at all the way I would have liked it to, especially in regard to people who were so much a part of my career and so near to me as friends as you Otto and Rommy, for instance.

I am quite sure that you would understand this without my writing but I am writing to clinch it.

Love to all.

P.S. I have lost 17 pounds—on purpose—and I am growing very pretty.

Jerome Kern to Oscar Hammerstein, June 7, 1944

Dear Oscar:

Of course I know pretty well how much some of the pinpricks in that Life story must have made you wince. There were certain things in it that made me want to wring Mrs. Francis Silly[6] Wickware's insensitive thick neck.

I wonder whether it was her or the editor who thought it nice and sly to juxtapose the two sentences under the board meeting picture: "Hammerstein helps fix members' share in earnings. He is in the top bracket".

This little furtive follow-up of all the too many references to earnings certainly left a coppery taste in the mouth.

The idiotic cuckoo completely missed what I assume to be your little whimsy. The librettist is invariably subjugated by the composer when the latter is alive, hence it is not Bizet's CARMEN JONES, it is Hammerstein's CARMEN JONES.

Why don't they give the subject, if he's important enough to write about, the opportunity of proofreading?

The best thing about the wholly misconceived, horribly belated salute to you was the warmth of your note in reference to it—that and the postscript.

Which reminds me that I forgot to crow a little bit to you in my recent ones. On May 18th it was just on year since I used tobacco in <u>any shape or form</u>!! Also on purpose, not by doctor's orders or through failing health or any infirmity. Just wanted to see which of us was the boss.

I won.

But I'm getting fat as hell.

Any more thought to Marco Polo?

Love from us all,

Jerry

Oscar Hammerstein to Jerome Kern (excerpt), circa June, 1944

I read very carefully my adaptation of Marco Polo as far as it went and I fell in love with it all over again. I still think as before that this could be a very distinguished and unusual musical play. The structural problem is now

---

[6] *Life* magazine writer Francis Wickware's middle name was Sill.

very clear to me. Donn Byrne has given us material for two thirds of a play. One third must be invented. There is a big gap between the avowal of love by Marco and Goldenbells and his departure from China. Byrne skips right down to the finale and we suddenly find Goldenbells is no longer alive by appearing as a very lovely ghost. What actually happened of course, was that Marco was appointed by her father to escort her on a ship to a foreign realm where she was to marry a prince and on the way she died. Since nobody knows how, it would be my romantic belief that she tossed herself overboard outside the port of her future husband, Marco having been too honorable during the trip to betray her father's trust in him and really wring Goldenbells as she undoubtedly wanted to be wrung. This would also tie in with his great religious zeal.

This phase in Marco's journey is used by Eugene O'Neill in his play MARCO'S MILLIONS but his conception of the character is entirely different. He paints Marco as a kind of medieval Babbit who is so intent on making money and trading in the East that he never realizes the young princess' availability. This is a very unwelcome idea to me and would certainly be no good for a musical play. The voyage, however, if fitted in with Donn Byrne's characterization of the two people could be a beautiful interlude, at times gay and at the finish poignant and heartbreaking.

Jeanette MacDonald to Oscar Hammerstein, June 6, 1944

Dear Oscar:

Jerome Kern has just left after a very interesting conference—subject matter, the American opera idea.

I am hastening to write you about it as I am considerably thrilled to find him amenable to the whole proposition. I told him of our brief conference when I was in New York last January, and he said he would write to you to find out what reference book you found on the subject of Tabor and the "Doe"[7] mine. Naturally, I could not give him that information, but Jane

---

[7] Elizabeth McCourt Tabor, better known as Baby Doe, lived a life rich with scandal (1854–1935). Her husband, silver magnate and, briefly, U.S. Senator, Horace Tabor, one of the richest men in America, lost his fortune in the Panic of 1893. He died destitute a few years later. Baby Doe's struggles continued another forty years, until she was found frozen to death at eighty-one. Her story ultimately inspired the opera, *The Ballad of Baby Doe* (1956), with music by Douglas Moore and a libretto by John Latouche.

Cowl told me you had found several interesting books on the subject at the public library.

I did not mention having discussed any of this idea with Billy Rose, simply because, first, Billy definitely poo-pooed Kern as composer for an American opera. Secondly, I am afraid Billy is a little offended at me for not going in his "Seven Lively Arts"[8] and, third, Rose is quite against presentation at the Metropolitan. My feeling on the subject, along with yours and now Kern's, is that the Metropolitan prestige might have great merit in its serious acceptance by the musical world. However, Jerry hit one nail squarely on the head when he mentioned, "with such a combination, it is a natural."

I am really quite excited and pleased by Jerry's reaction, and hope his enthusiasm will not be dampened after he had read up on the subject matter. I am sure you will be hearing from him promptly. Incidentally, I would appreciate a word in reply as to your continued interest in the venture.

Jerry tells me you are recuperating from an operation, and I send my best wishes for a complete and speedy recovery. May I recommend recuperation in California? The climate is ideal you know! Give my best to Dorothy.

Sincerely,

Jeanette

Oscar Hammerstein to Jeanette MacDonald, July 6, 1944

Dear Jeanette:-

Jerry and I have had an exchange of letters about opera and you. We are naturally interested in both. It would be, however, dishonest not to tell you of the obstacles that beset the project.

In the first place, when I say opera I don't mean the Met because I don't believe that their methods down there could ever give us the results we

---

[8] *Seven Lively Arts* was an extravagant revue, produced by Billy Rose after buying and refurbishing the Ziegfeld Theatre. Despite songs by Cole Porter, a ballet by Stravinsky, sketches by Kaufman and Hart, and a cast that included Beatrice Lillie and Bert Lahr (and Susan Blanchard as one of the showgirls), it closed after 183 performances.

want. After hearing FALSTAFF sung in English by Tibbett and drowned out by Sir Thomas Beecham and not understanding a word I am discouraged about the Metropolitan. Their whole training and background is to put sound before meaning and the acoustics of the building conspire with them in this objective.

The other and more serious obstacle is my very full schedule. I have just begun to write a play which will not open in New York until next April. Following that I am writing a picture based on the biography of my grandfather and that is so important to me that it might very well consume all of the following year. I naturally don't expect [you] to wait around that long and that is why I am frankly warning you now what an unreliable fellow I am.

If you decide to go ahead with BABY DOE with anyone else I would naturally have no right to kick, nor would I. I would, however, regret very much not being in on it and if anything comes up that disturbs or changes the plans described above I will let you know immediately of my availability. Meanwhile, the best of luck to you.

As ever,

Both the Navy and the Army requested extra performances of *Oklahoma!* be added just to accommodate servicemen. Beginning on June 6 and continuing into March 1945, there were Tuesday matinees of *Oklahoma!* where the royalties had been waived and ticket prices were significantly reduced for members of the armed forces.

Oscar Hammerstein to D. C. Patterson, USNR, June 8, 1944

Dear Captain Patterson:-

I deeply appreciate your kind letter of June 7th. I stopped in at the matinee last Tuesday and felt as you did that the air was electric with a fine spirit which emanated from the audience, conveyed itself to the company, and then vibrated itself back to the audience. It was very thrilling and I am happy that the idea has turned out so well.

All good wishes to you.

Sincerely,

Mary Martin to Dorothy and Oscar Hammerstein, June 12, 1944

AM HAVING COCKTAILS AT COPACABANA TEN EAST 60TH STREET THIS FRIDAY FROM FIVE TO SEVEN. PLEASE COME AS I SO WANT YOU TO MEET DOLORES GRAY. ESPECIALLY WANT TO MEET WHAT I FEEL IS A MOST EXCITING YOUNG PERSONALITY BEFORE HER DEBUT THAT NIGHT. BEST

MARY MARTIN

Oscar Hammerstein to Abel Green, *Variety*, June 22, 1944

Dear Abel:-

In your drama critics' selection for the "Bests" of the season, don't you think it is an omission not to list the best lyrics as well as the best musical score and best scene designing?

I have noted this omission in the past two seasons and wondered about it. Last year I had a long meeting with myself and awarded me the prize and this year I gave it to Ogden Nash[9] but maybe I am biased and next year you want to let the critics decide.

Love and kisses,

Oscar Hammerstein to Furniss T. Peterson, June 25, 1944

Dear Mr. Peterson:-

I liked the lyrics you enclosed.

In answer to the third paragraph of your letter I don't think that the lyrics depend so much on "inner sanctum knowledge or connections". What lyrics really need is music. I take it that composers are few in your corner of Tucson Arizona so I am going to take the liberty of submitting your verses to a publisher here in New York and ask him if he likes them well enough to show them to a composer.

Let me know if this is all right with you.

Very truly yours,

[9] A popular poet of mostly humorous light verse, Nash wrote the lyrics for 1943's *Lady in the Dark*.

Deems Taylor, ASCAP, to Oscar Hammerstein, July 18, 1944

Dear Oscar:

Would you break down and sob your little heart out if I threw you off that Symphony Policy Committee and appointed Walter Kramer in your place?

I don't imagine that the business of the Committee is particularly up your alley, and it's a field in which Walter has had years of experience.

If this is okay by you, will you send me a formal resignation for the record?

Ever yours,

Deems

Deems Taylor,

President

Oscar Hammerstein to Deems Taylor, July 19, 1944

Dear Deems:-

I am enclosing my letter of resignation. I have no choice in the matter.

I know very well that your "request" is a thinly veiled demand backed up by the threat of that vindictive group at ASCAP headed by yourself which has been out to get me ever since I won the potato race at the ASCAP annual clambake at Staten Island in 1926.

I had looked upon my appointment on the Symphony Policy Committee as a chance to serve my organization and perhaps advance myself in the concert field. I realize now that I was set up as a straw man merely to be knocked down at the first opportunity. There is little that I can do about this and it is foolish for me even to be writing this letter. The steam roller you control is inexorable, irresistible, irrelevent [sic], incompetent and immaterial. I just wanted you to know that I am on to you.

Resentfully,

Oscar Hammerstein to Deems Taylor, July 19, 1944

Dear Deems:-

Owing to the press of many obligation piling up on my time this year, I would appreciate it very much if you would accept my resignation from the Symphony Policy Committee.

Very truly yours,

Deems Taylor to Oscar Hammerstein, July 25, 1944

Dear Oscar:

I am a little surprised, not to say hurt, by the tone of your letter of July 19th.

If I suggested your resignation from the Concert and Symphony Policy Committee, the suggestion was made only out of a sense of duty, of which I have a complete set.

Permit me to give you the background of this whole ugly business (as if you don't already know it). I have been told by people in a position to know, that you were planning to use your membership on the Concert and Symphony Policy Committee, as a pretext for writing the lyrics to Beethoven's "FIFTH SYMPHONY" and to sell a musical comedy libretto based on Bach's "B MINOR MASS".

Since you well know that both these assignments had already been promised to Pinky Herman, there was nothing left for me to do except to act, and act promptly.

I cannot help feeling that the spirit in which you have taken this thing is derogatory, unethical and lousy.

Hoping you are the same, I remain,

Tolerantly yours,

Deems

P.S. At the suggestion of my secretary, I am placing your letter and the carbon of my reply, in my personal files rather than in those of the Society, since she points out that some (I couldn't quite make out what she said) would be quite capable of taking both seriously.

D.T.

Hy Kraft was largely unlucky in his career as a playwright. It appears that Hammerstein helped underwrite Kraft's ambitions out of friendship and kindness.

Oscar Hammerstein to Hy Kraft, July 21, 1944

Dear Hy:-

In your last letter to me there was a kind of embarrassment at the necessity of getting down to cases and coming to anything like a specific business arrangement with me. I feel the same embarrassment and the same confidence that you have—that you and I would never come to any difference over a business arrangement. I, nevertheless, agree with Howard that it is desirable for us to put down some statements and they are these.

First, I agree to pay you $1,000 as an advance against royalty or any other type of remuneration you may eventually receive for your work on a version of DON QUIXOTE. You are to make a complete draft of your version which will be designed as a musical play not containing lyrics but with suggestions for song ideas or with scenes that can be converted into lyrics and be given musical treatment (I am already going into much more detail than I intended to but now that I have started it's fun) When you submit your manuscript to me if I don't like it and don't wish to proceed further with it all property in it reverts to you but you keep the grand. If I do like it then it is mine to produce as a musical play or picture. I would have the right to call in an additional collaborator—even me, maybe—and appoint whatever composer I see fit. I would, of course, want you to be pleased as far as these assignments are concerned.

If you do no further work than the draft you submit you will get 1% of the gross as royalty. If you proceed further in collaboration with another writer you will get 1½%. This is, of course, on the understanding that the royalty paid for the book, lyrics, and music would be somewhere between the usual royalty of 6 to 8%.

These terms are made as a suggestion to you and if there is anything about them that you don't like please tell me. The royalty on SHOW BOAT was 7% of which Jerry got 3, Edna got 1½, and I got 2½. The royalty that Dick and I receive now is 8%. In the case of the adaptation of GREEN GROW THE LILACS, Lynn Riggs got 1% for his play and Dick and I split the other 7.

I state these facts so that you can gauge the basis of my suggestion. It is very interesting—your setup with Harry Ruby and Guy Bolton—I certainly hope it materializes.

The thing I like about DON QUIXOTE is that the stakes are high. It is a chance not merely to come through with a hit—an objective not to be underrated of course—but it also has the makings of something really important in the theatre and worth getting excited about.

Go to it. Love to all,

Jerome Kern to Oscar Hammerstein, August 7, 1944

Dear Oscar:

I don't know the status of Show Boat revival. I even don't know whether you're still interested. I certainly don't know if you think anything of Gene Lockhart as Captain Andy. I made a pretty comprehensive report about his performance here to Howard, but sometimes Howard, before your very eyes, goes into the Vagueness, and goodness knows what he reported to you.

In brief, Lockhart had geniality, unction, the assurance of experience and training, and as I told you over the telephone at the time, he did as well as he could with the little help he got from stage management, the badly rehearsed ensemble, and the sound effects in the Trocadero scene, the last practically non-existent.

Anyway, the enclosed copy explains itself. I'll take time out to explain the why and wherefore.

I suffered so with Lester's ineptitude at the first performance here in Los Angeles that I just couldn't go back stage and compliment Carol Bruce, Lockhart and Todd Duncan, and ignored Hatfield and the gal who played Magnolia (I've forgotten the silly bitch's name). By the same token I couldn't put on two faces and compliment the incompetents, so I slunk off into the night.

Sooooo. . . . .

The next time I ran into Gene Lockhart who is an active member of the Players Club West Room, I tossed him a gushing orchid and said "How about you for New York?" (At that time [the] revival had plenty heat on.) Last Monday sitting around the pool table at this Beverly Hills branch of the Players, I saw him again, and, having embarked on a project, perforce had to see it through, so I asked him once more "Hey, what about New York?"

So that's the reason for the enclosed and why I can't give an imitation of four Hawaiians playing Joe Cook.

Hoping you are as carefree and lightheaded as I.

Hastily,

Jerry

Although Dwight Marfield never appeared in a Hammerstein show on Broadway, he and Oscar were at least occasional and warm correspondents. The following exchange was the result of an earlier letter from Marfield seeking career advice—both as an actor and songwriter—while performing in summer stock.

Oscar Hammerstein to Dwight Marfield (Grove Theatre, Nuangola, Pennsylvania) (excerpt), August 15, 1944

When in hell are you leaving Nuangola? When you do come back please come and see me and bring your song, too. I am anxious to have you meet the Theatre Guild people because there is a good chance of my carrying out my threat to develop a part for you in my version of LILIOM. I would appreciate a letter from you telling me about when you expect to return.

Dwight Marfield to Oscar Hammerstein, August 19, 1944

Dear Mr. Hammerstein,

Good. Fine. I am glad I am to meet the people early in the game, so you can tell them the part is being put in for me. Otherwise you can write the book and you can die and Mr. Rodgers can get amnesia and they can go ahead with it and they can say the part calls for a <u>short</u> man. ("We are negotiating with Wuzra[10] [*sic*] Stone as a matter of fact------what <u>did</u> you say was your last Broadway show, Mr. Marfield?")

Now as to the date of my return to New York,--I have been feeling the need of somebody's advice; and I might as well ask yours. This theatre keeps open as long as there is any business. Last year they kept it open into October and all the actors got pneumonia and died, which makes it cheaper because they can ship the corpses back by freight instead of having to buy seats for them. The Final Cause of my being here is simply to avoid the heat of the City. The Efficient Cause of my lingering on and fulfilling Newton's Law of Intertia is equally simple: it is the Equity ruling that, if I give notice, I have to pay my own fare back and my Stellvertreter's[11] fare out.

Now what would you do if you were me? Left to my own devices I shall possibly linger on until late September. I like the mountains; and nobody but you seems to give a damn if I ever come back.

Yours truly,

Dwight Marfield

P.S. In line with my permanent predilection for the merry-merry, I have augmented my performances here with the following musical contributions.

JANIE,. . . ..playing the colored houseman, I sang "I'm goin back to Shee-caw-go to get my good hambone boiled", off-stage.

LOST SHEEP . . . . . . playing an Anglican padre, I intoned "Life is chiefly froth and bubble," to a sort of improvised plainsong setting.

THE CHILDREN'S HOUR. . . . . . I restrained myself.

ANOTHER LOVE STORY . . . . . . playing John Asprey, I sang, "She only had an apple tree, but you, you've got an orchard," as I made my second act entrance.

BUT NOT GOODBYE. . . . . . I opened the show playing "Believe Me If All Those Endearing Young Charms" on the flute.

ARSENIC ET VIEUX DENTELLES . . . . . . .I sang "Night and Day Under the Hide of Me" as I lit the candles round the dramatic critic.

---

[10] Marfield likely meant the actor "Ezra Stone" and typed "Wuzra" either inadvertently or humorously.

[11] "Stellvertreter" means "proxy."

THE DOUGH GIRLS (now in rehearsal) . . . . . . after completing my representation of General Slade and changing into the habiliments of the Russian priest, I come forth and chant a portion of the Eastern Orthodox marriage service, according to the mode in which I learned it from a priest in Nanticoke.

D. H. M.

John Erskine had been an English professor of Oscar's at Columbia University. He was a driving force behind what came to be known as the "Great Books" movement, and a prolific author. Erskine was also a pianist and composer, and became the first president of the Juilliard School of Music, and director of the Metropolitan Opera Association.

Oscar Hammerstein to John Erskine, August 31, 1944

Dear Dr. Erskine:-

I have been in the country most of the time since I received your synopsis of the Mendelssohn biographical play. I shall be back in town in mid-September and would be delighted to have lunch with you and talk to you about it.

As to my own availability for taking an active part I cannot promise much because my present commitments take me forward for a full year—or maybe backward, there is no telling yet.

I am, however, interested in the idea and might be of some help to you in formulating production plans. Quite apart from this rather vague suggestion, it would be a nice experience to see you again after the many years that have intervened since I sat in Hamilton Hall and listened to you reading poetry. I told your daughter[12] the other day that up to that time I had never dreamed that the words in poems meant anything. I thought poetry was an association of words calculated to create rhythm and rhyme and very little more. To my amazement you proved to me that some of the poets actually meant to convey important thought and feelings.

If you will tell me where I can phone you when I come back I will suggest a time and place for our meeting.

Very truly yours,

Hammerstein's opinions were increasingly sought on all manner of topics.

---

[12] Erskine's daughter, Anna, was an actress in the 1930s, and in 1940 was an assistant to Josh Logan on a production of *Charley's Aunt*. She married the playwright Russel Crouse.

Oscar Hammerstein to Jack Goodman, Simon and Schuster, September 6, 1944

Dear Jack:-

This is what I have to say about radio, in halting and confused prose which you are to rhetoricize:-

Radio has done a fine job with music. It has brought the best music, played by the best orchestras and sung by the best singers, to millions who have never had access to it. In the field of "popular" music, however, we must raise an ungrateful protest. The dietetics are at fault. Radio strives to give us what we like but it gives us too much of it. The Hit Parade, an excellent program, carries on surveys which determine, not accurately but substantially, what are the ten favorite songs of the nation each week. There is no fault to find with this program, but there is an evil which stems from it. The producers of all other musical programs follow it up by giving us an overdose of songs we have endorsed. This sends them back on the Hit Parade the following week, stronger than ever. They are again played on the other programs only more than before! Thus, our favorite current melodies swing around and around this vicious circle until they drop dead with dizzy exhaustion. The surfeit of listener appetite in some cases reaches positive resentment of the song once loved. The cure for this is obvious but rather difficult to bring about. Briefly, what is needed is greater enterprise and courage on the part of the producers of musical programs. Instead of slavishly pressing through the bottleneck of three top tunes heard each Saturday night, they should frequently add new songs which in their opinion are good songs, prior to public endorsement. This would create more variety on the air. The listeners would continue to choose the songs they like, and they would reach the Hit Parade when they were liked enough, but they would not get the artificial overstimulation they get now.

The difficulty, of course, is that the average producer who desires to hold his job doesn't want to gamble on his own taste. It is much safer for him to use only the songs that have already found public favor. He can't go wrong in this way. Even if his sponsor doesn't like the songs the producer can counter with the statement that they are already popular and why argue with the public?

This is a very tough radio problem. Something should be done about it no matter how hard it is to do, because the repetition of three songs on practically all musical programs all day long, day after day, is a major flaw in radio entertainment.

O-O-O-O-O-O-O-O-O

I have just read this over and I am sure there must be some graphic way of saying the whole thing in five short sentences—and better, too.

All good wishes,

Sincerely,

Oscar Hammerstein to Alan Green, Writers' War Board, September 25, 1944

Dear Alan:-

My favorite sentence in your letter is, "In order to insure the success of this play it is being sponsored by a committee, etc."

This is a very good thing to know and probably explains why a great many plays have failed. They didn't have a committee to sponsor them.

I face this dilemma. I haven't time to be an active chairman and yet I do not like to be a chairman of something and take even that faint responsibility without having anything to say about the project for which I am faintly responsible. This means that I would rather not do it. It also means that if they look far and wide and can't find anybody else to do it then I will do it.

All good wishes to you.

Sincerely

In response to Oscar's letter in response to his letter, Alan Green replied: "I am writing the New York War Fund, telling them that you are loath to assume the Honorary Chairmanship for the reasons stated in your letter. The odds are that they'll come rushing back with a request that you take the job, loath or not."

Theresa Helburn (Theatre Guild) to Richard Rodgers and Oscar Hammerstein, October 5, 1944

Dear Oscar and Dick:

We have just seen a breakdown of the division of royalties and profits in case

LILIOM is a success and runs for a minimum of sixty weeks, and we are very depressed by the result.

If the play made a very good operating profit every week for sixty weeks, we would end up with $37,000 for all of our work, time, services, etc., including my services and Lawrence's services. You would end up with $163,000. If picture rights sell for $300,000 we would end up with a total from all sources of about $55,000 and you would end up with about $300,000.

In addition to suggesting the play and working on the production, we also have to bear the entire managerial responsibility, including that of getting out road companies, European companies, etc. and keeping them in good shape for years afterwards, which in our original proposal was to be borne equally between us. In the arrangement now suggested, you will receive your percentage merely as authors and for a certain amount of supervising services but not as managers. I understand, of course, that you do not want to be tied down to the managing responsibilities and all that is involved, but since you don't wish this, it seems to us that the adjustment suggested would make things a little less inequitable, and we feel that you must agree with the justice of this request.

Sincerely,

Terry

P.S. In considering the above, please bear in mind that we have turned down a number of other musical plays in order to concentrate our efforts with you and these included both BLOOMER GIRL and SONG OF NORWAY, and we only did SING OUT SWEET LAND because the music was old and we hoped to do it with you.

The following is stapled to the previous letter, not on stationery, in draft form with sections crossed out. Passages in italics are handwritten. Whether or not it was sent and, if so, with or without attachments is unclear. But it shows Hammerstein's great attention to the business side of his work.

Oscar Hammerstein to Theresa Helburn and Lawrence Langner (draft), circa October, 1944

Dear Terry and Lawrence:

The "breakdown" of figures on Liliom which depresses you are about as cock-eyed a set of fallacious statistics as anyone was ever depressed by.

There is no such thing as a show that runs at a gross of $30,000 a week for sixty weeks, and then decides to close.

You yourselves say: ". . . ..we would have to bear the entire responsibility of getting out road companies, European companies, etc. and keeping them in good shape for years afterwards-" Yet you are only paying yourselves off on the basis of one company for sixty weeks!

Why is a hit limited to 30,000 gross to-day? In a big house you can do 40,000 and get a profit of 10,000 a week—or more.

Even at 30,000 Oklahoma had been netting between 7,000 and 8,000— leaving out the National Company.

Comparison between authors' royalties and managerial profits always separate in favor of the former if you take the first 60 weeks of a musical hit's run. It is after that that profits overtake royalties.

You say: "In the arrangement now suggested you will receive your percentage merely (sic) as authors and for a certain amount of supervising services but not as managers." We think "a certain amount of supervising services" is hardly descriptive of the time and energy and experience expected of us in helping you produce a musical play.

In your anxiety to be depressed you even cast some doubt on whether you can get the play financed on a basis of not more than 50% to the investors. Are you really worried about this? Money seems easy to get for any show and we think our names with yours make it even easier. We have each already had several unsolicited requests by people to be permitted to put money in.

Not point to mention> 3 ½ (Incidentally you gave us a raise. 7 ½)

Beyond all these misconceptions of your plight there is the very important fact that this was not a deal we exacted from you by any grim bargaining. It was your own proposition made to us by people experienced in producing and familiar with the mathematical contingencies of all kinds of shows. It may be that at the time you were over-anxious to persuade us to write Liliom (We were lukewarm at first, you will remember) and that you over-rated the importance of signing us before some other manager wooed us away. Even understanding this, and forgiving it, we are disturbed that after we have worked on the play for four months, and rejected all other offers, the subject of terms is now reopened.

BUT—whether you are right or wrong, if you are dissatisfied or depressed and it is within our power to alleviate any hardship you believe exists, we will do all we can within the limits of what we think is fair to ourselves. We don't think reducing our share from 50% of the producers' share to 33 1/3 percent is fair. _____ *But –*

I Remember Mama opened on Broadway on October 19. It was the first show produced by Rodgers and Hammerstein. Based on the popular semi-autobiographical novel, *Mama's Bank Account* by Kathryn Forbes, Rodgers and Hammerstein commissioned the script from playwright John Van Druten who they also hired to direct. The show was a hit at 713 performances, and in 1948 it was adapted as a film starring Irene Dunne.

Peter Moen became indispensable to Oscar beginning in the mid-30s. Initially, he was Oscar's masseuse, chauffeur, and general helper. Later, Peter and his son, Walter, managed Highland Farm. It was Peter who had the famous exchange with Hammerstein, asking if Oscar could arrange tickets for Walter to see *Oklahoma!* after his upcoming wedding reception. Oscar agreed and asked when the wedding was to be. "The day you can get the tickets," Peter replied.

Oscar Hammerstein to Peter Moen, Highland Farm, October 19, 1944

Dear Peter:-

My play opens tonight and in a couple of weeks I am hoping to get down to the farm. Meanwhile, I wish you would send up to New York two broilers at the beginning of each week and a duck in the middle of each week. I think it would also be a good idea for you to mail us eggs as often as you can so that we do not have to buy them here in New York. I expect you, however, to take the eggs that you need for your own purposes first.

I am glad to hear that everything is all right at the farm. Miss Glatterman tells me she sent you a blank to fill out. This is for the insurance of the bull. Please fill this out and mail it to her as soon as you can. I miss the farm very much and am most anxious to see it again and incidentally get a good massage.

Kindest regards to Mrs. Moen and family.

Sincerely,

Toni Ward, William Morris Agency, to Oscar Hammerstein, October 27, 1944

Dear Mr. Hammerstein:

For days now I have been trying to reach you and your secretary has told me that she has left messages with you but unfortunately I have been unable to get you in.

I understand that at the moment you are going ahead with "Lilliom" [*sic*] and I want to talk to you about Shirley Booth who would like very much to be submitted for the part of "Julie".

Could I please get your reaction on this? Would it be possible for me to see you one day to talk to you about assisting in any casting on the play?

Very cordially,

Toni

Toni Ward

Oscar Hammerstein to Toni Ward, October 31, 1944

Dear Miss Ward:-

Shirley Booth, who is a very good friend of mine is also a very good actress and completely unsuited for the part of "Julie".

Very truly yours,

Shirley Booth was a wonderful character actress, excellent in both comedies and dramas, but she was not an ingénue. And while she starred in a few musicals, her voice was more duck than dulcet.

Oscar Hammerstein to Leighton Brill, October 31, 1944

Dear Leighton:-

Regarding Howard's opinion on GENTLEMEN UNAFRAID, he is wrong about Jerry. Jerry has definitely withdrawn. I congratulate you on your new work. It sounds fine.

It is true about Maggie. She has been home about a month. She is living with Mike and Alice at 161 West 54th St. if you would like to write her.

This takes care of the various paragraphs in your letter. As you have read, MAMA is a smash hit. It is selling out and looks as if it is in for a very big run. OKLAHOMA continues to be the biggest demand at the ticket agencies—5 to 1 for the nearest impediment and MAMA is the biggest dramatic draw. CARMEN JONES which was booked to go on the road this October just won't lower its grosses enough and so it looks as it if will stay on all through this season in New York. In December it will complete a year's run on Broadway which makes the ninth show I have written that has done this. I think this is a record.

Meanwhile, Dick and I are very busy getting back to our job of LILIOM which I don't think I can get ready for rehearsal before February. I had to take off a week—this week—to make some minor changes in the script of STATE FAIR. Walter Lang, who is directing it, came East to confer with us. They are really going ahead and shooting it as written and the thing I have to do this week involved only very small alterations.

The Hammerstein biography is warming up again as it does periodically and I might have some news on this soon. I am hoping to make this my next job after LILIOM. The idea would be to go down to Doylestown and stay there and do the whole job there next summer.

We are expecting Billy home for Christmas and maybe sooner. His ship is on a long trip now at the end of which he will be a chief. He would like very much to go into officers' training when he gets back on leave but this is a longshot probability.

Susan is rehearsing in Billy Rose's SEVEN LIVELY ARTS, the big revue with which he is reopening the Ziegfeld Theatre. In addition to Susan the cast boasts of Bea Lillie, Bert Lahr, Benny Goodman and Markova. Susan is one of twelve referred to as "Ladies of Fashion" or "Models"—the phrase "Show-girl" is being studiously avoided but that is what they are. Jimmy has gone away to George School which he likes very much. Jennifer is at Baldwin school. Mary is on a two-month vacation and the farm is closed except for Peter, who lives at the cottage and takes care of the Angus herd. We will all be down, however, over Christmas. Alice is doing playreading and research for me. Henry has just finished his naval V-12 course at Duke and is headed for pre-midshipman school in Asbury Park. Dorothy is working very hard but having little fun because of the constant irritation due to late deliveries and labor difficulties. This, I think, winds up my report on the family.

We saw the Redells last week and they have borne up wonderfully under the loss of Bill and seem now to have emerged from it. We saw Donald a few weeks ago and he looks fine. For the next few months he will be instructing in a southern air base. New York is wonderful. The theatre is booming and we are now having crisp autumn days such as you effete south-westerners cannot include in your celebrated climate—the fame of which is only partly justified.

Let me say again how happy I am that the thing you are doing seems to be clicking so well. What I like best is that irrespective of the success or failure of this present venture the assistant producer credit is bound to build into something for you and I think it is exactly what you ought to be doing. I think this is all I have to say except to send my love to you and Jean and that I miss you both.

Henry Lenahan to Oscar Hammerstein, November 3, 1944

My dear Mr. Hammerstein:

I tried to reach you on the phone a few times to talk about the classification of your play, "I REMEMBER MAMA", but [was unsuccessful and there is a concern on behalf of] the Catholic Theatre Movement. As you know, in a matter of this kind, a conversation is usually more complete and satisfactory than a letter.

I feel that you will be pleased to learn that our reviewers find "I REMEMBER MAMA" satisfactory and unobjectionable except for an instance of the disrespectful and irreverent use of the name of 'God'. Without this objectionable feature, the play could be given an "A" rating.

You will understand the spirit which prompts this letter and pardon me for taking your time. I thought you would like to know the above for your personal information.

With sincere best wishes, I am

Very truly yours,

Henry J. Lenahan

(Rev.) Henry J. Lenahan

DIRECTOR

THE CATHOLIC THEATRE MOVEMENT

Oscar Hammerstein to Reverend Henry J. Lenahan, November 9, 1944

Dear Father Lenahan:-

Thank you for your letter regarding I REMEMBER MAMA.

Mr. Rodgers and I have had several long talks about this subject with the author, Mr. Van Druten. We feel that the reaction to the line you refer to is a highly personalized one. We listened carefully to the audience and their laughter is of the most good-natured and hearty kind without any endorsement of profanity or irreverence. I know that you don't agree but it seems to us that certain lines spoken by certain characters which are consistent with those characters do not constitute a disrespectful attitude on the part of the author, actors or audience toward God. We recognize that willful irreverence is a highly undesirable thing in the theatre but we also feel it wrong to pass arbitrary rules that certain lines are profane whenever and however used irrespective of their context or the character who speaks them.

To us—I mean the three of us, Mr. Rodgers, Mr. Van Druten and myself—this line spoken by Uncle Chris under these circumstances has no profane, irreverent or disrespectful intent and although we respect your opinion deeply and appreciate your interest we should feel insincere in following your suggestion.

With sincere good wishes, I am very truly yours,

The Catholic Theatre Movement issued a "white list" naming plays appropriate for Catholics to attend. They explained their raison d'être thus: "the very existence of a White List will enforce the necessity of personal investigation into all forms of public amusement in order that he may be saved from exposing those near and dear to him to the dangers of contamination."

Jerome Kern to Oscar Hammerstein (excerpt), November 5, 1944

⊙ In addition to elimination of that "THE" (per my wire) may I change <u>mem o ry</u> to <u>mem'ry</u>?

Oscar Hammerstein to Jerome Kern, circa November 6, 1944

Dear Jerry:

BELATEDLY ANSWERING YOU [*sic*] LETTER YOU CAN DO ANYTHING YOU WANT WITH MEMORY EXCEPT TO ACCENT IT ON THE LAST SYLLABLE.

OSCAR

The exchange above regards the standalone song, "The Sweetest Sight That I Have Seen." Hammerstein wrote the lyrics for the chorus in 1939, after being inspired by "a pair of lovers on the beach . . . They both had white hair. His arm lay gently around her shoulder, and they gazed out at the silver Pacific, peace and contentment in their eyes." He wrote the lyric to a Kern melody he recalled from years before. The song wasn't published until 1945, and for that publication Hammerstein and Kern added a verse. Its last three lines are:

Lovingly letting my mem'ry stray,
I pause to recall the sweetest
Of all sights I've seen on the way.

Judy Holliday to Oscar Hammerstein, circa November, 1944

Dear Mr. Hammerstein,

As you know, I have been out here in the city of angels for a year now, remembering every day for a hundred different reasons the talk we had about Hollywood and its villainy.

With the exception of one swell month when I worked for George Cukor in "Winged Victory", (The Roxy—Dec. 7—Don't Miss It!) <u>everything</u> you warned me about has happened. And for the rest of the year I have been struggling with the giant strength of a minnow on a hook to escape that particular fur-lined limbo which is waiting just for me.

But the end is near in the shape of option time and I am reading of your plans for a musical "Liliom" and wondering how far it has been set and how legitimately Julie and Marie have to sing and whether you have any use for a sunkist ex-commedienne. (The one good thing that came out of this year was that I found out that I could act. I have a tearful little job to do in "Winged Victory" and I'm O.K.)

Meanwhile, as a last attempt to earn the salary they pay me, I am trying to persuade Fox to test me for the city girl in "State Fair". I don't know what sort of picture it's going to be,—Hammerstein and a Lang-Fox Technicolor musical seem to be at opposite poles—and I don't know how involved you are in it, but it would be fun to work with you, even by proxy, long distance and mental telepathy.

I know how ridiculously busy you are, but if you have the time, get your secretary to type something to me and you initial it. Or don't you know how we do things out here.

Love –

My new name is Judy Holliday!

635½ South La BreaLA

Oscar Hammerstein to Judy Holliday, November 9, 1944

Dear Judy:-

When are you coming East? If it is soon Dick Rodgers and I would like to hear you sing. The bad news is that both "Julie" and "Marie" have to sing "legitimate" but just how illegitimately you sing, I don't quite remember. It will be good to know.

I was amused by your letter. I used to live on La Brea myself.

All good wishes,

Judy Holliday as Julie Jordan is a less outrageous notion than Shirley Booth, but still far from right. She never quite lost her girl-from-Queens sensibility, making it hard to imagine her playing a somewhat shy New Englander. While her voice was more pleasant than Booth's, it was nowhere near the lyric soprano called for by Carousel's score. Holliday leapt to stardom in 1946 when she starred in Born Yesterday on Broadway.

Oscar Hammerstein to Jack Davies, November 14, 1944

Dear Mr. Davies:-

It was very kind of you to get the Army-Notre Dame tickets for me and I appreciate it deeply. My gratitude is not the least bit dimmed by the score. It was not your fault that the West Point backfield consisted of Tarzan, Dick Tracy and Superman.

With all good wishes.

Sincerely,

Oscar Hammerstein to Jerome Kern (excerpt), December 4, 1944

Dorothy tells me she is taking the Century on Friday and I may be on the train with her. I am going out to attend a party (birthday) of the OKLAHOMA Chicago Company. Last Saturday I went to the CARMEN JONES birthday party. All my children are growing up so fast.

The exchange below marks a sea change in the relationship between Oscar and his older son, Bill, no longer Billy. The two communicate as adults with mutual respect; Oscar's response reveals the degree to which he was following the war and harboring strong opinions about how it was being waged.

William Hammerstein to Oscar Hammerstein,
December 24, 1944

Dear Dad –

It's Christmas Eve Ho Ho. The only familiar things about it for me is the fact that I have a bad cold. I suppose that might be some sort of psychiatric suggestion but actually I think it's due to my getting caught in a draft (air not military). We arrived at the base today and two letters from you greeted me as well as one from Maggie and a couple from friends who have gone back to the States—one of them on his way out here again aboard a transport—as crew not passenger. The other has drawn the unthinkable duty aboard a fair weather training ship in Boston Harbor. Poor fellow. He was formerly our executive officer. A very nice chap and he deserves the break.

Was downhearted to learn that the possibility of my seeing CJ [*Carmen Jones*] has dimmed to virtual oblivion—at least as far as the original company is concerned. Perhaps I may see a revival in a few years. I do hope so. As it looks now I may be just in time to catch the last night of Oklahoma's third revival. Our motto, in case I haven't mentioned it, is "The Golden Gate by Forty Eight!" to which even more pessimistic wags have added " . . . and the Breadline of the Forty Nine". Admiral Nimitz' Xmas greetings to the Fleet mentions that our increased distance from home at this time is a measure of our success intimating that the further from home we get geographically the closer we get . . . shall we say . . . historically. A pretty good thought, anyway. Although my geographical distance from home is just about the same as it was last year. But in the wind are promises of a slight change of scene—not too far away. In time I shall be quite satisfied even if it means a little fireworks which I haven't seen in almost a year. I really need a change of some sort and it doesn't matter what sort—except, of course, that the only change which can really mean anything at all is the one which brings me home. Just so you don't think I've been making up this story of my not coming home—on arrival here today the first thing I heard was the wails of other QMs who have also heard the sad news. My friend Disbrow (the violinist CQM—don't remember if I mentioned him to you, but we have recently become very friendly and he is one of the nicest guys I've met in this Navy) has left—but his orders have been in for almost three months now and also his replacement. He was being kept aboard for reasons better known to his skipper and has finally been released. Thru my efforts with friend Wallsten he was able to get a fast ship to the coast and even now is probably disembarking. Saw Wallsten this afternoon, incidentally, and he has had an article published in Colliers—forget which issue. You might be interested in it as it deals with his tour thru NG with Judith Anderson and declares some conclusions about entertaining service men in battle areas. Notable among them (the conclusions) is one where he and I discussed after the J[ack]. Benny turkey which appeared here a few months ago. That is that girls, if they take part, should not be so damned sexy (in their get up) unless they intend to visit each tent and hut during the night, taking on all hands. What they do is bordering on the sadistic.

On the consent and waiver gismo which you enclosed in your letter I shall have to wait a week before signing it because it is dated 1945 and I'm afraid if I try to rub out the 5 and put in 4 I'll make a mess of it. Of course I could have the witness post-date it but it's so official looking that it frightens me so I'll just wait a week and then sign it and send to you—or better I wont bother you with it but send straight to Howard. You'd probably lose it anyway and have to send me another one. Of course I don't understand why they are just now getting around to settling up the estate but please don't try and explain. I'll accept it as fact knowing that Law like the Navy, is slow and roundabout in it's [sic] ways.

You wished me Merry Xmas for which I am grateful, and said we might have to start thinking of Easter as I once mentioned. When I mentioned it, it was as a grim sort of joke, but now it looks very much as if I won't even make Easter. Maybe my mother's birthday will become the feted day of homecoming.

And speaking of birthdays—please do me a big favor. Have the florist send Maggie a lot of beautiful flowers with a note which I shall enclose in this letter. Spend lots of money and be sure to let me know how much so I can send you the amount. I particularly do not want you to actually pay for them. In case you have forgotten the date of her birthday, it is Feb 14. Valentines Day which may or may not be significant or something or other. By lots of money I mean, say $25 or $30. Maybe that isn't so much or maybe it's a hell of a lot. I have no remote idea of the cost of flowers these days but I only know that I want her to have lots and lots of them all over the place. If that means $50 or $100 OK/ I'm a rich man and have no better way to spend it at the moment. Of course one of these days I'll get home and have to live on what I've got and then it will seem a terribly small amount. But I'll worry about that then. Meanwhile please give Maggie hundreds of flowers. Throw in some orchids and American Beauties and things. How I long to sit at a table covered with Damask and shining silver and flowers and finger bowls—to be dressed immaculately in soft linen and feel clean and pure—not to have sweat under my arms and my pants sticking to my legs—to smell a woman's perfume and to engage in an enjoyable conversation devoid of four letter smutty words, which seem to be necessary to verbal expression in the Navy.

Your list of shows with a year and more on Bway is very impressive and I had never realized that it constituted a record of any sort—but I take your word for it and admit it's quite a thing. Doesn't Jerry Kern run you a close second? Did the Princess Theatre shows ever run for over a year? Also impressive is your deal on the OH the 1st picture. From what you say I gather that it will be a couple of years or so before you finally get around to its shooting.

I'm waiting on tenterhooks (I must look up that word) for news of how Susan's test came out. Soon, no doubt, I shall see her picture hanging in tents and on outhouse walls in the jungle.

Maggie says she's seen you only three times since her return. This is not, I suppose, any fault of either of you, but I do wish you could see more of each other. There must be lots of things you could talk about and you've never really become well-acquainted with each other. I'm terribly sorry to hear that Dorothy has been unwell and it makes me very much ashamed that I've neglected writing to her. Please give her my love and hopes that she is soon her normal healthy-as-a-horse self. I'd hate to think that when I return to civilian life we all won't be able to have our old fast sets of doubles. Certainly the time could not be nigh that such things will be denied us. I've always kidded you about being old or doddering simply because you are both so young and lively and it never has really occurred to me that someday you may begin to show age. Now you are around fifty, aren't you? I shouldn't think anyway that you should stop being young until well into sixty. Then you can both settle into your chairs with a blanket around your legs and crack jokes for the rest of us to laugh at. Of course I expect I'll be old way before my time and when you're ninety and I'm in my late seventies you'll have to steady my hand as I pour the brandy and Dorothy will look broodingly around the room and suddenly bounce out of her wheel chair to change the whole place from Louis Quinze to something with applique or trompe d'oeil (D'oil—d'oeul) and Maggie will probably be voting Republican and persecuting minorities. Ahhhh life! Ahhhh Stashun Houze! It must be time for me to go to bed. I do go on. Good nite—a pox on Merry Christmas but love to all

Yr dting son –

Scrooge

P.S.

Why not have Maggie + Alice at the farm for a while? It would do them both good—they could probably help out Dorothy while she's resting. Don't say I suggested it.

Oscar Hammerstein to William Hammerstein, December 24, 1944

Dear Bill:

In receipt of your bad news about the delay of your leave, I don't know which whom I should most condone, you or us. Not being one for condoning, I'll just take it as it came, advising you and everyone else involved to do the same. C'est la guerre, and there is worse guerre than that going on. Maybe you'll be here in time to see Liliom. I am enclosing an interesting article by Olin Downes written after he has had lunch with Dick. Please return this to me. It will be the first important clipping I'll have to put in my Liliom book. Do you remember my bound copies of script and scores which I always present to Dorothy? I now add all notices and publicity, so that they make interesting and perhaps some day valuable souvenirs. I am also binding books containing personal publicity not specifically connected with any one show—like the story in LIFE, etc.

Answering the questions in your letter:

(1) Susan is a show girl. She neither sings nor dances. She wears Valentina clothes and walks across the stage occasionally, with eleven other beautiful girls. She gets $75 a week. You ask is she good or bad? She is good.

With her money she is going to pay for her own dramatic education. I am going to try to get her into The Academy. She will also take ballet and perhaps some singing, to place her speaking voice. All of this she will take care of out of her salary, and buy some war bonds besides.

These plans, however, await the result of a test she is having at 20th-Fox. If they like her, she may go straight to Hollywood which I believe to be her eventual destination. It may be a little soon, however. She will not be seventeen until next March.[13]

(2) My conversation with Cole was a matter of him stopping me on my way to the door of The Stork. The whole thing took only thirty seconds—enough to convince me that you would be home a few days later.

I promise to get a picture of Maggie to you.

I also promise to do my best to get her a job in N.Y. This will be harder.

She and Alice are coming over to Christmas dinner tomorrow. As I told you, we are having it in town this year. To-night (X. Eve) the traditional tree-dressing will take place with the traditional dressers on hand—Milton Cohen, Reggie, Jerry Watanbe, and all the Indians: Jimmy, Shawen, Jennifer, Sue, Henry and another sailor friend, Nora Howard, Dorothy and I. I don't do so much as I used to, so I don't get angry any more. I let the others worry. As I ran over the above names, certain newsy tid-bits occurred to me about several. Reggie: His wife leaves for Reno in a few days. Jerry: His mother will probably not realize her ambition to see England before she dies—cancer. She is over eighty, I believe. Henry: January 27, he goes to Columbia for four months, after which he is slated to get his commission if all goes well. His marks have all been very high. Nora: Stu is the pianist in the pic of "7 Lively Arts" He will also accompany Bea [Lillie] if she takes a Night Club job. But she probably won't because she can't keep any money anyway, what with the combined Brit. and Am. Taxes.

We have three openings to see this week, Dorothy and I. Wednesday The Guild opens a musical piece called Sing Out, Sweet Land. The music is all American Folk Songs. I saw it in Boston and I think it has a good chance. It has an amateurish quality which will be either the making

---

[13] Susan Jacobson Blanchard—Dorothy's daughter from her first marriage—did not appear in another Broadway show; however, she did go to Hollywood where she was cast in three films in 1947. In two of them her scenes were cut and in the third she was un-credited. She married Henry Fonda in 1950.

or the ruin of it. Depends a good deal on those old devil first-nighters. Thursday there is another musical show called "On the Town" about which the reports are good. It is written and devised by some newcomers: Jerry Robbins who electrified the ballet world last year with a great new ballet called "Fancy Free" and two others whose names I forget.[14] The only old-timer concerned is G. Abbott who directed it. On Friday we journey to Philadelphia where we see "Way Up in Central Park"[15] a new musical by Rommy and Dorothy and Herb Fields, produced by Michael Todd—and published, incidentally by Rodgers & Hammerstein, alias Williamson.[16] I am rooting hard for it, for Rommy more than anyone. I'd love to see him come back and fool the jivists.

Saturday morning we'll go from Phila. to Doylestown where we hope to stay for a solid month, with one or two days interruption only. During that delicious time I hope to finish Liliom. We are at present aiming for rehearsal starting February 12—(This, after all was a very good starting date for Honest Abe). I believe we will be ready with the libretto and score, but we may be held up by casting trouble.

The recent reverses on the European front have been very distressing. The worst part has been listening to the comments of armchair generals. I am sure we will not know the true cause of the surprise and the break-through for some time. It does seem that our Intelligence was not very accurate concerning German strength. But it is ridiculous for us to draw any conclusions or blame anyone until we know who to blame—if indeed anyone is to blame. I do blame—and bitterly—some very heroic and great and prominent Generals for making all their grandiose prophecies last August. No one asked them to predict the probable end of the war with Germany, but they did. Factory workers naturally started to leave war jobs and feather their peacetime nests. Then came the cry to get back to their jobs. Didn't they know there was a war going on?

[14] Really three: composer Leonard Bernstein, and the aforementioned book writers and lyricists Betty Comden and Adolph Green. *Fancy Free*, also with music by Bernstein, actually premiered in April 1944, not the previous year.

[15] *Up in Central Park* was a modest success. Its score includes the standard "Close as Pages in a Book."

[16] Rodgers and Hammerstein formed their own music publishing company in association with Max Dreyfus of Chappell. They named the company Williamson as both of their fathers were named William.

Well, the obvious answer is that the poor devils had just been told there wouldn't be a war going on for long. This has been the trouble since the war started. The people have been alternately cushioned and kicked until they haven't known where they stood at any time. If they had been consistently kicked, and never cushioned I do not believe they would have complained. They have been the victims of scientific "conditioning" by advertising-minded leaders.

Then there is the disappointing goings on in Greece, Italy, Belgian and Poland. I am not taking sides. I don't know what factions are right. I can see arguments for both views in each case. BUT—I see no justification for separate action by England, Russia and The United States, and the various bi-lateral agreements and old fashioned "balance of power" treaties that are being entered into. Looks like the old hooey. Well, so who thought we would emerge from this conflict into an Utopia? Not your aged father! Mankind is not of a piece, yet. It is a crazy-quilt. And all you can do with a crazy quilt is add a patch here and a patch there. The best thing an individual can do is to try to land on a color he likes. Of course, now and then a man comes along with a dye that would make it all one beautiful solid color. But the people who are in the business of manufacturing patches, usually manage to crucify him before he can un-cork his magic liquid.

With this complex and incomplete comparison I close, with

Love –

Dad

A Christmas card from Kathryn Forbes—the author of *Mama's Bank Account*—features a picture on the front of a girl angel holding a star.

Kathryn Forbes to Oscar Hammerstein, circa December, 1944

Dear Oscar:

Laugh if you will—but <u>this</u> angel made me think of you!.

K

Oscar Hammerstein to Kathryn Forbes, December 28, 1944

Dear Kathryn:-

I am inclined to agree with you about my resemblance to the angel although I believe my features to be more finely chiseled. She hasn't my thin, patrician nose nor my high intellectual forehead but she does carry a gold star that she apparently cherishes very dearly and this is the way I am with I REMEMBER MAMA.

Happy New Year to you.

Chapter Seven

1945 (and Smatterings from 1946 and 1947)

As 1945 began, *Oklahoma!* was in the second year of its smash Broadway run. One tour was now ensconced in Chicago, where it would run for 532 performances, and a second company was about to begin its national tour on January 8. *Carmen Jones* was still playing on Broadway, and the Rodgers and Hammerstein–produced *I Remember Mama* was going strong, *State Fair* was about to begin filming. Rodgers and Hammerstein's musical adaptation of *Liliom* would soon begin rehearsals. The war was turning the Allies' way; Bill Hammerstein was still aboard ship in the South Pacific; and on the home front Oscar continued working on several war-related committees. Highland Farm was home, not just to Oscar, Dorothy, Alice, Susan, Henry, and Jimmy, but various "adopted" people, including Shawen Lynch, the daughter of an English friend of Dorothy's, Margot Devauchier, the daughter of a French father and an American mother, and Jennifer Watanabe, the daughter of Dorothy's sister Doody. And in the summer of 1942, Jimmy's friend, Stephen Sondheim, then twelve, had begun "infiltrating" his way into the household and was now under Oscar's wing and influence.

Oscar Hammerstein to Leighton Brill (excerpt), January 8, 1945

We were disappointed at not having Billy home for Christmas but apparently chief quartermasters are in demand at the moment and the Navy isn't giving any of them leaves for some time. This is tough on Bill because he has already been overseas for twenty months and he is supposed to be eligible for a states' side leave after sixteen or eighteen months. Maggie is still here champing at the bit to get back to Red Cross work but tied down waiting for Billy.

This is about all the family news. Susan as you know made her debut in the SEVEN LIVELY ARTS with eleven other pretty girls who walk on turn around and walk off. Her brother, Henry, says that when she isn't on the show goes to pieces—and this is nearly true.

The Letters of Oscar Hammerstein II. Mark Eden Horowitz, Oxford University Press. © Mark Eden Horowitz 2022. DOI: 10.1093/oso/9780197538180.003.0007

I have seen CENTRAL PARK the new show which Rommy and Herbert and Dorothy Fields wrote. It is in Philadelphia and is doing very well. I like the songs and the book is fair. The cast is not quite as good as fair. I think, however, that it has a good chance. It opens here the end of the month. Our firm publishes the songs.

William Hammerstein to Oscar Hammerstein (excerpt), January 16, 1945

Dear Dad –

Here we are about to do some more travelling to new and interesting places. Just when we move I do not know altho we've been expecting to the past week. More than that I cannot say, of course, but I should think the conclusions are rather obvious. Since I don't expect to receive any mail for awhile and haven't had any in about three weeks I shall assume that had I had any there would have been one from you and so I answer it herewith which is a bonus because when I finally do receive it I will have to answer it again.

Last night I went ashore to a CB base and saw the best movie I've seen out here—Cabin in the Sky. Have you seen it? Ethel Waters is captivating and Rochester very good. There's a wonderful song which I don't remember from the show called De Consequences and another called Happiness is Just a Thing called Joe which Miss Waters sings to make your eyes water. The theatre in which I saw the picture was also the best I've seen out here altho it was very hard to get to it. It is situated in a gully—a natural amphi-theatre–a miniature Hollywood Bowl. The stage looked fairly substantial and I imagine when Irving Berlin gets up this way, which he will very soon, he will find little to complain of. Of course it can't begin to compare with the opera houses of Rome and Naples and Algiers and Cairo but it's almost big enough to do the show without compressing it as they had to at the base when I saw it a few weeks ago. Maggie has, I hope, read you my letter which related my meeting Mr. B. and other members of his company whom I had known before. Viz.—Max Showalter, Billy Josephi (or Joseffy), John Koenig and a fellow named Roger Kinney who used to sing with Ray Bloch on the Philip Moisher [Morris?] show. I met also a detestable individual named Ben Washer who was frightfully upset because New Guinea had not been civilized before he arrived to the extent of possessing a replica of the Centre Theatre. I noticed a strange thing in meeting those people. They all seemed like pansies to me. I'm sure they weren't (not <u>all</u> of them, anyway) but I decided that I've been away from theatre people for so long that I've become used to the tough talking rugged type of sailors with whom I live and gentility has come to seem soft and queer to me. Of course, maybe they <u>were</u> all pansies, but I doubt it. But it was a good show and I enjoyed it very much as did the entire audience.

William Hammerstein to Oscar Hammerstein (excerpt), January 29, 1945

So ----- now we are in the Phillipines [*sic*] (which I am allowed to tell you but not the exact location which is silly because you read the newspapers and you can see I have time to write you) and our duty is somewhat the same tho it promises to be duller—for awhile at least. By the time it gets more interesting I shall probably (I hope) be on my [way] home. The days and weeks are dragging more each day with the certainty of leaving. I don't know exactly what the transportation deal is out of here but I'm going ashore tomorrow and try and find what mud hole the air transp. office is located in. If not by air then we (the Chief Bosun and I) will try to make a deal with a merchant ship. That way we will be assured of a restful trip and enough good food to bring us back to full colored well filled men. The food situation as you may imagine, is pretty damn tough and getting worse. Our progress is so fast and our expansion as well, that it's an impossibility to keep fresh food flowing in. The job of transporting troops and munitions and equipment seems to be going ok and if we have to live on dried rations to make it end quicker that's ok by me. Our cook is a good baker and we have bread as long as we have flour—and I know what they meant when they said it was the staff of life. Other than bread we subsist mostly on salmon and beans and good old Navy coffee. Strong black Joe ground in the states. For a long time we had only Aussie coffee and I had to give up my morning cup—just couldn't stomach it. But I'm back to it again since we got the stateside stuff. No matter how tough the eats situation gets aboard ship there is always the small consolation that those poor bastards on the beach (Army, Navy and CBs) fare that much worse.

So that's the living situation. We still have a little beer left and we get two cans a day as long as it holds out. Ordinarily I should think that the islands could go far towards subsisting a good part of us here as there are many farms and rice fields but the jap left nothing in his wake but destruction and sadly happy looking people who daily are still coming down out of the hills with their dunnage and their little naked babies. They haven't even any clothes left and will trade all kinds of things for clothes and food. The girls will take mattress covers—will plead for them—from which they make very attractive form fitting dresses. An officer from another APC saw a sleazy looking wench walking down the street wearing a very fashionable looking print dress—on a double take he discovered that it was made from a regulation Navy officers bed spread with the anchor and the USN deftly removed. Dave, the SK, saw a man with a pair of shorts made from pillow ticking. Pretty sharp, too.

Our evening entertainment of which we have been deprived for about a year now, has begun again altho not nearly so well produced as of yore. Last night was the best so far tho none too good. Our old friend "Piss-call Charlie" came over for a look but I don't think he got to see very much (In case you are unfamiliar with the jargon from which this fellows name originates, a piss-call is a nocturnal awakening after which it is uncomfortable to go back to sleep without relieving oneself)

The clipping re: Dick's plans for music in "Carousell" [*sic*] was most interesting and I return it herewith as per your request.

Susan's success is amazing. I can remember when I was running my tail off working far into nights and dashing to Hell's Kitchen to get impossible things like a hurdy-gurdy which _must_ play "Poor Little Buttercup" and you wouldn't let me join equity because the minimum pay for ass't stage mgr. was too much, you thought, for a young punk of 20 or 21. I should have been beautiful and a good horse for Valentina's creations—yet. My present pay is more than I ever have earned and it still doesn't touch $75 a week. I hope the tyke sticks by her plans of sinking it into good dramatic education which she will certainly need if she is to carry on successfully in her new career. I wish her the greatest of histrionic achievements and I shall watch her carefully and I hope in admiration.

Happy to hear that Carmen has not yet packed up and please try and hold it thru March.

As to your getting Maggie a job as you said you'd try, I can see now why that is such a difficult thing. It's always hard to get someone a job when they don't want it. I've just had a letter from her in which she apprises me of the fact that she has slated herself for more overseas duty. At the time she wrote it she didn't know I was coming back so soon but she did know I was coming back in a matter of months and it was a great disappointment to me when I learned that she couldn't wait for me. I haven't yet answered her letter (which came three days ago) because I think it better that I cool off before I put things down on paper which I may regret. I think tomorrow I shall be ready to answer and perhaps I'll ignore the whole thing. I only hope now that she can delay her adventuresome plans long enough to spend my leave with me. I had also counted on her being with me in California while I await my new ship, which wait might be anything from a few weeks to a few months depending on whether I get an already commissioned ship or a new construction—but that, I suppose, is out now.

By now "Central Park" has opened and I share your hopes that it was successful. My best wishes please, to Dorothy and Rommy and Herb Fields.

Saw an article in Colliers about Arthur Schwartz and his activities at MGM (?). When the war is over he is going to have a visit from a certain young composer to whom he gave much encouragement some years ago. That is if my subsequent efforts prove to bear out that encouragement.

Your WWB meeting with "communication" people sounds very good and I hope its purpose succeeds. I've always felt badly about that sort of thing and I agree that it does much more harm than Father Coughlin or Hitler. It keeps alive the ancient prejudices which people would gladly forget if they weren't constantly reminded of them. The public mind is such an easy thing to educate why can't we educate it in the right way just as easily as we do the wrong way?

Yes—the world is a crazy-quilt but it threatens to become crazier still if developments continue as they go now. Neither did I expect a Utopia (alright—an Utopia) to emerge from the present contortions of the world but I certainly expected the people of the world to learn something and it doesn't looked [sic] as if they've learned very much. I don't expect this to be the last war of the world's history but it must, to my way of thinking, be the last one for a long time and this it cannot be unless it ends conclusively which I don't think it will. Mere military defeat means nothing. Dumbarton Oaks is a farce to me. An example of what we will do after the war in the countries we have defeated lies in our treatment of Italy and I think that stinks. Of all the bungled stupid jobs that stands out as the worst. The Greek situation I cannot understand at all and must reserve judgment. The Russians at the moment are 129 miles from Berlin. How will they handle Germany? I've an idea they will do a good job. Maybe I'm wrong. But somebody better start doing a good job somewhere or thousands of lives and gallons of blood and worlds of misery and suffering will have been for nothing but, at best, the "status quo" we heard so much about in the early days of the war.

I hope Mryrus of the Cotillion Room was right and it's amazing how close he is at that. If I should get home the third week in Feb (which, after all is not impossible even if I don't leave here until then) I shall go to him immediately and find out how long my next cruise will be—and Maggie's.

And that winds up tonights installment. Listen in next week at this same time. Will Billy get home in Feb? Will Liliom be a hit? Will Maggie join the paratroopers? Will MacArthur reach Manilla? Will Timoshenko reach Berlin? Will Susan reach for a Lucky instead of a sweet?

Goodnight and love-

Bill

As proof of the size and complexity of the Hammerstein household:

William Hammerstein to Oscar Hammerstein et al. (excerpt), January 29, 1945

Dear Dad and Dorothy and Alice and Maggie and Henry and Susan and Shawen and Jimmy and Jenny and Madame W. and Doodie and Jerry and Milton and Mary and Nora and Stu and Unk and Mimi –

The order of names has nothing at all to do with my preference except for one or two understandable cases who shall be nameless.

Photo 15 James and Dorothy Hammerstein, and Susan Blanchard, circa 1932.
Photograph courtesy of Oscar Andrew Hammerstein

Jack Yorke to Oscar Hammerstein (excerpt), January 29, 1945

Dear Mr. Hammerstein:

Mr. Paul Robeson has agreed to do a musical for me next year. We have agreed that an operetta, based on "Othello", would be an ideal vehicle for him, and he has given me the green light to go ahead with it. It is at his suggestion that I am writing to you. During one of our talks, I mentioned that I thought you and Dick were the only ones to do the book, music and lyrics. In this he wholeheartedly agreed with me. He says he knows you well, and that I should write to you with his full sanction.

Photo 16 James and William Hammerstein, Henry Jacobson, and Oscar Hammerstein II, circa 1933. Photograph courtesy of Oscar Andrew Hammerstein

Oscar Hammerstein to John Yorke, February 2, 1945

Dear Mr. Yorke:-

Thank you for your letter and for your kind confidence expressed in Dick Rodgers and me. The trouble with us is that we have too much to do. Our present plans jointly and separately take us right into the end of 1946.

As to the proposition of making an operetta out of OTHELLO I am in no position to give you my opinion because it is something that would take a great deal of study. Writing anything for Paul Robeson would be an agreeable task for me because of my admiration for him as an artist and my feeling of friendship for him as a man. I am sorry, however, but it doesn't look as if we can be of any help to you or him on this one.

All good wishes to you,

Sincerely

Paul Robeson starred in *Othello* on Broadway for 296 performances from October 1943 until July 1944. It remains the longest-running Shakespeare play in Broadway history. He then took the production on tour for nearly a year.

Hungarian-born playwright and author Ferenc Molnár immigrated to America in 1940 to escape persecution as a Jew in Eastern Europe during the war. Although *Liliom* was not a success in Hungary in its 1909 premier, it eventually became Molnár's most popular play. The Hungarian version of his book *The Captain of St. Margaret's* was published in 1926 and its English translation was released in 1945.

Oscar Hammerstein to Ferenc Molnár, February 2, 1945

Dear Mr. Molnar:-

I was delighted and charmed by THE CAPTAIN OF ST. MARGARET'S.

I am nearing the end of my task, adapting your play, and I have conflicting feelings about it. On the one hand, I feel it may be a very unusual and distinguished musical play and as such I hope that you will be pleased with it. On the other hand, I have fears that you will miss many values that you created which I, in my wisdom or ignorance have had to sacrifice for new values which I thought necessary to it in its musical form. Whatever happens, please forgive me and be assured that at any rate my intentions were good.

I hope I will be able to see you soon. I will telephone you as soon as I have time to breathe and strength to pick up a telephone.

With all good wishes,

Sincerely

Photo 17 Oscar Hammerstein II at his standing desk, 1945. Photograph
courtesy of Oscar Andrew Hammerstein

Despite setting the show on the Maine coast—and the resulting changed milieu and
occupations of its characters—*Carousel* was reasonably faithful to *Liliom*. *Carousel*
even retained Billy's suicide (although for the film they were forced to make his
death accidental). Among other alterations: the characters that became Carrie
and Mr. Snow were now more comic foils, and the character of Louise was made
more sympathetic. Hammerstein also removed social commentary related to anti-
Semitism. The most significant change was in the ending. In Hammerstein's version,
Billy is finally able to find a way to help his daughter.

Oscar Hammerstein to John Van Druten, February 2, 1945

Dear John:-

Under separate cover, I am sending you a published copy of CARMEN JONES to which, as one of its earliest cheerleaders you are surely entitled.

A letter to you has been on my daily agenda for four weeks but each day it has been crowded off by a man whose Hungarian name was Liliom (since he has come to this country he is called just plain Billy)

I don't know if anyone has written to you about the "Christmas Party" that Mady and Homolka gave to the company two weeks ago. It was upstairs at Sardi's and among other things there was lutefisk on the smorgasbord. The man who was serving it, dressed in the conventional chef's uniform said to me, "Would you care for some fish pudding?" and I felt like smiting the Philistine with a handful of this fish pudding. What he did to me was something like asking a child what he would like for Christmas from Mister S. Claus. The party was uneventful and a little on the staid side—at any rate that's how it was up to the time that the managers left. It was the first time I had seen the entire company together since the opening and it was also the first time I had ever seen them without their director whom I must say they seemed to need badly. I am sure you could have drawn more gaity [*sic*] out of them and perhaps your very presence would have turned the trick—or perhaps I am just being sentimental as songwriters are wont to be.

I suppose you would like a report on the performance of the play. We have made several little changes since you left. I hope you won't mind the cut Dick and I have made in the hospital scene—the line, "Then I treat you". It is true this was a laugh but we didn't think the right kind. At any rate we have compensated for this by adding a laugh in the second act. Thirkelson and Trina now have triplets. We had to put on a bigger baby carriage and since it wouldn't fit on the table, we have to wheel it on from the wings but it doesn't look bad—and what a belly laugh it is. Dick suggested making one of the tots a colored baby but I didn't think you would like this. It will also interest you to know that Cora's navel is back in the show. She came to us and asked us especially to let her restore it because her young man has just returned from the Italian campaign and he comes and sits in the third row every night. We thought, therefore, that patriotism as well as good business dictated this little change.

Outside of this the performance is pretty much as you left it. Otto has changed most of the lighting but the show looks much better. In fact, whatever we have done since you left has tended to brighten and lighten the entertainment. Going into the hotel lobby we no longer play the Viennese waltz. We have put in an Oklahoma medley which, while anachronistic, gives the scene a very much better start and cues Miss Brown into a little dance step which she has always wanted to interpolate.

Turning away from serious things we miss you very much. What are your plans? Are you going to cook yourself on the desert all spring or will you be a sport and come back here for the opening of "Carrousel" [*sic*] (Liliom) in New York about the last week in April or the first week in May? My suggestion is that you come here then and maybe I will be able to go back with you a few weeks later because it will be necessary for me to visit your very arid and justifiably maligned part of the country about the first of June.

I am offering odds of 20 to 1 you have already started on a new play and not having the brashness that a manager should really have I haven't the nerve to ask you, "Please, please, may Rodgers and Hammerstein produce it?"

Since we go into rehearsal in a week and since I haven't yet finished my play, you will probably not hear from me for some time but I look forward to hearing from you and I particularly would like to know your reaction to the little changes we have made in MAMA—not that we will do anything about it if you don't approve.

Meanwhile, Dick and I and the two Dorothys send our love.

Sincerely,

Marc Holstein to Oscar Hammerstein, February 2, 1945

Dear Oscar:-

I want to tell you how much I have enjoyed your article on Jerry. It is almost perfect—almost, hell it is perfect! It is familiar and intimate without being vulgar; tenderly affectionate without sentimentality; and it rings true. It has the integrity which is characteristic of both the author and his subject. Only those who know Jerry as intimately as we do can appreciate how completely you have caught the spirit of Ariel and Puck and Falstaff which has been blended in his make-up and I liked so much (and I love you for) the part you gave Eva. Nothing could be more effective than the five simple words with which your little essay ends. They express also (I need scarcely tell you) the sentiments of

Sincerely yours,

M. G. H.

Oscar Hammerstein to Marc Holstein, February 13, 1945

Dear Marc:-

Thank you for your nice letter. It made me a little ashamed that I had used up so many words to describe Jerry when you knocked him off so much better with only three; Ariel, Puck and Falstaff.

All good wishes,

Sincerely

Emma Hammerstein to Oscar Hammerstein, February 6, 1945

Dear Oscar 2nd:-

I have been very ill for over a year and suffered much of the time from acute and almost unbearable <u>pain</u> caused by diverticulitis of the colon. I was fleuroscoped [sic] + X-Rayed in New York Hospital 1 yr. ago last Sept. + that was the answer have been under their direction ever since regarding medicine, vitamins, diet, etc.

On Nov. 9th, 1942 at Lying-In <u>Hospital, N.Y.C.</u>, Dr. Stander, head Dr. there, performed a major operation on me, removing a very large tumor about 17 lbs., which was floating in the abdominal cavity + pressing on my vital organs.

For over a year I have not felt able to get about but have done so from mere "necessity"—always in agony.

Nearly 2 wks. ago, such an acute situation developed that I was compelled to go at once for treatment to a bladder-specialist, Dr. Leo Gibson, Medical Arts Bld. this city. Upon examination he told me I had a large tumor - I was in such agony that he advised me to go into the hospital that very day for an operation, but wanted <u>Dr.</u> Clark [?] bldg.., gerecologist [sic], to examine me + give his opinion. He Dr. Clark said I had a tumor in the abdomen as large as a person's head + that I had better get in the hospital for an operation right away—otherwise I might <u>at anytime</u>, have an emergency + that would not be so good. I have great difficulty in arising out of my chair + the pain in my left side is so acute that it takes a couple of minutes before I can straighten up + start to walk + my left arm is almost helpless + I haven't a soul to raise a hand to help me or wait on me or do anything—in my old age— I have hoped in some miraculous way to overcome it all. But, I'll have to face the music. Dr. Clark, connected with Syracuse Memorial Hospital, wants me to come in within the next week or two. His fee, private room, anesthetist, operating room, etc. + incidentals will amount to around $500.00. I just could not stand to have any others moaning + groaning or <u>snoring</u> around me—or even to have anyone except the Drs. + nurses speak even. I lie + suffer in quietude, myself, relax + rest + any aggravation of others around me would be unbearable as I am extremely nervous + sensitive to such things. After all you suffered through last summer, I am sure you understand.

The situation is this that I have to keep what I have on hand to pay income taxes + yet I should get into the hospital at once + cannot. Could you help me with this situation so that I may go in a few days + have the very necessary comfort of a private room?

Will you very kindly let me know at the earliest possible moment? Dr. Clark wrote Dr. Stander for details of 1942 operation. You can verify facts from him.

I am sorry to write you such a letter but I [?] am in a fox-hole + have to get out somehow.

I do hope you have fully recovered from your appendectomy + that you + yours are well and happy.

With very best wishes,

Sincerely yours,

Emma Hammerstein.

Oscar Hammerstein to Emma Hammerstein, February 14, 1945

Dear Emma Hammerstein:-

I deeply sympathize with you and I sincerely wish I could spare the money you request but I just can't. I am making a great deal of money but I am getting only about five cents on the dollar because of the tax rate. What I have left doesn't quite pay the expenses of my immediate family and I recently had to borrow money to pay my 1944 tax bill.

This is a strange state of affairs but it is nevertheless true. All good wishes to you,

Sincerely

Oscar Hammerstein to Richard Berger, RKO Pictures, February 14, 1945

Dear Dick:-

Please excuse the promptness with which I am returning the script of RIP VAN WINKLE. I have read it and I don't like it very much. I think if Rip Van Winkle is worth doing it is worth doing without having a shot in the arm of current social significance. It is an old classic fantasy and it is either worth repeating or it isn't. I don't mean that it should be done without the application of modern imagination but I think the way it is handled in this script is a misfit.

Nelli tells me the good news about how your affairs are progressing and I am really thrilled by it. After CARROUSEL [sic] (Liliom) opens here sometime near the end of April I expect to make a trip to the Coast to confer with Preminger for a week or so on the biography of my grandfather which I am doing for Fox. I look forward to seeing you then.

Meanwhile, best of luck and good wishes.

Sincerely,

Letter from Oscar Hammerstein to Abraham Mandlestam,
February 15, 1945

Dear Mandy:-

I am delighted with the pictures of I REMEMBER MAMA. It was most kind of you to send them to me.

As for the last paragraph of your letter asking me to forgive you for not having invested in OKLAHOMA I have never felt any resentment about this at all. I was only surprised that you didn't shoot yourself.

All good wishes to you,

Sincerely,

Oscar debated economics with his childhood friend Milton Kadison who worked on Wall Street. (They first met at summer camp; later Kadison dated Myra Finn, before she and Oscar married.)

Oscar Hammerstein to Milton Kadison, February 19, 1945

Dear Kaddy:-

On the third page of THE VALUE LINE there are these sentences:-

"There are only two ways in which this crisis could be relieved. The first is to reverse the tax policy, permitting the accumulation of any amount of capital tax-free, provided only that it be invested."[1]

Since this is the identical proposition that I originated when you were having lunch at my home several months ago and which you brushed off with the superiority of most Wall Street snobs I am surprised that you have the affrontery [sic] to send it to me now as a new idea from a financial expert.

---

[1] The Value Line: Investment Survey. Vol. IV No. 5, February 5, 1945.
  The section quoted in Hammerstein's letter is preceded by:
  "The significant thing, though, is that the New Deal Administration has at last come to grips with the crisis that its tax policy has created—the paralysis of equity financing."
  And is followed by:
  "The government's revenue in that case would have to come from the tax on the amount the individual spends for his creature comforts. If our Henry Ford should accumulate a fortune and reinvest it in his own industry, to that extent he would be serving the public."

When it comes to fundamental economic reform the poets have only to sit back and wait for the statisticians and jugglers in commerce to catch up with them. I am very happy to see that the boys downtown are beginning to see a glimmer of the very obvious remedy I had seen months ago.

Thanks for the endorsement.

Love and kisses

Oscar Hammerstein to Milton Kadison, March 6, 1945

Dear Kaddy:-

Unfortunately, I haven't kept the document of capitalist lip service which you sent me but I definitely remember that my very good financial device was used not as a straw man to be knocked down but as one of the two possible remedies. The writer even brought it back in his summing-up and had definitely not eliminated it from consideration.

I am further not impressed by your rattling off a series of economists in which you rather star one Lord Woolton,[2] whom I eliminate on the ground of scurvy motives. His owning one of the best racing stables in England is prima facie evidence that his whole view of economics and society is colored by the desire to buy oats for his horses leaving only cake to be eaten by the tenants on his neglected estates of which he is a notoriously absentee landlord.

As to that unworthy comment of yours on the word "effrontery" I should have better claimed your confidence than to have you think I had misspelled it. It was a lapse of Nelli's but I am not sure she has not invented a very much better word for my purposes since it is directly an "affrontery" for jerks like Bernhard,[3] Dahlberg,[4] and Hazlett[5] to be stealing my stuff.

---

[2] Frederick James Marquis, 1st Earl of Woolton, was Minister of Food in England during the War, where he established the rationing system. He then became Minister of Reconstruction in the War Cabinet.

[3] Arnold Bernhard was the founder of Value Line, an "investment research and financial publishing firm."

[4] Arthur Dahlberg was an economic consultant to the Hoover Administration and worked on the National Economic Recovery Plan for the Roosevelt Administration.

[5] Henry Hazlitt was the principal editorial writer on finances and economics for *The New York Times*, where he opposed the formation of both the World Bank and the International Monetary Fund.

I shall be delighted to write in your copy of CARMEN JONES and I have no doubt that some day the book will be rendered more valuable for being inscribed by a distinguished economist.

As ever

Luise Rainer was a German-born actress who immigrated to America in 1935. She won back-to-back Oscars for *The Great Ziegfeld* in 1936 and *The Good Earth* in 1937, after which her film career faltered.

Oscar Hammerstein to Luise Rainer, February 23, 1945

Dear Luise Rainer:-

I read THE MESSENGER with interest—in the light of the interpretation you wish to give it. I have talked it over with Dick Rodgers and while we both feel that the play might succeed, it is not sufficiently exciting to either one of us to make us want to produce it. This is not so much a reflection on the play as a statement of the peculiar position we are in as producers. Our only motive for producing a play is the pleasure we can get out of doing something of unusual quality and importance and we prefer to sit and wait until that kind of prospect allures us.

We both think that perhaps you can make a success out of THE MESSENGER and you have our best wishes in this project.

Sincerely,

Letter from Oscar Hammerstein to Myra Finn, February 23, 1945

Dear Mike:-

Thank you for the CARMEN JONES review which made me much less indignant than it did you. I wouldn't make a cause celebre out of such an insignificant book review tucked away in a paper of a very small circulation in spite of its excellence.

Immersed as I am in rehearsals, I wouldn't want to waste my energy stirring up a tempest in so small a teapot. This fellow would love that. It would make him much more important. I would prefer to leave him in the oblivion he so well deserves. Besides in any letter duels with newspaper men you can't possibly win because they always have the last word and if you write directly to the editor he nearly always backs up his men.

All good wishes,

Sincerely,

Letter from G. M. Loeb to Oscar Hammerstein, February 24, 1945

Dear Mr. Hammerstein :

I was fortunate to be present Wednesday afternoon at Mr Glaenzer's apartment when you rendered the lyrics to "Carrousel" [sic]. My partner, Mr J E Swan, introduced me but I had to leave after the first complete reading and playing of each number. I am a very amateur experimenter—I have a piece of "Sing Out Sweet Land" and may be offered a piece of Carrousel. If I was supposed to tell whether it will be a financial hit Wednesday, I am indeed an amateur.

However your lines intrigued me as being really marvelous and in full keeping with what anyone familiar with your sexcellent [sic] top quality work would expect. "Excellent", I mean the "s" is my bad typing but not a bad word for "Time" magazine or in a play.

Of course I have not seen the script but I note it must be changed a very great deal from the European atmosphere of Lilliom [sic].

In any event I am writing to suggest, if accuracy in your lyrics is desirable, that your staff check the mating habits of sheep. I put some sheep in up here when the war broke out and seemingly the females are in heat just once a year—autumn—and lambs are born only in late winter. By Easter they are in the language of the market place "spring baby lambs".

I do not think rams mate with ewes in June as they do in your lyrics but I am not really certain. We have been told to keep our rams separate at all times except when the ewes are in heat but we did not follow this precaution and in several years all mating seemed confined to September-October— no mounting whatsoever in June or if so no results.

I have often wondered what happened first—the lyrics or the music. But it seems in this the words must come first—leaving Mr. Rodgers to fit his tunes. I can visualize it as a most charming stage entertainment—light operetta. How much will be sung on the radio, or hummed by the public or played on records I do not know. In popular words it might be too good, or too highbrow to put it another way to earn filthy lucre.

In any event I enjoyed hearing it and look forward to the production. I enjoyed meeting you and am sorry that it was perforce so casual.

Sincerely yours,

G M Loeb

Letter from Oscar Hammerstein to G. M. Loeb, March 2, 1945

Dear Mr. Loeb:-

I was delighted with the parts of your letter praising my work and thrown into consternation by the unwelcome news about the eccentrically frigid behavior of ewes in June. I have since checked your statement and found it to be true. It looks very much as if in the interest of scientific honesty I shall have to abandon the verse dealing with sheep.

The play is shaping up very well in rehearsal and I hope that when you see it, it lives up to your expectations.

Thank you for your interest.

Sincerely,

The lyric in question refers to this quatrain from "June is Bustin' Out All Over":

> The sheep aren't sleepin' any more.
> All the rams that chase the ewe sheep,
> Are determined there'll be new sheep,
> And the ewe sheep aren't even keepin' score!

Oscar never did change the lyric. Loeb was not the only one to raise the issue. Hugh Fordin claims: "It was after the lyric was finished that Peter Moen pointed out to him that sheep do not mate in June; they mate in winter and bear their young in the spring. Oscar hated his lyrics to be inaccurate, but he let the stanza remain, explaining to purists, 'What you say about sheep may all be very true for most years, sir, but not in 1873. 1873 is my year and that year, curiously enough, the sheep mated in the spring.'"

Oscar Hammerstein to Samuel Taylor,[6] March 2, 1945

Dear Sam:-

I read your script last night and I have nearly the same reaction that I felt on reading your last one. Like the last one, it gives me a very positive confidence in your talent as a playwright but I find myself not interested in the subject matter and the characters you have chosen to write about. I think that this play is written very very much better than your last one not only in respect of the quality of its dialogue but also from a structural standpoint. I also feel that there is a strong likelihood that you will get this one produced and if it is produced, I certainly wouldn't bet against its success. I think it has more than a fair chance—given very skillful casting and direction.

But this letter is mainly about my personal opinion. For me, the characters are not sufficiently primitive or important to make the kind of play that excites me. There are times when I don't quite understand their switches. While the barrier between the two lovers is very clear and understandable they seem to shy away from each other quite arbitrarily at different times. Whenever she becomes understanding and willing he would pull a quick switch and dodge away. As soon as she would take "no" for an answer he would come back to her and she would dodge. This emotional see-saw would be quite consistent with some characters and in fact a play could be written on the very tendency in lovers. But in these people it seemed perverse and annoying to me—except in a very [few?] situations where I fully understood their reactions. I seem to be accusing you of obscuring and I have an uncomfortable feeling that I am being obscure myself. If you would like to take [*sic*] to me face to face and tell me I am crazy ring me up—Regent 4-1392—and come around to the house some evening. I am home nearly every night.

Sincerely,

P.S. I must add that I thought old man Leach was a wow. Do you think you could persuade G.B.S. to come over and play it?

---

[6] In 1950, Rodgers and Hammerstein produced Taylor's first play on Broadway, *The Happy Time*.

Oscar Hammerstein to Ham Fisher (author of the comic strip "Joe Palooka"), March 6, 1945

Dear Ham:-

Your syndicate very properly asked my permission for your use of part of the lyric of OKLAHOMA in your February 24th strip. I granted it but I didn't grant the permission to misquote the lyric—nor did I dream that an old lyric memorizer like you would bawl up the words in so foul a manner. It just makes me lose my faith in human nature and in the permanence of old institutions.

Love and kisses,

As ever,

The widely syndicated comic strip, *Joe Palooka*, featured, as creator Ham Fisher described him, "a big, good-natured prize fighter who didn't like to fight; a defender of little guys; a gentle knight." The lyric as it appeared in the comic strip was, "O-OK-LAHOMA WHERE THE WIND COMES FOLLOWIN' THE RAIN . . . OKLAHOMA OKAY." Fisher seems to have conflated two lines, and should have used either "Oklahoma, Where the wind comes sweepin' down the plain," or " . . . When the wind comes right behind the rain."

Barbara Clough, Dean, George School to Oscar Hammerstein, April 7, 1945

Dear Mr. Hammerstein:

I have your note of March 25 saying that you will be glad to have Jimmy and Steve come to New York on April 19 to see the opening of your new play. It is contrary to school policy to permit students to be absent from classes for such a reason.

I have not talked to Jimmy about the absence, but I have had several conversations with Steve. He proposes to leave George School after classes on Thursday, arriving in New York in time for the play and returning to George School by 8:30 Friday morning in time for assembly.

I understand that Jimmy must go to New York on Friday because of a dental appointment. Is it not expecting too much of the boy's time and energy to make two trips to New York in so short a time? Absence under these arrangements do not meet with the approval of the school, but on the other hand, we want to cooperate with parents' wishes and the desires of our students.

Will you please let me know how you feel about the matter.

Sincerely yours,

Barbara M. Clough, Dean

"Steve" is Stephen Sondheim. It's not clear whether or not Jimmy and/or Steve attended the Broadway opening of *Carousel*, but according to Sondheim, "When Jimmy was fourteen and I was fifteen and it was spring break at George School, Oscar took us to New Haven for the first-night performance." The first night in New Haven was March 22, Sondheim's fifteenth birthday.

Oscar Hammerstein to John Van Druten (excerpt), April 23, 1945

Carousel had a great opening and a wonderful press—all but Wilella Waldorf[7] who clings desperately to the protection of not liking anything so that she may like herself a little better than she knows she ought to. It is selling out. The line is long and winding and, all in all, we are what is pleasantly yclept[8] a smash. P.S. We did a great deal of work in Boston. We injected more of Billy and Julie into Act One. We shortened and dove-tailed Act Two, integrated the ballet, and entirely changed our conception of God. In fact we cut Him and Her out of the play and put in a little old man who is a keeper of Heaven's back door—a sort of service entrance St. Peter who speaks New England dialect.

World War II ended in Europe with Germany's surrender on May 8—VE Day (Victory in Europe).

[7] Wilella Waldorf was a drama editor and then drama critic for the *New York Post* from 1928 until 1946.
[8] An archaic term, it could be translated here as "called."

Judith Chase Churchill to Oscar Hammerstein (excerpt), May 18, 1945

I am preparing a light piece for THE LADIES' HOME JOURNAL which will present the ideas of a few outstanding men in literary, screen, stage and political fields in an amusing entertaining question: What would you do if you were running your house in the place of your wife?

Oscar Hammerstein to Judith Chase Churchill, June 1, 1945

Dear Miss Churchill:

If I were running my house, I would save the energy and shoe leather of the waitresses and the time of the guests by eliminating service plates that have to be removed one by one at the beginning of a meal. In fact, I would cut out the whole one-by-one business and serve all plates on one trip. I may as well confess that I feel very bitterly on this subject.

Very truly yours,

Oscar Hammerstein

Peter Moen[9] to Oscar Hammerstein, May 26, 1945

Dear Mr. Hammerstein:

Just a few lines from the Highland farm to give you first hand information about the situation as it stands here up to date. First let me tell you we are all fine and in good health.

Everything on the farm is in good shape, and we are going strong. But this is a very broad statement, so let me break it down into details, which are many.

I like to give you an account from each department on the Estate.

---

[9] Peter Moen's letters are rich with idiosyncratic spellings and an unusual script and lettering that shows his first language was Germanic.

1) Angus Department:

They are all doing fine, and are now in the field at all times.

No 79. did not come in with a calf as yet. But it does not worry me, because she is feeling fine, and it is no doubt due to miscalculation of time.

2) Chicken Department:

The Egg production have decreased to 24 eggs pr. day. But is expected.

3) Broiler department:

I sold 100 Broilers at ceiling price and have received check for $148- which I have this day depossited to your account.

The Electric freeser I have filled to the top and can not even gett one more in there, and it sure is a pleasure to look at. But let me ad one thing, it sure is a dirty job killing all thos chickens. Mrs. Moen and my self spendt 3 days on this tedious work. But when it is over we feel good.

Only hope you dont give them all away.

I believe I have about 50 left, and if I dont hear to the contrary, I shall dispose of them at ceiling prices.

4) Turkey department:

On May 18th I bought 25 Turkeys 8 weeks old at $2.80 each. average weight 5 lbs. all white. It is practically impossible to buy any so if you think I paid to much I can disspose of them at ones $5- each, the only bad feature of the transaction is, that I left for Newyork on May 19th and left Mr. Rohr in charge, on my return that evening I was minus two Turkeys. The blessed Dog had a Turkey dinner. But what could I say, we had a wonderful time in Newyork and we surely admire your wonderful show. But personaly I wished I had staid at home and saved the Turkeys.

5) Pig department:

On May 14th I bought for you acount 3 wonderfull Berkshire Pigs, vaccinated and Cutt. $14- each 10 weeks old, about 50 lbs each—They are doing fine, and I am sure you will like them.

6) Sheep department:

On May 24—I bought for your acount 2 sheeps and 1. Buck, also clasified as Berkshire at $19.50. each and they sure looks good, as I understand it we shall have an increase in that family next Easter.

7) Flower department.

I have planted all the plants that came out from the seeds Mrs. Hammerstein received from Australia, here is hoping they will trive in their new home.

8) Agriculture department.

The Cats are comming fine, also the "Corn is green" and seems to be coming along fine. I expect to cut the field in front of the house this comming week, and next the alfalphea field. I expect to sell the first cutting at $20 pr. ton right on the field.

I expect to gett Mary at N. Philadelphia Railroad station Tuesday morning 11.15. also I expect to gett Mr. Watanabe the following day.

As I understand it I must drive him to Baldwin scool for the graduation.

I cant understand how it can be done. But supoce protest is of no use. Mrs. Moen and the children joins me in appreciation for your kindnes letting us see your fine show. Our little home is not finished as yet. But we have lots of time. Would like very much to hear from you, in fact you might give me the gate in your letters, as I have been spending your Money freely. Inclosed please find Bills for the various items.

Including two weeks pay for Mr. Rohr.

Have a good time in Hollywood and give our greetings to Mrs. Hammerstein

With best wishes.

Peter Moen

Oscar Hammerstein to Peter Moen, May 31, 1945

Dear Peter:

I enjoyed receiving your letter and all the news you gave me. I hope by this time that 79 has had her calf. I approve of your selling the extra 50 chickens. Don't worry too much about the loss of the two turkeys, but I hope there is some way of keeping the dog away from them in the future. I approve of all the purchases you have made, and I'm looking forward to seeing the results when we get home---which I think will be about June 18th.

I am sending you a check to give to Rohr.

Am very happy that you enjoyed the show. Mrs. Hammerstein and I both send our regards to all of you.

Sincerely,

Oscar Hammerstein

Oscar Hammerstein to William Perlberg (Twentieth Century-Fox Film Corp.), June 4, 1945

Dear Bill:

As you know I ran "State Fair" yesterday and I think it might be a good idea if I put down on paper just what my impressions were.

Its virtues are obvious. It has the family interest and it has entertainment and an attractive background. It is a well produced picture. But it doesn't do any of us any good to stress the things we like. At this point, before you preview, I would prefer to tell you some of the things that disappoint me. My over-all disappointment was the fact that the story and the characters were presented with less realism than I had anticipated and the picture emerges as more of a "musical comedy" than I hoped it would be. I was happiest in the sequences that had to deal with Fay Bainter and Charlie Winninger, because their performances were more legitimate than were the performances of the four young characters. I believe that the two best spots in the picture are Fay Bainter's winning the mince meat prize and Charlie Winninger's "Blue Boy" getting the championship. I don't think these sequences could have been presented better than they were and I wish the whole picture had been done that way. The performances of all four of the young characters are too "sweet", and a little on the cute side. It is not constructive to discuss that now because that can't be changed. I do believe, however, that some of the quality of honest story interest which I miss could be rescued by restoring a few short scenes. (I know at the outset you have a terrific time problem and as I suggest the scenes you ought to put back, I am prepared to suggest what footage you can eliminate.)

1—I don't like cutting from the family's journey to the Fair to Wayne on the Midway. I think it is important to establish the family's headquarters at the Fair, outside their trailer. The scene between Margy and her mother with the music of the Fair over the shot and the barkers calling "Hurry! Hurry! Hurry!" and Margy's excitement and impatience to go to the Midway is all valuable. Without this scene and the other one establishing Winninger in the swine pavilion the picture seems to lose direction, with alternate sequences of Margy and Wayne roaming around the Midway by themselves, each picking up a boy-friend and girl-friend. The family interest gets lost for a long while and I believe the family is the biggest thing we have to sell in this picture. Maybe I can sum up my worry by saying that this picture cannot stand up against "Coney Island" on a purely entertainment basis and it must come through with a quality of its own to compensate. I have a feeling that the scenes that have been cut are the scenes that have quality and the "entertainment" scenes which are left turn it into a picture which competes with "Coney Island" in its own field—and loses out.

2—The second scene I miss is the Swine Pavilion scene where Bainter brings Winninger's lunch to him. I have two reasons for missing it. One is my desire to keep alive these characters and relieve the see-saw alternating of scenes between the Wayne and Margy stories. The other reason is that Blue Boy's collapse is not sufficiently dramatized without this scene. All that is left in your present version is that later we see "Blue Boy" lie down ill, and then Esmerelda comes in and he gets up. I don't think this is enough. The "Blue Boy"—Esmerelda story is so attractive and entertaining that a little building up will pay big dividends.

3—The next scene I miss is the scene at the showers where Wayne comes home after his first night out and his father meets him and tells him he turned down his bed. Here is another important "family" touch and lifts the characters out of the paste-board, musical comedy puppet class. I don't know how the scene came out in shooting, but I had great hopes for the street sequence where the two boys passed each other singing. To get any heartbreak at all out of the Wayne-Emily story I think it is necessary to see Wayne on this morning after the first night. All we have got to indicate the depth of the affair is the scene in the hotel corridor after he has hit the crooner on the nose. I happen to be scared to death of this scene. I think it will get "wrong" laughs from the audience. I am, as a matter of fact, worried about this whole sequence in the hotel. Wayne's singing of the song seems all right, but when they go into the verse, Emily sings much too glibly for a girl who has never read the words or music before and it again degenerates into musical comedy. While I like this verse, I would just as soon see it cut and go straight into the second refrain, duet arrangement. I don't know the picture well enough to know whether this can be done. I am just ad libbing it as a suggestion as I write to you.

4—In case you agree with me on any of these points and consider restoring some of this material, here are some of the things I think could conceivably be cut: Some of the Hoop-la scene. The Hoop-la man seemed to me to be too much of a heavy and too little a comedian, and I would personally welcome any cut you can make here. I think also that you might be able to cut down part of the scene between Wayne and the song plugger. I don't think the story about the poor song writer in Brooklyn will get over. It seemed funnier when I wrote it than it does now. These I realize are very small cuts. I am now going to make a suggestion that will probably be a very unpopular one. I would like to cut down the Iowa number as much as possible. It only comes to life for me when we cut to Winninger and Bainter and the rest of it is for the most part false gaiety and rather embarrassing. I know that this sequence was put on at great expense and with a great deal of effort and I know it will be argued that it gives the picture a production "lift", but I don't agree. I don't think the audience is as simple-minded as we think and I don't think that mere noise and action and crowds jumping around and singers and dancers clowning awkwardly has any entertainment value at all.

My last beef is the very finish of the picture. It was apparently thought that we should end singing something, but if this is entirely sound, I don't think you have hit upon the right way to carry it out. After the story is really ended it seemed awfully silly to me to have Dick Haymes suddenly start to sing, "It's a grand night for singing." Leaving out the fact that this happens to be a bright and sunny Sunday morning, the abrupt emergence to song here seemed like a very obvious attempt to give a singing actor something to do at the end of the picture. It seemed as if we were making an apology for not having a finish. If I am right, this is very serious, because it belittles the whole picture. I think it will be worth while for all of us to put our heads together and try to dope out a new finish. I originally wrote a long musical finale which Dick and I thought unusual and effective. I realize, however, that the reasons of both budget and footage which dictated the cutting of this finale were good ones. But I think perhaps we were all a little lazy; first in evolving the quick finish that we decided upon, and later in trying to fix it by having Haymes suddenly burst out with a very irrelevant plug for one of our song hits.

This has been a long essay and you must be good and sick of me by this time. If you want to talk to me about any of the points I have brought up, I will be glad to see you before I leave.

All good wishes,

Sincerely,

Regarding Oscar's concerns and suggestions, the final film shows very little was addressed. (1) The scene between Margy and her mother is in the film, but there is nothing establishing Winninger before we see Margy and Wayne wandering around the Midway by themselves. (2) There is no scene showing Bainter bringing Winninger his lunch. (3) In the shower scene the father does not meet the boy and tell him he made his bed for him. Two boys do not pass each other singing. The scene where the boy hits the crooner in the face, and the scene in the corridor afterward, are still there. Emily still sings glibly the verse for which she has never read the words or music. (4) Both the Hoop-la scene and the scene with the song plugger are still lengthy (though it's possible that these scenes are shorter than they were). The entire Iowa number is there including the crowd swing dancing after the singing. The film ends with Dick Haymes singing eight bars of "It's a Grand Night for Singing"—in the daytime.

Memo from Lawrence Langner, the Theatre Guild, to Theresa Helburn, Oscar Hammerstein, and Richard Rodgers, June 12, 1945

I have been very much disturbed about the pressure that is being put on all of us about OKLAHOMA! for Europe as well as England. There seem to be different people pressuring for OKLAHOMA! to go to Europe. I am all for having the soldiers over there get a chance to see OKLAHOMA! and Mr. Friedlander was on the phone with me yesterday and made the suggestion—which seems very practical to me— that, when the Pacific Company comes home in a couple of months, it should then be refurbished and improved and sent to Europe—that is, those members who want to go—rather than start all over again with a second company.

Now this proposal from England bothers me a good deal. It seems to be a combination of USO and London commercial production. Frankly, I would like to ask what we are going to do this fall—work for prestige or work for cash? Looking over the Guild books, by the time we have paid income tax there is very little left but prestige. The question is, do we want to go on working almost entirely for prestige or would we rather wait a year or so and get some money as well? I do think we have all had lots of prestige and I do think taxes are going to go down some a little later. When we talked about OKLAHOMA! some time ago, we all thought of it as something that we should try to work on a delaying principle—that is, spread it out as long as we could—and this is the reason why, instead of sending out a third company, we have sent out a second company and are trying to play it town after town with repeat engagements to build up over a number of years.

But there is another thing that bothers me. When we can't get a good company for New York City—with so many boys still in the Army—how the heck are we going to get a good company for England and who the heck is going to keep it up? Under the age situation, Jerry Whyte may be out of the Army within the next six months. To attempt to do an English company without him would, in my opinion, by [sic] suicidal, and to attempt to do such an English company with a lot of 4-F's would be equally suicidal. In my opinion, we can only do a fair to middling, or even a bad, job now. It will give us very little prestige. Later on, we can do a very good job and I think we will be able to keep some of the money.

Will you please all express to me your views regarding the present situation, because it may be that I am just discouraged with all the difficulties of keeping up the New York company in good shape.

LL.b

Arthur Hammerstein to Oscar Hammerstein (excerpt), July 4, 1945

Dear Oscar

I regret that words by wire passed between us that never should have happened although they were brought on by a sincere desire by me to see the name Hammerstein live "and properly" I cannot take all the blame for my end. That telegram in answer to mine in which I suggested Paul Muni to play my father, was the most insulting and disrespectful communication that could have been sent to me, Muni is a ham, I agree, show me an actor that hasn't _ham_ and you'll see an actor that hasn't succeeded. How much of ham did John Barrimore [sic] have? and Preminger statement that he wouldent [sic] direct if Muni was to play my father. Was my judgement always so bad that I never know how to cast a show.

Well all that is water under the bridge. I'am [sic] satisfied that its all off. I would of never allowed my father's life be fictionized [sic] and to be insulted twice by the same studio would be a little too much, you remember the trouble with Joe Schenk[?][10].

I wish that you would let the newspaper know that you didnt [sic] accept to do a play for Alice Fay[e] in place of the biography as was stated in the Chicago Tribune as was given out by the Fox people.

In conclusion I must tell you that as far as this bungled up misunderstanding is concerned, I am the same uncle as the day you spoke to me to start you off in the show busness [sic]. Your father asked me never to let you get into that damn show business. How wrong he was. When you were six your father said to me that you would do big things in your life but Reggie would always suck his thumb. How right he was.

Oscar Hammerstein to Rouben and Azadea Mamoulian, July 13, 1945

Dear Azadea and Rouben:-

Thank you very much for the birthday telegram. Its intent was clear but its specific meaning was obscure and I could only conclude that if all four of you were sober, the telegraph operator must have been drunk.

We all missed you both at the luncheon. Come home soon.

Love,

Oscar

---

[10] Joseph Schenk, second president of United Artists, became chairman of Twentieth Century-Fox—until 1936 when conviction for tax evasion interrupted his career.

The United States dropped an atomic bomb on Hiroshima on August 6, and on Nagasaki on August 9.

William Hammerstein to Oscar Hammerstein, August 11, 1945

Dear Pop-

I'm sitting in the Capt's chair on the bridge. We are underway + he'll be up here in a few minutes so I'll have to get out—quick.

The news as you know—has been hot the past couple of days. Just heard the text of our reply, the part which most impressed was "Please accept, sir, the renewed assurances of my highest consideration". I doubt seriously if Mr. J Byrnes has ever actually met the Swiss Minister. Even if he had met him once before, say, at a diplomatic ball in Luxembourg it seems unlikely that he proffered at that time his highest consideration. Therefore renewed assurances would seem out of place. Assurances—maybe—but not renewed ones.

I waste time on such idle prattle not because there aren't many things more interesting with which to fill the pages of a letter—but because they are things about which I cannot talk. Perhaps if the war should suddenly end the censorship regulations would be dropped + I could tell you all about the little cruise we're having. But as it is I can only say that I'm very, very tired. You may perhaps guess some of the rest.

All our thoughts at this time turn naturally to the speculations on the probable lapse of time between the cessation of hostilities—whenever that may be—+ the day they start handing out those lovely diplomas. I would like mine framed in something Grinling—Gibbinish[11] + I want Dorothy to decorate a room using it as a theme. Since it isn't particularly colorful the room should make an interesting study in black + white. Anyway, even if next week should find us politically at peace—I fear that there will be many months more for me to champ at my wearing bit. I should very much like to get out in time to stage manage Showboat. Now is the time for maybe—one of Howard's Admirals?? Or the one you gave my serial number to??

---

[11] Grinling Gibbons was a master wood carver in England in the late 1600s and early 1700s.

The Capt has arrived on the bridge. He's just the sort of a salty skipper that Dorothy would love. His language is most colorful. I wouldn't say it was dirty—colorful. I couldn't repeat in mixed company many examples of his bridge rhetoric—but still I don't consider it dirty. If his ship still had prospects of going into battle—which I don't believe it has now—I would feel fully confident with this man on the bridge—which is a high tribute from a sailor to his skipper. Looking at him right now one might find it hard to believe what I say—he has cold cream on his sunburnt nose—a not flattering condition.

It's a beautiful tragic day like others I have described to you in the past. A good day to be at sea. But the hour for hard work approaches + so I leaveth you.

My love + the enclosed carton for Dorothy.

Love,

Bill

William Hammerstein CQM

P.S.

Wrote another waltz—How's the lyric for the first one?

William Hammerstein to Oscar Hammerstein, August 18, 1945

Dear Dad –

Well, at this writing my future looks pretty rosy—and pretty immediate, too.

You may have heard of the new Navy point system. In fact it's doughnuts to Carousel tickets that my mother has already figured my points + told you how many I have. In case she hasn't—I have 45½ points as of 22 August. I need 44 to be eligible for discharge. At this moment it looks very much as if I'll be transferred as soon as we hit the states. Transferred, that is, to some distribution center or so-called "re-adjustment" center + then to go thru some sort of mustering out process. No telling how long that may take but it doesn't worry me. There are hitches, however. I'm trying to heed the advice in your last letter. I don't want to be over-pessimistic but I shy away from the rosy outlook—it's disappointed me too many times. Pessimism, you might say, is a weak man's defense against adversity. But we must look at said hitches. I will probably need a replacement. The Navy directive reads in a very ambiguous manner. Navy communications are not noted, at least with me, for being classical examples of rhetorical clarity. This order, which is 4 pages longs, is one of [the] most mystifying documents of Naval history. Anything can happen as a result. I may or may not have to await a replacement. If I do it will mean a Pacific cruise for an indefinite length of time. If I don't it will probably mean a discharge + my brown suit with the pin stripes within a few weeks. I can know no more than that until we hit the states. That will be ---- blank --- but soon. This censorship is silly now. I think the man who was supposed to call it off when the war ended has forgotten about it.

Now—what chances my getting the job of Asst. Stage Mgr. with Show Boat in the event that things turn out as well as I hope to God they do? Don't write your answer—but have it ready when the phone rings—please, it would be wonderful to walk into a job like that—an almost certain assurance of steady work for at least, I should say, a year—no? I'm ready + willing to go right to work as soon as I've had time to change from skivvies to underwear + from those lovely black ties you bought me on your birthday to some nice colorful paisleys or wide stripes which I shall steal from your closet while you aren't looking. I don't think I'd better try those bow ties just yet—it'll take a little more time to get that much adjusted.

I've written to Maggie telling her just how the situation stands—or rather how [it] fluctuates—+ asked her to do as she wishes—that is to come home now on the chance that I'll get out right away—or to wait until she has definite word that I am out or in the process of being discharged. She will undoubtedly choose the latter course + I hope I can send her a cable within a couple of weeks giving her the good word.

I haven't heard from Maggie now in 3 weeks. I don't understand the mail being held up that long. If I haven't heard at all by the time I return I shall cable her regardless of what news I may have. Perhaps I could phone her—but I haven't any idea what part of that hemisphere she's hanging out in. The last letter was written from London as she was packing to go to Paris. That was in the middle of July. I can't help worrying some when these things happen—+ what with that + the war over + this hot + cold prospect of discharge I've been pretty nervous lately. We've had some time to rest since it all happened + I haven't been able to make good use of it. The Chief PhM gave me some luminal the other night + even that didn't help much. Last evening I lay down at about 5:30 while waiting for someone to get out of the shower + I woke up at 11:30 then took the shower + didn't sleep until 0300 this morning. I've been smoking too much + my bowels haven't moved since the Japanese people bowed in shame before the Emperor. I suddenly hate bitterly my surroundings + am bothered by petty discomforts which have been an accepted part of my life the past almost 4 years. I haven't, however, come to the point where I've lost interest in my job. It doesn't mean as much to me + I don't particularly care how well things go but I've acquired I think, a quality of conscientious devotion to accepted duty. This I give you as a recommendation for the job I've asked for with Show Boat. This—and the fact that I've acquired mature authority. People obey me—they do things for me. Not always as well as I would like them done but that isn't altogether my fault. I yell at them sometimes but not often + not unless I think the situation calls for a display of impatience—as situations sometimes do. In the Navy I have always regarded my men as comparative to chorus girls + boys—+ in the theatre I expect to find the comparison holding true in the reverse. The only difference being that in the Navy one's orders are backed by the authority of discipline + regulation. It's much easier, for instance, to make people listen to what you say when they are lined up in two straight ranks + standing at attention then when they're just gathered around in a bunch.

These are all idle reflections on nothing in particular. I was, until a moment ago, completely alone in the CPO Quarters—a rare condition. It has changed now + I find the atmosphere not quite so conducive to letter writing.

So—g'bye for now and I'll see you soon. If I get any definite dope I'll keep you posted—writing either to you or to my mother.

Love to all + you—prediction of a full complement for Xmas dinner looks pretty good. It'll be a wonderfully happy event.

Love—Bill

William Hammerstein CQM

Fox released *State Fair* on August 30. World War II ended in Asia with the Japanese surrender on September 2—VJ Day.

Anita Loos is best remembered for *Gentlemen Prefer Blondes*, her 1925 novel which she turned into a play in 1926, then a film in 1928, and which she co-adapted as a musical in 1951. Loos sent a copy of her new play, *Happy Birthday*, to Rodgers and Hammerstein who enthusiastically agreed to produce it as their next show. It starred Helen Hayes, and Rouben Mamoulian was named director. Whatever film plans Mamoulian may have had at this point, his previous film was *Bells on Her Fingers* in 1942, and his next would be *Summer Holiday* in 1948; *Jumbo* wasn't filmed until 1962, and it was not directed by Mamoulian.

Oscar Hammerstein to Rouben Mamoulian, October 9, 1945

Dear Rouben:

Anita has rewritten the first act and Dick and I are both enthusiastic about what she has done. She has clarified all of the obscure scenes and characterizations which cluttered up her former version and she has eliminated the stunt which we feel took away from the fantasy in the second act. We have since persuaded her to take out the small scene which she had wedged into the act and it will now play in one scene and one set, without being broken unnecessarily.

She expects to have an improved second act this week and I honestly believe that we are not very far from a version with which we could go into rehearsal.

Speaking of rehearsals, their present starting date is September 1, 1946 and what we are all most interested in—Anita, Helen, Dick and I—is whether you will be able to clear your decks at Metro so that you can pilot us through to the New York opening.* I don't know whether you can or will commit yourself so far ahead, but there is no hesitation on our parts of committing ourselves to you.

Another thing we'd like to know—and we are blushing to mention such sordid details—is whether you can give us some idea of what in general your terms would be.

I have heard a rumor that your first picture at Metro will be "Jumbo". This is exciting to Dick because it is his score and to me because I think you would do a wonderful job on a circus story. I know you wouldn't keep much of the original, but you would wind up with something great.

We all miss you and Azadia very much and we hope there will be some miraculous chance that will bring you to New York this season. Why not come to do some circus research? The best chance we have of seeing you in California is the likelihood of Dorothy and me staying there a week or two on our way to Australia when we go there next April.

Please write as soon as you get a chance.

Love to both of you

Oscar

* Rehearsals—Sept. 1
Opening on road Oct. 1

" N. Y. Nov. 1

Rouben Mamoulian to Oscar Hammerstein, October 27, 1945

Dear Oscar:

Your very nice letter was forwarded to me to Palm Beach, where Azadia and I spent a fortnight lazily baking in the sun. The rest did us much good. The sun was hot, the nights cool and the skies beautiful. We thought and talked about you and Dorothy frequently and wished you were there with us. You would have enjoyed it. I sent you a brief card from there (with a box of desert dates—chewy sunshine!) saying I would write, but you may receive this letter first because of the mail.

I was glad to hear Anita has done such a nice job of rewriting her first act. Everything you say about it sounds good and right.

About making a commitment for the play—there is no hesitation with me, just as there isn't any with you. I am excited about the play, as you know, and enthusiastic about working with you and Dick again, and with Anita and Helen—what fun it will be! I would like to commit myself contractually as quickly as I committed myself emotionally, but I think I should first make sure that there is no possible clash with my obligations to Metro. I have to make a picture for them, after which I can do a play. I have not started working yet, you know—I "report" to the Studio on the first of November. "Jumbo" is not really set yet, and won't be until I can discuss things with them.

Offhand, I think the dates will work out perfectly and September first for the start of rehearsals should be fine. The only awkward thing would be if I finish my picture way ahead of that date—in which case I may have to either lose a lot of time, or if I make another one, make dead sure to be finished with it in good time to start working with you before September first. I think it is a good idea to discuss this with M.G.M. and if they feel, as I do, that this should work out without difficulty—I would be delighted to immediately sign on the dotted line with you all. If they find it difficult and not without reason to clear the question of dates at this time—then I should wait long enough to get out of my picture-subject and on the shooting day, at which time it will be quite easy and safe to gage the time and make the decision. So let me talk this over with them, and then write you more definitely. In reference to the "sordid details"—don't worry about those—we will be able to agree easily, I am sure. Will cover these when the question of dates is out of the way.

Your idea about my doing circus research in New York is "immense" and, believe me, I am going to keep it in the back of my mind (and not very far back). It would be wonderful for Azadia and me to spend a little time with you and Dorothy in New York.

In the meantime both of us are quite excited about your trip to Australia and the possibility of you and Dorothy spending some time here on the way. That is good news! If we don't get to New York, we'll have this to look forward to. How is "Show-Boat" coming along? You must be kept pretty busy with it.

Please give Azadia's and my affectionate greeting to Dick and Dorothy and to Anita and Helen. With all our love to both of you,

As ever,

Work began on the Jerome Kern biopic, *Till the Clouds Roll By*. Because Oscar is portrayed (briefly) in the film he was sent portions of the script for approval.

Oscar Hammerstein to Arthur Freed, MGM Studios,
October 16, 1945

Dear Arthur:

Al Lewis sent me the enclosed scenes in which I appear in your picture.

As you can assume, I have no desire to be anything but cooperative in this and if you want me to, I am willing to give you the clearance on these two scenes exactly as they are written but I have first made a few notes in the hope that you will act on them and have the author loosen up the dialogue a little bit. If you decide to do this, mail me the new scenes and I shall sign them promptly and return them to you.

Making us all speak so stiffly and formally, I believe, will make the scenes very dull—although it is not in my province to say so. It is yours. The only speech I have that I really couldn't consent to having me say is that "I came across a book that I think is going to make one of the great shows of all time." No librettist of over fourteen would think of saying such a thing.

Please forgive me for being such a busy-body.

The best to you.

Sincerely,

Oscar

Oscar Hammerstein, 2nd

The line Oscar objected to was changed to: "I'll tell you what brought me out here, Jerry, I came across a novel that I think's going to make a great show." Of course the novel in question was *Show Boat*. And it was Kern who had suggested it to Oscar. Shortly after filming began, Jerome Kern passed away on November 11. He was sixty years old. Oscar was by his side.

Theresa Helburn to Oscar Hammerstein, November 13, 1945

Dear Oscar:

I must send you a note to tell you how much my thoughts have been with you this week and how deeply sorry I am that Jerry Kern had to go, just at this time when he was starting such fresh, new adventures with you and with Dick.

I was perhaps more keenly aware than most people of just what you were going through with your old friend and collaborator, as my mother died in exactly the same way at exactly the same age. There were for me, however, two compensating thoughts—first, that she did not live on mentally crippled, and second that she never had to grow old, a thought that she always deeply resented. I wonder, was Jerry like that?

Perhaps it is odd for me to be writing you a letter of condolence, but I just couldn't help it.

Much love,

Terry

The "new adventure with you and with Dick" was *Annie Get Your Gun*. Rodgers and Hammerstein produced the show. The score was supposed to be written by Kern and Dorothy Fields; it was Fields who came up with the idea of a musical based on the life of Annie Oakley, With Kern's death, Irving Berlin took over writing the music and the lyrics. Dorothy and her brother wrote the libretto.

Oscar Hammerstein to Alice Hammerstein, November 17, 1945

Dearest Alice:

It is good to be down on the farm and away from the recent confusion and depression with which New York has been connoted the past ten days.

On Monday, November 5th I spoke to Jerry on the phone. His breakfast was just coming up to his room. I told him to have it at his leisure. There was no need to rush to the theatre. I would see him there at two P.M. when we were to audition some singers for the Show Boat chorus. He was bright and chipper over the phone—as he had been ever since his arrival in town. And his appearance had matched his spirit. His color was good. He looked healthy and rotund, as you had seem him a few weeks earlier on the west coast.

At One Thirty, Leighton called me at a Dramatists' Guild luncheon committee meeting. He said Ascap had phoned to report that a man with an Ascap card in his pocket with the name of Jerome Kern written on it had been stricken with some sort of attack on 57th Street and Park Avenue and that someone had called up and so informed Ascap. I told my office to phone every hospital in town. So Leighton, Billy and my secretary called them all, reporting to me twenty minutes later that Jerry was in none. Meanwhile, however, they had sent Willy Torpey (Assistant stage manager to Billy and an old retainer—do you know him?) over to the scene of the accident. He found out that Jerry had been taken to The City Hospital on Welfare Island. That's the island under the Queensboro Bridge where the jail used to be. It is now a free hospital.

I left the meeting, taking Dick with me. We all met over at the island and found Jerry unconscious in the neurological ward. He was getting oxygen and had been given excellent care. I immediately phoned Harold Hyman. Willie Krohn, Jerry's accountant and old friend arrived a few minutes later and he phoned Dr. Foster Kennedy, a friend of Jerry's and a distinguished neurologist who had attended him before. I phoned Eva. She was not in her hotel. I remembered that Dorothy Fields had said she would have lunch with her that day. I had Billy phone every restaurant I could think of. No luck.

Harold arrived and pronounced his condition very serious—a cerebral hemorrhage. Eva returned to her hotel and we located her. Willy Krohn went over to get her. Dr. Kennedy arrived and was still there when Eva got over. He was more hopeful than Harold and said it was not a hemorrhage but a spasm of a blood vessel in the brain and not nearly as dangerous.

(I forgot to mention that when I arrived there was a zealous priest hovering there to administer last rites. He asked me if it was true that Jerry had recently been converted and I said I was quite sure he had not)

Meanwhile, the New York police, having found Jerry's California address on the card had phoned the Los Angeles police who had phoned Betty. Later I phoned Betty to report Kennedy's optimistic diagnosis and a marked improvement in Jerry's condition. He had not become conscious but he was responsive when he heard my voice or Eva's. Eva told Betty it didn't look as if it would be necessary for her to come east but Betty wanted to, so she took a plane that evening. We met her the following evening at LaGuardia field—Dorothy, Dorothy Fields and I. There had been no change in Jerry meanwhile.

At two, the following morning, Betty and Eva phoned us and pleaded with us to use our influence to get Harold back on the case. They had phoned Kennedy repeatedly and had not been able to get him. We got Harold and went over to the island with him and stayed there until four. Harold told us the truth. It wasn't hopeless but it was close to it. And if he should come out of it, Harold couldn't say in what condition Jerry's brain or body might be for the rest of his life. We came back to town with Harold at four. I couldn't sleep for a long time. That was the night Jerry died as far as I was concerned. I was deeply affected and realized then that he had had a greater grip on my affections than I had known. It was more than losing a friend. It was like losing a brother. It was something else. It was a little like losing a wife. Collaboration, like marriage, leaves the two people concerned in possession of common bonds no other two people share.

Kennedy left for Chicago and stayed away two days but left two assistants in charge. Despite the fact that he and Harold disagreed on the cause of Jerry's condition, it was fortunate that they agreed on the treatment. There wasn't much treatment. Rest and quiet and watchfulness by nurse and Doctors. On Wednesday they moved him to Doctors' Hospital— in the same room you came to see me in last year. The move did him no harm, and no especial good. Dorothy and I took a room in the hospital near Eva and Betty's room. We remained constantly with them for three days. On Sunday he died. I was with him at the time. I went downstairs and told Eva. She took it wonderfully. She has not broken down once as far as I know. They were married thirty five years. That's a large foundation of tradition to suddenly crumble beneath you. But she has kept her balance somehow.

She asked me to speak at the services. I doubted whether I could go through with it, but agreed to try. I didn't quite make it. I sort of went to pieces at the end and never finished the last sentence. I enclose the brief speech I made.

I am of course proceeding with the production of Show Boat. We shall start rehearsals December 3, as planned, opening January fifth. It was hard for me to pick up these duties at first. Jerry's sudden and unnatural absence from the theatre depressed me. But I am emerging from this stage and hope this week-end in Doylestown will help me a great deal. To-morrow we are picking Jimmy up at George School and driving him over to The Columbia-Princeton game. We must both go into town on Monday but we are coming back Wednesday to have Thanksgiving here.

Eva gave me a beautiful gold watch she had given Jerry on his last birthday. She is very grateful to both of us. Dorothy was wonderful for her.

She and Dorothy Fields did more than any of her friends to keep her spirits up during that trying week.

Have you come to any decision regarding where you'll go after your six rollicking weeks in beautiful Las Vegas? Is it to be here or there?

I'm sorry this long letter could not be more sprightly, but I thought you would be curious about all this. Maybe my next letter will have brighter news for you.

Billy is working hard. The scene and costume designs for Show Boat look beautiful and I think we have a very good cast. Did I tell you that Jan Clayton is going to be Magnolia?

Now you write to me!

Love,

Dad

I have promised myself not to play upon your emotions—or on mine.

We, in this chapel, are Jerry's "family". We all knew him very well. Each of us knows what the other has lost.

I think he would have liked me to say a few simple words about him. I think he would not have liked me to offer you feeble bromides of consolation—butterfly winds of trite condolence to beat against the solid wall of our grief. He would have known our grief was real, and must be faced.

On the other hand, I think Jerry would have liked me to remind you that to-day's mourning and last week's vigil will soon recede from our memories, in favor of the bright recollections of him that belong to us.

At the moment, Jerry is playing "out of character". The masque of tragedy was never intended for him. His death yesterday and this reluctant epilogue will soon be refocused into their properly remote place in the picture. This episode will soon seem to us to be nothing more than a fantastic and dream-like intrusion on the gay reality that was Jerry's life.

His gayety is what we will remember most—the times he has made us laugh; the even greater fun of making <u>him</u> laugh. It's a strange adjective to apply to a man, but you'll all understand what I mean: Jerry was "cute". He was alert and alive. He "bounced". He stimulated everyone. He annoyed some. He never bored anyone at any time. There was a sharp edge to everything he thought or said.

We all know in our hearts that these few minutes we devote to him now are small drops in the ocean of our affections. Our real tribute will be paid over many years of remembering, or telling good stories about him, and thinking about him when we are by ourselves. We, in this chapel, will cherish our special knowledge of this world figure. We will remember a jaunty, happy man whose sixty years were crowded with success and fun and love. Let us thank whatever God we believe in that we shared some part of the good, bright life Jerry led on this earth.

On December 3, Oscar had begun rehearsals for a revival of *Show Boat*, under his direction. The show opened at the Ziegfeld Theatre on January 5, and ran for 418 performances. Jan Clayton left *Carousel* to play Magnolia *and* Kim in the production.

Oscar Hammerstein to Rouben Mamoulian, January 18, 1946

Dear Rouben:

First, I want to express my thanks to you and Azadia for the very handsome leather wallet you sent me for Christmas.

Next. I want to congratulate you on your choice of "Ah, Wilderness"[12] for your next picture. I have several times considered it for musical adaptation and once suggested it to Dick, but the quick Rodgers frown crossed his brow and I let it go.

Now that you have started, have you any idea at all when you will be finished with it? This is transparently a selfish question because I am thinking of the Anita Loos play and wondering if we can count on you.

"Show Boat" opened and scored very heavily. The critics were nearly all enthusiastic and business is booming. I am happy not only because of this but because the job is behind me and the load is off my shoulders. It was tough going, producing and directing and limping along without Jerry.

---

[12] *Ah, Wilderness!*, an uncharacteristic comedy by Eugene O'Neill, became the film musical *Summer Holiday* (1948). Directed by Mamoulian, its songs were written by Harry Warren and Ralph Blane.

Dorothy and I are crystallizing our plans for the Australian trip and it looks now as if we will be passing through your village toward the end of May. We both send our love to both of you.

As ever,

Oscar

OH/lz

P.S. I also want to thank you for your nice telegram on the opening night of "Show Boat". Dick wants to thank you too for sending him a telegram— even though he had nothing to do with it.

Oscar Hammerstein to Rouben Mamoulian, March 30, 1946

Dear Rouben:

We have been worried by our last talk with you regarding your compensation for directing "Happy Birthday".

We certainly have no desire to pay you less than you believe you are worth, nor do we want to be in the position of bargaining with you. We would be delighted if we could say: "Rouben, write your own ticket". And if this were an ordinary dramatic show with a simple set and a small cast, that is just what we would say. But what faces us in "Happy Birthday" is a production which will cost as much as a fair sized musical comedy and a payroll which will necessitate musical comedy grosses in order for us to pull out.

It occurs to us that when you, quite properly, made a distinction between a director's royalty on a musical show and on a dramatic play you may not have realized that this play is so hooked up that we must aim for grosses in the neighborhood of thirty-thousand dollars instead of sixteen-thousand or seventeen-thousand, which is the gross of a normal dramatic hit. With Helen (who is one of the few real stars left in our theatre who draw money) we have little doubt that we can command this kind of gross. If the public likes the play, those are the figures we will be dealing in. If they don't then it will be a failure and nobody can make any money.

We have talked the matter over carefully. What we definitely don't want to do is bargain with you. We want to offer you not the lowest price at which we think we can get you, but the highest price we think we can possibly afford to pay and if that doesn't satisfy you, we will still be good friends and that will be the end of it.

Here is an outline of the essential terms:

1 - 3% of the gross
2 - A fee of $5,000.00 to be paid during rehearsal (or before that if you wish)
3 - Your billing to be the same size type as ours and Anita's ad to appear whenever ours and/or hers appears.
4 - In the event of a second company, the same royalty of 3% if you stage it personally, 1½% if you do not stage it.
5 - Round trip transportation from California.

We make no disguise of how unhappy we will be if you don't do the play. We think this offer a very fair one and it is certainly much higher than we would make to anyone else. As far as we can find out, it is the highest royalty ever paid a dramatic show director—but why not?

Please let us hear your answer very soon.

All the best wishes.

As always,

Oscar

RH [*sic*]/z

P.S. I came to town today to see a new girl for "Show Boat" and hoped to speak to you personally about this. Unfortunately, I know you are tied up on your big opus today and I have to leave on the six o'clock train for New Haven.

Oscar and Dorothy sailed to Australia in May, partly prompted by Dorothy's desire to see her seventy-nine-year-old mother. On May 14, Oscar and Dorothy celebrated their seventeenth anniversary aboard the ship. And because it had been delayed for two weeks, on May 16 they missed the opening night of *Annie Get Your Gun*.

Howard Reinheimer to Oscar Hammerstein (in Melbourne), May 14, 1946

Dear Oscar:

Just a few jottings:

1. I received a letter today from Lawrence Langner enclosing copies and correspondence from the French owners of CHANTICLEER.

Apparently, there is no chance of making a deal as the owners' demands on motion picture and other world wide rights are not only very tough, but they have finally come out and stated that they don't want any musical show to be written on the property. That closes the book on that. I spoke to Dick Rodgers and he seemed very relieved as he likes the new project much better. I warned Dick that Lawrence thought he would make much better progress if he mentioned the names Rodgers and Hammerstein in the negotiations. I told Dick to say that even if that were so, they sounded so worrisome and troublesome, he preferred not to get mixed up with them.

- - -

May 27, 1946.

2. As I said in the earlier part of this letter, I suspected Langner would finally try to get a deal by disclosing that you and Dick were going to do it. Now the French owners are more interested than before. I had a phone call from Peter Davis at the Guild to the effect that they would like to send a cable and LeClaire has apparently indicated an interest on the following general terms:

1½% of the gross on first-class performances with a guarantee of $500 a week. $5,000 advance against royalties. Coupled with this would be a three month option (I assume the three months would be after the opening of the play but I am not sure) to purchase all the picture rights for $30,000.

May 28th, 1946.

I have been holding up these few jotting[s] until now.

1. Dick and I had a talk about the CHANTICLEER thing and he came to the conclusion that now was the time to acquaint the Guild with our position on the whole matter because surely we would not want them to make an offer which would involve commitments on their part, etc. Dick arranged to meet with Terry and tell her about the new play that you and he were working on. This he did and just called me to tell me he had lunch with her and Lawrence and explained the whole situation and told them not to go ahead on the CHANTICLEER thing. As usual, the Guild, of course, understood everything but were disappointed that the CHANTICLEER thing was not being pursued. They then asked Dick whether they could not participate in some fashion and Dick explained to them generally the problems which presented themselves if they could participate, but at any rate, he

could not give them any decision until he had gotten more material from you in the first place, and secondly there was no use in discussing the matter until you got back from Australia. I think that settles everything satisfactorily and we can talk about it when I see you on the Coast.

2. I got a call today from Doodie in which she says that you had promised to send Shawen Lynch to college; that Shawen has just been accepted at Barnard; and that she had to have $100 for matriculation fee or on account of tuition—I am not sure which. So I sent her the $100.

3. Regarding the Fox theatre project, I have been waiting to hear from Joe Moscowitz, who was going to take the matter up with Skouras. So far, Moscowitz has no work except that he informed me he understood there was a restriction against building a theatre on the 53rd Street side. I passed this along to Walter Redell, who told me there was such a restriction if the theatre was built entirely on the 53rd Street side, but that he was sure they could get a variance from the City provided the entrance on the 53rd Street side was only used as an emergency entrance and exit. I reported this to Joe and so far have not heard anything further from him.

4. Dick no doubt has kept you informed of the ANNIE business and there is very little I can tell you. I gather Dick has been very assiduous in his box office attendance and is keeping an eagle eye there to make sure they are really pushing the tickets for the dog summer months. Apparently the demand is great even though some of the reviews were not quite what we hoped for.

5. I don't know how much Dick has told you about it, but the Shubert situation has gone this far. The ice was finally broken when Weinstock called up Morrie Jacobs and said they had a $13,000 bill for repairs to the theatre and wanted to know what we intended doing about it. Morrie played dumb and turned Weinstock over to me. I, of course, told him that just as Shuberts have been waiting for their final figures on expenses, we had been waiting for ours and that they were not yet completed. I then told Weinstock they came to approximately $40,000 which was the closest estimate Morrie can give us (incidentally, I enclose a breakdown which you might be interested in seeing). At any rate, I explained in the friendliest spirit it was a matter I thought we should all discuss in a huddle so I had a meeting two days ago with Walter, Dick, Milton Weir and Elias Weinstock. At the meeting, Weir said they felt it was all our fault and we were responsible to them for the

$13,000, and I naturally countered with the statement that we differed with them on that score as our expert engineers (without mentioning names) had advised us it was not our fault at all and therefore that the Shuberts should bear their own losses and were responsible for ours besides. I was anxious to keep this on as friendly a basis as possible and if it is humanly possible to avoid a lawsuit to do so because unfortunately as you know we are going to be thrown back on the Shuberts for theatres not only in connection with this show but with Hayes and other shows to come. I don't mean by this that we should sit down and take it from them, but on the other hand, there is no use in getting into litigation without first showing a desire to cooperate on a fair solution of the problem. Dick agrees with me on this.

The next step at the meeting was that Milton Weir suggested as a formula for the handling of their damages, they felt it was fair that we should stand their part of the damages on the sharing basis—namely we should stand approximately 25% and they would stand the balance. Accompanying this was a further statement from him that he would like to know whether we had any formula we would like to submit as a counterproposition or any other type of formula we might have in mind. My guess is what he had in mind was we would pay 25% of their losses and they would pay 25% of ours, which would mean that they would like to see us stand 75% of the total aggregate loss. Since the actual cost of repairing the building ($13,000) is approximately 25% of the total aggregate of losses of both sides, it is my feeling that what Weir was playing for was a suggestion on our part that we would call off the whole argument by their paying for the theatre and we standing our own losses.

Well, since we had no formula to suggest at the time, I ducked the whole issue by suggesting an adjournment of the meeting for a few days until after we had had an opportunity to discuss the whole matter with Twentieth Century. I explained that Twentieth was vitally interested in view of its financial participation and that I would not dare suggest any form of compromise in view of a firm attitude expressed to me by Twentieth that we should do all possible to place our losses on the Shuberts since they were responsible. (This, of course, is not true, since Moscowitz had never made such a statement to us), but I thought it advisable to throw as much onus on the shoulders of Twentieth as we could possibly do. Our final figures will be finished by tomorrow and I have arranged with Moscowitz to meet with him and his Legal Department and our next meeting with Shuberts will probably be on about Monday, June 3rd.

6. The Equity situation stands just the way it was. I think it is best that we do nothing towards arbitration or otherwise until we have moved further along with our Shubert discussions.

7. Morrie gave me a rough idea of cost yesterday and hopes to have better figures by tomorrow. They run to about $300,000 to $310,000, including bonds, plus the $40,000 loss above referred to. So we would have come in just about as budgeted and if we get no adjustment on the loss or relief from Equity, it will come to about $350,000.

8. Your apartment lease has been closed up and everything is in order.

9. Regarding CARMEN JONES, I have had a couple of talks with Sam Katz by long distance and he is waiting to see us both when we get out West. I have also had several talks with Elliot Daitz and Billy's attorney and I have prepared Certificates of Incorporation and by-laws for the corporation which is to take over the picture rights. The name of the company will be Glenmore Productions, Inc. and will be organized as a Delaware corporation.

Bestest

Howard

P.S. I have just received notice of Equity's request for an arbitration.

The "Shubert situation" refers to the following: The premier of *Annie Get Your Gun* on Broadway was delayed by at least two weeks because of issues involving the set. The riggings in the Shubert-owned Imperial Theater were not strong enough to support their weight. There were great expenses incurred both in the delay and in retrofitting the theater. It's the only musical produced by Rodgers and Hammerstein on Broadway for which they did not write the score (they would go on to produce a few musicals by other songwriters in England). The reviews were largely favorable, with most of the hosannas directed at Ethel Merman as Annie Oakley. Irving Berlin's score—now widely regarded as his best—was unappreciated by some of the critics. But as Steven Suskin noted: "*Annie* was an immense hit, the second musical comedy to go over the 1,000-performance plateau. (Until *My Fair Lady* came along in 1956, the four longest-running musicals were *Oklahoma!*, *South Pacific*, *The King and I*, and *Annie*. All from Rodgers and Hammerstein!)"

Richard Rodgers to Oscar Hammerstein, May 18, 1946

SECOND NIGHT LIKE PHILADELPHIA LOVE

DICK

Richard Rodgers to Oscar Hammerstein, May 23, 1946

AUDIENCES BETTER THAN PHILADELPHIA COMPLETELY SOLD OUT JUNE ADVANCE ON SEVENTY FIVE LOVE

DICK

Richard Rodgers to Oscar Hammerstein (in Melbourne), June 11, 1946

UNION REFUSES TO ACCEPT NO LIGHTING CREDIT CLAUSE FOR MIELZINER MAMOULIAN HAS RESIGNED ARBITRARILY I WOULD LIKE TO SIGN LOGAN AS WOULD HOWARD HELEN AND ANITA PLEASE ANSWER

LOVE = DICK

Happy Birthday opened on October 31, 1946. It was directed by Josh Logan, and Jo Mielziner was credited for both lighting and set design.

At the start of 1946 Hammerstein had three Broadway shows still running from their original productions: *Oklahoma!*, *Carousel*, and *I Remember Mama*. During the course of the year *Annie Get Your Gun* and *Happy Birthday* opened, along with the Hammerstein-directed revival of *Show Boat*, and there were limited run productions of *Desert Song* and *Carmen Jones* at City Center. Altogether, Oscar had eight shows on Broadway in a single year that he wrote and/or produced.

Oscar Hammerstein to Kurt Weill, January 20, 1947

Dear Kurt:

Very few people were happier than I at the reception accorded "Street Scene". Everyone in town had closed the show before it opened and there is nothing so gratifying as seeing wise-guys fooled.

Dorothy and I would love to accept your invitation to see the play again. After we return from Boston, I'll call you up.

Congratulations and best wishes.

Sincerely,

Oscar

Street Scene was advertised as a "dramatic musical," while Weill, the composer, referred to it as an "American opera." Lyrics and libretto were by Langston Hughes and Elmer Rice, based on Rice's 1929 play in the vein of American Realism. Although the show was reasonably well-received by the critics it was less so by audiences; it ran for148 performances.

I have found very few letters from or to Hammerstein from 1946 through 1948. There's an argument to be made for giving 1947 short shrift. That was the year of *Allegro*, the first musical by Rodgers and Hammerstein not based on pre-existing material—and their first commercial failure. It was also Oscar's most personal musical, dealing with issues with which he himself struggled, making the disappointment all the more stinging.

Allegro was the third Rodgers and Hammerstein show produced by the Theatre Guild. Since the advent of *Oklahoma!*, Rodgers and Hammerstein had already produced four other shows themselves (*I Remember Mama*, *Annie Get Your Gun*, *Happy Birthday*, and *John Loves Mary*), but apparently, contractually, they owed the Theatre Guild a third show. In the case of *Carousel*, the Theatre Guild was billed as producers, but in point of fact Rodgers and Hammerstein acted as producers and had an unprecedented percentage of the weekly gross and profits. *Allegro* was conceived to use a comparatively spare and simple set, and one of its innovations was to use the equivalent of a Greek chorus to comment on and express the thoughts of the characters. It was also planned that a significant amount of dance would be used as an integral part of telling the story. As a result, Agnes de Mille was hired to both choreograph and direct the show; it was the first of only two Broadway show directed by de Mille (the second, *Come Summer*, closed in 1969 after seven performances). According to multiple accounts, de Mille was difficult to work with, sometimes cruel, and quickly overwhelmed by the demands of steering such a large show—a show that was being re-written during rehearsals and on the road. *Allegro* had its first out-of-town tryout in New Haven, September 1 through 6. It did not go well.

Joshua Logan directed the three previous shows produced by Rodgers and Hammerstein—*Annie Get Your Gun*, *Happy Birthday*, and *John Loves Mary*. His insights are fascinating, inspiring one to wonder, if he had directed *Allegro* . . .

Josh Logan to Oscar Hammerstein, September 4, 1947

Dear Oscar,

You asked me to come up this weekend and I will certainly do so. In the meantime I would like to get a few of my first impressions on paper. The audience told you that the show is great. They followed the story and were satisfied with it. Of course the treatment is still the big excitement. And even with the understandable mishaps of last night, it's a wonderful job on everyone's part.

The boy, Battles,[13] is the sensation of the evening to me. The softness I worried about is gone when I see him in the part. Jennie is wonderful too. I also liked the mother and think you will have a hard time getting anyone as lovely and gentle for the part. The father is attractive and manly. Perhaps with performance and work he can be pulled through okay, although his face when singing doesn't help the lyrics. He doesn't seem to mean the words.

I hesitate to tell you again how much I dislike the grandmother. I felt a real growing resistance to her in the audience and I believe this will increase. Perhaps this is not all the fault of the actress although I'm inclined to feel that most of it is. She's completely humorless, theatrical, in-love-with-her-own-voice and constantly boring. She really gets you off to a bad start with her singing of her first song. This is partly staging as she sings to the audience instead of the baby and never indicates that she knows what the lyrics mean. I talked to Herb Fields and Dorothy afterwards and learned that they disliked her too and had said so to Dick. Herb told me that Dick was very pleased with the grandmother. This really frightened me as I think she is a real menace to the show. She should either be changed or cut down or eliminated. You must decide which, but please do something drastic about her.

Aside from cuts, blends and making of points I feel the main things to work on are:

1. Grandmother
2. Get Joe on sooner.

---

[13] John Battles played the show's lead, Joseph Taylor, Jr. Battles had previously starred in *On the Town*; after *Allegro* his career shifted to Europe.

3. Get another song or idea for the "So Far" spot.
4. Get the show off to a better start.
5. Outside of "Money Isn't Everything," "Allegro," "One Foot Other Foot," I think all the songs are unexcitingly staged and performed. They get over because they are good songs but the full value is not yet realized— even the "Wedding" seemed muddy at the beginning.

Now if you can still stand I'd like to be more specific about these points and some others –

The beginning picture can be improved. It looks a little tawdry and cluttered as it is. Could the curtain go up on Marjorie in bed alone with a moment of music—perhaps she could sing to the baby—then give the chorus an entrance or have them behind the traveller for the first singing of Joe Taylor, Junior. Perhaps you could do the whole scene in front of the traveller except for the realization of the father's fantastic description of the town, closing the traveller as he pulls the thermometer from her mouth— this would eliminate the awkward exit of the chorus and give you a chance to play a more intimate scene without the great void behind this tender moment. This would also give you a chance to do the celebration of Joseph Taylor Jr. without having to depend on applause. They could sort of fade away if the traveller is closed on them slowly.

Perhaps the grandmother could sing to the baby without lifting it from the mother's side and they could both [step?] off on the platform when the applause comes at the end of "I've Seen It Happen Before," bringing on the chorus to cover the mother's change and establish the position of the baby in the audience.

Maybe the <u>cry of the baby from the audience mike</u> could start at this moment and the chorus could start the "Pretty Baby—Say Goo-Goo" speech as though speaking to that.

The March is wonderful as sung by the chorus but for a moment there is a hiatus between the dance and song,--I spoke to Dick on the phone. After the applause the singers could pick up "Now you can march around the yard" backing off to reveal the dancers.

The scene between the mother and father is too long—by this time the audience is getting hysterical to meet Joe. That's why the dance at the freshmen get-together seems endless and unemotional and away from the story—also why "A Fellow Needs A Girl" seems too long. Once Joe is on things are hot and wonderful.

I still think that a comedy scene with Joe and his girl in the mood of "I'm on the loose" should replace "So Far." I realize that Joe is going to sing again soon, but if he could have some good comedy in a song or a number ---. That girl is a bit player and we don't care about her at all but we do care about Joe and Charlie. Couldn't it be their moment instead of the girls' moment together with or without the girls, or Joe's with the girl. Also I don't like to see the song clowned in order to get laughs—in other words this spot should have a comedy lift, featuring someone we care about.

I feel that the freshman dance should last just long enough to put over the trick of how they are dancing and then into Joe's entrance.

Going back to the full stage classroom struck me as a retard. Couldn't the Tennyson poem be done in one and then open to the big stage for the return of Jenny?

Do you or Dick feel that the chorus sings too much of "You Are Never Away" before Joe sings it, thus robbing it of its full effect when he sings the whole thing?

The wedding is too long but will be dynamite.

The mother dying on stage is hard to take and hard to act. Couldn't it be revealed by Charlie and Joe's scene?

Could the Allegro dance which is great finish fast and have the slow movement in the middle?

Wouldn't the nurse be prettier and more sanitary with less hair?

Could Bigby-Denby be less of a caricature—the silly laughs out, for instance?

Ned Brinker would help the laugh on the J. P. Morgan joke if he didn't laugh so heartily but smiled weakly.

Mr. Lansdale's working too hard.

Buckley works too hard too. He gets the kind of laughs we used to get in the Triangle shows. Maybe someone else could to [sic; do?] the Coach— or Buckley—the confusion doesn't help.

DON'T READ THIS IF YOU GET MAD EASY.

Could Joe have a personal musical moment in the second act, maybe at the "Come Home" spot, just as he is beginning to mature and see himself. The mother comes in and robs him of his moment. I don't think this is fair to say now as "Come Home" was killed by the fire scare. It's just that I'm so fond of Joe, I hate to see other people taking over moments that should be his—he's the story and he's the best actor in the show.

I also feel that the elimination of the grandmother and mother in the departure-for-Chicago scene would help the mother's appearance in "Come Home". I remember that Dick always says that if you do everything everyone suggests in New Haven you would have to start all over again.

I think if you just get a smooth performance of the show as is, it's great enough for this world. It's just that I'm jealous as hell of the director that gets a chance to work on a show with the inspired conception this show has.

Please think of me while I'm in the Brevoort –

Best always,

Josh

Josh Logan to Oscar Hammerstein, September 6, 1947

Dear Oscar,

This is the letter that I didn't intend to write. But thinking over last night's show, I've decided that I must express myself once more about it.

I was actually disappointed last night and I couldn't put my finger on the reason until I thought it over. I still feel the same way as I did in the first letter but with these few changes: first of all, I saw the show all the way through without the hysteria of first night and the forgiveness of a first night audience. Last night struck me as [a] much more normal reaction to the show as is, and it wasn't good enough. I still feel this is greatly due to a poor performance of the really brilliant stuff in your first act, and a general heaviness in the performance and staging of the moving moments. The Grandmother's death is hurt greatly by the pause after her singing "All of a Sudden, All of a Sudden," and before the boys run in. Couldn't you black out on the grandmother, and have the boys run in shouting at the very moment—the grandmother could then walk of[f] back offstage, or merely stand there in a different colored light (not green or blue) while the next scene is played. This last seems to me a better idea as, in this way, she could be surrounded by the Chorus, and not just suddenly appear with them. This would mean that the Grandmother never moves from her spot during the scene with the two boys, the scene with the Mother and Father, and the scene with Jennie when she says "I'm sorry about your Grandmother." Also I believe that it would be a very smooth transition from the live Grandmother to the Grandmother's spirit, who remains with him even at the moment of her death. I[t?] would also save another entrance for her which is a little confusing as it stands. I think this would also give a symbolic quality to her joining the Chorus, which represent to me his subconscious mind or Id or Ego or whatever it is. In this way, the Mother's appearance as a spirit might be prepared for [*sic*; "far"?] better. These transitions are extremely important to work out as they are really confusing and emotionally shocking because of the confusion. For instance, at the moment of the child beginning to walk, when the spot on the Grandmother and Mother blacks out and they run offstage in half-light as the Chorus starts singing "Now You Can Go Wherever You Want," there is such a let-down that the Chorus gets off to a bad start. Couldn't they start this song while the Grandmother and Mother are still lighted, cross in front of them, obscuring them as the light fades on them rather than blacks out on them and the traveller closes slowly in front of them.

I am changing my mind about the scene between Beulah and Joe. I still feel that you must get all the comedy you can into the first act but if you are going to keep the song "So Far" which is a beautiful song, I think the scene should be played seriously and the song sung for its sentimental value and should not be clowned. If the girl that sings it is a sincere girl who is genuinely impressed by Joe and is not just a lay, the song might be used for plot value, showing that there were other girls that could have influenced Joe if he had not had this obsession about Jennie. In this case, I would let Charlie and Molly have the comedy scene and then show that the older sister is a cut above her younger sister or even better, just a girl friend or acquaintance of Molly who is genuinely fascinated by Joe and his career. In this way, you could show an adolescent love that might have started and taken Joe in another direction. In this case I would see Joe starting out to believe he is on the verge of another love, let him join in with her on the song, and give the impression that this is another direction that Joe could turn. At this point, Charlie and Molly might arrive with the idea that they're all going home and Charlie could give to Joe the letter from Jennie (which he's had in his pocket all the time and which might have been planted in the scene between Charlie and Molly and used as an excuse by Charlie to leave off love-making with Molly and go to find Joe). In the scene between the four of them, Beulah could still be singing "So Far," while Joe is reading the letter. When Joe discovers that Jennie has given up Bertram and is coming home, he drops Beulah like a hot-cake, and leaves Beulah to finish the song alone. This might be used as a chance to blend "So Far" with "You Were Never Away," that way showing the strength of his feeling for Jennie which smothers the embryonic affair. Perhaps the orchestra could start "You Were Never Away," drowning out the melody of "So Far," and could take Joe to the position he is in, standing in front of Jennie for the first time since her return from Europe. I wish you would consider this possibility of blending the two songs as you did several times in "Carousel." This, of course, would eliminate the return to the classroom and the reading of the Tennyson poem, which is, at the moment, a slight retrogression to me. It also does not come [across] as well in performance as it did in reading the script.

For awhile I considered suggesting the Beulah be Emily younger, that she could tell him in this scene that she is going to study medicine and that could be their bond. If this could be written so that it is not too much of a coincidence that she appears in Chicago (perhaps Charlie could hire her instead of Joe), there might be a plot value to planting her in the first act. This might also give a bigger kick to the wedding if we see him with a sympathetic girl and completely ignoring her as he marries Jennie. Of course, this would have to be carefully handled so that it would not make Joe a villain by hiring her as his nurse. A little interest on Charlie's part in her in the first act might confuse this, leading us to believe that the romance is to be between Charlie and Emily rather than between Joe and Emily. Of course there is one definite advantage to this suggestion—and that is that you would have a girl singing "So Far" that would mean something to the story instead of a girl in which we have no interest whatsoever.

Oscar, last night I told you that I found "Come Home" rather moving. On thinking this over and analyzing the story at the same time, I feel I was moved by the beautiful singing of the song and the contrast it gave to the Ya-ta-ta song and "Allegro." I am not suggesting that "Come Home" should be cut but merely used as a possible solution to Joe's dilemma at the moment; several thoughts could be going through his mind: he is unhappy and disgusted with the life he's living; the Mother appears to him and suggests that he go back to his father and start his medical career all over again; perhaps the strains of "You Were Never Away" and "One Foot—Other Foot" appear in rapid succession to be going through his mind. He is pulled in several directions at this moment instead of just one.

What I really feel is the most important problem to solve is the whole development of Joe's final decision. Throughout the play he has been weak, indecisive, influenced by everyone—his wife, grandmother, father and Charlie. Joe never really makes a strong move, I would love to see him become a proud, almost arrogant, male at the end of the show. His action as it stands now is a kind of cowardly retreat rather than a brave step. It takes no real courage to turn down a puppet position in a ridiculous hospital to go back to Security and paternal guidance—it's almost like a retreat to the womb and therefore does not have the lift that is [*sic*; "it"?] should have when Joe finally breaks off all shackles and becomes a man who makes his own decisions and sees his real purpose in life.

For this reason I would like to see him toy with the idea of going home and then, realizing how much more valuable he could be by taking over this large hospital and running it his own way for the genuinely sick and the needy, no matter who they are, reject this idea. He could even blackmail Lansdale (because of his relationship with Jennie) to give him the power to run the Chicago hospital as he sees fit and not as a sort of private hotel for semi-neurotics and spoiled rich people. This would need the plant of a fine epidemic or some other disorder in Chicago and his realization that he could help more people, more really sick people, there than by going back home. Also I feel that it would excuse him for not socking Lansdale in the jaw the moment he sees him. The Chorus could tell us, at the moment he sees Lansdale, what is going through Joe's mind. Joe could be already to fight Lansdale when he is stopped by the realization that he could really hit him harder by weakening his position in the hospital and, at the same time, achieve his (Joe's) purpose of turning this place into a genuinely humanitarian institution. When he goes to the dedication ceremony, he should already have made up his mind what he's going to do. When he gets a chance to speak, he can make a strong announcement to the reporters of the change in policy which shocks the Lansdale crowd. At Lansdale's objection he can force him to submission by sheer will and strength of purpose which is, in effect, blackmail.

Maybe it would be necessary to have a scene between Lansdale and Joe before the dedication and [*sic*; "in"] which the idea is planted in Lansdale's mind. And then at the dedication he is forced, in front of the crowd, to agree to it. I believe this can still be made to use the "One Foot—Other Foot" theme for the end of the show and the visual picture could be used too.

Believe me, Oscar, this is not idle playmaking on my part. Whether this is the solution or not, I feel that you are in more trouble than evidently most other people feel. I did not feel this as strongly on opening night, as a matter of fact I was so carried away by the warm reception of the audience and the enormity of the job that had been done that I felt the story carried better than I feel it does now. Friday night's audience was to me a much more normal one, and their reaction was tame where it should have been ecstatic. I feel that you must be ruthless in fixing this show. If it means changing the father, change him. Just fixing the show as it is and getting a smooth performance is not enough. It must be thoroughly satisfying with tremendous high spots and a thrilling finish before it can have the effect that you want it to have.

I'm afraid I have indicated to you and Dick that I am just a jealous bastard who feels that he's been left out of the show. I hope you believe that my jealousy is the jealousy for you two and your success. I have a much clearer idea of how to fix the show than I have been able to put on paper. And I would be able to tell it to you better with my voice than with a typewriter. Perhaps if you are interested I could come up to Boston for a night and fly back in the morning but I am not suggesting this unless you and Dick feel that the show needs as drastic work as I feel it needs.

I'm afraid that critically you will still be led to believe that the show is packing more dynamite with the audience than it actually does. As it stands now it will get some rave notices and hysterical enthusiasm of numbers of people. What I am talking about is the mass effect which I feel the show can have if the points are really made so that everyone understands and feels them. I beg you not to ridicule these suggestions or brush them aside until you have given me a chance to explain them more clearly. Please know that I care tremendously for you and Dick and for your show.

As ever,

Allegro opened on Broadway on October 10. The reviews were mixed, leaning toward the positive. Because of the show's extraordinary advance it had a modest run of 315 performances and purportedly made some money, it even sported a six-and-a-half month national tour. There was no London production and there has never been a Broadway revival. Hammerstein was haunted by the show's failure. In the months before he died he worked on a revised version of *Allegro* for television, believing he could now correct the show's flaws.

Shortly after *Allegro* opened, Oscar and Dorothy set sail on a Scandinavian vacation.

Oscar Hammerstein (on the *M. S. Gripsholm*, Swedish American Line) to Alice Hammerstein, November 10, 1947

Dearest Alice:

I am writing the day before we land. We should be there now but we are in 24 hours late. This was due to a strong headwind which we encountered the first two days and also to some engine trouble. We had several very rough days which didn't bother Dorothy or me but poor Pete [?] was laid low in his cabin for a solid week. I was talking to the ship's doctor one evening, in the bar, and he told me of a new seasickness prescriptive pill which had been given to the armies that had to cross the channel on D day. So I got him to send some of those pills down to Peter and they cured him right away.

A young man, a Swede, said he had met you at some party in New York when you were engaged to be married. I'm sorry I can't remember his name but I can't remember any Swedish names because they seem so much alike. They all end in "son" or "sen" and they all have B's and J's in the most unlikely places. We have met quite a few however and we like them very much. It has been a gay trip, lots of drinking and dancing late at night.

Yesterday I won the Ping Pong championship and was given a pretty silver goblet. It was a thrilling match. When I reached the finals I met a young American boy who was conceded by all—me, too—to be undefeatable. He's a very flashy player with a tricky serve that baffles everyone. I watched him play a few others and figured out that if I could receive it on a "pick-up" or half-volley it would redress the effect of the "stuff" he put on it. This proved to be a sound theory.

Feeling somewhat like David facing Goliath (I haven't played in so long that my old assurance had left me) I started in and found, to my surprise and to the surprise of the galley, too, that I was giving him a pretty good fight. He led all the way, of course, but I caught up to him and finally won the first set, 25–23. Then he slammed me all over the place and won the second 21–3; Then I held on quickly and won the third set 21–19; Then he beat me 21–17; So we squared off for the final set. He led all the way again and I was beginning to console myself that I had given him a good fight anyway. He had me 19–16 and then I won the next three points with the aid of some bold shots and quite a little luck (net shots and hits on the edge of the board.) It then got to be deuce again, and I won 23–21! I have devoted a lot of space to this but it was really dramatic and thrilling. I must say that I had some very lucky breaks. The boy is a better player than I. Anyway, I am now determined to set-up a good Ping Pong corner in the barn with properly arranged lights, and all. We never play basketball anymore and so will devote that room to Ping Pong, Badminton, and Shuffleboard.

The only work I did on the trip was to correct the script of Allegro so that I could airmail it to Alfred Knopf who is publishing it, but this was not much of a job. I have done a little reading and a great deal of sleeping—late morning rising, and afternoon naps. The food is wonderful. "Smörgasbord" in the bar every night. The Swedish drink "Aquavite"— often called "Schnapps" is very pleasant and Dorothy has become addicted to it as she did to "Tequila" in Mexico. She is a girl who goes for the "wine-of-the-country".

No more news from the ocean. I'll write to you next week from Denmark.

Love

Dad

P.S. Just saw that boy and asked his name. It is:

Sven Malmberg

**Oscar Hammerstein (Grand Hotel, Stockholm) to Alice
Hammerstein, November 19, 1947**

Dearest Alice:

I promised to write from each country but I missed out on Denmark. In fact to-day—eight days after leaving the ship—is the first chance I have had to sit down for a half hour and make with a pen.

We arrived in Gothenburg, Sweden, a day late on account of rough weather, head-winds, and one cylinder being out of commission (The Gripsholm is a motor ship).

That afternoon we inspected The Gothenburg City Theatre and The Concert Hall. They are the most modern and best designed theatrical buildings I have ever seen. I will give you the details during the Christmas holidays. There are too many to describe here. The State and the Cities contribute large sums to their theatre and the Scandinavian countries are very art and culture conscious. This development started long before their Socialist Governments were elected. It has been so for many years and State and City-endowed theatres of this kind are built under more politically conservative governments.

That evening we had dinner with the Baron and Baroness Von Essen and her father Axel Jonson (Yoncon) [?] who own the Swedish-American Steamship Line. Another guest was Lars Schmidt and his wife. He is a theatrical agent whom I may appoint as my representative here. It was a pleasant evening with marvelous food and lots of drinking. The "Vodka" of Scandinavia is a white drink called Aquavite, it's most often referred to as Schnapps. You have a chaser of beer with it, or mineral water. I like beer. We also had red wine and champagne and Swedish [?]. This list of drinks we have had at every lunch and dinner we have sat down to!

The Swedes are great ones for toasts and certain formal customs govern the toasts. The host toasts the guest of honor. Later in the evening the guest of honor lifts his glass and states how happy he is to be where he is and what an honored guest of honor he is. If an old man toasts you, you must answer him with another toast within three minutes. No one ever drinks alone. Throughout the dinner, if you feel like drinking you catch someone else's eye first, lift your glass, he lifts his and you both say "Skoal" (SKOLE TO YOU). After dinner you thank the hostess and kiss her.

The next morning Lars Schmidt drove us down to Denmark and that evening we were in Copenhagen. We had dinner with Mr. and Mrs. Holys Besk. (These Eversharp Pens! Here's another. I'll try the name again:) Holger Bech. He is a banker who also adapts and translates plays. He translated Porgy and Bess for Denmark. Also present were Mr. and Mrs. Gregord. He operates a theatre in Copenhagen, not a State Theatre.

After dinner we stopped in at his theatre and watched a half hour of the performance—a dramatic play. I, of course, could not understand a word, but it looked like good, realistic acting.

The next day we did a little unorganized sight-seeing and had lunch down by the fisherman's wharves—wonderful! (Not for you because you don't like fish)

That evening we saw the Ballet at the opera house. One modern Swedish ballet had very exciting music and original scenic and costume designs. The other was traditional. Both were too long. Parts were well danced.

The next day we took a ferry to Malmö to inspect another remarkable modern theatre. (Malmö is in Sweden so we were crossing the frontier again, Passports, money, declarations, etc. That afternoon we took the ferry back to Copenhagen and went through the whole thing again.)

We had dinner with Mr. and Mrs. Kjeld Abell. He is Denmark's best serious playwright. When the Germans occupied Denmark they immediately closed two of his plays because they were Anti-Nazi and they started looking for him. He blonded his graying hair, grew a moustache, dyed his eyebrows and wore glasses, and kept changing his residence. He worked in the resistance movement and successfully dodged the Gestapo throughout the entire duration of the occupation.

We liked these people very much and stayed up so late talking politics and drinking the while that I finished up the evening very drunk indeed. Dorothy will, with great delight, supply the details when she sees you.

The next day we flew up here to Stockholm. Peter took most of our luggage on the train. Peter has been living a life of his own, picking up people and having a wonderful time.

In Stockholm the same pattern has continued. We have been entertained a great deal, taken to "Skansen" a little exhibition and zoo and restaurant in the city park, and to "Brigadoon" which opened just before we got here (not very good) and another show. I have left out the business side of the trip because I am bored enough with it without describing it. I have been beat by agents and managers. They all want the rights to the shows, of course. The press I have handled in all the cities by seeing them all one time in one group. If I saw them separately I'd have no time for anything else.

This is the most beautiful city I have seen. Broad lakes and canals reach in from the Baltic sea and divide the town into sections. The public buildings therefore have either bodies of water or plazas in front of them. This hotel is on the water and on the opposite bank is the royal palace.

Yesterday I visited the summer palace at Drottningholm which has a theatre built in 1750 and preserved exactly as it was, scenery and all. Please ask me to tell you about this when I see you. I spent two hours there and I would like to come back and spend two weeks there. The soul of the theatre lives there. It is a fascinating museum.

To-day is our last day here and to-morrow morning at 8.15 we leave for Oslo. We don't arrive until 8.00 in the evening, but we are looking forward to a day's rest on the train. How we need it!

I am getting almost tired of eating and drinking and the austerity of England looms up as an attractive relief. It is true that they are on rations here, but somehow the rationed food seems more than enough.

We, as you may have gathered, like the Scandinavians very much. The most attractive of all is a composer named Sylvain.[14] He is the most successful of the popular Swedish composers, but he is so discouraged by European conditions that he is going to Tonga in the South Sea Islands and is going to try to live like Gauguin. This sounds serious but he is very amusing and hearty about it.

I must have left a good many details out of this narrative but I'm written out. I'll continue from Oslo.

Love

Dad

---

[14] Jules Sylvain, né Axel Stig Hansson, was a Swedish composer of film scores and operettas.

Chapter Eight
1949 (Preceded by a Smattering of Letters from 1948)

There are disappointingly few letters from 1948, but a handful among them are worthy of inclusion.

Agnes de Mille to Oscar Hammerstein (excerpt), February 2, 1948

I gave a rehearsal the other day to those benighted creatures we call our actors. I asked [John] Battles to stop singing his lines and to think about what he was saying—result: the play [*Allegro*] was fifteen minutes overtime—

Oklahoma! closed on Broadway on May 29, 1948, after a record-breaking 2,212 performances, an event acknowledged in Sondheim's reference to a black-edged condolence.

Stephen Sondheim (Beta Theta Pi) to Dorothy Hammerstein, June 1948

Dearest Dorothy-

I am very sorry to hear about the loss of your mother. Please accept my sincere sympathy. I heard about it from Mom and Sue, who were up here yesterday to see our show, "Night Must Fall," in which I had the lead. It was fun having them up, but I was sorry to hear the news.

Has Jim been accepted anywhere yet (college, that is)? I understand he's going to England this summer. How I envy him! What will you do, go over with him and Sue, or stay here, or what?

The Letters of Oscar Hammerstein II. Mark Eden Horowitz, Oxford University Press. © Mark Eden Horowitz 2022.
DOI: 10.1093/oso/9780197538180.003.0008

How's "Tales of the South Pacific" coming? Is Ockie still in the "groping" stage (to use his phrase)? By the way, tell him I meant to send a telegram of condolence edged in black, last Saturday night at 11:30.

The musical was a big success. We called it "Phinney's Rainbow," because the President of Williams is James Phinney Baxter III. We made just under $1,000 on the show, which is phenomenal for the theater (they've never made over $100 before). They're clamoring for another show, but I just have no ideas. I may adapt Ferenc Molnar's "Liliom" + turn it into a musical. It might be cute; what do you think?

I'll be out of here in 10 days—see you then. Take care of yourself + give my love to Ockie, Sue, + Shawen.

Love,

Steve

Billy Rose tends to be remembered as cocky and gruff, but this letter reveals an unexpected insecurity and his clear respect for Oscar.

Billy Rose to Oscar Hammerstein, July 12, 1948

Dear Oscar:

I wonder if you would do me a favor—a big, big favor.

As you know, I've worked on my book for a long time. Emotionally, its success means a great deal to me. The hollering of my publishers that it will sell a lot of copies doesn't excite me too much. They hollered just as loudly a year ago when it was a paste-up job.

To a certain extent, it's pre-sold. LOOK MAGAZINE paid a substantial sum for the pre-publication rights, and READER'S DIGEST has bought the condensation rights for their usual generous check. My own corporation is footing the bill for publishing and exploitation, and that means that the book won't be a secret.

But there are many things concerning "WINE, WOMEN AND WORDS" that I'm fuzzy about—sequence of chapters, the wisdom of including one or two of the chapters, certain episodes, some of the line writing, etcetera. I mailed the enclosed letter to Ben Hecht several days ago and sent him a set of galleys. His letter this morning was full of wisdom and good, tough professional criticism. He strongly urges that I write a final chapter—and this I decided to do a couple of weeks ago. He makes one or two other suggestions which are pretty radical.

Outside of Ben, you're the only friend I have whose judgment carries a lot of weight with me. Could you steal a few hours out of your busy life to read the galleys carefully, mark them up any way you see fit, and then send me a letter which would incorporate your ice-cold suggestions—the suggestions you would make if you were the publisher!

If you tell me you're too busy for this chore, of course I'll understand. But if you can find the time, I'd be very grateful. If you can, have your girl call Helen and we'll send a set of galleys over. But please, please— don't hesitate to bow out of this if you're too tied up. I will, of course, understand.

Affectionate regards,

Billy

BILLY ROSE

Allegro closed on July 10, 1948.

Shirley Potash was a friend of Susan's from California where she worked for the publicity department at Twentieth Century-Fox. She came east and stayed with the Hammersteins for a few months and, as Oscar worked on the script for *South Pacific*, she began transcribing his Dictabelts which led to her becoming a secretary/ assistant to Rodgers and Hammerstein. She later became an editor at *People* magazine and ended her career as an associate producer for ABC's *20/20*.

Shirley Potash to Oscar and Dorothy Hammerstein, October 5, 1948

Dear Mr. and Mrs. Hammerstein:

As I am infinitely more articulate at my typewriter, I thought a written acceptance of my job could much better express a very grateful heart. I know you won't regret your decision.

As for salary, I'm reluctant to ask for more than $2. per week. However, before you discover I'm not worth much more, would $60. a week be agreeable to you? As things progress, or retrogress, you can use your own judgment. I realize I will be doing some work I already know, but for what I expect to learn, I cannot accept payment. And there are several important things involved in this job that I'd rather not discuss in a material vein, because then I'd really feel odd about accepting emoluments of any kind.

You mentioned that I could use this position as a stepping stone if I choose. But I feel that the next step up from the Hammersteins will come when I'm receiving my business correspondence in care of St. Peter or his Shivkih equivalent.

Before I become completely carried away, when would you like me to start? I'm sure you can reach me somewhere on the third floor at 157 East most anytime.

Loving thanks,

Shirley

P. G. Wodehouse to Oscar Hammerstein, October 12, 1948

Dear Osc.

Thanks most awfully. Your letter tells me just what I want to know.

I hope 'Pacific' is shaping well. It ought to be a wonderful show.

And now I have gone and let myself be talked into appearing in Television ! ! ! I'm like your Oklahoma girl who couldn't say No.

So long

Yours ever

Plum

I didn't realize till I'd finished this that the three paragraphs in my letter rhyme. It's practically a lyric.

Lars Schmidt was a Swedish producer who brought American plays to Scandinavia and Europe. In 1948 he acquired the Nordic rights to *Oklahoma!*, *Carousel*, and *Allegro*, and later added *Annie Get Your Gun* and *South Pacific* to his roster. In addition to Rodgers and Hammerstein, Schmidt was an ardent promoter of Tennessee Williams' plays and, between 1959 and 1967, he mounted twenty-two productions of *My Fair Lady* in nine Scandinavian and European countries.

Oscar Hammerstein to Lars Schmidt, October 25, 1948

Dear Lars:

I was distressed by your phone call because a request from a man playing the lead in "Oklahoma" to pad his part by singing a number from "Carrousel," [*sic*] and his receiving any encouragement whatever from the management or you implies that "Oklahoma" may be produced in Sweden with as little understanding as was "Brigadoon."

"Oklahoma" is not an operetta like the "Beggar's Student" or "Prince of Pilsen." It is not a vehicle for deep-chested baritones to display their voices. It is a small human story, a sketch of characters, and a swift moving symbol of the spirit of the pioneer America about 1900. If it is done in any way except the fresh and simple and honest manner in which you saw it in London or New York, it will be a dismal failure. Its only chance is for it to be done in the American manner and not in the European manner.

This, naturally, applies to all our plays in all the Scandinavian countries. If your phone call meant what I think it means, we are off to a very bad start. I hope that I am wrong in my fears.

All the best to you.

Sincerely,

Oscar Hammerstein, II

Howard Reinheimer to Richard Rodgers and Oscar Hammerstein, December 12, 1948

Dear Dick and Oscar:

What further decision have you made regarding the name of the Play? I made a copyright search of the title. This revealed that the only prior use of the title "SOUTH PACIFIC" was a musical play produced in New Haven December 29, 1943. I gather that the play was not presented any other place, but I am checking on it.

It is my belief that this limited use would not foreclose our using the title but since "SOUTH PACIFIC" is such a generic term, it is entirely possible that we might have problems concerning the use of this title by others. It would fall in the same groove and give rise to the same problems as the title "OKLAHOMA."

I would like to discuss this further with you if you are "sold" on the use of the title.

Sincerely,

Howard

HOWARD E. REINHEIMER

Leland Hayward was a Hollywood agent with a who's who roster of clients. He produced four plays on Broadway prior to *South Pacific*: *A Bell for Adano*, *State of the Union*, *Mister Roberts*, and *Anne of the Thousand Days*. Josh Logan co-wrote and directed *Mister Roberts* (and William Hammerstein served as production stage manager). It was Hayward who first saw the theatrical possibilities in James Michener's collection of short stories, *Tales of the South Pacific* and had approached Michener about the rights. The producing credits for *South Pacific* would read: Produced by Richard Rodgers and Oscar Hammerstein II in association with Leland Hayward and Joshua Logan. Behind-the-scenes issues regarding credit and compensation grew contentious.

Leland Hayward to Richard Rodgers and Oscar Hammerstein, December 23, 1948

Dear Dick and Oscar,

Now that the dust has settled somewhat and the Jamaican sunshine has unruffled my nerves to the extent where my brain is active again I feel that I should try to make one point clear to you both before we go any further with this venture.

I feel that first last and always "Pacific" is the primary consideration. As you both know I am sure, I have looked forward for a long time to working with you both and have realized that my contribution to the play would be mainly to make the going as smooth for you both and for Josh as it was possible for me to do. As all of us know, any emotional turmoil only makes things tougher and if Josh's feeling toward me complicates things for you in any way you must tell me honestly and quickly so that I can get out and the play can go ahead. I think I am as anxious as any of you to see the story done for I have believed in it for a long time and I would feel very, very badly if I were the one to hinder its progress.

I keep thinking that when I get back to New York next week I will find that all the things Josh said were part of a bad dream and that our plans will go smoothly ahead. But in the case that that isnt [*sic*] true and you feel or he feels that the situation between us will hinder the production, you must allow me to withdraw.

I think and hope that there is enough good will between us so that personal feelings can be eliminated and that you two reach a decision which is based on the play and nothing else.

Whatever you decide will be completely understood by me.

Best always,

Leland

Also Merry Christmas + Happy New Year to you + Dorothy from Nancy + Myself –

Leland Hayward to Richard Rodgers, Oscar Hammerstein and Joshua Logan, January 1, 1949

RECEIVED YOUR CABLE STOP FIRST I HEREBY WITHDRAW AS COPRODUCER OF SOUTH PACIFIC SECOND THIS HAS NOTHING TO DO WITH BUSINESS DETAILS WHICH I HAVE ASKED LEW WASSERMAN TO TAKE UP WITH LOGAN. THIRD I HAVE ALREADY TOLD YOU THREE THAT I NEVER HAD ANY INTENTION OR THOUGHT OF DOING ANY PLAY THAT COULD POSSIBLY CONFLICT WITH SOUTH PACIFIC FOURTH AS BOTH DICK AND OSCAR SAID TO ME ON TELEPHONE IN HAVANA NONE OF YOU HAVE ANY RIGHT ANYWAY TO TAKE POSITION THAT I COULDN'T DO ANYTHING ELSE BUT SOUTH PACIFIC WITH OR WITHOUT CONFLICT FIFTH I AM WITHDRAWING PURELY BECAUSE IT HAS BECOME TOO UNPLEASANT FOR EVERYONE CONCERNED SIXTH I MUST INSIST NO PRESS RELEASE ON THIS MATTER BE GIVEN OUT BEFORE MY RETURN SUNDAY AND THAT THIS PRESS RELEASE BE GIVEN OUT BY ME SEVENTH HAPPY NEW YEAR

LELAND HAYWARD

Richard Rodgers, Oscar Hammerstein and Josh Logan to Leland Hayward, January 2, 1949

LELAND HAYWARD SUNSET LODGE MONTEGO BAY JAMAICA (BWI)

SINCE THE CONFLICT CAUSED BY YOUR DOING TWO PLAYS AT THE SAME TIME IS THE ONLY COMPLAINT WE HAVE EVER EXPRESSED WE ARE SURPRISED THAT YOU ELIMINATE THIS CONFLICT AS THE REAL CAUSE OF YOUR RESIGNATION AND BASE IT ON THE GROUND OF UNPLEASANT RELATIONS OF WHICH WE HAVE NEVER BEEN AWARE. REGARDING ITEM THREE OF YOUR CABLEGRAM YOU STILL AVOID ANSWERING OUR SPECIFIC FEAR THAT THE KINGSLEY PLAY WILL GO INTO REHEARSAL BEFORE WE OPEN IN NEW YORK. ITEM FOUR IN YOUR CABLEGRAM IS A MISQUOTATION REGARDING ANY PUBLICITY RELEASE WE WILL OF COURSE MAKE NONE WITHOUT CONSULTING YOU AND INSIST THAT YOU MAKE NONE WITHOUT CONSULTING US REGARDING ITEM SEVEN HAPPY NEW YEAR TO YOU TOO.

DICK OSCAR AND JOSH

Oscar Hammerstein to Lawrence Schwab (excerpt), January 12, 1949

Josh and I have just finished what I call the "first draft of the fifth draft," and while it looks at the moment as if it were a little longer than "Parsifal," it does seem to have great strength and vitality. You can never make safe prophecy of the quality of entertainment, but at the present moment it entertains us.

Oscar Hammerstein to Agnes de Mille, January 14, 1949

Dear Agnes:

Please be patient with me about the Australian and South African rights, and take my word that you will get all that is coming to you. The only reason you have received nothing from South Africa is that, so far, we have received nothing from South Africa. As far as the contract is concerned, it is not entirely Reinheimer's fault as I had undertaken to talk to the Guild about framing a contract, and I delayed a long time. I have, however, spoken to Lawrence, and I hope to get this all cleaned up for you very soon. Meanwhile, as far as money is concerned, you have my personal word that you will get exactly what I promised you.

In the brief seconds I spoke to you the other night, I did not tell you how much I admired your skillful production of "The Rape of Lucretia." I thought it one of the most interesting and graceful directorial jobs I have ever seen in the theatre. I thought, also, that the lyrics of the beautifully written text came over very clearly, and I loathed most of the music. There is no reason why a Roman play should have a score that sounded as if it were limited to the confinements of the Greek scale.

Love,

Oscar Hammerstein, II

In a 1979 *New York Times* interview, Agnes de Mille spoke of her experience with the original production of *Oklahoma!* and Rodgers and Hammerstein: "Dick Rodgers went to bat for me twice. He went to the Theatre Guild, who produced it, and said, 'You've got to give her something.' So I got $50 a week. I asked them would they make it $75 and they refused me. Then it was changed to one half of one percent after five years. On 'Carousel' I got one half of one percent." In a January 18 letter to Hammerstein, de Mille wrote: "I have just heard from my Danish friend that a production of 'Oklahoma' is playing in Malmo, Sweden. How about this? My old teach, Sven Aage Larsen, has done the choreography after memorizing it here. Nice work! Dan informs me that a production is pending in Copenhagen. Do you know anything about this?"

Oscar Hammerstein to Agnes de Mille, January 20, 1949

Dear Agnes:

I am returning Erik Kristen's[1] letter. We have no control of this or, for that matter, any of those Swedish productions. I don't know of any way to do this since none of us is willing to go out to these various ends of the earth to supervise. We have to put it in the hands of the best people available and

---

[1] Erik Kristen was a dancer in the original production of *Oklahoma!*

hope they will do as well as possible. I am told by my agent in Scandanavia [*sic*], that "Oklahoma!" has broken all records in Malmoe. The money hasn't come in yet, but when it does we will see that you get some. Another company opened in Helsinki, and one is pending in Copenhagen and another in Olso. Do not, however, order any new pianos or Cadillacs on the strength of this news. When these various kronen are translated into dollars, what you wind up with is oodles of gratification and about one oodle of cash.

Love,

Oscar Hammerstein, II

After seeing *Allegro*, one G. M. Philpott wrote to Rodgers and Hammerstein on January 17: "Not only was this good theater, but it was the most penetrating commentary on our civilization that I have seen and I want to thank both of you for a most enjoyable experience."

Oscar Hammerstein to G. M. Philpott, January 21, 1949

Dear Mr. Philpott:

I am very happy that you thought so well of "Allegro," and I am deeply grateful to you for taking the trouble to write me about it. Of all my plays, this one stands very high in my affection, and I believe very fervently in what it has to say. I am always gratified to receive a sincere endorsement like yours.

With all good wishes to you.

Sincerely,

Oscar Hammerstein

Josh Logan to Oscar Hammerstein, January 27, 1949

NO MATTER HOW LARGE THE TYPE, THE THRILL AND HONOR OF BEING COAUTHOR WITH YOU COULDN'T BE LARGER. I GRATEFULLY ACCEPT YOUR DECISION. IT MAY BE SMALL TYPE TO YOU BUT ITS BIG TYPE TO ME. I PRAY OSCAR THAT THIS FEELING OF PENALTY WILL BE FORGOTTEN SOME DAY PERHAPS THE DAY THAT OPERATION SOUTH PACIFIC IS

SUCH A SUCCESS THAT ANY SACRIFICE WILL HAVE BEEN
WORTHWHILE=

JOSH=

Logan's gratitude soon tempered. Oscar (in consultation with Rodgers and
Reinheimer) agreed to give Logan co-credit for writing the book for *South Pacific*,
but on posters and programs his name appeared in smaller type than Rodgers and
Hammerstein (although his billing as director was in large type); he did not to share
in any of the author's royalties, and Rodgers and Hammerstein controlled the copyright and ownership of the show. Logan was left embittered, although he and his
wife, Netta, maintained their friendship with Oscar and Dorothy. However, having
directed four original Broadway productions for Rodgers and Hammerstein, he
never again directed a new show for them (though they did approach him about
at least one other possible new show). He did continue working on *South* Pacific,
rehearsing with new cast members on Broadway, and directing the national tour,
the London production, and the film.

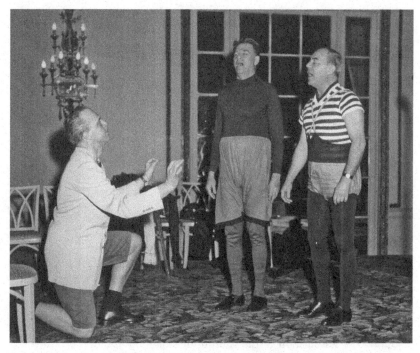

Photo 18 Josh Logan "directing" Oscar Hammerstein II and Richard Rodgers

Stephen Sondheim (Williams College) to Oscar Hammerstein, February 2, 1949

Dear Mr. H.—

Would you be so kind as to make a memo to the effect that the Adams Memorial Theatre of Williams College would be much obliged if they could get their grubby hands on any and all of the curtain materials, drapes, etc., which will be free of earthly bonds when "Annie Get Your Gun" closes?

We will be happy to defray shipping expenses and will make the aforesaid items cheerful and comfortable in their new home. We need them for the forthcoming musical smash hit by that renowned composer of intellectual, abstruse and unhummable music—one Stephen Sondheim.

Many thanks, and please let us know when and if it is possible.

All love to Dorothy, and once more, best of luck with Pinza, Martin and company.

Steve

Oscar Hammerstein to Stephen Sondheim, February 7, 1949

Dear Stevie:

There is a good chance that you can have the pink scene from "Annie Get Your Gun." All other curtains, drapes, and soft material we shall store. I suggest some responsible Williams man, alumnus, or member of the Williams Club from New York get in touch with our Morrie Jacobs (general manager of R. & H.), and arrange for the carting shipment and paying for same. The show closes this Saturday night and quick action is of the essence.

Love,

Oscar Hammerstein to David L. Meyer, February 7, 1949

Dear Dave:

Are you going to make me write you a long letter to talk you into joining the Association of the Alumni of Columbia College, or are you going to come across with the five bucks just so that you will have no further trouble from me.

All the best.

As ever,

Oscar Hammerstein, II

Annie Get Your Gun closed on Broadway on February 12.

Oscar Hammerstein to James Hammerstein (excerpt), February 17, 1949

We were both very happy about your marks, and I think it would be wonderful if you would set them as a new standard to meet and, possibly, surpass. This sounds a little like the speech of a football coach between the halves, and I am a little sorry I started it.

I was interested in one paragraph of your letter. I quote: "I meant to call you last Sunday, but I had to rush and deposit the girls safely back at College, and didn't get back until late." I haven't time to explore all the possibilities of this sentence, but I am intrigued by the fact that you had to <u>rush</u> and deposit the girls <u>safely</u> back at College—one wonders why, if you had to rush to get them safely back, you "didn't get back until late," and one almost fears for the girls' safety.

Jeffrey Bocca, *Sunday Empire News*, February 23, 1949, with Oscar Hammerstein's response

IN ANSWER TO FOLLOWING CABLE BOCCA READ TO SHIRLEY POTASH VIA PHONE:

PLEASE GET CONCISE COMMENT OSCAR HAMMERSTEIN ON OKLAHOMA TOMORROW BEATING DRURY LANE'S RECORD RUN PREVIOUSLY HELD BY ROSE MARIE. (SIGNED) FOREIGN SERVICE—SUNDAY EMPIRE NEWS

O.H.'S MESSAGE:

I WAS VERY PROUD OF ROSE MARIE'S RECORD. AS LONG AS IT HAD TO BE BEATEN, I AM GLAD OKLAHOMA WAS THE SHOW TO DO IT. I CONSIDER DRURY LANE THE FINEST THEATRE IN THE WORLD IN WHICH TO PRODUCE A MUSICAL PLAY. IN SPITE OF ITS CAPACITY, IT HAS AN INTIMACY AND WARMTH THAT HELPS ANY PLAY PRODUCED THERE. I SEND MY SALUTATION, CONGRATULATIONS, FELICITATIONS AND GOOD WISHES TO THE COMPANY FOR A CONTINUED LONG RUN.

Oscar Hammerstein to James Hammerstein, March 1, 1949

Dear Jimmy:

This will have to be a very quick note, but I do want to ask you one question. Did you finally go to the consultant you were supposed to see about your failing in Greek? From what I gathered out of the communication, you were supposed to see him whether your next marks were better or not, and he seemed to feel neglected.

You say your music teacher seems to be pleased at your slow improvement, so I assume he doesn't like students who go too fast.

Love,

Howard Reinheimer to Richard Rodgers, Oscar Hammerstein, and Leland Hayward, March 6, 1949

Gentlemen:

Just a note to tell you that Michener's agent telephoned and asked that I convey the message that Michener is deeply appreciative of the unusual courtesy which was extended to him in permitting him to participate in the financing of the show by means of funds advanced by the Producers.

Sincerely,

Howard E Reinheimer

Josh Logan, in New Haven, to Oscar Hammerstein, circa
March 6, 1949

Dear Oscar:

Thank you for the show + the fine time I had working with you—and the credit sharing and all the boosts and gooses. For god's sake don't lets make too quick decisions tomorrow night. I don't want to know what anyone thinks except you and Dick and the audience as a whole. If there's any difference of opinion please lets give the thing under dispute another chance. At this point, I'm afraid my pal Leland becomes the little hysterical man whose here. Any moment of doubt on anyone's part will be aired aloud. Please be careful of his helpful hints. Last year after one tryout of [Mister] Roberts in New Haven, I was told to throw out the final touches-. Please let's not use words like Shubert Operetta about this show—I will fix <u>anything</u> in this show—toward the happiness of all three of us but I cannot give full satisfaction to Leland, Nancy, Gilbert Miller, Howard Cullman, Howard Reinheimer, Lew Wasserman, Morrie Schrier, and people of that kidney,-

Thanks + good luck

Josh

South Pacific began its out-of-town tryouts in New Haven on March 7, 1949. Gilbert Miller was a noted theater owner and producer. Howard Cullman was an investor in Broadway shows who, much to his later regret, had decided against investing in *Oklahoma!* Lew Wasserman was chairman and chief executive of the talent agency MCA. Morrie Schrier was Logan's lawyer.

Stephen Sondheim to Oscar Hammerstein, March 7, 1949

ALL BEST WISHES FOR ANOTHER SUCCESS. DO YOU NEED A GOOD BARITONE? LOVE TO YOU AND DOROTHY-

STEVE

Eslanda Robeson to Oscar Hammerstein, March 9, 1949

My dear Mr. Hammerstein:

All during the long drive back to Enfield last night, I thought about your SOUTH PACIFIC. What a beautiful accomplishment that is! Its quite impossible to discuss it. There it is, and WHAM. You go out satisfied, having had a wonderful time in the theatre, no hold barred. The curtain when the four stays there, a la family, was full of imagination and impact. I congratulate you once again. You may be amused to hear that when I got home, at 3 in the morning, I sat me down then and there and wrote to Paul at length about the play, and assuring him that with this kind of thing coming up, he may be able to come home and find something he can get his teeth into, after all. He is at present on tour in concert, in England, meeting with fabulous success everywhere. Even the two concerts for Albert Hall in London have been sold out, complete with standingroom!!

And please, may I make one small suggestion, very respectfully? In thinking back over the play, it troubled me a little that the Negro soldier was ALWAYS jitterbugging. It is very possible that I am unduly sensitive racially, but so are a lot of us, and it would help enormously that if just once, he appeared with his comrades NOT cutting up. I agree that he does it beautifully, and that you-all probably hadn't thought of the sum total of the impression, and even that I may be wrong. Could be.

Cordially, I salute you.

Eslanda Robeson

Mrs. Paul Robeson.

Now don't misunderstand me. The jitterbugging is marvelous, and belongs here, but I'd like to see him once NOT do it.

Oscar Hammerstein to Mrs. Paul Robeson, March 14, 1949

Dear Mrs. Robeson:

Thank you very much for your letter, and the gratifying comment therein. Since you have seen the play, and before I received your letter, we have inserted an episode in which Arnie Savage is <u>not</u> jitterbugging.

I am looking forward to being able to read your book when I get some free time here in Boston this week.

Thank you again, and all best wishes.

Sincerely,

Oscar Hammerstein, II

Agnes de Mille to Oscar Hammerstein, March 12, 1949

Dear Oscar –

I hear such things about "Pacific" as has never been rumored before. I rejoice for you, because I remember your plodding up and down the lawn in Doylestown in turmoil of spirit. I loved you as I saw you wearing down the grass day after day.

I think people have given up hoping you'll make a mistake and some sort of flop- Right now I think they're giving up that idea, and will relax and lean on you from here on out as our chiefest national pride and spiritual comfort. You fill hungers; and now we can be sure where to turn. My heart expands tremendously to recognize this –

Devotedly,

Agnes

South Pacific continued its out-of-town tryouts, opening in Boston on March 15.

Agnes de Mille to Oscar Hammerstein (in Boston),
March 15, 1949

DEAR OSCAR WHAT MORE CAN I SAY MY BOSOM CONTINUES TO SWELL WITH PRIDE LOVE

=AGNES

Oscar Hammerstein to Agnes de Mille, March 18, 1949

Dear Agnes:

Thank you for your Boston letter. I think I am proudest of these words of yours than of any tribute of any kind I have ever had.

Love,

Oscar Hammerstein, II

Oscar Hammerstein to Leighton Brill, March 18, 1949

Dear Leighton:

The show is, at this point, the strongest show that I have ever seen. The comment is almost unbelievable, and it is impossible to have any fears for the New York opening.

Reggie came up to New Haven last Thursday night (March 10th) with Milton Cohen, and during the intermission complained of dizziness, and then dropped to the floor. He was taken backstage and we sent for an ambulance. Over at the hospital, the doctors went ahead on the assumption that it was a heart attack. He had no pain, however, and was at no time unconscious. At about 2:00 a.m. he became nauseous and threw up a great deal of blood. The diagnosis was then changed to internal hemorrhage from an ulcer. Three years ago, Harold had told him he had an ulcer but Reggie, having little respect for the degree of M.D., ignored Harold's diagnosis and diet, and cured himself with a package of Tums. This is the result. He had a second hemorrhage on the next day, and we were all pretty worried. But now, one week later, he seems to have passed the danger mark. He is still in the New Haven hospital. I have just hung up the receiver after talking to him. He has started to eat again, and they believe he will be strong enough to return to New York this coming Sunday.

That's all the news. I sent Alice the Boston notices. Call her up and she will give them to you.

Love,

Oscar Hammerstein, II

Oscar Hammerstein to Joel Raphaelson (*The Harvard Crimson*), March 22, 1949

Dear Joel Raphaelson:

In your "South Pacific" notice you assume that I had invented the story of the Frenchman and the American Navy nurse. You probably had read the paper edition of the book, which did not include this story. The original edition, however, contained it. The title was "Our Heroine," so it's Michener's story—not mine. I thought your criticism very well written and, in many respects, a better analysis than many of the daily papers contained.

Please give my kindest regards to your mother and father when you write to them—unless, like my son James, you don't write to them, in which case remember me to them when you see them.

Best wishes.

Sincerely,

Oscar Hammerstein, II

Joel Raphaelson to Oscar Hammerstein, March 24, 1949

Dear Mr. Hammerstein:

Thank you for your very kind letter. I did read "Tales Of The South Pacific" in the paper editions, so I missed the story called "Our Heroine." I regret the error---and I hope it was the worst I made. For the fact that still another of Michener's stories has been worked into "South Pacific" increases, rather than diminishes, my admiration for the remarkable things you and Joshua Logan have done with the book.

I enclose a second article of mine about "South Pacific." It is a sort of Harvard equivalent of a New York critic's Sunday article. It was written several days ago. Yesterday I saw the play for the second time, and some of my convictions are shaken, particularly the one concerning "Younger Than Springtime." And I understand that Elinor Hughes in the Boston Herald also did not care for "You've Got To Be Taught;" her concurrence shakes my conviction on that point. And I'm beginning to think that the first scene, which I called "woefully slow" in the review that has already mysteriously got into your hands, is one of the finer things in "South Pacific."

So perhaps it is a perfect play. At any rate, I shall certainly never become a drama critic. It is too hard to be fair to your own opinion in the short space that newspapers allow, and in the short amount of time, let alone to be fair to the play you are writing about.

It seemed to me yesterday afternoon that Pinza's diction in "Some Enchanted Evening" was much clearer than it was on the second night, although the word "room" still gets lost, and although some people around me had difficulty with "stranger." (I was sitting in the back row of the first balcony.) And the words of "Happy Talk" are extremely difficult to hear, which is a shame, since they are among the most engaging in the play, as I have discovered from the sheet music.

Please forgive my prolixity. I have been so taken by "South Pacific" that once I start talking about it I have trouble stopping.

I shall certainly send your regards to my parents. I do write to them, although when I was at George School, I didn't. Perhaps, if your son is still there, this somehow accounts for his silence, and you can look forward to the day when he will be as loquacious a correspondent as I am.

Best of luck with "South Pacific" in New York.

Sincerely,

Joel Raphaelson

From the beginning, the song "You've Got to Be Carefully Taught" elicited strong reactions.

Thomas McWhorter to Oscar Hammerstein (Boston), April 2, 1949

Dear Mr. Hammerstein:

I was fortunate enough to have seen your wonderful new show, South Pacific, last night and I was amazed that I am forced to agree with the critics that the perfection which you attained in Oklahoma! was, in this case, surpassed.

It is not necessary for me to tell you how good it really is, and if it were just another good show I would not bother to write. But this is a great show, Mr. Hammerstein—and therein lies the difference.

If you will accept the sincere and earnest opinion of a layman and theatre-goer though, there is one way in which it can be improved: Please eliminate that song by the Lieutenant in the last act which deals with something on the order of "They have to be very carefully schooled". It is not necessary to carry the point or "message" of the play (if you insist on having a "message" in it), and it seems out of place. It gives the audience the same let-down feeling as if the show were abruptly halted for a double-barrel three-minute commercial. It is like drinking a scotch-and-soda and suddenly swallowing the ice cube! You could not have interrupted the beautiful flow of entertainment any more effectively had you stopped the show for a VD lecture. Of course nobody would question the lofty purpose of a VD lecture, but if it is out of place it should not be presented.

My point is that that particular song weakens not only the show as a whole but also weakens your "message". Up to that point the question had been dealt with subtly and with good taste. It says nothing that isn't said in every paper, magazine, book of fiction and radio broadcast. The theme is wearing thin. Admittedly the song ties in with the plot of the story, but it is too blunt—too much like pure, harsh, propaganda.

Examine which deals with this same theme most effectively : Madam Butterfly or Finian's Rainbow? The latter had a beautiful score that made people enjoy it in spite of its heavy propaganda. But it flopped in London. It will not go into the records as a great play or musical even though I believe the score deserved it. Do you?

And then, too, by and large, people go to a musical to be entertained— not harangued to. That song is a harangue—presumably for the benefit of the moron who did not get the point from the events in the play which preceeded it (and followed it).

The above criticisms I offer in all sincerity, and I offer it only because South Pacific is my musical, It gave me a thrill I had never before experienced in the theatre, except from La Boheme.

Sincerely yours,

Thos. McWhorter

Lieut.Comdr.,USN

Oscar Hammerstein to Thomas McWhorter, April 11, 1949

Dear Lieutenant Commander McWhorter:

Thank you for your letter of April 2nd. I am very happy that you like "South Pacific" so well, and I am grateful for your interest in suggesting the elimination of "You've Got To Be Taught." Please forgive me for not agreeing with you.

I am most anxious to make the point not only that prejudice exists and is a problem, but that its birth lies in teaching and not in the fallacious belief that there are basic biological, physiological and mental differences between races.

I would like to note that your comparison of "Madam Butterfly" with "Finian's Rainbow" is not very sound. I was in London when "Finian's Rainbow" failed. It was due entirely to bad casting and bad production. If you ascribe "Madam Butterfly's" long life to the absence of propaganda, I would also say that Puccini's brilliant score had a great deal to do with its continued success.

I believe I get the point of your letter very clearly and I realize very well the dangers of overstating the case. But I just feel that the case is not fully stated without this song. I wish it were true that all these things are accepted by the public. You say "the theme is wearing thin," but in spite of this, I see progress being made only very slowly.

Thank you again for your letter.

Sincerely,

Oscar Hammerstein, II

South Pacific opened on Broadway on April 7, 1949. It was Rodgers and Hammerstein's most highly anticipated show and one whose success, both critically and with audiences, exceeded expectations. An immediate hit, its innovations and unusual qualities may be missed or overlooked. Not atypical for Rodgers and Hammerstein, it featured two love stories, but what was unusual was that neither of them was comic, and one of them featured an older couple, and the other a mixed race couple whose relationship ends tragically. It was a contemporary show, not a period piece, set less than ten years earlier, about experiences well known to its audiences. And it had a serious point to make about the poison of prejudice

South Pacific featured the established Broadway star, Mary Martin, and the opera star Ezio Pinza. There was no named choreographer, and the little dancing that there was felt spontaneous and improvised. (It's interesting that Rodgers and Hammerstein went from a show directed by a choreographer to one with musical staging by a director.)

James Michener to Oscar Hammerstein, April 7, 1949

FROM ONE BUCK'S COUNTY FARMER TO ANOTHER, I THINK THIS IS A TERRIFIC EVENING. MY MOST HEART-FELT APPRECIATION-

JAMES A MICHENER=

Oscar Hammerstein to James Michener, April 12, 1949

Dear Jim:

Thank you for your kind opening night wire. If you'll ever come down to Pennsylvania and light there long enough for me to talk to you, I will someday tell you how grateful I am to you for entrusting your fine work to me.

All the best wishes to you and your wife.

Sincerely,

Set designer Jo Mielziner applied the "lap dissolves" he had introduced in *Allegro*. This staging innovation enabled seamlessly moving from scene to scene in a cinematic way—without bringing the curtain down between scenes to change the sets. Given *Allegro*'s troubled reception, few noticed Mielziner's revolutionary methods, but with *South Pacific* they became influential.

Note from Jo Mielziner to Oscar Hammerstein, April 7, 1949

All my thanks Oscar –

It's a joy + a privilege to be your designer

Jo

Oscar Hammerstein to Jo Mielziner, April 15, 1949

Dear Jo:

Thank you for your note on opening night. I don't know how to describe your contribution to the success of "South Pacific." I only shudder if I try to imagine the play without your ingenuity and rare craftsmanship. It was a pleasure, as always, to work with you.

Gratefully,

Oscar Hammerstein, II

Francis S. Milton to Oscar Hammerstein, circa April, 1949

Dear Mr. Hammerstein,

A copy of "Some Enchanted Evening", which I purchased at Carl Fischer Music Store, contains the following lines:

Some enchanted evening

You may see a stranger across a

crowded room

And somehow you know,

You know even then –

That somewhere you'll see him again

And again.

As the phrase "you may see" implies the future, as does "some", it is difficult to see how you arrive at the use of the present tense for the phrases "And somehow you know" and "you know even then".

Perhaps there is an explanation which the viewing of "South Pacific" will reveal. However, if the explanation is that the song is sung by an uneducated person I doubt that he would use the word "enchanted."

I expect to be worried by this minor point for many years to come— every time I hear "Some Enchanted Evening."

Sincerely,

Francis S. Milton

Oscar Hammerstein to Francis S. Milton, April 8, 1949

Dear Mrs. Milton:

In my conception, the words of "Some Enchanted Evening" are philosophical, relating to any time at all, and not prophetic. In other words, on some enchanted evening, any evening at all, one may—is likely to—see a stranger and at that time (even then), somehow one knows that she will see him again—tomorrow, the next day, or sometime in the future. I hope this will decrease your worry to some extent and if it doesn't, just turn off your radio—this may be a good idea anyway.

Thank you for your interest.

All good wishes to you.

Sincerely,

Oscar Hammerstein, II

E. Y. "Yip" Harburg to Oscar Hammerstein, April 8, 1949

THIS IS A SALUTE TO PERFECTION BRAVO AND HALLELUJAH AND THANKS FOR IGNITING ME.

YIP HARBURG

Oscar received a congratulatory letter from a Hilda Geers, which closed with: "I have never seen anything to equal it and while I'm sure you will go on giving us great performances nothing can ever be better than 'South Pacific'—and I might add no one is nicer than you—You know I knew you 'when.'

Oscar Hammerstein to Hilda F. Geers, April 12, 1949

Dear Hilda:

It was very sweet of you to write me about "South Pacific." When you say you knew me when, I presume "when" means when you and I were dancing partners and could do no better than win second prize. So, you see, I knew you when too, and I don't think that was any more my fault than yours. I danced just as well as you did, but you were prettier.

All the best to you.

Sincerely,

Oscar Hammerstein, II

Harold Hyman, a childhood friend of Oscar's, became the family's doctor.

**Harold Hyman, MD to Oscar Hammerstein, April 21, 1949;
enclosing a letter from Arthur Hammerstein to Harold Hyman,
April 17, 1949**

Dear Oc:

Please read this and send it back to me unless you would like to preserve it.

Ever yours,

HTP

Harold Thomas Hyman, M.D.

Dear Harold

I thank you for your report on my rejuvenation and your suggestion as to my diet, I will carry out your order to the letter.

If you know some dame that has invested long wants and desirous of buying a couple of real milkers, Iam [*sic*] your man, I'am tired of sailors following me on the beach.

I'am happy to have lived to see Oscar get out of that ten year slump but what came out of it the greatest living writer manager. I felt those failures as though they were my own. Your statement was not exaggerated when you write that Iam his father. I have been so ever since my brother gave me that title upon his death.

After the curtain droped [*sic*] on that eventful opening night of South Pacific all I could hear was his fathers last words to me—don't let Oscar ever get into the show business—if only he would have looked down that night. It was the night of <u>my</u> life for their now lives the greatest Hammerstein. Iam not taken much to sentiment, but that night I was born over. Instead of all the sentiment a joke would have sufficed but your closeness to Oscar gave me satisfaction and relief.

Remember me to your clever wife.

Sincerely

Arthur

Shirley Potash to Oscar Hammerstein (excerpt), April 22, 1949

Dear Boss:

Just had to tell you the following: Goddard [Lieberson] called again. He said that Rodgers, Hayward, and Logan left Columbia drunk with power after listening to the records. He also said that Dick, "who looks like he's at Rabbi Wise's funeral, even in his happiest moments, didn't even find one spot where someone might be accused of breathing incorrectly." And he said that practically every word on [the] record can be understood perfectly (and he's tried it on several people who haven't seen the show), the only exception being "Joe[2] DiMaggio's glove" from you-know-what. And as Goddard put it, "You'd have to be a friend of DiMaggio's to understand that, or you'd have to see the show twelve times. . . .." I think he's a very funny man.

Matthew Huttner, writing an article for *Esquire* magazine about women composers, asked Oscar, "as one of our foremost composers" to answer the questions:

(1) Why in your opinion are there so few outstanding female composers?
(2) Whom do you consider now to be the top female composer in America?

---

[2] The actual lyric from the song "Bloody Mary" does not include "Joe," merely "Her skin is tender as DiMaggio's glove."

(3) What do you consider to be the basic requirements for composing good popular music?

(4) Do you think that women can develop these requirements to the same extent
as men?

Oscar Hammerstein to Matthew Huttner, May 4, 1949

Dear Mr. Huttner:

With no wish to be uncooperative, here are the only answers I can
make to your four questions:

1. I don't know.
2. I don't know.
3. Sincerity.
4. I don't know.

Incidentally, I am not—as you described me in your first paragraph—"one
of our foremost composers." I am not a composer at all.

Very truly yours,

Oscar Hammerstein, II

Myra Finn to Oscar Hammerstein, circa April 1949

Dear Oc,

It is difficult for me to tell you how much I enjoyed S. P. the other
night. It is easily the most satisfactory evening in the theatre I've
ever spent.

If satisfactory seems a weasel word I'm sorry, but it does express
what I mean. The whole thing was so <u>easy</u> to see + hear. Never a moment
of strain or embarrassment. Several things impressed me particularly.
In the first place, not stressing Pinza as an opera star, is, I believe, something that few people would have the confidence + restraint to do. He is
perfect. It's odd to want to describe a middle aged somewhat portly man
as "cute", but that is just what I want to do!

I also want to give vent to my pleasure at sitting a whole evening
in the theatre with no restless sitting in the dark between scenes. How
simply that is done, + what a <u>satisfactory</u> innovation it is.

One thing I am curious about tho. In the reviews I read no one even hinted at your wonderful propaganda song. It is beautifully done + came as a complete surprise to me.

You notice I don't mention Mary Martin. Anything I might say about her would sound like the mouthings of an adolescent.

I loved the whole thing – + should like to see it again. Let me know when I may –

Yrs

Mike

P.S. I see I forgot to say "thank you" after all. Thank you.

Photo 19 Mary Martin in *South Pacific*

There is a long tradition of marketing and endorsements of products associated with show business and stars. In the teens Vernon (and particularly) Irene Castle lent their names and images to any manner of things including dolls, cigars, cosmetics, and clothes. With *South Pacific* there was an explosion of what was then referred to as "commercial tie-ups"—to the extent that managing such things ultimately became a full-time staff position. Prior to *South Pacific* I am not aware of any actual product placement *in* a Broadway show.

Milton Biow[3] to Oscar Hammerstein, May 4, 1949

Dear Okie:

In "South Pacific" I have three great problems:

They're using Coca Cola bottles, we handle Pepsi-Cola; they're using Rheingold Beer, we handle Ruppert; they're using some cigarette—not Philip Morris.

The only client smart enough to see it quickly—or at all—was Al Lyon.

What can I do to get Philip Morris used? Can you help me—or tell me how I can help myself?

Greetings.

Cordially,

Milt

Oscar Hammerstein to Milton Biow, May 18, 1949

Dear Milt:

I am a little embarrassed because both you and Al Lyon have thanked me for putting the Philip Morris package in the show, and that was not done.

I had sent word down to the stage manager to do this, and you had been told about it and assumed that this was equivalent to a fait accompli. The facts are, I have since learned, that our general manager—who has

---

[3] Milton Biow was one of the seminal figures in the advertising business, forming an agency in 1917 that later was credited as being the first to do national ad campaigns on radio and television.

always taken charge of all these things in all our shows, had made a deal with Chesterfield and that is why they are in the show. It is hard to back out on that now because it was a bonafide agreement made by our representative. I am sorry I can't do anything about this. We'll just have to be on our toes quicker the next time.

Love,

Oscar Hammerstein, II

Oscar Hammerstein to Josh Logan, May 8, 1949

Dear Josh:

It was good to hear from you from the ship, and a nice warm feeling of good humor and sentiment emerged from your misspelled letter and lodged itself in me.

I do hope we meet somewhere but, at the moment, we have no definite plans. The most likely place, of course, would be in England in July. The season ends, of course, with the Goodwood racing meeting, but I can't meet you there because some time ago my grey topper was disfigured by Jim and Susan in a hastily produced charade honoring one of my birthdays. We may, therefore, have to meet you at Lyon's Corner House.

The news from here is all better than good. The advance hovers somewhere between four hundred thousand and five hundred thousand dollars, the audience hovers up around the chandeliers throughout most of the performance and Pinza continues to hover over Mary Martin to everyone's delight and, perhaps, his own private frustration.

The music sales this week will catch up and pass the total music sales of "Kiss Me Kate," since its opening, and from several sources we have learned that the albums, in the first few days, have already surpassed the total sale of albums of "KMK."

Dick tells me that the Spewacks saw "South Pacific" the other night, came to Mary's dressing room afterwards, heard a great deal of gushing from other people, remained after those other people had left, spent twenty minutes with Mary, Dick H and Dick R and left without having said one word about "South Pacific." This is some kind of world's record for keeping the wrong balance in the air without dropping it.

We had a swell time in Florida. Larry and Mildred both send their love. We flew to Bimini for two days, went out in a glass-bottom boat and did some fishing from it. This was a humiliating experience because we could look through the glass bottom and see the fish nibbling away our bait. The score ended in a shut-out for the fish, but the air and the sun were lovely. The air was invigorating and the sun was enervating, and this ended in a tie. For another two days we went into the Everglades under the auspices of the Audubon Society and studied wild life. I have learned to identify the Roseate Spoonbill, the Louisiana Heron, the Snowy Egret, and at some distance I can tell a vulture from an eagle because when they soar, an eagle's wings are flattened out, the vulture's wings form an obverse V. I've also met a bird called the Man o' War who lives on fish but can't catch them himself, and so he gets his food by scaring smaller birds to drop their fish. My two day study only reinforced my theory that birds have been misunderstood for many years. They have been built up by poets and sentimental naturalists to connote gentleness and beauty when, as a matter of fact, they are the most predatory, vicious and murderous living beings, and as for their beauty, they have it only when they are far away. Close up, their mean, small, reptilian eyes give them away. I have turned this material over to Philip Wylie, whose talent for invective is superior to my own, and he is working on it. I warned him that this was an unpopular idea, but he said that is what attracted him about it.

My fretting son was up for dinner last night, and he is torn between the worries of all the replacements in "Mister Roberts" and the thrill of having been given this responsibility. Piercing his protective pessimism, which he wears as a Turkish woman wears her veil, I am led to suspect that he is secretly elated and optimistic about all the people he is working with. I have an idea that this is a great experience for him and that he is going to do a very good job.

I have an idea that there is any number of attractive and trifling data I could add to this letter, but I am trying not to think of these because my morning is spent, my energy is waning and your time, at the moment, is too valuable to waste because you are spending it on pleasure. With this somewhat pompous and unconvincing excuse for closing a letter, I close with love to you both from both of us.

As ever,

Oscar Hammerstein, II

Thomas Heggen was the author of the novel *Mister Roberts* and co-wrote the play adaptation with Josh Logan, who also directed. On May 19, at the age of thirty, Heggen was found dead in his bathtub. Some speculated that his death was a suicide, while others vehemently objected. Intentional or not, a combination of alcohol and medication contributed to his drowning.

Oscar Hammerstein to Josh Logan, June 3, 1949

Dear Josh:

I felt impelled to write to you two weeks ago, until I started to compose a letter and felt that nothing I could say about Tom Heggen would help you any, and that I could only accentuate the shock and grief you must feel. Not having known him as a friend, my grief was small compared to my fury and impatience with whatever strange and warped thinking deprived the world of the contribution he may have given it later. I have tried to analyze the source of this tragedy, and I can only put it under the general heading of a lack of faith in the world as the wonderful place it is to live in. The failure to recognize this obvious fact and the tendency to becloud it by overstressing what is wrong, seems to me the greatest handicap that exists against the generation which in other respects seem in every way superior to other generations. I can't say more on this subject without writing a book or a play and perhaps that's what I ought to do.

I had John Swope come over today to photograph, of all things, my hands. This is because somebody wrote to me and said she wanted to draw them and add them to a collection of hands she has drawn. She said she needed a photograph of mine, and it was one of those requests too bizarre to refuse.

John told me you were enroute to Paris, where you would stay a couple of weeks and go on to London. There is still a twenty-to-one chance that Dorothy and I might meet you there (I mean twenty-to-one against). It depends on a great many inconsistent and paradoxical considerations. Shirley frowned as I dictated that last sentence, and I wonder why.

Yesterday Dick and I were honored at the Columbia commencement, by each being awarded a Medal of Excellence, together with two other alumni. I wore a cap and gown for the first time since I graduated in 1916. I also wore my B.A. loop or whatever they call that thing they throw over your head. It is no use denying that I felt very important indeed, and I don't see how judges can mete out pure justice in robes like these because one feels over-confident of one's opinions and has not the proper humility for clear thinking. Dick and I were pikers, because at the same exercises Helen Hayes was given a degree of Doctor of Laws, and I think I shall never forget how pretty she looked in her cap and gown as she received her citation.- not a bit like Portia, but more like the Barnard seniors. She seemed, however, much more frankly delighted than they were. At the alumni luncheon she made a darling speech. What a girl!

Pinza has been out twice with laryngitis, but he is back now. John Swope told me that his Dorothy had seen the play the other night, arriving as the curtain was rising. She had not heard the announcement and sat through the whole show entranced with Dick Eastham who she thought was Pinza. I don't believe he is that good, but he is an exceptionally fine understudy. And each night, entering a few minutes after the groans with which the audience greeted the stark announcement of Pinza's illness, he never failed to win them over so that by the time he sang the waltz, he received an ovation.

The columnists are busy, and so are all the inside dopesters, with the most fantastic rumors that ever surrounded a show. It is said that Pinza has never had laryngitis but is a temperamental opera star who just appears when he feels like it. It is said that he and Mary are carrying on a hot backstage romance and those who hear this take it up from there and invent their own details. It is said that Pinza has had nothing wrong with his throat but he thinks there is, and he must constantly attend a psychiatrist to be told that he can sing. Applause is not apparently enough. Then there is the big ticket speculators scandal which has its various versions. I do not subscribe to the theory that all kinds of publicity is good for plays, and I think that this is bad publicity. I think it is harming the play quite as much as a hundred small boys with bean shooters can harm the hull of a dreadnought.

I sat through the show last week and can report to you that it is in very fine shape indeed, that I made only a few notes and they were of such a character that I could delegate John Fearnley[4] to relay them to the cast.

I also sat through a performance of all the understudies this week and within the limits of what can be expected from understudies, I think that we are very well protected. Sandy, I am sure, would make a big hit with the

---

[4] John Fearnley, the stage manager for *Carousel*, subsequently became the casting director for Rodgers and Hammerstein, at least through *Pipe Dream*. He was considered a critical member of their support team.

audience, although the play would suffer a good deal in the eyes and ears of anyone who had ever seen Mary play the part. Sandy's chief handicap is her youth. She doesn't look too young, but she "talks" too young—if you get what I mean.

Last night, the Schwabs came in from Montauk Point and we went out with the Hallidays. Mary is looking wonderful and fairly sailing. I was dancing with her and she said, "Nobody could have expected this kind of success, could they?" I said, "Nobody but Josh, but he used to get a little tight and say, 'Let's face it, this is going to be the Goddamndest show that was ever done.'" There is so much more gossip.

Shirley broke her foot, but will soon get rid of her cast. Susan is dancing around the house in strange costumes. And Jimmy arrived today from North Carolina with, I believe, an impressive row of "C's" on his report card, and a record of having underestimated his budget three times during the last term. It is obvious that somewhere in Chapel Hill he has something "to put on a clean white suit for."[5]

Love to you both from both of us.

As ever,

Oscar Hammerstein, II

Laurence Schwab to Oscar Hammerstein, June 3, 1949

Dear Mr. Hammerstein:

Tonking is a Northeastern Province of French Indo-China. The Province of Kwang-Si and Wan-Nan of China proper border it to the north. The chief population is Ammanese, but Chinese undoubtedly infiltrate.

Kindly inform Bloody Mary and daughter of their heritage.

Sincerely,

Laurence Schwab.

RESEARCH EXPERT FOR

LAZY AUTHORS.

---

[5] Oscar is quoting from his own song, "There is Nothin' Like a Dame": "We got nothing to put on a clean white suit for, / What we need is what there ain't no substitute for".

Incidentally it has just occurred to us that you boys ought to remember a certain play—the initials are E.W. [East Wind]—which was laid in a place called Indo-China. There are 108,000 reasons.

Oscar Hammerstein to Laurence Schwab, June 7, 1949

Dear Larry:

Thank you for your research. I followed your suggestion and informed Bloody Mary and her daughter of their heritage. It turns out that all this time they thought they were Koreans.

Looking forward to seeing you soon, on a dune, in the light of the moon.

Please excuse me if I stop this letter abruptly. I have just got an idea for a song.

Love from us both.

As ever,

Oscar Hammerstein, II

Afro-American Newspapers to Oscar Hammerstein, June 15, 1949

SINCE CBS FORBIDS OFFENSIVE RACIAL EPITHETS IN SONGS HOW ABOUT ELIMINATING DARKY FROM OLD MAN RIVER.

REPLY DPR COLLECT

Oscar Hammerstein to Afro-American Newspapers, June 16, 1949

GENTLEMEN:

IN ANSWER TO YOUR TELEGRAM SUGGESTING ELIMINATING DARKY FROM OL' MAN RIVER THIS IS NOT MY WORD BUT IS THE INVENTION OF SOME SINGERS. THE MODERN LYRICS IN OL' MAN RIVER AS USED IN THE RECENT PRODUCTION OF SHOWBOAT IS "COLORED FOLKS WORK ON THE MISSISSIPPI."

VERY TRULY YOURS

OSCAR HAMMERSTEIN II

A fan of Oscar's who wrote him occasional letters, asked about the "haunting song" "Bali Ha'I,'" specifically wanting to know what "Ha'I" is an abbreviation for.

Oscar Hammerstein's secretary to Walter Ayling, June 29, 1949

Mr. Hammerstein received your letter of June 21st. . . .and in answer to your question concerning the song "Bali Ha'i", the latter word, in rough translation, means "on the sea" in Chinese . . . a la Shanghai.

I hope this is the information you wanted.

Best wishes.

Sincerely,

Sec'y

Leland Hayward to Oscar Hammerstein (excerpt), June 22, 1949

We had dinner with [Maurice] Chevalier the other night and I hit him with the idea of doing "South Pacific" in Paris. He doesn't know the score so I have sent for some records for him. He looks absolutely sensational. I doubt if he would ever stay put long enough for a run, but I think we ought to all come over here and do "South Pacific". I think it could be regulated so you could gross as much as $25,000 a week. The Folies Bergeres grosses about $20,000, and I really think it would run in Paris forever, and we could all make a lot of francs, which would be quite useless since neither Dorothy or Nan care anything about Paris or clothes or furniture or jewels. But actually, just to spread American culture seems to be kind of our duty. Actually, I am going around to look over two or three theatres with a guy and figure out about grosses and stages, etc. It would be a terrible sacrifice on Dorothy's part to have to come over with you but maybe she would be willing to make it.

Oscar Hammerstein to Josh Logan, July 6, 1949

Dear Josh,

This is the first letter I have tried to write you on my new dictaphone. I have, however, been using the dictaphone for about a month or so. I have bought two sending machines, one for the country and one for the city— and then there was one receiving machine for Shirley to use in town.

Following your last letter I visited South Pacific and watched Myron McCormick. I found his performance excellent in every respect. It is true I saw only the first act. I shall try to catch the second act this week. The rest of the performance was fine—even thrilling. I don't know whether it has improved. I certainly feel that the audiences have. That night, during the act, the audience behaved like a large group of people who had all met somewhere else and said, "Let's all go over to the Majestic Theatre and get drunk." Their behavior was irrational . . . they jumped at every joke and every note of the music like fish to bait they loved and didn't care whether they got hooked or not. (I feel that that last sentence would have been constructed more neatly if I had been writing with a pencil instead of dictating in this devil machine.) When Mary sang "Wonderful Guy", she did not quite get out the last note before they burst in with applause. Then she walked over to the hat - like a barefoot boy with feet of vanilla - and the applause grew in volume and intensity. At the end of the song when all the girls join her, the applause was deafening and a couple of whistles could be heard. This, of course, lasted and carried over into the entrance of the girls with, some more to spare. When Mary reappeared and started to do the turns across the stage, there were definite whistles and it sounded more like a football game than a show. I am not sure but what, in some way, we have combined all man's emotions into that play so that the reactions are somewhat like the combination of a big football game and a bull fight and grand opera and tragedy and comedy, the thrills of first love, fireworks on the Fourth of July and a soupcon of that exaltation which the Wright Brothers must have felt when their first mechanical kite left the ground. Now I'm drunk!

Not so happy is my report on the tedious work I have been doing trying to get the script ready for publication. I have always liked Charlie Atkin and have considered him a fairly capable stage manager. I did not know, however, that he was possessed of a talent of a very special kind. In doing over the script, he has, with unerring accuracy, managed to eliminate every stage direction which should have been preserved for the printed version . . . and he has, with equal care, left in all the stage directions which are no longer of any use to us—where we have changed the direction. You remember the careful description which opened the second act? That is out . . . and he has substituted merely a list of names of the girls and boys who appear in that. This is very useful for him in running this company, but it will be of little interest to people who read the printed version of South Pacific and it won't be very much use to stage managers who do the show with other companies.

Actually, Charlie has made an excellent script for the running of this particular stage at the Majestic for this particular company. All the names are in and at the back of the book he has a very complete light play and costume plot. His cues are also in very good shape throughout the script, but this is a special thing. He doesn't want anyone else ever to run a stage of this company and he doesn't want anyone to read the book. I have been on this work for about three weeks now—a little more, perhaps. The fact that these three weeks happen to have been the worst hot spell I can remember since I have been living in the eastern United States has not helped any. Part of the job I have done on airplanes. . . .Last week we made a flying trip first to Chicago to visit my uncle for two days and then to Los Angeles where I accepted an invitation to make a speech to the Screen Writers Guild and award a prize for "Snake Pit." My real interest, however, was to make the speech and represent the Author's League as its president and try to establish better relations between the two bodies. I think in some measure I accomplished this. Dorothy went with me and we stopped with Charlie Brackett and had a very pleasant three days with him. We also saw Alice in her new home with her new husband and she cooked a dinner for us of which she and we were all very proud. We were gone only six days all together. While I was out there, I heard a story which touched me deeply. Cole Porter arrived a month or so ago and gave presents to about 50 of his friends—an album of South Pacific to each. This is my idea of a gentleman, a sportsman and an artist.

My other mission out there was to interview small male moppets for "The Happy Time." I auditioned about eight and found one who is quite promising. (Who is the little English boy who made such a success in some picture that has something to do with an embassy? With these definite inquiries, you should be able to trace him for me when you get to England and let me know what you think of him.) In our explorations so far I find that boys of thirteen seem to take a big jump and are far ahead of boys of twelve and eleven. The trouble with casting a boy of thirteen for the part is that he soon becomes fourteen and starts to look like an old man.

Otherwise, I have occupied myself preparing a selection of my lyrics which Simon and Schuster are going to print in the form of a book of poems. I am going to write a foreword explaining my own appraisal of them as lyrics for the theatre, rather than poems to be considered divorced from the dramatic and musical content. I am also going to write an afterword for the book and discuss lyric writing in general with some particular references to the lyrics included in the book. And I am also going to use some of my worst early efforts so that young men may be encouraged. I think this should be done by everyone who attains any success at all. The trouble is that most successful men scare the hell out of young men by appearing to have been perfect from the very start. I think their early imperfections are very important- to guide and encourage young men who wish to follow them in whatever profession they have been making their success.

I was very happy at your report that Emlyn Williams has finished a play and that you like it. I demand a copy at once to mutilate, maim or nibble as I see fit. Dick and Dorothy Rodgers sold their Fairfield house with the intention of buying a new one on Long Island. They have wound up buying a new one ten miles from their old one in Fairfield. It is a very beautiful place, a lovely big house with nicely laid-out gardens, a swimming pool and a tennis court . . . and a fine meadow in which to place croquet course. I have just heard the bell on the Dictaphone. What a good idea! It is like a factory whistle. I gather up my pail and my lunchbox and start home to the wife.

Love to yours,

The Happy Time by Samuel Taylor was the fifth show produced but not written by Rodgers and Hammerstein. The promising "moppet" was Bobby Henrey in the film The Fallen Idol. The part ultimately went to Johnny Stewart who went on to originate the role of Prince Chulalongkorn in The King and I.

Jean Darling, the original Carrie Pipperidge in Carousel, in a letter to Oscar wrote: "Read that you and Dick are doing 'The Happy Time' this fall and I was wondering if there'll be a part I can read for. I do hope there is something for me."

Oscar Hammerstein to Jean Darling, August 3, 1949

Dear Jean:

We haven't seriously approached the casting problems of "The Happy Time," because nothing can be done until we find a 12-year-old brat who can act. When you return to New York why don't you phone us. Maybe we'll have some news for you then.

Love

Oscar Hammerstein, II

Oscar Hammerstein to Mrs. Herman L. Fox, August 6, 1949

Dear Mrs. Fox:

The interesting comment about "New Moon"[6] is that we produced it in Philadelphia and it was a hopeless flop. I heard a couple coming out of the theatre before the curtain was down one night, and the woman said to the man, "They can never fix this one if they work for the rest of their lives." We closed the show after two weeks in Philadelphia, and we wrote a new libretto keeping very little of the old one. We also wrote a new score. What was left of the original production was the scenery and costumes. We also gave it a new cast. We re-opened the play in Cleveland eight months later, and then we played Pittsburgh and then brought it to New York, where it became one of the biggest operetta vehicles ever produced here. It has been playing on and off all over the world ever since, which means for the past twenty-one years.

I'm afraid I haven't time to give you all the material you would like on the other plays, but it seems to me that you have all I could tell you if you have read the Saturday Evening Post and Colliers articles.

Very truly yours,

Oscar Hammerstein, II

Rodgers and Hammerstein's success as producers guaranteed a steady flow of scripts submitted for consideration. The script sent in by Jessyca Russell is variously described in her cover letter as a "melodrama," "gangster fare," and "cops and robbers on stage." Jack Gaver was a drama critic and Broadway columnist for United Press International; he also became Russell's husband.

Oscar Hammerstein to Jessyca Russell, August 6, 1949

Dear Jessyca:

Thank you for sending me Jack's [Gaver] script. And please excuse the delay in sending my comment—my various duties involving the Author's

---

[6] *The New Moon* opened in 1928 and ran for 509 performances. With music by Sigmund Romberg, the score includes four classic songs: "Softly, As in a Morning Sunrise," "Stouthearted Men," "One Kiss," and "Lover, Come Back to Me."

League, ASCAP and Dick's and my future production schedule has left me with little time to read manuscripts.

My judgment on these types of plays is not very good because I do not like them, even though they are hits. I would, therefore, not be very much of an asset in producing one of them. I hope that it will be produced, and I wish Jack and his collaborator the best of luck.

While I'm distributing good wishes, have a few yourself.

Sincerely,

Oscar Hammerstein, II

Oscar Hammerstein to James Geller (excerpt), August 6, 1949

You have struck the wrong man. My allergy to plays about Hollywood is unique and extraordinary. I'll be happy to read the other play Dudley has written if you will send it to me.

Oscar Hammerstein to Helen Vail, August 6, 1949

Dear Miss Vail:

I have read "Reno Ranch." The background is a good one. I think your story is lacking in dramatic variation, and naive in its approach to the problems and characters that make up the Reno scene. I have an idea that since you were designing this story for a play you tried to make it "light." It is my opinion that the story of musical plays should be very sturdy. I think perhaps you should use this material for a musical play with the same serious and genuine approach you would give it if you were writing a "straight" play.

It was kind of you to submit your manuscript to me. I wish you the very best of luck with it.

Sincerely,

Oscar Hammerstein, II

P.S. "Reno Ranch" is herewith enclosed.

OH, II

Oscar Hammerstein to Wolcott Gibbs, August 13, 1949

Dear Wolcott Gibbs:

This is to thank you for your graceful appraisal of my lyrics to appear soon in Cosmopolitan. It was kind of you to undertake this assignment, and I am proud of your comments. I value these the more because your article is neither gushing nor patronizing and has the ring of honesty. This, to be sure, is no new quality in your work. Your comments on "Allegro" had the same ring of honesty. Disagreeing with many of them, as I did, I nevertheless respected them—or grew to respect them after that first quick homicidal impulse left me.

All the best to you,

Sincerely,

Oscar Hammerstein, II

Oscar Hammerstein to Robert Behr, August 16, 1949

Dear Bob:

In the last line of your letter to me you say you believe in "Bandana", Mr. Hammerstein. I hope you will share my belief. The question is What is this "Bandana"? that you hope I believe in. It is not a finished play. It is a very full scenario of the first act of a play. One can be interested or not interested in this portion of a work, but what kind of belief can one have in it. Belief in it as what . . . as something that may turn out to be something some day.

In an earlier paragraph you say that throughout this last arduous year there have been many times when it seemed that the play was ready for me to read, but that despite the advice of friends, you did not give it to me. But, Bob, this is not a play yet. This is still what it was eighteen months or two years ago when you first submitted [it] to me. It is an idea for a play. As I vaguely remember what you first told me, this is an improvement on that idea and this is as far as you have gotten in all that time. I take for granted the truth of your suggestion that in this time you have met many problems not only literary, dramaturgic, and musical, but also social and economic. I am sorry that you have had these handicaps, but I cannot share these troubles with you. I have too many problems of my own and of other people to whom I am already attached. I don't wish to take on any more.

Let me give you the best advice you have ever had. Stop talking about this play and write it . . . finish it and then submit it to me. By finishing a play, I mean writing the dialogue, the directions, the lyrics, the music. Write it all as well as you can and as completely as you can and then I will read it. This is what all writers must do eventually if they want to be writers. Stop talking this over with your friends and with me. Go ahead and do the job as well as you can.

If I thought you had no talent or even if I thought this particular idea was a hopeless one, I would not give you this advice. I believe that you have the start of a good story here, but it is one that depends entirely on treatment. Some of your detailed description suggests that you have in mind just how to treat it. Well, why not do it. Go ahead and write it, Bob. . . .write it.

All the best wishes to you.

Sincerely,

Oscar Hammerstein II

Oscar Hammerstein to Dorothy and Howard Lindsay, September 19, 1949

Dear Dorothy and Howard:

Your surrey is on my mantel, and it is hard for me to imagine what the mantel looked like before it was there. It now looks so essential to my study. Not only does it recall "Oklahoma," but it has for me a much more powerful and basic nostalgia. I cannot help feeling that this toy and I are about the same age. I had iron fire engines and milk wagons and light artillery pieces. And when I look at this one, I am sitting on the floor in a Harlem apartment on a rainy day. It was very sweet of you to think of us when you found this treasure, and I don't know what you could have given us that I would like more. Best wishes for a successful and happy tour, and love from us both.

As ever,

Oscar Hammerstein, II

Howard Lindsay was an actor, director, and playwright, largely in collaboration with Russel Crouse (they later wrote the script for *The Sound of Music*). Lindsay's wife was the actress Dorothy Stickney (they played the King and Queen in Rodgers and Hammerstein's *Cinderella*). At the time of this letter, they had recently completed their Broadway run in *Life with Mother*.

Oscar Hammerstein to John Crosby, New York Herald Tribune, September 20, 1949

Dear John Crosby:

As your constant reader and occasional admirer, I must take issue with your condemnation of a line in the lyric of "They Didn't Believe Me." You say: "The song contains the most awkward line ever written by Oscar Hammerstein—'and I'm certainly going to tell them.'" I find it an especially graceful line, very much in character with the spirit of the song and easy to sing—even fun to sing.

The merit of the line is, of course, a matter of opinion. You don't like it and I do. Neither of us can prove the other is wrong. I can, however, prove beyond all shadow of a doubt that this is not the most awkward line I have ever written. I didn't write it.

All good wishes anyway.

Sincerely,

Oscar Hammerstein, II

The Kern song "They Didn't Believe Me," from the 1914 musical *The Girl from Utah*, boasts a lyric by Herbert Reynolds. The published lyric actually reads: "And I cert-n'ly am goin' to tell them." However, almost from the beginning, singers have adopted the far more graceful "and I'm certainly going to tell them"—often using the contraction "gonna."

Hammerstein was often approached by friends and colleagues for input into their own productions, and Rodgers and Hammerstein were also approached as potential investors in shows in addition to their own productions. Prior to producing *Gentlemen Prefer Blondes*, Herman Levin had produced shows as diverse as the Harold Rome revue, *Call Me Mister*, Sartre's *No Exit*, and Shakespeare's *Richard III*. After *Gentlemen Prefer Blondes* he had his greatest success with *My Fair Lady*.

Oscar Hammerstein to Herman Levin, September 30, 1949

Dear Herman:

I have re-read "Gentlemen Prefer Blondes," and send you these reactions for what they are worth.

All the best to you.

Sincerely,

Oscar Hammerstein, II

Notes on "Gentlemen Prefer Blondes"

The adagio act is a fine idea but I think it is essential to introduce some of these characters before we see them in the scene which leads up to their dance. The more they can be integrated in the story the better.

Scene where Esmond gets the wire from his father; this is under-written. The reaction is too smooth and the solution too quick. It is not believable this way.

The shortness of the second act is a great worry, I think. There are some very good moments in it, especially the first scene, and perhaps that can be extended and made into a very much longer one than appears in the script.

Second scene Act II: in the taxicab is not only short but very weak indeed. The scene is obviously written only to cue in the song "You Say You Care." I know it is difficult to add much thickness to this story of Dorothy and Henry's but I think it should be done in some way.

The theory of the final scene is very good but it is good enough to be written more completely and with more subtlety. I think the old man capitulates too quickly. There is a definite feeling of 'hurry up, we must get the curtain down here' and I don't think that should be present in a scene which has so much amusement and ingenuity in its conception. The play will not be long and there is no need to hurry up. The scene ought to be written for all it is worth and the character of Esmond's father given more dimension.

Regarding the casting as announced in the paper so far: George Givot . . . When Herman spoke to me about Givot, I thought it was a good idea because I have for a long time thought that George could play a part. He is a funny man and he can sing and he is good-looking. On reading over the play I am just wondering if he can be straight enough because this is essentially a straight part and not one for a comedian. The things that happen around him are funny but they are funny mainly because he _is_ a straight man, a kind of a sympathetic and attractive goof with no harm in his soul and with a real love for Lorelei. I hope Givot will not try to be funny if he is cast in the part. The general list of names seems to me susceptible to the criticism that it may be cast too broadly. Rex Evans is just a very trite rubber-stamp example of English gentleman. Alice Pierce, whenever I have seen her, has been very broad, indeed, and I don't know if I'm going to be prepared to believe either of these two people unless they are held down very sternly by Jack Wilson. Perhaps my conception of the play is too legit-imate but the leading part of Lorelei is going to be played very legitimately by Carol Channing because she is a fine actress. There is going to be nothing unbelievable in her portrayal of the part and I hope her efforts will not be cancelled off by too many clownish characterizations around her.

Oscar Hammerstein to Irving Berlin, October 3, 1949

Dear Irving:

Sven-Olaf Sandberg, a singer whom I met in Sweden when I was there a couple of years ago, sent me a record he made of "They Say It's Wonderful" and "The Girl That I Marry." I am sending the record on to you because I think you will be pleased with it. I don't understand Swedish any more than you do, but it sounds as if they did a good clean job with the lyric translation.

I am delighted to hear of "Miss Liberty's" success.

Love to Ellin and yourself,

As ever,

Oscar Hammerstein, II

Irving Berlin to Oscar Hammerstein, October 4, 1949

Dear Oscar:

Many thanks for sending me that record of "They Say It's Wonderful" and "The Girl That I Marry" sung by Sven-Olaf Sandberg. I'm crazy about this guy's voice and I agree it sounds like a good translation. I'm particularly impressed with the phrasing.

By the way, Irving Hoffman let me read your foreword for the Simon and Schuster book of your lyrics (I understand you didn't object to this) and I think it's swell. Coupled with the lyrics to be published in this book, I'm certain it will be a big hit.

Thanks for your kind words about "Miss Liberty". It really is surprising how well the show has been doing considering the terrible notices we got. Our advance isn't as good as we would wish, but I still feel we'll come out of it with some kind of a hit and pay off.

It was nice hearing from you. Love to you and Dorothy from us.

Always,

Irving

Oscar Hammerstein to Leah Salisbury, October 6, 1949

Dear Miss Salisbury:

I am returning the Gow-d'Usseau play for only one reason. I don't like it. Because of my admiration for the talent of these two men I feel resentment that they have used up any of it on a story and a group of characters who seem to me so unimportant—as well as irritating. I hope I am wrong and I wish them the best of luck.

Sincerely,

Oscar Hammerstein, II

James Gow and Arnaud D'Usseau had written the plays *Tomorrow the World* (1943), about an American couple who adopted a German boy and then had to deal with his Nazi upbringing, and *Deep Are the Roots* (1945), about a Black soldier who returns to the south after World War II and begins a romantic relationship with the daughter of a Senator, for whom his mother had been a servant. Both plays were successes, the latter directed by Elia Kazan.

Drama critic and author Gilbert Gabriel, as a newcomer to the Authors League, following up on a conversation they'd had, wrote Oscar a letter asking about the League's acceptance of a practice he found unacceptable: "The ticket-agency racket has always been a private, profit-snatching enterprise. It is now in such bad odor that the city administration, plus all branches of the theatre, would like to see it altered."

Oscar Hammerstein to Gilbert W. Gabriel, October 13, 1949

Dear Gil:

Your letter effects me as a whirling dervish would be effected if someone should take a tuft of his hair and twist him around so that he might spin faster and longer. At our next meeting let me give you a brief dissertation on the ticket business as I know it. I wish I knew more about it or less about it, but I will tell you what I know.

All the best.

Sincerely,

Oscar Hammerstein, II

Oscar Hammerstein to Billy Rose, October 19, 1949

Dear Billy:

Mike Mok passed on three questions to me which he didn't feel he could answer (this is in connection with a questionnaire you sent him on which you're basing your Reader's Digest piece). In answer to the first question, the weekly net of "South Pacific" ranges between ten and eleven thousand dollars a week. The second question, "How much money has 'Oklahoma!' earned to date for the producers and backers?" My estimate would be somewhere over four million dollars by this time. The answer to the third question, "What is the biggest firm offer made by the movies for the rights to 'Oklahoma!'?" is a tough one because we have never really had a firm offer. We have merely told them it was not for sale. The movie companies make it a practice now to call up Howard Reinheimer every few months and ask if there is any change, and he always says no. There have been however, conversations implying that we could get over three million dollars, and in another instance it was suggested that we might get all the profits. It would be untruthful, however, to say that either of these was a firm offer. They were "feelers." These conversations took place during the first four years of the run, not during the last two years when the picture market has dropped. This gives rise to a natural question: Is the value as great as it was? I think there are two answers. The first is that if we sold the property four years from now, when it is ten years old, if we got less than we would have got a few years ago, we would still be getting more because we could not have kept that when added to the early income that the play was making. The other answer is, however, that from present indications the major road rights will be alive and kicking for many years to come, and bringing us all a greater income than we could derive from any capital sum they could possibly give us. There is a third answer and that is, the longer a play is popular, the more valuable it becomes for pictures. "Ben Hur" ran for twenty-six seasons and then had several revivals, and after that the General Lew Wallace estate finally sold it to Metro for half the profits. The picture grossed ten million dollars which was way ahead of anything before "Gone With The Wind" came along (I would check these figures with Nick Schenk).

The bottom line of all this is, of course, that Dick and I have the movie rights to "Oklahoma!," "Carousel," and "South Pacific" in our safe and instead of selling them, we have the makings of a nice little new movie company of our own, starting off with these three properties.

Hope we see you soon.

Love,

Harry Ruby to Oscar Hammerstein, October 31, 1949

Dear Oscar:

Yours of the 28th in re the song you hum better than you play. There were three lyrics. One was called: Moonlight on the Meadow. This one, when you heard it, a few years ago, you swore you had nothing to do with. There was another you worked on with Bert. I have forgotten it; I can't find it. But I do recall that we were not too hot about it. The third, A KISS TO BUILD A DREAM ON, between us, was yours alone. Having a rather treacherous memory along certain lines, I can assure you I am not mistaken.

Under the circumstances, I thought it only fair to arrange the credits as I did. However, if you want them changed, you can do what you like.

I have not heard from Abe Olman—Robbins Music Corp., since he left. I was wondering whether you had heard from him. No doubt you hadn't—up to the time you wrote the letter.

Tonight—at my age—which shall be nameless, I am going to a Halloween party at Groucho's. About forty of us, all old enough to be somebody's grandfather, will be dressed—that is, in masquerade. I was going to go as a middle-aged Jew, but none of the costume companies has that kind of get-up.

Halloween, while not as sacred as Yum Kipper [*sic*], is nevertheless a very important Jewish holiday. It commemorated the birthday of Meyer Halloween, who distinguished himself as a notary public during the Thirty Years War. According to the little I know about it, gentlemen of a certain religious persuasion, are not allowed to pass counterfeit money until sundown. But it is all right to attend a harlequinade at Groucho's house—which is no worse than passing counterfeit money. AMEN!

Rumor has it that they'll never get Max Gordon again—and that he has $100,000 stashed away in Millie's name. I don't know how that leaked out, considering that Max has told it to everyone he knows.

Please give our very best to Dorothy and you.

Sincerely,

Harry

P.S. The rehearsal for THREE LITTLE WORDS[7] starts today.

Oscar Hammerstein to Harry Ruby, November 7, 1949

Dear Harry:

I will take your word about the song and let you handle the whole thing. I have not heard from Abe Olman.

---

[7] *Three Little Words* was a biopic of Bert Kalmar and Harry Ruby.

What I am mainly interested in is how the Halloween party came out. I was most interested in your description of how the holiday started and I have no further questions on it.

There was undoubtedly a leak in Max Gordon's office. People all over town know the grosses and the net profits of "The Women" when it played Curran's in San Francisco in 1936.

Bob Milford tells me he was in Max's office, and while he was there, Max spoke to Douglas in Washington and gave him a message to give to "Winnie". He then called up Baruch and discussed devaluation with him, and left Bob abruptly because he had an appointment with the mayor. During the conversations, Bob had noticed him writing something on a pad. After Max left Bob could not restrain his curiosity and walked over to the desk to see what Max had written. It was just one word—potroast. It is easy to deduce that he had a date to go to Luchow's that night.

Love to you and Eileen,

"Douglas" refers to General Douglas MacArthur; "Winnie" is Winston Churchill; "Baruch" is Bernard Baruch who, among other things, was a financial advisor to President Roosevelt.

Oscar Hammerstein to Hy Kraft (excerpt), November 12, 1949

Confidentially, "Oklahoma!" is not for sale. Tell everyone!

Oscar Hammerstein to Irene Gallagher, November 30, 1949

Subject: Letter from Nash Airflyte Magazine requesting permission to quote line of "Ol' Man River."

Dear Irene:

You may tell the Nash Airflyte Magazine that it is o.k. to use the words "Fish Gotta Swim, Birds Gotta Fly" in the context they submitted. You may also inform them that these words are not from "Ol' Man River." They are from a song called "Can't Help Lovin' Dat Man." In "Ol' Man River" there is nothing about either swimming or flying. It is mostly rolling.

Love,

In his autobiography, *Musical Stages*, Richard Rodgers wrote: "For the first time in our career, a project was submitted by someone who wanted to play the leading role. Early in 1950 we received a call from Fanny Holtzmann, Gertrude Lawrence's lawyer, asking if we would be interested in writing and producing a musical adaptation of *Anna and the King of Siam*." Although they may not have given the property serious consideration prior to its proposal by Holtzmann, it had, in fact, already been proposed.

William Morris (William Morris Agency) to Oscar Hammerstein, December 8, 1949

Dear Oscar:

Would you be interested in "Anna and the King of Siam" as a book for your adaptation to a musical play?

I am sending a copy herewith for your recollection. With personal best wishes, as ever,

Sincerely,

Bill

Morris

Oscar Hammerstein to Leighton Brill, December 10, 1949

Dear Leighton:

Send me sketches and all the material you have so that I know what the revue is about. A complication has come into our lives. Dick and I find now that we cannot invest in a show without taking on the responsibility of pulling in a lot of other investors. A legend of infallibility has sprung up which gives us the Midas touch and while, of course, this is nonsense to anybody who really knows the uncertainties of show business, the unjustified responsibility can, nevertheless, not be laughed off. We know now when we put up a few thousand dollars of our money we are also putting up several thousand of other peoples money who copy us and, therefore, we have to be very careful indeed. There is no such thing as "taking a flyer" anymore. That is why I must not do anything about your show before I can see whether or not I can come in.

Going to another paragraph in your letter,[8] there is absolutely no truth in anything you read in any Los Angeles paper about anything to do with "South Pacific." We are not making any picture production. Maybe in thirty years—not very much sooner. The one thing that is true is that the National Company will be coming out there this summer. It is equally true that you will be there on the first night. How could you doubt it?

Love,

Oscar Hammerstein, II

It was notoriously difficult to get tickets for *South Pacific*, leading to innumerable complaints. In the letter below Oscar responds to a woman who was horrified to discover that there was such a thing as house seats—that not all ticket buyers had an exactly equal chance to get tickets.

Oscar Hammerstein to Mary Zales, December 12, 1949

Dear Miss Zales:

Regarding your letter and the episode at the box-office, I can interpret it only as something that is quite normal and, I believe, natural. Mr. Rodgers and I, and our two co-producers, and the two stars in the production keep back a limited number of seats each night which we use to accommodate our close friends and business associates. We wrote the play and produced it, and I cannot see anything disgraceful in our reserving the privilege of favoring our friends. There are over 1,600 seats in the house. Mr. Rodgers and I keep out eight each. The rest are on sale at the box-office for patrons who write in, and at the various ticket agencies. The play is so great a success that all three of these mediums are quickly exhausted, and it is difficult to get tickets. Please forgive us for writing and producing such a successful play. I am sorry that you were unsuccessful in getting tickets on the day you went there for the day you asked for. I suggest that if you write in you may have better luck. We reserve certain weeks for mail orders. As I have said before, there are a little over 1,600 seats a night. We can neither increase the

---

[8] Brill's incoming letter included: "Have had a call from the Disney Studios, that you are going to make an independent production of South Pacific (movies), they would like you to look into their facilities. Would you like me to check on this for you?"

number of these seats nor the number of days in the year. As for our holding a few back for our own use and to accommodate our friends, I do not see how you interpret that as "playing politics."

Very truly yours,

Oscar Hammerstein, II

Oscar Hammerstein to Harry Mestayer, December 12, 1949

Dear Harry:

I'm so sorry to hear of your recent hard luck. Here is the $55.00 you need. Please don't make any attempt about paying it back. Take it as a Christmas gift from an old friend.

All the best.

As ever,

Oscar Hammerstein, II

As reported in *The New York Times* on November 27: "The firm of Rodgers and Hammerstein took an option on Irving Elman's dramatization of Sholom Aleichem's 'Tevye's Daughters.'" There's no indication that this was for them to adapt the stories or the play as a musical, although that prospect is a tantalizing one. In 1964 *Tevye's Daughters* became the basis for *Fiddler on the Roof.* But what if . . . ?

Memorandum from Irving Cohen to Richard Rodgers and Oscar Hammerstein, December 12, 1949

Re: TEVYE'S DAUGHTERS

Dear Dick and Oscar:-

I thought you might be interested in the status of the above-entitled property.

I have secured all the necessary agreements from Irving Elman and the heirs of the Estate of Sholom [*sic*] Aleichem, as well as the publishers.

Irving Elman's rights were imperfect, and it was necessary for me to secure additional rights in order to vest you with complete rights of production and to share subsidiary rights.

All agreements have been signed and now require your signature. Elman has also agreed to permit Williamson to publish the score. I will submit agreements to you for signature in the next day or so.

With kindest personal regards.

Sincerely yours.

Irving

Oscar Hammerstein and Richard Rodgers to Josh Logan, December 19, 1949

DEAR JOSH: ANXIOUS TO LEARN WHAT YOU THINK OF "TEVYE'S DAUGHTERS." WHEN AND WHERE CAN WE PHONE YOU.

LOVE,

OSCAR AND DICK

Josh Logan to Richard Rodgers and Oscar Hammerstein, December 26, 1949

FEEL I AM NOT RIGHT FOR TEVYE VERY RICH MATERIAL BUT I DO NOT FEEL FORM HAS BEEN FOUND TO TELL STORY DO NOT CARE ENOUGH ABOUT TEVYE'S FATE WOULD LOVE TO DO ANOTHER SHOW WITH YOU BUT DO NOT THINK THIS THE ONE LOVE TO ALL=

JOSH

Myra Finn to Oscar Hammerstein, circa December, 1949

Dear Oc –

I can be pretty stupid at times. One of my chief reasons for asking you to call me, completely left my mind as we became involved in World

Federation. So rather than risk another hiatus of several days I take this method to inform you of a decision I have made.

After keeping faithfully a promise you extracted from me about 20 years ago, I am about to reneg [*sic*] on it. You probably, with your happy facility for only remembering pleasant things do not recall that you told me "First nights belong to me." Theatre, that is. I reluctantly agreed + as time went on, didn't even miss them. However, 20 years ago I had no idea that such a promise would ever involve Billy. So this is to tell you that starting Dec 22,[9] any show with which Billy is connected—+ you are not—I intend to be present at the opening. I hardly think you can resent that. I am just as proud of him as you can be, + certainly would enjoy speaking personally to his friends + mentors.

This letter is just to avoid any such imbroglio as was caused by the Kadison wedding last summer.

Feeling sure you will understand my sentiments

I am

As ever

Mike

---

[9] This was the opening night for the Garson Kanin play *Rat Race*, for which Billy was the Production Associate.

Chapter Nine
1950

The year began with only one Rodgers and Hammerstein show on Broadway, *South Pacific*. They were preparing to produce two plays by others—*The Happy Time* and *The Heart of the Matter*—and were inches away from beginning work on their next musical, *The King and I*. On January 17, Oscar was elected to the highly prestigious National Institute of Arts and Letters (a precursor of the present-day American Academy and Institute of Arts and Letters).

Oscar Hammerstein to Herman Levin, January 1, 1950

Dear Herman:

I saw the show [*Gentlemen Prefer Blondes*] for the second time last week and enjoyed it very much, but there is one blot on it so easy to remove that I don't understand why you haven't done something about it. After Channing finishes "Diamonds Are A Girl's Best Friend," there is only one possible thing to follow it with—a blackout. If Helen Hayes, Ezio Pinza and whatever stars you can think of made an entrance following that number, nobody would listen to what they had to say. How then can you expect them to do anything but cough—as they do immediately they see two sub-plot characters stroll on to play an unimportant scene, and follow it with a reprise. Believe me, Herman, the show falls from one of its highest peaks to one of the lowest valleys in the space of a split second when those two people enter, and a lull is nothing to introduce when you are approaching the end of your second act. I imagine that the original purpose of this reprise was to plug the song, but this is a very expensive plug indeed, and an unfair burden to impose on a musical play. The songs are there only to serve the play, and not vice versa.

If I seem didactic and pompous about this, I am sorry. But it is an offensive thing to me as a showman to see so unnecessary an excrescence on so agreeable a surface. Please forgive the intrusion. It is a gesture of friendship to you all.

The Letters of Oscar Hammerstein II. Mark Eden Horowitz, Oxford University Press. © Mark Eden Horowitz 2022.
DOI: 10.1093/oso/9780197538180.003.0009

Happy New Year and love from Dorothy and me.

As ever,

Oscar Hammerstein, II

The surprising thing about the letter above is that it was written nearly a month after the show opened, on December 8, 1949.

Leighton Brill was preparing to produce a musical revue in Los Angeles titled *Of All Things*. Brill engaged composer Maurice Engleman and lyricist and writer Alan Alch—"the boys" as described by Oscar—to write the show's songs and sketches.

Oscar Hammerstein to Leighton Brill, January 3, 1950

Dear Leighton:

The boys spent an afternoon going over their material. I like them both very much personally, and there is a good chance that they will probably develop into important contributors to our theatre. I told them that they should make their next project a book show. As you know, I have little sense of what makes a good review [*sic*; revue], because as far as I'm concerned nothing makes a good review. I sat through "Touch and Go" the other night wondering why I hadn't stayed home, and it is a big hit. That part of the material I heard for your show seemed no worse, and no better (except that these boys write much better songs than are in "Touch and Go"[1]). The sketches seem fair, but neither hilariously funny or startlingly original. This is an admission that my lack of enthusiasm for this is no different than my lack of enthusiasm for all the run-of-the-mill reviews that I have seen, and it should in no way deter you from your project. I heartily approve of what you are doing and I wish you the very best of luck—as you well know. I can't recommend to Dick that our firm take any part in it because we should really feel that anything we go into is something great and carrying with it the chances for either a big financial success or, at least, a chance for cultural or artistic value.

[1] *Touch and Go* was a Broadway musical revue, written by Jean and Walter Kerr, with music by Jay Gorney. It opened in March of 1949 and ran for 176 performances.

I must, however, get back to the two young men who, I believe, under your guidance may soon be doing fine things. They should work more along the lines of "Enter Spring." This is by far the best song, the one with the finest quality.

A comment about your budget—or rather, a question: Is it possible for you to have this kind of budget and at the same time employ Actors' Equity people. I note that all the minimums and rules of Actors' Equity are ignored, as well as those of the Dramatists Guild. I assume that you have checked all this and in some way these kind of things can be done on the coast.

I didn't act on your suggestion regarding Chappell's, and I told the boys why. There is no point in it. They are in a much stronger position once they have had a production. Then they can sign a real contract with the publishing house. Right now I don't believe they can sign any kind of contract. Publishers, like agents, only hop on the bandwagons after they've started to move.

I am really rooting hard for you, Leighton, and I hope you put this over and we all wish you a Happy New Year and send our love.

As ever.

Oscar Hammerstein, II

P.S. Those fruits you sent are wonderful and would raise hell with my diet, if I were on one.

OH, II

Oscar Hammerstein (New Haven) to Arthur Hammerstein (excerpt), January 3, 1950

We open [*The Happy Time*] here, in New Haven, on Thursday night, January 5th. I will send you the notices, of course, and from Boston as well. Right now I can tell you that I'm very much afraid that our first act lacks substance. Our second act seems fine and most of the cast are very good indeed. I have already got the author [Samuel Taylor] busy trying to give weight to the first act and not to depend too much on charm.

Oscar Hammerstein to Jean Fly, January 9, 1950

Dear Jean:

Thank you for the beautiful corsage. I will wear it with my blue. I think you know it. It's a little number I had on when we had dinner together that night, and you admired it. It is not a new suit, but I wear it on opening nights and on the road. Much as I prize the flower, it is a poor substitute for having you and Ted in the audience on a Boston opening. We will send you a full report.

Love to you both.

As ever,

Oscar Hammerstein, II

Oscar Hammerstein to Lawrence Langner (Theatre Guild), January 11, 1950

Dear Lawrence:

I am returning your script of "Come Back, Little Sheba" under separate cover. Dick and I will be very glad to avail ourselves of your kind offer to let us have 1% each. We shall buy the 2% as a corporation, and I will instruct the Reinheimer office to get in touch with you about this.

I think it is a true and heartbreaking play, and I hope that it will be very successful, not only because of my friendship for the producers, but also because human sympathy and understanding for unfortunate people is the greatest thing the theatre can accomplish.

Love,

Oscar Hammerstein, II

Come Back, Little Sheba opened on Broadway on February 15. The first play written by William Inge, the drama starred Shirley Booth and ran for 191 performances. Booth won a Tony for her Broadway performance, and an Oscar for the subsequent film.

Oscar Hammerstein (Boston) to Arthur Hammerstein,
January 11, 1950

Dear Uncle Arthur:

We have a strange problem with this show. It is a combination of a tender human comedy and a big laughing farce and, if you will notice, several of the Boston critics took exception to this combination. The principal critic, Elliot Norton, was the only one who gave it an unqualified rave. In New Haven the show was packed with many more laughs than we had anticipated, and in Boston at the opening night, it was received with much more interest in the dramatic side and less demonstrativeness on the comedy side. I am inclined to think this is closer to the way New York will receive it, and during our two weeks up here we will try to work in this direction—without losing the good laughs.

The second night audience in Boston were, as usual, more like New Haven, and I am convinced that this is a great audience show. The only thing to worry about is that first night in New York when the cast can be thrown off their balance so far by not hearing the laughs of a normal audience.

I suppose that by now you are beginning to shape up your benefit. I hope you repeat the success you have every year. After we get back to New York, and the show has opened, I will write to you or call you up. How soon do you get your telephone?

I was almost forgetting the big news. Reggie is to be married again! The date is February 11th, and this time he is marrying a very fine girl. I wish he had met her first.

Dorothy joins me in sending our love to you and your Dorothy.

Oscar Hammerstein, II

Beatrice Lillie to Dorothy Hammerstein, January 20, 1950

Darling Dorothy,

It made me very happy to receive a letter from you. As far as I'm concerned you can have all my paintings.

Here we are in Portland . . . snowed in. 'Spect to be back in New York in about six weeks where I certainly hope I can see more of you, if it's not a rude answer.

What about that Laton [*sic*] Brill marrying Xenia Banks who is in our show. She is really a very, very nice girl and I feel that they will be very happy. It certainly was a surprise.

Now then get your husband in a corner and ask him what about "Mary Poppins" or the "Brass Boot Knob".

Also what about your daughter? When is it taking place?

All my love,

Bees Knees

Australian by birth, Dorothy Hammerstein left Melbourne at twenty-two, went briefly to England, and then came to New York where she was quickly cast in *André Charlot's Revue of 1924*. The show's stars were Lillie, Gertrude Lawrence, and Jack Buchanan. It was there that Dorothy and Bea formed what would be a life-long friendship. Ironically, around the same time that Lillie was suggesting that Oscar transform *Mary Poppins* into a musical, Oscar's protégé, Stephen Sondheim, was attempting his own musical version.

The Happy Time opened on Broadway on January 24.

Ernest Martin to Oscar Hammerstein, January 25, 1950

Dear Oscar:

Thank you very much for your company and for the show last evening.

It's obviously off to a strong start and I'm sure you'll be pleased when the final accounting is made.

We would like very much to have you read a first act draft of "Guys and Dolls", which I hope to be able to put into your hands sometime next week. I'll call you as soon as it is ready.

As I mentioned last night, owing to our dissatisfaction with candidates for the male lead, as well as the need for perfection in all other departments, we undoubtedly will not be able to open the show in New York in May and may even delay until early fall. We are going ahead with our plans at full speed nonetheless, and are making good progress, including the getting of money.

In regard to the latter, we are holding open an amount equal to that which you and Dick put into "Where's Charley?" until such a time as you have had enough evidence on paper to have an estimate of the show. Naturally, we would like to have you with us again but I don't want you to feel that your not doing so would cause us unusual difficulty. Word about the show has gotten around and the money is not a problem.

Thanks again to you and your wife for last evening. It was fun getting to see something of you and your family.

Fondly,

Ernie

Guys and Dolls, produced by Cy Feuer and Ernest Martin, with a sparkling score by Frank Loesser, opened in November of 1950. An immediate and oft revived hit, it ran for 1,200 performances. *Where's Charley*, also produced by Feur and Martin, and also with a score by Loesser, opened in October 1948 and ran for 792 performances.

Jo Mielziner to Richard Rodgers and Oscar Hammerstein, February 17, 1950

Dear Dick and Oscar,

I have had some correspondence from both the Theatre Guild and from Prince Littler in London regarding the use of my blueprints and color sketches of CAROUSEL. Since they are unwilling to make a deal with me which would cover additional work on my part the present situation is as follows: Littler will receive from me all blueprints and color sketches as they were at the time we went into production. I bring this up because as you will recall much of the second act material came to me while we were executing the first act. This resulted in a certain brevity in some of the sketches and a good deal of work was done by personal contact in the studios.

From my own personal experience in London it's hard enough to get scenery and lighting executed to the level of our standards when the designer is there personally. In the case of CAROUSEL, I strongly recommend that you and/or the Guild have somebody supervise this production on the technical side during the execution of the settings. There is a tendency on the part of English craftsmen to redraw American designs to fit the British sight-line problems in a manner which is not always pleasing. Because of the whole experience I had with Tennessee Williams' GLASS MENAGERIE and A STREETCAR NAMED DESIRE (even though I supervised the building and painting of the latter) I have decided not to put my name on English productions on which I cannot have close control of the building, painting and lighting.

I am eagerly looking forward to seeing your Graham Greene dramatization. I liked the book so much.

With warm regards to you both.

Yours, as ever,

Jo

Jo Mielziner

Rodgers and Hammerstein produced a play version of Graham Greene's 1948 novel, *The Heart of the Matter*, with a script by Greene and Basil Dean. It opened in Boston on February 20, and it closed there on March 4. Rodgers describes it as the only production with which he was associated that never opened in New York. Rodgers and Hammerstein were producing *The Happy Time* and *The Heart of the Matter* almost simultaneously. As Rodgers explained: "In a way, *South Pacific* presented Oscar and me with a problem similar to the one we'd had to face after *Oklahoma!* opened. With the show obviously set to run for years, we saw no point in competing with ourselves by following it up with another musical of our own. Therefore we did as before: we turned to producing other people's plays."

Mildred Knopf (Mrs. Edwin Knopf) to Oscar Hammerstein, February 19, 1950

Dear Oscar, -

Last night I had an idea for you and Dick and I must say that I got so excited I could scarcely sleep. Why not "Uncle Tom's Cabin?" Please say you'll tuck the idea away in the back of your head and think about it!

I believe that "my client" Miss Dunne felt "real bad" this A.M. when she read that you had cast the part of Anna. Is't true? –

My dearest love to Dorothy and to yourself. I always miss you both –consistently.

Devotedly ever,

Mildred

Oscar Hammerstein to Mildred Knopf (Mrs. Edwin Knopf), February 27, 1950

Dear Mildred:

"Uncle Tom's Cabin" was musicalized once under the title "Topsy and Eva." It had a very successful run on the coast and didn't do well in the East. The Duncan Sisters played "Topsy" and "Eva." Paul Robeson's wife and someone else have collaborated on another version, bringing it "up to date" according to their own philosophy. I have read it and it is interesting, but far too diffuse. Thank you for the suggestion. I will take a look at the original when I get time. I believe it would have to be written from an approach very different from Mrs. Stowe's viewpoint.

The part of "Anna" has not been filled. Gertie Lawrence suggested the story to us and we are in the process of negotiating with her—quite a complicated process. Does Irene really want to come back to the stage? I mean, really? It would be very interesting for Dick and me to know this, whether for "Anna" or for anything else.

Love,

Oscar Hammerstein, II

Harriet Beecher Stowe's novel *Uncle Tom's Cabin* features in the Margaret Landon novel, *Anna and the King of Siam* (1944); one of the King's wives even adopts "Harriet Beecher Stowe" as part of her English name. In *The King and I*, Oscar gave that interest to the character of Tuptim, which then sets up the choice of *Uncle Tom's Cabin* as the source material for the ballet-within-the-show, "The Small House of Uncle Thomas." Irene Dunne played Anna in the 1946 film of *Anna and the King of Siam* (with Rex Harrison as the King).

In a February 20 letter to "Dick and Oscar," Clare Boothe Luce submitted an outline for a "straight comedy" called *Married from Home* (or *Our Wedding Day*), for Rodgers and Hammerstein to consider producing. The majority of her short cover letter is spent singing the praises of *South Pacific*.

Oscar Hammerstein to Clare Boothe Luce[2], March 8, 1950

Dear Clare Luce:

Dick and I have read your scenario and we both believe it would make a charming light musical comedy. At the time we spoke to you we had already started to explore an offer to do a musical version of "Anna and the King of Siam." Since then we have become more deeply involved in it and also very enthusiastic about it. This, I am afraid, would knock us out of the running for a year and make our services to your manuscript too remote to be of much value to you.

I am grateful to have had the chance to read this story and I want also to express my thanks for your pamphlet entitled "The Twilight of God," which I have read with very real interest. I believe that I can say that I am much closer to agreeing with your conclusions than I am to an endorsement of all the steps by which you reached them. Some of them violate the laws of logic which I learned under Professor Cooley in Philosophy A-1 at Columbia back in 1915. So many things, however, have changed since then, why should a law of logic remain immutable? I am substantially friendly to the aims of your pamphlet and that is surely the important thing to say.

All my best wishes to you.,

Sincerely,

Oscar Hammerstein, II

---

[2] Among Clare Boothe Luce's notable achievements were: an editor for *Vogue* and *Vanity Fair*, Congresswoman from Connecticut (1943–47), and Ambassador to Italy (1953–56). She is best remembered for her play (subsequently filmed), *The Women*. *Married from Home* came to naught.

**Oscar Hammerstein to Jean Ely (Mrs. Edward Stevenson Ely),
February 25, 1950**

Dear Jean:

Something slipped up. You said that your carnation would off-set any "contretemps." I firmly believe it would have fulfilled its mission, only your carnation arrived a day early. I wore it to the dress rehearsal and the dress rehearsal was fine. The next night we opened. I wore another carnation and never have I seen so many "contretemps" in one evening. Please get your dates straight the next time.

I am deeply and sincerely and affectionately grateful for your thoughtfulness and your own deep and sincere affection which I cherish.

Love from us both to both of youse.

As ever,

Oscar Hammerstein, II

**Oscar Hammerstein to Arthur Hammerstein, (excerpt)
March 3, 1950**

How did your show[3] come off. Ours didn't or, rather, it's coming off rather quickly this Saturday night. It needed so much re-writing that we couldn't have accomplished it without staying out on the road a long time, and doing this would have cost too much money. I'll write you more about it in a later letter.

**Note from Richard Rodgers to Oscar Hammerstein, March 9,
1950, enclosing letters from a Virginia [?], March 7, 1950, and
Donald Mosty, March 8, 1950**

Dear Oscar,

For whatever these are worth.

Love,

Dick

Gentlemen:

---

[3] For several years, Arthur Hammerstein volunteered for the Annual Under-Privileged Child Benefit in Palm Beach, Florida. He regularly sought Oscar's help in corralling talent to perform.

Apropos of the report about "Anna and the King of Siam" becoming a musical. Please won't you give us a star who can sing? Gertrude Lawrence may be charming—but did you listen to the broadcast Sunday night? The vocal interludes were pathetic. And a heroine under 50 would be more appealing to the public.

Very Truly,

Virginia

Dear Sirs:-

Gratuitous advice is never popular, and when offered to men who are proven masters of their field, it becomes downright rude. So please, gentlemen, consider the following remarks in the light of an opinion that many of us have, and about which we feel so strongly that we must express it—and I was elected spokesman.

We were excited to read that ANNA AND THE KING OF SIAM is being considered as a musical—if it materializes, can't we have it REALLY musical? We feel like hounds to say it, because Gertrude Lawrence has given us many happy hours in the theatre, but Time is no respecter of persons, and (let's face it) is catching up with her. She could put over a song, without much voice, but now even this no longer seems true. If you heard the U.S. Steel hour on Sunday night, you will get our point. With constant study, the dear woman could not produce real music. And how about giving a gifted American a break for a change? Surely you can find a soprano with charm, and not depend merely on a Name for box office receipts. You have done it before.

Very sincerely,

Donald Mosty

Gertrude Lawrence's career began in her girlhood in the early 1900s in England, but it was *Andre Charlot's Revue of 1924* that brought her to Broadway and fame. She starred in both musicals and straight plays and had a primary partnership with Noel Coward, who wrote his greatest success, *Private Lives*, for Lawrence to co-star in with him. Although Lawrence's voice was not a great one, and was less than ideal on recording or radio, seeing her on stage made all the difference. As Rodgers wrote: "Though I had known all along that her singing would be a problem, I also knew something about Gertrude Lawrence: she had a radiance that could light up an entire stage. Even during rehearsals it was obvious that she would be magnificent in the role of Anna. I also felt that her intrinsic style and feeling for music could compensate for her faulty pitch, and most of the time it did."

Oscar Hammerstein to Hy Kraft, March 9, 1950

Dear Hy:

Your invitation to stop with you this Spring is a kind one and a very attractive one. It is very doubtful, however, if we are coming. Our present plans, immediately following the launching of "South Pacific" in Cleveland on April 24th, are to go to London to help out with the production of "Carousel" which follows "Oklahoma!" at the Drury Lane. If those plans change, we shall be dashing out to avail ourselves of the advantages listed in your letter.

I'm glad to hear that you've finished the book for your new musical. Keep me posted on its progress towards production.

On the Cole Porter show,[4] I know nothing except what I've read in the paper, and what I've read in the paper indicates that it's kind of a madhouse. They have accepted Dwight Taylor's version and they have rejected Comden and Green's version, and there is vague talk of lawsuits, and I don't know who the villains are, the authors or the producers.

Dick and I are batting .500 this season. "The Happy Time" is a solid hit, and "The Heart of the Matter," at this writing, is a solid flop. We closed it after one week in Boston. There is a good play here if the authors will do a complete re-writing job, and we are storing the production awaiting their completion of this.

Dick and I have nearly completed negotiations for the musical stage rights to "Anna and the King of Siam," and I have already started to work on it.

Three weeks ago Reggie was married. Ten days ago Henry was married, and next month Billy is going to be married. Sometime during the

---

[4] Cole Porter's *Out of This World* opened in December 1950, with a script credited to Dwight Taylor and Reginald Lawrence. Problems extended beyond the script, and George Abbott was brought in to take over directing duties from Agnes de Mille. Charlotte Greenwood received the best notices.

year Susan will be married. Beyond these statistics I have no startling news about the family. We spoke to Jimmy at North Carolina last night and he said he had slept only six hours in three days. Knowing that his exams are coming up I could sympathize with him as a diligent student. It turned out, however, that all his waking hours in those three days had been devoted to finishing the writing of a new musical show for the Sound and Fury Club of North Carolina University. That may, or may not, be a more worthy object than the credits he would have gained had he passed the examinations I think he is about to flunk—who can tell.

Love to you all,

Oscar Hammerstein, II

Oscar Hammerstein to Mary Cremme, March 14, 1950

Dear Miss Cremme:

To your great surprise I have remembered to send you a story. It isn't about me, but you said it didn't have to be:

Allan [sic] Lerner, who I believe to be the best of our young librettists, had struggled for several years to write a Broadway success. With his collaborator, composer Fritz Loewe, he wrote a musical play that finally reached the professional stage. It failed. They then wrote another, and it enjoyed a fair run. Then, finally, they wrote "Brigadoon." The night it opened in New York City, Allan called up his father who was in Florida and told him that the play was a hit. Mr. Lerner, Sr., returned from the phone to his card game and announced to his friends around the table the good news that Allan had just told him. One of the friends said, "That boy of yours is certainly lucky." "Yes," Mr. Lerner answered, "and it's a funny thing about Allan, the harder he works, the luckier he gets."

Any good?

Very truly yours,

Oscar Hammerstein, II

Brigadoon was the fourth Broadway musical with book and lyrics by Alan Jay Lerner and music by Frederick Loewe. Their first collaboration was *The Life of the Party* (1942), followed by the Broadway shows *What's Up?* (1943), *The Day Before Spring*

(1945), then *Brigadoon* (1947). They would go on to write *Paint Your Wagon*, *My Fair Lady*, *Camelot*, and *Gigi*.

G. M. Loeb to Oscar Hammerstein, March 16, 1950

Dear Mr. Hammerstein:

Somehow, when I picked up the VARIETY and looked at the front page, Wednesday, March 15, which tells about SOUTH PACIFIC being the one-year Broadway champion, I got a shock seeing that your top ticket was $6.00 and way back in 1927, your top ticket for SHOWBOAT was $6.00.

Is there anything in the world that cost $6.00 in 1947 [*sic*] that still costs $6.00 in 1950? I notice that the gross of SOUTH PACIFIC at its $6 top was $2,635,000 and I imagine the audience paid nearer $10 million. With our big chain of offices, it seems we're buying SOUTH PACIFIC seats almost every week. The lowest price we've been able to get them at has been around $30 and we've paid as much as $50. We tell people to write to the box office, but when they find out they have to wait, they just won't do it and it's their money, so we have to follow their instructions.

However, I still think that with productions costing more, actors getting more, musicians getting more, heating, cooling, rent and everything else up, tickets ought to be more. The way to do it is to put them up by $1.00 every three months until you get them where supply and demand appear to be in balance.

After the OPA went off at the Waldorf, minute steak was $2.50 and the next week it was $3.00 and it's been inching up ever since until now it's $5.00. Likewise, you may have noticed the same thing happen imperceptibly with your heating oil bill if you use heating oil intown [*sic*] or in Pennsylvania and possibly you noticed how imperceptibly gasoline went up, but up it went.

Personally, I've been a great plugger for more variation in prices, depending upon location in the house, such as I found most prevalent in Germany before the war. There isn't any reason in the world to have an orchestra price and a mezzanine price. I should think that the orchestra could be split into anywhere from 3 to 6 different price zones.

I hope you'll get a chance to read that book I sent you by hand a few weeks ago –"... & Co."

Very truly yours,

G M Loeb

Oscar Hammerstein to G. M. Loeb, March 21, 1950

Dear Mr. Loeb:

Your letter proves something strange to me. You and I are the only ones who believe this. I have been talking it up for some time. Part of the ticket scandal is due, undoubtedly, to the fact that we charge too little. Our price is so far below the supply and demand price that someone else is bound to profit by it if we don't. A great man[y] of the theatre's ills are due to the fact that admission prices have not been scaled to meet the enormous increase in costs.

The strange part of all this is that one is continually hearing pleas for a lowering of the admission scale, and many of these come from showmen. At this moment, all I can do is agree with you. There is very little sentiment on our side. The managers are, at the moment, concentrating on lowering costs and while they are doing that, it is no time to increase admission prices. I believe, however, that these prices should be increased commensurately with the extent of whatever failure we have in lowering the costs.

At the beginning of your letter you are surprised to learn that the price of "Show Boat" in 1920 [sic] was no less than for "South Pacific" in 1950. The joke is that "Show Boat" cost more. The article in Variety was inaccurate. The gross price for "Show Boat" was $6.60, with 10% tax. "South Pacific" charges $5.00, and with 20% tax the gross is $6.00.

Thank you again for your continued interest.

Very truly yours,

Oscar Hammerstein, II

Oscar Hammerstein to James Hammerstein, March 24, 1950

March 24, 1950

Dear Jimmy:

This is what I think about the car:

1. You say it will be good to help you "get around the campus". I have been on that campus and it looks to me as if many generations of healthy and able-bodied young men have got around it without automobiles. This must also include faculty members, very few of whom can afford automobiles.

2. What else can you do with the car except get around the campus? You can have fun with it. I am all for fun, but I don't think you have time for this kind of fun. You are not very well up in your school work. You have just flunked one out of three courses. You are very busy in extra-curricular activities—so busy with your playwriting that you have not been able so far to go out for tennis. You cannot, therefore, possibly have any fun with a car without encroaching on the time when you should be doing these other things for which you haven't enough time anyway.

3. I think the main attraction of this whole project is the "idea" of having a car. I don't believe you have thought it through.

4. You have the idea that you would be buying it and supporting it with your own money (incidentally don't forget the supporting part; you have not finished with the financial problem when you have bought the car). What do you mean by your own money? One fund is a fund set aside by Jerome Kern for your education. It so happens that we do not have to draw upon that, but perhaps you might later on. Surely he did not put by some money every month for you in the hopes that it would buy you a car. Your other sources of wealth are your interests in "South Pacific" and "The Happy Time". We put up the money for these investments for you in hopes that, if the shows were successful, they might build up a small fortune for you. This is exactly what they are doing because the investments have turned out to be good ones. There was never any intention of getting some extra money so that you could buy a car. It has been our dream that you keep, at any rate the "South Pacific" money intact, because if you do, you will wind up with a very fine nest-egg by the time you get out of college, and it will grow considerably, even after that.

5. I have great fears that this is a turning point toward self-indulgence, and might set a pattern very dangerous for your future.

6. In spite of all these heavy words. I still say you can make up your own mind. I have expressed my views and expressed them rather strongly. I may also say that Mother agrees with me, after having given the matter further consideration—even though she was somewhat encouraging to you before, but please believe this is not a command. If you decide to buy a car after all the evidence is in, and after measuring your own opinion and your own knowledge against the ones I have expressed, there will be no come-back from me. I will assume you have given it very careful thought and have made your own decision, and I will also assume that it is a wise decision, and made honestly. This statement sounds like almost an empty gesture after the vehement views I have expressed, but it is not. If you decide to buy a car we will make the funds available to you out of your show money.

We are just leaving for the farm now. When I spoke to you last night you didn't tell me whether or not you had yet received your razor. If you haven't received it let me know. It was air-mailed to you on Tuesday.

Love from us all.

Oscar Hammerstein to Mary Martin, March 28, 1950

Dear Mary:

Thank you for the neckties. Thank you for the record. And thank you for being a "Honey Bun" and for singing "A Wonderful Guy" the way you do, and for keeping your scalp clean, for being a great star without ever acting like one, and for being a sweet girl and always acting like one.

Love,

Oscar Hammerstein, II

Oscar Hammerstein to Hy Kraft, March 28, 1950

Dear Hy:

I have read "Just For Laughs," and it lives up to its title. This involves criticism as well as commendation. I think you have provided ample opportunity for Phil Silvers to be funny, and I am sure he will be in this part. I would have liked, however, to have seen more flesh on the bones of the story. I know that the characters in a show of this kind do not have to experience the love throes of Tristan and Isolde, but I think you could dig a little deeper into their emotions than you do. The first brief meeting of Cliff and Sally, on which they make a date, is hardly the foundation for a crisis when Sally breaks that date for the perfectly sound reason of wanting to make a good living. I think they should have more background to their story before this happens. I think also that you might improve the suspense of this story (which, at the moment, is nil) by pulling in another cutie for Cliff to play around with. This is conventional, but might be useful. If you don't like it, try to find something that is less conventional but, nonetheless, useful. I even think that the story between Betty and Russ could be improved. I don't know how, because I haven't had time to think about it, but it just seems too bare.

Summing up, I think that you have rich characters and plenty of comedy, and that you have neglected plot situations and the development of those that you have. One thing that I am sure you can do: You can make the Phil Silvers part really in love with Sally. In this way, there will be greater suspense over the Sally-Cliff story, and when she marries Cliff, Phil can take it pretty big and when a comedian bumps into a real dramatic situation it is always a very welcome thing with the audience. I like the way you have him taking it, and his message to his mother, but all along the line there was very little implication that he had any feeling for Sally. I don't mean to suggest that he, for one moment, should let Sally invade his thoughts so far as to exclude his own ego, but it should be clear to the audience that within the limitation of this kind of man, he is in love.

I am delighted that you have Johnny Mercer to write the lyrics and I think Phil is perfect casting for the lead. When do you think you will go into production? Please keep me posted.

I am now quite certain that I will not be in California for the opening of "South Pacific." We have booked passage on the Mauretania April 28th. "Carousel" is going into rehearsal shortly after we arrive, and opens at the Drury Lane about June 6th, after which we will come back to New York.

Love from us both to Reata, Jill and you.

As ever,

Oscar Hammerstein, II

P.S. I am returning the script under separate cover.

O.H., II

Just For Laughs became the musical *Top Banana*, with songs by Johnny Mercer. It opened on Broadway November 1, 1951, and starred Phil Silvers.

Oscar Hammerstein to Robert Dolan, April 7, 1950

Dear Bobby:

It was good to hear from you, and I suppose I have to thank your new apartment which has given you the elbow room you apparently need in which to type a friendly letter to a man. This, of course, proves that your typing technique is faulty. The proper form is with elbows close into the hips, very much as one holds himself while riding a horse. Since your form is probably bad on a horse too, I shall not press a subject about which you may be very sensitive.

I am glad you look back on the evening you spent with us with some pleasure, because I have worried a great deal about it, being somewhat ashamed at losing my temper with Henry. What disturbed me was that it must have seemed to you like some deep seeded [*sic*] stepfather-stepson animosity which in truth does not exist at all. There is great mutual affection between us.

It was good to read your approval of my foreword,[5] and shrewd of you to guess all the while I was writing it I wanted to extend it into a full book. My greatest problem was keeping it down (sounds like a man with ptomaine poisoning).

It is true we are going to England April 28th, to sit in on the rehearsals of "Carousel."

I am delighted with the success of "Texas [Li'l Darlin,"] but much less flabbergasted than you are. It compares very favorably with most of the other things in town.

Love to you both,

Oscar Hammerstein, II

---

[5] Refers to Oscar's book, *Lyrics*—lyrics for seventy-two of his songs, preceded by a forty-five-page "Notes on Lyrics."

P. G. Wodehouse to Oscar Hammerstein, April 10, 1950

Dear Oscar.

Would you have time before you sail for England to have a look at a three act one set comedy I have written—nine characters, all American except an English butler—scene, Hollywood? Star part for a man.

Edward Everett Horton is very interested in it, so is Guthrie McClintic. They have both made suggestions for improvements, and I have rewritten it and am taking it to the typist today. It ought to be ready by the end of the week.

I shall quite understand if you are too busy, but if you aren't, will you give me a ring and I will leave the script at the office.

Best wishes

Yours ever

Plum

Letter from Oscar Hammerstein to P. G. Wodehouse, April 14, 1950

Dear Plum:

I would be delighted to read your script, but I must tell you in advance that not [sic] matter how much I like it I don't see how Dick and I can fit any additional project into next season's plans. This is a great pity, because when I hear of a play set in Hollywood with an all American cast except for one English butler, and this play is by you, I am beginning to chuckle already.

All the best.

As ever,

Oscar Hammerstein, II

Oscar Hammerstein to Cynny [?], April 11, 1950

Dear Cynny:

I was bowled over by the slippers. They are by far the most beautiful slippers I have ever owned, and this is saying a great deal because I have made it a point to collect handsome slippers from all parts of the world. These are just wonderful, and they do something for my feet. What the right slipper does for my right foot is to pinch it a little, but this is not your fault because you had a perfect right to assume that both my feet were the same size. I don't think anything can be done about it because I am sure the slipper will stretch.

In case you think there is a frivolous note in this letter (I don't, but Shirley's attitude has been very strange during my dictation), I want you to be assured of my deep sincerity when I tell you that I appreciate not only the beauty of your work, but your extreme kindness in taking so much time as this job must have taken. I further compliment you on your discretion in giving me a present in return for "South Pacific" tickets. Most people make the mistake of looking upon Shirley as their benefactor, and as you have probably noticed, her desk is showered daily with gifts from all kinds of people. (It may be that you have not noticed this because her desk is normally so littered, that baubles from Cartier's and Van Cleef and Arpel's can easily be covered over. Sometimes they slide off onto the floor—where the wastebasket should be. Shirley has just said, "My desk has been very clean lately, if you've noticed." I haven't.)

I don't know how to adequately show my appreciation. I have suggested to Dorothy that she cease to deposit all rent checks for the following year, but while she is a sweet-natured person there is a mercenary streak in her which she finds difficult to conquer. I can only suggest that you request more tickets. After all, if Shirley has her clientele, there is no reason why I shouldn't have mine.

All best wishes to you and Chapin.

Larry Spier, who worked for Rodgers and Hammerstein's music publishing wing, Williamson Music, wrote Oscar a letter in which he asked: "I was kinda wondrin' if, through the years, there wasn't a favorite song(s) of yours which for some reason or other never became popular. Perhaps I could do something with it today. Let me know."

Oscar Hammerstein to Larry Spier, April 19, 1950

Dear Larry:

You are right. The song is "The Folks Who Live on the Hill" from "High, Wide and Handsome."

All the best.

Sincerely,

Oscar Hammerstein, II

South Pacific won the 1950 Pulitzer Prize for Drama. This was the second musical to win the award, but the first time the composer was included. (*Oklahoma!* was awarded a Special Pulitzer, not for Drama.)

Stephen Sondheim to Oscar Hammerstein, May 3, 1950

CONGRATULATIONS RE JOE PULITZER. ALSO BEST WISHES FOR GOOD TRIP AND SUCCESSFUL OPENING LOVE=

STEVE

Oscar Hammerstein to Sam and Rae Goldsmith, May 4, 1950

Dear Sam and Rae:

It was very sweet of you to send me the candy. Since I am on a diet at the moment it created a stern temptation to me, and what do you think I did? I yielded.

All the best to you both.

As ever,

Oscar Hammerstein II

Milton Cohen to Oscar Hammerstein, May 8, 1950

Dear Oc,
I sent the champagne for your dinner,
In hopes that you had picked a winner;
And that you might enjoy a toast,
To the horse you thought could beat "Your Host".
But had I known "Oil Cap." would fail
I would have ordered gingerale.
For after you had heard the worst,
It would suffice to quench your thirst.
However, things are now quite clear,
Although the cost to me was dear,
For ne'r again will I take losses
On Your gol danged GRAY HORSES.
    Love to you and Dorothy,
    Milton

Oscar Hammerstein to Milton Cohen, May 15, 1950

Dear Milton:

Several months ago I was minding my own business with not a thought of the Kentucky Derby, and certainly no knowledge that a gray horse was running. It was you who brought Oil Capitol into my life, and it was you who put through the extraordinary deal of making a bet at 3½ to 1 so far ahead of the rest. I now receive a poem from you implying that I started the whole thing. You will shortly hear from my solicitors, Chumbley, Metcalfe, Worcester and Buggs, 42 Ginsburg Street, London W.1.

With all good wishes,

Oscar Hammerstein, II

What follows is one of the most fascinating exchanges of letters in the Hammerstein Collection, clearly articulating two sides of the issue of when, how, why, and if changes should be permitted in an already produced work. It's an argument that will continue as long as there is theater.

Josh Logan to Oscar Hammerstein, May 17, 1950

Don't read this at one sitting or you'll miss tea.

Dear Oscar:

If they were trying to elect the most charming bastard (emphasis on the word "charming") in the world, I'd vote for you. If you ever find that it is too difficult to make a living writing lyrics, I'm sure you could get a job anywhere luring birds from trees or selling rugs to Arabians, or just simple jobs like making black white, for instance.

You are right. I am "tetchy" on the subject of changes, and yet I am very glad I am because by using the word "distrust", that ugly word, I sparked that wonderful letter from you. Probably if we live to be a thousand, you and I will never agree on what is and what is not a change in a theatrical production. The things I consider to be simply sticking-close-to-the-original might seem to be "changes" to other eyes.

For instance, in going through the play now with Ray Middleton, I have found numbers of places where words were altered from your original writing of the first scene or later on from some line or piece of direction that you and I had planned during our days in Doylestown, alterations made to accommodate the limitations in speech of our leading man, Ezio Pinza. He was unable to do certain things, say certain lines, and so we put them into a form that he could speak, but not necessarily into the form we wanted or thought was best. As an example, do you remember the line, "He was the town bully," which you originally wrote in the first draft of your first scene? Mary Martin had asked if we could reinstate it. I had even forgotten that it was there. It is so much better than, "He was a terrifying bully," for which we finally settled because Ezio could not make the word "town" understandable.

Again, I found that I had been the victim of Ezio's desire to pace about the stage and make a lot of movement during the long speech which tells the story of his background in France and how he killed the man. I found that the stage managers had carefully plotted out his pace upstage, his great melodramatic shrug and slap of the thighs when the man fell dead in the cobblestone streets of his French town. I suddenly realized that this was not my original direction. It was Ezio's conceit because he wanted "to do something", "to be active" during a speech which has so much more power if it is spoken quietly while standing still or squatting casually next to Nellie, drawing pictures in the sand, as I had originally planned it. This is also the reason why a great deal of the kissing, the chasing, is in the stage manager's script—things I never wanted and I am sure none of us wanted, but we compromised on them because Ezio wanted them so badly. It seems to me that in trying to go back to the very origin of the scene with two other actors, Dick Eastham and Ray Middleton, that I am not making changes at all, but simply eliminating changes that had been made in spite of me.

Since writing to you, in which I was going to list all the changes I have put into the second company, I have discovered in working with Ray Middleton that there are many changes that Mary Martin herself wants eliminated—things Ezio had allowed to get into the play. Although Mary talked about how badly Dick Eastham was changed, she does not realize that Dick Eastham was in the process of going back to the original. I think that you will find that I have been trying to stay nearer to the Emile De Becque that you originally conceived. The kind of wolfish, grandpa satyr quality that Emile was in Ezio's hands in which he makes love to the audience and sticks his tongue down Mary's throat, is eliminated—maybe to the disappointment of some women. The wonderful urbanity that he had because of his accent and background, Ray will never have because he does not posses these qualities. He will be gentle, forceful and I think the most dramatic exponent of Emile De Becque's character that we have ever had—not the most charming.

Incidentally, his accent is going to be okay. I have had him out to my house this weekend and we have gone over every word and taken each word apart. Nedda read Nellie Forbush and I just worked with Ray on his speech. He has a wonderful ear and his background of studying French in preparation for operatic roles is coming to his aid. I think we've got the real French "R" and some of the careful use of "TH" that Emile should have, and I think we are going to have a creditable performance by the time you get back from Europe. Perhaps it will take a little longer than that. Ray is very nervous about going in and trying to remember the accent and all the other things he has to remember while he has the opening night nerves or the nerves that are going to come from the first two or three days rehearsal. And Mary does not want to rehearse too much as it tires her. Thank God she didn't try to do PETER PAN.

You were very flattering to me with your figure of speech in which you called me a "polo player", but I would like to tell you that much as I appreciate your nice remarks about me, I have a deep feeling and conviction on the subject of creation in direction which I have had over a number of years that seem to be at variance with yours on the surface. That is why I am "tetchy", as you call it.

I believe fundamentally that if we could ever speak the same language on this subject or if you sat through every rehearsal with me of a duplicate company from the beginning that you would see exactly what I am driving at. I do not recreate merely to whet my jaded appetite or to keep myself from being bored at rehearsal. I am constantly searching for truth. I want to improve, to perfect, to fill up holes that seem to have always been unfilled in the original piece because I lacked an idea for them at the time.

There were two big changes in the second company which I think bettered the story.

One was Emile De Becque's full realization of the sting of Nellie's race prejudice—the devastating quality of it which I think you have wonderfully dramatized in your lyric to "I Was Cheated Before" which will deepen the entire play at that point and give "This Nearly Was Mine" its proper setting and final emotional fulfillment. I believe that by the time Dick Eastham and Ray have sung this song that there will be much more charged emotion in the audience at this point than there ever was during Pinza's singing of a kind of concert piece which no one quite understood. The wonderful subjunctive quality of your lyric of the verse is coming through thrillingly and I know that you will find a satisfaction as a lyric writer that you have never felt at that moment in the play. Dick's music is more thrilling, too, I feel. Emile's lonely remembrance of things that are never going to take place in the future is a dramatic musical peak rather than merely a tonal one.

The second big change is the new cure for Nellie's reprise of "Some Enchanted Evening" on the beach.

As I recall, I have a very corny habit of using the word "remember" as a crutch. I don't think you wrote those "remembers". Whenever I saw them in the show I felt that they were my doing, and therefore I was trying to eliminate the word when we went into "Some Enchanted Evening" originally when she says, "the officers' club dance—remember?" and changing it to "wasn't it?" The other, going into the reprise on the beach, I am sure is an improvement although I am not sure Mary Martin will do it because she has seen Janet Blair do it and I am sure she will be suspicious that it is being foisted off on her. However, we haven't gotten to that point yet and I am certainly not going to press it because I don't care that much. I simply feel it would be better and more satisfying artistically than the thing I resorted to in the original staging of the scene.

As for the smaller variations in the show, they must seem to be changes simply because they were recreations from scratch. I had no one around who knew the show intimately. I started rehearsal on the second company of SOUTH PACIFIC with a new stage manager, new actors and myself. None of us remembered exactly what the moves were or the groupings of the original company. And I had never plotted them out exactly in the original company. I explained generally what the mood of the scene was, got everybody to be in as much of a creative state of mind as possible, and then let the movements take care of themselves; that is, the sitting downs and the standing ups and the groupings of the men and the girls. Whenever somebody got an idea, I would put that into the show. This I did also with the second company because I have always done that and it never occurred to me that anyone would object. When I tried to duplicate exactly, I wasted time. John Fearnley, as many times as he has seen the show, cannot absolutely duplicate it: "Where does she look at him? On which step does he pause?" It wasn't until we got Mary Martin on the stage recently that we knew exactly where Emile stood at every point. Even Charlie Atkin, who knows it as well as he does, and Billie Worth and Webb Tilton, who imitate Pinza and Martin, could not tell us exactly at which point Mary looked at Ezio or he looked at her. Only Mary could tell us this and Mary can only do it when she gets on the stage and something does not occur exactly as it has the night before.

However, in working on the second company I didn't even try to do this. I merely tried to stage the show again as fast and quickly and efficiently as I possibly could. I treated all the actors as though they were creating the parts for the first time and tried to give them my idea of Emile De Becque, of Nellie, of Billis, Bloody Mary and so forth, and let them at it. I gave Diosa Costello things that I had tried to give Juanita Hall but which she had not been able to grasp. I immediately saw that the sheer innocence of Juanita Hall's face, that moon face, was not going to be Diosa's and that probably I must make her much more the crafty woman of Michener's story and which we eliminated because we knew Juanita Hall could not do it. This I do not really consider a change but merely a recreation from the original.

I tried a couple of changes in Billis simply because I had always been disappointed in the laughter at those moments in the original New York play and I had never had a decent idea to cover them. . . .the business of the shirt in Billis' face after "minor tears and burns", and the salute business (which did not work) after Harbison looked at him. Generally, Myron McCormick got the laugh by rolling his eyes upward. This piece of business often went overboard and I was trying to find something that could not look like just sheer hamming and would be something definite we could rely on as a laugh. It turned out that my second idea of the salute was a failure and it was dropped.

The other changes I will list quickly:

1. The extra drum rolls for the start of Alligator, which I thought was a more gentle transition and which you changed back, I understand, when I went to Cuba. It was probably better the original way. I had just always felt it was too much of a shock and seemed a little too much like revue technique.

2. I eliminated Billis' little dance and the extra repeat of the singing of "Bali H'ai" because I thought the joke was over. This was substituted for, I believe, by a line which you finally wrote, "Primitive but astonishing".

3. The addition of the words "mark my words" after "He'll never make Captain", which seemed to make the line stand out a little more and I think gets a better laugh.

4. The lines about Admiral Nimitz which I believe you and Dick wrote and you may or may not have eliminated.

5. The fact that Emile turns the children together so he can get in between them and sing front and then pick up the little girl instead of the little boy. This occurs twice in the play, once in the first scene and then in the final scene.

6. The drum roll which precedes the orchestral reprise of "Some Enchanted Evening" during which Emile pantomimes his surprise at seeing Nellie. In the New York company I have eliminated the drum roll because Dick Rodgers was worried about it and substituted an increase in volume in the airplane noise which for my purpose does the same thing. The reason for this change is because I have had numbers of people tell me

that they thought from Emile's behavior that he knew Nellie was up at his place and was not surprised to see her.

There are all the changes I can remember. Perhaps you can remember many more, but I have searched my brain and none occur to me. They are far less when I look them over than in any other second company I have ever staged, and I am still puzzled why I am on this subject, but I am so I would like to finish if you can stand to read any more.

Since you were doing ALLEGRO at the time I was staging the second company of ANNIE GET YOUR GUN, you probably do not remember how enormously different that company was to the one originally in New York. We gave Annie much more to do and Frank Butler much less, and lines, crosses, business were changed throughout. Yet I am sure that the eventual show was to the casual eye the exact duplicate of New York because it had the same final effect. Mary Martin could not do certain things that Ethel did and therefore I attacked the whole part of Annie from a different direction. I took advantage of Mary's ingenue qualities; for example, I added a little waltz step in the middle of "I Got Lost In His Arms" pantomime.

Going back over the shows that I have staged and second companies that I have staged myself, I have always tried to recreate the play from the original script and to make the actors have the feeling that they are starting from scratch rather than trying to walk a narrow pattern that was set by the other company. At the same time, I have tried to keep the same characterizations, the same feeling, the same effect of emotion and of laughter that was in the original. I don't think there was any change that was made that wasn't made to intensify or to deepen the effect or to get closer to the original writing. They were never changes in the sense that the play was distorted or moved into a different sphere or trifled with.

One of the reasons I used the word "distrust", which is a word that began to occur to me from that first run-through of SOUTH PACIFIC in front of the audience, was because I had a feeling that eventually the show would be the same in its big, over-all effect, and that the little details that go into this over-all effect were simply incidental and could be changed back or changed even to a third or fourth way in order to get that final effect. Just as the key changes and the fact that the girls are given more to sing in "I'm Gonna Wash That Man Right Out of My Hair" will not change the final musical effect.

These are things that we as creators of the play see very clearly, but the average audience simply realizes that the dynamics are the same, its interest is held, it's laughing and crying as much as it did at the original product.

My biggest example of this whole scheme, which is not a discovery of mine, I hope you know, is on MISTER ROBERTS. I have made numbers of direction and line changes on MISTER ROBERTS since the opening, some of them because actors have changed and some of them because time has changed—because we are further away from the Second World War, because some of the G.I. expressions have become dated and not as funny as they were when we originally opened, because some of them are absolutely impossible to remember now that we are further away and our audiences are further away from the G.I. jokes. And yet I believe MISTER ROBERTS is the same play today as it was two weeks after we opened in New York. But we have been constantly searching for a deeper truth to the play, and I believe have kept its effect the same by constant changes—and I say changes meaning changes from what is bad to what is good—from what is tentative to what is sure. For rules of where to stop we have relied on our own taste: Fonda's, Leland's and mine.

Now you have my statement or credo, or whatever you might call it. Perhaps you are right. Perhaps I should stick to the original. Perhaps I am over-creative and can work only in a creative mood; and therefore when a thing has been set, as SOUTH PACIFIC was set, it might be a good idea for whatever replacements are made or new companies formed, to have them done by the stage manager or by someone who will stick to the original and duplicate it. I can't believe that this is a good plan, but if you feel it is a good plan, believe me I am certainly going to abide by it because I respect you and admire you and I know that your experience in the theatre is beyond any that I have had. You have been through too many companies, too many creations in the theatre, not to know what you are talking about.

I am sorry that I have not convinced you in the time that we have worked together that my theories of the theatre and the theories of direction, especially on second companies and replacements are the preferable ones, because I believe that in not convincing you I lose a certain fight I have waged about these companies and replacements. And yet, I also see very clearly that when a thing becomes magic and beautiful in one way, that it would be wonderful to be able to freeze it at that point and keep it.

My point is that I don't believe it can be done. I don't think that the living theatre can stay the way it is. I think that time changes the play itself;

that things become just chemically different every time a play gets in front of an audience, and therefore I believe that a stage manager cannot duplicate. No one can duplicate, not even the greatest of all—the camera—because I don't think you can duplicate the audience nor can you duplicate the effect an audience has upon a work of art.

For instance, I believe that Charlie Chaplin's CITY LIGHTS, as wonderful and as brilliant as it is now, is both hurt and helped by the fact that it is exactly as it was originally. It is more nostalgic and some things are very funny today that were not funny then, and other things do not get laughs at all. It's not the same. I believe, however, that if Charlie Chaplin could recreate CITY LIGHTS today he would have even a bigger work of art better suited to the audience today rather than something that will grow quaint some day.

One of the best bits of news that we have on SOUTH PACIFIC is that Dick is going to work carefully with Ray on the keys and is also going to supervise the orchestral rehearsal before he goes to Europe. I feel in this way we are going to have a very much fresher singing of the score by Ray than we would have if it were going to be left in my hands and Dell'Isola's.

Oscar, I am thrilled to hear that you liked the run-through of CAROUSEL, as CAROUSEL is one of the greatest things that has ever been written in our theatre. I just hope that the English production is up to it. I have played the score over and over all these years and I have even now a new 33 RPM recording of the score and I still think that lyrically and musically it's about tops in my experience. And that includes SOUTH PACIFIC, which, wonderful as it is, never moved me as much as moments of CAROUSEL, which I think is a high achievement and one that should make you both live forever in the history of our theatre.

Please give my love to Dorothy. I'm awfully sorry that we're not going to be in England together. I would love to wander around London a bit with both of you and learn some of the things that you know about that wonderful city.

Billy visited us with his new family and he looks wonderful to me—glowing and happy and on his way to great success. I know that you already are proud of him, but you will be more so as these years go by.

Best always, and thanks always.

Josh

P.S. Attended Dick's 25th Anniversary Party today. Kids from the shows sang the G. G.[6] score. It is still fresh + the jokes are still good. I think it was charmingly done + I believe everyone was happy including Dick who must have suffered a bit during a bass rendition of "Ole Man Rodgers—His Songs Keep Rollin' Along."

Just for the record I'm sending a copy of this letter to Dick + Leland as they are in on the changes too. Maybe we can have this correspondence bound like G.B.S. [George Bernard Shaw] to Ellen Terry.

Oscar Hammerstein to Josh Logan, May 31, 1950

Dear Josh:

Commenting on the first paragraph of your letter dated May 17th, I wish to say that it is not difficult to charm birds off trees. All you do is spread out some food and water for them and they come. My method for selling rugs to Arabians is merely to mark the price down so it becomes attractive to them. The point is that charm is not so much a matter of style as substance. Many charmers are given credit for elaborate deception, but all they are doing is serving up the food attractively. Taking it on that basis, you are not a bad "charmer" yourself, and I can find nothing in your letter with which I disagree. I don't think I could justify a prescription of unalterable rigidity in a work of art in the theatre, either as to performance or text, but I think it most important to remember that when you decide to depart from the original form and break the crystal, you are entering a danger zone and caution is the word. If you are on top the Empire State Building and walking eight feet away from the parapet, you are in no danger at all. If you decide to go over to the parapet and lean over, you may see a great many things and have a better time, but at that point you must decide how far it is safe to lean. The stakes are very high.

Let us look at grand opera. God knows my fingers itch to change not only the productions of opera, but the texts, to make some sensible cuts. They have been kept in too rigid a form for many years now. One thing, however, can be said for them. They live. They go on. In their imperfect and quickly dated form they go on, and there is no proof that in the hands of smart alecks

---

[6] "G. G." probably refers to the 1925 *Garrick Gaieties.*

like you, and me they might not have gone on. Some serious mistakes might have been made in the desire to effect perfectly logical changes.

Once you start making changes it becomes almost a compulsion to make further changes, to lean over the parapet too far. Shakespeare has lived for many years without changes in the text except for cuts, but performances of Shakespeare, however, have been changed a great deal again and again, but the text has been kept sacred. No sane man adds or subtracts words within the lines, although now and then scenes are cut. The most extreme example is Gilbert and Sullivan. Here the text is kept inviolate. Now what of the production, and the direction, and the performance? In the cases where liberties have been taken, mainly in the United States, Gilbert and Sullivan can become very dull. The most successful performances of Gilbert and Sullivan are the D'Oyly Carte presentations and these happen to be the productions that adhere religiously to Gilbert's original direction and conception. I advance this example not as positive proof that this should be done with all works because I do not believe it should be done with all works, but I do advance it as an indication, a very strong indication, that the longevity of a work depends a great deal on the maintainence [sic] of the original form, and if variations are to be made, they should be made slight and made with great care indeed. Making changes can so easily become an accumulative pastime, not only on the part of one who makes them, but— and this is the main danger—those who follow are likely to be encouraged too much to make further changes. "Oh!," say they, "you can make changes, can you? Well, now I'll try my hand." And after a succession of directors who have not had the sacredness of the original work drummed into them and the inviolability of the original conception, all add their own and put their dirty little fingers in the pie and what have you got—Hollywood!

Dorothy and I agree that we are having our best visit of all to London. We have seen so many people whom we like very much, and spend a good deal of time in the country and have got around in the city to interesting places with interesting people, and have gone off by ourselves on occasion too. It has just been wonderful. I'm afraid I've done very little on "Carousel," except go in now and then and make notes with Shirley and give them to Jerry Whyte who has done a very capable job. The secondary parts recruited here in England are not much better than adequate, but the Americans who came over are playing it beautifully and I think we shall come off fine. I hope so because I love "Carousel" so very much. Dick and Dorothy arrive this morning. As a matter of fact, Dorothy and I are going over to the Savoy in a few minutes to meet them. We are, as you know, going to Paris for four or five days after the opening here and then sailing back on the Queen Mary, arriving June 21st, soon after which I hope we'll see you and Nedda and have a good time together. My fingers are crossed for the opening of Ray Middleton, but I'm sure he is going to be great. Good luck on it and thanks for the wonderful work Dick tells me you have done on this job.

Love,

Oscar Hammerstein to Jimmy Dyrenforth, May 22, 1950

Dear Jimmy:

I am sorry that you have had so many vicissitudes with the production of your play. I am even more sorry that Dick and I are not now in a position to give you any help. We have no frozen pounds here. They have all been transferred into dollars.

A personal note of advice: Don't you think you should write a new play and not drag out too many months and wear out too many hopes on this one? You describe many reasons given by many people for not doing it, but it has been my experience that when people like a script all reasons for not doing it quickly fade. To be quite honest with you, I don't remember the story of your play, although it probably would come back to me if I saw the first page, but reading between the lines of your letter it would seem to me that you have a lame duck on your hands. Don't give your life to it. Start something fresh. (If you have already done this, this whole letter is, of course, automatically cancelled.)

All good wishes to you.

Sincerely,

Oscar Hammerstein, II

Oscar Hammerstein to Howard Reinheimer, June 1, 1950

Dear Howard:

Dick is over here now and we are in the homestretch. If the play doesn't get over it will be merely because the London public does not want so serious a musical play, but from my conversations with most people I don't think this is so.

I am enclosing the draft of a contract made out by Ricketts, the purpose of which is to give Williamson the right to handle radio and television rights of our American group of plays over here. Obviously he has made a contract much too broad and much too inclusive. In the first place, it should be limited to England, and in the second place, it shouldn't be a question of their getting specific rights. I know that you would make these comments anyway. I am anticipating them and telling Ricketts what I think, but I wish you would write and suggest a contract of your own. The object is this: lots of money is dribbling away from us, not only me, but Frank Mandel, and Harbach, Rodgers and Hart and all of the Americans in our group because Shubert sets up that he owns radio rights and he gets paid for them all the time. Ricketts says it is just a crime and I think so too. He says what he lacks when he wants to fight them is a document, some kind of title, and that is what he is after. It just happens that he has given himself too much title in this suggested draft. I would welcome any suggestion you might make, and if you could airmail it back, he and I can discuss it before I leave England which will be June 10th.

The copy of the contract with Shuberts that you sent me clearly states their right to share in radio rights. It is equally clear, however, that we have the right, and we only have the right to handle the radio rights. This is a thing that must be got over in the instrument that Ricketts could handle. The income to Williamson might be quite small. I think they would be entitled to a ten per cent commission, but I think it would be very important for Williamson to start to become this kind of power on this side of the Atlantic, and it surely would result in being a power. It shouldn't be hard to sell to those who are not in Williamson because it is a service whereby they will be getting some income, however small, where before they were getting nothing at all. Another paragraph of your contract disturbs me, and it seems to be one that we have forgotten in connection with Tom Arnold's skating show, "Rose-Marie on Ice" (how final that sounds, "On Ice"). Have we violated our agreement to give Shubert the first refusal on a legitimate stage venture? This is a legitimate stage venture. What else is it? It is not repertory, or stock, or amateur, and have we violated our contract in not giving him a chance to do it first, even though we know he would [not?] have done it.

I feel very strongly that we should go into business more, in a bigger way here, and that we should produce our own plays, and that we should use some of Williamson's money as it comes in. We have already missed an opportunity to do that last year and given money to the government which we could have used, for instance, for the purchase of the English rights to "The Happy Time." We could have given an advance for that and had a piece of it without it costing us anything. I will discuss all this when I see you.

I am sorry this letter must be so brief and end here, but I have to dash off to rehearsal. I will call you on the telephone after we open. Love to Ellie and yourself from all of us.

As ever,

Oscar Hammerstein, II

Carousel opened in London on June 7. (Presumably the dating on the letter below is an error.)

Oscar Hammerstein (London) to Arthur Hammerstein (excerpt), June 7, 1950

We open "Carousel" tomorrow night. The company is very good and the production looks beautiful in the Drury Lane. I am, however, very doubtful about the reception we will get because I'm not at all sure that the London public will accept the fantasy in the last act, and I think also that the play might be a little too serious for them. However, I can do nothing about that. I know we are giving them the best possible production.

Referring to *Gentlemen Prefer Blondes*:

Herman Levin to Oscar Hammerstein, June 14, 1950

Dear Oscar:

At long last, the reprise of "You Say You Care" is out. I thought you would like to know.

With my best to you and to Dorothy –

Sincerely,

Herman

Oscar Hammerstein to Herman Levin, June 22, 1950

Dear Herman:

Congratulations on the death of the reprise. After such a long illness it is a mercy.

All the best.

Oscar Hammerstein II

Oscar Hammerstein to Basil Dean, June 26, 1950

Dear Basil:

Coming over on the Queen Mary I read your script [*The Heart of the Matter*] slowly and carefully and with great interest. I think it is a definite improvement. I like best the new first scene which clarifies the background of the story, and some of the characters. I like very much the first love scene between Scobie and Helen, and the father-daughter implications at the finish of the scene. I also feel that you have improved the ending of the play, and given the audience a loop-hole for believing in the penitence and possible salvation of Scobie.

I wish I were enthusiastic enough to say: "Go ahead and we'll back you with the London production," but I am not. Dick and I have discussed this at great length, and we cannot get away from the fact that we haven't sufficient belief in this play to associate ourselves with you in an English production. How much this opinion is colored by the previous production in Boston it is hard to say, but we have lost our taste and affection for the story. It is quite possible that if we were reading this version for the first time we should feel very differently about it. Unable, however, to escape our prejudice, we cannot bring ourselves to the idea of trailing along behind a production in which we not only have not the proper enthusiasm, but in which we seem to have little faith.

We hope with all our hearts we are wrong about this, and that some more cool-headed, unbiased, and shrewd partner will come along and back you, and make a lot of money out of the play, but we are definitely not your boys on this one.

Best of luck to you in your South African enterprise. We hope that "Hassan" repeats its former English success. If you come to New York later this summer as you said you might, we look forward to seeing you.

All the best.

Sincerely,

Oscar Hammerstein

Norman Krasna to Oscar Hammerstein, June 28, 1950

Dear Oscar:

I just saw "South Pacific."

Well, it's uneven. It starts great, and gets better. Fortunately there is no way to cure this.

I think you have written a genuine, full-blown, honest-to-God masterpiece.

For you to attempt another show to either surpass, equal or approximate "South Pacific" is nothing but arrogance and bad taste.

Member, Local Fan Club,

Oscar Hammerstein to Norman Krasna,[7] July 10, 1950

Dear Norman:

Thank you for your brief and kind critique of our little charade. Quite apart from your gratifying comment, it was good to hear from you again after this long time.

All the best.

As ever,

Oscar Hammerstein II

---

[7] In 1947 Rodgers and Hammerstein produced Krasna's play, *John Loves Mary*.

Oscar Hammerstein to Mary Martin, July 13, 1950

Dear Mary:

Thank you very much for the singing telegram. The young woman did not sing it as well as you could have, but I realized that at the moment you were very busy warbling "Honeybun"—a most taxing aria.

Love to you and Dick –

Oscar Hammerstein, II

Oscar Hammerstein to Louis B. Mayer (MGM), August 4, 1950

Dear L.B.:

Just before leaving California I noted an announcement in the Examiner that Republic would make a picture called "Wings Over the South Pacific," and that they had registered the title with your Association. I am bringing this to your attention because I think these situations have a basic concern for all of us.

I am not anxious to get involved in an unpleasant lawsuit, nor am I at all certain that I could prevail upon the courts to enjoin Republic from the use of this title. I might win on the ground of unfair competition. I don't know. One thing, however, is certain: The title, "Wings Over the South Pacific" is an obvious attempt to cash in on the amazing popularity of our play, and I maintain that such a practice is injurious not only to the owners of a particular theatrical property, but also to the entire picture business. Every good theatrical property is potentially a good picture property, and cutting in on valuable titles must eventually damage, to some extent, their picture value.

One consideration that increases the mischief is that the exhibitors of a picture called "Wings Over the South Pacific" are quite likely to bill the words "South Pacific" much larger than "Over the." Irrespective of Republic's good faith and belief that they have created a new and original title, there is a limit to the control they can exert on exhibitors' exploitation.

I am appealing to you, as one of influence and weight in your Association, not only to attempt to discourage this inroad on the title value of "South Pacific," but to establish a principle against all such inroads on all theatrical and literary properties which are destined someday to become picture properties.

Deeply confident in our friendship, I am sure that I could persuade you to take some steps in this direction as a personal favor to me, but I believe this goes beyond our friendship and beyond this individual instance, and it is on this broader basis that I prefer to suggest that you take some action.

Dorothy and I both enjoyed seeing you and Lorena again. I hope the four of us can get together soon on your next eastern visit.

As ever,

Oscar Hammerstein, II

Oscar Hammerstein to Louis B. Mayer, August 14, 1950

Dear L.B.:

Mr. Yates just phoned me and suggested that he change his title to "Wings Over the Pacific," a solution highly satisfactory to us and, I think, no way injurious to him because it seems to me like a better title than the other. At any rate, it makes all the difference in the world to us because it is the two words, "South Pacific," which is our trademark.

Dick and I are both deeply and sincerely grateful to you for your kindness and your prompt and efficient help in this matter. I cannot truthfully say that I was surprised at this, but the lack of surprise in no way lessens my gratitude.

Dorothy wants to join me in sending our love to you and Lorena.

As ever,

Oscar Hammerstein, II

Lester Markel of the *New York Times* inquired of Oscar: "How would you like to do a piece on what makes for a successful musical comedy?"

Oscar Hammerstein to Lester Markel, August 9, 1950

Dear Lester:

I am so busy trying to turn one out ("Anna and the King of Siam"), that I haven't time to write about how it's done and, at the moment, I don't feel at all sure that I know how it's done.

All the best,

Oscar, Hammerstein, II

Oscar Hammerstein to Maxwell Anderson, August 9, 1950

Dear Max:

I have read your statement about Russia, and I applaud its courage and clarity. I am not, however, ready to reject completely the hope that we can do anything but fight them. I admit there is almost no chance of talking out a peace, but I am unwilling, at this point, to make an unofficial decleration [*sic*] of war. "We shall all be on the front lines before this thing ends, whether we like it or not." I am not sure of this, nor am I willing to say it.

I have been working very hard the past two years as a United World Federalist. We believe that Russia, and all countries, should be invited into a Federation of Nations. This may be a technical position because it is almost certain that she would refuse such an invitation, and we will be thrown into a power struggle—the one that you say is already upon us. I am very nearly in agreement with you, but just one little step behind and unable, at this time, to take a position inconsistent with my long range philosophy.

I am anxious that you do not take this to be any dreamy advocacy of disarmament, or bare-breasted exposure to Russian attack. I know that we of the free nations must build up our military and naval strength. I would add that it is high time we built up our diplomatic strength. We have been making criminally stupid mistakes in the East. I believe, also, that a great deterrent to war would be a development of Truman's Point Four Program. In our military rivalry with Russia, we at least have an atomic bomb. In our diplomatic rivalry, we have nothing but sound and fury. I think there is still a chance for us to beat Russia in the chess game, although, at the moment, we are in a very bad position. I would like to emphasize the necessity of fighting on this ground, even more than with arms.

I hope we can sit down together and talk about all this sometime.

All the best,

Oscar Hammerstein II

Oscar Hammerstein to Ruth Mitchell, October 5, 1950

Dear Ruth:

I appreciate how disappointed you must have been to hear that we had engaged Jerry Whyte as stage manager for "Anna," and I am very sorry about this. I know that you had your heart set on the job, but there were a great many considerations and votes weighing in his favor. I have never been sure that "this is a man's world," but back-stage certainly is. I know that there is no manager in the business any better than you, but it is very hard to buck the tide of prejudice against women stage managers for big musical shows. I surely hope we can give you a chance at a really attractive job someday, and the sooner, the better.

We are working hard up here on "Burning Bright." It is impossible to estimate its commercial chances, but I believe it has a good chance of becoming one of the most important plays of this season.

Love from us all,

Ruth Mitchell ultimately became a stage manager for *The King and I*. Her extraordinary list of credits went on to include: stage manager for *Bells are Ringing*; production stage manager for *West Side Story, Gypsy, Fiorello, Forum, She Loves Me*, and *Fiddler on the Roof*. She took the title of "produced in association with Hal Prince" for *Cabaret, Company, Follies, A Little Night Music*; and then as "assistant to Hal Prince" for *Sweeney Todd, The Phantom of the Opera*, and *Kiss of the Spider Woman*. Mitchell's last Broadway credit was for Prince's 1994 revival of Hammerstein and Kern's *Show Boat*.

Production costs for *The King and I* were greater than those for any previous Rodgers and Hammerstein show. They might have gone even higher had one notion of Hammerstein's been adopted.

Jo Mielziner to Oscar Hammerstein, October 9, 1950

Subject: Elephants

In a conversation today with Mr. Fairfield Osborn, president of the N. Y. Zoological Society, and his chief assistant in charge of maintenance of animals, a man by the name of Crandell, the following information was revealed:

It is their experience that elephants do not work well alone—that even with a pair of elephants they are not too happy or as easily persuaded to do a routine as when they are working in a herd (such as large circular elephant herd).

It takes several roust-abouts to handle even the tamest elephant because of their enormous strength and weight.

The problem of the reinforcement of stage floors was brought up as an elephant often shifts his weight so that it is not evenly distributed on his four feet. The heavy construction of all platforms, and ramps, would necessitate a great added burden to both scene trouping and scene shifting.

Elephants are extremely sensitive to temperature. Not only the exposure to winter climate in Northern States would be a hazard, but even if this problem were solved with closed vans the sudden exposure to the heat of back stage lights might cause serious trouble.

Elephants are not easily persuaded to accept the sudden noise of audience applause and blinding lights without much preparation and long association with surroundings that are familiar to them.

Cost of even a young bull or cow would start at $3500 a piece.

The Zoological Society said that if we were willing to solve the above listed problems and face the risk that you recommend Henry Trafflich, Fulton St. N.Y. a dealer in circus animals. The Society said that if an elephant purchased by the management was no longer of service the Society might, provided the animal was in a healthy state, buy him for nominal amount.

I know Mr. Osborn personally and I think his opinions were straight forward and unprejudiced, while if we go to the animal dealer, Mr. Trefflich, I'm afraid we will get a lot of sales talk and not an honest opinion.

J.M.

Jo Mielziner to Oscar Hammerstein, October 16, 1950

Dear Oscar,

I have completed my research background on ANNA AND THE KING OF SIAM and I am beginning to get a mechanical solution to the whole production which I think will fit into a workable scheme with one exception. The deck of the steamer is the problem which is troubling me. In analyzing the requirements for this scene, I am disturbed by the fact that a greater part of this is better played with the actors facing the audience. If, as you indicate, the vista of approaching Bangkok is upstage, it seems to me the scene begs for a spectacular or very important "scenic effect". I feel that the treatment for all the other scenes in the production should be approached from an angle of interpretation in simple terms of what in actual life is rather overly ornate a style of architecture. Now, if we handled the scenic solution to the scene about ship in a realistic manner it would not be in keeping. How would you feel about a device that would reverse the situation aboard ship? In other words, we see not a large set but a portion of the sailing steamer which allows the action to be 95% towards the audience. Even little Louis, although occasionally rushing upstage to perhaps an elevated portion to get a better look, would really be seeing the approach of Bangkok out somewhere in the audience. By lighting effects on the bottom of the sails, I think I could give the sense of both movement and the suggestion of the glow or torches when the crelahome [*sic*] and his party board the ship.

To really achieve a tremendously effective scenic stunt would, I am convinced, set a visual key out of keeping with the remainder of the production.

I hope my memo to you on the emotional idiosyncrasies of the elephant did not get to you just at the point when you had decided to use a live animal in the show.

I hope I have a chance to see you tonight at the dress rehearsal of BURNING BRIGHT.

Yours, as ever,

Jo o-o-o-o-o-o-o-[drawing of an elephant]

Burning Bright, written by John Steinbeck and produced by Rodgers and Hammerstein, opened on Broadway on October 18.

Oscar Hammerstein to Stephen Sondheim, October 20, 1950

Dear Stevie:

Thank you for your opening night telegram. We are still flickering.

All the best to you.

Oscar Hammerstein II

Oscar Hammerstein to Gerald Waxman, October 20, 1950

Dear Mr. Waxman:

Thank you for your interesting letter about "Burning Bright". As a matter of fact your suggestion for the handling of the second act curtain was the original way in which Steinbeck wrote the play. Joe Saul got the idea himself, but it seemed to Steinbeck, and to all of us, that this was very contrived and gratuitous. I am inclined to agree with you that the way it is now being played is also a contrivance, but at least the motivation comes from somewhere, and in the other instance it seemed to come from nowhere. This is not a complete answer to you because I fully realize that your point is that it would be coming from Joe Saul's character. It may be that this revision was a mistake.

That play has been a most interesting one to produce because opinions on it vary so widely. There are those who are impressed deeply by it, both intellectually and emotionally—as you have been, and there are others who reject it completely. I am sorry to report to you that among these are most of the New York critics. The play opened in New York Wednesday night, October 18th, and with two exceptions received very poor notices. It is not possible at this point to predict whether it will survive them.

At any rate, I am very grateful for your interest, and I am glad that you wrote your letter. I see no reason why you should have been the least bit diffident about expressing your opinion to me. I would like more of this from the theatre-going public. It would be healthy for all of us.

All good wishes to you.

Sincerely,

Oscar Hammerstein II

Robert Lantz (Gale Agency) to Oscar Hammerstein, October 23, 1950

Dear Mr. Hammerstein:

I spoke to your secretary this afternoon, and she told me that it will be difficult to see you before you leave for the country tomorrow.

The matter I wanted to discuss with you on behalf of Miss Hedy Lamarr concerns "THE LITTLE PRINCE" by Antoine de Saint-Exupery. Miss Lamarr has bought the stage and movie rights to this book, which she loves very much. She was wondering whether you knew it, and whether you and Mr. Rodgers would be interested in it as a possible musical. She is a great fan of yours and especially asked me to tell you that.

If you do not know the book, I shall be very glad to send you a copy. It is a very short book, and whatever you may decide about it, I am sure you will enjoy reading it.

Of course, if you and Mr. Rodgers would be interested in it at all, Miss Lamarr would be more than delighted to come East to discuss this with you further and tell you what her particular ideas and plans for it are.

Hoping to hear from you soon, and with kindest regards,

Very sincerely yours,

GALE AGENCY, INC.

Robert Lantz

Oscar Hammerstein to Robert Lantz, October 26, 1950

Dear Mr. Lantz:

Your letter regarding "The Little Prince" by Antoine de Saint-Exupery is most interesting but we are in no position to discuss anything like that for some time. We are at the moment busily engaged in writing an adaptation of "Anna and the King of Siam" which will not come to New York before April, and further commitments take us through next season. I am sure that

Miss Lamarr would not want to wait that long. Thank you very much for submitting the idea to us.

All good wishes.

Sincerely,

Oscar Hammerstein II

John Steinbeck to Richard Rodgers and Oscar Hammerstein, October 26, 1950

Dear Dick and Oscar:

I want to say now that I can think of no care, nor consideration nor thought which might have been used which was not. It was a beautiful production. The failure was the play, and, since I still think it is a good play, even I can take no blame. I'm sorry that money was lost. That is the only thing that was. I enjoyed and learned. But I did not learn to do it differently than it was done.

At the risk of being sentimental (and who isn't) I liked every part of it, and I thank you for the association.

I seem to thrive on opposition. I never felt better or more alive in my life. For all my life I have been practicing to do a certain book and now I am ready for it and will get to it right off. And don't think it won't be kicked to pieces also. Everything I have ever done has been attacked. And in a way I imagine that is good. At least I do not get lulled into a success pattern. And I do not think this is the end of B.B.

Finally I am proud of the association with Rodgers and Hammerstein. That means much more to me than a simple success would have. I have my motto painted over my door— "Si no quieres vola—curdado de las alas." [If you do not want to fly—curled wings.] It works.

John.

Burning Bright closed on October 28, after thirteen performances.

Oscar Hammerstein to Irving Berlin, November 1, 1950

Dear Irving:

Dorothy and I saw "Call Me Madam" two nights ago. This was our first visit and we both thoroughly enjoyed it from curtain to curtain.

While the show was on the road I heard gloomy reports about it, and indeed the first encouraging thing I heard came from Dick Rodgers, who saw it on its last night in Boston. He was the first one to tell me that he thought it was a great show—without any reservations—and that he particularly admired the score. He said you had five wonderful numbers, wasn't that enough for any score, and I agreed that it was. Having seen it myself now, I endorse his opinion.

My purpose in writing to you is not merely to report what Dick thought, or to tell you what I thought, because neither of these opinions is very important right now. The play is a solid, smashing success. I just wish to say it deserves to be. It has no weakness. I think that the book is consistently entertaining and engaging, and has a great deal of charm. I think that Paul Lukas is a sincere performer and of great value to the play, even if he is not a good singer. I have never liked Merman so well—not even in "Annie Get Your Gun", because in addition to her usual vitality, she exhibits a sweetness in this play, both in the dialogue and the singing. I just had a wonderful time all through the evening and so did Dorothy, and so will millions of people. My congratulations to you, and continued admiration.

All my best wishes.

Sincerely,

Oscar

Oscar Hammerstein to Elna Laun, November 8, 1950

Dear Miss Laun:

We would not be interested at this time in a production of a Yiddish translation of "Oklahoma!"

Thank you for your interest.

Very truly yours,

Oscar Hammerstein II

Leland Hayward, with Jerome Robbins, to Oscar Hammerstein
(transcribed from a recording), November 11, 1950

Dear Oscar:

I am writing this from the hotel in Paris. Jerry Robbins is with me. I thought perhaps he could talk to you a few minutes on this record and give you his feelings and impressions and emotions about "Anna". He saw some native dancers here that he wants to talk to you about, and he is full of good ideas and hot notions about the whole project, so wait a minute and I'll introduce you to Jerome Robbins.

Hello Mr. Hammerstein, first of all I want to tell you how really very very excited I am about the show. The bad part of it is that I haven't gotten it out of my mind since I've gotten here and it keeps obsessing all my time. Last night I went to see some Indonesian dancing at the legation here. There was some Java, Sumatra, Bali, Celebes and I saw some wonderful things which started me thinking of how they could possibly be used in the show. These are all just ideas and kind of off the top of my head, but I wanted to tell you about them. One thing I saw that I was particularly impressed by was a dance between a man and a woman, in which the woman did very little. Most of the time she just stood with her eyes cast down, and sort of presented herself to the man who was standing across on the other side of the stage, who was watching her. The music was very exciting, not loud, but rhythmic and pulsating, and he, while he was watching her would only very slowly move his head, somewhat bird-like, somewhat snake-like. It was terrifically sexy. It was almost as if he had been touching her all over, and this distance between them pointed this up all the more and I was immediately struck by the parallel between this dance and the story of "Anna and the King of Siam" in their personal relationship—that there was no contact between them but that this thing was going on all the time. I was speaking to Leland tonight about it, and he said it would be wonderful if there was some way of using this, and he said "Well perhaps at one point when he is giving her dictation, that this dance is going on as part of the King's entertainment." I have a lot of thoughts about the dancing in this show. From what I have seen the tone of it should be very quiet. It should not be balletic in any sense at all. It should be based completely on native material, mostly as far as the range of movement is concerned. I don't think it should be large or extravagant. I think the figures each should be crystal and jewel-like, and performed with great dignity and great elegance, and that the humor should come out of basically just the juxtaposition of what they are dancing about and the manner they dance it with, rather than any broad or farcical elements whatsoever. The only ideas I had that may be interesting or amusing is that perhaps Anna has helped them only at certain moments or have given them ideas about theatre such as the scene in the western civilization rather than the eastern. For instance what I think would be very lovely and very beautiful is if she had rigged up this faked paper snow to come down at one point, which would float gently down and which the dancers themselves would move through. I think that could be very exciting.

The next thing that I tell you is not because of any particular ambitions I have concerning the show. I am completely pleased to do just the ballet, but in reading the script over and over I felt very much that all the movement should be of a particular style, and maybe by this time you have arrived at the same idea yourself. I think that the entrance of the servants and the entrance of the children and the manner of the deportment around the court should all be of one style which should really be connected with the ballet ultimately, not that it leads up to it, but that it is all of one piece. I am very excited about the script. I think it's a wonderful script. When first I read it I was very tired and didn't want to think of work, and then over the days I think I slowly haunted Leland about it.

I saw a girl here, a singer, who I spoke to Leland about concerning the role of Tuptim. I am going to take Leland up to see her, and see how he likes her. I don't know to what degree you've got on with your casting at all. I spoke to Howard Hoyt and I told him to contact Johnny Fearnley as far as looking around for material such as it is in New York now, of Siamese and Oriental dancing, so that all that would be prepared when I came back. The ballet, as I mentioned earlier, I do not see as a huge overpowering number of people. I think it should be like a polished jewel, delicately performed and intimately done. The music interests me as to what will be used there, because the music that I have heard here plays a very important part, the percussion, quality, the nasal singing quality, and all that is indicated in the script, but I did not know how far you were planning to go on this. I'd be very interested to hear what your view is on the subject. I can't think of anything else right now. If I do I'll jot it down and try to make a lot of notes and ask Leland to do this for me again. I'm very flattered and honored that

I have been asked to do this, and I am certainly very happy to be working with you all on it.

Oscar, this is Leland again. If you want to you can write Jerry a dictaphone record for him to play here on my machine. He's really so God damn excited about the thing that he's driving me crazy about it. Now, wait, he has one other thing he wants to say to you. Jerry kind of did the dance that he described to you a few minutes ago on this record for me, kind of a rough outline of it, and by God, it's wild and exciting because the thing about it is that apparently in all these Siamese or these Oriental dances there is practically no movement of the body. It's a very very slight movement, and when they move just one finger or toe, or flick an eyelash, it['s] a terrific wallop. It's done with great quiet. It's got Jerry very excited over the dramatic import of such a dance, and that's all he wanted me to tell you. I hope everything went well in Minneapolis and Chicago, and that the show got off to a great opening in Chicago, and, I've got a few more seconds here on the record so I'll just tell you we had a good trip over, very quiet. Both Nan and I were so damned exhausted we couldn't get out of bed, and I got a terrible disease. I wore some new silk socks to Dick's party which apparently the dye in them was poison, or anyway it was poison for me, and I got an allergy in my feet. They're full of blisters and all puffed up, so I couldn't get out of bed, which was a very good thing because I slept all the way across the ocean, and we've been in Paris a few days now, and actually Nan and I haven't been out of the hotel room but twice to get something to eat, and we've just slept the clock around the rest of the time. We're going over to London on Monday to look at "Roberts" and "Accolade" and do all those kind of chores. If you've got anything you want me to do for you in London I'll be there from Monday the 13th I guess it is until about the 23rd. I'll be at Claridges Hotel. You can cable me there if there's anything I can do for you or Dick, or anything in connection with the theatre. If you want me to go look at a theatre in London, or do anything about the "Pacific" thing while I'm there, just shoot me a cable and I'll be very happy to do it. Please give your Dorothy our love. By the way, how's your new granddaughter? We saw Billy down at the boat. He came down to see us off, and I had a feeling that Billy was very disappointed that he hadn't had a son instead of a daughter, but I told him he had plenty of opportunity to eventually accomplish that aim, and I hope you are pleased with your new granddaughter. Take care, Oscar, and we'll see you very soon. Love from us both.

Oscar Hammerstein to Betty Borchardt, November 16, 1950

Dear Miss Borchardt:

Thank you for your letter and the envelope enclosing your interesting photographs. Regarding my coming play, "Anna and the King of Siam" I am afraid there will be nothing in that for you because you are too tall to play any of the parts. All of the female parts, outside of Gertrude Lawrence's star part, are Siamese women, and they as you know are all very small. I think you would like to know my general impression of you from hearing you sing the other day. I think you have a very sweet voice, that it needs further training, and that beyond that you need training and experience in the actual projection of a song. You were more impressive in singing "Granada" than when you tackled the song with the English lyric. I felt that your singing was lacking in the emotional appreciation of the lyric that a singer should give a song. The words did not seem to be felt deeply by you. There is no use just singing notes. The better singers give every possible value to the lyric. I don't believe these comments should discourage you. You are still young and you have time to develop your talent. The one thing that you must remember is that you have chosen a difficult career. It is not a matter of getting up and singing for one manager and falling into a good job immediately. You must sing for many until you land in the right spot, and all the time that you are waiting you must work and perfect your singing voice and develop your theatrical imagination, study other singers—successful singers, and watch how carefully they put value into their songs.

Beyond this advice I can tell you nothing at the moment, but I shall be pleased to hear you again at some future time when you think you have improved.

All good wishes to you.

Sincerely,

Oscar Hammerstein II

The King and I was the only Broadway *musical* directed by John Van Druten. He went on to write and direct two more plays—*I Am a Camera* and *I've Got Sixpence*—before he passed away in 1957. (*I Am a Camera* was later adapted into the musical *Cabaret*.)

John Van Druten to Oscar Hammerstein, November 29, 1950

Dear Oscar,

A brief line of report. I saw Irene Sharaff on Saturday, and recognized her instantly in the lobby of her hotel from your description of her as looking remotely Siamese. She had strange pearl pins in her hair, and a very odd make-up! She showed me the sketches she had done, and I thought most of them very good. I was not sure of the Kralahome's coat that she had drawn: I think I would prefer him to be more naked.

She had a couple of queries on the script. One, which had already occurred to me, was over Anna's undressing, in her soliloquy. She seemed to feel, as I did, that Anna cannot take off her hoop-skirt and then get it on again, decently and conveniently. I think this needs some thinking about. The other was over the scene in Scene 6 where the King is concerned about the Kralahome seeing the wives in their night-clothes. In the first place, she tells me that Siamese do not HAVE night-clothes; and secondly, that the Kralahome would have seen them all in all stages of undress—breasts bare etc.—anyway. I suggested she bring this up with you when she sees you.

I have read quite a lot of the book, and am going on with it. You will find it hard to re-name Son-klin (the mother of Prince Chulalongkorn) with the name of the real mother. The Prince's real mother was the dead queen who was being cremated when Anna arrived! (See the book on Page 44.) I gather she had only been dead a few months, but I prefer your four years! I cannot think we need be so exact and factual, anyway. Irene S. told me that the present Royal family dislike the whole idea of Grand-daddy (or is it Great Grand-daddy?) being put on the stage, and hope it will all be very wrong and inexact anyway!

I do find both Anna and Louis perfectly maddening in print—Louis especially, with his habit of burying his tear-ridden face perpetually in Anna's skirts. I do realize, of course, that Anna is a Victorian Lady, and we cannot escape that. However, it HAS occurred to me that we might as well make perhaps something more of a point of it—and of her hot temper, as well. I have therefore very slightly sketched in a few lines in the opening scene, where—via Captain Orton—we let on that we know what we are doing, and that ladylikeness and hot temper are Anna's faults rather than her virtues, and that she does TRY and overcome them from time to time. I don't know if it comes off at all—and it isn't very strong—but I am enclosing the pages of Scene 1 (without any of the stage business) for you to look at. I do believe in this way—and perhaps we might even go a little further—we can cover ourselves and Anna's slight skirt-pulling prissiness a little bit. I shall be very glad to hear what you feel about it all.

I think that is all for now. I got down here yesterday. It is hot and lovely. I slept out in the garden after lunch to-day. I do seem to have left New York at exactly the right time, and I wish you could be out here, too. If you can and would care to come, just send me a wire and COME.

Have you given any further thought to Alan Napier as Sir Edward Ramsay? You might make some enquiries about him. I can get into touch with him out here. But there may well be someone just as good in the East.

All the best for now. I look forward to all the new pages, and to getting really going later on with everything. It all excites me a lot. I did not see Gertie, as I read that she had gone with Daphne du Maurier to Florida for two weeks.

Best to Dick, and both Dorothys,

Yours,

John

Oscar Hammerstein to John Van Druten, December 5, 1950

Dear John:

Thank you for your letter and the script of Scene 1. I am very soon sending you a new copy of Scene 1 which contains all the cuts we had previously agreed upon, and most of the changes that you have suggested. I inserted a reason why the Captain thought that Anna had a quick temper, otherwise the implication is that he is an old friend of the family, and knows more about her character than ordinarily he would. I don't know if you think my reason for his knowing about her temper is a good one, but we must have some reason.

Regarding Irene Sharaff's worries, I think they are little ones. If Anna cannot take off her hoop skirt let her leave it on. We shall take off some petticoats and undress the top of her down to her guimpe.[8] As for

---

[8] A kind of blouse, or covering for the neck and chest.

the King's concern about the Kralahome's seeing the wives in their night clothes, when as a matter of fact they have no night clothes, let us welcome this as a chance to cut. The King will exhibit no concern and we will save four or five lines. I have found out the real name of Chulalongkorn's mother, and it looks like a hard one to pronounce, but I am going to find out from the Siamese if it is really hard or not. After she dies, the Prince was brought up by a great-aunt, who had also brought up his mother. We might use her, or we might keep Son Klin and not have her [as] the mother of the Prince. All that we would lose is the second act speech about Anna not being fair to her son, but her protest could be on behalf of all the children, she being a kind of head nurse and head wife. Tell me what you think of this.

Your invitation to come out is most attractive, and I would fly there like a shot, only I must report I have had a very tough time with the lyrics so far. They have not come very well. I can tell you that I think I have sketched in Anna's background rather well in lyrics leading up to the song "Tom and I". I am about to embark on the King's song, "Something I Nearly Think I am Not Sure etc." "Tom and I" held me back a long time. I am glad to be past it. I am spending all my days on the lyrics now, and at night when I am not too tired, I go back to the script. I have so far only made the cuts and changes in the first two scenes. You shall be hearing from me anon.

Love from us all.

John Van Druten to Oscar Hammerstein, December 8, 1950

My dear Oscar,

The re-typed version of Scene 1 came this noon. Thank you very much. I am sorry to find that it is still eleven pages, but of course if one will go on adding things . . .

I am glad that you kept my ladylike and hot-tempered bits. I am a bit sorry that the line about "Kings don't, usually" has gone. I have a strong suspicion that Gertie could get a nice laugh out of it. There was no letter to cover it, so I don't know if you want me to go on through the script in this way, but I probably will do so for my own amusement in the next few days. I am really coming to life again, and feeling full of bounce and vitality.

I suppose you read that poor Colin Keith-Johnston has left the Cornell show. How about HIM for Sir Edward, if he would take it for the work it would probably give him? [*sic*]

All my best to you all. Everything good.

Yours always,

John

Oscar Hammerstein to John Van Druten, December 12, 1950

Dear John:

I have no violent prejudice against "Kings don't, usually". I think, however, that it is at best a very small giggle, and that the idea that Kings don't usually is implicit in what she has just said. You may have that for Saturday afternoon in New Haven, if you like.

I think it is an excellent idea for you to go ahead through the script in the way that you have been doing. I am going to send out the cut and changed versions of the scenes to you as I finish them. I think that scene one will come to ten pages instead of eleven, if you agree to the additional cuts I indicated in the copy I sent you. We have already thought of Colin Keith-Johnston for the part of Sir Edward, and Johnny Fearnley is approaching him.

All the best,

As ever,

Oscar Hammerstein II

Oscar was asked for a favorite recipe to be included in a *Celebrity Cook Book* being compiled to benefit the Damon Runyon Cancer Fund.

Oscar Hammerstein to Mrs. M. Brookfield Michael, December 11, 1950

Dear Mrs. Michael:

I have no favorite recipe. I eat everything that is put in front of me.

Sincerely,

Oscar Hammerstein II

Oscar Hammerstein to Arthur Hammerstein, December 12, 1950

Dear Uncle Arthur:

Thank you for your check. I haven't any news to report to you. Freed, as you know, is coming east after the holidays, and I will spend some time with him at that time, and see if we can't get a definite decision about the biography.

I am going along very slowly with my lyrics. It gets tougher and tougher because I have to try to make them better and better. However, it will be no hardship for me to make a few phone calls for you in connection with the benefit during the month of January, even though I will still be hard at work on these lyrics. We go into rehearsal January 26th and will open in New Haven February 26th.

The Chinese situation has not curtailed our efforts in World Government. As a matter of fact this might be a very good time for us to interest people who see what a terrible, and what a silly thing war is, when it is right on top of them. You understand, of course, that our overall and long range plans do not have anything to do with disarmament. We believe in a big army, and navy, and air force. Right now, the bigger the better. We have to protect ourselves until we can get a World Government. I read in the paper this morning that Lloyds of London has offered fifty to one against a world war before next September 21st. This is something, anyway.

If our state department and our people could only get it through their heads that this is not a football game, and doesn't have to be won by any particular score on any particular field, but a problem in which all of us ought to jump in and invite all other nations to come with us, we might get somewhere. I am afraid, however, that our leadership hasn't the proper wisdom or courage, and what discourages me even more, I see nobody in the Republican party who might be any better equipped than the people in the Democratic party who have made so many mistakes. Every time I begin to think that maybe Truman isn't so bad after all, he writes a letter.

We all send our love to you and Dorothy and wish you a merry Christmas and a happy New Year.

Oscar Hammerstein to Dorothy Fields, December 26, 1950

Dear Dorothy:

Things are looking up. Not only do I like the candy much better than the cookies, but it seems to me that this candy is fresher than the cookies were. A quick look at them also convinces me that a few hours devoted to them can attain better results weight gaining than the cookies could have given me. I don't know whether I am an envious and covetous man by nature, but even this year I think Dorothy's present is better. I love the color and the cut, and I love the flair and shape of it. When Dorothy put it [on] my comment was that if she were a bell she would ring.

Merry Christmas, Happy New Year, and love to you all.

Oscar Hammerstein to Mary Martin and Richard Halliday, December 26, 1950

Dear Mary and Dick:

At last I am a Knight of the Garter, and as the owner of the two most adorned legs in town, I wish to thank you both. No longer can they call me "old wrinkle socks".

Merry Christmas, Happy New Year, and love to you all.

Chapter Ten
1951

As 1951 began, Rodgers and Hammerstein had two shows on Broadway, *South Pacific*—the hottest ticket on Broadway—and the play *The Happy Time*, produced by R & H. Meanwhile, *Carousel* was playing in London's West End, and a national tour of *Oklahoma!* was still making its rounds.

America was some six months into the Korean War, and, in late January, the United States tested a one-kiloton nuclear bomb in Nevada. During World War II Hammerstein and Rex Stout were both active members of the Writers War Board. Stout also led the Society for the Prevention of World War III, an organization that joined with other groups to form the United World Federalists, of which Hammerstein became an ardent member. The United World Federalists advocated the expansion of the United Nations' authority to enforce the rule of international law in order to prevent future wars.

Oscar Hammerstein to Rex Stout, January 11, 1951

Dear Rex:

An idea for the bulletin. One of the questions we all hear most is: "Is it not too late to talk about World Government now, when we are already at war? Do we lay low now and wait for this war to be over and renew our activities in this direction?" The article would of course point out that this is the best time of all, when the horrors and the ridiculous cruelty of war is right at our door; to work as hard as we can on any method that we know to stop this in the future. I have expressed all this very clumsily but I am pretty sure you get the idea, and in the hands of one of our literati, I am sure it might turn into a cogent and important paragraph.

A second idea. A paragraph on the assumption that one gleans from the newspapers these days; that the solution to all our troubles is the creation of a powerful Army, Navy and Air Force for defense or eventual victory over Russia—we would state our belief that it is necessary to create such a force. (CF Hammerstein Minute Man speech written by Rex Stout) but that

The Letters of Oscar Hammerstein II. Mark Eden Horowitz, Oxford University Press. © Mark Eden Horowitz 2022.
DOI: 10.1093/oso/9780197538180.003.0010

more than this is the necessity of concomitant effort to develop the only possible plan for eliminating the necessity of such large defense forces in the future.

I realize that this last will seem elementary to many of the bulletin readers, and perhaps so will the first paragraph, yet I think that these two things are basic mistakes and we should provide our readers with answers when they meet these questions from the schmo friends, of whom there are many. Laura Hobson seems to have more than anyone. She is always quoting them, and I don't see why she has them in her house.

Love to all.

Having completed a script for *The King and I*, Hammerstein sent a copy to Margaret Landon, the author of the 1944 novel *Anna and the King of Siam*, on which the musical was based.

Oscar Hammerstein to Helen Strauss (William Morris Agency), January 16, 1951

Dear Miss Strauss:

I am sorry that Miss Landon didn't like my play, but I cannot help feeling that there is much more to my script than meets her eye. I hope that when she comes up to New York to see it on the stage, that she will be pleasantly surprised.

Sincerely,

Oscar Hammerstein II

Josh Logan to Richard Rodgers and Oscar Hammerstein, January 18, 1951

Dear Dick and Oscar:

It's three o'clock in the morning and I am still sitting here in my living room, completely knocked out, with my mind crawling, thinking about the tremendous emotional kick I got out of hearing the score last evening.

I could, of course, sit back and say that this is the most wonderful thing I have ever heard in my life, and I'm not sure that it isn't. I'm sure of a few things that are absolute perfection and I have several doubts about others, and I thought I might as well express them to you rather than keep them quiet, and you can either throw this letter away or take some of it and use it, or do what you will.

First of all, I think both musically and lyrically that HELLO YOUNG LOVERS is the greatest single dramatic song that I have ever heard in my life, and probably ever will. Up to this point my favorite had been that soliloquy in CAROUSEL, or perhaps IF I LOVED YOU, but this one seems to me at this moment to top both of them.

I am also completely crazy about THE WAITING SONG, THE PUZZLEMENT SONG and ANNA'S SOLILOQUY where she gets an imaginary kick from the king at the end. All four of these things seem to me to be highlights in a show and four such highlights should make this show worth going to see for anyone, just for them alone.

Now for my few reservations.

Number one, I was disappointed in the song between Tuptim and the boy—the duet, I mean—not Tuptim's LORD AND MASTER song, which I thought was wonderful. It's THE SHADOW SONG; I'm not exactly sure of the title. But may I express myself on it this way. There are so many moments in the show of frustrated love that it would be a great and welcome thing, and wonderful contrast, if there could be a really elated, sexy song between these two exciting young people. Somehow, the song has a kind of darkness about it, both lyrically and musically. There is an emotional life and a kind of fulfillment in YOUNGER THAN SPRINGTIME that would be very helpful from these two kids. I know that they can't go off dancing together. In other words, it is not a song that I would find easy to stage if I were the director.

Number two, I am also a little bit worried to hear that there is going to be no mass singing in the first act, and no dancing except for a tiny bit at the opening. May I make a suggestion? Is it possible in the schoolroom scene when the children are learning that they could be given a dancing lesson by Gertie and a gay, happy dancing song with a lot of kids singing with her? If this could be inserted and give some chance for a little more fun in this act.

It would be nice to have something quite Western, as for instance a polka or gallop or whatever could be done in that period.

And now, Dick and Oscar, perhaps I am wrong, but I feel that THE PATROL somehow robs the beginning of HELLO YOUNG LOVERS in which her tale is translated by Sonklin, because somehow I feel that musically it is not as much of a contrast as it could be to THE PATROL. Dick, when you spoke to me you said that you were trying to figure out a way of not doing any Oriental music and you had found a way of doing it comically. I have a feeling that delicate and charming as THE PATROL is itself, that somehow there could be more melody to it, another section with upbeat major or double time or something more Richard Rodgers and less a kind of Oriental comment. It might not be understood as it is as satirical. Perhaps if I heard this orchestrated I would feel absolutely different.

In other words, and to sum up, my whole reservations come from the fact that the great moments of your score are so great that of necessity they are fairly similar. There are two angry fighting songs which remind me of each other and yet are wonderfully different . . . WAITING and THE SOLILOQUY. And there are three songs in which women sing about men who are not on the stage. Therefore, anything that can be done to bring some gay, elated or bright musical moments without dissonance, I think should be studied. I would also like to say that any moment that the Western type of music is used as opposed to the Eastern type, would be a welcome contrast.

Now I would like to close by saying that if you do nothing that I say you will still have a great work of art and a great theatrical achievement and an enormous success. I am proud to have been able to hear this score and I am proud that you are my friends and that I know you and can brag about that fact to other people.

Best Always,

Logan's suggestion to add a "gay, happy dancing song" for Anna and the children in the first act was realized in the song "Getting to Know You." However, Rodgers credits Gertrude Lawrence for making the suggestion when they were out-of-town in Boston in March.

Oscar Hammerstein to Laurence Schwab, January 31, 1951

Dear Larry:

I have just finished your book and enjoyed it very much indeed. This is a fairly big thing for me to say because this is the type of book I never read. I am not an addict of true adventure stories or tales of illogical gallantry, and yet I liked this story of yours very much. I think what caught me was the result of your very complete research, which created a background of reality and interesting information.

What I didn't like was your treatment of the English characters. Not the damning factual evidence which you produced. There is no doubt that you have the goods on the English merchants in China of that period, but since they are the natural heavies of this story, I think they should have been characterized better. I would not ask for any punches to be pulled or any whitewashing, but I would ask that among them there would be a few intelligent villains, and possibly one or two virtuous men. As it was, they were all singularly alike, and could all have been played by either one of the Grossmith brothers—or by Lou Holtz imitating the Grossmith brothers. These are hard words but I make my attack aggressive because I think this is a hole in your novel, and a very vital one. The English element here is terribly important. Their trade in tea mixed up with their trade in dope is the dramatic side of your novel, and I think it should be projected better and seem as authentic in your treatment as the facts undoubtedly are.

I think all of your descriptions of the various scraps that ensue are exciting and brilliantly devised. The color and the background jump out at you and leave memories after you put the book down, and the cast of characters seems to me very well chosen.

I do have a general feeling regarding the dialogue that is in dialect, the same feeling I have about four English characters—in regard to your Frenchman and your Italian cook. Maybe this is a special prejudice of mine, but I think the dialogue and the idiom used in many places is trite and smacking a little of the Dick Tracy school. There is no reason why this should be, and if you agreed with me you could fix it quite easily. I don't think this side of the writing is up to the rest of the writing, the conception of the episodes or the prose descriptions.

One more little criticism—and I am very proud of this one because it is technical, and I am amused by it because you put me in the position of making it. Do you remember when we took that trip into the Everglades and did some bird watching? I remember distinctly that the naturalists told us that the Man O' War bird was a kind of <u>highjacker</u>. He waited for other birds to swoop down into the water and come up with a fish, then he would scare the birds away and catch the fish in mid-air when they dropped it from fright. He had to do this because he could not go down into the water himself to get the fish. He could not do this because he could not take off from the water. If a Man O' War bird lands on the water he's stuck, and yet on page 149 you describe them as taking off from the water. T-t-t-t-t!

In spite of these sharp criticisms, I must tell you that I am excited about this book, and I am curious to know what you are doing about it. What are your plans? Have you interested a publisher? To what extent? Please tell me all about it, and meanwhile my love to Mildred and you.

P.S. I have heard that St. Petersburg didn't pan out. I hope you are not too concerned about this. You ought to regard that music circus business as a sideline, and don't let it encroach too much on the much more important job of making this book as good as you can, and then starting a second one.

Schwab died on May 29, 1951, leaving his book unfinished.

Alice Meyer and Ilene Spack (Weinreb), circa February, 1951

Dear Mr. Hammerstein,

We have just come home from South Pacific. In talking it over, we began to compare it with your other productions. Two of us felt that "Carousel" could never be surpassed, but we have read unfavorable criticisms and talked to people who were either neutral or made adverse comments about the production. We would like to know what you consider to be your best work.

Sincerely yours,

Alice Meyer

Ilene Spack

Oscar Hammerstein to Alice Meyer and Ilene Spack,
February 16, 1951

Dear Misses Meyer and Spack:

I really have no favorite plays. I like some for some things and others for others. It is like having a large family of children and liking them all, but for different reasons—and not liking a few, also for different reasons. Thank you for your interest.

Sincerely,

Oscar Hammerstein II

The King and I began out-of-town tryouts in New Haven on February 26.

Robert Dolan to Oscar Hammerstein, February 27, 1951

Tuesday Morning

8:30 A. M.

Dear Oscar: -

Taking 9:00 A.M. train to town. (Have to be in by 10:30.).

Can't get over some of the beautiful writing done by both you and Dick. Planning to send you letter from N.Y. C. with whatever notes I have. Throw them in the waste basket if you don't like them.

Had no idea I was to be your guest in matter of tickets. Many many thanks. It was a beautiful show.

Bobby Dolan –

February Twenty Seventh

1   9   5   1

Dear Oscar:-

Here, for what they are worth, are some notes I made on the show.

I loved the writing, your book and lyrics and Dick's music. I think you can both be proud. Hardly any of my notes concern the writing. This show represents a real striking out for new forms on Dick's part and I think he has been very successful. I thought the show was well conducted, that Russell did a fine job and that the orchestral combination was very ingenious.

Do you think Gertrude Lawrence's conception of the part should be such a young character? Her manner of speech and her hair-do, especially, give me the feeling that she would like to be thought young. This not only seems unnecessary for such a fine performer as she but also I think it does the show considerable harm. Anna would find a warmer relationship with the King if she were to meet him a little closer to his age-bracket. I am aware that she has often been accused of being "cute" but I am also aware of her performance in "Fumed Oak" so I know that she is a fine actress and if she were made to understand that the younger she makes herself the worse it is for the part she would give the best performance of her life. I don't know whether I'm very clear about this but I feel it very deeply. She seems to be singing pretty well and more on pitch than is her custom. Both in the scenes and the songs she covers a little too much territory on the stage . . . walking back and forth. This seems such a trivial note to make but it really did bother me. It certainly provides action but I think it interferes with the establishment of an undercurrent of electricity between Anna & the King.

Yule [sic] Brynner was a very fortunate choice for the part. I don't think there is ever a reason to wonder whether he will take the show away from Lawrence. For all I know he may even have the larger part but she is the better performer and that counts. I was wondering whether his performance couldn't stand a little more progression. Say, for instance that he clearly establishes at the outset that he is a King, a man with a mind of his own, and occasionally has fits of temper throughout the show, but saves the full strength of his rage for the whip scene. There were many times in the show when he seemed to be stoop-shouldered and crouching and bending his knees. Perhaps he ought to avoid this if he is to be every inch a King most of the evening. Even when he gets mad he should not lose his dignity as a King. It is too bad he isn't a better singer so that he could do full justice to the Puzzlement number. From where I sat the weakness of the number seemed to be his performance (I didn't catch all the lyrics). Other than the usual remedies such as playing softer, or thinning out the orchestration, or bringing him down front more I wouldn't know what to suggest here. Perhaps there are cuts in the lyric that you would know about.

I'm damned if I can understand how a good actor like Murvyn Vye can be so far away from a character. His voice and accent (or lack of it) seem wrong. He is the only one in Siam who doesn't talk like the rest of the Siamese. And the accent he uses has too many American overtones to make me think he would ever be right for the part. Someone with the unction of Cedric Hardwicke or Joe Schildkraut or Arnold Moss would provide a quiet force in contrast to the King. Also Murvyn has a different physical build than any other Siamese shown on the stage.

In many ways Dorothy Sarnoff is wonderful in the part. But she needs much work on diction. It is so hard to understand her lyrics. This is not as serious as it sounds. I've seen people with worse diction brought around in a few days of painstaking work. As for Doretta Morrow, I haven't a complaint. I think she's excellent. Now to the songs.

I WHISTLE A HAPPY TUNE ... A wonderful number. Don't see how it can be done any better.

MY LORD AND MASTER ... Not catching all this lyric. I am not sure whether the lyric is identical with that used in the reprise with Phra Maha Rot. If it is then it is all the more reason that we understand the two distinct moods she uses to sing the number proper and the reprise.

WAITING . . . This is a good way to have her meet the King and I thought it was fine.

SCENE . . . The idea of this lyric and the manner of projecting it and Dick's usage of two keys are all wonderful. When you are looking for cuts in the show stay away from this spot.

HELLO, YOUNG LOVERS ... Just about as beautiful a song (lyrically and musically) as I've ever heard. The writing of the song made me cry. Isn't this one of the spots where Gertrude Lawrence moves about a little more than necessary?

THE ROYAL SIAMESE CHILDREN . . . Working with children is no easy matter. At the opening the audience laughed a few times during this number. I couldn't catch all the lyrics so I am not able to judge it.

A PUZZLEMENT ... Dick provided this lyric with a very clever music setting. If I remember correctly this is one number that is a little heavy in orchestration in one or two spots. There is a musical phrase that closes one strain with a descending melody (I think in major thirds) that was spanking fresh. But, I think it was only used once. I have no doubt that this number and the reprise that follows is a "trouble spot". The King is going to need some direction here that will help him feel more at home.

SHALL I TELL YOU WHAT I THINK OF YOU . . . There doesn't seem to be enough light and shade in Lawrence's performance here. Also it is overloaded with movement, which makes it difficult to follow the lyric.

SOMETHING WONDERFUL . . . A truly beautiful song. If Sarnoff will work on diction here it will be a perfect spot. This, to me, is a new idea for a lyric and certainly an ingenious though simple melody.

****

The dramatic climax of Act I is a perfectly valid one. We are expected to be filled with anticipation for the meeting with Sir Edward Ramsay. Will the King be considered barbaric or civilized? But when Sir Edward walks on the stage one doesn't worry any more. We have spent a whole act with the King and at a glance it is obvious that he has more on the ball than Sir Edward will ever have. This actor gives us a musical comedy Ambassador. That is very dangerous. Sir Edward must have all the dignity and importance that can be found in an actor. I don't think this fellow is right for the part.

****

WE KISS IN A SHADOW . . . The boy who sings this number, for some reason or other, never reaches the audience. So long as you can afford to give these people a small amount of time on the stage I think you might consider re-casting this part with a boy who, after he has subjected himself to a Siamese haircut, still comes off as a pretty attractive specimen worthy of the gifts God gave Doretta Morrow.

THE SMALL HOUSE OF UNCLE THOMAS . . . A very beautiful thought-out number that belongs intrinsically in this show. I liked it very much but not as much as the audience did. Perhaps my complaint is one of length. You've probably made cuts in it already. Aren't Tospy, Eva and Simon introduced twice? Maybe, the first introduction could be eliminated.

SHALL WE DANCE . . . There's nothing to be said about a number that stops the show. Except, perhaps, that it should be considered a warning signal. It seemed to suggest either that the audience was hungry for something like this (and perhaps should have had it's [sic] equivalent earlier) or that they simply wanted to see those two people become closer friends. If it's the latter than you have no worry at all. I think it is essential to pin down the dialogue and business down to specific numbers of bars so that the music can fade and swell in the right places without interfering with the dialogue.

****

Here is my most important suggestion about the book. In the scene where the King is about to whip the slave some things bothered me. First of all I thought too many subjects were discussed there. Second after Anna says "No I won't go I'm going to stay here and watch you do the whipping" the King finds he can't whip the girl and exits. Now Anna has a scene with Murvyn which, for some reason or other, is not clear to the audience. It's clear to me but not to them, I think. He tells her that she should go as she is no help to Siam. What about this suggestion: play [the] scene as is up to his preparing to whip the girl. Then, instead of throwing the whip away, he finds he can't whip her and orders her, Murvyn and the attendants to leave. Then he turns on Anna, (they being the only two on the stage), and says "You were saying you wanted to go back to your country. Well, go. You are no help here. You have done nothing but weaken me. In Siam the people get their strength from their King. If he is weak, Siam is weak. Now go . . . please go." (I'm surely not trying to write dialogue but it is the best way I know to describe the scene. I had been discussing this scene with George Oppenheimer and he felt this would not only be a little clearer, but give added strength to the scene that follows in her bedroom. This plan is his idea and I must say that it seems to have some merit.)

****

NOW YOU LEAVE . . . I loved the music to this number but I didn't catch all the lyric. I really can't judge it.

I don't imagine I've been much help Oscar. And I wouldn't be surprised if you had all these notes already. Nan and I were very grateful for having seen it. What I didn't say at the outset is that there is no doubt in my mind everything you need for a fine wonderful show is already there in the writing. I would be amazed if cutting and polishing didn't solve most of the problems.

A month or so ago we were discussing the supposed love story between Ingrid Bergman and Bing Crosby in Bells of St. Mary's. You felt there might be a parallel with the story of Anna & the King. I agree and am more deeply convinced of it than ever after having seen the show. But I firmly believe that the direction of Lawrence and Brynner must be geared with that idea constantly in mind. It's there in the script and the songs and it is up to them to see that no action on the stage interferes with it.

It's an adult, literate and artistic show. So much thought and work poured into a show deserves to have the public pour their life's savings into the St. James' box office.

Sincerely,

Bobby –

Oscar Hammerstein to Robert Dolan, March 26, 1951

Dear Bobby:

Thank you for your long letter written to me at New Haven, and high time I thanked you too. I was very happy that the play made so deep an impression on you. We have, I believe, improved it a great deal since you've seen it. I hope you have another chance to see it before you go back to the west coast. If you have not already left New York at the time you get this letter, will you please call me up. I would very much like to see you.

All the best.

As ever,

Oscar Hammerstein II

Gertrude Lawrence to Oscar Hammerstein, circa March, 1951

Dearest Occie

Please I beg you put back the chess scene for the reading of that most important letter until you can get some further cuts elsewhere.

My change means- hair, shoes—underclothes, hat, coat + dress, + I am so wet after the Polka + the whipping scene that last night they had to rip me out of the Ball Gown. It is impossible also to be in any mood for the reading of such a letter, apart from the fact that we all feel pretty stupid standing in a front cloth for it like the "Brooklyn Comedy 4." I stand for ages waiting for the reprise of Lovers while Tuptim + her chappie plan their escape + Tiang spies around—why not make a decent cut there?

Anyhow—please, give me a break on that letter scene for these two shows today. I am sure you will have some better cuts by rehearsal tomorrow.

We rang down at 11.12 last night, so we are "making progress."

Fondly

‚Anna'

The King and I opened on Broadway on March 29.

Sigmund Romberg to Oscar Hammerstein, March 30, 1951

Dear Oscar:

I not only want to thank you for the tickets you sent me, but also to tell you what a great kick I got out of watching the opening night performance of "THE KING AND I".

That is a monumental piece of work you have done. In fact, it is difficult for me to find just the right words to tell you how I feel. I think that to be in a position to write what you want to write, when you want to write it, is reaching the highest pinnacle of one's ambition, and just that puts you, in my estimation, in a unique class, leading all other men in your field bar none.

With my love, as ever

Sincerely,

Rommy

SIGMUND ROMBERG

P.S. On Monday April 9th I am expecting to meet you down at the bar of the Ritz Tower, at seven o'clock. Then we will have dinner and come back to my apartment for some bridge.

Ruth Cosgrove was a publicist based in New York, but who primarily represented motion picture studios. In 1953 she married the comedian Milton Berle.

Ruth Cosgrove to Oscar Hammerstein, March 30, 1951

Dear Mr. H,

I loved The King and I. You and Mr. Rodgers made it a beautiful, lovely and poignant play and I sat there full of such pride for both of you.

I hate the people who insist on making comparisons, but I'll join them only long enough to say that The King and I had the same sad beauty that you gave to Carousel. Hello, Young Lovers is one of the most beautiful lyrics I've ever heard, and that loud noise you heard was my heart breaking.

I can't possibly let you know what a thrill it was to be at the opening, and my deepest gratitude to you for inviting me.

Nothing but love and affection for you always.

Ruth

Ruth Cosgrove

As Chief Custodian of Variations of Titles on Anna and The King of Siam it occurs to me how wonderful it will look and sound when you do it in Paris. . . .Le Roi et Moi.

Oscar received a fan letter dated March 26, during the show's out-of-town tryout, positive, but for one criticism: ". . . many with whom I have spoken agree with me that the line 'Etc etc etc' is quite overworked and could almost be called trite. When the King gets it off the first time it is good and very well done. I wish that you could cut down the number of times that it is used to about three or four, spread them out a bit but give up a few of them."

Oscar Hammerstein to Mrs. William P. Everts, circa April, 1951

Dear Mrs. Everts:

Thank you for your letter of March 26th. We have often discussed the repetition of the "etceteras" and wondered why the audience seemed tireless in laughing at them no matter how many times they were repeated. Otherwise we should have cut out more of them. I agree with you, however, that two or three more could still be cut out to the advantage of the play, and I shall do this. I am very grateful for your interest and your praise. The play has become an immediate success of very large proportion, I believe, since the New York opening.

All good wishes to you.

Sincerely,

Oscar Hammerstein II

Oscar Hammerstein to Ruth Cosgrove, April 3, 1951

Dear Ruth:

Thank you for your nice letter. I am very happy that you liked the play so well. I also like your translation for the French title, but I think there is a grave danger that following the model "Annie du Far West" they may call this one "Anna de Far East". I hope you will do your best to stop this. The whole idea of the Paris presentation is a little frightening, and I am very glad that Josephine Baker has returned to America, for she would have been the obvious Tuptim, and I believe the balance of the play might have been thrown off by this casting. This is as far as I wish my imagination to dwell on the whole thing at this moment. I am trying to rest, you see. Deliberately shutting Paris from my brain, I leap to the Siamese version of "The King and I", and think about the ballet. How about one of their traditional Siamese plays done in the manner of Michael Todd? This should be electrifying to the Bangkok first nighters, (there would be no second night).

All the best to you.

Oscar Hammerstein II

Dorothy Fields to Oscar Hammerstein, circa March, 1951

Oscar darling:

Above everything else I have seen, I most admire and love "The King and I". It is beautiful, touching, charming and funny. I must admit that when I went across the street to see Mary—because I am leaving for the coast tomorrow—I was streaked with mascara. I don't ever hope to attain anything so beautiful as you do in words, but by God, I'm going to try. The audience reaction was simply wonderful. They applauded after every song very heartily, and the final curtain was a triumph.

My love and thanks to you.

Dorothy

Oscar Hammerstein to Gertrude Lawrence, April 3, 1951

Dearest Mrs. Anna:

I have on former occasion announced gratitude on you for bestowing of gold lucky piece, for holding of in palm of hand, etcetera, etcetera, etcetera. This is my official and documentary expression of thanking you for generous behavior. This does not, however, give you right to ask me for new cue to "Young Lovers" of which I have already give exhorbitant [sic] sum. Please accept felicitous assurance of admiration, devotion and—forgive my broken English—

Love,

Oscar Mongkuy

Gertrude Lawrence to Oscar Hammerstein, April 10, 1951

Dearest Oscar/

I expect you have been discussing my apparently incredibly bad manners in not having written to thank you for everything, including the Kelly concoction!!!

I cannot repeat such remarks as "there are no words, nor thanks" which some one wrote me, as I am not quite sure how the remark was meant to be taken—also because there are words which I do want to say.

"Getting to Know You" has been a most warm and remarkable milestone in my career—and your great patience, and understanding has caused me constant solace, at times when, being a bit of a perfectionist + therefore very sensitive of my shortcomings, I have often felt inadequate to the task. Believe me Oscar, I have learned to love you in a very deep and lasting fashion, and am extremely proud to have been part of your great success with "The King + I". My deepest gratitude for your constant kindness + consideration.

Ever devotedly

Mrs Anna

Basil Rathbone to Oscar Hammerstein, April 25, 1951

Dear Oscar, Where exactly can you + Dick Rogers [sic] go after "The King + I"! It topps [sic] everything + how do you top "it"!

I suppose in many ways this is a silly letter yet a "desperate" man can do some pretty silly things! Believe-it-or-not I am still "Stage Struck" which the critic Colemen noted when he secured me for appearing in "The Gioconda Smile"! Pictures, Radio + now T.V.—ah practical solutions to one's practical problems, but just a resistance—there is no joy in such living. I merely note that my friend Paul Lukas + now Mr. Brunner [sic] (+ what a performance!) make legitimate acting performances in plays with music. With "the legit", so-called, in its present doldrums it would seem that if one wished to continue one's career in the theatre the only way is via the play with music. I have no idea what you + Dick Rogers have in mind next, if anything - but couldn't we lunch or let me come to the office + talk with you both. Q.E.D. I want to be in your next show! What an idea! I'm crazy? Why? I even have a voice! having sung all my life + it would take very little work to put me in shape to compete with most singers, with obvious exceptions!! And I have an idea for you + for me! of course you may ignore this epistle as the daydreams of a madman—don't do that! Anyway it would be fun to see you again.

I am going to St. Louis to lecture on Friday—god help me—I'll be back Sunday.

Ouida joins me in good wishes always

Yours + Sincerely

Basil Rathbone

In a July letter to Eva Kern about a planned Broadway revival of *Music in the Air*, Hammerstein wrote: "We have signed Basil Rathbone for the Carmanatti part."

Somewhere things went wrong; in an August letter to Rathbone, Oscar wrote: "I sincerely hope that this honest disagreement that you and I have had about the management of the play, and its opening, will have nothing to do either with our friendship or our prospects of working together again at some other time, because I would like to do this very much." Dennis King replaced Rathbone.

Dr. Alfred Cohn to Oscar Hammerstein, May 10, 1951

Dear Mr. Hammerstein, - (and may Mr. Rodgers be included?)

Yesterday, to the King and I, I took a treasure of delighted and contented memories I had gathered them over the years. I took with me also—to be tested curiously—what Mr. Brooks Atkinson has written about the new play. When we came away, I said to my wife, has a play of such insight and value and tenderness and beauty—or better—have plays like this by Rodgers and Hammerstein been written except, in a different key, by Gilbert and Sullivan? No one else has. And doesn't this play transcend the others? Has not this one dared more greatly and trusted the perceptions of to-day's audience greatly more than has any other one?

I agree with Mr. Atkinson. The books and the motion picture of this story do not matter. These sources play no more necessary role than in W.S.'s plays, the Gesta Romanorum or Holinshed's chronicles. This play is a creation as are the Merchant of Venice or Richard III, creations.

You seem to have managed with the greatest skill, the speed of motion of a passionate story. The tempo is just right. And the music is a triumph in itself alone, but naturally as part of a whole, intricate + subtle + powerful. Melody and rhythm and tone kept reminding me beautifully of the Orient. I remembered my sojourn in Bangkok + the East.

I should like to have discovered the novelty of the play by myself without the help of Mr. Atkinson, but for that I was too late. And yet I was glad I had heard Mr. Brynner on the radio, Sunday a week ago. I liked and believed in his reflections on the character of the King. But the way he played the King surprised me that is why, as a second reason, I have wanted to write this letter—Mr. Brynner was authentic—no doubt about that—but I think the unity of his tone was disturbed. I asked myself, is as much of the King's harshness and vehemence as this necessary? Of course I saw the dramatic problem. The point needed to be made. Men as brutal as

he have turned up farther away from the jungle, historically + geographically, Richard III + Mussolini. This King's access to the manner of the awakened world was meager—less than that of Peter the Great. The news had
come. His intelligence and the stimulus of Anna make his ambition wax—
mightily. Obviously, it was too much. He had to die. But she, so exquisite,
so basically gentle, so cultivated, can she really have been captivated and
captured? Such things happen in psychopathia sexualis, but was this that?
I have never seen Gertrude Lawrence more captivating, more winning,
more feminine. I resisted a little, but enough to raise the question—Would
not the verisimilitude of the King have been conveyed more convinc-
ingly has his regal masculinity been less close to being starkly brutal? Like
Hashimura Togo, I ask to know.

One more thing—the ballet enchanted but disturbed me. Having
seen the ballet at Angkor, the form was familiar. This one was charming
in feeling and technique but, I thought, the burlesque was a little
exaggerated.

If it seems I want to paint the lily, it is no doubt a lily I want to see
painted. The tale, the method, the sobriety, the beauty, the music, the scene,
taken together, made a moving whole. You have created a play, delightfully
provocative and have provided another treasured memory.

Sincerely yours,

Alfred E Cohn

P.S.

I notice that I have written too long a letter but, indirectly, that is not
my fault.

Oscar Hammerstein to Dr. Alfred Cohn, May 21, 1951

Dear Dr. Cohn:

Thank you for your letter of May 10th. Dick Rodgers and I are both delighted to receive such a warm tribute. Your point about the King's characterization is very interesting. I would say that his harshness and vehemence
were dynamically necessary to the play. I feel also that Anna was attracted
to him in spite of this surface because she saw through it, understood the
struggle inside him, his ambitions to improve his land and adopt what was

good in western culture, pitted against an inconsistent unwillingness to give away any of his kingly power, his birthright.

About the ballet: I think that if we had hewn to the traditional line more authentically it would have been much less entertaining to western eyes and ears—even, perhaps, a little dull. I don't know. This is a fine balance to strike, and often one underestimates public reception of things that are real and honest. Sometimes one overestimates it. You can never be sure.

Thank you again for your interest and kindness.

All good wishes to you.

Sincerely,

Oscar Hammerstein II

Oscar Hammerstein to Arthur Freed (MGM), May 23, 1951

DEAR ARTHUR: I THINK SHOW BOAT WILL BE A DAZZLING SUCCESS. I AM GOING TO PHONE YOU SOON AND TALK TO YOU ABOUT IT. CONGRATULATIONS.

OSCAR

Oscar Hammerstein to Eva Kern Byron, May 23, 1951

DEAR EVA [Kern]: I HAVE SEEN SHOW BOAT. I THINK IT WILL BE A VERY SUCCESSFUL PICTURE. IT DOES NOT CAPTURE THE SPIRIT OF THE PLAY, BUT IT HAS ITS OWN CHARACTER, AND I BELIEVE IT SUCCEEDED IN WHAT IT SET OUT TO DO. I LIKED THE CAST AND I THINK THEIR TALENTS WERE EXPLOITED WITH GREAT SHOWMANSHIP. I WILL SEE RUSSELL MARKERT WHEN HE CALLS ME. LOVE

OSCAR

The 1951 film re-make of *Show Boat* was released in September, so it must have been an early cut or preview that Oscar saw. Directed by George Sidney and starring Kathryn Grayson, Howard Keel, and Ava Gardner, the film was MGM'd into something bright and colorful.

Oscar Hammerstein to John Van Druten, June 5, 1951

Dear John:

Having read that the new production of "Bell, Book and Candle" has been put off, I assume that you are not returning to the east as soon as you had planned, and I think therefore that I should send you a report on "The King and I".

The only bad news is what you have probably already read—that Johnny Stewart has left us and he is doing a picture in Hollywood. After what looked like a hopeless search, we have found another boy. We have not found another Johnny Stewart for the simple reason that Johnny Stewart is probably one of the best actors in the country today, and I include actors of all ages. The boy we chose for the part is Jackie Collins. He is pretty good now, and I believe he will become very good, but never Johnny. He is a sensitive and sincere boy, and he takes direction intelligently. We put him in last Wednesday matinee. It is true that he left out a great many things that I told him, but that was due to nervousness. I understand he is much better now. I will see him again this week. Our most difficult job is to get him to stand up straight with his chin up, in the regal manner of Johnny Stewart. I am sure this is not a vain hope, and that we shall be able to get him to do this when he is less occupied with the lines themselves. He reads the part very well indeed, and the play suffers only when you think of Johnny as a standard for Chulalongkorn.

Better news. Last week I sat through the performance in row 4, and had a wonderful time. In every way I think the play has improved. The characterizations have been enriched. No changes have been made, but the actors just seemed to have eased into their roles better, and I couldn't find any places where we had lost ground. I did make some notes, but they were superficial. Gertrude is magnificent. None of the nonsense that we were warned about has shown up in her performance so far. She seems very deeply aware of the character of Anna, and the danger of Gertrude Lawrence intruding herself into it. The advance sale is making all the boys around the box office very happy indeed, and they tell me that we are the hottest ticket in town. I do not find this hard to believe because I have never had such enthusiastic reactions for any play with which I have been connected. Friends, and people I have never seen before, or heard of, come up to me and drool. They also write letters which are most extravagant.

I still don't believe that this play has as broad a base of popularity as "South Pacific", but it is clear by now that those who are struck with it are struck more deeply and become more devoted, even than those devotees of "South Pacific". There seems to be a general gratitude on the assumption of intelligence we have imparted to the public. (I do not like that last sentence, because I don't think you impart assumptions to people, but you know what I mean, and I just don't feel like re-composing the sentence. Just give me a C- for composition.) Anyway, I feel very happy because of the kind of people who like this play, and because of what they say. I am sure that you, too, have had the same experience with your friends and people of the theatre. I have heard indirect reports of glowing comments from Hollywood by those returning to New York.

Business in general is very bad indeed. Four musical plays are selling out at the moment; "Call Me Madam", "Guys and Dolls", "The King and I" and "South Pacific". One dramatic play is selling out. This is "The Moon is Blue". After that, the record dips to alarmingly bad business. I suppose this is what makes our box office boys so jubilant about our own strength.

Were you here when Len Mence had his heart attack. It looked very bad for awhile, but he is mending well and should be back in the cast within two weeks. He wrote me a letter from the hospital saying that he was understudying two nurses and a doctor.

But enough of this. What are you up to now? I ask the question for a simple reason. I am what Dorothy frequently calls me, a "a nosey-Parker".

She sends her love, as do I.

Oscar Hammerstein II

Oscar Hammerstein to Sherman Ewing, June 5, 1951

Dear Sherman:

I have read your play at last. Please forgive me for not giving you quicker service on this job. I just couldn't get to it because of a flood of pressing duties that came upon me following the opening of "The King and I". I always naively look forward to a rest after a play is produced, and somehow or the other I always become busier in a different way.

If you had told me the story of "White Collar Girl" before you started to write it, I would have said: "This is a very good story, and well worth writing". I still believe this. My quarrel with the play is its too obvious treatment. I do not always believe that the characters are saying the words you put in their mouths. I think you are illustrating your points in a too cut and dried manner, as far as characterization and dialogue are concerned. I think the theme is wonderful and fairly original as far as stage themes are concerned. I think that the story you have chosen to illustrate your theme is a good one—mathematically sound. I just don't believe you have been settled enough in conceiving and developing the characters you have chosen. The tantalizing part of it is that they are well chosen and promising characters.

Have you shown this play to any producers yet? I would be interested to hear their reactions. It is a tempting play, but I believe it needs no piece-work or casual structural re-building. If I am right, it needs a complete re-writing of interior treatment—character and dialogue.

I am starting to repeat myself so I had better quit.

Love to you both.

Oscar Hammerstein II

A letter from a disappointed patron began: "Mrs. Rosenthal and I saw about 60% of your very excellent 'The King and I' on May 28th—a reason, we sat in these seats" (the ticket stubs were stapled to the letter). After a more detailed description of their difficulties, the letter closed with:

"Continued success in your grand shows—I hope the rest of 'The King and I' was as splendid as the parts we saw!"

Oscar Hammerstein to Herbert Rosenthal, June 12, 1951

Dear Mr. Rosenthal:

I am sorry that you did not like your seats in the St. James Theatre on May 28th. After receiving your letter I paid a visit to the theatre and sat in your seats, and it is true that on the same side of the stage on which you sat, there are details that must have been missed. This, however, I am afraid is true of every theatre in New York. There are some seats on the extreme side from which the entire performance is not always visible. Mindful of this, we, in directing plays, always move important scenes toward the center of the stage. This has been done for so long that it has become traditional. I know of no way out of this except to reduce the number of seats in all the theatres in New York, and there are practical objections to this because, as it is, our capacities are too small to meet rising costs. The public, of course, knows that when they sit on the extreme right or left, they will miss a few details, but I agree with you that they should not be assured of a perfect view by the box office, and if they told you this at the St. James, then they are at fault. These men are not my employees. They are employed by Mr. Lee Shubert, who controls and manages this house, among others, but I shall speak to them and report your letter to them. In the English theatres there is a diagram of all the seats right on the window of the box office, and the customer can see exactly where he is going to sit by tracing the location of his ticket. I believe this should be done in our theatres, too.

Again let me express my sincere regret that you did not see every detail of "The King and I". I am glad that you enjoyed what you saw, and I assure you that there is very little that you did not see—I mean very little of real importance to the plot. I will admit, of course, that the narrator of the ballet, who is the character Tuptim, is important, but here we have a severe stage management problem. The center of the stage must be cleared for the ballet, and the narrator must of necessity stay on the extreme end of the proscenium. In closing, let me thank you for the kind and tolerant tone of your letter, although it contained a complaint, and a justified one.

All good wishes to you.

Sincerely,

Oscar Hammerstein II

Oscar Hammerstein to Cecil E. Hinkel, June 28, 1951

Dear Mr. Hinkel:

Your letter to me, while quite understandable, is based on the false supposition that I have enough money to loan you, and all the other people who make similar requests. The fact is, that at the end of the year I have just about enough money to pay all my bills, because while I make a great deal, I am also taxed a great deal, and the only benevolences I can allow myself are those which are tax deductible. I don't know whether you will understand this situation or not, but you must take my word for it that I get at least one request like yours in the mail every day. There is really no more reason why I should grant yours, and not the others. I don't know you and I have never heard of you before, but I am certainly willing to believe that you are worthy of the loan, if I could afford to make it. I wish you the very best of luck, and since you say you have friends who would loan you the money, I really do not see why you don't appeal to them. If they know you and like you, they have much more reason to give it to you than I have.

All good wishes to you.

Sincerely,

Oscar Hammerstein II

Of all the works Rodgers and Hammerstein considered adapting as a musical and then abandoned, none is more alluring to imagine than what they might have done with George Bernard Shaw's *Pygmalion*. Of course, in 1956 Alan Jay Lerner and Frederick Loewe turned it into the musical *My Fair Lady*, and unofficially took over the Rodgers and Hammerstein mantle as musical theater's preeminent songwriting team. Theater legend has it that Rodgers and Hammerstein struggled with their adaptation and eventually decided they couldn't figure out how to do it. As far as I can tell, the legend is false. Rodgers and Hammerstein indeed considered the project, but I've found no evidence that any work was actually done on trying to adapt it—there are no notes, sketches, outlines, or drafts in Hammerstein's papers. What seems ultimately to have caused them to abandon the project were their difficulties in dealing with the producer Gabriel Pascal, who owned the rights and whose demands proved untenable and the association undesirable. Pascal died in 1954, which is, perhaps, one of the reasons Lerner and Loewe may have had an easier time of it. But to show how seriously they considered the show, there's a July 1 letter from Lisa Kirk in which she thanks Oscar for their recent talk, and provocatively adds: "I'm so happy that you are going to talk to Dick about the possibility of me for Pygmalion. Just thinking about it gives me goose bumps—I guess I'm a 'cockeyed-optimist'!— or is it a cockneyed-optimist!!—All kidding aside, the thought of your doing this show is thrilling."

Gertrude Lawrence was plagued by ill-health almost from the beginning of *The King and I*. As early as February there were discussions about whether or not to take out an insurance policy on her. Oscar's personal physician, Dr. Harold Hyman, was involved in Lawrence's care and at one point wrote to Oscar: "I have no alternative but to attest, on behalf of my colleague, that extensive medical services, requiring a high degree of skill and discretion, were rendered, and that it was my under-standing that the 'team' acted on behalf of the producers. Surely the first call to see G.L. came from you; and the urgent telephonic request to leave for New Haven was received, by Ben, from Dick. Our reports were made to, and in behalf of, the producers, according to our understanding, since G.L. had her own physician, to whom I reported, and her own laryngologist, whom she visited even while Sam was treating her."

Oscar Hammerstein to Dr. Harold Hyman, July 3, 1951

Dear Harold:

Since receiving your letter I have learned that the whole affair has been settled and that the doctors are being paid, half by Gertie and half by R. & H.

In your letter you seem to share Gertie's lawyer's assumption that we had retained you and were, therefore, responsible. Your assumption was fair enough but his was not. The actual circumstances were that John Fearnley, our Casting Director, called up and told me that Gertie had asked me to suggest a doctor. I was rather surprised that she had no physician of her own, and no nose and throat man, but I, of course, suggested you. And then, at her behest I suppose, Fearnley called you and the rest went on automatically. That is why I told you that in the last analysis I would certainly be financially responsible if there was no way of working it out.

Dick and I have managed many stars and many actors and actresses now, and no one so far has asked us to pay their doctors bills. Mary Martin has been sick, Helen Hayes has been sick, Pinza has been sick, and no one ever asked us to pay a doctor. When this issue arose, however, I told Howard that I believed in view of the pressure of opening a play, and in view of the fact that if Gertie had been sick and we were not opening, her expenses would not have become so high, that it was fair for us to pay half. And so there is the whole thing, and I am glad it's over.

See you soon.

Love,

Oscar Hammerstein II

Josh Logan to Oscar Hammerstein, July 30, 1951

Dear Dick and Oscar:

These are some notes I made during a discussion of SOUTH PACIFIC with Peter Glenville. He is the English director who did THE INNOCENTS here and who directed a number of successes in England. I think he is a very brilliant man and knows both the American and English publics. Here are the suggestions he made:

1. He thinks we should charge a guinea rather than a pound for the stalls downstairs and that there must be some fifteen-shilling seats. He says that a guinea, even though it is more than a pound, somehow sounds less as the English public is used to paying even two guineas for Flagstad concerts, and Charles Cochran always used to charge a guinea for his opening nights. I don't know the subtle difference, but he feels this very definitely. I pass it on for your consideration.

2. He is very strong in his feeling that Cable should not be a Britisher, for the following reasons. He says it would not flatter the British, that this character shows the most weakness of any in the show, and they would take his sleeping with Liat and then refusing to marry her as if it were some comment on the British character. He feels they would resent Cable if he were a Britisher. However, he does think we could make it very clear that Cable is of good family and has gone to expensive schools.

3. He thinks that the most difficult thing in SOUTH PACIFIC for the British to accept is the race problem aspect of the show, and he feels that Nellie becomes very unsympathetic to the British when she turns down Emile because he has loved a Polynesian woman. He suggests that we make the Polynesian woman Emile's housekeeper who died when the second child was born, and that there was very little sentimental relationship between the two, Emile and his housekeeper; it was simply a matter of necessity. This, he thinks, would make the situation much stronger to the British mind. He says that even though the British practise [*sic*] race prejudice in the colonies, they think of themselves as knights in armor where America is concerned and do not go along with us or sympathize with our race problems at all.

Best,

Josh

Oscar Hammerstein to Agnes de Mille, August 7, 1951

Dear Agnes:

I have just finished your book.[1] I liked it very much. It is what I have been hoping someone would some day do—write a clear and unaffected picture of experiences in the theatre. You describe what is perhaps only a corner of the theatre, but what is there is authentic and true in focus. You have done the same, only to a much greater extent, with the ballet. I say this, although I don't know as much about the ballet as I do about the theatre. At any rate, everything about the book rings true.

The writing is, as you perhaps know, uneven, and sometimes it is very difficult for me to understand how the same woman, who is guilty of such laziness as referring to her mother as someone with "all the stability of Gibraltar. She was a rock . . . ", can, in the very next sentence say a beautiful and simple thing like, "It was as though the shadow of her father stood behind her and quietly laid his hand on her shoulder". I dare say that I must overlook all the typographical errors as something that awaits the proofreader, and I hope that there will be some further editing. I have the idea that too much "footage" is devoted to Cecil deMille, who certainly belongs in the picture, and certainly is entitled to a good bit of attention, but I wonder if he should have so much—whether he doesn't throw things off balance in the first third of the book, which is, of course, about you and your career and the roots of it. He is a part of the roots. It sometimes looks as if he is going to be the whole book. I don't feel violently about this because at the end it all resolves, and I realize why the book is constructed as it is, and why Cecil is in there promi-nently. It is just a question of the degree of prominence he should have.

When you are going over it do a little further polishing, before it gets to the proof page stage, look for some scene in a dressing room—I forget whose dressing room—in which you say something like "People running in and out of her dressing room like a French farce". Of course you don't mean that the people are like a French farce. You mean that they are doing this as in a French farce. I also remember a "from whence" which offends me especially, because every time *I* see it used I translate it. Whence means from where, and from whence means from from where, which is very silly indeed. I think it is used somewhere about your father, and I think it is

---

[1] De Mille's memoir, *Dance to the Piper*, was published in January 1952.

something like "from whence came the sound of tennis balls". I am not sure about this. I know that you know better, because you use whence properly in several other places.

These didactic chidings are minor things, and very unimportant alongside of my major reaction to the book. It is an honest story about a girl who is intensely interesting, and, quite incidentally, turns out to be a success story, and this does not hurt it a bit. I am very happy that you finished exactly where you did. If you had carried it on from success to success it would have become one of those songwriter concerts where they say, "And then I wrote . . .". While telling of your career and the people who were part of it, you make many wise comments, and you have thrown a clear light on the vague gropings of creative dancers. "Vague gropings" is unworthy of your high ends, and blood and sweat and soul that are being pried loose from yourself in your work. I am quite sincere when I tell you that I am determined to read this book again, more slowly and more carefully. I think there is a great deal in it from which I can turn a profit, and apply the profit to my own work.

Congratulations and love.

Oscar Hammerstein II

Oscar Hammerstein to Jack Goodman (Simon & Schuster), August 8, 1951

Dear Jack:

The chess set is just wonderful. The pieces are just the right weight for me, and perfectly balanced, and they fit into the squares as if they were made for them. I expect to play the game of my life on this board, and I surely look forward to taking you on—but without the confidence you assume I have. I started chess late in life, and my teacher was an eleven year old boy. It took me three years to be able to beat him, and now we play pretty even. (Of course he is much older now, and something of a genius—I hope.) I look forward to seeing you soon, and I hope the Rodgers and Hart Song Book is the great success that it should be.

All the best.

As ever.

Oscar Hammerstein II

The "eleven year old boy" was Stephen Sondheim.

In his memoir, Richard Rodgers wrote of *South Pacific*: "All that marred the show's run was the frequency of Mr. Pinza's absences. He loved basking in the adulation bestowed on him as a middle-aged matinee idol, but he never could be counted on to show up for performances. He couldn't wait for his year-long contract to expire, and the minute it was up, he was on a plane for Hollywood—where he made two of the deadliest bombs ever released." But it seems that, at least for a while, Mary Martin held out hope that Pinza would join her in the London production. Martin left the Broadway production while it was still selling out on Broadway in order to star in the show in London.

Oscar Hammerstein to Mary Martin (in Edinburgh), August 16, 1951

DEAR MARY:

PINZA SIGNED WITH MGM YESTERDAY FOR PICTURE TO BE DONE IN MARCH. HE HAS TOLD US HE CANNOT GIVE US MORE THAN FOUR MONTHS AT THE VERY MOST SO I AM AFRAID THIS IS THE ANSWER. DON'T WORRY—EVERYTHING IS GOING TO BE WONDERFUL NOVEMBER FIRST.

LOVE

OSCAR

Mary Martin to Oscar Hammerstein, August 17, 1951

Dear Oscar:

Thank you for your cable. Of course Ezio couldn't be considered for 3 or 4 months –

Does that mean you'll <u>have</u> to have Wilbur? I just can't get excited—and <u>you</u> know I'm a worrier—but would you mind letting me know anything, everything—<u>I am practical too</u> and maybe I could get all the worrying over with before we reach London.

Richard says he sent both your office on Madison and Mike Mok a copy of our trip-schedule—He's written our secretary to send another as soon as she gets back from her vacation—but Mok could give you his.

You know I love S. P. and you!

We are being gay –

Love –

Always

Mary

P.S. [?] Josh?

Oscar Hammerstein to Mary Martin (in Dublin), August 27, 1951

Dear Mary:

In answer to your question, "Do we <u>have</u> to have Wilbur?", yes—we do. You say you can't get excited about him, but isn't the truth really that you couldn't get excited about anybody except Ezio in this part—that is, anybody that we know about? Of all the people we have auditioned so far, you may be surprised to know that Wilbur is not only the best, but seems to stand head and shoulders over all the others. He has gained a great deal in stature and poise since shows like "Up in Central Park" and "Mexican Hayride", and speaking of those shows, to be fair to Wilbur they didn't have parts like Emile deBecque in them. He really encouraged all four of us when we heard him play the first scene the other day. I don't want to oversell him to you, but I am sure you are going to be very pleasantly surprised when you start to rehearse with him—always granting in advance that he is not Pinza, but then no one is.

I had an alarming call from Louis Calta of the Times the other day. Somehow or other he had got a rumor that you did not like Wilbur Evans. He said "I thought this was fantastic when I heard it and so I called you about it to check". I said it is fantastic—we would not think of asking Mary to play with anyone of whom she did not approve. I am telling you this so that if anything comes up you will be quick to make a complete denial of any displeasure or even doubt about Wilbur, because this would be very bad public relations for the show, and you, and all of us.

Dorothy and I deeply envy you and Dick going through Scotland. We are both half Scotch ourselves, and don't see why you should get there ahead of us. Our grandparents were there first. How we'd love to be making that trip, but the fact is [MISSING WORDS] a lot, and the best thing we have to look forward to is England, which isn't bad either. We'll all have a wonderful time in London, I know, and we're going to have a helluva show and a wonderful opening night.

Love to you from us all.

As ever,

Oscar Hammerstein II

Mary Martin (in London) to Oscar Hammerstein, September 23, 1951

Oscar—I love you! You're always so clear. Just love your letter of August 27th—because of the change of schedule. You're exactly right when you say—"isn't the truth really that you cant get excited about anybody except Ezio" Yes!—But I love you too because you always seem to see the over-all, the big picture. Of course I can't get excited about Wilbur [Evans]—but I have seen him now—we've had tea together + He does look so very much better. He does have the enthusiasm and the interest. He will be a good worker and I am really and truly a Cock-eyed Optimist about him + I do agree it's going to be wonderful ------- because ---- I had the biggest thrill last night. Went to the Drury Lane—saw Carousel from every part of the house including the gallery + Really what a wonderful, wonderful theatre! I've never seen a show there before and now I know what you've known all along—it shows a play off to its very very best. It gave me confidence—it erased all my worries and fears. I just can't wait!!!! And [I] know you'd be proud to see Carousel there now. It looked wonderful—the cast gave their very very best—and the audience loved every second.

About Louis Calta calling you—am pretty sure he must have been trying to "get" a story—it must have been his own hunch. I haven't said or written to anyone about Wilbur—I really know its best to keep that kind of thing to ones-self. In fact I've told everyone here—including the newspapers—that he's half Ronald Colman—half Errol Flynn. We have had <u>only</u> good "public relations"—and long shall it be—in fact let's pray—for always –

Give our love to your dearest Dorothy—Can't wait until we see the sight of you both!!

Love

Mary –

Denis P. S. Conan Doyle to Oscar Hammerstein, August 16, 1951

Dear Mr. Hammerstein,

I am allowing myself to approach you because I know so well your great reputation and because you have given me, as well as countless thousands of your other admirers, an unforgettable evening. Unfortunately I have never had the pleasure of meeting you nor am I approaching anybody who knows you for a letter of introduction. I am acting as my own Sherlock Holmes and am trying to find you myself, to ask you if the following proposition would interest you.

The great English showman and theatrical producer, Sir Charles Cochran, came twice to Paris from England in order to approach me with regard to the possibility of producing a musical play based on the immortal character of Sherlock Holmes, the literary creation of my father, the late Sir Arthur Conan Doyle. He was particularly anxious to adapt for that purpose one story which he considered preeminently qualified to succeed in that particular form. The story in question is "A SCANDAL IN BOHEMIA", which briefly is as follows. Sherlock Holmes never loved a woman, he always remained impervious to their charms, with one singular exception, a Hungarian opera singer named Irene Adler who gained his interest and admiration and to whom he always referred as "THE woman". She is the central female character in this particular story, and in the course of all the sixty different Sherlock Holmes stories she was the only woman adversary who ever defeated Holmes. In this story, Irene Adler had had a love affair with the King of Bohemia, a huge figure of a man who later calls on Holmes at his famous Baker Street rooms in London with the object of retaining his services for the purpose of recovering from Irene Adler, who at that time was living in

London, a certain compromising photograph of her with himself which had been taken during their love affair. The reason for the King's anxiety to recover this photograph was the fact that he was anxious to marry a Princess from a neighbouring State and Irene Adler, out of jealousy, had threatened to send this photograph to the King's royal fiancée, which he realized would definitely ruin his chance of marriage. Holmes promises to do his best. He has no respect for Irene Adler, and treats her superficially as being a cheap woman. Nevertheless, she eludes him, until one day, Holmes, by an exceedingly clever and ingenious deception, succeeds in entering Irene Adler's house in disguise and in getting her to disclose to him unwittingly the secret hiding place where she keeps the photograph. The following day he returns to her house, and succeeds in opening the hidden panel in Irene Adler's perfumed closet. After opening the envelope after his escape from her house, however, Holmes finds not the long sought photograph of Irene Adler with the King of Bohemia, but a photograph of the lady herself alone, in a beautiful evening dress, inscribed "To Mr. Sherlock Holmes, with all my good wishes". With the photograph, Holmes also finds a letter from her addressed to him in which she tells him that although she is keeping the compromising photograph as protection against any revengeful move which the King might be tempted to make in the future, he has nothing to fear from her if he leaves her alone.

The day Holmes finds this photograph, Irene Adler leaves her house and disappears from London. The reason for this is that before definitely deciding to send the compromising photograph to the King's fiancée, she has consulted a London lawyer to ask his advice as to how she could best make use of it. This lawyer, a very handsome young man, is horrified at what she proposes to do and he persuades her that, however much she may have been wronged by the King, she should not take this vindictive step which would probably ruin the lives of two people. Irene Adler comes under the good influence of this young lawyer, falls in love with him, and marries and goes away with him.

On the eve of his wedding, the grateful King comes to Sherlock Holmes's rooms again and asks him to name anything he wishes, however great, that is within his power to bestow, as a reward for his services. Sherlock Holmes replies that the only reward he wishes is to be allowed to keep the inscribed photograph from Irene Adler, to which the King agrees.

Holmes's exact feelings towards Irene Adler are never defined, and the intriguing question as to whether or not he has developed a romantic feeling for her is left in abeyance and unanswered. It is sure, however, that she was the only woman in his life who ever really interested, intrigued or moved him to any emotion at all.

That is a brief and very inadequate résumé of the story which Cochran was so anxious to produce as a musical play, first in London and later in New York. He had provisionally selected an excellent cast with Ilona Massey as Irene Adler and Georges Guetary as Holmes. The décor was to be entrusted to Cecil Beaton, or another, and Christian Dior agreed to design and produce all the dresses, which was particularly pleasing to Cochran owing to the fact that one of the biggest scenes which he had envisaged for this play was to have been a Court Ball in old Prague in which the romance between Irene Adler and the King of Bohemia was to have been shown among suitable music and a magnificent array of dresses of the period. It was not Cochran's intention for Holmes to sing on the stage, but the other leading characters would have done so. Unfortunately, this most interesting project failed to materialize on account of the fact that Sir Charles Cochran suddenly died.

I am writing to ask you whether you and Mr. Rodgers would be interested in producing a musical play based on this wonderful story of my father. I wish you would let me have your full and frank reactions. If you are not interested, I should greatly value and appreciate your advice as to whom I should approach in the matter in America, both as regards the production side and also regarding the adaptation and music. I should like to add that at no time since my father wrote the world-famous stories has the moment been so propitious as it is now for the appearance of a Sherlock Holmes theatrical production, in view of the enormous and widely-publicised [sic] success of the Sherlock Holmes Exhibition in Baker Street, which is an official part of the Festival of Britain, and also because of the fact that the family intends to send an original and unique Sherlock Holmes Exhibition to the United States this winter for a protracted nation-wide tour of all the leading American cities.

Yours sincerely,

Denis P.S. Conan Doyle

Oscar Hammerstein to Denis P.S. Conan Doyle, August 28, 1951

Dear Mr. Conan Doyle:

Thank you very much for your interesting letter of August 16th. It would seem that "A Scandal in Bohemia" might prove to be a very good musical play. Mr. Rodgers and I are unfortunately occupied with too many commitments at the moment to consider anything further, and I suggest that you submit your ideas to someone else. I assume that you have already considered the eligible producers, authors and composers in England. Here in the United States I should think the most likely producers to approach would be Mr. Max Gordon, The Lyceum Theatre, New York, The Theatre Guild, 23 West 53rd Street, Mr. George Abbott, 630 Fifth Avenue, and Mr. Leland Hayward, 655 Madison Avenue.

Thank you again for making the suggestion to us, and all good wishes to you in this project.

Sincerely,

Oscar Hammerstein II

Michener supplied the following notes for possible script changes to accommodate British audiences for the upcoming London production of *South Pacific*. The notes may also have been helpful for the production that opened in Melbourne in 1952.

James Michener to Oscar Hammerstein, September 5, 1951

Dear Oscar,

Concerning the New Zealanders and Americans in the South Pacific, I offer these brief notes: (1) N.Z. troops served throughout the area in closest contact with our troops. As contrasted to the Australians, who were supplied by Australian and British sources, N.Z. troops used American equipment throughout. This meant that they were in constant contact with American supply units. In aviation particularly this liaison was close. (2) Enzedders, as they were called, did, of course, use their own uniforms. So far as I can recall the Enzed enlisted man was distinguished by wearing shorts longer than ours, stockings usually up to the knee, T-shirts whose sleeves came down to the last two inches above the elbow, blunt-toed shoes. I cannot recall the caps. (3) It would be entirely probable that Lieut. Buzz Adams could have been an Enzedder. N.Z. air units used our strips and we theirs. They conducted every kind of aerial operation that we did. It was especially common for them to engage in trips like the one with Emile DeDecque [*sic*]. However, when Captain Brackett says, "A Marine, assigned to me?" he would not use the word Enzedda. American officers always called officers New Zealanders, but our enlisted men might call other enlisted men Enzedders. The word <u>limey</u> would <u>not</u> be used. Nor would Anzac. (4) Some of the force of Buzz Adams' attitudes toward color would be lost if a New Zealander were used; but it could still be there. The force would be identical if an Australian were used, but it would have been unlikely that an Australian would have been integrated with our <u>air</u> forces or reconnaissance teams in military status. Only civilian, or a civilian in temporary U.S. navy uniform and status. Therefore the idea is [*sic*] of using an Australian would not be wise. (5) I served with New Zealanders for two years, knew them well, and can vouch for the above information. (6) Incidentally, nurses could have been and sometimes were New Zealand girls. And canteen girls most often were. Entertainers, too.

Warmest regards,

Jim Michener

For the London production of *South Pacific*, the credits read: "Staged by Joshua Logan/Reproduced by Jerome Whyte." Whyte went on to alternate between production supervisor in New York and heading Rodgers and Hammerstein's London production firm, Williamson Music Ltd. Frank Rich in a 2001 article in *The New York Times*, "Oh, What a Miserable Mornin'," wrote of Rodgers: "He had no close friends, except Jerry Whyte, a former Prohibition rumrunner who served as Rodgers's general factotum and procurer of chorus girls."

Jerry Whyte to Richard Rodgers and Oscar Hammerstein, September 14, 1951

Dear Dick and Oc,

I returned from Berlin last night after witnessing something I wouldn't have missed for the world, and am only sorry that you too could not have seen what happened when "Oklahoma" was presented before an audience of over 2,000, of which less than 20 were English and American civilians and Army personnel.

Every point, dialogue, music and lyrics were just devoured. The applause at the end of each number was just thunderous. Considering the limited back-stage space the production looked remarkably well. We were very fortunate to have Lem Ayers supervising the construction and painting. Just to get an idea of what we were up against, the Titania-Palast was a former film house, with no facilities to fly anything. In order to facilitate the changes, travellers was [sic] closed in, and a crew of stage hands rolled the drops, tied them off and re-hung whatever necessary for the following scene.

I must say that stage staff were one of the finest groups of technicians and co-operative workers I have ever seen. They so impressed our six department heads that our boys asked the entire staff to luncheon which, quite understandably, the local men found hard to believe. If the entire world could only work that way, we would be much better off.

At the end of the first act Peter Davies and myself were taken to one of the large public television screens. There are two in different sectors of the American Zone, both within a quarter of a mile of the Russian Zone—we visited the one at Potsdamstrasse, and I will try to describe what I saw.

An eighteen-foot square screen set in a field partially cleared of the rubble; outlined against the back of the screen a skeleton of a structure— all that remains of what was supposed to be, at the request of Hitler, a tourist bureau and information centre. There were, I should say, roughly 1,000 people viewing the show, sitting on rocks, their bicycles or just on the ground. You see, there are usually no restrictions forbidding people of the Eastern Zone to come across, and it is the feeling of the Military High Command in Germany that by the end of the engagement in Berlin there is no telling how many people will have viewed it from these two screens so near to the Russian Zone.

In addition to these two screens, there were approximately eighty smaller sets in various shops throughout the major streets. We also drove past there, and in front of each I dare say there were anything between twenty-five and fifty people viewing the show on small screens. It is my opinion the propaganda value of this thing is unlimited, and I was glad to have been on the spot to see what may have been a momentous occasion.

As for the security measures taken during the televising, it was as though atomic work was going on! The two cameras, which were set up on high pedestals right and left in the auditorium were manned by television technicians, and the control room too were limited to nothing but the television personnel set up by Supreme Headquarters. They were guarded by local and military police, and I myself, together with Davies, had great difficulty in being admitted. There is no doubt in my mind that your requests for protection, reproduction and copyright, are being protected to the fullest degree.

The destruction and rubble still remaining is beyond description. I was advised that 86% of the entire city of Berlin was destroyed. It's a sight that I will long remember, and I hope to God nothing like that ever happens again in this world.

I enclose herewith two of the write-ups and hope you can get someone to translate them for you, also a couple of programmes.

Mary and Dick arrived in London last night, and we are meeting at the Press Conference arranged by MacQueen Pope at Drury Lane.

Kindest regards and love to the two Dorothys and yourselves.

As ever,

Oscar Hammerstein to Joe Ruggere, September 25, 1951

Dear Mr. Ruggere:

Thank you for writing me and suggesting we make a musical play out of "Little Abner". As a matter of fact, about four years ago I had a conference with Al Capp in Boston and Joshua Logan, who is very anxious to do this very thing—nothing came of it. Perhaps something will some day. Thank you very much for your interest.

All good wishes to you.

Sincerely,

Oscar Hammerstein II

On October 8, a revival of *Music in the Air* opened on Broadway. It was directed by Oscar, and produced by his brother, Reggie. The cast included Dennis King, Conrad Nagel, and Charles Winninger. It ran for fifty-six performances.

South Pacific opened in London on November 1. It starred Mary Martin and Wilbur Evans. (Martin's son, Larry Hagman, played a Seabee.)

Mary Martin to Oscar Hammerstein, circa November 2, 1951

Darling Dick and Oscar—Your beautiful flowers warmed our glowing hearts! Oh! It is good to be in our second "home" again—Everything is even more wonderful than we had hoped and prayed and dreamed about—These dear people—that exciting Theatre—Jerry Whyte acting as host and friend—Can't wait till you both get here and we're all together in the thrilling adventure –

Our love –

Mary and Richard

Evelyn Laye was an English performer who starred in operettas and musical comedies musicals. She made her Broadway debut in Noel Coward's *Bittersweet* in 1929 and starred in a handful of films in the 1930s, but by 1951 her star was shining a little less brightly—certainly not at the wattage of Gertrude Lawrence.

Oscar Hammerstein to Evelyn Laye (in Australia), November 6, 1951

Dear Evelyn,

Thank you for your telegram. Why don't you come home through the States and see the show? At the moment Gertie wants to play it here in London and all over the United States but you never know how these things will turn out and if you come to New York to see the play, then we would see you and this would be a very fine thing for both of us.

Love,

Sigmund Romberg died on November 9, at the age of sixty-four. Romberg and Oscar collaborated on five Broadway operettas: *The Desert Song, New Moon, East Wind, May Wine,* and *Sunny River,* and three film musicals: *Viennese Nights, Children of Dreams,* and *The Night is Young.*

Harold Thomas Hyman, M. D. to Oscar Hammerstein (excerpt), November 13, 1951

Dear Oc:

I thought you and Dorothy would like to hear what little I know of Rommie's [Sigmund Romberg's] death. I examined him two weeks ago and he was his usual jovial self. He remained so almost to the moment of his death which probably occurred from a massive intra-cranial hemorrhage much like the one that struck down Jerry [Kern]—and, curiously enough, also at 57th Street and Park Avenue.

He was talking to Lillian and a friend of her's [*sic*] in Lillian's bedroom when the papers came. A few minutes before 11:00, he started for the bathroom with his paper and apparently unbuttoned his trousers but not his shorts before he died. Lillian, of course, was unaware of what had happened and it was not until almost three-quarters of an hour later that she decided to see what was keeping him so long and found him on the floor. It was a wonderful way to make the transition from life to death and certainly better than the lingering that Jerry went through.

Lillian wanted you to deliver the eulogy but Otto Harbach was substituted. Lillian, by the way, has been simply wonderful, illustrating again how extraordinarily well people face real situations.

There is very little important news of Bucks County. "Mrs. Big" is spectacular—but that is not news. She is now the possessor of a mink coat but whether she will ever wear it is to be another question. When the weather is clement she does not need it—and when it is inclement she is afraid to expose it. However, should we get a clement/inclement day, I imagine she will trot herself forth.

Oscar Hammerstein to Howard Reinheimer, November 19, 1951

Dear Howard,

The trip I made to Barcelona with Lars Schmidt was profitless unless you consider it a profit to find out that Musical Comedy in Spain is a "dead pigion." [sic] We learned that the interest of that portion of the public which can afford to pay for theatre is confined pretty much to Opera and Ballet. No one seems to care for the lighter musical theatre and there seems to be little producing and performing talent in this field. One entertainment that purported to be a musical play was the worst thing I have ever seen on any stage, no one in the cast or chorus could sing or dance. The Spanish people whom we consulted said this was a typical and representative production. When one considers that condition in the light of the few dollars that could be made out of a full house of pesetas it doesn't seem worth anybody's time to try to promote a theatrical venture in this country, so the Spanish trip has only this negative result, I am sorry to say.

I stopped off in Paris on the way back to London and had a talk with Miles Herbert and Paule Ganne. They have no further news of possible productions but I instructed them both to step-up their search for possible adaptors for any manuscripts there, these foreign productions stand or fall on the translations as you well know.

I also saw a singing girl I liked very much in Paris, her name is Damy Douberson.

Now I am back in London where I expect to brush up the performance of "South Pacific" and pursue the Pygmalion matter, luckily they are playing it at a house in Wimbledon so I shall be able to see it in front of an audience.

I will be home a week from today.

Love from Dorothy and me.

Sincerely,

Gabriel Pascal to Oscar Hammerstein, November 26, 1951

RE: "PYGMALION"

My dear Mr. Hammerstein:

I wanted to write to you last week in London, but knowing that you arrive tomorrow morning I write to you on Mr. Louis Lurie's advice now, and

I hope that your partner Mr. Rodgers and your lawyer Mr. Reinheimer will not resent my direct approach to you, while they are in negotiations with my lawyers Irwin Margulies and Edwin Davis.

According to my dear friend Lurie there would be no differences with your legal advisor Howard Reinheimer to accept the one-half money in the production, and according to my English lawyer Edwin Davis there is no more difference to have the second five years from the trustee, thanks to the clever suggestion of Mr. Reinheimer.

The only difference between my group and your group is the question of the billing. Before you left for England, you remember our personal talk in your house, when I told you that if Bernard Shaw would be alive, he would not allow me to make the deal if I am not presenting with you, the play. Even in his own conception, PYGMALION was too much associated with my name in the public mind, and I told you then how grateful I would be, even if you broke your own company's tradition, and you and Mr. Rodgers would agree that my name should be associated with both of your names presenting this property.

I told you in all sincerity and humbleness that I agree that on Broadway my name means very little, and that you are giants compared to me in your field, but I worked very hard since my boyhood for my name, as you worked for yours, and with the help of God it reached world fame.

Now when RKO will spend hundreds of thousands of dollars on publicity on my name, and on my last picture, ANDROCLES AND THE LION for next season; that it would be even a commercial asset to join my name to both of yours on the same billing.

I understood that time that you had nothing against my personal request. In contrary, you favored it, and would convince your partners Mr. Rodgers and Mr. Reinheimer to accept your recommendation. You can imagine how surprised I was when Mr. Reinheimer sent me the copy of your cable.

To be brief, I am asking you again as a personal favor, in the spirit of G.B.S. to accept and recommend to your partners this special desire of mine, and I am certain that the three of you will never regret it.

With my most affectionate regards,

Yours ever,

Gabriel Pascal

Irene Dunne to Oscar Hammerstein and Richard Rodgers,
November 27, 1951

Dear Oscar and Dick:

Thanks so much for the invitation to play "Anna" on the Coast next summer. Might be interested in doing it if I thought I could do the picture at a later date. Maybe you could tell me if this is at all possible.

Of course instead of Anna and even the movie I still would rather have a part in a new Rodgers and Hammerstein show next year. But at any rate do let me know about the possibility of the film, and I will reply very promptly.

I may be in New York for a week in January. Do you plan to be there at that time?

Best always,

Irene ---

Oscar Hammerstein and Richard Rodgers to Irene Dunne,
December 7, 1951

Dear Irene:

Thank you for your letter of November 27th. We just got back from England, and that is why we have been so long in answering you. It is fascinating to think of the possibility of your doing Anna on the coast next summer. The commitment of the picture to you would not be difficult for us, and actually very attractive, if we had any idea when we were going to do the picture. But as you know, we are putting all our picture rights to all our properties in a safe and keeping them until we can use them with more profit than we could now. That makes the whole proposition so remote that it would not be a very good thing for either us or you to make any commitments in this regard. We are happy to hear that you are coming to New York in January, and I hope you will let one of us know before you come, and where you will be, so that we can arrange to see you, an event to which we both look forward.

Merry Christmas and love.

Richard Rodgers

Oscar Hammerstein II

Clifton Fadiman, who had been the host the CBS quiz program, *Information, Please*, was now the host of *This Is Show Business*.

Oscar Hammerstein to Clifton Fadiman, December 10, 1951

Dear Kip:

I thought your piece on "musical comedy's decade of realism, from Pal Joey to The King and I" was a particularly good one, and while I am at it, and have a few extra posies handy, I should like to toss them for the now very smooth and mellow "This Is Show Business". Since returning from England I have caught a couple of them, and believe that I detect in its master of ceremonies a greater warmth and glow of contentment than has ever emanated from him in previous performances. Possibly, for professional reasons, he turns it on a bit, but the funny part about these things is that you can't turn them on unless they're there in the first place. Let us all meet soon and get into a fight about this.

Love to you and Annalee from both of us.

Sincerely,

Oscar Hammerstein II

In answer to a perennial question:

Oscar Hammerstein to Gladys R. Neuser, December 19, 1951

Dear Miss Neuser:

Ideas for our songs come from the story we are working on at the moment—the story and its characters and the situations in which they find themselves, and just as the dialogue tries to tell that story, so do the lyrics, and in this way we evolve song titles and subjects. The "popular songwriter", who doesn't write for plays, must necessarily get his ideas independent of stories and characters, and therefore he invents them, or draws from his own emotions and his life experiences. I think this is harder to do, and I have never tried it.

I enclose the autographed picture as you requested.

Best wishes to you.

Sincerely,

Oscar Hammerstein II

Oscar Hammerstein to Mrs. William F. Wolter, December 20, 1951

Dear Mrs. Wolter:

Thank you for suggesting to us the idea of doing a musical play on the life of Robert Schumann. I am afraid Mr. Rodgers would not be interested in taking another composer's music and adapting it, and for my part, when you say: "The life of Robert and Clara Schumann is a natural for the old style music play", you make a very complete and sweeping condemnation, because we have no intention of writing "an old style musical play".

In spite of this cool reception to your idea, we are most warmly grateful to you for your interest in submitting it to us.

All good wishes.

Sincerely,

Oscar Hammerstein II

At the time of this letter, Erich Leinsdorf was the music director for the Rochester Philharmonic Orchestra. He had previously conducted for the Metropolitan Opera and was briefly music director for the Cleveland Orchestra during the war. He went on to become music director for the Boston Symphony among other achievements.

Erich Leinsdorf to Oscar Hammerstein, December 23, 1951

Dear Mr. Hammerstein:

Calling you in Doylestown on a wrong number and finding out from Milton Kadison that you were in Florida I resort to this old-fashioned way of telling you that I found the King and I, which we saw last night, about the finest and most enjoyable show imaginable. To produce with so much sophistication a completely naïve effect is true Art in my book. We saw the two principal roles played by the understudies which showed again that a real theatrical work needs the stars only for original publicity but not for any definite improvements. My own reaction to the evening was that of a child who had just lived through a fascinating, charming and poetic fairy tale.

If the music were equal to the words, the production and the staging it would be too much.

It seems to me that the plays which have as their central characters an incongruous couple (South Pac. and this one) solve one of the eternal quests in the theatre, to find plausible conflicts which are new and moving.

I consider the King and I so far the finest contribution you have made to the theatre. If you are in search of a new venture I wish you would look through Stefan Zweig's libretto (after Ben Jonson) which he wrote for Richard Strauss and which became eventually an abortion of an Opera called The Silent Women (Die schweigsame Frau.) You can surely get the score and/or libretto of that work from Boosey-Hawkes 30 West 57.

I have a sneaking suspicion that this may be your dish.

With best wishes for the New Year etcetera etcetera

Yours

E Leinsdorf

The musical *Wish You Were Here* was co-produced, co-written, directed, and choreographed by Josh Logan, although Jerome Robbins was brought in as a show doctor. Harold Rome composed the score. The show opened on June 25, 1952, and, though the reviews were largely unfavorable, it ran for a respectable 598 performances. Its success has largely been attributed to three things: Eddie Fisher's hit recording of the title song, a working swimming pool on the stage, and excerpts from the show performed on the Ed Sullivan show. It didn't hurt that the show featured a young and good-looking cast often clad in bathing suits.

Oscar Hammerstein to Josh Logan, December 24, 1951

Dear Josh:

I have just finished reading "Wish You Were Here". Granting its obvious virtues: youth, a warmth and touching sentiment in the love story, amusing characters, sympathetic characters and suggestions of a very good laughing show, and also the element of sex interest—which is a whole lot for a show to have—let me now list my worries: it's too long, but much too long. There are too many scenes, too many sets, and too many songs used to tell the story. Teddy becomes annoying because she so suddenly turns, first in the scene with Chic, and then with Pinky. She seemed to be suddenly and almost too late defending her honor, thereby bewildering the young men. I think Chic, too, is more unreasonable than credible in the first breakup scene. Now there happen to be three breakup scenes—the one on Eagle Rock, the one in which he finds Teddy in Chic's room, and then the last one. I think if there was some way in the second act of merging Chic's two discoveries where the evidence seems to be piled up against Teddy, if this could be done in one scene instead of two, it would be better. I also think that in each case the explanations which satisfy Chic's worries, are too easily accepted by him. I think all the reconciliations are unconvincing, as if you became bored with them and said: "Well, this will be all right. Now they like each other again, now we build up to the next crisis again". The crises are built up much better than the solutions. My last worry is the basketball game. I assume you have thought this out and have a way of working it. I don't see how it can work at all. I don't see how it can look like a basketball game with two baskets on a stage. No basketball court is that small, and everybody knows that. I also think it's going to be [a] terrible mess and a rough-house unless you have something up your sleeve that I cannot find in the script.

I think that without any delay you should have this typed by Rialto in the usual way, so that you get a better line on the length. It is now all double space, but I think you will find it very long even in the conventional setup. I just have a feeling that you are profligate with scenes and words and music, and that now you ought to bravely shave things down to the proper economy. I think you have all the elements of entertainment and of a big success in this play, but there is more drudgery, more problem solving, more of the less attractive work to do. I think however that drudgery now will prevent panic in Philadelphia.

Merry Christmas to you all.

Chapter Eleven
1952

The King and I and *South Pacific* were still going strong on Broadway, as was *South Pacific* in its national tour and in London. The national tour of *Oklahoma!* was still winding its way across the country. The United States continued to be embroiled in the Korean War. Rodgers and Hammerstein had nothing new on the horizon, and Oscar was still very good at sending out thank-you notes.

Oscar Hammerstein to Marge and Dubbie, January 2, 1952

Dear Marge and Dubbie:

The shirt is a humdinger, and will add luster to my already brilliant wardrobe, and enable me to make more dazzling changes during the hot summer days on Highland Farm. Love to both of you and Roy and the kids.

We are all well here, and have had the usual confused and exciting Christmas and New Year's. Tonight is New Year's Eve and I am trying to get all my letters finished before the year begins. Dorothy and I are alone, and with all due respect to the family, we are not sorry. The last of them departed today. We loved having them, and we also like very much not having them for just a couple of days.

Please tell Roy that one woman met another woman in the street, and said: "What have you done to your hair? It looks terrible. It looks like a wig". The second woman said: "It is a wig". The first woman said: "You'd never know it".

With these happy Christmas thoughts and forecasts for the new year, I close.

As ever,

Oscar Hammerstein II

The Letters of Oscar Hammerstein II. Mark Eden Horowitz, Oxford University Press. © Mark Eden Horowitz 2022.
DOI: 10.1093/oso/9780197538180.003.0011

Oscar Hammerstein to Milton and Melise Biow, January 2, 1952

Dear Milton and Melise:

I love my cushion with the quotation from my lyric on it. It's a kind of paradoxical thing, because with a cushion like this I shall probably write no more lyrics. It will be more fun to rest.

All my love and best wishes to you both for a happy new year.

As ever,

Oscar Hammerstein II

Oscar Hammerstein to Agnes de Mille, January 2, 1952

Dear Agnes:

The old pictures are just wonderful. I don't blame you for your reluctance in letting them go, but don't think you'll ever get them back.

I hope we will see you very soon, because I want to discuss "Paint Your Wagon".[1] I think it contains some of your best work for the theatre. I think the whole production was skirting very close to real greatness, but the author didn't keep his eye on the ball, and he hit it out of bounds.

I have written a very tasty review of your book, and I believe it will [be] in next Sunday's Tribune. I will be sore if it isn't because they gave me a deadline this Monday.

Love to you both and best wishes for a happy new year.

Sincerely,

Oscar Hammerstein II

---

[1] *Paint Your Wagon* opened in November 1951 and ran for a disappointing 157 performances. In his review of the show, Walter Kerr wrote: "Twice in the first act Agnes de Mille catches hold of a striking mood. At the opening of the second act Miss de Mille cuts loose with a roaring dance-hall fandango, and she follows it almost immediately with an exquisitely touching number called 'Another Autumn.' But the rest of *Paint Your Wagon* is a much too earnest proposition."

Oscar Hammerstein to Gordon Manning, Collier's Magazine, January 3, 1952

Dear Mr. Manning:

Here is the verse from the Bible which I would like to contribute to your symposium as my favorite.

John I—chapter 2—Verses 10 and 11

"He that loveth his brother abideth in the light, and there is none occasion of stumbling in him. But he that hateth his brother is in darkness, and walketh in darkness, and knoweth not whither he goeth, because that darkness hath blinded his eyes".

All good wishes to you.

Sincerely,

Oscar Hammerstein II

The Fourposter is a two-character play by Jan de Hartog. It was directed on Broadway by José Ferrer and starred the actual married couple Hume Cronyn and Jessica Tandy. On a single set—featuring a large bed—the play follows a married couple through the ups-and-downs of their marriage, beginning with their honeymoon and ending with their preparing to move out of their home thirty-five years later.

Oscar Hammerstein to Hume and Jessica Cronyn, José Ferrer, and Jan de Hartog, January 6, 1952

Dear Hume and Jessica Cronyn, Jose Ferrer, and Jan de Hartog:

We saw "Fourposter" last night through a film of tears, the most satisfying kind of tears because they were inspired not by sadness or solemnity, but by the recognition of the beauty that lies in all the married lives of all the stumbling, bumbling human beings who try to do their best with each other. Their combined intelligence is pitifully inadequate for the terrifying problems that beset them, but having that incredibly hardy love that some couples share, they attain a kind of shaky and incomplete conquest over life. They may well call this happiness, and be proud to have won it. No wonder everyone cries. Everyone laughs, too, as far as we could see and hear, sitting in the audience last night, and everyone leaves the theatre, as we did, with pride in the nobility of average people, and deep gratitude toward the four of you, who made such a beautiful evening possible.

All our best wishes.

Sincerely,

José Ferrer to Oscar and Dorothy Hammerstein, January 15, 1952

Dear Oscar and Dorothy,

As you know probably better than I do, when you do a play you not only hope it will be a success, but you hope that a few people will understand what you intended—and will love it for the qualities that you saw in the original when you read the script and that you tried to express to the best of your ability out of respect for the author, and with the collaboration of the actors.

I can only tell you that your letter makes me realize that, from the standpoint of imparting to the audience the same emotion that I experienced and still do from THE FOURPOSTER, directing it was much more than a commercially worthwhile effort. You have made it for me a memorable and justifiable experience in the warm reflection of your own generous personalities.

Thanks from the bottom of my heart, and God bless you both.

Affectionately,

<u>Jose</u>.

French actor Roger Rico was brought in to replace Ezio Pinza as Emile de Becque in *South Pacific*—with disastrous results. He was ultimately fired because much of his English remained unintelligible, about which there were multiple complaints by his co-star Martha Wright. But the press portrayed his firing as retribution for an incident that had taken place at the Stork Club, where Rico and his wife had taken the Black star Josephine Baker as their guest. The Club served the Ricos their dinner but did not serve Baker. Outraged, Rico called his lawyer and a deputy police commissioner; the incident led to complaints by the NAACP and picketers outside the club.

Roland H. Wolpert to Oscar Hammerstein, January 17, 1952

Dear Mr. Hammerstein:

Not too long ago I mentioned to my wife, "What a wonderful thing it must be to be Oscar Hammerstein." I meant it. I admired you as both a fine human being and as an artist.

I hear now that you fired an actor because he dared to speak out against racial intolerance.

I hope it isn't true. I'd swear that from what I know about you, it wasn't true.

And yet the actor has been fired and the accusations persist.

The point is, if true, if the Oscar Hammerstein of 1952 can be forced to acquiesce to so cowardly an act, when can any human being be free to act in accordance with his own basic sense of decency?

Roland H. Wolpert

Oscar Hammerstein to Roland H. Wolpert, January 21, 1952

Dear Mr. Wolpert:

Mr. Rico is no longer in the cast of "South Pacific" for one simple reason. For eight months his English did not improve. In fact, it became more obscure, and the people who paid to see "South Pacific" were not getting a fair deal, and so we replaced him. Any suggestion that we took him out of the cast because of his stand on racial intolerance is fantastic and unjust and evil. The play itself is an argument for racial tolerance, and so is my next play, "The King and I". So is every speech I have ever made. On March 6th I am co-chairmanning a meeting with Lena Horne at Madison Square Garden under the auspices of the National Association for the Advancement of Colored People. I have no patience with anyone so thoughtless and cruel as to make an assumption like this, entirely against the evidence of my life and work. Thank you for doubting this careless rumor, conceived by some clown and kept alive by a chain of idiots, and thank you for writing to me to receive my side of the case.

Very truly yours,

Oscar Hammerstein II

From a letter Josh Logan wrote to a "Ginette" and copied to Oscar: "Actually, we are paying Roger $2500 not to play Emile de Becque. We are hoping that in order to leave the country he will make a settlement for a little less than the $90,000 which is due him per contract, but even at that, since he has left the show the performance has improved so enormously and the audience reception is so much better than it was while he was playing that it is worth it to us."

The Rico incident is also discussed in the wide-ranging letter below. But it opens with responses to several suggestions that Mary Martin and Richard Halliday gave Oscar of works he might adapt as musicals to star Mary. Regarding Marguerite Courtney, she was writing a biography of her mother, the stage star Laurette Taylor. In 1963 Martin starred in the musical *Jennie*, which was *very* loosely based on Taylor's life.

Oscar Hammerstein to Mary Martin and Richard Halliday, January 24, 1952

Dear Mary and Dick:

I have read the original book by Hudson, and don't see how I could make a musical play of "Green Mansions". Meanwhile, I have sent to Metro and asked them if they would send me the script you mentioned by Theodore Reeves. I have also asked them to send me whatever version they have of "Forever". I'll send for "Love Affair" too, over at R.K.O. I remember liking it very much. The last sequence is a tough one to get by—I mean when she is in the wheel chair—but it's worth another study.

Regarding Marguerite Courtney's letter, I don't know what there is to say except to tell her that we were interested, and would like to see her final version. Her letter implies that we may have to wait quite some time. When I go out to California this spring, I will make it my business to see her and have a long talk with her. If she hasn't written her material by that time, I will try to get it verbally so that I will know more about the second half of the story. Meanwhile it seems to me that we cannot afford to wait for this without scrounging around for more ideas. I mean all of us—you and Mary and Dick and me. Keep shooting suggestions at me. I love it.

We are all delighted with the amazing business being done at the Lane. It is too bad in a way that we cannot send full statements to the critics each week, so that they can be further mystified by the gullibility of the British public, and their stubborn refusal to agree with these learned gentlemen.

The New York theatrical season has not brought up many pearls. Dorothy and I loved "The Fourposter" with Hume Cronyn and Jessica Tandy giving perfect performances in a really lovely play, and the best musical to open so far is "Pal Joey", the production of which is much better than the first production. It is a solid hit, and deservedly so. "Paint Your Wagon" just missed being a great play, but I am afraid it missed by too much. It is still doing business, mostly because of theatre parties. I would not predict a very solid run for this one. Agnes deMille's work is just great, but Alan Lerner did not get much further than writing a sketch or plan for a good musical play. Possibly he is doing too much picture work. In the second act of this play, Jim Barton sings a lovely song called "I Was Born Under a Wandering Star", where it tells how he must always roam, and cannot ever stay in one place. In the next scene the gold runs out of the hills, and the mines seem to dry up, and everybody leaves town, making it a ghost town—everybody except Jim Barton, who says: "This is my town, and I can't move"—this is the same man who only ten minutes ago was "Born Under a Wandering Star".

Dorothy Rodgers is back in the hospital, but this time the news is much more encouraging. They have conducted further tests on her, and think they have found that after all the trouble is a muscular contraction in the back. She is getting shots for this, and seems to be feeling very much better.

My own Dorothy has not been up to snuff, and is now having tests to see if it is gall bladder trouble. Whatever it is, it is not serious, and only a slight discomfiture. We are going to Washington next week, where I must do some political work for the Authors League and A.S.C.A.P., and we are stopping with the Spenders—the Australian Embassy, where Dorothy decorated.

We have finally become too discouraged with Roger Rico, whose English got worse and worse, and whose performance seemed less clear and more annoying to the audience as he went along. We have put in his understudy, George Britton, who is really one of the best deBecques we have had. Rico, you remember, was in a big fuss at the Stork Club a few months ago, when he and his wife took Josephine Baker there and didn't get good service. There is a nasty whispering campaign, which I am quite sure he has started, which takes the position that we fired him because of the bad publicity arising from his stand on the Negro question. This is a pretty ironical accusation to point at us, but I am sure there are some shmos in town who are only too willing to believe it.

I don't know exactly what his plans are, but I have a strong hunch that he and Madame will want to go back to France this summer. In this case I know he will be responsible to you for the balance of his rent, but I think we might be able to help him and you with another tenant. It seems to us that it would be an ideal place for Gertie Lawrence. Please tell me what you think of this, and whether you would like me to look into it for you—and for us too. It might persuade her not to spend as much time up on the Cape as her contract at present calls for—a six week vacation. We are scared to death of this gap in the play's continuity. "The King and I" is still very strong, and has maintained its big advance. I guess it is the most solid success in town, not excluding "Guys and Dolls", and I would like to keep it so as long as we can.

In your next letter I would like a report of how Heller[2] is doing with her dancing, and any other tid-bits that you have about that young lady—and for that matter, even about yourselves.

Dorothy is out of the house at the moment, but I know she would be pretty sore if I didn't include her when I send our dearest love to you both.

As ever,

Oscar Hammerstein II

Richard Rodgers to Oscar Hammerstein, January 28, 1952

Dear Oscar,

In looking through portfolios in my library, I find that we have quite a number of unused songs. I think that we might go into this together in the near future and decide whether there is enough usable material to

---

[2] Heller Halliday is Mary Martin and Richard Halliday's daughter.

round out a score for a possible full length stock or stage presentation of STATE FAIR.[3]

Love,

Oscar Hammerstein to Dr. Daniel Schneider (excerpt), February 6, 1952

Thank you very much for sending me your book which I look forward to reading as soon as I can find time to sit down in the traditional armchair. The armchair is easier to find than the time.

There were enormous difficulties arranging permissions for American performers to play on British stages, and even when permissions were arranged, they were usually for limited periods of time. The lone exception seems to have been Mary Martin for *South Pacific*.

Jerry Whyte (in London) to Richard Rodgers and Oscar Hammerstein (excerpts), February 9, 1952

Dear Dick and Oc,

After several meetings and trying every form of persuasion unsuccessfully, RAY WALSTON[4] will terminate his contract here after the performance April 12th. I don't think there is a possible replacement here and I don't even think it advisable to try the understudy for a performance because Mary Martin has taken a dislike to him. Naturally I will be on the look out for any possibilities but I think it will be necessary to bring a man from America.

The labour permits have been extended for the seven American artists until March 31st. As you may or may not remember a query was raised regarding Muriel Smith, Wilbur Evans and Archie Savage as to what we plan to do after March 31st. I believe this was started by the understudies or agents of Muriel Smith and Wilbur Evans, however, I have contacted one of the most important men in Labour Relations and he has given me assurance that the thing will be straightened out. I told Prince about this

---

[3] *State Fair* was re-made as a film in 1962. It included five new songs, all of them with lyrics by Rodgers. The show made it to Broadway in 1996 and included songs from the Rodgers and Hammerstein trunk.

[4] Walston played Luther Billis in *South Pacific* in London and recreated the role in the film.

situation and this man, Mr. Selby, does all of his work too so I am really not too concerned.

- - - - - - -

As you can well imagine the death of the King[5] was a terrible shock to the nation. Naturally the matinee and night performance were cancelled, the patrons who came to the theatre were given the choice of a refund or exchanging seats for a future date, better than ninety percent of them booked in advance which is a clear indication of the strength of the show. The performance Thursday night was absolute capacity which surprised everyone and of course naturally last night was capacity. Our advance continues to climb and as of last week it was £25,598 which was £267 more than the previous week.

- - - - - - -

Regarding possible Kings for "The King and I"—Olaf Ollsen is N.G., but Herbert Lom[6] looks quite exciting. His interpretation might be a bit different but he looks as though he could be awfully good.

Oscar Hammerstein to Paul T. Hurt, Jr., February 12, 1952

Dear Mr. Hurt:

I cannot give you permission to use the album of "South Pacific" in the way that you describe. Once we open the gates, our copyright will be generally abused all over the world. I suggest, however, that if you forget that you wrote me this letter, I will forget that I turned you down. Then you might go ahead and do it, and once it was done I am quite sure I would not try to put you and the Cub Scouts in jail. The main point is legally I do not wish to grant you the permission. If you go ahead "illegally" I would hope that you respect my wishes not to quote this letter to anyone, so that they would do it too. I don't want this kind of thing to spread. That is my main concern.

Very truly yours,

Oscar Hammerstein

---

[5] King George VI of the United Kingdom died on February 6.
[6] In a July 4, 2019 email to this compiler, Stephen Sondheim wrote: "according to Dorothy (Hammerstein), Lom was Oscar's favorite King."

Oscar Hammerstein to Tom Arnold (excerpt), February 12, 1952

The King's death has had a deep effect upon the American people, and there has been more space in the newspapers on this subject than on any other that I can remember for a very long time. The silver lining, is, of course, the accession to the throne of a very attractive and intelligent young woman who has it in her to become a great Queen.[7]

Barbara (an employee of Rodgers and Hammerstein) to Oscar Hammerstein, February 15, 1952

Dear Mr. Hammerstein:

This is just to let you know that I finally caught up with Harry Belefonte [sic] last night, at the Blue Angel—and it was well worth the hunt, or chase, or whatever it was. He is a most exciting performer, and that face is just as "beautiful" as it was in the picture you sent me. I have one big fear as far as his ever playing the King is concerned—and that is I'm afraid there could be no doubt but that he is colored. The terrible lighting at the Blue Angel could have accentuated this. Anyway, he is going to audition for you next Thursday.

Sincerely,

Barbara

Oscar Hammerstein to Jerry Whyte (in London), February 15, 1952

Dear Jerry:

Here is a letter with nothing in it, but it is in answer to the parting crack in your letter to the effect that you "hope all is well in New York, seems as though you had been gone for ages, especially considering the fact that you haven't heard from either one of us". Well, now you are hearing, but there is not much news. The good news is that Yul and Gertie are both back in the show. The bad news is that Yul's voice is already wearing kind of raw because he is not saving it very much.

---

[7] Queen Elizabeth II of the United Kingdom.

We are trying to talk McCormick[8] into going over to London. Keep your fingers crossed. You will probably know about it before you get this letter.

I was surprised to note that our business was so good after the death of the King. I had expected a very big falling off.

We are all going out to Chicago today to get the show ready for its road tour. It will leave Chicago at the end of next week. Dick and I are going along to help, and to see that Josh doesn't write a completely new version. Business has been excellent out there since we put up the "last weeks" notice. Business in New York is very bad this week.

If this isn't a nothing letter, what is? Anyway, now you have officially heard from one of us. Always be assured that in our grim, silent, inarticulate way, we all love you very much.

Oscar Hammerstein to Theresa Helburn and Lawrence Langner (Theatre Guild), February 15, 1952

Dear Terry and Lawrence:

I want to thank you for being so kind as to give [me] two seats for "Jane",[9] which Dorothy and I saw last night. The depth of my gratitude is not so great as to force me into saying that I liked the play, but I did think that it was cast and produced beautifully, and I was having a wonderful time all during the first act. Then it seemed to blow out through the stage door like so many English comedies. I hope I am wrong and that the critics are right about this, because you got wonderful notices. The audience certainly seemed to enjoy the play last night.

Love,

Oscar Hammerstein II

Congressman Charles Deane of North Carolina met Hammerstein at a Congressional Subcommittee hearing chaired by Congressman Joseph R. Bryson of North Carolina,

---

[8] Myron McCormick was the original Luther Billis on Broadway.
[9] *Jane* was a play by S. N. Behrman, based on a story by W. Somerset Maugham. Directed by Cyril Ritchard, it starred Edna Best and Basil Rathbone, and ran for 100 performances.

at which Oscar was testifying regarding an upcoming bill. Deane wrote Oscar a letter passionately advocating for the cause/organization Moral Re-Armament (MRA) and a musical, *Jotham Valley*, which advocated its principles: absolute honesty, absolute purity, absolute unselfishness, and absolute love. He also asked for Oscar's guidance or assistance in promoting the songs.

Oscar Hammerstein to the Congressman Charles B. Deane, February 15, 1952

Dear Charles Deane:

Thank you for your letter of February 6th, and the enclosed music from "Jotham Valley". I have gone over all of the songs and found some of them very good indeed. Of course, I think that when you have a play filled with songs like this the motive becomes so obvious that the objective is almost destroyed. I myself have frequently written songs of optimism and gaiety with themes very similar to these, but they have been in plays with stories that had other values in them, and songs that were not all pointed in the same direction, and it is my belief that this is one reason why so many propaganda plays fail, however worthy the philosophy may be that inspires them. It is hard for me to judge whether they can be exploited on the air or by records, but I note that the publisher is a very good one, and it is much more in the line of Carl Fischer Incorporated to attend to the exploitation of music than it would be in my line. I don't even exploit my own. My publisher attends to all that. It is a separate talent and craft.

I was interested to hear of your "testimonial" for Moral Re-Armament, and what contact with it achieved for you. I believe this, of course, and think that the more we all believe and trust in these values the better the world will be.

Thank you again for writing to me. I appreciated hearing from you.

All good wishes.

Sincerely,

Oscar Hammerstein II

Walter White, NAACP, to Oscar Hammerstein, March 7, 1952

I HAVE OFTEN SUFFERED FROM LACK OF COMMAND OF THE
ENGLISH LANGUAGE TO EXPRESS WHAT WAS DEEP IN MY HEART.
BUT NEVER SO MUCH AS TODAY IN TELLING YOU HOW MUCH
WE APPRECIATE NOT ONLY WHAT YOU DID BUT THE SPIRIT IN
WHICH YOU HELPED TO MAKE LAST NIGHT'S MADISON SQUARE
GARDEN SHOW ONE OF THE GREATEST IN HISTORY. NOTHING
JIMMIE BYRNES OR HERMAN TALMADGE[10] OR ANYBODY ELSE
CAN DO TO HURT HEREAFTER CAN POSSIBLY MATCH THE SENSE
OF ASSURANCE THAT HUMAN DECENCY STILL EXISTS WHICH
YOU HAVE GIVEN US. MY WARMEST THANKS IN WHICH ALL THE
NAACP JOINS-

WALTER WHITE=

**J. N. Ferryman, Asst. Professor of Social Science, University
of Colorado to Oscar Hammerstein, March 12, 1952**

Dear Mr. Hammerstein,

Your name has become a part of a study[11] in the meaning of democracy which is being made at the University of Colorado. In its initial stage,
this study has sampled the opinion of farm, labor and business groups
throughout the state of Colorado. As a part of the study each person
questioned was put in this situation: "Think in terms of a displaced person
coming to the United States from an iron curtain country. If you had it
within your power to ask any living American to sit down with this immigrant and his family and explain to them the difference between life here
and life behind the iron curtain, whom would you choose?"

As the second step in this study, we are following up on these selections,
and are writing to all those persons suggested as "most desirable spokesman"

---

[10] James F. Byrnes, of South Carolina, was variously a Congressman, Senator, Secretary of State,
Associate Justice of the Supreme Court, and Governor. Byrnes fought anti-lynching legislation and
opposed *Brown v. the Board of Education*. Herman Talmadge, Governor of Georgia (1945–1948), was
a staunch segregationist who, as a Senator, vehemently opposed the Civil Rights Act of 1964.
[11] The study, "On the Meaning of 'Democracy,'" was published in *The Public Opinion Quarterly* 17,
no. 1 (Spring, 1953), and under the auspices of the American Association for Public Opinion Research.

by at least one member of each of the three different economic groups. You are one of ninety seven persons so selected. We would, therefore, like to request an answer from you which we may, in turn, pass on to the people of our state who are thinking together, with renewed dedication, upon the meaning of freedom. What specific examples would you use to show the meaning of our way of life to a foreigner who had never experienced it?

This study is being conducted through the cooperation of the Colorado Federation of Labor, the Colorado State Grange, and the Colorado Junior Chamber of Commerce. It is totally financed by a research grant from the University of Colorado, but is the sole responsibility of the undersigned. The two basic purposes of the study are as follows: first, to stimulate sincere thought and discussion throughout the state on the real meanings of democracy; second, to observe whether the term, "American way of life" means the same to all of us, regardless of what economic and social part of that life we occupy.

I am sure it is obvious from the above how much your cooperation would add to the meaning of the study. If you wish it, we shall be pleased to send you a copy of the findings when they are completed.

Sincerely,

J. N. Ferryman

Asst. Professor of Social Science

Study Director

Oscar Hammerstein to Dr. J. N. Ferryman, March 19, 1952

Dear Dr. Ferryman:

I am answering your letter in which you ask me to tell you what I should do to show the meaning of our way of life to a foreigner from an "iron curtain country".

I would put before him a series of conflicting newspaper articles, editorials and public utterances, and I would take him on a visit to several of our churches, plays and movies. He would thus receive an impression of the varied views and tempers that influence our thought.

I would ask him to read our Constitution and our Bill of Rights, and I would then acknowledge to him that while all Americans subscribe to these principles, not all live up to them. The foreigner must not be given an idealized picture of us. He must be told of our imperfections, and made aware that we know our shortcomings and have the courage to admit them, and the right to discuss them.

I would do my best to make it clear to him that the blessings of life in a free democracy lie not in achieved perfection, nor in an enforced loyalty to a fiction that perfection exists. The essence of democratic life is the chance for people to better understand themselves as individuals and as a group; the chance to continue an improvement by trial and error, having the humility and the strength to acknowledge error, and the will and the power to keep trying.

Very truly yours,

Oscar Hammerstein II

Oscar Hammerstein to Walter Knapp, March 14, 1952

Dear Walter:

Forgive me for not answering your letter sooner. To tell you the truth, I thought I had answered it. This happens to me quite often now, and implies that maybe you are right about my age, and I am mistaken. (You will remember that I am under the impression that I am fifty six years old, and you have a theory that I am five or six years older than that). When I received your card, I looked in my folder of unanswered letters, and there, lo and behold, was yours. I am particularly sorry because when I read it over I find that you have given me two invitations, one for June 27th and the other for March 23rd, when you are celebrating your forty year anniversary. I would love to come to this, but this is also Jimmy's birthday, and we expect Jimmy to be drafted soon, and we think we'd better spend this birthday with him, so let's aim for the boat race on June 27th. Let me also congratulate you both on reaching the forty year mark. This is a rare achievement these days.

Thank you for the suggestions[12] for musical adaptation, but I feel that we have done our "western" and should turn to things quite different.

---

[12] Knapp's suggestion: "I notice that Rodgers + you are doing a little groping around and I know that you wont pay any attention to me but here are two suggestions that might be of interest, 'The Squaw Man' + 'the Great Divide' both of which would have nothing to do with 'Oklahoma.'"

In "The King and I" we have just done the "eastern" and pretty soon we will be running out of directions, and may have to come back to the west. We are toying with a half of an idea at the moment, but we have not developed it very far at this point. The trouble is that Dick and I are both so busy with other things, managing the companies we have, and taking part in all the outside activities which [we] are trying to gradually eliminate. The days go by very fast, and they are filled with a number of things that are the results of having said yes to easy requests a few months ahead of that. Suddenly they pile up on you, and you find you are accomplishing nothing except making personal appearances here and there. I spoke up at the Yale Dramatic School last week, and two weeks before that I played Swarthmore. I enjoy doing these things, but they are beginning to cut in on my real professional work too much, and I am going to cut it all out.

Arthur got over the weakness that he had six weeks ago, and he sounded fine on the phone yesterday. He's all pepped up now about dictating on his tape recorder the story of his life. He started off dictating to a local stenographer in Palm Beach, but she couldn't take it after the first day. The next time he called her up to come over, she said, "Will your wife be there?" He said: "Christ! I'm seventy nine. What are you worried about?" But I gather from him that some of the words he had to use in telling the story of his life were highly censorable, and embarrassing to a strange young woman. Incidentally, we have made a deal, although this is not signed yet, for the movie production of my grandfather's life. This is something Arthur has wanted to have done for a long time, but no sooner does it look as if it's going through, than he has to turn to his own life. I am sure if it is ever written in dramatic form it will have to have private showings, and can never reach the screen except in a highly cleaned up version.

Billy, who as you know is out at Paramount starting out as a producer, likes it very much out there and has bought a house in the valley. He claims that he can bring up his three children (he adopted his wife's two) much better than here in the east, and I agree with him. The public schools are better, and you can get more for your money to bring up a family out there.

Alice has adopted a very sweet kid, who was one of the kids that Dorothy and I and Pearl Buck and a few others are interested in, in Pennsylvania. It is called Welcome House, and it is for children who are half Asian and half American. This little girl is half Japanese. And so here I am the grandfather of a half Japanese baby. She is one of the most alert and enchanting kids I ever saw. Billy's baby is coming along fine, but I haven't seen her in nearly a year now. Dorothy now is also a grandmother. Henry's baby is over a year old. Rounding out the report, Susan's marriage to Hank Fonda is very successful, and altogether everything is fine with all of us. In a few weeks Dorothy and Dick Rodgers and Dorothy and I are going to Nassau. Dorothy Rodgers has been very ill for nearly a year now, and that would be a good place for her to recuperate, and a good place for Dick and me to get away from this rat race and start in to work on something that counts. I think we'll stay about a month. Later on, Dorothy and I will fly to California for a week to see Billy and his wife, and outside of that I don't see any trips looming up, and I don't see why we can't keep our date on June 27th.

Love to you both from both of us.

As ever,

Oscar Hammerstein II

Oscar Hammerstein to Richard Halliday (London), March 18, 1952

Dear Dick:

I have read the M.G.M. version of "Green Mansions", and while this makes it much easier to visualize a possible stage production, I still would be very much afraid to embark on it. "Forever" is still the elusive "nearly good idea" it has always been, and my reactions to it today are exactly what they were about twelve years ago when someone submitted it to me in Hollywood. The Leo McCarey story is delightful for the first half, and then becomes somber and goes downhill toward the end, not that it isn't a big lift when Boyer finally finds Dunne, but it is awfully hard to block out the shadow of being crippled that hangs over the end of the story.

I have been reading digests of the world's best stories, and considering all kinds of historical characters. I have been reading poems with the idea that possibly a story might be suggested by a great poem, and I have been assiduously reading the reviews of the latest books published. I have so far found nothing that excites me or would excite you, and yet I am sure that if we all keep plugging we will be bound to finally light on that big idea. I have even been trying to work out an original plot (the nerve of him!) and although I have hit on something that interests me, it so far doesn't seem to suggest a starring part for Mary.

I hate to write this account of failure, but it is very important that I keep you posted about this so that you will be apprised of what a bad risk I seem to be for you. The one faint gleam I can send you today is that a playwright—who must be nameless for the moment—has told Dick and me that he has an idea for you, and that he would like to work it out with us, and we are going to meet him and discuss it with him next week. If anyone like him came up with a big idea, I would of course be most happy to collaborate with him. You might bear this in mind if anybody brings anything to you. I would be perfectly content to write the lyrics and help out on the book, and not demand full credit—much as I would prefer it.

There is a picture of Mary in the Sunday Times, in connection with a story about the Gershwin album that she made. Her face looked so American that it made me homesick, even though I am in New York and she is in London. If you can unravel this, it means something.

Dorothy Rodgers is out of the hospital, and she and Dick and my Dorothy and I intend to go away together for about a month somewhere where there is sun. It will do both of the girls good, and possibly Dick and I can meet each other and get to know each other and perhaps get some work done together. Here in New York it is just hell. I have had to swear off making any more speeches or doing any more good. Last week I spoke on the theatre at the P.E.N. Club, and up at New Haven at the Yale Drama Department, and two weeks before that I played Swarthmore. Goodbye to all that, and to all my committees and everything else. I am really rarin' to get going on some songs and snappy dialogue. Wish me luck.

Josh has made big improvements in the first act of "Wish You Were Here". They go into rehearsal in about three weeks. From what he tells me his cast looks very good.

Don't think I couldn't go on and on as far as material is concerned, but I have to go to a committee meeting!

Love to you both from both of us.

Oscar Hammerstein II

P.S. I just realized that "both of us" could mean Dorothy and I or Dick and I. Let it go both ways.

Oscar Hammerstein to Jerry Whyte (excerpt), March 24, 1952

Now to get to the important part of my letter. An artist's model reported at the artist's studio as usual one morning, and the artist said: "Gosh, I'm tired today. I don't feel like painting. I was up late last night and I feel lousy. Let us just have a cup of coffee". So they were having a cup of coffee, when he heard a noise on the stairs, and he says: "Quick! That's my wife! Quick! Take your clothes off!"

Oscar Hammerstein to Mary Martin and Richard Halliday (London) (excerpt), March 31, 1952

Dear Mary and Dick:

In answer to a question in your last letter, I (Oscar) have read "Sappho", and I think perhaps it would make a good story for Kit Cornell. We (Dick and Oscar) might be more excited about it if we had already found a story for Mary Martin, who is the star we happen to have in our care. Speaking of her, we are anxious to know as soon as we can what, if any, are her desires for next winter.

Have you any ideas now about whether you want to leave the London "South Pacific" company at the end of your contract, or stay on through another season? We know this depends on several things— the presence or absence of a new play to do; the situation surrounding Heller's dancing career; last, and perhaps the most important, whether you feel it would be fun to stay through another season, or not fun. We hate to be trying to tie you down to a decision this far ahead, but it is terribly important that we know as soon as possible. If you decide not to stay, you must admit in all modesty that it is no cinch to find someone to sell to the London public following (to quote another fellow's song) irreplaceable you. You have probably heard of the sensational repetition of the 100,000 pound buy for the second six months of this year. This means that the time is not far off when we shall be starting to build up a new advance for the third six months, and the public will have to know whom it is buying—Mary Martin or Jennie Ersatz. (Please burn this letter after you read it. We would hate Jennie ever to find out about the above sentence).

Since it doesn't look as if we can have a play ready by next November, we hope to have Mary remain at the Drury Lane, and not Jennie. Can you give us any inkling at this time how you feel about all this? The four of us, Dick, Oscar and two Dorothys are entraining for Palm Beach today, and we expect to stay [. . .] [The second page of this letter has been lost.]

Oscar Hammerstein to Madge and Cyril Ritchard, March 31, 1952

Dear Madge and Cyril:

Thank you for the book. I don't promise to read it this week, because it is my intention to go out on to the hot sands and become burnt to a crisp on my first day there. I will then be so physically paralyzed and mentally stultified by the sun that I shall not be functioning normally before about a week. Then, if I can summon the energy to pick up the book, I shall. I may not be able to turn more than a few pages the first day, but I shall get better each day, and I am quite sure that within two weeks I shall have mastered the thing. This is nice to look forward to, and I am indebted to you for the anticipation. It doesn't look as if we shall see you before you go to England, and on that supposition I am wishing you great success there. I am hoping that the cottage will be a wonderful thrill for you to get back into, and I hope that the play will get over with more than that. I hope that they will say of Cyril: "This is all right about a limited engagement for the play, but what about the Ritchard fellow? Why can't we have him stay over for another?" "Oh!" will come the quick answer: "He has previous commitments in the states, and may be there for an indefinite period". I hope this all comes true and that we will see you at the end of the summer here for an indefinite period in a crashing new success. Am I not in an expansive mood this morning?

Love to you both.

Oscar Hammerstein II

The following letter starts by talking about the presidency of ASCAP, which was offered to Oscar but which he turned down. In Wolfie Gilbert's letter to Oscar he wrote: "Let us finecomb our membership, and if necessary amend its bylaws so that any man measuring up to the job, even though he is not a member of the Board, would be eligible." With Oscar turning down the position, Ruby believed the presidency should be retained by Otto Harbach.

Oscar Hammerstein to Harry Ruby, April 29, 1952

Dear Harry:

On the same day that I received a letter from you I received a letter from Wolfie Gilbert saying the same thing. I want you to know that I couldn't agree with you more in the theory that we should rescind the resolution and re-elect Otto Harbach. I have told Wolfie, and I am telling you to get all the fellows you can to send wires to their friends on the Board, urging them to accomplish this elimination of a resolution which is very much in our way.

I don't think I ever congratulated you on the success of our song, and on the achievement of its being one of the five candidates for the Academy Award. I cannot help feeling that we would have won the statuette if you had been on your toes rounding up votes out there, passing out a few cigars and kissing an occasional baby. But the trouble with you is that you are an idealistic dreamer, staying home and letting your fingers move idly across the ivories, and now and then going out into the garden to look after your prize carnations. This is not the way to win Academy Awards, and I hope you have learned your lesson.

Four weeks ago Dick and I and our wives went down to Palm Beach, and we made up our minds that we would come back with a completely developed story for our next play. We came back with four sunburns.

Love to Eileen and you.

Oscar Hammerstein II

Harry Ruby to Oscar Hammerstein, May 1, 1952

Dear Oscar:

I am not using my best paper for a reply to yours of the 29th, which, if examined closely, could pass as, well, to put it politely, adverse criticism.

But, first, a word about your attitude on ASCAP matter Re: The next president. I am so happy you see it as you do. I just dashed off a hot—but tactful—letter to Cunningham, who, as you may know, is a really nice person.

I cannot say this for some of the others [*sic*] lads who lunch daily at the Paddock, which place I have called: Miasma Beach—which I hope is not too clever. (I shall not mention names—except on request.)

In closing that part of this letter, I do hope that the resolution is suspended for this term, to allow the retention of Otto. (By the way, I think the other fellers here have written—or wired—to other members of the board. That, I believe is being taken care of)

Now, to get back to your letter all about "our" song, as you call it, despite the fact that all you wrote of it is the lyric, I do not agree that it was I who loused up getting the statuette. The four hundred dollars I spent on cigars, alone, which were handed out to babies, is only a small fraction of what this thing cost me.

For ten nights running, prior to the night of the Academy Award Affair, I dined three hundred persons at the better cafes. Three hundred persons a night, for ten nights, runs into the kind of money Berlin gets for agreeing to do a picture if he likes it, which is not applied to the sum he gets for doing the job.

He now charges ten dollars for coming to the phone when friends call. But that is only for local calls. For the use of a vamp, of a song he has no use for, he gets $50,000, tax free, and room and board for a year. I understand you gotta hand it to him.

"Our" song would have won that Award (seriously), had there not been three song[s] up for it at the same studio: MGM. People around here were betting we'd get it. Maybe they were trying to be polite and kind, but Carmichael and Mercer said we should have won. Maybe next time . . . when you, Dick and I do a song for MGM. . . And it's Goddam nice of you to do it, because you and Dick don't need me. See you in June

Sincerely,

Harry

"Our" song was "A Kiss to Build a Dream On," written for but not used in the film *A Night at the Opera* in 1935. It was unearthed in 1949 and placed in the 1951 film *The Strip*. Louis Armstrong's subsequent recording sold over 500,000 copies by the end of January 1952, becoming his biggest hit to date. Nominated for an Oscar, the song lost out to Johnny Mercer and Hoagy Carmichael's "In the Cool, Cool, Cool of the Evening".

Oscar Hammerstein to Marc Connelly, April 29, 1952

Dear Marc:

I have a letter [from you] written as Secretary of the National Institute [of Arts and Letters] containing a nomination blank. I think it is high time that Dick Rodgers was elected in the music group, but I don't believe I am the one to propose him. I know that [Douglas?] Moore is very much for him, and it seems to me that Virgil Thomson is against him. If you think, as I do, that Dick should be in it, would you consider speaking to Moore and asking him to propose Dick? If you don't agree with me let me know and I will try some other channel. I am under the impression, however, that we have talked about this before, and that you feel as I do.

All the best to you.

As ever,

Oscar Hammerstein II

Marc Connelly to Oscar Hammerstein, May 5, 1952

Dear Oscar:

Dick's name has already been proposed by Deems [Taylor] and seconded by me, and by this time, I'm sure Douglas Moore's name will also be on the nomination. This time I think we will have practically unanimous support.

As ever,

Marc

Marc Connelly

After reading in *Collier's* that Oscar's favorite bible passage was John 2:10,11, Pastor Ivan Hagedorn of Philadelphia, hoping to write a sermon about it, wrote Oscar asking for the reason behind his selection.

Oscar Hammerstein to Rev. Ivan H. Hagedorn, May 14, 1952

Dear Dr. Hagedorn:

The Bible passage quoted in Collier's is one of my favorites because it states a truth which could solve so many problems that exist in the world today, and eliminate so much of its strife. We cannot possibly attain security or happiness without really believing and practicing brotherhood. The belief and practice of universal distrust and fear and hatred are accomplishing more toward our destruction than any other warped thinking that I can imagine.

I hope these observations may be of some use to you.

Very truly yours,

Oscar Hammerstein II

The letter below was probably in response to a rumor that "You've Got to Be Carefully Taught" would have to be cut from a hoped-for production of *South Pacific* in South Africa, where apartheid had begun in 1948, and where the first apartheid law was enacted in 1949—the Prohibition of Mixed Marriages Act. This was followed in 1950 with the Immorality Amendment Act, which made it illegal for South Africans to marry or have sexual relations across racial lines.

Oscar Hammerstein to Herbert Kretzmer, *Sunday Express*, South Africa, May 5, 1952

Dear Mr. Kretzmer:

Mr. Rodgers turned your letter over to me, feeling that as author of the book and lyrics it was more in my province than in his to answer your question. It is a very simple answer. If "South Pacific" is to be produced in South Africa the text will not be altered. It will be exactly as you saw it in London.

You refer to a "censor" in your letter. It is my understanding that there is no official censor in South Africa. Any request for alterations must therefore come from some other source. As far as I am concerned, no pressure could influence me to make any changes that would water down the plot or theme or characterizations of this play. I have already made this very clear to the producers.

In writing this letter to you I am assuming that you literally mean the sentence: "Your comment would be used only if there is censor trouble". I don't think it would be fair to the producers to stir up controversy and hurt the play's chances. I believe with the deepest conviction that if they produce the play, they will not deliberately break faith with me. But if any power tries to force them to do this, I want to know about it.

Thank you for your interest in writing to Mr. Rodgers and making the inquiry that has given me the chance to state our position to you.

With all good wishes.

Sincerely,

Oscar Hammerstein II

Oscar Hammerstein to Hume Cronyn, May 6, 1952

Dear Hume:

I finally read "Mr. Arcularis",[13] and I can understand the fascination it has for you. I warned you that I was weak on fantasy, and a great deal of the play is obscure to me. I mean there are scenes the purpose of which I do not understand. In fact, if there is a major theme in the play, I do not understand this either. Quite apart, however, from my vague intellectual response to the play, I found it irresistible emotionally. I read it lying in bed, and Arcularis' creepy visits to the coffin in the ice box made me so cold that Dorothy thought she had a chill.

You asked me to ignore the prologue and epilogue, but I didn't ignore them, and I am not sure that one should. For us literal-minded fellows it

---

[13] "Mr. Arcularis" began life as a short story by Conrad Aiken, who adapted it as a play in 1957. The story begins and ends with Mr. Arcularis in an operating room. The body of the story has him on a "ship" that turns out to be dream taking place during surgery—a surgery which, it seems, he will not survive.

creates a point of reference which we badly need. We say: "Ah!" This is the suspension between life and death, the rambling foggy thoughts of a patient under an anesthetic, having an operation that finally proves fatal to him. Without these two poles to lead away from and arrive at, I would be much more lost than I was.

There is beyond any doubt fine quality in the writing, and an unusual opportunity for the man who plays Mr. Arcularis. Miss Snell is a lovely character and will prove in production more important than she looks in the manuscript, because she is the "bright spot".

I just took a quick look inside the script and find that when I say "prologue and epilogue" I was not talking about the same things you were talking about. I thought the prologue and epilogue were the scenes in the operating theatre. But I find they are the rather cryptic dialogues that precede and follow the scenes in the operating theatre. Now I agree with you completely. These should be cut. They are the kind of footnotes that require footnotes.

I am off to Washington now to try to persuade the lawmakers there to permit moppets to appear on the stage.

All good wishes to you and Jessica.

Sincerely,

Oscar Hammerstein II

Oscar Hammerstein to Dorothy Hammerstein for their 23rd Wedding Anniversary, May 14, 1952

My dearest darling bady wife:

This is a note to go with your morning corsage and your evening corsage ---

I love you more deeply than ever. Our lives are two strands that have become so tightly braided together as to be one strand, stronger and stouter, inseparable and unbreakable. There could be no happiness for me except in this sweet bondage.

Your legal husband and eternal lova [sic] –

Ockie

Here we have reference to the birth pangs of what will become *Me And Juliet,* Rodgers and Hammerstein's sixth Broadway musical.

Oscar Hammerstein to Mary Martin and Richard Halliday (in London), May 15, 1952

Dear Mary and Dick:

There is an article in Variety this week that says that Dick and I are trying to develop a musical play with a backstage story. This much of the article is true, and nothing else in it is true. The reason I am hastening to tell you this is that one of the things it says is that this story is designed as a starring vehicle for Mary, and this is not true. This story—as far as it has been designed, and it is not very far—has no parts in it that would be suitable for a star, male or female.

We are still looking anxiously for something that we think would be a suitable vehicle for Mary, but we haven't found anything yet about which we are enthusiastic enough. If we decide to proceed with the story we are beginning to work out, that has nothing to do with our other project for Mary. One would not eliminate the other.

I hope you had a wonderful vacation in Sicily. I wish Dorothy and I could fly over there just to hear you tell us about it and to see you again. It looked for a while as if we might be able to squeeze this in early in the summer, but now it doesn't look so much that way. Heigh-ho!

I saw Jim Michener down at the Bucks County three weeks ago and he reported to me on his visit to London, his delight with the performance he saw there, and the pleasant time he had with you.

Business at the Majestic has fallen off quite sharply, but this is seasonal. I expect we'll have a rough summer, but if we survive it, then I should predict that we would run throughout next season into May or June.[14] "The King and I" is still selling out and is a very strong ticket.

This is about all the gossip and chit-chat I can think of at the moment. I would like to get some of the same from you, and soon.

Love from us all.

[14] *South Pacific* ran until January 16, 1954.

Gertrude Lawrence's recurring ill-health became increasingly problematic, but when Rodgers and Hammerstein expressed their concerns they were largely dismissed by Lawrence, her agent, and her doctor. A handwritten note at the bottom of this letter to Gertrude Lawrence reads: "Not mailed".

Richard Rodgers and Oscar Hammerstein to Gertrude Lawrence, May 20, 1952

Dear Gertrude:

We are sorry that you were unable to see us either Monday or Tuesday, because we were anxious to record with you our deep concern over what seems to us a crisis in your theatrical career. We have expressed our feelings to Fanny and David Holtzmann, but they apparently are not in agreement with us—or perhaps they misunderstood us.

You are still playing the part of Anna magnificently, perhaps even better than you played it when we opened. Your singing of the score, however, has deteriorated to an alarming extent. We don't think you know this, and it is no fun to be the ones to tell you the news, but somebody has to. Eight times a week you are losing the respect of fifteen hundred people. This is a serious thing to be happening to one of the great women of our theatre, and it would be dishonest and unfriendly of us to stand by any longer without making you aware of the tarnish you are putting on your past triumphs, and your future prospects. Whether you want to face up to this problem, or allow the situation to drift on as it is doing, is a decision you will have to make.

It may be that you will resent our telling you this. If you do it will be childish on your part. We have neither motive nor desire to worry you. We are trying to protect you from a danger that faces you, and at the moment, as we do this, we are the best friends you have.

Our love, always.

Richard Rodgers

Oscar Hammerstein II

Gertrude Lawrence to Oscar Hammerstein, May 22, 1952

Dearest Oscar.

I am sending this note to you + hope you will pass the word on to Dick.

I was sorry not to get a chat with you on Monday night—but only caught a fleeting glimpse of you as I dashed by to change, + when next I emerged you had gone.

This beastly damp + humid spell has given me a slight chill + last evening I sent for Doctors Rubin + Richard + they both decided that I had better shut up shop for the day, + brought me home. However.! I hope to return on Friday night and see the week out.

Meantime, maybe next week you + Dick would care to have that drink with Richard + me back here at the house after the play some evening—as you know it takes <u>hours</u> for me to prepare to present myself in public after the play, whereas we can come back here with me in full war paint.

I am sorry to be away but happy that Connies[15] sister will get a chance to see her as "Anna." Maybe it will enhance her opinion of these U.S. which I believe she can't understand at all!!

I hate just lying here, + get very restless for the gang at the St. James— but, unlike the Chinese, we only pay doctors when we are sick!!!

If you feel like calling me on Tuesday from the Country I shall be here –

Love to you + Dorothy

"Mrs Anna"

May 22.52.

<u>P.S.</u>

Incidentally, I would like your office to find out how the rumour reached Miss Hopper that I was permanently leaving the play. Perhaps you could instruct M. M.[16] to straighten her out on this matter.

---

[15] Constance Carpenter was Lawrence's understudy in *The King and I*, and after Lawrence's death became her replacement for most of the rest of the run.

[16] Michael Mok handled publicity and public relations for Rodgers and Hammerstein.

Howard Reinheimer to Richard Rodgers and Oscar Hammerstein, May 24, 1952

Re: "SOUTH PACIFIC"—South Africa

Dear Dick and Oscar:

I have just had word from South Africa that because of the conditions down there, it is not possible for them to present SOUTH PACIFIC at the present time.

Sincerely,

Howard

HOWARD E. REINHEIMER.

John Hersey's Pulitzer prize–winning novel *A Bell for Adano* is set in a town on the Italian coast, occupied by the Allies in 1943. According to a review in *Time* magazine: "The mood of *A Bell for Adano* is bitter. Its humor is raucous and wild . . . At its best it is a superb piece of reporting. Read unimaginatively, it is a deadly account of U.S. official incompetence. Stripped of its humor, it is the story of a battle for democracy." In December, 1944 a play of the novel opened on Broadway, written by Paul Osborn, and produced by Leland Hayward. A film version opened in June 1945. (It's not clear who Joe is in the letter below.)

Oscar Hammerstein to John Hersey, May 24, 1952

Dear John:

I have read Joe's letter to Luise Sillcox, and I am returning it herewith. It is difficult for me to be very intelligent about this. One thing I am certain of. "A Bell for Adano" would not make a typical musical comedy, but it is quite obvious that Joe doesn't think so either. He is submitting his idea as a musical play that would be nearly an opera, perhaps, and that gives rise to the question of the quality of adaptation. It would have to aim high. Let us assume that Joe, who seems to feel this very deeply can do his part. The next question is who will do the music and the lyrics. We are rich in songwriters, but very poor in real composers, or lyricists who can write a score of any quality for this kind of undertaking, and I think it would be a fair question for you to ask—who had he in mind to do the music and the lyrics. On the basic story change which he suggests, (having Joppolo unmarried, and therefore free for a love story with Tina that had some chance of a happy ending) you are of course a much better judge than I because it is your story.

One suggestion. In case you decide to go ahead with it, it might not be a bad idea, if Paul Osborn is willing, to have the book written by Paul and Joe in collaboration. I still think, however, that the main problem is the score. Fritz Loewe might do it. If he and Alan Lerner, his collaborator, would do the score, it might be fine, Lerner, however, usually likes to do the book too.

These random and somewhat flabby reactions are about all I can give you. I wish I could be more definite and brilliant about it.

All good wishes.

Sincerely,

Oscar Hammerstein II

Richard Halliday to Oscar Hammerstein, May 27, 1952

Dear Oscar,

The best news is that you have started to work on a new project. Very many thanks for sending us this long-awaited good news. Our very best wish is with you every second of the way.

We feel as though we are standing on the corner of 44th Street and Broadway. My sister and her husband are here—Cheryl Crawford has just left, Abel Green just arrived, and Gabriel Pascal has flown in to talk about PYGMALION with Lerner and Lowe [sic] doing the job. (Mary wonders what's the matter that everyone except us seems to see this as a likely possibility). Then John Byram and Dick Watts arrive next week and I believe Lawrence Langner too. In order to keep the Anglo-American spirit alive, Mary and Noel are to rehearse again for a British-American benefit.

The one visitor, a friend of yours, who worries me is—Robert Menzies.[17] He came to see SOUTH PACIFIC last Saturday, the night he

---

[17] Sir Robert Menzies was the Prime Minister of Australia.

arrived. He has asked Mary to bring the whole family to live with him in Australia. In the meantime they have reached the exchanging-photo period. If he hadn't introduced his attractive wife to Mary—and if he hadn't been so obvious that the thought Mary should go to Australia to play S.P.— then—I'd really be worried.

Heller has just had her first foot injury! That is something to worry about. She had to see a doctor twice. She couldn't do her ballet for one whole day. But the doctor gave her permission to dance today—so Heller's world is full of nothing but sunshine again.

If you and Dorothy would come over we'd promise to give up every American and Australian too—we'd arrange your life so you'd have peace and quiet for nothing but writing! In the meantime, we hope you two are having wonderfully good days down on the farm.

Our love is with you –

Always –

Dick

Oscar Hammerstein to Eva Kern Byron, May 29, 1952

Dear Eva:

Howard has told me something about the "Show Boat" situation. The copyright renewal is of course in Edna's hands, and it is true that she can give out licenses without our songs. This might be a dubious right for her because the songs have become so identified with the property. On the other hand it is true that we have no legal right to her property unless she assents that we do. Since most of the income for the rest of the life of the copyright renewal will be in so-called subsidiary rights, radio, television, pictures etc., with perhaps an occasional stage revival, I am in sympathy with her desire to increase her original share, because she was the creator of the story and the characters. I understand that it was her suggestion that we each take one third. We can either follow this simple course, or we can go into shaded fractions which I believe in the long run will not mean very much one way or the other to anybody. And so I don't care very much what is finally decided upon. In the original instance Jerry and I made separate deals with Ziegfeld, and at that time Jerry commanded more than I could.

When we last revived the show, however, Jerry recognized the fact that there wasn't very much theory on which to base this inequality, and we divided evenly. I think that if you will sit down with a pencil and paper and imagine probable fees that we might get for performances, you will find that the small fractional differences will not accomplish anything except to complicate bookkeeping. If, for instance, a radio performance of "Show Boat" earned $2100, we would each get $700 on an equal division. If, on the other hand, Edna sticking to her demand for one third got $700, and the rest were divided $720 to you and $680 to me, I don't think that over many years of license releases this discrepancy will make you or your estate rich or me or my estate poor.

These are my only observations. I don't [think] that the subtlety of division is nearly as important as our straightening this out in some way so that this valuable property can be made available to people who want to use it.

Our plans for coming to the coast are now very uncertain, although I am very anxious to come out sometime this summer, if it's only for a week. When we decide we can get away you will be the first to know, and we shall certainly keep some time for you.

All our love to all of you.

Oscar Hammerstein II

Oscar Hammerstein to Herbert Gellendre, June 20, 1952

Dear Mr. Gellendre:

We are in receipt of your prospectus, regarding your production, "Everyman". Two years ago Mr. Rodgers and I adopted a policy of not investing in any productions which we did not ourselves control. One of our main reasons for this decision was based on the fact that our presence among a list of investors was used as an encouragement to other investors, and this was based on an exaggerated idea of our theatrical wisdom. Too many people reason that if Rodgers and Hammerstein were in a play it had an abnormal chance of success. We know this to be untrue, and we felt too responsible for influencing strangers whom we had no desire to influence. The same principle is true even though the net proceeds of your project are to be devoted to a charity. We are not sufficiently familiar with your property to endorse it, and we know that our names on it carry and endorsement far beyond the importance it should have. We are sorry not to be able to accommodate you in this instance, and we are sincerely grateful to you for giving us the opportunity to come in.

Very truly yours,

Oscar Hammerstein II

In June, Virginia Carrick of G. P. Putnam's Sons, wrote to inquire if Oscar would be interested in talking to the publishing house about his autobiography. "After all," she reasoned, "you did write a song called 'Why Was I Born?' which is of course a perfect title for your story." In his initial response, Oscar wrote: "I don't see how I can possibly budget the time to write an autobiography—not for several years, anyway. But let me say that your title is a brilliant suggestion. I hope I remember it when I finally get around to the job, and I hope I remember that you were the one who suggested it." To which Carrick replied: "In the meantime would your time budget permit you to have a drink with me at your convenience? It would be fun to be among the several publishers with whom you have discussed your autobiography, particularly if some day I have to give up the title to one of them. But I hope it won't come to that."

Oscar Hammerstein to Virginia B. Carrick, G. P. Putnam's Sons, July 3, 1952

Dear Mrs. Carrick:

Thank you for your letter. I would like very much to sit down and talk over with you a book which I shall probably never write. If you are willing to waste your time this way, so am I. I think it is wonderful to talk over books that are not going to be written. You have a good deal of the pleasure of preparing a book and not the pain of going through with it. At the moment I am staying in the country trying to write a play. When I come to town for a longer stretch, I will phone you.

All good wishes.

Sincerely,

Oscar Hammerstein II

Oscar Hammerstein to Richard Halliday, July 10, 1952

Dear Dick:

It was good to hear from you, and while you have told me that I don't have to answer your letter right away, I am answering it immediately after reading it and the enclosures, Mrs. Courtney's letter, and Miss Eustis's "The Return to Love".

1. Your letter I am forwarding to Dick Rodgers, because I know he will be very proud of what you said about him.
2. I am glad to hear that Mrs. Courtney is getting on with it and that she believes the middle and last parts will be even better than the first. This is what Dick Rodgers had hoped when I submitted my digest of the first part to him.
3. "The Return to Love". This is all news to me. I thought love had been going on all this time, and here I am told that since Elizabethan times it has been out of favor. We popular songwriters have been fooling a lot of people, or they have been kidding us.

In spite of the fact that I think the facts in the article are exaggerated, the theme is one with which I completely agree. The distinction between mere sex and love is an important one to make, but I don't think it is quite so much of a discovery as Miss Eustis thinks it is. There is a play I know, for instance, in which two people do fall head over heels in love with each other at first sight, even though the man is much older than the woman, and there is no psychoanalysis involved, and then in the same play a young man starts with sheer sex with the Tonkinese girl, and the sheer sex evolves itself into a very deep love for which he is willing to throw over everything. Unfortunately he dies and is never put to the test.

This doesn't say that another play shouldn't be written about this subject—lots of plays. I wish with all my heart that we could find one, and I have a deep conviction that we will. The only trouble is that we haven't found one so far. Let's all keep working on this.

Michael Mok gives me glowing reports of Mary, her performance and herself, and I am hearing the same from all people who come from London. This makes me very happy to hear, as I am also happy to hear that you have improved your condition, which was not so good for a while. Let's keep it good now. We all miss you very much, and I wish to heaven there was some way of my flying over there during the summer, but at the moment I wouldn't know how to find the time to fly to Hoboken to watch the ferries come in and go out—a thing I would dearly love to do—well not <u>dearly</u> but it would be a nice diversion.

I am knee deep in our new play. I have written seventy five rough pages—perhaps the roughest pages you ever saw. Next week Dorothy and I are going up to spend the week with Jean and Ted Ely in Annisquam, and I am going to try to smooth out the roughness while I am there. This would mean that I would come back with a first act (only dialogue, no lyrics).

"Wish You Were Here", as you know by now, got very bad notices, but it is going along at a fairly good clip, not selling out, but doing business that might indicate that it will run for some time and perhaps surprise a great many people. Josh has worked gallantly on it, and is still working on it.

We have an improvement at Doylestown. We have put in a swimming pool, and I now do so much floating about in it that I wonder how I got along for so long. Dear me, how do the poor people live?

I feel that I am beginning to ramble, and so I will stop. Dorothy keeps bobbing in and out and keeps telling me to be sure to send her love, so I now do this very thing. It is always wonderful to know that I haven't forgotten to do something.

Dorothy sends her love, so there!

So do I!

Oscar Hammerstein II

Oscar's 57th birthday was on July 12.

Oscar Hammerstein to The Court of Siam, c/o "King and I" Co., St. James Theater, July 1952

Most Honorable Court of Siam:

I wish to make many, many thanks for birthday telegram I shall have received on birthday. In humble gratitude I bow like toad, and send all my love, good wishes, et cetera, et cetera, et cetera.

Oscar Hammerstein II

In honor of Hammerstein's birthday, a concert of songs by Hammerstein and Kern was presented at Lewisohn Stadium, with 19,000 in attendance. The Stadium closed their season three weeks later with a Rodgers and Hammerstein concert, with 17,000 in attendance.

Oscar Hammerstein to Stephen Sondheim, July 14, 1952

Dear Stevie:

Thank you for your birthday telegram. Your wishes for dry weather came true, and the concert seemed to me to be a very successful one. The lyrics were balled up in only two songs this time, but I had my revenge. When singers forget lyrics of songs as old and well known as these, not only does the author wince, but the entire stadium winces, and I am sure the singer receives a scar from which she never recovers. Good!

Love,

Oscar Hammerstein II

A report was sent to Hammerstein regarding changes made to a production of *Carousel* at the Starlight Theatre in Kansas City. Richard Berger, the theater's producer, responded by telegram with: "Dear Oscar Please accept my abject apologies and assurance that all cuts will be reinstated immediately. Must admit I planned some minor deletions which in all honesty thought would enhance presentation of Carousel in outdoor theatre Our audience start to leave theatre at shortly after eleven oclock in order to make bus connections and I thought it better to have show end at this time rather than have droves of people walk out before it was over."

Oscar Hammerstein to Richard Berger, Starlight Theatre, July 25, 1952

Dear Dick:

Thank you for your wire. It is very reassuring to hear from you that you have restored the script to the way it was. I too am sorry that we had to hear it second hand, and I would have been glad to discuss cuts with you to get it down to playing time. I cannot for the life of me, however, understand why the playing time should dictate the insertion of a line like: "Get in the house—get in bed—keep warm" after Julie has told Billy she is going to have a baby.

"Carousel" is a very delicate play, not as sturdy as "Rose Marie" or "Desert Song", and I think it need[s] very sympathetic treatment. I am sure that as a producer you are giving it just that. But when I heard about the changes I blew my top.

Best wishes to you for a great success with the play, and with all the rest of your projects this summer.

Sincerely,

Oscar Hammerstein II

Richard Rodgers to Oscar Hammerstein, enclosing a letter from John Steinbeck, July 29, 1952

Dear Oscar,

I know that you and I discussed the enclosed and I also know that you had very cogent arguments against John's idea. I just can't remember them at the moment. I also know that it doesn't interest me very much. Do you think you can recall what you told me and write to John?

Love,

Dick

July 4, 1952

Positano, Italy

Dear Dick and Oscar: Here's four months of our six month trip gone and I don't know where it has gone. We have been all over hell and gone. Elaine is doing it up in her usual efficient way. She knows twice as much about churches as the pope and he owns them. I'm pretty lazy about these things. Even pictures and statues which I like I can get kind of constipated on. It may be heresy to say but I think this can even happen to Elaine. She passed a twelfth century church the other day without hardly twitching.

You know it is said in lumber camps that you usually log in the whore house and screw in the woods. I've been brooding here on an obscure beach in Italy. It's fourth of July and I haven't even a squib to set off. I know the mayor and I'm going to ask him for a few sticks of dynamite. We'll see if he can get them for us. I think we are home sick but we aren't going to admit it to anybody. And we will be back on sept first.

What I have been brooding about is you two. Can't get the King and I out of my mind, the dignity it has and the stature and the tenderness and the reaching in both music and theme. I guess everybody tells you what to write. So I'm going to join the unselect group and tell you what to write. Boilleau[18] [sic] said there were three creatures worthy of literature, Kings Gods and Heros [sic]. You can kind of transcribe that to mean that the only men worthy of literature are men who make their mark on the souls of men. We have one in our country who above all others has done this. everybody has had a crack at him and I don't think anyone has done it yet. I begin to think you can't get deep into people without music. I mean the story of Abraham Lincoln. Its the whole country and the mark of him is just as deep or deeper now that it ever was. And nobody could do that story like you two. And there is no story I would rather help with. I think of it in this unique American form which you have so developed, the play with music. I think of the story not as being complicated or fancy but very simple First act, the lean ugly man who loved a girl who died, who made the American dream, who made jokes and loved to dance and was a horseman and a wrestler and a hell of a good lawyer. Who debated with Douglas. Can't you see the Lincoln Douglas debate in music? Then the first act ends with the election to the Presidency. The second is the years of the war and the saddness [sic] and the death of his son and and [sic] his fancy crazy wife and always the girl who died. And this act would end with the victory which he felt not as a victory. And then the short third act, the attempt to heal the nation, and his dream of his own death and perhaps a last scene, the opening of Our American Cousin and the assassination. No detail, just rough form and the chance to give the nation great music based on itself and the chance to restate to the nation what it is about now in its time of fear and uncertainty. Lord I would like to work on that book. No one has really put it down and it is all there dramatically, beginning middle and end. Think about it will you? It's not a short thing. It maybe should take a long time. And I can't think of anything better to do for you nor for me. That's all, now I've told you and I won't haunt you with it but I hope the subject begins to haunt both of you.

---

[18] Nicolas Boileau-Despréaux, French poet and critic, 1636–1711.

Monday we go back to Rome and up to Paris for Bastille day. Our center or base is the Lancaster Hotel Rue de Berri Paris. I would love to hear from you. We are really getting a yearning for that ugly skyline and our ugly friends and our children. Sometimes we don't see a paper for weeks on end. We know nothing that has happened. Hope you are all well. We love you and miss you. Forever our love to all Dorothys. And we'll hope to see you as soon after Sept 1st as we can.

I've got a new long book[19] coming out about then. And I think it is good. It had better be or I will have been wasting my time for a good forty years.

so long

John

P.S. As in greek tragedy, the audience already knows this story. There should be a minimum of explanation

Oscar Hammerstein to John Steinbeck, August 5, 1952

Dear John:

Each of us thought that the other had answered your July 4th letter from Italy, so both of us are now making apologies to you for the long delay.

We can give you no definite reaction to your idea for doing a musical play about Abraham Lincoln. It is a path that many have trod, and the three of us, of course, would have to conceive of some way to tread it more excitingly than it has ever been done before. You no doubt have some feeling about how this could be done, and I think the best thing is for us to wait until you come here, so that the three of us can sit down and discuss it very carefully.

There is only one definite answer about one thing in your letter that we can give you. You say: "Can't you see the Lincoln Douglas debate in music?" The answer is no, we can't, but we are not adamant, and maybe you can show us how this is possible. All the other things you say about its possibilities are of course true, and we are in no way prejudiced against the idea

---

[19] *East of Eden.*

of doing this particular biography. Yet, even as I tell you this I feel that I am dipping my pen in cold water as I write. Why is this? I think perhaps that my instinct, and Dick's as well, as that the thing has been done just too often. Instincts, however, are not always the final and correct answer, and we shall keep our minds open. The most attractive part of it all at the moment is the idea of doing anything at all in collaboration with you. This attracts us both very much. So let us talk, first about Lincoln, and if that doesn't work, let us talk about something else. I think the three of us might turn out a very good musical play, and if we didn't, I think the three of us would have a very good time working together.

It's good to hear that you and Elaine will be back with us soon. Please let us know when you get here.

Love to you both from all four of us.

Oscar Hammerstein II

Attached to the carbon of the letter below is an article titled "Sittin' Starin' N' Rockin'," by Hugh Scott. Its opening paragraph reads: "Next to a lullaby, the most tranquil item in today's nervous world is an organization called the Sittin' Starin' N' Rockin' Club. Its 2500 members never fret about meetings or committees or annual reports, nor do they worry about dues or don'ts. The single thing requested of them is that they spend some fragment of each day placidly in a convenient rocking chair."

Oscar Hammerstein to Tom Saxe, July 31, 1952

Dear Tom Saxe:

Thank you for your letters and your gifts. My gratitude is mixed with guilt, because I feel not as qualified for membership in your excellent organization as I should be. I own a rocking chair, and I do sit and rock and stare across a quiet meadow, but not, I am afraid, as often as you would like me to. Quite disloyal to your philosophy, I often sneak upstairs and get in a few hours work in my study. I thought I should get this off my chest. If the club takes disciplinary measures for such cases as these, I am of course willing to face them.

All good wishes to you.

Sincerely,

Oscar Hammerstein II

Leighton Brill was now Executive Producer at Melody Fair, a tent theater in Toronto, Canada.

Oscar Hammerstein to Leighton Brill, Melody Fair, July 31, 1952

Dear Leighton:

Dick sent me this clipping with a question: "Why don't they give us better billing?" It's not a bad question, not only for the benefit of Rodgers and Hammerstein, but for the benefit of Melody Fair. It seems to me that our names could be used to better advantage, because they are a much bigger draw than any other names that you have in much larger type. This is no contractual complaint. This is a suggestion that we are business-getting names, and it would be good to use them.

Let me add that this is not a big worry, but the beef was made by Dick, and I thought I would report it to you.

Best wishes for your continued success, and love from us all.

Oscar Hammerstein II

Screenwriter Harry Kurnitz, working on his biopic of the Australian soprano, Nellie Melba, wrote Oscar: "Naturally, your sainted grandfather figures prominently in the screenplay so you can alert the family lawyers to stand by with injunctions, torts, writs of attainder or whatever is your favorite legal club. Our research department (an idiot girl by Thomas Hardy out of Mary Webb) has cracked under my passion for authentic detail and I am high and dry on one significant point: did the late great impresario speak with an accent? . . . All I really need is a 'yes or no' to the question but if time hangs heavy on your hands why not do us a forty or fifty page outline, with seven or eight songs."

Oscar Hammerstein to Harry Kurnitz, July 31, 1952

Dear Harry:

I have consulted my Uncle Arthur regarding his father's manner of speaking English. Arthur, who didn't like him, and now at the age of eighty still has a frightened look in his eye when he speaks of him, admits that the old man did speak a very beautiful cultivated English, with only a very slight accent betraying that he was born in Germany.

My friendly attitude in giving you this information is not to be considered indicative of any disposition to deal lightly with you in the courts. I have sold my biography of my grandfather to Louis Mayer. His lawyers and mine will be ready for you. All ports, both sea and air, will be watched. I suggest that you make no attempt to return to this country.

Dorothy sends her best, as do I—(without, of course, "prejudice to my cause".)

Oscar Hammerstein II

Oscar Hammerstein to Jerry Watanabe, August 6, 1952

Dear Jerry:

I enjoyed your letter and the pamphlet on fruit and vegetable juices. When I see you I will explain to you what I think this kind of diet would do to me. Or maybe I can make it pretty clear now by just telling you that if I took too many vegetable and fruit juices during the day, I should have to move my Dictaphone, typewriter and rhyming dictionary into the bathroom and keep them there. I am unnusually [sic] susceptible to this kind of thing.

I am disappointed that so far I have not been able to come up and see you. I have been working very hard down on the farm, and as you know, done a little travelling. I was out at Arthur's last weekend and I am afraid poor Dorothy is having a tough time with him. He is getting very demanding and complaining, as some old people become, and he has an idea that Dorothy has no right ever to cross him or contradict him, or forbid him to do anything at all. He is very lonely, because he has no one to talk to except Dorothy with whom he fights continually. I know that my short visit did him a lot of good, my treatment consisting merely in sitting down and letting him talk to me all day long for a day and a half. Physically he seems very well. He has no complaints, no pains, no medication to speak of, but he is thrashing out blindly in resistance to old age and the weaknesses and disabilities that come with it. He still does some work in his shop, and is working even now on a new invention—a device for [?] to do away with the soap dish. But he cannot achieve the same highly accurate work he used to perform with his machines. He doesn't read much and it bothers him that he doesn't remember things even a few seconds after he has started to write them down. I explained to him that I had the same trouble and that he shouldn't worry about this.

I am delighted to hear reports from Doodie that you're getting along so well. This is wonderful and exciting news. I am coming to town next week and I am hoping that in some way I can squeeze in a few hours, and maybe take you over in a game of chess. I'll phone next week and let you know if this is possible.

I expected to stay down in the country this week but I had to run in yesterday to audition Julie Wilson as a possible successor to Mary Martin in London. She gave a very good audition and I think she will be the girl, but we are keeping this confidential for the time being—until we can get our permit for her to go into England and work. Last night Dorothy and I and Eve and the Rodgers went down to the Waldorf to see the Spanish troupe who are there. They are very good indeed. It is a band of very fine instrumentalists, most of whom are also good vocalists, and it is very fast moving.

That's all the news. Hope to see you next week.

Love from us all.

Oscar Hammerstein to Dick Campbell, August 6, 1952

Dear Dick:

I have read your friend's play, "Roughshod Up The Mountain", and I agree with you that this author has talent for characterization and that he has chosen a good theme about which to write a play. His fault lies in repetition and "over-planting". He seems to feel that the characters must come in and explain everything to the audience, and he does not yet know how much the audience picks up by indirect implications, and how they prefer to find out things by action and observation of character rather than hearing the characters tell them just what is going on, and just specifically what they are thinking. The manuscript, then, is a long way from being a play, but it has dialogue that is colorful and that has an authentic feeling to it. What this man needs is what so many of our young playwrights need—a chance to have experimental productions in front of an audience, so that they can learn how smart an audience is. (And also how much does have to be explained to them.) There are small movements in this direction, the New Dramatists being one, but so far they are a drop in the bucket. I am hoping that more help is going to be created for the young playwright, and later I intend to become active myself in this direction.

Thank you for letting me read the play, and all good wishes.

Sincerely,

Oscar Hammerstein II

Harry Ruby to Oscar Hammerstein, August 7, 1952

Dear Oscar:

First, if you can give us any suggestions as to casting, as you suggested that night in your own parlor, I'd like it very much. Right now, we have no one, which is a good start. What do you think of the Avon Comedy four to play the romantic lead?

Getting a show on, as you probably have read, is not easy. It seems that people who have more money than they know what to do with, don't do anything with it. A wire to Henry Ford, Jr., who is the son of Henry Ford, Sr., went unanswered; which surprised me.

Eileen says it could be because he has never heard of me. That is ridiculous. I drove one of his Dad's cars back in 1920. It's just that when they get big they forget.

Millions are being spent by the Rockefeller Foundation to find a cure for the common cold. Who in his right mind, would invest in a common cold when he can put the same amount of money in a show? Who ever heard of a man winding up with a dame backing a common cold?

There are so many things that I'd like explained before I move on to parts unknown. I watched both conventions and now I know that the apes from which we're descended are still with us. I hope to live long enough to see the end of conventions and a prison sentence for "Humorists" who call you on the phone to tell you a joke. It may be far off, but someday they'll make life uncomfortable for people who tell jokes.

Anyway, if you can spare an hour one of these days, I'd like to play my score for you. It is entirely different from the one I played for you a few years back. Only two songs remain from that version. I guess it ain't fair to ask you to go through this, but there are certain guys a writer likes to play for. If you wrote songs you'd understand this.

Sincerely,

Harry

Oscar Hammerstein to Harry Ruby, August 13, 1952

Dear Harry:

I am going back to the country today, but I would like to hear your score as soon as I can. Will you phone me in town, Templeton 8-0430, next Wednesday morning? We can make a date then. I can hardly believe what you tell me about Henry Ford Jr. People indeed have short memories. I don't blame you for being not only surprised but resentful. I wouldn't blame you if you got so sore that you wouldn't send him another telegram, but I know what kind of a guy you are. The thirst for revenge can occupy but a small place in your heart, and then only for a short while. If Henry Ford Jr. came up to you tomorrow and offered to put up all the dough for your show, I bet you'd say let bygones be bygones and let him do it. I wouldn't think this was very wise of you, but I would like you for it.

All the best.

Oscar Hammerstein II

Deems Taylor sent Oscar a draft of his book (sections at a time), *Some Enchanted Evenings: The Story of Rodgers and Hammerstein*, for his input. In his accompanying cover letter Taylor wrote: "Part Three of the book you have read. Here, also, is Part Four, the concluding chapter. Not that it's any of your business, but you might as well read that, too. After all—who knows?—you might find it over-complimentary—and I might assassinate Stalin."

Oscar Hammerstein to Deems Taylor, September 3, 1952

Dear Deems:

Part four may be none of my business, but it is just as well that you gave me a peek. On page 33 you say: "Would Rodgers have thought of the music for 'Getting To Know You' with its provocative opening triplets if he had not had Hammerstein's lyric before him?" The answer is he would and did. In fact, he wrote that tune three or four years before Hammerstein's words, "getting to know you", inspired it. You'd better lay off that one:

On page 36 I would suggest that "There's Nothing Like a Dame", put forward as an example of my comic songs in "Oklahoma" is ill chosen, since it was in "South Pacific".

As for the rest of Part Four, it seemed fine. It is true that here and there I thought you had a tendency to be over-extravagant in your admiration, but who am I to argue with you? You are probably right.

All in all, I think you have done a fine job. I must tell you my favorite line of all—the most perceptive description of me that I have ever read— "craggy looking, with an air that is deceptively easy-going". I am still chuckling. I almost hope that the sale of the book will be small. I don't want too many people to know this.

All the best to you.

As ever,

P.S. The sign for the office is a big hit. We are all very grateful.

On August 16, Gertrude Lawrence fainted backstage after a matinee performance of *The King and I*. A few days later she was admitted at the New York-Presbyterian Hospital for tests, and diagnosed with hepatitis. She was scheduled for exploratory surgery, but the morning of the surgery she became comatose, and she passed away suddenly on September 6, at the age of fifty-four. An autopsy revealed that she had widespread abdominal and liver cancer.

John Van Druten to Oscar Hammerstein, September 6, 1952

VERY SHOCKED BY NEWS. MUCH SYMPATHY TO YOU AND DICK SHALL BE BACK SEPT 18 ANYTHING I CAN DO PLEASE CALL ON ME-

JOHN VANDRUTEN

Oscar met Reverend Slee years earlier when Slee was Executive Director of the Anzac Club. In a letter to Oscar he wrote: "I have been inspired to write you to ask you if it would be possible to rearrange ['You'll Never Walk Alone'] for a sacred anthem, involving words that would be Biblical? I know that you [have] a deep religious sense and therefor I am appealing to you for this. If it is not possible to rearrange the lyrics with sacred words would it be convenient to set to music some sacred psalm or Biblical verse for an anthem?"

Oscar Hammerstein to Reverend J. F. Slee, Church of the Ascension, September 11, 1952

Dear Doctor Slee:

Thank you for your letter of August 29th. I am very happy to know that you think so well of our song, "You'll Never Walk Alone". As the author of the words I am afraid I would not like anyone else's words to be set to the music. The song as it is is used on many occasions almost as if it were a hymn, although I realize it is neither sacred nor Biblical. I am afraid there would be legal complication in any procedure like the one you suggest, and quite apart from that, I feel myself sentimentally and temperamentally averse to it. Nevertheless, I am very proud that you thought of the song in this connection.

All good wishes to you.

Sincerely,

Oscar Hammerstein II

Oscar Hammerstein to James Carhartt, September 15, 1952

Dear Mr. Carhartt:

I do remember you very well as the man who wrote the lyrics for Celeste, which both Dick Rodgers and I admired. I am sorry to hear that

you are broke, and sorry that I can't come through with some great big gesture to aid you, but I am sending you two hundred dollars in the hope that
this small sum might be just the little needed to ward off the last straw, and
that the camel's back can be kept intact for the purpose of finishing the work
he is doing. This is an awkward comparison which I am now sorry I got
into, but I haven't time to improve on it or start a new letter. Good luck to
you, and don't bother to write any eloquent letter of thanks. Just acknowledge that you received the money. You haven't time for long letters now.
You've got other work to do. Finish that job and make it a big hit.

My best wishes to you.

Sincerely,

Oscar Hammerstein II

Josh Logan desperately wanted Rodgers and Hammerstein to musicalize French
author Marcel Pagnol's "Marseilles trilogy": *Marius*, *Fanny*, and *César*—first produced as plays and then films. But David Merrick had the rights, and, while he
was willing to share them with Rodgers and Hammerstein as co-producers, he
wasn't willing to release them entirely. Merrick was so passionate about *Fanny*'s
possibilities as a musical that he flew to France three times in order to secure
permission. But Merrick's personality and behavior riled—he didn't just ruffle
feathers, he plucked and singed them—and an enmity developed between him
and Rodgers. Harold Rome ended up writing the score (one of his best), but one
can imagine it would have been an ideal story for Rodgers and Hammerstein.
(Florence Henderson, not Mary Martin, starred in *Fanny*; Henderson was some
twenty years Martin's junior.)

Josh Logan (London) to Richard Rodgers and Oscar Hammerstein, September 22, 1952

(By dictaphone)

Dear Dick and Oscar:

We are almost at the end of our trip. I'm in London now and Nedda
and I are seeing as many plays as we possibly can. We have had a fine visit
with Mary and Dick and also with Emlyn and Molly and all our English
friends.

While I was in France I went down to Monte Carlo and met Marcel
Pagnol, as probably you have heard from David Merrick. I was so impressed

with him and with the whole idea of the show that I thought it was worthwhile taking one more crack at trying to settle something between you and Merrick and me, and seeing if we couldn't get together and make this wonderful show come off.

While I was at Mary and Dick's the other night I told them the story of FANNY. Both of their eyes began to show that they were being as moved by the story as we were when we saw it. At the end of the story, Mary and Dick both said that it sounded exactly like something that she would love to do, and may only hope and pray that you two would do the score.

With Mary as Fanny, I would think we could use the ending of CESAR, the picture you did not see, and bring the story twenty years later with the similar time lapse you had in SHOW BOAT, Oscar.

The only reason I bring this up is that Marcel Pagnol tells me that the audiences always felt a great desire to see Fanny and Marius get together, and they would ask the ushers and doormen when the next bit of the story was going to be dramatized as they felt the story was unfinished. I can't help but feel that this is a possible anti-climax; however, it is very cleverly done and it might be worth your examining the picture of CESAR and our all talking about it together if you are interested in the thing at all.

Leland tells me, Dick, that he has talked to you about the idea of doing TRILBY, and I think that is possibly a good idea; however, I am so full of the FANNY story that I can't feel myself getting excited about anything else at the moment.

Meantime, I hope that you and Merrick can come to some sort of an agreement and that we won't all find ourselves crucified by that awful negotiations with lawyers and such.

We have had a lovely trip and both Nedda and I are very rested in spite of the hurried nature of our visit here and in Paris. We got a wonderful rest on the beaches in Portugal and in Madrid before we got here.

I saw SOUTH PACIFIC the other night and I thought it was in extremely good shape, as I told Jerry Whyte.

Dick, you would be very proud of little Chin Yu as Liat. She is perfectly charming and is by far the best since Betta. She dances beautifully and plays the part with real emotion.

I like the Billis. He isn't at all like any of the other Billises but he is very legitimate and gets good laughs, and I think the audience likes him enormously.

Mary is still wonderful, of course—and I am again impressed by the wonder of that great Drury Lane Theatre. I've never seen anything like it and I suppose the world never will.

Oscar, we saw your pretty little New Zealand cousin, Miss Pope, who was with Heller Halliday. She sent you and Dorothy her love.

Mary's son Larry is now an Airman Third Class, having gone through basic training in the American Air Force over here. He will be stationed in England for three years and then one year in America before he is let out of the service. He is enormously improved, I think—speaks with a very tough American accent and is much more mature than when I last saw him. He has just turned twenty one and is a very good looking kid.

Heller is loving the Sadlers Wells School, so Mary is going to come back here to study for the rest of the year and not come home until June, except for the week she is there doing the song for the picture. You'll hear everything from her so I might as well not write any more about it now, so let's hope we can all get together on the wonderful Pagnol story.

Love to both Dorothys and all your families from Nedda and me.

Best,

Oscar Hammerstein to Anne Glatterman, October 16, 1952

Dear Anne:

When I was in the office yesterday on a weekly legal job, I learned quite accidentally of your mother's death. I was deeply sorry, and while I know that you can assume my sympathy for you, I was anxious to write to you and state it. There are no effective words you can say at a time like this. The one who is bereaved has to accept whatever has happened and make the adjustments that are necessary, which I know you will do bravely in spite of your grief.

Love,

Oscar Hammerstein II

Felicia Lamport was a columnist, poet, and satirist. Her first book, *Mink on Weekdays (Ermine on Sunday)*, was a best-selling memoir of her childhood in a wealthy, New York, Jewish family.

Oscar Hammerstein to Felicia Lamport, October 24, 1952

Dear Felicia Lamport:

I have read "Mink on Weekdays" and I feel that you have done quite well in getting the book into play form. I have not read it more than once and so can give you no careful analysis. My impressions are that it is too long and that you still have a good deal of work to do to sharpen it up and make it move better. But I think this would be a waste of time unless at this juncture you interested some very good actress who could play the part of Kay. The play will stand or fall as a characterization, just as "Life With Father" did. The plot will never be the attraction. Have you a play agent? I think you should get one, and I think you should find out if he agrees with me that the proper approach for selling this play would be to interest the artist first, and then present the producer with a package—artist and play.

I wonder if Dorothy Stickney could do it? She might. Whether or not her performance as "Mother" in "Life With Father" would be a help or a deterent [*sic*] for this play I do not know. She of course would not be playing a part anything like the way she played "Mother" because the characters are quite different. I just mention her because she is a good actress and she is looking for a play, and if, even before you appoint an agent, you would like me to, I should be very happy to send your script to Dorothy. Just let me know if you would like me to do this.

I believe I told you that Dick and I have retired from production—as far as other people's plays are concerned, and that is why you see no reference in this letter as to whether or not I would like to produce it. Perhaps I had better put a reference in. It is this: If I were an active producer at the moment, I would seriously re-read and study your play because the first reading suggests that it might be one of those "sleepers" with a slight plot, but with a very attractive character dominating, and then after the second or third reading I should probably make certain recommendations to you, or perhaps even before doing this I would search around as I advise you to do, for the right woman to play it.

Let me say also that for a girl who has never before written a play, you have been very shrewd and sensible in your adaptation of this story.

All good wishes to you.

Sincerely,

Oscar Hammerstein II

Although Rodgers and Hammerstein initially supported Dwight Eisenhower's bid for the presidency, as Rodgers put it, "when he failed to take a stand against the contemptible behavior of Senator Joseph McCarthy . . . I switched my support to Adlai Stevenson." Stevenson invigorated the liberal wing of the Democratic party, but with the anti-communist fervor of the McCarthy era still holding sway, Stevenson was demonized by many on the right. When Rodgers and Hammerstein openly supported Stevenson, some of that enmity was directed at them.

Mary Smith to Richard Rodgers and Oscar Hammerstein, October 29, 1952

Dear Dick Rogers [sic] and Oscar Hammerstein:

Last night I witnessed the death of two brilliant men—and a little of my heart dies with them—and as I sit here trying to write a fitting obituary I'm holding back the tears for all the beautiful—beautiful music and lyrics that died with you. I ask myself 'why'—why should two men—two men who symbolize in the minds of thousands of people all that is fine and stimulating—the feeling that only great music can bring—why should you support a form of government whose every action has been corruption—greed—graft and finally reached the peak in ultimate wick[ed]ness in the needless bloodshed of our youth. How can you sleep at night?

I took no notice of the Hollywood characters that stood beside you on that platform last night—we expect that sort of thing from them -. Hollywood has long been an unlimited source for Commies and trash—as every intelligent American can tell you. There are exceptions—but they are very few. But you two—you are enshrined in peoples hearts—a special place where we keep the really good things—it is inconceivable that our idols have feet of clay. A man just can't write the haunting tender melody of "Hello, Young Lovers"- or the touching beautiful lyrics of "Oh, What a Beautiful Morning" and not have a deep understanding of the whole rotten mess our country is in. Your hearts and your minds can't be at peace with the sentiments you expressed on that platform last night. And you'll never write another worth-while lyric or compose another line of great music until you are at peace with yourselves. I wonder—is it Democratic prosper[i]ty you seek—the thirty pieces of silver—Look closely at every bit of money you spend—money reaped from the socalled prosper[i]ty—Oh yes—it keeps your theatres crowded—your royalties rolling in—Look closely at every bit of money you receive from this prosper[i]ty—you might see a tiny drop of blood on every bill—blood from some boy in Korea—needless blood shed in a hopeless war.

Today I have gathered up all your wonderful music—some are so old they are almost collectors items—treasured down throught [*sic*] the years— to be passed on to another generation—or so I thought—gathered them and placed them in the fireplace—and touched a match to them—and I warmed my hands near the blaze—but inside I was very—very cold in- deed. Cremation isn't a beautiful sight—and I had just cremated two people I loved very much for a long—long time.

Mary Smith –

Aspiring songwriter Bert Landon complained to Oscar that a music publisher named Shapiro had just rejected his song "When We Were Lovers" because he felt that the word "lovers" implied more than just sweethearts. According to Shapiro, "lovers" meant "sweethearts in bed." Landon says he brought up Oscar's song, "Hello, Young Lovers," to the publisher, who dismissed the example be- cause the song was from a "musical comedy." Landon seeks Oscar's agreement that the publisher is wrong.

Oscar Hammerstein to Bert Landon, November 20[?], 1952

Dear Mr. Landon:

You can add "Lover Come Back to Me" and "Goodbye My Lover, Goodbye", and you can gather all kinds of evidence to prove Mr. Shapiro wrong in his theory. The trouble is you cannot make him publish your song if he doesn't want to publish it. I find that publishers have the strangest theories and superstitions about what you can say in a song and what you can't say. My only advice is to carefully forget what they tell you, and to keep on writing to please yourself. This gives you no guarantee of success, but I think it's your only chance.

All good wishes to you.

Sincerely,

Oscar Hammerstein II

Walter White, executive secretary for the National Association for the Advancement of Colored People, wrote Oscar that he had "been nominated to fill the vacancy on our Board of Directors created by Louis Wright's death . . . I am writing now to ask you if you will accept the nomination and serve if elected."

Oscar Hammerstein to Walter White, NAACP, November 20, 1952

Dear Walter:

I am indeed honored by the information in your letter, and terribly disturbed because I don't see how I can conscientiously accept this honor. There are several boards of which I am already a member that I am neglecting shamelessly, and it would be dishonest of me to take on more duties when I cannot discharge the ones I have. This is a most unwelcome decision for me to make because of all the activities I am part of, there is none closer to my heart than the NAACP.

If it was a matter of having my name on your board it would be different, but I know that what you want and what you need is a worker, and that is what I would like to be if I could—not just a figurehead.

Please understand my feelings in this matter, and transmit them to the others.

I hope we will be able to see you and Poppy soon. Love to you both.

Oscar Hammerstein II

Oscar Hammerstein to Howard Reinheimer, November 24, 1952

Dear Howard:

1. Has Al Siegel finished getting the figures on the Shubert stock situation for "Rose Marie" etc? He was just finishing this up each time I inquired about it during the last year.
2. Has Anne Glatterman cleared up the French royalty situation and paid off Frank and the two widows? The last four times I spoke to her she was just about to do it.
3. My will?
4. Louis Mayer?
5. Myra Finn annual gift?
6. Cass Canfield, George Bye, Deems Taylor?

This will be the first of a weekly reminder.

Love to you all.

Oscar Hammerstein II

Oscar Hammerstein to Hy Kraft, November 28, 1952

Dear Hy:

You started your last letter with a statement that I owed you a letter. This letter will only technically discharge the debt, for I am crowding it into a very few minutes' time that I am grabbing, if you can make out this sentence, all well and good, but don't spend too much time on it.

I am very glad that you enjoyed "South Pacific" again, and I agree with you when you praise Jerry [Whyte]. I think he is a great asset to us.

I have finished the second draft of dialogue for my new play [*Me and Juliet*], and I am now starting on the lyrics. We shall go into rehearsal on March 19th. We are playing six weeks on the road and coming into New York on June 4th—that is if I can ever get these damn lyrics written.

I took the election in my stride and instead of railing against the decision, I tried to dope out why the people were right—on the assumption that they always are. I believe that their mass wisdom was greater than mine or yours or the other [Adlai] Stevenson followers, who in their enthusiasm for such a rare thing as he—a politician with honesty and courage, who could also be articulate—we overlooked what the majority did not overlook: the growing staleness of the Democratic party, the ostrich attitude to the corruption in Washington, and a natural instinct which told them that it was indeed time for a change, not only to clean out some of the old fellows, but to give the new fellows a chance to prove if they were right or wrong. I believe that they will prove that they were wrong.

I have no faith in the honesty of the Republican party or the soundness of their international policy or their ability to realize that you can't go back to the old ways of William Howard Taft (which Robert Taft certainly believes). But it is just about time to test out their boasts about how much better they could run this government. If they justify them, more power to them. If they don't, they'll be out in four years. I understand that Stevenson is prepared to start reorganizing the Democratic party. He emerged from this election the most popular defeated candidate in the history of the United States. I don't hear a word against him from any quarter, from the press or in private conversation. I think we have here the makings of one of our greatest men. I have been told that since the election he has received seventy thousand letters from all over the country. Just friendly endorsements and letters of consolation. I have heard that he is answering every one of them himself. This will take some time, and I don't suppose his return to the practice of law will start for several months.

The theatrical season so far has neither been better nor worse than usual. A big comedy hit opened a few nights ago. It is called "The Seven Year Itch" and it was written by a young man whom I met when he was one or two days old. He is the son of one of my best friends. His name is George Axelrod. "Time of the Cuckoo" with Shirley Booth seems to be doing well. "Bernardine" by Mary Chase is a hit. Charlie Friedman's "My Darlin' Aida" got a bad press, but it looks to me like it's finding a good public. I think it has a chance to survive. Its grosses have been good so far because they have sold many parties, but the talk I hear is reassuring. "An Evening With Beatrice Lillie" is a hit, and a very amusing evening it is even though she doesn't use any new material. Moss Hart's new play [*The Climate of Eden*] failed after two weeks, but it was a very honorable failure. He had undertaken something with great courage, a very difficult play to write, and even though it missed there is certainly no disgrace involved. It was a good try. "Dial M For Murder" seems to be the most satisfying play of all. I haven't heard a word against it. It's a solid smash. Why am I saying all this? You probably get Variety every week.

Family report: The Fondas go on tour with "Point of No Return" next week. They wind up in California where I believe Hank will do the picture "Mr. Roberts". Billy phoned me from California a few days ago, and his experiences at Paramount are a little on the dull side. I don't think things look too good out there for him—not at that studio, anyway. Maybe I am wrong, and please don't report this to any Paramount representatives in London. They might write to Hollywood and by accident one of their letters might be read. Jimmy, who has been stage manager with "Fourposter" for the last several months, is switching over to a new play, a musical adaptation of "What Every Woman Knows" called "Maggie". They go into rehearsal in a few weeks. Alice has finished the lyrics for her play, but her producer has not finished raising the money. Henry is doing very well with Milton Biow, but my only informant is Milton. Henry will say nothing. Reggie bought a play last week. He liked the script very much and I liked the script very much too, and after that nobody liked it. We are the only two people in the world who like this play, and he has about decided that he shouldn't buck the entire population of the country and stubbornly stick to what he and I think. I think he is right. Dorothy is very well and looking very well. Jerry Watanabe is doing remarkably well. He has gained fifteen pounds in the last two months. It is quite encouraging, but it is still in the crossing of fingers department.

Both Dorothy and I are delighted that you have fallen in love with England. I would have been very disappointed in you if you had not. Have a good time and let me hear from you soon.

Love to you both.

Oscar Hammerstein to Stanley Pargellis, The Newbury Library, December 17, 1952

Dear Mr. Pargellis:

I enjoyed Adlai Stevenson's talk on Lloyd Lewis in your Bulletin, and as a matter of fact I enjoyed the whole volume. Is every issue of your Bulletin as good as this one? I congratulate you. This is nothing like the usual dry job that is done with organs of this kind.

I have also read your dissertation on conservatism. It seems to me entirely a question of semantics. Many of the characteristics and virtues that you attribute to your conservative, I would attribute to what I call a liberal. You rang in a new one on me—"rationalist". I don't think I like him very much. He seemed to be a boneyard into which you threw everything that did not belong to your beloved conservative.

The older I grow the more impressed I am with the truth of trite sayings, which by now have been rendered nearly useless because they have been said too much, and people have forgotten the literal inspiration of their first launchings. For instance, take the expression "It takes all kinds of people to make up a world". Nobody makes any avowed denial of this statement, but on the other hand very few really subscribe to it. Most people believe that if it takes all kinds of people to make up a world, a great many of those people should be left in the background. Many believe that only their kind of people make up a world, or are needed to make up a world, and the others are superfluous burdens. Now, actually it is very very true that it takes all kinds of people to make up a world. Not only are the conservative and liberal needed, but the reactionary and the radical too. I have no interest in choosing my own category, and I am quite willing to join all their clubs and attend their meetings when I feel like it, and vote yea or nay when I feel like it. I prefer to avoid loyalty to any of these crowds. But if one feels the need of attaching one's self to a category, that is all right too—providing he admits the essential necessity of the existence of the others' existence.

This does not alter the fact that you were substantially right when you called me a conservative. I have always been so by behavior, whatever philosophies and theories I have had intellectually, or whatever indignations I have felt emotionally. When I was a child I did not have any of the instincts for a rebellion that most children have. If I heard a rule, I obeyed it. I think that psychologists regard this as a very bad sign. Maybe it is, but anyway that's what I was—a milksop.

I enjoyed our talk very much indeed, and look forward to the next one.

All good wishes to you and Mrs. Pargellis.

Sincerely,

Oscar Hammerstein II

Oscar Hammerstein to Theresa Helburn, December 22, 1952

Thank you for your verses, Terry.

Now in answer may I say

Two can write in rhythm merry.

Every doggerel has his day.

Love and merry

Christmas Terry.

Oscar Hammerstein to the Kiwanis Club, West Palm Beach, December 30, 1952

Gentlemen:

In my recent very brief visit to Palm Beach, I had a talk with my uncle, Arthur Hammerstein, about the problems of your annual benefit. He told me that his health would not permit him to be active in any more of these entertainments which he has helped you put on for the last twenty seven years, and I thoroughly agreed with him. Since in the past few years I have been assisting him to whatever extent I could, I thought I had better tell you what my position and thoughts are in this matter.

I am writing and preparing for production a new play to go into rehearsal in February or March, and it will be impossible for me to be of much use to you if you put on a benefit this year. As a matter of fact, the way my obligations are piling up in the theatre, (I not only write plays, but I produce them, and I have a backlog of motion picture versions of these plays which I must soon start to handle) I don't think it is possible for me to promise any help to you for some time to come, and it would be dishonest of me to allow you to place any reliance on me. Parenthetically, I want to point out to you that I have not been of any great help in these past years. Whenever I called up an actor for you, his first reaction was deep disappointment that I was not offering him a job in a play, and for this reason I was not very successful in persuading many of them to go down to play a benefit. My phone call was always a letdown for them.

This brings me to the main purpose of my letter, and that is to attempt to dissuade you from raising money in this way. I think you should find another way. I know that I am not down there with you, and don't know your problems as you do, but I do know the problems of theatrical benefits from my experience up north and elsewhere in the country. Even when the grosses attained are as large as you could expect them to be, the net is dwindling fast. Benefits are suffering from the same handicaps that the entire theatre is suffering from. Costs are getting too high, and now, as you know, the actors' organizations are telling them to take fees for benefits, and are forbidding them to perform without salary. This practice is becoming universal, and their fees will go up, not down. (It will probably be a wrench to some of you to give up this long established custom, which is almost an institution in your community, but after all, your object is to raise money for the underprivileged children, and it is your duty to find out the best way to do this. I do not believe that the small amount that you will be able to raise nowadays would justify the effort of putting on a big show, and I urge you to invent some other method for raising money).

Please excuse me for butting in and presuming to tell you what to do, but since I have been in a second hand way interested in your project for the last few years as an assistant to my uncle, I thought I might be permitted to speak my piece and tell you what I thought about all this.

My best wishes to you for your project this year, whatever it is.

Sincerely,

Oscar Hammerstein II

Carol Parodneck was a high school student who wrote Oscar a series of questions, prefaced with: "I am interested in the mechanics that go into the production of a play and I hope that you will be kind enough to answer a few of my questions regarding this subject."

Oscar Hammerstein to Carol Parodneck, December 31, 1952

Dear Miss Parodneck:

The questions you ask cannot all be answered very directly or simply.

1. What governs your decision when picking an actor or an actress for a major part?

So many things. Their voice projection, both in speaking and singing. The way they look and how their general type is suited to the part I am trying to fill.

2. How soon in rehearsal is it evident when a performer is not right for his or her part?

It may be in the first ten minutes. It may be in the second week. It may not show in rehearsals at all, and we may have faith in the actor's ability to fill a part right up till after the opening when he or she has appeared in front of an audience. There is no rule for a thing like this.

3. How are rehearsals organized?

This is too detailed a question for me to answer fully, and indeed there is no specific answer because it depends on the director. Various directors organize rehearsals in various ways. The first week the dancing and singing ensembles are rehearsed in separate groups while the cast is rehearsed by the stage director in the dialogue scenes, and then later the various units are brought together.

4. What happens when in the choice of leading actors or actresses an understudy in rehearsal appears to be more suited for the part, but is unknown in name?

Nothing happens if the leading actor has already been signed to play the part. To put him out of the part would constitute a breach of contract, but if it is a contract that includes two weeks' notice, and the understudy is obviously much better, the chances are the understudy will replace the original player. This too depends on personalities and the temperaments involved, and the degree of difference between the players.

5. Does the understudy go through the entire routine of rehearsal?

Sometimes yes, sometimes no. Sometimes the understudies are not chosen until after the play opens on the road.

6. In a musical production, which are written first, the lyrics or the music?

There is no set rule for this. Sometimes the music first, sometimes the lyric first.

7. When a play does not receive favorable reviews on an out of town try, does that always mean that it is not considered for Broadway?

It almost never means that it is not considered for Broadway. The notices out of town have very little to do with the decision of the producer and the playwright whether or not to open on Broadway. It is audience reaction that decides them, and also their own reactions. Sometimes they are surprised by a play. It is not nearly as good as they thought it was.

8. When choosing a play for production, what are the governing factors?

It would take me about one month to answer this question, and I haven't a month's time to devote to you. I would say in general that the main governing factor is that a producer or author should like the idea himself very much indeed before going ahead with it. That is the one major governing factor. If you don't like it, it's foolish to do it. It's foolish to try to guess what the public will like. You can only consult your own taste, your own feeling.

9. What is the percentage of plays produced written by authors on request or chosen from plays already written?

This is an impossible question. I don't know what the percentage is.

10. What part does a writer play in the production of his work?

It all depends on the writer. More and more it seems to me that the writer is one of the chief factors in production. The Dramatists Minimum Basic Contract provides for the author's approval of all casting and the employment of directors, and in the case of musicals, musical conductors and dance directors. I would say he plays a very important part, if he wants to.

All good wishes to you.

Sincerely,

Oscar Hammerstein II

Chapter Twelve
1953

Oklahoma! continued to tour the country and *South Pacific* was still playing on Broadway, in London, and on its national tour. *The King and I* continued its Broadway reign. Oscar was at work on the lyrics and libretto for his sixth Broadway musical with Richard Rodgers, *Me and Juliet.*

Oscar Hammerstein to Rita Sargent, January 3, 1953

Dear Rita:

Thank you for your thoughtful kindness for sending me the handkerchiefs which, believe it or not I need. Why does a man always need handkerchiefs? Some of them are lost in the laundry, but I know that many of them can be found in old bathrobes and overcoats out of season. Anyway, these were very welcome and were particularly pretty ones.

All good wishes to you for the New Year.

Sincerely,

Oscar Hammerstein II

Oscar Hammerstein to Murray Matheson, January 3, 1953

Dear Murray:

Thank you for the multiple gifts. We enjoyed opening it and seeing all the various goodies, and our enjoyment of the passion fruit and the honey from Australia will continue into the New Year—but not very far. (This is no reflection on the quantity of the provisions, but rather a comment on the speed and greed of our eating).

Love and best wishes for the New Year.

Oscar Hammerstein II

The Letters of Oscar Hammerstein II. Mark Eden Horowitz, Oxford University Press. © Mark Eden Horowitz 2022.
DOI: 10.1093/oso/9780197538180.003.0012

Oscar Hammerstein to Billy Rose, January 3, 1953

Dear Billy:

Thank you for the wonderful bottle of assorted liquers [*sic*]. I have read in the papers that you were sailing for Europe last Friday, and if that is so this letter will seem strangely unimportant to you when you arrive home and go through your pile of mail—like writing on a stone found in the tomb of Tutankhamen.

All good wishes for a Happy New Year to you.

Sincerely,

Oscar Hammerstein II

Oscar Hammerstein to Stephen Sondheim, January 3, 1953

Dear Steve:

Thank you for the shoelace on which I am to found my fortune in modern music.[1] With my talent and determination, youth and grit, I expect to take this and build it into a bedlam.

Love and best wishes for the New Year.

Oscar Hammerstein II

Oscar Hammerstein to Howard Turtle (The Kansas City Star), January 7, 1953

Dear Mr. Turtle:

I believe that Mr. George DeHaven's home talent enterprise is an important contribution to the living theatre. The centralization of the professional theatre in Broadway is an evil, and I am afraid a necessary and a natural one, but everything possible must be done to stimulate activity in cities throughout the country that are far from Broadway. Mr. DeHaven has given us one of the few practical answers to the problem.

---

[1] Sondheim does not recall what this particular gift was, but when asked about it he replied: "The only connection I can make is that I spent a number of years after graduation educating him in 'modern' music, which he'd loathed (i.e., Stravinsky, Bartok, et al.) by giving him a recording every holiday. I started his education with the Ravel Trio (!)."

All good wishes to you.

Sincerely,

Oscar Hammerstein II

Oscar Hammerstein to George Rosenfeld (United World Federalists), January 8, 1953

Dear Mr. Rosenfeld:

No, I cannot give you a song. In the first place I am too busy finishing up the songs for my new play—and I will not be finished with them in time for rehearsals. In the second place I don't believe songs about big political issues can be written in this way. They bob up by accident, but I do not know how I would sit down and say: "Now I will write a song about world federalism". Songs must be simple and emotional, and when they try to deal with a question as complex as world federalism (in its present state) they become editorials, and editorials make very bad singing.

It is true that I am going to do my best to be with you on April 29th if my play is in such condition that I can leave it for one evening.

All good wishes to you,

Sincerely,

Oscar Hammerstein II

George P. Nigh, House of Representatives, State of Oklahoma, to Richard Rodgers and Oscar Hammerstein, January 21, 1953

Gentlemen:

As a proud citizen of the State of Oklahoma, may I take this belated means of expressing my sincere appreciation for the wonderful credit you have brought to our state, Oklahoma.

Without resorting to superfluous flattery, I would like to state that your stage production has done more than all our combined Chambers of Commerce' since Statehood.

I would like to receive from you the necessary permission, if possible, to introduce in the House of Representatives of the State of Oklahoma, the resolution making the song "Oklahoma" from the stage production, the official song of the "OK" state. There is great sentiment for this action among House members, and particularly among our young and progressive citizens.

If you see fit to allow me this great privilege, I would consider it an honor to introduce said proposal.

Hoping to have a favorable replay from you soon, I am

Sincerely yours,

(Signed) George P. Nigh,

Rep., Pittsburg County, Okla.

Handwritten at the bottom of the letter is a note, probably in Rodgers' hand: "If O.K. with O.H., please accept or ask O.H. to do so. Probably the latter."

Oscar Hammerstein to George P. Nigh, House of Representatives, State of Oklahoma, February 5, 1953

Dear Mr. Nigh:

In reply to your letter of January 21st, Mr. Rodgers and I would be delighted to permit you to introduce into the House of Representatives of the State of Oklahoma the resolution making the song "Oklahoma" the official song of the "OK" state. We would consider this a great honor to our song.

All good wishes to you.

Sincerely,

Oscar Hammerstein II

Oscar Hammerstein to Mary Martin (excerpt), January 22, 1953

The book of "Me and Juliet" is finished—or at any rate the present version is finished. Dick and I have written four songs, and I am hard at work on the rest of the lyrics now. We go into rehearsal March 19th, and I can promise you now with every confidence that all the lyrics will not be finished by then.

Oscar Hammerstein to Arthur Hammerstein (excerpt), January 30, 1953

I am moving ahead with my lyrics, but very slowly. Somehow or other, however, I know that when we open in Cleveland all the songs will be written. The one thing I do know is that they won't be written when we go into rehearsal because they never are. I always have four or five songs left over to write while the company is rehearsing. Remember when we used to do shows together we very seldom had the second act written.

Oscar Hammerstein to Ray Bolger, February 2, 1953

Dear Ray:

I have heard that you are still going to be in Florida on the 23rd of February and thereabouts, and it encouraged me to send you this letter to ask you if you could possibly appear on the Kiwanis benefit for underpriviledged [sic] children at Palm Beach. This is a show started many years ago by Sam Harris, John Golden and Arthur Hammerstein. Arthur and John still run it and I sort of help out from this end. Nobody knows better than I do how well you deserve a rest in Florida, and how justified you would be in turning me down because of all the other benefits you so generously work for during the year. That is why I think it is fairer for me to write to you and give you a chance to think it over first, instead of calling you on the phone and hitting you on the head with it. But Ray, if you can possibly do this, (the benefit will be on February 23rd) the mere announcement of your name around this time would insure the sale of all the tickets for the show. Do you think you can give your kindness one more little push and come up to Palm Beach for this event? I don't have to tell you about the worthiness of the cause. You are familiar with that, I am sure. It is one of the best things of this kind that we are doing in our country.

Please let me hear from you soon. All the best [to] you.

Sincerely,

Oscar Hammerstein II

A nearly identical letter was addressed to Dorothy Sarnoff.

Katharine Brown (MCA) to Mary Steel, c/o Oscar Hammerstein, February 5, 1953

Dear Mary:

I'm enclosing herewith a copy of the teletype which I sent to the Coast today in reference to SABRINA FAIR. I think Mr. Hammerstein might like to know exactly what was said.

Cordially,

Kay

KATHARINE BROWN

CITRON—COAST:

RODGERS & HAMMERSTEIN WILL PERMIT EXPLORATION DEAL SAM TAYLOR PLAY BUT FEEL STRONGLY THEIR NAME NOT BE USED AS PART OF SELL. IT IS MATTER OF RECORD THEY HAVE OPTION ON PLAY BUT OPTION IS NEVER COMMITMENT TO PRODUCE. THERE [*sic*] INTEREST IN HEPBURN FOR PLAY VERY STRONG.

KAYBROWN

Rodgers and Hammerstein produced Samuel Taylor's first Broadway play, *The Happy Time*, in 1950. In May 1952 they paid $2,500 to Taylor as an advance for *Sabrina Fair*, his third Broadway play, which would open in November 1953. What's fascinating about the above telegram is its mention of Audrey Hepburn. At the time of the telegram, Hepburn had had one previous role on Broadway, in the play *Gigi*, which had closed in May 1952. Her first starring role in a film—*Roman Holiday*—wasn't to be released until September. While she did not star in *Sabrina Fair* on Broadway, she did indeed star in the film, now titled *Sabrina*, which opened in 1954. All this suggests Rodgers and Hammerstein's prescience with regarding to casting.

Arthur Godfrey was a widely popular and influential host and entertainer, first on radio, then on television. The Mariners were an integrated vocal quartet made up of two Black and two white singers. The four men had been in the Coast Guard together during World War II. Singing gospel and popular music, Godfrey featured the group regularly, first on his radio and then his television programs.

Oscar Hammerstein to Arthur Godfrey (CBS), February 5, 1953

Dear Arthur:

On the night of March 24th at Madison Square Garden, the National Association for the Advancement of Colored People are going to have a big show. I am co-chairman with Lena Horne. The Mariners have consented to appear, and I am writing to ask you if there is any chance on earth of the rest of your show, including you, coming over and making it the brilliant evening I would like it to be. The NAACP is a great organization. The work they do is about as important as anything else that I know of. Nobody knows better than I how many demands of this kind are made on you, and how impossible it is to accept all of them, however worthy the cause involved may be. But Arthur, this is a great cause and a cause that needs our help very badly, and the sacrifice I am asking you to make and the service I am asking you to give is requested of you only after very sober consideration by me. I hope you can find it in your heart to do it.

All good wishes.

Sincerely,

Oscar Hammerstein II

Oscar Hammerstein to Nora Errante, February 12, 1953

Dear Mrs. Errante:

I receive many letters like yours, and I am always very disturbed that I cannot give them satisfactory answers. The music business has been shamefully neglectful of its duty to provide some means of appraising the work of new songwriters. Many publishing companies do not look at new material for fear of plagiarism suits, and this is also true of many authors like myself. My lawyer will not permit me to look at any new material. I can only advise you to have copies of your manuscript made and send them to some of the best publishers, cross your fingers and hope that someone will read them and like them. Of course, people who come to live in New York have a better chance of landing their songs with a publisher because they establish personal contacts, and after a good deal of trampling the streets and knocking on doors, they sometimes get in. But for a writer like yourself, living out of town, it is very difficult and I am sorry to say that very little is being done about it.

With all good wishes to you, and hoping that you may in some way obtain a hearing for your song, I am

Sincerely,

Oscar Hammerstein II

Photo 20 Gertrude Lawrence singing "Hello, Young Lovers" in *The King and I*, circa 1951

John Cornell was one of the stage managers for *The King and I* on Broadway—along with Jerry Whyte and Ruth Mitchell. "Connie" is Constance Carpenter who had been Gertrude Lawrence's understudy and took over the role from August 1952 through December 1953.

Oscar Hammerstein to John Cornell, St. James Theatre, February 13, 1953

Dear John:

As I told you last night the performance on the whole seemed very good indeed, well balanced and well paced, and no signs of any real slipping. These are the notes I took:

<u>Act 1, Scene 1:</u> When Connie sang "I Whistle a Happy Tune" she was masked by the boy's head. If she will just have him sit a little bit more upstage on the trunk and see that his head is not in front of her head as she sings toward the side of the house that is stage left, she will be all right. This is a simple matter.

Please tell Connie that she should be more firm with the Kralahome on these two speeches that follow each other. When she says: "I expect a bargain to be kept on both sides" she had a sort of pleading gesture last night. She leaned forward as if she didn't expect it at all, but was asking them to be done. I think she should be straightened out when she says this, and also when she says: "For the time being" there should be a note of defiance and a challenge and the statement of an issue for the audience to watch. There shouldn't be any quavering in the voice, or any suggestion that she is just whistling in the dark. This is the firm side of Anna, and this is the place to show it.

There was something wrong with the exit on this scene, but I was writing my notes and didn't look up at the beginning of it. I wish you would go out front and see what it is. It wasn't definite, Connie's starting to cross and then stopping and then starting to whistle. I knew that by the time I looked up things weren't going the way they ought to be. Maybe the men have spread out too much. The whole thing seemed indefinite. Take a look at this.

At the beginning of Scene 2, John, the Prime Minister, is much too heavy when he barks out at the king that Anna has been here two or three weeks and he's been having trouble with her. I don't know why he barks that out so. It makes him look weaker, not stronger. This schoolteacher who has been giving him trouble should be to him only a thing that can be slapped down easily at any moment by a great wave of his lazy paw. He makes it look as if she has been harrowing him. That is not the proper dramatic relationship at this point. She has been a nuisance. That is the idea, and it should be said quietly, not barked.

Has Terry[2] done something to her makeup? Her face looked a little dirty, as if she were trying to age it and put hollows into her cheeks. I don't think this is at all necessary.

Please forward my suggestion to Connie that instead of imagining the young lovers being down at about where the horn section is, that it would be better if they were out, if she called out into the night, out into the front. She may answer that she has always been doing this. I don't know, but if she has I think it's wrong. I think the lovers ought to be somewhere on the first balcony. They are all the young lovers in the world she is really talking to. The song is bigger than that. She makes it small by singing down to the orchestra pit on her left.

Please ask Freddy Dvonch[3] if he didn't think the tempo of "Hello, Young Lovers" was just a little on the slow side last night. I had that impression.

There is an overlapping of speeches, and they should slow up at this point where Louis points to Siam and the Prince says: "Siam is not so small" and he says: "Look at England". All that was too quick in there. Take a look at that tonight.

Reprise of "Puzzlement" by the two kids. I could not hear the cue to it. The boy is very indistinct—the little boy who plays Louis. I wish you would work on him a lot. Right through the play he is indistinct. Is this because of his effort to simulate an English accent? I would rather sacrifice some accent in favor of clarity.

Suggest to Terry for me that when she says: "It must not sound like advice" she would get a much bigger laugh if she turns away from Anna when she says it. Instead of saying that to Anna and then turning on the next speech, if when Anna says: "Does he want me to advise him?" she turns away embarrassed and says: "It must not sound like advice" out toward the audience, the laugh will be bigger and no less legitimate.

On the subject of Terry I am terribly discouraged. I thought I made it very clear to her the last time we rehearsed that she should not chew up

---

[2] Refers to Terry Saunders, who played Lady Thiang.
[3] Frederick Dvonch was the music director for *The King and I*.

her lines so, that she should not read them so loudly, not so vehemently, not hit the audience on the head with every word that she utters. When she does this you cannot hear the words because they don't sound like words. They sound like sounds that are chopped out from somewhere, coming up from her stomach and forcing their way out through her throat. I know that she does not have to deliver lines this way because at rehearsal we corrected them. She said she understood me, and she quieted down, and the scene sounded like a scene. I have no fault to find with the way she sings a song, which I think is superb, not only vocally but dramatically. It would be just twice as effective if this were the culmination of her emotional upset, if she hadn't been so violent all through the scene, if we had only seen her try to repress her emotion, but she lets it out full force and vitiates it so that you stop listening to her, partly because you can't hear her, and partly because every line is delivered with the same maniacal intensity. Ask her for God's sake to quiet down and play that scene, and all her scenes like a human being. I am deeply concerned about this.

Act Two—The Ballet: Stephanie[4] was unclear when describing Eva's death, when describing how Buddha wants her to come up and personally thank him. The girls are loud here, but Stephanie is [neither?] loud enough or definite enough. Tell her, however, that I thought her delivery of the whole Uncle Tom's Cabin narration was much better than it used to be.

Please tell Connie that in the cue to "Shall We Dance?" I would like to see her eyes raise up from the black shoes to the white waistcoat and then to the face. She doesn't do these three steps. She looks down at the black shoes and then it becomes less definite when her eyes rise from the shoes to the waistcoat to the face.

And these are all the notes I took. I thought Yul was fine and didn't have so many of those spots where he becomes unclear and too fast. In fact, I don't know when his performance was better. I want to congratulate you and Ruth on the way the show has been kept up, and I had a very good time.

All the best.

Oscar Hammerstein II

---

[4] Stephanie Augustine played Tuptim.

Constance Hope, representing Jeanette MacDonald, wrote Oscar to see if he and Rodgers would be interested in adapting *Traviata* as a vehicle for MacDonald for Broadway—a colloquial version in English.

Oscar Hammerstein to Constance Hope, February 25, 1953

Dear Miss Hope:

Doing TRAVIATA would not attract Dick Rodgers and me because Verdi has already taken care of Rodgers' department, so what would there be left for him to do?

If someone else has already made this adaptation, I will be very glad to read it when it is finished. We might be interested in such a script as producers, even though it is not naturally within our scope as writers.

Very truly yours,

Oscar Hammerstein II

Oscar Hammerstein to Hy Kraft (excerpt), February 19, 1953

I have finished eight songs, and have another eight to write, and we go into rehearsal March 19th, and so I shall keep my record for never having a show finished when we go into rehearsal—a clean and unblemished record. I know that I cannot write eight songs between now and then. I hope however to have them all done before we open in Cleveland a month later. I shall keep you posted on these important details.

"Wonderful Town",[5] that adaptation of "My Sister Eileen" opens here in a week. All the reports from the road are glowing and it looks like a sure hit. I am particularly glad on this account because of Jerry Chodorov, who has needed a hit for some time, and we like to have our Bucks County neighbors prosperous and happy.

Jule Stein's [*sic*] "Hazel Flagg" sent in terrible reports from the road wherever it played, but it has opened in New York and seems to be a hit. "Maggie", the adaptation of "What Every Woman Knows" opens tonight in New York.

---

[5] *Wonderful Town* was a hit with music by Leonard Bernstein, lyrics by Betty Comden and Adolph Green, a book by Joseph Fields and Jerome Chodorov, and direction by George Abbott, it starred Rosalind Russell. It ran for 559 performances.

I am not hopeful for it. I saw it on the road and they could have made it into a very big hit, but I think they blew their road tour and didn't do the work they should have done—anyway, they didn't take my advice, so I am pretty sore. This isn't strictly true. The advice I gave them the first week they ignored, but in the last five days they came around to it and did many of the things I had told them to do, too late I am afraid. Jimmy is assistant stage manager with this show. He also has put his money in it because he had great confidence in it. He's pretty sore too, but he has had good business experience, and has got a good view of show business in the less smooth and scientific side.

Billy has settled with Paramount. I mean he is out and has got a good piece of change, enough to tide him over for at least a year. So now he is looking around for something, but looking carefully, because he doesn't face hunger for some time. He spent a few weeks with us in New York recently, but he has gone back. Hollywood is more topsy-turvy then ever because of the three dimension movies that everybody is announcing. I told Billy to start a whispering campaign to add to the confusion. I would like him to get it known quietly that Einstein is working on a fourth dimension film. This ought to finish them.

Agnes de Mille to Oscar Hammerstein, February 20, 1953

Dear Oscar:

Thank you so much for your note. It was sweet of you to write.

As for "Maggie", I specified that I would need a new choreographer and a week's deferment of opening date. They could furnish me with neither so I declined the risk. I never saw such a bouquet of degenerate and un-disciplined young men gathered around a piano in my life. The composer, who seemed to be in five sections, travelled nebular fashion and the central boy wore a scarlet waistcoat and his hairdo was Mamie Eisenhower's. I turned to Don Walker and said, "I do not believe my eyes," and he replied, "Neither do I but one grows accustomed to it." Well, I was afraid of that. I was afraid I might grow accustomed to something or other of what was going on. Every single musical number needed to be completely restaged and that wonderful girl kept from bleating like a sheep stuck in a gate. I think Fearnley is very largely to blame. At the first run-through he should have thrown Graham out on her well-turned little ass and got in some professionals. The cast as I talked to them was desperate. It is a pity because some of the play was very moving. Now we come to that, it appears that Sir J. M. Barrie knew his job. Ah, well, there is no substitute I have found for virility, discipline, or courage.

This is my valentine to you, dear Oscar.

Love,

Agnes

Maggie, based on Barrie's *What Every Woman Knows*, had songs by William Roy; Don Walker was the orchestrator and June Graham the choreographer. John Fearnley, a stage manager for Rodgers and Hammerstein and responsible for much of their casting, was one of the show's producers; James Hammerstein was one of the show's stage managers and, likely, a reason behind Oscar's interest in the show. It seems de Mille was asked to come onboard either as a play doctor or to take over direction altogether. The show ran for five performances.

Philip Kadison[6] to Oscar Hammerstein, February 22, 1953

Dear Oscar,

Conscience wouldn't permit me to leave this letter unwritten. Because, in absentia, you are the most soothing influence possible on Christopher. He may be screaming his lungs out for some reason or other, and this he can do, but let either one of us sing Dites-Moi, and he coos. In the beginning, after Fay had stumbled on this bonanza, I refused to believe it. But one day I was left alone with him, and the trouble started. He wouldn't eat or nothin'. He would just scream.

So, for laughs I sang the song. Perfection. I next merely hummed the melody. Bedlam. Then, to make sure, I sang the words to the Star Spangled Banner, or whatever it was. Perfection again. So it's gotta be the words and nothing more. Don't tell Dick, it may upset him.

Well, many thanks, and our gratitude. Perhaps some day Christopher will thank you himself, on our behalf.

Best to Dorothy and yourself,

Philip

---

[6] Philip Kadison was the son of Oscar's good friends, Milton and Lily Kadison.

Oscar Hammerstein to Philip Kadison, February 25, 1953

Dear Phil:

It is high time that you broke down and acknowledged your indebtedness to me. I can remember a little over four years ago, stamping up and down over the fields and hills of Pennsylvania trying to bat out some words to keep your kid quiet, and you must remember that this had to be done from a very small reservoir of French words. In fact, these are about the only words I know, and it was just luck that I put them all together—well, not luck. I worked very hard on them. But all this time I have been wondering why you have never said anything about it. Anyway the belated gratitude is welcome to me.

Love to you and Fay.

As ever,

Oscar Hammerstein II

One theater-goer's criticism of *South Pacific* was not related to "You've Got to Be Carefully Taught," but rather focused on another song: ". . . after leading one to expect that it was written around an ideal love affair, as introduced by the enchanting song, 'Some Enchanted Evening', you developed a love affair which was not at all 'ideal'!" Her concern is not the fact that Emile had been married to a native woman " . . . and had two little dark-skinned children . . . " but that when asked to tell her about his life, "he with-held the thing she would have wanted, or rather needed, to know, and which, he must have realized, she would have to know in the end!"

Oscar Hammerstein to Susan Eastman Watson, March 16, 1953

Dear Mrs. Watson:

Thank you for your letter of March 2nd and your interesting comments on "South Pacific". It was my conception that Emile was worried about confessing to Nellie the fact that he had killed a man. He did not know her well then, did not dream that her prejudice extended as far as it did, and did not feel guilty about his past life with a Polynesian woman. I don't think he willfully held back information that at that time he thought she would consider important. He had been so well conditioned to that point of view. His one worry in that first scene is how to tell the woman he loves and wants to marry that he once killed a man.

Thank you very much for your interest, and your comments on the silly Georgia episode.

Very truly yours,

Oscar Hammerstein II

That "silly Georgia episode" refers to a shocking event. As described in a UP story:

Two Georgia legislators who denounced the musical "South Pacific" as propaganda, vowed today to introduce bills to outlaw movies, plays and musicals having "an underlying philosophy inspired by Moscow." State Rep. David C. Jones and State Sen. John D. Shepard issued a statement . . . [saying] their charge of propaganda referred particularly to the song "You've Got To Be Taught" which, [they] said, urged justification of interracial marriage. "To us that is very offensive, . . . Intermarriage produces half breeds. And half breeds are not conducive to the higher type of society. We in the South are a proud and progressive people. Half breeds cannot be proud. In the South we have pure blood lines and we intend to keep it that way."

Writer, J. C. Furnas, while working on his book, *Goodbye Uncle Tom's Cabin*, wrote to Oscar inquiring what reactions he had received to "The Small House of Uncle Thomas Ballet" from *The King and I*. Furnas noted that:

The story of the ballet, for instance, is by no means that of the book or the more widely used stage-versions—perhaps people with long memories and literal minds have been objecting that it wasn't Simon Legree who pursued Eliza across the ice? If so, that would indicate an interesting survival of acquaintance with the originals. Or, in view of the way many modern Negroes feel about the implications of Uncle Tom as folk-figure, you may have been receiving reactions unfavorable to the abstraction of that folk-figure in the ballet.

Oscar Hammerstein to J. C. Furnas, March 23, 1953

Dear Mr. Furnas:

Beyond the general praise for the Uncle Tom's Cabin ballet as a very entertaining portion of "The King and I", I had no comments whatever, political, social or philosophical. I believe that the conception of a young Oriental girl's adaptation of "Uncle Tom's Cabin" in the 1860's is so bizarre and stylized as to be beyond the pale of literal consideration.

Very truly yours,

Oscar Hammerstein II

Oscar Hammerstein to Hy and Rita Kraft, March 16, 1953

Dear Hy and Reata:

The Italian slippers have come. They fit me perfectly and I find them serviceable in my occupation of creeping around the house so no one will hear me while I eavesdrop on their conversation. I go into rehearsal in three days. I still have three songs to write and numerous bits and pieces to clear up, and that is why this letter must end right here at this very period.

Except for love to you both,

Working on his dissertation, "Restatement of the Play Script in Musical Theater Terms Exemplified by Oscar Hammerstein II," Charles Einach, a student at Syracuse University, wrote Oscar a letter, asking which version(s) of *Carmen* he consulted in the writing of *Carmen Jones*, and how the song "Nobody Else But Me" functioned when it was added to the 1946 revival of *Show Boat*.

Oscar Hammerstein to Charles Einach, March 19, 1953

Dear Mr. Einach:

In writing "Carmen Jones" I consulted the French text and the English translation in the published score. I also read Prosper Merimee's book, and that is about all. I found out later that there had been an interesting translation by the Galsworthys, but Deems Taylor sent that to me some time after the play had opened.

Regarding "Nobody Else But Me", after the opening in New York it was cut because it seemed that today the last scene where everyone gets old had better be as short as possible. It was the only part of the play that did not seem to me to hold up. The spot in which "Nobody Else But Me" was sung in New York filled in an old spot in the original which was taken up by Norma Terris' imitations. As Kim she imitated some of the famous stars of the day. This was a talent unique to Norma, and not part of the libretto proper. In London we had another song to take this place called "Dance Away the Night". It perhaps would never have been a musical spot had it not been for Norma's talent for imitation when we put on the original production. Your suggestion that I might send any statement regarding my method or theory of libretto restatement comes at a time when I am too busy to do anything except my present job. I go into rehearsal this week, but I suggest that you get a copy of my book called "Lyrics" in which I have written quite a full foreword about the construction of musical plays. This was published by Simon and Schuster. I hope this letter will be of some help to you.

All good wishes.

Sincerely,

Oscar Hammerstein II

Oscar was masterful at defusing awkward situations, camouflaging the vinegar with honey.

Richard Rodgers and Oscar Hammerstein to Mary Martin and Richard Halliday, March 20, 1953

Dear Mary and Dick:

We have heard from Bill McCaffrey that your television appearance with Ezio has been called off, and we would like to make it clear to you that much as we would have enjoyed listening to a re-broadcast of the original program which you and Ezio did a few years ago, we had to consider the fact that other ears beside ours would hear it. The result would be injurious to the two companies of "South Pacific" now playing in the United States, and the emphasis on what the play was when you and Ezio were both in it would be humiliating to the people who are now carrying on for us. With your good theatrical common sense we know that you both realize the validity of our concern. We thought, however, that [we] had better state it because things that happen thousands of miles away are often misunderstood. How soon are you going to eliminate those thousands of miles? Make it quick!

Love from us both.

Richard Rodgers

Oscar Hammerstein II

Although he enjoyed *The King and I* very much, one question frustrated R. Kaplan, and "aroused discussion and even some resentment" with his theater-going companion: "did Anna love the King or was she falling in love with the King? By way of definition, let us describe love in the physical or corporal sense as contrasted with the spiritual or non-physical sense. Was Anna's regard for the King . . . based upon her affection for him as an honest, likeable person . . . or as a man with whom she could have or might have gone to bed with."

Oscar Hammerstein to R. Kaplan, April 9, 1953

Dear Mr. Kaplan:

I think that Anna and the King are really in love with each other as man and woman, but I don't believe that either one of them knows it. Working together as they did, and influencing each other as much as they did, there has always seemed to me a suggestion of something more than an intellectual and spiritual bond between them. When you put the question bluntly—"Was he [a] man with whom she could have or might have gone to bed with?"—I don't believe she might have, but I believe that she could have had she not been a Victorian, had he not been Oriental, and had all the conditions that surrounded their life together been changed. I feel that I am getting obscure, but what I really mean to say is that they felt this attraction but were inhibited, not only from expressing it to each other, but each to himself. When they dance the polka they come closest to feeling and showing this desire.

Thank you very much for your interest in this fascinating subject. Please understand that my answer does not purport to be an accurate and specific one. There is a great deal of room for opinion in this story, and no one will ever be able to prove anything.

All good wishes to you.

Sincerely,

Oscar Hammerstein II

Oscar Hammerstein to John Cornell, April 9, 1953

Dear John:

I may not be able to get in again before we go on the road, and there are some notes I want to establish with you.

1. Why has not the first curtain been remedied according to our discussion? Louis still leaves Anna too soon when he sees the four men standing there, and so we do not get any picture of the mother and son starting to march by, whistling bravely. That is the way it was set. Louis should not break until after they have walked a few steps. He now dashes right over.

2. Louis must either be forced to talk louder and more distinctly or we must replace him.

3. What happened to the twins? If we can't get twins that look identical, we should get two that are not identical. The joke is still good if we have two the same size. No one told me anything about the elimination of the twins, or was one boy off that night? Please let me know about this.

3. [*sic*] What happed to the two bird girls in the parade crossing in the second act?

4. When Chulalongkorn says "Siam not so small" it is impossible to hear the word "Siam" because he says "Siam" while everybody else is making a noise. If he will just wait one beat his line will come out. "Not so small" is not a very interesting thing for the audience to hear. What they should hear is "Siam not so small!"

5. Please tell Connie that when she says: "So do I" at the end of the whipping scene I cannot hear her. This is a very important line. After he says: "I wish you never come to Siam" she must answer with great feeling, from the bottom of her heart: "So do I. Oh, so do I!" as she goes off. She throws this away too much.

6. I stopped in to see Alfred[7] at the matinee, as you know, and what I told him was to be more worried during the first part of "Puzzlement", and I also corrected his gesture on "From bee to bee to bee". That was all we discussed. I just wanted to keep you up with everything.

All the best to you.

Sincerely,

Oscar Hammerstein II

John Cornell to Oscar Hammerstein, April 10, 1953

Dear Mr. Hammerstein:

Many thanks for your letter and notes on "The King and I". I have taken care of them with the company members involved.

As for your questions, I did correct the curtain of the first scene when you first brought it to my attention. Dickie unaccountably slipped back, more from nerves, I think, than carelessness. I have rehearsed him several times since Monday for audibility and I believe he can now be heard. He is a very sensitive little boy and I would hate to lose him sooner than we must because of growth. I will keep after him.

The twins have not been eliminated; I certainly would have told you if they had. They were on vacation this week, and will be back Monday. When I agreed to this week, Yul was expecting to leave on March 15th. When the date changed, I thought of keeping them, but it was their school holidays, family plans had been made, etc., and it didn't seem too important. I told John Van Druten and Alfred about it some time ago.

The birds were a slip. One of the girls was very ill with flu and couldn't make it; the other—now very red-faced—was telling Ruth how good she thought Alfred was.

Incidentally, John Van Druten thought that Yuriko did not dance that night, because he missed her humor. (She did dance.) I want you to know

---

[7] Alfred Drake was Rodgers and Hammerstein's first choice to play the King, but he turned the part down. According to Hugh Fordin it was because he felt the King did not have enough to sing, but Rodgers in his memoir says it was because Drake could not commit to more than six months and had additional demands. Drake did take over for Yul Brynner for several weeks while Brynner went on vacation and, according to Rodgers, was wonderful.

that she too had flu, and barely made the performance at all. I hope you will not judge her on that night, as she is generally a meticulous and conscientious artist, and a real inspiration to the others.

Alfred improves in both appearance and performance. There is only one Yul, but this change has had a beneficial effect in causing the rest of the cast to re-study their own conceptions.

Sincerely yours,

John

John Cornell

Me and Juliet began out-of-town tryouts in Cleveland on April 20 and in Boston on May 23.

Oscar Hammerstein (in Boston) to William F. McDermott (*The Cleveland Plain Dealer*), May 19, 1953

Dear Bill:

I think we have fixed the missing step in the love story which was bothering you.

After the scene where Larry rehearses Jeanie and for the first time evokes some interest from her, and after the scene in which Bob has threatened him, we have the Alley Scene. This takes place several months later and in the middle of the scene Jeanie is heard singing offstage and everyone in the Alley looks off. They exchange understanding looks with one another and assume innocent postures and expressions as she comes in singing dreamily "Marriage Type Love". She sees them all, greets them happily and goes into the theater still singing. Then one of the girls comes in and informs the gossipy stage troupe that she just saw Larry and Jeanie in a chili joint together and that when they left they separated and went to the theater on opposite sides of the street. The whole company are apparently in on the "secret" and approve of this development. Then Larry passes through, whistling, closely observed and understood by everyone. After he goes, there is a discussion about what might happen when Bob finds out about them. This seems to ease the leap into the love scene in the dressing room and I think you would be very satisfied with it.

We have done some other useful work. I think the first five minutes are now clearer and the story gets on its feet quicker. The best change of all is in the first "Me and Juliet" sequence in which we make it clear to the audience that the play within the play in [*sic*] intended as a human and humorous allegory rather than a big, beautiful, soggy spectacle, as it was when you saw it. Bob Alton is now very busy on polishing his dances—notably the ballet in the second act, and we all think we are about ready to go into New York.

My kindest regards to your wife and you.

Sincerely,

Oscar Hammerstein II

Oscar Hammerstein to the Editor of the *Tulsa Tribune*,
May 27, 1953

Dear Sir:

David Milstein of your city has forwarded to me the copy of an editorial which appeared in your paper on May 14th, 1953. Delighted as I am with the praise you accord our song "Oklahoma!" I am deeply disturbed by a series of inaccurate statements which you have made regarding our copyright control over its uses. Mr. Rodgers and I are most anxious to have it known that you are wrong in your assumptions that the Central High School "Daze" could not use the song without prior permission. It is equally untrue that the Philharmonic orchestra could not play it without paying a fee. Concert fees are paid to ASCAP by the concert hall in which music is used. The individual orchestras do not pay. It is not true that a dance orchestra could not use it at the University of Oklahoma's Junior Prom, or that the University of Tulsa's choir couldn't sing it at a concert without permission and paying a royalty fee.

The only restriction to be observed is that the song should not be used against any dramatic background. It may not be dramatized by playing a scene from "Oklahoma!" or even inserted in a scene of any other play or story. That is all.

So tell your readers, and all the people of Oklahoma that not only may they play it and sing it anywhere and everywhere to their hearts content, but that we want them and urge them to do so. Songwriters write songs for people to sing, and nothing makes them happier than to know that their song is being sung. Mr. Rodgers and I are very proud that our song has been adopted by your state. Play it and sing it loud and long and often!

All good wishes to you.

Sincerely,

Oscar Hammerstein II

Me and Juliet opened on Broadway on May 28. The reviews were uniformly bad. In the *New York Times* Brooks Atkinson wrote: "All the things everyone loves in a Rodgers and Hammerstein show struggle with a book that has no velocity. To tell the truth, *Me and Juliet* looks a little like a rehearsal—beautiful, talented, full of good things, but still disorganized. As the tired sages of show business invariably remark as though one phrase could solve everything: 'It needs work.'" Despite the reviews, *Me and Juliet* survived for 358 performances and actually made a modest profit. (*RCA* had capitalized the production in exchange for a 50 percent interest and rights to the cast recording.) The score generated one standard, "No Other Love," a haunting tango whose music came from the television documentary *Victory at Sea*.

George Abbott[8] to Oscar Hammerstein, May 29, 1953

Dear Oscar –

I have developed such an affection for this enterprise that I was bleeding a bit from last night's reaction. Your note was balm to my wounds –

Yours

George

Irene Sharaff to Oscar Hammerstein, May 31, 1953

Dear Oscar:

Thank you for the bouquet and thank you for your very kind note on the opening night. I am so proud to have had the chance to work with you again and this is, above all, a fan letter because it's a grand show and people

---

[8] *Me and Juliet* was the only Rodgers and Hammerstein show directed by Abbott, although he had previously directed five Rodgers and Hart shows.

come out of the theater feeling good and having had fun. I'm sure I'm one of the many who have been moved by your view of the theater in the show. You make it a friendly and wonderful profession, which it can be, and it is impressive that a play about the theater can be so free of the seamy and less pleasant sides. It shows what a big person you are and what a good thing for us you are around!

Love

<u>Irene</u>

The Levittown in Bucks County, Pennsylvania, was the second one built, the first being in New York. Others followed. Levittowns were developments of thousands of homes—mass-produced suburbs—built so efficiently that they were comparatively affordable with required modest down payments. The letter below was a sample letter that may or may not have been sent, but in 1954 Oscar definitely sent letters on the topic of racial exclusion in housing to dozens of prominent figures (as you'll see). Thurman Arnold had been Assistant District Attorney in charge of Antitrust under FDR, Associate Justice of the U.S. Court of Appeals for the D.C., a professor at Yale, and in 1946 became a founding partner in the law firm Arnold & Porter.

Oscar Hammerstein to Thurman Arnold, circa June, 1953

<u>SAMPLE LETTER</u>

Dear Thurman,

We are having growing pains in Bucks County. It looks like those pains may hurt American democracy, possibly the whole free world. I wonder if you would care to unsheathe your pen and help us avoid the worst hurt.

Between 1950 and 1955 the population of this county, which began with William Penn, will double. Some 300 new industries have indicated plans to move in next door to our $500,000,000 Fairless Works of the United States Steel Corporation. Levitt & Sons, Inc. are constructing 16,000 homes on acres which recently yielded only spinach. In the face of this industrial and human onslaught, our basic facilities are overtaxed. But more important, our democratic principles are being severely tested, too.

Bucks County has lived by the constitutional provisions calling for equality of opportunity. According to all the evidence several thousand

Negro citizens will soon be employed in area industries. Yet today they cannot buy a home either at Levittown or Fairless Hills, the main low-cost developments. Employers have only slowly begun to fill jobs purely on the basis of ability. Happily, our schools tend to remain unharmed by what could become first-class prejudice if some of us fail to stand up against it.

The question is, of course, how to stand up against the prejudice which lies at the root of housing segregation, unequal job opportunities, etc. A few of us thought that if we had written answers from 100 or so thoughtful Americans, the collective results might give us more powerful leverage in strengthening democracy here.

1. How important to our nation's future do you think is our basic premise that "all men are created equal"?

2. Do you regard racial equality and understanding as matters of grave importance to the future of mankind?

3. If you were teaching in our schools, how would you teach our boys and girls to accept and to live by the American precepts of equality?

4. If you were teaching here and saw several striking examples of segregation nearby, how would you teach our boys and girls equality?

Unless you indicate to the contrary, I want to feel free to quote your materials on behalf of democracy everywhere and our young people here. Thank you sincerely for your early and thoughtful help. A few of us here feel that there are few things more worthwhile than speaking out when fundamental democratic rights are challenged.

Cordially,

Oscar Hammerstein, 2nd

Oscar Hammerstein to Goodman Ace,[9] NBC, July 1, 1953

Dear Goodman Ace:

Thank you for telling me what you and Jane thought of "Me and Juliet", and don't think I wasn't happy to hear it. The critics were thrown off their

---

[9] Goodman Ace was a comic writer and performer on radio and television.

balance a bit, and built up some kind of strange resentment against Dick and me having the right to a "lighter moment". Fortunately nobody else seemed to object, and I am glad that you were one of these.

All the best to you.

Sincerely,

Oscar Hammerstein II

Oscar Hammerstein to Robert Breen, July 2, 1953

Dear Mr. Breen:

Thank you for an exciting evening. Your production of "Porgy and Bess" is a vibrating, dynamic and moving experience. Obviously a labor of love, it is filled with understanding and fine theatrical invention. I found the company excellent, my only criticism of their performances being that in general they tended toward a lack of clear definition in delivering their lyrics. They seemed more interested in sound than in meaning. In spots this is desirable, but most of the time I found this disturbing, possibly because of my special interest in lyrics.

Again thank you, and I am more than ever receptive to the "Carmen Jones" project in the event that you study it further and hit upon an approach which is attractive to both of us.

All good wishes to you.

Sincerely,

Oscar Hammerstein II

Oscar Hammerstein to Hy Kraft, July 3, 1953

Dear Hy:

About two weeks ago I wrote a letter to you on my Dictaphone, but the Dictaphone wasn't doing very well at that time and a couple of records went for nothing. I became so incensed at technocracy that I said to hell with it, and several very fine letters were snatched from posterity's eager arms.

Having recovered from my temper I now take transmitter in hand (a new one) to tell you what I told you in the former ill-starred dictation:

The notices on "Me and Juliet" were as you probably have heard or read—mixed. No, I would say not mixed but unanimously lukewarm. The boys seem to be thrown by the kind of play it was, which was simply a musical comedy, lacking the depth and breadth of our more recent ones. We were sure it was a very good musical comedy, and have been since vindicated by the public, who enjoy it and are coming to the tune of $58,000 gross a week. This is standing room at $7.00, so that commercial side of it seems to be all right, and I believe we will quite rapidly get back our $350,000 investment. My own reaction to the notices is strange because I cannot help but feel flattered by the great expectations the boys have for us, and their criticism was based on these. To this extent I think they were justified. Had I my last year and a half to live over again I think I should not have started on this project, but have used the time better on a more important theme. It may, however, have been important, as Dick and I thought at the time, for us to change our pace, both for our own benefit and for the benefit of whatever public we have. Anyway, enough about po' li'l ol' me. How is your project getting along?

Don't bother to answer because you can do it right to my face in a few weeks, I hope. Dorothy and I are sitting here, each on his own tenderhook [sic], waiting to hear from Jerome Whyte. As soon as he has lined up what he considered good prospects for "The King and I" he is going to let me know and we are coming over, although only for a few days, and we will be able to see very few people, but among these will be guess who.

Dorothy joins me in sending our love to you both.

The following is a reply to a letter from a Robert Goldman that included this: "I have just graduated from Princeton University and am anxious to find a place in the theatre . . . I want to get started on something right away. I was president of the Triangle Club at college and produced a very successful show. I feel I can be of help to somebody in the theatre world who might need a young man with a talent for fresh ideas, as well as an eagerness to do all the legwork required."

Oscar Hammerstein to Robert S. Goldman, July 7, 1953

Dear Mr. Goldman:

Thank you for your interesting letter. There is no opening in our organization at the moment, but if one should develop I will send for you. This kind of promise always sounds very feeble. As a matter of fact, it is. I am well aware, however, that the theatre needs young men of your background and your ambition, and I will do whatever I can to help you get into the theatre. Meanwhile, the only thing I can suggest is for you to pound pavements very determinedly and try to get a job for next season. I have always believed that stage manager work is the best way to start. My two sons are both stage managers now, as I was when I was younger.

Beyond this I have no suggestion, but please keep battering at the doors of managers, mine as well as others. If you keep it up long enough you will get in.

All my best wishes to you.

Sincerely,

Oscar Hammerstein II

Barbara Miles and Ronald Sumner to Oscar Hammerstein, July 28, 1953

Dear Mr. Hammerstein,

We feel somewhat like the school-child who has found an error that the teacher didn't notice. It is with this certain amount of satisfaction, although not necessarily happily, that we would like to call to your attention an error which we noticed in one of the sequences in Me and Juliet.

Perhaps you have already discovered it, and decided to let it go through anyway, or perhaps, as we hope, this is a revelation to you. In either event, in the "Intermission Talk" number, one of the female patrons sings a few of the songs from the first act, which she has just seen, of "Me and Juliet." One of the numbers which she tried, albeit unsuccessfully, is "It's Me." However, "It's Me" is not in "Me and Juliet." As we need hardly remind you, it is done by Joan McCracken and Isabel Bigley in the dressing room sequence.

I think we shall treasure this always as our favorite, prized theatre boner.

While your attention is still ours, we would like to ask a question which has bothered us for the last two years. In The King and I, shortly after Tuptim's unsuccessful attempt to escape, the news is brought to the King that Lun Tha has been captured and is dead. But you never stated how he died. Were we to assume that he had been executed on the spot? If you meant to leave it to our imaginations, be assured that our two imaginations have played thoughtfully with the question for some time now. [CUT OFF] or comment would be highly appreciated.

We could hardly write these words to you without taking advantage of the opportunity to express the overwhelming respect and love that we have for the works that you and Mr. Rodgers have given to the American theatre. You couldn't possibly receive too much praise for the plays that you have written. There aren't ten seconds in South Pacific that aren't pure beauty and enjoyment. In the absence of perfection, South Pacific will do.

And The King and I is certainly not far behind it as America's second greatest musical.

Thank you very much for having permitted the error in Me and Juliet which presented us with this opportunity of communicating with you.

Very sincerely yours,

Barbara L. Miles

Ronald Sumner

Oscar Hammerstein to Barbara Miles, July 28, 1953

Dear Miss Miles:

You are quite right in pointing out the error in "Me and Juliet". I wrote the lyric for "Intermission Talk" during rehearsals and didn't discover the mistake I had made until we were on the road working on the show. It was one of those things that I intended to fix when I got around to it, but there were so many more important revisions to make that I never did get around to it, and in fact never did believe that anyone would be keen enough to catch me at it, but of course in time some one does, and we are always learning this lesson over and over again. I hope you will confine my secret to a few thousand of your most intimate friends. This is not the kind of think I like to have bruited about.

As to your second question in "The King and I", you may fill in how Lun Tha was killed. My own feeling is that he was not killed in any formal execution. I think he was killed trying to escape from the little sailing boat on which he was caught. He was a gallant fellow, and would not be killed without putting up a fight. In scenes of high melodramatic content, it is best not to put in details which slow up the action and tend to transform emotional reaction to intellectual analysis. Furthermore, if it [is?] assumed that people are killed very quickly and readily for offenses like this, it will also be assumed that Tuptim herself will be very quickly dispatched. She assumes this when she says: "Then I will soon be with him". As she is dragged off into the wings she screeches, and very likely that is when it happens.

I am touched by your deep interest in my work, and I am most grateful for your letter.

All good wishes to you.

Sincerely,

Oscar Hammerstein II

In a letter to Oscar, Lawrence Langner wrote: "The recent events in Russia, which I prophesized in my preface to SUSANNAH AND THE ELDERS,[10] has made me wonder whether this would not make the timely book of a musical as you suggested once before. It is curious how these dictatorships tend to follow the same pattern as was set by the American comedy. The play was about the revolt of the younger generation against the older generation's dictatorship, although it was treated in comedy terms. I do hope you will consider this as a possible book."

Oscar Hammerstein to Lawrence Langner (The Theatre Guild) (excerpt), July 28, 1953

Thank you for your letter of July 22nd, and your suggestion about "Susannah and the Elders". I can give you no logical or detailed reason why this should not be made into a musical comedy, because as you pointed out I thought so at the time I saw it, and I can give you no logical reason why I shouldn't do it, except that I don't feel the urge to. It just doesn't seem like

---

[10] Langner co-wrote the play *Susanna and the Elders* with his wife, Armina Marshall. It premiered on Broadway in 1940.

an attractive thing for me to put my mind to at this moment. As a writer yourself I think you will understand this explanation—without reason— better than any other.

Leighton Brill to Oscar Hammerstein (excerpt), July 29, 1953

In "Music in the Air" I have made a big change. In the dressing room scene Bruno, Frieda and Anna do a comedy version of "The Song is You". At the end of the scene I have a couple of lines—"Where is that little girl, Sieglinde", "Where is the school-teacher, Karl", "Back in Edendorf teaching school, Sieglinde is there too" etc., etc., "and Weber will publish Walther's number and they'll play it at the wedding". Then I cut to a corridor with all the happy peasants. At the end of the wedding ceremony Sieglinde and Karl are being blessed, they go into "We belong Together", the postman comes in with published scores of "I've Told Every Little Star" and distributes them. Black out at the end of this and back to my arena stage where Bruno and Frieda go on with "I Love You, I love you, I love you" and into chorus of "Song is You", clinch, and curtain. It works out extremely well.

P.S. Is there any truth in the rumour that Phil and Alice have adopted a Chinese baby?

Oscar Hammerstein to Leighton Brill (excerpt), August 1, 1953

Anent your postscript, it is not true that Phil and Alice have adopted a Chinese baby. What is true is that about eighteen months ago they did adopt a baby who is half American and half Japanese—one of the babies in Welcome House, the organization which Pearl Buck and Dorothy and I and several other people around here have [been] interested in for several years. Melinda is two years old this Monday, and she is a remarkable child—one of the most alert and brightest and enchanting kids I have ever seen. Of my various grandchildren, adopted, step and all varieties, there is none I love better than Melinda.

I have found no evidence of it in the correspondence, but a significant experience in Oscar's life began in July when his passport was due for renewal and, because of speculations that he had been a member of the Communist Party, he was permitted to obtain only a limited passport that would cover the next six months while an investigation took place. His contributions to and membership of various organization had proven suspect, as had his support of Paul Robeson's right to express unpopular beliefs. It was a dark experience that Oscar handled with grace and dignity, as he continued to support friends who were blacklisted.

Oscar was sent proofs of the jacket for the soon-to-be-released book, *Some Enchanted Evenings*, for any responses he might have. He had some.

Oscar Hammerstein to Frank S. MacGregor, Harper & Brother, August 2, 1953

Dear Mr. MacGregor:

I believe Lynn Farnol, representing me, has already got in touch with your office and told you of the one exception I take to the copy for the jacket. It is foolish to say "—in a saga of entertainment history that runs from the 'Garrick Gaieties' of 1925 to the epochal 'Oklahoma!', 'South Pacific' etc . . . " By the time 1925 had rolled around, I had had eleven shows produced, one of them being "Wildflower", which ran more than a year in New York, and another being "Rose Marie", which is still running as a very lively stock property. I suggested that our careers be designated as having started when they did start, with the Columbia Varsity shows. I imagine that by this time this objection and suggestion have already been relayed to you. I am sure you will see the good sense of the point I make. Thank you very much for your courtesy and understanding in this matter.

Very truly yours,

Oscar Hammerstein II

Climb High was the fourth and the last of the "assignments" Oscar gave Sondheim to hone his skills in writing musicals. This assignment was to write an original musical. The previous assignments had been to adapt a play he liked (*Beggar on Horseback*), a play he liked but thought flawed (*High Tor*), and to adapt a novel or short story/stories (*Mary Poppins*). Sondheim began working on *Climb High* during his senior year of college and had been working on it for two or three years. Oscar's letter was accompanied by the script Sondheim gave him, now heavily annotated by Hammerstein.

Oscar Hammerstein to Stephen Sondheim, August 6, 1953

Dear Stevie:

Regarding "Climb High", not only did we like the original conception, but only a couple of months ago when you restated your theme it sounded good then. At the time I suggested that it was perhaps the prologue that started us off not liking the boy, whereas if you told the story in its proper chronology, without flashbacks, you could get the audience to like him and go with him, as with a son, and be anxious when he went off the track all through the play. Then it would be taking the form of a conventional "race". I think as I look back on it that you have fallen down badly with your other characters with whom he comes in contact. They all seem shallow wisecracking young people. You know a lot of young people who are nicer than these. I don't think a play should be filled only with nice people, but it is good to have a variety, and some characters who are foils for others.

Going back to the beginning, however, there is no doubt that a story can be told about a man who instead of learning how to use the tools of his craft, learns only how to put on the proper costume for it, thinking that he is going on a shortcut, and finding in the end that you must always go back and learn how to use those tools. It is as if a caddy on a golf course practices with whatever he can, with whatever clubs he can afford to buy or borrow or steal, whereas another comes out in just the proper kind of slacks or shorts, and well tailored shirt and shiny clubs, and never learns to hit a ball. This is your story and it is perfectly sound. In fact it is the story of "Death of a Salesman". The salesman, however, had a wife who was very real, long-suffering but really strong and loyal to a touching degree. He had sons who were jerks, but you could trace their jerkism to the salesman himself. He had passed on his phoniness to them. The friend next door was a nice feller and so was his son. The salesman kept deceiving himself and deceiving fewer and fewer other people until finally he couldn't even deceive himself any more, and so he killed himself. This is a good straight, strong, honest treatment of the same theme.

I would like to talk this over with you at great length (not the salesman, but your play) when you return, or if I go out there—whichever comes first.

The story of the Mizners is of course good material. I agree with your analysis of Wilson. When he cheated he was cheating cheats. His view of life and his behavior may well have been more logical than those of "normal" people. Certainly he was a most entertaining figure. Would your idea be to get any rights from the estates or from Alva Johnson, or to use only factual material and build your own story? The decision whether to make it a biography or a fiction inspired by Mizner is a big one to make. At this moment I don't know which would be the best.

I have shown your letter to Dorothy and I wouldn't be surprised if it resulted in a letter to you. She writes to everyone else in the world, why not you?

Love from us both.

Oscar

The story of the Mizners relates to another project that Sondheim hoped might be his next musical. This was to be based on the life of Wilson Mizner— gambler, confidence man, boxing promoter, playwright and screenwriter, raconteur, and infamous seller of swamp land in Florida—and his brother, Addison, a respected architect, brought down by his brother. Alva Johnson had written a dual biography, *The Legendary Mizners*, a book that Sondheim was thinking of optioning.

Oscar Hammerstein to John Peter, *Look Magazine*,
August 6, 1953

Dear Mr. Peter:

Replying to your letter of July 29th requesting a comment for your feature, tentatively titled "New Era Living", I submit the following:

The biggest changes in our lives during the last quarter of a century have been wrought by the amazing advances in communications. Planes flying faster, sights and sounds coming clearer over air waves have brought us all closer together.

What will happen to us in the next twenty five years will depend on how we choose to use these communications. What shall we communicate? How much good sense? How much nonsense? How much kindness? How much cruelty?

The progress of science can be of little good to us unless we make commensurate progress in the art of human understanding.

I hope this answers your need.

All good wishes to you.

Sincerely,

Oscar Hammerstein II

Richard Rodgers and Oscar Hammerstein to Agnes de Mille, August 10, 1953

MISS AGNES DEMILLE

THE THEATRE GUILD HAS RELINQUISHED ALL ITS RIGHTS AND INTERESTS IN OKLAHOMA AND WE ARE REPRODUCING THE PLAY UNDER OUR OWN MANAGEMENT OPENING CITY CENTER THEATRE AUGUST THIRTYFIRST. IT IS OUR WISH TO ACCORD YOU APPROPRIATE RECOGNITION BY REASON OF THE ORIGINAL PRODUCTION BOTH BILLING WISE AND MONETARILY AND WE WOULD LIKE TO TRY TO PUT DOWN ARRANGEMENTS WITH YOU ON PAPER AT THE EARLIEST POSSIBLE TIME. OUR FIRST DISPLAY AD OF THE NEW PRODUCTION WHICH WILL APPEAR IN NEWYORK PAPERS ON SUNDAY GOES TO PRESS THIS THURSDAY. WE DO NOT LIKE TO USE YOUR NAME EXCEPT WITH YOUR CONSENT SINCE WE HAVE NO CONTRACT WITH YOU. WE WOULD SUGGEST THAT PENDING OUR DISCUSSING THE WHOLE MATTER YOU GIVE US THIS APPROVAL BY WIRING US TO THIS EFFECT WITHOUT PREJUDICE TO OUR RESPECTIVE RIGHTS.

DICK AND OSCAR

A cover note stapled to the front of this telegram reads: "PLEASE CALL ME AFTER YOU READ THIS/HOWARD," suggesting that Howard Reinheimer actually wrote the telegram. The City Center production of *Oklahoma!* ran for forty performances, and featured Florence Henderson as Laurey, and Barbara Cook as Ado Annie. But the telegram to de Mille may have been as much about setting the stage for their plans for a film, as it was about the City Center production.

Oscar Hammerstein to Arthur Hammerstein (excerpt)
August 20, 1953

Dick and I have purchased all rights to "Oklahoma" from the Theatre Guild, not only the picture rights, but the stock and amateur rights (which I think will go on forever). We are now selling the picture rights to our company, and we are already deep in conference with the director, Fred Zinnemann, to plan the picture. I think we will start rehearsals in February and go before the cameras in March. I will let you know more about this later.

Oscar Hammerstein to Richard Rodgers, August 24, 1953

Dear Dick:

Regarding the synopsis of "Colombe" by Anouilh which is being produced by Bob Joseph with Julie Harris, and regarding your general question: "What is your feeling about our making investments in outside productions at this time?" I think that we ought to make investments if we like a play a great deal, but I think we should always read the play. We are not like other angels who can be told the play is not to be read. We are on the inside, and I don't see why we should put any money in anything that we don't know a great deal about. I suggest that you ask Joseph to send you the script when it is finished.

In general I don't think we ought to let it get about that we're investing in plays. I just think that we ought to be a little less rigid than we were a couple of years ago. It is a nuisance to be appealed to all the time. It is still true that when we invest we are taking on a responsibility beyond other investors because we are encouraging further investment. I don't see, however, why this should block us from making extra money or helping along a project that seems worthy of help. If you disagree with any of this, let's talk it over the next time we meet.

Love,

Oscar Hammerstein to Leighton Brill, *Melody Fair* (excerpt), August 24, 1953

In your last letter to me commenting on the changes in "Music in the Air" you say: "You evidently did not have my letter in front of you when you wrote your scathing comments." Well, I did have your letter in front of me, and I have it in front of me now, and this is what it says: "In "Music in the Air" I have made a big change. In the dressing room scene Bruno, Frieda and Anna do a comedy version of the Song is You". (I assume you mean the usual version.) "At the end of the scene I have a couple of lines—"Where is that little girl, Sieglinde", "Where is the school-teacher, Karl", "Back in Edendorf teaching school, Sieglinde is there too" etc., etc., "and Weber will publish Walther's number and they'll play it at the wedding". "Then I cut to a corridor with all the happy peasants. At the end of the wedding ceremony Sieglinde and Karl are being blessed, they go into "We belong Together", the postman comes in with published scores etc." Well, all I can say is that this sounds good and lousy to me, and in some cases baffling. I don't know what "a corridor full of happy peasants" means. I have never seen happy peasants meeting in a corridor. What corridor? Is it a corridor in a public building, a hotel, a hospital? Or is it just a corridor of a set which was in some other show that you played there this summer.

Let us suppose it didn't sound lousy, and let's suppose that it wasn't. How can you calmly tell me that you have made these changes without ever having asked me if you can make them? They are very radical changes indeed, and I am telling you what I told Dick Berger a year ago. If you can't play my plays without changes, don't play them. If you think changes should be made, tell me about them and give me a chance to consent to them.

Regarding the information you say you have received about the summer theatre production of "Carousel", this was staged by Billy Hammerstein and it has broken records every place it has played. It has also received very fine notices. I don't doubt that a few people whom you have bumped into told you that they didn't like it. That may be quite possible. I have not seen it myself. I have heard only good reports on it, and one of the cast I have taken away to play in the road company of "Oklahoma!" She is one of the most talented girls we have come across in a long time, Barbara Cook. Do you know her?

Oscar Hammerstein to Deems Taylor, August 27, 1953

Dear Deems:

I think the book is swell. I have been all through it, and to prove that I didn't skip any let me call your attention to a strange statement on page 20: "The successful musical comedies of the period, shows such as "The Vagabond King", "The Student Prince", "Rose Marie", "Princess Flavia", had one thing in common. Their setting was anywhere but America." Like Canada,[11] for instance?

I am, however, in no mood to cavil because I am very happy with your job, and proud to be part of the subject matter.

All the best to you.

As ever,

Oscar Hammerstein II

New York Mayor Vincent Impellitteri declared August 31 through September 6, "Rodgers & Hammerstein Week" in honor of their having four musicals running in New York simultaneously—*South Pacific*, *The King and I*, and *Me and Juliet* on Broadway, and *Oklahoma!* at City Center.

After years of holding fast, suddenly Rodgers and Hammerstein opened the sluice gates allowing film versions of their musicals. Four films would be released within four years, all of them released by Twentieth Century-Fox: *Oklahoma!* (1955), *Carousel* (1956), *The King and I* (1956), and *South Pacific* (1958).

Howard Reinheimer to Oscar Hammerstein, September 23, 1953

Dear Oscar:

Things have been so busy here—particularly with Dick getting ready to go off a week from today, that I have not had any time to write you—besides there has been practically nothing that could not wait for a fuller discussion when I see you in London. Hence, I will limit this note to merely a few jottings.

---

[11] *Rose Marie* was set in Canada.

1. Looks like Ellie may fly after all so, unless there is a change of heart, there will be two of us arriving on the Ambassador on Saturday morning, October 3rd. Of course, anything can happen to change her plans, but in any event I will be there.

2. My cable to you about THE KING AND I motion picture is due to the fact that Moscowitz has been applying the pressure by saying that his people insist that we adhere to the October 1st deadline. He rightly says that according to the contract and the extensions he gave us, we must offer the property to 20th Century by October 1st, although they naturally would like to sit down and talk about a proposition whereby we would be associated with the making of the picture.

So that you are better informed as to the legal situation, our contract obligation is to offer the property at an all-cash price—release date to be one year after closing of all American companies, but not later than April 1, 1956 (this would include England).

If 20th Century rejects the offer, we can make a like offer to any <u>outside</u> company and close the deal at the same price or better, but if we can only get a lower price elsewhere, 20th Century has first option to buy at such lower price.

3. While we own the picture rights to <u>our</u> version including music and lyrics, our rights are limited to one picture and then only for 10 years. So you see we are rather boxed in since 20th Century is applying the screws. I am meeting with Joe tomorrow in an effort to postpone the date, but I may be compelled to quote a price to him before October 1st, in which event we are all agreed we should suggest between $400,000 and $500,000. My thought is that if we agree on the value of the property, I may be able to postpone decisions as to how the picture is to be made—cinemascope, regular 35 mm., or possibly, as may very probably happen, through a licensing of Todd AO.[12] The fact that the picture cannot be released until a year and [a] half after OKLAHOMA opens gives us some edge in negotiations. You will hear further from me in this regard.

---

[12] Mike Todd co-founded the company Todd-AO (the "AO" represented their partners, the American Optical Company), which also represented a new process for projecting a remarkably rich 70 mm print on a 128-degree curved screen—if one wished. *Oklahoma!* was the first film released using this process.

4. Schenk is coming to New York; Todd has not yet returned and the annual meeting is set for a week from today. The fur should fly by then since George Skouras anticipates troubles from Todd, even to the extent of Todd possibly trying to block the financing deal. More about that too, when I see you.

5. The DeMille deal has been closed on a basis of $35,000 for 20 weeks in California, plus free consultation services before her contract begins.

6. Saw the ROBE in cinemascope. The opening which was attended by every notable in the picture business including exhibitors, distributors, etc. showed no enthusiasm whatsoever and left the theatre completely without applauding. Personally, I thought the picture was very good and that cinemascope was quite good, but showed no pliability—particularly in intimate scenes. Those on the inside call it just another wide screen effort although the newspapers for the most part (New York Times excepted) were glowing in their plaudits. The result has been that the Roxy is doing the biggest business they have ever done—over $260,000 the first week and from outward appearances 20th Century is riding high. However, as a tip-off on what the insiders think, the morning after the picture opened at the Roxy 20th Century stock dropped from 17 to 15½--although the market was strong that day. Since then the stock has remained the same, but I have a hunch that some insiders are supporting it, since every day that stock has dropped another point or so, but seemed to recover at the close of the market.

7. Regarding Williamson, I had a very pleasant meeting with Max and Sidney Wattenberg at which Max said that it was a fait accompli to turn over the stock immediately and work out the details along the formula as follows:

(a) You and Dick to extend your employment contract with Williamson and the Chappell management for an extended period of time.

(b) The OKLAHOMA contract with Crawford and the CAROUSEL contract with T. B. Harms [will] be cancelled.

(c) For the balance of the present period of your contract (i.e. until 1962 or the death of either Max or Louis [Dreyfus], whichever date is earlier), Chappell to receive as a management fee percentage of sales and/or profits which would approximate what it is now receiving from various sources, including its earning on 50% of the stock.

(d) When Max and Louis are no longer in the picture, this management percentage would be materially dropped even though a new manager, satisfactory to you and Dick, would come into the picture.

(e) If such new manager proves unsatisfactory to you both, you can cancel the whole deal by paying a still lesser percentage of profits to Chappell for the balance of your extended term. This last sum is primarily a deterrent against your arbitrarily cancelling out the Chappell deal. I told Max that we would all discuss this in London—and it looks as though, subject to working out fair figures, the deal can be closed as above outlined.

That's all for the time being—see you a week from Friday.

Sincerely,

Howard

Howard E. Reinheimer

HER:lk

Rushing this to catch the airmail. So excuse any mistakes

HER

Leonard Dinnerstein to Oscar Hammerstein, September 25, 1953

Dear Sir:

I am a student at City College. I have just started work on a long essay entitled, "The Theme of Brotherhood and Tolerance in the Plays of Oscar Hammerstein II." Could you please send a personal statement on the subject?

Yours truly,

Leonard Dinnerstein

The King and I opened in London on October 8.

Oscar Hammerstein to Leonard Dinnerstein, October 28, 1953

Dear Mr. Dinnerstein:

I suppose that my best personal statements on the subject of brotherhood and tolerance are in the plays that you intend to deal with. I am very happy that you are writing this essay because none of the references to this theme in my plays is accidental. They are quite deliberate and conscious. I believe that the introduction of this theme in plays is more effective than plays that are written obviously to propagate these virtues. The public resists direct propaganda—in our country, anyway.

All good wishes to you.

Sincerely,

Oscar Hammerstein II

Howard Reinheimer to Richard Rodgers and Oscar Hammerstein, October 14, 1953

Re: GONE WITH THE WIND

Dear Dick and Oscar:

In accordance with our conversation in London, I telephoned J. Robert Rubin at Metro on my return and informed him that primarily by reason of the situation regarding the motion picture rights, you would not be interested in doing a musical play of the above.

Sincerely,

Howard E. Reinheimer.

Oscar Hammerstein to Jerry [possibly Watanabe], October 26, 1953

Dear Jerry:

Thank you for the cuttings. I enjoyed the one about autumn and the furniture moving, and as I told you, it was wonderful to get the world series cuttings in England because there was no news of the series at all over there. I think it remiss of the British papers not to have at least two lines about the foremost sporting event of the American year, but remiss they were. Did you see the fight the other night? I am sorry I didn't have a chance to look at it. It must have been a pretty good one to watch. It seems to me that Randy Turpin[13] has gone sour temperamentally, and he might have beaten Bobo if he had trained properly.

I am writing to you because I have not been able to see you so far, and this next week looks like a tough one for me. I am not even sure that you enjoy visitors because of the difficulty you have in talking now, so I think perhaps we'll carry on a correspondence for a while. I would, however, like to stop in and see you, if only for a few minutes. I just want assurance that you think this is a good idea, and I don't want to impose myself on you if it is a bore to you. I am hoping very hard that your condition will soon take a turn for the better, and that you will work your way out of this trouble which I believe you have met so gallantly, and been so patient about.

It is good to be back on the farm. The cattle seem in fine condition, and everything is lovely here except that the leaves have piled up and gotten very dry and are not very pretty. I bought two cows in England, a heifer of the Gammer family, which is considered pretty fine stuff and always goes for very big money in the sales here. Any cow with the name of Gammer gets a very big price. In fact very few owners are willing to sell their Gammers, so I paid $6,000 for this one! I got another one, a very fine breed—Georgina— for $600, and this is a real bargain. The seller also agreed to transport cows over here and pay for their expenses in quarantine. This amounts to about $1000 for the two cows. You see, they must go to Scotland first and be quarenteed [*sic*] there for two months. Then they sail across to Canada and stay there for two months before they are permitted to cross our sacred borders. I imagine this is mostly for the hoof and mouth disease prevention. We are off to a cattle sale in Lancaster, Pa. tomorrow, where we are entering a pretty good cow. It is also a show.

There is not much more news except that Dick and I are getting into harness slowly. Our chief problem at the moment is to try to find a cast for the picture version of "Oklahoma!" and so far we have not been lucky at all. We haven't cast one part, but we will now concentrate on this job.

---

[13] On October 21, Randy Turpin, who was British, fought Bobo Olson at Madison Square Garden for the Middleweight boxing title.

Meanwhile we are looking for a play to do. God knows why because it seems we have enough to do without a new play. It is just habit, I suppose.

Let me know if I may drop in for a few minutes.

Love to all.

In June of 1941 Rodgers first wrote Oscar, asking whether he'd be willing to collaborate with him and Larry Hart on a musical version of Edna Ferber's novel *Saratoga Trunk*. In February 1942 Oscar and Kern discussed doing the show. Now in 1953 the possibility is raised again, this time by Ferber and Moss Hart. Although Rodgers and Hammerstein declined in favor of what would become *Pipe Dream*, they wrote a detailed response to an outline they were sent.

Richard Rodgers and Oscar Hammerstein to Edna Ferber and Moss Hart, November 3, 1953

Dear Edna and Moss:

We are confident that "Saratoga Trunk", built along the outline you have started, can be a big hit and a beautiful show. For several reasons, however, the other story we have been considering is more interesting to us. It will be a more radical departure from the previous stories and groups of characters with which we have dealt. We don't think its chances of being successful are any greater than the chances of your play—perhaps not as good. We just feel more like working on that one, and that perhaps is the best if not the most analytical way of putting it. It would have been a lot of fun for the four of us to work together on a play, so let us do it some time on some other play.

We have gone over your outline quite carefully since you presented it to us the other day, and for whatever you think they are worth, we would like to submit these comments to you:

The first scene and the conception of the "Song of Recognition" should work out perfectly. Both Kaka and Cupide should have a good part of this because they know more about it than Clio. It would be good to have this identified as a trio, so that the "Revenge Song" would stand out as her solo. This is in many ways, as you know, the most important song in the show because it sets her and justifies and motivates all her behavior for the length of the play.

We are not so sure about the opening of Scene 2 because it is just an atmosphere song, and once the story is on its way it might seem to be only an attractive intermission. You mention that there has been no opening chorus, and this then would be it, but since it is no longer an opening, why the chorus? A comparable instance might be the male chorus of "Dames" in "South Pacific", after a quiet duet opening, but "Dames" was not just a folk song of the South Sea Islands, as this is a Creole song of New Orleans. "Dames" was an expression of the loneliness and sex hunger of these men. The equivalent should be true here if you are going to sing a choral rendition of a song. If it is a Creole folk song, it should have some application to the general situation or to the mood of one of the characters at the moment.

It seems to us, in fact, that this whole Scene 2 does not advance the story enough to justify itself. At the end of Scene 1 Clio has expressed her intentions. Shouldn't the next thing we see be the activation of those intentions? Couldn't whatever you have in Scene 2, that you feel necessary, be included in Scene 1? We have a feeling of padding as far as scenes and sets are concerned around this spot. Should there be a church scene <u>and</u> an outdoor market scene? Is it possible to have the church across the way from the restaurant so that you can see her coming out of church and going toward the restaurant, and soon meeting Clint?

We may be missing something, but it seems that Scene 2 and Scene 3 both finish without having made a long enough stride. If this is true there will be a kind of flat feeling when these curtains close, however beautiful the inner content might have been.

It seems to us that Clint should have a moment alone to set himself straight with the audience before Clio comes on—something equivalent to Gaylord Ravenal singing "Who Cares If My Boat Goes Upstream"—before he sees Magnolia. This is of course not at all essential. It might be interesting enough to have a stranger staring at her and have the audience just as ignorant of his background as she is. The main advantage of giving him a song before she comes on is a purely theatrical one, rather than a dramatic one, to get him off on the right foot with the audience, and let them know that he has a fine voice.

We think the "Food Song" is wonderful, and a fine chance for both lyric writer and composer.

Scene 5 is swell, with a very good finish.

Ditto for Scene 6. (A suggestion about the song that Cupide and Clint sing: Cupide is glib in his philosophy about women, but now and then the lyric writer should insert a pathetic reminder that for him it is all hearsay. He cannot have had any experience of his own. It can be very touching to realize that Cupide is a thwarted romantic.)

Scene 7. The wisdom of having a ballet is something you should discuss carefully. It is linked with the general policy of whether you want to have a big show with a large ensemble, or a small but elegant show. We both lean toward the latter, but it is not a decision to be made hurriedly. The story content of this scene is very important, and should play very well. Clio's scene with her half sister is very dramatic. The only hard part of the scene is the ballet, and what it is about. If you have a formal ballet like "Swan Lake", it may get over on its sheer virtuosity, and then again it may be another one of those "attractive intermissions".

The rest of the act seems just wonderful—interesting, romantic and dramatic. The only reservation we suggest for this portion is a doubt about the number, "Not Me", merely because it seems to be so much like the number "Revenge". Is it not better to stick to reprising "Revenge" (which has to be a very strong song anyway). "Not Me" seems to be just a corollary to "Revenge".

The second act seems at its best when it is leaning hard on the relationship between Clio and Clint. We feel only mildly involved with the business of cutting a dash at Saratoga. A little of this will go a long way, we think. We don't mean that we are not interested in Clio's determination to cop a rich husband, but if Clio's radical decision to walk to the Springs instead of driving to the Springs created a sensation with the Saratogans of that era, we don't think it is going to create much of a sensation with an audience of this era.

This is a well rounded out love story. A man who was a drifter finds himself going out to win a fortune for only one reason—a girl who wants a fortune. A handsome adventurer is suddenly a nice ordinary man in love, a guy doing it all for a doll. The girl, a money mad and spurious aristocrat, realizes that she is ready to throw all of that up for a man, and she makes the decision before she knows that the man is going to be a millionaire. We think there is a danger in cluttering up this good human finish with too much attention to the frills and fripperies of Saratoga. Clint's return, bloody and unbowed and victorious, and Clio embracing him, must not suffer because it is felt necessary to show a big ensemble event in the Saratoga hotel wherein the heroine has to create a sensation for society. The importance of this big party scene is the phrase you use in the last sentence of your outline: "This song burns Clio's bridges behind her". The words to this song can do a great deal in determining the extent of the audience's satisfaction with this story. The more we feel what has gone on in Clio's heart before this decision, the better. What goes on in the minds of the Saratogans should not be emphasized too much because the audience just does not care enough about this. They will care about these two people.

Looking over this, we realize that it all could seem very didactic and pompous to you, but please don't believe that it is either. These are hastily written and not very carefully composed notes, expressing our instinctive reactions to the story, and not pretending to be the result of thorough analysis. We thought we saw a few danger signals, and if we didn't tell you about them it would not be very friendly of us.

Our best wishes for the project, and our love to you both.

Dick + Oscar

Richard Rodgers

Oscar Hammerstein II

Oscar Hammerstein to Lynn Farnol, November 9, 1953

Dear Lynn:

Thank you for your letter of November 3rd regarding NBC Lecture Hall. Please tell them that I shall not be able to accept their kind offer. And for your information, Lynn, let me tell you of a resolution I have made. (I am going to take a sabbatical—not from work, but from public appearances of all kinds.) After this month (I am going to accept no commitments from any people or organization, however worthy the cause. It will seriously endanger my health if I go on doing things as I have been, and I <u>know</u> that I am seriously endangering my professional output.) These things are using up my time and my energy and my ingenuity, which I think might all be better placed in my work. I would like you to tell this to anyone who comes to you asking for my services. I can make this decision and carry it out with a clear conscience because I have been doing a lot of work for a lot of causes, and I think I am entitled to a layoff, don't you.

All good wishes.

As ever,

Richard Rodgers and Oscar Hammerstein to Jerry Whyte,
November 9, 1953

Dear Jerry:

We understand you are coming back to the States soon, and after you have had a short rest here, we have a job for you. We would like you to go to the West Indies (islands to be chosen later) and do a little scouting for us in connection with two projects.

1. We are thinking seriously of adapting a story by John Steinbeck which is more or less a sequel to his previous book, "Cannery Row". We are not quite sure whether we want to keep the story in California, near Monterey, as he has it, and this atmosphere might be more suitable for music. We will tell you something about the story when we see you, and with this in mind we would like you to go down there and find out what you can—a kind of research expedition for us.

2. While you are there you might be considering that locale for "South Pacific". We are a little ignorant about these islands and don't know whether you can get the same kind of scenery that you would get in the south Pacific Islands, but if we could, it would be we believe much more economical to send a company there on location when we do "South Pacific" then all the way across the Pacific. This is of course a more remote venture, but we may do the picture right after we've done "Oklahoma!" and it isn't too soon to learn the answer to this important question.

Let us know when you are coming, and we will have a conference about this soon after your arrival.

All our best wishes to you.

Sincerely,

Richard Rodgers

Oscar Hammerstein II

Hy Kraft wrote Oscar a letter with an idea he has for a new musical, *The Royal Flush*. He is excited by the idea of casting it with Vivian Blaine, Sam Levene, and Stubby Kaye—three of the original stars of *Guys and Dolls*—hoping to re-capture lightning in a bottle. As he puts it: "Suddenly the idea jelled once I hit on the juxtaposition of these three people vis-à-vis royalty. I know this is a solid premise and extremely timely and lends itself to the basic elements of a musical . . . Commercially, we take quick advantage of the three years they've all been with 'Guys and Dolls'. Surely, there's a ready made audience in New York for them when they return to the states in the Fall."

Oscar Hammerstein to Hy Kraft (excerpt), November 20, 1953

You English are too impetuous for me. I open a letter written on blue paper, and I am plunged into a quick and telegraphic scenario which goes by like a cop's motorcycle, and then I read it over again. Skipping down to the last question: "Would Rodgers and Hammerstein be interested?" Dick and I are still holding to the policy of not producing other people's shows because we don't find time to produce our own. I think that your idea may be a good one. I don't think that the names involved are as important as you do. I don't think Broadway is waiting for these three people to come back together unless they come back together in a wonderful story, so it goes back to the story. When you develop it a little more I'd be glad to read it and give you my reaction to it.

As you may have read by now Dick and I are going to do a musical adaptation of John Steinbeck's "Cannery Row" and a sequel which he is now writing to it. What I mean by that is that we have access to both the sequel and the original. I am very excited about this and about the group of characters and the background, and I have an idea we can do something with it—something that is quite different from anything we have so far tried.

In a letter from Billy Rose, he writes: "Some months back, Robert Breen told me that he had seen the concert version of CARMEN JONES—the one headed by Muriel Rahn—in Chicago. He said he thought it was fifth rate in every respect, and could only hurt a possible revival . . . I'm sure the income derived from this version of a show which meant so much to both of us emotionally is a minor one to you these days. The time isn't far off, as I see it, when there might again be a large audience for a first rate revival of CARMEN JONES, and this bad little salesman can only hurt."

Oscar Hammerstein to Billy Rose, November 20, 1953

Dear Billy:

Thank you for your letter and the news about the Muriel Rahn production of "Carmen Jones". I did not give Campbell this right in order to make money. You know it doesn't do me any good to make even a little money. I can't keep it any more than I can keep big money because somehow they add it all up together and you can't separate it. My motive was to let these poor people get a little employment. The project has brought them in a living, I suppose, for the last three seasons. I agree with you, however, that if it is as bad as we are hearing, it is becoming injurious to the property, and I will withhold the license from them after they complete this present short season. (I think they go out for about ten weeks and play mostly universities.)

I had a talk with Otto Preminger before he left for Europe and he is going to get in touch with us as soon as he gets back. He seems really serious about doing it as a picture, and he tells me he has some interesting ideas for its production on the screen. We'll all get together about this after he comes back.

All good wishes.

As ever,

Oscar Hammerstein II

Preminger produced and directed the film of *Carmen Jones* and, remarkably, it was released eleven months after Oscar's letter.

Howard Reinheimer to Richard Rodgers and Oscar
Hammerstein, November 11, 1953

Dear Dick and Oscar:

I have been in touch from time to time with ABC regarding their proposal to set up a Rodgers & Hammerstein television company.

Since you are now working on so many other things, don't you think I had better tell them definitely that at least for a year you won't be doing anything along those lines?

Sincerely,

Howard

The following letter was sent to Josh Logan, while Logan, who suffered from bi-polar disorder, was in the hospital, recuperating from one of his two nervous breakdowns. Its chattiness is its kindness.

Oscar Hammerstein to Josh Logan, November 28, 1953

Dear Josh:

It is thanksgiving day (should I have used capital letter? I think no) I am considering the turkey we ate at two P. M.—it is now 10 P. M. and the fact that I am still "considering" it is significant. Last week he was one of these singularly unattractive fowls huddled with his friends on their wire perch, gobbling angrily when I approached, and turning blue about the head. I stuffed so large a part of him into me to-day that for a while I was afraid I was turning blue about the head. I didn't dare look into the mirror to check.

You often hear people say that they could not kill and eat something they had seen grow up on a farm. I can understand this kind of sentimental attitude towards a soft-eyed calf, a playful lamb or even a pig who has the kind of busy-body personality you can't forget. But turkeys were made for man to eat, and for no other reason. They are silly-looking, suspicious and unheroic birds who take on glory only after they have been cooked, stuffed and placed on a table. And they so stultify the inside of those who eat them that Thanksgiving Day letters are the dullest letters written in all the year. Apology preamble over!

Maybe I feel dull because I have just read such a bright quotation from a man whose wit I envy, Gilbert K. Chesterton. Here is what he said: "Angels can fly because they take themselves lightly," --- Isn't that great?

Does it make you sore when you see words like that and realize the awful truth that you did not write them? Magazine articles call me that "nice, modest, unenvious O. H." When will they discover the scowl behind that benign mask? I confide to you that I loathe G. K. C. for having found these words and put them together. There they were all the time and I might have done the same.

I am going to get up early to-morrow morning and try to juggle as many words as I know and assemble them into a great epigram—but to-morrow, not to-day.

Social note: Wonderful news—Paul Eirle[?] and Ginette Liederman[?] are coming over—December 11th, I think. They will stop with us for three days, fly to Hollywood and then spend another week or so in New York, on their way back. Dorothy and I saw Ginette on one of her quick dashes to London. (Speaking of London "The King and I" got over in a big way. It is the best company we've had)

We spoke to Nedda to-day and she said she would meet them at the airport and take them to your place for the first night. This will save us the necessity of coming into town on a Sunday. Then, on Monday she'll bring them down and deposit them on 63rd St. with us.

Another Social Note: The Rodgers and Hammersteins' went down to Washington last week-end when we presented a T.V. show on the occasion of a dinner for President Eisenhower—of all Presidents! This indicated no change in our political views but we were both happy to show that, unlike the Roosevelt and Truman haters who never let up in their jeers, we respect the chief executive office after the election is over. I think it is important to do this. We had a good bill—Ethel Merman, Helen Hayes, Lucille Ball and Desi Arnaz, Eddie Fisher, etc. Do you get Northern television shows down there? Maybe you saw it.

I was delighted to be told that I could write to you, even though I seem to be wasting the chance on rather unsensational material. The turkey is not entirely to blame. There isn't really any startling or important news.

Write to me when you can. I will write again soon whether or not I hear from you. The farm is more wonderful and peaceful than ever. I don't know but what I like it better in winter than in summer. If simple life is what one comes to the country for then the winter is the simplest time. The summer is perhaps a little too gaudy some days.

Dorothy and I look forward to having you and Nedda here as soon as you can come. If, before that time, you want visitors, just say the word. I didn't mean just in Connecticut—Louisiana is only a few hours more away from Pa. If one "took oneself lightly" he wouldn't even need a plane—Damn that Chesterton!

Love from us both –

Oscar

Billie Burke—Florenz Ziegfeld's widow and an actress best remembered for playing Glinda the Good Witch in *The Wizard of Oz*—wrote Oscar for his help arranging for "a proper resting place for [Ziegfeld] at Forest Lawn . . . I thought if you knew about this long cherished desire of mine to see a resting place for Flo more in keeping with his standing in the theatre—you might see your way to doing something about it—"

Oscar Hammerstein to Billie Burke, December 3, 1953

Dear Billie Burke:

Thank you very much for your letter. I was glad to hear from you, and did not in any way consider it an imposition for you to come to me with your problem (as you seemed to fear).

We all have varying senses of values and ideas of what is important and what is not. I have never felt it important for anyone to have a "resting place" after they died. There is no monument that can be erected to Flo that would be as lasting as the great things he has done in the American theatre, the people whose careers he started or influenced, people who in turn have influenced others and helped them on their way. He is indeed "The Great Ziegfeld" and nobody will ever take his place, which was unique. I do not urge that you agree with me that this is the important "monument", but I could not with any heart try to promote a piece of stone or bronze to take the place of the great facts of his accomplishments, and the memories we have of them.

Answering an implied question in your letter, my relations with Flo were always of the most pleasant. We were good friends, and I don't know whether he admired me, but I had a deep admiration for him and his work.

Thank you for writing to me. I feel complimented that you have turned to me, and sorry that I cannot in all honesty be of any help to you in this undertaking.

All good wishes.

Sincerely,

After George M. Cohan's death, a memorial committee was established to commission a statue in his honor. Hammerstein was the committee's second chairman, and saw the project through to its dedication in Duffy Square in 1959. Why Oscar was more sympathetic toward Cohan's cause than Ziegfeld's remains a mystery.

Oscar Hammerstein to Sherman Billingsley, The Stork Club, December 10, 1953

Dear Sherman:

Thank you for the Vintage Cologne. It's obviously too good to be sprayed all over me. I shall probably use it as a liqueur.

Best wishes for a Merry Christmas and a Happy New Year.

As ever,

Oscar Hammerstein II

Oscar Hammerstein to George Axelrod,[14] December 18, 1953

Dear George:

You're a hell of a rich playwright now, and charities are deductible, as your lawyer must have told you. The Federation of Jewish Philanthropies of New York has to raise $16,950,000 this year. I don't know if you are familiar with their work, but take my word for it, they do wonderful work

---

[14] George Axelrod was the son of Oscar's Columbia classmate and close friend, Herman Axelrod. George's play, *The Seven Year Itch*, opened in November 1952 and was an immediate hit. At 1,141 performances, it became the longest running play of the 1950s.

running among other things one hundred and sixteen hospitals and welfare agencies. How about five hundred bucks? Four hundred? . . . Anything, of course, that you feel that you can give will be deeply appreciated, and no money can be better spent.

All the best to you.

Your aging uncle,

Oscar Hammerstein II

Oscar Hammerstein to Billy Rose, December 22, 1953

Dear Billy:

One year you rolled around with $3000 for Federation of Jewish Philanthropies, and then you clammed up. This year they have to raise $16,950,000, which is $2,450,000 more than last year. You know about this crowd, and you know it isn't one of those rackets. It takes care of 116 hospitals and welfare agencies, and it's really a wonderful organization and one that has to be supported—especially by New Yorkers, and if you aren't a New Yorker, who is? What do you say?

All good holiday wishes.

As ever,

Oscar Hammerstein II

P.S. As you have probably heard, I am nuts about "Kismet", and we are arranging with Charlie Lederer to produce it in London. I think this is a theatrical property which might be much greater than any of you connected with it realizes. If it is properly managed it will run at your theatre for God only knows how long. It should then go out on the road for a long life, and be part of the stock catalogue for many, many years. It is "The Desert Song" of 1953, and while that may not seem terribly flattering today, "The Desert Song" was a great old warhorse in its day, and is still galloping strongly. This is getting to be a long postscript, and I don't want to take you[r] mind off the first part of the letter.

Kismet as a musical was conceived by Edwin Lester. It premiered at the Los Angeles Light Opera and its sister house in San Francisco in the summer of 1953. It opened on Broadway in December 1953, won the Tony for best musical and ran for 583 performances. It opened in the West End in April 1955 but not, it appears, under the auspices of Rodgers and Hammerstein or their Williamson Music subsidiary. They did produce several non-Rodgers and Hammerstein plays and musicals in the West End, including *The Pajama Game*, *Damn Yankees*, *Teahouse of the August Moon*, *The Desperate Hours*, *The Seven Year Itch*, and *A Shot in the Dark*. At least one of the reasons behind these productions was the difficulties they faced taking the profits from their own shows out of England.

Chapter Thirteen
1954

Begun in October, 1943, the national tour of *Oklahoma!* is finally winding down; it will close in Philadelphia in May. *South Pacific* will close on Broadway on January 16, after 1,925 performances, while its national tour will continue into 1955. *The King and I* will close on Broadway on March 20, its national tour beginning on the 22, and the London production will run into January of 1956. *Me and Juliet* closes on April 3; there will be no tour and no London production. Much of Rodgers and Hammerstein's attention through the coming year will be on the filming of *Oklahoma!* Their next musical, *Pipe Dream*, won't open until November 1955.

The year starts with Christmas thank yous . . .

Oscar Hammerstein to Dorothy Fields, January 3, 1954

Dear Dorothy:

It seems that you sent me another present as well as the iron, and Dorothy says I must thank you for that too. Why didn't you quit when you were even? Why did you take another chance? Anyway, you came out all right again because the shoe shiner is a big success. (Did you really send me this too?) It gives me a very dainty feeling in the morning when I put on my farm shoes and have that sweet little red pompom revolve over them, giving then a sheen and a gleam that I could see my face in if I could bend over that far.

More love and more wishes for a Happy New Year.

As ever,

Oscar Hammerstein to "Master" Stuart Scadron, January 4, 1954

Dear Stuart:

Thank you and your family for the very handsome shirt. That's number one. Number two, let me congratulate you on your debut as an actor in the

The Letters of Oscar Hammerstein II. Mark Eden Horowitz, Oxford University Press. © Mark Eden Horowitz 2022.
DOI: 10.1093/oso/9780197538180.003.0013

production "The Little Fir Tree". I am sorry I was not there to see the play. I looked in all the papers but there were no write-ups. You ought to get after your press agent and tell him to get on the ball.

Love and Happy New Year to all of you from your affectionate Episcopal, Jewish, Mohammedan godfather.

Oscar Hammerstein II

. . . and fundraising letters . . .

Oscar Hammerstein to Harold Rome, January 19, 1954

Dear Harold:

How about a donation for Federation of Jewish Philanthropies this year? You have donated before and then fell off the wagon, and I wonder if I can't pull you on again. This year is a particularly important one. We are trying to raise two and a half million more than usual, bringing it up to sixteen million. I don't have to dwell on the importance of this work. It is one of the really good and necessary charities.

The theatre has been making a very poor showing this year, but now we are making progress in raising old donations and getting new ones. I don't know what heading I'll put you under, but you can name your own title. Just cough up with as good a check as you think you can give me.

Switching the subject suddenly and without a cue, when am I going to hear that score?[1] I cannot rely on Josh's limited vocal attainments for much longer.

Love to you and Florence.

Oscar Hammerstein II

. . . and advice:

---

[1] *Fanny*—the show Logan had desperately hoped Rodgers and Hammerstein would write.

Oscar Hammerstein to Stanley Rich, January 21, 1954

Dear Mr. Rich:

I will not be able to see you because I am going down to Pennsylvania this afternoon to stay on my farm and work on my new show for several months.

I am always dismayed at receiving letters like yours—and I receive a great many—because it is very hard to know what to tell lyric writers except to continue to write lyrics, to find a composer, and then to find a publisher. I would not suggest that you go along too far without a composer because lyrics without music are even worse than music without lyrics. I mean they are hard to sell or to interest people. There is, unfortunately, no little musical theatre that I know of. I feel as I write letters like these that the whole theatre and the music publishing world is deeply at fault in not having any machinery for helping ambitious writers of music and lyrics. Somehow or other people do get their work produced. It is done by a combination of talent and un-remitting industry and patience. My only advice to you is to get yourself a composer and be sure that you like him and his music, and start writing songs with him. If you have an idea for a play, write the whole play with songs in it.

This advice is even more difficult to follow if you live in Lime Rock, Connecticut, because you are away from the base of all these activities, which is New York.

The only good thing I can tell you is that in the last analysis the quality of what you write will get you where you want to go, if it is good. There is a great desire, a great need for good songs, and if you can write one, it will find its way to publication and performance. You ask me to prove this. I cannot. It is just my belief.

All my best wishes to you.

Oscar Hammerstein to Nedda and Josh Logan, January 30, 1954

Dear Nedda and Josh:

I read the review of Clarence Derwent's[2] book with tears rolling down my cheeks. He has crowned his career with one of the greatest services one

---

[2] Clarence Derwent was a British-born actor whose Broadway career began in the teens and, though he seems to have worked fairly steadily, it was in productions that ran toward the mediocre.

could do for mankind. He has written a book which is obviously the harmless substitute for sleeping pills which we have all been awaiting. If you have any stock in those big chemical firms that put out those pills, sell now before the second edition!

Love,

Harry N. Sperber, a friend of a friend of Oscar's, sent him the following questions (which he indicates he's also sending to 150 "world famous persons"):

(1) As a child, did you dream of becoming what you are today?
(2) If not, what did you hope to grow up to be?
(3) What caused you to take the road of life which you have chosen?

Oscar Hammerstein to Harry N. Sperber, February 12, 1954

Dear Mr. Sperber:

I am sorry that I can give you no answers that can be of much use to you in the list you are compiling. As a child I did not dream of becoming what I am, nor do I remember hoping to grow up to be anything in particular, except possibly a professional baseball player. Those are the answers to the first two questions. The third question cannot be answered very simply. As you know, I come from a theatrical family who gravitate toward the theatre no matter what they start to do first. I was brought up seeing most of the plays that came to Broadway, and at least one vaudeville show every week. I went to Columbia to study law, but became interested in the Varsity shows there, and in the family manner, "gravitated".

Very truly yours,

Oscar Hammerstein II

Oscar Hammerstein to Arthur Hammerstein (excerpt), February 12, 1954

"The King and I" goes out on the road the end of March, just completing a three year run in New York. I expect it to do very big business on the road.

He was in five Broadway shows in 1925 alone. He was the president of Actor's Equity from 1946 to 1952. His memoir was titled: *The Derwent Story: My First Fifty Years in the Theatre in England and America.*

In fact, out on the coast we have some very big guarantees lined up already. We play the summer out there and then go down to the state fair in Dallas, Texas, where we have a very big guarantee. Then we move up to Chicago and try to play there as long as we can.[3]

"Me and Juliet" does not act like a champion. We have got back the $330,000 investment, and have made some, but I don't expect this to be a real smash like the others.

Dorothy and I may fly over to London for just a few days in April to see the opening of "Teahouse of the August Moon" over there. Dick and I and Louis Dreyfus acquired the English [rights] to this play, which is a big hit in New York this year. We also bought the musical version of "Kismet", which I think will be great for London.[4] But we won't produce that there until after "The King and I" has finished at Drury Lane, and that may be two, and even three years. The way it is going now there is no telling how long it will run. It's a real sensational hit. I like the company over there better than the company we have here—except for Brynner.

We have been making alterations on the farm, giving me a new dressing room for my morning massage, and more closet room for my clothes. Like all those jobs, it came to much more than I thought it was going to come. If the carpenter's bill doesn't surprise you, the plumber's will, and that's the way it goes.

Oscar Hammerstein to Paul Blanshard, George School, February 25, 1954

Dear Paul:

Here is a rough draft of a letter, which I would like very much to discuss with you after you have read it. I am flying to California on Sunday, February 28th, but I shall be gone only a week. Please get in touch with me after that.

All good wishes.

Sincerely,

Oscar Hammerstein II

---

[3] *The King and I* national tour ran for twenty-five weeks in Chicago, opening November 22.
[4] *Kismet* ran for 648 performances in the West End, as opposed to 583 on Broadway. It opened in April of 1955; Jack Hylton is the named producer.

Dear _____ :

Within the past two years United States Steel has built the largest steel mill in the country near Morrisville, Pennsylvania. Other plants for products that use steel have been and will be built in the near future, thereby creating new employment for more than a hundred thousand people so far.* To house prospective employees, thousands of homes have been erected. These have all been restricted to white residents.

When the steel executives were approached and asked to give a portion of these new jobs to Negros their answer was that there were not enough Negros available living in the neighborhood.

The builders of the new developments were approached and asked to permit Negros to live in these new developments, and their answer was that the steel people were not employing enough to make it worth while.

The builders also answered that they couldn't possibly permit Negros to purchase houses among the white section as it would immediately reduce the value of the property and start a great deal of trouble.

This letter is not an attack on either United States Steel or the builders of new residences in this area. Their actions result not necessarily from their own privately held beliefs, but from a regard for what they consider to be a general belief. The purpose of this letter is to find out how actual is this condition. Is it still true that property must go down in the neighborhood as soon as a Negro family moves in? Is this a myth or a fact? If it is a myth it is important that we expose it. If it is a fact it is important that we destroy it and turn it into a myth.

I am gathering opinions from people who are highly respected in our country. I therefore am asking for yours. First I will tell you mine, so that you may know to what extent our opinions coincide or differ.

It seems obvious to me that the real estate problem is a self-propelled one. If a Negro family takes a house on your block, why should the value of yours and all other residences deteriorate? If you and the rest of your neighbors continue to live there, it would be the same pleasant row of houses it has always been. But if you fall into a panic inspired by an anachronistic prejudice and fear of the new family, and if you start moving away, then of course the properties will go down because they will be thrown upon the market quickly. Under such circumstances new purchasers are frightened off. It is the panic from an ugly illusion that reduces real estate values, and not the mere fact of a new resident whose skin is darker than his neighbors.

If the new resident has a disorderly and slovenly family, it will not be good for the street. This would be equally true if he were white. If the new resident who is colored has a well behaved and well bred family, no one on the block is really injured.

You may think I believe this because I want to believe it. Of course I want to. But it has much more support than a mere desire on my part to respect the human race. The human race has already provided a good factual basis for my belief.

HERE INSERT STATISTICAL DATA.

Will you please write to me and tell me what you think of all this? I know you are busy, but I think that we are all obligated to give some time to this question It is a basic one. IT must be faced, and we have [no] excuse whatever for letting it drift on as it has drifted in this new and important industrial community at Morrisville, Pennsylvania.

I would like very much a letter from you with permission to quote you. If, however, for any reason, you desire not to be quoted, I would still like an expression from you, and will respect any limitation you place on my right to publicize it.

Very truly yours,

Oscar Hammerstein II

* Is this figure correct?

Oscar Hammerstein to Reverend Edward Conway, February 26, 1954

Dear Father Conway:

I have read only the first three scenes of "The Girl From Green Bay". Plays are difficult to read. People frequently make mistakes, liking some plays which fail, and not liking others which eventually succeed. I don't think this is difficult, however, to appraise. It is completely silly and unplayable. Feeling nothing but the kindest intentions toward any friend of yours, I implore the author to spend no more time on this project, and certainly no money—not her own or anybody else's.

My best wishes to you always.

Oscar Hammerstein II

Regarding the purchase of the French rights for *The King and I*, Anatole Heller, of the Bureau Artistique International, wrote to Howard Reinheimer: "I have meanwhile contacted here the, I think, best two French playwrights for the translation and adaptation. They are Jacques Deval and Marcel Achard. Both of them immediately pointed out that it is absolutely out of the question to locate the action of the French version in Siam. With the present political situation in respect to Indo-China, this would mean, in their opinion, to go straight to a sure flop. I had, from the beginning, the same fear in a less sharp form, therefore we should have the right to change the script insofar as 'Siam' should become an unnamed Asiatic kingdom."

Oscar Hammerstein to Howard Reinheimer, March 11, 1954

Dear Howard:

Regarding Anatole Heller and "The King and I" in Paris, I think that if he and the French public are so dumb, that we might as well forget about it. I am not willing to refer to Siam as an unnamed Asiatic kingdom. I think the play is sheer nonsense if it isn't about a real place.

Howard Reinheimer to Richard Rodgers and Oscar Hammerstein, March 24, 1954; enclosing a letter from James Michener, March 17, 1954

Dear Dick and Oscar:

I wrote to Michener again asking him for his opinion as to whether the United States—Japanese conflict was something that should be considered before making a deal with Japan. The enclosed letter is self-explanatory but leads nowhere.

May I suggest that one of you speak to Michener directly on the telephone and then let me know whether or not I should proceed definitely to close a deal.

Sincerely yours,

Howard

Howard E. Reinheimer

Enclosed letter from James Michener to Howard Reinheimer, March 17, 1954

Dear Mr. Reinheimer:

You raised a most difficult point in your letter of March 11th. I cannot even give an opinion as to whether SOUTH PACIFIC ought to be presented in Japan at this time. Let me share with you my thoughts, however:

1) Almost anything American that is presented in Japan at this time will call for considerable and noisy left-wing objection. Whether the material offered is good or bad, constructive or destructive, it is going to get savage treatment from these few, and insofar as there is anything in it which might legitimately draw their fire, to that extent their completely ridiculous additional charges will gain weight.

2) On recent trips to Japan I have been badgered by almost every major producer or movie company to:

(a) Write an original movie.

(b) Sell SAYONARA[5] for immediate stage production.

(c) Let Rodgers and Hammerstein release South Pacific.

(d) Act in Japanese movies.

(e) Release all of my works for immediate publication in Japan.

Everything I have released has been pasted by the left-wing and they have been fiendishly clever in picking out some weak spot in everything I have

---

[5] *Sayonara* was a 1953 novel by Michener. The story of an interracial romance was adapted into a highly successful film in 1957. It was directed by Josh Logan who immediately after directed the film of *South Pacific*.

done and making a big thing of it. On the other hand, from commitments offered me on my last trip alone, I could probably work in Japan exclusively for the next four years (I accepted none of them). I also know that the magazine which is currently serializing SAYONARA has increased its circulation 25%, which is astounding for the Japanese market. The magazine's editors themselves have advised me of this.

3) I would not suppose that any work of art would be criticized one way or another because it dealt with the general United States-Japanese conflict. Moving pictures of this kind, unless they were in outrageous bad taste, have been among the most successful in post-war Japan. Two young men I know have made a fortune out of peddling old American war newsreels.

I'm afraid I don't know what conclusions I myself would draw from the above evidence.

Sincerely,

Jim Michener

Oscar Hammerstein to Howard Reinheimer, March 30, 1954

Dear Howard:

Regarding the Japanese situation, after reading Michener's letter and thinking it over, I think we'd better forget about it.

As ever,

In March Edna Ferber wrote: "I am completely baffled by the SHOWBOAT [sic] City Center production plans. Here, according to your son William, is an operatic performance of SHOW BOAT (whatever that means) which won't be as good as the performance by the better company and better rehearsed company of the operetta season which comes later; and no Burl Ives in the first two operatic performances. This will, I suppose, get the reviews. My mind refuses to make any adjustment to this somewhat bewildering situation, but I am delighted to know that SHOW BOAT is being done at all."

Oscar Hammerstein to Edna Ferber, April 1, 1954

Dear Edna:

I don't blame you for being baffled by the City Center "Show Boat" production, but I believe I can make things just a little clearer to you. The "operatic" performance of "Show Boat" will be no different from the usual version except that the cast will favor singing rather than acting, since some of them are in the opera troupe. The reason for this is that the "operetta" season was made possible by putting "Show Boat" into the "opera" repertory, there being no allocation of funds for an operetta season. The money made from "Show Boat" will finance the operetta season, which consists of only two other plays, "Fledermaus" and "Carousel". They already have a production for "Fledermaus" and so I take it that "Carousel" will be the single new expense to the City Center Company. I am sorry I started to explain this to you because I am finding it very hard to understand myself. It seems that a certain fund, given by some generous civic-minded soul provides only for opera productions. "Show Boat" can be originally financed as an opera, but not as an operetta. Then after being financed, can suddenly be turned into an operetta, to the surprise of nobody at all.

The "Opera" performance will be reviewed by music critics, not by play critics.

I am exhausted!

Love,

After reading and re-reading an article Oscar wrote on "World Government" that had been published in the *Saturday Review Reader* several months prior, private Warren Moskowitz reached out to Oscar in a lengthy letter, asking: "Why don't we get behind a movement to educate the American people and the world of the functions of the U.N. and on the purposes of limited world government . . . What can we do, Mr. Hammerstein? Certainly we have an obligation to our consciences to do something _ _ _at least to speak out."

Oscar Hammerstein to Pvt. Warren Moskowitz, May 27, 1954

Dear Mr. Moskowitz:

Thank you for your letter. The United World Federalists are continuing in the directions you suggest. I must admit that at the present time we are meeting with more apathy than ever, but I hope this is only a passing phase. It seems surprising that with the threat of the A bomb and the H bomb and now the cobalt bomb that there is not a growing desire to engage in some constructive work toward peace, but a great many people seem to think it's easier to drift into war and wholesale destruction.

I am sorry I have not a more encouraging report, but I think we are at a very low point now and things may get better later on. Would you like to join the United World Federalists. I would be glad to send you a membership blank and arrange for you to receive the literature that we put out. The important thing for us all is to stick to our ideals and to keep working for them, even against discouragements which may be only temporary.

With every good wish, and thank you for your interest.

Very truly yours,

Oscar Hammerstein II

Oscar Hammerstein to Yul Brynner (in Cincinnati), April 19, 1954

Dear Yul:

Please forgive me for not writing to you sooner. Since I saw you I have been whirling around the country, to Hollywood and back. I worked there all day long every day, and I am just getting my breath and taking care of my mail.

I read your notes very carefully, and I have this to say: I agree with everything on the page. I think, moreover, that these notes reveal not only a thorough understanding of the play—which I knew you had—but a most subtle appreciation of Anna's character. Surely you cannot know the King any better than you know her. This is of course not surprising because the two of them are so interdependent on each other.

On the basis of these notes, I not only grant you permission to work with Pat,[6] but I urge you to, and I hope that she will respond as she ought to, and as I think she will. I think it is very nice of you to be making this offer, and I am sure that it can do the play nothing but good.

I'll see you on the coast.

All good wishes to you.

Sincerely,

---

[6] Patricia Morison played Anna in *The King and I* on Broadway and in the national tour with Brynner.

Rudolf Bing, General Manager, Metropolitan Opera Association to Oscar Hammerstein, April 23, 1954

CONFIDENTIAL

Dear Mr. Hammerstein:

How very nice of you to have written! My wife and I greatly regretted that you could not come but we hope to have you at the box more frequently next season.

There is one matter of great importance to me which I would like to discuss with you at your earliest convenience. Unfortunately, I am now on tour with the Company and in New York only on occasional "in between" days. I think, therefore, I had better give you, in a few lines, my idea so that you may think it over and then let me know whether you are willing to discuss it further with me when I am in New York next time which will be between May 8th and 13th.

I would very much like for the season after next, that is the season 1955-56 to produce an Offenbach operetta and I wonder whether you might be interested in adapting or rewriting book and lyrics somewhat on the lines that Garson Kanin and Howard Dietz, four years ago, adapted and rewrote "Fledermaus". I am particularly anxious to find a vehicle for Rise Stevens who has not had any new role in New York for quite a few years and who, I think, could adapt herself excellently to the style and requirements of such a work. I am thinking of "The Duchess of Gerolstein" but would be perfectly willing to consider another Offenbach work if you have a preference.

The main thing is that you should let me know whether in principle you would be willing to consider such a suggestion. If you are interested, please telephone Mr. John Gutman at my office who will then make every effort to send you a score and libretto as quickly as possible.

I look forward with great interest to hearing from you and would hope very much that you could see your way to agree to such a collaboration which I would greatly enjoy.

With king regards,

Yours sincerely,

Rudolf Bing

Oscar Hammerstein to Rudolph Bing, April 29, 1954

Dear Mr. Bing:

Your suggestion that I adapt an Offenbach operetta for you is a very attractive one, but I am afraid there is no chance for me to accept it. Dick Rodgers and I are working on a new play now, and somehow or other, while writing it we must also supervise the filming of "Oklahoma!" this summer. If we can get these two things done within the next twelve or fourteen months we shall be very happy indeed. I cannot therefore consider anything else for some time.

My best wishes to you for a pleasant summer.

Sincerely

Oscar Hammerstein II

Oscar Hammerstein to Marshall Field, Jr., *Chicago Sun-Times*, April 28, 1954

Dear Marshall:

Thank you for giving me the chance to read Dulles'[7] article in "Foreign Affairs". I am sending the volume back as you requested.

I found his description of the new look clear enough. I don't think it added anything to my former understanding of the theory, and I still think it is essentially "a theory". Recent developments in Indo-China seem to strengthen my opinion. There has been some talk by Nixon of our sending troops there. I do not hear anything about dropping bombs anywhere else, and I am very glad that I have not heard this, but if in a crisis of this kind we are still talking about whether or not to send troops, what is new about this "look"? It seems that we are discussing this as if the question were: Will it be another Korea, or will it not be? If we decided on the former course, we would have to go back to the old look, increase our appropriations for ground troops, increase our taxes to pay for them, and be right back where we were.

---

[7] John Foster Dulles was Secretary of State under President Eisenhower. A vociferous anti-Communist, Dulles was a principal architect of America's Cold War strategies and positions.

I am not going to criticize Dulles on the unfair basis upon which Acheson was criticized. I believe both men have faced the most difficult diplomatic problems in the history of civilized man. I don't expect miracles from either one, and I resent any claim of miracles accomplished by Dulles when he is facing the same troubles that Acheson faced, and seems to be no more a genius than was Acheson. I think both men are very intelligent and good men. I think that the new look will turn out to be the old look, or perhaps no look at all.

With this cryptic finish (which I would have difficulty in explaining myself) I will close my letter, echoing the same hope you expressed, that we shall all meet soon again.

All good wishes.

Sincerely,

Oscar Hammerstein II

Oscar Hammerstein to Dorothy Hammerstein, May 14, 1954

For
Dorothy,
My darling wife
On our twenty-fifth wedding anniversary
Three pieces of silver are bestowed
With my worship for her beauty
My gratitude for her bounty
And all the love in my heart.
They are to be used by her
For the purchase of real estate,
Objects of art, clothes, gems,
    Trinkets, fripperies or, indeed,
Anything but china.
From
Her devoted and happy husband,
Ockie

Oscar Hammerstein to John Steinbeck, May 28, 1954

Dear John:

Here are the first two scenes of "Pipe Dream" which, as you have read in your American papers is an adaptation of a new book by John Steinbeck called "Sweet Thursday".

It may seem as if I have done very little since the last installment your read, but in addition to finishing the second scene, I have also gone back and filled in all the lyrics. Lyrics take me a longer time than dialogue—especially when most of the dialogue is lifted bodily from "Sweet Thursday".

Before going on to the next scene, which will be in the Western Biological Laboratory, I am going to insert an intermediate scene between these two. It will be (1) for the purpose of making a scene change and (2) to prepare the audience for the flophouse, which is a rather bizarre and unusual community to jump an audience into without preparation. If you have read "Cannery Row" or "Sweet Thursday" you will understand, but there may be one or two people out front who only go to shows and at home look only at television screens, and will not have read the two books. So for their benefit I will put in a little scene and try to make it as entertaining as possible, while giving them the information I believe they will need.

Dick has now started to set these lyrics to music. He has been waiting for me to give him several lyrics at once so that he can achieve a balance for the score, and a variety of tempo and treatment. I haven't heard any music yet because I don't believe he has finished any of it. When I say he has started I mean today he has started. He is up in Fairfield and I am in Doylestown as I dictate this letter into my trusty Dictaphone.

You will find in the same large envelope another mysterious manuscript in which I wistfully hope to interest you. It is an undertaking by Robert Fulton (to set your curiosity at rest immediately he is indeed a great great etc. grandson of the inventor of "Fulton's Folly"). He is a United World Federalist, but this undertaking is under aegis of The Institute For International Order, which roughly speaking is the tax-deductible branch of the UWF. Bob has interested the Ford Foundation in this project. He tells me that he understands the United Nations had a similar idea for which they had enlisted your services and that it fell through.

I hope you will have the time to read through this brochure, and let me know whether you would be one of the contributors. I have assured Bob that I would be a kind of coordinator if we lined up enough good writers, and that my coordination would include editing to some extent, and whatever consultative value I could give to the television production.

On next Monday, May 31st, I am flying out to the coast to work on the production of "Oklahoma!" I am flying back the following Saturday so that I can help out with the United World Federalist dinner that Sunday night, June 6th. I am staying east until June 10th, because on June 9th Dorothy and I—really Dorothy with me kibitzing—are (is) staging a big fashion show for Welcome House, and trying to raise a few thousand dollars for them down here on the farm. She expects about fifteen hundred people, I think. On the tenth we both go back to California to stay. We have taken a house on Readcrest Drive (9360 Readcrest Drive, Beverly Hills) where we will stay well into October. My routine will be to devote the mornings (9 to 12:30) to "Pipe Dream" and the afternoons to "Oklahoma!" I will train my colleagues to leave me alone in the mornings. In the evenings I will tell everybody that I am working on "Pipe Dream" so that I don't have to go to those parties, but what I shall really be doing I hope is to go to bed at about 9:30 and get some rest. I hope Dorothy and I will both have the character to stick to this schedule. During most of the month of July we shall be in Arizona on the outdoor shooting.

I feel that I must be starting to bore you with these details. The source of my feeling is that I am beginning to bore myself.

We had an audition yesterday, and Harold Clurman[8] told me [about] the letter he had received from you. I am very glad you wrote to him because it apparently had a deep effect on him—of gratitude and confidence and security, which your endorsement gave him. I believe that Harold

---

[8] Harold Clurman was a drama critic, one of the co-founders of the Group Theatre, and directed some forty plays on Broadway, including premieres of works by Clifford Odets, William Inge, Arthur Miller, Carson McCullers, Lillian Hellman, and Tennessee Williams. *Pipe Dream* was the one Broadway musical he directed (*Johnny Johnson* is described as a "play with music").

may give us a very fine and sensitive job. I am trying now to condition him into looking for singers who can act well enough, rather than actors who can sing well enough. Both Dick and I feel optimistic about casting, even though we have so far decided on only one. The characters are so definitely drawn that I don't believe they will present a problem beyond the normal problem that is always there in seeking perfect casting.

As a matter of fact, casting has never been so difficult for me as it was when Elaine[9] was with the Guild. She always outplayed the people she was auditioning, and it was very difficult for me to keep my mind on the subject. Elaine is perhaps the most arresting figure on the stage in my memory and the most skillful scene-stealer. I don't think for a moment that this was unconscious on her part. I believe there was a real spirit of competition always present. Again and again I had the feeling that I was watching a sparring partner knock out the training champ, or the pacer outdistance the training runner. Fearnley is more self-effacing, but now we are having trouble even with him. He has bought himself a pair of grey silk pants, and they pick up highlights and glare back at the candidates. The sheen on the spears of those Assyrians was dull compared to Johnny's legs.

He is now out in Hollywood too, and auditions from now on will be of Barbara Wolferman,[10] for Barbara Wolferman and by Barbara Wolferman.

Our [anniversary] party was a big success—anyway, we liked it, and the word-of-mouth seems very good—at any rate what has come back to us. We were both sorry you couldn't be there to help us celebrate.

If you think that I am beginning to ramble on, you have no idea of how far I could go, because I am in a dangerously rambling mood. Feeling the danger acutely, I shall flee suddenly.

Love to you both.

---

[9] Elaine Steinbeck, *née* Anderson had been an actress and stage manager; she was an assistant stage manager on the original production of *Oklahoma!* She married John Steinbeck in 1950.
[10] Barbara Wolferman was assistant casting director for *Me and Juliet* and *Pipe Dream*.

P.S. Among the writers who have already promised to do programs for "The Thirteen" are Christopher LaFarce, Fanny Hurst, Cleveland Amory, Rex Stout, Robert Raynolds, Harry Overstreet and Mrs. Overstreet.

John Steinbeck (in Paris) to Oscar Hammerstein (in Beverly Hills), June 14, 1954

Dear Oscar,

Your letter, three scenes and brochure arrived a couple of days ago and I must say we are delighted with the scenes and the lyrics. What a good writer you are ! I think I understand your small intra-scene very well. It could be somewhat a shock to come across the Palace Flophouse without an introduction. The lyrics delight us ! Ma Soubrette read the scenes to us with feeling that would have destroyed you. I will be very happy not to hear what Dicky does with the lovely lyrics. I agree with you about Elaine. Sometimes I even feel that she is capable of catching flies extracurricularly but that is alright too. At least there are no flies on her. I am delighted that you are finally going to be in Hollywood, a goal toward which you so long worked !! It gives me a good feeling to know that virtue is sometimes rewarded in this world.

We are well and happy here and they have not put us in jail for it yet. The letter to Harold Clurman was heartfelt.

I come now to the undertaking by Robert Fulton. I didn't know that the plan of the United Nations had fallen through, although I should have known. A great many people promised to work but at the last moment I was told that they did not. I wrote a piece for them and read it on tape for them for broadcast which if they have not used it, might serve your purpose, perhaps with animated cartoons as a background. This material will be in the hands of Gerald Kean in Ben Con's office of the United Nations. I am quite sure that he would release it to you if you wish. And I believe that it is a better job than I could do offhand at the moment. Will you listen to it and let me know. Of course, you know I will do anything farther in my power to help along this cause.

The children arrived this week and I don't know whether a childless man like you will understand our enthusiasm ! This is the longest letter I am likely to write for the rest of the summer. Please do keep in touch and know that, happy as we are here, we will be delighted when we are all together again in the Ritz Hotel. Please ask Morrie Jacobs not to forget Elaine's $ 1000.- in the show and ask him if he wants it now. I can have my agent send it if he does.

Love to Dorothy and of course to yourself and do bore me again with the long letter when you have a moment.

Oscar Hammerstein to J. Lee, Weller, Son & Grinsted, June 8, 1954

Dear Mr. Lee:

The Gammer heifer arrived in reasonably good shape after her journeys, and we are taking good care of her and she seems to be happy in her new home.

I lack papers on her. I have so far received no registration or pedigree records. I know that there are some papers filed at the border, and it may be that I shall still receive some from the insurance agents, but as yet they have not come.

You can see why it is important to me to have her English registration so that I can register her over here.

Beyond the registration information, I am most anxious to get the heifer's pedigree for at least four or five generations back, because since the lines are not well known here, the more chance I have of having recognizable names the better, and the more names I have the more likelihood there is of my being able to show some that are known here. I would appreciate very much your getting this information to me, together with all details of any prizes or honors or prices in connection with the other members of this cow's immediate family. Please let me hear from you as soon as you can, and tell Mr. Cresswell for me that the cow has been received in good condition.

With all best wishes.

Sincerely,

Jeanne Bal[11] to Oscar Hammerstein, July 13, 1954

Dear Mr. Hammerstein,

I would like you to know that I feel that you did the best thing in not signing me for another year. Based upon what you have seen. Unfortunately you have not seen my performance since you worked with me in Hershey.

I realize now what my basic problem as an actress was and Mr. Hammerstein, no one worked on that problem except you. I honestly feel that I have not only successfully maintained the performance you saw after we worked together but that I have steadily improved and am continuing to improve. I feel that I am much better than I was in Detroit and you liked me then.

I understand that the reason that you and Mr. Rodgers let me go was because I failed to maintain direction. I would like an opportunity to prove that I have not only retained your direction but have improved beyond it within the pattern you set.

At this late date I realize there is no chance of my continuing in the part of "Nellie", so this letter is not an effort to keep my job. I am, however, concerned over leaving your employ without taking along your professional goodwill. My only interest is in showing you that I can now consistantly [sic] play a good "Nellie".

I have a plan that will only take one hour of your time. I realize that it is impossible for either you or Mr. Rodgers to come here and see me. But I can come to the coast and see you. I could bring a script and John Fearnley could read with me. I would like to do the first scene for you because that has always been the scene you liked me in least. I will gladly do any or every scene for you but I feel that the first will prove my point.

I can come out over any weekend convenient with you and still make my performance in good time.

I am writing this letter to you because it was you who last viewed my performance and worked with me.

---

[11] Jeanne Bal was the fourth Nellie to appear in the national tour of *South Pacific*, from July 1953 to July 1954. She went on to appear in several dozen television shows between 1955 and 1970.

Mr. Rodgers and John Fearnley worked with me on previous visits and the performance you saw in Hershey contained all of their correction.

I know only too well that my performance slipped, at which time I wrote Mr. Rodgers and asked for help, which I received from both he and Johnny. They were right in their correction because you did not change any of them except the first scene exit and one line in the beach scene. You went further and worked on my basic problem as an actress which ruined my "Nellie". In other words, I slipped only once and was completely fixed only once. I realize that this is once too often but I would like to keep the record straight. I am not likely to slip in this direction again with any part.

I would like an opportunity to do the first scene for you and Mr Rodgers so that you both, while you are together, might see your direction in effect.

As I said, my only interest is in leaving your employ with your professional goodwill.

What do you say Mr. Hammerstein?

Sincerely,

Jeannie Bal

Oscar Hammerstein to Jeanne Bal, July 18, 1954

Dear Jeannie:

If you and Ross are motoring out to California this summer for the fun of it I would be delighted to see you, but please don't make the trip for this reason alone because giving one performance in front of us would not prove your point. It is a question of giving many performances in succession with a company and in front of an audience.

Without this demonstration, however, I am perfectly willing to believe that your experience of the past year has indeed taught you to sustain a performance, and that the next chance you get you will succeed. I know that you were impressed with the talk we had in Hershey and if you will remember what I told you, you will not go wrong.

I believe that it is best for you to play another part now. You have got all you can out of "Nellie". Look around now and get yourself a new role.

Don't insist on its being a lead just because you have been playing a lead, and don't insist on the billing you have been getting. The only important thing for you is to find a character colorful enough to be effective. You are young and now you have had a very valuable experience. When we gave you the job you were only young. Go to it now. We have great confidence in you.

Our best to Ross and yourself.

Sincerely,

Oscar Hammerstein, II

Oklahoma! began filming its exterior scenes on July 14, continuing for seven weeks in Arizona and New Mexico. Interiors were then filmed at the MGM studios and wrapped on December 6.

Oscar Hammerstein to Dr. Harold Hyman, July 24, 1954

Dear Harold:

I was glad to get your letter and happy that you are so interested in SWEET THURSDAY. I don't suppose that I shall ever be able to bring out in the play all the things you see in the book but I am having a very good time with it and I think it may turn out very well.

We have been in Arizona for two weeks and except for a few quick trips to Hollywood we shall be here until about August 20th. Rain has interrupted our shooting a good deal but what we have on film so far looks fine.

Dorothy and I are enjoying our simple life living in a motel in Nogales. Every morning I try very hard to get Dorothy to let me cook breakfast but she always insists that she should be the one and I, being the better natured of the two, step aside!

I don't know when we will see you in Doylestown but if I can find a week anywhere within the next two months we will fly east and sneak down for a few days.

Please convey my sympathy to Marion for the vissitudes [*sic*] of the Dodgers. I am torn between sorrow for her and joy for Reggie.

We are flying up to Hollywood tonight and we're going to spend Sunday and Monday there. Alice, Phil and Melinda are stopping at our house before returning east. Billy is out here too so we will have kind of a reunion.

Love to you both,

Oscar Hammerstein, II

Oscar Hammerstein to John Steinbeck (in Paris), July 29, 1954

Dear John:

I hope you were not too disappointed on receiving the cable we sent you today. It took us several weeks to make up our minds, but for some time our subconscious knew very well that we were kidding ourselves. Oddly enough, our worries have nothing to do with any anxiety about finishing the adaptation. It was the time necessary for production which worried us. I shall not be back in New York until November 1st, and assuming that we could finish the book and score by January 1st, there was just no time at all to give this production of PIPE DREAM the care it needs. Our duties toward OKLAHOMA will extend beyond the shooting period (which will not be over until November 10th). They include cutting, exploitation and management.

Producing PIPE DREAM the following autumn can do nothing but benefit this project. I am sure you will understand this.

I hope you and Elaine and the family are having a wonderful summer in Europe. If you are not, and would like to charter a plane and come to Nogales, Arizona, you will be very welcome. Dorothy and I are living in a motel here, leading an extremely simple life and loving it.

We both send our love to you.

Oscar

Oscar Hammerstein, II

Norman J. Zierold to Oscar Hammerstein (excerpt), July 30, 1954

This is a humble request for one word from you, namely, the saddest word in the English language. What is it in your opinion?...

I'm a student at the University of Iowa, working my way through college not by selling magazines, but by writing for them. My work has appeared in the Kiwanis Magazine, the American Mercury, Popular Mechanics, and others. By now you've guessed that I'd like to build a feature around "The Saddest Word in the English Language"

My plan is to make the article largely pictorial---a photo of each person contacted, two or three salient biographical facts, "the saddest word," as each individual sees it, and his comment if he has any. I will do no interpreting whatsoever of quoted remarks.

Oscar Hammerstein to Norman Zierold, August 7, 1954

Dear Mr. Zierold:

The saddest word I know is "but".

Very truly yours,

Oscar Hammerstein, II

Oscar Hammerstein to John Steinbeck (in Paris), August 12, 1954

Dear John:

Thank you for your sympathetic and understanding letter regarding our decision to postpone. It was no surprise to me but a pleasant endorsement of a belief in you.

The element of surprise in your letter was the second paragraph in which you turned down my handsome invitation to Nogales, admitting, unblushingly, that you preferred Paris, followed by a trip to Italy and Greece. This betrays a sense of values difficult for me to understand, but as the not-yet-popular song says: "It takes all kinds of people to make a world".

Now about this third paragraph, these weekly pieces for Figaro etc. , are they in French or am I over-rating you? I hope so.

We are well satisfied with the way the picture is progressing, in spite of the fact that we've been held back a great deal by rain. It has not been so hot here. I wish only that the sky would stop perspiring and give us a chance to do same. It costs a great deal of money to send an army of technicians and actors out to a location in the morning and have them come back empty handed and wet to the skin at night.

Today, on August 12th, we have every intention of sending Elaine a cable on her birthday, two days hence, but in case we flop, this is a documented record of intent and a retroactive expression of good wishes for the day, which shall have passed by the time this letter arrives. When I start to write involved sentences like this I always know it is time to stop.

Our love to you both on all days as well as birthdays.

Sincerely,

Oscar

Oscar Hammerstein, II

Oscar Hammerstein to Max Gordon, August 25, 1954

Dear Max:

I am writing to you now for no particular reason except that I suddenly miss you and would like to say "hello" and to give you the report that I am just finishing a stay of almost two months in Arizona where we have been on location with OKLAHOMA! I believe we are getting some great stuff on film, but Zanuck always says that too! It has rained here nearly every day and all I can say is that the stuff we get had better be great because we could produce all the plays on Broadway for the next two seasons with the money that is going into this picture.

We return to California this Saturday August 28th and you can reach me at MGM Studios any time.

Dorothy and I have both enjoyed Arizona and will tell you all about it when we see you. At the moment it doesn't look as if we can get back to New York until the latter part of October.

Love to Millie and yourself.

As ever,

Oscar Hammerstein, II

Josh Logan to Oscar Hammerstein, September 1, 1954

Dear Oscar:

Half way through my rehearsals of FANNY, I suddenly felt compelled to write you because I have just read again your introduction to CARMEN JONES, which, as you know, is one of my favorite shows, ever.

I hear wonderful reports about OKLAHOMA. Nancy tells me that Leland and she saw several thousand feet of it and that it was the most tremendous experience they'd almost ever had. They have a feeling that it's going to be one of the biggest sensations in all show business. "It is a new kind of show business" to quote them. Naturally, I am terribly happy for you as I know this will mean an enormous amount to you both financially and what is more important, artistically.

Oscar, I thought a great deal about you during the last few months, while I was working on FANNY and I have kept your words of advice on the script close to my ear. I still feel that you will be borne out when you said originally that you thought it would be a "block-buster". It certainly looks like it to me now and I am on my fifteenth day of rehearsal. We had one run through of the first act and it has an enormous emotional kick to it. Harold has written some more songs and we've put rhythm under some of the ones you've heard and the whole score seems to have a variety that might have seemed to be missing when it was first heard.

WELCOME HOME is a sensation when Pinza sings it—and speaking of sensations Pinza is going to be, I feel, the sensation of the entire show. Even though Slezak is superb and perhaps is holding back at rehearsals waiting to use his lethal weapon when he reaches an audience, I don't think he can take the show away from Pinza, as Pinza is IT. As Slezak said, "Most actors to play this part would have to black up—use burnt cork, Pinza is already black".

Of course, the big news about any show is the discoveries and I think Florence Henderson is sent from heaven to us to play Fanny. She is all that a twenty-year-old girl could be plus the fact that she has a slight feeling of maturity. As Slezak says, she is not a girl, she is a little woman. And Bill Tabbert is a young prince who has had the spell lifted which was put on him by an evil genie at his childhood. He is radiant and loose and free, moves beautifully and of course that tenor voice is something beyond compare.

We have had a bit of trouble with the part of Honorine, but I think we have hit the right woman so far. The first idea, Jennie Goldstein, was good except that she just plain couldn't lose her Second Avenue accent. It wasn't Jewish, it was just New York with those double "t"s—and she should be a whale of a success in a Broadway musical if she could be correctly cast.

Marie Powers, who only flew over from Nice to replace her is even more of a disappointment because she is, as you say in your introduction to CARMEN JONES, a product of the singing teachers, she can't read just an ordinary straight line. I think we are going to replace them with a woman named Zamah Cunningham, who is real, and a good actress and has enormous breasts which have a lot to do with the success of Honorine, if I am to believe the French pictures. She is a bit like Mother Earth but she is also capable of a roll in the hay with a Senagalese soldier in Barbantine's warehouse.

And just so you won't get too worried about me, I must report that we have an Egyptian belly dancer in the show a young girl names Nejla Ates which translated from the Turkish means "sunset fire". She plays a dancer at one of the dives in Marseille where Marius goes to get his berth on the ship and later appears in Fanny's hallucinations in the second act, which have been worked out as a sort of ballet opera, a play within a play, which allows us to use our crowd of singers and dancers in exotic costumes. We have eliminated all the business of the child's dreaming. We have a tremendous ending now and I am very excited about the whole thing, as you can see. This is just a note to tell you about my progress and hope that you think of Nedda and me when you are talking with Dorothy, as we are real friends of yours and tremendous admirers, and we are so happy about the reports of OKLAHOMA.

I am delighted Mary Martin is bringing in PETER PAN which from all reports can be fixed. Unfortunately, she needed some professional help or a boss to help her, didn't she.

Leland had us all worried but I am delighted to hear that he is giving up some of these wild schemes of his and is going to be put in irons for a while by Nancy.

I hope MISTER ROBERTS will be a great picture and I am sure that John Ford will do everything to make it one. I also trust Hank Fonda to be our guardian angel on the script.

Oscar I certainly hope that you and I will get a chance before we get much older to get together again. I still have a feeling that we can achieve something together that would be a miracle. I don't know whether it should be in movies, or television or on the stage, but I have a feeling it should be in the musical theatre and perhaps in the operatic field. If you agree with me I should certainly like to know it.

Best love to everyone, to Dick and Dorothy and all of your co-workers.

Josh

Oscar Hammerstein to Josh Logan, September 3, 1954

Dear Josh:

I loved getting your letter. I have been wondering about FANNY and feeling vaguely disloyal because I am unable to hop a plane and run in on at least one rehearsal before you open.

All that you say sounds fine. I am particularly glad to hear that you think Pinza will come out on top because I think this would be a little better than if Slezak were to swamp him. Slezak is a formidable actor and I still think he will be hard to head off in the stretch. With Florence Henderson and Bill Tabbert pleasing you so well I don't see how it can be anything but a wonderful show. As for "sunset fire" I knew from the day that you put the rose between Helen Hayes' teeth that this was the beginning of a great career and that you would go up and up from there. Don't let people tell you that a little cultural element like a belly dancer will take the play over the heads of the public. They are grateful for a chance to study the primitive abdominal rhythms of the East and as long as you have plenty of entertainment to sugar-coat an academic touch like this it won't hurt a bit.

Dick and I saw PETER PAN Tuesday night and we and the two Dorothys liked it very much and think it has a fine chance. They have two sore spots, one is a little beyond the middle of the play when they are in their underground home. It goes a little too deep underground and needs pulling up with one lively dance number, and the elimination of some of the time given to serious sentiment. At the end of the second act, however, when Mary asks the audience if they believe in fairies the emotional quality falters for some reason I have not been able to analyze. I am going back to study this. This moment should be sure fire. I have the idea that perhaps

Mary goes at it too eagerly, too dramatically, and not with sufficient tenderness. It is as if (speaking in picture terms) she jumped a few frames to cut down to the finish.

Their other problem is a much needed telescoping of the last fifteen minutes down to about six or seven. I don't see why this cannot be done. Julie [sic] Styne, Betty Comden and Adolph Green have already interpolated one charming song and they are working on six more. I don't know what they can do with six but one great one would be fine.

I just had an S.O.S. from Dick to run over to the Sound Stage where he is pre-recording PORE JUD so I haven't time to give you as elaborate and enthusiastic endorsement of your last paragraph as it deserves. Let me just say yes, yes, yes, yes, I want this to happen.

Love to you and Netta[12] and extravagant wishes for "FANNY".

Oscar Hammerstein, II

Fanny opened on November 4 to mixed reviews but had a successful run of 888 performances. The primary complaints suggest that the show was overproduced, that a fairly simple and tender story was thrown off balance by Logan and producer David Merrick's efforts to make it a more colorful spectacle. Slezak and Pinza's performances were well received.

Peter Pan opened on October 20. It was profitable, despite the fact that it ran for only 149 performances, but its short run was planned from the start, as it culminated in a live telecast starring Mary Martin. The score was initially by Moose Charlap and Carolyn Leigh, but Jule Styne, Betty Comden, and Adolph Green were brought in and wrote several additional songs.

Oscar Hammerstein to Hal Levy, October 12, 1954

Dear Hal Levy:

I needed no expression of gratitude from you because I had a great time the other night, and far from being fatigued found myself stimulated throughout the evening.

---

[12] The original letter is in the Joshua Logan Collection where Hammerstein has personally corrected the spelling of "Nedda", drawing a line to a note that reads "She is not quite so famous out here." As Nedda Harrington she had a respectable career on stage and in film.

I am very grateful to you for the kind things you said to me in your letter of October 6th and doubt very much if I deserve them. As for the jar of marmalade you sent me, please tell your mother that no man deserves anything as good as that. In spite of my unworthiness, however, I am knocking off a good portion for every breakfast and enjoying it to the full. Please don't let it get around that this was my profit for the evening because if the government sleuths should get at it they would immediately establish a 200% tax on it! Please thank your mother for me and remember me to your class and tell them how much I enjoyed being with them.

With every good wish.

Sincerely,

Oscar Hammerstein, II

Howard Reinheimer to Richard Rodgers, copied to Oscar Hammerstein, October 29, 1954

Re: King & I—Rex Harrison

Dear Dick:

As you have already noted from the Photostat, which I sent you yesterday, Harrison is absolutely taboo for a replacement. This situation arose from a very acrimonious affair between Harrison and Zanuck several years ago. Oscar suggested that time is a great healer of tempers and that possibly Zanuck many not be so heated today as he was when our contract was originally signed. Accordingly, I spoke to Joe Moskowitz today. Joe is going to the Coast next week, and when he gets there, he will discuss the matter with Zanuck. He thinks it is possible that Zanuck may have cooled off by now and would give an O.K. if you and Oscar wanted Rex. In the meantime, I told Moskowitz that we would do nothing about contacting Harrison pending word from him.

Sincerely,

HER

HOWARD E. REINHEIMER

Rex Harrison played the King in the 1946 film *Anna and the King of Siam*, and Rodgers and Hammerstein discussed casting him in their musical version. Harrison was a star of both stage and screen, though not one known for doing musicals. That would change in 1956 when he starred in Lerner and Loewe's *My Fair Lady*, but at the time of this letter his ability to pull off a musical was unknown. Although in retrospect Yul Brynner was the obvious choice to reprise his part in the film, at the time he had played only a minor part in one minor film.

Richard Rodgers to Oscar Hammerstein, October 29, 1954

ROUGH DRAFT

Dear Oscar:

These are my thoughts in general concerning THE KING AND I.

For the most part I agree with Darryl's comments regarding length. I think that to attempt to release this picture in anything not less than two hours would be disastrous. One of the reasons his present picture script is so over length is because, it seems to me, the author has retained practically the entire play script and has reinstated most of the original picture script, to say nothing of anything original he may have added, which I am not in a position to identify, When the material involved in this rather long score is also added, the total is a staggering one. Whether or not whole sections can be eliminated is a question, but certainly there are long discussions that you and I did not find necessary in the theatre. For instance, on page 34 we have a discussion between Chulalongkorn and Anna which is not vital to the play, and this carries over through page 35 and 36 with Anna and the Kralahome. Also, for instance, on page 43 running into page 44 the same is true of the dialogue between Anna and the King. We get the same thing three times to establish the fact that ANNA is annoying the King about his promise: first, the little China house, second, the child's recitation, and third all the kids singing No Place Like Home. Surely, one of these would do by itself. On page 79 once again the undergarment thing is over-written. I question, on page 86, whether or not we need quite so much between Sir Edward and Anna.

The above are symptoms of the disease that Darryl finds in the script.

When he speaks about cuts in the score I am not sure he is without justification here as well. In the interest of doing a good job with material such as "Hello Young Lovers" and "Puzzlement" I would be willing to sacrifice "Lord and Master", but there is very little in the score that I would like to see go in favor of another plot song such as the new one suggested in this script. If the score is too long as it is, surely we won't help it by adding to it.

I am not against it, but I think we should reopen the question of putting "Hello Young Lovers" in the first scene and "Whistle a Happy Tune" in the second one. My worry, chiefly, is that we start off rather darkly and that "Lovers", being a slow song, may give the audience an impression that they're in a slow picture. "Whistle A Happy Tune", on the other hand, would give them a contrary feeling but would establish a facet of Anna's character, which is just as important to the play as her attachment to her late husband.

Do you think it wise to eliminate the musical device we had in the play for the Siamese language? The author may have had the feeling that the picture would demand too much of the same sort of thing. I don't like to surrender a device that has as much charm as this unless it is really necessary.

I think it is probably not too early to start talking to Jerry Robbins about doing the picture. It may even be too late.

The dramatic and pictorial values of the elephant device are remarkably good. I think that in the play it was always a little unclear as to why the King had to die. In this version his insecurity obviously forces him into an act of bravado which ends in a fatal injury. The source of his insecurity is the same in both versions but in this one it is clear and immediately dramatic.

Now for a few brief and not awfully important questions.

The last speech on page 2: I would suggest that the speech be inverted and that it read "It doesn't matter what kind of country Siam is, Captain Orton, I'll have a means of livelihood and a home of my own . . . a place to bring up my little boy to be as much like his father as possible". Its present form seems abrupt and expository.

The dissolve going from page 11 to page 12 leads me to believe that this scene shows immediately the scene on board ship. If this is the case I don't know how we get to sunlight so suddenly. However, if there is supposed to be a time lapse I think we need a device to show it.

Page 16—the bit about Anna being 150 years old evades me.

Page 25—if we keep "Lord and Master" I like it in this position very much.

Page 132—I think we ought to discuss the advisability of having the voices sing "Wonderful" at the end of the picture.

Do you think there is any wisdom in bringing up the question of doing this in Todd-AO or will this be so antipathetic to 20th Century's CinemaScope ambitions that they will not be able to consider it at all?

The film of *The King and I* was released in June of 1956. Its running time is variously counted as 133 or 144 minutes, depending on whether the showing includes the "Overture," "Entr'acte" and "Exit Music." Four songs from the stage production were cut: "My Lord and Master," "Shall I Tell You What I Think of You," "Western People Funny," and "I Have Dreamed." The film was directed by Walter Lang, who previously directed *State Fair*. The screenplay was by Ernest Lehman, who went on to do the screenplays for *West Side Story* and *The Sound of Music*. Jerome Robbins recreated his choreography. At one point there were plans for the King's death to be the result of his being gored by a white elephant.

Eleanor Weitzell McMahon spoke to Oscar at a United World Federalist dinner and in a follow-up letter she sent him a series of questions in lieu of an interview. Among her questions: "Do you believe that songwriters unconsciously reflect the values of their society, or do they consciously attempt to select themes which the public has already accepted? Do they lead, follow, or what? . . . How common are songs which deliberately attempt to lead or arouse public opinion, and how popular are such songs compared with those which simply reflect current thought? . . . "

Oscar Hammerstein to Eleanor McMahon, November 19, 1954

Dear Miss McMahon:

I have written in answers to your questionnaire which I have enclosed. In general, there is only one rule, that is for a songwriter to find some thing to say and say it as well as he can.

Your questions show a tendency to believe in polls and statistics. I don't, and I don't believe that a songwriter whose one motive is to guess what the public wants and try to give it to them will wind up anywhere at all. The song must be a sincere expression by someone of something which he considers important or heartwarming or amusing. Whether the public will agree with him must be left to fate.

Very truly yours,

Oscar Hammerstein, II

Prince Littler, Managing Director, Theatre Royal, Drury Lane to Oscar Hammerstein, November 17, 1954

My dear Dick and Oscar,

"THE KING AND I"

At a Meeting of the Board of the above Company this week several of my colleagues expressed dismay and considerable anxiety over the announcement that Miss Valerie Hobson[13] was to be married and leave the cast in January.

You will remember that when our recent Library deal was renewed, the Libraries were told of the arrangements that had just been completed for both Miss Valerie Hobson and Mr. Herbert Lom, and I am sure that if either of these artistes left the cast, they would feel that they had not had a fair deal.

Personally, I feel that Miss Hobson had so much publicity at the opening that her name is linked with the show, and I shall indeed be sorry to see her leave the cast, and trust that you will use your very best endeavours to retain her services as long as is practicable.

I feel that with the heavy costs of production for such a musical as "THE KING AND I" the principals also have a duty to us so that we may have an opportunity of recouping this heavy expenditure together with a reasonable return, and it is quite obvious that if one of our stars leave the production it cannot be otherwise than harmful.

---

[13] Hobson was an Irish-born film star who appeared in nearly fifty films between 1932 and 1954. *The King and I* was her final role. She opened the show in London in October 1953 and stayed until May 1955. On New Year's Eve 1954, she married John Profumo, a member of Parliament and the Secretary of State for War. In 1961 Profumo had an affair with the young model Christine Keeler who, it turned out, was also having an affair with a Soviet naval attaché. When the news broke in 1963, the scandal—the "Profumo Affair"—rocked the UK and helped bring down the Conservative government.

I would raise no difficulty if Miss Hobson wanted to have two weeks holiday for her honeymoon providing it was made quite clear at the time that she would return to fulfill the remainder of her contract as I should not want to be difficult with such a charming woman. At the same time one has to consider our obligations to ourselves, the Libraries and the general public.

Kindest regards to you both.

Yours sincerely,

<u>Prince</u>

Oscar Hammerstein draft letter to Valerie Hobson, circa November, 1954

Dear Valerie,

This is an extraordinarily difficult letter to write but it has to be done and you must be as patient and understanding as possible.

We have just received a letter from Prince Littler telling us that the Drury Lane company had a Board Meeting at which dismay and anxiety were expressed over the announcement that was made that you were to be married and leave the play in January. Prince points out to us that the Libraries made a deal on the assumption that both you and Herbert Lom were staying with the cast and his fear is that if either or you should leave it, both the theatre and the management of the play would be placed in an embarrassing and even difficult position. He feels that nobody could reasonably object to your taking a fortnight holiday for a honeymoon and says that he "should not want to be difficult with such a charming woman".

In all of the above we must concur. There is an obligation to our business friends in the Libraries, to the co-owners of the theatre and to our partners in the production. Beyond and above these considerations, there is a debt to the public which has been extraordinarily good to all of us. Insofar as you yourself are concerned, you have made such a great personal success and have so charmed the London public that it has now become an onus which only you can carry. You must do your best to sort out the various issues involved in this situation and you must try to realize that all of us, especially Prince and we two, have given this considerable and deep thought. This may be gratuitous and we hope that you won't mind our saying it, but a public that has treated all of us so nobly must be treated equally well by us all.

We send you our fondest regards.

Affectionately,

R.R.

O.H.

The above letter appears to be the first of two drafts. There's no indication whether the second or any other letter was ever sent. On the first letter there is a question mark next to the first paragraph; there are additional notes in the margin which appear to inform the draft below.

Oscar Hammerstein draft letter to Valerie Hobson, circa November, 1954

Dear Valerie:

It boils down to this: A very nice girl is soon to be married and, as the King of Siam might say, "all of her friends are happy thereof". There is a complication. The girl is a very important star in a very important West End attraction. A star is not merely an actress playing a part. She has responsibilities to her fellow artists whose current professional destinies and incomes are involved with hers. She has obligations to those who have invested time and talent and money in the attraction in which she stars. They in turn have obligations toward the owner of the theatre, and the libraries who have bought tickets in advance on the representation that she was to remain in the cast. And all—star, management and theatre owner—have a very deep obligation to the public who have thus far supported them so royally. This trust cannot be lightly held. Before reaching the phase where legal rights are stressed there are strong moral rights which must be considered, and we urge you to be mindful of these.

Our delay in writing this letter (for which we must apologize) has been caused by our anxiety to be fair and more than fair to you. If it were possible to give you exactly what you want and still be honest with the London public, the theatre, the company and all others involved, we would cheerfully give it to you. But we have conceived of no way to do this. The difficulties are not theoretical. There are already signs at the box office of The Lane of a reluctance to book after Christmas. This is surely due to the uncertainty established in the minds of the public regarding your continuance in the show. The announcement of your desire to retire from the theatre has naturally received wide publicity.

We have a letter from Prince Littler telling us that the Drury Lane company had a board meeting at which "dismay and anxiety were expressed" over the announcement that was made that you were to be married and leave the play in January. He points out to us that the libraries made a deal on the assumption that both you and Herbert were staying with the cast, and his fear is that if either of you should leave it, both the theatre and the management of the play would be placed in an embarrassing and even difficult position. He says:

"I feel that with the heavy costs of production for such a musical as "The King and I", the principals also have a duty to us, so that we may have an opportunity of recouping the heavy expense together with a reasonable return, and it is quite obvious that if one of our stars leave the production it cannot be otherwise than harmful. I would raise no difficulty if Miss Hobson wanted to have two weeks holiday for her honeymoon, providing it was made clear at the time that she would return to fulfill the remainder of her contract, as I should not want to be difficult with such a charming woman".

In all of this we concur. We would be glad to grant you a vacation for the honeymoon of what we hope will be a very happy marriage. We have nothing but good will toward you, and good wishes for your future, but we think that in the flush of your new excitement you were premature and a little reckless in making announcements of retirement long before the expiration of your contract. Such an announcement made, not by a girl playing a part in a show, but by a very important star, was highhanded and not very well thought out. Under the circumstances it may have been forgiveable [sic], and so we forgive you. But we cannot see what possible reason exists for us to go so far as to collaborate with you in breaking faith with our business associates, "The King and I" company and the public.

We are sure that in spite of your disappointment you will understand the good sense in this letter. We know you to be an intelligent and conscientious lady of the theatre and there is no reason to expect you, in the last analysis, not to behave like one.

Our sincere good wishes and love.

Oscar Hammerstein (draft letter) to Mr. Draper, circa November 1954

Dear Mr. Draper:

We have very carefully considered the suggestion in your letter of November 10th that we open the picture version of "Oklahoma" in Oklahoma City. The reasons you advance are very sound, and furthermore we are sentimentally inclined in that direction. Our colleagues, however, who are in charge of distributing the film, believe that there is nothing like a New York opening for launching a picture of any kind. In fact, they are already committed to this in the case of "Oklahoma". Beyond the normal motion picture reasons, in this particular case there is the consideration of equipment for a new process. The Todd A-O process will require an elaborate installation in the Rivoli Theatre in New York. The succeeding installations will be less elaborate and less expensive, but the initial one will involve such an investment as to make it impractical for a theatre in Oklahoma City. This as we say will not be true of succeeding presentations, but the inaugural investment will be very difficult to retrieve in a city of 300,000, even considering the other populations you would draw on.

This is a very reluctant decision that we report to you, but we are afraid that it is an essential one. Thank you for your suggestion.

We send you our best wishes.

Sincerely,

The model letter below was sent to dozens of prominent Americans. It was not, so far as I can tell, at the behest of any other individual or organization.

Oscar Hammerstein to "John Doe", December 20, 1954

Mr. John Doe
100 Main Street
Podunk, Michigan

Dear Mr. Doe:

Do you believe that the simple fact of a negro family moving into a neighborhood reduces realty values there?

Or do you believe this is an outdated theory that should be and can be exploded now?

Within the past three years, twenty odd miles from my home in Bucks County, Pennsylvania, the United States Steel Corporation has built the largest integrated steel mill in the country. Other plants involving products that use steel are rapidly rising near the mill. Since March, 1952, the number of factory jobs in that part of the country has more than doubled. Some twenty thousand new homes have been or are being built to house prospective employees. The sale of these homes, however, has been restricted to white residents.

From the beginning, United States Steel executives were urged to continue here the excellent practice established by them in their other plants—the practice of hiring in merit and irrespective of color. Their answer was that not enough qualified Negroes had applied from the neighborhood. It was quite true. Not many prospective Negro workers lived in that neighborhood. It was also true that not enough prospective white workers lived in that neighborhood, but homes were built for them!

This letter is not an attack on the United States Steel Corporation, nor on any of the various individuals or companies behind the home-building projects in this area. It is granted that their actions result not necessarily from their own beliefs, but from a regard for what they consider to be the beliefs of the general public. This letter seeks to find out what are "the beliefs of the general public". I am gathering opinions from Americans who have demonstrated their interest in human relations. I am therefore asking for your opinion. First let me tell you my own, so that you may know how we coincide or differ on this subject.

I believe that the real estate problem is a self-propelled one. It is obvious that the simple act of a negro moving into a house in your neighborhood does not automatically reduce property values. If you and your neighbors continue to live there, it will remain the same pleasant residential section it has always been. If, on the other hand, you and your neighbors fall into a panic inspired by fear or prejudice, put your homes up for sale and start an impulsive exodus, then of course values will decline. It is this traditional panic of the white property owner which affects values—not the skin coloring of the new neighbor.

If this neighbor, regardless of his color, is disorderly, it will not be good for your area. If the new resident who is colored is as well behaved and well bred as you want all your neighbors to be, no one and no property will be injured.

On the item of property values, a national study made in recent years disclosed that the Negro takes good care of property if it is in good repair when obtained. A Federal Housing authority shows that Negroes have a slightly better record of maintenance and payment than whites earning comparable incomes. There are numerous examples of public housing developments which have successfully operated with residents who are both white and colored. There are a few private developments (and they are increasing all the time) which have been built and operated on this policy and without any violent signs of racial tension. There is a development in Bucks County called the Concord Park Homes, a project of one hundred and forty units. Before it was started rival builders predicted certain trouble, and they also said the property values would be reduced serious by this policy. Their prophesies have not proved true.

What are your thoughts on this subject? Will you please write and tell me? I know you are busy, but I think we are all obligated to give some time to this question. It must be faced. No thoughtful American in any part of the country can afford not to face it. We cannot stand by and let the matter of segregated housing drift on as it has in the new and important industrial area recently established in Bucks County, Pennsylvania, U.S.A. Something must be done to avert a repetition of a mistake so tragically unjust as this one.

I would like very much to receive a letter from you with permission to quote you. If, however, for any reason you desire not to be quoted, I would still like an expression from you, and will respect any limitation you please on my right to publicize your words.

Very truly yours,

Oscar Hammerstein II

Oscar created two compilations of excerpts from twenty-eight of the responses he received. Those selected included Francis Biddle, Bernard Baruch, Curtis Bok, Norman Cousins, James Michener, Newbold Morris, Elmer Rice, Eleanor Roosevelt, Lessing Rosenwald, Budd Schulberg, and Bruno Walter. I assume Oscar's intent was to make his study public in some forum, perhaps in a newspaper or magazine. However, I've found no evidence that he succeeded, though he certainly must have shared it with individuals and organizations. The complete letters (and more that were not chosen for excerpts) are found among his papers.

George Skouras to Oscar Hammerstein, December 21, 1954

Dear Oscar:

Yesterday I saw the Dream Ballet number, I went to Arthur Hornblow's office and told him that in my opinion it lifts the value of the picture by about 40%. I don't want to bore you by attempting to tell you why the ballet is so great, but it brings out the depraved sex villainy of Judd and, being within the story, it makes the story itself strong and virile.

The Smokehouse Scene in my opinion is sublime, but I was annoyed and depressed by Eddie Albert's part as the Peddler, particularly his voice. In my opinion, his effort to speak with a Middle East accent is just a flop and I am afraid the critics will pick on it. To avoid that, I wonder if it is within the realm of possibility, taking into considerations contracts and other obligations, to dub in somebody else's voice for Albert's, which would be more convincing and more in the feeling of the character that you have created or, at least as I understand him to be.

I am sending this to you as a suggestion and if you think it is impossible, throw my letter in the basket and forget it.

With my best wishes.

Sincerely,

George

George P. Skouras

Oscar Hammerstein to George Skouras, December 28, 1954

Dear George:

I am very happy that you like the ballet so well, and that you now see how the picture gains momentum and substance and dramatic interest as it goes on.

I discussed your idea about dubbing in Eddie Albert's part with Freddie Zinnemann who has been spending Christmas with me. He does not think that would be practical, or an improvement on what we have.

I am looking forward to seeing you soon on your return from Rome. Meanwhile, a very Happy New Year to you.

Sincerely,

Oscar Hammerstein II

Arthur Hammerstein to Oscar Hammerstein, December 22, 1954

Dear Oscar:

Thanks for calling me on my Birthday. I feel much better after having talked to you about the manuscript, and to know you will take over for me and be sure that the book is made right. I'm not well enough to go to New York to fight it out with Jimmy [Vincent Sheean] and Simon and Schuster. I hate to give up but I'm really very tired. If Jimmy can't do justice to the story it's better to discard the whole thing, unless you will write it.

You will remember, Oscar, that three years ago Schuster came down here to see me and get the story of my father's life direct from me. I talked to him for three hours, about the tragedies, humor and sacrifice of a man who devoted his life to give the public music—grand opera was discussed very little. As you know, Schuster was so enthusiastic about what I told him that I doubted his sincerity, until he assured me that he thought it a great story and wanted to publish it—what happed to Jimmy that he missed the boat completely?

Enclosed are Chapters VII through XV. I have made very few notes in these chapters. For your convenience in checking my notations I have made a list of the pages on which they appear and attached it to the first page of Chapter VII. When you talk to Jimmy you will know if Chapter XV concludes the book. I think it should be added that after the death of my fa-ther Jimmy Walker wanted to call Times Square Hammerstein Square, and that I built the Hammerstein Theatre in memory of O.H. (with stained glass windows depicting all the operas that he had created in America, etc. etc.)

On the whole, I am greatly disappointed in Jimmy's manuscript. It was my understanding that he was not going to handle the biography strictly as such but would build up the story of my father's love of music, where it came from in the family, and how it ruined his life by trying to educate the public to grand opera. I never wanted the book to be "funny", on the other hand there are so many humorous incidents omitted, from both the research work and those I gave Jimmy, which intermingled with the drama, would make a terrific story. There seems to be so little about the Old Man, in comparison to the pages of research about opera, opera singers and conductors, that if all this is put in a section to itself I doubt if Jimmy will have enough left to make a book.

Why did the Old Man sacrifice himself and others for opera? Was it for his own pleasure or for the benefit of the public? Wouldn't he be in the same category as other great philanthropists, such as Marconi, Edison and Hudson, to name a few? It seems to me that his was an ever greater sacrifice—these other men stood to be financially successful in their endeavors, while my father didn't have a chance to succeed financially (and he knew it).

So much space is devoted to Mary Garden that it seems almost as much a biography of her as of O.H. I would like to put the record straight that she was not the "savior" of the Old Man's years in opera. She was lucky that he picked her from the Opera Comique to come to America. What did she had [sic] to lose? Nothing! Other singers drew and even larger crowd, such as Cavalieri, Melba, Tetrazzine and Renaud. There wasn't a night Cavalieri played Tales of Hoffman that she didn't turn them away—that much credit she deserves. Mary Garden thought we had brought Cavalieri to the opera house to play her roles and that's what made the trouble between her and the Old Man. Although she was wrong about this it wasn't a bad thought because we had to change our repertoire on account of Garden's illness.

If Simon feels that the public already has too many books about opera singers, why all this about Garden?

Many is the time it was necessary for Coini and I to stay up the entire night to change the repertoire for the next performance because Garden would give us such little notice that she would not go on. My thanks for this from the Old Man was an accusation that I was "drunk again" because of my red eyes and tiredness from lack of sleep. Coini and I were careful not to let him know ahead of time that Mary Garden could not go on because he would have substituted a fat dame in her place.

My father's weakness for fat women proved disastrous on more than one occasion. He got rid of petite Anna Held and put in obese Alice Rose to play the doll in La Poupee (at the Olympia). Needless to point out the full house soon dwindled to practically no one.

When Jimmy was at the farm the last time I was there he talked of making Caruso's refusal to come with us the big climax—I found nothing but a mention of it . . . . . .

Jimmy has a copy of the book of research I have, yet he omitted many interesting and important incidences. Neither did he use the humorous or dramatic events I gave him in conversation. I refer briefly to a few of them:

1. When the panic was on in 1907 the President of the Lincoln Trust Company, a friend of my father's, called him on the phone and asked if he could make a deposit in order to help regain the confidence of the public and stop the rush on the bank. The Old Man gathered together his subscription money and all of it in the box office, totally $50,000, and deposited the whole amount. When this was rumored the run on the bank was stopped and his money was safe, too, though he took the chance of losing all of it to help his friend.

2. O. H. was asked by reporters, "With what are you going to open the London Opera House?" The Old Man's answer, "With debts!"

3. The Old Man cabeled [sic] me from London when we were building the Philadelphia Opera House, the only reason to remind me, "Don't forget the flagpole."

4. At the time he built the Lexington Theatre he designed it for an opera house—he gave me "hell" for permitting my name to be on the contract with the Metropolitan, prohibiting us from giving opera for a period of ten years. He could have produced opera under my name!

5. Jimmy was to get the name of the tenor whom O.H. took from the Academy of Music in New York (the Academy of Music had to close when he left them for us). The first night he opened in Rigoletto he started to sing Aida—we finally found out he was crazy and had to let him go.

6. Ask Jimmy _why_ he didn't use the incident of the time I found the Old Man grappling with the conductor in his office at Manhattan. It was time for the orchestra to begin—I asked Coini where the conductor was and he told me to go to my father's office. I had just come from a meeting at the Metropolitan where I was informed they wanted my father to direct the German and Italian operas at the Metropolitan and the French operas at the Manhattan. My elation of carrying the good news to the Old Man turned to disgust when I found him fighting with his conductor—at curtain time— because he had learned through his detective that the other man had been out with d'Alvarez the night before.

7. When we were building the Olympia I asked O.H. why he gave the order for elevators to Otis when the ABC[14] firm quoted us much less. His answer, "I wasn't going to pay for them, anyway, and Otis can afford to lose."

8. An incident that could have been made extremely funny, but was only commented on, was the time the butler took away Campanini's food— as hungry as he was he was too polite to eat while meeting guests at Mrs. Mackay's (though all the others were eating). Much more importance should have been given to Mrs. Mackay, including the emerald she gave Campanini, etc.

Jimmy has done the same thing as the other authors who attempted my father's biography—giving all research and no story. The gamble O.H. made for grand opera should be wonderful reading from beginning to end—but the "old Man" should be paramount throughout, not the operas and singers _he_ made famous.

There are innumerable other stories that should be told, in addition to the above; for instance, Jimmy should have enlarged upon all the other data about Koster & Bials, and the fight in the street between O.H. and Kessler. There was the Harlem situation; the foreclosure of the Olympia by the New York Life; Cavalieri and the Vanderbilts; the weakness for fat women, etc. etc. etc . . . .

We have enough material about O.H. to make a more interesting story than was ever written by Hemingway or James Hilton. We didn't need a writer of Jimmy's capabilities to look up research and quote from it—anyone could do that. There are rare sparks through the manuscript

---

[14] There was an A. B. See Electric Elevator Company.

to prove that Jimmy might have given us what we expected of him. When I read the first few chapters I thought a certain amount of quoting from the record was necessary to get into the story—but it never came—it was a continuation of quoting from the record, which is extremely dry reading, even to me!

I'm counting on you to insist that Jimmy fulfill his promise that we will have a good book. We can have little hope from this first draft.

Best wishes for a Happy New Year.

As ever, Your Uncle,

Arthur

AH/j

Encls.

Oscar has marked up Arthur's letter in a way that suggests there are particular points he intends to bring to Sheean's attention.

Oscar Hammerstein to Kenneth Tynan, The Observer, London, December 29, 1954

Dear Kenneth Tynan:

Your piece about Bea entitled "Precious Lillie" is, I believe, the best description of a comic artist I have ever read. In an essay which dealt with "the futility of the English language as a means of communication" you quite paradoxically illustrated its efficiency. My congratulations to you!

All good wishes for the new year.

Sincerely,

Oscar Hammerstein II

Chapter Fourteen

1955

For the first time in twelve years, no Rodgers and Hammerstein shows are currently playing on Broadway. *The King and I* is still going strong in London, and its U.S. national tour will run through the year. Shooting for the *Oklahoma!* film has been completed, but months of editing and preparation lie ahead. Oscar and Dick are working on their next musical, *Pipe Dream* (working title, *Sweet Thursday*). Preparations are also underway for the films of *Carousel* and *The King and I*, both of which will be released in 1956.

Oscar Hammerstein to Charles Brackett, Twentieth Century-Fox Studios, January 6, 1955

Dear Charlie:

Yul Brynner called me up from Chicago yesterday where "The King and I" is playing, and expressed a great desire to read the script, which I had told him was very good. I can see no harm in letting him have it. He is a very intelligent man and it would be interesting to have his views on it. I think he will be very enthusiastic about it. I told him I would write to you and ask you to send him a copy. He can be reached at the Shubert Theatre in Chicago.

Dorothy and I and the Rodgers expect to be out in California during the month of February, and we look forward to seeing you then.

Love to Muffy.

Charles Brackett to Oscar Hammerstein, January 11, 1955

Dear Oc:

There is a studio policy, which has become firm as steel within the last few days, that no script shall be shown to an actor until a director has been assigned to a project and done his final work on it. This may sound petty

The Letters of Oscar Hammerstein II. Mark Eden Horowitz, Oxford University Press. © Mark Eden Horowitz 2022.
DOI: 10.1093/oso/9780197538180.003.0014

and capricious, but if you've read the recent movie columns you'll know that Bette Davis has just issued an ultimatum that she would play the first script submitted her on SIR WALTER RALEIGH, without one change, and nothing else.

The first script in question was an absolute B picture number, with a well written Queen Elizabeth moving among pale stencils. You can imagine our consequent frenzy.

If it's a real point that Brynner should see the script, write me another and more urgent letter now and I'll arrange it.

I can't tell you with what pleasure Muffie and I look forward to seeing you and Dorothy in February. I think Muff has written to say how glorious Dorothy's Christmas wassail was.

Yours always,

Chas.

Oscar Hammerstein to Yul Brynner (in Chicago), January 18, 1955

Dear Yul:

Here is an excerpt of a letter I have received from Charles Brackett:

"There is a studio policy, which has become firm as steel within the last few days, that no script shall be shown to an actor until a director has been assigned to a project and done his final work on it. This may sound petty and capricious, but if you've read the recent movie columns you'll know that Bette Davis has just issued an ultimatum the she would play the first script submitted her on SIR WALTER RALEIGH, without one change, and nothing else.

The first script in question was an absolute B picture number, with a well written Queen Elizabeth moving among pale stencils. You can imagine our consequent frenzy".

It seems to me, Yul, that they are going through one of their phases again, when they have been frightened by something, and when they are making big rules which they keep for a few weeks. I suggest that we let the excitement die down, and then I will repeat my request that they send you a copy of "The King and I" picture version.

Meanwhile I hope that you and Virginia and Rocky are keeping well.

With all good wishes.

Oscar Hammerstein to Charles Brackett, January 18, 1955

Dear Charlie:

Thank you for your letter. I have forwarded the information to Yul, and unless he gets hysterical, we can let it coast for a while.

I don't think it would do any harm to send him the script, but I can appreciate the reason for the rule and its present rigid obedience.

Our love to you and Muffie.

The following letter is in response to a draft of an article for *Coronet Magazine* promoting the upcoming release of the film of *Oklahoma!*

Oscar Hammerstein to Nicholas Matsoukas, Magna Theatre Corporation, January 18, 1955

Dear Nick:

If you have a copy of the article you sent me, I will refer to the anecdotes I think are suitable and those which are not. I will not comment on the one I have used in our article because obviously we think that was good.

On page 5 I like the story of the direct telephone wire connection between Nogales and California. Also the "La Paloma" story.

On page 6, the middle paragraph, I think we should soft-pedal all the talk about the people of Oklahoma feeling that their state has been bypassed. Let them make that noise. I don't see why we should.

In the next paragraph on page 6, I think the corn story is all right, but at no time should we make a gag of it. For instance, I don't like the last sentence of this paragraph which is on page 7: "this makes our musical story the only motion picture that grew its own corn". Corn has an unfortunate connotation in our slang. Let us be sure we mean the vegetable when we say corn.

On page 7 I don't like the last two paragraphs; Fred Zinnemann talking about Agnes' mind as imagining the ballet. When people see the picture they should have the illusion that it is Laurey's dream and not Agnes deMille's choreography. Dick Rodgers and I don't like backstage stuff in pictures or the theatre, or anything that takes away from the audience's illusion.

The next paragraph about the dialect is very gaggy and unprofessional.

On page 8 I like the line attributed to Arthur Hornblow: "It's a tiny little place with a population of seventeen people and thirty two cameras".

The next paragraph seems amusing to me, and while funny, no reflection on the picture.

The next paragraph about Peter Hurd I believe is very interesting.

The next paragraph with the gag and pun "moovies" I think is terrible.

On page 9 the paragraph about Irving Sindler is all right, but it seems to be a very small joke and very unprofessional. I don't object to it, however.

The next paragraph says that the corn was seven feet eight inches off the ground. I would consider that it was nearer sixteen feet than seven. Seven feet eight is not very high corn. This corn was the highest I ever saw.

The haircut isn't bad. It could be funnier though.

The next paragraph I don't think is at all funny, and the last paragraph I hate, and I would like to tell you why. It makes us look as if we were not very careful about our props. I think anything that makes us look frivolous toward anachronisms and accurate period stuff is bad for the picture.

On page 1- in the first paragraph, I don't object to the Spanish American War poster.

The next paragraph, however, I don't think is funny at all.

I don't know why I started on page 5, but I did. So now I will go back to page 1.

I don't think much of the gag in the fourth paragraph about taking our money to the bank in trucks.

In the last paragraph, the story about my ad in Variety[1] has been done to death. I think we could lay off of it now.

Best wishes.

Sincerely,

Oscar Hammerstein II

There were ongoing complaints that at many performances of *The King and I* during its national tour, Yul Brynner omitted his song "A Puzzlement."

Oscar Hammerstein to Melville D. Hartman, January 19, 1955

Dear Mr. Hartman:

Thank you for writing to me about your experience with "The King and I". It is not a rare one. Mr. Brynner has frequently omitted the number when he has been worried about his throat. I too have noticed that he sometimes shouts the dialogue on these very nights, but he believes that singing the song is a greater strain than playing the part all evening. I happen not to agree with him, and perhaps you as a physician will not agree with him, but men get strange ideas about themselves, and if they are actors, this proclivity is accented.

I am sorry that I can make no suggestion to you beyond the offer our manager, Harold Goldberg, made that you come to the show some night as our guest and hope that Mr. Brynner will do the puzzlement number on that night.

With all good wishes.

Sincerely,

Oscar Hammerstein II

---

[1] After *Oklahoma!* opened on Broadway, ending a decade of poorly received shows by Oscar, he ran a quarter-page ad in the holiday issue of *Variety* listing five of his flop shows and the number of weeks they ran—ranging from three to seven—closing with "I've Done It Before And I Can Do It Again!"

**Oscar Hammerstein to Harold Goldberg, Shubert Theatre,
Chicago, January 19, 1955**

Dear Harold:

Dr. Melville D. Hartman has written to me after receiving his letter
from you. I am sending you a copy of his letter to me as well as my answer.
If he gets in touch with you, give him a treat as you suggested in your own
letter.

Of course he is absolutely right, and Yul is very unfair to the public
and to the show and to the management in these frequent omissions of
"Puzzlement". I do not, however, know what to do about it. We never have
been able to solve this.

Dorothy joins me in sending our love to you and Ellen.

As ever,

Oscar Hammerstein II

Uncle Arthur wrote to Oscar saying, "I'm looking forward to seeing the movie
DEEP IN MY HEART as I have been told someone portrays you in the story."
The film is a highly fictionalized biopic of Sigmund Romberg and seems largely
designed to allow a series of stars to perform the best-known Romberg songs.
Released in December 1954, the film starred José Ferrer as Romberg; Mitchell
Kowall played the minor part of Oscar.

**Oscar Hammerstein to Arthur Hammerstein (excerpt),
January 24, 1955**

I have seen "Deep In My Heart", and the young man who portrays me is
all right, only he parts his hair on the wrong side. For a while I considered suing Metro-Goldwyn-Mayer for this libel but decided not to. It is
not a bad picture—a little schmalzy, but the musical numbers are handled very well.

Here are three representative responses Oscar sent to those who replied to his letter
regarding segregated housing (dated December 20, 1954).

Oscar Hammerstein to Frank Aydelotte, Institute for Advanced Study, Princeton, January 25, 1955

Dear Mr. Aydelotte:

Thank you for your letter of December 28th, answering my letter regarding the segregation evil as it affects the Negro housing problem. I am sorry that I did not write my letter clearly enough for you to understand. I really was not consulting you as a real estate expert, because I am well aware that that is not your calling. The main point I wished to make was that while the advent of a colored tenant or resident in a white section was assumed to lower property values, this process might well be due to an unjustified panic on the part of the white real estate owners, and that perhaps if we eliminated this bugbear, we might go far to effecting a cure to the trouble. Of course I cannot guarantee that this is so, nor did I ask for a guarantee from you.

The general response to my letter was gratifying indeed. Some very sensible and concrete suggestions were made. These I am passing on to the Bucks County Council of Human Relations for further exploration. If we make any further progress in this direction, I shall take the liberty of reporting it to you. Meanwhile, if you have any further suggestions, I shall be very happy to receive them from you.

My best wishes.

Sincerely,

Oscar Hammerstein to Newbold Morris, January 25, 1955

Dear Mr. Morris:

Thank you for your prompt answer to my letter regarding the Negro housing problem, and please forgive me for my not so prompt acknowledgement.

I wrote to a hundred representative Americans with the primary purpose of finding the extent of their interest in this problem. The results have been most gratifying. Nearly every one of the answers have, like yours, expressed a deep interest in the problem, coupled with an intelligent and realistic recognition of the difficulties.

Some very sensible and concrete suggestions were made. These I am passing on to the Bucks County Council of Human Relations for further exploration. If we make any further progress in this direction, I shall take the liberty of reporting it to you. Meanwhile, if you have any further suggestions, I shall be very happy to receive them from you.

My best wishes.

Sincerely,

P.S. I was particularly interested in the copy of your transcribed remarks on the occasion of your casting your vote in opposition to the Metropolitan Life Insurance Company housing project at the Board of Estimate meeting Thursday, June 3, 1943. There is very good sense here, and I am not surprised that later on it had its effect.

O.H.

Oscar Hammerstein to Harry A. Bullis, General Mills, Inc.,
January 25, 1955

Dear Mr. Bullis:

Thank you for answering my letter regarding the racial segregation problem and its effect on the housing and employment situation in the area being developed by the United States Steel Corporation near Morrisville, Pennsylvania. I have an idea that you misunderstood the intent of my letter. The last sentence of your answer reads: "In my opinion, controversies of this sort are best solved by education, tolerance and mutual understanding rather than by taking violent issue with misunderstanding, which only results in making it wider". I want you to know that I agree with your statement completely, and that if my letter implied inflammatory intentions on my part, then it must have been badly written. I wrote to a hundred people asking for their opinions and general philosophies on this question. Their answers were very gratifying indeed, and were all in the direction of "education, tolerance and mutual understanding." These three fine things are achieved by communication with one another—not by the "no comment" policy.

Very truly yours,

Oscar Hammerstein II

Mrs. Evan J. (Hannah) Morris to Oscar Hammerstein, January 27, 1955

Dear Mr. Hammerstein,

I am a member of a Drama Group, twenty in number and our members include business, professional women and wives of professors at Cornell University.

We believe that you have launched a new era in the American theater so, we are studying the history of your lives, as told in Deems Taylor book, "Some Enchanted Evenings".

I am to present the next program in our series on Feb. 21st and would be so very grateful if you could take the time and send me an answer to the following questions.

1. What do you consider your worst failure on the stage?

2. What is your most successful play from stage appeal and financial angle?

3. Have you ever thought of producing a movie of your most interesting lives? You should, if you have not, for it surely would be an inspiration for generations to come.

Thank you, very much.

Sincerely,

Mrs. Evan J. Morris

P. S. Any other information you care to give me will be most appreciated.

Oscar Hammerstein to Mrs. Evan J. Morris, February 9, 1955

Dear Mrs. Morris:

Here are my answers to your three questions:

1. My worst failure was called "Ball At The Savoy". It was produced at the Drury Lane Theatre in London, and was an adaptation of a German musical comedy.

2. "Oklahoma!"

3. No, we have not. Whenever movie companies have suggested this, my answer is always: "Over my dead body!" I mean this literally. The time for a biographical picture about a man is after he is dead and finished his life. If I saw a picture of myself now, it would make me feel dead.

Thank you very much for your interest in our work.

Sincerely,

Oscar Hammerstein II

Leland Hayward to Oscar Hammerstein, February 2, 1955

Dear Dick and Oscar:

I would have telephoned you before this but have really been frantically trying to finish up "Mister Roberts".[2] We are faced with the same problem that you guys are, i.e., shipping it by March 1st and this means endless, endless hours in the dubbing and cutting rooms.

I saw about eight reels of "Oklahoma" late last week. I know that Josh has talked to you because he told me he had spoken to you on the phone. Billy Wilder saw it as well as Jack Warner, Steve Trilling and half a dozen of the technical men here from the studio.

We saw among other things "Oh, What a Beautiful Morning", "Surrey", "People Will Say We're in Love", half of the ballet, "Oklahoma", the Smokehouse scene with "Poor Jud", etc. We did not see "Many a New Day" which I hear is so wonderful.

First of all, about the picture: all I can say is I think it's superb. I like it better than I ever did the play. Perhaps this is because it's so much easier to see and hear it than ever before. Oscar, your words and lyrics come through so brilliantly that they really made a terribly deep, deep impression on me. They seem so much clearer than on the stage. I was crazy about the people in the picture: Gordon MacRae, Charlotte Greenwood, Shirley Jones and Rod Steiger who, I think, is absolutely superb. To me he gave Jud an entirely new dimension and therefore the story itself seemed better than ever before. That was certainly a brilliant piece of casting. We saw very little of

---

[2] The film of *Mister Roberts*, produced by Hayward, as was the play, was released in July of 1955.

Gloria Grahame and Eddie Albert. I'm not talking about the process now but just the picture itself. It seemed to me you achieved brilliantly what you set out to do, i.e., to make a great motion picture of "Oklahoma". I can't imagine it being anything but an absolute sensation when it opens.

Now about the process [Todd-AO]: as you both know I have been a devotee of it since the first time I saw it in Buffalo over a year ago so it was no surprise to me to find out how good it is. I just don't see how CinemaScope or VistaVision or anything else could possibly stand up against it. It's a million light years ahead of anything else and I think the fact that you've been able to use it as brilliantly as you have, with all the problems and uncertainties of something new like that, is a terrific credit to you and to Arthur and to Freddie Zinnemann and everyone else.

I didn't tell anyone but Arthur but I feel that you should have taken more advantage of the participation thing in the runaway of the surrey. There is only one real participation shot which is the one going through the trees and I think it would have been wild and exciting if you had had a couple more during the chase like that.

I just think it's great. Incidentally, so did the people here at Warners. Bill Mueller and George Groves who are the technical guys were crazy about it. Of course the primary reason for Billy Wilder and my seeing it was its connection with the proposal to make SPIRIT OF ST. LOUIS[3] in Todd-AO. We had to decide by January 31st to enter into an agreement by that date because of the equipment problem. Mr. Woodbridge was extremely fair about any contract proposition and in fact went so far as to make it possible to give us an escape clause in case the technical problems which we were faced with could not be met. There were three principal technical problems that worried us; the matter of optical reduction, the matter of transparencies, and the matter of miniatures because we felt that in the case of SPIRIT OF ST. LOUIS it would be impossible to make a second negative as you did in the case of OKLAHOMA because of so much of the picture being made from an airplane and the technical problems inherent therein in trying to duplicate them.

---

[3] Hayward produced *The Spirit of St. Louis*, a biopic of Charles Lindbergh starring Jimmy Stewart and directed by Billy Wilder. It was released in 1957—in CinemaScope.

Both Bill and I also talked to Professor O'Brian O'Brien [*sic*] about these problems. We saw the roll of film that was optically reduced and certainly the quality photographically of the optical reduction was fine.

However, in that particular roll there was no allowance made for reduction from 30 frames per second to 24 frames per second and this problem in conjunction with the matter of synchronizing sound when reduced from the Todd size to standard does impose difficult problems. Apparently the theory now is that every fifth frame can be dropped from the Todd film to make it come down to 24 frames per second. Professor O'Brien told us that he eventually would have the problem licked in some other technical way that I don't know but there are certain shots where taking out every fifth frame would probably result in some jumpiness.

The matter of transparencies is also pretty much up in the air. There seems to be no doubt that it can eventually be done successfully but with SPIRIT OF ST. LOUIS we are faced with the necessity of knowing we can do them and fairly soon.

After a very thorough analysis by the Warners technical fellows they felt that it would be impossible by January 31st to make a firm commitment with these problems staring us in the face and certainly Warner and everyone else felt that unless we were sure we were going to go ahead with the process it would be unfair to make an agreement that might not be executed.

The additional consideration, of course, was the knowledge that it would increase the cost of the picture radically particularly since we were sure we would have to do some of it over by both methods. So, on Monday we regretfully told Arthur and Lew Wasserman told Woodbridge that we couldn't go ahead.

Both Billy and I feel pretty depressed about this but it's obviously impossible for us to force Warners to go ahead when they have some valid arguments on their side. I'm sure that in a couple of months we'll be around begging again. Woodbridge indicated to Wasserman that there might be additional equipment available anyway in the next couple of months. However, I thought I should write you a personal letter about this matter and explain it fully to both of you.

When the hell are either of you coming out here? I don't see why I should be suffering day and night in a dubbing room while you two live it up in New York.

We are almost through with "Roberts" and are having another preview tomorrow night and that I hope will wind it up. I must say we have all been terribly pleased with the three previews we've had. The reaction has been sensational.

Affections,

leland

Oscar Hammerstein to Leland Hayward, February 10, 1955

Dear Leland:

Thank you for your letter. Your enthusiasm about "Oklahoma!" made us very happy indeed. We understand clearly why you have decided not to use Todd A-O for the "Spirit of St. Louis", and at the same time we are very sorry about it because we think the process would have been great for the picture and vice versa.

Needless to say we are delighted at the news on "Mister Roberts". Josh had already told me about the first preview, and now you have told us about all three and it sounds like a smasheroo.

We have changed our plans and do not expect to come out to the coast for a while. I don't believe we will come out until the Todd A-O version is dubbed.

Dorothy and I are going down to Jamaica tomorrow. She has had a cold in the head, or rather three or four colds in the head one right after the other, and I think a little sun is what we have to give her, so we are leaving for a short stay. We won't stay more than ten days.

The book of "Pipe Dream" is finished. At least this particular draft is finished, and now we are working on the songs. It is a nice feeling to have this much done so far ahead of rehearsal time, which will not be until September 22nd.

Dorothy just came into the room and I said: "Any message for Nancy and Leland?" and she said: "Just give them my love, that's all". So I hereby give you her love and mine too, and herewith make my exit after a rather dull scene.

Oscar Hammerstein to Yul Brynner (in Chicago), February 2, 1955

Dear Yul:

Forgive me for not writing you sooner after your phone call. You put up a difficult decision for Dick and me to make, and we have talked it over very carefully. It is unlikely that we will ask you to return to the show immediately after the DeMille picture [*The Ten Commandments*] to play the three (or is it four?) weeks that you will owe us. On the other hand, it is very difficult to know at this early date where the show will be next July or what will be best for it.

We can assure you of this, that by the end of March when you leave us, we will be much better able to predict the future fate of the company and how we shall be booking it. So let us wait until then, and we shall try to give you a very definite answer at that time. Meanwhile, be assured that we will do our best to spare you any unnecessary or unreasonable hardship, no matter what our contractual rights may be.

Best wishes from us both.

Oscar Hammerstein II

Leighton Brill wrote Oscar of his decision to leave his wife: "It is with sincere regret that I have to tell you 'Brill is at it again'. Last Sunday I was forced to get out from under and I have left Kathryn. The whole damn thing was just too much and I couldn't take it . . . In regard to Kathryn, the difference in ages proved an insurmountable barrier. I admire her talent and have done and will do everything in the future to put her across. . . just wanted to let you know and will write to you in more detail when I know what the hell I am about."

Oscar Hammerstein to Leighton Brill, February 10, 1955

Dear Leighton:

Thank you for writing to me with unwelcome news, which, however, you and I had anticipated. There is no use hanging on to something that will not work. It just gets worse and worse.

You have said you will write to me later and tell me more when you know "what the hell you are about". About forty years ago you started weeping on my shoulder about l'affaire Ruth Schloss, and it has been going on for a long time. The shoulder is still there. Go ahead.

Let me know when you are coming to New York.

Love,

I. H. Prinzmetal to Oscar Hammerstein, March 14, 1955

Dear Mr. Hammerstein:

Gary Cooper, who is my client, became very excited about the possibilities for motion pictures of "SWEET THURSDAY", particularly with himself in the role of "Doc". He likes the idea even if it means that it will be a musical for the screen (he is taking his singing quite seriously).

I know this is quite premature but he felt that we should register this interest with you. This includes the possibility of joining with you in the motion picture set-up if it has not already been done, or participating in the purchase of motion picture rights.

Naturally, it also includes the possibility of investment in the stage production, although I am sure you would not be looking for funds for this purpose.

Gary has never gone as far towards a role or property for himself as in this case and anything that he can do now to participate in this project would be of real interest to him.

Sincerely,

I. H. Prinzmetal

Oscar Hammerstein to I. H. Prinzmetal, March 24, 1955

Dear Mr. Prinzmetal:

Thank you for your letter of March 14th in which you state the very gratifying interest Gary Cooper has shown in John Steinbeck's book, "Sweet Thursday". Dick Rodgers and I are very glad to know of his interest, and it will certainly be met with reciprocal interest on our part when the time comes for planning a picture based on our play. The play will of course be musical, and we expect to bring it into New York early next December. If it is successful, then it will be some time before we will want to do it as a picture. Whenever that time comes, however, we shall approach Mr. Cooper and discuss the project with him. We are happy to hear that he is "taking his singing quite seriously".

Financing for the stage production is completed and there is no way of taking in any more investors. We are, however, flattered by your confidence in us.

All good wishes.

Sincerely,

Oscar Hammerstein II

Samuel Chotzinoff, National Broadcasting Company to Oscar Hammerstein, March 16, 1955

Dear Mr. Hammerstein:

The year 1956 will mark the 200th anniversary of the birth of Mozart, and in connection with this bicentennial, the NBC Opera Theatre is planning a production of "The Magic Flute".

I have long wanted you to help us in our efforts to create an American "School" of Opera, and I feel that this might be the moment I have been waiting for.

A new English version of the "Magic Flute" really needs a poet rather than a mere Translator.

Goethe was so fascinated by this libretto that he wrote his one addition called, "Magic Flute" Part II. Why don't you write "Part III"?

Yours very truly,

Samuel Chotzinoff

General Music Director

Oscar Hammerstein to Samuel Chotzinoff, March 21, 1955

Dear Mr. Chotzinoff:

Thank you for your letter of March 16th, and for the flattery of suggesting that I write a "Part III" of the "Magic Flute". In the paragraph preceding this suggestion you said: "A new English version of the "Magic Flute" really needs a poet rather than a mere translator". I think it needs a magician. The "Magic Flute" is, in my opinion, one of the most mixed up and unintelligible libretti that I know of—and it has many rivals in the operatic catalogue. I think that the score of the "Magic Flute" should have a completely new libretto set to its beautiful notes, but if I undertook this job I would have little time left for Dick Rodgers. So I am declining with gratitude for your confidence in me.

All this is beside the point. When are you going to proceed with your autobiography? Blanche Knopf sent me a copy of "The Lost Paradise" and I enjoyed it more than any book I have read in years. You must go on with this. You can't leave me hanging around outside that concert hall waiting for you to come out, and to follow you wherever you go from there. Get back to work, and stop all this nonsense with N.B.C.

Sincerely, and with deep admiration,

Oscar Hammerstein II

Oscar Hammerstein to Charles Atkin,[4] March 22, 1955

Dear Charlie:

I read "The Passionate Men" with sustained interest throughout. I believe, however, that it's a very doubtful undertaking. I think it would play slowly, and it certainly plays on one key throughout. It is a play of well

---

[4] Charles Atkin was a stage manager for *Annie Get Your Gun, South Pacific, Me and Juliet*, and *Pipe Dream*. He had also appeared as an actor in Hammerstein's *Knights of Song*.

bred bickering—not always so well bred, but always in elegantly expressed English. There are a few anachronisms in the phrasing, but I don't believe these are important and could easily be eliminated.

I enjoyed reading it, but I am always fearful of plays with historical characters with the magnitude of these. It is almost impossible to believe in a cast of actors who are playing such gigantic figures as Jefferson, Washington, Hamilton and Burr. Maybe I am wrong. I hope I am. Thank you for letting me read it.

Kindest regards.

Oscar Hammerstein II

Josh Logan to Oscar Hammerstein, March 22, 1955

Dear Oscar:

I am going to call you in a few minutes, but I thought I'd put down a few notes about PIPE DREAM in case I get confused over the telephone and not say what I really feel.

First of all, I think you have an enormous hit. I haven't been this excited about anything you've written since THE KING AND I. As you know, I found it very difficult to talk about ME AND JULIET.

This is a wonderful job, Oscar, both in the book and lyrics, and I think that with Helen Traubel in it it could be one of the things to see for years to come. It's very touching and there's wonderful entertainment all through it, and once it gets started there seems to be no stopping it.

When I say "once it gets started", I mean that I found the very first scene a little difficult to follow emotionally. There seem to be several reasons for it as I read the scene over.

First of all, I don't think that Doc is sufficiently dramatized in this scene. Perhaps you don't wish to put in too much exposition, but you have such an interesting character in Hazel and such another interesting one in Suzy that it seems you could easily tell more about Doc between them, so that when he makes his statement that he's going to write a paper, we as the audience know that this is the first time he has ever said such a thing.

I think Hazel, in explaining Doc to Suzy, could tell the audience a lot more about him than we know—and therefore we would enjoy the drama of the scene when he says he's going to write the paper. I would like to know whether Doc is a poor man, a rich man; I'd like to know the fact that he doesn't like to work for people; that he actually does a rather menial job in collecting these things but has a kind of aspiration to do more and the ability to do more. The sooner we know this, the more effective the story is, and it seems to me that we don't get that until after Fauna is in and after we have seen more of Cannery Row.

Also, it seems to me that the scene with Hazel and Doc is a little rushed, and when he sings ALL KINDS OF PEOPLE it's a little too soon. I am not quite acquainted with the people when this song starts. I wish I knew where I was and who they were who were singing in order to fully enjoy it.

Another thing that has occurred to me: do you need to see the girl who was sleeping with him? I realize why she's there. It's to prove his masculinity and all that, but couldn't it be done just as easily by Hazel seeing the girl leaving in the yellow convertible and talking about her to Doc? Somehow, the idea of her dressing and undressing there is sordid and makes me dislike Doc for a moment. I would like to see him first as a lonely man.

The reprise of ALL KINDS OF PEOPLE could come a little later in the scene, couldn't it? Perhaps Hazel could sing it to Suzy about Doc.

But to sum up my feelings, it is at the beginning of the play I would like to know more about Doc, about Cannery Row, and about the people around—even if they're just suggested.

I think whatever problems you have are within the first thirty pages of the script. Just getting acquainted with them in the proper order and dramatizing Doc's problem. Whenever Fauna is on stage the whole thing is a dream, and I think BUM'S OPERA is one of the most delightful things I have ever read—and I haven't even heard the music, which should add delight on delight.

My deep and strong congratulations to you, Oscar. I really admire you for handling this material the way you have. It really has raised it much higher than it was in the original, in my estimation.

It was wonderful to see you and Dorothy the other weekend and I hope we can see each other many, many times in the years to come.

Love from us both.

Oscar Hammerstein to Josh Logan, April 2, 1955

Dear Josh:

Thank you for your letter, both letters, and especially the first one which was long and complete, and which I found very helpful—especially your comments on the first scene, all of which I intend to work on.

Dorothy and I had a wonderful time at your house two weeks ago and we are so glad to have finally worked in the long delayed visit.

Best of luck and love to you both.

Always,

Oscar

Douglas MacArthur was a five-star general and a controversial figure. He was Chief of Staff of the Army from 1930 until he retired in 1937. With the advent of World War II he was recalled to active duty in 1941 and made commander of the U.S. forces in the Far East, where he was charged with responding to the Japanese attack on Pearl Harbor and their invasion of the Philippines. He led the Allied victory over Japan and, despite the fact that the casualties under his command had been devastating, he was largely treated as a hero after the war. When the Korean War began in 1950, MacArthur was placed in charge of the United Nations forces there. However, his unwillingness to conduct a limited war provoked Chinese intervention, and when he publicly voiced his opposition to the war strategy approved by the Joint Chiefs of Staff, President Truman relieved him of his command. MacArthur's exchanges with Oscar reveal a more thoughtful, less bellicose man, than one might expect.

Oscar Hammerstein, Roger Stevens, and Norman Cousins
to General Douglas MacArthur, March 23, 1955

Dear General MacArthur:

We read with excitement and gratification your Los Angeles speech of January 26. Your inspiring plea for the abolition of war is a provocative challenge.

We are deeply interested in advancing your view and would be honored to have an appointment with you at your earliest convenience to discuss this important matter.

Sincerely,

Oscar Hammerstein II

Roger Stevens

Norman Cousins

General Douglas MacArthur to Oscar Hammerstein, March 29, 1955

Dear Mr. Hammerstein:

I am most grateful for your letter of the 23rd noting approbation of the point of view on the abolition of war expressed in my recent Los Angeles address and I wish you would convey my thanks to your distinguished cosigners. It did not however present any new thought but merely reiterated a conviction advanced by me from the battleship Missouri immediately following the surrender of Japan on September 2, 1945—a conviction conceived in the war born devastation of that Island Empire and heightened thereafter, as, in keeping with our Christian leanings, we the victor assumed the burden of rebuilding in peace that of the vanquished which we had destroyed in war.

Only the cynic will challenge the philosophy that the utter futility of war in its present scale of mass destruction dictates its abolition, but unfortunately cynicism plays a mighty, sometimes indeed a predominant role, in the fashioning of events which guide the world. But cynicism fortunately is largely confined to the upper strata of society and forms little part in the thinking of the great masses. Such thinking is more often attuned to practical necessity and reality. And there is no doubt but that if the issue of war or peace were left to the free will of the masses they would rule out war with practical unanimity. The question is how to mobilize that will and clothe it with at least a veto control upon the madness of leaders for the personal power which springs from the threat of war.

From a life time of service in foreign lands which has given me the opportunity to assess human philosophy in its manifold influence upon divergent sectors of the human race, I have come to realize that what reaches closest to a common aspiration of all mankind is the protective shield of constitutional law—a device which has grown to be universally recognized by all people of all races as the ultimate safeguard against arbitrary despotism of rights and liberties of the individual. So true is this that even the despot seeks refuge behind so-called peoples' constitutions in order to allay, however the artifice employed, public demand for such protection. And experience, the great teacher, has shown that seldom do a people unsubjugated by foreign bayonets, fail zealously to guard with all the strength their constitutional guarantees to life and liberty, even against the oppressive tactics of their own rulers.

Thus in Japan, a nation steeped in the norms and precepts of a feudalistic past, the people avidly and with increasing devotion, hold to their constitution gained through the ashes of war and defeat and even their leaders dare not seek change which under its terms rests solely with the people.

In the light of such observations and experiences, I have come to the personal conclusion that the abolition of war must ultimately rest upon a constitutionally mandated liberty guaranteed to the people—a liberty to be free of war which the people themselves will stoutly defend, and free from the confiscatory taxation to which the preparation for war inevitably leads. Therein would lie a system of universal inspection by the people themselves, upon whose predominant self interest would rest the avoidance of steps which lead to war.

The natural question which then arises is how all of this is to be brought about. To which I would repeat the axiom that there must always be a first in all things. In this, our great and powerful nation should be the first. Equipped as is no other nation or combination of nations successfully to wage modern war, it should show itself through dynamic leadership no less equipped to lead the world down the noble but highly practical road toward universal peace. In my opinion this well might be done through a ringing affirmation by a leader in public authority endowed with the necessary vision and moral courage of our readiness to abolish war by placing the issue of war or peace squarely into the hands of the people through constitutional guarantees against war or the concomitant taxation for the maintenance of war making power, subject of course to similar guarantees being accorded at least to the peoples comprising the other major nations of the earth. We would thereby challenge all other nations to meet us on so high a moral plane. By so doing our own moral positions would stand out as a beacon to summon all men of good will everywhere to join with us. In due course I am confident the pressure of other peoples upon their leaders would bring about another grand alliance, but this one not joined together for the massive prosecution of war but rather dedicated to the bringing about of universal peace.

I have gone into this more thoroughly than I had intended and should prefer to leave it there without attempting to pursue it in greater detail at this time, as without public authority I obviously can exercise but little public influence.

Most cordially,

Douglas MacArthur

Oscar Hammerstein to General Douglas MacArthur, March 31, 1955

DEAR GENERAL MACARTHUR SEEMS TO ME THAT YOUR LETTER PURELY AS A DEFINITION BOTH OF HOPE AND PURPOSE FOR THE HUMAN COMMUNITY IS SOMETHING OF A MASTERPIECE IT PROVIDES AN ELOQUENT STATEMENT OF POLICY AND ASPIRATION AS I READ IT I KEEP WISHING THAT WHAT YOU WROTE MIGHT BE MADE AVAILABLE TO ALL PEOPLES EVERYWHERE. I WOULD LIKE TO MEET WITH YOU AS QUICKLY AS POSSIBLE FOR THE PURPOSE OF DISCUSSING SOME SPECIFIC PLAN TO GIVE YOUR IDEAS IMPORTANT NONPARTISANT [sic] CIRCULATION. LET ME KNOW WHEN WE CAN GET TOGETHER NEXT WEEK AT YOUR CONVENIENCE

SINCERELY

OSCAR HAMMERSTEIN 2ND

Oscar Hammerstein to General Douglas MacArthur,
April 13, 1955

Dear General MacArthur:

Just before I left your apartment last Tuesday we were discussing the difficulty of getting radio and television coverage for speeches, however vital the subject, and however important the speakers were.

Knowing this to be true, but feeling that I must try in some way to circulate the important thing you have to say on this most vital of all subjects, world peace, I looked into our chances for getting it before the public with the help of the networks.

The results of my one man investigation are to me encouraging. I have been given a firm promise by C.B.S. that if you were to be our principal speaker at the World Federalists dinner on May 21st, they will give us a half hour on radio on that night. They will also give us fifteen minutes of television time. They cannot give it to us on that night, which is a Saturday, and impossible to clear, but on the following afternoon, which is Sunday. We would have from 3:15 to 3:30 on Sunday afternoon, and this is an excellent time for getting wide attention all over the country.

It is my belief that once this coverage were committed, it would be almost automatic that we would get newsreel representation on many TV newscasts and also in motion picture theatres.

When I invited you to speak at this meeting I had little heart in trying to persuade you to go to all this trouble in order to reach the ears of five of six hundred people. Now, however, I come with an important offer which I can with deep sincerity urge upon you. Assured of an audience of many millions of Americans, this is the greatest single step we could make toward bringing home to them the importance of permanent world peace. You could impress upon them the one big vital truth that you gave me last Tuesday, the thought I have been carrying with me ever since, namely that it is not enough for the people to realize that we can get peace only through enforceable world law, but they must let their leaders know that they believe this.

I am afraid we may never get another chance like this. It is only because of your unique position of honor in our country, and because of the affection all Americans hold for you, that a network would grant us this time. Please let me know if you will do this.

My very best wishes to you.

Oscar Hammerstein II

P.S. I shall be in town up to 1 PM tomorrow, (Thursday). I can be reached at Templeton 8-0430.

Herbert Lom, while playing in *The King and I* in London, wrote to Oscar: "I should like to enlist your help with [the] enclosed property (NAMOUNA[5]), the rights of which I acquired recently. I very much hope that you will find time to read NAMOUNA and give me your opinion as to its possibilities as a musical; what should be done to it, whether perhaps you feel like recommending somebody to write the book and music etc. I am bold enough to suggest that you yourself might perhaps want to take some kind of interest in it—but if this is not possible, I shall be very happy, dear Oscar, just to have a few hints from you. I am also prepared to be told by you that the whole thing should be completely re-written before being thrown into the waste-paper basket."

Oscar Hammerstein to Herbert Lom, April 5, 1955

Dear Herbert:

I have read "Namouna". I can see why the critics said that this play lacked music, and that it suggested material for an operetta. I too can see how it could be made into an operetta of sorts, but I am not the right man to consider this kind of property. My own policy is to look for properties that don't seem to be ideal for musical adaptation and then try to meet the challenge and turn them into a musical with some unusual character to them. The trouble with working on a musical which everyone says "should be made into a musical" is that you are likely to wind up with something very obvious and perhaps old fashioned. The story of "The King and I" is about a prim but strong willed English governess and a royal Oriental. The theme is liberalism versus absolute monarchy. "South Pacific", both in main plot and sub-plot deals with the racial question. In "Carousel" the hero commits suicide, and in "Oklahoma!" he commits manslaughter a few minutes before

---

[5] A play by the popular French playwright and screenwriter, Jacques Deval.

the curtain. These are all very unpromising premises on which to build a musical play. My objection to "Namouna" is that it is too "promising".

I do not, however, advise you to abandon it if you are very taken with it. I am by no means certain that it could not be built into a very successful musical play. I am just telling you why I would not like to work on it myself. I suggest that Vivian Ellis would write a delightful score for this piece, and that perhaps the librettist should be a playwright rather than one who has had too much experience with musicals. This would take away a kind of "operetta taint" and might give you a much more original approach from the standpoint of musical comedy.

I feel that all this has not been very helpful to you, but it's about all I can say right now except to express my regret at the news in your letter that you are soon leaving our company at the Lane. With so rare a "King" and so charming and talented an "I" taken from the cast, I wonder what will become of us.

All my best wishes to you.

Sincerely,

Oscar Hammerstein to Mr. Sidney C. Lund, April 14, 1955

Dear Mr. Lund:

Here is the message you requested for your United World Federalist dinner on April 28th.

My best wishes to you.

Sincerely,

Oscar Hammerstein II

When small boys fight with each other in a school yard, we do not put them in jail. We do not exert any law or force, beyond the usual chastisements. If, however, these small boys grow up and have firearms and threaten to use them, law must be invoked and enforced to stop them. Compared to what war would be in the hydrogen age, the campaigns of Caesar and Napoleon, and even the first two world wars, were like schoolyard fights between small boys. Those conflicts were settled by "normal chastisements"— reparations, reapportionment of territories and populations, patched-up peace agreements. That day is over. In a third world war there wouldn't be much left of the populations and their wealth and the territories in dispute. We have in our hands now weapons which must not be used. We cannot gamble the existence of our civilization on the unpredictable whims of international anarchy, we must have world law, and a means to enforce it.

The people know this, but they are waiting for their leaders to do something about it. The leaders know it too, but feel uncertain about the support of the people. It is the job of the World Federalists to somehow get their message to the people so that they can declare themselves to their leaders and urge them toward the only possible path to peace—world law.

An initial paragraph was crossed through, but in a note in the margin Hammerstein wrote: "BUT SAVE FOR ME". The excised paragraph reads: "An anarchist is considered by all of us to be a pretty dangerous fellow, a violent man who wants no government at all. No man running on an anarchist ticket could be elected to any office in this country. We would not trust the safety of a nation or a state or even a very small town to a man who did not believe in law and order. We do, nevertheless, put our trust in anarchy to preserve the security of all the people on earth. When people resist the idea of enforceable law among nations, let them realize they are anarchists because that is exactly what they are."

Oscar Hammerstein to Christopher La Farge,[6] April 21, 1955

Dear Kipper:

I have read your play [*Happily Ever After*] with a great deal of enjoyment. I think, however, that it is a play which is better in the reading than it would be in the playing. I would be hard put to it to explain to you just what I mean by this. It is something I feel rather than think. Stage dialogue must continually be climbing up hill, reaching one peak and then proceeding to another. The dialogue in this play rests on a series of plateaus and stays on each one for a long time.

Thank you for sending me the play.

My best wishes to you.

As ever,

Oscar Hammerstein II

---

[6] Christopher La Farge was the author of a handful of novels, three of them in verse. During World War II, he was an active member of the Writers' War Board.

Oscar Hammerstein to Patricia Esther Gilbert, April 21, 1955

Dear Miss Gilbert:

Thank you for your letter of April 2nd. In answer to your question, "is there nothing a good American can do to promote the cause of peace?" I will tell you what I do. I work with the United World Federalists, an organization designed to do all it can to strengthen the United Nations so that it may become an effective lawmaking body empowered to establish law against war which all nations, large and small, must obey, and equipped with an international police force to enforce such a law. I know of no way except this for achieving eventual and permanent world peace. It will be a long, hard struggle to achieve this ideal, but if we don't start on it some time, we shall never finish it. No one believes that order can be maintained in a small town without a court of justice and a police force. We do, however, expect the world to keep peace without any law or law enforcement. Anarchy is a very unpopular word, and yet this is the word which describes the state of international affairs.

Of late this idea has received endorsements from conservative leaders like General MacArthur (in his speech at Los Angeles about two months ago), Chief Justice Warren, General Sarnoff and Henry Luce. At some time or another all our leaders have said that world law was the only road to peace—President Eisenhower, Secretary of State Dulles, Harry Truman, Adlai Stevenson, Winston Churchill and most of the great leaders in Europe. They seem, however, to be waiting for some sign from the people, their constituents. They have not had this sign, and that is why action has been limited to philosophical statements on the issue, so that what "a good American can do to promote the peace" is specifically to do what he can to extend the strength of the United Nations far beyond its present capacities. There is a tendency on the part of many of our legislators to sneer at the weakness of the United Nations. I agree with them, and with all of their allegations about its weakness. They, however, wish to scrap it because it is weak. I believe it should be made stronger because it is weak.

With all good wishes to you.

Sincerely,

Oscar Hammerstein II

Harry Ruby to Oscar Hammerstein, April 23, 1955

Dear Oscar:

For four days, before I left N. Y., I was stuck in a room at the Gotham Hotel—wrestling with what my medico said was flu. Two days after I returned to B. H., Calif., I was knocked flat on my well-rounded by a thing entitled: lobar pneumonia, which kept me bedded down for over two weeks. I am telling you this only because of a couple of things that happened which I think are noteworthy.

The sincere concern on the part of my good friends, 1300 in all, was very heartening. There was barely enough room in the house for the flowers, books, candy, and other things that were sent me. The phone rang without letup; sometimes there were as many as forty calls in a row—with only a fraction of a second between calls. Eileen, the nurse, or the maid took the calls until I got well enough to do it myself.

We all know that friends who call mean well, that they have the interest of the patient at heart—and all that, but the following dialogue, almost the same, word-for-word, can get slightly monotonous after the 20th call:

"How are you?"
"Much better, thanks."
"Is there anything I can do?"
"No, thanks, not a thing."
"Are you sure?"
"Yes I am, thanks."
"If there's something I can do,
will you call me?"
"Yes."
"Promise?"
"Yes." - Etc.

One day, when I got weary of the talk on both ends of the phone, I said, in answer to: "Is there anything I can do?," "Yes, there is. Send me a certified check for ten thousand dollars." Within forty eight hours of the time of that call, I received checks totaling $70,000. Unless I was wrong about you, Max Dreyfus, and Dick Rodgers, I'm a cinch to wind up with an even hundred grand.

The following is one of those things they call miracles: On the third night of my illness, while still in a feverish state, I saw standing by my bed an apparition-like figure bathed in a soft, greyish blue light. "Who are you?" I whispered. The figure replied: "I am the father." I then asked: "Where are the Son and the Holy Ghost?" The figure replied: "They're out of town."— and was no more. Things like this kind of make you think.

Please give my best to Dorothy.

Sincerely,

Harry

P.S.: Feeling fine now. Another week's rest and I'll start dashing off those hit songs—which can get very boring.

Darryl F. Zanuck, Vice-President in Charge of Production, Twentieth Century-Fox Film Corp. to Oscar Hammerstein, May 12, 1955

Dear Oscar:

Many thanks for your note. I am of course delighted with your reaction on CAROUSEL. We are now doing the revisions and minor adjustments.

On the subject of THE KING AND I, I am studying the Tuptim role. If we can get Dorothy Dandridge to play it, it will add a fortune to the gross, particularly in Europe where in CARMEN JONES she has scored the greatest success of any actress in recent years. It has been pointed out to me by our foreign managers that Deborah Kerr is only mildly popular in Europe and has only been in one real success. They have also pointed out that Yul Brynner is totally unknown to the theatre-going public. Dorothy Dandridge in the cast, if she will play the role, would be of enormous benefit to us.

I hope that we can clear up all of the technical matters with CAROUSEL. I say this because after studying the script again I realize that 95% of the picture is exterior and therefore it must be made sometime late this summer while the weather is still good, as we will want to go on location to take full advantage of CinemaScope.

This presents a problem from the standpoint of casting. To get good people we have to work far in advance. I have analyzed everything and I believe that Frank Sinatra will win another Academy award in CAROUSEL. I think that he was born to play this role. He has all of the necessary larceny and yet he has the tenderness and he has developed into a remarkable actor, which has already won him one Academy award. He is hounding me because he has so many other offers and he wants to leave free time in case we decide to take him.

I think perhaps if we played him opposite the young girl you have in OKLAHOMA this might be an ideal combination.

Please let me hear from you.

Best always,

Darryl.

Oscar Hammerstein to Darryl F. Zanuck, May 17, 1955

Dear Darryl:

Thank you for your letter of May 12th. I agree with you completely about Dorothy Dandridge, and I hope you will be able to get her for the part of Tuptim.

The "Carousel" situation should be cleared up within a week and I will let you know as soon as this has been done. Everything has been agreed upon, and it is a matter of drawing up papers.

I was surprised to learn that you expected to produce it so soon. It seems like a big order to organize a production this quickly, but I guess you are the man who can do it.

Regarding Sinatra, both Dick and I are inclined to agree with you that he would be a very interesting and off-beat approach to the casting of Billy Bigelow. Neither of us would object to your signing him. We think, however, that you ought to take one look at Gordon MacRae in "Oklahoma!" I know that up to now he has been a very unexciting singing leading man, but he comes into his own in this picture, and we believe he will be a very important star after it opens.

The idea of Shirley Jones (the lead in "Oklahoma!") is a very good one. We are sending her over to Paris in the stage production of "Oklahoma!", which will be given in connection with the festival known as "Salute to France", a series of American art and cultural exhibitions to be given in Paris this summer. This involves her going into rehearsal this week, May 19th, and opening in Paris June 20th. After playing two weeks there, we plan to send her to Italy with the company. If you decided to use her in "Carousel" we might have to cancel her Italian part of the run, and therefore we would all have to make up our minds about this pretty soon.

Let us hear from you.

P.S. In writing to me it is well to send a copy to 10 East 63rd and another copy to Doylestown, Pennsylvania. I go back and forth a good deal and I am never quite sure on what days I will be in what place.

Darryl F. Zanuck to Oscar Hammerstein, May 20, 1955

Dear Oscar:

Many thanks for your letter. I am delighted that both Dick and you like the idea of Frank Sinatra as much as we do for CAROUSEL. I think it would be a terrible mistake for us to use the same cast that you have in OKLAHOMA. In all probability CAROUSEL will be in the majority of the theatres in the United States before OKLAHOMA. As I understand it OKLAHOMA will open in a number of legitimate road show engagements. The same thing in our new process may also happen to CAROUSEL but on this point we are not yet definite.

It is my opinion that the ideal cast for CAROUSEL would be Frank Sinatra and Jean Simmons. This is a so-called "motion picture cast." You have no idea how valuable this will be to us in Europe.

I have heard that Jean Simmons is simply sensational in GUYS AND DOLLS, and of course we know she is the perfect type, the right age, and she is an outstanding actress. She uses her own voice in GUYS AND DOLLS and does the two big numbers. In the case of CAROUSEL I assume we would have to dub her.

I can see no reason why we cannot be ready to start rehearsals and pre-recordings some time the end of July or in August. This will of course depend on the availability of the cast. This puts us in a position of being compelled to negotiate with them now.

From the standpoint of director what do you think of Henry King? He has just completed LOVE IS A MANY-SPLENDORED THING with William Holden and Jennifer Jones and I believe it is the finest directed picture we have had on this lot in five years and that it will be a strong contender for the Academy Award. He has a great background in both drama and musicals. Just think of a few of his credits: SONG OF BERNADETTE, ALEXANDER'S RAGTIME BAND, MARGIE, THE SNOWS OF KILIMANJARO. He is very sensitive with people. I think he might be a wonderful choice.

Best always,

Darryl.

Oscar Hammerstein to Darryl F. Zanuck, May 26, 1955

Dear Darryl:

Your ideas for casting "Carousel" sound very good to both of us. It also seems to me that Henry King, from his many and varied credits, would be a very good prospect for the directing job. Speaking of directors, have you settled on anyone for "The King and I"?

On receiving your letter I phoned my lawyer and told him to hurry up on the deal so we could come out in the open with the whole thing. Papers are being drawn up and he expects to have it concluded very soon, but I will keep after him because lawyers are notoriously slow about these things.

Dick joins me in sending our warmest regards to you.

Sincerely,

Oscar Hammerstein II

Dorothy Dandridge became a star as a result of *Carmen Jones*; she also became the first African American actress to be nominated for an Academy Award in a leading role. She *was* cast to play Tuptim, but withdrew on the advice of Otto Preminger (her *Carmen Jones* director, and now her lover), who felt she should take only leading roles. (The role of Tuptim went to Rita Moreno.) Deborah Kerr and Yul Brynner starred in the film. Both were nominated for Academy Awards; Brynner won for best actor.

Henry King directed the film of *Carousel*. Shirley Jones and Frank Sinatra were cast as the leads and even pre-recorded the songs. But arriving on set, Sinatra claimed that he was unaware that the film was being shot with two different kinds of cameras (for CinemaScope and CinemaScope 55) and that some scenes may have to be shot twice as a result. He left the set and quit the film. According to Jones, she later learned that Sinatra left at the insistence of his wife, Ava Gardner, who wanted him to join her on the set of the film she was making. Gordon MacRae was called in as a last-minute replacement.

Oscar Hammerstein to Josh Logan, June 1, 1955

Dear Josh:

I am writing to you about the Karamu Theatre in Cleveland. In 1915 Mr. and Mrs. Jelliffee, the founders, were searching for a way of integrating American white people and American negroes in an arts program. That was the motive. Since then, it has resulted not only in forwarding the cause of race equality, but in becoming one of the most important centers of theatrical achievement in Cleveland, and indeed in the country. I have attended some of Karamu's productions and they have amazing quality. I believe that their staging of Menotti's THE MEDIUM was the best I have ever seen.

Starting off in a little hut, they developed their plant into a theatre and arts and crafts building that cost over $600,000.

To complete their ultimate plan they are building additional units which at today's prices will cost another $600,000. Of this amount they have so far raised [?] in cash and have a pledge from the Rockefeller Foundation for another $100,000 providing they match it dollar for dollar by December 30th of this year.

I am appealing to my friends in the New York theatre world, especially those who are also friends of the philosophy that inspires the Karamu

Theatre. Will you send me a check for whatever you think you can afford? It is, of course, tax deductible.

All good wishes to you.

Sincerely,

Oscar

Oscar Hammerstein to Mrs. Wesley Towner, June 3, 1955

Dear Mrs. Towner:

Thank you for your letter of May 23rd and for your interest in the coming new play by Mr. Rodgers and me. The theatre ticket situation in New York is a very difficult one indeed. You suggest that if we had held out against theatre parties longer some other managers might have come along with us. Well, we held out for nine years and nobody came along with us. Furthermore, the public seems to like to buy their theatre tickets in this way.

Theatrical producers, like ourselves, are in a strange position. If a merchant has some rare article like a jewel or a handsome fur coat to sell that is better than any other jewel or fur coat in town, he charges more than anyone else and gets it, and all the profit goes to him. If a producer has the best show in town, his seats scale the same as those of every other producer, and the excess profits go to charity theatre parties or ticket speculators who have somehow got access to blocks of tickets on which they can profit. I say "somehow" because there are various ways, and they are difficult to detect. When we sell seats by mail we are careful not to sell more than blocks of four, and if we notice a series of checks from the same person with successive numbers on them, we do not honor the order at all because they obviously come from "diggers"—speculators.

Many attempts have been made to put a stop to this evil, but I am very pessimistic about the chances of stopping it as long as there is a large public of buyers willing to pay anything at all to entertain business associates who are coming to New York for a few days. The expense is deductible and, as you suggest, this crowds out the ligitimate [sic] New York theatre-goer like yourself. As in all black market operations I blame the buyer. When there are buyers willing to pay huge premiums over standard prices for anything, there will always be sellers created. I am more tolerant toward the sellers who are confronted with the temptation created by the buyers. Who are the sellers? Sometimes they are box office treasurers who work in league with the brokers and speculators. But I would not accuse one of them because I have never found any out in this kind of enterprise. It is sometimes suggested that the theatre owner is in league with the illigitimate sellers of tickets at a high premium. And it is sometimes also suggested that the producer is involved. I can tell you that Rodgers and Hammerstein have never been involved in any illigitimate ticket selling. Nevertheless our shows, when they are successful, have been veritable playgrounds for these illigitimate activities. If there was anything we could have done to stop it, we would have done it by now.

Our recent decision is based partly on the fact that we would just as soon see the premium go to a charity as to a speculator. In fact we would much rather see it go to a charity.

Mr. Rodgers and I write and produce for the pleasure it gives us, but this ticket side of the business is not fun at all, and for this very reason I find a letter like yours very disturbing.

I have received a few other requests like yours since the announcement of "Pipe Dream"- letters enclosing checks. I must turn them all down because I cannot set myself up as a supplementary ticket office and carry on the rest of my work at the same time. I am sure you will understand this. On the other hand, I find your letter so interesting and so indicative of your devotion to the theatre that I would like to see you get tickets for "Pipe Dream" on your birthday. I will destroy your check now. But in the fall, when we announce the sale of tickets and the scale of prices, and the theatre at which we will play, will you please write me another letter and remind of this letter, and my answer to it? Then I will try and make some of my house seats available to you for that night. It may be that that will be one of the evenings when a charity has taken over the house, but I am hoping to be able to hold back a few seats for my own personal use, and to accommodate my friends, and since it is your birthday, I will accommodate you on that night.

This is not a very constructive step in improving the conditions that disturb us, but it will at least fix you up for this particular evening.

My best wishes to you.

Sincerely,

Oscar Hammerstein II

With *Pipe Dream*, Rodgers and Hammerstein allowed group sales for theater parties for the first time. As it turned out, it was one of the reasons they were able to keep the show running as long as they did. One source states: "more than 70 performances were entirely sold to groups."

Junior high school student, Don Mitchell, wrote Oscar with a question that had "puzzled" him: ". . . what your definition of an educated person is." (He signs his letter, "Your friend.")

Oscar Hammerstein to Don L. Mitchell, June 28, 1955

Dear Don Mitchell:

You ask me a very difficult question because I believe that education is a relative matter. You are in high school, and compared to someone who is just starting grammar school you are an educated person. You are not, however, an educated person compared to someone who is about to graduate from college, and the graduates are not for the most part nearly so educated as the faculty who have taught them.

I think for all practical purposes a man is educated when he can read and write, and understand what he is reading and express his thoughts clearly in writing. This I think is the basic minimum. After that all education is an elaboration on these two accomplishments.

My best wishes to you.

Sincerely,

Oscar Hammerstein II

Oscar Hammerstein to Michael Todd, June 25, 1955

Dear Mike:

Thank you very much for the two handsomely bound copies of the books you are adapting for Todd-AO. I am faced with the choice of reading "War and Peace" or finishing the play I am working on. I think I will finish the play and read "War and Peace" after we have opened in New York. By that time you may have the movie script finished, and I will read that instead. Don't tell Tolstoy!

All the best to you.

Sincerely,

Oscar Hammerstein II

The following letter was forwarded to Oscar regarding the screenplay for *Carousel*. The Motion Picture Production Code[7]—a.k.a. the Hays Code—was a set of guidelines the film industry in the United States was supposed to use to censor themselves, in order to avoid censorship by outside authorities. The standards changed over time, but were in place from 1934 to 1968.

Geoffrey M. Shurlock, Motion Picture Association of America, Inc., Production Code Administration to Mr. Frank McCarthy, Twentieth Century-Fox Film Corp., June 27, 1955

Dear Mr. McCarthy:

We have read the final script, dated June 13, 1955, for your forthcoming production R-H PROJECT. While this story seems to be basically acceptable under the requirements of the Production Code, this present version contains certain important unacceptable elements, as well several lesser details which are in violation of the Code.

The suicide of Billy Bigelow violates that portion of the Code which states that suicide " . . . should never be justified or glorified or used to defeat the due processes of law". We will be unable to approve any indication that Billy took his own life to avoid being captured by the police.

Because of the sympathetic nature of the characters involved, we feel that Billy and Jigger should not be planning the cold-blooded murder of Mr. Bascombe. Under the circumstances, this seems to be too casual a dismissal of a serious criminal act to be acceptable under the Code. It would be well to confine the crime to theft, simply dropping the idea of attempting to kill Bascombe.

Going through the script, page by page, we direct your attention to details related to above mentioned problems, as well as certain other items.

Page 8: The girls on the platform should not be performing any type of "bumps and grinds" number.

Page 11: We ask that you eliminate the expression, "little tart".

---

[7] The code was both specific and broad. Its resolutions began with: "that those things which are included in the following list shall not appear in pictures produced by the members of this Association, irrespective of the manner in which they are treated: 1. Pointed profanity—by either title or lip—this includes the words God, Lord, Jesus, Christ (unless they be used reverently in connection with proper religious ceremonies), Hell, S.O.B., damn, Gawd, and every other profane and vulgar expression."

Page 12: Please avoid any suggestion that the "flashy type" of girls are prostitutes.

Page 18: The line, "I'll bet you do", is unacceptably pointed and should be changed.

Page 22: The following dialogue is unduly blunt and we ask that it be eliminated. "What you think I want with two of you? I meant that one of you was to wait. The other can go home".

Page 32: It will be of the utmost importance that you avoid any unduly suggestive termination to this love scene.

Page 36: The same applies to the bedroom scene involving Billy and Julie at the bottom of this page.

Page 42: The line, " . . . comfort they ken only get in port", is unacceptable and should be changed.

Page 45: The following lyrics are unacceptably pointed and we ask that they be changed. "All the boys are feeling lusty, And the girls ain't even puttin' up a fight".

Page 47: As previously mentioned, it is our opinion that you should eliminate the indication that Jigger and Billy are planning to murder Bascombe.

Page 57: The line, "I know what you want", is unacceptable and could not be approved.

Page 63: The use of the word, "dam", on this page should be eliminated.

Page 64: The same applies to the expression, "What the hell".

Page 65: The expression, "By God", is irreverent and should be eliminated.

Page 70: The toilet gag found in the lyrics sung by Jigger[8] could not be approved.

Page 74: The action at the bottom of this page in which the men "offer assistance", could not be approved.

---

[8] In "Blow High, Blow Low," Jigger sings: "Your boat will seem to be / Like a dear little baby in her bassinet, and her little behind / Is kind of inclined to be wet!"

Page 78: The dialogue, "quick or nothin'", is unacceptable and should be eliminated.

Page 81: Please eliminate the scene in which Jigger is shown patting Carrie's posterior.

Page 86: We cannot approve the words, "Gawd-knows-whatin' all night".

Page 89: We again direct your attention to the discussion of the planned killing. We feel it should be eliminated.

Page 94: As noted above, we will not be able to approve the indication that Billy takes his life in order to escape being captured.

Page 108: The following line of dialogue might prove objectionable and we recommend that it be changed. "If I had more sense I wouldn't have nine children".

We will be glad to read revisions overcoming the above mentioned difficulties. However, in any event, as you know, our final judgement will be based upon the finished picture.

Cordially yours,

G. M. Shurlock

Oscar Hammerstein to Henry Ephron,[9] July 20, 1955

Dear Henry:

Here is a list of the suggested changes for censorship purposes which we discussed on the phone today:

Instead of "There's a hell of a lot of stars in the sky",

"Why, y'can't even count the stars in the sky".

Instead of "skinny-lipped virgin" change to

"skinny lipped lady" with a "reading" on "lady" which you describe as "a lorgnette reading"

---

[9] Henry and Phoebe Ephron wrote the screenplay for *Carousel*.

Page 45, new verse instead of "lusty" verse in "June".

"June is bustin' out all over,
The moonlight is shinin' on the shore,
And the girls who were contrary
With the boys in January
Aren't nearly so contrary any more".

Page 65, in "Soliloquy", in case you are forbidden to use the words "by God", repeat "I'll try" three times.

Page 70, use the "crsyanthemum [*sic*] spout" verse instead of the one about the baby's behind.

Page 86, instead of "and God knows what'in' all night",

"and no more readin' at night"
or
"and not much sleepin' at night".

I think we agreed that this last was not very good and it would be better if you can hold on to the line we have, or change it to "and who knows whatin' all night".

I hope you win all your other arguments with the censors.

All good wishes.

Oscar Hammerstein II

Josh Logan to Oscar Hammerstein, June 29, 1955

Dear Oscar,

There is really no particular excuse for my writing you this letter except that I thought of you so much yesterday while working on a scene in PICNIC.[10] I suddenly felt myself blushing and wondered why. It was as though you were peeking over my shoulder with that penetratingly smug grin of yours and stating: "Why don't you have her put the flower in her mouth? After all, it's just as original to have Rosalind Russell doing it as to have Helen Hayes."

---

[10] *Picnic* was first a hit play by William Inge. It opened on Broadway in February 1953, with Josh Logan directing. Logan also directed the film, which previewed in December of 1955.

The fact is that I was photographing a scene that had a slightly Carmenesque quality to it, and I felt guilty and the guilt went right back to you. The reason I am writing is to let you know that I know it's corny before you see it and tell me. I am putting it bluntly, but that's the way certain people have to be handled.

Seriously, I want you to know what a wonderful time I am having working on this picture. I feel as happy and secure as at any time of my life. Everyone has treated me well. The film seems almost as good to other people as it does to me. And I am working with a cast that, so far as I am concerned, has never been equaled, with the possible exception of PACIFIC and ROBERTS. There was something about Kansas, the grain elevators, the backyards, the clouds, and the peoples' faces that gave a lot of quality to our scenes. I really have great hopes for this picture and feel it might be one of the best things I've ever done.

I don't know whether your experience was the same as mine in coming back to Hollywood, but I found it so much easier than I had expected it would be. These people give you so much help, and a director has at least a few moments to catch his breath while the cameraman is lighting and while various sets are being assembled, which seems to take some of the emotional burden away from the day.

I was very excited about Bill Holden's and Rosalind Russell's performances in the picture. But I think the outstanding discovery will be Kim Novak, who plays the pretty girl. I was worried about her, as you probably remember, but now I have no more worries. I think she was the ideal choice for the part.

Nedda and I miss seeing you and hearing news of you. I hope that you are getting along well with the lyrics on PIPE DREAM. I'm sure it will be a fascinating experience and a successful one for you. I am so sorry I missed seeing you when you made the short visit, but I'm hoping that before the summer is over, we will be able to meet either in New York or somewhere in between.

If you have a minute, drop me a line.

Best to your family,

Josh

Oscar Hammerstein to Josh Logan, July 11, 1955

Dear Josh:

I was very happy to receive your letter. It is a long time since we have seen each other, and I have wondered often about how you were getting along on "Picnic" and how you were liking directing a picture. I was also very gratified to realize that the mere memory of me talked you out of putting a rose in the mouth of Rosalind Russell. The question remains, what did my ghost fail to accomplish? Did it stop you from having Roz put one hand above her head and the other in front of her and snap her fingers as if she had castanets? Did she do anything at all with a rose? For instance, did she pick one off a rambler on the porch and throw it at him? Did she crook her arm like an imaginary basket and with her other hand toss cornballs out of it as she danced around? And if you made any of these mistakes, is there a way to eliminate them, or did you shoot the scene willfully in such a fashion that it cannot be cut? I can see you glaring at my ghost and saying: "I am burning all my bridges behind me! This is the way it must be whether you like it or not!"

There is no use for me to worry about all this three thousand miles away, but when you say "a scene that had a slightly Carmensque quality to it", what the hell do you expect me to do? Coming from you those are the most ominous words I have seen since I read what the scientists first told us about the potentials of the hydrogen bomb. Here I am minding my own business and trying to finish the lyrics of "Pipe Dream" and now you've got me worried about what went on on a certain set in Kansas a month or so ago. If you are really in a hole and sorry you did this, my only suggestion is that you take a closeup that you can cut to whenever the dance gets too Carmenesque. How about a closeup of the ex-president[11] of Actor's Equity with his hands tucked into his shirt sleeves and nodding in the enigmatic way of the wise Oriental. You might even give him a line as he nods— "Schoolteacher flesh"—and you could leave it to the audience to decide whether he was speaking of her manner or whether it was not intended to be in dialect and he was referring to the covering on her bones.

Outside of this scene, I have no doubts whatsoever about this picture. I think it is going to be just great, and I cannot tell you how happy I am

---

[11] The much ridiculed Clarence Derwent.

that you have got your feet wet as a movie director with such a fine story as this, and with such a group of characters. I gather from your letter that you are excited about the cast, and if you are excited about them, so am I. They sound wonderful. When do you think you will be showing any of it? And when do you think you are coming back east?

Our plans are to go into rehearsal September 22nd, which means we shall be in New Haven around that date in October, where we play for one week and then go to Boston for four. No matter how many lyrics I write I always seem to have six more to write. Months go by and people ask me how many more songs I have to write and I always say six and it is always true, and yet I keep writing more all the time. Could I be in a squirrel cage without knowing it?

What are your plans for next year? Are you going to direct that play for the Guild? Are you going ahead with "Sayonara"?

Tomorrow is my birthday. I shall be sixty years old. Reggie and Billy and Henry, Phil and Alice and Jimmy have chartered a fishing boat on the Sound, and they are taking me for a sail for my birthday. We expect to have lots of fun.

Dorothy toyed with the idea of giving me a surprise party, and then she very wisely got cold feet and asked me how I would have liked a surprise party and I told her: "No, please don't give me a surprise party. Wait until I am sixty-five and then don't give me one". So we are going fishing.

The day before the 4th of July it was over ninety and I played tennis and felt fine until I went into the pool that evening before going to bed and felt an unaccustomed chill. I then found out that I had a fever, and the fever stayed with me for four days while I did nothing except drink juices. It finally left me. I at no time felt any discomfort or any pain, but the thermometer kept registering from 100 to 102 degrees. I have concluded that my thermometer was sick, and I have sent it to the medicine closet for an extended rest.

Dorothy and I miss you and Nedda very much and we think you ought to make a bee-line for Doylestown when you come back. I will be in the throes of finishing up the rehearsal script and trying to finish the lyrics— and failing. It might be relaxing for you to sit there and laugh at me.

Love,

Steinbeck wrote to Hammerstein asking for an "extra share" in *Pipe Dream* for Elaine, going on to say: "I do know I am going to see a lot of rehearsal. I have never seen one put together. Harold Clurman assures me that it does not make him a bit nervous to be watched. In fact he likes it. Remember the time with Guthrie? That was the nearest to the Eleusis[12] I have ever been."

Oscar Hammerstein to John Steinbeck, July 11, 1955

Dear John:

It was very good to hear from you.

Regarding your desire to have two shares of "Pipe Dream", the one is already in the bag because you spoke to me about [it] over a year ago and this was to be for Elaine, and I believe you were going to surprise her. The other one may be harder for us to manage. We are setting up the finances now, and after Howard Reinheimer and our business manager and then finally Dick and I have had a go at it, I will let you know the result. We shall certainly try our best to give you two, but you certainly have one already. You've had it for a year.

I am very glad to hear that you are going to kibitz at rehearsals, but don't kid yourself that you can pose as an innocent bystander once you are there. In the first place, when it comes to this story and this group of characters, you have no innocence whatsoever. In the second place, if you are standing by, you will be pulled by the scruff of the neck right into the center of things. I take back this threat. It sounds too much as if I am trying to frighten you away, and anxiously I [am] trying to "draw you in". I meant to be much more subtle. Make out like I didn't say any of this. Come into our parlor—I mean our auditorium—and sit down and watch us. We won't bother you at all. It will be as relaxing as all get-out for you.

Love to Elaine and you from both of us.

P.S. Tomorrow is my birthday. All my children have chipped in and chartered a fishing boat and we are going to sail around Long Island Sound.

---

[12] The site of secret religious rites in ancient Greece.

I don't know what their plans are, but if on July 12th you see a strange looking boat with some strange looking kind of people waving at nobody around the shores of Sag Harbor, it was us taking a chance that that might be you and Elaine on the beach.

A fan wrote Hammerstein suggesting a change to the end of the lyric for "All the Things You Are," where the original reads:

Someday my happy arms will hold you,
And someday I'll know that moment divine
When all the things you are are mine.

Oscar Hammerstein to William Demastus (excerpt), July 13, 1955

"Sublime" won't do in "All The Things You Are" because the word in that spot must rhyme with "mine". The last line of the song, "When all the things you are are mine" is the most important line in the song. It rounds out the whole idea and I could not sacrifice it any more than I could rhyme "mine" with "sublime".

Oscar Hammerstein to Ruth Whitney, *Better Living*, July 14, 1955

Dear Miss Whitney:

I find it impossible to accede to the many requests I get similar to the one in your letter of July 8th.

As for this particular question that you ask: "What Makes a Home?" I am sure that I could not write a paragraph about this because I could never think of a better answer than one word. My answer to the question: "What makes a home?" would have to be "people". What else?

All good wishes to you.

Sincerely,

Oscar Hammerstein II

Oscar Hammerstein to the Alfred P. Sloan Foundation,
July 26, 1955

Dear Sirs:

I am writing to introduce to you Welcome House, Inc., in the belief that its work will interest the Alfred P. Sloan Foundation.

You may not be aware of a peculiarly promising group of American children, who are nevertheless, also peculiarly needy. They are children in the United States of Asian or part-Asian ancestry, who through some misfortune are homeless and without parents. Agencies usually refuse children with Asian blood even though they are American by birth, on the grounds that such children are too difficult to place for adoption.

A group of Americans became convinced some years ago that this situation could and should be changed, especially now, when the peoples of Asia need to be convinced of the values of our American way of life. We therefore established Welcome House, a child welfare and adoption agency, devoted to American children of Asian or part-Asian ancestry. Our program is two-fold:

1. To work with other child welfare agencies to find good homes for American-Asian children.

2. When another agency is unable to place the child even with our help, we will accept the child and plan for his adoption.

Welcome House, Inc., is now in its sixth successful year. We have cared for thirty-three children this year, and we must care for others who are waiting.

Such work needs money. Any question you would like to ask, we shall be glad to answer. Please advise us as to how to make proper application to your board.

Yours sincerely,

Oscar Hammerstein II

President

Oscar Hammerstein to Josh Logan, September 19, 1955

Dear Josh:

That little clipping you sent me about l'affaire Gropper-Minchenburg[13] is a magnificent illustration of Robert Burns' well stated conviction that the best laid plans of mice and men gang aft agley.[14] I had originally planted Rocky Marciano in the apartment next to Gropper, and I had even taught him to play chopsticks so as to annoy Gropper just at those times when he was working and turning out things like "The King and I". It was no easy task to teach Rocky chopsticks because he is quite unmusical. Then comes the agley part. Archie Moore, all the way out in San Francisco, defeats Bobo Olsen and becomes a contender for the championship. A lot of money-grubbing promoters get together and match Rocky with Archie Moore. The next step is that Rocky Marciano is sent up to Grossinger's to train, and without telling me anything about it leaves his sparring partner's nephew to do the job that he had promised that he would do. Quite apart from Minchenberg's small stature, it is a notorious fact that the nephews of sparring partners have very small, square brains. This explains the imbroglio (a word which Mary cannot spell unless she looks it up in the dictionary). In fact, it is the worst thing of this kind which has happened to me since Basil Dean's production of "The Heart of the Matter", which, as you remember, was an imbroglio that ganged agley, one of the most beatable combinations ever devised.

In expressing my gratitude to you for sending me a copy of "The Derwent Story" I must also add that this is one of the most unfriendly gestures ever made, and is a subtle though obvious plot to handicap "Pipe Dream" in the fear that it might come in as a competitor with

---

[13] Milton Gropper was a playwright with a string of failures. A classmate of Oscar's at Columbia, they collaborated on two unsuccessful shows in 1924. Years later, when Gropper fell on hard times, and as a kindness, Oscar hired Gropper for odd jobs, "to make digests of new novels and stories or do research." After *The King and I* opened, Gropper sued Oscar for nearly $250,000, claiming he had collaborated on the book and lyrics, and there was an agreement giving him a share of the royalties in exchange for taking no credit. It was a terrible experience for Oscar. Gropper and Minchenberg lived in adjacent penthouses, and had a fistfight because Minchenberg disturbed Gropper by playing the piano too loudly.

[14] From the Robert Burns poem "To A Mouse," translated as: "The best-laid scheme of mice and men / Go oft awry, / And leave us nought but grief and pain, / For promised joy!"

"Fanny". What is the matter with you? Haven't you been running long enough? And isn't there room for two big hits on Broadway? Think of how you timed this thing! It arrived on the morning before I go into rehearsal when I am trying to write comedy verses for Hazel's song in the second act. Lo and behold I receive a volume which is much funnier than anything I can hope to write. It not only undermines my confidence, but it tempts me. I must drop everything and read "The Derwent Story" immediately. Well, all right, you've caught me. I rush to my Dictaphone to tell you my impressions. I hope before reading the following you will pick up your copy, which I imagine is already pretty well thumbed. On the third page of photographs there is a picture of a so called Fluff. Look at it carefully and see if you don't detect what happened to Fluff in 1936 when our hero was playing "Lady Precious Stream" with Constance Carpenter. Admitting that Fluff was a pretty old dog by this time and probably had to be put away, I think it was a little heartless of Clarence to have converted him into that remarkable set of whiskers he is wearing. This of course was one of the depression years, and perhaps therefore we may forgive him for making a muff out of Fluff. For many reasons this "Lady Precious Stream" page is the most interesting of all. In his picture with Constance Carpenter he is wearing a beard as no actor, or indeed any person, has ever worn it before or since. The whiskers grow out of the top of his mouth instead of from his chin. I have heard two versions explaining this. One is that his enunciation was so succinct that the director felt a little blurring would be all to the good. I called up Constance Carpenter and other members of the cast, and I got a different explanation. It seems they had all signed a round-robin and presented it to the stage manager as a kind of ultimatum. They refused to go on with him unless he wore his thick beard covering his mouth as well as his chin. Explanation: this was that unfortunate halitosis through which he went. The latter explanation is supported by the picture next to the one with Connie. This is Clarence without the beard, next to Elfrida. Both look as if they are about to throw up.

One more interesting comment about this particular page—you will note that Connie has her hands clasped and inside her kimono sleeves. There is no picture of Clarence up to this time with his hands in this posture. Undoubtedly he took the hint from Connie, and although he built every subsequent characterization on this trick, he has never given her sufficient credit.

I have studied all the pictures to detect the source and the rise of the Chinese influence, and I have concluded that this did not come naturally to Clarence, that he sort of absorbed it from other actors as he went along. Take the picture of Whitford Kane, who played with him in Mrs. Bandmann-Palmer's company. There again Whitford's hands are clasped, and on the same page a picture of Clarence shows him with one arm up and his hand on his lapel, a sort of tentative step toward the imitation of Whitford, later to become the imitation of Connie. Two pages later, playing with Sir Godfrey Tearle in an early silent movie made by Gaumont Studios, we have Clarence with lace sleeves and the two hands sort of creeping together but not quite meeting. On this same page of the Conway-Tearle production is a picture of two tramps, and the question caption on the picture is: "Which is Derwent?" The obvious answer is: "I don't care." Two pages later, as Gratiano and Slender and Sartorius, he is going through a kind of campy period, and this laps over into the next page when he is playing in "Buddha" with Ruby Miller in 1914. He is still a little campy, and this handicapped him in playing a sultan. It nearly drove Roby crazy. Several pages later, skipping way down to the early 1930s, I find for the first time he was in a work of mine, the motion picture "Life of the Vernon Castles". He is holding up a warning index finger to Ginger Rogers. I don't remember what the scene was about, but this tableau makes me faintly sorry that I wrote it.

I would like to go over this collection with you some time and discuss these pictures more intimately. There are some strange ramifications which stem from them. For instance, why is Aline MacMahon in "The Madwoman of Chaillot" disguised as Blanche Yurka? What had Clarence just done with Denise Darcel which makes him look so roguish in the picture taken with him. Why did Dick Rodgers sneak away to his fifteenth anniversary and not tell me he was going? Who won the chess game with Melville Cooper?

So this is why I do not go into rehearsal tomorrow with all the verses for Hazel's song completed. Thank you, Josh Logan!

Love,

Arthur Freed to Oscar Hammerstein, August 18, 1955

DEAR OSCAR: "OKLAHOMA" IS A WONDERFUL POETIC AND STUNNING MOTION PICTURE. THE RODGERS AND HAMMERSTEIN SONGS COME TO YOU ONE AFTER ANOTHER

AND BRINGS TEARS OF JOY TO YOUR EYES. THERE IS NO COMPETITION TO THIS KIND OF ELOQUENCE AND THE BRILLIANT RECORDING AND NATURAL PRESENTATION WILL MAKE MOTION PICTURE HISTORY IN EVEN A GREATER WAY THAN THEY MADE THEATRICAL HISTORY. FROM THE BOTTOM OF MY HEART I AM SO HAPPY FOR YOU AND DICK. A HEART FULL OF APPLAUSE=

ARTHUR FREED=

Oscar Hammerstein to Arthur Freed, August 1955

Your telegram was a thrill to Dick and me. First because we respect your opinion, and second because we know you are an honest guy and don't blow blow [sic] off steam for no reason at all. Nothing could make us happier than this kind of reaction from you. Our best always.

Oscar

John Steinbeck to Richard Rodgers, forwarded to Oscar Hammerstein, August 18, 1955

Dear Dick

This is a subject that has come up often, but this is the first time I have ever brought it up. For a number of years a number of people have played and more than played with the idea of making a truly American Folk-opera of Mice and Men. Aaron Copland for one. Frank Loesser took it to work on for over a year and then brought it back saying it scared him too much. I mention it to you because of something you said recently about being ready or anxious for a tragic theme. I have felt this myself and I am glad that you do. I only suggest that you might consider my story because it does have the following qualifications. It is strictly American. It is very tight in form. It's characterizations are exact but lyric so that their expression might easily be in terms of music. It is very well known all over the world. Its structure is musical, with theme, variations and repeated theme, and last but most important, no one could do it like you and Oscar. Further it would continue the form that you and Oscar invented with Oklahoma, the play with music continuing both plot and theme. As a matter of fact this invention of yours is the only American contribution to any of the arts. Everything else we have taken from European prototypes.

I offer this as something to think about. If you think it stinks as an idea that is fine. The only thing that occurs to me, and that quite selfishly, is that some one is going to do it sometime, and no one could do it as you could. May I suggest you reread it with your musical antennae extended. It could be a long term project and nothing would please me more.

or forget it.

love

John

Oscar Hammerstein to John Steinbeck, August 24, 1955

Dear John:

Dick turned over your letter to me—the one you wrote to him about "Of Mice and Men". I would like to study it when I get a chance. I am of course familiar with the play, but never thought of it in terms of music. The first reaction I get is that it should be something close to real opera, not a musical comedy or even a musical play. I am flattered by your willingness to entrust it to us, and as soon as I get your "Sweet Thursday" off my neck, I will try to give it some time and sincere thought.

Love from all of us to you and your girl.

Fred Zinnemann was the director for the film of *Oklahoma!* Three of his previous films were *High Noon*, *Member of the Wedding*, and *From Here to Eternity*. Arthur Hornblow, Jr., the film's producer, had worked with Oscar on *Swing High, Swing Low*, and *High, Wide and Handsome*.

Oscar Hammerstein to Nicholas Matsoukas (excerpt), August 27, 1955

I think that you should do a little thinking about how to publicize Fred Zinnemann and Arthur Hornblow who up to now have not been treated very well. This is not your fault because they have been in Europe and Dick and I are naturally better copy. Therefore we have to push them a little bit.

I think they deserve more space than they have got, and if the press is not disposed to do it, we ought to prod them a little bit. Freddie Zinnemann should not be hard because he has such a brilliant record in the past few years, but Arthur Hornblow should get everything that is due him.

One other subject: I was talking to Henry Woodbridge on the phone the other day and he recalled a phrase that I used out on the coast last week, "emotional participation". He thought that this was terribly important to put into the heads of people, and especially critics, before we open. I think this is important too. I find that newspaper men read newspapers and believe them more than anybody, and if we could make them conscious of what we're driving at, namely that this is not merely participation in the sense of spectacle, but participation emotionally, I think it would be a very good thing. I would be glad to discuss this with you some time.

Oscar Hammerstein to Arthur Hornblow, August 27, 1955

Dear Arthur:

Thank you for your interesting and chatty letter about Venice. It fills me with envy, but it is a friendly kind of envy, meaning "wish I were there", not "wish you were not there". I am very happy to hear of your having a good time because you have been so long delayed in having it. It is Michael Todd now who is having his troubles with Kingsberg. It is flying into the eyes of both, and unfortunately does not seem to get into their mouths for even a temporary clogging.

Reports keep coming to me from the coast of extravagant predictions for the future of the Todd-AO version of "Oklahoma!" and quite soberly I am inclined to agree with all of them.

The one thing that disturbs me is something that perhaps we can rectify. I have been thinking it over very seriously ever since I saw the picture and I now forward the problem to you in the hopes that while you are lying in the sand and the gentle waters of the Adriatic are caressing your toes, an idea might occur to you.

This is what happens. We strike a beautiful chord of music, the lights come up on a lyric cavern of corn, the camera passes through the corn, the audience gasps and applauds—yes, even the jaded press. Following is a lone solitary rider in the distance and he starts to ride to the camera. Boy! What a picture it is already! We are away! We are off to the races! Then what happens? A list of lousy titles! Leave out the fact that the main title has not yet been made presentable. That is not what I am concerned with. It will be presentable some day. But by the time you've got down to telling the audience who was the assistant to the eyebrow curler you have lost your start. You might almost as well not have had that corn shot. This does not ruin the picture. It merely throws away the first big punch we have, and dissipates its thrilling effect. Do you know any reason why we shouldn't run the titles against any old mat? I don't care what the mat is. Maybe no mat at all. Run them against the last minute or minute and ten seconds, or whatever length they run, while the overture is still playing. Then stop, then start, do the picture as we planned it. Corn—Curly— "Beautiful Morning!" In this way you are still getting dividends from that first shot while you are going through the comparatively slow part of the lead into the surrey song. It seems to me we can use this hangover of excitement through what really is the blandest part of the picture. I can see no technical reason why this should not be done, and could not be done before we open. I am a little hesitant, however, to go ahead without first asking you if you can think of any bugs in the idea and, even more important, whether you can think of a positive plan for achieving the effect I am groping for. How about, for instance, travelling titles going across the big screen from left to right?

Sorry to bother your vacation with any professional question whatever, and yet I know you would want me to under the circumstances. If you would like to talk to me on the phone about this, I would be glad to phone you if you will cable your phone number and when and where you will be, and at what time you would like me to phone you.

Love to Bubbles and yourself from all of us.

Oscar Hammerstein to Arthur Hornblow, September 13, 1955

Dear Arthur:

Thank you for your long letter from Montecatini Terme. As I read it I felt guilty at having introduced this kind of worry into your vacation. I can reward you with good news. It looks as if we can fix this thing up. I have been in touch with Johnny Green on the coast. Some re-recording will be necessary, and it will consist of the following:

The overture will continue to the last two bars of "People Will Say We're in Love" and then two new bars will be scored to connect it up with the music which is now under the long shot of the valley. In other words, the beginning of the title music. This will continue down to the last two bars of the "Surrey" and will wind up with a big cadence for a finish. Then the corn music will start. We will go into the corn shot, and will need just a little new music to get from there into the long short of Curley leading up to his singing of "Oh, What A Beautiful Mornin'".

Freddie arrived in Los Angeles after I talked to Johnny and I got him and Johnny Briskin together to arrange the ways and means.

As for the visual side of the question, I am going over to Fort Lee today to look at a title that was made on black cards for protection some time ago. It was made with the same red lettering that we now have superimposed over the landscape shots. I must say I am disposed to like this title even before I see it because I have no interest whatever in knocking the audience off its feet by means of titles. They have had the most ingenious novelties hurled at them, and I don't think they mean anything at all. When the picture is a bit of fluff and wants to be started off with some ingenious trick, they may be of some use. I think this kind of thing is of no use to us. I regard the title as something that we have to get behind us before the picture starts so that it doesn't interfere with the picture. Actually, the effectiveness of these titles as credits will be enhanced a great deal if there is nothing else to look at while they are being shown on the screen. I had a feeling that the title and the landscape were competitors in the version that we now have. One wanted to see the beautiful pictures and didn't read the titles very carefully. Meanwhile the beautiful pictures were being spoiled by placards in front of them.

Freddie suggested over the phone that if the titles on the plain black background didn't look right we could put blue behind it. This of course would involve re-photographing and printing the title.

Another argument for the plain backing to the title I think is the fact that these titles are backed up by very exciting musical accompaniment.

The people are in the theatre, having listened to a fine overture, and then given a chance to read the credits to more good music, and they know the picture has not started yet. They don't expect to be emotionally moved by the title, nor do we need a title to excite their interest in "Oklahoma!" They have come there because they are very interested. Following this—even if they had the pants bored off them—comes the corn shot, and at that moment all doubts have vanished. They know they are looking at something great. If we follow this reaction immediately with our story and our characters, we are well on the way to a fine evening for the audience.

Freddie ran the picture last Friday and is in complete agreement on this title question. His reaction to the picture was very good, although more reserved than mine. He still clings to the idea that Jud is too tame in the first few reels—you remember the controversy over the scene where Jud tells her she has to go with him tonight. He finds the first reel a little on the bland side. This is true. We rely almost completely on charm and the introduction of the characters whom we want the audience to fall in love with, and the singing of two now famous songs, "Beautiful Mornin'" and "Surrey". I don't believe that dramatic conflict must start in a story immediately the curtain rises, but if this kind of opening is harder to get away with on the screen than on the stage, it makes even more urgent the necessity of taking advantage of a punch like the corn shot and riding on it into the mild scenes, which gives them some momentum for a while. You are quite right about the present version of the title not really affecting the picture in any serious way. All the people who have seen it are very enthusiastic about it. The only point about this title—and I will leave the subject after this—is that we are not fatally wounded by it, but we have a chance to be gloriously helped by it if we don't dissipate it as we now do.

Freddie thinks that the best people in the picture are Shirley and Rod Steiger. He doesn't mention Gordon. Josh Logan, who was crazy about the picture, thinks that Gordon is the best thing in it and, while he likes Shirley, has a feeling that she could have been a little better in the numbers.

My own reaction to this picture is almost completely emotional. I can stand off and criticize many things and wish that we had done many things differently—particularly the number "Oklahoma" and the duet, "People Will Say We're in Love". But the picture seems to be a great experience, great in the sense that the Mississippi River is a great river in spite of an occasional orange rind and some old whiskey bottles one might see floating down it.

We ran a few reels of O'Brian's print the other day over at Fort Lee and, as he said, his optical printer being more sensitive, has picked up some of the marks from negative handling that the contact print did not pick up at all. Each of the two reels we saw had a little "rain" in it. Neither Skouras nor I nor for that matter Dick who is a little more finicky about these things, we [sic] seriously disturbed by the marks. On the other hand, if they ran right through the whole film they might be very disturbing indeed. We are seriously considering the whole question of lacquering the negative. I will let you know how these talks come out. There seems to be some new process by Eastman which is much better than the old and less satisfactory experiments with lacquering.

This Sunday Dick and I are going to the Rivoli and we are going to run O'Brian's print from the top projector and the contact print from the lower balcony projector to compare the effect of the two on a temporary screen. (Speaking of screens, the American Optical people still believe there is a good chance we might get their new one in time for the opening.)

Enough of all this. Dick and I are within a week of starting rehearsals for "Pipe Dream" and we are nearly finished with it. If you miss the "Oklahoma!" opening, be sure that [you] and Bubbles are here for the opening of "Pipe Dream" anyway.

Love to you both.

In mid-September, Richard Rodgers was diagnosed with cancer of the "gum posterior of the last tooth". He attended the morning of the first day of rehearsal for *Pipe Dream* on September 21, and had his surgery the following day, a surgery which entailed the removal of the malignancy, several lymph glands, part of his jaw, and the loss of all of his teeth on that side of his jaw. He returned to work ten days later.

Photo 21 Richard Rodgers and Oscar Hammerstein II attending the premiere of *Oklahoma!* in Oklahoma City, November 1946. Associated Press Wire Photo. From the Richard Rodgers Collection, Library of Congress

Photo 22 Richard Rodgers, Fred Zinnemann, Dr. Brian O'Brien, and Oscar Hammerstein II, at the *Oklahoma!* film preview, Rivoli Theater, Broadway. Associated Press Wire Photo. November, 1956. From the Richard Rodgers Collection, Library of Congress

Oscar Hammerstein to Johnny Green (excerpt), October 6, 1955

Dick is coming along fabulously. He has attended rehearsals for two hours each day for the past five days, and his return to action has already had a great effect on the company. He has told them how to sing songs as only he can tell them, and the whole project has taken on new life. Rehearsals are going well, although the book has progressed faster than the numbers, partly because of Dick's absence and partly because our choreographer[15] is a little new at the game. His ideas, however, are very good. Our cast looks fine, and at the moment I feel very confident that "Pipe Dream" has a good chance to be a big hit.

Oscar Hammerstein to Oscar Schisgall, October 6, 1955

Dear Oscar Schisgall:

Answering your question on the phone this morning, this is my try at it:

The songs that have endured over the years are almost always songs that are easy to sing and easy to listen to. To be easy to listen to a song must have the element of some basic truth in it. The truth must be expressed very simply by the words, and usually it states an experience or thought with which the listener can identify himself. The melody should not be too difficult to be absorbed and appreciated by ears that have no elaborate musical cultivation.

In addition to the above qualities, a song, to be "easy to sing", should have words that are not only clear in their meaning, but written with some awareness of phonetic clarity. Many beautiful lines of poetry would not be beautiful lines when sung because of too many sibilants or tongue-twisting phrases contained in them. Good, popular and lasting lyrics do no use fancy words, nor words difficult to pronounce, nor words difficult to understand on first hearing.

I am dissatisfied with this definition because it sounds too academic, but it's the best I can do with the time I have to give you at the moment.

---

[15] Boris Runanin.

What the above description leaves out is the heart and soul which must be in a good song, the intangible and untechnical "feeling" that some songwriters have transmitted to the singing and listening public. This has to do with truth and sincerity and bigness of heart, and cannot be defined.

My best wishes to you.

Sincerely,

Oscar Hammerstein II

Arthur Hammerstein passed away on October 12 at the age of eighty-three.

As work continued on the screenplay for *The King and I*, there were ongoing discussions as to whether the King's death would be caused by his being gored by a white elephant or, as it was in the stage version, a poor heart (whose weakness may have been exacerbated by his shame at appearing weak in front of Anna and his subjects). Ultimately, the stage version was retained, some say at Brynner's insistence.

Oscar Hammerstein to Charles Brackett, Twentieth Century-Fox Film Corp., October 18, 1955

Dear Charlie:

I have not had time to read the script carefully, but I have carefully read the pages you mentioned in your letter having to do with the "elephant story". It seems to me that it is handled very well indeed, and it should work this way. I agree with you that Scene 80 is a dubious one to insert. I have a very specific reason for this. The one danger of this whole setup is a feeling of deprivation the audience may have at not seeing the King's struggle with the elephant. If you insert Shot 80 you are enhancing this risk by practically promising them to see the King approach in the next shot—or to walk into this one. If, on the other hand, you go from the King's statement that he is going to deal with the elephant straight to the news that he has been hurt, it seems to me perfectly good story-telling, and fairer treatment of the audience. Lady Thiang's speech on 107 is very essential, and I think that it is phrased about as well as it can be—better than I could do it anyway. It is not quite fair to refer to this as a "factual account". She is not only telling Anna that the King has been mortally wounded, but she is telling Anna that she (Lady Thiang) knows why he took the risk, and it is her way of exerting pressure on Anna to come to see him because she has some responsibility for the event.

The launching of "Oklahoma!" and the critical final week of rehearsals of "Pipe Dream" and the death of my Uncle Arthur (to whom I was very close) have crowded my life during the past few days, and are my excuse for not finding the hour and a half necessary to carefully read "The King and I" from cover to cover. I will try my best to do this before we leave for New Haven tomorrow, and if I have any further comments I will send them to you.

My best to you always.

Pipe Dream began out-of-town tryouts in New Haven on October 22, moved to Boston on November 1, and opened on Broadway November 30. The reviews strained to be kind. The show ran for 246 performances, then all but disappeared— there was no tour, no London production, no film, not even a hit song to enter the repertoire. It's the only Rodgers and Hammerstein show that did not make back its investment. Rodgers wrote: *"Pipe Dream* was universally accepted as the weakest musical Oscar and I had ever done together. . . . We had simply gone too far away from what was expected. . . . We were well aware that it was something of a mood piece with little real conflict, and that we weren't as well acquainted as we might have been with bums, drifters and happy houses of prostitution."

Josh Logan to Oscar Hammerstein, December 1, 1955

Dear Oscar:

I am leaving for Columbus in a minute, but I have been thinking about our conversation and I am trying to pin down the feeling I have about the split between the boy and girl in PIPE DREAM.

Since you had not suggested the split at the end of the first act, it seems to me that the sooner you have it start after the second act curtain, the better. Certainly I do not suggest that you do it before that wonderful Best House song, but is there anything to this idea:

Suppose Suzy comes out of her bedroom and the very first thing she says is "I'm never going to see Doc again as long as I live!" and explains her feeling and doubts to Fauna at that moment. Fauna, in some kind of desperation to avoid Suzy bringing down this disaster on herself, talks her into appearing at the party, simply as a way of getting Suzy to see Doc again. In this way she hopes that Doc will be so bowled over by the beauty of Suzy that he will propose to her on the spot. But Suzy does not know this; however, everyone else <u>does</u> know it. And while Suzy is singing the song to the crowd, the crowd, forewarned by Fauna, is looking at Doc for his reaction. Suzy, seeing this situation, is covered with embarrassment and then flies into a rage at Doc and everybody—but, <u>we</u> <u>know</u> why she is putting on this scene because of the explanation she has given in the earlier part of the act.

I am unable to supply the reason, but you know those reasons; it's just that I have never heard it clearly spoken in the play, in either version.

Another reason why I would like to see the explanation of Suzy's attitude come early in the act is that when she has on the bright dress and with all the people standing around, it is such a theatrical moment in itself that it blurs her true, deep doubts about herself and her relation with Doc, and somehow seems trumped up there whereas after their night of love in which he did not make a pass, it might come more definitely out of her character.

In talking this over with me, Nedda has come up with another idea which I think should be examined: the fact that Doc did not make a pass at Suzy might be the basis of her doubt about his love for her or any possibility of ever having any love for her.

At the end of the first act she has practically proposed an affair with him by going off to the sand dunes with him. Now, the fact that he does not take advantage of this offer and merely says he is lonely might give her the feeling that he fundamentally despises her or is repelled by her. If this could be put across to the audience, this would give great pathos to her situation in the bridal dress that it does not have now.

Now, on the subject of cutting, Oscar, may I urge you to examine the first part of the first act for some eliminations if possible.

Wouldn't the Home Song of the Girl's be more effective if it were in a shorter form? It is a beautiful song but it is enormously effective in one chorus, and even if a reprise is necessary, could it be a shorter version; for instance, the last half or the last phrases even. I have a feeling that the audience is in the "yes, yes, go on" state of mind at this point. The atmosphere has been brilliantly told up until then and they are anxious for Story to commence.

Another thing that is a terrific letdown is when the sheriff is seen walking along amiably and singing. This is what gives a kind of feeling that all these people are in love with human nature, which gives a softness at this moment which is dangerous. I would rather see this scene treated melodramatically or silently rather than in this amiable way. Rufus Smit, unfortunately is not a very interesting or arresting man and the less he has to do, the better I think for your play. It also seems to be a stall for scenery changing rather than an exciting contribution to the evening.

Actually, if there is any way you can eliminate some elements, even if it were a question of curtailing numbers and not finishing them completely, it would be helpful for propelling the evening a little more forward. Everything seems to be finished and sung in its fullest form, with no promise that something else is coming. Could some of them be treated without applause, for instance, and made to seem a little more fragmentary? There is an awful lot to swallow in the first setting, and then the next move is not strong enough to promise you anything else. The moment you're in the flop house, of course, you start sailing.

Now, the next danger spot is the first third of the second act, which could all be told in a much shorter form and you would have a better chance with the last part of your show, which now comes so late it is hard to whip up excitement again on the Doc-Suzy split because the audience is slightly in the same mood as the lyrics of the song which say, "let's stop horsing around."

Now, Oscar, here is another fantastic suggestion, and I only mean to throw it at you.

Would it be possible to get The Next Time It Happens early in the second act, even if it were done in the wedding dress someplace—instead of or in addition to Will You Marry Me?—so that you could go to your finale quickly after "Stand up to the girl." That is a marvelous moment, Oscar, full of excitement and promise with all those people singing, and somehow almost everything after that is anti-climactic.

Oscar, these suggestions are thrown at you hastily, but I feel there are things to do to this show that will make it into the same kind of show only more effectively realized. I would love to talk to you and Dick about it any time next week, and would be happy to meet you at any time or place you suggest.

Don't forget, Oscar, that whatever you do, it is worth it because this can be one of your greatest successes and there is absolutely no reason why a small amount of work cannot bring it fully realized to every audience that sees it. Even if you do nothing, it is a wonderful piece of work; unfortunately, it seems a little like what they call in Hollywood a rough cut, which means, as you remember, a cut where there is too much footage but you want to see all of your scenes and then decide later how to get it down to length.

Love to Dorothy.

Josh

Dictated;

not read.

P. S. If any of this is unclear to you, please save the letter and I think I can elucidate when we talk.

J.

Rodgers and Hammerstein continued to work on *Pipe Dream* after it opened but, always looking forward, preparations were being made to film *South Pacific*.

Oscar Hammerstein to John Fearnley, December 16, 1955

Dear John:

The more I look into it the more it seems to me that the West Indies might be very feasible for location in which to film "South Pacific". The islands do not seem to differ very much in appearance from the actual South

Pacific islands, and being more accessible it might turn out to be a substantial economical gain for the picture if we were to shoot it there.

Bear in mind not only the "Half Moon Bay" background which we talked about with the curving beach and the line of palm trees, but also bear in mind the practicability of quartering a good-sized company of actors and technicians near by. I found an ideal place in Jamaica last year as you know, but it would have been impossible to accommodate the company near enough to this location. I think their comfort is very important, not only to themselves but to the eventual quality of the picture. You don't get good performances out of dissatisfied, uncomfortable people.

If you find any locations that you like, be sure to take photographs so that we can submit them to whatever director we appoint, and also find out all about the transportation there from New York and Hollywood and how much it would cost.

I hope you come back with something.

Sincerely,

Chapter Fifteen
1956

Oscar Hammerstein to Reverend Theodore Speers, January 4, 1956

Dear Dr. Speers:

May I, as a professional giver-awayer at weddings, pay tribute to you as a presiding minister? It was a great relief not to hear the mournful melody intoned by many of your colleagues on these occasions. You spoke with the honest inflections of a man who felt and meant what he said. There is more to this than merely pleasing the ears of listeners. I am sure that a service of this kind gets through to the bride and the bridegroom and imprints its meaning on their memories. Being, as you are, a dealer in words, it was a refreshing experience to me to hear them delivered as words—not as mere music.

My best wishes to you.

Sincerely,

Oscar Hammerstein to George Skouras, January 5, 1956

Dear George:

I enclose two ads that I saw in this morning's papers. One, in which Todd-AO appears encircled by the O in Oklahoma seems to be much nearer the proper emphasis as far as picture and process are concerned. Our only suggestion in this ad is that our own names be in as heavy type as Todd-AO. You will note that only our initials are in that kind of type and the other letters are thinned out. The second ad, in which Todd-AO is in letters just as large as the title of the picture is, I believe, a very stupid ad, and ill-advised. It belittles the picture in that it puts it on an equal footing with a process which has been very badly received in the newspapers. The bad reception, due to reasons that we all well know,

The Letters of Oscar Hammerstein II. Mark Eden Horowitz, Oxford University Press. © Mark Eden Horowitz 2022.
DOI: 10.1093/oso/9780197538180.003.0015

would be no reason to soft-pedal the process. Certainly we are as anxious as you to feature it. But to feature it on an equal footing with the title is to me very bad advertising and bad business. People are going to see a picture called "Oklahoma!" based on a very famous play. They are going there secondarily (very secondarily) from curiosity about a new process. Your survey showed this relationship very clearly. The picture is overwhelmingly the attraction, and the process is a small added attraction. I think you should tell your advertising department that we are selling tickets for a picture. The audience is composed not of technicians, but of people who are interested in the love story of Curly and Laurey. I think this is an atrocious ad, and so does Dick.

All good wishes.

Oscar Hammerstein to Cheryl Crawford, January 6, 1956

Dear Cheryl:

I called you up several times this week but we never could connect. I wanted to thank you very much for sending me the book by Colette, which I found thoroughly enchanting. I don't know how to make it into a musical play. I always feel that the only justification for adaptation into another medium is the feeling that you can improve upon the original in some way. I don't know what I could do with this to make it better, and I feel that I might lose a great deal of what is already there.

It was kind of you to give me a chance to read this.

All good wishes for the new year.

Sincerely,

We don't know which Colette book producer Cheryl Crawford sent to Oscar. It's unlikely it was *Gigi*, as Oscar surely knew the work from Anita Loos's 1951 Broadway adaptation.

The London production of *The King and I* closed on January 14.

The film of *Carousel* opened on February 16. Though well reviewed at the time, the film is generally regarded as one of the lesser of the Rodgers and Hammerstein film adaptations.

Oscar Hammerstein to Harry Ruby (excerpt), February 23, 1956

I was very happy to hear from you and I am also happy to tell you that the rumor in the clipping that you sent has no basis of truth. The presidency of ASCAP is something I don't need and being a figurehead is something I need even less. Furthermore, the presidency of ASCAP needs a man who is not at all like a certain man who thinks he needs it and this is the broadest hint I will give you as to how I will vote next month and, furthermore, I would not like to be quoted.

Oscar Hammerstein to Billy Rose, April 4, 1956

Dear Billy,

I make it a policy not to write letters of condolence when people lose relatives or others who are dear to them. I have my own philosophy about this and think that letters of condolence are a polite intrusion on real grief.

I don't know, therefore, why I feel like breaking my rule and writing to you a letter of sympathy on the loss of your Mt. Kisco home, but the sight of the ruins on television so depressed me and my knowledge of your sense of loss is so vivid that I felt impelled to write to tell you how sorry I am about the whole thing. Knowing you, I am sure that something even more imposing and wonderful will arise from those ashes, but meanwhile I know that it has been tough for you to bear.

I told Dorothy I was going to write you a letter about this and she asked me to say "Me, too" for her.

All the best to you.

As ever,

Oscar Hammerstein to Elmer Rice, April 13, 1956

Dear Elmer:

Dick and I have re-read and re-studied very carefully the musical possibilities of DREAM GIRL.[1] There is little doubt in our minds that it can be

---

[1] *Dream Girl* became the basis of the 1965 musical, *Skyscraper*. With a book by Peter Stone, and a score by Jimmy Van Heusen and Sammy Cahn, it starred Julie Harris.

turned into a musical, but it just doesn't happen to be the kind of play we feel like doing right now. I believe that you as an author can understand this kind of reaction better than a layman who might consider it a very foolish answer. We feel like doing another kind of musical play, but we don't even know what kind we are looking for. We won't know until we find it. Thank you very much for submitting it to us.

I suggest that you go to Alan Lerner, who is certainly one of the brightest minds in the musical field today. It might very well appeal to him and if it did, I think he would do a very good job on it with one composer or another.

All the best from both of us.

Oscar Hammerstein to Carl G. Wonnberger, April 23, 1956

Dear Mr. Wonnberger:

Thank you for your letter about the film version of "Carousel". I am grateful for your interest in our work and for the time you devoted to writing me your views on the film. I am sorry you don't like it and found so much to irritate you. I cannot agree with all of your criticisms. I have a few reservations of my own, but I thought that all considered as a whole the film was a creditable version of the story. It is apparently pleasing audiences all over the country. That is no reason, however, why it should please you as well. You are certainly entitled to your own standards, and I find it gratifying to note that they are so high when you judge our plays.

My best wishes to you.

Sincerely,

Oscar Hammerstein II

Oscar Hammerstein to Doran Hurley, April 24, 1956

Dear Mr. Hurley:

My friend Monsignor Funcke of Hogansburg, New York has suggested to me that a book by you entitled "Monsignor"[2] might be turned into a very unusual and interesting musical play by Mr. Rodgers and me. He adds that

---

[2] *Monsignor* was published in 1936. Its *New York Times* review begins: "In 'Monsignor,' Doran Hurley has written the story of an inner conflict, the struggle in the divided nature of an able and

it might take a miracle to achieve this end. Since Mr. Rodgers and I like to undertake difficult tasks, I am have [*sic*] tempted to write you and ask if you can send me a copy of your book, and further, if you would be disposed to let us adapt it if we thought it was a good idea for us. I realize that copies of the book are rare, and I would take very good care of it if you sent me one.

My best wishes to you.

Sincerely,

Oscar Hammerstein II

Josh Logan (at Twentieth Century-Fox Film Corp.) to Oscar Hammerstein, May 9, 1956

Dear Oscar:

Thank you so much for your letter which enclosed Kenneth Tynan's piece on MIDDLE OF THE NIGHT. It's very flattering to have your play liked by anyone as tough as Tynan.

I miss New York at times but mostly I am so absorbed in working in this fascinating medium that I don't get too blue. It's very exhilarating, this movie business, especially when the material and cast is good. I think Marilyn Monroe is a delightful actress and she is a sweet girl and I am enjoying working with her. Also Don Murray is apt to make a big hit in this show [*Bus Stop*].

Are you working on the new show? The rumor that you are going to do STATE FAIR sounds like fun.

Would love to hear from you if you have a minute. Nedda is in New York for a few days on a rush business trip trying to help me resign Eddie Robinson but she will be back Friday.

What do you think of MY FAIR LADY and MOST HAPPY FELLA? Have you seen them yet?

Love to Dorothy and you from all of us.

Sincerely,

Josh

---

powerful prelate between the urge for personal power and a no less fundamental desire for spiritual grace."

Oscar Hammerstein to Josh Logan, May 15, 1956

Dear Josh,

The rumor about STATE FAIR had foundation, but not any more. We decided that it would be too much like a warmed over job for us to be doing right now.

Answering your question about my opinion of MY FAIR LADY and MOST HAPPY FELLA, I loved them both. FAIR LADY is completely charming and an incredibly skillful job by Alan Lerner. It's a perfectly produced show and I think you will eat up every minute of it. MOST HAPPY FELLA is not everybody's dish. Some people have a great many reservations against it and they usually involve a mixture of opera and musical comedy. I was able to accept this combination for the most part, although there were times when Frank [Loesser], under the impression that he was writing an opera, kept repeating certain passages and delaying the conclusion of scenes long after they had been concluded. This also had the effect of frustrating me when I was interested enough in the story to want to see what would happen next. "Next" wasn't soon enough. I also found the third act dipping off and not as well rounded out as the play was. The over-all effect on me, however, was a very good one and I found very exciting moments in the play and plenty of reasons for going back and seeing it again. I am sure you are going to get very varied reports on this one.

When are you coming home?

Love to you and Nedda from Dorothy and me.

As ever,

Josh Logan directed and produced the Paddy Chayefsky play, *Middle of the Night*, which opened February 8, 1956. At the time of the letter, Logan was directing Marilyn Monroe and Don Murray in a film version of the William Inge play, *Bus Stop*. Rodgers and Hammerstein had considered doing a stage adaptation of *State Fair*. *My Fair Lady* had opened on March 15, and would run a record-breaking 2,717 performances. In Rodgers' memoir he wrote: "*My Fair Lady* glided, waltzed and skipped into town to win immediate acceptance as a classic of the musical theatre. Not only was it a rich and endearing work, it also served to establish Julie Andrews as Broadway's most radiant new star. There wasn't a composer or lyricist who didn't start dreaming of songs for her to sing or roles for her to play." Rodgers and Hammerstein did not have

to wait long. Later that summer they were approached to write a television adaptation of *Cinderella* to star Andrews. As Rodgers said, "Casting her as Cinderella was
like casting Ethel Merman as Annie Oakley. It was right right from the start." Frank
Loesser's *The Most Happy Fella* opened on May 3. In three acts and over forty numbers, it was, if anything, an overabundance of riches.

Oscar Hammerstein to Dick Campbell,[3] May 22, 1956

Dear Dick:

There is a fallacy in your attitude toward "Carmen Jones". You have
come to regard yourself as a kind of middleman manager, with some kind
of priority on the property. The engagements you speak of in stock are
engagements that we are quite capable ourselves of contracting for. I am in
no disagreement with my lawyers in their stated policy to you. They take
care of my stock bookings for this and all my other attractions.

For some time I permitted you to take out a very small concert company and play it in small theatres. I do not think this has improved the
standing of my property at all. I much prefer larger productions which
other theatres are willing to grant me. When you say that the City Center
production has knocked you out of the Carter Theatre in Washington this
summer, this is not true. You have been knocked out of nothing. If the
Carter Barron Theatre wants to play "Carmen Jones", they must come to
me, not you. I think the Reinheimer office has given you good advice in
advising you to "find something new" as you say. I think you have been
leaning on this attraction too long, and I think you have come to look upon
it as something in which you have a pseudo property right. The property
belongs to the copyright owner, who wishes to dispose of it in any way that
seems advisable.

My best wishes to you and Muriel.

Sincerely,

Oscar wrote several letters similar to the one below.

---

[3] Dick Campbell was a Black actor, producer, and director, and a passionate and effective advocate
for Black artists in the theater and television; he was co-founder of the Negro Actors Guild. He was
married to Muriel Rahn, the original Carmen in *Carmen Jones*.

Oscar Hammerstein to Josh Logan, June 1, 1956

Dear Joshua:

George M. Cohan, one of the greatest names in the American theatre during the first three decades of this century, is to have a statue erected to him. The site is on Broadway, just where he belongs. It will be just south of Father Duffy Square. This has already been approved by Commissioner Robert Moses. Architectural plans are on the drawing boards, and the sculptor is working on the design for the statue.

The George M. Cohan Memorial Committee is being formed. It already includes Irving Berlin, Herbert Bayard Swope, Father George B. Ford and Governor Averell Harriman. As chairman of this committee, I am very anxious to have your name on it also. Your acceptance will involve no sacrifice of any time on your part.

The cooperation of Mayor Robert F. Wagner and other city officials has been assured in honoring George M. Cohan. The city is also honoring our theatre.

I hope to have your acceptance as soon as possible.

All good wishes.

Sincerely,

Oscar

Oscar Hammerstein II

Josh Logan to Oscar Hammerstein, June 11, 1956

Dear Oscar:

I received your letter of June 1st asking that my name be on a committee to help erect a statue of George M. Cohan. I am terribly sorry not to be able to join this committee but I have just started a committee of my own which is the committee for not putting up a statue of George M. Cohan.

I don't think it is my prejudice against anything Irish but I have always been repelled by George Cohan and all he represented that was selfish and egotistical in our theatre. I do respect his talent and his songs and even his plays, but I would not be an enthusiastic member of the committee. When you are doing it for Clarence Derwent please call on me again. He may not be as talented but he's nicer.

Best,

P.S. This is a personal letter + if you publish it I'll say it was written by Milton Grofeply.

As a producer, George M. Cohan was a fierce opponent of the Actors' Equity Association. The organization was created in 1913 and had their first strike in 1919, seeking recognition as a labor union. The formation of the union and the strike were in response to practices such as not compensating actors for rehearsal time, canceled performances, and added matinees, and forcing them to pay for their own costumes and travel expenses. Despite being a performer himself, Cohan never joined Equity, and through his opposition to the organization, the strike and, apparently, most of its goals, he earned the enmity of many in the theater community— some with long memories.

John Steinbeck to Oscar Hammerstein, June 6, 1956

Dear Oscar:

I don't think I could be called show business' brightest ornament and I did not know Geo. M. Cohen [sic] and I don't care much for statues unless they were carved by Michael Angelo, but if you want me to be on this committee I shall be very glad to. From what I have read and heard Cohen himself would have been very much in favor of a statue to himself and that is no bad thing. Walt Whitman spent the subscription money gathered by his friends to pay the grocery bill for a tomb for himself with marble floor show. I guess different people have different impulses but I do think that any one who seriously says he doesn't want to be remembered is either nuts or a liar. I think Buck Crouse had the most graceful and perhaps the truest desire of all when he said he would like to be remembered as Timmy's father. Our eminent American novelists who are presently fighting for billing on a tombstone, seem to have forgotten, Immortality as it was known in classical times is no longer valid. That kind went out with the Paper or papyrus shortage and small percentage of education. Now, I mean in our era, so much is happening in our knowledge of the physical world that it is almost impossible to keep up and there is increasingly little time to look back except perhaps nostalgically and that is for the old and the peedoff.

We have missed you and Dorothy. I don't go in to town much now. I find I can work out here and I want to get one more little book finished before I go to the conventions. And I can do it too with my new invention. I have a station wagon. In the back seat and attached to the back of the front seat I have a little folding desk. It holds a typewriter. Early in the morning I drive out to the ocean and park and stay until I get my day's stint done. No one can interrupt me because no one knows where I am. I don't even know where I am going when I start. When the sun comes in I turn the car and I [center?] the window to the breeze. I have a tiny set of files and a box of paper stock. It is almost ideal. I built the desk myself and it works. There is a red winged black bird perched on my radiator now looking in at me. What a way to live.

Hope to see you soon and meanwhile, by all means put me on this committee if you wish. Be sure though that I promise not to do any work of any kind. Love to Dorothy.

John

Oscar Hammerstein to John Steinbeck, June 12, 1956

Dear John:

Thank you for accepting the position of trust, honor and patriotism which I have so generously offered you. You will just love serving on the committee because we are going to have no meetings and do no work whatever. Your only obligation is to learn how to spell the name of the man whose statue we are sponsoring. He spells it C—O—H—A—N, thereby establishing him as an Irish-American from Providence, and no branch whatever of the famous Jewish clan. He had an interesting idea on this subject. He named a great many of his plays by Irish names—"Little Nelly Kelly", "Rosie O'Reilly" etc. He said that this would attract Irish attendance, and the Jews came to the theatre anyway.

Since you are the busy one these days and I am not, I shall wait to hear from you when you and Elaine come to town and tell us when you can see us.

Love to you both from both of us.

Oscar Hammerstein to Elizabeth Rider Montgomery,[4]
June 12, 1956

Dear Miss Montgomery:

I have read the excerpts from your book, "The Story Behind Popular Songs". Following your suggestion that I correct whatever is wrong, these are the observations I have made while reading the material:

ROMBERG

Page 2. It didn't happen that way at all. "The Desert Song" started by my reading an account in the newspaper of the Riff trouble in Morocco. I gave it to Frank Mandel and Frank and I started to write the story, having evoked Romberg's enthusiasm to do the score. After we got under way we then went to Otto and invited him into the collaboration. The three of us worked on the book and Otto Harbach and I collaborated on the lyrics. The production was by Schwab and Mandel.

FRIML

You do not mention Herbert Stothard [sic], whose name was also on "Rose Marie" as a composer with Rudolph Friml. They did not work together. They wrote separate songs. The most prominent ones were written by Friml—"Indian Love Call", "Rose Marie", "Totem Tom Tom", "The Mounties" etc. Herbert Stothard did several others and pulled the whole score together, incidental music, finales, etc.

KERN

Page 2. You must add as one of his collaborators Guy Bolton, who wrote all the books for the Princess Theatre plays with Kern. Wodehouse wrote the lyrics.

Page 3. He was neither gentle nor soft-voiced.

Page. 4. I think when you say in the third paragraph on this page that "Kern bought a book", you mean he read a book. He could not very well have bought it before the meeting with Edna Ferber which you describe.

---

[4] Elizabeth Rider Montgomery was a prolific author of children's books in addition to co-authoring many of the "Dick and Jane" primers. *The Story Behind Popular Songs* was published in 1958.

Page 8. It is not true that I was anxious to have a play produced by someone other than my uncle. I had already succeeded in this achievement when I wrote "Sunny" with Jerome Kern, which was produced by Charles Dillingham, and I had also produced "Desert Song" with Schwab and Mandel. Also, it is not true that Florenz Ziegfeld hated the name of Hammerstein. You are over-dramatizing here. The truth of the matter is this: When Jerome Kern read half of "Show Boat" he called me up and told me he had a play with a million dollar title, that he had only read half of it but that he wanted to do it with me. I then bought a copy and read it and, as you say, we each did independent scenarios and found that we had practically the same layout for the story. In the same day that Kern called me up he also called up Ziegfeld and enlisted his interest. It was only after several months, when we had practically finished the play and it looked as if Ziegfeld were stalling us and not intending to do the play that season, that we took the play to Arthur Hammerstein. Arthur wanted to do it, but he too was tied up with another play first. We finally went back to Ziegfeld and it was produced by him, as you know.

RODGERS AND HAMMERSTEIN

Page 9. Although it is true that I am very slow in my lyric writing, it so happens that your story about "Oh, What a Beautiful Morning" is spoiled because this is one of the few songs that I wrote quickly. I would say that I finished it in about three days.

I am afraid that it will be hard for us to come together during your stay in New York because on those dates I am going to be down on my farm in Pennsylvania. I wish you the best of luck in your undertaking.

Sincerely,

Oscar Hammerstein II

Oscar Hammerstein to Leo McCarey, June 28, 1956

Dear Leo:

As a matter of fact, Dick and I did run "Love Affair" (16 millimeter home projector) about four months ago. I had remembered the picture with great affection, and we considered it seriously as a possible musical play. I find it hard to adapt the last part to music—after she has been crippled. Dick likes this part the best and doesn't think the first part will hold up. I like the first part the best. It's a kind of a deadlock, isn't it?

Thank you for writing and suggesting it, and best wishes from both of us to you always.

Leo McCarey co-authored, produced, and directed the 1939 film, *Love Affair*, which starred Irene Dunne and Charles Boyer. McCarey took on the same jobs for the 1957 re-make, re-titled *An Affair to Remember*, which starred Deborah Kerr and Cary Grant.

Pipe Dream closed on Broadway on June 30.

Oscar Hammerstein to Judith Chase Churchill (for *McCall's* magazine), July 10, 1956

Dear Miss Churchill:

Subject: My secret ambition.

Answer: None.

Sorry.

Regarding the film of *The King and I*:

Oscar Hammerstein to Fletcher R. Andrews, July 11, 1956

Dear Mr. Andrews:

First let me thank you for your very gratifying interest in my work.

Now to answer your questions: The songs omitted had to be eliminated to bring it within playing time. The picture runs two hours and thirteen minutes, and this is a long time to sit in a theatre without any chance of getting up. Some pictures run longer, but usually they seem too long. In the case of "Oklahoma!" we inserted an intermission and it seems to work very well, but most picture producers do not believe in this and apparently 20th Century Fox doesn't think it is a good idea.

Anna's soliloquy, "Shall I Tell You What I Think of You?", which you regard as "the most regrettable omission", was eliminated not because of the time, but because somehow or other they could not get an effective rendition of it. I don't know whether this was the fault of the singing artist or the director or the music department. I was not in Hollywood during the shooting of the picture.

The song by Lady Thiang (the title to which you do not remember) was "Western People Funny". Personally, I do not feel that this was much of a loss.

I believe that there was another voice[5] dubbed in for Miss Kerr's songs. I am not sure whether this was true of the entire musical program because Miss Kerr has a voice. Sometimes the star sings most of the song and high notes are dubbed in, but more often the entire song is sung by another voice when there is any supplemental dubbing.

I agree with you on the excellent production that Fox gave "The King and I", and while I regret some of the omissions, I understand the reason for them.

My thanks again to you and your wife for caring so much about it, and also for your taking the trouble to write to me.

With every good wish for a pleasant summer.

Sincerely,

**Oscar Hammerstein to Philip K. Scheuer, *Los Angeles Times*,
July 14, 1956**

Dear Phil:

I read with great interest and gratification your piece in the Times entitled "R and H musicals take on added stature in films". Your plea to make more use of "cinematic techniques" is an interesting one. The producers, directors and screen playwrights involved all made efforts to introduce more movie feeling into "Oklahoma!", "Carousel" and "The King and I". Most of these sequences were cut because they seemed ineffective

---

[5] Marni Nixon famously dubbed Deborah Kerr's singing voice in the film.

in the scripts. The few of them that were kept and used were only fairly successful. It may be that strong musical plays attain a crystalized form that is hard to break through or reshape. If the score [is popular?] enough one doesn't dare omit numbers which the public are sure to be looking for. Solid stories are hard to open up so that room can be made for extended fanciful dance sequences. I myself am grateful for this. I do not like extended dance sequences unless they carry on the story or underline the thoughts or emotions of a character as they do in "Oklahoma!"

"South Pacific" is a different cup of tea. "South Pacific" will not only lend itself to cinematic techniques. It is in its present form nearly a motion picture. Even on the stage [it] achieved something like a lap dissolve in going from one scene to another. The vast spaces of the Pacific Ocean and the beauty of the Pacific Islands are waiting there eager to make a real movie out of "South Pacific", just as Doc Scheuer has ordered.

Thank you for your interest and for the nice things you have said about us.

Best wishes to you always.

Oscar Hammerstein to Shirley Potash, July 17, 1956

Dear Shirley:

Well, you did it! I thought there was no sarsaparilla left north of the Mason Dixon Line, and yet you came up with all those pint bottles! If you will ask your bootlegger to get in touch with me, I would be happy to give him a standing order.

I have always followed the policy of complimenting you as little as possible because I think it is bad for you, but on this occasion I cannot refrain from saying that it was very kind and sweet of you not only to remember my birthday, but also my predilection for this now practically illegal drink.

Love from us all.

(Your old—I mean

former—boss)

Oscar Hammerstein to Leighton Brill, July 17, 1956

Dear Leighton:

I am very happy to hear you are contemplating the establishment of a music circus in Anaheim on or about the grounds of Disneyland.

These music circuses have been successful in almost every locality where they have been started, and in the last few years they have sprouted up all over the country. They are, in my opinion, a very good thing for the American musical theatre. They bring to smaller communities a variety of "live theatre" production which they could not otherwise receive. Instead of elaborate scenery, which such organizations could not afford, they substitute the audience's imagination, and in most cases this is much better. In these days when touring companies are very difficult to sustain even in large cities, and impossible to gear for the smaller ones, the circus seems to me the answer. They, more than any other institution, are now keeping our American musical theatre alive. Since our musical theatre is the best in the world, it is well worth keeping alive, and therefore my best wishes go with you in this new project.

For quite selfish reasons I am also glad that you happen to be mixed up in this because it is an assurance to me that my plays as well as the works of others will be well done. Your feeling for musical productions and your long experience, first with me and later on your own, qualify you for this job as few others are qualified.

Good luck to you and love from us all.

Oscar Hammerstein to William [Hammerstein?], August 3, 1956

Dear Bill:

Langston Hughes came up to see me yesterday and we had a nice talk about the play. He has already made cuts which he estimates to eliminate a half hour out of the play. I have not seen them. They are interior cuts, chopping off lines and with no entire scenes eliminated. I think that is the right way to cut the play. He seems very anxious to have you direct it, and I told him that I thought that you would, and that I hoped you would.

He brought along another manuscript called "Tambourines to Glory" which is directed at the religious racket in Harlem. It is an interesting subject matter, but I doubt if this play does justice to it. I read it last night.

That's all for now. How about you?

Love,

Oscar Hammerstein to Otto Harbach "on His Eighty-third Birthday," August 18, 1956

Dear Otto:

In sending you birthday congratulations I cannot help congratulating myself on having known you for so many birthdays. One of my recollections of this treasured friendship is the thing you said on a day thirty summers ago when we were sitting in your garden at Mamaroneck, trying to write a lyric together. I believe it was for THE DESERT SONG. We were stuck. We had been rejecting each other's ideas for a couple of hours. Every road we had explored had become a dead end. We sat in mute frustration, staring in opposite directions. Then you broke the silence: "Oscar," you said, "We are not going to create this song. This song exists right now. It is somewhere in the world. Our job is to find it."

By the same token, Otto, I am not creating a tribute to you on your birthday. The tribute exists. It is therefore very easy to find. I don't have to make up good things to say about you. You radiate good things, and all your friends have to do is to catch them and hold them up for you to see, so that like Jack Horner you can say: "What a good boy am I!" Since you are too modest ever to say this, I will say it for you. "What a good boy are you!"

To those of us who know you well it seems reduntant [sic] to offer you the trite traditional "happy birthday" wish. In the first place, it is your nature to be happy. In the second place, you have so many reasons to be happy. From one birthday to another you have been adding pleasure and beauty to the world around you. Your professional life has been brilliantly successful. You have been the foremost librettist in the American theatre, and you have been the guiding star to many younger writers who have followed you. None of these is so indebted to you as I am.

It is impossible to estimate the extent of your effect upon our theatre, impossible to measure in applause or laughs or dollars, but we who have worked beside you know that you have left a mark that will never be erased.

Even more difficult is the task of estimating your influence upon those who have had the rare blessings of your friendship. Leaving out the direct help you have given to those who needed it—money, advice, encouragement—the important fact is that a man like you enriches his world merely by living in it. The knowledge that right here in our town we have a man whose thoughts are clear and just, whose instincts are unselfish, whose actions are kind and constructive—this knowledge is a tonic to everyone who possesses it. It is an asset on the balance sheet of the human race that offsets many discouraging liabilities. You have infused some of your wisdom and your virtue into many people. Your kindness and patience have traveled and will live long. Keep well and stay with us for many more years, Otto, brightening the darker and colder corners of our lives with the light of your good sense and the warmth of your good heart.

Always your good friend and pupil,

OSCAR

Oscar Hammerstein to Walter Knapp, September 24, 1956

Dear Walter:

Thank you for your letter of September 13th. You have asked for some news of the family, and there is very specific news to tell you. A week ago last Friday Jimmy and his wife had their first baby. Pooling all our grandchildren together, Dorothy and I now have ten, but this is the first one that we have had that is directly ours together. Also it is the first male child of this new generation, and the only current custodian of the name of Hammerstein. Also his name is Oscar (the third, that is). Therefore it is a cause of much happiness and celebration.

I am glad that you are holding up the Stevenson banner in your Republican desert out there. I am doing a little work on his behalf myself, trying to write out a little paragraph in a speech here and there, and help organize dinners and so forth. I am not going to be able to vote this year, however, because we are going to Australia on October 23rd. The State of Pennsylvania does not permit absentee votes except on the part of members of the armed services or people who are confined to sickbeds and hospitals.

Dorothy and I will be away for seven weeks. We are going to stop for six days in Hawaii where I expect to do some location work on "South Pacific", which we hope to shoot as a picture next summer. Josh Logan will direct it, as he did the play. After Hawaii we go straight to Australia, stop a few days in Sydney and then arrive in Melbourne in time for the "Melbourne Cup", which is a horse race Dorothy has been telling me about ever since I met her. It had better be good, and I had better make a lot of money on it. We will then stay for the Olympic Games and be in this country on December 14th.

Meanwhile I have started with Dick on a musical version of "Cinderella" which we are going to do as a spectacular on television, either at the end of February or the beginning of March. Julie Andrews, the star of "My Fair Lady", will be Cinderella. We are going to stick pretty closely to the classical story, the only difference being that this will be done to music. They will sing practically all of it. There will be music playing during every minute of the hour and a half telecast. It is really going to be a small opera, but we will shun that word because it frightens people.

Billy is in London at the moment, having been chosen as the director of the English version of "Fanny". Robert Morley will play the Walter Slezak part over there, and it will open at the Drury Lane at the end of October. Billy is doing very well now and seems to be in a good deal of demand as a director and producer. Within a year or so I think he will blossom into something important in the theatre. Alice and Phil and Henry and Joan all seem very happy. Alice and Phil have two children. Henry and Joan have three. Susan, having fixed up a lovely apartment in New York, has now sublet it and is going to Paris for six months to study French and have her child started in French, and incidentally have a very good time too, I suppose. Reg, having successfully put on "Show Boat" at Jones Beach this summer, is once again a country boy taking it easy in Doylestown and enjoying it.

I am sorry that you and Marian have had such a lousy sequence of breaks, and I hope that luck will turn the other way soon. I have "a feeling" that it will, whatever that is worth.

Love to you both from both of us.

As ever,

Oscar Hammerstein to Milton Kadison, September 26, 1956

Dear Kaddy:

Thank you for your letter and the exciting enclosure about the saga of Pfizer. I don't believe I grasped all the details connected with Pfizer's meteoric rise in the world of commercial chemistry, but I gathered that this is a hell of a company.

The villain in the Erich Leinsdorf production of "Orpheus" seems to be the author, Eric Bentley. I am not surprised. He is one of those academic critics who write books on how impossible all modern playwrights are. As a matter of fact, he admires no one very much after Eschylus [sic]. Like Kronenberger, whose sentiments are similar, he is a feeble playwright when he starts to compete with these poor modern hacks. I don't maintain that a critic should be a good playwright, but I am always surprised that when these fellows with normally high standards try their hand, they write not only bad plays, but cheap ones. Ah well!

Love to all.

Laurence Schwab to Oscar Hammerstein, September 26, 1956

Dear Oscar,

A few weeks ago I wrote you making a large request. I know it may have seemed a strong presumption on my part—I know it was terribly difficult for me to write. Before I attempt to arrange other ways of obtaining the money I wish you would let me know your feelings. A rejection will certainly be understood by me.

I'd appreciate a reflection of your attitude towards this jam I've gotten into.

Thanks.

Best,

Larry

Oscar Hammerstein to Laurence Schwab, October 2, 1956

Dear Larry:

I was under the impression that I had answered your letter, and I am sorry that I have kept you in suspense. It seems to me that while the fee that your lawyer wishes to charge you may be perfectly reasonable, I don't see why he shouldn't accept payment from you in installments out of your salary each week.

Answering the last sentence of your recent letter, "I'd appreciate a reflection of your attitude towards this jam I'm gotten into." I have no wish to censor you. It seems to be the result of a very unfortunate accident and very understandable, a strange combination of bad breaks following one upon the other. The only fault I can find with you is that having gotten into the jam, you have no money set by for this or any other kind of emergency. You have been earning a very good salary for a long time now, and your only dependent is yourself. Not to have laid something by seems immature, and I think that from here in, after you have dug yourself out of this financial scrape, you had better see to it that [you] put aside something every week out of your earnings. You never know what catastrophe or misfortune might overtake you at any time. It might be something like this, or you might even get married some day!

Your affectionate and Dutch uncle,

Oscar Hammerstein to Edward R. Murrow, Columbia Broadcasting System, September 27, 1956

Dear Ed:

I understand you are doing a program on Suez, to which I look forward with great excitement. I was wondering if, in the course of the program, you had had a chance to deal with what I consider the most important feature of the situation. It relates to our little talk on "Person to Person" on international anarchy. In other words, living in a world without any law or order, a nation—and even a small nation like Egypt—can suddenly say "I am no longer going to live up to my contract." Instead of having a court into which

the contractual parties can hurl him, we have a world thrown into immediate and complete confusion. We have international conferences. We have
threats of gunboat diplomacy. We have threats of boycott. We bluff, we negotiate. Russia, India, the United States, Great Britain and France summon
their conflicting philosophies and collide with one another in a disgraceful
free-for-all. A world of sovereign nations, without any enforceable law to
guide them is an idiotic spectacle.

I now descend from my soapbox with the fervent hope that you perhaps may step on to it some day. You are the man who could do something
about this.

All good wishes to you.

As ever.

In July of 1956, Egyptian President Nasser nationalized the Suez Canal in response
to the UK and the United States withdrawing support for the construction of the
Aswan Dam in response to warming relations between Egypt and the Soviet Union.
At the same time, Egypt closed the Straits of Tiran to Israeli ships, leading to the
"Suez Crisis" and France, Israel, and the UK invading Egypt. The crisis was resolved
with a United Nations peacekeeping force, its first.

BMI—Broadcast Music, Inc.—was founded in 1939 by the National Association
of Broadcasters, with the primary intent of giving radio stations an alternative to
having to pay ASCAP-represented composers the royalties they were demanding for
the licensing of their music. It gave the radio stations leverage, and also gave them
the ability to favor BMI-represented composers on their radio stations.

Oscar Hammerstein to Abel Green, *Variety*, September 27, 1956

Dear Abel:

I did not understand the word "backfire" on the first page of Variety.
Without challenging the figures for the moment, I submit to you that the
figures make no difference. The principle involved is, should the companies
which own and control the principal media of exploiting songs be in a position to exploit their own songs at the expense of others? It is a simple matter
of unfair competition. If only five percent of the performances on the air
were BMI, and that five percent was the result of undue plugging by the
owners of the songs, who also own the airwaves, it would still in my opinion

be an outrage. There is no reason why ASCAP should not have competition. Unfair competition is what the songwriters are talking about. And when I say songwriters I don't mean ASCAP at all. I mean all songwriters outside the orbit and the employment of the broadcaster-owned publishing companies.

I will always love you anyway.

A Tree Grows in Brooklyn was a bestselling semi-autobiographical novel by Betty Smith. Published in 1943, it told of a young girl growing up poor in Brooklyn in the 1900s and teens. A successful film version was released in 1945, and a musical version opened on Broadway in 1951. The score was by Arthur Schwartz and Dorothy Fields, but audiences found the show too wistful and sad, and the script—co-written by the director, George Abbott—threw the story off balance to favor of the colorful aunt, played by Shirley Booth. The show struggled through 267 performances. The film musical discussed below was never made.

Oscar Hammerstein to Charles Brackett, Twentieth Century-Fox Films, October 3, 1956

Dear Charlie:

I ran "A Tree Grows in Brooklyn" yesterday. I did not see the very finish because I had to rush away to make an appointment for which I was late, but I saw practically the whole picture.

I think you can make a wonderful musical out of it. It is a tender and beautiful and human story set against an earthy background. (I realize that "earthy" is a strange adjective to apply to pavement and bricks, but you know what I mean.)

I never read the book, but having seen the musical play and this picture yesterday, I realize that there are two handicaps to be aware of. They are the chief characters, Katie and Johnny. In both the picture and the play I found them two great big bores. The point is that they don't have to be. It is a question of writing them with more subtlety. Possibly Betty Smith found it difficult to write honestly about her father and mother. She has too much affection for her father and too much resentment toward her mother. The result is that he is just too damn sweet for words, and she is a complete and consistently unattractive scold.

The father and daughter relationship is perhaps the best thing in it, but here again in the writing it gets so coy that I want to walk away from it.

Why then do I say I think you can make a great musical out of it? It is because I think the characters—imagining them written with more subtlety and understanding, and being given more variety and dimension—are good characters. The relationships between them are fine and natural and believable. I am complaining merely on the emphasis, the overemphasis on the salient quality of each. This one is a hard woman. This one is a soft man. This little girl is a bookworm.

The right kind of songs will of course give shadings to the characters and create a greater sympathy and understanding for them. It will not be hard to introduce songs. Watching the picture yesterday, I could see a chance for a good "gossip theme" for the insurance man. He can retail the doings of the neighborhood in verse, and it could be very humorous and attractive. There would of course be a father and daughter theme which would deal in fantasies and make-believe. A love song between Katie and Johnny the night he comes home, the night she waits up for him. Possibly you would show a shot of Johnny performing at that wedding party that he went to that night, showing that hardly anybody listened to him as he sang, and then tying it up with his description of the affair when he came home.

While I thought the musical play fell far short of the possibilities of the story, and while I believe that they over-developed the part of Cissie in order to satisfy Shirley Booth, I nevertheless missed some of the solid comedy scenes that belonged to Cissie and to Cissie's house—especially the false pregnancy scene. Was that invented by the musical comedy authors, or was it in the book?

It occurs to me, Charlie, that you would have an easier time with this musical version if you could acquire the rights to the play version. Some of the songs were good, especially the gay and humorous ones. If you had access to these and had the right to add anything else you pleased, I believe it could only enrich the final version that you would create.

Furthermore, acquiring the rights to the stage play would eliminate the chance of lawsuits in this quarter. It is going to be very difficult for you to musicalize the story without seeming to have crossed their version somewhere or other. Your search for musical devices may very well lead you into the same roads that they travelled before, and very confusing issues may develop.

Since they cannot market their version elsewhere, I should think that the price paid for their material would not be excessive and in the end would eliminate possible embarrassment and indeed help the whole project.

Here endeth my random reflections on "A Tree Grows In Brooklyn".

Best wishes to you.

Always,

Oscar Hammerstein to Max Gordon, October 22, 1956

Dear Max:

I have been thinking about your play [*Everybody Loves Me*] a great deal since I saw the runthrough [*sic*] on Friday. I have been hanging around rehearsals long enough to know that on the fifth day, when actors are holding parts in their hands and thinking of positions, it is pretty hard to get anything like a final characterization from any one of them, and certainly the director can achieve very little in the way of pace and composition.

On the other hand, there is great danger in making too many allowances and in assuming this or that is going to be "all right later on". A rehearsal like that can show basic tendencies, and the basic tendency in Pat Harrington's performance alarms me deeply.

A play can be killed in the first minute and a half, and that play was killed for me the other day in less than that time. As soon as I heard the low, meek tones and saw the sad face on Pat Harrington, I was sunk, and so I believe was the play. My advice to you and Bob [Sinclair] is DON'T WAIT FOR PRINCETON! By that I don't mean that you should fire Harrington tomorrow. But if you cannot get a comic performance out of him, and a performance that will start the play off in the right mood, then fire him and don't wait for Princeton. I don't think there is anything more important for Bob to do now than to find out whether he can get this man to tell the audience what kind of play this really is when the curtain goes up. He is in command for quite some time. What kind of play is it? It is unquestionably a character comedy, a very good comedy built around an interesting central figure, with well drawn characters surrounding him. It is neither a slap-bang farce nor is it an O'Neill tragedy. It is a human comedy. But a comedy!

The seriousness of what Harrington did to me the other day was not merely the deficiency of an actor not playing a part well. He set the tone of the whole play, misled me, the audience, and threw the rest of the cast into the dumps. They never came up. I don't believe that the part is that of a poor meek little man. He is meek enough not to answer Gordie back when Gordie insults him. Gordie is his meal ticket. But this type of stooge is very seldom meek when he is around other people and when the boss is not looking or listening. The authors seem to know this. They have written him that way. He makes a pass at Gordie's girl when Gordie isn't around. He poses as an expert on show business and he really believes he is an expert. Secretly this kind of man often believes he has more talent than the boss but just doesn't have the breaks. But Harrington plays the part as if the boss is always looking and ready to jump on him. He plays the part of a poor beaten man who was brought up in an orphan asylum and kicked around all his life, and has given up and decided to take everybody's insults with humble resignation. This is not funny! I think there would be some value in having him start off very cockily—even if the authors had to do a little re-writing. Then you would see the contrast after Gordie comes in and he clams up and becomes the stooge.

I firmly believe that he slows up the pace and brings down the volume to a degree that might bring disaster upon you, so DON'T WAIT FOR PRINCETON!

I would like you to show this to Bob for whatever it may be worth to him, and at the same time thank him for his courtesy in allowing me to see the runthrough. I admired the progress he has made mechanically, and it seemed to me that he is all ready to leap into the critical second week of re-hearsal and start to attain characterizations from his people. I thought the cast were all very good indeed (with that one glaring exception, who may after all be fixed up). I don't think the little girl could be improved upon. I think Temple [Texas] is giving a very well balanced performance in a part that is very difficult to balance. She shouldn't be tarty, and on the other hand she shouldn't act like a graduate of Miss Finch's Young Ladies Seminary. She lands between the two extremes very well, I believe. (I thought Bob, if he will forgive my impertinence, that in the first scene she had her back to too large a part of the house. I started sitting over on the extreme right. She made her entrance and sat in a chair with her back three quarters to the audience. I moved to the center so that I could see her face. And I didn't see her face. Since she is a new character getting established, this may be a handicap—unless you have done this deliberately for some good reason that I wasn't conscious of.)

I think all the character men are fine, the young boy is perfect, and nobody could have been chosen for the principal part who could have come near Jack Carson. I think he played much lower than he will eventually play, but that is all part of the first week unfamiliarity. You have the cast to give this play all the bounce that it ought to have.

There is no reason why this play, in the hands of you and Bob, couldn't turn out to be a solid winner. Only remember—D.W.F.P.

Love and good luck to you all.

Pat Harrington was not replaced. *Everybody Loves Me* did not make it to Broadway.

There's comparatively little correspondence between Rodgers and Hammerstein, probably because they would work together or just a phone call apart. A rich exception is a handful of letters exchanged while Oscar and Dorothy were attending the 1956 Summer Olympics in Melbourne. Oscar was still at work on the book and lyrics for *Cinderella*, their upcoming television musical. (Because of the reversal of seasons in the Southern hemisphere, the 1956 Summer Games were held from November 22 through December 8.)

Oscar Hammerstein (in Melbourne) to Richard Rodgers, November 10, 1956

Dear Dick:

I have a pretty good rough draft of "The Prince Is Giving a Ball", the long "montage" number. I'll be sending you the finished number in a week or ten days.

I've been brooding about a line in "Do I Love You Because You're Beautiful?" I don't like "Am I making believe, etc?" "Making believe"

(Outside of the fact that I cashed in on that phrase some years ago) seems an unimportant expression in this connection. How about this?

Am I telling my heart I see in you

A girl too lovely to be really true?

Let me know what you think.

The last time we went over this number, I suggested that you stay up on the higher notes, going into the phrase: "Are you the sweet invention, etc.?" First, you said you had wanted to finish in minor, then you said you could do what I was asking for and still finish in minor.

Now I have a new idea. Would it not be more exciting and psychologically sounder to finish the refrain in major, even though you have started in minor? It is my conception that although the last line is a question, the lover really believes she is "as beautiful as she seems". So after starting with doubt (Minor key) the major finish would imply: "Oh, hell, I love you and I really think in my heart of hearts that you are as beautiful as you seem." This is based, of course, on the assumption that it is not musically ungrammatical to start with minor and finish with major.

One thing is sure. My instinct is groping around for more of a lift at the finish than we have.

Last Monday, before we left Sydney, Skouras and Irving phoned me about Josh's doing Sayonara before S.P. (Let me tell you that Skouras on the phone, eleven thousand miles away, is one continuous hum of static.)

I airmailed a letter to Josh expressing concern particularly about Paul Osborn. (Josh had always said he would do Sayonara first if he could cast it.) I told him that if Paul had to go back on Sayonara for final scripting it would throw us badly because we must have a rough screenplay in December, not only for budget purposes but for scheduling to accommodate possible date conflicts with either of the two stars, to say nothing of the time urgency in arranging for the housing facilities on location, wherever we go. In the Hawaian [sic] islands we would certainly have to do this many months ahead.

I haven't heard from Josh yet. Have you?

We are having a great time. The hospitality is a little more elaborate and more frequent than I would like, but we're managing it pretty well.

This hotel is opposite a park—like the Ritz in Boston—and I go out there to work every morning. In the afternoon we go racing or play tennis at Marjorie's. The evenings are pretty well booked. All the favors Dorothy has performed for dozens of Australians passing through New York have now bounced back on us. Fortunately, however, this is an early to bed city, and that saves us.

I have a part-time secretary but she isn't around to-day so, as you can plainly see, I have typed this myself. Be grateful that I didn't write it long-hand. I'm forgetting a lot of things I meant to discuss, but I can always write again.

Love to Dorothy and You

Oc

P.S. Please send the Vanity notice of Max Gordon's opening at Princeton (Nov. 8) and send me any news you may have of their project.

Richard Rodgers to Oscar Hammerstein, November 19, 1956

Dear Oscar:

I have your November 10 letter and since today is the 19th, it apparently takes quite a while to get in contact with you.

I have no particular qualms about using the line "Am I making believe, etc.?". It occurs to me that this is simply a part of the language and it is not connected with you any more than it is with dozens of other authors. I am not devoted to the line "A Girl Too Lovely To Be Really True", for the simple reason I am not devoted to splitting infinitives.

Apparently, you don't remember you gave me a pretty good briefing on the subject of going into a climax on the phrase "Are You The Sweet Invention etc.". At the time I agreed that you were absolutely right and I changed the tune to subscribe to your suggestion. It still reaches higher for its climax and ends in major rather than minor. There is absolutely nothing ungrammatical about ending in major when you start in minor. It is quite conventional and extraordinarily effective. I think you will find you have the lift at the finish that you expected.

Since I wrote to you a few days ago, there has been no further news about S.P. We will be looking at people a little later in the week and I will have news for you then.

The household news is excellent and I find myself at the height of my vigor and possibilities. The repercussions from Sirmay and Dreyfus are heartening, to say the least. Enclosed is Variety clipping you requested (Max Gordon's show), but he tells me on the phone that they got a bad beating in Philadelphia, to such an extent that he is not even sure he wants to bring it in to New York or not. I am deeply disturbed about this for his sake as I know this can have a violent effect on his future behavior. Leave us hope.

You sound as if you are having a wonderful time. Certainly you deserve it! This is also true of us. Let's all keep it up.

Love,

Oscar Hammerstein (in Melbourne) to Richard Rodgers, November 26, 1956

Dear Dick: I enclose an Australian Hit Parade report—shows that we have two out of the seven, first and third, and up to this week we had been running one, two.

The games are wonderful. I go every day. The first day however, when there was no competition was the most thrilling. First there was emotional value in the spectacle of the greatest young athletes of sixty eight countries marching in and standing before you; then the entrance of the runner, one of a long relay that had carried the torch all the way from Greece; the Olympic oath; the opening of the games by The Duke of Edinburgh. The whole experience left us all wilted and drained. Every one [sic] felt like going home and flopping into bed, and guess who did.

The town has gone very social to celebrate the games and there are big shindigs every night. I am wearing tails as often as black tie and my Adams apple has raised a protective callous so that I don't mind so much any more.

I'm still getting in two hours work every morning, two days of tennis a week and an occasional race meeting—a good full life.

You know my new schedule—Dec 11 with Josh, home the evening of December 12, lunch with you at 12.30 I hope? Possible work on the project afterwards, I also hope.

Love to all,

Oscar

Oscar Hammerstein to Richard Rodgers, November 28, 1956

Dear Dick:

Last night I saw the picture, "The King And I" again. This morning I am convinced that this is our best work. I have a kind of humble feeling of not knowing how we did it. It has more wisdom as well as heart than any other musical play by anybody. It will remain "modern" long after any of our other plays. It seems to me to be far in advance of them in its mental and emotional adulthood.

This was not the opening of a run. It was a special charity show—Jewish, what else?—and nevertheless the audience was most enthusiastic, applauding nearly all the numbers, the applause growing in volume and spontaneity as the film progressed. The actual run will not begin in Melbourne until Christmas. It opens earlier in Sydney, December 13.

My reason for wanting to change "make believe" was not chiefly because of my earlier use of the phrase. In my letter to you I mentioned that only parenthetically. I think it is a "little" phrase and I think "Telling my heart" has more emotional importance. You, apparently, don't because you didn't even mention it. Let us wait until we get together which will be in two weeks. I don't share your split infinitive phobia but I tried very hard to dodge "really" and couldn't get out of it. I even considered asking you to eliminate the two notes and substitute a long one thus: "A girl too lovely to be true" but feared it was less interesting musically.

I wrote Max a letter and emphasized the fact that he wasn't alone in being wrong. You and I liked the play and Bob came all the way from the coast to do it. If you run into him you might take the same tack.

I'm having a good time but I'm getting about ready for that fast trot back to the stables, the familiar stall and the home-cooked oats. See you soon. Love to you both –

Oscar

Richard Rodgers to Oscar Hammerstein, December 3, 1956

Dear Oscar,

Possibly this note will miss you, but I'll take my chance. As I said in my last communication, once you and I sit down in a room and discuss those matters of syllables and notes there isn't the remotest possibility of disagreement. I can change the melody line to conform to what you

Photo 23 Oscar Hammerstein II and Richard Rodgers. Photograph by G. Maillarde Kesslere, B. P. From the Oscar Hammerstein II Collection, Library of Congress

would like to do quite easily and I know that you have ways of avoiding a split infinitive. In any event, it will be good to have you back and sit down and talk things over.

I have not only finished everything with the exception of "Impossible", and that problem I discussed with my last note to you, but all my manuscripts are in Sirmay's hands and have already been copied. I think possibly only once before in my career have I been so caught up with myself.

Your news about your fun in Melbourne is very gratifying. Please enjoy yourself up to the last possible moment.

Love to Dorothy and you.

And thank you for the Christmas presents . . .

Oscar Hammerstein to Murray [?], December 27, 1956

Dear Murray:

I have them on even now, and I as I dictate these words into my Dictaphone I am looking down with admiration at my well turned ankle. A chain stitch seems to do something for my ankle, but it is equally fair to say that my ankle does something for the socks. Do you pay fees to gentlemen models? Or, by giving me these socks to wear are you tricking me into modeling them for nothing? All right, I will fall for your trick. Keep sending them to me. In case you have forgotten I had received from you a black pair, a white pair and a grey pair. Skip the pink.

Love from us both and best wishes from us both for a happy New Year.

Sincerely,

Oscar Hammerstein to Cyril [Ritchard?], December 27, 1956

Dear Cyril:

Thank you for the wonderful clothes brush. I know that this kind does the job better than any other and I will have no excuse from now on to go around with lint and old pencil shavings on my coat as you usually see me.

I would like also to take this opportunity to thank you for the magnificent scarf you gave Dorothy. I am sure that scarf is not the right word. It's too big for a scarf, but I mean that thing you gave her. I thank not only on her behalf but on my own because it is a feast to my eyes and I find it very becoming on her.

I am sorry that we were not able to see you cavorting in "Perichole," but I hope we'll catch you at it later in the season. Meanwhile our love and best wishes for a happy and successful New Year,

Chapter Sixteen
1957

Oscar Hammerstein to Mildred [?], January 3, 1957

Dear Mildred:

Thank you for Bentley's book.[1] I haven't read it yet, but some day when I feel in the mood for flagullation [*sic*] I will start it. That is the way this opinionated little pipsqueak always affects me. Don't accept this as a criticism of the gift. I think it is good for us to have these irritating experiences once in a while—like scrubbing yourself with a very stiff brush.

Best wishes to you for a Happy New Year.

Love

In 1954, Sandy Wilson's *The Boy Friend*, took the West End by storm. It was by turns a satire, homage, and parody of 1920s musicals such as those created by Rodgers and Hart and the "Princess shows" by Guy Bolton, P.G. Wodehouse, and Jerome Kern. The latter were modestly produced musicals most of which were staged at the Princess Theatre. *The Boy Friend* opened on Broadway in September 1954, introducing Julie Andrews as a newfound star.

Oscar Hammerstein to Guy Bolton and P. G. Wodehouse, January 28, 1957

Dear Guy and Plum:

Please forgive me for keeping your script so long and for not answering you sooner. One thing that has delayed me was my feeling that I haven't a very intelligent list of comments to make. I find it difficult to be "oriented"

---

[1] The book is likely Eric Bentley's *The Playwright as Thinker*.

The Letters of Oscar Hammerstein II. Mark Eden Horowitz, Oxford University Press. © Mark Eden Horowitz 2022.
DOI: 10.1093/oso/9780197538180.003.0016

in the script. I know the songs are great, and I see nothing wrong with the plot nor the entertainment possibilities that are suggested by it. But in spite of your wild desire not to have another "Boy Friend" I find myself haunted by that very play. I know this is nothing like it, and I know that you have a story and a score that can stand on its own feet. Yet the mere fact that you make a point of this being "an old time show" in the prologue seems to set the audience up for a "Boy Friend" attitude.

I took the liberty of giving the script to Dick Rodgers in hopes that he might come up with a more constructive reaction than mine. It was, however, quite the same reaction. I don't know what the answer is. I think perhaps that attractive as the prologue is, it might be better if you just chucked it and presented the play on its own values. I think perhaps there is a danger in some lines that seem to have a flip quality of the old days, i.e. the fifth line on page 1-26.

Jeff

But the old story, I suppose; don't expect good cookers to be good lookers.

Maybe this is too typical of the snappy dialogue of the period, and maybe you should just write the play "straight". The story is funny, the characters are attractive and the songs are bound to be fine. I know very well that this has none of the absurdities of "Boy Friend" and yet somehow it seems to me that you have fallen in the middle, somewhere between "The Boy Friend" and a show that can stand on its own today without reference to a former period, either by direct suggestion as in the prologue, or in the style of the dialogue.

This is a fumbling and unconstructive criticism, I am afraid. That is because I can't find myself in the state of reception to say "I like it" or "I don't like it". I don't think you have succeeded in telling an audience just how to approach the play. There is so much of it that is obviously right, and something about it that is - not so obviously - wrong. "Well!" I can hear one of you saying to the other, "that's the last time we will give a play to that bumble-head to read."

Anyway; I've done the best I could, and I wish you both the best of luck.

As always,

Oscar

Guy Bolton to Oscar Hammerstein, February 7, 1957

Dear Oscar,

It was immensely kind of you to take so much trouble in analysing [*sic*] the Princess resurrection. I think you are completely right and I question whether it would be possible to present such a show as anything but a satire of the musical of its period.

There was one of the series that never arrived at completion that was a much more modern idea and it is just possible that it might be worth while to see if that could be brought to life. I shall bear in mind what you have said when weighing the problems involved.

I now have to tell you a sad piece of news that has just come to me in this morning's mail: Graham John[2] is dead. Bay says in her letter, 'please tell Oscar. He was very kind to Graham and he might like to know how warmly Graham felt toward him.'

He had a tumor on the brain, much the same thing that George Gershwin suffered from, and was operated on in London last week. He died of heart failure after the conclusion of the operation.

If you should want to drop a line to Bay –

Her address is:

Turtulla,

Ardee,

County Louth,

Eire.

With every good wish and renewed thanks.

Yours as ever,

Guy

---

[2] Graham John was a British librettist and lyricist. Among his shows were the 1928 West End musical, *Blue Eyes*, starring Evelyn Laye, with music by Kern, and book and lyrics by Bolton and John.

After a nightmare experience in the West End negotiating permissions (and denials) for American actors to appear in *South Pacific* (only the casting of Mary Martin went easily), Oscar argued for more author/producer control of casting foreign performers in shows in the States. Here, two theatrical unions—The Dramatists Guild and Actors' Equity—were at loggerheads. The debate still rages today.

Oscar Hammerstein to the Council of Actors' Equity Association, circa January, 1957

Ladies and Gentlemen:

I read your letter regarding the alien actor problem to the Dramatists Guild Council January 3rd, 1957. Coming as it does after many months of amiable and reasonable discussions, exchanges of letters, and earnest attempts at mutual understanding, we find it discouraging proof of an attitude which cannot be reconciled with our own. Those members of your Council who have been, from the first, determined to encroach upon our right to cast our own plays seem, at last, to have prevailed.

The present ruling to which you are now so earnestly devoted puts your Council in the position of over-ruling the judgment of the dramatist and the manager as to what are the essential qualifications needed for a part in the plays they write and produce. It is quite true that the old 60/40 did, in principle, curtail our freedom to cast as we liked. But it gave us enough leeway in which to make our own decisions regarding the most important parts. The new ruling deprives us of any casting rights beyond those you desire to grant us in plays where foreign characterizations are required.

Whenever we have protested against the excessive control which your new ruling gave you, you have pointed out to us that in the past your Council has been reasonable and even lenient in permitting the admission of foreign players. We have acknowledged this in all our meetings with you. Now again, we note that [in] your letter of December 6th you say: "As for the administration of the present rule, we point with pride to the fair and equitable manner in which we have exercised our prerogatives . . ." A few days later you denied the management and the authors of "My Fair Lady" the right to employ three very important players for three very important parts, players who were chosen after months of exhaustive auditions. Complete proof of these auditions were submitted to you by the management. We don't think you can "point with pride" to this decision because it was an extremely unreasonable and arrogant one. This is my opinion, the opinion of our Council and, I am sure, would be the opinion of all producers, critics and patrons of the theatre. This ill considered decision gives us very little assurance, in fact it gives us well justified fears for the future administration of the power which you have chosen to assume.

In view of my admiration for your organization and the high regard in which all of us on the Council have always held you, it is depressing to find ourselves on opposite sides from you on an issue so vitally important to the theatre, both as an art and an industry. Your obvious determination, however, to place your casting judgment above ours, leaves us no choice. We think you are wrong. We are against you, and we shall stand against you as firmly as we possibly can. We shall express our opposition as openly and eloquently as we can. We shall make our opposition as effective as we can make it. We shall use whatever power we have and whatever ingenuity we have to reverse what we consider an unsound and unfair policy.

Sincerely and regretfully,

Oscar Hammerstein II

President, Dramatists Guild

The above letter is a heavily edited draft, a version of which may or may not have been sent.

It's surprising that Josh Logan seems to have had so little final say in casting the film of *South Pacific* that he was about to direct. (At the time of this correspondence, Logan was in Japan directing the film *Sayonara*.)

Josh Logan to Oscar Hammerstein (excerpt), February 15, 1957

I have heard nothing about the results of the location search by 20th Century. It is very important that some advance work be done on that if we are to start by July 1st.

John F. tells me you have signed Ray Walston + I read in the columns that Mitzi Gaynor is set. I hope so as I would be thrilled with that casting. I am sure that I can do a big job with Mitzi—she really excites me in the part. And Ray—well he's the top Billis ever—

Oscar Hammerstein to Josh Logan, February 27, 1957

Dear Josh:

Thank you for your letter of February 15th from Japan. I note that you will be in the [U.S.] east from about April 8th for ten days, and I will keep my own schedule open during that time so that I can spend as much time with you as you are able to spend with me. We shall of course be in touch with each other during the month of March once you arrive back in the country. The purpose of this letter is mainly to bring you up to date, a sort of progress report.

1. The location crew are in the Hawaiian Islands now. I believe they have been there for about a week.

2. Mitzi Gaynor has been signed.

3. Ray Walston has been signed, or at any rate an agreement has been reached pending some billing difference. (He was insisting on third billing after Mitzi Gaynor, and we maintained we could not give him that until after we see who is going to play the part of Cable.)

4. John Kerr has expressed interest in the part of Cable and is now reading the script.

5. Juanita Hall is of course available. We have not yet signed her because we are in a little doubt about her voice. Dick was disturbed by the vibrato when she sang for us at the office. We are going to make a short vocal test over at Fox's eastern studios to see how much worse the vibrato will sound in a mike. I personally do not anticipate any serious worry from this quarter, and anyway we can always have the standard clause giving us the right to dub in a voice if necessary.

6. Brazzi: We just played an Italian record made by him, and his voice did not sound good at all. Dick and I both liked it when we heard it downstairs in the living room about two years ago, but on this record it was not at all reassuring, and we must be prepared to dub in a voice for him if he cannot do any better than shown on this record. We have so far only a letter contract with him (which is of course binding on us both) but when the full contract is made out we will be sure to have the dubbing clause in there to protect ourselves.

7. We have not approached Russ Brown yet for Brackett because we thought we should wait until you came back and had a talk about other possibilities. Russ will not run away from us meanwhile Dick has brought up the subject of Martie Woolfson, and I don't see why he should not be a candidate too. There is something unusual about his height, and something very forceful in his performance. He is not the usual movie "Captain". Somehow his appearance makes him look more real because he is so atypical.

8. Regarding your cutter, Walter Thompson, I see no reason why you shouldn't have him if you want him.

9. Paul's script seems to me to be in very good shape. He is deep in his rehearsals now, in fact very near the out of town opening. It seems to me that when you come here in April we can all sit down together and work out the final script. Not all of the things that we talked about in the Beverly Hills Hotel panned out as we anticipated. But after some juggling around I think Paul came up with what looks to me like a script you could really start to shoot with tomorrow. I don't doubt, however, that we shall get some new ideas after having been away from it several months. I think, as a matter of fact, this is going to help all three of us. I have no doubt that we'll wind up with a wonderful shooting script.

I was very happy to hear that you had finally decided to do Jimmy and Barbara's play. I have read the new version and I think it's nearly twice as good as the first version. I think its commercial chances have been enhanced greatly, and it has lost none of its original sensitivity.

I can hardly wait until I can see "Sayonara". All you say about it sounds very exciting.

We have gone into rehearsal with "Cinderella" and our performance will be March 31st, Sunday, 8:00 o'clock Eastern Standard Time. I hope you will be able to see it. We have a very fine cast, and it all feels good at this point.

I hope you will phone me soon after you arrive in California—after you have caught up on your sleep, perhaps. I shall be in New York all the time now up until the television performance, so you can call me here at the New York house.

Dorothy and I send our love to you and Nedda.

Oscar Hammerstein to Jerome Whyte (in London), February 19, 1957

Dear Jerry:

I enclose a letter I have received from Hy. Is there any way in which you can handle this for me? I suggest that you ask him for the latest version of his script and read it, and if you sincerely believe it has a chance in London, I think that we, on your recommendation, would invest a thousand pounds. If you don't think so, please get in touch with Hy and double-talk your way out of the whole thing so as to save me the embarrassment of turning him down. You might tell him that we are putting everything into "Damn Yankees" and everything else has been sent to America, or something like that.

On the other hand, if you like it well enough you might cable Dick and me and we'll take it up with him.

I'm sorry to saddle you with this unwelcome job, but I don't see how I can handle it myself.

Since time seems to be of the essence, I hope you will get in touch with Hy right away.

All the best,

As ever,

E. Maurice "Buddy" Adler was a producer at Twentieth Century Fox Films who, in 1957, replaced Darryl Zanuck as head of production. Adler was the producer for *South Pacific*.

Oscar Hammerstein to Buddy Adler, Twentieth Century-Fox Films, February 19, 1957

Dear Buddy:

You'll remember that on my way to Australia I stopped off in Hawaii and spent several days in the plane of a friend flying very low over the coastlines of Kauai and Maui. I did not visit any other islands except, of course, the one on which Honolulu is situated, Oahu.

The most promising locations I saw from the plane were on Kauai, and the enclosed map indicates my findings.

At the top of the map I have indicated two possible coves into which the PBY plane might slip, disembarking Cable and deBecque. I think the best one was Hanalei Bay. It so happened that just around the corner (to the left on the map) there were hills from which it might be believable that the Japs could be training their guns on Billis out in the rubber boat—the "diversionary action" which goes on while the other two are being landed. I realize that this could be tricked and that you wouldn't actually have to have this geographical setup. But it so happens that this seems to be just right, and the right distance, and possibly it would lend reality to the whole episode. As you see, over to the right and still on top of the map I found another possible cove in Anahola Bay and several beaches with palms along the edge which seem to be close to what we were searching for. The part that I marked "jungle" in the Kawaihau District might be the area we would use to indicate the jungle in which deBecque and Cable were hiding, and over which the Japanese planes would fly. It is very thick in there.

I realize that your experts will be much better at this job than I was in my amateur way, but if this information gives them any start I am sending it to you hoping that it may be of some help.

I have been told that the weather is bad on Kauai, but mainly up in the hills, and that it is much better along the shore.

I am sure that your men will look at other islands, and perhaps they will find better places than I did.

The one thing I saw nowhere was anything that looked like Bali H'ai. Even if we surrendered the two volcano effect, I saw nothing that came up out of the water and looked at all magic or mysterious or romantic.

Anyway, here is the result of my amateur effort for what it is worth. Wish the boys good luck and happy hunting. The sooner they set out the better. It is getting very late.

I have had a cable from Josh saying that he expects to be back the end of February or the first week in March. He will no doubt get in touch with you as soon as he arrives.

Dick and I are both very happy to have you with us on this job, and we want to express our gratitude for all you have done so far, and all we hope you are going to do.

Sincerely,

Oscar Hammerstein to Nell and Lynn Farnol, February 22, 1957

Dear Nell and Lynn:

Your kind letter was sufficiently gratifying, and a needless reward for our hospitality because your presence at the farm made our weekend so happy.

Then along comes that nectar erroneously called Scotch.[3] We each had an inch of it with no ice, no water and no soda, and that is the way we shall drink it for the rest of our lives. Any foreign matter added to such golden liquid would be sacrilege. It is really a wonderful Scotch. I don't pretend to know anything about Scotch. I only feel that when I drink that, I do know a lot about Scotch. Something tells me this is the best of all. We really got a great pleasure out of our drink, and will dole it out to ourselves, and possibly to no one else at all, as long as the bottle lasts.

Thank you, thank you, thank you!

Our love and best wishes to both of you.

Oscar Hammerstein to Buddy Adler and Josh Logan, March 7, 1957

Dear Buddy and Josh:

I have just spoken to Jim Michener on the phone regarding the possibility of finding an island somewhere outside of the Hawaiian Islands which would suit the description of Bali H'ai.

The actual island he had in mind when he named it Bali H'ai was Atchin and Vao. They are off the island of Malekula, which is north of New Caledonia.

---

[3] A note accompanying the Scotch reads: "the last bottle of Glen Grant Scotch malt whiskey in New York."

He also mentioned Aoba, which is about 150 miles north of Noumea in the New Hebrides. He thinks there may be others in the New Hebrides, and he also thinks that perhaps there would [be] some islands off Fiji.

Take it from there, boys!

All the best.

Oscar Hammerstein to George Skouras (copied to Richard Rodgers and Irving Cohen), March 8, 1957

Dear George:

Josh Logan is back from Japan and had a meeting the night before last with Buddy Adler, Sid Rogel, Al Newman and the art director. It was a long meeting at which they considered all problems very thoroughly.

The first problem they had to consider was Josh's obligations to "Sayonara". He is obligated to Goetz until June 1st, and believes he will be needed all that time to complete the shooting, the cutting and processing and previewing of "Sayonara".

The next problem has to deal with the enormous and thorough preparation necessary to a project like "South Pacific". The fact that 95% of the picture is going to be shot on the Hawaiian Islands means that they must leave for there completely prepared in every respect, well rehearsed and with every pre-recording made in advance.

Josh is willing to start rehearsals and pre-recording on June 15th. He wanted twelve weeks for these purposes, but Buddy, Al Newman and Sid Rogel cut him down to eight. They all agree, however, that eight weeks will be needed before any of the departments will feel safely prepared for departure to Hawaii.

In addition to the rehearsing and recording during these eight weeks, there are of course many other details that will require Josh's time—sketches from the art department, how to "dress up" various locations, etc, etc. (Actually this would not be nearly time enough for all this were we not certain that we can "steal" a little time from Josh during his work on "Sayonara" to engage in various consultations with our technicians.)

This makes the shooting date August 15th in Hawaii. I know this is disappointing to you, as it is to me, but we cannot add any months to the calendar, and we must face the fact that Logan is doing this other picture. As it is, I am a little uneasy about his bouncing from one job right into another without more than two weeks or ten days break.

I cannot disagree with such experts as Adler, Logan, Rogel, Al Newman and the art director when they present a solid front and say that eight weeks preparation is a minimum time.

It is always important to have a picture released as soon as possible, but it is not so important as making the picture a great picture. No chances must be taken on that score.

The estimated shooting schedule is sixty days in Hawaii and five days in the studio. We have a good chance of holding to this schedule because Josh is a fast director and shoots in all kinds of weather.

Fox are giving us Leon Chamroy as cameraman. He is the best they have, and is one of the best in Hollywood. He shot "The King and I" and has won about fifteen Academy Awards. To save time, we will put him to work very soon, putting him on a plane with Todd-AO cameras and sending him to the Islands to take point-of-view shots which we need for the picture.

The location team, now in Hawaii where they have been for about ten days, will soon be back with all the results of their trip.

Provisions are being made for housing the company. The late shooting date gives us an advantage in this department because there is not such a rush of visitors during this time as earlier in the summer.

During the eight weeks of rehearsal and recording Fox Studio is turning over its entire music department to us and giving us the rehearsal stages.

Fox is working out a breakdown of schedules for each character, and will send it to us next week so that we can determine the starting dates of their contracts. This of course is very important in relation to the actors who get the big money.

An assistant director has already been appointed to work with Josh. His name is Kadish. He will coordinate all the technical details for the production.

So far we have signed, as you know, Brazzi for deBecque, Mitzi Gaynor for Nellie, Ray Walston for Billis and Juanita Hall for Bloody Mary. Our only important and difficult role to fill now is that of Cable. The other[s] will be quite easy, and we should spend very little money on them.

One other assistant to Josh is being appointed. He will help Josh out with the dances—especially the native dances on Hawaii.

This brings you up to date on all present plans. It's a long time since we've seen [each other?]. Maybe Dick and I can steal away from rehearsals for a little while next week and we can sit down and talk over everything.

All my best wishes to you.

Sincerely,

Oscar Hammerstein to Pfc Jack Perfect (excerpt), March 14, 1957

Answering your questions: I never write music.

Sometimes I write the words first and Mr. Rodgers sets music to my words, but very often he writes the melody first and I set words to his melody.

I never get an inspiration for a song out of nowhere, and all my songs are inspired by the story and the characters I am writing about.

Cinderella was broadcast live on CBS on March 31st. The show aired (in the Eastern through Mountain time zones) to a staggering and record-breaking audience, estimated at more than 107 million viewers, in (estimates vary) 18,864,000 to 24.2 million households, representing some 60 percent of the country's entire population at the time. In his memoir Rodgers noted that the broadcast occurred on the fourteenth anniversary of the opening of Oklahoma!, and in that show's original, five year Broadway run, it was seen by a little more than four million people, and ten years on the road garnered close to eight million more. Julie Andrews was universally praised, and reviews for the show itself were good, but not spectacular. The show became a cultural mainstay with two television remakes, versions staged around the world, including London, Australia, and Japan, a 2013 Broadway production, and an untold number of amateur and other mountings. Unfortunately, I have found no correspondence reacting to the broadcast.

Asked to contribute "a few paragraphs of your thoughts on 'Book Learning' for inclusion in a book I am doing, 'My Best Advice'," Oscar responded with:

Oscar Hammerstein to Lloyd Foster, Jr., April 9, 1957

Dear Mr. Foster:

Here is my "best advice".

Develop the habit of being honest with yourself. The extent to which you may succeed with this difficult undertaking will measure your success in being honest with other people. The extent of your honesty with other people will measure the extent of your happiness, repose and gratification in life.

Being honest includes toughness and courage, courage for instance to admit what you are afraid of. Only when you admit the existence of a fear to yourself can you start making any advance toward conquering that fear. Honesty to yourself involves the finding out what you really want in life as well as the things you really do not want. The truth about yourself is hard to find, but it is your duty to seek it out. On no other basis can you erect a good life. Too many of us build our lives on self-created fantasies about ourselves. An admirable instance of this common and tragic mistake is Mr. Arthur Miller's play, "Death of a Salesman".

I hope this will serve you in your book.

Sincerely

Oscar Hammerstein to Jodie Hanemann (University of Florida), May 3, 1957

Dear Miss Hanemann:

Beyond the pleasure of receiving a letter from the daughter of an old adagio partner is the embarrassment of realizing that I have no "favorite" artist, painting or piece of sculpture. Since you are an art major, I am afraid this will shock and disappoint you. I am frequently shocked and disappointed when I meet a painter or a sculptor who has no favorite musical play. But that's the way it is.

I remember when I was making the grand tour of Europe as a youth (even before I met your father) I stood before "The Night Watch" in a museum in Amsterdam and was reverently impressed. If you must have an answer, then say I'm just a fool for Rembrandt. If this seems just too corny, why don't you merely insert the name of your own favorite artist, painting or piece of sculpture. I will be very happy to endorse you, and in fact will be surprised by my own good taste.

Best wishes to your father and mother and you.

Sincerely,

Oscar Hammerstein to Marc Connelly,[4] May 21, 1957

Dear Marc:

I know that "Hunter's Moon" has been a long labor of constant love, and the script is ample proof of the care and affection you have lavished on it. It is a gentle, sensitive work. These words are written as an admiring fellow-author. You have, however, approached me as a prospective producer. And as such I must say that I do not think that the play is a promising theatrical investment, either in New York or in London. Statements like this by cautious entrepreneurs are being disproved all the time, as I hope this one will be.

All good wishes to you.

Always,

Italian actor Rossano Brazzi was cast to play the French planter, Emile deBecque in the *South Pacific* film, where his singing was dubbed by the American operatic bass, Giorgio Tozzi.

Oscar Hammerstein to Rossano Brazzi, May 28, 1957

Dear Rossano Brazzi:

With the shooting date of "South Pacific" approaching so quickly, Richard Rodgers and I are indeed happy to know that we will have you with us playing the part of Emile deBecque. We know that you will give a

---

[4] Marc Connelly was the author of *The Green Pastures*, and co-author, with George S. Kaufman, of *Beggar on Horseback*. *Hunter's Moon* never made it to Broadway.

superb interpretation of this role. In regard to your singing the score, however, we have serious doubts. We have given careful study to some of your recordings, and have had consultations with the 20th Century Fox music head, Mr. Alfred Newman. It seems to all of us that while your voice is pleasing, its quality cannot measure up to the quality we know we will get from your dramatic performance. We all think it would be a pity for you to succeed so brilliantly in one department and open yourself to criticism in the other department. Joshua Logan, who will direct you, and Buddy Adler, who will produce, feel strongly that we should have another voice dubbed in for the singing. This, as you know, has been done very successfully with a great many other stars, and it has turned out well in all cases.

We all hope and feel that you will agree with us that this course will result in a more satisfying success for you and the picture.

We look forward to seeing you soon. Dick joins me in sending best wishes to you for a restful holiday before you join us in what we believe may be the greatest musical picture ever produced.

Sincerely,

Oscar Hammerstein to Bernard A. Davey, Jr., Testimonials Unlimited, July 9, 1957

Dear Mr. Davey:

I do not, as a matter of policy, consent to have my name used in advertisements suggesting that I endorse any products. In addition to this consideration, I couldn't possibly have my name on a hat band because I never wear a hat.

All good wishes to you.

Sincerely,

Oscar Hammerstein to Hy Kraft, July 17, 1957

Dear Hy:

Thank you for sending me the synopsis of PARIS LEGEND. It seems to me that the content and the spirit of your treatment falls into the pattern of operetta. I am interested only in a story with honest human interest. Your story has a bizarre and irresponsible approach which might well create a successful operetta, but I do not want to write a successful operetta. I want to write about people I believe in and think I understand.

In short, the way I try to find a musical play, and am trying now, is to pretend that I am looking for material for a straight play without music. When anyone comes to me with an idea that looks obviously to be good material for a musical comedy, I run like a thief. (This is the reason why I ran from "Pygmalion".)

I hope this terse rejection will not discourage you from submitting any other ideas that may come to you. We are still looking and looking hard.

Love to you and Reata.

As ever,

Oscar Hammerstein (in Beverly Hills) to Richard Rodgers, July 27, 1957

Dear Dick:

Not a great deal was recorded this past week. Two very vital renditions did get on the soundtracks, however—"Dames" + "Bloody Mary". The rest of the time was devoted to making costume and make-up tests. I took no part in these but am, of course, going to check on the results with Josh [Logan] + Buddy [Adler].

We saw South Pacific[5] downtown—an extraordinary company. Tozzi's voice is better than Pinza's and the applause he gets on "Enchanted Evening" is as great. Pinza never put over "This Nearly Was Mine" like this guy and Josh and I both feel that we never heard a reception to this song like the thunderclap it gets here. As you may have read in Variety we are beating the business of "My Fair Lady." I asked Ed Lester how this was possible. We were standing on the [?] stage of the Philharmonic. He pointed up to seats that were up under the ceiling and along the side of the house. "There are about four hundred bad seats in this house that we don't try to sell," he said. "People insist on buying them for South Pacific." It appears that with these

---

[5] Mary Martin and Giorgio Tozzi starred in a production of *South Pacific* at the Philharmonic Auditorium in Los Angeles, from July 8 until August 10. Martin was forty-three.

four hundred the capacity is 2600. Normally they consider the capacity 2200 and a "sell-out" is when they sell 2200 tickets.

Mary and Dick are cool to us. We have all noticed it. Sweet as they are in most things they are blinded about this one thing. They don't realize that she is not young enough to play Nellie in the movie. This is regrettable. Age is not, in my opinion, the only deterrent. I did not like her performance, although, god knows, the audience did. She was "cute"—very much as Peter Pan is! The little dry crack in her voice was over-used. The comedy was well served. The emotional quality—much of it—was lost. It was more of a Martha Wright Nellie than a Mary Martin portrayal.

When I went back to the studio next day I was happy to look at and listen to Mitzi Gaynor. I think she is going to be just great.

Josh and I have had no opportunity to pursue the original story any further, but I have done some work on it. I believe this must be considered as a long-pull investment. He will direct Jimmy [Hammerstein] + Barbara's [Wolferman] play [Blue Denim] after South Pacific. This takes him through the early spring (March) 1958. He has another obligation to contend with, a picture at Metro. So the writing of a book could not start until next summer. Then perhaps you and I could work on the score while he was doing his M.G.M. stint and we could produce it after that.

A few other things have come up—two books sent by Joe Fields, properties he has bought for himself but which he would like to do with us if we wanted to do them. Another book has been sent by a man named Irving Bucher[?]. One more thing, an idea for an original story that Ernie Martin has submitted to me. Like the original with Josh it is still embryonic but I think worth pursuing.

All these things have "far future" written on them but that doesn't disturb me if it doesn't disturb you. I have an urge and an eagerness to have a play and perhaps two plays lined up, but I have no impatience whatever about getting them "on". The time to produce them is after they are written. The important thing—I think—is to have something we want to write.

I went over my personal income figures with my accountant before I left New York. They must be similar to yours. The income, without a major theatrical company running for us, was staggering. God knows we don't need money! And now the picture of South Pacific will be released within the year and this could easily be a financial block-buster.

So I am reminding myself and you that we have no time pressure—only our fervent desire to write something when we find something we want to write and to produce it when we damn please!

I expect to be back in New York two weeks from to-day—August 10th. If we fly on Aug 9th I'll see you on the tenth. If we fly on Aug 10th I'll see you on the following Wednesday, Aug 13th. It will depend on how the pre-recording schedule is adhered to. Josh + the company are due to leave here August 9th.

Many dozens of people have asked about you and send their love.

Dorothy and I send our love, too—a lot of it.

Oscar

Oscar Hammerstein to Richard Rodgers, July 29, 1957

Dear Dick:

When I wrote you yesterday I forgot to tell you that Louis Dreyfus phoned last week and asked if they could release in England, "All At Once You Love Her." Teddy Holmes keeps asking for it, in the belief that he could make it a big hit there. Since it seems far from likely that "Pipe Dream" will ever reach England, I told him to go ahead. I was sure you would agree that we might as well have a song hit in England, if we can.

Speaking of song hits, it has occurred to me that when South Pacific is released we should lean heavily on "Younger Than Springtime" + "Happy Talk." They were shoved[?] under by "Enchanted Evening," "Wonderful Guy" + "Bali H'ai." These are already big hits and can take care of themselves. The other two are great songs and should be pushed, I think.

Cases in point: "Only Make Believe" didn't take its place alongside the others until the second time around. The "delayed take" of "You'll Never Walk Alone" is another example.

I'll talk to you about this when I come home –

Love,

Oscar

Oscar Hammerstein to Richard Rodgers, August 22, 1957

Dear Dick: Just leaving for the airport to enplane for Kauai.

The news is not all good. I didn't like Josh's first day of shooting—"Wash that man"—Mitzi was tres gai but completely missing giving the impression of whistling in the dark or "dancing with tears in her eyes"—Josh's fault. I am sure—really first-day—shooting complications. Buddy reported my reaction by phone and Josh agrees. It will be re-shot to-morrow while I am there, unless waiting would delay us. He is trying to move things ahead for to-day's shooting.

His other stuff is just wonderful. The audience of a thousand sailors for "Honey Bun" etc is thrilling and funny. The second unit stuff—embarkation and beach landings at dawn is great. Long after we have had our use of these shots, we will be renting them to other companies, I think. Same goes for our Fiji shots (not that we are in that business).

George Skouras, Julia and Odyssia are on our plane to-day. Are you green with envy?

DRUM SONG:

Joe seems content to collaborate with me on the book and have us do all the producing. His lawyer may later ask for some profit sharing but so far Joe has not. I think he is entitled to something for acquiring the book first but will wait til he opens the subject.

Complication: He had in fact shaken hands with Buddy Adler on a pre-production deal. Buddy maintains Joe has moral commitment, but wants no unpleasantness with you and me. We're all very friendly about it. Irving Cohen was here at the time and promises to talk to Joe Moskowitz[?] next week in N. Y. I think the conclusion is easy to predict. Joe, who prides himself on being a tough bargainer will not accede to what Irving + Howard ask and the deal will be off—as we want it to be.

Morally Buddy is [?] a point against Joe, because no terms had been discussed with the handshake. Fox would not hesitate to walk away from a handshake if the terms were not satisfactory, and there is no reason why Joe shouldn't do the same. Further, it is now a musical venture, which changes the whole complexion.

The fact is Buddy is nuts for this property, possibly he's the most enthusiastic of all. He also keeps saying that you and I are in the Fox "family". So does Spyro. I agree and I told him that if anything could be done, any company [?] for stage + screen on Flower Drum Song we'd be happy. But Irving is not optimistic. All they can give us is money which we don't need. And we would have to surrender some freedom in handling the property.

Mr. Lee, the author of the novel gets 1%. I have not discussed figures with Joe.

Joe promises to start immediately on a tentative lay-out so we'll have something to start with when we meet again, on my return.

So we're really in business.

I'll write from Kauai

Love from both of us –

Oscar

Oscar Hammerstein to Josh Logan, September 4, 1957

Dear Josh:

First I must report my reactions to "WONDERFUL GUY". I ran it in 35mm yesterday morning and I cried. And I ran it in TODD-AO yesterday evening and the same thing happened to me. I don't know when I have seen anything so gay and true and touching. I am very grateful to you and Mitzi and Leon for what you did with this song.

Now, what you want to hear the most is my reaction to the light change and the gauzy frame coming into the songs. Your urged me before I left Hawaii to be "definite" about it. I am sorry that I cannot be definite or clean-cut in reporting my reaction. I think, however, that I can tell you what is good about it and what is doubtful in my mind. The conception of the device is wonderful and it is my belief that it can work. I think a great deal will depend upon the subtlty [sic] with which the music will steal in to accompany each light change. I regret that the change does not start sooner and take longer in its final achievement before the singing begins ("ENCHANTED EVENING").

Buddy feels strongly, that when the gauzy framework surrounds a long or medium shot that it seems like bad photography. Most of the technicians agree with him. I defended the effect by saying that once we had established the device for the song and then continued to use it in other songs that it will be quite clear to an audience that it is not an accident or a photographic defect.

I do agree with Buddy, however, that the framework is at its best when it comes deeply into both sides and frames a close shot in the center of the picture. That was why Leon's test was so good. That couldn't possibly look like an accident to anyone because the only clear part was her closeup and the rest of the screen was in a mystic fog.

I was very uncomfortable, however, in a close shot of Mitzi in "WONDERFUL GUY" when she stretched out both arms and they pierced the "gauze". I was also jarred when she walked through it from the side. It seems to me, that if it is to be a frame it must be only that and not a part of the action of any character. I've been trying to think of what songs will be done in this way while you are on location and the only one, I believe is "HAPPY TALK". According to a conversation you and I had, you would certainly not use this device on earthy numbers like "DAMES" and "BLOODY MARY". Of course, when it comes to "BALI HA'I", the sky is the limit on theatrical effects and the light changes you describe to me I know will be wonderful. On the gauze frame I think you should bear in mind the things I have pointed out. That it does not look good when people walk through it or throw their arms or legs in the air and it is more effective when it comes deeply into the sides rather than when it looks like a fade off on the edge of the screen. It might be that in the case of "BALI HA'I" that where the lighting is so extravagant and the action and movement so continuous that the gauze effect might be in your way.

I think I am voicing Buddy's opinion as well as my own except that he veers more to the conservative fear of it and would prefer that you discontinue using the gauze effect. (I know that gauze effect is not a good description but you know what I mean.)

This is not a simple question to answer. This could be wonderful and truly blazing and on the other hand there is some merit in asking the question, why should we stick our necks out too far, when by simply not sticking them out we are going to have a smashing success. I don't hold with this as a sound philosophy of show business. I believe in taking chances as you do. On the other hand, I see no reason why we shouldn't take every precaution to protect ourselves in case we are wrong.

I again saw "WASH THAT MAN", this time on the big TODD-A-O screen and was again impressed by the almost unbelievable improvement over the first try. I saw for the first time the reprise of "SOME ENCHANTED EVENING" and I loved every minute of it. Brazzi is out of sync in some of it but I hope we have enough to cut around this. At the very worst, a retake of this 2 shot would not be a great problem. Fred Hines the sound man was worried, not only because of synchronization but because it seemed to him that Brazzi was not moving his lips enough throughout the song to be making the sounds coming from the singer Tozzi. I am about to take my plane for New York and will be unable to read or sign this letter.

I don't want to confuse you about "WONDERFUL GUY". The complaint about Mitzi's hands going into the gauze will not hurt the number because there are so many shots you can use instead at this particular point. As a matter of fact, as good as the closeup is, I think what you will be using most is the medium and long shot because she is such a wonderful figure on the beach against the blue water and the white spray on the black rocks behind her. GOD what a number!

Love to Nedda, the family and the company.

Sincerely,

Oscar

Oscar Hammerstein to Clifton Fadiman, September 9, 1957

Dear Kip:

It is a long time since you so kindly sent me an inscribed copy of "Any Number Can Play". I could have and should have sat down and thanked you on the day I received the book, but I thought that perhaps it would be better to read it first and then thank you. This is always a mistake because I never read a book as soon as I think I am going to. At any rate I got my chance when I started to fly to California, thence to Hawaii and then back again, and I didn't need all those trips only one of them in which to read and finish and enjoy the book very much. In addition to a great deal of graceful entertainment I find some alarming truths in the book. You don't state them in any scary way, and I think this is a good idea. When Upton Sinclair shouts "fire!" you put your hands on your ears because he shouts so loud that you cannot believe any conflagration can be as big and dangerous as he says it is. When you, Clifton Fadiman, whisper "fire –" the reader pricks up his ears and wonders whether it isn't worse than you are telling him.

Anyway, that is the reaction of one of your devoted readers, and another reaction is gratitude to you for having written the book and then for having sent him a copy.

Love to Analee and the family from Dorothy and me.

As ever,

Josh Logan to Oscar Hammerstein, September 12, 1957

Dear Oscar:

I am dictating this on the Bali H'ai beach while we are preparing a shot of Cable and Billis arriving by boat, with the island in the background and the outrigger canoes in the foreground. It is a beautiful day and we have already got a number of superb shots of Bali H'ai—but not the approach to the island, and I am not going to rest easily until we have them. The rest of the shots could be taken on a bad day or even reproduced on the back lot.

The main purpose of this letter is to thank you from the bottom of my heart for the letter which finally got to me which you dictated in Hollywood. I was living in a kind of hell because I had not received a report from you on what you had seen, and I kept getting very negative reports from the studio on our work. It seems that the usual thing had happened: Buddy had allowed himself to be influenced by all of the little technicians, and there was a general negative feeling coming through the grapevine to us. This was most disturbing to me and to Leon Shamroy, as, not having heard from you, we were beginning to feel that you agreed with them.

Fortunately, a set of dailies came through, the film on the singing of Some Enchanted Evening was done with the fog which is much more pronounced, and the yellow filter, and I can tell you now that they are history-making dailies. The only thing the matter with them is that in a couple of years we will hate them because so many people will be copying them! I can only describe them to you by saying that they are the most romantic scenes I have ever seen on film. They are something like a sanguine drawing or a copper etching. Nellie's face is soft around the edges, her lips, eyes and nose are clear—but the whole effect is of great beauty. There is even a suggestion of "evening" in the shots which adds to the meaning of the song.

I am sure that if you had seen these dailies you would never hesitate again about this technique we are employing. In fact, what it is, Oscar, is something that photographers have tried for for years but never could understand the way of doing. Generally, because they want to give mood to a song, they have pulled back to show a lot of scenery [such as during] If I Loved You in CAROUSEL or the peach-picking bit during People Will Say We're In Love. Now, with this fogged edge and the change of color, we are able to move very close to the actor's face and still get a great deal of mood; therefore, we can see the eyes, the mouth clearly and can understand what the actor is thinking and feeling while he is singing the song, and yet there is enough around the face to give it mood without showing a lot of scenery. I hope I am making myself clear; at least I understand what I am saying!

Oscar, your paragraph in which you say that it is important for people to take chances struck me, as you can imagine, right where I live. I am not going off half-cocked. I am working with the best cameraman in the business—we both agree on what we are doing—and I am sure the end results will be very special.

The worries you had—walking through the edges of the fog or Nellie's hands extending through the fog—can easily be eliminated by editing; and as you know, this fog effect is only going to be used in our most romantic scenes, never the realistic or comedy scenes. Bali H'ai will be shot only with yellow filter and never fogged edges because it is romantic enough with the smoke in the background and the atmosphere of the whole place. Naturally, though, on the song Bali H'ai we will go all out, as you suggest.

At any rate, what I am trying to say is thank you for being strong, clear, and above all for being what I call a true artist—which you have never shown better than in your letter to me. I admire strength, especially on the positive side, as I have found throughout my life that most people can be strong negatively . . . but few can be strong positively. Anyone can criticize; few can encourage.

Love to Dorothy. Hope to hear from you soon.

Josh

Dictated;

not read.

Oscar Hammerstein to Josh Logan, September 24, 1957

Dear Josh:

I was happy to get your letter of September 12th. Just before receiving it I ran some assembled material in New York without sound. I saw the arrival of Bali H'ai with Billis and Cable walking ahead of the curious throng. Unfortunately I did not have sound, and was trying to dope out what Billis and Cable were saying to each other. It looked magnificent even though it was a small screen.

I also saw the interrogation scene and the reprise of "Some Enchanted Evening" and "Wonderful Guy". It is not a final cut but it is beginning to look wonderful already. I am very happy with everything I have seen so far.

My plans are to come out to the coast at about the same time as your return from Hawaii. I believe something happens to a company when they return from locations, and it might be good for me to be there and help along the adjustment if I can. I feel very vague as I say this, but it is more of a hunch than a reasoned decision. I believe I am also thinking of a possible outbreak from Brazzi at that time, and I think I should be there to help Buddy and you quell that if it arises.

I saw Dick yesterday, a day after he had had minor surgery—a hernia which he has had for some time, and which the doctors thought might be fixed up now since he is in the hospital anyway. He came through very well and really looked wonderful when I saw him. He goes out a great deal now, sees shows, even rehearsed "Carousel" at a runthrough [sic] and is leading much more of a normal life except that he must always return to the hospital. They do not want him to go to either of his homes. The source of all the trouble remains something of a puzzle, although there are a score of amateur psychologists all jumping in with various theories at the moment.

I believe we are going to conclude the deal with Joe Fields whereby we will write and produce a musical version of "The Flower Drum Song". Joe would do the book with me.

The story that I was working on with Feuer and Martin is still a possibility. Feuer and Martin even went so far as to announce it the other day, but this was with my permission because there was a story in the newspapers which was very much like the central situation in ours. The newspaper story was a true one. It still, however, is in the conversation stage and is likely to remain so for some time.

Dorothy and I went down to Philadelphia to see "West Side Story"[6] and it looks like the season's first big smash. It will open this Thursday in New York. The critics in both Washington and Philadelphia were raves without exception. The audience loved the show the night I saw it and so did Dorothy and I. This is very interesting because it is really a tragedy, almost as complete as "Romeo and Juliet" is. Everyone concerned with the play has done a brilliant job. It is uneven but adventurous and fresh in its approach, especially in the handling of the dances by Jerry Robbins. He has managed to get principals who can sing and dance too. Everyone in the company dances. I think you will be interested in this show when you return.

Dorothy just had a big bout with flu. Everyone always asks me: "Is it Asian flu?" and I bow my head, ashamed of myself and of her too and say: "No." There seems to be a general idea that if you haven't got Asian flu you just haven't got nothin'. But she had something just the same, no matter what you call it. It was 104 degree fever and a great deal of discomfort, swollen gland and headaches. She is all right now and just needs a rest.

And that is as much material as you have time to read now because you are not getting those long stretches of rain any more which gave you so much time for reading and writing.

There is one other idea. I ran some of the candid movies that were being taken for publicity. That shot of you and me in the rain underneath the oilskin is strange indeed. It is not clear that we are listening to music, and we both look bemused, as if the rain had gone to our heads and we had

---

[6] Oscar had encouraged Sondheim to take the job as (co-)lyricist on *West Side Story*, convincing him that collaborating with Leonard Bernstein, Jerome Robbins, and Arthur Laurents was too great an opportunity to pass up. According to Hugh Fordin, "When Oscar couldn't attend a rehearsal of the entire show, a special run-through was staged for him prior to the Philadelphia break-in."

water on the brain. Lots of the other shots are funny and amusing and especially interesting to those of us who are in them and know all the other people. It should wind up as a pretty good thing for the public to see. I have never seen anything like it before.

Love to Nedda and the kids. Looking forward to seeing you all soon.

In his July 27 letter to Rodgers, Oscar had counseled patience in choosing their next project, as a few possibilities were being considered. Two months later they seem to have settled firmly on *Flower Drum Song*. The book would be co-written with Joseph Fields, and the show produced by Rodgers and Hammerstein in association with Fields. Fields had previously written the books for *Wonderful Town* and *Gentlemen Prefer Blondes*.

Oscar Hammerstein to Irving Brown, Chappell & Company, September 9, 1957

Dear Irving:

Such permissions as those requested by the Westchester Christian Church are usually granted by Max Dreyfus and me both agreeing. In this case it is all right with me for them to make the quotations described in their letter, but only on condition that they quote correctly. In their letter they misquote by writing:

"When shivering in my shoes—"

The word is "while", "While shivering in my shoes—"

In their quotation of "You'll Never Walk Alone" they have a strange way of spelling the same word differently. In the fifth line they say:

"Walk on through the wind, walk on thru the rain—"

I would prefer to have them use the conventional spelling throughout, and that goes for "Tho your dreams be tossed and blown—" I don't like this spelling, and I certainly don't like any inconsistency in spelling.

Furthermore, they have left out two words in the next to last line. The line is:

"Walk on, walk on with hope in your heart and you'll never walk alone—"

They have only one "walk on".

I wish you would adopt it as a policy if these problems come before you again to always compare what they say they wish to quote with the actual lines as written in our scores.

The upshot of this letter, then, is to say that they can quote, but the quotations must be exact, and if they haven't got a published copy from which to quote, send them one, or send them at least a corrected type-written copy.

All good wishes to you.

Sincerely,

In August Oscar wrote a piece for the *New York Herald Tribune* titled, "Is It Really YOUR Hit Parade?," that began:

Things may be looking up for people who like good songs, and like to decide for themselves what songs are good. Last week, U.S. Sen. George A. Smathers of Florida introduced a bill prohibiting all broadcasters from owning record companies or music publishing firms. In his speech on the Senate floor, he stated that the people have been denied the freedom to choose their own music. He said that broadcasters' ownership of 2,000 song-publishing firms (Broadcast Music, Inc.) along with their ownership of the Victor and Columbia recording companies "constitutes a massive interlocking combination not in the public interest. The public today is a captive audience. It is being force-fed a brand of music not always to its liking."

In response Oscar received a letter from Glen Harmon, Vice President and General Manager of the Louisville, Kentucky radio station, WINN. Harmon's letter began:

In all of my twenty-four years of experience in radio, I have never read a bigger or more damnable lie, from a man who has derived his entire livelihood from music . . . It is rather strange indeed that a man of your position would strike out at the hand that has fed him for, lo, these many years. Perhaps, your memory is short on the giant dracula of monopoly that was ASCAP when it controlled the radio broadcast industry before 1940.

Oscar Hammerstein to Glen A. Harmon, WINN, Louisville, September 18, 1957

Dear Mr. Harmon:

I have not time to deal with all the inaccuracies that characterize your letter of September 11th, but I really must straighten you out on a few things. In the first place, I am not a man who has "derived his entire livelihood from music". The bulk of my income has come from royalties and profits resulting from stage presentations throughout this country and abroad. Second to this source is the sale of the picture rights to my plays. "Music", as you understand it, accounts for only a small share of my earnings.

I am not "striking out at the hand that has fed me for lo these many years". I am merely trying to tie the hands that are beating me and other songwriters over the head.

Leaving aside the strange confusion you have with the character "Dracula" and the word "monopoly" (Dracula was merely a weird kind of murderer. He was not, as I recall, a monopoly) I must admit that my memory is short if, as you say, ASCAP ever "controlled the radio broadcast industry before 1940". Perhaps it is your memory that is too imaginative and colorful. Your industry proved in that very same year that ASCAP did not control it. You took our music off the air, and when a new contract was made, you reduced its terms. It was poor "Dracula" who got the kicking around that time.

I am surprised that only 63% of the logged music on your station during the month of August was by ASCAP writers. The figures usually put out by the broadcasters are 85% for ASCAP and 15% for all other music. Your station seems more zealous than the average in its affection for BMI music.

We know, of course, that some preponderance of the music played on the air has been written by members of ASCAP because we who are in this voluntary membership organization have built an impressive catalogue over the years and have developed almost all of America's most important composers and authors. What disturbs us is that we don't seem to be getting our share in the performance of new songs. In the seventeen years of its existence BMI seems to have a remarkable percentage of new songs most played on the air. Yet in all this time very few of these new songs alleged to be so popular have enjoyed any life at all after the brief months of their exploitation, and none of the composers and authors of these songs have turned out to be Gershwins or Kerns or Berlins or Frank Loessers. This fact raises suspicions in the first place as to how much the public really liked them.

I note you have "twenty four years in the broadcasting business". I think that by this time you should realize the true legal position of ASCAP in regard to your accusation that it is a monopoly. In 1940 ASCAP signed a consent decree with the Department of Justice, a legal assurance you have been enjoying ever since. If ever we were a monopoly, our wings have been clipped. We could not go back to the situation of 1940 if we wanted to. It surprises me, under the circumstances, that you still look upon us as "Dracula".

It may help you to understand our fears today if you look back upon your fears of 1940. We are now afraid that you are too powerful for us. All the stock in Broadcast Music Incorporated is owned by broadcasters. The two largest recording companies are owned by the two largest networks. The disc jockeys who place the records on the machines in the various broadcasting stations are employed by the broadcasters. This seems to us an alarming interlocking of song control. It has awakened the concern of Senator Smathers and Congressman Celler and his committee. It has brought protests from some important groups and from many important citizens.

How justified our fears may be will be decided in the courts, or perhaps in congressional hearings or in the Department of Justice. Meanwhile it behooves all of us to examine the situation carefully and think clearly, and not sound off carelessly or indiscriminately at one another. You describe your station as "a little 250-watt station in the backwoods of Kentucky". I consider your station very important, as I consider all stations in the United States of great importance, wielding great power in their community and charged with serious responsibilities. It is my aim, and I hope it is yours, to achieve a more intelligent, more common-sense basis for harmony between the music world and the broadcasting world. I see no reason why that should not be done eventually, and I hope eventually means soon.

Very truly yours,

Josh Logan to Oscar Hammerstein (excerpts),
September 20, 1957

We finished Bali H'ai, including one shot which was taken from a reef by Ray Kellogg (it was to be a painted-in shot showing all of Bali H'ai with the boat approaching). After the picture had been taken, the camera was knocked over by an enormous wave that came from nowhere. The whole camera, tripod, and magazine went into the water. For a while it seemed a great tragedy to us, but a bit of the film was taken out and developed here in black-and-white, and at this moment it seems okay. There was no sign of streaking. At any rate, we have sent the film back to be processed and we will know if it is good or bad before we leave here.

I think you will like the Bali H'ai sequence. The walks up through the tropical foliage that Bloody Mary and Cable take, and the corresponding run-throughs of Liat running to meet Cable are most beautiful in the Gauguin tradition.

Now we are on Bloody Mary's beach. Today we finished all the shots on the pier, which includes Cable's entrance with Buzz Adams on a rubber boat, and a beautiful shot where he stops in the foreground on the pier and looks at Bloody Mary's beach as well as de Becque's house up on the hill. A pre-dawn shot photographed through a light lavender filter shows de Becque and Cable, Adams, Harbison and Brackett in the scene just before the takeoff. I think you will like the shot where the camera moves past them all and focuses on a collection of trash—coconuts, beer cans, soaked newspapers, etc.—It is Billis, and suddenly the trash moves off at a great speed, and through the water you can see [the] swimmer's arms and legs.

We are going back up to the Burkmyer estate for one half day more of shooting. This is because we liked the night shots so very much that we thought we ought to take a few more before moving in for the close shots in the studio.

- - -

I am happy to report that John Kerr looks very good and has contributed a great deal to the part of Cable already. Little France Nuyen acts like a professional; when she has to look, see, register happiness, it comes bubbling out of her and shines from her face. Haven't seen Mitzi for several days as she has been in Honolulu, but Brazzi is very happy—and his wife has lost 35 pounds. I must say this is hard to believe, but he says it is quite obvious.

- - -

I am sure you will like the effect Leon used in Bali H'ai—shooting through a deep purple-pink filter on Cable walking through the girls after having left Liat. Torches are flaming at the side of the pier, and Bloody Mary steps into the shot and says, "Is gonna be my son-in-law."

In other words, Oscar, I am still very excited about our work and feel that the picture is going to be visually one of the most beautiful ever made. Also, I am more and more impressed with the authenticity of our casting. It is bound to bring results. I wrote a lot of this to Dick but thought I could be more specific with you as you had been here and could better understand the situation.

The morale is still very high here, although I think the crew is longing to get home. If we have good luck on Bloody Mary's beach we should make it around the first week in October. At first, I was planning to film a great deal of Bloody Mary's beach back at the studio, but now that the set has been dressed it looks so wonderful that I feel we would lose a great deal by not knocking it off here. I do think the fact that we have rehearsed it so thoroughly will make us move pretty fast.

In response to Oscar's August 26 article in the *New York Herald Tribune*, they published a riposte by Carl Haverlin, President of BMI. Confused by the back-and-forth arguments, Lester Markel of *The New York Times* sought clarification from Oscar, who supplied it.

Oscar Hammerstein to Lester Markel, *New York Times*, September 27, 1957

Dear Lester:

I don't blame you for being puzzled by the BMI controversy. Here is a brief rundown:

In 1940 two things happened. The networks, fearing that ASCAP had a monopoly of music and could therefore dictate its terms, formed an organization called Broadcast Music, Incorporated, so that they would have a source for music of their own set up in competition with ASCAP. All the stock in BMI is owned by the broadcasters. The publishers within the group are subsidized by guarantees.

The other thing that happened was that the Department of Justice also considered ASCAP a monopoly. The Board of Directors did not contest an "information" filed by the Department of Justice in Milwaukee and signed a consent decree under which it agreed to limit its powers.

How much of a monopoly we were was proven in 1940. The broadcasters threw us off the air and kept us off until we were forced to go back to them and sign a new contract at a rate considerably lower than our former contract. Some monopoly.

The consent decree has been operating for seventeen years or so, and under it there are certain assurances that the broadcasters have. Any time they think we are asking for too much money they can go to the courts and have the courts decide whether or not our request is fair. Our writers may license [to] the broadcasters directly if they wish. There is no exclusivity in the contract. Publishers may divide into separate corporate entities and thus belong to both BMI and ASCAP, and many do.

In spite of these assurances the broadcasters have built their own organization steadily and made it so strong that the shoe is now on the other foot. We fear the monopolistic strength of BMI, and I believe with much greater reason than they ever feared us. The source of their strength is that they are in a position to decide what new songs can be made popular. Today the publicity of a number starts with a record. (In this connection please note that the two biggest record companies are controlled by the two biggest broadcasting networks.) After a record is cut it is sent out to the disc jockeys all over the country. The disc jockeys who are employed by the owners of the broadcasting stations, who in turn own all the stock in BMI, are the ones who decide what records to broadcast to their listeners. We have evidence of cases in which they have been instructed to play BMI music and not ASCAP music. Even where specific evidence is not available, you can imagine that there is a strong and natural tendency to play the music that the boss owns rather than outside music.

When these records are played enough times to justify their "popularity" they move up to the networks where they are sung, often by the recording artists who made the record in the first place, who when they give a live performance are plugging the sales of their record. Many of these performers have interests in BMI publishing firms. Many of them have not. All of them are interested in making popular records and selling them. Record sales become reflected in the sales of sheet music, and the first thing you know "Your Hit Parade" is flooded by "Their Music". The process is not without variation. Now and then an ASCAP song is written that is so strong that it creates its own demand, and it is of course played on the stations and networks. It is also true that of the popular standard numbers that are played again and again through the years 85% are ASCAP songs. These are the figures of the broadcasters. This can hardly be avoided because we do have the best writers in America, who have created the popular music literature in America. This raises an interesting point. If the BMI songs that have flooded the market for the past seventeen years had been really as "popular" as they were claimed to be and as their performances indicated that they were, why have they not lived? Why have they not taken their places alongside of ASCAP popular standards and become a permanent part of America's song catalogue? Why have practically all of them died following their three or four months exploitation on the air? Could it be that there was something phoney [*sic*] about their "popularity"?

Although by their own admission 85% of the music played on the air is ASCAP music and 15% BMI, the broadcasters pay in fees to BMI an amount which is 40% of what they pay ASCAP. 85 to 15 performances, 60 to 40 payment.

When I was testifying in examination before trial, I was asked self-serving questions by the opposing attorneys. This is customary. Thus when I was asked for evidence of discrimination by broadcasting stations or record companies "of my own knowledge" my only honest answer could have been that "of my own knowledge" I had no such evidence. I have never been present at the moment of a discriminatory act. I do have knowledge, however, of ample evidence gathered by other people and brought to light during the Congressional hearings. It is pretty strong stuff.

Beyond what evidence there may be, there remains the alarming existence of this powerful setup. The essence of the Sherman-Clayton Anti-Trust Act is that a monopoly should be broken when it becomes so powerful as to be dangerous. It is not necessary to prove abuse of the power. The mere existence of the power is the peril and the reason for its elimination.

I believe that since the broadcasters are in the music business and own stock in a group of music publishing companies, they are placed in the position of being an alarming threat to all songwriters who are not in their group. They, as owners of the music, can decide what songs the two biggest recording companies will make, and what records will be put on the machines of the broadcasting stations. When songs without merit are placed on these machines they naturally and automatically are keeping off songs that might have superior merit. When merit ceases to be the criterion, not only does the independent songwriter suffer, but the public is being deprived of a right to hear songs in fair competition and to choose the ones they like best.

I hope this letter will help clear things up for you. If you want to go further into it, I'll be happy to treat you to lunch.

All good wishes.

As ever,

Oscar Hammerstein II

Oscar Hammerstein to Roger L. Stevens,[7] October 1, 1957

Dear Roger:

Thank you very much for having Dorothy and me at your lovely party last week and again congratulations on the success of "West Side Story". I also congratulate you on your courage in making the play possible. This is a great way to start off a new season.

All good wishes.

Sincerely

Oscar Hammerstein to Goddard Lieberson, Columbia Records, October 4, 1957

Dear Goddard:

I think we are in the midst of a semantic misunderstanding. Country music that really comes out of the country, and folk songs that really come from folks are compositions with which I have no quarrel. I have, however, heard the phrase "country music" applied to the junk that is being written today in imitation of country music. I have heard these things on the air, and I have heard them make the Hit Parade, and I have heard them called

---

[7] Roger Stevens, Hal Prince, and Robert E. Griffith were the producers of *West Side Story*.

country music. These imitations that are sometimes even unconscious satires are a degradation [*sic*] of American songwriting with which I have no patience. Illiteracy in music and words has no charm or worth unless it is the genuine illiteracy of an ignorant man who is nevertheless a natural poet. The bums who say: "Let's write some country music" and then invent the illiteracy and the stupidity and the trite rhymes and the undistinguished music in order to simulate "country music" and folk songs, are just bums and will never be anything else.

I want to assure you that I was making no implication of your motivation. I know that you wrote a sincere article, and my only fears were that it would be misunderstood and taken as an encouragement to turn out more of that unspeakable trash.

We are going to California next week, to stay only about a week. I hope that if all four of us can be caught in the same city at the same time that we can have dinner together some night. I will ask Dorothy to call up Brigitta.

Love to you both.

**Henry Allen Moe, John Simon Guggenheim Memorial
Foundation to Oscar Hammerstein, November 21, 1957**

Dear Mr. Hammerstein:

May I have your judgment of Mr. Joseph Auslander's[8] ability as a poet? He has applied for a Fellowship and referred me to you.

Mr. Auslander is considerably older than the group of persons this Foundation was set up specially to assist; but with reference to him, as with reference to all candidates, the primary question is: Is he first-rate?

As always, anything you say will be held in the strictest confidence.

Thank you

Sincerely yours,

Henry Allen Moe

---

[8] Joseph Auslander was the first United States Poet Laureate, 1937–1941.

Oscar Hammerstein to Henry Allen Moe, John Simon Guggenheim Memorial Foundation, circa November 1957

To be asked point blank whether any individual is a "first-rate poet" is a shattering experience. It forces me immediately to ask myself if I can define poetry. I suppose that when I use the word I know what I mean, but I am not at all sure that my conception would coincide with many others. As to what is first-class poetry, that surely is a matter of varied and conflicting opinion.

Within what I take to be the framework of your question, I most sincerely believe that Joseph Auslander is a poet with honest feelings who has the gift to express them honestly and simply. I have read many of his poems with great enjoyment. I have been at various times touched and amused and exhilarated by his work. I admire his feeling for form. I believe also that at a time when perhaps too many poets are leaning toward free verse and avoiding the discipline of meter and rhyme, it is a good thing to encourage one who faces these disciplines. There is room for all kinds of poetry, free verse, blank verse and rhymed verse. As a good craftsman in the latter field I think Mr. Auslander well deserves help from your foundation.

Sincerely,

Oscar Hammerstein to Brooks Atkinson, November 22, 1957

Dear Brooks:

Thank you for your pages from the New Statesman.

If Bevan[9] gets in, as seems most likely, there is a good chance that England will make this decision. The chain reaction that will follow staggers the imagination. Through my cloud of fears shines a very faint silver lining—the relief of knowing that here will be a decision that must bring results, that the ice will be broken. The fact that giant floes may be headed straight in our direction is a prospect not to be belittled, but anything seems better than the solid freeze that has blocked all action.

---

[9] Aneurin "Nye" Bevan was a UK Member of Parliament, representing the left wing faction of the Labour Party. In 1957, he reversed course on the issue of nuclear weapons, arguing against nuclear disarmament. It was later claimed he changed after talks with members of the Soviet government, who argued if the British kept their nuclear weapons, they could be used as a bargaining chip with the United States.

I think that I wish that the English would do this. I think I would welcome anything that will force us to discard stale assumptions and to create new and bold approaches to international problems.

Since my trip to California cheated me out of our last luncheon date, perhaps we should make another one and talk over some of these matters. I am going back to California on December 1st, but when I return after about a week I will call you up.

All good wishes.

Oscar Hammerstein to Robert Dolan, November 25, 1957

Dear Bobby:

Dick and I some time ago adopted a policy of not going into plays produced by other people because our presence in the list of investors suggested an endorsement of the project far beyond any logical reason. Believing this to be a responsibility we didn't want to take on, we decided to stay out of everything with very few exceptions. An example of an exception is that we are taking a unit each in Jimmy Hammerstein's play because my staying out of a play produced by my son would have the opposite effect of suggesting that I thought it was lousy. I am sure that you will understand the reason behind our policy, and I certainly regret it in this case because I would like to cast a vote for you in anything you do.

Let's get together soon.

Love,

Oscar Hammerstein to John S. Robling, December 19, 1957

Dear Mr. Robling:

I enclose a brief article for your use during National Library Week. I am sorry that I am sending it after the December 20th deadline, but it was impossible for me to make this date.

Very truly yours.

Beyond the pleasure, the emotional or mental stimulation that a book gives a reader, there is a most important by-product that modern literature provides. This is the material supplied by books to dramatists, librettists, composers and screen playwrights. I would say that of all the screen plays produced the best are those made from stories previously printed. Many of our best plays are adaptations from books, and in the field of musical plays I can give first-hand evidence of their value. Among the books I have converted into libretti for musical plays have been "Show Boat" by Edna Ferber, "State Fair" by Philip Stong (a screen musical), "Tales of the South Pacific" by James Michener, ("South Pacific"); "Anna and the King of Siam" by Margaret Landon, ("The King and I"); "Sweet Thursday" by John Steinbeck, ("Pipe Dream"); and at the moment Joseph Fields and I are adapting C.Y. Lee's "The Flower Drum Song". All these have music by Richard Rodgers except "Show Boat" which I wrote with Jerome Kern.

The composer and librettist are fortunate indeed if they can build their complicated musical and dramatic edifices on the solid ground of a well written novel. They start off with a treasury of well defined, well studied characters, in situations that have already been tried out on the reading public and found to be interesting. What the novelist has said on the printed page the composer and lyricist can place into their own medium of song, create color, interpret and, in some instances, add dimension to character and story. The process is not very often one of addition. Usually a play which cannot run more than two and a half hours and must be expressed mainly in music, becomes a kind of distillation of the original work. Sometimes two or three characters may be moulded [sic] into one for the stage. There is time only to deal with the basic essential elements. Yet there is no substitute for the richness and completeness with which the original author provides the adaptor. The adaptor cannot use all the material in the book, but all the material is at his disposal and ready to be absorbed by him. A craftsman in his own right, it is his function to recreate in his own world and with his own tools the characters and situations created by the original author.

Oddly enough, the adaptation does not seem to become a commercial competitor of the original, but rather a stimulant to increased readership.

Oscar Hammerstein to Dorothy Hammerstein, circa
December 25, 1957

This pumpkin wouldn't be a coach,

It turned into a diamond bloach!

Melly Chlistmas and

All the love of P.F.

There are a handful of notes and cards to Dorothy where Oscar refers to himself as "Plince Fort" and where he distorts words as above, reminiscent of children's mispronunciations. The brooch was obviously inspired by *Cinderella*.

Chapter Seventeen
1958

Oscar Hammerstein to Robert J. Johnson,
January 8, 1958

Dear Mr. Johnson:

I am afraid that I have no opinion on what music will be in five, ten or twenty years. I have the impression that the youth of our nation know a great deal more music than the previous generations, and that their taste will be more sophisticated. If this is so, then the composers will surely rise to meet this taste.

I am not in the least concerned with the dangers of "rock and roll" because in the next twenty years there will be other primitive beats and arrangements, and people will again be alarmed. All these phases are harmless at the worst, and at best are sometimes helpful in developing music. Jazz, swing, rock and roll, bop, are all styles rather than music per se. They are a way of treating composition, not a way of composing.

I have a feeling, rather than an opinion, that music written in America is going to be of higher quality in these coming years.

I hope this comment will be of some help to you.

Very truly yours,

Oscar Hammerstein to Father Edward A. Conway,[1]
January 10, 1958

Dear Ned:

Thank you for your Christmas card and your good wishes for my survival. As you say, "we tried". I read with continued amazement the various

---

[1] Father Conway, a Jesuit priest and director of the Creighton University Center for Peace Research. An advocate for the formation of the UN, he campaigned for international cooperation in arms control.

The Letters of Oscar Hammerstein II. Mark Eden Horowitz, Oxford University Press. © Mark Eden Horowitz 2022.
DOI: 10.1093/oso/9780197538180.003.0017

suggestions for an answer to the Sputnik, for increased armament budgets, for more disarmament conferences—all within the framework of international anarchy. It is as if there was already in existence a world law—just one, and an unbreakable one. This law declares that there shall be no world law, and that no one should even discuss the development of law and order among nations. This game we play, with all our lives at stake, has to be played within a territory as rigidly marked as a baseball diamond. World law and order is beyond the foul line, a dead ball.

Dorothy joins me in sending our love and good wishes.

As ever.

Richard Rodgers to Oscar Hammerstein (excerpts), January 24, 1958

I had lunch with her [Thana Skouras's] father yesterday and he put in a strong pitch to get me to go to California and sit with Al Newman[2] for three weeks while Al scores the picture. This suggestion I find impractical, unnecessary and embarrassing. I can't imagine holding Al's hand while he does what he knows how to do better than anyone else in the business. I explained this gently to George [Skouras], who seemed to understand. He came back to the office with me and showed me the figures comparing AROUND THE WORLD Todd AO versus 35 m.m. I had seen these before with you and him, but I couldn't spoil his fun.

I went to see AS YOU LIKE IT done by the Shakespearean Festival people the other night. It was simply wonderful and I conceived what turned out to be a very successful gimmick which I put into operation immediately rather than making a simple donation, as you and I discussed it, of $2,500. There was prominent space in yesterday's paper announcing that Rodgers and Hammerstein would match every $100. contribution with $100. of its own. I had already told Joe Papp that $2,500. was our limit, but we deliberately left this out of the announcement as we didn't want to discourage any contributions. This morning's mail alone brought in $900. from the outside.

---

[2] Alfred Newman was the conductor and music supervisor on the film of *South Pacific* and composed most of the underscore. He wrote music for over 200 films and also served as some combination of composer, conductor, and music supervisor. Newman was nominated for an unprecedented forty-five Oscars, winning nine.

I have the beginning of a cute tune for the first song[3] in case nothing occurs to you that you find exciting.

Oscar Hammerstein (in Montego Bay, Jamaica) to Richard Rodgers, January 25, 1958

Dear Dick:

No news and no song. This is no place to work. But it is such a wonderful place not to work that I have decided to enjoy it to the full on its own terms and store up enough energy—and guilt—to equip me for a big dive when I get home.

I'll call you Friday morning (Jan 31) We have a lunch date but if you want to meet me sooner I'll be at the office about eleven (coming from the barbers) Since I've got these projected meetings after lunch, you'd be free to go up to the country if you'd planned a week-end in Southport.

We're all in good shape, sunburned, stupefied and contented. Dining with Adele Astaire to-night who sends her love to you. So does Dorothy. So do I.

Oscar

Plans for *The Sound of Music* began over a year and ten months before the show opened—before work had barely begun on *Flower Drum Song*. The show was brought to Rodgers and Hammerstein by Mary Martin and Richard Halliday who, with Leland Hayward's help, acquired the rights to the West German film, *The Trapp Family/Die Trapp Familie*, and permission from the Trapp family. The initial idea was to do the show as a play incorporating songs from the Trapp Family Singers repertoire. But when approached to write an original song or two for the show, Rodgers and Hammerstein demurred, saying that rather than mix old and new they thought it better to either only use the traditional songs, or to write an entirely new score. Martin, Halliday, and Hayward were enthusiastic about having an all-new score—if it were written by Rodgers and Hammerstein. Rodgers and

---

[3] The "first song" in *Flower Drum Song* is the haunting "You Are Beautiful." So the "cute tune" is probably something else.

Hammerstein would only do it if they could wait to begin work until after *Flower Drum Song*. All parties agreed.

Sister Gregory was a Dominican nun and a theater professor at Rosary College (now Dominican University) who began a friendship with Mary Martin in 1949—the result of a letter Sr. Gregory wrote Martin after seeing her in *South Pacific*. When work began on the show, Martin sought out Sr. Gregory for her perspective and advice. Sr. Gregory's responses were initially forwarded to Oscar, but eventually she and Oscar (and Dorothy) developed their own direct friendship and correspondence.

Sister Gregory Duffy to Mary Martin and Richard Halliday, forwarded to Oscar Hammerstein, February 23, 1958

My dears:

What wonderful news! I'd read you were considering the Trapp story but had no idea anything was settled. It should make enchanting theatre. I found the book delightful and thoroughly enjoyed the family in concert.

You are right, it seems to me, in believing that Maria's struggle to know her vocation in life is very much the heart of the matter. However, I sense that you are a little afraid of the material. You mustn't be!

If you trust it honestly and artistically it is bound to be good theatre. For many reasons there will be a temptation to hedge a bit or to sentimen- talize—please don't! That would result in a Bells of Saint Mary's, Heaven Knows Mr. Allison sort of thing that is dishonest, inartistic, and (for me at least) slightly nauseating. It is understandable that you should be a bit wary about handling the convent angle because most people—Catholics and non-Catholics alike—are more or less confused about the subject. You realize, too, that no matter how you treat it there will be a certain amount of criticism—but that would be true about almost any subject you might choose. You are persons of integrity as well as sensitive artists, if you are true to yourselves, Maria will emerge a flesh and blood woman, radiating simplicity, warmth, generosity, tenderness and humor.

The whole purpose of life, it seems to me, is pin-pointed in Maria's struggle to choose between two vocations. Like every adult human being, she must find the answer to the question: "What does God want me to do with my life? How does He wish me to spend my love?"

Many people believe one is attracted to the religious vocation because he or she is either afraid of life or incapable of love. Actually, the majority are drawn to it because they are keenly appreciative of the gift of life and have a tremendous capacity to love. The center of that love is God, and from that center it flows out into all areas of life. Most of us (we lucky ones, at least), were born of love and found great happiness and security in the family of which we were a part. We know from long experience the joy of that particular vocation, and it is natural and right that the majority should choose it because it promises the greatest human happiness this side of paradise. However, for some few, the feeling will persist that another vocation might offer greater scope for the love they feel. In time, such a person usually decides to settle the question by giving religious life a try, and if she is a woman, will enter the religious community that attracts her and for which she is most fitted. Although religious throughout the world are identical in the basic purpose of their existence, they differ greatly in rules, customs, dress, work, and manner of living.

At first, the girl becomes a postulant, which simply means that for a time she will be <u>observing</u> convent life from the inside, without actually being a part of it. She usually wears a uniform of sorts, although there is no hard and fast rule about it, this uniform usually differs from the habit of the community. The postulant is a completely human person and brings into the convent all the characteristics and personality traits she has developed throughout the years. She tries to determine [if] she is compatible with religious life, or, if through training, she can be made so. Usually she finds she must change herself a bit, and if she dislikes the idea, is always free to leave.

After about a year, the postulant and the superiors who have been in charge of her, determine whether or not she should go on. In our community, at the end of the year, the postulant is sent home on a vacation—wearing secular clothes, of course—and is urged to take up her old life, do all the things that formerly delighted her, weigh the old freedom against the the [sic] life she has seen in the convent, and then decide whether or not she wishes to return.

If the postulant still desires to embrace the religious life, and her superiors agree she has the potential, she becomes a <u>novice</u>. This means that she is formally given the habit of the community, assumes a religious name, and begins the life of the Sisters. However, she does not take the vows of religion. The novitiate is a time of testing, and the novice is completely cut off from her old life (few letters, no visitors, etc.) and is subjected to intense discipline. She rises, breathes, prays, works, sleeps, and plays by the bell! However, if at any time she feels she's had it, she is free to leave at once; or if her superiors discover that for any of a number of reasons she would not make a good religious, she is sent away. From about a third to one half of those who decide to try the life either leave or are sent away before the end of the novitiate.

If, however, a person has discovered that her love for God is the very core of her life, and if she is approved by the community, she finally becomes a true member of the religious by taking the three vows, but only for a limited number of years. The number differs from group to group, but is usually from three to ten. It is the vows, I think, that are most misunderstood by outsiders.

The first vow one takes is that of <u>Poverty</u>—and by it, one renounces the right of ownership, not because he feels material things are not good, but simply because he feels he can work and move more freely in the service of God. Anything he needs for himself or for his work, he simply asks for and receives; the kind and amount depending on the work he does.

For example: In my studio are innumerable books, records, a radio, record-player, TV set, and so forth, because my particular work as a teacher demands them. However, if tomorrow my superiors were to decide I could serve better in another capacity, I would be ready to leave Rosary in a few hours, taking with me only strictly personal articles, no more than would fit in my trunk and traveling bags. The Vow of Poverty does not mean living without things we need or like, but rather using them in a detached sort of way and being able to give them up cheerfully on a moment's notice, if asked to do so.

The second vow is that of <u>Chastity</u>—and by it one offers his or her body to God and dedicates it to His service, rather than using it as a channel of love, for husband, wife or family. A religious is neither afraid of sex nor disgusted with it, but rather recognizes it as one of God's greatest gifts, and therefore, in consecrating it to His service, one reflects the measure of one's love. Certainly one would not offer as a gift something he considered shoddy!

The third vow is that of <u>Obedience</u>—and by it one offers his freedom of action to God. It is by far the most difficult of the three, because one says, in effect, "I will obey my religious superior because in those commands I see reflected God's will for me." Because we are human beings who differ from one another in many ways, there can be definite personality conflicts between superiors and subjects, but because all are at least <u>trying</u> to live in affection and concord, there is actually very little friction.

After one has lived under the vows for a given number of years, a nun is again given the opportunity to leave if she wishes. In fact, some communities never allow their Sisters to take permanent vows, but they must renew them from time to time. In most cases, however, after one has lived under vows for from three to ten years, one is allowed to take them for life. However, if with the passage of time a Sister feels she would rather live outside the convent, she can apply for a dispensation from the vows and in a matter of a few months would be perfectly free to leave. At no time in the life of a religious is it necessary "to leap over the wall"—the door is always open.

That is a brief (and thoroughly inadequate) explanation of the machinery of religious life. When Maria Trapp entered the convent as a postulant, she was a perfectly normal girl, bringing with her the impulses and attitudes of any healthy young person. By observing life in the convent (and by experiencing its discipline) she was attempting to determine whether or not it was the life she was intended to live. From the book I gather that she was a bit immature and not yet sure of the meaning of life and love. Certainly she had no realization of romantic love. By the way, no vow is valid unless a person completely understands what he or she is doing; that is why most communities prefer candidates who have enjoyed life and thoroughly understand it, because they are perfectly aware of what they are leaving and what they are getting in exchange. Although Maria had a deep love for God, her superior recognized her immaturity—she was more child than woman, and therefore not ready to make a choice that would ultimately involve the emotions of an adult woman. That is probably why she was sent to the Von Trapp home—a way of marking time—because while there, she was not actually a postulant.

The very generosity and capacity for love that had attracted her to the religious life in the first place, began to deepen and expand. For the first time, perhaps, she knew a man as a friend, and slowly began to be attracted to him, perhaps began to love him.

In other words, she began to mature, and because the experience was new and a little frightening, she ran back to the place that symbolized peace and security for her.

Now Maria was in a position to make an honest choice, because she could understand the power of human love as well as spiritual love. This was the moment her superior had been waiting for, because now Maria could answer the question: "How does God wish me to use my capacity to love?" And her answer was: to spend it in the heart of the Trapp family. In fact to become the heart of the Trapp family. There was no stigma attached to the choice. It was not a declaration that she loved God less and people more, but rather, a recognition of the road she was meant to travel from the beginning. That sure knowledge was the core of her life from that moment on, and helped her to develop into the magnificent woman she was. Mary will be particularly equipped to understand and project her, because she, too, has a special capacity to love.

You will need someone to clarify technical points for you, but not to determine how Maria should be portrayed. It would seem that a priest would be of much more help to you than a sister, because we would tend to look at the thing from our own particular point of view, and in the light of our individual experience.

Also, most nuns are pretty reticent about discussing themselves or their lives with strangers. For example: I could no more have written this letter to Mr. Crouse, let us say, than you could discuss the intimacy of your love for one another with the person who happened to sit next to you on a train. Because we are friends and I have learned to trust you and love you, it is possible for me to share with you, at least to a degree, the most important thing in my life.

A priest, on the other hand, has observed different communities of sisters doing many types of work and living under a variety of rules and regulations. He knows the reactions of people toward them and would have more freedom in working with you than would a nun. For example, he could meet with you at times and in places that would be impossible for one of us. Most important of all, he would have his finger on the pulse of important ecclesiastics in the New York area. You will have no problem in representing the Church accurately, because the Church, believe it or not, is amazingly liberal and tolerant; it is rather certain individuals within the Church who constitute the problem.

I do have what might be called a "fraternal twin", a Dominican like myself. About sixteen years ago, I audited a course in Principles of Drama taught by Father Brendan Larnen, and was tremendously impressed with his keen mind and careful scholarship. Although I haven't seen him since, from time to time, I've read articles and book reviews he has written, and we have many mutual friends. Father Larnen has a deep interest in and knowledge of the arts, theatre included. In fact, I've heard he has attempted a play or two, but as a mutual friend confided, "He always gives the line to the wrong character." He is a gentle, balanced person, who possesses a sense of humor and is one with whom you could freely discuss any problem. Since he is a trained theologian, he would know the answers to your questions, or at least know where to find them. However, if you feel you would rather work with a sister, I'll try to locate one for you. Sisters with theatre training, ironically enough, are much easier to find in the other sections of the country—although few and far between everywhere, they are much more so in the East. In case you are interested, Father Larnen's address is:

Reverend Brendan Larnen, O.P.
St. Vincent Ferrer Priory
869 Lexington Avenue
New York City, New York

It would seem that most of the South Pacific crowd is involved in this new project, plus the gifted Lindsay and Crouse. You know, I hope, that if I can be of assistance to you ever, you need only ask. However, I am equipped to give little but my prayers and those, very fervent ones, are yours daily. Your happiness and success are dear to me. God bless and keep you.

Your devoted,

/s/ Sister Gregory

Raymond Koff, a student at Adelphi University, wrote Oscar for his input for a paper he was writing about the influence of popular music on public opinion: "I have come upon the notion that most of the lyrics of popular music places a premium on instability. Frustration, uncertainty and insecurity are apparently highly emphasized in popular music. Escapism into a dream world of wishful thinking about idealized love, and of vague, unreal sentiment largely divorced from reality has become the vogue. Since you are undoubtedly America's foremost lyricist, I am extremely interested in your feelings toward this conception . . . if you could possibly take a few moments to comment on this notion I would be sincerely grateful."

Oscar Hammerstein to Raymond Koff, February 26, 1958

Dear Mr. Koff:

I have not the time to write a very complete set of impressions on the subject of your letter. I can only say that I do not think that "most of the lyrics of popular music place a premium on instability." I think that all kinds of songs are being written today, and I think this is true of all times. I don't believe there has been any great or permanent change or trend in songs. We always have a share of sentimental songs about romantic love, and we always have a share of frenetic songs about dancing very fast and getting very excited. Writers keep on writing pretty much what people keep on thinking and feeling. People keep thinking and feeling pretty much the same things. Sometimes there is a change of emphasis, but it doesn't last long. I think that you can adopt almost any hypothesis if you look hard enough. It is like finding quotations in the Bible to suit your purposes.

I realize that this is the kind of letter which is of no help to you whatever, but this is the only kind of letter I know how to write on this subject.

Best wishes to you.

Sincerely,

The film of *South Pacific* premiered on March 19. The movie was a box office hit and became the highest grossing film of 1958. And the film's soundtrack reigned at number one on the charts for seven months. Despite its successes, the film received mixed reviews and was only nominated for three comparatively minor Oscars, only winning one, for Sound (that year *Gigi* won nine). Much of the criticism was related to the color filters used in filming several of the scenes—mostly songs—which proved odd and distracting. Because the filters were used in the filming itself, there was no way to change or remove the effect later.

Oscar Hammerstein to Louis B. Minter,[4] March 26, 1958

Dear Mr. Minter:

Among the many letters I have received, all congratulating me on the Mike Wallace program,[5] and from all kinds of people, friends and strangers, business men, professional men, housewives, a very good cross-section of the country, I have received only one letter in criticism, and that is from you.

I find some of your statements about me quite flattering. I am glad to think that you consider me a "charming, kind, gentlemanly genius" and "a man of great soul and integrity". These are very fine things to be. You also consider me "a typical 'Free Thinker' who doesn't think." This, I take it, implies that you, a hard-headed and logical attorney, consider me a rather fuzzy-headed and uninformed idealist. I have read your letter twice and find it filled with false assumptions, with conclusions having no basis of fact, and with a kind of hysteria that seems to beset many over-anxious conservatives today.

At the end of your first paragraph you say: "Please, Mr. H., say it isn't so. Please tell us that you ARE a patriotic American; that you are not only opposed to Communism, but cannot feel kindly toward anyone who deliberately becomes a communist." The fact is that I said very clearly on Mr. Wallace's program that I am opposed to Communism and that my political views and Mr. Robeson's were very far apart. I made this very clear. I then said that I would not, however, sit in judgment on Mr. Robeson because of the unfairness of which he has been a victim. Earlier in the paragraph you say "Perhaps you would get mad if you could not stay in the same hotel as your troupe members, but can that possibly justify IN YOUR MIND, a man becoming a communist, who had been able, by virtue of the freedom of America, to become an All-American tackle, a foremost singing star and wealthy?"

The fact is that I did not "justify in my mind" a man becoming a Communist. And incidentally, I would disagree with you that "by virtue of the freedom of America" he was able "to become an All-American tackle,

---

[4] Minter was an attorney in Hollywood, a partner in the firm Minter and Feder. His letter came to Oscar via ASCAP.

[5] On March 15, Oscar was the guest on the ABC television show, *The Mike Wallace Interview.*

a foremost singing star and wealthy". Lots of people have the freedom of America and do not become All-American tackles, and lots of people who have benefit of the freedom of America are tone deaf and do not become singing stars. It is this strange lack of logic in your letter which puzzles me and makes me wonder why the law attracts you as a profession.

The discussion of a budget is pretty complicated for you or me, but I would like to remind you that when the United States takes out a loan it is not an "unsecured loan". I believe it has the best security that exists on earth today—the great wealth of this great country.

I don't believe you and I would ever agree on some of the broad statements you make about labor being on top and the Democratic party being the Labor party and the Republican party being the business party.

The second from the last paragraph of your letter, on Page 2, is full of ironic paradox. In condemning liberals as being reformers and emotional, you yourself are being so emotional that you neglect to make any attempt to substantiate your statements. You say that all the things that liberals believe in seek "violent self-expression" and that "it is high time for conservatives to write, and even scream". It seems to me that you and many conservatives are distinctly the emotional type and that you are screaming all the time, as in this letter.

I think it is good to be dissatisfied with things as they are. Otherwise we would never make any progress. I think it would be a good thing if wealth could be more equally distributed, but I recognize that this is a difficult thing to bring about, and a difficult condition to maintain. I do not say: "Down with the old and up with the new" unless I believe that the new is an improvement. And I don't believe I have ever been guilty of violent self-expression, nor do I think that all liberals are.

On this subject, I believe that if you had listened more carefully to the telecast you would have remembered that when Mike Wallace asked me if I was for some kind of modified Socialism, I said I thought we were indeed and for some time had been living under a kind [of] modified Socialism. He then said: "Do you want it to go any further?" and I said: "No".

I studied law for two years at Columbia University, and then went into the theatre. As I read your letter I wonder whether I should have remained in law and whether you shouldn't have written musical comedies.

In closing this letter I must give you some very bad news. Of all the letters and phone calls I have received approving and enthusiastically praising me for this half-hour's interview, the most praised portion of all was "how I handled the Paul Robeson question". This approval came, not from Communists, but from people who had listened carefully and soberly to what I had to say.

Thank you for writing to me. I am sorry that you were troubled by the telecast, but I would like to reassure you that your worry seems to have been caused not by what I said, but what you <u>thought</u> I said.

My best wishes to you.

Sincerely,

Born in China, Chin Yang Lee immigrated to the United States in 1943. He was working as a teacher, translator, and journalist while he wrote his first novel, *The Flower Drum Song*. The book was published in 1957 and became a bestseller.

C. Y. Lee to Oscar Hammerstein, March 31, 1958

March 31, 1958

Dear Mr. Hammerstein:

I am very happy to learn from Joe that you have already completed three songs. It is wonderful news that everything is sailing so smoothly. There are a number of talents here who are anxiously awaiting an audition.

Joe says that you want to know something about flower drum. It is an ancient instrument, but not too different from a bongo. It's about two feet long, with a face the size of a dinner plate. Roughly it looks like a miniature beer barrel. There is a good picture of it on the cover of "The Flower Drum and Other Chinese Songs", published in 1943 by the John Day Co. The drum is slung over the shoulder of a pretty girl, who beats it with a stick. You may also find some suggestions about costume in that cover picture.

[Hand-drawn picture of a flower drum]

By the way, have you received a copy of my second novel "The Lover's Paint"? If not, please let me know.

Best regards.

Sincerely,

<u>C.Y.</u>

Please say hello to Mrs. Hammerstein for me.

In a 2003 interview, speaking of Rodgers and Hammerstein and *Flower Drum Song*, Lee said:

I remember during the tryout, I did not sit very close to Rodgers and Hammerstein. But I wanted to. I was a playwriting student at Yale, and I thought I could learn a lot by watching them. So I followed them around. I found out how Hammerstein discovered the flaws during the rehearsals for the tryout. Hammerstein wouldn't watch. He kept his eyes closed and would listen for the chairs. If the chairs squeaked too much, he knew the audience was restless; he knew there was something wrong. He did not pay attention to the stage. He would tell the secretary to mark it and say, yes, I have to change the number. Even during the tryout period in New York, they were still changing it. I remember they thought one number was not very good. The chairs squeaked too much. So Hammerstein took two nights to change one number. He was a slow worker. Two nights, and he wrote a new song . . . It was called "Don't Marry Me."

Oscar Hammerstein to Josh Logan, March 28, 1958

Dear Josh:

The picture is doing fine business. It is not selling out, but the business is solid and the word of mouth seems very good. Yesterday we ran an ad in the evening Telegram that was a half a page on two pages. In other words it crossed over two pages and was very effective. It contained some wonderful quotes from the criticisms. Sunday we are running a whole page ad in the Times and it looks great. This too has the quotes in it.

It may interest you to know that in a little box in the Tribune this morning there is an announcement that William Zinsser[6] is going to be

---

[6] In his *New York Herald Tribune* review of *South Pacific*, William Zinsser wrote: "20th Century Fox has wrapped a fancy package—and lost the story inside . . . The songs are graceful and tender, even at shattering volume. But the move is a victim of an old Hollywood fallacy: that if a production is 'big' enough, it's bound to be great."

henceforth on the editorial staff and that Beckley will be the film reviewer. So this gets him off your neck. I understand that the Reids were all very upset with Zinnser's notice because they loved the picture. I don't suppose there is any causal connection between this fact and the switch of his journalistic duties. I hope not, because I am all for freedom of speech, even for critics.

Ed Sullivan ran your information that we were making cuts in the picture. It didn't look like good publicity to any of us. Somehow or other any suggestion of acknowledged imperfections looks bad. Furthermore, if cuts are going to be made, there is a tendency to wait until they get in so the best version can be seen. I think we should soft-pedal this and go ahead and make our cuts.

I had a talk with Buddy [Adler] on the phone a couple of days ago and he is moving ahead with the cuts. He has sent for Bob Simpson to return from his vacation, poor guy!

I went to last Saturday's matinee and made a lot of notes—almost all of them were the ones that you and I had gone over together. When I saw Mitzi's face with the wet hair singing the verse of the reprise of "Some Enchanted Evening" I got cold feet on that cut. But we are going ahead with it anyway to look at it. There may be a way of preserving the verse without the chorus.

We have opened in Chicago, Philadelphia and Miami. I have had no reports except on Chicago, which I hear is great with all the notices good. This is only a second-hand report from Skouras. I imagine I will know more about all this in a couple of days.

Skouras also showed me a letter from Goldman in Philadelphia, the theater owner, who makes ecstatic predications about the picture after the press preview there. So do the press, I understand.

The controversy on the color filters still rages. Most of the reactions I have heard are on the wrong side, although there are some very articulate approvals. They seem to be outnumbered by those who believe that the color changes are a distraction.

Meanwhile I hope the colors on Montego Bay are a consistent gold and that you and Nedda are basking in it and having a wonderful time and a very well deserved rest. We look forward to seeing you as soon as you come back.

Love from us all.

Robert Dolan to Oscar Hammerstein, April 2, 1958

Dear Oscar:-

It occurred to me that you probably wouldn't be getting to the Trapp family project for quite some time and when you did you might forget some of the points we discussed. If it's any help to you I thought I'd jot down the few notes I made, plus one or two others that came to me after I left you. You can put this away in a file and look at it later on when you get into active work.

1 . . . How to stage vocals (group) whose special appeal is a unique blend of part-writing. If there is physical separation between the singers the blend seems to go out the window. If there is movement in addition to separation, the results are often disastrous. If they are bunched together and do not move much it is ideal musically but static visually. Also, the interesting thing about the Trapp Family musically was that they had a blend all their own. That is why people paid to see them. How well that can be duplicated by singers who are also going to have to act is a question. Of course, they could sing in a motionless grouping while someone else interpreted the music visually but such a staging cannot be repeated too often. I realize that you are not planning to give a concert of group singing but, rather, are telling a story about people, but, this group singing of theirs is a basic part of that story and that's why these problems are important.

2 . . . How receptive an American audience would be to a story showing the Germanic way of life . . . their kind of humor, clothes, their habit of discussing individual problems in mass family meetings.

3 . . . Mother's relentless way of pushing ahead under the cloak of good manners.

4 . . . The non-dramatic character of the Baron.

5 . . . The particular kind of music for which the Trapp family is famous. In this regard I would hesitate to blend an original score with Mozart,

Haydn, Palestrina or folk music. I think it is safer to make the score exclusively original.

6 . . . The very American Mary Martin playing the very Austrian Baroness. I can understand how an actress like Mary would want to take on such a challenge but, she has gone beyond her milieu before and failed . . . notably in a Noel Coward show in London.

Finally, you and Dick have already done a show about a woman who becomes a governess to a man's children. What made that story come alive was the fact that the man was quite a man equally, if not more, interesting than the woman.

I recall reading about a book that came out last year that was a lengthy correspondence between a remarkable nun and George Bernard Shaw. The book got wonderful write-ups and I have a feeling it contains a great deal of interesting material on the subject of the layman's questions about the religious life.

If, when you get to the writing, I am not in New York, by all means contact my sister yourself. Her name is Sister Mary Caroline and she is Dean at Notre Dame College, Staten Island. Her phone number is Gibraltar 7-4343.

I very much enjoyed our lunch and I hope we can do it again soon. Am amassing the data on American Express and, as soon as it is all together, Howard and I will get together with you and brief you.

Best,

Bobby

The first stage version of Rodgers and Hammerstein's *Cinderella* was produced by Harold Fielding and opened at the London Coliseum in December 1958 and ran through the holiday season. However, this wasn't exactly Rodgers and Hammerstein's *Cinderella*, but a traditional British pantomime version that used the Rodgers and Hammerstein songs and added a few of their more obscure numbers. Fielding put together a lavish production, designed to appeal to British audiences. The stepsisters were played by well-known male comic performers in drag (travesty), and the character of Buttons was played by pop star Tommy Steele (Buttons is a servant in Cinderella's household who has an unreciprocated crush on her and helps her along the way). The character of Dandini is a valet to the Prince. Fielding's production featured a large cast and orchestra, spectacular sets, and even a flock of live geese.

Oscar Hammerstein to Harold Fielding, June 4, 1958

Dear Mr. Fielding:

I have received the outline for your treatment of "Cinderella" and studied it carefully. Since it is a very bare outline, I am "flying blind" so to speak, and I am not at all sure that some of my suggestions for songs will be suitable.

The first thing to do is for you and Teddy Holmes to get copies of the scores of "Me and Juliet" and "Pipe Dream". He has these scores at Chappell.

If you can have a copy of your outline before you, I will refer to the number of the scene according to your own numerical system:

Act One, Scene 1, Item 2—Dandini's opening song. I suggest that a possible opening number would be "Keep It Gay" from "Me and Juliet", Page 53 in the score.

Act One, Scene 2, Item 5—Button's opening song—"Sweet Thursday" from "Pipe Dream", Page 88.

Act One, Scene 1, Item 6—The Prince's opening song—"Keep It Gay" from "Me and Juliet", Page 53. (Whichever spot you think is best for this song. I think it would be excellent right here, and perhaps the Prince and Dandini could sing it together.)

Act One, Scene 7, Item 1—Number for the Prince, "The Man I Used To Be" from "Pipe Dream", Page 78.

Act Two, Scene 2, Item 5—Prince. Here too is a possible spot for "The Man I Used to Be". (It seems to me that the Prince is a little overburdened with numbers if you use all the spots indicated in your outline.)

Act Two, Scene 5, Item 2—"If I Weren't King"—This never reached the performance. The lyric was in the first script I sent you, which was not our final performing script. No music was ever set to this lyric because Dick and I decided it was a rather weak comedy effort. I am sending you a copy of the script as it was finally performed, and this is more dependable that the first one you received.

Act Two, Scene 9, Item 1—Buttons—"Thinkin'", from "Pipe Dream", Page 170.

In addition to these suggestions for the spots indicated in your outline, I recommend that you look over some other songs that might be available for other spots. For instance, "Suzy Is a Good Thing" from "Pipe Dream", Page 98. By substituting the name 'Cindy', for 'Suzy', this might be a very effective number for Cinderella and Buttons.

For Cinderella—"I'm Your Girl" from "Me and Juliet", Page 165. (This would have to be sung to the Prince in absentia, down near the end of the play when she thinks she has no hope of ever being found by him, but she sings to him in her imagination.)

Buttons—"Lopsided Bus" from "Pipe Dream", Page 43.

The Ugly Sister—"Bum's Opera" from "Pipe Dream", Page 63.

"   "The Tide Pool" from "Pipe Dream", Page 24.

Prince—"Will You Marry Me?" From "Pipe Dream", Page 164, (after he has found her).

In some cases minor changes might have to be made to avoid anachronism or eliminate dialect which would not be consistent.

I am most anxious to hear from you soon and receive your comments on these possible suggestions made, I am afraid, at random, because I am not sufficiently familiar with the play.

Please tell me if someone has been assigned to write the new version and, as work is completed, I suggest you send it to me as quickly as possible so that I can give you whatever comments or suggestions I may have.

Best wishes to you.

Sincerely,

Harold Fielding to Oscar Hammerstein, June 17, 1958

Dear Mr. Hammerstein:

Thank you very much for your letter of June 4, regarding "Cinderella", which I have received via Teddy Holmes, and also for the letter of Agreement which has been received from your attorneys via Chappell and Co. Ltd.

I have been most pleased to accept the Agreement in principle, although I have felt it necessary to raise a number of points of detail in a letter which I have sent to Chappell's and which will no doubt be forwarded to your Attorneys.

We have already done a great deal of work on the book, and under separate airmail cover I have sent you a copy of a dummy book which has been prepared by our producer, Freddie Carpenter. I would stress that this is merely intended to show the general shape of the show. Mr. Carpenter has linked your scenes and songs with dialogue taken from other pantomime scripts, and it is intended to have all this "borrowed" dialogue re-written, but preserving the same general line. The dummy script, however, will serve a very useful purpose in helping us all to see where we are going. I am not asking for your approval of this script, except as a general outline.

We have now reached a point in our thinking over here where I feel it would be very useful if Freddie Carpenter could fly over to see you and Mr. Rodgers. He has several important points which I think cannot be easily settled in letters. These include:

(a) Is the Prince to be played by a woman[7] (as is usual in British pantomime) or a man? (This materially affects the construction of the book).

(b) Should the comics be confined strictly to the material in the book, or can we allow one or two "gaps" where they may work their own material? (This has an important bearing on copyright which I have raised in my letter to Chappell's).

(c) Can we permit Tommy Steele to use two or three of his well-established song successes[8] in his own act, somewhat along the lines of Sammy Davis's spot in "Mr. Wonderful"?

You will also see from the attached musical break-down that there are three important song spots which Freddie Carpenter (working with Teddy Holmes) has not felt able to fill from the scores of "Allegro", "Me and Juliet" and "Pipe Dream".

[7] For this production they cast the baritone heart-throb Bruce Trent.
[8] At least one Tommy Steele number was interpolated into the score.

I know well that you and Mr. Rodgers cannot spare much time from working on your new show, but it would be most helpful to us if you could see Freddie Carpenter, and I am suggesting that he should fly over in the first week of July if that would be convenient to you. I am sure that you could settle all his problems very quickly, probably within a couple of days, but correspondence on these production points might stretch out into weeks without either side fully understanding the other's point of view. Moreover, if these matters are settled at a personal interview, I shall then feel assured that we are working along lines which will secure your ultimate approval.

With best wishes,

Yours sincerely,

Harold Fielding

The show ended up interpolating three Rodgers and Hammerstein songs from *Me and Juliet*: "Marriage Type Love," "No Other Love," and "A Very Special Day."

Oscar Hammerstein to Julius Hoffman, United Business Men's Association, June 19, 1958

Dear Mr. Hoffman:

My anecdote:

When "Oklahoma!" was at the height of its run in New York and tickets were in great demand, a young farmer[9] from my part of Pennsylvania got in touch with me and asked me if I could possibly help him get two seats for "Oklahoma!" so that on the day that he got married he could take his bride into New York and take her to the show. I said that I would try to help him get the tickets, and I asked him what day he intended to be married. He said: "Well, you tell me what night you can get the tickets, and I'll be married on that day."

Very truly yours,

---

[9] Walter Moen, son of Oscar's farm manager, Peter.

Oscar Hammerstein to Henry Simon, Simon & Schuster,
July 7, 1958

Dear Henry:

I have read Newman Levy's text for the song book and I think it does its job well in that it will help the reader understand how the songs were cued into the various plays. I made a few notes, and here they are:

In the reference to "Pipe Dream," Page 3. Shubert Theatre is not spelled with a "c". That is the composer.

I don't like it said that we thought "Pipe Dream" a better play than the critics thought it was. I don't believe we have ever said that, and I don't believe we think it. We try to avoid exhibiting this kind of sorehead attitude, and I would be much happier if this were cut out.

"Oklahoma!", pages 4 and 6, the character is Aunt Eller, not Ellen.

"Carousel". It is true that putting "Liliom" into New England was Dick's idea. I think the dialogue ascribed to him is a little phony—"I've got it!" I think a mere statement that he had this idea and that we all liked it would be better than "I've got it!"

"Carousel", page 5. The lyric is "I never <u>knew</u> how to get money", not "know".

"South Pacific", page 1. "Hammerstein added plot and situation of his own." This rather neglects Joshua Logan, who wrote the book with me. I think perhaps you should say Hammerstein and Logan.

Page 5, the title of the song is "This Nearly Was Mine", not "This Almost Was Mine".

Page 2 and 6, the song is "Dites Moi", not "Mois".

(I am quite sure that your proofreader would have caught most of these things, but I might as well record them while I am writing you.)

"The King and I", page 2. You will note that throughout these articles, Dick seems to play a more prominent part than I in making decisions. Newman Levy also quotes him several times, and I am given the feeling that I am sort of a junior partner. On this particular page, for instance, it is Rodgers who whispers "There's our King" when we see Yul Brynner.

Well, as a matter of fact, we both recognized immediately that that was our King, and it really wasn't Dick who turned to me and said it. I think I spoke first. Although this doesn't make any difference, it seems me that in this one place, perhaps, we do not have to ascribe the discovery to Dick. He has enough credit in the course of the articles, and I have little enough. Maybe I should say "There's our King". As a matter of fact what I did say was "Papa, I want him."

I do not think it is true that "Gertrude Lawrence played "The King and I" up to the last six months of its run. I believe she played about a year and a half of the three year run. This of course could be looked up. It is not important but it might just as well be accurate.

Page 4. I have not discussed this with Dick, but I wondered if it is a good idea to call the "March" a Prokofieff type march. It seems to me that it is a wonderful Rodgers march, with really no debt to any other composer.

Pages 4 and 5. The character is not Lady Thiana, but Lady Thiang.

I do hope you will be able to fix the jacket design as we discussed it. Those letters are really very hard to see. As for the other illustrations, I thought they were very gay and colorful and suitable to the song material. I am certainly looking forward to the publication.

Best wishes.

Sincerely,

In July, Oscar had gall bladder surgery that involved a four-week hospital stay. Reggie Hammerstein passed away on August 9.

Oscar Hammerstein to Ward Morehouse (excerpt), September 9, 1958

I have my back to the wall right now in the task of finishing the songs for THE FLOWER DRUM SONG which goes into rehearsals September 25th. I have lost so much time in the hospital that I am way behind in my schedule. I have been working down here but next week I'm coming up to New York to be near things as we approach rehearsals. For a while I must keep my nose to the grindstone and no other. After I come up for air I hope we can all get together.

Film and television director Edward Buzzell wrote Oscar: "I am taking the liberty of sending you an idea that could utilize all your old properties—the hits, the near-hits and the misses—and many other plays available for live or tape television. It is a long-shot that you might be able to devote some of your time to this sort of project, but the Rodgers and Hammerstein name would give it the dignity and prestige needed to attract the proper interest."

Oscar Hammerstein to Edward Buzzell, Edward Buzzell Productions, Ltd. (excerpt), September 22, 1958

Dick and I have consistently turned down all ideas which contemplated using our names as producers of a television show. We have been given many flattering offers and have even been told that we would not have to devote any time to it—just cash in our names!

This is precisely what we do not want to do. Our names are good because we stand behind them and work behind them, and on the day that we farm them out to somebody for use they will start to dwindle in their importance.

Oscar Hammerstein to Dinah Shore (addressed to Mrs. George Montgomery), October 6, 1958

Dear Dinah:

Some time ago I wrote you a fan letter about the way you sang "Hello Young Lovers." Since then you have sung many of my songs and I have quelled the impulse to write to you saying to myself—"I cannot keep writing to her everytime she sings the song well because she always does."

Now I am forced to break my silence because I sat dewy-eyed listening to you sing "Something Wonderful" last night, and I can't remember when I ever heard man, woman or child sing a song with such compassionate understanding, grace, and empathy.

While flinging compliments, let me say I thought the show was about as successfully produced as any television show I have ever seen. Its humor was original and its smoothness amazing considering the fact that it was the first of a new series.

Congratulations to you, and thank you, thank you, thank you for "Something Wonderful."

Dorothy joins me in sending love to you. I hope that the next time you come to New York, you will let us know.

As ever.

Flower Drum Song began its out-of-town tryout in Boston on October 27.

Oscar Hammerstein to Eddie Benjamin, November 29, 1958

Dear Eddie:

It was good to hear from you, and very gratifying to learn that you liked "SOUTH PACIFIC". I, too, consider it a very fine picture version of the play. Among New Yorkers who saw the play originally it seems impossible to break down their loyalty to Mary Martin and Ezio Pinza. In fact, when roles are identified with fine artists like these, it is always difficult to accept any others in the same part.

I remember years ago when Peggy Wood played "BITTER SWEET" in London, and Evelyn Laye played it over here. It was an invariable experience that the people who had seen Peggy first thought she was far superior to Evelyn Laye, and those who saw Evelyn first felt that she was the only possible girl for that part.

Luckily, the people who have seen SOUTH PACIFIC with Mary Martin and Ezio Pinza are a handful compared to the total movie-going public, and the business that the picture is doing reflects this fact. We have had very long runs in all the cities we have opened in. It is now becoming established as a great success in England and will soon hit the European cities on the TOD[D]-A-O screen.

Since the bars seem to be coming down in Russia it may be that we shall be able to send it to Russia too. I agree with you that it would be fine to get it over there, and fine for the Russians to see that we have the courage to deal even with race problems in musical plays.

Answering your paragraph which starts with the question "how am I?", I am fine now and for the first time getting back my normal strength and vitality. I had two operations. In the first one they took out my gall bladder, and then that started a complication which resulted in a second operation on my prostate. I had no time to take a long convalescence because I had to plunge immediately into completing the lyrics and book of "FLOWER DRUM SONG" which opens in New York this coming Monday, December 1st. This wasn't so foolish a thing to do as it sounds because I believe putting my mind on writing the show put my mind off my body and helped me perhaps to get better more quickly than I would have otherwise.

Incidentally, FLOWER DRUM SONG, although it has not yet opened in New York, looks like a very solid success. At any rate it was in Boston!

I didn't have my diverticular taken out because I don't think you can do that; you'd have to take out a great many other things with it. I do, however, think that that was the real trouble and I am following a rather strict diet of no roughage now. The operations had one good effect—they took 20 lbs. away from me; I have gained back 10 but intend to hold the line at that point, and I find myself quite often admiring my image in the mirror. All my clothes have been taken in and it seems to me that I look quite beautiful.

Dorothy and I send our love to you and Blanche, and I surely hope you will let me know the next time you come up to New York, and let me make my house seats available to you for FLOWER DRUM SONG.

As ever,

Oscar

Flower Drum opened on Broadway on December 1. Despite its Chinese-American exoticisms, Flower Drum Song is the closest Rodgers and Hammerstein came to writing a traditional musical comedy. The show was a success with a 602-performance run and a film to follow. The reviews were generally kind. For example, from John Chapman in the New York Daily Post: "another notable work by the outstanding craftsmen of our musical theater, and it is unlike anything they have attempted before . . . a lovely show, an outstanding one in theme and treatment. But I shouldn't go to it expecting to be bowled over by sensation, it is a sweet, gentle story, sweetly and gently treated."

Richard Detwiler, The Wool Bureau Incorporated, to Oscar Hammerstein, December 4, 1958

Dear Mr. Hammerstein,

I went to The Flower Drum Song the other night expecting an enchanted evening. It turned into a night of horror when the players started burning holes in my livelihood with invidious references to how easily wool burns.

Please try burning this Countess Mara[10] of delicate wool challis. You can make a hole in it. You can produce a little char, and innocuous ash. But nobody's neck is going to go up in flames. Wool doesn't flame, it doesn't melt, it doesn't have to be flameproofed. As our technical man says, wool doesn't propagate a flame.

If you'd rather wear the tie without a hole in it, please try burning the woolen swatch instead.

Aside from that, I loved the play.

Sincerely yours,

Richard M. Detwiler

Director of Publicity

Oscar Hammerstein to Richard M. Detwiler, December 12, 1958

Dear Mr. Detweiler:

I am sorry to have caused you all that horror and thank you for the tie.

Our character, Old Master Wang, knows nothing about wool and was interested only in destroying a Western coat which was uncomfortable for him. In alibi-ing his destruction as an "accident" he said that wool burned easily. Of course this was an outright and unforgivable lie.

I shall talk this over with the character and see if he will eat his words.

My best wishes to you.

Sincerely,

Oscar Hammerstein

---

[10] Countess Mara was a high-end Italian fashion house known for their neckties. Challis is a lightweight woven fabric.

Oscar received a lovely, long letter from Dorothy Derry Shaw. It begins as a more general fan letter, but quickly focuses on *Flower Drum Song* and her speculations on how it will be musicalized. Here is a sampling from the letter:

It will, perhaps, be a long time until we have the pleasure of seeing "The Flower Drum Song". But I want to tell you of the interesting adventures that I am having with C.Y. Lee's lovely story. As a hobby, I review books and talk to women's groups on various topics. Currently, it is Mr. Lee's book and with it I offer a series of "Guesses" as to what the great Rodgers and Hammerstein team will be doing with it on stage. . . I guess:

1. The music will be fresh and unusual, inspired by the ancient folk-songs of China. Apparently simple, these melodies are really intricate, and the Flower Drum songs must have offered a real challenge to the composer.

2. The characters are fascinating, unforgettable. It will be most interesting to see which of the Wangs will be the Hero of the musical show: Young Master Wang whose complicated love life affords rich materials for the story line, or Old Master Wang whose character and personality and behavior compel our respect and amusement to a point of deep affection.

Oscar Hammerstein to Dorothy Derry Shaw, December 4, 1958

Dear Mrs. Shaw:

Thank you very much indeed for your letter and for the great interest that you have in our work. Your 'guesses' on FLOWER DRUM SONG are very shrewd. I will go through them one by one and tell you how close you came.

1. The actual Flower Drum songs were not adaptable for the purpose of the American musical stage, and we made up one of our own which sounds "traditional" but is really not. Mr. Rodgers did not use any Chinese music whatever as the basis for his score but there is a good deal of Chinese color in the orchestrations.

2. The story is mainly about Young Master Wang rather than Old Master Wang because we wish to emphasize a stronger love story than the book contained. We therefore brought in the character of Mei Lei very early in the story, instead of late. (In the book she comes in in the last quarter.) The character of the old man is, however, a dominant figure, and his relationship with his son is perhaps the most interesting element in the play.

3. Not only is "Grant Avenue" a personality in its own right, but we have actually written a song called "Grant Avenue".

4. It is indeed a colorful show. The designers, Oliver Smith on scenery and Irene [Sharaff] on costumes have done a beautiful job.

5. I don't know if we have quite caught the "delicate shapeliness" of the book's dialogue, or the "exotic stylized quality that glimmers through the action" but we have tried and, in some measure, we have succeeded.

6. We did not deal with political questions, and Communism is of course not mentioned at all since it is not an essential part of the book, - of the original book. The social theme, however, of Western assimilation is very important to our story.

7. I think we have succeeded in stating Mr. Lee's attitude as an American Chinese: he thinks so, too.

8. This point of yours is a very shrewd one, I think, and I believe we have dealt with the "ancient culture shining through the busy walking-and-talking on Grant Avenue".

9. The most important outcome of our production, of our producing this play is, I believe, your point of Americans feeling closer to Chinese. Without making any special comment we told this simple story about a Chinese family which could well be told about an American family, and it makes us all feel closer. Further, since the cast are made up almost entirely of Oriental people, the audience gets to know them and feels less self-conscious about differences as the evening goes on. We have a very charming cast who speak very well for the Oriental side of the world.

Again, thank you for your interest in us. It is gratifying to get letters like yours. They give us the enthusiasm we need for continuing our work.

Best wishes to you,

Sincerely,

Chapter Eighteen
1959

Turning their attention to what will become *The Sound of Music*, Rodgers and Hammerstein had yet another title under consideration.

Howard Reinheimer to Oscar Hammerstein, February 6, 1959

Re: TRAPP FAMILY ("Love Song"—Title)

Dear Dick and Oscar:

I am in receipt of the enclosed research covering the use of the above title for the forthcoming musical play. The title has been used so many times for various literary and musical properties, that it is doubtful whether a very successful play would be sufficient to create any type of secondary meaning that could entitle you to stop unscrupulous competition.

You might note that so far as America is concerned the only play produced was in April 1925. I am quite sure that there would be no secondary meaning attached to that production which could cause any trouble.

I note, however, the Pirandello play which was not only produced in Europe in 1931 but was also the basis for a German motion picture. This might possibly create a priority of rights which could occasion trouble in some foreign countries. I would not know to what extent the stage and motion picture production might create some foreign proprietary interest in the title.

You will further note that over 300 musical compositions have already been copyrighted under that name. I am afraid that this would make it completely impractical for you to have any controls of a song in the play entitled "Love Song", and you would find many unscrupulous publishers and writers capitalizing on your play if successful.

PLEASE, PLEASE, PLEASE get a new title!

Sincerely,

Howard

The Letters of Oscar Hammerstein II. Mark Eden Horowitz, Oxford University Press. © Mark Eden Horowitz 2022.
DOI: 10.1093/oso/9780197538180.003.0018

Oscar Hammerstein to Carol Geiger, February 25, 1959

Dear Miss Geiger:

I do think that all students should be taught Latin in school. It is the foundation of many modern languages. I believe that it has helped me in my understanding of English, and I believe that it was good mental training for me to have studied Latin in school and college. It was the means also of acquainting me with a literature I might have ignored. The works of Caesar, Cicero, Virgil and Horace have beauty, majesty and eloquence. I am very much against the elimination of Latin from the regular courses of any school.

All good wishes to you.

Sincerely,

Working on his Master's thesis at the University of Kansas City, Missouri, Dean Peskin included Oscar as one of the recipients of a letter he wrote "to the world's leading citizens." He goes on at some length, but his primary question is: "Because it is my belief that you are one of the most powerful individuals in the world today and because power is known to men in varying forms I wish to propose a question on the basis of the following proposition . . . , as one who is the possessor of power, what does this power mean to you?"

Oscar Hammerstein to Dean B. Peskin, March 4, 1959

Dear Mr. Peskin:

Answering the question in your letter, I must say that I never think of myself as being a man of great power. I know that songs I write are sung and heard by many people, and that therefore some of the words I think of may influence. "Influence" and "persuasion" are perhaps better words to describe whatever weapons I have. Somewhere in the word "power" there lurks the element of "force". I never think of myself as being in a position to force people to do anything, nor have I any inclination in this direction. If some men enjoy the possession of power, and are preoccupied with the problem of how and when to use it, I am not one of these. The question in your letter, in fact, is a completely new one in my life. I have never once thought of myself as possessing power, and therefore it could never have meant anything to me.

My best wishes to you for the success of your thesis.

Sincerely,

Richard Rodgers to Oscar Hammerstein (excerpt), March 13, 1959

This is principally to tell you there isn't anything much to tell you. You've read about the weather and you know that two tremendous hits, SWEET BIRD and RAISIN have opened. Business in general is so poor that these two did not sell out last night. I need hardly tell you that FLOWER DRUM SONG did. Ed Kenney is back and in good form, although the situation is hopeless with his mother.

Leland tells me that the Hallidays are violently opposed to putting Jerry [Whyte] on the show. Apparently there was some sort of run-in in London with SOUTH PACIFIC. Jerry doesn't know what it was, but Leland and I feel that under the circumstances it would be awkward and would put us in an untenable position to force the issue. Leland understands, however, that we are deeply concerned over the mechanical supervision of a show like this, especially where Oliver Smith and a very difficult backstage situation are concerned. I think we'll have to get some suggestions from Leland as to a solution.

Oscar Hammerstein to Dania Krupska,[1] March 21, 1959

Dear Dania:

There was a Dream Ballet indicated in the original script of Oklahoma and it involved many of the play's characters. The form in which it reached the stage, however, was the result not only of Agnes's editing of my clumsy scenario, but also of many details that were her own contributions—the dance hall girls, Curly's defeat by Jud, the manner of "substitution". While it

---

[1] Dania Krupska was a dancer in *Oklahoma!* and *The King and I* and an assistant to Agnes de Mille on *Allegro* and other shows and ballets. Among the shows she choreographed were *The Most Happy Fella* and Rodgers' penultimate show, *Rex*.

is true that the Ballet and all dances have become a part of the play and belong to the owners of the play, they do not belong to you and if you restage any of Agnes's original work, you must of course acknowledge this, and give her the credit due her (which I know you want to do). I don't see how you, as a choreographer can possibly stage the Dream Ballet in its present plot significance without encroaching on Agnes's version.

I was surprised to hear that any stock production has been made in which Agnes's dances had not been used. It would be interesting to see some of the other versions.

Congratulations on the new baby, about whom I had not heard, and good luck to you in your summer work.

Dorothy and I both send our love –

Oscar Hammerstein to Dorothy Hammerstein, circa March 1959

To a certain lady I met on the deck of the Olympic thirty-two years ago and who dealt my heart a blow from which it has never recovered!

Your Ockie

Oscar Hammerstein to Jule Styne, April 22, 1959

Dear Jule:

I am having trouble getting the last $10,000 for the George M. Cohan Memorial. You are on the committee, but you have so far not made any donation. (You of course were not obligated to.)

I saw "Gypsy" last week and loved it. I also think you are about to make a lot of dough. Would you like to break down and send me a check?

All the best,

Oscar Hammerstein to Hy Kraft (excerpt), May 7, 1959

I am busy working on a new musical play for Mary Martin, to open next fall. Everything is going well here. The whole family is well (at the latest checkup). And Vice President Nixon is very busy working his fingernails to the bone, welding the brightest God-damned halo you have ever seen. Don't laugh. He may get away with it.

Oscar Hammerstein to Tennessee Williams, June 3, 1959

Dear Tennessee Williams:

There appeared in Ed Sullivan's column a week or so back a mis-quotation of a speech I made in Philadelphia. To read it one might think that I had made an attack upon your work, or at least expressed some disapproval of what you are doing. Nothing could be further from my intentions. I am an awe-struck admirer of your talent. You and I may be on opposite sides as philosophers, you more preoccupied with the seamy side of life, I with the brighter side. But I believe we should go our separate ways and follow our separate inclinations without feeling it necessary to disapprove of each other.

I ran into Josh Logan who asked me about the material in Ed Sullivan's column. I explained to him that it was an inaccurate version of what I had said, and I told him that I had thought of writing to you about it. He then urged me to do so.

You may not even have read the column, or if you did might not have attached much importance to it. I don't suppose it is important, but I felt that I should clear it up for my own sake.

With best wishes to you.

Sincerely

Oscar Hammerstein II

The aforementioned Ed Sullivan column, "Li'l Old New York," appeared in *the New York Daily News* on May 23. Sullivan wrote:

"If Tennessee Williams writes about a tree on a hillside, invariably the tree is old and twisted. The background is utterly desolate. While that is an accurate report, why forget the same [tree?] in the spring when God's miracle of rebirth [greens?] that same tree with tiny flowers and the background becomes appealingly green? Or why not describe the third stage when the magnificently rooted tree is bearing apples or cherries?" That [same?] inquiry was [made?] by Oscar Hammerstein 2nd at the Philadelphia banquet which honored him in the crowded grand ballroom at the Belvedere-Stratford. Most of us are betrayed into the same effort which entraps Tennessee Williams representing the dull side of the coin rather than the brighter side. Hammerstein himself is a Pollyanna, which underscores the validity of his observation. In point of moral courage there is nobody in the world theater who surpasses Oscar . . . So when, Hammerstein, full of hope and enthusiasm reminds us that a desolate orchard later becomes a growing testament to the miracle of God, let's listen to Oscar rather than Tennessee Williams, who I think is a cockeyed pessimist.

Leland Hayward to Richard Halliday (in Brazil), copied to Oscar Hammerstein, May 28, 1959

MOST SUCCESSFUL PRODUCTION MEETING YESTERDAY FROM AUTHORS DONOHUE OLIVER HERMAN BLUM MYSELF STOP COMPLETED ROUGH FIRST DRAFT AND NEXT WEEK STOP HEARD FIRST SONG SOUND OF MUSIC ABSOLUTELY KILLING BEST THING THEY HAVE WRITTEN IN TEN YEARS CONCEPT SHOW THRILLING OLIVER[2] BRILLIANT MANY DECISIONS REACHED PENDING YOUR APPROVAL JOE LAYTON CHOREOGRAPHY AND STAGING MUSIC NUMBERS ALL ENTHUSIASTIC LUCINDA BALLARD COSTUMES EXCEPT MARY'S EVERYONE'S FEELING LUCINDA DREADFUL NUISANCE BUT UNTOUCHABLE FOR CHARACTER WORK STOP MARVELOUS GIRL ELLEN HANLEY NOW REPLACING POLLY BERGEN FIRST IMPRESSIONS[3] FOR ELSA[4] STOP NO OTHER CASTING EVEN CLOSE STOP WILL KNOW MIDDLE NEXT WEEK BLACKTONS[5] AVAILABILITY ONE YEAR BUT NINETY PERCENT SURE NOW DICK OSCAR MYSELF VERY ANXIOUS FOR JAY PARTICULARLY FOR CHORAL WORK WITH KIDS PLACE CABLE "HAYWIRE" APPROVAL OF ABOVE STOP THANKS FOR YOUR CABLE OPENING GYPSY ITS SENSATION LOVE TO BOTH

LELAND

[2] Oliver Smith, set designer.
[3] *First Impressions* was a musical based on *Pride and Prejudice*.
[4] Marion Marlowe ended up playing Elsa. Ellen Hanley appeared in *Fiorello!* Instead.
[5] Instead of Jay Blackton, Frederick Dvonch became the music director for *The Sound of Music*.

Oscar Hammerstein to Ted Wing, June 3, 1959

Dear Ted:

Thank you for your letter of June 2nd and your kindness in inviting me to write a pageant for the City of Atlanta. Your confidence in me is misplaced. I cannot write a pageant because I hate pageants. I have never seen one that was not dull and ponderous.

David Selznick has been trying to interest me in a stage version of "Gone With The Wind" for several years, but it seems to me that the picture did such a good job I would not like to go into competition with it. Incidentally, no matter who you get to adapt "Gone With The Wind" into a pageant, I suggest you look into the legal rights because you might run into some trouble with Selznick.

Anyway I am very grateful to you for thinking of me in this connection, and I wish the greatest success to the project. I realize that even though I do not like pageants many people do and they are performed very successfully every year.

My best wishes to you always.

Josh Logan to Dorothy Hammerstein (excerpt), June 23, 1959

What a thoughtful and dear gesture—to send me Lady Task's letter. For some reason the criticisms of South Pacific (movie) have hurt more than usual. I tried so hard to make it great. But it's almost impossible to compete with a memory and the memory of S.P. was so strong with everyone. The whole world was directing it for themselves. Casting it too. Naturally my work didn't compare with their own. But now that the returns are coming in—especially those from England I'm feeling a bit better . . .

Presumably written after hearing some of the songs for *The Sound of Music*:

Mary Martin and Richard Halliday to Richard Rodgers and Oscar Hammerstein, June 24, 1959

NO WONDER YOU ARE TWO WONDERFULLY DEAR AND GREAT GENTLEMEN WE ARE SINGING QUOTE THE WHOLE DAY

LONG UNQUOTE AND WILL BE SINGING OF OUR LOVE AND ADMIRATION AND GRATITUDE TO YOU BOTH ALWAYS AND ALWAYS-

MARY AND DICK=

Oscar Hammerstein to Mary Martin and Richard Halliday, June 30, 1959

Dear Mary and Dick:

No royalty statements that we may ever get from this show can reward us as did your wonderful telegram. Thank you.

Love,

Myra Finn to Oscar Hammerstein, circa July 1, 1959

Dear Oc –

In my state of semi-coma this morning I omitted a few things I wanted to ask you-

Did you know that "Ball at the Savoy" has been produced in Moscow?

Do you know that there is a revolting rock + roll record made out of "Indian Love" which is sung by a girl with a horrible voice + the lyrics have been changed to make them sexy + suggestive?

Do you know about a book called the "In + Out" Book in which it states that "O H always was, is, and always will be out" what ever that means.

Do you know that in Plummy's[6] last book he has used the lyrics (part of them) of "Old Man River" to make them sound anti negro? page 6 I believe –

Where are the Knapps?

With all this good news I close.

Yours

Mike

---

[6] P. G. Wodehouse.

Oscar Hammerstein to Myra Finn, July 7, 1959

Dear Mike:

Taking up your letter categorically—I did not know that "Ball At The Savoy" has been produced in Moscow, but I don't believe I had anything to do with European rights, and if I did, I can't collect from Russia anyway so I think I'll just forget about that one.

I have not heard about the "Indian Love Call" record, but there is nothing I can do about that either—except to try not to hear it.

I have heard about the "In And Out" book and I am very happy to be out.

I had not heard about Plum's book and the "Ol' Man River". I will look this up.

In answer to your question "Where are the Knapps?" I enclose a photograph of their house in Vermont. It is a chicken farm only they have no chickens yet because business is so bad. It is a very hard place to get to. When I was in Boston the last time I tried to figure out a way. It would be at least four or four and a half hours drive from Boston, and there is no way of my getting a chance to spend nine hours on the road in order to spend an hour with them. So we couldn't work it out. I spoke to them on the 'phone. In a letter soon after, they sent me the enclosed photograph of their villa.

Thank you for the informative letter. I will be seeing you soon.

Oscar Hammerstein to Jeremy Pope, July 14, 1959

Dear Jeremy:

I am sorry that I have taken so long to answer your letter. I am very busy at the moment writing the songs for a new play which goes into rehearsal in September. I am, as usual, behind my schedule.

I think that the lyric for your song is very trite. It is not enough unlike many other songs, either in form or in the treatment of the theme. I, therefore, think that very few publishers would evince any interest at all.

You should forget all the songs that you have ever heard, and write one that is all your own.

Looking over the manuscripts again, I find that there are three songs in all, and all about the same subject: Someone has lost his love and is crying to her about it. I must confess to a personal prejudice toward all these songs. I don't believe they are real. I don't believe that anyone who ever took this attitude after being thrown over has ever succeeded in getting back into the good graces of the one who jilted him. If she jilted him because he was boring, God how boring he is now that he starts to cry about it.

I am aware of the success of many so called "torch songs." These, however, are laments delivered not to the one who has turned the singer down. They are more like soliloquies or confidences exchanged with friends, not direct pleas and protests by the jilted to the jiltor.

I am sorry that I cannot give you a more enthusiastic appraisal, but I know that you don't want anything but an honest opinion.

My best wishes to your family.

As ever

Oscar Hammerstein II

Oscar Hammerstein to Margot Wattles (excerpt), July 15, 1959

I am busy working on my new play "The Sound of Music" in which Mary Martin will be starred. We go into rehearsal on September 1st and open in New York on November 12th. I am working well and I am in danger of having all my songs finished by the time we get into rehearsal—a fact I have never once accomplished in my 42 years' experience with the professional theatre.

Oscar Hammerstein to Albert Sirmay, July 16, 1959

Dear Albert:

Thank you for sending over the scores of FLOWER DRUM SONG. I shall be ordering more later. I glanced through it and it seems like a very good job.

I object very strenuously to the back page where the vocal scores of ALLEGRO, CAROUSEL, KING AND I, ME AND JULIET, OKLAHOMA!, and SOUTH PACIFIC are all advertised, and the credit for the composing is given to Rodgers and no credit is given to Hammerstein for the lyrics which are certainly part of the score. The only instance in which for some reason I was given credit was ME AND JULIET, which is the least distinguished of all the scores. I note, too, that this is also done in the case of SHOW BOAT and MUSIC IN THE AIR, where Kern has apparently done the whole thing. I am good and sick of this custom of only mentioning the composer in connection with vocal scores. The word "vocal" implies that there are words as well as music, and in the future I want equal credit with whatever composer I work with. I think it is high time this damn nonsense was stopped. I have put up with it all my life and I am getting too old to put up with it any further.

All good wishes to you.

Sincerely

Albert Sirmay to Oscar Hammerstein, July 20, 1959

Dear Oscar:

I cannot tell you how much we regret the aggravation caused you by the obsolete back page on the vocal score of Flower Drum Song.

If you look at the new edition of the Show Boat vocal score you will notice that there is no back page listing at all. When Flower Drum Song went to the printer they were instructed to leave the back page blank. This order was unfortunately ignored and they deliberately added the faulty back page.

Your point concerning equal credit to you and the composer is the most natural thing in the world and any violation of this principle is sheer stupidity. In giving credit to you on just one vocal score: "Me and Juliet" is an unforgivable mistake.

Please be assured that I will make it my business that no more blunders of this kind will happen in the future.

I'm sending you three copies of the new printing of the Show Boat vocal score and I hope there will be no trouble with it.

Again expressing how sorry we are about this immensely disturbing incident I am,

Yours as always.

Alb. Sirmay

Oscar Hammerstein to Albert Sirmay, July 29, 1959

Dear Albert:

Thank you for the scores of "Flower Drum Song" and "Show Boat". I do not prefer a blank page to a page advertising all the other scores. I would much prefer a page advertising scores which gave equal credit to the librettist as well as the composer.

Before you start to print proofs of the songs, it might be an economy if you send me the piano copies so that I can make corrections in them. There are a few mistakes already, and I find that very often mistakes that are in the original copies have a way of staying in.

At the concert the other night I heard one of these original mistakes, and I wonder if we are still printing copies with this mistake on it. It is in "You Are Beautiful". The verse should start: "Along the Hwang Ho Valley", not "Along the Hwang Ho River". The word "ho" in Chinese means river, so Hwang Ho River means Hwang River River. I wish you would tell Irving to tell singers at the concerts who sing to use the corrected version.

I am looking forward to getting the piano copies so that I can send them back to you corrected, and that will prevent one set of corrections in the proofs.

All good wishes.

As ever,

Richard Halliday to Hayward, Rodgers, Hammerstein, Lindsay, Crouse, and Vincent Donehue, July 21, 1959

Re: Notes re phone conversation with Baroness Von Trapp, 7:00 P.M., July 20th.

From the Baroness, "Reading the first scene twice is one of the highlights of my life for me. But I have two great wishes:

1) Please rectify my husband's picture. Now he looks like a Prussian officer. He's so marshalling—so much a marshall [*sic*]. He wasn't like this. This is what comes out and it is not his true nature.

2) The second request: that scene where the girl tells Maria that their father is in love with her. This is false. It does not ring true for anyone.

May I tell you how it really happened? . . . The truth is that the three youngest—4. 6. 8 year-olds—had heard that I might be going back to the convent. So the three of them went to their father and said, 'If you don't marry Maria, she'll go back to the convent! You have to marry her!' Their father said, 'But I don't know whether she likes me!' They came running through the house to me where I was standing on a ladder, cleaning the chandelier (we had a German housekeeper and whatever she told me to do, I did)—they rushed up to me and said, 'Maria, do you like our father?' I said, 'Of course I do.' So they went back to their father and told him. Later he came to me. I was holding a very expensive flower vase, and he said to me, 'Maria, thank you.' I said, 'Thank me? For what?' He said, 'Well, aren't we engaged?' . . . And BOOM went the vase!"

Baroness' comments on character of Maria:

"I think, after reading the whole script through, I honestly feel the picture of Maria is more on the sentimental side all the way through. She isn't really a tomboy. I don't want to upset anybody but anything on the line of her sliding down the bannister - you'll have to do something. She has to be a little rowdy. We don't really get that impression from the script. There is no conflict in her character, or maybe the word is contrast. She is sweet and kind and gentle and lovely—but no tomboy. She sings without permission, loudly, but that is sweet, too."

Baroness quite insistent on coming down to New York for meeting, preferably tomorrow (Tuesday), but Halliday dissuaded her.

She mentioned several times wanting "a reason to come to New York." Halliday told her he felt it important at this stage that he and Mary go there to see her, and she agreed. She asked if Donahue would come. Halliday said, "He said he must come." She also asked about Lindsay and Crouse, saying "Why don't you work on them tomorrow?"

The Baroness added, "I don't want my husband to look like a Prussian general, not too severe. It should be brought out a little more definitely that this is not his true nature—he treats the children the way he does because that's the way he treats his sailors, that's the reason for the whistle he uses, he doesn't know any other way. He must say himself that he knows he's wrong, but doesn't know what else to do." The Baroness added, "If I could only explain my husband to Lindsay and Crouse. My husband's character is not quite right and Maria is not quite right. Again, my husband must not be too severe. He does come through that way in the script. He becomes nice too late, after we've been told that he is only severe—Prussian-navy like. We've had no chance to see even a glimpse that basically he is a kind man, until so late, while all the time he did have a good, kind nature. He was born with that."

Richard Halliday to Hayward, Rodgers, Hammerstein, Lindsay, Crouse, and Vincent Donehue, July 22, 1959, forwarding a letter from Sister Gregory, July 20, 1959

Attached is a letter from Sister Gregory, written after reading the script.

Believe we all will find constructive suggestions here, especially regarding moments and attitudes dealing with nuns and their lives in the convent.

Richard Halliday

My dears:

Thank you so very much for sending the script—I enjoyed it tremendously! I could kiss you all on both cheeks for your portrayal of the Sisters—you have avoided both extremes and hit straight down the middle! For me the characters are honest, human and almost completely believable. Realizing how much thought and time has gone into the script, I know that you have a good reason for every word and every line, so please treat the following comments in the light of someone coming to the script cold and simply thinking aloud as she goes along.

1-35: The Sisters involved in this scene seem to belong to the Abbess' advisory council. Because of their offices, the Mistress of Postulants and Mistress of Novices would be members of that group. Since Rafaela seems to understand Maria very well and is very fond of her, perhaps she could be indicated as Mistress of Postulants. This would explain why her voice carries unusual weight with the Abbess.

1-3-6: I like Berthe's line, ". . . .the religious life is no place for the pious." It should raise a chuckle. Perhaps the meaning would be clarified if the next line read: "You mean the sentimentally pious, Sister Berthe," followed by Rafaela's line, "Yes, she does tend to pray—well, dramatically and pretentiously." Or something of the sort.

1-3-7: In formal conversation one would always use the title, "Reverend Mother." However, in informal conversation or when one wishes to show affection, one would omit the Reverend. Berthe might say, "Mother is being very kind." However, if you wish to point up Berthe's personality—a stickler for the letter of the law—she would certainly retain the full title.

1-3-7: "And under her wimple she has curlers in her hair." This line bothers me because it drastically changes the image I've formed of Maria—that of an untrammeled youngster, something of a tomboy, and completely unconscious of her physical beauty and the power that beauty could exert. That very unawareness gives impact to a line in the wedding scene. Would such a child be vain enough to wear curlers in her hair? Would she not be more likely to have uncombed, wind-blown hair?

1-3-8: Please don't have them giggle! Chuckle—laugh—and even explode with laughter, but not giggle. When laughter wells up we are inclined to either smile or go all the way and laugh whole-heartedly.

1-3-10: When the Abbess rises she might well finger her rosary but I doubt very much that she would kneel on the priedieu. This is the kind of decision she has to make many times a day and a "shortie" prayer would be all the time she could give to her simple decisions throughout the day.

1-3-11: We rarely, if ever, refer to "saying our beads;" it is rather, "saying or praying our rosary."

1-3-15: I like this scene very much! However, after Maria signifies her obedience by kissing the ring and the Abbess has accepted it by placing the sign of the cross on the forehead, I think the Abbess would in some way express her tenderness for and understanding of this child. An American Dominican would certainly caress her in no uncertain terms but I suppose a German Benedictine would not. However, could the same effect be given if, after the sign of the cross and the God bless you line, the Abbess would cup Maria's face in her hands and show her understanding of the child's need by anticipating the request and saying: "My child, you have my permission to sing." NO? Well, anyway, some expression of tenderness and love.

1-6-35: In our formal prayers Thou and Thy are frequently used. However, when we pray informally, which is much of the time, we more or less talk to God as we would a good and close friend—after all, that is what He is. At those times we would use the intimate You. I think Maria would use You and Your in her prayer because it is a simple, warm conversation with God.

I-6-36: Because we believe in the Divinity of Christ, we would refer to Him as the Divine Son rather than Holy Son.

In this next bit I am probably way out in left field! Somewhere between pages 1-7-53 and 1-8-63, I think there is an obligatory scene missing. After the Captain's line, "You shouldn't have done this to me," and before Brigitta's "Because he's in love with you," I think a scene, a song, something is needed to show what is happening. Maria is awakening physically and emotionally, and although unaware of the cause of the strange feelings within her, would show some of the turbulence that marks emotional growth. Maria has tremendous capacity for love and when she begins to awaken, it would not be a placid experience. The fact that she is totally unconscious of what is taking place adds impact to her fright and flight when Brigetta drops her emotional bomb. On the other hand, the Captain is an older, experienced, sophisticated man who has kept his emotions on ice for some time and is in the process of finding a wife with his head rather than with his heart. Wouldn't he be a bit disturbed when his iron will begins to weaken and he realizes he is attracted to a woman—child, almost—who is years younger than he and a postulant to boot? Perhaps he doesn't fully realize what is happening, either. But I want to see something happening between these two that is unrelated to what they feel for the children. I don't think such a scene would detract from the mutual recognition of love on page 2-1-12, but would prepare us for it. Perhaps I have too great a taste for dramatic conflict—dialogue and characterization are never enough—I want to see the basic conflict thru dramatic action. Please don't shoot, I'll give up quietly!

1-9-66: Even in convents that are cloistered and in which very strict rules for silence exist, one can always speak out of necessity or charity. Since Sister Rafaela comes to the office of the Abbess on business, it would not be necessary to ask permission to speak—that is implied if the Abbess admits her.

1-9-65: The Postulant does not receive a habit—that is reserved for a solemn ceremony when she becomes a Novice. The girl would be given a Postulant's Uniform.

1-9-69: This scene is beautiful! However, because of the depth of her feelings, Maria might drop the Mother Abbess and use the more affectionate Mother.

2-2-13: It has long been the custom at Rosary for graduates to visit the college with their wedding parties on the way from the Church to the reception. The Sisters who have been particularly close to the girl and those under whom she has majored, make a definite effort to greet her and her bridal group—since we average about five or six a week we can't see them all. Such moments are deeply moving because we see a girl whose intellectual curiosity we have stimulated, whose mind we have helped train, and whose heart and soul we have tried to enrich, standing on the threshold of fulfillment. Although she receives a Sacrament when she is married, we do not when we take the vows of religion. We have tried to help her recognize the tremendous potential of her womanhood and the power and beauty of the Sacrament she has received.

Although all the Sacraments are channels of grace to the soul, it is most wonderfully evident in matrimony because the very purpose and office of this Sacrament is to infuse human love with aspects of the divine. We have taught her that marital love is a unique blending of the spiritual, physical, intellectual and emotional aspects of her being and will penetrate the entire personality, and that when that love sweeps on to its complete fulfillment, her body and that of her husband become sacramental, each a channel of grace for the other. We look at this bride and see the child we have guided and loved ready to begin the work for which she was born—that of pouring out her love on her husband, children, home. We know that she will experience sorrow as well as joy and we would shield her from grief if we could. While our hearts almost break with love for and pride in her, we smile, arrange her veil or train for a picture, look at her ring and bouquet, and say something completely ordinary, like, "You look beautiful, dear," or "You're a lucky boy, Joe." Yet in our hearts we are praying, "Dear God, make them happy and please let him be gentle with her."

Sometimes I think I simply cannot go thru it again and could almost pray not to love them so much—because a little of ourselves, of our hearts and minds, goes out with each one of them and remains with them always. And something of them remains with us and binds them to us with affection throughout the years. You have caught a reflection of all this in your wedding scene, I don't know quite how you managed—how could you know in order to make it so natural, so right?

When Sister Rafaela feels the material in the slip, it is not the richness that impresses her, she has become accustomed to rich material in the vestments used in Chapel—she is rather covering a deeper emotion by doing something very ordinary with her hands. I don't think Maria would ask permission to say she is beautiful. After all, she is no longer subject to the Abbess, Might it not be more natural for her when she sees herself reflected in all the radiance of her love and happiness, to break out spontaneously with, "Why, Mother, I look beautiful!" And the Abbess might lighten the moment, yet reflect her own feeling by breaking in with, "Do not be vain, my daughter. Let me say if for you. You are indeed beautiful, my dear!" The lifted eyebrow on "This is lovely but isn't it a ---?" line on the previous page also might be reaching for light to cover deeper emotions. On the other hand, Berthe might actually mean it.

2-2-15: Sister Rafaela's line is not clear to me. Does she mean that it is a wonderful experience for Maria to have found her true place in life? The vision phrase is ambiguous but perhaps the song to follow clarifies it.

2-6-40: I love the ending of the script and find it completely satisfying, but I cut my literary teeth on the Atlantic and the New Yorker. I wonder if Saturday Evening Post devotees who have never heard of the Trapp family might ask: "What's with the mountain bit? Did they make it or didn't they?" However, if the music is in a triumphant strain they certainly should get the message.

These comments must seem rather silly and amateurish. However, I deliberately refrained from thinking them over—they are first impressions, nothing more. You have been patient to stay with me so long. As always, my dearest love and fervent prayers. God keep you.

/s/ Sister Gregory

Oscar Hammerstein to Howard Lindsay and Russel Crouse, July 29, 1959

Dear Howard and Russel:

I enclose cues to "My Favorite Things", "You Are Sixteen" and "The Lonely Goatherd".

On page 1-3-8, will you please eliminate the direction about giggling, to please Sister Gregory. Will you also correct the spelling of one word. It should be "flibbertijib[b]et". This is a word in the dictionary, and this is how it is spelled, but everybody who has re-typed it or put it into a music manuscript so far has considered that I have made a mistake, and writes it in two words just as you see it now in the script. Everyone seems to think (as I did) that this is a New England colloquialism. Actually, it is a good old English word.

On page 1-3-15. I think the direction should read that Maria sings the last part of the song. We can decide later how much she should sing here. Obviously it shouldn't be the whole song.

I enclose also a number sequence for the script, but I have done only the first act because I haven't enough to put into the second act, and so many things are undecided regarding titles.

I am staying in New York this weekend in case you should want to get in touch with me about anything.

Love to the whole Annisquam chapter.

As ever,

A Jack Perfect contacted Oscar with a suggestion: "Have you ever thought of writing a musical that would have two endings, one happy and the other sad? On alternate performances, you would alternate the endings. The first act for all performances would be identical and just the action in the second act would make it happy or tragedy. The songs in the first act - same, but different songs in the second act or possibly just different words."

Oscar Hammerstein to Jack Perfect, August 13, 1959

Dear Mr. Perfect:

Thank you very much for submitting your ingenious idea for a musical with two endings. As far as I am concerned it is so difficult to write a musical with one ending that I wouldn't even start on the project you suggest, even though I consider it very original and enterprising of you.

Thank you very much for your interest in my work.

Sincerely,

Richard Halliday notes, re. phone conversation with Sister
Gregory, August 4, 1959

As the script is now, the Captain is cold. He is almost unattractive until very late in the play.

Anything that's attractive about the Captain is told us, we never see it. Elsa tells us. The housekeeper tells us, "He never used to be that way". Maria tells us when she tells the Abbess. But we never see it ourselves. I think you have to prepare the audience for the change.

In "South Pacific" we were prepared for the change in Nellie. She was fun from the beginning. So is Maria. And her scene with the children is delightful. But the Captain—Of course, the actor can do a great deal, but I didn't find it in the script.

That's why a scene seems needed where we could see something underneath that cold exterior—it's only at the end of the play where he becomes attractive.

Even when he's with the children alone, after Maria leaves, there doesn't seem to be any warmth. Here and all the way along, everyone is more astute, more intelligent than he is. He seems to have to be told the score.

The only scene where I think he is even likeable is the last scene—after they're married. It's unbelievable that anyone could change him so quickly—it's not there in the script . . . In the cold script, I just couldn't like him. I wasn't prepared for his change. And I don't want to be "told" about him—I want to see for myself. I hope that if they do write a new scene, we will see some of the potential in the man.

In the Captain there isn't anything human.

As a woman, I'd much rather get my hands on Max!

Just to test it, I had two of the Sisters read a part of the script—to get their reactions—to be sure it wasn't prejudice on my part. Their reaction was: "He's cold—just cold."

The very fact that Maria had the temerity to give him back the whistle—she must see under that coldness, something—at that point we're almost willing to go along with her—she's astute—there's something there we don't see—but we've got to see!

Any man who has a basic something about him would be disturbed about the children being alone. He says to the housekeeper—a line that bothers me very much—"I'm going tomorrow if we can get a governess." A normal father would not do that. He would at least find out what kind of a governess he was getting. People will react against that. You know how we are with children and dogs! . . . The Captain's never home except when they change governesses. Why?

Every time we see the Captain, he's negative—but when people talk about him, they're (He's) positive.

I don't care how much you grieve over the loss of a wife, he shows no tenderness ever. In the scene with that delightful little child—if we could just see once where he broke through his guard. I want to see him when his guard is down, because none of us can keep it up 24 hours a day. Sometime when he's alone and he "loo[k]s astounded", he should show weakness, in a movement perhaps. I want to see his guard down before Maria gives her life and her love to him—I want to know that he is capable of tenderness. Maria is a child and therefore follows her heart.

Think the opening is just magnificent. I don't think I've ever seen a character set so quickly and so perfectly. In "The Nun's Story" for instance, the nuns weren't happy. Your story tells the story of those who are. Thos[e] of us who are happy haven't time to write a book about it!

Moss Hart's highly regarded memoir, *Act One*, was published in 1959.

Oscar Hammerstein to Moss Hart, August 6, 1959

Dear Moss:

The other day Dorothy said: "Did you write to Moss about his book?" I said: "Of course I did! I wrote to him when he sent it to us and thanked him for the inscription." Then in the middle of that night I woke up and realized that maybe this was not so. I then asked my secretary to look over my letter files and she reported that I had not written to you. Now you have left for Europe, but I want this letter to be waiting for you when you return.

1. I did receive your book, and was delighted and flattered by your inscription to Dorothy and me.

2. I have read the book and like it very much indeed. I think it is an honest account of things that have happened to you and how you reacted to them. I also think it contains important and fascinating information to people outside the theatre, revealing what goes on inside the theatre.

3. Don't let the intermission last too long. I am very anxious to go back and read the second act.

I hope you and Kitty have a good time while you're away and then come back and have the same good time you always seem to be having here. After you come back let us share some of it with you.

Love to both of you from both of us.

Having appeared in several Hammerstein musicals, most recently *The King and I*, Len Mence inquired whether there might be a part for him in *The Sound of Music*. Oscar replied:

Oscar Hammerstein to Len Mence, August 27, 1959

Dear Len:

No dice. There are one or two character parts which I don't believe are very well suited to you, but Lindsay and Crouse and the director had dozens of candidates anyway and since I am writing only the lyrics for this play and these were non-singing parts, I did not have much to say about them.

If during rehearsals some of these people fall down, I will get in touch with you immediately and see if I can pry you into the organization.

I don't like doing shows without you because in all my experience I have never enjoyed cutting anybody's parts the way I have enjoyed cutting yours.

If nothing happens I hope to see you soon anyway. Dorothy sends her love as I do.

As ever

Oscar Hammerstein to Harry Ruby, September 1, 1959

Dear Harry:

I was glad to get your letter of August 25th and to hear about a new record of "A KISS TO BUILD A DREAM ON." This is a stubborn kind of song which keeps being reborn every once in a while. I hope this will be as successful as the Armstrong revival.

I attended George Meyer's[7] funeral service yesterday. Stanley Adams delivered a short Eulogy in good taste and with good sense. Barry Duff who is an old pal of George's at the Friar's gave a wonderful little thumbnail sketch of George. It was warm and human and true. Then, as usual, the Rabbi came along and never having met George in his life proceeds to describe somebody else and took about twenty minutes to do it. I think he used the material that applied to some successful industralist [sic] and pillar of society over whose obsequies he had presided the week before. Anyway he was certainly talking about a fellow who never heard of the Belmont Race Track.

I looked over at the family and they were all weeping. They were all believing what the Rabbi was saying and wondering perhaps why they had been so blind all their lives as not to have discovered these solid and very dull qualities in George.

Rehearsals of "The Sound of Music" begin this morning. I think this will be the 46th time I have sat down with a cast to a first reading of a play I have written—not counting plays we have produced or foreign companies of plays. I guess this makes me a veteran. I feel like one too; otherwise I would not be calm enough to be dictating letters this morning.

Love to you and Eileen from both of us.

As ever,

Sister Gregory to Mary Martin and Richard Halliday, September 17, 1959, forwarded to Oscar Hammerstein (excerpt)

My dears,

The statement that I was disappointed not to have heard some of the lyrics and music from the show was <u>not</u> a subtle hint for you to send it to me— scout's honor! During these busy and hectic days <u>please</u> don't worry about my hearing the music. It will do me good to "compose my soul in patience" until the recordings are released—and what a wonderful day <u>that</u> will be!

However, I was most pleased to hear, CLIMB EVERY MOUNTAIN. It's a beautiful song and drove me to the Chapel, (relax chums, I'm sure it will not effect [sic] your audiences in the same way). It made me acutely aware

---

[7] George Meyer was a songwriter whose most successful period had been the teens and twenties. His best remembered song is undoubtedly "For Me and My Gal."

of how tremendously fortunate are those who find the dream that will absorb all their love, and finding it, embrace it to the end. Anyone would have made book at about fifteen hundred to one against me ever finding this one—everything in my education, environment, and temperament would seem to have militated against it. How from all the gay, glittering and gilded avenues that beckoned I found the secluded by-way that has brought such unbelievable happiness for over twenty years, only God knows. So I just had to dash into Chapel, give Him a quick but heart-felt "thank-you" and ask that all the youngsters I love so devotedly not only find their dreams but also have the courage to follow them—wherever they lead.

I like the way the music begins on a low, muted tone and builds toward the exaultation [sic] of the last measures. As usual, Mr. Rodgers has done a beautiful job. However, it was the lyric that sent me to the Chapel. Hammerstein lyrics, (even the pre-Rodgers ones), are a unique combination of simplicity, sincerity, a sort of humorous tenderness, and exquisite imagery. Although reminiscent of Christopher Fry, Mr. Hammerstein's images are less studied and seem perfectly yet effortlessly to express what we ordinary souls feel but cannot communicate. At the moment dozens of unforgettable ones leap to mind, such as "the corn is as high as an elephant's eye", "June is bustin out all over", "I'm as normal as blue-berry pie", "Though your dreams be tossed and blown", "a bird who is bound he'll be heard is throwing his heart at the sky", "the tide's creepin in on the beach like a thief, afraid to be caught stealing the land"—and practically every line in YOUNGER THAN SPRINGTIME. Perhaps I lack objectivity, but it would seem that some of his most delicate and expressive images are to be found in THE SOUND OF MUSIC, but I'll spare you any more quotes. However, I cannot resist adding that, although anyone who hears them responds to Mr. Hammerstein's lyrics, only thoughtful, mature, and literate people can truly appreciate their depth and poetic beauty. Since I have a passion for poetry and frequently have to resort to a Geiger counter in order to discover the meaning in much contemporary work, it's a joy for me to listen to something that is both poetic and intelligible. In case you've missed my message—I like CLIMB EVERY MOUNTAIN! Without question, Mr. "H" probably could have been a first-class poet, if he chose—and, just as probably, would have starved to death!

There are some discrepancies regarding Oscar's ill-health and the timing of things. In his memoirs, Rodgers says that Oscar had not been feeling well for a while, "complaining of discomfort," and "in September, just before rehearsals began he was operated on for an ulcer." But in Fordin's biography he says that rehearsals began the last week of August and Oscar went for his regular physical, having no complaints, other than mentioning that he would wake up hungry in the middle of the night and a glass of milk would fix the problem. Suspecting an ulcer, his doctor ordered X-rays and other tests and ended with a diagnosis of stomach cancer. Oscar had surgery on September 19. The surgery revealed that his cancer was stage IV and they removed three-quarters of his stomach. The surgeon said it was likely that Oscar had six months to a year left to live. The family decided that Oscar should not be told that his condition was terminal. His doctor believed Oscar knew but chose not to discuss it.

Oscar was hospitalized until October 4, thereby missing the out-of-town tryout for *The Sound of Music* in New Haven on October 3.

Oscar Hammerstein to *The Sound of Music* Company, in New Haven, circa October 2nd, 1959

YOUR TREE OF MY FAVORITE THINGS IS THE BRIGHTEST AND SHINIEST THING IN MY ROOM, BLOOMING AS IT IS WITH KINDNESS AND THOUGHTFULNESS. I LOVE YOU ALL AND WISH YOU GREAT SUCCESS MONDAY NIGHT. YOU ARE FORGIVEN IN ADVANCE FOR ANY MISTAKES –

EXCEPT IN A LYRIC.

OSCAR HAMMERSTEIN

Harry Ruby to Oscar Hammerstein, October 6, 1959

Dear Oscar:

I am writing to acknowledge a letter from a very lovely Lady called— the distaff side of the family. This is an indirect way of doing it, but I am one guy wot does not live by rules. All through the years, while others were turning out hits, I wrote flops, just to be different.

Being different, is a way of standing out—in lieu of doing something good. Some do it by going for days without shaving; others by drinking his fellow men under the table; and some, who have no sense of humor, try to be fun by using four-letter words in mixed company. And so ends my short-but-dull discourse.

Now then, a day before I received Dorothy's letter, there came a long distance phone call from Lillian Romberg. (It was the 3rd game of the World Series, to be exact). Lillian said you would be going home the next day, that all was well, etc., etc., which was such good news . . . same as the news in Dorothy's letter. Let us say that Lillian's call, and the Dodgers winning the third game of the Series 3 to 1, was strictly coincidental—the kind of situation writers used to get away with in the movies.

Have been in post-operative situations six times, I can tell you how to pass the time away. Catch up on your reading. Start with BEN HUR, which is about a certain me, the Lord God, and a chariot. One of these days they will do a remake of that story and wind up with a ball game. I do believe people are getting tired of that chariot race.

You might take a look at Edward Bellmay's [sic] (Did I louse that one up. I think it is Bellamy.) . . . LOOKING BACKWARD—or Hecht's A JEW IN LOVE, which is a touching, tender and human story about a Jew who is in love. It came very near stopping all Jews from falling in love.

Newton's "Principia." Isaac Newton, you may recall, was the first man to make an apple fall to the ground. Before he did it, they said it couldn't be done.

I am sure you have read Plutarch's Lives. However, in the latest edition, revised just seven years ago, there is a chapter on Geo. Jessel. If you haven't got this classic, Plutarch's, you can have mine. Mine comes in nine volumes.. signed by Plutarch. . . in fact, it was one of the rare editions hard to come by. It was inscribed by Plutarch to Leo Durocher.

Well, I think I will put an end to this trivia. But not before I dash off a poem. This is an ode to two persons I shan't give the names of, but they belong to ASCAP.

For every Svengali there's a Trilby-

There's always been and there always will be.

J. Harrison Ruby

Forgive me if I have bored you. Please tell Dorothy thanks for her letter. How nice of her to write with all she has to do. And now to trek Coliseumward for the fifth—and maybe last—game of the Series.

Sincerely,

Harry

P.S.:

This is the neatest letter I have ever typed.

Oscar Hammerstein to Harry Ruby, October 9, 1959

Dear Harry:

Thank you for your letter which I enjoyed a great deal. The most attractive reading you mentioned was Plutarch's Lives with a new chapter on George Jessel. This I would like to see. A little less than a month ago George was in town and helped me out at the dedication of the George M. Cohan statue. It was quite a night on Broadway. They roped off Duffy Square and about 10,000 people gathered around, and at the end of the ceremonies George led them all, singing "Give My Regards to Broadway", and it was fine. During the two and a half years that I was engaged in the struggle of raising a not very large sum of money for the memorial, I found a great many people who didn't like George M. Cohan as a person. Of course if we erected statues to people because there were nice fellows, there would probably be no statues at all. Almost everyone I can think of who had statues had them for achievements and in spite of some pretty bad reports on their personal lives. Anyway, Cohan's statues [sic] looks very good to me right there on Broadway where he belongs. The tribute came to him about fifteen or twenty years too late, I think, and that was one reason why we had difficulty in swinging it.

I am back from the hospital and getting stronger every day, looking forward to joining the new play in Boston at the end of next week. I hear great reports on it and expect to enjoy myself when I see it.

Dorothy and I send our love to you and Eileen.

Oscar Hammerstein to Mrs. Bishop, October 6, 1959

Dear Mrs. Bishop:

It was very kind of you to write to me, and I enjoyed your letter—the news of KARAMU,[8] your comments on world affairs, disarmament, and the chance for world peace.

Senator Humphrey is pretty close to being a World Federalist, although I don't believe he would plead guilty if confronted with the charge at the moment. I would be tempted to support him for President on the basis of his views on world peace and World Law. I have little confidence that he would be elected if nominated.

---

[8] Karamu House, founded in Cleveland in 1915, is the oldest African-American theater in the United States.

The American people, when voting for a President, seem to vote as much for a "personality" as for a man and his views. When plain-looking men attain the Presidency, it is only because they were Vice-Presidents (Coolidge and Truman). The elected ones are all men who might also be chosen for leading men or character leads in plays. They have commanding personalities. Even Harding was a very handsome and striking looking man. Roosevelt, Eisenhower, McKinley, Theodore Roosevelt, Cleveland— and going back much further—Lincoln, Andrew Jackson and George Washington, all had commanding presence.

It is something we seem to demand. It is the only thing that I think our good friend Adlai Stevenson has not got. He has everything else that I would like in a President, but his is not the strong proud-looking father the public seems to want. He is a highly intelligent and rather jolly uncle.

I have left the hospital and I am home resting and being fed six meals a day. In two weeks, I expect to join "The Sound of Music" which will be in Boston at that time. It has already opened in new Haven and I have had very optimistic reports about it.

We open in New York on November 12th, and a few weeks later Dorothy and I expect to be in Round Hill [Jamaica]. We both send our best wishes to you and your husband and your nice neighbors.

Sincerely

Howard Reinheimer to Louis Dreyfus, copied to Richard Rodgers and Oscar Hammerstein, October 8, 1959

RE: "SOUND OF MUSIC"

Dear Louis:

You are probably completely up to date with respect to the above play and its reception in New Haven so I can't say anything other than that the word-of-mouth, the reviews, etc. etc. have been perfectly wonderful. How it will be received next week in Boston or on the New York opening is something that none of us can foretell at this moment but it looks extremely good.

Although ordinarily it is early to take up and discuss the English rights we have a feeling that we should put ourselves on record with Hayward and

Halliday, who control the production, to the effect that Williamson def-initely wants to produce the play in England. While, of course, Rodgers and Hammerstein have a very important voice with respect to the English produc-tion the making of the deal for England really vests with Hayward and Halliday.

Prince Littler and Binky Beaumont saw the show in New Haven last night and our hunch is they would like to get in on the English production.

With this in mind Dick and Oscar feel that we should not let any grass grow under our feet but should definitely announce our desire for Williamson to produce the play before Hayward and Halliday proceed with any discussions with Beaumont and Prince. I know you will approve of this procedure. We can always decide at a later date to what extent, if any, we would let others participate in the English production.

Sincerely,

After leaving the hospital, Oscar recuperated at home for ten days, but he did make it to Boston, where the show opened on October 13. It was in Boston that Rodgers and Hammerstein wrote their last song together, "Edelweiss." According to Fordin, Oscar worked on the song starting on October 15, and com-pleted it on October 21.

Harry Ruby to Oscar Hammerstein, October 15, 1959

Dear Oscar:

Except for knowing the exact location of the trees, telegraph poles, and lampposts in the neighborhood, dogs leave this world knowing no more than they did when they came into it. Alas! The same can be said about most human beings—and I am sorry to have to include you and Dick in this category.

I had lunch with Ben Feiner today. He told me what an enormous hit "THE SOUND OF MUSIC" is. But he also told me what it is about: A girl in a Convent, Hitlerism, etc. Now then, when will you fellows learn that you cannot make a successful musical out of such subjects?

I thought you learned your lessons with OKLAHOMA and CAROUSEL. But no! You go right on being stubborn—you won't listen—you (plural) just haven't got open minds.

Let's take the first named: OKLAHOMA. What made you fellers think you could put over a hit musical without a line of chorus girls doing a fast number for the opening? How in hell did you ever dare to think that they would go for an old woman sitting down front, center, churning butter while a man sang a song, a waltz yet, offstage?

Evidently it made no impression—being as how you went on to write another show called: CAROUSEL, where the hero was shot—or stabbed—to death right in the middle of the show. A child could have told you that wouldn't work. It stands to reason that—if the headman in a show is knocked off so early in a show—or knocked off at all—the opus falls apart.

How long are you fellers gonna go on taking people for fools? But why should I let myself get so exercised about something that doesn't concern me? I can hear you say: "What in hell do you know about show business?" I know this. I saw OKLAHOMA the first week it opened in N. Y. and predicted it wouldn't last more than five years on Broadway. Be big enough to admit I was right.

Anyway,

Sincerely

Harry

Elliot Norton to Oscar Hammerstein, November 7, 1959

Dear Oscar,

I am sorry not to have seen you again before you left but happy to learn from Dick you are making good progress.

I saw the show again and although I still have the same reservations, I am sure it will be one of the biggest popular hits you have ever had. May I say I also believe that the lyrics in this case are some of the finest, simplest and most beautiful you or anyone else has ever written.

With my best wishes for your rapid recovery.

Sincerely,

Elliot N.

Elliot Norton

Oscar Hammerstein to Elliot Norton, November 10, 1959

Dear Elliot:

Thank you for your letter. I am in much better shape than I was when you last saw me. I have been given permission to get off my diet, and quite apart from enjoying my meals more, I am getting a big psychological lift from not feeling like an invalid any more.

I am worried by your "reservations" for two reasons. First, I am not sure what they are because you have not been as specifically analytical as usual. I gather, however, that you feel an overall corniness. The second reason for my worry is that I am afraid that whatever it is that bothers you will be sure to bother one or more of the New York critics.

I feel as you do about the ultimate popularity of the play. It seems to be one of the best audience plays I have ever had any experience with.

What I must talk to you about some time is "J.B."[9] I saw your telecast last Tuesday with Archie MacLeish and Basil Rathbone. Your praise was so high, in fact stratospheric, that I felt the unpleasant harbinger of the first nasty debate that you and I have ever had. It is possible that I have missed many of the qualities which you discover in the play. I could find no justification for the circus framework. It seemed to me like an arbitrary theatrical affectation. As for the central figure, alongside the biblical Job, who is magnificent and noble and strong, Archie MacLeish's Job seemed a paranoid cry-baby.

Obviously this fierce discussion cannot be carried on by mail, but let's put it on the agenda for our next meeting. It may not be fierce at all. You may have a few well-chosen and monumental words that can convert me quickly.

If you and Florence plan to come down to New York this winter, please let us know beforehand so that we can have a meal together.

Dorothy and I send our love to you both.

As ever,

---

[9] *J.B.* was a play by Archibald MacLeish; it opened on Broadway in December 1958, and went on to win the Pulitzer Prize for drama. Written in free verse, it's a modern retelling of the Biblical story of Job.

The Sound of Music opened on Broadway on November 16. The reviews were mixed, with many carping about the show's sentimentality and over-sweetness. But the show had a "record-breaking" advance and audiences embraced it from the beginning. The show was a hit, running for 1,423 performances. To the surprise of many, it ran even longer in the West End—2,385 performances.

Roy Winsor to Oscar Hammerstein, November 18, 1959

Dear Mr. Hammerstein:

It seem a very long time ago that, as Milton Biow's Television Director, I visited you in Doylestown to have you opinionate about I, Bonino. (This by way of introduction).

My purpose in writing this note is to say how much I enjoyed Sound of Music, and to protest the tragic ignorance, personal pique, or girlish envy, that is apparent in little destructive remarks of several of the critics.

Chapman is a non-perceptive ass to want to see the Trapp family in America! Is it possible for so influential a writer not to infer that the material selected was selected?!

And for Atkinson to lament the "clichés of operetta" without realizing, as dean of critics, that your musical biography could hardly accommodate four Brownshirts singing "Lidice[10] is dead, let's pock up its head", is absurd.

Kerr? Of course the story is sentimental. So is Christmas with Dickens. If Kerr does not like Barrie, others may not like Fire Island. This criticism is not objective. It's egocentric. (I won't buy the Cadillac because the white wall is smudged!).

Only Watts refused to find flaws based on personal rather than professional judgment.

There. I have said it all. To repeat, there is no real purpose in all of this. I have no axe to grind, no play to sell. It irritated me, however, to read the

---

[10] Probably refers to the Nazi Lidice massacre in 1942 where, in retribution for the assassination of the SS official Reinhard Heydrich, the town of Lidice was all but destroyed, all males over fifteen were killed, and most of the remainder sent to concentration or extermination camps.

reviews. These "men of measured merriment" seem to contribute only to their own vanity, not to the theatre.

Congratulations on your wonderful evening in the theatre. And thank you for letting me fulminate.

Cordially,

Roy Winsor

Oscar Hammerstein to Roy Winsor, November 25, 1959

Dear Roy Winsor:-

Thank you for your letter of November 18th. I am very happy that you liked the show so well. It is a particular pet of mine and I am happy to see how it affects audiences every night. It is the only play with which I have ever been connected which is not only applauded at the final curtain but is always cheered.

I, too, was irritated by some of the critics' comments but not to the extent that you were. I appreciate your irritation, however, and thank you for it.

Best wishes

Phyllis Rich Bradley to Oscar Hammerstein, November 19, 1959

Dear Sir,

"On what meat does this our Caesar feed that he is grown so great" as to issue and order "people who write for tickets shall not stipulate date or location."

Since the weary evening I spent at Oklahoma I have never been to another of your productions. However as a long time member of the theatre going public I resent a producer presuming to dictate to his prospective audiences.

Yours truly,

Phyllis Rich Bradley

Oscar Hammerstein to Phyllis Rich Bradley, November 24, 1959

Dear Mrs. Bradley:

The advertisement for "The Sound of Music" to which I think you have reference represented an attempt on the part of my business manager to save the public time and trouble. Since we have come into New York with an advance sale of over two million dollars, there are very few locations left in the Theatre for the next seven months. To avoid the nuisance of people writing in for dates that we cannot fill, we suggested that they write in without specifying date or location and we could then do the best we could.

There is no wish to dictate to the public. How could we. No one has to write in, and no one has to see our play. You inform me that you have not seen any of my plays since "Oklahoma!" and that was in 1943. It is strange but I wasn't even aware of your absence from my other plays and if you had not told me of it I would never have known.

Very truly yours

Oscar Hammerstein to Walter and Marion Knapp, December 7, 1959

Dear Walter and Marion:

The show has opened in New York and I believe it will be a very big hit. Of course there is no doubt about the next eight months because we are all sold out and there is therefore no doubt about getting our money back. Judging by the way it's going with audiences, I think it will run a very long time. I'll be disappointed if it runs for less than three years in New York especially if Mary Martin stays with it.

Most of the notices were fine—2 or 2 [sic] exceptions, and at least one, The New Yorker, was really bad, but I've been getting bad treatment from this young man [Kenneth Tynan] for a long time. I don't think that he and I have the same ideas of what a good show is, especially musicals.

Dorothy and I are off to Jamaica next week and never have I looked forward to anything with more relief. In the first place we get out of all the Christmas business (not Dorothy, because she has been buying presents for the past year and has finished her job) but it will be quiet there over

Christmas and New Years and I don't expect to do anything except lie on the beach in the morning and play tennis in the afternoon. I am all well again but need some exercise to harden me up. We have grass courts down at Round Hill and they are much more fun to play on and not so hard on these old feet.

After we come back to New York we will remain here about six weeks and then we go to London to produce "Flower Drum Song" over there. We go into rehearsal the end of February. Outside of this, I have no professional plans. I would like to take a good long rest before starting anything else.

My yearly report on the family:

Billy is working in television. His steady job is with the Colgate Commercial, but in addition to this he has the right to take outside assignments and he is now producing a Christmas show for CBS which will be on the air on December 10th. It has to do with the winter quarters of the Circus and he is down in Florida now working on it.

Alice is a contented matron and mother in New Rochelle. She is very busy working on a charity show at the moment and on the side bringing up those two lovely children she adopted. Her husband, Phil, is working on TV commercials for an advertising firm.

Jimmy is still the stage manager of "Flower Drum Song" but this is a side line now. His chief interest in life is the construction of a ski run. He and a group of fellows are putting up a ski run with ski lifts on a site that is only two and a half hours from New York and it should do very well. All these places are doing well, but his being so close to New York should really get off to a quick start. A lot of money had to be raised and he raised most of it and did all by himself and am I proud of this. He seems to like being a promoter and perhaps has something of his great-grandfather in him. (I hope he hasn't too much of him in him.)

Susan and her daughter Amy are coming down with us to the farm this evening—our last weekend for sometime. Amy is a cute kid about five years old and a handful.

Henry is a great success as an advertising man. He is Vice-President of the firm he is with and making a very large salary. He is turning out to be a fine boy. He has a lovely wife and four children—two girls and two boys. With Billy's three daughters, Alice's son and daughter, Jimmy's son and Susan's daughter, we now have eleven grand-children between us. No wonder we are going away for the holidays!

I miss seeing you both and I tried to consider some way of getting up from Boston but I really was not well enough to make that kind of round trip at this time. I hope that you can sell that house for the purely selfish reason that I would like to get a chance to see you, and living where you are, you're just about inaccessible.

Quickly running over the list of your old friends, I can report that Dorothy Dalton Hammerstein seems to be in fine shape. She is still living in Florida, but I believe she will soon take a house in Scarsdale or near there so that she could see more of Carol and her grandchild Dorothy. Carol seems to be happily married to an advertising man John Schneider and as I tell you about these children whom you probably still visualize as little moppets I must remind you that they are all about to enter middle age. Ax seems to be the same and still looks the same as ever. I have not seen Myra in several mothers [sic] but I have talked to her on the phone and I get reports of course from Alice and Bill. Her health seems to be much better than it was and she sounds all right over the phone.

I wish you both a Merry Christmas and a really happy New Year. By "really happy" I mean I hope you will be able to sell your house and get out of there.

Dorothy sends her love to you both and so do I.

As ever

Oscar Hammerstein to Harold Fielding, December 10, 1959

Dear Harold:

I re-read "Victoria Regina" and found it, as always, delightful. For your present purposes, I am afraid I found it too delightful, because I don't see what we can do to make it any better. These scenes have the fascination of an object that you see with a microscope. They are so small and delicate and perfect, one wonders how to add the weight of music, singing and pageantry without spoiling the whole thing.

I think there are serious questions that arise in the consideration of this project. I note that the Lord Chamberlain did not permit the production originally in England because Victoria was a royal personage so recently alive that it seemed bad taste to portray her on the stage at that time. I assume he has changed his mind since then, and that you have looked into this side of the picture.

But it gives rise to the basic question: Should the actress who plays Victoria also be a singer? Will it take away from subtlety of the characterization? Can a singer be found who is a good enough actress to command the respect that one must command playing this part? (Julie Andrews might do it).

I think that Dick Rodgers and I are especially sensitive to these questions because we are American and not English. The whole project frightens us, to be truthful.

We do not, however, want to shut the door tight. Our suggestion is this: We shall both be in London during the month of March supervising the production of "Flower Drum Song". If by that time you have consulted an important British playwright, who might have a solution to the problems I pose, we would be very glad at that time to sit down with him and you and discuss the situation again. It is, of course, understood that if meanwhile you find others who you think might do a good job on the songs, you are perfectly free to do so. In other words we do not feel that you must hold this open for us, but if it is still open at the time we come to London, we shall be glad to talk to you about it.

We are both delighted with the advance in Bristol. Congratulations!

All good wishes to you.

Sincerely,

Oscar and Dorothy left for Jamaica on December 12 with plans to return on January 10. They were joined by the family for Christmas, but the vacation was largely intended for rest and recuperation. Oscar did, however, work on a treatment for a new film version of *State Fair*.

Oscar Hammerstein to Ira Gershwin, December 14, 1959

Dear Ira:

I had assumed that I had thanked you for your book [*Lyrics on Several Occasions*] and for the very kind inscription you wrote in it. Waking up with a start one morning and doubting whether I had written the letter, and yet telling myself that I knew I had, I asked my secretary about it and she said that I had not. This is a rather long preamble and a kind of apology to have delayed my expression of thanks for this kind gesture.

Thank you also for writing the book. It is a way of telling the public something about which they know very little—the work and worry that goes into a song. I believe all these accounts are written gracefully, intelligently and entertainingly, and I am very glad such a book exists.

Reading over the lyrics again reminded me of how good you are at this job and how much I envy you for some of the "nifties" that you have pulled off in your time.

Dorothy joins me in sending our love to you, and congratulations on a job well done.

Sincerely,

Oscar Hammerstein to Lynn Farnol, December 14, 1959

Dear Lynn:

Last night (Friday) I went to the Lunt-Fontanne and with all the others made a tape for MONITOR which will run on Christmas night and will purport to come from the theatre at that time. It has since occurred to me that if it is public knowledge that I am in Jamaica at that time, here will be another unimportant, but quite inexcusable, deceit on the public on the part of Radio and me.

I would like, therefore, to have you tell Frank Goodman who, I believe started the thing, to have me eliminated from the Broadcast. The only alternative would be to take some of the things out of it, and admit that I had made it about Christmas previous to Christmas night. (I don't think they would want to do this as it will raise a question about the whole Broadcast.)

I thought of this last night (Friday) and made some jokes about it, but since thinking it over, I don't think it's such a joke. I am very anxious not to be a party to any deceit, even a minor deceit, of the public by Radio. I am sorry I did not take a firmer stand about it last night (Friday), then I would not have to bother you with this, but since I didn't, will you take care of this while I am away?

All good wishes and love to you and Nell from both of us.

Richard Rodgers to Oscar Hammerstein, December 23, 1959

Dear Oscar:

You've read about our crippling snow storm and I will relate it immediately to our projects. We are already sixteen hundred dollars better than last week at the St. James* [*Flower Drum Song*] in spite of the snow but last week was bad enough to allow plenty of room for improvement. I have now met and talked with the English versions of Mioshi and Sezuki. They are both delightful to look at and talk to and I'll hear the Mioshi girl sing next week, probably. The Sezuki one is as cute as they come but I won't hear her as she takes off almost immediately for her home in Hawaii. Anita Darian went on Monday permanently in Arabella Hong's part. Her dialogue projection and appearance can be improved easily but her voice is exquisite and we now have our best, by far, rendition of the song ["Love, Look Away"]. The commander—master of ceremonies is a 14-carat stinker in the part. We'll have to get rid of him some way. There are no other problems there worthy of note.

All THE SOUND OF MUSIC news is wonderful. Our intake is within ten thousand a week of our gross so it becomes apparent that we're in for a very long stay. The performances as of last night were just wonderful as was the audience reaction. Dave Kapp has taken "Favorite Things" from his choral album and released it as a single. He tells me it is a very big hit and this is in the face of very poor single-record sales in general. One dealer in Detroit phoned an order of one thousand copies "assorted" yesterday. The feeling that this is going to turn out to be one of our most popular scores is unavoidable and who's trying to avoid it.

Howard reports that you and Dorothy are in wonderful shape. This is fine news and I hope you'll both take advantage of the fact that there is nothing up here that is in any way burdensome. Just have a good time and come back when you're ready. We'll be happy to see you. Dorothy and I send our best love.

Affectionately,

Dick

* Mat. Today, Wednesday, completely sold out, 2nd balcony and all

Richard Rodgers to Oscar Hammerstein, December 24, 1959

Dear Oscar,

Here is a brief weekend report. The day before Christmas the sheet music sales were 1,500 assorted copies and this, of course, is only [for] a half week. The total for the week is over 5,000 copies and we all think that's wonderful. So much for publishing.

The St. James [*Flower Drum Song*] at the moment is about $3,000. ahead of last week and Morrie tells me he thinks the rest of the week will be better. Everything at the Lunt [*The Sound of Music*] is wonderful.

ABC has now come up with a new "documentary" idea for me to think about. I was right a couple of months ago when I told you I thought the Archie MacLeish thing would fall through. Now it appears ABC has bought the television rights to all of Winston Churchill's work and life. They think they would like me to do the same sort of job that I did for "Victory at Sea". It might be a good idea for me to do it[11] so that I can keep busy during the comparatively uncreative period immediately ahead. Naturally, if I were to close a deal with then, I wouldn't allow it to interfere with STATE FAIR or anything that you and I might consider.

Christmas, cold weather and slush are around us and under us, but things in general are fine.

Best love from Dorothy and me to you both.

Affectionately,

Dick.

---

[11] Rodgers wrote the background score for *Winston Churchill—The Valiant Years*, which aired on ABC beginning in November of 1960.

Chapter Nineteen
1960

Flower Drum Song was still running on Broadway (its run ends on May 7), and preparations were underway for the West End production, which opened on March 14. *The Sound of Music* was still in its prime on Broadway. Oscar was at work on a planned film remake of *State Fair*, and a hoped-for television production of *Allegro*.

Richard Rodgers to Oscar Hammerstein, January 4, 1960

Dear Oscar,

I have just received your December 31st letter regarding a script writer for the new STATE FAIR. Howard is more than slightly inaccurate when he says that I am "willing to leave the entire discretion in the hands of Twentieth". I'd hardly be of a disposition to put Twentieth in your place regarding decisions of this nature (or any other). I still feel that Twentieth Century ought to know what they are doing and we ought to take their suggestions seriously just as I take your objections to their suggestions seriously. I have just sent a wire to Howard in California saying the following:

"Oscar feels strongly that other names besides Delmar Daves and Sonya Levien[1] should be submitted to us by Twentieth Century. Please let me have your thoughts."

The ALLEGRO information is very exciting to me and CBS is anxious to have some word from us. In any event there is nothing to be done about it until you get back from Jamaica and we can sit down and discuss it.

Report from the St. James [*Flower Drum Song*]: the general level of the performance has gone up at least 75% with Cely Carrillo playing the part. She looks sweet enough to eat, acts more than capably, has a charming voice and can be heard. I am making an adjustment in the key of "Miracles" as it is at present too low for her and I feel she can be more effective. Jack Soo

---

[1] Sonya Levien did write the screen adaptation for the 1962 remake of *State Fair*.

The Letters of Oscar Hammerstein II. Mark Eden Horowitz, Oxford University Press. © Mark Eden Horowitz 2022.
DOI: 10.1093/oso/9780197538180.003.0019

gets belly laughs and I am afraid the new Commodore Low is not merely a bust – he's a whole statue. We are taking this up vigorously, as Jimmy will tell you.

Joe Fields is interested in doing a musical version of Phil Barry's HOLIDAY with us. He is sending us each a copy of the script. I was non-committal. For your information I learned in rapid succession that he doesn't like TAKE ME ALONG, FIORELLO, MUSIC MAN or Lindsay and Crouse. I didn't ask him how he felt about Marion.

Business this week is supposed to be terrible, but we'll never know it at the Lunt-Fontanne [*The Sound of Music*]. All last week without benefit of benefits the performances went wonderfully and everybody did well. This morning first mail at Chappell's brought orders for 1,500 copies. Max is very happy and Louis is unintelligible.

The newest joke going around concerns the three most over-rated things in the world: home cooking, home loving and McCann Erickson.[2]

Now about your sweet invitation to Dorothy and me to go to Jamaica with you just before going to London. We are both afraid to say yes. Neither one of us is awfully anxious to be away from home that much. You will recall that we hope to go from London to Italy and spend some time on the continent. This is probably different from your plans and accounts for the difference in our feelings. We both hate, however, to think that your going back to Jamaica would be stymied by our not going with you, but you asked me to tell you what we "really want to do" and this just about sums it up.

ANDERSONVILLE[3] opened last week and we went to see it Saturday night. I can't imagine how they'll be able to give a performance this evening as the actors chewed all the scenery to bits on Saturday. It's a pretty fair play outrageously hurled at the audience.

New Year's Eve was silly and it's nice to be back with something like a normal routine.

---

[2] McCann Erickson is one of the oldest and most esteemed advertising agencies.
[3] *The Andersonville Trial*, a play by Saul Levitt, is the story of a war-crimes trial of the commander of a notorious Confederate POW camp. José Ferrer directed a cast that included George C. Scott.

Have a wonderful time for the last of your Jamaica stay and come home where you will be more than welcome.

Love to you both from Dorothy and me.

Dick

Barbara Kruse, a freshman at the Hyde Park Junior High School in Las Vegas, wrote Oscar a letter as part of a school project, asking: "In your opinion, what do you think is the greatest need today, to elevate and edify youth?"

Oscar Hammerstein to Barbara Kruse, January 15, 1960

Dear Miss Kruse:

Your question cannot be answered very briefly, and I haven't time to give it the thought it deserves. If you want a quick and very incomplete general answer, I would say that the greatest need today, to elevate and edify youth, is to direct them back to elementary and very old-fashioned principles, to stress the importance of honesty and faith in goodness and respect for elders. I would cover all these admonitions with a general one: "not to be afraid of being corny". It doesn't seem to me that the new stuff introduced to take the place of corn has been very good for us.

My best wishes to you for the success of your enterprise.

Sincerely,

Elliot Norton to Oscar Hammerstein, January 25, 1960

Dear Oscar,

Thanks for the excellent lunch and the pleasant discussion of Saturday.

It is good to see you completely well again; it seems to me your recovery was not only rapid but also complete; you look wonderful.

I'm glad you're going to do "Allegro" on TV – without the divorce! Perhaps at this time it will be more widely acceptable. I have often thought about the play, and came to the conclusion long since that perhaps your thinking was ahead of its time. Perhaps there are now more playgoers ready to accept what you have to say.

I hope you don't stay away from the theater too long, but I am sure you are right in giving a lot of thought to your next play. Right or wrong, the public have now come to think of anything with which you and Dick are associated as a Rodgers and Hammerstein creation; and from such a work they expect not a conventional musical comedy or operetta, however good of its kind it may be, but something far truer and closer to life. You were the men who changed the popular musical theater; you can't very well go back to the old devices. The libretto of "South Pacific" was so sound and so true in and of itself that it was included in at least one anthology of "straight plays". After that, we expected only work along similar high lines, even when it was produced not by you but by your associates. It's too bad that more people don't know that Lindsay and Crouse wrote the libretto of "The Sound of Music" – but they don't. They attribute it to you.

I will look forward to seeing you when you come up to Brandeis.

My best to you and Dorothy,

Elliot N.

Oscar Hammerstein to Gordon and Margot, January 26, 1960

Dear Gordon and Margot:

The coat is beautiful, and I am now going out to buy a guitar so I can understudy Theodore Bikel. Dorothy thinks that I look like a Nazi in the coat, and this is probably due to my German blood which I have tried to keep hidden until now. The coat shows it up. On these cold days in New York when I like to keep the window of my study open, the coat is warm and I feel very elegant in it. Thank you both very much.

Dorothy at the moment is down with some virus business, but it is not serious and I don't believe it will lay her low very long. She is a hard girl to keep in bed.

Everyone else is fine. I hope we will see you in London in March. Love to you all from both of us.

Sincerely,

Oscar Hammerstein to Alec McGowan, February 1, 1960

Dear Mr. McGowan:

I have many times disapproved of some of the procedures of the House Un-American Activities Committee. I believe, however, that for a group of citizens to attempt [to prevent] its hearings is not only hopeless, but highly improper, and I will not lend my name to any such project. Whatever their intentions may be regarding an examination of the five young people you speak of, and however unjust may be their intentions, I consider it quite beyond my province and yours to block a congressional committee from carrying out what it supposes to be its function. If what they are doing is illegal, then the question must be taken into the courts.

Very truly yours,

Oscar Hammerstein to Thomas deWitt Walsh, February 3, 1960

Dear Tom:

I have read "THE STARS BETWEEN" and while it is obvious that you have worked very hard on it, and that much of the work you have done is good, I just don't think that the play would have any chance in present Broadway competition. I don't find myself quite believing in any of the characters, and while some people may differ with me regarding the necessity of believability in musical comedies, I don't know of any really big ones that have not had good basic stories.

I think that in your anxiety to make the dialogue entertaining you have made it artificial and theatrical. This is applicable to almost all the characters.

The best thing in the play is the eighth number of Act One, "I Am Your Old Man". I mention this not only because I am glad to be able to point out a positive virtue in your work, but also because this is an indication of what I think the play --- and indeed every play --- needs. This is a sincere and human statement by a human being, by a father to a son. I find it very touching and honest and the kind of writing that I like.

I am not going to submit the play to my sons, Jimmy and Billy, because I know their tastes so well that I am sure they would not be interested in producing it.

I am sorry to be so discouraging, but it would be decidedly unfriendly to be less than honest. We are looking upon this as a prospective professional production to be presented on Broadway. The standards are high, the requirements are stiff, and having a flop is no fun for anybody. I have great respect for you and your collaborator, as I have for anyone who starts and finishes a full manuscript of a play. This accomplishment is not to be underrated. My congratulation on the completion of the effort and I am by no means hopeless about you as a prospective librettist. I am hopeless about this particular play.

Best wishes.

Oscar Hammerstein to Anne Glatterman (Reinheimer & Cohen), February 4, 1960

Dear Anne:

Regarding your inquiry on an off-Broadway production of VERY WARM FOR MAY: I am indeed against it. The show is not good enough to revive, on or off Broadway.

Love,

Oscar Hammerstein to Dolores Bergin, February 5, 1960

Dear Miss Bergin:

Thank you very much for your letter. "My Favorite Things" happens to be the song from "Sound of Music" which Mr. Rodgers and I like best. I am happy to know of your interest in our work and very grateful to you for taking the time to write.

All good wishes.

Sincerely,

Oscar Hammerstein to Frank Scully, *Variety*, February 12, 1960

Dear Frank:

I quote from your recent article in "Variety":

"Of course, it is a matter of record that Oscar Hammerstein 2d. credits Larry Hart in 1918 with teaching him about interior rhymes, feminine rhymes, triple rhymes, and false rhymes . . . "

A matter of what record? I never said it, it isn't true. Where did you get the "record"? Larry and I were very good friends and worked together in Varsity shows at Columbia, but we never gave each other lessons in anything. He was a master of interior rhymes, triple rhymes, and ingenious rhymes. My own songs are noted rather for an absence of rhymes --- even at the ends of lines.

Your piece on Ira's book was a very good one and would have made me rush out to buy a copy had not the author already very generously sent me one for free.

Best wishes to you.

Sincerely,

Harry Sosnik was a music director and conductor who had worked on the CBS "General Foods 25th Anniversary Show: A Salute to Rodgers & Hammerstein." In preparing a television special on Vincent Youmans, Sosnik wrote Oscar, asking for any anecdotes or human interest vignettes he might share about working with Youmans—something that would make a human interest story to be included during the program. Oscar had collaborated with Youmans on three musicals in the 1920s: *Wildflower, Mary Jane McKane,* and *Rainbow.* Neither the shows nor the songs they included have had any ongoing life. Youmans' life and career were all too brief—he died of tuberculosis at forty-six, and his composing career covered only thirteen years. But Youmans was one of the great songwriters, with standards that include: "Tea for Two," "I Want to Be Happy," "More Than You Know," "Through the Years," and "Without a Song."

Oscar Hammerstein to Harry Sosnik, February 19, 1960

Dear Harry:

Vincent Youmans worked harder on verses than any composer I've ever known. He didn't dash them off as mere preludes to refrains, but painstakingly worked them out and would never turn them in to his collaborator until he had done all that he possibly could to make them perfect. In the first play we did together, "Wildflower", he had still not given me a verse to one of the songs three days before we opened in Wilkesbarre [*sic*], Pennsylvania. This gave his lyric writers, Otto Harbach and me, a very short time to set words, rehearse them, and produce the number in time for the opening. It also gave the orchestrator very little time to make his arrangement. Nevertheless, Vincent just could not bat out something that was merely serviceable, even under the pressure of an imminent opening. I believe the originality of his verses shows the loving care which he put into them.

The other surprising thing about Vincent was his desire to do so many things beside write music. He was fascinated by the theatre and had high ambitions to be a producer, to own a theatre, and later a string of theatres. He liked to delve into the problems of scene and costume design, lyric writing, stage direction, and choreography. He was a composer of rare talent. That should have been enough to fill his life. But it wasn't. As his friend, I always resented the time and energy he wasted on these other activities. When one thinks of the rich catalogue of melody which he created in a very short time, one wishes greedily that more hours of those few precious years had been devoted to creating more songs.

All good wishes to you, Harry, for the success of your program.

Sincerely

Oscar Hammerstein to Eugene Gorman, February 16, 1960

Dear Gene:

I was touched by your letter and very grateful for your concern and for your simple expression of real friendship.

Last September, after I had started rehearsals for my last play "Sound of Music", I didn't feel up to snuff and went to my doctor who had me X-rayed. The X-ray showed a cancerous tumor in my stomach. I forthwith went into the hospital and had a good portion of my stomach removed. Two and a half weeks later I was able to rejoin my show in its pre-Broadway tour in Boston and I went right back to work. Luckily, the show was in very good shape and didn't need much heroic attention, but I did whatever was needed. I have been improving ever since. After the opening (a great success, which didn't hurt my physical condition any), Dorothy and I went down to our cottage in Jamaica and stayed a month. We both came back feeling very fit and that is the way I am now.

In a few weeks we are going to London to produce "The Flower Drum Song" (I don't know if that is a new title to you, but that is the show that opened a year and a half ago in New York and is still prospering here.)

So you see, everything is going well now and I am back to living my normal life, even swimming and playing tennis.

Thank you for all the very kind things you said in your letter. Dorothy and I both send warmest regards to you.

As ever,

Joseph Lang (Vice President of Columbia College), in a vituperative letter to Oscar, whom he addresses as "Ock" (suggesting they had been childhood friends), excoriates him for the "pure unadulterated treacle" that is *The Sound of Music*.

Oscar Hammerstein to Joseph Lang, February 17, 1960

Dear Joe:

I found your letter interesting for many reasons. What fascinates me is your certainty. You don't express a mere opinion, but state your reactions as if they were incontrovertible facts the belief in which must be shared by all. In your last paragraph you say " . . . do you expect us to settle for the cardboard figures that grace the 'Sound of Music'? . . . It is not enough to give us the undeniably marvelous Mary Martin back again; we must have her in a part worthy of her. No, we don't expect a masterpiece every year; we do expect something better than 'Sound of Music' from the two men who have practically revolutionized our musical theatre."

Who the hell is "we"? You and a very small minority who agree with you? It is certainly not the people who see the show every night and rush to the box office to buy tickets for future performances, nor the strangers who fill my desk with letters thanking me for the beautiful evening they have spent, nor those who stop me on the street and thank me, nor the people who are buying sheet music and show albums in record-breaking proportions. I do not say that they are right and you are wrong. There is no right or wrong in these matters. The taste of various members in an audience is widely divergent and each is entitled to his own opinion. No one, however, is entitled to make the sweeping ex cathedra statements you make, with the air of finality and over-confidence you exhibit.

I will not begin to correct you in the many misquotations which characterize the first page of your letter, but I would like to straighten you out on one paragraph that is full of wise-guy conclusions. We were not looking around desperately for a Mary Martin vehicle. We were not looking for something sure-fire because people who are really in the show business know that there is no such thing. As a matter of fact, Mary Martin found this property first and then invited us into it. We accepted the invitation because we liked the story very much. We didn't see it as the bromide you so flippantly describe. We didn't remember any other musical plays which dealt with a postulant who had made up her mind to take the veil and then had fallen in love with a man. We thought it a very original situation that when her problems were put before the mother superior, the Mother advised her to go back to the man. We, in our innocence, considered this a very original turn of plot and a situation of great human interest. We think our collaborators have told the story well in dialogue and that we have written one of our best scores to back up this story. All of us --- the star, the authors, the director, and the producers --- entered into this project loving it very much and wanting to do it. It has turned out to be a very big success. That does not mean that you should endorse it or like it. Nor are we obliged to agree with you that it is unadulterated treacle. I guess that's where we ought to leave it.

Sincerely,

In response to Oscar's letter, Mr. Lang doubled down: "When you ask 'who the hell is we', I refrain from making the obvious rejoinder, Brooks Atkinson and I–(although

I will admit that Mr. Atkinson and I have had some private correspondence about the play)–nor will I be flippant and reply that the pronoun 'we' refers to the critics who called your opus 'Little Women with music', and me. I will just defend myself by saying that 'we' is purely editorial."

Oscar Hammerstein to Joseph Lang, March 7, 1960

Dear Joe:

Having been forty-two years in the business I know what a minority and a majority is. If a majority of an audience doesn't like a play they go out and tell others, and they tell them in very loud voices. Even if a large minority doesn't like a play it is reflected in the box office. The reception that our play receives nightly and the reaction at the box office is complete and incontestable proof to anyone who has been in show business for any length of time that the vast majority of those who see the show, like it. That a minority do not like it is, of course, obvious. It is equally obvious to me that they are a small minority, otherwise we would not be doing so well.

As for your comparisons with our five best plays, I cannot argue with you. I am very fond of all these works myself---perhaps inordinately fond of them. I do not, however, write one play in competition with another. If I were afraid to compete with former works I would have stopped in 1927 after I wrote "Show Boat". My policy is merely to find something I like and do the best work I can on it and hope for the best.

I am off to London now to produce "Flower Drum Song" there. Best wishes to you.

Sincerely,

Oscar Hammerstein to Lydia Angelosante, February 25, 1960

Lydia Angelosante:

I don't know of any formula for success. No matter what one's vocation is, he must work very hard and believe in what he is doing. That is all I know about the subject.

My best wishes to you.

Sincerely

A group of schoolchildren were asked to write letters to Oscar. Here is one example:

Sandra to Oscar Hammerstein, circa February 1960

Sandra

Room 7

Grade 4

Dear Mr. Hammerstein,

I like do re me becaus I like the tune and the words. Our whole school knows do re me even the gindirgarders and the first grades too. We have a grade choir and we all love do re me. To me do re me is cute.

One of your do re me

Lovers,

Sandra

Oscar Hammerstein to Hayes Gordon[4] (in New South Wales, Australia) (excerpt), March 10, 1960:

I don't think "Pipe Dream" would be a success over there. As far as that is concerned, it was not a success here and I think for good reasons. I do not, therefore, encourage you to cast any blissful eye on it.

Flower Drum Song opened in London on March 24. Oscar and Richard Rodgers and both Dorothys were in attendance.

Having read an article which ridiculed songs like "You'll Never Walk Alone," Reverend Edward Upson Cowles wrote Oscar to praise the song—a "great favorite" of his and a group of men who sing monthly at the parsonage—one he associates with Jesus' words "Lo, I am with you always." But, he asks, what did Hammerstein "have in mind" when he wrote the lyric?

---

[4] Hayes Gordon OBE, AO, founded the Ensemble Theatre in 1958. It is now Australia's longest continuously running theatre group.

Oscar Hammerstein to Reverend Edward Upson Cowles,
April 6, 1960

Dear Mr. Cowles:

It is difficult for me to add any interpretation to my lyric "You'll Never Walk Alone" beyond what the words say. The last line is "Walk on, walk on with hope in your heart, and you'll never walk alone". For the word "hope" you could substitute "faith" or you could substitute "God". I mean exactly what the words say and I can't think of a single footnote that would be necessary to explain my theme more specifically. I am sure that this is the way you understand the song and the way I would want you to.

Thank you very much for your interest in my work.

Very truly yours,

Dorothy Hammerstein (in London) to Sister Gregory,
March 16, 1960

My dear Sister Gregory – We loved getting your letter which was forwarded to us here. Our anniversary is May 14th so we are going to keep your letter and read it again on that date. Thank you for the good wishes and for your affection. We have been here for nine days and return to New York on April 4th. We are here for the London production of Flower Drum Song which opens on March 24th. On the 23rd there will be a charity preview which Princess Margaret is going to attend. All this sounds nothing at all like what I would like to say to you. We saw you for such a little time and yet we talk about you a lot. We think you are cute and funny and also what you say and think can make us cry. I am grateful that you are praying for us – please pray extra hard for Oscar because he has been so ill. I don't talk about his illness to him but I worry about his well-being without letting him know about it. We've all had "tummy trouble" since we've been here but when he has it it is more worrying. I do hope that we see you again soon. It would be good to talk to you.

Most lovingly

Dorothy + Oscar

Oscar Hammerstein to Richard Rodgers (in Venice),
April 7, 1960

Dear Dick:

We are back home after a pleasant and uneventful flight.

I heard the recording [London cast recording of *Flower Drum Song*] last Friday and liked it very much. It lacks the polish of a Goddard Lieberson recording, but it makes up for this in what I thought was great vitality. They do the whole routine of "Grant Avenue" with background noises, shouting, very spirited playing by the orchestra (augmented by twelve violins and some brass), and the whole thing adds up to what I think will be a very successful album in England. The definition of the lyrics was fine. Kevin Scott sang "You Are Beautiful" very well except that he had a tendency to go back to the "triplets"---not all the way, just part of the way. The Joan Pethers recording of "Love Look Away" was not as bad as they seemed to fear it would be. Its fault is that her vibrato is more pronounced on microphone than it is in the theatre.

When I left London the show was in the same state as when I spoke to you last in Rome. The reports are that it is going very well with the audience and they are buying steadily in advance. With the exception of the Wednesday matinees, we have standees every night.

I am enclosing a list of cablegrams that I answered on your behalf and mine after you left for Italy. I forged your name on most of these, using one pen for your name and another pen for mine.

I had a long talk with Lynn Farnol yesterday. He strongly recommends the June 6th dinner from the advertising men, in which all three networks seem to be concerned. Incidentally, June 6th is the opening date of "Flower Drum Song" in Los Angeles. If we didn't want to accept the advertisers' invitation, we could use the possibility of our going to Los Angeles as an alibi. It seems easier, however, to stay here and go to dinner than fly to Los Angeles and see that show again. What do you think?

I also told Lynn Farnol about the Jimmy Roosevelt project, which is now a definite date --- September 18th. He had known nothing about it.

I am looking over understudy material for "Flower Drum Song". Had one session yesterday and am going down for another today. This is Wednesday matinee and I am going to put in "You've Got Two Noses".

Max Dreyfus tells me that when Lent came and the snows came, the usual ten thousand copies a week receded to five thousand copies a week, which is about the rate at which we are going now. As he says, this means it is very much alive although not what it was. He tells me that the performances are very numerous on the air. I am going to have lunch with him next week. He is having one of those local operations this week.

I saw Howard after he returned from the coast. The "Flower Drum Song" deal is very hot and looks as if it will go through. We are trying to work out some kind of billing where you and I can be alone without dragging along a third party. It seems to me that we ought to be able to work this out because, if Joe does the screen play, he can be compensated in billing in that direction.

There is also great interest in "Sound of Music" from two quarters – Jack Warner and Universal. I told Howard that if the Universal deal included Doris Day, I was very leery about her playing the part. I realize that right now she is one of the hottest stars on the screen. But we are not producing the picture right now. I think she is a little too old to play the part now, and how old will she be before we are able to release it is more than anyone can say. I certainly wouldn't like to be committed to her or to anyone at this juncture. I think that we should be adamant about having nothing but young girls play the part from now on, in pictures, in London, on the road.

The last week in London flew by and I found myself busier than I was before we opened, because I had put off so many people with the rehearsal alibi before that. Anyway, it's over, and while I did enjoy myself, I am glad to be back[.] Dorothy and I both send our love to both of you and hope that you are having a wonderful time.

Love,

Had the following letter been written in previous years I would not have included it. No film seems ever to have been made and to read this degree of critical detail on an unknown work may seem tedious. But the fact that Oscar went to such thoughtful and generous effort at this point in his life seems so revealing of the man that its inclusion felt important and necessary.

Oscar Hammerstein to George Skouras, April 12, 1960

Dear George:

I have just finished reading "At This Sign". It is the kind of script that should be read over several times and studied carefully, but here are my impressions after one reading:

Constantine has three enemies who must be disposed of in the course of his career, Galerius, Maxentius and Licinius. All are pictured as weaklings. An elementary rule of story suspense is that the opposition to the hero should be strong. If it is weak, there is no suspense at all. How can an audience get excited about the trials of a hero if he is told in advance that the opposition is easy to push over?

I think this is an obvious fault and further, a very easy one to fix. Let us start with Galerius. All right, he is a tyrant and a drunken sensualist. Such men, however, can be made to look very dangerous. The script says, "He rises somewhat unsteadily to his feet and struggles in his stupor to withdraw his short ceremonial sword from its scabbard." Then Galerius says, "Hundreds of people around me --- and I must do everything myself." This is an ineffectual, old-fashioned line, always used to make a fool out of the man who says it. The script then goes on to say "He at last frees the sword from its scabbard and lurches uncertainly down the steps, a picture of futility in authority."

Why make him a picture of futility? Why not have him galvanized into action and angry determination when he hears that Constantine has escaped? Let him raise hell with the slave who brings the news and with the courtiers around him, and let him give directions to pursue Constantine, making it clear that he will do everything within his power to get Constantine back and put him in a better guarded dungeon than before. He cannot afford to let Constantine escape. He must get him back!

I would suggest cutting the attendant's line, "We cannot pursue him, my lord. He has hamstrung our fastest horses." In the first place, no one is going to believe that a man who has just escaped jail has had time to hamstring all the horses in the kingdom. It is a silly line and an unbelievable one, and furthermore, it soothes the audience instead of exciting them. It tells them, Don't worry, Constantine is going to get away; he has the only fast horse in the kingdom. This is the opposite of what the audience ought to be told if you want them to be interested and anxious while they continue to look upon Constantine's daring escape.

The next tyrant to deal with is Maxentius. I realize that it is necessary for Constantine to defy him and get away with it. In this way, he acquires Josephus as his lifelong and loyal friend, and also he impresses Fausta. It could however be made clearer to the audience that Maxentius dares not oppose Constantine, the son of the emperor, but is nevertheless a man to be reckoned with. After Constantine goes, it might be a good idea for Maxentius to adopt some specific plan or trick to get even with Constantine. He may even start planning the organization of the huge army which will meet the emperor when he returns. (At this point he would not know that the emperor at that time will be the son and not the father.) I would suggest also that Livia and Fausta do not dare make such a fool of Maxentius to his face. As it is now, after Constantine goes, the two women score off Maxentius and are openly impudent to him. I believe they should feel scorn for him but not dare to express it.

The way Maxentius is drawn now, in the early part of the script, completely nullifies the suspense one should feel in the latter part of the script when he goes out on the bridge to meet Constantine in combat. If you are told in the earlier part that he is an ineffectual weakling, where is the excitement when he comes out on the bridge to meet Constantine? He should either be painted as a great warrior in combat (in spite of his other faults), or as a very tricky man who is likely to pull some kind of ruse on Constantine when he meets him on the bridge.

Jumping ahead, for the moment, to the bridge episode, there are some things about it I don't understand. In the first place, how is the audience to know that Constantine is signaling to Maxentius that he wants to decide the conflict by single combat? It says so in the script, but there is nothing to tell the audience what these signals mean. In the second place, if Maxentius outnumbers Constantine by three to one, why does he consent to throw away those odds and meet Constantine in single combat? It seems a very dumb thing for a smart man to do. It seems as if he is doing it merely because the authors want him to do it. If this single combat decision was an historical fact, I am sure something has been left out of history, because the episode doesn't make sense.

I am disturbed on page 46 by the abruptness immediately following Constantius' meeting with a son he has not seen for a long time. Constantius says, "My son". He then turns to his generals and introduces him, "My lords, this is my son, Constantine". And that is all that happens between father and son after all these years. Constantius turns to Constantine and says, "We are checking our last details. Tomorrow we will smash the British strength forever", and they go back to the table to go on with the battle plans. Leaving out the unfortunate wording "Checking our last details", which is so modern and colloquial, I don't see why this meeting is made to take place right in the midst of an important council of war on the eve of the battle. Why not play a scene well worthy of such a reunion in which the son might report to his father the welfare of his mother, whom he has just visited, of his own wife and son, and some reference to the tyrants Galerius and Maxentius? In other words, play a scene here and not be in such a hurry to get on with the story and neglect what should be a big moment. After the scene between father and son, you could then dissolve to the council of war and Constantine can be there with the generals looking over the maps and so forth.

I am also disturbed at this council of war scene by the fact that it seems too easy for Constantine. It seems unbelievable that at a meeting of seasoned generals one little squirt comes in and says, "Why not do this, have the cavalry come in from both sides, etc."; and have the emperor say, "That's fine, we'll do it." It gives the whole battle a feeling of unimportance and unreality. The audience feels that wars are not won that way. Constantius himself is presumably a fine tactician. The whole crowd of them are belittled if a young man comes in with one smart-aleck idea which is immediately accepted. I would find the whole thing more believable if they explained this tactic to Constantine and if he begged to be allowed to lead one of the divisions of the cavalry from one of the hills. His father and the generals nod their assent and he is overjoyed. This seems to me to be good enough for him. And I would believe that the whole thing is happening.

You may consider me too literal and too much a stickler for reality, but I am hitting at a basic fault that appears several times in this script. There is such an eagerness to get on with the action and break into spectacular battle scenes and so forth, that the human side is neglected. If the human side is neglected, the battle doesn't mean a damn thing.

I would like to say at this point that compared to the previous script that I read, vast improvements have been made, especially at this very spot.

There is now a relation between father and son. And when the old man is killed, it means much more than it did in the previous script.

On page 137 there is a close shot of Alexander's study in Alexandria. That's what the script says, but here is a new character in a new place. How does the action and how does the dialogue tell us that this is Alexander in Alexandria? Who are these people? There is no way of telling. The audience doesn't know where they are nor in what relation to the story this new group of characters are to be accepted.

I think that this conclusion of the story is very powerful. I am not prepared to say if or how it should be cut, but it does seem quite long to me. Nevertheless, this is not a real worry because the substance is there and the final conversion of Constantine is a most dramatic and affecting finish.

I do not quite understand his wife being there. Where does she come from? Where does she go? Why does she go? Is she real or is she a vision? I don't know whether it is the fault of the script or something I missed in the reading, but I felt uncertain about this element. I wonder if it is a good idea to bring her back into the story. It seems to me like an attempt to tie up all the pieces a little too neatly. The big over-all dramatic fact is the conversion of Constantine. His wife has become a very small detail in this big and colorful tapestry. It seems a little "Hollywood-y" to bring her back here and sort of square things up with her.

I made a few notes on dialogue. Some of it I found pretentious. Much of it I found very good indeed. I don't think at this point the words are a thing to worry about --- although they must be worried about later. The main question is, have you a story to tell? I am sure that you have. My frankness and bluntness in this critical letter must not be taken to mean that I don't like the project. I think there are strong and great possibilities in it. Now is the time to make sure that the foundation is well-constructed.

As I admitted at the beginning of the letter, one should read and study this script more than once. That is why I only tentatively suggest that you and the authors take a good look at the whole Licinius episode to see whether you could not do without it. It seems that three tyrants may be one too many. I found myself a little bored at this part of the script. The only value I see in it is that it gives Crispus a chance to do something and show his prowess as a naval commander. But I did not enjoy Licinius groveling before Constantine. Maybe it is necessary to have this element in the story. I am not sure. I just throw out the suggestion that you might study it.

Thank you for giving me a chance to read the script. I wish with all my heart that this work you are putting into it will be crowned with success. Best to you always.

Oscar Hammerstein to Marian and Walter Knapp, April 27, 1960

Dear Marian and Walter:

A few weeks ago we returned from England, where "Flower Drum Song" was successfully launched. When I say "successfully", I mean only the people who buy seats and help it to sell out every night. The critics thought it was just terrible. But since they have thought nearly everything I have ever done there was terrible, it doesn't make very much difference. Outside of the critics in London, I still love everything else there and we had a very good time.

This, I suppose, is my report on the family which I occasionally send you:

Jimmy has had a busy year launching a new ski area in the Catskills, only two and a half hours from New York. It is a wonderful hill and he has his ski lifts up there, but he has a long way to go and needs more money to float it for continuation next. I don't know whether or not he'll make it, but if he doesn't, somebody is going to make money on that project some day. Skiing is getting to be a very big business as you Northern New Englanders know.

Billy has still got a job in television and so has Phil Mathias, Alice's husband. Henry is doing very well in the advertising business and making more money than anybody. Susan is in love with a Canadian actor and that about rounds up the report.

Dorothy and I are both well. I have gotten over all effects of my last operation and now go into the swimming pool every morning (I started April 11th and there's no heat in the pool).

I am not planning any new show at the moment and this is the first time in a long time that I have been in that position. I kind of like the position.

I like getting up in the morning with no anxiety whatever and no songs to write. I don't know how long this feeling will keep up, but I am not fever-ishly looking around for anything. I do manage to keep pretty busy anyway without writing anything new because the old things take up a lot of my time, as do all the committees that I seem to be on.

I had lunch with Ax the other day and must report to you that he has still not changed one bit --- either in appearance or in thought or speech. He is, of course, very much wrapped up in George's career (in case you don't recognize the name of "George", it is "Ginty"). Ax himself has bought a house very far East of New York and divided it into two apartments, one of which he occupies himself. The other he is trying to rent. For some reason or other, he has not had much success with renting it. I am sure, however, that he will come out alright. Ax is doing a lot of painting now and may have a one-man show in about a year and a half.

I don't seem to have as much news for you as I thought I had, unless I start in on the grandchildren, and if I do, it'll take me two or three hours to finish up. It is not that I am a doting grandfather, but I find grand-children and the way their parents bring them up are a most compli-cated and frustrating subject. I am not, however, complaining very much because I let everything take its natural course, and the natural course of everything leads straight to confusion. Perhaps the most interesting thing to say about them is that my oldest, Billy's oldest daughter, is sev-enteen and I can still trim her in tennis although she is Number Two on the George School Girl's Team. You remember tennis don't you Walter? It is played with a racket --- an oval on a handle – with a cross-lattice of catgut. It is a game only for spry young men like myself and you wouldn't know about it. As a kind of a hedge against the time when I am not quite so spry, we have laid out a very nice croquet course on the Farm, and we play quite a little of that.

We both miss you very much and wish there was some way of seeing you. Maybe there will be at some time when I can go up to Boston and not be busy on a show. We'd make a special trip. That is, unless you have some good luck and sell the place.

Now you write to me and tell me all your news and I promise not to wait so long next time before writing. Love to you both.

Oscar Hammerstein to Cheryl J. Spear, April 27, 1960

Dear Miss Spear:

You have written me a letter with three questions. They are: When the king danced with Anna, did he do so because

a. He liked the Western custom of couples dancing together;

b. He had fallen in love with her;

c. He was jealous because she had danced with the Kralahome.

a. It is clearly stated in the play that he did not approve of the custom in the West of couples dancing together;

b. I don't believe he had fallen in love with Anna, or if he had, he certainly had not admitted it to himself. I believe he was attracted by her and I believe had it not been for many bars of race, religion and civilization that they might very well have fallen in love. Let us say that they were subconsciously in love with each other.

c. I was not aware she had ever danced with the Kralahome. This is an off-stage event that must have been seen by you and your classmates, not by me.

Best wishes to you.

Sincerely.

Oscar Hammerstein to Joseph Auslander, May 31, 1960

Dear Joe:

I do not as a rule write to bereaved friends, as I consider such letters an intrusion rather than a kindness. A loss[5] like yours deserves the honor of complete and honest grief, unmarred by the fly specks of futile condolences.

I know that you will ride your sorrow courageously until it has spent itself, until at any rate your eyes become clear enough to see that you are left with the blessing of Audrey's son.

---

[5] Auslander's wife, the Pulitzer Prize-winning poet, Audrey Wurdermann, died May 20; she was forty-nine.

We read the report in "Time" magazine after returning from a trip, during which time we had not read any daily papers. It was Dorothy who thought I should break my rule and write to you. Please let me know if either of us can be of any assistance. We both send our love.

As ever,

Prugh Roeser to Oscar Hammerstein, May 31, 1960

Dear Mr. Hammerstein:

Recently, my class studied yours and Mr. Rodgers' play "The King and I." In the discussion of the musical, the King's relationships [sic] with Anna caused a rather heated controversy. Some members thought that the King regarded Anna as just another woman—like any one of his wives. Others contended that he was in love with Anna, but that she did not return his love. Could you, as co-author of the play, straighten out our thinking?

Thank you,

Prugh Roeser

Oscar Hammerstein to Prugh Roeser, June 7, 1960

Dear Prugh Roeser:

The relationship between Anna and the King was the element which interested me most and the main reason for writing the play. It is not, however, a definite thing and perhaps must remain a mystery, since it was a thing known only to each of the characters and perhaps not one that they admitted even to themselves. It is my belief that each had a strong attraction for the other, mentally and physically. Certainly the King did not regard Anna as "just another woman". His letter, written to her before his death, is ample proof of that.

Also, before his death there is a scene between Anna and her son, Louis, and when Louis says, "You liked him very much, didn't you, Mother?" and Anna answers that she "liked him very much indeed", that I think was as close as a Victorian Welshwoman would come to admitting the deep affection that she harbored for the Oriental king. Their story is neither a love story nor a story without love. There is a wide margin of uncertainty into which the audience can write whatever they please.

Very truly yours,

Oscar Hammerstein to James C. S. Yang, June 8, 1960

Dear Mr. Yang:

I have thought a great deal about the problem you discuss in your letter. I don't understand your own suggested recommendations. They seem very vague to me. I myself have been for some time a United World Federalist. We believe that the only solution is enforceable world law: a world court that is really a world court, and a world police force to enforce the decisions of that court. We are in favor of extending the power and the scope of the United Nations to effect this kind of organization. We meet with great opposition from people who tell us this is not practical. We think that this is the only practical approach to world peace and not to face up to the problems of achieving this very difficult goal is merely running away from the danger.

I certainly agree with all your fears and with your desire to think of some remedy for the grave dangers we face. Not enough people are trying to think of anything. They are merely wringing their hands or walking blindfolded.

Thank you very much for writing to me.

Very truly yours,

A labor dispute between Actors Equity and the League of New York Theatres resulted in a Broadway blackout from June 2 through June 13. The issues included salaries, road salaries, rehearsal pay, per diems on the road, welfare, and pensions. David Merrick was among those negotiating on behalf of the producers. The blackout caused the closing of a revival of *Finian's Rainbow* and other shows, and possibly the early demise of *Once Upon a Mattress*.

Oscar Hammerstein to Alice Hughes, King Features Syndicate,
June 9, 1960

Dear Miss Hughes:

Your letter, suggesting that we make a separate contract with Actor's Equity "on the Equity terms, whatever they are", is undoubtedly a well-intentioned appeal. We are afraid, however, that it is based on a broad misconception of the present economic status of the theatre. This is not the day for any producer, however high-minded and sympathetic he may be, to agree with the terms of Actor's Equity, or any other union, "whatever they are". The costs of running a show have now reached a point so alarmingly high that there is scarcely any motive for private capital to remain in the business.

We don't believe in a socialized theatre, run and controlled by the state, but that may be what the theatre will be driven to in this country.

There are two points in your letter which I must contradict. You say "$120 is scarcely more than a secretary gets nowadays". Miss Hughes, it is more than a secretary gets nowadays, and much more. Remember that we are talking about a minimum salary, not the salary for any special talent. Some secretaries get $200 a week, some actors get $6000 a week. We are not talking about them. We are talking about minimum salaries.

In carrying on the comparison with the secretary, you might also remember that she works about 40 hours a week and sometimes more when called upon. The actor works 24 hours a week, except when there are special rehearsals called, and they do not occur very often once a show is running.

In your last paragraph you quote Brooks Atkinson as saying he has heard that "it is the producers' intention to stay closed till Labor Day, as business is off anyhow during the summer." This is nonsense. Business is off for the flops, which will close anyway. Plays that are running at a profit and trying to get their money back, certainly do not want to close during the summer. "The Sound of Music" and 9 or 10 other plays are losing a great deal every week they are laid off and it is money that may never come back to them. So when you say you are shocked and aghast at the cynicism of this attitude, you are being shocked and aghast at an attitude that does not exist.

We, on our part, are depressed by a cynicism that too readily assumes the producers to be a group of untutored louts, without integrity, without human compassion, without love for the theatre or for anyone else.

All the people of the theatre are lovers of the theatre. They are all wed to it. They all marry it for love. Some make some money too. Of all the different groups, the producers make the least money and get nearly no love at all.

We appreciate your motives for writing to us, and we are very grateful for your high opinion of us. It must be clear to you, however, that we are not the men to appeal to as potential defectors from the producers' cause. We want very much to have peace in the theatre, but not at the prices quoted. We believe we are in a last ditch fight to preserve free enterprise on Broadway.

Very truly yours,

Oscar Hammerstein to Sister Gregory, June 20, 1960

Dear Sister Gregory:

Thank you for your thoughtful letter inspired by the recent unpleasantness between actors and producers. There was really no trouble or strain in our "family". We were on different sides of the fence, but we did not glare at each other.

Speaking for myself, I was bored by the whole thing, as I am bored by most labor disputes. I do not belittle the issues involved, but I believe that men always behave childishly in these situations, sometimes causing a conflict far beyond the issues themselves.

At the first meetings, they pound their fists on the tables, wave their arms and shout that neither side will give in an inch. Unfortunately, they both believe this, no matter how many times they go through the futile ceremonies. Then nobody speaks to anybody else for a long time – not until three or four days before the deadline. Then both sides become concerned and meet again, but their personal relationships by that time have so deteriorated that it is very difficult to discuss the terms with coolness or reason. Then someone makes a threat and another makes a counter-threat and so it goes until the very last minute. At the very last minute, it is sometimes settled with both sides dissatisfied. Sometimes, as in the past experience, it goes beyond the last minute and people are thrown out of employment and other people are affected by it. This is almost routine in every labor dispute and it is high time that someone devised a more civilized and grown-up method of discussing these very real differences.

The thing that troubles me is that this attitude extends to conflicts more important than labor strife. It extends to international conflicts and today threatens the very existence of our civilization and perhaps most of our lives. I don't believe we can ever eliminate disagreement, and I don't believe that we should. The thing for us to concentrate on is our attitude toward disagreement, our intolerance, our violence, our stupidity.

Here endeth my sermon for today. Dorothy wishes me to tell you that she too is grateful for your kind letter. We are always delighted to hear from you and send you our warmest good wishes and our love.

A Robert Kitchen wrote Oscar, drawing his attention to the story "The Light in the Piazza" by Elizabeth Spencer, which had appeared in the June 15 issue of the *New Yorker*.

Oscar Hammerstein to Robert Kitchen, July 6, 1960

Dear Mr. Kitchen:

Thank you for your tip on the story in the New Yorker, "The Light in the Piazza".[6] It is a charming story and a tantalizing one. It is difficult for me to get out of my head, and difficult for me to make up my mind about. It would be difficult, I believe, for us to adapt it as a musical play, but it is a tempter.

Thank you very much for your kindness and your interest in suggesting it to me, Best wishes to you.

Sincerely,

---

[6] *The Light in the Piazza* did become a musical, with a score by Richard Rodgers' grandson, Adam Guettel. The source was recommended to Adam by his mother, Mary Rodgers.

According to Hugh Fordin, on July 7, Oscar's doctor, Ben Kean, told Oscar that X-rays showed that his cancer had returned and he suggested a course of chemotherapy. Oscar decided against it.

Oscar Hammerstein to Buddy Adler, Twentieth Century-Fox, July 12, 1960

Dear Buddy: I have to cancel my trip to the Coast. I haven't been feeling very strongly lately and so I went to the doctor. My blood count has gone down considerably and I seem to be suffering a kind of delayed reaction from my operation last September. In other words, I bounced back very fast, but now the normal symptoms have caught up to me. I am getting B-12 shots and I am also on a diet which involves five meals a day. My stomach, being much smaller than it was, cannot absorb three square meals at only three sittings. The doctor want[s] me to stay around here until he stabilizes my new eating habits or, as he mystically expresses it, my "post-gastrectomy regimen".

I tell you all these sordid details because I am self-conscious about having asked you to organize a big meeting for me on the Coast and then suddenly being forced to call the whole thing off.

This leads me to the suggestion that when and if it is convenient, it would be fine if Charlie Brackett and Mr. Breen could come East to confer with Dick and me when they think they are ready to discuss the new layout, with particular reference to new songs. I think that all would agree that it would be a great mistake for them to go too far before talking to us. The new songs should be part of the new architecture and it would be very difficult to wedge them in once you get to the stage of dialogue or even a rough dialogue version. I think that when you on the Coast are convinced that you have a good design for the new screen play, that that will be the time for us all to get together.

As for "The Sound of Music", I can only suggest that on one of these trips during which you whiz through New York if you will give me a little advance notice, I shall be prepared to spend a few hours with you whenever you say you can. There is one thing we feel strongly about in the casting of the picture. The lead should be a really young girl. It is the essence of the story that a young girl finds herself in charge of seven children and in love with a man quite a bit older than herself. I realize that that has not been true in the casting of our original New York Company, but in that case we had a brilliant stage star, and the audience is willing to pretend for the sake of spending a great evening with a personality like Mary Martin. Pictures are more realistic.

For instance, I know that Doris Day was very anxious to star in "The Sound of Music". We have two counts against her: We think she is a little old for it now and that in three years from now when it is released she will be older. We also think that Doris is a real Middle-Western corn-fed American girl with no hope of ever appearing like an Austrian postulant.

I am sorry that I had to make this switch, but it was unavoidable. Please tell Charlie to let me know when he thinks he will be able to come with Breen. Dorothy and I send our love to Anita and you.

As ever,

Oscar turned sixty-five on July 12. There was a small dinner with family and close friends, including Stephen Sondheim.

Josh Logan (in France) to Oscar Hammerstein, July 21, 1960

Dear Oscar:

The papers tell me that you had a wonderful birthday party and Nedda and I have been talking of you and Dorothy a lot. We are enjoying ourselves enormously here in Paris and earlier in Marseille, but we do miss seeing our friends.

FANNY is going to be, I am sure, the best thing I have ever done, in movies that is. I think I have learned more about the camera and I have the opportunity of supervising the final cutting and the time to do so which, you know, was my one great disappointment in SOUTH PACIFIC. I also have one really true genius working with me and that is Jack Cardiff, the cameraman, a delightful fellow and one with impeccable taste.

Surely, we could not have a better cast than we have for this picture. Leslie Caron was born to play FANNY and she is most intelligent, cooperative and enthusiastic, this is a rare quality and helps me look forward [to] our day's work with excitement rather than fear. Horst Buchholz is an extremely young actor and I think is going to make a big hit as Marius. Chevalier, of course, is a dream of charm and talent, naturally. His role of Panisse is going to bring him into a prominence as an actor that he never had. We also have Boyer who has dignity and authority as Marius' father. Baccaloni as the ferry-boat captain and a marvelous French actress named Georgette Anys, who weighs about 300 pounds and has the face of a doll to play Fanny's mother.

Marseille was an exciting and emotional place. We got many shots of the local people there as well as the busy harbor, in the constant smell of fish. This, I feel, will make our picture a real experience for the American picture-goers.

We are now living in a beautiful apartment on the Avenue d'Iena. Tom and Sue are with us as well as our couple from Connecticut, Carl and Selma. It makes life very pleasant but, as you know, the biggest contributor to happiness is working on a story that is as rewarding as FANNY.

Emlyn Williams, Molly and Margalo Gilmour [sic; Gillmore] are coming over next week to spend their bank holidays with us. As we have six bedrooms, we can take care of them easily. It will be fun to hear the latest gossip from London. Russel Crouse was here the other day and tells me of this fabulous movie sale of SOUND OF MUSIC. Leland and Variety agreed that it is the only seller on Broadway now. You are most fortunate in these difficult days to have it and the FLOWER DRUM SONG.

How I wish we could do a show together before too many years pass! How often Nedda and I have regretted that you and Dick did not do FANNY. If you get any ideas, please let me know. I agree with you, I only want to work on something that really excites me.

Nedda sends love to you and Dorothy and to all your family and please let us hear from one of you when you have the time and energy.

We will be back around the middle of September. Meanwhile, our address is:

54 AVENUE D'IENA

PARIS

Josh

Oscar Hammerstein to Josh Logan, July 28, 1960

Dear Josh:

It was good to hear from you and we are very excited about all that you say about "Fanny". It sounds wonderful and I cannot wait to see it.

I have not been very well. A kind of delayed "take" following my operation last September has found me with a low blood count and sadly lacking in my usual energy. However since I have nothing to do but take care of myself, that's what I'm doing. We are spending a great deal of the summer in Doylestown, and I am enjoying it. This week I have spent with Dick and Charlie Brackett (producer) and Dick Breen (screen playwright) conferring about the re-make of "State Fair" for Twentieth Century. Dick and I will write two or three new songs after we all create the new layout.

We have one or two new ideas for a new show but nothing worth talking about yet. I agree with you that it would be wonderful for us all to get together on something.

It seems a very long time indeed since we spent an evening with you and Nedda, and I hope that as soon as you come back you will ring us up and we can arrange a revival meeting. Love to you both.

As always,

In response to an inquiry:

Oscar Hammerstein to John Greer, August 4, 1960

Dear Mr. Greer:

I have no motto in life.

Very truly yours,

The following is the last letter I have seen written by Oscar Hammerstein. The fact that it accompanies a donation seems significant.

Oscar Hammerstein to John F. B. Mitchell, Jr., President,
New York State Branch, United World Federalists,
August 10, 1960

Dear Mr. Mitchell:

Thank you very much indeed for your letter of July 27th. I am in agreement with your ideas, and am enclosing my contribution of $50.00 toward the realization of the Committee.

Best wishes to you.

Sincerely

Oscar Hammerstein II passed away at Highland Farm on August 23 at the age of sixty-five.

Dorothy Hammerstein received hundreds of condolence letters, cards, and telegrams after Oscar died. They came from friends, family, colleagues, and complete strangers whose lives were touched by Oscar and his work. It is impossible to provide a truly representative sample, but the letters below will have to do.

Maria Augusta Trapp to Dorothy Hammerstein,
August 22,[7] 1960

Dear Mrs. Hammerstein,

The day before yesterday Richard Halliday called me and told me how sick your dear husband was. I wanted to send a telegram immediately but Richard thought a letter would be better so I wrote with a trembling heart. For one or another unaccountable reason the letter was not mailed right away and now he is reading it from the other world. I enclose it to you anyhow because this is how I felt and how I now feel for you. I remember only so well that there is absolutely nothing anybody can say which would really reach one's heart in these days but let me assure you that our prayers are with him and with you, not only today but from now on.

I met your husband only two short times but that was enough for me to remember him always as the one who not only wrote but lived the

---

[7] The date on this letter is probably a mistake.

words: "--- and love in your heart wasn't put there to stay, love isn't love until you give it away."

With heartfelt love and sympathy

Maria Trapp

Samuel Taylor to Dorothy Hammerstein, August 24, 1960

Dear Dorothy:

News comes late here in Maine, and all the more painful because we didn't know that Oscar was ill.

He was the only man I ever wanted to turn to when I felt unsure, and he never failed me. I shall miss him selfishly, and I feel sorry for everyone who didn't have the experience of him that I did. Not those who know him; they had him. It's the ones who didn't know him who should mourn for what they've missed.

Suzanne sends her love and her heartfelt sympathy, and so do I.

Yours always,

Sam

Siegfried Herzig to Dorothy Hammerstein, August 26, 1960

Dear Dorothy:

Mine is just a small voice amid all the great tributes, but I speak as one who knew Oscar for over fifty-five years—ever since he was voted the most popular boy at Weingart Institute (he was a swell tennis player there, too.) Ours was a loose friendship through the years, but I always knew it was there—such as on the morning I woke up to a flop called "Vickie". Oscar was on the telephone (and who else but he would telephone you after a flop.) He was inviting me to lunch to tell me not to be discouraged and try it again. Just a year later, when after taking his advice, it looked as if I had it made, he called again to say: "When you open in Philadelphia, I'll be there in case you need me." How typical—always to be there when he was needed!

One more thing, Dorothy. Both Betty and I feel there's also a wonderful Mrs. Oscar Hammerstein and we hope that friendship will always be there too.

Love and you know what we mean –

Sig x

Agnes de Mille (Prude) to Dorothy Hammerstein, September 8, 1960

Dearest-

This is a terribly hard letter to write – and yet it seems to write itself. As I speak of Oscar, love and memory flood my heart as they have done since I knew him. . . . He was one of the chief influences of my adult life and every thought of him cuts deep.

It is to him I owe the change in my fortune, for it was he and noone [*sic*] else who got me "Oklahoma!" His was the recognition that found me out. I had had sixteen years of un-success and might but for him have had sixteen more and so closed my life with none of my chief gifts realized. This is a thought [that] gives me pause. It was he and noone else made it possible for me to do the stronger and more mature work in "Carousel" and opened still wider doors for me in "Allegro." . . . . But beyond this there is so much more. This hardly touches what I owe him. There is hardly a new experience I meet but I hear his voice, I recall some bit of wisdom or wit, some enchanting nonsense, some caution to hold steady, some reaffirmation of the faith by which I set my course.

I have seen very few of the tributes, because I have been in the woods, and papers are not to be had. . . I wonder, have many people spoken of his compassion? I know they have praised his great gifts but just as his writing brought lucidity and tenderness with the craft his presence brought humanity with its practices.

It has grieved me to the heart being apart from not being as close to him, these past years as formerly. This, I suppose, is the way of life, but I regret the lost experiences. I used to turn to him for everything, as you probably know, advice, comfort, reaffirmation, admiration. Oh – as I write, so much, so very much comes back: his criticism of my book which he read through in manuscript, his visits to the Henry George school with you (both acts of intense generosity.) Jonathan's chess lessons, tennis and talks about Shakespeare with Walter, and then the costume parades, the auditions, the times I was stuck in a dance in the attic of the Guild and he straightened me out, the times I was stuck in the basement, the time he took me in his arms and said the "Allegro" ballet made him weep, the trips everywhere, his championing me in conferences, in interviews, in articles, the long deep heart-searching conversations about everything, every thing.

As a professional I weep the termination of his work, but oh! what a heritage he left us! How bonny and wise, how darling and deft, how inescapable so many of his lyrics! Has anyone compared him to Robert Burns? He is quite different, but equally beloved, as he also will go into our language, with the very fiber of it. Girls and boys are going to talk with his words, with his point of view, long hence, and may perhaps not be aware whom they quote. He will be in the air they breathe, he will shape their memories, their perception, everything they see + taste. Above all these things they cherish they will always have him.

I've kept every word he ever wrote me. I imagine many people have done so. He is an absolutely indestructable [*sic*] piece of our lives, and I am grateful for every minute I had with him.

Darling – when you can let us see you. I love you very much.

Devotedly

Agnes

Dorothy Hammerstein to Sister Gregory, September 16, 1960

Dear Sister Gregory – You wrote to me on August 24th which seems years ago already. On Sept. 2nd I went to the cottage in Jamaica with three of the children for ten days mostly to escape the telephone and all the wonderful people who wanted to come and see us. I don't know why the latter is so nerve wracking one's instinct is not to discuss ones troubles but somehow one feels one ought to, to make the other person feel better. We found ourselves comforting others which perhaps is the very best thing that could happen. Not one of us (meaning the children + me) seemed inconsolable – perhaps that will come. Whether Oscar imbued us with such strength I don't know and I don't really understand it yet. We had thirty one years of very close involvement with each other. I had tremendous respect for him but also a protective feeling and now I have no regrets for things that might have been or might not have been – no feelings of guilt – only pride in our life together. The worst thing really is not being able to tell him everything that is funny or interesting. I hate him to be missing things. Perhaps because so many people from everywhere loved him and told us so helps us to feel less lonely. I don't know. As you said before I do not understand this sense of security. But we all have it. He must be responsible for this in some way. He had such admiration for you. We talked about you a lot and he used to quote your letters especially the one you wrote about marriage. That made him cry. There is so much to do in the near future. The children are being so wonderful + help me. You are a darling to invite me to Rosemary College and maybe someday I will remind you about it.

My most affectionate + grateful thoughts to you with this.

Dorothy

Dr. Benjamin Kean to Dorothy Hammerstein,
September 16, 1960

Dear Dorothy:

I have delayed writing because it is so difficult to say what one feels.

In almost twenty five years of medicine I have not seen anyone handle so difficult a personal situation so well as you.

At one of his last visits to my office I told Oscar, despite all other recommendations to the contrary, I would suggest that he take a course of X-ray therapy. The next day he came back with these words,

"Ben, I have considered very carefully your recommendation. In this showdown I must really decide whether to die, possibly a little later in the hospital, or on Dorothy's pillow. I'm really lucky and never knew how much until now."

Ben

Dorothy Hammerstein to Dr. Benjamin Kean,
September 18, 1960

Dear Ben – Thank you very much for your kind letter which I received yesterday—It was not difficult really to behave well under the recent circumstances. Oscar and I had a wonderful thirty-one years together with very few sour notes and so there are no regrets for what might have been and he left us all with emotional strength and balance – This is how things seem now and I think it will last – He was too young, too good, and most undeserving of his illness but he told me that we have so much to be grateful for, that to whine and cry would be pure greediness-

Thank you for your understanding + care of our darling Oscar –

Sincerely always

<u>Dorothy</u>

Photo 24 Oscar Hammerstein II, circa 1915. White Studio

Permissions Acknowledgments

Letter from George Abbott used by permission of Temple University

Letter from Afro-American Newspapers used courtesy of the AFRO American Newspapers

Letter from Herman Axelrod used by permission of Steve Axelrod

Letter from Edward Benjamin used by permission of William Benjamin

Letter from Rudolf Bing used by permission of the Metropolitan Opera

Letter from Milton Biow used by permission of Matthew Broderick

Letter from Charles Brackett used by permission of the Estate of Charles W. Brackett

Letter from Katharine Brown used by permission of Kate R. Barrett

Letters from William Cagney used by permission of the William J. Cagney Trust

Letter from Samuel Chotzinoff used by permission of Robin Chotzinoff

Letter from Judith Chase Churchill used by permission of John M. Churchill

Letter from Barbara Clough used by permission of George School

Letters from Betty Comden and Adolph Green used by permission with special thanks to Amanda Green and the Estate of Betty Comden Kyle

Letter from Marc Connelly used by permission of the Dramatists Guild Foundation

Letter from Ruth Cosgrove used by permission of William Berle

Letter from Richard Detwiler used by permission of Anne Detwiler Crecraft

Letter from Leonard Dinnerstein used by permission of Julie and Myra Dinnerstein

Letters from Robert Dolan used by permission of Casey Dolan and Robert Dolan

Letter from Alfred Drake used by permission of Candace Wainwright

Letters from Sister Gregory Duffy used by permission of Toni Harris, Prioress, Dominican Sisters of Sinsinawa

Letter from Irene Dunne used by permission of Mark Shinnick

Letters from Edna Ferber used by permission of the Trustee for the Edna Ferber Estate

Letter from José Ferrer used by permission of Stella Ferrer

Letter from Harold Fielding used by permission of Sharon Oxenbury Adams (Fielding Estate)

Letters from Myra Finn used by permission of Pat Benner

Letter from Dorothy Fields used by permission of David Lahm

Letters from Arthur Freed used by permission of Steve Saltzman

Index

Bolded page numbers indicate letters written to or by the associated name. Page numbers in italics indicate photographs

Abbott, George, 214, 376, 596, **697**, 865
ABC, 725
Abell, Kjeld, 443
Abingdon, Bill, 66, 73
Abraham, Paul, 65
Academy Awards, 163, 220, 632–33
Ace, Goodman, **699–700**
Achard, Marcel, 738
Acheson, Dean, 745
Act One, 967–68
Actors' Equity, 429, 504, 851, **880–81**, 1010–13
Adams, Alva, **179–80**
Adams, Frank, **319**
Adams, Stanley, 969
Adams, Timothy, **326**
Adler, Buddy, **884–86**, **886–67**, 887, 888, 892, 893, 896–97, 898, 902, 932, **1014–15**
Afro-American Newspapers, **480**
"Ah Still Suits Me," 112
Ah, Wilderness, 423
Ahlert, Fred, 285
Akins, Zoe, 101, 106
Akron Club, 184
Albert, Eddie, 772–73
Alch, Alan, 503
Aleichem, Sholom, 499
Alexander's Ragtime Band, 163, 167
Alfred P. Sloan Foundation, **824**
"All At Once You Love Her," 895
"All Kinds of People," 796
"All the Things You Are," xii, 180, 212, 215, 216, 236, 823
Allegro, 431, 441, 445, 447, 454, 487, 531, 937, 987, 988, 1020, 1021
  Logan on, 432–40
Alsberg, Henry G., 19

Alter, Louis, 41
Alton, Robert, 224, 225
Alvine, Glendon, 154
Always You, 6
American Jubilee, 183
American Theater Wing War Service, 225, 226, 233
America's Sweetheart, 47
Ames, Winthrop, 51
And the Angels Sing, 278
Anderson, Hans Christian, 32
Anderson, John, 181
Anderson, John Murray, 286
Anderson, Maxwell, 126–27, **543–44**
Andersonville Trial, The, 988
André Charlot's Revue of 1924, 148, 507, 513
Andrews, Fletcher R., **855–56**
Andrews, Julie, 848–49, 861, 877
Androcles and the Lion, 603
Angelosante, Lydia, **997**
Angelus, Muriel, 267
animation, 169
Anna and the King of Siam (film), 510, 514, 762
Anna and the King of Siam (Landon novel), 497, 510, 514, 562. *See also King and I, The*
Annie de Far East, 575
Annie Get Your Gun, viii, 419, 425, 427–30, 431, 456, 457, 531, 550, 849
Anouilh, Jean, 610
Ansky, S., 18
Any Number Can Play, 899–900
Anys, Georgette, 1016
Applause, 126
Applebaum, Stella, **341**
Arlen, Harold, 163, 291
Armstrong, Louis, 291, 968

Arnold, Thurman, **698–99**
Arnold, Tom, **620**
Around the World, 919
ASCAP, ix, 166, 208, 213, 231, 262, 269, 270, 285, 297, 352–54, 419–20, 496, 616, 630–32, 696–97, 845, 864–65, 905–07, 909–11
Astaire, Adele, 920
Astaire, Fred, 73, 91, 135, 139, 284
Astor, Lady Nancy, 149
At the Sign, 1002–06
Ates, Nejla, 758
Atkin, Charles, 482, 529, 794–95
Atkinson, Brooks, **42–43**, 180, 578, 697, **914–15**, 978, 997, 1011
Augustine, Stephanie, 684
Auslander, Joseph, 913–14, **1008–09**
Australia, 425, 452, 596–97, 861, 872
Authors League, 277, 483, 485–86, 493, 616
Away We Go!, 278. *See also Oklahoma!*
Axelrod, Betty, 89
Axelrod, George, 667, **728–29**, 1007
Axelrod, Herman, 4, **5**, 1007
Aydelotte, Frank, **784**
Ayers, Lemuel, 598
Ayling, Walter, **481**

Babes on Broadway, 199
Baby Doe, 348, 350
Bainter, Fay, 342, 408
Baker, Josephine, 575, 613, 617
Bal, Jeanne, **751–53**
"Bali Ha'i," 481, 530, 895, 898, 903, 908, 909
Ball at the Savoy, viii, 62, 65–66, 73, 786, 954–55
Ballard, Lucinda, 952
Ballerina, 60
Ballyhoo of 1930, 41–43
Band Wagon, The, 88
Banks, Xenia, 507
Baravalle, Victor, 90, 95, 120
Barnes, Margaret Ayer, 114
Barries, James M., 687
Barrymore, John, 410
Barsony, Rosy, 66
Barton, Jim, 264

Batman, The, 252–53
Battles, John, 432, 445
Beaton, Cecil, 595
Beau Brummell, 71, 174–75, 176
Beaumont, Hugh "Binkie," 975
Bech, Holger, 443
Beck, Martin, 60
Beecham, Sir Thomas, 337, 350
Behr, Robert, **487–88**
Beisman, Paul, 188, **242**
Belafonte, Harry, 620
Bell for Adano, A, 640–41
Belle of New York, The, 305
Bells of St. Mary's, The, 571
Ben Hur, 494
Benchley, Robert, 181
Benjamin, Edward, **194–96**, 197, **942–43**
Bennet, Arnold, 94
Bennett, Robert Russell, 95, 165, **223–24**, **242**, 245, 250, 273, 275
Benny, Jack, 372
Benthem, M. S., 248, 251
Bentley, Eric, 862, 877
Berg, David, **231–32**
Bergen, Edgar, 139
Bergen, Polly, 952
Berger, Richard, 137, **145–46**, 152, 156, **188, 242**, 285, **647–48**
Bergin, Dolores, **992**
Bergman, Ingrid, 571
Berlin, Ellin Mackay, 29–30
Berlin, Irving, vii, viii, 29–30, 36, 222, 380, 419, 429, **491–92, 550**, 907
Berman, Pandro S., **147–48**
Bernhard, Arnold, 395
Bernstein, Leonard, 18
Berry, W. H., 71
Bess, Demaree, 317–19
Betty Lee, 13
Between the Devil, 135
Bevan, Aneurin, 914
"Bill," 106, 118, 120, 246
Billingsley, Sherman, **728**
Bing, Rudolf, **743–44**
Biow, Milton, 474–75, **611**, 668, 978
Bittersweet, 43, 189, 942
Bizet, Georges, xii, 223, 224, 319, 347
Black Majesty, 116, 121

Blackton, Jay, 952
Blair, Janet, 529
Blanchard, Susan (stepdaughter), x, 22, 26, 135, 178, 182, 193, 366, 373, 374–75, 379, *385*, 447, 515, 627, 668, 861, 981, 1006
Blanshard, Paul, **735–37**
Bledsoe, Jules, 247
"Bloody Mary," 471, 893, 898
Blossom Time, 164
Blue Denim, 894
Blum, Ralph, **92–93**, **95–96**, 98, **269–70**, **278**
Blumenthal, A. C., 60
BMI, 864–65, 905–07, 909–11
Bocca, Jeffrey, **457–48**
Bohème, La, 86, 258, 465
Boles, John, 111
Bolger, Ray, 146, **678**
Bolton, Guy, 22, 355, 853, **877–79**
Booth, Shirley, 364–65, 370, 505, 667, 865, 866
Borchardt, Betty, **554**
Bowles, Paul, 260
Boy Friend, The, 877, 878
Boyar, Ben, 145
Boyer, Charles, 1016
Boykin, Edward, 136
"Boys and Girls Like You and Me," 331–33
Brackett, Charles, 483, **778–79**, **780**, **837– 38**, **865–67**, 1014–15, 1017
Bradley, Phyllis Rich, **979–80**
Brass Boot Knob, 507
Brazzi, Rossano, 882, 889, **891–92**, 899, 902, 908
Breen, Dick, 1014–15, 1014, 1017
Breen, Robert, **700**, 724
Brigadoon, 444, 449, 515–16
Brill, Leighton "Goofy," 38, 41, **65–74**, 108, **110–13**, 115, 136, 150, **163**, **173–74**, 177, **209**, **221–23**, **252–53**, **275–76**, **277**, **300–01**, 329, **365–66**, **379–80**, 419–20, **462**, **497–98**, **503–04**, 507, **652**, **705**, **711**, 791, **792**, **858**
Britton Pamela, 306, 317
Britton, George, 616–17
Broadway Melody, 99
Broderick, Helen, 100

Brown, Ada, 109
Brown, Anne, **254–56**
Brown, Irving, **904–05**
Brown, Katharine, **679**
Brown, Lew, 47
Brown, Russ, 883
Bruce, Carol, 264, 355
Bruce, Nigel, **159–62**
Bryant, Louis, 17
Brynner, Yul, 568, 572, 577, 578, 684, 694–95, 735, **742**, 762, 778, **779–80**, 782–83, **791**, 807, 837, 939–40
Buchanan, Jack, 135, 148, 507
Buck, Gene, 231
Buck, Pearl, ix, 626, 705
Bullis, Harry A., **785–86**
Buloff, Joseph, *280*
"Bums' Opera," 796
Burke, Billie, **727–28**
Burning Bright, 544, 546–47, 549
Burns, Bob, 343
Burns, David, 306
Burns, Robert, 1021
Bus Stop, 847, 848
Buzzell, Edward, **941**
Byington, Spring, 342, 343
Byrnes, James F., 411, 623

Cabin in the Sky, 253, 254, 290–91, 301, 380
Cabot family, 122
Caesar, Irving, 231, 233, 237, 238
Cagney, James, 320–21
Cagney, William, **320–22**
Call Me Madam, 550, 582
Calta, Louis, 591, 592
Calthrop, Gladys, 72
Camille, 51
Cammarano, Salvadore, 258
Campanini, Cleofonte, 776
Campbell, Dick, **654–55**, **849**
Campi, Dr. John G., 124
"Can I Forget You," 134
"Can't Help Lovin' Dat Man," xi, 496
Cannery Row, 722, 723, 746
Cantor, Eddie, 243
Capp, Al, 599
Captain of St. Margaret's, The, 387–88
Cardiff, Jack, 1015

Carhartt, James, **658–59**
Carlisle (Hart), Kitty, 146
Carmen, xii, 85, 223, 262, 269, 312, 690
Carmen Jones, xii, 18, 85, 88, 184, 210,
    223–24, 242, 245, 254, 257–58, 262,
    267, 269, 271–72, 273–75, 284, 286,
    289–90, 297, 298–99, 307–10, 312,
    319, 327, 328, 340, 365, 370, 389, 396,
    429, 430, 690, 699, 724, 807, 810, 849
Caron, Leslie, 1015
Carousel, xiii, xvi, 126, 291, 314–17, 326–
    27, 329, 337, 347, 364, 369–70, 379,
    382, 387–88, 389, 390, 397–98, 401,
    430, 431, 437, 453, 533, 535, 566, 574,
    647–48, 711, 714, 741, 802, 939, 975–
    76, 1020. *See also Liliom*
Carousel (film), 494, 712, 778, 807–11,
    815–18, 844, 846
Carousel (London), 508–09, 514, 520,
    536–37, 538, 561, 592
Carpenter, Constance, 639, 681–84, 693,
    826
Carpenter, Freddie, 937, 938
Carpenter, Janet, 89
Carrick, Virginia, **644**
Carrillo, Cely, 987
Carson, Doris, 65
Carson, Jack, 869
Carter, Tim, 259
casting, xii, 43–44, 46, 69, 73, 97–101,
    108–11, 138, 143, 145–46, 147, 150,
    151–52, 170, 221, 222, 224, 236–37,
    238, 240, 243, 245–52, 253, 254, 256,
    260–61, 263–67, 268, 272, 273–75,
    285, 313, 317, 320–24, 327, 329–30,
    337, 341–43, 355–56, 364, 369–70,
    410, 481, 482, 483, 484, 491, 510,
    513–14, 554, 556, 558, 581, 590–93,
    600, 604, 618, 619, 620, 621, 629–30,
    636, 654, 671–72, 717, 723, 747–48,
    757–58, 761, 765–69, 772–73, 792–
    93, 807–11, 880–81, 889, 942, 952,
    968, 985, 1001, 1014–15
Castle, Irene, 139, 474
Castle, Vernon, 135, 139, 474
Cat and the Fiddle, The, 88
Catholic Theatre Movement, The, 366–68
cattle, x, 344, 403–04, 717, 750

Cavalcade, 55, 250
Cavalieri, Lina, 774
censorship. *See* Motion Picture
    Association
Center Theatre, 140–41, 142
Chamberlain, Neville, 149
Champagne and Orchids, 81, 88
Chamroy, Leon, 888
Channing, Carol, 491, 502
Chanticleer, 425–26
Chaplin, Charlie, 533
Chapman, John, 943, 978
Chappell & Co., 714–15, 904, 935, 936–37,
    988
Charlot, Andre, 147–48
Charpentier, Gustave, 258
Chauvelot, Robert, 175
Chauve-Souris, Le, 13, 14
Chertok, Jack, **85–86**
Chesterfield, Lord Philip Stanhope, 155,
    156
Chesterton, Gilbert K., 726, 727
Chevalier, Maurice, 481, 1016
Chodorov, Jerome, 685
Chotzinoff, Samuel, **793–94**
Christians, Maddy, 327, 389
Christie, Audrey, 145
Chu-Chin Chow, 50–51, 56
Churchill, Judith Chase, **402**, 855
Cinderella, 163
Cinderella (panto), 934–38
Cinderella (television), vii, 489, 849, 869–
    70, 871, 873, 874–75, 883, 889, 917
CinemaScope/CinemaScope 55, 764, 788,
    807, 811
Citizen Kane, 283–84
City Center, viii, 430, 710, 712, 740–41
City Lights, 533
Civil War, 142–43
Clark, Bobby, 247, 249, 250, 251
Clayton, Jan, 422, 423
Climate of Eden, The, 667
"Climb Every Mountain," 969–70
Climb High, 706–08
Clough, Barbara, 134, **400–01**
Clurman, Harold, 747–48, 822
Cochran, Charles, 587, 593, 595
Cohan, George M., 201, 320, 321, 728

Cohan memorial, George M., 728, 850–52, 950, 973
Cohen, Irving, **499–500**, **887–89**, 896–97
Cohen, Milton, 462, **525**
Cohn, Dr. Alfred, **579–80**
Coini, Jacques, 774–75, 776
Colette, 844
Collier, Constance, 106
Collins, Frank, 66
Collins, Jackie, 581
Colman, Ronald, 170
Colombe, 610
Columbia Law, viii, 1, 36, 734, 929
Columbia Pictures, 135, 138, 253, 283
Columbia University, 1, 4, 6, 322, 358, 456–57, 477–78, 511, 993
Columbia University Players, 184
Comden, Betty, **323–24**, 514, 760
Come Back, Little Sheba, 505
"Come Home," 435, 437–38
Concord Park Homes, 771
Connecticut Yankee, A, 300
Connelly, Marc, **633**, **891**
Conway, Edward A., **737–38**, **918–19**
Cook, Barbara, 710
Cook, Joe, 262
Cooley, Professor, 511
Cooper, Gary, 792–93
Copland, Aaron, 259, 828
Cornell, John, 681, **682–84**, **693–95**
Cornell, Kit, 629
Cosgrove, Ruth, 573, **574**, **575**
Costello, Diosa, 529
Coughlin, Father Charles E., 383
Count of Luxembourg, 113
Countess Maritza, 10, 227
Courtney, Marguerite, 615, 645
Cousins, Norman, **797–98**
Cover Girl, 283–84, 336
Coward, Noel, 43, 55, 72, 311, 513, 641, 932
Cowl, Jane, 348–49
Cowles, Edward Upson, 998, **999**
Cradle Will Rock, The, 135
Crawford, Cheryl, 207–08, 209, 210, 213, 221, 641, **844**
Cremme, Mary, **515–16**
Crisham, Wally, 65

Cronyn, Hume, **612–13**, 616, **635–36**
Crosby, Bing, 238, 571
Crosby, John, **489**
Crosland, Alan[?], 37
Crouse, Anna Erskine,
Crouse, Russel, 222, 489, 926, **958–65**, 968, 988, 990, 1016
Crowther, Bosley, 183
Cukor, George, 369
Cullman, Howard, **345–46**, 459
Cummings, Jack, 234
Cunningham, Zamah, 758
Curran, Homer, 170

D'Usseau, Arnaud, 492–93
Dahlberg, Arthur, 395
Daitz, Elliot, 429
Damn Yankees, 730, 884
"Dance Away the Night," 691
"Dance, Little Lady," 311
Dance to the Piper, 588n.
Dancing in the Streets, 265
Dandridge, Dorothy, 807, 810–11
Darian, Anita, 985
Darling, Jean, **484**
Daves, Delmar, 987
Davey, Jr., Bernard A., **892**
Davies, Jack, **370**
Davies, Peter, 598
Davis, Bette, 779–80
Davis, Edwin, 603
Davis, Peter, 426
Day, Doris, 1001, 1015
Day, Edith, 9, 29
Dean, Basil, 508, **539–40**, 825
Dean, Frances, 69
Deane, Congressman Charles, 621, **622**
Death of a Salesman, 900
Deep In My Heart, 783
de Hartog, Jan, **612–13**
"De Land o' Good Times," 137, 311
De Lisle, Claude Joseph Rouget, 226
de Mille (Prude), Agnes, 286, **289–90**, 304, 331, 445, **452–53**, **461–62**, **588–89**, 611, 616, **709**, 710, 781, 949–50, **1020–21**
DeHaven, George, 675
Dell'Isola, Salvatore, 533

Demastus, William, **823**
Denes, Oskar, 66
Denmark, Copenhagen, 443, 453
Derwent, Clarence, 733–34, 825–27
Desert Song, The, 7, 21, 22, 23, 47, 52, 430, 648, 729, 853–54, 859
Desperate Hours, The, 730
De Sylva, Buddy, 47, 266, 278
Detwiler, Richard, **944**
Deval, Jacques, 738, 802
Devauchier, Margot, 379
Dewey, Thomas E., 339
Dewood, Lorraine, 195
Dial M for Murder, 667–68
"Diamonds Are a Girl's Best Friend," 502
Dictaphones, 447, 481, 484, 700–01
Dietrich, Marlene, 262, 265
Dietz, Howard, 308, 743
Dillinghanm, Charles, 11, 54, 844
Dinnerstein, Leonard, **715–16**
Dior, Christian, 595
Disney, Walt, 168
"Dites-Moi Pourquoi," 687–88, 939
"Do I Love You Because You're Beautiful?," 869–70, 871, 873
"Do-Re-Mi," 998
Dodgeson, Peggy, 301
dogs, 155, 253, 403, 405
Dolan, Robert, **521**, **567–72**, **915**, **933–34**
Don Quixote, 354–55
Donahue, Walter, 306
Donehue, Vincent J., 952, **958–64**
Donn-Byrne, Brian Oswald, 86, 88, 348
Donohue, Jack, 17
"Don't Marry Me," 931
Douberson, Damy, 602
Doublas, Milton, 209
Doughgirls, The, 276, 277
Douglas, Margaret, 327
Downes, Olin, 374
Doyle, Arthur Conan, 593
Doyle, Denis P. S. Conan, **593–96**
Doyle, Jack, 69
Drake, Alfred, 187, 275, *281*, 293, 317, **340**, 694–95
Dramatists' Guild, The, ix, 209, 323, 419, 504, 880–81
Draper, Mr., **769**

"Dream Ballet" (*Oklahoma!*), 772–73, 781, 949–50
Dream Girl, 845–46
Dreyfus, Jean, 70
Dreyfus, Louis, 10, 69, **128**, 714–15, 895, **974–75**, 988
Dreyfus, Max, 214, 714–15, 904, 988
Drury Lane, 55, 69, 74, 457–58, 514, 520, 538, 592, 599, 616, 661, 735, 765–69, 861
Dubin, Al, 163
Duchess of Gerolstein, The, 743
Duff, Barry, 969
Duke, Vernon, 291, 308
Dulles, John Foster, 744–45, 805
Dumbarton Oaks, 384
Duncan, Todd, **254–56**, **273–75**, 355
Dunne, Irene, 80, 104, **105**, 107, 111, 134, 164, 363, 510, **604–05**
Durbin, Deanna, 168, 238, 252
Dvonch, Frederick, 683
Dybbuk, The, 18–20
Dyrenforth, Jimmy, **536**

East is West, 26
East Wind, 54
Eastham, Dick, 478, 527–28
Ebsen, Buddy, 99, 103, 146, **147**
Eburne, Maude, 111
Ed Sullivan Theatre, 345
Ed Wynn Revue, 13
Eddy, Nelson, 81, 88, 89, 109, 110, 111, 115, 183, 252
"Edelweiss," 975
Edna His Wife, 114
Einach, Charles, **690–91**
Eisenhower, Dwight D., 663, 626, 805, 974
elephants, 545–46
Elizabeth II, Queen, 620
Ellis, Charles, *49*, 66
Ellis, Mary, 66, 67
Ellis, Vivian, 803
Elman, Irving, 499–500
Ely, Jean, **512**
Engleman, Maurice, 503–04
Ephraim, Mr. and Mrs. Lee, 29
Ephron, Henry, **817–18**
Ernst, Morris, 60
Errante, Nora, **680–81**

Erskine, John, **358**
"Et cetera"s, 574
Evans, Rex, 491
Evans, Wilbur, 590–93, 600, 619
Everts, Mrs. William P., **574–75**
Everybody Loves Me, 867–69
Everyman, 643
Ewell, Tom, 191
Ewing, Sherman, **582–83**

Fabulous Invalid, The, 166
Fadiman, Clifton, 258, 329, **605, 899–900**
Fairless Hills, 699
Falstaff, 337, 350
Fancy Free, 376
Fanny, 659–60, 757–60, 826, 861, 1015–16
Farnol, Lynn, 706, **721–22, 886, 984–85**, 1000
Farnol, Nell, **886**
Father of the Blues, 226
Faust (opera), 85
Faye, Alice, 342, 343, 410
Fearnley, John, 478, 558, 586, 686–87, 748, 752, **841–42**
Fears, Peggy, 60
February Hill, 114
Federation of Jewish Philanthropies, The, 728–29, 732
Feldmun-Blum Corporation, 92, 95
"Fellow Needs a Girl, A" 434
Ferber, Edna, 21, 45–46, 47, **60–61, 185–87**, 205, 208, 218, 222, **245–46, 247–48**, **251–52, 302–04**, 355, 642–43, **714–21**, **740–41**, 853
Ferrer, José, 612–13
Ferryman, J. N., **623–25**
Feuer and Martin, 508
Feuer, Cy, 508, 903
Fiddler on the Roof, 499
Field, Jr., Marshall, **744–45**
Fielding, Harold, 934, **935–38**, 982–83
Fields, Dorothy, 276, 376, 380, 419, 420, 422, 432, **560, 575–76, 731**, 865
Fields, Herbert, 113, 276, 376, 380, 419, 432
Fields, Joseph, 276, 277, 894, 896–97, 903, 904, 988
Fields, W. C., 113
Fight for Freedom, 221–22

film industry. *See* Hollywood
Fine, Sylvia, 222
Finian's Rainbow, 465, 466
Finlayson, Jimmy, 69
Finn, Myra "Mike". *See* Hammerstein, Myra
Firefly, The, 4
First National, 37
Fisher, Ham, **400**
Fitzgerald, Leo, 221, 285
Florsheim, Sidney, 344
Flower Drum Song, 896–97, 903, 904, 920, 930–31, 940, 942, 943–46, 949, 956–58, 981, 983, 985–86, 987–88, 995, 998, 1000–01, 1006
Fly, Jean, **505**
"Folks Who Live on the Hill, The," 134, 524
Folies Bergère, 5, 481
Follow Thru, 53
Fonda, Henry, 532, 627, 668, 759
Foran, Dick, 306
Forbes, Kathryn, 363, **377–78**
Forbidden Melody, 153
Fordin, Hugh, xix, 1, 2, 4, 223, 281–82, 970–71, 975
Forever, 615, 627
"Forever and a Day," 200
Foster, Jr., Lloyd, **890**
Fourposter, The, 612–13, 616, 668
Fox, Janet, 252
Fox, Mrs. Herman L., **485**
Fox theatre project, 427
France, 5, 54, 226, 602, 666, 738
Frank, George, 96, 113, 163, **170, 232**
Freed, Arthur, **199**, 234–35, 250, 253, 254, 256, 270–71, 286, 290–91, 299–300, 305, 331–33, 418, 580, 827–28
Freedley, Vinton, 214, **217–18**, 219, 220, 221
Friedman, Charles, 286
Friml, Rudolf, 4, 853
Fry, Christopher, 970
FTP (Federal Theatre Project), 179–80
Fulton, Robert, 746–47, 749
Funcke, Walter, 846
Furnas, J. C., 689–90
Furs and Frills, 4

Gable, Clark, 285, 314
Gabriel, Gilbert, W., **493**

Gallagher, Irene, **496**
"Gallavantin' Aroun'," 106–07, 118, 119
Gangs All Here, The, 44, 45, 191
Ganne, Paule, 602
Garbo, Greta, 176
Garde, Betty, 275, **282**
Garden, Mary, 774
Garland, Judy, 199, 208, 290, 332
Garrick Gaieties, 259
Gateson Marjorie/Marjory, 136
Gaver, Jack, 485
Gay Divorce, A, 73
Gay Divorcee, The, 91
Gay Hussars, The, 227
Gaynor, Mitzi, 881, 882, 889, 894, 897, 898, 899, 932
Geers, Hilda, 469, **470, 908**
Geiger, Carol, **948**
Gellendre, Herbert, **643–44**
Geller, James, **486**
Gensler, Lewis, **191–92**
Gentlemen Prefer Blondes, 415, 490–91, 502–03, 538–39, 904
Gentlemen Unafraid, xi–xii, 136–37, 140–47, 149–50, 152–54, 163, 165, 212–13, 214, 220, 365
George and Margaret, 131
George School, 366, 400–01, 464
George VI, King, 29, 619, 620
Gershwin, George, 12, 18, 25, 210, 242, 339, 879, 907
Gershwin, Ira, vii, 163, **210–11,** 283–84, 330, 907, **984,** 993
Gershwin, Leonore "Lee," 283–84
Gest, Morris, 51
"Getting to Know You," 564, 576, 657
Giacosa, Giuseppe, 258
Gibbons, Helen Davenport, 175
Gibbs, Wolcott, **487**
Gielgud, John, 69
Gilbert and Sullivan, 154, 159–62, 249, 535, 578
Gilbert, L. Wolfe, 630–31
Gilbert, Patricia, Esther, **805**
Gilliland, Helen, 71
Gilmore, Max E., 246, 247
Girton, Tom, **194**
Give Us This Night, 93–94
Givot, George, 491

Gladstone, Peter, **232**
Glaenzer, Jules, 302, 303, 397
Glass Menagerie, The, 509
Glatterman, Anne, 113, **279,** 364, 661, 666, **992**
Gleeson, Helen, 252
Glenmore Productions, Inc., 429
Glenville, Peter, 587
Glorious Morning, 163
"Go in and out the Window," 42
Godfrey, Arthur, 679, **680**
Goldberg, Harold, **783**
Goldberg, Rube, 87
Golden Bells, 86, 165, *See also Marco Polo*
Golden Dawn, 36, 227
Goldman, Robert S., 701, **702**
Goldsmith, Sam and Rae, 524
Goldstein, Jennie, 756
Goldstone, Nat, 218, 261
Goldwyn Follies, 139
Gone with the Wind, 142–43, 494, 716, 953
Good Companions, 68
"Good Girl," 243
Good News, 52
Good-bye Again, 91
"Goodbye Mama (I'm Off to Yokohama)," 225
Goodman, Benny, 366
Goodman, Jack, **359–60, 589**
Gordon, Hayes, **998**
Gordon, Max, 56, 60, 74, 87, 88, 89, 91, **140–41,** 142, **144–45,** 149, **187, 188–89,** 190, 191, 192, **198–200,** 213, 214, 224, 235, 242, 254, **278,** 495, 496, 596, **756, 867–69,** 871, 873
Gorman, Eugene, **994–95**
Gothenburg City Theatre, 442
Gould, Morton, 329
Gow, James, 492–93
Grady, Hugh, 7, 19
Graham, June, 686–87
Granger, Lester, **256–57**
"Grant Avenue," 946, 1000
Gray, Dolores, 263–64, 352
Grayson, Kathryn, 236, 313, 329–30, 341, 343, 580
Great Waltz, The, 90, 146, 163
Green, Abel, **351,** 641, **864–65**
Green, Adolph, **323–24,** 514, 760

Green, Alan, **360**
Green, Johnny, 222, 832, 836
Green, Paul, 304
Green Grow the Lilacs, 259–60, 261, 262,
    265, 267, 268, 271, 275, 299, 303, 355.
    See also *Oklahoma!*
Green Mansions, 615, 627
Green Pastures, 244
Green Peach, The, 11, 12–18. See also *Song
    of the Flame*
Greene, Graham, 509
Greenwood, Charlotte, **260, 261**, 317, 787
Greer, John, **1017**
Gregord, Mr. and Mrs., 443
Gregory Duffy, Sister, **921–26, 960–64**,
    965, 966–67, **969–70, 999, 1102–13**,
    1021–22
Gregory, Pfc. D., **333–34**
Grimm, Brothers, 32
Grofé, Ferde, 260
Gropper, Milton, 825
Group Theatre, The, 134–35
Grünwald, Alfred, 65
Gueteray, Georges, 595
Guggenheim Memorial Foundation, John
    Simon, 913–14
Guiterman, Henry Rosenwald, 6
Gumm, Harold, 274
Guthrie, Woody, 259
Guys and Dolls, 507–08, 617, 723, 809
Gypsy, 950, 952

H.M.S. Pinafore, 159–60
Haas, Dolly, 138
Hackney, H. H., **344**
Hagedorn, Ivan H., **634**
Hagman, Larry, 661
Hall, Al, 139
Hall Johnson Negro Choir, 244
Hall, Juanita, 529–30, 882, 889
Hall, Natalie, 327
Halliday, Heller, 617, 642, 661
Halliday, Richard, 263, **265–66**, 475, 479,
    560, 599, **615–17, 629–30, 637, 641–
    42, 645–46**, 659–60, **691**, 894, 920,
    921–26, 949, **952, 953–54, 958–64**,
    966–67, 975, 1018
Hamilton, Arthur, 126
Hammer, Alvin, **323–4**

Hammerstein (Mathias), Alice
    (daughter), ix, 7, 55, 56, 58, 62, 77–78,
    81, 135, 156–57, 177, **181–82**, 193,
    233, 253, 278, 325, 366, 375, **409–10,
    419–23, 440–44**, 483, 626, 705, 821,
    861, 981, 1006
Hammerstein, Alice Nimmo (mother), 1
Hammerstein, Anna "Mousie" Nimmo
    (stepmother), 1, **2**, 136, 152, 178, 182
Hammerstein, Arthur (uncle), viii, xvi, 1,
    4, 5, **7–8**, *8*, 9, **18–20**, 23, 24, 51, **74**,
    147, 151, 156, **165–66**, 170, **192–93**,
    207–09, 227, **233–34, 284–85, 310**,
    312–13, 328–29, 345, **470–71, 504**,
    506, 512, 538, 559, 626, 652, 653–54,
    670, **678, 710, 734–35, 773–77, 783**,
    837, 838, 854
Hammerstein, Dorothy Blanchard
    (Jacobson) (second wife), ix, *20, 21*,
    22–35, 50, 56, 93, 114, 135, **177–79**,
    183, 193, 233, 276, 282, 325, 366, 370,
    374, *385*, 411, 421–22, **445–46, 506–
    07**, 560, 616, 627, **636**, 646, 668, 705,
    745, 821, 860–61, 903, **917**, 950, **953**,
    980, **999, 1016–23**
Hammerstein, Dorothy Dalton (Arthur's
    wife), 328, 653, 982
Hammerstein, Emma Swift (step-
    grandmother), **124–25**, 180, **391–93**
Hammerstein, Fedor, **63–65**
Hammerstein, Gustav, 171
Hammerstein, James "Jimmy" (son), 50,
    51, 135, 178, 182, 193, 233, 325, 366,
    385, 386, 400–01, 421, **457, 458**, 463,
    464, 479, 515, **518–19**, 668, 686–87,
    821, 860, 894, 915, 981, 1006
Hammerstein, Maggie Garland (daughter-
    in-law), 300–01, 339, **341**, 365, 371,
    372–73, 374, 375, 379, 383, 413
Hammerstein, Myra "Mike" Finn (first
    wife). ix, 1, **3**, 5, 6, 11, 19–20, 22, **53–
    63, 74–75, 77–78, 80, 81–85, 88**, 113,
    157–59, 177, **257–58, 287–88, 396–
    97, 472–73, 500–01**, 666, **954–55**
Hammerstein I, Oscar (grandfather), 1, 63,
    85, 289, 296, 345, 652–53
    plans for a biography or a biopic of: 156,
    170, 271, 350, 373, 393, 409–10, 626,
    653, 773–77

Hammerstein II, Oscar, *xxi*, 3, *20, 21, 307,*
386, 388, 455, 835, 874, 1023
ambitions of, 54, 734
giving advice, 38–40, 57–59, 62–63,
75–76, 155–58, 197, 228–29, 232,
244–45, 310–12, 351, 356, 359, 399,
405–08, 418, 449, 484, 486, 487–88,
490–91, 502, 503–04, 518–20, 536,
539, 554, 565–66, 583, 588–89, 605,
608–09, 621, 635–36, 640–41, 654–
55, 662–63, 664–65, 670–71, 680–81,
700, 702, 707–08, 714–21, 733,
737–38, 752–53, 802–03, 804, 863,
865–69, 877–78, 890, 955–56, 989,
991–92, 997, 1002–06
on audiences, 181, 205–07, 279, 430,
475, 482, 506, 538, 547, 582, 612–13,
701, 833, 980, 996–97, 1006
on birds, 476
feelings about changes in scripts or
direction, 194, 534–35, 647–48, 658, 711
on child-rearing/as a parent, 56–59,
62–63, 77–78, 81, 82–84, 155–58,
177–78, 181–82, 457, 458, 518–19
actively collaborating/on collaboration,
13–18, 90, 101, 104, 105, 106–08, 115–
16, 117–19, 131–34, 136–37, 138, 149–
50, 166–69, 227, 230–31, 239, 314–17,
327, 347–48, 368, 405–08, 555–58, 746,
837–38, 869–75, 964–65
congratulations from, 199, 430, 550,
605, 612–13, 700, 843, 859–60, 899–
900, 941–42, 967–68
on country music, 912–13
on critics, 181, 196–97, 205–07, 396–97,
401, 430, 487, 489, 547, 672–73, 699–
700, 701, 980, 1006
death of and letters of condolence,
1018–23
defensiveness of, 41–43, 258, 303–04,
351, 449, 487, 614, 706, 939–40, 941,
957, 993, 997–98
education, definition of, 814
on economics and financial policy,
394–96
finances of, 54–55, 57, 74–75, 77–78,
87, 88, 91, 92, 113, 146, 165, 239, 255,

269–71, 279, 287–88, 296–97, 325,
343, 393, 584–85, 894
fear of flying, 62
health of, 326, 340, 341, 821, 940, 941–42,
970–71, 995, 999, 1006, 1014, 1017
on honesty to the public, 984–85
on investing in shows, 497, 643–44, 710,
915
on importance of learning Latin, 948
on saving his letters, 217
on literature as source material for
shows, 915–16
love letters by, 22–35, 636, 745, 917, 950
on lyrics, 398–99, 469, 483–84, 489, 559,
605, 764–65, 817–18, 823, 854, 859,
869–70, 873, 889, 904–05, 926, 984, 993
on music, 43, 918
on being over-extended, 323, 326, 328,
360, 485–86, 721–22
on poetry, 358, 914
on political and social issues, 317–19,
182, 376–77, 543–44, 559, 561–62,
624–25, 634, 663, 666–67, 668–69,
680, 697–98, 708–09, 716, 735–37,
741–42, 744–45, 770–72, 784–85,
797–98, 800–02, 803–04, 805, 824,
863–64, 914–15, 918–19, 928–30,
973–74, 1010, 1013
on being powerful, 948–49, 991
research for plays and musicals by,
12, 17, 43, 67–74, 136–37, 398, 545,
596–97, 930
resentments of, 242, 939–40, 957
reporting on Scandinavian trip,
440–45
on what makes a good song, 836–37
thanks, letters of, 3–4, 6, 139, 335–
36, 410, 462, 467, 468, 480, 487,
505, 519, 523, 524, 541, 542, 560,
589, 610–11, 618, 674–75, 690,
728, 731–32, 814, 857, 877, 886,
899–900, 984, 990
desire to write a great war song, 200–01,
225–26, 233–34, 859–60, 875–76
on writing, 43, 559, 605, 676, 678, 685,
690, 695–96, 764–65, 804, 821, 844,
889

Hammerstein, Reggie (brother), 1, 65, 69, 135, **143–44**, **145**, **146**, **150**, **152**, 178, 181, 193, 225, 233, 277, **325**, **327–29**, **333**, **337**, 375, 459, 506, 514, 600, 668, 821, 861, 940

Hammerstein, Stella (aunt), **288–89**, **295–96**

Hammerstein, William (father), 1, 4, 296, 471

Hammerstein, William "Bill/Billy" (son), ix, 5, 6, 55, 58–59, 62–63, 77–78, 82–84, 135, **154–57**, 157–58, 177, 193, 225, 232, 233, 276, 277, **280–81**, **298–99**, 300, 325, 329, 345, 365, **371–77**, 379, **380–84**, *386*, **411–14**, 420, 476, 501, 514, 626, 627, 668, 686, 711, 740, 821, **858–59**, 861, 981, 1006

Hammerstein's Theatre, 345–46, 774

Hampton, Hope, 10, 11

Handy, W. C., 226–27

Hanemann, Jodie, **890–91**

Hanley, Ellen, 952

"Happiness is a Thing Called Joe," 380

Happy Birthday, 415–17, 423, 424–25, 428, 430, 431

"Happy Talk," 464, 895, 898

Happy Time, The, 483, 484, 502, 504, 506, 507, 508, 514, 538, 561

Harbach, Otto, xi, 4, **7–8**, **9–18**, 19, **38–41**, *41*, **75–76**, 79, 90, 135, **136–37**, 139, **149–50**, 153, 165, 212, 213, 217, 227, 231, 246, 250, **310–12**, 346, 537, 631, 632, 853, **859–60**, 994

Harburg, E. Y. "Yip," 163, 291, **469**

Harmon, Glen, 905, **906–07**

Harrington, Pat, 867–69

Harrison, Rex, 510, 761–62

Hart, Lorenz, vii, 88, 126, 184, 185, 187, 259, 260, 299–300, 329, 537, 714, 993

Hart, Moss, 36, 127, 140, 222, 667, **714–21**, **967–68**

Hartman, Melville D., **783**, 784

Haskall, Jack, 10, 143

Hayes, Helen, **196–97**, 415, 417, 424, 428, 430, 478, 502, 586, 759

Hayfoot, Strawfoot, xi, 136, 217, 264, 310–12

Haymes, Dick, 342, 407

Hayward, Leland, **450–52**, **458**, 459, 471, **481**, 532, **551–53**, 596, 640, 660, 757, 758, **787–91**, 920, 949, **952**, 974–75, 1016

Hayworth, Rita, 284

Hazel Flagg, 685

Hazlitt, Henry, 395

Healy, Dan, 143

Hearst, William Randolph, 283–84

Heart of a City, 192

Heart of the Matter, The, 502, 508, 512, 514, 539, 825

Hecht, Ben, **205–07**, 446–47

Heggen, Thomas, 477

Helburn, Theresa, 259, 260, **291–95**, **314–17**, **326–27**, **330**, **361–63**, **408–09**, **418–19**, **621**, **670**

Heller, Anatole, 738

Hellman, Lillian, **323**

"Hello, Young Lovers," 563, 564, 569, 574, 576, 664, 683, 763, 941

Henderson, Florence, 710

Henderson, Ray, 47

Henrey, Bobby, 484

Hepburn, Audrey, 679

Herbert, Miles, 602

Hersey, John, **640–41**

Herzig, Sig, 163, **279**, 282, **1019–20**

Heyward, Dorothy, 259

Heyward, DuBose, 210, 259

High, Wide, and Handsome, 126–27, 134, 524

Highland Farm, x, 183, *184*, 191, 233, 261, 276, 344, 363–64, 379, 402–05, 717, 727

Hilliam, B. B., 71

Hines, Fred, 899

Hinkel, Cecil E., **584–85**

Hirschfeld, Al, 138

Hitler, Adolph, 152, 201, 227, 383

Hobson, Valerie, 765, **766–69**

Hoffman, Irving, 492

Hoffman, Julius, **938**

Hoffmannstahl, Hugo von, 258

Holden, William, 819

Holiday, 988

Holland, Charles, 254

Holliday, Judy (Tuvim), **323–24**, 325, **369–70**
Hollywood, 36–40, 55, 74–75, 77–78, 80, 81, 84–85, 87, 88, 89–121, 126–27, 135, 139, 145, 146, 147–48, 163, 165–66, 168–69, 186, 208, 218–20, 221, 234–36, 269–71, 278, 283–84, 305, 313, 320–25, 329–30, 331–32, 337, 393, 405–08, 410, 417–18, 493–94, 580, 604, 627, 653, 686, 712–14, 716, 717, 724, 753, 755–56, 760, 761–64, 769, 772–73, 778–82, 787–91, 807–11, 815–21, 827–28, 829–34, 837–38, 841–42, 843–44, 847, 855–57, 881–83, 884–89, 891–92, 893–99, 908–09, 919, 927, 931–32, 1001, 1014–15
Hollywood Anti-Nazi League, ix, 123, 149, 290–91, 299–300
Hollywood Bowl Opera Association, 194
Holm, Celeste, *280*
Holman, Russel, **94–95**
Holmes, Teddy, 895, 935, 936
Holstein, Marc, **390–91**
Holtzmann, Fanny, 497, 638
Home Front, The. *See* World War II
Home, James, 1, 4, 184
"Honey Bun," 541, 896
Hope, Constance, **685**
Hopkins, Arthur, 51
Hornblow, Jr., Arthur, 781, 788, 829, **830–34**
Horne, Lena, 291, 339, *345*, 614
Horton, Edward Everett, 522
House Un-American Activities Committee (HUAC), 123, 991
How Green Was My Valley, 267
Hughes, Alice, **1011–12**
Hughes, Elinor, 463
Hughes, Langston, 431, 858–59
Humphrey, Hubert, 973
"Hundred Million Miracles, A," 987
Hunter's Moon, 891
Hurley, Doran, 846
Hurt, Jr., Paul T., **619**
Huttner, Matthew, 471, **472**
Hyman, Bernie (Ben), 177
Hyman, Harold, 420–21, 462, **470**, 485–86, **586, 601, 753–54**

"I Am So Eager," 215
"I Cain't Say No," xiii
"I Enjoy Being a Girl," xiii
"I Hear Music," 216, 217
I Remember Mama, viii, 363, 365, 366–68, 378, 379, 389–90, 431
"I Was Born Under a Wand'rin' Star," 616
"I Whistle a Happy Tune, 569, 682, 763
"I Wish Dad Dere Wasn't No War," xii
"I Won't Dance," 67, 212
"If I Loved You," 563
"If I Weren't King," 935
Illica, Luigi, 258
"I'm Gonna Wash That Man Right Outa My Hair," 531, 896, 899
"I'm One of God's Children (Who Hasn't Got Wings)," 41
Impellitteri, Vincent, 712
Imperial Palace, 94
"Impossible," 875
"In Egern on the Tegern See," 216
"Indian Love Call," 9, 115, 853, 954–55
Information Please, 258–59
Inge, William, 505
Ingram, Rex, 291
Institute for International Order, The, 746
integrated housing. *See* segregated housing
"Intermission Talk," 702, 703
"Is it Really YOUR Hit Parade" (article), 905
Israels, Josef, **334–36**
"It Ain't Necessarily So," 210
"It's a Grand Night for Singing," 407, 408
"It's Me," 702

Jacobs, Morrie, 427, 456
Jacobson, Henry (Dorothy Hammerstein's first husband), 22, 33
Jacobson, Henry Blanchard (stepson), x, 22, 135, 178, 182, **297–98**, 366, 375, 379, *386*, 514, 521, 627, 668, 821, 861, 981, 1006
Jane, 621
Janis, Elsie, 243
Janssen, Werner, 246
Japan, 738–40
J.B., 977
Jessel, George, 973

Joe Palooka (comic strip), 400
John, Graham, 879
John 2:10, 11, 612, 634
John Loves Mary, viii, 431
Johnny Was a Lady, 228–29
Johnson, Hall, **244–45**
Johnson, Robert J., **918**
Jones, Allan, 108, 111, 189
Jones, Shirley, 787, 809, 810, 811, 833
Jonssen, Axel, 442
Jotham Valley, 622
Jubilee, 140
Julius Caesar, 135
Jumbo, 415, 416, 417
"June is Bustin' Out All Over," 397–98, 818
Junior Miss, 242, 276
Just for Laughs, 519–21. *See also Top*
    Banana

Kadish, Ben, 888
Kadison, Milton, 5, **394–96**, 607, **862**
Kadison, Philip, **687–88**
Kahn, Otto, 14
Kálmán, Emmerich, 227, **228–29**
Kalmar, Bert, 240
Kaplan, R., **692**
Kapp, Dave, 985
Karamu House/Karamu Theatre, 811–12,
    973
Karloff, Boris, 170
Katja the Dancer, 11
Katz, Sam, 88, 89, 90, 221, 429
Kaufman, George S., 36, 127, 134, **202–03**,
    204, 221–22, 225
Kean, Ben, 1014, **1022–23**
Keith-Johnston, Colin, 558
Kelly, Gene, 236, 284, 336
Kelly, Patsy, 103–04
Kennedy, Foster, 420–21
Kenney, Ed, 949
Kenyon, Nancy, 237, 247
Kern (Shaw), Betty, 282, 299, 420–21
Kern (Byron), Eva, **50**, 93, 128, 282, 420,
    420–21, 577, **580**, **642–43**
Kern, Jerome, xi, xiv, 7, 21, 25, 30, 34, 36,
    45–46, 47, **50–51**, 56, 60, 66, 74, 76,
    79, **80–81**, 86, 89–90, 91, **92–93**, 96,
    103, 104, 105, 106, 107, 113, 127–28,

132–33, 134, 135, 136, 139, 141, 151,
    153, 163, **164–65**, **166–69**, *167*, 170,
    177, **179**, 180, 183, 190, **200–01**,
    208, 209, **211–20**, 223, 227, **229–31**,
    234–39, 242, **243–44**, **246–47**, 248–
    51, 253, **263–65**, 271, **282–83**, 284,
    285–86, 302, **338–39**, **346–48**, 349,
    355–56, 365, **368**, **370**, 373, 390–91,
    417, 489, 601, 642–43, 714, 853–54,
    877, 907
  death of, 418–23
Kerr, Deborah, 807, 811, 856
Kerr, John, 882, 908
King, Dennis, 71, 578, 600
King, Henry, 810
King and I, The, xiii, 429, 497, 502, 509–10,
    511, 513–14, 543, 544, 546, 551–58,
    562–64, 567–80, 581–82, 585–86,
    607, 610, 617, 620, 637, 638–39, 681–
    84, 692–95, 703, 704, 731, 734–35,
    738, 742, 782–83, 791, 802, 825, 932,
    939–40, 1008, 1009–10
King and I, The (film), 604, 712, 713,
    762–64, 778–80, 810, 811, 837–38,
    855–56, 873, 888
King and I, The (London), 600, 619, 691,
    726, 731, 735, 766–69, 778, 803, 844
Kirk, Lisa, 585
Kismet, 211, 729–30, 735
Kiss Me Kate, 475
"Kiss to Build a Dream On, A," 240, 494–95,
    632–33, 968
Kitchen, Robert, **1013**
Kiwanis Club, West Palm Beach, **670–71**,
    678
Knapp, Marion, **135–36**, 955, **980–82**,
    1006–07
Knapp, Walter, **135–36**, **625–27**, **860–61**,
    955, **980–82**, **1006–07**
Knight, Esmond, 69
Knights of Song, 154, 159–62, 163, 165
Knopf, Blanche, 794
Knopf, Edwin H., **123**
Knopf, Mildred, **509–10**
Koenig, Bill, 37, 38
Koff, Raymond, 926, **927**
Kohler, Fred, 111
Komroff, Manuel, 50

Korda, Alexander, 117
Korngold. Erich, 86, 93–94
Kraft, Hy, 134–35, 149, 227, 338, 343, 354–55,
    496, 514–15, 519–20, 666–67, 685–86,
    690, 700–01, 723, 884, 892–93, 50–51
Kraft, Rita, 690
Kramer, Walter, 352
Krasna, Norman, 540
Kretzmer, Herbert, 634–35
Kristen, Erik, 453
Krohn, William, 420
Kronenberger, Louis, 862
Krupska, Dania, 949–50
Kruse, Barbara, 989
Kurnitz, Harry, 652–53

Lady Be Good, 183
Lady in the Dark, 211
Lady Objects, The, 138, 163
Laemmle, Carl, 92
Laemmle, Jr., Carl, 92, 93, 97–99, 103–5
La Farge, Christopher, 804
Lahr, Bert, 366
Lamarr, Heddy, 548–49
Lamour, Dorothy, 278
Lamport, Felicia, 662–63
"Land of Good Time, The," 137
Landis, Jessie Royce, 327
Landon, Bert, 664–65
Landon, Margaret, 510, 562
Lang, Joseph, 995–97
Lang, Walter, 365, 764
Langner, Lawrence, 259, 291–95, 326–27,
    337, 361, 362–63, 408–09, 425–26,
    453, 505, 641, 704–05
Lantz, Robert, 548–49
Larnen, Brendan, 926
Larsen, Sven Aage, 453163

"Last Time I Saw Paris, The," vii, xii, 183,
    191, 200, 220
Latouche, John, 301–02
Laun, Elna, 550
Lawrence, Gertrude, 65, 148, 329, 497,
    507, 510, 513–14, 553, 556, 564, 568,
    569, 570, 572–73, 576–77, 579, 581,
    585–86, 600, 617, 621, 638–39, 657–
    58, 681, 681, 940

Laye, Evelyn, 29, 43–44, 46, 135, 600, 942
Layton, Joe, 952
League of New York Theatres, 110–13
Lebaron, William, 94
Lederer, Charles, 729
Lee, C. Y (Chin Yang), 897, 930–31, 945,
    946
Lee, J., 750
Lehman, Ernest, 764
Leinsdorf, Erich, 246, 606–07, 862
Le Maire, Rufus, 147
Lenahan, Henry, 366–68
Lerner, Alan Jay, 36, 515–16, 585, 616, 641,
    846, 848
LeRoy, Mervyn, 146
Lester, Edwin, 164, 169–70, 210–11, 212,
    215, 217, 219, 223, 230, 237, 239,
    243–44, 355, 729, 893
"Let's Quite Pretending" (article), 317–19
"Let's Say Good-Night," 26
Levien, Sonya, 984
Levin, Herman, 490–91, 502–03, 538–39
Levittown, 697–98
Levy, Hal, 760–61
Levy, Newman, 939
Lewis, Al, 418
Lewis, Lloyd, 142–43, 162
Lexington Theatre, 775
Libedinsky, Yuri, 17
Library of Congress, xv, xx
Lieberson, Goddard, 471, 912, 1000
Life (magazine), 343, 346
"Life's Full of Consequence," 380
"Light in the Piazza, The," 1013
L'il Abner, 599
Lilac Time, 71
Liliom, 314–17, 326–27, 338, 341, 356,
    361–63, 365, 369, 374, 376, 379,
    387–88, 389, 390, 397, 446. See also
    Carousel
Lillie, Bea, 148, 366, 375, 506–07, 667
Lily of the Valley, 205–07
Lincoln, Abraham, 649, 650–51
Lindsay, Dorothy, see Stickney, Dorothy
Lindsay, Howard, 222, 488, 489, 926, 958–
    65, 968, 988, 990
Little Prince, The, 548
Littler, Prince, 618–19, 765–66, 768, 975

Liverights Book Store, **114**
Lockhart, Gene, 355–56
Lockridge, Richard, 181
Loeb, G. M., **397–98, 516–17**
Loesser, Frank, 508, 828, 848, 907
Loewe, Frederick, 515–16, 585, 641
Logan, Josh, xv, 430, 431, **432–39, 451–52,**
    454–55, *455*, **459,** 471, **475–76, 477–**
    79, 481–84, 500, 526–36, 562–64,
    587, 597, 599, 607, **608–09,** 621,
    659–61, 725–27, 733–34, 757–60,
    795–97, 811–12, 818–21, 825–27,
    833, **838–41, 847–48, 850–51,** 870,
    881–83, 886–87, 887–89, 892, 893,
    896, **897–99, 900–04, 908–09, 931–**
    33, 939, 951, **953, 1015–17**
Logan, Nedda, **733–34**
Löhner-Beda, Fritz, 65
Lom, Herbert, 619, 768, **802–03**
London theatre. *See* West End
"Lonely Feet," 67
Long, Avon, 210
Loos, Anita, 415, 416, 423, 425, 430
Loring, Charles, 286
Los Angeles Civic Light Opera, 164, 211,
    223, 244
"Lost Chord, The," 161
Lost Paradise, The, 794
Louise, 86, 258
Love Affair, 615, 854–55
"Love Look Away," 985, 1000
Love Me Tonight, 126
Love Song (early title for *The Sound of*
    Music), 947
Luce, Clare Boothe, **511**
Lukas, Paul, 550, 577
Lund, Sidney C., **803–04**
Lynch, Shwawen, 379, 427
Lyon, Al, 474
Lyons, Arthur, 248, 264
Lyrics on Several Occasions, 984

MacArthur, Douglas, **797–802**, 805
Macauley, Richard, 168
MacClintock, 91
MacDonald, Jeanette, 81, 88, 89, 115, 168,
    183, **348–50,** 685
MacGowan, Jack, 234–35

MacGregor, Frank S., **706**
Mack, Charles, 310
Mackay, Mr. & Mrs. Clarence, 29–30, 776
Mackaye, Dorothy, 17
MacLeish, Archibald,
MacMurray, Fred, 278
MacRae, Gordon, 787, 808, 811, 833
Madama Butterfly, 86, 465, 466
Maggie, 668, 685–87
Magic Flute, The, 793–94
Mahoney, Francis X., *49*, 98
"Make Believe," xi, 117, 119, 285, 895
"Make Way for Tomorrow," 286
Malmberg, Sven, 441
Mama's Bank Account, 363. *See also I*
    Remember Mama
Mamoulian, Azadea, **410**
Mamoulian, Rouben, xv, **126–27,** *280*, 291,
    292–95, 309, **410, 423–25,** 430
Mandel, Frank, 24, 29, 46, 47, 49, 52, 54,
    108, **308,** 537, 853–54
Mandelstam, Abraham, **394**
Manges, Horace, 288
Mankiewicz, Herman, 4, 283–84
Mann, Thomas, 149
Manning, Gordon, **612**
Manning, Hope, 150
Mannix, Eddie, 88, 89, 230
"Many a New Day," 335
March, Frederick, 111
"March of the Siamese Children," 940
Marco Polo, 86, 91, 114, 338, 339, 347–48.
    See also Golden Bells; Messer Marco
    Polo
Marco's Millions, 348
Mardi Gras, 188
Marfield, Dwight, **356–58**
Margetson, Arthur, 66
Margulies, Irwin, 603
"Maria," 961, 965
Mariners, The, 679–80
"Marines Hymn," 234
Mariza, 10–11, 12
Markel, Lester, 542, **543, 909–12**
Married from Home, 511
"Marseillaise, La," 226
Marseilles trilogy, 659–60
Marsh, Howard, *48*, 50, 247, 252

Marsh, Vera, 110
Martin, Ernest, **507–08**, 894, 903
Martin (Halliday), Mary, 36, 238, 263, 264, 265–66, 285, 290, 329, **351**, 467, 473, *473*, 475, 478, 479, 482, **519**, 526–29, 531, **541**, **560**, 586, **590–93**, 599, **600**, **615–17**, 618, 628, **629–30**, **637**, 645, 654, 659–61, **677–78**, **691**, 758–60, 894, 920, **921–26**, 932, 942, 949, 950, **953–54**, 995–96, 2014
Marx, Groucho, 495
Marx Brothers, 240
Mary Poppins, 507, 706
Massey, Ilona, 595
Matheson, Murray, **674**
Mathias, Phil, 861, 981, 1006
Matsoukas, Nicholas, **780–82**, **829–30**
May Wine, 108, 114
Mayer, Louis B., 80, 88, 89–90, 190, 230, 253, 270, 271, 275, 285, 290, **541–42**, 653
Maytime, 90, 167
McCarey, Leo, 627, **854–55**
McCarthy, Frank, **815–17**
McCarthy, Joseph, 663
McClintic, Guthrie, 522
McCormick, Myron, 482, 530, 621
McCormick, Robert R., 226, 317, 318
McDaniel, Hattie, 109
McDermott, William F., **695–96**
McGowan, Alec, **991**
McGuire, Bill, 26
McLeod, Mr. (NBC), **51–53**
McMahon, Eleanor, **764–65**
McWatters, Miss, 327
McWhorter, Thomas, **464–66**
Me and Juliet, 637, 646, 666, 674, 677–78, 685, 690, 695–96, 697–98, 699–700, 701, 702, 703, 731, 735, 795, 935–37, 938, 957
Meador, George, 327
Medium, The, 811
Meet Me in St. Louis, 290, 331–33
Mellen, Bill, 32–33
Mendelssohn, Felix, 358
Mence, Len, 150, **151–52**, **266–67**, 582, **968**
Menzies, Robert, 641

Mercer, Frances, 247
Mercer, Johnny, 163, 520–21
Mercury Theatre Group, The, 135
Merman, Ethel, 276, 429, 531, 550, 849
Merrick, David, 659–60, 760
Merry Widow, The, 10, 266
Merson, Billy, 9
Mescal, John, 112
Messenger, The, 396
Messer Marco Polo, 86, 87, 88. *See also Marco Polo*
Mestayer, Harry, 151, **499**
Metropolitan Opera, 273, 349–50
Mexican Hayride, 330, 591
Meyer, Alice, **566–67**
Meyer, David L., **456–57**
Meyer, George, 969
MGM, 56, 75–76, 87, 88, 89–90, 145, 146, 147, 183, 208, 218, 220, 221, 230, 235, 245, 247, 248, 270, 275, 286, 329, 331–32, 383, 417, 418, 494, 541–42, 580, 590, 627, 632, 716, 756, 894
Michael, Mrs. M. Brookfield, **558**
Michener, James, ix, 450, 463, **467**, 529, **596–97**, 637, 738, **739–40**
Middle of the Night, 847
Middleton, Ray, 526–28
Mielziner, Jo, 430, **468**, **508–09**, **545–46**
Mike Wallace Interview, The, 928–29
Miles, Barbara, **702–04**
Milestones, 167
Milford, Bob, 496
Miller, Alice Duer, 162–63, **163**
Miller, Gilbert, 459
Milstein, David, 696
Milton, Francis S., **468–69**
Mink on Weekdays, 662
Minnelli, Vincente, 290, 291, 333
Minter, Louis B., **928–30**
Miranda, Carmen, 194–95
Miss Liberty, 491–92
"Mist is Over the Moon, A," 163
Mister Roberts, 450, 476, 477, 532, 668, 787, 790, 819
Mitchell, Don L., **814**
Mitchell, John F. B., **1018**
Mitchell, Ruth, **544**, 681
Mizner, Wilson and Addison, 708

Moe, Henry Allen, **913–14**
Moen, Peter, 276, **363–64**, 366, 398, **402–05**
Moen, Walter, 363, 938
Mok, Mike, 493, 591, 645
Molloy, J. Carroll, **203–04**
Molnár, Ferenc, 314, **387**
Monsignor, 846–47
Monroe, Marilyn, 847
Montgomery, Elizabeth Rider, **853–54**
"Moonlight on the Meadow," 494
Moore, Douglas, 633
Moore, John, **198**
Mora, Helena, 263
Moral Re-Armament, 622
Moran, George, 310
Morehouse, Ward, **940**
Moreno, Rita, 811
Morgan, Frank, 266
Morgan, Helen, *49*, 57, 103, 128, 181, 218,
     246, 252
Morgenthau, Jr., Henry, 236, 275
Morner, Stanley, 164
Morris, Hannah, **786–87**
Morris, Newbold, **784–5**
Morris, William, **497**
Morrison, Patricia, 742
Morrow, Doretta, 569, 570
Moscowitz, Joe, 761
Mosely, Lois, 246
Moscowitz, Joe, 427, 429, 896
Moskowitz, Warren, **741–42**
Most Happy Fella, The, 847–48, 849
Mosty, Donald, **513**
Motion Picture Association. . . Production
     Code Admin., 815–17
Motley Group, The, 69
Mozart, Amadeus, 793–94
Mr. Arcularis, **635–36**
Muni, Paul, 410
Muny, The. *See* St. Louis Municipal Opera
     Theatre
Murfin, Jane, 138–39
Murrow, Edward R., **863–64**
music circuses, 858
"Music Goes Round and Round," 131
Music in the Air, viii, xiii, 60, 61, 66, 81,
     165, 211–12, 214–17, 219, 223, 230,
     237, 239, 243, 577–78, 600, 705, 711

Music War Committee, ix, 277
My Darlin' Aida, 667
My Fair Lady, 323, 429, 448, 585, 762, 847–
     48, 861, 880–81, 893
"My Favorite Things," 985, 992
"My Lord and Master," 563, 569, 764
My Sister Eileen, 242, 267, 276, 685

NAACP, ix, 613, 614, 617, 623, 665, 680
Namouna, 802–03
Napier, Alan, 556
Nash, Ogden, 351
Nathan, George Jean, 330
National Institute of Arts and Letters, 502,
     633
National Urban League, 254–57
Naughty Marietta, 102, 111
Nazism, 63
NBC Opera Theatre, 793
NBC, 51
Neuser, Gladys R., **605–06**
New Dramatists, 655
New Era Living,
New Moon, The, 29, 36, 47, 53, 88, 183,
     242, 485
New Orleans, 187, 188, 195
New York Shakespeare Festival, 919
New York War Fund, 360
Newberry, Barbara, 73–74
Newman, Alfred, 887, 888, 892, 919
Nigh, George P., **676–78**
"Night and Day," 73
Night Watch, The (painting), 890
Nimitz, Admiral Chester W., 371
Nixon, Richard, 951
"No Other Love," 697
"Nobody Else But Me," 690–91
Nordheimer, Alice, **171–73**
Norton, Elliot, 506, **976–77**, **989–90**
Notes on Lyrics,
Novak, Kim, 819
Novarro, Ramon, 80
Novello, Ivor, 69
"Now You Leave," 571
Nun's Story, The, 967
Nuyen, France, 908
Nye, Gerald, 317, 318
Nymph Errant, 65

Oakland, Ben, 138
O'Brien, Brian, 789, 834, *835*
Of All Things, 503–04
Of Mice and Men, 828–29
Of Thee I Sing, 339
Offenbach, Jacques, 743
Oh, Boy!, 231
"Oh, What a Beautiful Mornin," 282, 335,
    664, 831, 832, 833, 854
O'Keefe, Walter, 207, 208
Oklahoma!, xi, xii, xiii, 22, 88, 126, 259–61,
    268, 271, 277, 278–82, 284, 291–95,
    297, 299, 301–04, 309, 312–13, 320–
    23, 330, 339, 341, 350, 355, 363, 365,
    379, 394, 400, 408–09, 429, 445, 449,
    452–54, 488, 493, 524, 709–10, 712,
    714, 787, 802–03, 809, 828, 889, 938,
    949–50, 975–76, 979–80, 1020. *See
    also Green Grow the Lilacs*
  box social scene/custom, 302–04
  cast recording, 333, 334–36
  national tour, 305–06, 309, 337, 370,
    379, 610, 731
"Oklahoma," 400, 676–77, 696–97, 834
Oklahoma! (film), viii, 320–23, 493–94,
    496, 709–10, 712, 713–14, 717, 731,
    744, 747–48, 753, 754, 755–56, 757,
    760, 769, 772–73, 778, 780–82, 787–
    88, 790, 809, 827–28, 829–34, 843–
    44, 855, 856–57
Oklahoma! (London, and Europe), 9, 408–
    09, 514, 597–99
Oklahoma! (Yiddish translation), 550
Oklahoma, relations with the state of, 676–
    77, 696–97, 769, 780
"Ol' Man River," xi, xiii, 97, 119, 129–31,
    251, 480, 496, 954–55
Oldham, Derek, 71
Oliver, Edna May, 49, 99, **100**, 105, 109,
    164, 218, 246, 249
Ollsen, Olaf, 619
Olman, Abe, 495
Olympia Theatre, New York, 776
Olympics in Melbourne, 1956 Summer,
    869, 872
On the Town, 325, 376
On Your Way, 1
"One Foot, Other Foot," 438, 439

One Night of Love, 138
One Touch of Venus, 290
O'Neill, Eugene, 259, 348
opera, 85–86, 258, 337, 348–50, 535, 607,
    685, 740–41, 743, 774–76, 793–94,
    828–29
Oppenheimer, George, 571
Orpheous, 862
Orsatti, Frank, 190, 191, 218–19, 235, **253**,
    254, 270, **299–300**
Osborn, Paul, 640–41, 870, 883
Othello, 340, 385–87
"Our Heroine" (story), 463
Our Show Boat, 128
Our Town, 329
Out of This World, 514
OWI (United States Office of War
    Information), 276

Pagliacci, 86
Pagnol, Marcel, 659–61
Paint Your Wagon, 611, 616
Pajama Game, The, 730
Pal Joey, 314, 616
Panama Hattie, 213, 234
Papp, Joseph, 919
Paramount Pictures (Studio), 94, 686
Pargellis, Stanley, **668–69**
Paris Legend, 892–93
Paris on Broadway, 138
Parker, Dorothy (Mrs. Alan Campbell), 203
Parodneck, Carol, **671–73**
Parsons, Louella, 262, 265
Parvati; A Romance of Present Day India, 175
Pascal, Gabriel, 585, **602–03**, 641
Passionate Men, The, 794–95
Pasternak, Joe, 220
"Patrol, The," 564
Patterson, D. C., **350**
Patterson, Elisabeth, 105
Paul, Eva, 298–99
Peace Pirate, 1
Peardon, Patricia, 326
Pearl Harbor, 196, 198, 225, 317
Pearl, Jack, 151
Peck, Gregory, 105, 252
Peinzmetal, I. H.,
"People Will Say We're in Love," 334, 834

Perfect, Jack, **889, 955**
Perlberg, William, **138–39, 313, 329–30,**
    336, 341–43, 405–08
Peskin, Dean B., **948–49**
Peter, John, **708–09**
Peter Pan, 527, 758–60, 894
Peterson, Furniss T., 351
Pethers, Joan, 1000
Philpott, G. M., 454
Phinney's Rainbow, 446
Pi Lambda Pi, 6
Picnic (film), 818–20
Pidgeon, Walter, 105
Pierce, Alice, 491
ping-pong, 440–41
Pins and Needles, 135
Pinza, Ezio, 464, 467, 472, *473*, 475, 478,
    502, 526–27, 586, 590, 613, 691, 757,
    759, 893, 942
Pipe Dream, 718, 722, 731, 746–47, 749,
    754, 778, 790, 792–93, 795–97, 813–
    14, 819, 820–21, 822, 825–26, 834,
    836, 838–41, 855, 895, 935–37, 939,
    998
Pollak, Robert, **337**
"Poor Jud is Daid," 760
Pope, Jeremy, **955–56**
Pope, MacQueen, 599
Poppy Girl, The, 7–8
Porgy and Bess, 126, 208, 209–11, 214, 247,
    259, 273, 274, 304, 308, 335, 700
Porgy, 259
Porter, Cole, vii, 140, 265, 483, 514
Potash, Shirley, **447–48**, 457, **471**, 479,
    481, 523, 535, 857
Powell, Eleanor, 236
Powers, Marie, 758
Preminger, Otto, 393, 410, **724**, 811
"Prince is Giving A Ball, The," 869
Princess Theatre shows, 853, 877
Prinzmetal, I. H., **792–93**
product placement, 474–75
Prude, Walter, 290
Puccini, Giacomo, 86, 258
Puck, Eva, *49*, 248, 251
Pulitzer Prize, 339–40, 341, 524
"Puzzlement, A," xiii, 557, 563, 568, 569,
    683, 763, 782–83

Pygmalion, 585, 602–03, 641, 893

Queen Christina, 175–76
Queen o' Hearts, 191

race and racism, 142–43, 254–56, 300–01,
    331, 383, 460–61, 466, 480, 587, 613–
    14, 617, 623, 626, 634–35, 640, 665,
    680, 688–89, 697–98, 705, 735–37,
    770–72, 783–85, 824, 942
radio, 51–52, 60, 359–60, 864–65, 905–07,
    909–12, 946, 984–85
Rahn, Muriel, 724
Rain, 262, 265, 308
Rainbow, 36, 268
Rainer, Luise, **396**
Rainger, Ralph, 163
Raitt, John, 337
Ralph, Jessie, 109
Randall, Carl, 73–74
Rape of Lucretia, The, 453
Rapf, Harry, 80
Raphaelson, Joel, **463–64**
Rasely, George, 327
Rathbone, Basil, **577**, 577–78
Rathbone, Ouida, 241
recordings, 319, 333, 334–36, 471, 475,
    483, 619, 905–07, 909–12, 985, 1000
Red Wagon, 68
Redell, Walter, 427
Redell family, 366
Reed, Napoleon, 271, **272**
Reeves, Theodore, 615
Reinhardt, Max, 151
Reinheimer, Howard, viii, ix, 22, 23, **36–**
    38, 55, 56, 60, 75, 79, **86–87, 89–92**,
    96, **113–14, 129–31**, 140, **141–42**,
    153–54, 214, 219, 230, 239, 243, 244,
    250, 271, 288, **296–97**, 354, 355, 365,
    425–29, 449–50, 453, 455, **458**, 459,
    493, 505, **536–38, 602**, 603, **640**, 642,
    666, 712–15, 716, 725, 738–40, 761,
    822, **947, 974–75**, 987, 1001
Rembrandt, 891
Reno Ranch, 486
requests for assistance/money, 63–64, 124–25,
    171–73, 180, 288–89, 391–93, 499, 584–
    85, 658–59, 862–63

Return to Love, The, 645
Revuers, The, **323–4**
Reynolds, Herbert, 489
Rhodes, Ila, 248
Rice, Elmer, 431, **845–46**
Rich, Stanley, **738**
Ricketts, 537
Rico, Roger, 613–15, 616–17
Riggs, Lynn, 259, 260, 265, **279**, 299, 355
Rip Van Winkle, 338, 393
Ritchard, Cyril and Madge, **630**, **875–76**
RKO Pictures, 147–48, 393, 603, 615
Roach, Katherine, 250
"Road to Glory, The," 137
Robbins, Jack, 90
Robbins, Jerome, 376, **551–53**, 607, 763, 764, 903
Robbins, Music Corp., 495
Robe, The, 714
Roberta, 88, 91, 162, 164, 167, 170, 208, 246
Roberts, Joan, 275, *281*, 293
Robeson, Eslanda, **460–61**, 930
Robeson, Paul, 45, 46, 57, 97–98, 103, 106, 109, 112, **116–17**, 221, 238, 245, 247, 251, 266, 385–87, 460, 706
Robin, Leo, 163
Robinson, Earl, 222, 259
Robling, John S., **915–16**
Rockefellers, 88
Rodgers, Dorothy, 484, 616, 627, 628
Rodgers, Richard, viii, 88, 126, 184, **185**, **186**, 187, 211, 259, 260, 262, 266, 268, 278, 282, **291–94**, 304, 305, **306**, *307*, 313, **314–17**, 325, **326–27**, 328, 330, 337, 338, 340, 342, 355, **361**, 365, 367, 374, 382, 385, 396, **408–09**, 416, 420, 423, 424, 426, **430**, 432, 434, 439, **449–52**, 453, 455, *455*, **458**, 459, 471, 475, 477–78, 484, 497, **499–500**, 505, **508–09**, **512–13**, 513–14, 522, 528, 530, 534, 536, 537, 539, 550, 564, 567–68, 569, 577, 578, 579, **587**, 590, 595, 596, **597–99**, 603, **604**, 606, **617–18**, 626, 627, 631, 633, 634, **638–89**, 639, 643, **648–49**, 651, 652, 658, 662, **663–64**, **676–77**, 685, 687, **691**, 696–97, 701, 703, **709**, **710**, **716**, 717,

718–21, **722–23**, **725**, 735, **738–40**, 744, 746, 751–52, 760, **761**, **762–64**, 791, 793, 808–09, 812–13, 822, 827–28, **828–29**, 834, *835*, 836, 844, 848–49, 854–55, 861, **869–75**, *874*, 878, 882, 884, **887–89**, **893–97**, 902, 909, **919–20**, 935, 938, 939–40, 941, **947**, **949**, 952, **953–54**, **958–64**, 970, 983, **985–86**, **987–89**, **1000–01**, 1017
Rodgers & Hammerstein, viii, 65, 265, 363, 376, 390, 415, 419, 426, 429, 431, 447, 456, 484, 485, 499, 511, 546, 549, 561, 597, 643, 679, 685, 710, 712, 723, 730, 781, 854, 856
Rodgers & Hammerstein Television Company, 725, 813
Rodgers and Hammerstein Song Book, The, 939–40
Roeser, Prugh, **1009–10**
Rogel, Sid, 887, 888
Rogers, Ginger, 168
Roi at Moi, Le, 574
Romberg, Lillian, 601, 971–72
Romberg, Sigmund, 7, 25, 36, 38, 44, **53**, 108, 114, 145, 173, **174–76**, *176*, 183, **190–91**, 192, **199**, 242, 339, 346, 376, 380, **573**, 601, 853
Rombert, Hugo, 246
Rome, Harold, 222, 225, 607, 659, **732**
Romeo and Juliet, 69, 93, 99, 109, 903
Rooney, Mickey, 170, 236
Roosevelt, Franklin Delano, 75, 226, 298, 319, 726
Rose, Billy, **189–90**, 208, 209, 214, 219, 220, 221, 230, **269**, 272, 273, 275, 284, 286, 290, 349, 366, **446–47**, **493–94**, **675**, **724**, **729**, 845
Rose-Marie, 7, 8–9, 12, 21, 88, 115, 162, 194, 457–58, 666, 706, 712, 853
Rose-Marie on Ice, 537
Rosenfeld, George, **676**
Rosenkavalier, Der, 258
Rosenthal, Herbert, **583–84**
Rosenwald, Mrs., **6**
Ross, Lanny, 138, 249
Roughshod Up the Mountain, 654
Roy, William, 686–87
Royal Flush, The, 723

Ruby, Harry, 152, **240–41**, 355, **494–96**, 631–32, **655–56**, 806–07, 845, 968–69, 971–73, **975–76**
Ruggere, Joe, **599**
Ruggles, Charlie, 222, **268–69**
Run, Little Chillun, 244–45
Runanin, Boris, 836
Ruskin, Harry, 41
Russell, Jessyca, **485–86**
Russell, Rosalind, 818, 819, 820
Russia, 942, 955
Russian Diary of an Englishman, The, 17
Russian Revolution, 16–17

Sabrina Fair, 679
saddest word, the, 754–55
Saint-Exupery, Antoine de, 548
St. Louis Blues, 227
St. Louis Municipal Opera Theatre (The Muny), 137, 183, 187, 188, 190, 195, 208
Salisbury, Leah, **493**
San Francisco Civic Light Opera, 211
Sandberg, Sven-Olaf, 491–92
Sang, Leonard, 306
Sappho, 629
Saratoga Trunk, 185, 186, 208, 209, 214, 217–18, 219, 221, 230, 248, 718–21
Sargent, Rita, **674**
Sarnoff, Dorothy, 569, 570
Saul, Joe, 547
Saunders, Terry, 683
Saunders of the River, 97
Savage, Arnie, 461, 618
Savory, Gerald, 131, **132–34**
Saxe, Tom, **651**
Sayonara, 739–40, 821, 870, 883, 887
Scadron, Stuart, **731–32**
"Scandal in Bohemia, A" (story), 593–96
Schenk, Joseph, 410
Schenk, Nick, 494
Scheuer, Philip K., 856–57
Schisgall, Oscar, **836**
Schmidt, Lars, 442, 448, **449**, 602
Schneider, Dr. Daniel, **618**
Schrier, Morrie, 459
Schumann, Robert and Clara, 606
Schwab, Laurence, 29, 46, 47, 49, 52, 54, **122–23**, 147, 154, **224–26**, **268**,

326, **452**, **479–80**, **565–66**, 853–54, **862–63**
Schwartz, Arthur, 183, 283–84, **339–40**, 383, 865
Scott, Allan, 90
Scott, Kevin, 1000
Screen Writers Guild, 483
Scully, Frank, **993**
Secret Code, The, 253
Segal, Vivienne, 146, 317, 329
segregated housing, 697–98, 735–37, 770–72, 783–85
Selznick, David O., 953
Serlin, Oscar[?], 338
Seton, Bruce, 71
Seven Lively Arts, 349, 366, 375, 379
Seven Year Itch, The, 667, 730
Shakespeare, William, 26, 100, 535
Shall I Tell You What I Think of You?," 563, 564, 764, 856
"Shall We Dance," 570–71, 674, 1008
Sharaff, Irene, 555, 556, **697–98**
Shaw, Artie, 299
Shaw, Dorothy Derry, **945–46**
Shaw, George Bernard, 259, 399, 585, 603, 934
Shea, Joseph, **320–23**
Sheean, Vincent "Jimmy", 773–77
Sherlock Holmes, 159, 593–96
Sherwood, Robert, 276
Shore, Dinah, 238, 243, 245, 246, 247, 249, 251, 285, **941–42**
Short, Hassard, 286
Shot in the Dark, A, 730
Show Boat, viii, x–xi, xiii, xvi, 18, 21–22, 23, 43, 71, 167, 218, 227, 280, 302, 323, 335, 354–55, 418, 516, 517, 690–91, 854, 997
Show Boat (1929 film), 45
Show Boat (1936 film), 92–121
Show Boat (1951 film), 580
Show Boat (London), 29
Show Boat (novel), 60–61
Show Boat (revivals), 45, 46, 57, 61, 164–65, 169–70, 205, 207–08, 209, 210, 211, 213–14, 219, 221, 230, 237–39, 240, 242, 245–52, 256, 262, 263–65, 275, 285, 305, 339, 355, 419, 421, 423, 480, 642–43, 740–41

Show Boat (sequel), 45, 46, 47–48
Showalter, Max, 380
shows proposed but not pursued, 50–51,
   68, 86–88, 90, 94–95, 114, 116–17,
   122, 131–33, 174–76, 191, 234–36,
   268, 278, 325, 338, 339, 347–50,
   354–55, 358, 386–87, 393, 396, 423,
   425–26, 499–500, 507, 511, 522, 539,
   548–49, 585, 593–96, 599, 606, 615,
   527–28, 649–51, 659–60, 662, 685,
   710, 716, 718–21, 723, 743–44, 793–
   94, 802–03, 828–29, 844, 845–47,
   854–55, 884, 891, 893, 953, 988, 1013
Shubert. J. J., 174–75, 188, 193, 204–05,
   209, 267
Shubert, Lee, 189, 204, 207, 209, 231, 584
Shuberts, the, xvi, 54, 151, 170, 188, 204,
   209, 214, 221, 230, 427–29, 537, 666
Shurlock, Geoffrey M., **815–17**
Shurr, Louie, 111
Sidell sisters, 250
Silent Women, The, 607
Sillcox, Luise, 640
Silvers, Phil, 519–21
Silvers, Sid, 152
Simmons, Jean, 809
Simon, Henry, **939–40**
Sinatra, Frank, 808–09, 811
Sinclair, Upton, 900
Sing Out, Sweet Land, 361, 375, 397
Sirmay, Albert "Doc," 872, 875, **956–58**
Sir Walter Raleigh, 779
Six Red Months in Russia, 17
Skelton, Red, 150
Skouras, George, 427, 714, **773–74**, 834,
   843–44, 887–89, 896, 919, **1002–02**
Skouras, Thana, 919
Slee, Reverend J. F., 658
Slezak, Walter, 327, 757, 759
Sloane, Grena, 246, 247
"Small House of Uncle Thomas, The," 570,
   579, 580, 674, 689–90
Smathers, George A., 907
Smith, Dr. (of ASCAP), 213
Smith, Eleanor, 60, 68
Smith, Mary, **663–64**
Smith, Muriel, 618
Smith, Oliver, 952

Smith, Queenie, 109, 110, 111
Snow White and the Seven Dwarfs, 169
So Big, 205, 302, 303
"So Far," 433, 436, 437
Society for the Prevention of World War
   III, 561
"Soliloquy," xiii, 818
"Some Enchanted Evening," 464, 468–69,
   528, 893, 895, 897, 899, 902, 982, 932
Some Enchanted Evenings, 656–57, 706,
   712, 786
Something for the Boys, 276
"Something Wonderful," 570, 942
Sondheim, Stephen, x, 50, 379, 400–01,
   445–46, 456, 459, 507, **524, 547,** 589,
   647, 675, 706–07, **707–08,** 1015
Sometime, 5
"Song is You, The," 212, 705
Song of Norway, 211
Song of the Flame, 12, 36, 242. *See also*
   Green Peach, The
Song of the West, 36
Soo, Jack, 987–88
Sosnik, Harry, 993, **994**
Sothern, Ann, 236
Sound of Music, The, 489, 764, 920–26,
   933–34, 947, 949, 952, 953–54, 956,
   958–65, 968, 969–70, **971,** 974–80,
   985, 986, 987, 988, 995–97, 1001,
   1011, 1014–15, 1016
"Sound of Music, The," 952, 970
South Africa, 452, 634–35, 640
South Pacific, xiii, 429, 446, 447, 449–52,
   454–55, 458–71, 472–75, 478–81,
   482–83, 493–94, 498–99, 502, 509,
   516, 517, 523, 524, 526–33, 540, 541–
   42, 561, 566, 582, 607, 610, 613–15,
   610, 634–35, 637, 640, 641, 646, 688–
   90, 691, 703, 731, 751–52, 802, 819,
   926, 939, 942, 966, 990
South Pacific (film), 494, 498, 712, 722,
   841–42, 857, 861, 871, 881–82 884–
   89, 891–92, 893–96, 897–99, 908–09,
   919, 927, 921–32, 942, 953, 1015
South Pacific (London), 587, 590–93, 596–
   97, 600, 610, 616, 618–19, 621, 629–
   30, 646, 654, 660–61, 731, 880, 949
South Pacific (tour), 514

Spack (Weinreb), Ilene, 566-67
Spain, 602
Spear, Cheryl J., 1008
Speers, Theodore, 843
Spencer, Kenneth, 254
Sperber, Harry N., 734
Spewack, Sam and Bella, 204, 222, 475
Spier, Larry, 523-24, 524
Spirit of St. Louis, The, 788-89
Spring 1600, 69
Spring is Here, 268
Springtime in the Rockies, 261
Stage Door Canteen, 225, 226, 233
Star and Garter, 251
Star-Spangled Banner, The, 341
State Fair, 313, 320-24, 326, 329-30, 336,
    337, 341-43, 365, 369, 379, 405-08,
    617-18, 847-48, 983, 986, 987, 1014,
    1017
Steel, Mary, 679
Steele, Tommy, 934
Steiger, Rod, 787, 833
Steinbeck, Elaine Anderson, 748, 749, 756,
    822
Steinbeck, John, 546-47, 549, 648-51,
    722, 723, 746-50, 754, 755-56, 822-
    23, 827-28, 851-52
Stevens, Risë, 743
Stevens, Roger, 797-98, 912
Stevenson, Adlai, 663, 666-67, 668, 805, 974
Stewart, Johnny, 484, 581
Stickney (Lindsay), Dorothy, 488, 489, 662
Stockwell, Harry, 306
Stone, Harlan Fiske, 331
Stormy Weather, 134
Story Behind Popular Songs, The, 853-54
Story of Vernon and Irene Castle, 135, 139,
    148
Stothart, Herbert, 6, 7, 9, 19, 223, 227, 242,
    337, 853
Stout, Rex, 277, 317-19, 561-62
"Stouthearted Men," 233
Stowe, Harriet Beecher, 510
Strauss, Helen, 562
Strauss II, Johann, 90, 146
Strauss, Richard, 258, 607
Street Scene, 430-31
Streetcar Named Desire, A, 509

Styne, Jule, 685, 760, 950
Suez Canal crisis, 863-64
Sullivan, Arthur, 159-62
Sullivan, Ed, 932, 951-52
Summer Breeze, 88
Sumner, Ronald, 702-03
Sunny, 7, 26, 36, 38, 68, 223, 854
Sunny River, 88, 183, 187-90, 195, 196-99
"Surrey with the Fringe on the Top, The,"
    334, 833
Susannah and the Elders, 704-05
Suskin, Steven, 429
Swarthout, Gladys, 93-94, 113
Sweden, Gothenburg, Malmö, &
    Stockholm, 442, 443-44, 453-54
Sweet Adeline, 34, 74, 81, 230
Sweet Thursday, 746, 753, 778, 792-93,
    829. See also Pipe Dream
"Sweetest Sight That I Have Seen, The," 368
Swing It, Susan, 122
Swope, John, 477, 478
Sylva, Margaret, 151
Sylvain, Jules, 444
Symphony Policy Committee (ASCAP),
    352-54

T. B. Harms, 250, 714
Tabbert, William, 757, 759
Tabor, Elizabeth McCourt "Baby Doe,"
    348, 50
Tales of the South Pacific, 446, 450, 463
Talmadge, Herman, 623
Tambourines to Glory, 859
Tandy, Jessica, 616
Taylor, Deems, 231, 262, 304, 307-08, 312,
    352-54, 504, 633, 656, 657, 690, 712,
    786
Taylor, Dwight, 514
Taylor, Kent, 111
Taylor, Laurette, 615
Taylor, Samuel, 399, 484, 514, 679, 1019
Teahouse of the August Moon, The, 730, 735
television, 181, 691, 725, 726, 941, 987
"Tennessee Fish Fry," 183
Tennent, H. M., 69, 72
Terris, Norma, 48, 49, 57, 146, 152, 252,
    690-91
Tevye's Daughters, 499-500

Texas *Li'l Darlin'*, 521
Thalberg, Irving, 56, 88, 90, 99
Theatre Guild, The, viii, 259–60, 262, 268,
    271, 277, 278, 291–95, 313, 314, 326,
    338, 361, 375, 408–09, 426, 431, 453,
    505, 709–10, 748
"There is Nothin' Like a Dame," 657, 893, 898
"They Didn't Believe Me," 489
"This is London," 191
This is Show Business, 605
This is the Army, 380–81
"This Nearly Was Mine," 528, 893
Thomas, John Charles, 212, 217, 223
Thompson, Walter, 883
Thomson, Virgil, 633
Thousands Cheer, 313
Three Little Words, 495
Three Men on a Horse, 181
Three Sisters, The, 36, 66–74, 75, 76, 79,
    154, 230, 260
Through the Russian Revolution, 17
"Throw Out the Window," 42
Tibbett, Lawrence, 337, 350
ticket difficulties/scandal, 363, 478, 493,
    498–99, 516–17, 523, 583–84, 812–
    13, 938, 979–80
Tickle Me, 7
"Till Good Luck Comes My Way," 102, 110
Till the Clouds Roll By, 417–18
Time of the Cuckoo, The, 667
Titlon, Webb, 529
Tobias, Charles, 201
Todd, Michael, 276, 281, 376, 575, 714,
    814, 830
Todd-AO, 713, 764, 769, 788–89, 814, 830,
    897, 899, 919
Top Banana, 134, 519–21. *See also Just for
    Laughs*
Top Hat, 91
Topsy and Eva, 146
Torpey, William, 420
Tosca, 86
Tote Stadt, Die, 86
Touch and Go, 503
Towner, Mrs. Wesley, **812–13**
Tozzi, Giorgio, 893
Trapp Family Singers, 933
Trapp Family, The/Trapp Familie, Die, 920

Trapp, Maria Augusta Von, 920, 958–60,
    1018–19
Traubel, Helen, 795
Traviata, La, 685
Tree Grows in Brooklyn, A, 865–67
Trilby, 660
Trovatore, Il, 258
Truex, Ernest, 252
Truman, Harry S., 726, 797, 805
Tulsa Tribune, **696–97**
Turtle, Harold, **675–76**
Twentieth Century-Fox, 81, 168, 290, 313, 336,
    338, 341, 342, 405, 428, 447, 712–14, 778,
    807, 815, 837, 855, 865, 882, 884, 888,
    892, 896–97, 987, 1014, 1017
"Twilight of God, The" (pamphlet), 511
Two Thieves, 50, 329
Tynan, Kenneth, **777**, 980
Tyres, John, 285
Tyson, Jack, 59

Uncle Tom's Cabin, 509–10, 689–90
Unger, Gladys, 174
United States Steel Corporation, 697, 736,
    770
United World Federalists, ix, 543–44, 561,
    676, 741–42, 746–47, 749, 797–98,
    800–01, 803–04, 805, 863–64, 918–
    19, 973, 1010, 1018
Universal Studios (Pictures), 92, 97, 100,
    1001
Up in Central Park, 376, 380, 591
Urban, Gretl, 250
Urban, Joseph, 249

Vail, Helen, **486**
Value Line, The, 394–95
Van Druten, John, 363, 367, **389–90**, 554,
    555–58, 581–82, 658, 694
Van Vechten, Carl, **170–71**
Varden, Evelyn, 327
Vardi, David, 19
Variety ad, 782
Verdi, Giuseppe, 258, 685
Very Warm for May, viii, 88, 166, 173–74, 177,
    180, 181, 188, 234, 237, 239, 291, 992
Victoria Regina, 982–83
Victory at Sea, 986

Viennese Nights, 36, 38–39
Vitaphone, 36
"Vodka," 12
Von Essen, Baron and Baroness, 442
Vye, Murvyn, 569

"Waiting," 563, 564, 569
Wald, Jerry, 165, 168, 241
Waldorf, Wilella, 401
Walker, Don, 686–77
Walker, Jimmy, 329, 773–74
Wallace, Mike, 928, 930
Wallsten, Robert, 372
Walsh, Thomas deWitt, **991–92**
Walston, Ray, 618, 881, 882, 889
war songs, 200–01, 225–26, 233–34
Ward, Toni, **364**
Warner Bros., 36, 37, 81, 186, 205, 208,
    788–89
Warner, Jack L., 36, 37, 149, 185, 186, 787,
    1001
Washer, Ben, 380
Wasserman, Lew, 451, 459, 789
Watanabe, Eleanor "Doodie" Blanchard
    (Dorothy's sister), 233, 239, 375, 427
Watanabe, Jennifer, 379
Watanabe, Jerry, **121**, 233, 239, **653–54**,
    716–18
Waters, Ethel, 143, 380
Watson, Susan Eastman, **688–89**
Wattenberg, Sidney, 250, 714
Wattles, Margot, **956**
Waxman, Abe P., **307–08**
Waxman, Gerald, **547**
"We Kiss in a Shadow," 563, 570
Week, A, 17
Weill, Kurt, 222, 259, 289–90, **430–31**
Weinstock, Elias, 427
Weir, Milton, 427
Weiss, J. Purdy, 203–04
Welchman, Harry, 71
"Welcome Home," 757
Welcome House, ix, 626, 705, 824
West End, The, 8–9, 12, 19, 29, 65–74, 75,
    131, 408–09, 457–58, 508–09, 514,
    536–38, 553, 618, 621, 729–30, 735,
    765–69, 880, 974–75, 978, 983, 995,
    998, 1000

West Side Story, 764, 903, 912
"Western People Funny," 764, 856
Westley, Helen, 109
Westport County Playhouse,
Whale, James, 95, **99**, **101–03**, **106–10**,
    108–10, 111, 112, **115–16**, **117–21**
"What a Pretty Girl," 137
What Every Woman Knows, 668, 685, 687
Wheeler, Burton, 317, 318
Where Do We Go From Here, 163
Where's Charley?, 508
"Where's the Mate for Me?," 102
White, George, 56
White, Mrs., **3–4**
White, Sammy, 103–04, 109, 111, 164, 248, 251
White, Walter, **623**, **665**
White Collar Girl, 583
Whiteman, Paul, 329
Whitney, Ruth, **823**
Whoopee (film), 45
Whyte, Jerry, 306, 309, 409, 535, 544,
    597–99, **618–19**, **629**, 666, 681, 691,
    722–23, **884**, 949
Wickware, Frances Sill, 347
Wilcoxon, Henry, 69
Wilder, Billy, 787, 788
Wildflower, 7, 8, 19, 223, 242, 706, 994
Wilk, Jacob, 185
Wilkins, Herbert, 59
William Morris Agency, 247, 364, 497, 562
Williams College, 456
Williams, Albert Rhys, 17
Williams, Emlyn, 484
Williams, Tennessee, 448, 509, **951**, 952
Williamson Music, Ltd., viii, 376, 500,
    537–38, 597, 714, 730
Wilson, Jack, 491
Wilson, Julie, 654
Wiman, Dwight Deere, 145, 214, 221, 300
Winchell, Walter, 281
Wine, Women and Words, 446–47
Wing, Ted, **953**
Winged Victory, 369
Wings Over the Pacific, 541
Wings Over the South Pacific, 541
Winninger, Charles, **49**, 57, 110, 112, 164,
    221, 222, 236, 238, 245, 247, 251, 252,
    266, 268–69, 285, 405, 406, 600

Winsor, Roy, **978–79**
Winston, Bruce, 65, **139–40**
Winston Churchill—The Valiant
   Years, 986
Wish You Were Here, 607–09, 628, 646
Wizard of Oz, The, 146
Wodehouse, P. G., **448**, **522**, 853, **877–78**
Wolcott, Alexander, 90
Wolferman, Barbara, 748, 894
Wolpert, Roland H., **614**
Wolter, Mrs. William F., **606**
Women, The, 145, 496
"Wonderful Guy, A," 482, 519, 895, 897,
   898, 899, 902
Wonderful Town, 685, 904
Wonnberger, Carl G., **846**
Wood, Peggy, 942
Woodbridge, Henry, 789, 830
Woolfson, Martin, 883
World War I, 4–5, 6, 231
World War II, things related to/affected by,
   xi, xiv, 63, 149, 152, 171–73, 183, 191,
   193, 196, 197, 200–04, 217, 221–22,
   225–26, 227, 232, 233–34, 256–57,
   275–76, 277, 317–19, 322, 325, 331,
   334, 336, 345, 350, 376–77, 379, 381–
   84, 408–09, 411–14, 443, 797
World's Fair, 1939 New York, 183
Worth, Billie, 529
WPA (Works Progress Administration),
   179–80
Wright, Martha, 613, 894
Writers War Board, ix, 276, 277, 317–19,
   331, 360, 383, 561
Writers' Board for World Government, 277
Wyckoff, Evelyn, 306, 317
Wylie, Philip, 476

Yang, James C. S., **1010**
Yankee Doodle Dandy, 320–21
Yokel, Alex, 213, 221
Yolanda and the Thief, 299–300
Yorke, Jack, **385–87**
"You Are Beautiful," 958, 1000
"You Are Love," 118, 120
"You Are Never Away," 434, 437, 438
You Can't Take It with You, 127, 167
"You Say You Care," 538–39
You Were Never Lovelier, 283–84
"You'll Never Walk Alone," 658, 895, 904–
   05, 998–99
"You've Got to Be Carefully Taught," xiii,
   463, 464–65, 473, 634, 688–89
Youmans, Vincent, 223, 242, 993–94
Young, Carleton Scott, 247
Young, Nancy Kenyon, 237, 247
Younger Than Springtime, 463, 895, 970
Your Hit Parade, The, 359, 905, 910
"Yukon Jake" case, 130
Yule, Joe, 236
Yuriko, 695–96

Zales, Mary, **498–99**
Zanuck, Darryl, 37, 191, 313, 756, 761,
   762–63, **807–10**
Ziegfeld, Florenz, 21, 24, 26, **43–49**, 51, 54,
   56, 57, 60, 148, 250, 727–28, 854
Ziegfeld Follies, 43, 242
Ziegfeld Theatre, 325, 366
Zierold, Norman J., **754–55**
Zinnemann, Fred, 710, 773, 781, 788,
   829–30, 832–33, *835*
Zinsser, William, 931–32
Zorina, Vera, 268
Zweig, Stefan, 607